CONTEMPORARY FASHION

OTHER ART TITLES FROM ST. JAMES PRESS

Contemporary Architects

Contemporary Artists

Contemporary Designers

Contemporary Masterworks

Contemporary Photographers

Contemporary Women Artists

International Dictionary of Architects and Architecture

International Dictionary of Art and Artists

St. James Guide to Black Artists

St. James Guide to Hispanic Artists

St. James Guide to Native North American Artists

St. James Modern Masterpieces

CONTEMPORARY FASHION

SECOND EDITION

Editor:
Taryn Benbow-Pfalzgraf

ST. JAMES PRESS

GALE GROUP

THOMSON LEARNING

Detroit • New York • San Diego • San Francisco
Boston • New Haven, Conn. • Waterville, Maine
London • Munich

STAFF

Taryn Benbow-Pfalzgraf, *Editor*

Kristin Hart, *Project Coordinator*

Erin Bealmear, Joann Cerrito, Jim Craddock, Stephen Cusack, Miranda H. Ferrara, Melissa Hill, Margaret Mazurkiewicz, Carol A. Schwartz, Christine Tomassini, Michael J. Tyrkus, *St. James Press Staff*

Peter M. Gareffa, *Managing Editor, St. James Press*

Mary Beth Trimper, *Manager, Composition and Electronic Prepress*
Evi Seoud, *Assistant Manager, Composition Purchasing and Electronic Prepress*
Dorothy Maki, *Manufacturing Manager*
Rhonda Williams, *Print Buyer*

Barbara J. Yarrow, *Manager, Imaging and Multimedia Content*
Dean Dauphinais, *Senior Editor, Imaging and Multimedia Content*
Leitha Etheridge-Sims, Mary K. Grimes, David G. Oblender, *Image Catalogers*
Lezlie Light, *Imaging Coordinator*
Randy Bassett, *Imaging Supervisor*
Dan Newell, *Imaging Specialist*

Mike Logusz, *Graphic Artist*

Maria L. Franklin, *Manager, Rights & Permissions*
Shalice Shah-Caldwell, *Permissions Associate*

Cover photo: Design by Roberto Capucci, ca. 1980-97 © Massimo Listri/CORBIS.

Library of Congress Catalog Cataloging-in-Publication Data
Contemporary fashion / editor, Taryn Benbow-Pfalzgraf.—2nd ed.
p. cm.
Includes bibliographical references and index.
ISBN 1-55862-348-5
1. Fashion designers—Biographical—Encyclopedias. 2. Costume design—History—20th century—Encyclopedias. 3. Fashion—History—20th century—Encyclopedias. I. Benbow-Pfalzgraf, Taryn.

TT505.A1 C66 2002
746.9'2'0922—dc21

2002017801

Printed in the United States of America

St. James Press is an imprint of Gale
Gale and Design is a trademark used herein under license
10 9 8 7 6 5 4 3 2

CONTENTS

EDITOR'S NOTE FROM THE FIRST EDITION

This volume is dedicated to Colin Naylor (1944–92), who initiated its publication and was editor until his early death. Colin's distinguished contributions to the arts—as editor of *Art & Artists* and as editor of indispensable reference volumes published by St. James Press and the Gale Group—resonate with his lively sense of the role of contemporary arts. I had the privilege of writing for him at *Art & Artists* decades ago and began on this volume in order to be involved again with an old friend and an inspiring editor. While he is not present for its outcome, *Contemporary Fashion* will always bear Colin's sense of adventure, scope of interest, and unceasing imagination. *Contemporary Fashion* is, I hope, no less Colin's book and dream for his absence upon its fulfillment.

Contemporary Fashion seeks to provide information on and assessment of fashion designers active during the period from 1945 to the present. International in scope in accordance with fashion's wide resourcing and dissemination, this volume attempts to provide dependable information and substantive critical appraisal in a field often prone to excessive praise and hyperbolic language. Each entry consists of a personal and professional biography; bibliographic citations by and about the designer; when possible, a statement by the designer on his or her work and/or design philosophy; and a concise, informative essay. The book's emphasis is on design creativity and distinction; in instances of a corporation, family business, design house, or other collective enterprise, we have attempted to hone in on the distinguishing attributes of the design tradition. Much literature from specialized periodicals is assimilated in the critical essays and listed in the bibliographies, offering the reader access to a wide variety and deep concentration of specialized literature.

Special appreciation is owed to the designers and design houses who generously supplied statements, information, and visual documentation. Virtually everyone in the civilized world talks about fashion. It is an area in which most of us consider ourselves knowledgeable, if only as a function of making our own clothing decisions on a daily basis. *Contemporary Fashion* gives value to the data and ideas of fashion discussion; it is intended to aid the discourse about apparel and edify the lively fashion conversation. *Contemporary Fashion* is to stand as a solid reference where no other comparable volumes exist and to make a contribution to fashion study and its allied expressions.

—Richard Martin (1947–99)

EDITOR'S NOTE FROM THE CURRENT EDITION

I have been happy to perpetuate a project beloved by both Colin Naylor (1944–92) and Richard Martin (1947–99), and believe each would be pleased with *Contemporary Fashion, 2nd Edition*. Unique to the second volume is an advisory board of industry professionals, who helped select the new designers and companies added to the previous edition's international mix. Additionally, the number of photographs is more than double the original, so readers and researchers may experience both a written and visual record of this evolving field.

Contemporary Fashion, 2nd Edition, like its predecessor, is filled with informative essays mirroring the many facets of the fashion world, including extended biographical headers with website addresses whenever available, and extensive bibliographic listings. Those involved with this book have striven to be as current as possible, and developments were added up to the moment the book went into publication.

This edition would not have been possible without Kristin Hart, who offered advice and unflinching support; Barbara Coster, who tackles whatever is thrown her way; Karen Raugust, who always comes through, with good results; Jocelyn Prucha, for diving repeatedly into murky waters for up-to-the-second information; Peter Gareffa, for offering me another opportunity; and to the beloveds, who made working this hard worthwhile: John, Jordyn, Wylie, Foley, and Hadley.

Lastly, a technical note: to save space and the mindless repetition of periodicals used throughout the publications sections, abbreviations were used for the *Daily News Record* (as *DNR*) and *Women's Wear Daily* (*WWD*). Discerning readers may also note in most cases when *Vogue* is listed, it is accompanied by the city of its publication (Paris, Milan, etc.), except when issued from New York.

—Taryn Benbow-Pfalzgraf

INTRODUCTION

Fashion is often perceived as frivolous, irrational, and dictatorial. Changes in fashion strike many people as mysterious, arbitrary, and senseless—except as part of a conspiracy to trick "fashion victims" into buying unnecessary new clothes. In 19th-century America, dress reformers argued that contemporary fashion was created by a cabal of male couturiers and Parisian courtesans, who sought to become rich by promoting immoral styles. Although courtesans are no longer significant trendsetters, designers are still widely regarded as dictators devoted to the planned obsolescence of successive absurd and expensive clothing styles. Conversely, the fashion press tends to characterize favored designers as "geniuses" whose creations arise independently of socioeconomic forces or cultural trends. Although more flattering, this latter view of the design process is no more accurate than the antifashion critique.

Years ago, when Richard Martin edited the first edition of *Contemporary Fashion,* he was one of a very few scholars who took fashion seriously. Throughout his career as an author and curator, Richard argued that fashion should be acknowledged as one of the visual arts. He was well aware that fashion's association with the female body and with the ephemeral, as well as its reputation as a commercial enterprise, had contributed to its lesser reputation in comparison with the arts identified with men. But he insisted that, on the contrary, fashion played a singularly important role in modern culture. With the publication of *Contemporary Fashion,* he sought to provide substantial documentation on the work of a wide range of fashion designers, believing this would empower readers to recognize how fashion provides insight into issues such as self-expression, body image, gender, sexuality, class, and the manifold relationships between high art and popular culture.

Richard was a friend and mentor, and I am honored to provide an introduction to this latest edition of *Contemporary Fashion,* which includes a number of new and revised essays. Like the first edition, it seeks to provide reliable information on the most important fashion designers active from 1945 to the present. Since contemporary fashion is very much a global phenomenon, the book is international in scope. Organized alphabetically, it consists of essays on individual designers (from Armani, Balenciaga, and Chanel through Westwood, Yamamoto, and Zoran) written by scholars or critics in the field of fashion history. Each entry includes biographical information, as well as a critical assessment of the designer's contributions to fashion, and a bibliography to facilitate further research. Thanks in part to Richard's work, fashion is now increasingly regarded as a legitimate area of research, and fashion designers receive greater recognition as creative individuals working within a complex and valuable tradition.

—Dr. Valerie Steele, Chief Curator and Acting Director,
The Museum at the Fashion Institute of Technology

ADVISERS

Dr. Leslie Davis Burns
Bobbin Educator of the Year, 2001
Author & Professor
Apparel, Interiors, Housing & Merchandising
Oregon State University

Christina Lindholm
Chair, Fashion Design & Merchandising
Virginia Commonwealth University

Cindy Marek
Offshore Manager
HMX Tailored (a division of Hartmarx)

Susan Reitman
Professor of Textiles
Fashion Institute of Technology

Dr. Valerie Steele
Chief Curator and Acting Director
The Museum at the Fashion Institute of Technology

CONTRIBUTORS

Kevin Almond
Rebecca Arnold
Andrea Arsenault

Therese Duzinkiewicz Baker
Sydonie Benét
Whitney Blausen
Sarah Bodine
Carol Mary Brown
Kim Brown
Jane Burns

Marianne T. Carlano
Barbara Cavaliere
Hazel Clark
Debra Regan Cleveland
Linda Coleing
Elizabeth A. Coleman
Arlene C. Cooper
Caroline Cox
Andrew Cunningham

Fred Dennis
Janette Goff Dixon
Jean L. Druesedow

Doreen Ehrlich
Mary C. Elliott
Jodi Essey-Stapleton

Alan J. Flux

Mary Ellen Gordon
Lisa Groshong
Roberta Hochberger Gruber

Yoko Hamada
Chris Hill
Nancy House

Diana Idzelis

Owen James

Betty Kirke

Darcy Lewis
Christina Lindholm
Brian Louwers

Daryl F. Mallett
Janet Markarian
Lisa Marsh
Kathleen Bonann Marshall
Richard Martin
Elian McCready
Kimbally A. Medeiros
Sally Ann Melia
Christine Miner Minderovic
Sally A. Myers

Janet Ozzard

Kathleen Paton
Angela Pattison

Karen Raugust
Donna W. Reamy
Jessica Reisman
Nelly Rhodes
Alan E. Rosenberg

Susan Salter
Sandra Schroeder
Margo Seaman
Molly Severson
Dennita Sewell
Madelyn Shaw
Gillion Skellenger
Mary Ellen Snodgrass
Carrie Snyder
Megan Stacy
Montse Stanley
Valerie Steele

Teal Triggs

Vicki Vasilopoulos
Gregory Votolato

Myra J. Walker
Melinda L. Watt
Catherine Woram

CONTEMPORARY FASHION

LIST OF ENTRANTS

Joseph Abboud
Abercrombie & Fitch Company
Adolfo
Adri
Gilbert Adrian
Miguel Adrover
Agnés B.
Akira
Azzedine Alaïa
Walter Albini
Victor Alfaro
Linda Allard
Ally Capellino
Sir Hardy Amies
John Anthony
Aquascutum, Ltd.
Junichi Arai
Giorgio Armani
Laura Ashley
Christian Aujard
Sylvia Ayton
Jacques Azagury
Max Azria

Badgley Mischka
Cristobal Balenciaga
Pierre Balmain
Banana Republic
Jeff Banks
Jeffrey Banks
Jhane Barnes
Sheridan Barnett
Rocco Barocco
Scott Barrie
John Bartlett
Franck Joseph Bastille
Geoffrey Beene
Bellville Sassoon-Lorcan Mullany
Benetton SpA
Patirizio Bertelli
Laura Biagiotti
Bianchini-Férier
Dirk Bikkembergs
Sandy Black
Manolo Blahnik
Alistair Blair
Bill Blass
Blumarine
Bodymap
Willy Bogner
Marc Bohan
Tom Brigance
Brioni
Donald Brooks
Brooks Brothers
Liza Bruce

Bruno Magli
Burberry
Stephen Burrows
Byblos

Jean Cacharel
Calugi e Giannelli
Roberto Capucci
Pierre Cardin
Hattie Carnegie
Carven
Joe Casely-Hayford
Bonnie Cashin
Oleg Cassini
Jean-Charles de Castelbajac
Catalina Sportswear
Jean Baptiste Caumont
Nino Cerruti
Sal Cesarani
Hussein Chalayan
Champion Products Inc.
Gabrielle "Coco" Chanel
Caroline Charles
Chloé
Jimmy Choo
Liz Claiborne
Ossie Clark
Robert Clergerie
Kenneth Cole
Cole Haan
Cole of California
Nick Coleman
Sybil Connolly
Jasper Conran
Corneliani SpA
Giorgio Correggiari
Victor Costa
Paul Costelloe
André Courrèges
Enrico Coveri
Patrick Cox
C.P. Company
Jules-François Crahay
Angela Cummings

Lilly Daché
Wendy Dagworthy
Sarah Dallas
Danskin
Oscar de la Renta
Louis Dell'Olio
Ann Demeulemeester
Myrène de Prémonville
Jacqueline de Ribes
Elisabeth de Senneville
Jean Dessès

Christian Dior
Dolce & Gabbana
Adolfo Domínguez
Dorothée Bis
Randolph Duke

Eddie Bauer
Mark Eisen
Alber Elbaz
Perry Ellis
David and Elizabeth Emanuel
English Eccentrics
Ermenegildo Zegna Group
Erreuno SCM SpA
Escada
Esprit Holdings, Inc.
Jacques Esterel
Luis Estévez
Joseph Ettedgui

Alberto Fabiani
Fabrice
Nicole Farhi
Kaffe Fassett
Jacques Fath
Fendi
Han Feng
Fenn Wright Manson
Louis Féraud
Salvatore Ferragamo
Gianfranco Ferré
Alberta Ferretti
Andrew Fezza
David Fielden
Elio Fiorucci
John Flett
Alan Flusser
Anne Fogarty
Brigid Foley
Fontana
Tom Ford
Mariano Fortuny
Diane Freis
French Connection
Bella Freud
Giuliano Fujiwara

James Galanos
Irene Galitzine
John Galliano
The Gap
Sandra Garratt
Jean-Paul Gaultier
Genny Holding SpA
Georges Rech
Rudi Gernreich

Mary Quant

Paco Rabanne
Sir Edward Rayne
Red or Dead
Tracy Reese
René Lezard
Maurice Rentner
Mary Ann Restivo
Zandra Rhodes
John Richmond
Patricia Roberts
Bill Robinson
Marcel Rochas
Rodier
Carolyne Roehm
Christian Francis Roth
Maggy Rouf
Cynthia Rowley
Cinzia Ruggeri
Sonia Rykiel

Gloria Sachs
Yves Saint Laurent
Saks Fifth Avenue
Fernando Sanchez
Jil Sander
Giorgio Sant'Angelo
Arnold Scaasi
Jean-Louis Scherrer
Elsa Schiaparelli
Carolyn Schnurer
Mila Schön
Ronaldus Shamask
David Shilling
Simonetta
Adele Simpson
Martine Sitbon
Sophie Sitbon
Hedi Slimane
Graham Smith
Paul Smith
Willi Smith
Per Spook
Stephen Sprouse
George Peter Stavropoulos
Stefanel SpA
Cynthia Steffe
Robert Stock
Helen Storey
Strenesse Group
Jill Stuart
Anna Sui
Alfred Sung
Sybilla

Vivienne Tam
Tamotsu
William Tang
Gustave Tassell
Chantal Thomass
Vicky Tiel
Tiffany & Company
Jacques Tiffeau
Tiktiner
Timney Fowler Ltd.
Ted Tinling
Zang Toi
Isabel Toledo
Yuki Torii
Torrente
Transport
Philip Treacy
Pauline Trigère
Trussardi, SpA
Sally Tuffin
Richard Tyler

Patricia Underwood
Emanuel Ungaro
Kay Unger

Valentina
Valentino
Koos van den Akker
Joan Vass
Philippe Venet
Gian Marco Venturi
Joaquim Verdù
Roberto Verino
Donatella Versace
Gianni Versace
Sally Victor
Victoria's Secret
Victorio y Lucchino
Viktor & Rolf
Madeleine Vionnet
Adrienne Vittadini
Roger Vivier
Michaele Vollbracht
Diane Von Furstenberg

Catherine Walker
Vera Wang
Chester Weinberg
John Weitz
Vivienne Westwood
Whistles
Workers for Freedom

Kansai Yamamoto
Yohji Yamamoto
David Yurman

Zoran

A

ABBOUD, Joseph

American designer

Born: Boston, Massachusetts, 5 May 1950. **Education:** Studied comparative literature, University of Massachusetts, Boston, 1968–72; also studied at the Sorbonne. **Family:** Married Lynn Weinstein, 6 June 1976; children: Lila, Ari. **Career:** Buyer, then director of merchandise, Louis of Boston, 1968–80; designer, Southwick, 1980; associate director of menswear design, Polo/Ralph Lauren, New York, 1980–84; launched signature menswear collection, 1986; designer, Barry Bricken, New York, 1987–88. J.A. (Joseph Abboud) Apparel Corporation, a joint venture with GFT USA, formed, 1988; Joseph Abboud Womenswear and menswear collection of tailored clothing and furnishings introduced, 1990; opened first retail store, Boston, 1990; collections first shown in Europe, 1990; JA II line introduced, 1991; fragrance line introduced in Japan, 1992, in America, 1993; introduced J.O.E. (Just One Earth) sportswear line, 1992; designed wardrobes for male television announcers for 1992 Winter Olympics, Albertville, France, 1992; Joseph Abboud Environments bed and bath collection launched, 1993; Joseph Abboud fragrance launched, 1994; formed Joseph Abboud Worldwide to oversee labels and licensing, 1996; forged strategic partnership with GFT, 1997; introduced black label line for men, 1999; company acquired by GFT for $65 million, 2000. **Awards:** Cutty Sark award, 1988; Woolmark award, 1988; Menswear Designer of the Year award from Council of Fashion Designers of America Award, 1989, 1990; honored by Japanese Government in conjunction with the Association of Total Fashion in Osaka, 1993; Special Achievement award from Neckwear Association of America Inc., 1994. **Address:** 650 Fifth Avenue, New York, New York 10019, USA.

Publications

On ABBOUD:

Articles

Dolce, Joe, "Last of the Updated Traditional," in *Connoisseur* (New York), March 1987.

Saunders, Peggy, "Joseph Abboud," in *Boston Business,* July/August 1987.

"A Man's Style Book, Joseph Abboud," in *Esquire* (New York), September 1987.

de Caro, Frank, "Men in Style: A Designer to Watch," in the *Baltimore Sun,* 24 September 1987.

"Designers Are Made as Well as Born," in *Forbes* (New York), 11 July 1988.

Carloni, Maria Vittoria, "Da commesso a mito," in *Panorama,* 27 November 1988.

LaFerla, Ruth, "Past as Prologue," in *New York Times Magazine,* 19 February 1989.

Wayne, Hollis, "Fashion Forward—the 90s," in *Playboy* (Chicago), March 1989.

Stern, Ellen, "Joseph Abboud, Down to Earth," in *GQ* (New York), October 1989.

"The Word to Men: Hang Looser," in *People Weekly* (Chicago), Spring 1990.

Burns, Robert, "Abboud Takes on Classics in a Big Way," in *Los Angeles Times,* 8 June 1990.

Hatfield, Julie, "Abboud Brings Worldly Styles Home," in *Boston Globe,* 5 September 1990.

Conover, Kirsten A., "Abboud Sets Tone for '90s Menswear," in *Christian Science Monitor* (Boston), 5 November 1990.

Roosa, Nancy, "Much Abboud about Clothing," in *Boston,* January 1991.

Fenichell, Stephen, "The Look of the Nineties: Four Designers Lead the Way," in *Connoisseur* (New York), March 1991.

Hancox, Clara, "And Now, the First Joe Abboud," in *Daily News Record,* 15 July 1991.

"Joseph Abboud's Next Step," in *Esquire* (New York), August 1992.

Beatty, Jack, "The Transatlantic Look," in *Atlantic Monthly,* December 1995.

Gault, Ylonda, "Fashion's Marathoner," in *Crain's New York Business*, 14 July 1997.

Gellers, Stan, "Joseph Abboud Goes for the Gold with Black Label Clothing," in *Daily News Record*, 9 June 1999.

Dodd, Annmarie, "Abboud Sells to GFT for $65 Million," in *Daily News Record*, 21 June 2000.

Curan, Catherine, "GFT Sews up Abboud Brand," in *Crain's New York Business*, 17 July 2000.

Lohrer, Robert, "Joseph Abboud Faces a Rich Future," in *Daily News Record*, 19 July 2000.

* * *

Joseph Abboud has said that his clothing is as much about lifestyle as design. Since 1986, after breaking away from Ralph Lauren, he has filled a niche in the fashion world with his creations for men and, more recently, for women as well. For the contemporary individual seeking a façade that is as casual, elegant, and as international as the accompanying life, the Abboud wardrobe offers comfort, beauty, and a modernity that is equally suitable in New York, Milan, or Australia. Abboud was the first menswear designer in the United States to revolutionize the concept of American style.

Born in Boston, Abboud is hardly provincial. Something of an outsider, he did not come to fashion through the usual design school training and had no pre-established world in which to fit. Instead he

Joseph Abboud adjusting an item from his spring 2001 collection. © AP/Wide World Photos.

made his own. His approach to fashion was via studies in comparative literature, followed by study at the Sorbonne in Paris. His fall 1990 menswear collection Grand Tour pays homage to that experience with its romantic 1930s and 1940s designs, reminiscent of Hemingway, while his own rich ethnic background provided the depth of appreciation for global culture inherent in his work. Coming of age in the 1960s, Abboud began collecting early Turkish *kilims* (flat woven rugs) with their salient handcrafted quality and stylized geometric patterns. These motifs form a recurring theme in his work, from the handknit sweaters to the machine-knit shirts. The rugs themselves, in muted earthtones, complement the calm, natural environment of the Abboud stores. For Abboud, the presentation of the clothing mimics the aesthetics of the garments: soft, casual, and elegant in its simplicity.

Color, texture, and the cut of Abboud fashions express a style that lies between, and sometimes overlaps, that of Ralph Lauren and Giorgio Armani. The palette of the Joseph Abboud and the 1992 J.O.E. (Just One Earth) lines for both sexes is more subtle than the traditional Anglo-American colors of the preppie or Sloane Ranger genre, yet more varied in tone and hue than the sublimely unstated Armani colors. Neutrals from burnt sienna to cream, stucco, straw, and the colors of winter birch, together with naturals such as indigo and faded burgundy, are examples of some of the most alluring of Abboud dyestuffs.

The Pacific Northwest Collection, fall 1987, manifested rich hues, from black to maroon, but even these were harmonious, never ostentatious. The black of his leather jackets, fall 1992, appears like soft patches of the night sky due to the suppleness and unique surface treatment of the skins. The fabrics for Abboud designs represent the artist's diligent search for the world's finest materials and craftsmanship. His respect for textile traditions does not mean that his work is retrospective but that his inventiveness is grounded in the integrity of the classics. His interpretation of tweed, for example, although based on fine Scottish wool weavings, which he compares to the most beautiful artistic landscapes, differs from the conventional Harris-type tweed. Silk, alpaca, or llama are occasionally combined with the traditional wool to yield a lighter fabric.

Unique and demanding in his working methods, Abboud is at the forefront of contemporary fashion-fabric design. His fabrics drape with a grace and elegance that is enhanced by the oversize cut and fluid lines of his suits. His characteristically full, double-pleated trousers, for example, are luxurious. The romantic malt mohair gossamer-like fabrics for women in the fall 1993 collection are cut simply with no extraneous details. Even the intricate embroideries that ornament the surfaces of many of his most memorable designs, from North African suede vests with a Kashmiri *boteh* design to the jewel-like beadwork for evening, have a wearability uncommon in the contemporary artistic fashion.

Nature is Abboud's muse. Beyond the obvious J.O.E. line appellation, the theme of the bucolic environment provides inspiration for the garments. Country stone walls, pebbles on a beach, the light and earthtones of the Southwest are interpreted in exquisitely cut fabrics that embrace the body with a style that becomes an individual's second skin.

Abboud's easy, elegant style had translated into a $100 million business by 1997, with overseas sales accounting for about 35 percent of turnover. It was considered a healthy operation, but did not reach the heights of some of his better-known peers. In 1998 Abboud sought to boost his profile by entering into a strategic alliance with his 10-year licensee GFT USA, a subsidiary of the Italian company Holding de Participazioni Industriali (HdP). With the move, he hoped to increase synergies between Joseph Abboud Worldwide and GFT's J.A. Apparel subsidiary, both formed in 1996. The two businesses developed an integrated management structure and increased coordination among licensees.

Abboud launched an upscale black label line for men over 35 in 1999, intending to supplement his existing upper-moderate tailored clothing business. The products are sold in the designer's own shops and about 40 select doors at 10 leading retailers. They are manufactured in the U.S. using European fabrics.

In 2000 Abboud further cemented his relationship with GFT when the latter purchased Abboud's label and licensing rights for $65 million. Abboud plans to continue as creative director and chairman emeritus for at least five years. The Abboud labels generated an estimated $250 million in sales in 2000, with about 80 percent of that business from GFT, which produces and distributes Abboud's black and diamond label tailored clothing, sportswear and golfwear. The remaining sales come from 27 other licensees; Abboud's licensed lines include fragrances, furs, coats, lounge- and sleepwear, swimwear, timepieces, and home furnishings.

The GFT acquisition will enable expansion in key areas such as international distribution, golf, and women's wear, as well as boosting the company's retailing operation and enhancing the Joseph Abboud Environments bed and bath collection. GFT and Abboud are also considering the introduction of new collections, such as one geared toward younger men.

Abboud's business, at times, has been overshadowed by trendier labels such as Tommy Hilfiger, as well as by Italian designers who appeal to the same clientele. But his customer base—which includes several high-profile sports anchors and news anchor Bryant Gumbel—has long been loyal his earthy colors, use of texture, and his ability to combine the classic with the modern.

—Marianne T. Carlano; updated by Karen Raugust

ABERCROMBIE & FITCH COMPANY

American sportswear and outerwear retailer

Founded: in 1892 by David Abercrombie to sell camping supplies; joined by Ezra Fitch to become Abercrombie & Fitch, providing exclusive outdoor needs, including clothing and equipment. **Company History:** Moved to new Madison Avenue digs, 1917; filed for bankruptcy, 1977; bought by Oshman's Sporting Goods, 1978; bought by The Limited, 1988; Michael Jeffries became CEO, 1992; back in black ink, 1995; went public, 1996; spun off by Limited, 1998; introduced children's stores, 1998; launched Hollister stores, for younger teens, 2000; also publishes *A&F Quarterly* catalogue/magazine. **Company Address:** 6301 Fitch Path, New Albany, OH 43054 USA. **Company Website:** www.abercrombie.com.

Publications

On ABERCROMBIE & FITCH:

Articles

Paris, Ellen, "Endangered Species? Abercrombie & Fitch," in *Forbes,* 9 March 1987.

Brady, James, "Abercrombie & Fitch Forgets Its Days of Hem & Wolfie," in *Advertising Age,* 31 August 1998.

Cuneo, Alice Z., "Abercrombie Helps Revive Moribund Brand via Frat Chic," in *Advertising Age,* 14 September 1998.

"Fashion's Frat Boy," in *Newsweek,* 13 September 1999.

Young, Vicki M., "Catalogue Controversy Rages on as More States Criticize A&F," in *Women's Wear Daily,* 8 December 1999.

Goldstein, Lauren, "The Alpha Teenager," in *Forbes,* 20 December 1999.

Perman, Stacy, "Abercrombie's Beefcake Brigade," in *Time,* 14 February 2000.

Margaret McKegney, Margaret, "Brands Remain in the Closet for Gay TV Show," in *Ad Age Global,* December 2000.

Wilson, Eric, "A&F: The Butts Start Here," in *Women's Wear Daily,* 5 February 2001.

Elliott, Stuart, "Bowing to Nation's Mood, Retailer Cancels Issue of Racy Catalogue," in the *New York Times,* 17 October 2001.

* * *

Although Abercrombie & Fitch (A&F) has been around for about 110 years, most of its current customers could care less that it outfitted legendary explorers like arctic explorer Richard Byrd. The firm's clientèle is predominantly Generation X and Y, and the Abercrombie logo has gone way beyond its sturdy apparel and into the realm of cool.

Abercrombie & Fitch has come back from the brink of extinction several times since its founding in 1892 by David Abercrombie. Originally created to sell camping gear, Abercrombie met up with lawyer Ezra Fitch and expanded the business to include a myriad of products for the rugged outdoorsmen of the time. Yet A&F didn't cater to just anyone with a yen for adventure, but only to those who could afford to pay premium prices for high-quality goods. Among the firm's early adventurers were Rough Rider Teddy Roosevelt, Byrd, Charles "Lucky" Lindbergh, and Amelia Earhart; the next generation included Winston Guest and macho sportsman and writer Ernest Hemingway.

The company did a bumper business until the 1960s, when flower power and environmental awareness began to seep into the American consciousness. Abercrombie & Fitch's atmospheric stores, with mounted animal heads and stuffed dead animals, were soon out of sync with a country awash in change and protest. The majority of A&F merchandise catered to hunting and fishing enthusiasts, and blood sports lost their popularity as the decade ended and the 1970s began. Although the firm valiantly tried to expand its wares to appeal to more customers, A&F filed for Chapter 11 in 1977.

Oshman's Sporting Goods bought A&F in 1978 and hoped to parlay its fame into a broad mix of sporting goods and apparel, as well as a wide range of other products. The rescue failed, despite repeated attempts to revive the Abercrombie cachet. In 1988, clothier The Limited Inc. acquired the struggling A&F for $47 million, along with its 27 stores. The Limited, however, was an evolving retailer itself, having bought Victoria's Secret, Penhaligon's, Henri Bendel, and others in quick succession. The future of A&F, however, came in the form of Michael Jeffries, who took the reins as chief executive in 1992, when there were 35 rather unimpressive A&F stores dotting the nation. Jeffries had an unusual way of conducting business, from his 29-page employee manual to his maniacal detailing of each and every store.

Jeffries' know-how and marketing savvy were put to the test. He drastically overhauled Abercrombie's image to appeal to a younger, hipper crowd, doing away with anything but apparel and accessories. Jeffries wanted to entice the collegiate crowd into A&F and did so with creative advertising and making each A&F store a cool place to visit and spend money, with blaring popular music and a sales staff with attitude. By 1995 the retailer was not only in the black but a true cultural phenomenon. Abercrombie's logoed t-shirts and cargo pants became the must-have apparel for teenagers on up, which happened to be the fastest growing segment in retail.

To keep the momentum going, Jeffries initiated the *A&F Quarterly* (a slick magazine-like catalogue they call the "magalogue") and aggressive advertising. Both measures received much attention but brought the ire of parents, advocacy groups, and politicians when some of the material offered drinking tips and some content was deemed pornographic. Like Calvin Klein before him, Jeffries had pushed the envelope too far but had no remorse or plans to change his ways. In 1999 the company ran its first television ads, and the company hit a staggering milestone—breaking the $1-billion sales threshold.

By the end of the 20th century, the A&F magalogue was marketed only to more mature kids (18 and older with an ID to prove it) because of its emphasis on sex and "college-age" pursuits like partying. The younger crowd, of course, and virtually anyone buying Abercrombie had already bought the image along with the jeans, baggy pants, cargo shorts, and t-shirts. Though sales remained relatively solid, A&F had its share of troubles in the new millennium. Stock prices tumbled, its television ads didn't quite hit the mark, and as always, the firm continued to receive criticism for its *A&F Quarterly*. Oddly, in an instance when Jeffries could have reached millions of television viewers with his products, he refused to allow A&F clothing to appear in Showtime's *Queer As Folk* series—featuring young, hip, sexually active teens and adults doing all the things A&F showcased in its magalogue, with the exception that these pretty boys and girls were gay.

By 2001 Abercrombie had attempted to delineate its customers into three categories: for the younger or preteen crowd, it had launched Abercrombie stores in 1998; for teens and high schoolers, there was the newly introduced Hollister Co. in 2000; and older, college-aged buyers remained prime targets of traditional A&F stores. The latter group was also those to whom *A&F Quarterly* was addressed, but Jeffries seemed to have gone too far with the 2001 issue featuring the usual bevy of naked males and females. Bowing to pressure Jeffries pulled the issue, titled *XXX,* despite pleas that the magalogue was wrapped in plastic (like *Playboy*) and sold only to those with proof of their age.

Abercrombie & Fitch has proven itself a purveyor of more than just style, but of fashion advocating a particular lifestyle. Some quarrel with the firm's message and methods, but millions continue to pay premium prices for the simple apparel emblazoned with its name.

—Nelly Rhodes

ADOLFO

American designer

Born: Adolfo F. Sardiña in Cardenas, Cuba, 15 February 1933; immigrated to New York, 1948, naturalized, 1958. **Education:** B.A., St. Ignacious de Loyola Jesuit School, Havana, 1950. **Military Service:** Served in the U.S. Navy. **Career:** Apprentice millinery designer, Bergdorf Goodman, 1948–51; apprentice milliner at Cristobal Balenciaga Salon, Paris, 1950–52, and at Bergdorf Goodman, New York; designed millinery as Adolfo of Emmé, 1951–58; also worked as unpaid apprentice for Chanel fashion house, Paris, 1956–57; apprenticed in Paris with Balenciaga; established own millinery salon in New York, 1962, later expanded into women's custom clothing; designer, Adolfo Menswear and Adolfo Scarves, from 1978; perfume *Adolfo* launched, 1978; closed custom workroom to concentrate on his Adolfo Enterprises licensing business, 1993; debuted limited collection through Castleberry, 1995. **Exhibitions:** *Fashion: An Anthology,* Victoria & Albert Museum, London, 1971. **Collections:** Metropolitan Museum of Art, New York; Smithsonian Institution, Washington, D.C.; Dallas Museum of Fine Arts; Los Angeles County Museum of Art. **Awards:** Coty Fashion award, New York, 1955, 1969; Neiman Marcus award, 1956. **Member:** Council of Fashion Designers of America.

Publications

On ADOLFO:

Books

Morris, Bernadine, and Barbara Walz, *The Fashion Makers,* New York, 1978.

Diamonstein, Barbaralee, *Fashion: The Inside Story,* New York, 1985.

Milbank, Caroline Rennolds, *New York Fashion: The Evolution of American Style,* New York, 1989.

Stegemeyer, Anne, *Who's Who in Fashion, Third Edition,* New York, 1996.

Articles

"Adolfo," in *Current Biography* (New York), November 1972.

Standhill, Francesca, "The World of Adolfo," in *Architectural Digest,* December 1980.

"Oh Come All Ye Faithful to Adolfo," in *Chicago Tribune,* 19 June 1985.

"In Tune on Upscale Adolfo Dresses: The Illustrious," in *Chicago Tribune,* 22 June 1986.

Morris, Bernadine, "Adolfo in New York: A Richly Evocative Private Realm for the Celebrated Couturier," in *Architectural Digest,* September 1989.

Friedman, Arthur, "Always Adolfo," in *Women's Wear Daily,* 21 July 1992.
———, "Adolfo Closing His RTW Salon After 25 Years: Golden Era Ends," in *Women's Wear Daily,* 18 March 1993.
Schiro Anne-Marie, "Adolfo Decides It's Time to Stop Designing," in the *New York Times,* 19 March 1993.
"Adieu Adolfo," in *Chicago Tribune,* 24 March 1993.

*

To make clothes that are long-lasting and with subtle changes from season to season—this is my philosophy.

—Adolfo

* * *

In April of 1993, Adolfo closed his salon on New York's East 57th Street, after more than 25 years producing his classically elegant knit suits, dresses, and eveningwear. The outcry from his clientèle was emotional and indicative of the devotion his clothes inspired in his "ladies," including C.Z. Guest ("It's just a tragedy for me. He has such great taste, style, and manners…I've been wearing his clothes for years; they suit my lifestyle. He designs for a certain way of life that all these new designers don't seem to comprehend."); Jean Tailer ("I'm devastated…. He's the sweetest, most talented man. With Adolfo, you always have the right thing to wear."), and scores of others, such as Nancy Reagan, the Duchess of Windsor, Noreen Drexel, and Pat Mosbacher.

These loyal clients were among the many who returned to Adolfo season after season for clothes they could wear year after year, clothes that looked stylish and felt comfortable, style and comfort being the essence of his customers' elegant and effortless lifestyle.

Adolfo began his career as a milliner in the early 1950s, a time when hat designers were accorded as much respect and attention as dress designers. By 1955 he had received the Coty Fashion award for his innovative, often dramatic hat designs for Emmé Millinery. In 1962 Adolfo opened his own salon and began to design clothes to show with his hat collection. During this period, as women gradually began to wear hats less often, Adolfo's hat designs became progressively bolder. His design point of view held that hats should be worn as an accessory rather than a necessity, and this attitude was carried over into his clothing designs as well.

Adolfo's clothes of the late 1960s had the idiosyncratic quality characteristic of the period and, more importantly, each piece stood out on its own as a special item. This concept of design was incongruous with the American sportswear idea of coordinated separates but was consistent with the sensibility of his wealthy customers who regarded clothes, like precious jewelry, as adornments and indicators of their social status. Among the garments that captured the attention of clients and press during this period were felt capes, red, yellow, or purple velvet bolero jackets embroidered with jet beads and black braid, studded lace-up peasant vests, low-cut floral overalls worn over organdy blouses, and extravagant patchwork evening looks.

Adolfo remarked, in 1968, "Today, one has to dress in bits and pieces—the more the merrier." By 1969 he described his clothes as being "for a woman's fun and fantasy moods—I don't think the classic is appealing to people any more." Just one year later, however, he changed his point of view and at the same time increased the focus of his knits, which had been introduced in 1969. In a review of Adolfo's fall 1970 collection, Eugenia Sheppard, writing in the *New York Post,* declared "he has completely abandoned the costume look of previous years." Adolfo was always responsive to his customers' needs and this sudden change of direction probably reflected their reaction to the social upheavals and excesses of the last years of the 1960s.

By the early 1970s the 1930s look, inspired by films such as *Bonnie and Clyde* and *The Damned,* swept over fashion, drowning out the kooky individualism of seasons past. His explorations of this look led Adolfo, in 1973, to hit on what would become his signature item. Taking his cue from Coco Chanel's cardigan style suits of the 1930s, Adolfo translated the textured tweed into a pebbly knit, added a matching silk blouse, and came up with a formula his clients returned to over and over again until his retirement. These revivals of a classic became classics in their own right and the look became associated in America with Adolfo as much as with Chanel. Adolfo's collections were not limited to suits. When other American designers abandoned dresses for day in favor of sportswear separates, Adolfo continued to provide his customers with printed silk dresses appropriate for luncheons and other dressy daytime occasions. Adolfo's clients also relied on him for splendid eveningwear combining luxury with practicality. Typical evening looks included sweater knit tops with full satin or taffeta skirts, fur trimmed knit cardigans, silk pyjamas, and angora caftans.

After closing his salon to concentrate on marketing his licensed products, including perfumes, menswearm, furs, handbags, sportswear, and hats, Adolfo made numerous appearances at departments stores and on QVC to promote his name and products in the early and mid-1990s, which were valued at some $5-million annually. In late 1995, he returned to designing, with a limited collection sponsored by Castleberry.

The designer himself once remarked that "an Adolfo lady should look simple, classic, and comfortable." He brought modest and characteristically American design ideals to a higher level of luxury and charm, combining quality and style with comfort and ease. While in some fashion circles, seeing women similarily dressed was a serious fashion *faux pas,* with Adolfo designs, women were thrilled to see their high-brow selections reflected in social scene mirrors. According to the *Chicago Tribune* in 1986, "Adolfo Ladies revel in duplication, triplication, quadruplication and more—much, much more." All because, as Jean Tailer told the *Tribune,* "we all feel a security blanket in getting the best of the collection." Adolfo provided, as the *Tribune* aptly called it, a "social security," to his ladies and they gave him loyalty, devotion, and upwards of $2500 per suit.

—Alan E. Rosenberg; updated by Nelly Rhodes

ADRI

American designer

Born: Mary Adrienne Steckling in St. Joseph, Missouri, 7 November 1934. **Education:** Attended St. Joseph Junior College, 1953; studied retailing and design, Washington University (School of Fine Arts), St.

Adri, 1967: jersey minipants suit and shoes decorated with nail heads. © AP/Wide World Photos.

Louis, 1954–55, and fashion design at Parsons School of Design, New York, 1955–56; studied at the New School for Social Research, New York, 1956–57. **Family:** Married Fabio Coen, 1982. **Career:** Guest editor, *Mademoiselle,* college issue, 1955; design assistant for Oleg Cassini, Inc., New York, 1957–58; design assistant, later designer, B.H. Wragge, New York, 1960–67; opened Adri Designs Inc., 1966–67; formed Design Establishment, Inc. with Leonard Sunshine and the Anne Fogarty Co., New York, for the Clothes Circuit by Adri and Collector's Items by Adri division of Anne Fogarty, 1968–72; partner with William Parnes in Adri label for Paul Parnes's Adri Sporthoughts Ltd., 1972–74; designed for Ben Shaw company, 1975–76; Adri for Royal Robes, leisurewear, under license, 1976–77; Jerry Silverman Sport by Adri label, 1977–78; ADRI label collection for Jones New York, 1978–79; ADRI collection marketed by Habitat Industries, 1980–83; began as critic, Parsons School of Design, 1982; Japanese licensee N. Nomura & Co. Ltd, 1982–87; ADRI Collection marketed by Adri Clotheslab, 1983–87. Created Adri designer patterns for Vogue, 1982; designed several sportswear collections a year, selling to smaller specialty stores and private customers; joined Parsons School of Design faculty, 1991; corporate name changed to Adri Studio Ltd., 1994. **Exhibitions:** *Innovative Contemporary Fashion: Adri and McCardell,* Smithsonian Institution, Washington, D.C., 1971; various shows, Fashion Institute of Technology, New York City. **Awards:** Coty American Fashion Critics "Winnie" award, 1982; "International Best Five," Asahi Shimbun, Tokyo, 1986. **Member:** Council of Fashion Designers of America. **Address:** 143 West 20th Street, New York, NY, 10011, USA.

Publications

On ADRI:

Books

Lambert, Eleanor, *World of Fashion: People, Places, Resources,* New York, 1976.

Morris, Bernadine, and Barbara Walz, *The Fashion Makers,* New York, 1978.

Stegemeyer, Anne, *Who's Who in Fashion, Third Edition,* New York, 1996.

Articles

"The Find: Adri," in *Women's Wear Daily* (New York), 7 November 1966.

"Adri Opens the Door," in *Women's Wear Daily* (New York), 30 October 1968.

Banik, Sheila, "The Adventures of Adri: A Designer Goes From Wragge to Riches," in *Savvy* (New York), October 1980.

Burggraf, Helen, "Adri: Soft and Easy Designs for the Fast-Paced 1980s," in *New York Apparel News,* Spring 1982.

Morris, Bernadine, "Banks and Adri Win Coty Awards and Cheers," in the *New York Times,* 25 September 1982.

———, "From Ellis, a Casual Whimsicality," in the *New York Times,* 27 October 1982.

———, "A Sportswear Preview: Fall on Seventh Avenue," in the *New York Times,* 5 April 1983.

*

I believe in a "design continuum" of clothing that is essentially modern, that reflects the changing patterns of living, evolving gradually but continually.

Good design can be directional *and* timeless, functional and innovative in the tradition of American sportswear, and responsive to the needs of a woman equally committed to professional responsibilities and an enduring personal style.

—Adri

* * *

From the moment she fell in love with her first Claire McCardell dress while still a teenager—a dress she copied for herself many times because it fit her so well—Adri (Adrienne Steckling-Coen) idolized McCardell who, coincidentally, was one of her lecturers at the Parsons School of Design in New York. Adri's early years with B.H. Wragge taught her the principles of tailoring and mix-and-match separates, long a staple of American sportswear. Designing for Anne Fogarty reinforced the feminine focus of Adri's design philosophy. Always, she returned to McCardell's tenet of form following function. Shapes were simple, skimming the body without extraneous detail or fussiness, often based on the practicality of athletic wear. While McCardell favored dresses, Adri emphasized trousers, later designing skirt-length trousers, or culottes, for variety.

From the beginning Adri utilized soft, pliable fabrics such as knits, jerseys, crêpe de Chine, challis, and leather. Her clothes were identified by their floaty qualities and she maintained that this softness made them easy to wear and provided relief from the frequent harshness of modern life. They were also ideal for tall, long-limbed, slender figures like her own. During the late 1960s Adri presented V-necked short dresses with high waists or wrapped fronts, in solid colored synthetic jerseys. Natural fibers, such as unbleached linen, came of use in the 1970s and knits continued to be staples for Adri skirts, trousers, and tunics in various lengths. By 1980 a typical Adri evening look consisted of silk trousers topped by a strapless chenille top and fluid lace jacket.

Interchangeable neutral solids such as beige, black, and white were combined with bold primary colors so Adri's customers could collect the separates throughout the years and create their own ensembles, without having to purchase a new wardrobe each year. The simple timelessness of the designs, as well as their easy cut and fit, made this possible. Prices were in the moderate to better sportswear range.

Adri wore her own apparel to accept her Coty award in 1982: a belted silver-grey (she called it "platinum") mohair sweater over midcalf culottes made of grey suede. Soon afterwards she branched out into menswear, creating unisex sweaters, cardigans, and vests. Evening looks continued to be based on day shapes, but fabricated of highly colored striped shiny rayon or mohair. Pullovers, jackets, and vests were frequently long, and Adri kept experimenting with new materials, such as eelskin, for her contrasting boldly colored belts, or handloomed Japanese fabrics with interesting textures. A touch of the opulent 1980s was evident in her use of tapestry jackets to be worn with velvet trousers, as well as damask and silk Jacquard.

Clothes like these can be easily adapted for homesewers, and Adri contracted with Vogue Patterns during the mid-1980s for a relationship that continued into the 1990s. The same McCardell-inspired sporty yet fluid lines were evident; shirtwaist dresses with topstitching detail, softly gathered jackets, shaped hemlines with gracefully flounced skirts, cummerbund accents to shorten the appearance of tall, slim figures, gently gathered waists, and easy wrap dresses were some of the offerings available to seamstresses wishing to recreate Adri's classic multifunctional designs.

Since changing her corporate name to Adri Studio Ltd. in 1994, Adri has continued to design small collections. Hard at work in her New York studio, she has focused on designer collections exclusively. With her Egyptian partner, Nadia Abdella, Adri continues to fashion the fluid, timeless pieces for which she has always been known. "The concept," she says, "remains the same." This design concept was always, she noted, a very flexible, contemporary one and has continued into the 21st century quite successfully. She creates one exclusive designer collection a season that is both wholesale and retail. The Adri collections are available through exclusive stores and show in private clubs, such as The Ruins in San Francisco. This approach, both simple and consistent, and the adaptable charm and enduring quality of an Adri garment, have created a niche for the designer and, "It's working," she says.

—Therese Duzinkiewicz Baker; updated by Jessica Reisman

ADRIAN, Gilbert

American designer

Born: Gilbert Adrian Greenburgh in Naugatuck, Connecticut, 3 March 1903. **Education:** Studied at Parsons School of Design, New York and Paris, circa 1921–22. **Family:** Married Janet Gaynor in 1939; son: Robin. **Career:** Film and theater designer, New York, 1921–28; designer, MGM studios, Hollywood, 1928–39; ready-to-wear and custom clothing salon established, Beverly Hills, 1942–52; fragrances *Saint* and *Sinner* introduced, 1946; opened New York boutique, 1948; retired to Brasilia, Brazil, 1952–58; film designer, Los Angeles, 1958–59. **Exhibitions:** Retrospective, Los Angeles County Museum, circa 1967; retrospective, Fashion Institute of Technology, New York, 1971. **Awards:** Coty American Fashion Critics award, 1944. **Died:** 14 September 1959 in Los Angelos, California.

Joan Crawford modeling "Change," a two-piece silk dinner dress with gold paillettes designed by Gilbert Adrian for the film *Humoresque* (1946). © Bettmann/CORBIS.

Publications

By ADRIAN:

Articles

"Do American Women Want Clothes?" in *Harper's Bazaar* (New York), February 1934.

"Garbo as Camille," in *Vogue* (New York), 15 November 1936.

Gilbert Adrian, ca. 1935. © Bettmann/CORBIS.

"Clothes," in Stephen Watts, ed., *Behind the Screen: How Films Are Made,* London, 1938.

On ADRIAN:

Books

Powdermaker, Hortense, *The Dream Factory,* Boston, 1950.

Riley, Robert, *The Fashion Makers,* New York, 1968.

Lee, Sarah Tomerlin, ed., *American Fashion,* New York, 1975.

———, *American Fashion: The Life and Lines of Adrian, Mainbocher, McCardell, Norell, Trigère*, New York, 1975.

Lambert, Eleanor, *The World of Fashion: People, Places, Resources,* New York and London, 1976.

Pritchard, Susan, *Film Costume: An Annotated Bibliography,* Metuchen, New Jersey and London, 1981.

Milbank, Caroline Rennolds, *Couture: The Great Designers,* New York, 1985.

Maeder, Edward, et al., *Hollywood and History: Costume Design in Film,* New York, 1987.

Milbank, Caroline Rennolds, *New York Fashion: The Evolution of American Style,* New York, 1989.

Leese, Elizabeth, *Costume Design in the Movies,* New York, 1991.

Stegemeyer, Anne, *Who's Who in Fashion, Third Edition,* New York, 1996.

Gutner, Howard, *Gowns by Adrian: The MGM Years, 1928–1941*, New York, 2001.

Articles

Gordon, James, "One Man Who Suits Women," in *American Magazine* (Philadelphia), March 1946.

Obituary, the *New York Times,* 14 September 1959.

Sims, Joseph, "Adrian–American Artist and Designer," in *Costume,* 1974.

Kinsey, Sally Buchanan, "Gilbert Adrian: Creating the Hollywood Dream Style," in *Fiberarts* (Asheville, North Carolina), May/June 1987.

Lambert, Gavin, "Janet Gaynor and Adrian," in *Architectural Digest* (Los Angeles), April 1992.

* * *

By the time MGM costumer Gilbert Adrian went into business for himself in the middle of World War II, his potential customers were already familiar with his work. For over a decade American women had been wearing copies of the clothes he had designed for some of the most famous movie stars of all time. Adrian's ability to develop a screen character through the progression of costumes, be they period or modern, was translated into dressing the newly modern career women while men were away at war.

Adrian was primarily an artist, having trained in France, and was able to perceive Greta Garbo's true personality—aloof, mysterious, earthy—and change the way the studios dressed her; insisting upon genuine silks, laces, and jewels to lend authenticity to her performances. For all the stars he dressed, Adrian believed the quality of materials worn by a woman affected how she behaved in the clothes, even if the details were not immediately obvious. He brought the same philosophy to his custom and ready-to-wear creations. Of course the copies MGM permitted to be made of Adrian's costumes, timed to coincide with the releases of the films, were not always of the same fine quality as the originals, but the overall look was what women were after. While films provided a great escape from the dreariness of the American Depression, the famous white organdy dress with wide ruffled sleeves that Adrian designed for Joan Crawford in the movie *Letty Lynton* offered cheer and flattery. Macy's New York department store alone sold nearly half a million copies in 1932. The artist's eye perceived the need to balance Crawford's wide hips, and the broad shouldered typical "Adrian silhouette" triggered a fashion revolution in America and abroad.

For Jean Harlow in *Dinner at Eight,* Adrian created another widely copied sheer white bias-cut satin ballgown. Though Madeleine Vionnet invented the bias cut and Elsa Schiaparelli was credited with padded shoulders, at least in Europe, Adrian had the awareness to bring high fashion and glamour to the screen. Joan Crawford praised Adrian's emphasis on simplicity to make a dramatic point, as in the suits she wore in her later films. Even in lavishly costumed period dramas, Adrian was able to stop short of excess. Often, as in Garbo's *Mata Hari,* the character's evolution into purity of spirit would be expressed through increased simplicity of costume. Adrian's understanding of light and shadow made possible clothing that, due to clarity of line, looked as well in monochrome film as later black-and-white photographs of his commercial designs would show. His eye for perfect cut was impeccable. A day suit consisting of a beige wool jacket trimmed with loops of black braid, paired with a slim black skirt, black gloves, and beige cartwheel hat, looks as crisp and smart today as it did when featured in *Vogue* in 1946. Fluid floor-length crêpe gowns were dramatically yet whimsically decorated with asymmetrical motifs of horses, cherubs, or piano keys, or his taste for modern art would be indulged in gowns made up of abstract jigsaw puzzle shapes in several colors.

Just as in films Adrian worked within themes, so did his collections for Adrian, Ltd. develop according to such themes as gothic, Grecian, Persian, Spanish, or Americana. For the latter he appliquéd Pennsylvania Dutch designs on gowns and made tailored suits and bustled evening gowns out of checked gingham, echoing the gingham checks worn by Judy Garland in *The Wizard of Oz.* Adrian costumed Garbo as the essence of romance in *Camille,* not only in 19th-century crinolines, but in white nightgown (which could have been any female viewer's late day dinner dress) for the film's death scene. For his average American customer, Adrian recommended clothes like the "costumes worn by the heroines of light comedies…in moderate-sized towns." Katharine Hepburn in *The Philadelphia Story* was dressed by Adrian as the ideal girl next door, while conservative Norma Shearer mirrored the sophisticated simplicity of Adrian's future well-heeled Beverly Hills clients in *The Women.*

The spare, padded-shouldered, narrow waisted and skirted silhouette of the 1940s was the ideal medium for Adrian's artistry with fabric, while conforming to the wartime L-85 restrictions on materials—the U.S. government limitation on the amount of fabric used in a civilian garment for public consumption. The color inserts, appliqués, mitering of striped fabrics and combinations of materials in one ensemble allowed for savings in rationed fabrics, while creating the trademark Adrian look which was desired then and is still sought after by vintage clothing collectors. Old-time movie glamor would resurface in some of Adrian's elegant columns of crêpe, diagonally embellished by headed bands of ancient motifs, or thick gilt embroidery on dark backgrounds. Diagonal lines and asymmetry also lent interest, as in a short-sleeved wartime suit sewn of half plaid and half wool—completed by a hat trimmed in plaid edging. Having grown up observing his father's millinery trade, Adrian had included hats in his movie costuming and his designs, such as Garbo's slouch, cloche, and Eugenie, were widely copied in the 1930s.

Adrian unsuccessfully resisted Dior's round-shouldered New Look. Men returned from the war, and women returned to the home. Decades later, with the resurgence of women into the workforce, Adrian's broad shouldered looks enabled women to compete confidently with men, as designers resurrected the masterpieces of this truly American fashion virtuoso.

—Therese Duzinkiewicz Baker

ADROVER, Miguel

Spanish designer

Born: Majorca, Spain, December 1965. **Education:** Left school at the age of 12 to work on the family farm. **Career:** Teamed with American tailor Douglas Hobbs to launch clothing line Dugg, 1995; opened boutique, Horn, in New York's East Village, 1995–99; launched first collection Manaus-Chiapas-NYC, 1999; launched second collection, Midtown, 2000; received financial backing from the Pegasus Apparel Group to produce Miguel Adrover line, 2000. **Awards:** Council of Fashion Designers, Best New Designer of the Year, 2000.

Miguel Adrover, spring 2001 collection. © Fashion Syndicate Press.

Publications

On ADROVER:

Articles

Hume, Marion, "Miguel Takes Manhattan," in *Harper's Bazaar,* May 2000.

Bee, Deborah, "Uniform Chic Puts Avant Garde Into Everyday Wear," in *The Guardian,* 19 September 2000.

Moore, Beth, "Rebel Designers Deconstruct Fashion Genres, Assumptions," in the *Los Angeles Times,* 22 September 2000.

Goldstein, Lauren, "From New York, Miguel Adrover's Moneyed Moment," in *Time,* October 2000.

Jones, Rose Apodace, "Educating Adrover," in *Women's Wear Daily,* 2 October 2000.

Wilson, Eric, "The School of Miguel," in *Women's Wear Daily,* 2 February 2001.

McCants, Leonard, and Julee Greenberg, "Gritty and Pretty: A New Niche Emerges in NYC's East Village," in *Women's Wear Daily,* 13 February 2001.

Miguel Adrover, fall 2001 collection. © Fashion Syndicate Press.

Menkes, Suzy, "Adrover's Egyptian Odyssey," in the *International Herald Tribune,* 13 February 2001.

Porter, Charlie, "Designer Storms Fashion Desert," in *The Guardian,* 13 February 2001.

Thurman, Judith, "Combat Fatique," in the *New Yorker,* March 2001.

Collins, James, "One Year Later," in the *New Yorker,* April 2001.

Morra, Bernadette, "Designer Gives New Life to Old Classics," in the *Toronto Star,* 21 September 2001.

* * *

Miguel Adrover is a self-trained fashion designer who quit school at the age of 12 to work on the family farm located on the island of Majorca, Spain, in a small village called Calonge. His first inspiration into the fashion world came when he visited London as a teenager, where he was exposed to punk rock and the New Romantics. In his village, he became the one who was always into the latest music and punky clothes. He served in the army in his late teens and upon discharge ran a bar in Spain.

On his first visit to New York in 1991, Adrover decided to stay. He worked as a janitor and lived in a tiny basement apartment. Four years later, in 1995, he befriended a Native American tailor, Douglas Hobbs, and together they made and sold t-shirts. The same year, they opened the Horn boutique in New York's East Village. Horn soon became the playing ground for young designers from New York and London who didn't have any other place to show their clothes. These designers included Alexander McQueen, Bernadette Corporation, and Bless. Horn also carried labels such as Dugg, Bruce, and As Four. Adrover and Hobbs closed the boutique in March 1999 to concentrate on designing women's clothing.

With many friends but little money, Adrover turned out his first collection, Manaus-Chiapas NYC, at a Latin theater in New York's Lower East Side in the summer of 1999. The collection was about the journey of a woman, kicked out of her surroundings, who is struggling yet nonetheless very strong. Adrover received some favorable press, but could not afford and did not attempt to market the clothes since he had only $5 in his pocket. Although he was a newcomer to the world of fashion, he was seen as a rising star after his showing.

His second show, for fall 2000, took place in a rundown theater in the Lower East Side in February and was titled "Midtown." Adrover wanted to show the paradox of different classes of people mixing on the sidewalks of New York City, where one finds middle-class, homeless, and upper-class people. The show's theme was his interpretation of pedestrians on the streets, and drew many of the fashion world's most important people, including Anna Wintour, chief editor of American *Vogue,* and Cathy Horyn, fashion journalist for the *New York Times.* The Midtown showing had been financed by *Vogue,* who paid Adrover a settlement of $12,000 after his samples were stolen from the magazine's offices.

The collection was made up of borrowed classics from past designers which Adrover turned into works of art, using deconstruction and reconstruction. He flipped Burberry macs inside out, took a Louis Vuitton bag and made it into a miniskirt, and transformed writer and neighbor Quentin Crisp's mattress into an overcoat. The coat has become somewhat of a legend in itself—since everyone who worked on it developed a terrible rash.

After the Midtown show, Adrover was suddenly the next superstar fashion designer. He was soon signed by the Pegasus Group, and Judith Thurman of the *New Yorker* called him "a phenom." The eponymous Miguel Adrover collection debuted in May 2000 to high praise and was sold to stores worldwide. Adrover went to Italy to buy his fabrics, from old bolts of cloth, for the 36-piece collection. Adrover's designs can now be found in stores in the U.S., Europe, and the Far East.

In February 2001, Adrover showed his fourth collection, "Meeteast," an Egyptian-inspired presentation for which he spend six weeks in Egypt in order to develop ideas. The showing was a trip around the Arab world, filled with exotic designs, and like his previous collections, received much media hype—though not all positive. Meeteast was somewhat of an oddity in the fashion world, featuring military looks with traditional Arab, colonial, and missionary garments. Models wore harem pants, tunics, and supple knits; some fabrics had been soaked in the Nile River to alter their color while also allowing Adrover to make a political statement about the Third World.

Adrover is a rising star in the fashion industry, another retelling in the classic story of the American dream. "I would love to be considered a classic," the designer told *W* magazine, yet his version of "classic" would surely have a twist, as he aspires to be "a modern classic, an abstract classic."

—Donna W. Reamy

AGHION, Gaby

See CHLOÉ

AGNÈS B.

French designer

Born: Born Agnès Troublé in Versailles, France, 26 November 1942. **Family:** Married Christian Bourgois, 1958 (divorced); two additional marriages and divorces; five children. **Career:** Junior fashion editor, *Elle* magazine, Paris, 1964; designer, press attaché, and buyer for Dorothée Bis, Paris, 1965–66; freelance designer for Limitex, Pierre d'Alby, V de V, and Eversbin, Paris, 1966–75; set up CMC (Comptoir Mondial de Création) holding company for Agnès B., 1975; established first Agnès B. boutique in Les Halles, Paris, April 1975; opened second-hand shop in same street as boutique, 1977; created American subsidiary of CMC and first American boutique in Soho, New York, 1980; opened men's and children's boutique Agnès B. Enfant, Paris, 1981; license with Les Trois Suisses for mail order of selected items, 1982; opened Agnès B. Lolita boutique for teenagers, also opened La Galerie du Jour art gallery/bookshop, Paris, with ex-husband, 1984; launched Le B perfume, skincare and cosmetics products, and a maternity collection, 1987; launched ranges of sunglasses and watches, 1989; launched Le petit b.b. perfume for children, 1990; launched Courant d'air perfume, 1992; established many shops in France and worldwide, including Japan, London, and the United States. **Collections:** Musée des Arts de la Mode, Paris; Musée du Louvre, Paris. **Awards:** Order of Merit for Export, Paris. **Address:** 17 rue Dieu, 75010 Paris, France.

Publications

On AGNÈS B.:

Books

Stegemeyer, Anne, *Who's Who in Fashion, Third Edition,* New York, 1996.

Articles

Voight, R., "Success Par Excellence," in *Passion* (Paris), March 1983.

Jonah, Kathleen, "How to Live Straight from the Heart," in *Self,* October 1983.

Petkanas, Christopher, "Agnès B. from A to Z," in *Women's Wear Daily,* 22 April 1985.

Bleichroeder, Ingrid, "A Certain Style: Agnès B," in *Vogue* (London), January 1986.

"Agnès B.," in *Cosmopolitan* (London), September 1987.

Tretlack, Philippe, "Agnès B: Chez les Soviets," in *Elle* (Paris), 26 October 1987.

"Agnès B. Good," in the *Daily News Record* (New York), 2 May 1988.

Bucket, Debbie, "French Dressers," in *Clothes Show* (London), March 1989.

Tredre, Roger, "A Design Plan for No Seasons," in *The Independent* (London), 16 November 1989.

Weisman, Katherine, "Success Is the Key of Agnès B.," in *Women's Wear Daily,* 15 December 1994.

Socha, Miles, "French Fashion Retailer Agnès B. Plans to Open Its Eighth U.S. Store," in the *Daily News Record,* 13 November 1996.

Edelson, Sharon, "Agnès B.: Will She Play the Midwest?" in *Women's Wear Daily,* 14 November 1996.

Larson, Soren, "Agnès B.'s Stealth Launch," in *Women's Wear Daily,* 7 February 1997.

Levine, Lisbeth, "French Connection: Parisian Designer's Trend-Defying Fashions Put the Accent on Personal Style," in *Chicago Tribune,* 30 March 1997

Attias, Laurie, "B.-Watch," in *ARTnews,* Summer, 2000.

* * *

Agnès B. (the B stands for Bourgois, from her first marriage) is a French sportswear designer who has catapulted herself to fame by challenging the need for fashion in clothing design. She denies that clothes must be stylized, highly detailed, and ephemeral in order to catch the public imagination. Her ascent began in the mid-1970s when, after only a few years in the fashion business, first as junior editor at *Elle* magazine and then briefly as an assistant to Dorothée Bis, she opened her own boutique in a converted butcher shop in Les Halles, Paris, to sell recut and redyed French workers' uniforms, black leather blazers, and t-shirts in striped rugby fabric. Her reputation grew as one of the first young French clothing designers to sell fashion to those who did not want to look too fashionable. In fact, her clothes, while identifiably French in their no-nonsense cut, simple subdued colors (often black), and casual mood, have a timeless quality that keeps them current. The wrinkling common to natural materials and the already-worn look that characterized the hippie ethos were translated by Agnès B. into a timeless chic, combining common sense with flair.

In the age of name identification and personal marketing, Agnès B. is as respected for her business sense as for her relaxed fashion designs. The spontaneous, childlike hand with which she quickly fashioned the logo for her stores belies a sophisticated business sense. Retaining her own independent boutique rather than being swallowed up in larger department stores, she astutely perceived that the nondesign of her clothes was too inconspicuous, and that they would blend in with other, trendier lines, and be lost. She opened over a dozen shops in France, of which seven are in Paris, with branches in Amsterdam, London, Tokyo, and the United States (including Boston, Chicago, Los Angeles, and New York).

Her understated approach to design for real people (men and children, as well as women) extends to her shows, which she has called working sessions, where professional models are rarely used, and her stores, in which casual and friendly salespeople mix their own antique or mod clothes with her separates. All the stores exude the same comfortable look, with pale wooden floors, white walls, and the occasional decorative tile. The flimsy curtain that separates the display area from the communal dressing rooms is an implication of the marginal distinction between Agnès B. clothes and what everyone else is wearing.

Agnès B. has managed to keep her family-run business a success for several reasons. Her designs reflect the lives of her customers, speaking more to purpose than to style. She generally produces two collections per year but adds regularly to the collections throughout the year. She keeps the business organized by using a computerized management method of production, delivery, and inventory and keeps the boutiques and stores happy by delivering frequently and consistently. Her customers remain content because the quality of the clothing is consistent. Interestingly, unlike most designers, she keeps some items in her collection for several seasons; "You can't destabilize the client.... Customers want to see some constant pieces." Her clientèle includes women, men, and children and have been described as "cultish."

Her designs have been popular in Europe, the Far East, and in several cities in the United States. In the early 1990s, she expanded her American market, and by 1996, she had a total of eight stores in the U.S., with plans to open several more. By 1997 there were 93 worldwide stores, generating some $260 million annually. Next came the opening of a new store in Chicago, Illinois, and the launch of a beauty products line of skin care, makeup, and four fragrances to the U.S. market. Agnès B. is known for her display windows, which are characteristically devoid of mannequins—where she merely hangs the clothes on hangers and the accessories are strewn about. She also includes movie posters in the display, which have become one of her trademarks.

Agnès B. strikes a commercial and creative balance—a radical chic. "I have no desire to dress an elite," she states. "It's all a game. I work as if I were still in my grandmother's attic, dressing up. Clothes aren't everything. When they become too important, when they hide the person wearing them, then I don't like them. Clothes should make you feel happy, relaxed, and ready to tackle other problems."

—Sarah Bodine; updated by Christine Miner Minderovic

AKIRA

Japanese designer

Born: Maki Akira, Oita, Japan, circa 1949. **Education:** Graduated from Oita University; worked for and studied fashion with Reiko Minami, Tokyo. **Career:** Moved to New York, 1974; tailor, Halston, 1976–81; showed first own collection, 1982; began designing wedding dresses for high-end department stores, from late 1990s.

Publications

On AKIRA:

Articles

Morris, Bernadine, "Bolder Designs for Evening," in the *New York Times,* 27 August 1985.

Hyde, Ann, "Akira on Bias," in *Threads* (Newtown, Connecticut), October/November 1991.

Horyn, Cathy, "Saying 'I Do' to a Radical Gown," in the *New York Times,* 4 January 2000.

"Akira," available online at First View Collections Online, www.firstview.com, 30 September 2001.

"Fashion Victim," available online at www.fashionvictim.com, 30 September 2001.

* * *

In the romantic imagination, the artist thrives on alienation, a critical distancing of an "other." Akira is of two worlds. In Japan, he is addressed by his surname, Maki; in America, he uses his first name, Akira. These are social conventions of two cultures, but they are also the theses and antitheses propagating Akira's fashion. An American designer when he designs ready-to-wear clothing in Japan, Akira is conversely viewed in America as a Japanese designer working for the American custom market. He is, however, both and neither; his state is only relaxed elegance. After studying and first designing in Japan, he came to New York to work with Halston, having been inspired by the work of Halston he found in American fashion magazines.

After working with Halston until 1981, when Akira established his own business, he has become a designer of two identities, with businesses in two countries and a single design philosophy, a synthesis of East and West. In Akira's custom business in New York, he creates out of the distilled, almost astringent principles of design he has maintained since working for Halston, with stress on bias cut, quality materials, color, and timeless elegance. His American custom clients come to him for a sense of personal comfort and self-assured dignity. While some of his American dresses, often bridal gowns, are adorned with beadwork and other decoration, their principle is in the cut. His is the abiding modernist conviction of truth to material and essential geometries of cut that animated Halston. An external simplicity, like that of a composed Japanese interior or a modern Western painting, is achieved through decisive reductivism and the primacy of the fabric.

In his Japanese productions, Akira creats clothing for young women of Japan no less elegant than their American counterparts but perhaps more fashion forward. His suits for daywear and early evening emphasize a comfortable, soft shaping inspired in part by Claude Montana. American sportswear inspirations for the collection in Japan, like Claire McCardell, help create what Akira has acknowledged is a "very American look" reflective of the emergence of Japanese women in the 1980s and 1990s into active, comfortable American lifestyles.

Ann Hyde, writing in the October/November 1991 issue *Threads,* pointed to the seeming contradiction between Akira's intellect in design and his sensuous achievement. "He is a rationalist at heart," states Hyde, referring to his intense interest in the underlying mathematics and geometry of garments, but he is also a designer of supreme elegance and grace. The unifying factor, like that of Renaissance architecture, is proportion, indivisibly a coolly mathematical calculation and a supremely romantic sensibility.

Citing that he learned from Halston the value of the designer looking in the mirror, seeing front, back, and side in cubist simultaneity and seeing thereby the garment as paramount—not the wearer—Akira points out that the mirror's impression is more canny than the human eye in discerning proportion and balance. Working in the custom design studio of Halston and in his own design business in New York reinforced Akira's principle of design specific to the client but generic to the design ideal in proportion. The same idea is carried through in the ready-to-wear collections in Japan.

Bias has always been an essential feature of Akira's designs, allowing both his design primacy and comfort in wearing. Recalling Halston's layered chiffons as "outrageously beautiful" in color and draping, Akira has used bias to wrap the form, conceiving of fashion not as a series of planes but as continuous volume realized three-dimensionally in the twist and torque of bias. Some collections were inspired by Byzantine art and Turkish culture; others by early Netherlands paintings, especially the work of Jan van Eyck.

Akira's good business sense has kept him afloat in the high flux of the fashion world as it reached an end of a strong economy and a sure decline in client investment in luxury clothes, furs, and accessories. The 21st century found him supplying high-end, avant-garde bridal gowns to Barneys New York, the prewedding mecca of the smart set. Within the new bridal salon, a source of a new trend toward chic understated wedding wear, Akira's line rubbed hangers with the likes of Vera Wang, Jil Sander, Christian Lacroix, and Geoffrey Beene.

If East and West, reason and style have been the antipodes of Akira's work, there is careful synthesis in Akira's garments in both the 20th and 21st centuries. It is an impressive joining of Japanese formality, American simplicity, the restraint of design, and the universal common sense of comfortable, wearable, and yet beautiful clothing.

—Richard Martin; updated by Mary Ellen Snodgrass

ALAÏA, Azzedine

French designer

Born: Tunis, Tunisia, circa 1940. **Education:** Studied sculpture, École des Beaux-Arts, Tunis. **Career:** Dressmaker's assistant, Tunis; dressed private clients before moving to Paris, 1957; part-time design assistant, Guy Laroche, Thierry Mugler, 1957–59; au pair/dressmaker for the Marquise de Mazan, 1957–60, and for Comtesse Nicole de Blégiers, 1960–65; designer, custom clothing, from 1960; introduced ready-to-wear line, Paris, 1980, and New York, 1982; opened boutiques, Beverly Hills, 1983, Paris, 1985, and New York, 1988–92.

Azzedine Alaïa in 1986. © CORBIS.

Exhibitions: *Retrospective*, Bordeaux Museum of Modern Art, 1984–85; *Retrospective*, New York, 2000. **Awards:** French Ministry of Culture Designer of the Year award, 1985. **Address:**18 rue de la Verrerie, 75004 Paris, France.

PUBLICATIONS

By ALAÏA:

Books

Alaïa, Azzedine, and Michel Tournier, *Alaïa,* Göttingen, Germany, 1990.

Parent, Marc (ed.), *Stella,* New York, 2001; Introduction by Alaïa Azzedine.

On ALAÏA:

Books

Howell, Georgina, *Sultans of Style: Thirty Years of Fashion and Passion 1960–1990,* London, 1990.

Stegemeyer, Anne, *Who's Who in Fashion, Third Edition,* New York, 1996.

Articles

McCall, Patricia, "Expanded Horizons for Azzedine Alaïa," in the *New York Times Magazine,* 5 September 1982.

"Now that Fit is It, No One Shapes Up Better than French Designer Azzedine Alaïa," in *People,* 27 December 1982.

Morris, Bernadine, "The Directions of the Innovations," in the *New York Times Magazine,* 27 February 1983.

Talley, Andre Leon, "Azzedine Alaïa," in *Interview,* June 1983.

"Stirrups Sport Style: Trousers Worn with Glamour and Ease," in *Vogue,* September 1984.

"Fashion Meets the Body: Azzedine Alaïa on Splendid Form," in *Vogue* (London), July 1985.

Ettlinger, Catherine, "This Man Has Brought Back the Body," in *Mademoiselle,* October 1985.

Salholz, Eloise, "The Man Who Loves Women," in *Newsweek,* 21 October 1985.

White, Lesley, "At Long Last Alaïa, the Chic of Araby," in *Elle* (London), November 1985.

Buck, Joan Juliet, "Body Genius: Designer Azzedine Alaïa," in *Vogue,* November 1985.

"The Azzedine Mystique," in *Vogue,* February 1986.

Arroyuelo, Javier, "L'art de vivre d'Azzedine Alaïa," in *Vogue* (Paris), March 1986.

Dryansky, G. Y., "An Eye for Allure," in *Connoisseur,* August 1986.

Worthington, Christa, "The Rise and Fall of Azzedine Alaïa," in *Women's Wear Daily,* 17 October 1986.

"Trois Créateurs: Leur Classiques, Azzedine Alaïa, la Perfection des Lignes," in *Elle* (Paris), 10 November 1986.

"Alaïa: La Passion du Vert," in *Elle* (Paris), March 1987.

Gross, Michael, "The Evolution of Alaïa: A New Ease Takes Over," in the *New York Times,* 31 March 1987.

Drier, Deborah, "The Defiant Ones," in *Art in America* (New York), September 1987.

"Alaïa: The Total Look," in *Elle* (Paris), 26 October 1987.

"Finally Alaïa Shows—to Mixed Reaction," in *Women's Wear Daily,* 13 November 1987.
"The New Spirit of Azzedine Alaïa," in *Vogue,* February 1988.
"La Femme un peu Provocante d'Alaïa," in *Elle* (Paris), 4 April 1988.
"Atmosphère Alaïa," in *Vogue* (Paris), August 1988.
"Alaïa e Gaultier: Due Stilisti a Confronto," in *Vogue* (Milan), October 1988.
"24 Heures de la Vie d'un Tailleur," in *Elle* (Paris), 24 October 1988.
Nonkin, Leslie, "Azzedine Addicts: Affection Turns to Affliction for Alaïa's Curvaceous Clothes," in *Vogue,* November 1988.
"Le Printemps d'Azzedine Alaïa," in *Elle* (Paris), 20 February 1989.
Maiberger, Elise, "Azzedine Alaïa's Late Late Show," in *Vogue* (London), March 1989.
Scott, Jan, "Call This Man Alaïa," in *Paris Passion,* March/April 1989.
"All About Alaïa," in *Elle* (New York), April 1989.
Gross, Michael, "Azzedine When He Sizzles," in *New York,* 15 May 1989.
Radakovich, Anka, "Downtown Chic," in *Harper's Bazaar,* November 1989.
Howell, Georgina, "The Titan of Tight," in *Vogue,* March 1990.
Roberts, Michael, "Alaïa, Alaïa, Style on Fire," in the *Sunday Times Magazine* (London), 25 March 1990.
Lennard, Jonathan, "Alaïa," in *Paris Passion,* July 1990.
Howell, Georgina, "Acting Up for Azzedine," in the *Sunday Times Magazine* (London), 7 October 1990.
Schnabel, Julian, "Azzedine Alaïa," in *Interview* (New York), October 1990.
Schiro, Anne-Marie, "Alaïa for the Slim and Curvaceous," in the *New York Times,* 5 April 1992.
Lindbergh, Peter, "Such Allure, Such Alaïa," in *Interview,* June 1992.
"Azzedine Alaïa," in *Current Biography,* October 1992.
Donovan, Carrie, "Alaïa's Devoted Fans," in the *New York Times,* 15 December 1992.
Spindler, Amy, "Alaïa and Léger Loosen Up a Bit," in the *New York Times,* 20 March 1993.
"Boiled Becomes Cool," in the *New York Times,* 3 April 1994.
Sischy, Ingrid, "The Outsider," in the *New Yorker,* 7 November 1994.
Horyn, Cathy, "Meeting the Enemy: Overstimulation," in the *New York Times,* 7 March 2000.
———, "Genius Has a Habit of Showing Up Every so Often," in the *New York Times,* 2 May 2000.
Middleton, William, and Craig McDean, "Giant," in *Harper's Bazaar,* August 2000.
Horyn, Cathy, "For Alaïa, a Retrospective and a New Deal," in the *New York Times,* 23 September 2000.

* * *

Dubbed the King of Cling by the fashion press in the 1980s, Azzedine Alaïa inspired a host of looks energizing High Street fashion, including the stretch mini, Lycra cycling shorts, and the bodysuit. His designs were renowned for displaying the female body and, accordingly, bedecked the bodies of off-duty top models and stars such as Tina Turner, Raquel Welch, Madonna, Brigitte Nielson, Naomi Campbell, and Stephanie Seymour. Alaïa's clothes caught the mood of the times when many women had turned to exercise and a new, muscled body shape had begun to appear in the pages of fashion magazines. Many women wanted to flaunt their newly-toned bodies, helped by recent developments in fabric construction that enabled designers to create clothing to accentuate the female form in a way unprecedented in European fashion.

Prior to his success in the 1980s, Alaïa studied sculpture at the School of Beaux-Arts in Tunis. He moved to Paris in 1957 and lived in a tiny apartment on the Left Bank, paying his rent and bills by babysitting while pursuing his dreams. He apprenticed to Christian Dior for five days before landing a two-year stint (1957–59) as a part-time design assistant for Guy Laroche and Thierry Mugler. He also served as an au pair and dressmaker for the likes of the Marquise de Mazan and the Comtesse Nicole de Blégiers (1957–65). He began designing private works in 1960, and his elite clientele eventually expanded to include Greta Garbo, Claudette Colbert, Cécile de Rothschild, and French film star Arletty.

Following in the footsteps of the ancien régime of Parisian haute couture, Alaïa is a perfectionist about cut, drape, and construction, preferring to work directly on the body to achieve a perfect fit. Tailoring is his great strength—he does all his own cutting—and although his clothes appear very simple, they are complex in structure. Some garments contain up to 40 individual pieces linked together to form a complex mesh that moves and undulates with the body. The beauty of his design comes from the shape and fit of the garments, enhanced by his innovative use of crisscross seaming.

His method of clothing construction includes repeated fitting and cutting on the body. His technique of sculpting and draping perhaps comes naturally to him, since he studied sculpture at L'École des Beaux-Arts in Tunis, but also owes much to Madeleine Vionnet, the great *tailleur* of the 1920s, famed for the intricacies of her bias-cut crêpe dresses that molded closely to the body. Vionnet applied the delicate techniques of lingerie sewing to outerwear, as has Alaïa, who combines the stitching and seaming normally used in corsetry to achieve the perfect fit of his clothes. Combined with elasticated fabrics for maximum body exposure, his garments hold and control the body, yet retain their shape.

Although, at first sight, Alaïa's clothes seem to cling to the natural silhouette of the wearer, they actually create a second skin, holding in and shaping the body by techniques of construction such as faggoting. This body consciousness is further enhanced by using materials such as stretch lace over flesh-colored fabric to give an illusion, rather than the reality, of nudity.

Alaïa introduced his first ready-to-wear collection of minimalist clothes in 1980 and continued to work privately for individual customers until the mid-1980s. Although his clothes are indebted to the perfection of the female body and indeed, at times, expose great expanses of skin, he manages to avoid vulgarity with muted colors and expert tailoring. He introduced riveted leather, industrial zippers, and a wide range of fabrics, including lace, leather, polymers, silk jersey, and tweed.

Sometime in the mid-1990s, Alaïa vanished from the fashion scene, although in an August 2000 interview in *Harper's Bazaar,* Alaïa insists he "never went anywhere." In 2000, he burst back into the limelight with a new collection. The new look was a drastic departure from his previous sexy, on-the-edge designs. This collection, described as "much more sober, almost Amish in comparison" by critics, has as its centerpiece the pleat, accentuated by long, Alpine-inspired flower-printed skirts, girly knit dresses, and bead-bedecked leather pleated kilt-style skirts. His classic designs of the

1980s are also being adapted by designers such as Helmut Lang, Marc Jacobs, Narciso Rodriguez, Nicolas Ghesquíre, and Rei Kawakubo for the likes of Louis Vuitton, Balenciaga, and Loewe. Alaïa also had a retrospective exhibition in September 2000, with an all-star cast turning out to honor him, including fellow designer Calvin Klein, supermodels Stephanie Seymour, Iman, Heidi Klum, and Naomi Campbell, as well as Jocelyne Wildenstein, Polly Mellen, Kate Betts, Daryl Kerrigan, Amanda Lepore, David LaChapelle, and Sigourney Weaver.

In a surprising move, Alaïa joined forces with Miuccia Prada's label as a designer, joining Lang, and Prada herself. Alaïa will continue to handle all distribution in France from his boutique in Paris, and Prada will handle his worldwide distribution.

Alaïa shows regularly but nevertheless seems above the whims and vagaries of the fashion world, producing timeless garments, rather than designing new looks from season to season, and inspiring the adulation of enthusiastic collectors that was once reserved for Mariano Fortuny.

—Caroline Cox; updated by Daryl F. Mallett

ALBINI, Walter

Italian designer

Born: Born Gualtiero Albini in Busto Arsizio, near Milan, 9 March 1941. **Education:** Studied fashion and costume design, Istituto Statale di Belle Arti e Moda, Turin, 1959–61. **Career:** Illustrator for *Novità* and *Corriere Lombardo* periodicals, Milan, and freelance sketch artist, Paris, 1961–64; freelance designer for Krizia, Billy Ballo, Basile, Callaghan, Escargots, Mister Fox, Diamantis, Trell, Mario Ferari, Lanerossi, Kriziamaglia, Montedoro, and Princess Luciana, Milan, 1964–83; established Walter Albini fashion house, Milan, 1965; signature ready-to-wear collection introduced, 1978; Walter Albini Fashions branches established, London, Rome, Venice. **Died:** 31 May 1983, in Milan.

Publications

On ALBINI:

Books

Vercelloni, Isa, and Flavio Lucchini, *Milano Fashion,* Milan, 1975.

Mulassano, Adriana, *The Who's Who of Italian Fashion,* Florence, 1979.

Soli, Pia, *Il genio antipatico,* Venice, 1984.

Buiazzi, Graziella, ed., *La moda italiana: Dall'antimoda allo stilismo,* Milan, 1987.

Bianchino, Gloria, and Bonizza Giordani Aragno, *Walter Albini,* Parma, 1988.

Sozzani, Carla, and Anna Masucci, *Walter Albini,* Milan, 1990.

Articles

"Walter Albini," in the *Sunday Times* (London), 15 October 1972.

"In Focus: Walter Albini," in *International Textiles* (London), No. 523, 1975.

Etherington-Smith, Meredith, "Albini's New Image," in *GQ* (New York), October 1976.

"Walter Albini, the Designer's Designer," in *Manufacturing Clothier,* 1976.

"Lo stile multimaglia in sfumature rare," in *Vogue* (Milan), October 1978.

"Walter Albini: Italian RTW Designer is Dead," in *Women's Wear Daily* (New York), 3 June 1983.

"Walter Albini, Men's Wear Innovator, Dies at 42," in the *Daily News Record,* 3 June 1983.

Skellenger, Gillion, "Walter Albini," in *Contemporary Designers,* London, 1990.

* * *

In William Shakespeare's *Richard II,* "report of fashions in proud Italy" are the vanguard for what comes to England only in "base imitation." Walter Albini epitomized the brilliant epoch of Italian fashion in the 1970s, when it seized the international imagination. At least as much as any other designer, if not more, Albini had the Italian spirit *con brio.* Journalists compared him to Yves Saint Laurent and Karl Lagerfeld, designers whose careers outlasted Albini's flash of brilliance. Albini brought his obsession with the 1920s and 1930s to the elongated line and youthful energy of the 1970s; his collections of 1969 and 1970 tell the story of his encapsulation of the time: Gymnasium and Gypsy and China in 1969; Antique Market, the Pre-Raphaelites, Safari, Military, and Polaroid in 1970.

Sadly, Albini so brilliantly embodied the 1970s for Italy (as one would perhaps say of Halston in the U.S.) because of the détente of his work by 1980 and his death in 1983, just after his forty-second birthday. Isa Vercelloni and Flavio Lucchini, in their 1975 book, *Milano Fashion,* described Albini's mercurial yet gifted personality and habits: "From adolescence he still retained the capacity of dreaming, but with the ability of giving body or a semblance of reality to his world of dreams. He had the rare quality of even doing this without spoiling it. This is why women like his dresses so much. They recognize immediately that imagination is given power."

It was a wide-ranging imagination, indicative of the 1970s in its travelogue-inspired wanderlust, that captured the vivacity of Diana Vreeland's *Vogue* of the 1960s. Like Vreeland, Albini loved the 1920s and extolled the freedom of women and reminded them of their liberation during that period. Also like Vreeland, Albini was smitten with North Africa and the potential for exoticism. He played with paisley and was fascinated by the pattern and design asymmetry as well as the mysterious women of China. His pragmatic exoticism is evident in a spring 1980 t-blouse and party skirt combination, described in a *Harper's Bazaar* March 1980 ad as "the mystique of madras. A bit sophisticated for midnight at the oasis…but divine for sunset on the patio."

So many collections were produced in his own name and others between the late 1960s and 1980 that he touched upon many themes, but he returned consistently to the 1920s and 1930s. He had moved to Paris because of a lifetime preoccupation with Chanel, whom he had glimpsed during her late years, but he more substantively used her as a touchstone for his collections. His fall 1978 knits, as photographed by

David Bailey, intensified the luxury of Chanel tailoring, although slightly oversized, in a palette of bronze and browns. For his Mister Fox line in beautiful geometrics, he approximated Sonia Delaunay, but echoed the feeling of Chanel. His movie and fashion magazine passions would encompass Katharine Hepburn and Marlene Dietrich, but for Albini these merely confirmed the role of Chanel in freeing women to be comfortable in sportswear- and menswear-derived styles that were luxuriously tailored for women.

Besides Chanel, Albini's other passion was for ancient Egypt, for which he felt mystical affinity and which served as an inspiration for his men's and women's fashions—especially his fashion drawings. By the mid-1970s, Albini's style was predominately an amalgam of ancient Egyptian motifs (although often attributed elsewhere in the East) and Chanel, using the Chanel suits and proportions with the accommodations of wrapping *à la Egyptienne* and the excuses of Venice, North Africa, and India for billowing harem pants and other pantaloons of which Chanel would scarcely have approved. In 1978 a riding skirt, with its fluid drape, was teamed with a short cropped jacket, combining tradition with contemporary 1970s style.

In some ways, Albini was the precursor of Gianni Versace. His intensely personal style respected many historical exemplars and was passionately defended and highly expressive. Like Versace, Albini combined a studious infatuation with the past with a passion for his own synthesis of styles and a comprehensive style attainment and conviction that was his own; he created this with a fervor approaching fanaticism that reinforced the sense of abiding adolescence and keenest ebullience for the work.

Vercelloni and Lucchini asked Albini what his motto was; he said, "Enjoy today and leave unpleasant things for tomorrow." For Albini and the extravagant fashion he created, fate held no tomorrow and no unpleasantness.

—Richard Martin

Victor Alfaro, fall 2001 collection. © AP/Wide World Photos/ Fashion Wire Daily.

ALFARO, Victor

American designer

Born: Chihuahua, Mexico, 26 May 1963; immigrated to the U.S., 1981. **Education:** Attended University of Texas, 1982; graduated from Fashion Institute of Technology, 1987. **Career:** Assistant to Mary Ann Restivo, late 1980s, and Joseph Abboud, 1990; established own business, early 1990s. **Awards:** Vidal Sassoon Excellence in New Design, 1993; Omni-Mexican award for Best Latin American Designer, 1994; Dallas Fashion award, 1994; Council of Fashion Designers of America New Fashion Talent award, 1994. **Address:** 130 Barrow Street, New York, NY 10014, USA.

Publications

On ALFARO:

Books

Stegemeyer, Anne, *Who's Who in Fashion, Third Edition,* New York, 1996.

Articles

Hochswender, Woody, "Patterns: An American Alaïa," in the *New York Times,* 7 April 1992.

———, "Tufts and Tacks, Bells and Beads," in the *New York Times,* 9 April 1992.

Lee, Ricky, "New York to Mexico," in the *New York Times,* 2 August 1992.

Fischer, Laura, "The Thrill of Victor," in *Avenue* (New York), March 1993.

Spindler, Amy M., "For Next Wave, Attitude Counts," in the *New York Times,* 2 April 1993.

———, "Fresh Talents Dig Up Tasty Design," in the *New York Times,* 5 November 1993.

Foley, Bridget, "Alfaro Sprouts," in *W,* March 1994.

"Alfaro: Beyond the Pale," in *Women's Wear Daily,* 9 August 1994.

Torkells, Erik, "The Night is Young," in *Town & Country,* September 1994.

"New York: Victor Alfaro," in *Women's Wear Daily,* 4 November 1994.

Spindler, Amy M., "Learning from Las Vegas and Show World," in the *New York Times,* 5 November 1994.

Victor Alfaro, fall 2000 collection. © Reuters NewMedia Inc./ CORBIS.

Min, Janice, and Allison Lynn, "Fitting Pretty: Going for Sheer Glamor, Designer Victor Alfaro Gives Grunge the Gate," in *People,* 20 March 1995.

"Rising Star," in *Women's Wear Daily,* September 1994.

"New York Comes Alive," in *Women's Wear Daily,* 1 April 1996.

White, Constance C. R. "No Show Due to Lack of Finances," in the *New York Times,* 8 April 1997.

"Milan Haute Hippies and Good Sports," in *Women's Wear Daily,* 9 March 1998.

Conti, Samantha, "New Deals Focus on Control of Brand," in *Women's Wear Daily,* 27 May 1998.

"Alfaro, Gilmar to Launch Line," in *Women's Wear Daily,* 7 December 1999.

* * *

Victor Alfaro, known for his "come hither" designs, claims the only fashion design training he has ever had was poring through fashion magazines. Born and raised in Mexico, Alfaro moved to the U.S. as an exchange student to perfect his English and to study communications at the University of Texas. At the time, fashion design was "just a fantasy," but later he applied to the Fashion Institute of Technology in New York City. After graduating in 1987, Alfaro worked as an apprentice designer, and by the mid-1990s, at the age of 30, he had become recognized as one of the leading designers in the United States.

Bare simplicity and an equally frank sexuality inform Alfaro's dresses for cocktail and evening. Bridget Foley predicted in March 1994 *W* article, "The heir apparent to Oscar and Bill? Perhaps. Victor Alfaro may be New York's next great eveningwear designer." If Alfaro is the torchbearer of style for New York nights, his role betokens a shifting sensibility, one that pointedly exalts the body, seeks out youth, and takes risks. Skilled in the vocabulary of separates (he worked for Mary Ann Restivo and Joseph Abboud), Alfaro eagerly draws upon the street for inspiration and demands a body consciousness that have made some call him the American Alaïa. In early recognition as a designer for celebrities, photographed by Francesco Scavullo for *Cosmopolitan* covers in New York, Alfaro flirted with attention-getting vulgarity, though his collections have come to represent a more natural but nonetheless willfully seductive sensuality.

Amy Spindler, in an April 1993 piece for the *New York Times,* commented, "Victor Alfaro's clothes come with plenty of attitude." The attitude is, of course, of postfeminist women's individuality and options, including a very 1990s' reexamination of the possibilities of seductive, relatively bare clothing in the most luxurious fabrics. One needs a self-confidence approaching attitude to wear dresses and outfits of such body-revealing form, but one also needs a distinct segregation of Alfaro's partywear from day-to-day clothing. His clothes are not for the timid, but neither are they for showgirls. Spindler refers to his "sex-kitten clothes," but their relative austerity, depending entirely upon textile and shape, keeps them from being vitiated by Las Vegas.

Alfaro does however raise provocative issues of women's overt and self-assured physicality and sexuality more than of sexual license. To be sure, short skirts, bared shoulders, lace in direct contact with skin, leather, and sheer skimming fabrics suggest fetishes, but there is always something strangely wholesome about Alfaro's sensibility. Singer Mariah Carey is quoted as saying very aptly that Alfaro's "clothes are fierce." Their ferocity resides in the fact that they define strong women.

According to Ricky Lee (*New York Times,* 2 August 1992), Alfaro was counseled by one buyer from Chicago that in order to succeed, he should add more suits to his line. But Alfaro rightly declined, knowing he was not creating professional clothes nor daywear basics. He eschews sobriety and, with it, tailoring. Rather, he was responding to sexuality's siren and creating the sexiest siren dresses for young New Yorkers of the 1990s. He is dressmaker to the legendary Generation X. Alfaro was defining a strong personal style and a clientèle that is generationally, visually, and libidinously nurtured on MTV and informed by multicultural street smarts. Woody Hochswender reporting for the *New York Times* in April 1992, found Alfaro's collection "suggested sex—in a voice loud enough to clear a disco. There were lace chaps and fake snake chaps, worn over bodysuits. Skintight snakeskin jeans were zipped all the way from front to back, reason unknown. Rib-knit sweater dresses were worn with harnesses of metal mesh, Mr. Alfaro's version of the bondage look sweeping fashion."

Explaining his relative restraint and deliberate avoidance of vulgarity in his fall/winter 1993–94 collection to Foley, Alfaro said, "I didn't want it to look cheap. Buyers see every trick in the book, and they want clothes that are wearable." Alfaro has consistently made unencumbered clothing, emphasizing minimalist sensibility and cut and employing luxurious materials. In these characteristics, he is a designer in the great American tradition. His distinctive deviation from this tradition might seem to be his hot sexuality, the body-tracing and body-revealing simplicity of his clothes—but again and again, 20th-century American designers have been dressing advanced new women of ever-increasing power and self-assurance.

In 1996 *Women's Wear Daily* claimed Alfaro's collection was his "best ever." The same year, he designed a line of coats, manufactured by Mohl Furs, featuring an ink-dyed Persian lamb pea coat, a leather trench coat, and a camel hair coat lined with mink inspired by photography of Jacques-Henri Lartigue. Despite his talent and popularity, Alfaro was experiencing financial difficulties and seeking financial backing. He entered into a licensing agreement with Italian manufacturer Gilmar in 1998 which allowed him to make long-term plans, be more involved in the manufacture of his garments, and to have a ready place in the European fashion scene.

His first collection shown under the agreement with Gilmar was well received. Merging Milanese chic with American-styled sportswear, Alfaro created a less revealing collection he "claimed to have started with the idea of a rich hippie, but in the end, this collection had little to do with a redux of counterculture references." True, his pieces were more boxy and full than his previous lines, but keeping to his unique and sensuous style, Alfaro added rabbit mules as a finishing touch. For the fall of 2000, Alfaro and Gilmar debuted their new line, Vic., which sells for nearly half the price of Alfaro's signature line. Alfaro told *Women's Wear Daily* (7 December 1999), "The Vic. line will be a little bit more on the fashion side and forward. It's still a designer collection; it's just another one of my personalities."

Alfaro is creating the postfeminist fashion sensibility, consummately beautiful in execution, infinitely skilled in construction, and assertively avant-garde. Even as some critics dismiss his work as offensive, Alfaro is a true fashion risk-taker and visionary. He is defining and dressing today, and will dress hereafter, the bravest woman of the future.

—Richard Martin; updated by Christine Miner Minderovic

ALLARD, Linda

American designer

Born: Akron, Ohio, 27 May 1940; grew up in Doylestown. **Education:** Studied fine arts, Kent State University (Ohio), 1958–62. **Family:** Married Herbert Gallen, 2000. **Career:** Design assistant, Ellen Tracy, New York, 1962–64, then director of design, from 1964; Linda Allard label introduced, 1984; design critic, Fashion Institute of Technology, New York; visiting professor, International Academy of Merchandising and Design, Chicago; board of directors, Kent State University. **Member:** Fashion Group International, Inc., Council of Fashion Designers of America. **Awards:** Dallas Fashion award, 1986, 1987, 1994. **Address:** 575 Seventh Avenue, New York, NY 10018, USA. **Website:** www.ellentracy.com.

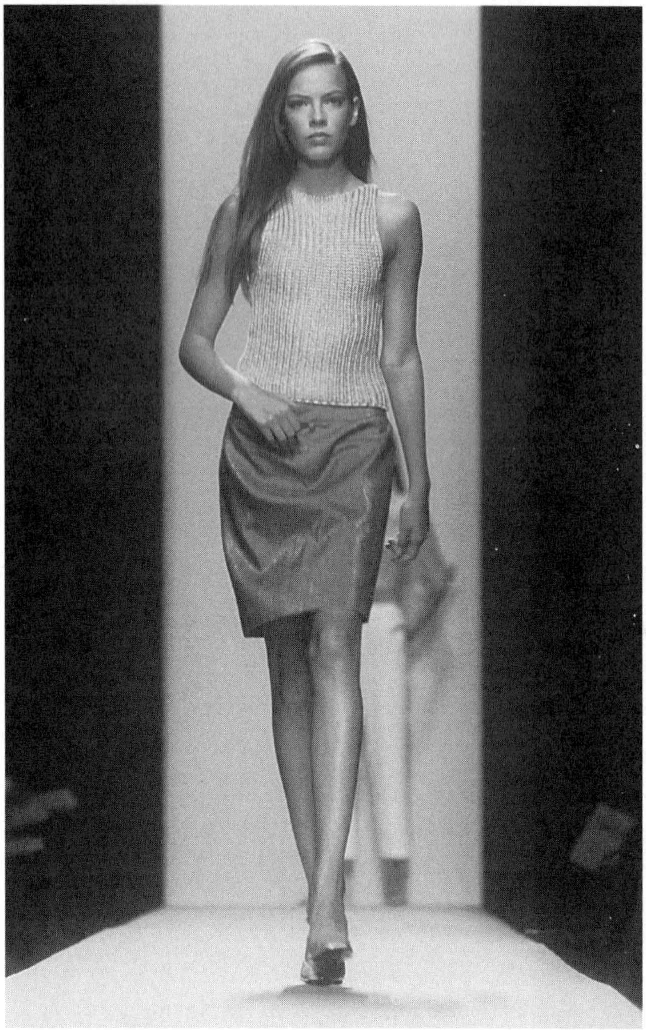

Linda Allard, designed for Ellen Tracy's spring 2000 collection. © Fashion Syndicate Press.

PUBLICATIONS

On ALLARD:

Books

Stegemeyer, Anne, *Who's Who in Fashion, Third Edition,* New York, 1996.

Articles

Daria, Irene, "Linda Allard: Growing up with Ellen Tracy," in *Women's Wear Daily,* 2 June 1986.
Caminiti, Susan, "A.K.A. Ellen Tracy," in *Savvy,* October 1988.
Kantrowitz, Barbara, "The Real Designer Behind that Ellen Tracy Label," in *Newsweek,* 24 October 1988.
"Linda Allard," in *Accessories,* December 1988.
Ozzard, Janet, "The Prime of Linda Allard," in *Women's Wear Daily,* 14 December 1994.
Schiro, Anne-Marie, "Designed for Retailers and Real Women," in the *New York Times,* 5 April 1995.
"Comfort Zone," in *Women's Wear Daily,* 18 February 1999.

Linda Allard, designed for Ellen Tracy's spring 2000 collection. © Fashion Syndicate Press.

Socha, Miles, "Ellen Tracy Has a New Bridal Line," in *W,* March 2000.

* * *

Linda Allard is the woman behind Ellen Tracy. In fact, there is no Ellen Tracy—there never was. The company was founded in 1949 by Herbert Gallen, a juniors blouse manufacturer, who invented the name Ellen Tracy for his fledgling firm. Gallen hired Allard in 1962, fresh out of college, as a design assistant. She quickly expanded the line to include trousers and jackets. Two years later, she was made director of design, and a new Ellen Tracy was born. Since then, under Allard's artistic leadership, Ellen Tracy has become synonymous with top-quality fabrics, clean lines, and the concept of a complete wardrobe for the working woman.

Allard grew up in Doyleston, Ohio, in a 100-year-old farmhouse with five brothers and sisters. Allard was taught to sew at a young age by her mother, and quickly began designing garments for her dolls. "Even before I could sew, I was always designing clothes for my paper dolls," she said. After receiving a fine arts degree from Kent State University in 1962, she moved to New York, where she received her first job offer from Gallen.

Shortly after Allard joined the firm, Ellen Tracy moved away from junior clothing to apparel designed for the newly established female workforce of the 1960s. Allard was one of the first designers to address the shifting demographics, creating a professional look, stylish yet appropriate for the workplace. Eventually, by the mid-1970s, the company moved into the bridge market. The bridge collections (which filled the gap between upper-end designer lines and mass-market brands) have since become the fastest growing area of the women's fashion market, key to Ellen Tracy's success, with the company's volume nearly tripling over the following decade.

As the creative force behind Ellen Tracy, Allard transformed the company into one of the key anchor designers in the bridge market. To give the collection more of a designer feel, Allard's name was placed on the Ellen Tracy label in 1984. Nonetheless, Allard believes high fashion has little relevance to most women's lives. "The extreme end of fashion is overrated," she has commented. "It gets a lot of coverage by the press, but it doesn't mean anything to a lot of women. We mean more to real women."

In the 21st century, working with a 12-person design team, Allard was responsible for the entire Ellen Tracy line. To her, designing begins with an emphasis on high-quality fabrics and specific color grouping: "We start with color and a sense of the flavor of the collection. Will it be fluid or rigid, soft and slouchy or tailored? The focus is on easy dressing and effortless shapes. We develop the fabrics first, finding the texture that expresses the attitude we feel, and then comes the styling. Fabrics make the collection unique." There are three Ellen Tracy collections each year. To ensure the clothes work well with each other, each garment is sold separately. "The modern woman buys a wardrobe of jackets that work well in a variety of pairings," Allard explained.

Ellen Tracy, Inc. has grown to be one of the top 10 womens' clothing companies in the United States. After 50 years, Ellen Tracy remains a dominant label and can be found at prominent department stores such as Lord & Taylor, Neiman Marcus, Bloomingdale's, Macy's, and Saks Fifth Avenue. Perhaps the essential element for its success is customer loyalty. Ellen Tracy has been able to identify its primary customers, largely made up of career women, and Allard keeps design and quality consistent. As Allard told Janet Ozzard of *Women's Wear Daily,* "We deal in investment clothing, although we do try to offer some fashion because our customer does demand [it.] I think it's one of the reasons we keep constant: we study our customer, we have the same viewpoint. I design for a woman who has a career or a profession and wants to feel fabulous in her clothes, but it isn't the be-all and end-all of her world."

The increase in sales and popularity of Allard's designs was also due to the growing need for stylish, comfortable, and no-nonsense wardrobes, since the number of women who hold professional jobs has increased dramatically. Allard's designs are not necessarily considered to be cutting edge; she merely includes up-to-date styling and leaves out any, as *Women's Wear Daily* described, "glitz or sleaze."

Another key element to Allard's success has been her ability to diversify. Allard launched a petites division in 1981 and four years later debuted a successful dress unit. To cater to the more leisure-oriented customer, Ellen Tracy introduced its latest expansion, a sportswear line called Company, in the fall of 1991. Allard said her intent is to provide "the same level of quality for the woman who doesn't need strictly career clothes, or whose career offers more fashion choices than the tailored suits we're known for." In 1992 a fragrance line was launched, followed by the introduction of plus-size clothing and a collection of sophisticated evening dresses. Ellen Tracy also has licensing agreements to produce scarves, shoes, eyewear, hosiery, and handbags.

Allard lives and works in Manhattan and spends weekends in her new country home in Connecticut, set on 60 acres of rolling countryside. She designed the house with her brother, David, an architect. The house is a 5,500-square-foot Palladian-inspired villa, complete with studio and guest quarters. "When we were designing my new house," Allard explained, "I challenged my architect brother to take strong classical designs of the past and make them livable for today."

When asked in an interview with *Women's Wear Daily* if there was a missing ingredient in her life, she replied, "I've always thought about the idea of having children, but I think children need to be nurtured, and I don't think you can do that from five to six at night." Additionally, she commented, "From the age of ten I always wanted to design. I never excluded having a family, but my work is so demanding. I'm happy I have a lot of nieces and nephews, so I can enjoy family life and kids." Allard did make room for a husband, however: on New Year's Eve 1999, Herbert Gallen, Ellen Tracy's company chairman, proposed to Allard, who said "Yes."

—Janet Markarian; updated by Christine Miner Minderovic

ALLY CAPELLINO

British design firm

Founded: by Middlesex Polytechnic graduates Alison Lloyd and Johnathan "Jono"Platt in 1979. **Company History:** After graduation, they worked for Courtaulds, then Platt worked for Betty Jackson and Lloyd made hats and jewelry at home; designed accessories, selling to Miss Selfridges chain, 1979; developed clothing range, 1980; critically acclaimed collection for Olympic Games, Moscow, 1980; introduced childrenswear line, Mini Capellino, 1981; menswear line launched, 1986; signed licensing agreement with CGO Co., Japan, 1987; opened flagship store, Soho, London, 1988; launched diffusion sportswear line, Hearts of Oak, 1990; signed agreement with textile firm Coats Viyella for promotion and marketing, 1992; design consultants to the firm, from 1992; introduced Ally-T range of t-shirts, 1993; worked with Irish Linen Guild, 1993; collaborated with Jones Bootmaker to develop dual label shoes, 1994. **Company Address:** N1R, Metropolitan Wharf, Wapping Wall, London E1 9SS, England.

Publications

On ALLY CAPELLINO:

Articles

"Influences: Ally Capellino," in *Women's Journal* (London), April 1985.

Tyrrel, Rebecca, "Rival Look on the City Streets," in the *Sunday Times Magazine* (London), 4 September 1988.

"No Business Like Show Business," in *Fashion Weekly* (London), 9 March 1989.

Dutt, Robin, "Ally Capellino," in *Clothes Show* (London), October/November 1989.

Fallon, James, "Irish Linen Makers in Clover," in *Women's Wear Daily,* 22 February 1994.

"Retailers Spring Season Moving Slowly," in *Women's Wear Daily,* 30 March 1995.

Chappell, Helen, "Causes to Die for Darling," in *New Statesman & Society,* 3 May 1996.

* * *

In the early 1990s a truce seemed to have been called between British fashion designers and clothing manufacturers. Large manufacturers such as Coats Viyella and Courtaulds had previously viewed the fashion designer as a suspicious entity. A change in consumer needs and public taste, however, forced many companies to rethink their strategies. High Street retailers began demanding short runs of stock in response to swiftly changing trends, which reflected designers' needs for small quantities of items difficult and expensive to produce. Ally Capellino is one of the designer names to bridge the gap between these problems.

In 1992 Ally Capellino signed an agreement with Coats Viyella, Britain's largest textile company, to promote and market their brand name and give them access to Coats Viyella's design and production facilities, among the most advanced in technological development in the world. In return Ally Capellino would bring a more fashion-oriented handwriting to the business through by acting as design consultants. This would, in turn, hopefully avert the criticism aimed at British clothing manufacturers for producing unadventurous products.

Ally Capellino was founded in 1979 by Alison Lloyd and Jono Platt, creating a name based on Alison and the Italian word for "small cap," or *capellino.* Both were graduates from the B.A. fashion course at Middlesex Polytechnic and they initially sold accessories to British fashion chains Miss Selfridge and Elle. The company developed a distinctive clothing line that included a children's line, menswear and womenswear, with simple, well-cut lines and cotton separates. This was developed and sold to an international market, predominantly in Italy, the U.S. and Japan.

In 1987 the firm signed a licensing contract with the GCO Company in Japan, which aimed to achieve optimum positioning of the label in terms of retail, public relations, and advertising exposure. This was followed, in 1988, by the opening of the Ally Capellino store in Soho, London, which developed into an emporium for clothing, childrenswear, and lifestyle items. Hearts of Oak, a diffusion sportswear collection, was introduced in 1990, followed by the launch of Ally-T, a unisex range of t-shirts, in 1993.

Alison Lloyd sees herself as one of a new breed of fashion designers, far more commercially and market-orientated, as she said when interviewed in the *Independent,* in London: "We are sensible rather than outrageous. We have made many mistakes in the past, but we have learned from them, and we made them with our own money rather than relying on handouts." This is a very positive attitude in light of the agreement made between the company and Coats Viyella. Many previous associations between industrial giants and designer names have become stifling rather than creative. Ally Capellino wanted to retain its independence but capitalize on the commerciality of their association.

Ally Capellino seemed to have found the perfect solution to a classic problem and managed to establish a business association which recognized the fact that designer fashion represented just the tip of a multibillion-pound industry, in terms of prestige and kudos. Ally Capellino continued to create attractive, comfortable wear in the middle and later 1990s, with innovations such as using Irish linen and lace in 1994 and 1995; contributing to a fashion show benefit for the London Zoo's endangered species along with fellow designers Paul Costelloe and Zandra Rhodes in 1996; and mixing fashion with politics by dressing Cherie Blair in the last few years of the 20th century.

—Kevin Almond; updated by Owen James

AMIES, Sir Hardy

British designer

Born: Edwin Hardy Amies in London, 17 July 1909. **Education:** Studied at Brentwood School to 1927. **Career:** School teacher, Antibes, 1927; office assistant, Bendorf, Germany, 1928–30; trainee, W. & T. Avery Ltd., Birmingham, England, 1930–34; managing designer, Lachasse, 1934, managing director, 1935–39; served in the British Army Intelligence Corps, 1939–45; lieutenant colonel; head of Special Forces Commission to Belgium, 1944; designed for Worth and for the British government Utility Scheme during the war; established own couture business, Hardy Amies Ltd., 1946; introduced ready-made line, 1950; dressmaker by appointment for HM Queen Elizabeth II, England, from 1955; added menswear, 1959; firm owned by Debenhams, 1973–81, repurchased by Amies, 1981; also designed menswear for Hepworths, from 1961; vice-chairman, 1954–56, and chairman, 1959–60, Incorporated Society of London Fashion Designers. **Exhibitions:** *Court Couture 1992*, exhibition at Kensington Palace, London. **Awards:** Named Officier de l'Ordre de la Couronne, Belgium, 1946; Royal Warrant awarded, 1955; *Harper's Bazaar* award, 1962; Caswell-Massey International award, 1962, 1964, 1968; *Ambassador* Magazine award, 1964; the *Sunday Times* special award, London, 1965; Commander of the Royal Victorian Order, 1977; Personnalité de l'Année (Haute Couture), Paris, 1986; British Fashion Council Hall of Fame award, 1989; Knight Commander of the Victorian Order, 1989. **Address:** Hardy Amies Ltd., 14 Savile Row, London W1X 2JN, England.

Publications

By AMIES:

Books

Here Lived..., Cambridge, 1948.
Just So Far, London, 1954.
The ABC of Men's Fashion, London, 1964.
Still Here, London, 1984.
The Englishman's Suit, London, 1994.

Articles

"A Century of Fashion," in the *RSA Journal* (London), March 1989.

On AMIES:

Books

Lambert, Eleanor, *World of Fashion: People, Places, Resources,* New York and London, 1976.
McDowell, Colin, *A Hundred Years of Royal Style,* London, 1985.
Milbank, Caroline Rennolds, *Couture: The Great Designers,* New York, 1985.
Stegemeyer, Anne, *Who's Who in Fashion, Third Edition,* New York, 1996.

Articles

"Hardy Country," in *Vogue* (London), March 1975.
Boyd, Ann, "Hardy Amies, Haute Couturier," in *The Observer* (London), 3 February 1980.
Hauptfuhrer, Fred, "Oh, Those Polka Dots! Oh, Those Bows! Hardy Amies Designs Queen Elizabeth's Clothes," in *People,* 8 October 1984.
"Happy Birthday Mr. Amies," in *Vogue* (London), July 1989.
Ginsburg, Madeleine, "Tailor-made," in *Country Life* (London), 13 July 1989.

Sir Hardy Amies, 1955: lamé suit with mink collar. © Hulton-Deutsch Collection/CORBIS.

Design by Sir Hardy Amies, ca. 1951. © Norman Parkinson Limited/Fiona Cowan/CORBIS.

Lambert, Elizabeth, and Derry Moore, "The Reign of Hardy Amies: The Queen's Couturier in London and Gloucestershire," in *Architectual Digest* (Los Angeles), September 1989.

"Hardy Perennial," in *Fashion Weekly* (London), 19 October 1989.

"What's a Couturier to Do?" in *Chicago Tribune,* 21 May 1990.

"Royal Attire on Exhibit in London Palace," in *Chicago Tribune,* 20 September 1992.

"The Englishman's Suit," in the *Economist* (U.S.), 16 July 1994.

Williams, Hugo, "The Englishman's Suit: A Personal View of its History, its Place in the World Today, its Future and the Accessories which Support It," in the *Times Literary Supplement (TLS),* 22 July 1994.

* * *

Hardy Amies began his career as a couturier when he was brought in as managing designer at Lachasse, in London, after the departure in 1933 of Digby Morton. He acknowledges that by examining the models left by Morton he learned the construction of tailored suits. The 1930s was an auspicious time for the new generation of London couture houses emerging, for British tailored suit reigned supreme in America. Amies' contribution to the construction of the tailored suit for women was to lower the waistline of the jacket, which he believed Morton had always set too high, thus giving the "total effect of a more important-looking suit." His fashion philosophy, that elegant clothes must have a low waistline, characterized his work ever since and his clothes have always been just above the hipline rather than on the natural waistline. Working on his theory that fashion design should be a process of "evolution rather than revolution," Amies has conceded that his duty as a designer was to vary the cut and design of the tailored suit to make it as feminine as possible, without departing from the canons of good tailoring.

Like his counterparts in the London couture, Amies' work was always tempered by the requirements of the private couture customer who formed the majority of his business. Unlike the Paris couture houses who enjoyed the support of large textile firms and saw the link with couture as a beneficial form of publicity, as well as backing from the French Government for its *industrie de luxe,* the London couture houses did not benefit from such aid. The main role of the London couture, according to Amies, was not to create avant-garde clothes for publicity purposes but to design for the individual customer.

Amies is perhaps best known for his work for Queen Elizabeth II for whom he began a long association as a royal dressmaker in 1950 when he made several outfits for the then Princess Elizabeth's royal tour to Canada. Although the couture side of the Hardy Amies business was traditionally its less financially successful area, it has nonetheless given his house a degree of respectability as a royal warrant holder. One of his best known creations is the gown he designed in 1977 for Queen Elizabeth's Silver Jubilee portrait which, he said, was "immortalized on a thousand biscuit tins." While Amies' royal patronage clearly enforced his international image, his menswear and related fashion spinoffs (such as licenses) were by far his most sucessful enterprise. His small leather goods, ties, knitwear, and shirts, produced and sold under licensing agreements in various countries including America, Canada, Australia, and Japan, made the Hardy Amies label a household name.

Another side of Amies' work is in corporate uniform designing for the service industries, such as hotels and airlines, where his reputation both as a designer of tailored clothes and his royal association have undoubtedly made him an appealing choice.

Amies weathered the transformation of London's fashion image as the home of the thoroughbred tailored suit to a veritable melting pot of creativity, during a career that spanned more than fifty years. And even after his retirement in 1994, he remained one of Britain's best known establishment designers. Though he has admitted "I'm absolutely astonished at my success," and downplayed his talent, everyone agrees Hardy Aimes has inimitable style.

—Catherine Woram; updated by Nelly Rhodes

ANSELM, Marilyn and Yoram

See HOBBS, LTD

ANTHONY, John

American designer

Born: Gianantonio Iorio in New York City, 28 April 1938. **Education:** Studied at the Academia delle Belle Arti, Rome, 1956–57; graduated from Fashion Institute of Technology, New York, 1959. **Family:** Married Molly Anthony; children: Mark. **Career:** Designer, Devonbrook, New York, 1959–68; designer, Adolph Zelinka, 1968–70; established John Anthony Inc., New York, 1971–79; custom tailoring, from 1986; debuted ready-to-wear collections, 1994, 1996, and 2001. **Exhibitions:** Riverside Theatre and the Center for the Arts, Palm Beach, Florida, 2001. **Awards:** Maison Blanche award, New Orleans, 1964; Silver Cup award, Kaufmann's Department Stores, Pittsburgh, 1964; Mortimer C. Ritter award, Fashion Institute of Technology, New York, 1964; Coty American Fashion Critics "Winnie" award, 1972; Coty Return award, 1976.

Publications

On ANTHONY:

Books

Morris, Bernadine, and Barbara Walz, *The Fashion Makers,* New York, 1978.

Milbank, Caroline Rennolds, *New York Fashion: The Evolution of American Style,* New York, 1989.

Stegemeyer, Anne, *Who's Who in Fashion, Third Edition,* New York, 1996.

Articles

Morris, Bernadine, "Evening Dresses: Taking it Easy," in the *New York Times,* 5 June 1984.

———, "In Two New Couture Collections, Glamor is a Theme," in the *New York Times,* 30 June 1987.

———, "Dressing Up, and Down," in the *New York Times,* 19 September 1989.

Heimel, Cynthia, "Service, Fit, Original Design are What Make the New American Couturiers Hot," in *Vogue,* January 1990.

Morris, Bernadine, "The Rebirth of New York Couture," in the *New York Times,* 1 May 1990.
Larmoth, Jeanine, "Haute Couture American Style: The Free Spirit," in *Town & Country,* May 1991.
Morris, Bernadine, "Dramatic Tailoring for Day and Night," in the *New York Times,* 17 September 1991.
———, "A Compromise Made of Jersey," in the *New York Times,* 15 September 1992.
"John Anthony Back in Wholesale," in *Women's Wear Daily,* 26 April 1994.
"Anthony's New Venture: Ready-to-Wear," in *Women's Wear Daily,* 4 May 1994.
Vienne, Veronique, "The Chivalrous Couturier," in *Town & Country,* September 1995.
La Ferla, Ruth, "A Fashion Show to Chamber Music," in the *New York Times,* 17 September 2000.
Canupp, Shelley, "So Haute...John Anthony," in the *Palm Beach Press Journal,* 15 February 2001.

* * *

Born Gianantonio Iorio in Queens, New York, to a metalworker, John Anthony has evolved into a dress designer who uses the most luxurious fabrics in the simplest shapes with unequalled taste. Educated at the Academia delle Belle Arti in Rome, and the Fashion Institute of Technology, Anthony worked for several wholesale companies before opening his own house with the manufacturer Robert Levine in 1971. He immediately marketed his look towards the top end of ready-to-wear, establishing a glossy, up-to-the-minute fashion image and selling to leading retail stores.

Anthony's first collection was an edited Marlene Dietrich look, featuring masculine tailoring in pinstripe and herringbone wools, softened with blouses underneath, or pleated and smocked crêpe dresses. By 1976, he was showing the soft, liquid separates that became his trademark; ice cream colors seemed to melt into clothes that were so light they almost floated. Anthony believes designing clothes is a fusion of function and purpose. The function appears to be his logical, wearable approach; the purpose lies in his pared-down minimalist ideas. He edits collections down to their bare essentials and, while other designers often show over 100 styles per collection, he makes his statement in half this number. His subtle, understated clothes are designed for a young, sophisticated woman. He uses natural fabrics like wool, crêpe, chiffon, jersey, satin, and menswear fabrics. He is particularly noted for his cardigan sweaters or pullovers, teamed with skirts and his elegant gala evening gowns, in contradictory daywear fabrics.

His modern understatements have brought him commissions from high-profile clients like the wives of U.S. presidents, including Betty Ford, Rosalynn Carter, and Jacqueline Kennedy Onassis, who needed to attract attention through impeccable taste rather than outrageous overstatement. Performers Lena Horne, Audrey Meadows, and Julie Andrews were also among his customers through the years. Muted color is another strong feature of Anthony's work. He believes the color palette in a collection should intermingle, so one item can easily go with everything else. His first collection was predominantly black with white, navy, and red. He claims to hate shock colors like turquoise or fuschia, and has usually been faithful to a range of beiges, christened with names such as peanut and cinnamon.

Anthony considers the designer's job as one to make things easy for the customer. Yet behind this ease lies a renowned skill for cutting, tailoring, and overall dedication to developing a specialist style, which has won the designer Coty awards. He was one of the first designers to promote the idea of easy-to-travel clothes that could be rolled up in a ball and thrown into a suitcase with no danger of wrinkling. Anthony recommends his customer buy a few things that work for her each season, then interchange and adapt these garments to create several different looks.

For the fall 1994 season, Anthony released his first ready-to-wear collection in nearly a decade, called John Anthony Couture. Featuring coats, suits, day dresses, and cocktail and evening dresses consisting of lamb-trimmed brown wool, navy mandarin-collared pantsuits, and little wool jersey dresses with full, above-the-knee skirts, the collection pieces wholesaled at $500 to $1,900. Showing his charitable side, Anthony's show was a benefit for pediatric cancer patients at Sloane Kettering Memorial Hospital. The spring collection featured, according to *Women's Wear Daily,* "A line dresses in red silk for day, evening columns in white taffeta and silk and two stunning ball gowns, one a whirl of strapless tulle, the other a pale pink silk gown overlaid with black lace."

Anthony's masterpieces have traditionally sold in the higher-end marketplace, with a coat going for $6,000, a suit for $8,000, and an evening gown for $20,000, but the line he released in 2001 featured sizes up to 16 and the price tags range from $1,800 to $5,000, putting his works within reach of the average upper middle-class consumer.

—Kevin Almond; updated by Daryl F. Mallett

APOSTOLOPOULIS, Nikos

See NIKOS

AQUASCUTUM, LTD.

British ready-to-wear firm

Founded: by John Emary in London, 1851. **Company History:** Early firsts include rain-repellent woollen cloth, the raglan sleeve, and the trench coat. Manufacturer of outerwear, from 1851; introduced womenswear, 1909; New York showroom opened, 1948; manufacturing outlet in Canada opened, 1949; Manchester and Bristol shops opened, 1950s; added suits for men, 1951; introduced full line of women's fashions, 1986; granted royal warrants, 1897, 1902, 1903, 1911, 1929, 1949, 1952. **Awards:** Clothing Oscar, 1958; Queen's award for Export Achievement, 1966, 1967, 1971, 1976, 1979, 1990; British Knitting and Clothing Export Council Export award, 1986. **Company Address:** 100 Regent St., London W1A 2AQ, England.

Publications

By AQUASCUTUM LTD.:

Books

The Story of Aquascutum, London, 1959.
The Aquascutum Story, London, 1976, 1991.
The Aquascutum Heritage, London, 1984.

Design by Aquascutum, Ltd., ca. 1951. © Norman Parkinson Limited/Fiona Cowan/CORBIS.

On AQUASCUTUM LTD.:

Books

Bentley, Nicolas, *A Man's Clothes,* London, 1952.
Adburgham, Alison, *Shops and Shopping,* London, 1964.
Hobhouse, Hermione, *A History of Regent Street,* London, 1975.

Articles

"Aquascutum—100 Years Proof," in *Vogue* (London), March 1976.
"Purses, Umbrellas, and Gloves, Oh My!" in *Chicago Tribune,* 20 July 1988.
York, Peter, and Page Hill Starzinger, "Americans Have Often Taken Fashion Inspiration from the British," in *Vogue* (New York), February 1990.
Fallon, James, "Aquascutum Accepts $121m Buyout Offer," in the *Daily News Record* (New York), 25 April 1990.
Taylor, John, "The Aquascutum Heritage," in *British Style*, No. 3, 1990.
Skolnik, Lisa, "Let Raindrops Keep Falling—Women are Ready With Their Trenches," in *Chicago Tribune,* 12 April 2000.

* * *

Aquascutum's distinctive name is two Latin words meaning "watershield"—a name which has become synonymous with the best of traditional British clothing. Aquascutum originated as a name for the finely tailored coats made of showerproof natural fabrics developed by a small tailoring firm based in London's Regent Street. They were ideal protection from England's inclement weather, and, like many ostensibly functional items of clothing and footwear, the Aquascutum raincoat or cape also achieved high fashion status, worn even in fine weather. Today's equivalent may be seen in the likes of the Burberry jacket, originally created for outdoor enthusiasts of fishing and hunting, but as likely to be seen worn over a city suit as on the moors. Timberland boots and Levis were also developed originally as workwear but have achieved cult fashion status.

A royal customer has always been an important asset to any business, and Aquascutum was fortunate in attracting the custom of Edward VII, Prince of Wales, who wore both greatcoats and capes made of the miraculously rain-repellent cloth. In 1897 the company was awarded its first royal warrant as "Waterproofers" to HRH The Prince of Wales.

For the first 50 years of business, Aquascutum was involved solely in the production of clothing for gentlemen. In 1909 the company launched its first collection of womenswear, prompted by the increasing popularity of sportswear for women. The often-romanticized imaged of the landed gentlemen and his tweed-clad lady have become potent symbols of English culture, and a persistent element in Britain's international fashion image. It is interesting to note that when fashion designer Katherine Hamnett first showed her collection in Paris in 1989, *Le Figaro* remarked upon the fact that England now produced clothes other than cashmere sweaters and raincoats. In this light it is understandable that, when foreigners refer to English style, they are usually implying the quintessentially English look of companies such as Aquascutum or Burberry, rather than the avant-garde style of contemporary designers. Aquascutum represents the traditional image of thoroughly good British taste which lent itself perfectly to the sporting events that dominated the English Season.

While Aquascutum is perhaps best recognized for its clothing, it is in fact the company's technical achievements in the textiles field that are most remarkable. The 1950s were an important period for the company in terms of textile developments. In 1955 Aquascutum introduced an iridescent-toned cotton gabardine for men's and women's raincoats. Three years later they launched a black evening coat made of showerproof wool and mohair fabric which won the company a clothing Oscar. In 1959 a rainproof cloth (called Aqua 5) was introduced which eliminated the need for reproofing after dry cleaning, which resulted in worldwide acclaim for Aquascutum. The company's breakthroughs in textile development, including more recent work with microfibers, found the new fabrics incorporated into both the menswear and womenswear collections.

Aquascutum continued to produce an extensive collection of clothing and accessories for men and women, with a full range of womenswear introduced in 1986. A high profile client soon emerged in the person of Prime Minister Margaret Thatcher, dressed exclusively by the company for years during her terms in office. Aquascutum also introduced accessories, including handbags and travel bags, umbrellas, hats, scarves, and small leather goods, many of which bear the company's coat of arms. In the first part of the 21st century, trench coats were suddenly back at the height of fashion, with Aquascutum and its longtime rival, Burberrys, once again at the forefront of the industry.

Viscount Thurso wearing an Aquascutum Ltd.-designed ensemble, ca. 1985. © Norman Parkinson Limited/Fiona Cowan/CORBIS.

As a company that originated producing clothing to protect its wearer from an unruly native climate, Aquascutum became a recognized brand label at international level. Though generally considered "conservative" fashion, dressing royalty and government officials, or "vintage" by others, Aquascutum outerwear has endured for 150 years and will never be out of style.

—Catherine Woram; updated by Nelly Rhodes

ARAI, Junichi

Japanese textile designer

Born: Kiryu City, Gunma Prefecture, 13 March 1932. **Education:** Trained in weaving at his father's textile factory, 1950–55; also studied at the Theater Arts Institute, Tokyo, 1953. **Family:** Married Riko Tanagawa, 1958; children: Motomi, Mari. **Career:** formed Tomodachi Za puppet theater group, 1950; independent textile designer in Tokyo, from 1955; developed new metallic yarn techniques, 1955–66; worked with fashion designers Rei Kawakubo, Issey Miyake, Shin Hosokawa, and others, from 1970; produced computer-designed woven fabrics, from 1979; founded Anthology studio, 1979, and Arai Creation System company, 1987; opened Nuno fabrics shop, Tokyo, 1984; advisor, Yuki Tsumugi Producers Assn., Japanese Ministry of Trade, and International Wool Secretariat, from 1987; teaches at Otsuka Textile Design Institute. **Exhibitions:** Gen Gallery, Tokyo, 1983; Nichifutsu Gallery, Kyoto, 1984; Sagacho Exhibition Space, Tokyo, 1984; Shimin Gallery, Sapporo, 1985; Axis Gallery, Tokyo, 1986; Rhode Island School of Design, Providence, 1988; *Hand and Technology: Textiles by Junichi Arai 1992,* Yurakucho Asashi Gallery, Asashi, Japan; Pacific Art Center, Los Angeles, 1993; *Junichi: Glistening Fabrics,* Kemper Museum of Contemporary Art, Kansas City, Missouri, 1997. **Awards:** Mainichi Fashion award, Tokyo, 1983; Honorary Royal Designer for Industry, London, 1987. **Address:** Shinsyuku Kiryu-city, Gunma-pref 376, Japan.

Publications

By ARAI:

Articles

"Nuno Choryu," in *Ginka Bunka Shuppan,* No. 63, 1985.

On ARAI:

Books

Tulokas, Maria, ed., *Fabrics for the 1980s* (exhibition catalogue), Providence, RI, 1985.

Sutton, Ann, and Diane Saheenan, *Ideas in Weaving,* Loveland, CO, and London, 1989.

Arai, Junichi, et al., *Hand and Technology: Textiles by Junichi Arai 1992* (exhibition catalogue), Asashi, Japan, 1992.

Articles

Tulokas, Maria, "Textiles for the Eighties," in *Textilforum* (Hanover, Germany), September 1985.

Cannarella, D., "Fabric About Fabric," in *Threads* (Newtown, CT), November 1985.

Popham, P., "Man of Cloth," in *Blueprint* (London), December/ January 1987–88.

Tulokas, Maria, "Textiles by Junichi Arai, 1979–1988," in *Textilforum* (Hanover, Germany), June 1989.

"Junichi Arai," in the *New York Times,* 16 April 1990.

MacIsaac, Heather Smith, "Arai Arrives: Japanese Textile Designer Junichi Arai Makes His American Debut," in *House & Garden,* August 1990.

"Junichi Arai and Reiko Sudo," in *Design Journal,* No. 42, 1991.

Livingston, David, "Junichi Arai's Creations Provoke, Mystify," in the *Toronto Globe and Mail,* 16 January 1992.

Pollock, Naomi R., "Dream Weavers," in *Metropolis,* September 1992.

Louie, Elaine, "A Fabric that is Light, in Both Senses," in the *New York Times,* 25 March 1993.

Self, Dana, "Junichi Arai: Glistening Fabrics," available online at www.Kemperart.org, 17 July 2001.

"Quality Fabric of the Month," available online at Textile Industries, www.textileindustries.com, 18 July 2001.

"Tsunami: Yardage Exhibit," online at www.weavespindye.org, 18 July 2001.

* * *

Junichi Arai creates the stuff of dreams, fabrics never seen before. His work is a true collaboration: innovators in yarn and slit film production, in computers, and in loom technology are essential partners. But the finished product, the textiles "like stone" or "like clouds" created for Issey Miyake at his suggestion, or the fabrics Arai calls Spider Web, Titanium Poison, and Driving Rain, are pure Arai in inspiration, imagination, and execution. They could only have been created in Japan.

The great-grandson and grandson of spinners, and the son and nephew of weavers, Arai was born and raised in Kiryu, a historic textile center north of Tokyo. Steeped in Japanese textile tradition, he nevertheless dreamed of becoming an actor. Instead, at the age of 18, he began working in his father's factory, weaving obi and kimono cloth, including one that involved the twisting of gold or silver fibers around a core of silk yarn. The family firm also made synthetic and metallic fabrics for the U.S. cocktail dress market. In developing these fabrics, Arai acquired 36 patents. The eight years he spent helping run the business provided him with technical expertise but little satisfaction. It all paved the way, however, for his years of experimentation, teaching him the rules he would later break.

One of Arai's innovations is a burn-out process that dissolves the cotton covering from metallic thread, creating a new type of fabric. He also experimented with "melt-off," in which metal between two layers of lacquer in a slit film yarn is dissolved, producing an unusual, filmy fabric. Among his other creations are a stretchy yarn made of tightly coiled nylon covered by wool and another metallic fabric constructed from slit film polyester/silver yarn used in home furnishings. He has experimented with techniques such as using materials with different rates of shrinkage to create unusual puckers, then pulls in the fabric and transferring dye-embedded paper into wrinkled cloth—creating permanent folds of color.

Longtime colleague Reiko Sudo wrote in the exhibition catalogue for *Hand and Technology: Textiles by Junichi Arai 1992,* "He is truly the *enfant terrible* of Japanese textiles, delighting in snubbing convention, a naughty boy playing with ultra-high-tech toys." His genius consists of what Milton Sonday of the Cooper-Hewitt Museum in New York termed "pushing the limits" of both new and traditional technology, having the vision to take it one step further, or to combine fibers and technologies in new ways. The digital computer is his drawing board, freeing him to explore design possibilities and select the best ones. With it and the Jacquard loom, Arai hopes someday to create a fabric whose pattern changes as subtly as the days in a lifetime, never exactly repeating. For one exhibition, Arai concentrated on the combination of high technology and handcraft, using two different kinds of warp and weft, woven by the same machine, and limiting himself to two weave structures.

In a review of an Arai exhibit at the Kemper Museum of Contemporary Art in Kansas City, Missouri, in 1997 Curator Dana Self emphasized Arai's insistence that fabrics must resemble human skin in their flexibility and combinations of earthly elements, while possessing an ability to reshape themselves and retain their original essence. Arai, Self wrote, "merges traditional and nontraditional, simplicity and complexity," and draws on centuries of Japanese textile tradition. According to Self, he also understands that "textiles and clothing reverberate with ideas about how we clothe ourselves, how certain fabrics make us feel physically and emotionally, and how fabrics and clothing function in our culture."

Fashion designers like Miyake, Rei Kawakubo, and Yoshiki Hishinuma, a former Miyake apprentice, are among the collaborators whose imaginations Arai has challenged. Some of his fabrics are suitable for home furnishings; these are sold in Nuno showrooms in Tokyo, New York, Los Angeles, and Chicago. End use, however, is not really an Arai concern. In fact, some of his fabrics may only be suitable for museum installations, but that is quite beside the point of his work. Tiny print at the bottom of a hang tag, from a scarf purchased in an Issey Miyake boutique, whispers, "This work is the product of a weaving technology invented by Junichi Arai." As an innovator in weaving technology and the creation of new fabrics, he has no equal; in his work, the future is now.

—Arlene C. Cooper; updated by Sally A. Myers

ARMANI, Giorgio

Italian designer

Born: Piacenza, Italy, 11 July 1934. **Education:** Studied medicine, University of Bologna, 1952–53; also studied photography. **Military Service:** Served in the Italian Army, 1953–54. **Family:** Life partner, Sergio Galeotti (died 1985). **Career:** Window display designer, La Rinascente department stores, 1954; stylist, menswear buyer, La Rinascente stores, 1954–60; menswear designer, Nino Cerruti, 1960–70; freelance designer, 1970–75; first Armani menswear collection, 1974; introduced womenswear, 1975; launched Emporio Armani and Armani Jeans, 1981; Mani womenswear debuted, mid-1980s; Giorgio Armani Occhiali and Giorgio Armani Calze, 1987; sportswear range and Emporio Armani shops selling younger collection opened in London, 1989; Giorgio Armani USA formed, 1980; bought Antinea, 1990; AX, Armani Exchange, boutiques with lesser-priced basics opened in the U.S., 1991; acquired majority stake in Simint, 1996; bought Intai accessories producer, 1998; forged alliance with Ermenegildo Zegna, 2000; launched website, 2000; opened new Hong Kong and SoHo stores, 2001; fragrances include *Armani le Parfum,* 1982, *Armani Eau pour Homme,* 1984, and *Gio,* 1992; *Acqua di Gio,* 1995; *Emporio Armani* (his and hers), 1997; *Mania,* 2000. **Exhibitions:** *Intimate Architecture: Contemporary Clothing Design,* Massachusetts Institute of Technology, Cambridge, 1982; *Giorgio Armani: Images of Man,* Fashion Institute of Technology, New York, 1990–91, traveled to Tokyo, Paris, London; retrospective *Armani: 1972–92,* Palazzo Pitti, Florence, 1992; *Giorgio Armani,* 25-year retrospective, Guggenheim Museum, New York, 2000. **Awards:** Neiman Marcus award, 1979; Cutty Sark award, 1980, 1981, 1984; *Gentlemen's Quarterly* Manstyle award, 1982; Grand'Ufficiale dell'Ordine al Merito award, Italy, 1982; Gold Medal from Municipality of Piacenza, 1983; CFDA International Designer award, 1983, 1987; L'Occhio d'Oro award, 1984, 1986, 1987, 1988, 1994; Cutty Sark Men's Fashion award, 1985; Bath Museum of Costume Dress of the Year award, 1986; named Gran Cavaliere della Repubblica, Italy, 1987; Lifetime Achievement award, 1987; Christobal Balenciaga award, 1988; Media Key award, 1988; Woolmark award, 1989, 1992; Senken award, 1989; honorary doctorate, Royal College of Art, 1991; Fiorino d'Oro award, Florence, 1992; Golden Effie award, 1993; Aguja de Oro award, Spain, 1993; Academia del Profumo Award, Italy, 1993. **Address:** Via Borgonuovo 21, 20121 Milan, Italy. **Website:** www.giorgioarmani.com.

Giorgio Armani, fall/winter 2001 ready-to wear collection. © AFP/ CORBIS.

PUBLICATIONS

On ARMANI:

Books

Combray, Richard de, and Arturo Carlo Quintavalle, *Giorgio Armani,* Milan, 1982.
Hayden Gallery, Massachusetts Institute of Technology, *Intimate Architecture: Contemporary Clothing Design* [exhibition catalogue], Cambridge, MA., 1982.
Barbieri, Gian Paolo, *Artificial,* Paris, 1982.
Alfonsi, Maria-Vittoria, *Leaders in Fashion: I grandi personaggi della moda,* Bologna, 1983.
Milbank, Caroline Rennolds, *Couture: The Great Designers,* New York, 1985.
Perschetz, Lois, ed., *W, The Designing Life,* New York, 1987.
Coleridge, Nicholas, *The Fashion Conspiracy,* London, 1988.
Howell, Georgina, *Sultans of Style: 30 Years of Fashion and Passion 1960–1990,* London, 1990.
Martin, Richard, and Harold Koda, *Giorgio Armani: Images of Man,* New York, 1990.
White, Nicola, *Giorgio Armani,* New York, 2000.
Celant, Germano, and Harold Koda, New York & London, 2000.
Giorgio Armani: Twenty-Five Photographers, Ostfildern, 2001.
Giorgio Armani, Fundación del Museo Guggenheim, Bilboa, 2001.

Articles

Hamilton, Rita, "Giorgio Armani's Fine Italian Hand," in *Esquire* (New York), 22 May 1979.
"Giorgio Armani," in *Time,* May 1982.
Barbieri, Giampaolo, "La moda diventa arte," in *Amica* (Milan), December 1982.
Teston, E., "A Visit With Giorgio Armani," in *Architectural Digest,* May 1983.
"Armani: Success, Tailor Made," in *Vogue,* August 1984.
Mower, Sarah, "Giorgio Armani: A Man for All Seasons," in *Woman's Journal* (London), April 1986.

Thurman, Judith, "A Cut Above," in *Connoisseur* (New York), August 1986.
Romanelli, Marco, "Giorgio Armani: Il progetto dell'abito 1988," in *Domus* (Milan), January 1988.
Brantley, Ben, "The Armani Mystique," in *Vanity Fair,* June 1988.
Brantley, Bill, "The Emperor of New Clothes," in the *Daily Telegraph Weekend Magazine* (London), 17 December 1988.
Mower, Sarah, "Emperor Armani," in *Vogue* (London), January 1989.
Keers, Paul, "The Emporio of Style," in *GQ* (London), February/March 1989.
Kostner, Kevin, "The Emporio Strikes Back," in *Sky* (London), March 1989.
West, Carinthia, "Giorgio Armani," in *Marie Claire* (London), April 1989.
Cohen, Eddie Lee, "Giorgio Armani," in *Interior Design,* April 1989.
Furness, Janine, "Alluring Armani," in *Interior Design,* May 1989.
Cohen, Eddie Lee, "Emporio Armani," in *Interior Design,* September 1989.
Brampton, Sally, "Armani's Island," in *Elle Decoration* (London), Autumn 1989.
Howell, Georgina, "Armani: The Man Who Fell to Earth," in the *Sunday Times Magazine* (London), 18 February 1990.
Mardore, Lucienne, "La storia di Giorgio Armani," in *Marie Claire* (Paris), May 1990.
Borioli, Gisella, "Giorgio Armani: This is the Real Me," in *Donna* (Milan), October 1990.
LaFerla, Ruth, "Sizing Up Giorgio Armani," in the *New York Times Magazine,* 21 October 1990.
Gerrie, Anthea, "Giorgio Armani," in *Clothes Show* (London), June 1991.
Friend, Ted, "The Armani Edge," in *Vogue,* March 1992.
Doyle, Kevin, "Armani's True Confessions," in *Women's Wear Daily,* 25 June 1992.
Hutton, Lauren, "Giorgio Armani," in *Interview* (New York), April 1993.
Forden, Sara Gay, "Numero Uno: Giorgio Armani, the World's Most Successful Designer, Still Isn't Satisfied," in *Women's Wear Daily,* 26 October 1994.
Schiff, Stephen, "Lunch with Mr. Armani, Tea with Mr. Versace, Dinner with Mr. Valentino," in the *New Yorker,* 7 November 1994.
Menkes, Suzy, "Armani's Off-the-Rack Mozart," in the *International Herald Tribune,* 17 January 1995.
Forden, Sara Gay, "According to Armani," in *DNR,* 19 January 1995.
Spindler, Amy M. "Armani and Ferré: A Study in Contrast," in the *New York Times,* 11 March 1995.
Moin, David, Sharon Edelson, and Samantha Conti, "The Armani Blitz Begins (Giorgio Armani Stores in New York, New York)" in *Women's Wear Daily,* 9 September 1996.
Rawsthorn, Alice, "Master of the Cool Classic," in the *Financial Times,* 25 August 1997.
Socha, Miles, "Giorgio Armani," in *Women's Wear Daily,* 3 April 1998.
Conti, Samantha, "Giorgio Armani: The Changing Face of Elegance," in *Women's Wear Daily,* 23 June 1999.
Zargani, Luisa, "Armani and Zegna Form Joint Venture," in *Women's Wear Daily,* 25 July 2000.
Conti, Samantha, "At Home with Giorgio Armani," in *Women's Wear Daily,* 14 September 2000.
Heller, Richard, "Last Man Standing (Designer Giorgio Armani)," in *Forbes,* 12 November 2001.

* * *

Giorgio Armani is a design colonialist responsible for the creation of an aesthetic in both menswear and womenswear that had a firm grip on international style in the 1980s. Renowned for his use of fabric and expertise in tailoring, he is a world leader in menswear design responsible for the wide-shouldered look for executive women. His pared-down unstructured silhouette moved away from the standard tailored look epitomizing menswear since the 19th century; by eliminating interfaces, linings, and shoulder pads, Armani restructured the jacket, creating a softly tailored look.

Although Armani produces entire ranges of these functional, adaptable, flexible items of clothing that seem almost throwaway in their simplicity, they are, in fact, luxurious designs made of high-quality cloth. His clothes, however, although expensive, have their own understated glamour and could never be described as ostentatious. Neither trend nor tradition, the Armani style draws a fine line between the two. Eschewing change for its own sake, he believes in quality rather than invention. His collections are redefinitions of a

Giorgio Armani, spring/summer 2001 collection. © AP/Wide World Photos.

soft, unstructured style, playing with layers of texture and color but constantly renegotiating proportions. Elegant and understated, they have a timeless quality, a classicism often emphasized in nostalgic advertising campaigns by Italian photographer Aldo Fallai.

Born in Piacenza, Italy, in 1934, Armani's first taste of the fashion industry was with La Rinascente, a large Italian department store chain where in 1954 he worked on the window displays. He then transferred to the Office of Fashion and Style where he had an invaluable training in the use of fabrics and the importance of customer profiling and targeting. After seven years he left to design menswear for Nino Cerruti, and for a month worked in one of the firm's textile factories where he learned to appreciate fabric, the skills that went into its production, and the techniques of industrial tailoring.

In 1974 Armani launched his own label, which was to become incredibly successful—the biggest-selling line of European design in America. His first designs revolved around the refining of the male jacket, which he believed to be the most important invention in the history of dress, being both versatile and functional and suited to all social occasions. His idea was to instil the relaxation of sports clothing into its tailored lines. He later applied similar notions to womenswear, evolving a new manner of dress for women. He further developed a style for working women with an understated, almost androgynous chic.

In these years, Armani designs were very expensive, being made out of the most luxurious materials such as alpaca, cashmere, and suede. To expand his customer base and meet the increasing demands of a fashion conscious public for clothes with a designer label, he produced a cheaper womenswear range entitled Mani, made out of synthetics so advanced they could not be copied, together with the popular Emporio Armani range of sportswear. For men he produced definitive navy blazers, crumpled linen jackets, and leather separates, which he introduced in 1980, and oversized overcoats and raincoats. Impeccably tailored, with faltering cut, easy lines, and subtle textures, patterns, and colors, he introduced twists such as lowslung button placement on double-breasted suits for men and experimental blends of fabrics such as viscose with wool or linen with silk.

Like his contemporaries in the industry, Armani diversified into jeans, undergarments, neckwear, golf apparel, accessories, fragrances, and more recently, cosmetics. With more than a dozen clothing lines, the quality has not diminished, merely attracted a wider clientèle which in turn attracted the notice of luxury conglomerates LVMH and Gucci Group. Both approached Armani with acquisitive offers, but he refused. "Of course, I was flattered," he told Richard Heller of *Forbes* (12 November 2001), "But I decided to keep my independence." He is, indeed, one of a disappearing breed, without stockholders or backers to answer to—rather, he has increasingly bought his licensees and brought most Armani brand in-house.

If ever there was a doubt about how the world felt about Armani and his contributions to fashion, they were completley dispelled in November 2000 when the Guggenheim Museum threw a lavish gala to mark the opening of its Giorgio Armani retrospective in New York. Covering 25 years of Armani creativity and featuring 400 garments, the exhibition attracted a glittering crowd including Hollywood celebrities, athletes, and musicians. Giorgio Armani, now and forever, represents the finest in elegant, sophisticated style.

—Caroline Cox; updated by Nelly Rhodes

ASHLEY, Laura

Welsh designer

Born: Laura Mountney in Dowlais, Glamorgan, Wales, 7 September 1925. **Education:** Attended Marshall's School, Merthyr Tydfil, Wales, until 1932; mainly self-taught in design. **Military Service:** Served in the Women's Royal Naval Service. **Family:** Married Bernard Ashley, 1949; children: Jane, David, Nick, and Emma. **Career:** Worked as secretary, National Federation of Women's Institutes, London, 1945–52; founder/partner, with Bernard Ashley, Ashley-Mountney Ltd. printed textiles, 1954–68, in Kent, 1956–61, and in Carno, Wales, from 1961; opened first retail outlet, London, 1967; Laura Ashley Ltd. established, 1968; Geneva and Amsterdam stores opened, 1972; Paris, 1973; first U.S. shop, San Francisco, 1974; New York store opened, 1977; son Nick Ashley took over as design director, 1984; Laura Ashley Foundation created, 1984; company went public, 1985; shops topped 550 shops in 63 countries, 1993; Bernard Ashley resigned from board, 1998; stake (40-percent) of company sold to Malaysian United Industries, 1998; North American stores sold, 1999; flagship Regent Street store redone and reopened, 2000; plans for 100 home furnishings initiated, 2001. **Awards:** Queen's award for Export Achievement, 1977; Bernard Ashley knighted, 1987. **Died:** 17 September 1985, in Coventry, England. **Company Address:** 27 Bagley's Lane, Fulham, London SW6 2QA, England. **Company Website:** www.lauraashley.com.

PUBLICATIONS

By ASHLEY:

Books

Laura Ashley Home Furnishings 1981, Carno, Wales, 1981.
Laura Ashley Home Furnishings 1982, Carno, Wales, 1982.
Laura Ashley Home Furnishings 1983, Carno, Wales, 1983.
Laura Ashley Home Furnishings 1984, Carno, Wales, 1984.
Laura Ashley Home Decoration 1985, Carno, Wales, 1985.
Laura Ashley Book of Home Decorating (with Elizabeth Dickson), Carno, Wales, London & New York, 1985, 1988, 1990, 1997.
Laura Ashley Home Furnishings 1986, Carno, Wales, 1986.
Laura Ashley Home Furnishings 1987, Carno, Wales, 1987.
Laura Ashley Complete Guide to Home Decorating, Carno, Wales, 1987.
Laura Ashley at Home: Six Family Homes and Their Transformation (with Nick Ashley), London, 1988.
Laura Ashley Guide to Country Decorating (with Lorrie Mack and Lucinda Edgerton), London, 1992.
Leitch, Michael, *The Laura Ashley Book of Anniversary Delights,* 1993.
Laura Ashley Decorating with Fabric: A Room-by-Room Guide to Home Decorating (with Lorrie Mack and Diana Dodge), New York, 1995.
Berry, Susan, *Laura Ashley Decorating with Paper & Paint: A Room-by-Room Guide to Home Decorating,* New York, 1995.
———, *Laura Ashley: The Color Book, Using Color to Decorate Your Home,* New York & London, 1995.
Laura Ashley Decorating with Patterns & Textures: Using Color, Pattern, and Texture in the Home, London, 1996.

On ASHLEY:

Books

Carter, Ernestine, *Magic Names of Fashion,* Englewood Cliffs, New Jersey, 1980.

Dickson, Elizabeth, and Margaret Colvin, *The Laura Ashley Book of Home Decorating,* London, 1982; New York, 1984.

Gale, Iain, and Susan Irvine, *Laura Ashley Style,* New York & London, 1987.

Sebba, Anne, *Laura Ashley: A Life by Design,* London, 1990, 1991.

Evans, John, and Gabrielle Stoddard, *Laura Ashley: Fashion Designer,* Caerdydd, Wales, 1996.

Stegemeyer, Anne, *Who's Who in Fashion, Third Edition,* New York, 1996.

Articles

"Queen Victoriana," in *Sophisticat* (London), November 1974.

"The Laura Ashley Look," in *Brides* (London), Spring 1975.

Dumoulin, Marie-Claude, "Chez Laura Ashley," in *Elle* (Paris), 11 October 1976.

Gould, Rachael, "From Patchwork to a Small Print to World Wide: How the Laura Ashley Family Business Grew Up," in *Vogue* (London), 15 April 1980.

Cleave, Maureen, "Makers of Modern Fashion: Laura Ashley," in the *Observer* supplement, (London), 12 October 1980.

Sheffield, Robert, "The Twist in the Tail," in *Creative Review* (London), January 1984.

"Young Nick," in *She* (London), April 1984.

"Cut From the Same Cloth as Mom and Dad, Laura Ashley's Kids Get All Wrapped Up in the Family Business," in *People Weekly,* 24 September 1984.

Slesin, Suzanne, "Laura Ashley, British Designer, is Dead at 60," in the *New York Times,* 18 September 1985.

Dickson, Elizabeth, "Laura Ashley: Her Life and Gifts, by Those Who Knew Her," in the *Observer,* 22 September 1985.

Sulitzer, Paul-Loup, "Laura Ashley: Une impression d'éternité," in *Elle* (Paris), 4 August 1986.

"The Ashley Empire," in the *Sunday Express Magazine* (London), 25 September 1988.

Ducas, June, "Inside Story," in *Woman's Journal* (London), October 1988.

"Laura Ashley, A Licensing Legend," in *HFD—The Weekly Home Furnishings Newspaper,* 26 December 1988.

Finnerty, Anne, "Profile of Laura Ashley," in *Textile Outlook International* (London), January 1990.

Fernaud, Dierdre, and Margaret Park, "After Laura," in the *Sunday Times* (London), 4 February 1990.

Grieve, Amanda, "Clotheslines," in *Harpers & Queen* (London), April 1993.

Bain, Sally, "Life Begins at 40 for Laura Ashley," in *Marketing,* 13 May 1993.

Levine, Joshua, "Wilted Flowers: Laura Ashley Holdings Plc.," in *Forbes,* 10 April 1995.

Flynn, Julia, "Giving Laura Ashley a Yank: Anne Iverson Has Restored Profits and Refocused on the Home," in *Business Week,* 27 May 1996.

Lee, Julian, "The Floral Dance," in *Marketing,* 28 August 1997.

White, Constance C.R., "A Makeover for Laura Ashley," in the *New York Times,* 19 May 1998.

Hosenball, Mark, "Rendering Unto Laura," in *Newsweek,* 8 February 1999.

Smith, Alison, "Laura Ashley Shows Flower Power," in the *Financial Times,* 27 May 2001.

* * *

Welsh designer Laura Ashley developed and distilled the British romantic style of neo-Victorianism, reflecting past eras in clothing, textiles, accessories, and furnishings and did so demonstrating classic country styling. Her approach to design was inspired by her environment, the surrounding Welsh countryside, and her yearning to return to all things natural. Integrating ideas adopted from the designs and qualities of past eras, she combined elements to create a look of nostalgic simplicity and naive innocence. Floral sprigged cotton fabrics, often directly adapted and developed from 18th- and 19th-century patterns, paisleys, and tiny prints worked with romantic detailing to create a style that was original and easily recognized.

Ashley's style possessed old world charm with individual rustic freshness, reflected in traditional beliefs of bygone days. Victorian nightshirts, Edwardian-style dresses, the introduction of the long smock in 1968, delicately trimmed with lace, pin-tucked bodices, tiered skirts, and full puffed sleeves became her trademark, aimed at the middle market and retailed at affordable prices. Laura Ashley Ltd. rose from the modest beginnings of a small cottage industry, producing a simple range of printed headscarves and table mats in the Ashley kitchen, to the development of a company that became a huge enterprise of international renown. It was a fairy story in itself.

Ashley's self-taught skill produced ranges of womenswear, childrenswear, bridalwear, accessories, and furnishings. She established home interiors consisting of coordinated ranges of bed linens, wall tiles, curtains, cushions, and upholstery. Her brilliant concept of fabrics, her discerning research of past eras for new inspiration, and her study and reinterpretation of antique textiles led to the considerable success and endurance of the Laura Ashley label.

Traditional floral prints combined together, printed in two colors and various color combinations, distinguished her work. Through the technical expertise and experimentation of Bernard Ashley, Laura's husband and business partner, came new developments and improved machinery, which in turn extended versatility. New and subtle color combinations were produced, often to Laura's own design. Natural fibres, crisp cottons, and lawn fabrics expanded to include ranges in twill, silk, wool, crêpe, velvet, corduroy, and eventually jersey fabrics.

Along with the 1960s youth revolution came a move towards romanticism, conservation, and world peace, an alternative to modern living, pop culture, mass-produced clothing, and vivid Parisian fashions. Due to her convincing beliefs in past values, quality, and the revival of romantic simplicity, Ashley's success was overwhelming. Bernard's business acuity and Laura's determination led to the development of excellent marketing techniques. Retail settings, complementary to the old world style of neo-Victorianism, promoted a look of individuality and quality.

Throughout the 1980s the Laura Ashley style retained its unique and easily recognizable image, even after the real Laura Ashley's tragic death, after a fall, in September 1985. The Ashleys' son, Nick, took over as design director in the year before his mother's death, and the Laura Ashley style evolved, extending to all ranges to incorporate contemporary fashion ideas, including the introduction of jersey for practical and easy-to-wear clothing. In addition to Nick, the other

Ashley children, Jane, David, and Emma, all had roles within the family business.

In the 1990s the company lost its way; its lovely clothing was perceived as outdated and frumpy and the Laura Ashley image suffered considerably. Amid a series of executive changes, restructuring, and loss of market share in the years following founder Laura Ashley's death, the company finally regained its footing by retooling its image, updating its clothing, and expanding its home furnishings collection. A series of coffee-table books, which had been published annually in the late 1980s, grew to include how-to guides on home decorating in a myriad of styles from the *Laura Ashley Guide to Country Decorating* in 1992 to the *Laura Ashley Decorating with Patterns & Textures: Using Color, Pattern, and Texture in the Home,* in 1997.

Selling a 40-percent stake in the company to Malaysia United Industries in 1998, for $74 million, gave Laura Ashley a desperately needed infusion of cash. Next came the difficult decision to close many of its manufacturing facilities in Wales, then the sale of its underperforming North American stores to an investor group funded by Mayalsia United. By the start of the 21st century, Laura Ashley's Regent Street flagship store had reopened after a ceiling to floor refurbishment, and the company announced plans for its own website as well as opening 100 home furnishings stores by 2005. Rejuvenated and in the black after years of losses, Laura Ashley has regained its status, rediscovered its identity, and repositioned its signature style.

—Carol Mary Brown; updated by Nelly Rhodes

AUJARD, Christian

French designer

Born: Brittany in 1945. **Family:** Married Michele Domercq, 1972; children: Richard, Giles. **Career:** Worked as a delivery boy, stock clerk, then financial manager for Charles Maudret wholesale ready-to-wear firm, 1964–67; formed own ready-to-wear company with Michele Aujard, 1968; firm carried by Michele after Christian's death, 1977; first freestanding boutique opened, Paris, 1978; company purchased by Société Bic, 1983; fashions manufactured and distributed by Guy Laroche, and licensed to Japan's Itokin Group. **Died:** 8 March 1977, in Paris.

Publications

On AUJARD:

Articles

Hyde, Nina, "Continuing the Aujard Collection," in the *Washington Post,* 23 September 1978.

"Christian Aujard," in *Sir,* February 1982.

Palmieri, Jean E., "Barneys New York; Pioneering Designer Names for More Than Thirty Years," in *DNR,* 1 June 1995.

D'Aulnay, Sophie, "Alain Adjadj's Single-Minded Approach to French Retailing," in *DNR,* 7 August 1995.

Bow, Josephine, "The China Challenge: What it Takes to Enter Retailing in the World's Largest Potential Consumer Market," in *Women's Wear Daily,* 22 July 1997.

* * *

From the moment Christian Aujard premiered his first women's ready-to-wear collection in Paris, his designs were acclaimed for their youthful appeal, vibrant colors, and lively prints. The Aujard label quickly became recognized for its fresh attitude toward contemporary, updated sportswear. Aujard's first collection, directed towards the young, fashion-conscious consumer, successfully blended both classic and innovative elements into chic, wearable clothes, and thus instantly established his talent among the fashion world.

Michele Domercq, a former art student, began as Christian Aujard's designer of silks before becoming his wife and business partner. Combining her styling skills with his vision, the couple's ready-to-wear line for women took off as it was eagerly embraced by upmarket retailers, first in Europe and then in America. Aujard won acclaim for his upbeat attitude toward the tried-and-true, with youthful trench coats, blazers, trousers, pleated skirts, and shirtdresses. The clothes were tailored but relaxed, with features like elasticized waistbands and dolman sleeves that allowed ease of movement. Detailing was a focus, with interesting yokes and seams, and fagoting was a favored trim. Another Aujard hallmark was his use of natural fibers. Cotton, cashmere, linen, silk, wool tweed, crepe, and mohair—all found expression, as in his soft beige Honan silk blouson sweater and trousers of 1972.

In the 1960s and 1970s when women began to ask for access to the power traditionally enjoyed by men, designers answered with menswear styles for women, and Aujard's lines were no exception. But his menswear-inspired designs remained resolutely feminine, as seen in the bestselling Officer's Pantsuit. This ensemble, a double-breasted blazer over wide-legged trousers in a navy/white nautical palette, transformed the notion of an authoritative military uniform into a charming, yet provocative daytime look. Aujard also won much attention for his man-tailored oxford cloth shirts, crisp shirtdresses in dotted silk and wrinkled linen, and his double-faced beige wool wrap coat which reversed to tweed.

Women's eveningwear included elegant, refined short cocktail dresses of silk inset with bands of lace. The special domain of Michele, the silk clothes for evening were so successful she spun off a separate label under her own name. It was understood between the couple that Christian designed daywear and Michele designed eveningwear, and they often did not see each other's collections until they premiered.

Aujard ventured into men's ready-to-wear a few years after his womenswear. The collections for men featured both dress suits and casual separates, and continued the philosophy of elegant simplicity updated with youthful vigor. Vibrant, rich color, lively patterns, and prints became a signature, allowing men a wide range of fashion expression. Checks mixed with plaids and houndstooths, bright dotted patterns, and unexpected combinations created a cheerful, yet sophisticated look. In menswear, Aujard's typical attention to detail, use of fine materials, and witty attitude could be translated into a glamorous double-breasted suit of unexpected and dazzling white wool.

At the time of her husband's accidental death in March 1977, Michele took over the business and continued designing under the Christian Aujard name. At first she did not change the spirit of the Aujard collections, but by the late 1970s the lines were totally of her design. For both mens and womenswear she favored a mixture of textures and a palette of soft, saturated hues. Muted colors were chosen so that separates—jackets, sweaters, shirts, trousers, or skirts—would all coordinate. Crisp lines gave way to less constructed pieces in yielding fabrics like wool challis and satin. And while styling and managing the Aujard lines, Michele Aujard continued to oversee her own label.

The Aujard name continued to thrive as Michele invested ordinary styles with new life. For menswear she created wildly patterned waistcoats and drapy pleated pants, and she let color loose, using daring palettes considered taboo for men. She might mix violet, red, and emerald with gray, or playfully contrast textures, as in a rust tweed blazer against a persimmon satin shirt. Casual separates, such as a royal blue sport jacket over pale lemon trousers, glowed with intensity and radiated novelty, so that perceived boundaries between appropriate colors for men and women were blurred. The sweater woven with painterly motifs in brilliant color combinations also became a hallmark of Aujard.

The company's formula for success was its ability to push fashion limits while essentially remaining within the boundaries of convention. The Christian Aujard label has stood for sophisticated, affordable, and stylishly upbeat ready-to-wear clothing for men and women. On the label's longevity, French retailer Alain Adjadj told the *Daily News Record* (7 August 1995) sophisticated brands like Georges Rech and Christian Aujard, if marketed properly could certainly "relaunch the men's apparel business in France and [create] a worldwide boom."

—Kathleen Paton; updated by Sydonie Benét

AYTON, Sylvia

British designer

Born: Ilford, Essex, England, 27 November 1937. **Education:** Attended Walthamstow School of Art, 1953–57, and the Royal College of Art, London, 1957–60. **Career:** Freelance design work from 1959–63 included B.E.A. air hostess uniforms, 1959, clothing for B. Altman and Co. (New York), Count Down and Pallisades stores (London); worked at Costume Museum, Bath, England, 1960; designed hats for film *Freud,* 1960; formed partnership with Zandra Rhodes to open Fulham Road Clothes Shop, London, 1964; outerwear designer for the Wallis Fashion Group, Ltd., London, from 1969; freelance designer and pattern cutter for Keith Taylor, Ltd., London, 1975–80; part-time lecturer at Kingston Polytechnic (London), 1961–65, Ravensbourne College of Art and Design (London), 1961–67, Middlesex Polytechnic 1967–71; also external assessor for B.A. (Honors) fashion and textile courses, from 1976. **Awards:** Fellow, Royal Society of Arts, 1986; awarded MBE (Member of the British Empire), 1990. **Address:** c/o The Wallis Fashion Group Ltd., 22 Garrick Industrial Centre, Garrick Road, Hendon, London NW9 6AQ, England.

Publications

On AYTON:

Books

Mulvagh, Jane, *Vogue History of Twentieth-Century Fashion,* London, 1988.

Lebenthal, Joel, *Radical Rags: Fashions of the 1960s,* New York, 1990.

Debrett's *People of Today,* London, 1991.

Articles

Palen, Brenda, "Fashion on Fire," in *The Guardian* (London), September 1984.

Sinha, Pammi, and Chris Rivlin, "Describing the Fashion Design Process," [conference paper for the Second European Academy of Design Conference], Stockholm, 1997.

*

I design for a chain of High Street shops, so I sell to a very wide range of customers who expect well-designed, well-made and well-priced garments.

The coats and raincoats I design must be extremely "wantable." My aim is to make thousands of women feel wonderful by providing garments that are not too boring, too safe, or too extreme but sharp, minimal, very functional, uncontrived, all very easy but with an element of surprise. I am a perfectionist. I care desperately about the shapes and proportions of my designs. I care about every detail, every stitch, button, and buckle. If the design is easy on my eye, it will also please my customer.

I don't design to a theme or for myself. Most of my ideas evolve from season to season, or a new idea just flashes into my head. I am very aware of my customers' lifestyle, and, as fashion is constantly evolving, I must be aware of the changing needs of women, and yet remain creative, experimental, and forward thinking. I design for a type of woman, not for an age group, and I become that woman as I design. I believe there are basically three types of women—the feminine woman, the classic woman, the fashion woman—and I feel she stays that type all of her life, whether she is 16 or 60.

I adore designing. I am always enthusiastic about my work, and get great joy from seeing so many women wearing my clothes. It is my job and my joy to make her feel good and very special, and to encourage her to return to the shops to buy again and again.

—Sylvia Ayton

* * *

The name Sylvia Ayton probably means little to most British women, yet for the last several decades she has had a significant influence on what they wear. As outerwear designer for the Wallis Fashion Group, Ltd., Ayton produced fashion ranges in good quality fabrics at reasonable prices. Over the years, her coats and suits gained a rightful place in the forefront of High Street fashion.

Ayton's original ambition was to make women feel wonderful and special, as if each one were a "fairy princess." She dressed her first "fairy princesses" in the 1960s when she worked with Zandra Rhodes, Marion Foale, and Sally Tuffin. Some were private customers, but to her surprise, Ayton found that working for one person did not always provide satisfaction. During her career, she found the greatest fulfilment in designing a coat that will give pleasure to nearly 5,000 women. At Wallis, she produced two annual outerwear collections, mainly coats and suits. The cloth provided the starting point; each season came new fabrics and colors yet they had to be the right quality and price. These were used to create garments both fashionable but realistic—the typical Wallis customer was Ms. Average, but each woman had her own personality and lifestyle.

Ayton believed it most useful to divide women by type, rather than age group, categorizing them as "feminine," "classic," or "fashionable" types. This guided her attitude to her collections and dictated shapes and details. Each season, there were the classics: wool velour winter coats, gabardine trench styles, blousons. Of course there were always new ideas, unexpected twists, trims, or fabrics or completely experimental designs manufactured in small numbers for a few outlets. Alpaca wool coats, for example, were a luxury item featured only in a small number of shops. Ayton continually checked what customer were buying, and weekly sales figures provided an important guide. Sales influenced her ideas as much as the latest design intelligence.

Ayton has always been a realist who knows that business awareness is essential for a designer. This lesson was first learned in the 1960s when she opened the Fulham Road Clothes Shop with Zandra Rhodes, creating garments from fabric designed and printed by Rhodes. The press loved them, but their lack of backers, finance, and business sense proved fatal. For later designing, she thought like a buyer: pragmatic in seeking the best quality at a sensible price.

Ayton has worked unstintingly with British fashion design courses to instill high standards and to provide students with a realistic view of the industry. Annually, she organized placements in the Wallis design studio and pattern cutting rooms. Upholding standards is, in her view, essential. Having found her "fairy princess," she has spent years trying to teach young designers how to do the same.

Ayton visits Wallis clothing stores as often as possible to observe customers for herself, making her better able to create clothing for them when she returns to the design studio. She also collects fashion magazines from around the world and attends fabric fairs, usually in Europe, to keep at the forefront of the industry. Yet Ayton was never overly concerned with drawing up the newest, wildest outerwear on the market; instead, she focused on what clients will purchase. Her design process is cyclical, building upon the previous season as well as the last cold-weather season. She loses no time in warm weather, always looking ahead, researching markets and materials for the coming season as soon as production has begun on her previous work.

Working exclusively for a company label meant Ayton's name was not used to sell her designs. Her work, however, did not go unnoticed. She has received many awards, including the MBE for her services to fashion. The accolades are well deserved: as a designer Ayton has the right combination of qualities. She is a perfectionist and an idealist, but one with a very firm grasp of reality.

—Hazel Clark; updated by Carrie Snyder

AZAGURY, Jacques

French fashion designer working in London

Born: Casablanca, Morocco, 1956. **Education:** Studied at London College of Fashion, 1972–73; completed education at St. Martin's School of Art, London. **Career:** Worked for dress company in London's East End, 1972; began own business, 1975 (closed after one year; opened again, 1977); joined London Design Collections, 1978; judge, J&B Rare Designers Award, South Africa, 1997. **Address:** 50 Knightsbridge, London SW1, England.

Publications

On AZAGURY:

Articles

"How the Glamour Boys Are You," in *Cosmopolitan* (London), December 1987.

Dutt, Robin, "Jacques Azagury," in *Clothes Show* (London), April/May 1990.

Rodgers, Toni, "Double Vision," in *Elle* (London), March 1991.

"Relative Values," in the *Sunday Times Magazine* (London), 29 August 1993.

Watson, Ines, "Designs for High Living," in *Dispatch*, 12 December 1997.

* * *

Jacques Azagury is a designer of spectacular eveningwear for such high-profile clients as the Duchess of Kent, Joan Collins, Madonna, Emma Thompson, Elizabeth Taylor, Demi Moore, and Britain' First Lady, Cherie Blair. Azagury's reputation was enhanced when the late Diana, Princess of Wales, began to favor his designs. His glamorous style was perhaps best epitomized by the princess in the summer of 1994 when she walked out of the Ritz Hotel in London, to be met by the glare of the awaiting paparazzi, in a stunning Azagury black, graphite, and bugle bead sheath with sensuous side split.

Glamor and exoticism have always been part of the Azagury mystique. Born in Casablanca in 1956, he describes this environment as being exactly like a Hollywood film set. The precedent set by Ingrid Bergman in the film *Casablanca* or Lauren Bacall in *To Have and Have Not* established a culture that demanded a fabulously chic approach to dress. This was the ideal breeding ground for a fledgling fashion designer, and Azagury often attributes his sources of inspiration to a collection of photographs of his mother and her friends, lunching and partying in chic Casablancan style.

The Azagury family moved to London in the early 1960s so the children could benefit from an English education. His enthusiasm for fashion and style eventually led Jacques to study the subject at St. Martin's College of Art in London, which he entered at the young age of 13; after graduating, he quickly established his own label. Browns in London was one of the first high-fashion retail outlets to place an order. Joan Burstein, the owner of the boutique, recognized that the Azagury signature had an individual sophistication and luxury that easily complemented the slick appeal of her other labels, such as Claude Montana or Thierry Mugler.

Azagury began his own retail operation in London's Knightsbridge. As well as specializing in exclusive cocktail and special occasion wear for private clients, he also sells pieces to other fashion stores and top couture retailers throughout the UK. The operation is as chic as any Parisian couture salon and was complemented by Azagury's sister, Elizabeth, and her exclusive floristry business, Azagury Fleurs, which is run from the basement of the shop. His brother's shoe design label, Joseph Azagury, is run from premises nearby.

Azagury does not design for one particular type of woman, preferring to appeal to a huge cross-section from the ages of 13 to 60. He is adamant that what a woman does not want when purchasing eveningwear is fancy dress. Some eveningwear designers layer sequins, frills, ruching, and draping to create an overstated, unflattering fantasy, but Azagury uses sequins and frills with taste and discretion. The clothes never make major fashion statements but veer instead toward the classic and flattering. Their innovation and style come from Azagury's respect for cut and fit, and he devotes a great deal of time to getting this right.

In an article by Ines Watson (*Dispatch,* 12 December 1997), Azagury commented that Mrs. Blair, one of his most visible clients, "has great presence. She's now looking better than ever, she's affectionate, loves people and is always ready and willing to take suggestions." He reserves his deepest respect for the late Princess of Wales, of whom he said, "Dressing her was the highlight of my career. She was the most undemanding client and the best model that any designer could have. She was truly a lovely person, a gorgeous woman who will never be replaced. She would often phone me after an event where she wore one of my dresses, just to thank me. There aren't many people like that."

Azagury has survived and flourished in the ever-changing world of fashion because he insists upon perfect workmanship and continues to appeal to a broad-based international clientèle. He told Watson, "I found a great need for formal eveningwear that doesn't make the woman look like a grandmother. My designs are elegant and glamorous, yet they are still young." Additionally, he says he chooses only the best fabrics and never uses synthetics.

The Azagury family are a closely linked unit. As well as Elizabeth, two other sisters, Solange and Sylvia, and their father are involved in the companies. Creatively, what links the family together and motivates it is a united quest for design perfection. Grown-up, sexy sophistication sums up Jacques Azagury's style—never extreme but exquisitely made and fitted, whether it be a short, silver sequin cocktail dress, a crossover blouse in peacock silk, or a fabulously expensive full-length evening gown. Azagury never wants to compromise his look. "I don't like to see my clothes worn with other things," he declared in a *Clothes Show* magazine interview. He is protective of his designer's vision and does not want his customer to make sartorial mistakes, which epitomizes his continuing pursuit of chic and glamor in special occasion dressing.

—Kevin Almond; updated by Sally A. Myers

AZRIA, Max

American designer

Born: 1 January 1949, Sfax, Tunisia. **Education:** Dropped out of school to become a fashion entrepreneur. **Career:** Manufactured a variety of contemporary women's lines in Paris, 1970–81; founder/chief designer, Jess (U.S. retail stores carrying French-inspired women's ready-to-wear apparel), 1982–88; president/designer, and owner of BCBG Max Azria Group, including BCBG Max Azria (women's and men's designer label), Hervé Léger (French couture and deluxe ready-to-wear label), Parallel (contemporary label), and To The Max (young contemporary/better junior label), from 1989. **Awards:** California Designer of the Year, 1995; Atlanta Designer of the Year, 1996; Fashion Performance award, 1997; Seat on the Council of Fashion Designers of America, 1998; Divine Design's Women's Designer of the Year, 1998; Otis College of Art and Design's Fashion Achievement award, 2000; Top 50 Private Companies in Los Angeles, *Los Angeles Business Journal,* 2000. **Website:** www.BCBG.com.

Max Azria, designed for BCBG Max Azria's 2000 collection: silk chiffon dress with an organdy hat. © AP/Wide World Photos.

Publications

On AZRIA:

Books

Kronzek, Lynn C., *Los Angeles: Place of Possibilities,* Carlsbad, California, 1998.

Abramson, Susan, and Marcie Stuchin, *Shops & Boutiques 2000,* Glen Cover, New York, 1999.

Articles

"To the Max," in *Women's Wear Daily,* 23 September 1998.

Fox, Marisa, "Celebrities Put the Pizazz in New York Fashion Shows," in *Chicago Tribune,* 16 September 1999.

Servin, James, "Mad Max," in *Harper's Bazaar,* October 1999.

Davis, Boyd, "BCBG Max Azria," online at www.Fashion Windows.com, 25 October 1999.

Dam, Julie K. L., and Samantha Miller, "The Max Factor," in *People,* 22 November 1999.

Max Azria, designed for BCBG Max Azria's fall 2001 collection: silk chiffon beaded dress. © AFP/CORBIS.

Morgan, Erinn, "Bon Chic, Bon Genre: A Conversation With Max Azria," at www.2020mag.com, 1999.

* * *

Longtime entrepreneur Max Azria began his career in his adopted hometown of Paris in 1970 by designing a line of women's wear. In 1981 Azria moved to the U.S. and in 1982 launched Jess, a series of new-concept retail boutiques whose goal was to introduce chic French fashion to American women. By the time he launched the design house BCBG Max Azria in 1989, Azria had gained expertise in all aspects of the fashion business, including retail operations, accounting and finance, production, sales, merchandising, and design.

BCBG Max Azria is the means through which Azria has fulfilled a revolutionary goal: bringing high-style, high-quality fashions to American women at a fraction of the typical four-figure price. Named for the French phrase *bon chic, bon genre* (Parisian slang meaning "good style, good attitude"), Azria's brashness in building a global fashion empire in Los Angeles instead of New York can be interpreted as distinctly American. Observers have long commented on Azria's seemingly uncanny ability to make major fashion ideas accessible to the general marketplace.

Azria claims not to have had a mentor within the industry; however, he does cite two major design influences. "Audrey Hepburn's chic, clean, sophisticated style has been a continuous inspiration for my collections," he says. "Los Angeles itself is also one of my biggest influences. The city is the center of so many industries—entertainment, music and technology—that there is always something new to inspire me. This inspiration could be literal, like a specific film, or more general, like the continuous sunshine."

In true entrepreneurial fashion, Azria launched BCBG Max Azria with a handful of clothing items. Early successes included novel cashmere sweater sets and baby-doll dresses. Since then, he has developed a diverse array of collections for women, including evening dresses, denim, footwear, eyewear, swimwear, intimates, handbags, and small leather goods. For men, Azria has created casual wear, suits, outerwear, and footwear. In 2001, Azria announced a partnership with global consumer-product manufacturer Unilever to introduce a collection of fragrance and beauty products under the BCBG Max Azria label.

Azria has also diversified his holdings via branding in an attempt to become a true life-cycle nameplate—his customers range in age from 15 to about 60. In 1996, he launched To The Max, a junior sportswear line, and relaunched Parallel, a contemporary line. With his 1998 acquisition of Hervé Léger—known for its beautiful, seductive couture and deluxe ready-to-wear—Azria became the first American designer to own a major French couturier. In 2000, he formed a strategic alliance with Procter & Gamble to revitalize Rodeo Drive's unofficial landmark, Giorgio Beverly Hills. Azria now controls the boutique's retail operations and has created a more focused merchandising concept for upscale retailer.

Azria has become something of a retail giant. As of 2001, the company operated more than 150 of its own retail outlets worldwide. BCBG Max Azria's collections are sold in specialty stores throughout North America, as well as in in-store shops in major department stores, including Neiman Marcus, Bloomingdale's, Nordstrom, and Macy's.

Although Azria has always been happy to rely on celebrity customers—and there are many—to further his wares, he has also mastered another important tool in today's self-promotion arsenal: product placement. The stars of television shows as *Ally McBeal, Sex in the City, Friends,* and *Buffy the Vampire Slayer* are regularly seen sporting BCBG Max Azria apparel. Ironically, his core 25- to 40-year-old customers may tune out these television shows, but they're still buying Azria's designs. Azria singles out as his main competition some true fashion behemoths: Donna Karan, Calvin Klein, Ralph Lauren, Prada, LVMH, and the Gucci Group. These choices may evoke images of Azria playing David to the industry's Goliaths, but consider just how far BCBG Max Azria has come in little more than a decade. His rare combination of aggressive pricing, fresh interpretations of major trends, and effective self-promotion indicate that Azria will likely be able to go the distance with even his fiercest competitors.

—Darcy Lewis

B

B., AGNÈS

See AGNÈS B.

BACHELLERIE, Marithé

See GIRBAUD, Marithé & François

BADGLEY MISCHKA

American design team

Established: New York, in 1988, by Mark Badgley and James Mischka. *Badgley* born in East Saint Louis, Illinois, 12 January 1961; raised in Oregon; studied business, University of Southern California, to 1982; graduated from Parsons School of Design, New York, 1985. *Mischka* born in Burlington, Wisconsin, 23 December 1960; studied management and art history, Rice University, Houston, Texas, to 1982; graduated from Parsons School of Design, 1985. Before forming own company, Badgley designed for Jackie Rogers and Donna Karan, New York, 1985–88; Mischka designed for Willi Smith, New York, 1985–88. **Company History:** Acquired by Escada USA, 1992; introduced bridalwear, 1996; launched footwear line, 1999; opened first store, Beverly Hills, 2000. **Awards:** Mouton Cadet Young Designer award, 1989; Dallas International Apparel Mart Rising Star award, 1992; Marymount Designer[s] of the Year, 2001. **Company Address:** 525 Seventh Avenue, New York, NY 10018, U.S.A.

Badgley Mischka, fall 2001 collection: gold sparkle top over a leather skirt. © AP/Wide World Photos.

Publications

On BADGLEY MISCHKA:

Books

Stegemeyer, Anne, *Who's Who in Fashion, Third Edition,* New York, 1996.

Articles

Starzinger, Page Hill, "New Faces," in *Vogue,* March 1990.

"Badgley Mischka: A Single Focus," in *Women's Wear Daily,* 4 June 1990.

Kazanjian, Dodie, "Little Black Dress," in *Vogue* (New York), July 1991.

Lear, Frances, "Relevant Dress," in *Lear's* (New York), September 1991.

Barbee, Pat, "Glamor Boys: Badgley Mischka," in *Beverly Hills 213* (Los Angeles), 21 July 1993.

Friedman, Arthur, "Badgley Mischka: Into the Day," in *Women's Wear Daily,* 12 April 1994.

Torkells, Erik, "The Night is Young," in *Town & Country,* September 1994.

"Not Your Everyday Bride," in *Women's Wear Daily,* 11 December 1998.

Badgley Mischka, spring 2001 collection: silver sequined gown. © AP/Wide World Photos.

Boehning, Julie, "Lasting Charm: Badgley Mischka...," in *Footwear News,* 19 July 1999.

Young, Kristin, "Beverly Hills Opening for Badgley Mischka," in *Women's Wear Daily,* 8 June 2000.

"High Spirits...Badgley Mischka Got a Bit Lighter and Sportier," in *Women's Wear Daily,* 20 September 2000.

Jensen, Tanya, "Badgley Mischka's Midas Touch," from *Fashion Wire Daily,* 30 April 2001.

Ramey, Joanna, "Badgley, Mischka Honored in Washington," in *Women's Wear Daily,* 2 May 2001.

* * *

Designers Mark Badgley and James Mischka have said of their clothing, "one zip and you're glamorous." Their clothing radiates youthful confidence; fanciful but realistic, their designs recall the elegance of an age when one dressed for evening. The two young designers, who introduced their first collection in 1988 under the label Badgley Mischka in New York, have made glamour attainable by demystifying and simplifying it.

Uptown diners and downtown executives alike find something appropriate and pleasing in Badgley Mischka designs. Evening suits and dresses are refined and uncontrived—form-fitting wool jersey, cotton brocade, faille, embroidered lace, silk, and baby bouclé are used to create suits with long fitted jackets and pencil-thin or swingy full short skirts. One versatile wool jersey dress, perfect for career dressing, looks like two pieces, with a rib knit turtleneck and either a permanently pleated or straight wrap skirt, in gray or pale yellow.

The combination of fine crisp and softly draping fabrics (bouclé and silk, velvet trimmed wool, organza and silk chiffon) adds dimension and drama. Fitted, empire, or lowered, waistlines are superbly shaped. Expertly mixed cocktail dresses—with evocative cocktail names such as the Tom Collins, the Delmonico, the Bacardi—are off-the-shoulder, décolleté, bowed, lacy, or beaded and above the knee. All are subtly provocative, feminine, and flirtatious. Their bridal gowns cause women to swoon, such as the V-backed ivory lace and silk-crêpe dress, or the off-white silk brocade coatdress, with front wrap and jeweled buttons. Badgley Mischka bridal dresses are for the grown-up sweet tooth, confections allowing the beauty of the wearer to shine through the frills.

In July 1991 *Vogue*'s Dodie Kazanjian looked to six designers (including Bill Blass, Donna Karan, and Michael Kors) for the perfect "little black dress," and found it at Badgley Mischka. Frances Lear, writing in *Lear's* (September 1991), also chose a Badgley Mischka wool jersey as the magazine's "Relevant Dress," calling it "reminiscent of other seminal dresses, yet perfectly contemporary...as comfortable as your own skin." Such is the unerring sense of ease and balance in Badgley Mischka designs—they create something expertly vital without superfluidity or trendiness.

Lilly Daché, the great stylemaker of the 1950s once said, "real fashion begins with simplicity," and Badgley and Mischka employ this mandate, creating clothing that is not only beautifully made but beautiful to wear. By the end of the 20th century the designing duo dominated the eveningwear market, and had begun to make their mark on the bridalwear. Introduced in 1996, their gowns won raves from critics, stores, and brides-to-be.

In addition to eveningwear and bridal gowns, Badgley Mischka wanted to carve a niche in hip streetwear as well. While critics and celebrities crammed the runway for their opulently beaded gowns, many had little interest for the designers' more casual creations. Yet by 2000 their "tough chic" separates in colorful leather with chunky belts and bikerish cool garnered notice. *Women's Wear Daily* (20 September 2000) enthused, "Mark Badgley and James Mischka have lightened their touch considerably.... Hemlines rose, shapes got sportier and...though the overall effect was more buoyant, their signature sophistication remained. And it was nowhere more apparent than in the white leather-wrapped miniskirt worn with a gold knit t-shirt...and the flirty gold-accented halter dress—all of which fit to perfection."

Another milestone for the designers was opening their first store, in Beverly Hills, in fall 2000. The stylish Rodeo Drive boutique featured all of their signature creations, including their new footwear collection, launched the year before. The designers had plans for additional stores in New York and Florida, and had been negotiating a licensing agreement for a signature fragrance as well. And as if several starlets wearing their wares for the Academy Awards wasn't enough, Badgley and Mischka were awarded the Marymount Designer of the Year award from Marymount University in May 2001.

—Jane Burns; updated by Brian Louwers and Nelly Rhodes

BALENCIAGA, Cristobal

Spanish designer

Born: Guetaria, San Sebastian, 21 January 1895. **Education:** Studied needlework and dressmaking with his mother until 1910. **Career:** Established tailoring business, with sponsorship of the Marquesa de Casa Torres, San Sebastian, 1915–21; founder/designer, Elsa fashion house, Barcelona, 1922–31, and Madrid, 1932–37; director, Maison Balenciaga, Paris, 1937–40, 1945–68; spent war years in Madrid; fragrances include *le Dix,* 1948, *Quadreille,* 1955, and *Pour Homme,* introduced by House of Balenciaga, 1990; couture house closed, 1968; retired to Madrid, 1968–72; House of Balenciaga managed by German group Hoechst, 1972–86; Jacques Bogart S.A. purchased Balenciaga Couture et Parfums, 1986; couture discontinued and ready-to-wear collection launched under designer Michel Goma, 1987; reopening of Balenciaga stores launched, 1989; Josephus Melchior Thimister takes over as head designer, 1992–97; Balenciaga name rejuvenated with Nicolas Ghesquière as head designer, from 1997. **Exhibitions:** *Balenciaga,* Bellerive Museum, Zurich, 1970; *Fashion: An Anthology,* Victoria & Albert Museum, London, 1971; *The World of Balenciaga,* Metropolitan Museum of Art, New York, 1973; *El Mundo de Balenciaga,* Palacio de Bellas Artes, Madrid, 1974; *Hommage à Balenciaga,* Musée Historique des Tissus, Lyon, 1985; *Balenciaga,* Fashion Institute of Technology, New York, 1986; *Cristobal Balenciaga,* Fondation de la Mode, Tokyo, 1987; *Homage to Balenciaga,* Palacio de la Virreina, Barcelona, and Palacio Miramar, San Sebastian, Spain, 1987. **Awards:** Chevalier de la Légion d'Honneur; named Commander, L'Ordre d'Isabelle-la-Catholique. **Died:** 23 March 1972, in Valencia, Spain. **Company Address:** 12 rue François 1er, 75008, Paris, France. **Company Website:** www.balenciaga.net.

Cristobal Balenciaga, spring 2001 collection. © AP/Wide World Photos/Fashion Wire Daily.

Publications

On BALENCIAGA:

Books

Lyman, Ruth, *Paris Fashion: The Great Designers and Their Creations,* London, 1972.
Vreeland, Diana, *The World of Balenciaga* (exhibition catalogue), Metropolitan Museum of Art, New York, 1973.
Milbank, Caroline Rennolds, *Couture: The Great Designers,* New York, 1985.
Musée Historique des Tissus, *Hommage à Balenciaga* (exhibition catalogue), Lyon, 1985.
Fondation de la Mode, Tokyo, and Musée de la Mode et du Costume, Palais Galliera, *Cristobal Balenciaga* (exhibition catalogue), Paris & Tokyo, 1987.
Jouve, Marie-Andrée, and Jacqueline Demornex, *Balenciaga,* New York, 1989.
Howell, Georgina, *Sultans of Style: 30 Years of Fashion and Passion 1960–1990,* London, 1990.
Healy, Robin, *Balenciaga: Masterpieces of Fashion Design,* Melbourne, 1992.
Stegemeyer, Anne, *Who's Who in Fashion, Third Edition,* New York, 1996.
Jouve, Marie-Andrée, *Balenciaga,* New York, 1997.

Articles

"Cristobal Balenciaga," [obituary] in the *New York Times,* 25 March 1972.
"Cristobal Balenciaga: A Most Distinguished Couturier of His Time," in *The Times* (London), 25 March 1972.
Berenson, Ruth, "Balenciaga at the Met," in *National Review* (New York), 31 August 1973.
Mulvagh, Jane, "The Balenciaga Show," in *Vogue* (London), March 1985.
"Homage to Balenciaga," in *Art and Design,* October 1985.
Savage, Percy, "Balenciaga the Great," in the *Observer* (London), 13 October 1985.
Braux, Diane de, "L'Exposition en hommage à Balenciaga," in *Vogue* (Paris), December/January 1985/86.
"Nostra Lione: Grande esposizione consacrata a Balenciaga," in *Vogue* (Milan), February 1986.
Martin, Richard, "Balenciaga," in *American Fabrics and Fashions* (New York), September/October 1986.
Koda, Harold, "Balenciaga and the Art of Couture," in *Threads* (Newtown, Connecticut), June/July 1987.
Paquin, Paquita, "Le Ceremonial de Cristobal Balenciaga," in *Vogue* (Paris), November 1988.

Design by Cristobal Balenciaga, 1954. © Bettmann/CORBIS.

Baudet, Francois, "Leur maître à tous," in *Elle* (Paris), 19 December 1988.

McDowell, Colin, "Balenciaga: The Quiet Revolutionary," in *Vogue* (London), June 1989.

Howell, Georgina, "Balenciagas Are Forever," in the *Sunday Times Magazine* (London), 23 July 1989.

Auchincloss, Eve, "Balenciaga: Homage to the Greatest," in *Connoisseur* (New York), September 1989.

Morera, Daniela, "Balenciaga lo charme del silenzio: Il grande couturier spagnolo," in *Vogue* (Milan), September 1990.

Drake, Laurie, "Courreges and Balenciaga: Some of the Best Spring Fashion Bears the Signature—or the Spirit—of Two Great Designers," in *Vogue,* March 1991.

White, Edmund, "Cristobal Balenciaga: The Spanish Master at La Reynerie," in *Architectural Digest,* October 1994.

Horyn, Cathy, "Filling Balenciaga's Shoes a Hard Row to Clothe," in *Chicago Tribune,* 2 December 1999.

* * *

Cristobal Balenciaga's primary fashion achievement was in tailoring, the Spanish-born couturier was a virtuoso in knowing, comforting, and flattering the body. He could demonstrate tailoring proficiency in a tour de force one-seam coat, its shaping created from the innumerable darts and tucks shaping the single piece of fabric. His consummate tailoring was accompanied by a pictorial imagination that encouraged him to appropriate ideas of kimono and sari, return to the Spanish vernacular dress of billowing and adaptable volume, and create dresses with arcs that could swell with air as the figure moved. There was a traditional Picasso-Matisse question of postwar French fashion: who was greater, Dior or Balenciaga? Personal sensibility might support one or the other, but it is hard to imagine any equal to Balenciaga's elegance, then or since.

Balenciaga was a master of illusion. The waist could be strategically low, it could be brought up to the ribs, or it could be concealed in a tunic or the subtle opposition of a boxy top over a straight skirt. Balenciaga envisioned the garment as a three-dimensional form encircling the body, occasionally touching it and even grasping it, but also spiraling away so the contrast in construction was always between the apparent freedom of the garment and its body-defining moments. Moreover, he regularly contrasted razor-sharp cut, including instances of the garment's radical geometry, with soft fragile features.

A perfectionist who closed down his business in 1968 rather than see it be compromised in a fashion era he did not respect, Balenciaga projected ideal garments, but allowed for human imperfection. He was, in fact, an inexorable flatterer, a sycophant to the imperfect body. To throw back a rolled collar gives a flattering softness to the line of the neck into the body; his popular seven-eighths sleeve flattered women of a certain age, while the tent-like drape of coats and jackets were elegant on clients without perfect bodies. His fabrics had to stand up to his almost Cubist vocabulary of shapes, and he loved robust wools with texture, silk gazar for evening, corduroy (surprising in its inclusion in the couture), and textured silks.

Balenciaga's garments lack pretension; they were characterized by self-assured couture of simple appearance, austerity of details, and reserve in style. For the most part, the garments seemed simple. American manufacturers, for example, adored Balenciaga for his adaptability into simpler forms for the American mass market in suits and coats. The slight rise in the waistline at center front or the proportions of chemise tunic to skirt make Balenciaga clothing as harmonious as a musical composition, but the effect was always one of utmost insouciance and ease of style. Balenciaga delved deeply into traditional clothing, seeming to care more for regional dress than for any prior couture house.

As Marie-Andrée Jouve demonstrated in *Balenciaga,* (New York, 1989), his garments allude to Spanish vernacular costume and to Spanish art: his embroidery and jet-beaded evening coats, capelettes, and boleros are redolent of the *torero,* while his love of capes emanates from the romance of rustic apparel. Chemise, cape, and baby doll shapes might seem antithetical to the propensities of a master of tailoring, but Balenciaga's 1957 baby doll dress exemplifies the correlation he made between the two. The lace cage of the baby doll floats free from the body, suspended from the shoulders, but it is matched by the tailored dress beneath, providing a layered and analytical examination of the body within and the Cubist cone on the exterior, a tantalizing artistry of body form and perceived shape.

The principal forms for Balenciaga were the chemise, tunic, suit—with more or less boxy top—narrow skirt, and coats, often with astonishing sleeve treatments, suggesting an arm transfigured by the sculptor Brancusi into a puff or into almost total disappearance. Balenciaga perceived a silhouette that could be with or without arms, but never with the arms interfering. A famous Henry Clark photograph of a 1951 Balenciaga black silk suit focuses on silhouette: narrow and high waist with a pronounced flare of the peplum below and sleeves that billow from elbow to seven-eighths length; an Irving Penn photograph concentrates on the aptly named melon sleeve of a coat. Like a 20th-century artist, Balenciaga directed himself to a part of the body, giving us a selective, concentrated vision. His was not an all-over, all-equal vision, but a discriminating, problem-solving exploration of tailoring and picture-making details of dress. Balenciaga was so very like a 20th-century artist because in temperament, vocabulary, and attainment, he was one.

When Cristobal Balenciaga retired (though he briefly came out of retirement to design a wedding dress for Franco's granddaughter), his fashion empire was run by the German chemical group Hoechst. Balenciaga died in March 1972 and Hoechst managed the business until 1986 when Jacques Bogart S.A. acquired the company. Couture was discontinued in favor of ready-to-wear and the first Balenciaga collection, designed by Michel Goma, debuted in 1987. Over the next several years, the company began opening Balenciaga boutiques and brought in a new head designer, Josephus Thimister, in 1992. Dutch designer Thimister created predominately eveningwear and some Basque-flavored loungewear, but he left in 1997 and was replaced by a young designer named Nicolas Ghesquière.

Ghesquière had worked in Balenciaga's licensed clothing lines and while his ascension to head designer wasn't met with the enthusiasm of Givenchy's Alexander McQueen, or John Galliano taking over at Christian Dior, Ghesquière soon brought Balenciaga a welcome renaissance. His first collection, spring/summer 1998 attracted little attention, but his second showing garnered accolades from critics and fellow designers alike. Balenciaga in the 21st century is tremendously popular, featuring shades of original Cristobal Balenciaga designs with a Ghesquière twist. Sales under Ghesquière's reign have doubled in the last few years; the venerable Maison Balenciaga is alive and well, and its future is bright.

—Richard Martin; updated by Nelly Rhodes

BALMAIN, Pierre

French designer

Born: Saint-Jean-de-Maurienne, Savoie, 18 May 1914. **Education:** Studied architecture, École Nationale Supérieure des Beaux-Arts, Paris, 1933–34. **Military Service:** French Air Force, 1936–38, French Army Pioneer Corps, 1939–40. **Career:** Freelance sketch artist for Robert Piguet, Paris, 1934; assistant designer, Molyneux, Paris, 1934–38; designer, Lucien Lelong, Paris, 1939, 1941–45; founder/director, Maison Balmain, Paris, 1945–1982, Balmain Fashions, New York, 1951–55, Balmain Fashions, Caracas, 1954; director, Balmain S.A., Paris, 1977–82; ready-to-wear line launched, 1982; fragrances include *Vent Vert,* 1945, *Jolie Madame,* 1953, *Miss Balmain,* 1967, and *Ivoire,* 1980; fragrance business purchased by Revlon, 1960; also designed for the stage and films, from 1950. Company continued on

Pierre Balmain, fall/winter 2000–01 haute couture collection: fringed transparent top over silver metallic pants designed by Oscar de la Renta. © AFP/CORBIS.

Pierre Balmain, fall/winter 2001–02 ready-to-wear collection: knit top and embroidered skirt. © AP/Wide World Photos.

after his death in 1982. **Exhibitions:** *Pierre Balmain: 40 années de création,* Musée de la Mode et du Costume, Palais Galliera, Paris, 1985–86. **Awards:** Neiman Marcus award, Dallas, 1955; Knight of the Order of Dannebrog, Copenhagen, 1963; Cavaliere Ufficiale del Merito Italiano, Rome, 1966; Officier de la Légion d'Honneur, 1978; Vermillion Medal, City of Paris. **Died:** 29 June 1982, in Paris. **Company Address:** 44 rue François-1er, 75008 Paris, France.

Publications

By BALMAIN:

Books

My Years and Seasons, London, 1964.

On BALMAIN:

Books

Latour, Anny, *Kings of Fashion,* London, 1958.

Lynam, Ruth, ed., *Paris Fashion: The Great Designers and Their Creations,* London, 1972.

Milbank, Caroline Rennolds, *Couture: The Great Designers,* New York, 1985.

Musée de la Mode et du Costume, *Pierre Balmain: 40 années de création,* Paris, 1985.

Maeder, Edward, et al, *Hollywood and History: Costume Design in Film,* New York, 1987.

Guillen, Pierre-Yves, and Jacqueline Claude, *The Golden Thimble: French Haute Couture,* Paris, 1990.

Stegemeyer, Anne, *Who's Who in Fashion, Third Edition,* New York, 1996.

Articles

Verdier, Rosy, "Balmain: le décor total," in *L'Officiel* (Paris), April 1985.

"Le point sur les collections: Pierre Balmain," in *L'Officiel* (Paris), March 1986.

Janssen, Brigid, "A Fashionable Canadian Connection: Pierre Balmain's New Ownership," in *Maclean's,* 16 November 1987.

Duffy, Martha, "Mais oui! Oscar," in *Time,* 8 February 1993.

Bowles, Hamish, "Well Suited: Balmain Collection by Oscar de la Renta," in *Vogue,* May 1993.
Moukheiber, Zina, "The Face Behind the Perfume: Eric Fayer, Owner of Pierre Balmain," in *Forbes,* 27 September 1993.

* * *

French couturier Pierre Balmain believed "dressmaking is the architecture of movement." His mission, as he saw it, was to beautify the world like an architect, and the relationship between architecture and couture was emphasized throughout Balmain's career. He initially studied to be an architect, yet the beauty of couture, Balmain often argued, was when it was brought to life on the human form. He also believed "nothing is more important in a dress than its construction."

The House of Balmain opened, with great acclaim from the fashion press, in 1945. Alice B. Toklas wrote, "A dress is to once more become a thing of beauty, to express elegance and grace." Prior to opening his own house, Balmain apprenticed with couturier Edward Molyneux, in Paris, for five years. These years with Molyneux taught him about the business of couture, as Molyneux was at the height of his success during this time. Balmain defined him as a true creator and learned about the elegance of simplicity from Molyneux, which was so evident in Balmain's later designs under his own name.

After leaving Molyneux, Balmain joined the firm of Lucien Lelong, where he worked from 1939 to 1944 off and on during the war and the German Occupation. In 1941 the House of Lelong reopened and Balmain returned to work with a newly hired designer, Christian Dior. Balmain credited himself with the now famous "New Look" and cited his first collection (1945), pictured in American *Vogue,* as evidence. These designs did illustrate the feminine silhouette of longer, bell-shaped, higher bustlines, narrow shoulders, and smaller waists. The collections of Jacques Fath and Balenciaga were also reflective of the New Look silhouette with which Christian Dior was ultimately credited.

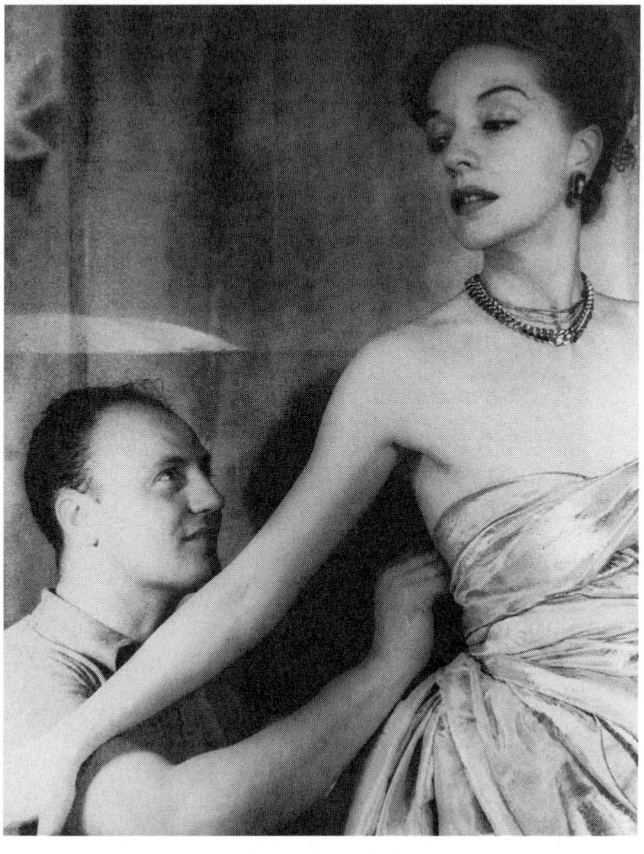

Pierre Balmain adjusting one of his evening dresses. © CORBIS.

Balmain believed that the ideal of elegance in clothing was achieved only through simplicity. He detested ornamentation for the sake of making a garment spectacular and offended the American fashion press by stating that Seventh Avenue fashion was vulgar. As a couturier he was not interested in fashion per se; rather he sought to dress women who appreciated an elegant appearance and possessed sophisticated style. Balmain once said, "Keep to the basic principles of fashion and you will always be in harmony with the latest trends without falling prey to them."

The basic Balmain silhouette for day was slim, with evening being full-skirted. He was credited with the popularization of the stole as an accessory for both day and evening. Balmain also used fur as trim throughout his collections. He was also remembered for his exquisite use of embroidered fabrics for evening.

After the war, Balmain toured the world giving lectures on the virtues of French fashion. He promoted the notion that French couture defined the ideal of elegance and refinement; his visits and lectures were intended to revive French haute couture, which had been virtually shut down during the war. As a result of Balmain's tours, he recognized the potential of the American market and opened a boutique in New York, offering his distinctly French fashions.

Balmain was one of the few French couturiers of his generation to also design for the theatre, ballet, and cinema, as well as for royalty. He was commissioned by Queen Sirikit of Thailand in 1960 to design her wardrobe for her official visit to the United States.

When Pierre Balmain died in 1982, his standards of elegance were still highly regarded in the world of couture. The tradition continued with Erik Mortensen, who had been with the company since the late 1940s, as head designer. In the late 1980s German-born Canadian financier Erich Fayer bought Ted Lapidus and perfumer Jacomo, then set his sights on Balmain. Fayer, along with Copeba, a Belgian investment firm, bought Balmain for around $30 million, which included reclaiming its fragrances from Revlon.

Fayer and Copeba soon parted ways after financial disputes and Fayer aggressively licensed the Balmain name, marketing champagne, rugs, furnishings, and virtually anything that could be sold under the Balmain brand. Balmain lost much of its cache, as well as many of its loyal customers and was put up for sale in 1989. Alain Chevalier bought Balmain in 1990 and brought in Hervé Pierre to lead the design team. After substantial losses and charges he looted the company of its assets, Fayer repurchased Balmain.

By late 1992 Balmain was poised for a welcome resurgence when American Oscar de la Renta was named its head designer. A star-studded gala in Paris marked de la Renta's official ascension to the post in January 1993, and his first collection for Balmain debuted the following February to rave reviews. Could an American designer bring the French Balmain back to its former glory in haute couture? Martha Duffy, writing for *Time* magazine in February 1993 said it succinctly, "If Balmain wants to catch up to the 1990s without leaping into the 21st century, the house made a very shrewd choice."

Balmain under the direction of de la Renta is a different couture house than when Pierre was at the helm, yet enduringly successful. The timeless elegance of Pierre Balmain's vision, however, lives on.

—Margo Seaman; updated by Nelly Rhodes

BANANA REPUBLIC

American clothing store chain and mail order company

Founded: by Mel and Patricia Ziegler in Mill Valley, California, in 1978. **Company History:** First Banana Republic Travel Bookstore opened, San Francisco, 1978; Travel Bookstore Catalogue first published, 1986; quarterly travel magazine, *Trips*, introduced, 1987; business acquired by The Gap, Inc., 1983; founding partners Mel and Patricia Ziegler resigned from firm, 1988. **Awards:** Direct Mail Marketing Association Gold Echo award, 1985, 1986; American Catalogue Gold award, 1987. **Company Address:** 1 Harrison Street, San Francisco, California, 94105, USA. **Company Website:** www.bananarepublic.com.

Publications

On BANANA REPUBLIC:

Books

Ziegler, Patricia, and Mel Ziegler, *Banana Republic Guide to Travel and Safari Clothing*, New York, 1986.

Articles

Gammon, Clive, "Banana Republic's Survival Chic is Winning Bunches of Trendy Buyers," in *Sports Illustrated* (New York), 19 August 1985.
Weil, Henry, "Keeping Up with the (Indiana) Joneses," in *Savvy* (New York), February 1986.
Grossberger, Lewis, "Yes, Do We Have Bananas!" in *Esquire* (New York), September 1986.
"From Jungle to Drawing Room," in the *Economist* (London), 14 March 1987.
"Banana Republic Founders Quit Firm," in *Women's Wear Daily,* 22 April 1988.
MacIntosh, Jeane, "Wall Street Eyes Banana Republic," *Women's Wear Daily,* 9 March 1989.
"Ripe Banana," in *Women's Wear Daily,* 17 March 1992.
Campbell, Roy H., "Banana Republic Stores Undergo a Fashion Makeover," Knight-Ridder/Tribune News Service, 10 December 1998.
Mullins, David Phillip, "Bananarama," *Footwear News,* 6 December 1999.
Tsui, Bonnie, "Banana Republic Bus Ad Campaign Shines," *Crain's New York Business,* 18 September 2000.
Jones, Rose Apodaca, "Messing With the Republic," *Women's Wear Daily,* 17 November 2000.
Articles also in *Newsweek,* 28 September 1987; *DNR,* 21 April 1988; *Women's Wear Daily,* 9 March 1989; and *San Francisco Business Times,* 18 August 2000.

* * *

Banana Republic was a creative fashion adventure in the United States that began when writer Mel Ziegler needed a new jacket. He wanted one without extraneous zippers or buttons, and not made in bright-colored polyester. While on assignment in Sydney, Australia, he bought three British Burma jackets. His wife Patricia, an artist, restyled the three jackets into one, using the various parts to make necessary repairs. She added elbow patches, horn buttons, and a wood buckle. Friends and acquaintances liked Mel's "new" jacket and inquired about purchasing one. It seems other people wanted clothing that was usable and stylish, without designer labels. Seeing a potential market, the Zieglers set off in search of army surplus and other items that could be converted into usable clothing. They traveled to South America, Africa, London, and Madrid, searching out usable goods. According to their book *Banana Republic Guide to Travel and Safari Clothing*, their motto became, "in surplus we trust."

Banana Republic display window featuring two ensembles, 1998. © Fashion Syndicate Press.

Display window at a Banana Republic store, 1998. © Fashion Syndicate Press.

At first they marketed their finds at flea markets, selling the surplus as it was or restyled. Basque sleeping bags became Basque sheepskin vests. Shirts with tattered collars were given new ones. Eventually the market grew so much the Zieglers moved into a storefront in Mill Valley, California. This became the second part of the Ziegler adventure in fashion and merchandising. Lacking funds for extensive decorating, they painted the walls in a zebra stripe, and added other decor to create the image of a jungle trading post. The background music was provided by their personal tapes of 1940s and 1950s jazz. The store was a dramatic, rather theatrical, setting for their surplus and redesigned articles of clothing.

The third part of this fashion adventure was the nontraditional catalogue the Zieglers developed to sell their product to both men and women. Again, due to limited funding, Patricia drew pictures of the clothes. Mel wrote text that went beyond bland descriptions of the clothes, to include their place of origin, or how to use the items.

Calling their enterprise Banana Republic to denote change, the Zieglers began a unique merchandising adventure. People liked the stylish, rugged surplus goods sold at relatively low cost. The business grew quickly, and in 1983 the Zieglers decided to sell Banana Republic to The Gap, Inc. The Gap provided the business know-how, which the Zieglers admittedly lacked, allowing the Zieglers to continue to concentrate on the creative end of the business, at which they excelled.

When demand outpaced the supply of surplus goods, Patricia designed clothing which was then manufactured for Banana Republic. The clothes and accessories were always stylish, comfortable, and high quality. The designs suggested travel, safari, and camping. The clothes were utilitarian, they could be dressed up or dressed down, and most articles were made of durable, natural, neutral-colored fabrics or fabrics that traveled well. Another likable feature of the company was customer service—free alterations were offered for much of the company's clothing. Walking into a Banana Republic store was like walking on to a movie set for a jungle outpost, an African hunting lodge, or British officers' club. Mock elephant tusks were hung and jeeps became part of the decor, as did old furniture and luggage. The Zieglers' original jazz collection was enhanced by animal sounds from the jungle.

The expanded catalogue had fashion descriptions written by a number of professional writers and journalists. The text included background stories, travel adventure vignettes, and endorsements written by famous people. Drawings were still used for the clothing but were now in color. In addition, photographs of people in various places, wearing the same or similar clothes were included. The catalogue had become an adventure to read.

Banana Republic emerged at a time when there was a general shift away from all-purpose department stores, towards smaller stores which concentrated on doing one thing well. They were one of the first stores to concentrate on clothing made of natural fabrics, in stylishly rugged designs. Catalogue selling was an integral part of their merchandising operation. Their customers were not concerned with the dictates of the fashion world. With Gap's input, sales increased dramatically and many new stores were opened. By 1986 Banana Republic was one of the hottest retail concepts, but the appeal for safari and khaki clothing was dwindling. By the end of the 1980s, new items, fabrics, and colors were introduced, but sales slowed even further and Gap announced plans to remodel and recreate all their stores. By early 1990 some of the stores were remodeled and stores were showing new merchandise. To maintain consumer traffic while changes took place, prices on remaining articles were substantially lowered and new merchandise was being introduced. New clothing, which featured brighter colors and a "cruise line" appeal were placed at the front of the store while the more traditional khaki apparel was placed in the back. Another big change was the disappearance of the theatrical props that had made the original stores unique.

With the changes, Banana Republic seemed to be back on track. The stores were less cluttered, were lighter and brighter, and the phrase, "Travel and Safari Clothing" was dropped from the name. Clothing articles included apparel for various occasions, including weekend wear, professional attire, and dressy casual items made of more luxuriant fabrics such as cashmere and suede. The change in decor, style, and fabrics was necessary given that many retailers were carrying travel-look attire such as cargo pants and Jeeps (or jeep-like vehicles) seemed to be parked in every other driveway. By the mid-1990s, following a growing trend, Banana Republic launched bath and body care products including a Banana Republic cologne and undergarments. Later, "whole concept stores" were created which included home accessories such as bedding, sofa pillows, candles, and picture frames. In 1996 Banana Republic opened stores exclusively for men and women.

In 1998 Banana Republic launched its most extensive marketing campaign, which included its first TV spots, print ads, magazine inserts, and outdoor kiosks. More interesting was the reintroduction of the catalogue—the first in over a decade. In addition to the catalogue, keeping customer service was kept in the forefront, with telephone order representatives called "style consultants." In the late 1990s, Banana Republic offered e-commerce, allowing customers to return articles at local stores rather than send them back through the post office. In 2000 Banana Republic reopened its flagship store in San Francisco on the corner of Grant Avenue and Sutter Street; this store offers valet parking, personal shoppers, and free cell-phone charging services.

Through Banana Republic, Mel and Patricia Ziegler filled a niche for comfortable, rugged, yet stylish clothes. They marketed their product through a catalogue that was interesting to read, and at stores that were an adventure to enter. Banana Republic has changed dramatically since the days when the Zieglers started the company; however, keeping with their original intent, customers are offered quality items and where customer service is still important.

—Nancy House; updated by Christine Miner Minderovic

BANKS, Jeff

British designer, retailer, and entrepreneur

Born: Ebbw Vale, Wales, 1943. **Education:** Studied textile and interior design, Camberwell School of Art, 1959–62, and St. Martin's School of Art, 1962–64. **Family:** Married Sandy Shaw (divorced). **Career:** Opened first shop, Clobber, 1964; freelance designer, Liberty, London, and Rembrandt manufacturers, 1975–78; designed bed linen collection, 1978; launched Warehouse chain of stores, 1978; initiated Warehouse Utility Clothing Company catalogue, early 1980s; host and co-producer, *The Clothes Show* for BBC television; designed clothes care products for Dexam International, 1998; created uniforms for Boots the Chemist, 1998; designed jewelry line for G&A, 1999; launched exclusive jewelry through QVC, 2000; developed uniforms for Abbey National, 2000; designed fashion concept for Sainsbury's, 2000. **Awards:** *Woman* magazine British Fashion award, 1979, 1982. **Address:** 21 D'Arblay St., London W1V 3FN, England.

Publications

On BANKS:

Articles

"Jeff Banks Designs," in the *Sunday Times* (London), 11 January 1976.
McCartney, Margaret, "Mr. Banks Bounces Back," in the *Sunday Times* (London), 11 January 1976.
McCormack, Mary, "Trend Setter," in *Annabel* (London), June 1983.
"Behind the Scenes–Fashion Line-up: The Entrepreneur," in *Living* (London), October 1983.
Hennessy, Val, "Banks, the Scruff Fashion Designer," in *You,* magazine of the *Mail on Sunday* (London), 11 December 1983.
Brooks, Barry, "Banking on Fashion," in *Creative Review* (London), October 1984.
"Influences: Jeff Banks," in *Women's Journal* (London), April 1985.
Mower, Sarah, "Dennis and the Menace," in *The Guardian* (London), 9 January 1986.
Rumbold, Judy, "Listening Banks," in *Company* (London), December 1986.
Robson, Julia, "Will Men Buy It?" in the *Sunday Telegraph Magazine* (London), 9 August 1987.
"Banks's Shock Exit," in *Drapers Record (DR): The Fashion Business* (London), 15 July 1989.
Brennon, Steve, "Banking on the Future," in *Fashion Weekly* (London), 26 October 1989.
McCooey, Meriel, "Be Prepared," in the *Sunday Times Magazine* (London), 15 April 1990.
Tredre, Roger, "Out of the Warehouse and into the News," in *The Independent* (London), 5 May 1990.
Barber, Richard, "Jeff Banks: Back Where He Belongs," in *Clothes Show* (London), March 1992.
"Boots Banks on £5.5 Million New Look," in *Community Pharmacy,* December 1998.

"G&A Creates Jeff Banks Jewelery Range," in *Duty-Free News International,* 5 March 1999.
"Abbeycrest Plans Designer Jewelry," in *The Financial Times* (London), 13 May 1999.

* * *

For many Britons Jeff Banks is the face of fashion. The television magazine he devised and hosts, *The Clothes Show,* has helped to democratize and demystify fashion. It spawned a monthly magazine, generated its own annual exhibition, and sponsored student fashion shows. The program epitomizes Banks' nonelitist attitude to fashion; his career has been devoted to making fashion available to a wide range of people.

Banks' greatest successes have been in the High Street: Clobber, his first London shop, carried the work of young designers such as Foale and Tuffin, and Janice Wainwright. Over ten years later, in the late 1970s, his Warehouse Utility Clothing company introduced designer looks at nondesigner prices. An initial setback—when the first London Warehouse shop and its contents were destroyed by fire—did not quell Banks' irrepressible energy. From their beginnings in London, the Warehouse shops have gained a national and international reputation. Started as a means of combatting wastage, the company utilized stocks of fabrics piling up in warehouses all over Europe. The resulting collections were retailed at almost wholesale prices. The shops, which have had a distinct design and style, sell only Warehouse merchandise, created by a team of designers. The interiors are minimal and logically planned, and the merchandise reflects the current fashion look, without being too extreme for the High Street. Ranges are regularly updated; the Warehouse equals lively, fresh ideas, translated into womenswear and the formula has proved attractive. Warehouse shops can be found in most major UK shopping venues, and in the mid-1980s outlets were opened in the United States.

The Warehouse concept helped to revolutionize shopping by post. Freemans, a traditional mail order company, launched Bymail, which brought the Warehouse style to a wider range of customers. The venture was a great success and was quickly followed by Classics Bymail and Men Bymail. With an emphasis on fabrics and cut, the classics included the perennial trenchcoat, suits, dresses, and separates in versatile and interchangeable dark and soft colors. The catalogues set new standards for mail order; created by top models, stylists, and photographers, the visually attractive spreads helped to sell the clothes. Like the shops, they had their imitators, both good and bad.

Sound team work has provided the essential backup for Banks' ideas, and he has inspired many people over the last several decades. Variety has been a mark of his career. As a designer, illustrator, retailer, manager, design director, consultant, and educator he has helped improve fashion attitudes and awareness. Business training is as important for him as design education, and he has made his views known by acting as a consultant and examiner for several British fashion degree courses. Fashion graduates are employed straight from college by Warehouse.

Banks' greatest achievement perhaps has been in promoting genuine fashion awareness, and he has the ability to fire up others with his own enthusiasm. In the early 21st century he continued to be a high-profile name in the industry, working to support British fashion by heading up, with others, Graduate Fashion Week, one of the main showcases for young UK talent. Banks also continued to create his own branded collections in apparel, accessories, and home furnishings. Additionally, he was active in designing custom uniforms for corporations.

Banks has created several licensed product lines for British manufacturers such as William Baird (apparel), Dexam International (clothes care products and storage boxes), Argos (china), and G&A and Abbeycrest (silver and gold jewelry). His products are sold through many distribution points, from mail-order catalogues to department stores including Marks & Spencer and Debenhams. His well-known brands include the high-end, classically styled Jeff Banks Collection, Jeff Banks Studio, and his lower- to mid-price range, Jeff Banks Ports of Call. The last is more exotic in styling, inspired by warm Southern cultures from around the world, such a Mexican-themed line of jewelry sold exclusively through home shopping network QVC. Banks is known for his inspired use of inexpensive fabrics, making fashionable, affordable apparel and accents available to young women.

Banks, through his consultancy, HQ, has also designed uniforms for many corporations. In 1998 he redesigned the uniforms worn by staff at the UK drugstore chain Boots the Chemist, creating outfits in lilac, white, green, and navy blue for 43,000 employees in 1,350 stores. In 2000 he designed uniforms for 9,500 workers at 800 branches of Abbey National, which were supplied by uniform maker InCorporateWear.

Banks signed a three-year partnership with the grocery store chain Sainsbury's in 2000, whereby he agreed to design a new in-store fashion concept for the retailer's large-format outlets. He created clothing collections for men and women and designed the boutique where the clothes are displayed, as well as supplying the visual merchandising and training Sainsbury's staff to sell the clothes.

Just as Banks was a pioneer in democratizing fashion through his appearances on British television, he has, through the Sainsbury's deal, become one of the first designers to translate fashion retailing to the supermarket setting. For three decades, Banks has made a significant impact on the British fashion industry and how it is perceived by the people of the United Kingdom.

—Hazel Clark; updated by Karen Raugust

BANKS, Jeffrey

American designer

Born: Washington D.C., 3 November 1955. **Education:** Studied at Pratt Institute, Brooklyn, New York, 1972–74; graduated from Parsons School of Design, New York, 1977. **Career:** Part-time assistant to Ralph Lauren, New York, 1972–74, and to Calvin Klein, 1974–76; designer, Nik Nik, 1976–77; designer in New York for Concorde International, Alixandre, Merona Sport, 1977–circa 1980; launched own menswear company, 1980; introduced boyswear collection, 1980; formed joint venture for designer line with Takihyo Inc., Hong Kong, 1988; design consultant, Herman Geist, New York, 1990; designer, Jeffrey Banks label for Hartz & Company, New York, beginning in 1984; Jeffrey Banks menswear, neckwear, and eyewear licensed for production in Japan, beginning in 1982; menswear consultant, Bloomingdale's, New York, beginning in 1993; extended sportswear collection with Johnnie Walker, 1998. **Awards:** Coty American Fashion Critics award, 1977, 1982; "Earnie" award for boyswear, 1980; Cutty Sark award, 1987. **Address:** 12 East 26th Street, New York, NY 10010, USA.

Publications

On BANKS:

Books

Trachtenberg, Jeffrey A., *Ralph Lauren: The Man Behind the Mystique,* New York, 1988.

On BANKS:

Articles

Bloom, Ellye, "Jeffrey Banks: To Boyswear with Love," in *Teens and Boys* (New York), October 1979.

Kleinfeld, N. R., "Jeffrey Banks Suits the Mood," in the *New York Times Magazine,* 2 March 1980.

Gruen, John, "The Designer's Eye for Timeless Fashion Photography," in *Architectural Digest,* September 1989.

Gite, Lloyd, "Breaking into the Fashion Biz," in *Black Enterprise* (New York), June 1997.

White, Constance C.R., "Patterns," in the *New York Times,* 16 June 1998.

Wells, Melanie, "Johnnie Walker's First Nips at Apparel Strut to Shelves," in *USA Today,* 19 October 1998.

* * *

At the age of 15, Jeffrey Banks was working as a salesman at the menswear store Britches of Georgetown, where he had already been a regular customer since he was 12. "He was surely the only high school student in Washington, D.C., with his own subscriptions to *Daily News Record* and *Women's Wear Daily,*" recounts Jeffrey Trachtenberg in *Ralph Lauren: The Man Behind the Mystique.* Banks is the consummate clothing aficionado and stylist, one who is positively obsessed with fashion. For some, apparel is simply the family business or narcissist's self-realization. For Banks, clothing is an ecstatic vocation.

A devoted movie fan since childhood, Banks has made his cinematic dream come true in clothing that evokes the golden age of Hollywood, in nuanced references to such stars as Audrey Hepburn (later a friend) and in a styling of menswear in the tradition of the debonair man about town. When Ralph Lauren visited Washington, Banks was chosen to pick him up at the airport. Fully dressed in Lauren clothing, Banks appeared as a precocious high school student and was asked by Lauren to come see him for a job when he came to New York for design school. While still in art school, Banks became Lauren's assistant and protégé in fulfillment of his interpretation of the traditional in menswear and in continuing development of his talents as a designer and stylist.

Banks subsequently designed furs for Alixandre, apprenticed with Calvin Klein, and designed for Merona sportswear. Even at Merona, his style was considered spectator sportswear, meaning the extended vision of sportswear but also the sportswear edited by Banks' keen eye to what is being worn and how it can be subtly improved. His deepest affection has always been, however, the romantic tradition of tailored clothing, a debonair style burnished by a sense of artisto nonchalance. In sportswear, Banks' strong sense of color is notable, but even for color his tailored clothing is his more natural medium. He calls himself a romanticist, but the term is weak for one so smitten by a passion for traditional clothing—a tradition that works for the most conservative gentleman but can be assembled with panache for the urbane sophisticate. Even more outside his own country, Banks' clothing in Japan epitomizes the grand sensibility of menswear brought into a fresh American focus.

Walt Whitman argued that American democracy promotes uniformity, even a sense of unimportance in individual citizens. American menswear in the second half of the 20th century was internationally effective in seeking distinction within the homogeneity of modern appearance. Designers such as Lauren and Banks addressed the social need for a traditional demeanor that would not disturb the standard of uniformity, albeit with a kind of smartness of detailing that is distinguished without being dandified. Both have, of course, learned a great deal from images in film and photography as well as keenly observing men of classic style. They then reinterpreted and refined that style.

Some would argue that a designer's transformative skill is honed in part by being an outsider—by observing that which cannot be possessed in its present form and by inherently needing and seeking change. Banks has given significant personal inflection to inbred, rarefied traditions of menswear, often connoting class. His customer—probably younger, because of his palette, than Lauren's—buys not to climb socially but to fit into a fantasy of best-dressed nattiness, perfect in effortless grooming, and informal high style.

Yet Banks' preppy, "dressed for success" image cannot be attributed to his look alone. The designer has more than just fashion sense; he has a proven business sense. He learned many things from his former mentor Ralph Lauren, and one was how to run a business. Although most designers tried to make it on their sketches, hoping to catch the eye of anyone who would look, Banks told *Black Enterprise* in June 1997, "Fashion is not art. It often comes very close, but at the end of the day it's commerce."

Planning and investing have been key elements to success for Banks. He may be one of a growing number of African American designers, but what separates him from others is his ability to secure sales of his designs to major department stores. Studies show African Americans spend more money on clothing than any other race, yet only a handful of African American designers have developed successful lines. Banks' $20 million companies, Jeffrey Banks Ltd. and Jeffrey Banks International, speak volumes.

After a lengthy hiatus, Banks came back in full swing in the fall of 1998. Teaming up with liquor company Johnnie Walker, Banks extended his line of rugged sportswear and accessories collection. Sold exclusively in Bloomingdales, the collection's signature trademark resembled a silhouette of a man in a top hat with a cane—not quite Johnnie Walker's ever-popular scotch liquor label. "That is the guy two years ago who wore his baseball cap backwards, drank beer out of a can and wore baggy jeans," Banks explained to the *New York Times.* "He now wears a $1,000 suit and is working on Wall Street, and he wants to look as good on the weekends as he does during the week."

—Richard Martin; updated by Diana Idzelis

BARNES, Jhane

American designer

Born: Jane Barnes in Phoenix, Maryland, 4 March 1954. **Education:** Graduated from Fashion Institute of Technology, New York, 1975. **Family:** Married Howard Ralph Feinberg, 1981 (divorced); married Katsuhiko Kawasaki, 1988. **Career:** Menswear company established as Jhane Barnes Ltd., 1977; president, Jane Barnes for ME, New York 1976–78, and Jhane Barnes Inc., from 1978; introduced women's collection, 1979; launched neckwear line, 1989; began designing home furnishing fabrics, 1989; footwear collection created, 1991; clothing licensed by American Fashion Company (San Diego, CA), from 1990; listed among the *Who's Who in America,* 1992; leatherwear licensed by Group Five Leather, (Minneapolis, MN), from 1994; launched first furniture collection for Bernhardt, 1995; created Jhane Barnes Textiles as a collaboration between Jhane Barnes, Inc. and Bernhardt Furniture Company, 1998; designed Orlando Magic basketball uniforms, 1998; opened second freestanding store, 1998; third store, 1999; fourth store, 2000; began formal alliance with furniture designer Herman Miller, June 2000. **Awards:** Coty American Fashion Critics award for Menswear 1980; Cutty Sark Most Prominent Designer award, 1980; Council of Fashion Designers of America (CFDA) Outstanding Menswear Designer, 1981; Cutty Sark Outstanding Designer award 1982; Coty Return Menswear award, 1984; Council of Fashion Designers of America award, 1981, 1984; Contract Textile award, American Society of Interior Designers 1983, 1984; Product Design award, Institute of Business Designers, 1983, 1984, 1985, 1986, 1989; American Association of Industrial Designers for Textile Collection, Gold award, 1990; Woolmark award, 1991; Resource Council Gold award, 1994; Best of NeoCon (National Exhibition of Contract Furniture) award, 1995, 1996; Good Design award, 1996; Neckwear Achievement award from the Neckwear Association of America, 1997; DuPont Antron Product Innovation award, First Place, 1998; Best of NeoCon award, 1998, 1999; Gold award for Textiles, 1999; Most Innovative award, 1999; Chicago Anthaneum Good Design award, Best of NeoCon award, 2000. **Address:** 575 Seventh Avenue, New York, NY 10018, USA. **Website:** www.jhanebarnes.com.

Publications

On BARNES:

Books

Stegemeyer, Anne, *Who's Who in Fashion, Second Edition,* New York, 1988.

———, *Who's Who in Fashion, Third Edition,* New York, 1996.

Articles

Burggraf, Helen, "Jhane Barnes," in *Men's Apparel News,* 14 October 1980.

Ettorre, Barbara, "Success Looms," in *Working Woman* (New York), June 1981.

"Jhane Barnes: A Material Force," in *GQ* (New York), November 1981.

Fendel, Alyson, "Jhane Barnes: 'For Inspiration I Look to the Future, Not the Past'," in *Apparel World,* 22 March 1982.

Groos, Michael, "Loosening Up: A New Look in Menswear for Fall," in the *New York Times,* 5 January 1988.

"The Americans: Jhane Barnes," in the *Daily News Record (DNR)* (New York), 15 August 1989.

"Tiny Pieces of Fabric," in the *New Yorker,* 29 October 1990.

Furman, Phyllis, "Resuiting American Men," in *Crain's New York Business,* 15 July 1991.

"Menswear Creator Jhane Barnes Makes her Case for Invention…the Technetronic Way," in *Chicago Tribune,* 11 September 1991.

"He's Got the Look…of Four Menswear Designers who are Showing and Telling Their Signature Looks for Spring," in *Chicago Tribune,* 25 March 1992.

Maycumber, Gray, "Fabrics a Weapon at Jhane Barnes: Designer Sees Textiles Winning Half the Men's Fashion Battle," in the *DNR,* 15 October 1992.

Agins, Teri, "Karan Gambles on Expanding Men's Line," in the *Wall Street Journal,* 9 February 1993.

"New York Reviews: Jhane Barnes," in *DNR,* 11 August 1994.

Savage, Todd, "Men's Fashion Designer Unveils Her Crossover Furniture Collection at NeoCon," in *Chicago Tribune,* 18 June 1995.

Geran, Monica, "MIC for Jhane Barnes (Matsuyama International Co. Clothing Store)," in *Interior Design,* May 1996.

Bucholz, Barbara B., "So This is Where You Work, Flexible, Genderless, Homier: Office Furnishings Adapt to Change," in *Chicago Tribune,* 1 September 1996.

———, "Best of Show, Buzz at NeoCon: the Interchangeable Office," in *Chicago Tribune,* 9 August 1998.

Strauss, Gary, "Casual Clothes by Intense Design, Jhane Barnes Wields Software to Weave Menswear Empire," in *USA Today,* 10 August 1999.

Bucholz, Barbara B., "Best & Raves, Two Judges Rate the Recent Winners for Office Furnishings," in *Chicago Tribune,* 26 September 1999.

Feldman, Melissa, "In Stitches," in *Interiors,* May 2000.

Swanson, James L., "Tactical Maneuvers Sighted: A Four Star General and Fabrics All-Star," in *Chicago Tribune,* 20 August 2000.

Rohrlich, Marianne, "Techno Fabrics Suffer Red Wine Stylishly," in the *New York Times,* 28 September 2000.

* * *

While trekking through the southwestern U.S., one might encounter increasingly intricate patterns within the simplicity of the unaffected surroundings. A convoluted pattern found on a leaf, perhaps, or the dewy complexities of a spider's web found in the early morn. Perhaps the sharp contrast of a red mountaintop against the azure sky, or the ripplings of a stone tossed into a puddle. Wherever we may find beauty in our natural world, Jhane Barnes strives and succeeds to assimilate the same into her concurrent design work. Her propensity towards nature is evident from her intricately patterned ties to a subtle environmentalist stand evident in minimal packaging and recycling-themed weekend wear.

While still in school, Jhane (then minus the "h") Barnes had thought to turn her talents toward the worlds of science or music. Realizing her talents didn't necessarily lie in those specialties, she set off for the Fashion Institute of Technology in New York. Fortuitously for the design world, Jhane landed her first big job in 1979, when a pair of trousers designed for a friend sparked the interest of an area retail executive to the tune of a $1,000-pair order. This charmed event triggered her formal debut into the world of retail fashion. No longer a plain Jane (she added the "h" to her name at the suggestion of an earlier partner), the transformation helped broaden her appeal and menswear marketability.

Work that started on a handloom during her early design years accelerated when Barnes discovered the mathematical design capabilities of the computer. With her computer, she has redefined the fashion textile, causing her already complex fabric design to explode within the boundaries of her own creative possibilities in revolutionary fabric design intricacies. Her use of the computer is so extensive in her design work that it has caught the attention of the mathematical world. Barnes was featured in a chapter of a McDougal Littell textbook entitled *Algebra II: Explorations and Applications,* in a section entitled "Sequences and Series: Fractals for Fashions." Barnes also is part of the Ohio Math Works, which prepares ninth-grade math students for the real world job application of their math studies.

The Jhane Barnes Menswear line is comfortable yet classy, with an eye towards the somewhat larger-framed physique. Barnes told the *Chicago Tribune,* "I tend to design for men with generous thighs and behinds." Her renowned clothing line has had a bit of assistance through advertisements placed in women's magazines, a growing trend among menwear desginers, including Perry Ellis and Phillips-Van Heusen. Stylish women seek out equally sophisticated clothing for the men in their lives, and where better to advertise than in magazines written by and for women.

The unique look of Barnes' apparel appeals to a distinctive type of clientèle. Even Nokia's chief designer Frank Nuovo, who turned the cellular phone into a fashion statement, joined the ranks of her admiring patronage. According to Katie Hafner of the *New York Times,* Nuovo was wearing a Jhane Barnes silk shirt during a 1999 interview. Other celebrities spotted wearing Barnes designs include Magic Johnson, Tony Danza, Billy Joel and his band leader, Mark Rivera, and Don Johnson on his *Nash Bridges* television series. Gary Strauss, writing for *USA Today* in August 1999 reported, "Barnes' clothing isn't for the fashion-timid or fashion challenged. The typical Jhane Barnes aficionado is affluent, self-assured and, unlike most fashion impaired men, likes being noticed."

Reflected in her menswear as well as her innovative furniture, which was unveiled in 1995, Barnes shows a flair for striking yet classically composed appearance in her design. Her furniture line has a clearly defined Japanese influence, and as Barnes told the *Chicago Tribune*'s Todd Savage in June 1995, "I've always loved Japanese architecture and been jealous that their traditional Japanese architecture is so modern. It's so much more modern and beautiful than even our Shaker. You can take an American antique, and it looks like an old antique out of another century, but you can take a Japanese antique and it looks timeless." A variety of elegantly simple chairs and sofas made their debut in her collection.

The timeless elegance observant in her work is an appealing factor indeed. Barnes works with natural colors, ranging from subtle to bold, and pairs it with arresting patterns. Bold stripes and computer-generated design are paired with the soft allure of natural color suited to a variety of preferences. The *Chicago Tribune* (August 9, 1998) commented that Barnes, "creates textiles that reflect the same quiet elegance as her clothing lines, but are practical for panels, walls, upholstery and drapery. She does them in slightly different colors to suit regional tastes." Barnes further explained, "New Yorkers like darker colors, Chicagoans more pattern, and those in Los Angeles want things lighter, brighter, and in larger patterns."

The design work of Barnes has become a fashion statement that will hold allure for many years to come. Her natural and ageless design approach has lent her exertions a classic tone with an architecturally digital feel. While she may not gain the appreciation of the masses, her unique combinations have done well and should continue to attract many loyal clients down the road. With such an innovative approach to textile design, the richness of Japanese architecture and Mother Nature for inspiration, one can only marvel at what the next Jhane Barnes design will reveal.

—Sandra Schroeder

BARNETT, Sheridan

British designer

Born: Bradford, England, 1951. **Education:** Studied at Hornsey and Chelsea Colleges of Art, 1969–73. **Career:** Pattern grader (with Ossie Clark and Celia Birtwell), then designer, Quorum, 1975–76; first collection under own label, 1976; designer, Barnett and Brown (with Sheilagh Brown), 1976–80; taught fashion at St. Martins School of Art, and textiles at Chelsea College of Art; freelance designer, Jaeger, Norman Hartnell, Salvador and Annalena, beginning in 1980; also designed own label range for Reldan. **Awards:** Bath Museum of Costume Dress of the Year award, 1983.

Publications

On BARNETT:

Articles

"Zandra Rhodes Conjures Medieval Spell in London," in *Women's Wear Daily,* 15 March 1983.

Brampton, Sally, "Showing the Rest of the World," in the *Observer* (London), 20 March 1983.

Petkanas, Christopher, "London: A Burst of Energy," in *Women's Wear Daily,* 11 October 1983.

"London Attracts U.S. Buyers," in *Women's Wear Daily,* 19 March 1984.

Jones, Mark, "Followers of Fashion," in *Creative Review* (London), December 1984.

Fallon, James, "Designers Set London Benefit to Fight Famine," in *Women's Wear Daily,* 6 August 1985.

———, "Designers Plan 'Fashion Aid' for Ethiopian Famine Relief," in *DNR,* 6 August 1985.

Kerrigan, Marybeth, and Etta Froio, "U.S. Stores Are Cool to London Styles, Prices," in *Women's Wear Daily,* 18 March 1986.

Mower, Sarah, "The Trick Up His Sleeve," in *The Guardian* (London), 21 August 1986.

Fallon, James, "House of Fraser to Open 1st London Unit," in *Women's Wear Daily,* 16 December 1986.

"Sheridan Barnett With a Twist," in *Vogue* (London), April 1987.

Fallon, James, "Hartnell Names Fratini to Design Spring 1990 Line," in *Women's Wear Daily,* 5 December 1989.

Thim, Dennis, "Bohan Nearing Deal to Design Hartnell Couture," in *Women's Wear Daily,* 19 June 1990.

Gabb, Annabella, "Blenheim's Traveling Show…," in *Management Today,* February 1991.

* * *

"We are dressmakers," insisted Sheridan Barnett in an interview with journalist Sarah Mower for *The Guardian* (21 August 1986). "I think it's ludicrous that designers should be made into superstars when they're just out of college. Nobody's a true dress designer until they've worked in the industry at least three years." Barnett passionately believes in the value of training, practice, and apprenticeship to the designer. To Barnett, design is a practical, problem-solving exercise that should be approached with organized discipline. He is not a prima donna, distracted by the whims and extravagances of an often superficial business. His first consideration is his customer and the practical needs they have, rather than the advancement or hype of his own name and talent. This could be one of the reasons why, outside the fashion business, Barnett is one of fashion's best kept secrets.

Barnett first produced a collection under his own label when he left the design group Quorum in 1976. His clothing was distributed by Lawrie Lewis, who went on to found Blenheim Dresswell in 1979. Along with designers like Hardy Amies, Jasper Conran, David Hicks, and Jean Muir, Barnett became known for making clothes for the woman of elegance and style. He quickly established a reputation for very wearable, simple, and affordable clothes and was always one step ahead of other designers, not only in ideas but also in his work. He introduced oversized jackets and ankle-length skirts a year ahead of the catwalk and two years before the High Street had caught on to the look. He also introduced silk pajamas before Parisian designers had even considered them. In many ways, he seemed to be developing a new modern formula to shape 1980s fashion and style. "It had to be interesting, well cut, original, comfortable—and a good fit," he declared.

Barnett aims for a sparseness of design, achieved through a process of elimination. His work has been described as "wearable and very clean, with good lines and beautiful fabrics," by Sheila Bernstein, vice president of Fashion Merchandising at AMC (*Women's Wear Daily,* 1 March 1983). His 1984 collection was inspired by the "unorthodox approach to dressing" of literary heroines Vita Sackville-West and Djuna Barnes. Removing the frills, trims, and fuss he claims to hate, Barnett believes customers should add their own style to the clothes to complete a look or change it from day to day. He strongly adheres to perfection in cut, sometimes spending a week over one sleeve, resetting it over a hundred times according to his perception of how it should fit. "Of course nothing's ever perfect," he has declared, emphasizing how a designer should never be satisfied, as it breeds complacency.

Barnett regards himself as a professional freelance designer, a position he feels strongly suits his temperament. Apart from his own label collections, however, he has collaborated in several successful design liaisons during his career. During the 1970s, he was in partnership with designer Sheilagh Brown, trading as Barnett and Brown and designing their own collections. During the 1980s, he produced ready-to-wear collections for Jaeger and Norman Hartnell (with Victor Edelstein, Allan McClure, and Allan McRae) as well as his own label range for Reldan (where he joined the likes of Mondi, Jaegar, Frank Usher, and Windsmoor, and had his work sold at stores like House of Fraser, owned by the Al-Fayed family); he also worked variously as a lecturer in fashion schools. The early 1990s saw Barnett take a position as designer for the Marks & Spencer supplier Claremont.

Barnett claims not to mind that he has not become a household name in Britain, as have designers such as Bruce Oldfield and Jean Muir. He is, however, regarded within the industry as one of the best designers around. Although he admits things may have been different had he worked in America, his love of London and British culture is a major influence in his work and something he would have had to sacrifice had he gone abroad. His contributions go beyond clothing; Barnett is also a philanthropist at heart, contributing to the Fashion Aid Show in 1985 to help raise money for famine relief in Ethiopia. Barnett joined Zandra Rhodes, Katherine Hamnett, Jasper Conran, Bruce Oldfield, Rifat Ozbeck, Betty Jackson, Wendy Dagworthy, and Issey Miyake, among others. He also taught design at Central St. Martins College of Art & Design, where he numbered among his students Juan Carlos Antonio (John) Galliano, who would go on to his own success, selling his graduating collection, Les Incroyables, to the likes of Diana Ross, and would eventually design for Christian Dior.

Sheridan Barnett's ultimate contribution to fashion is the longevity his clothes have and his simplistic taste and style. He has remained a rare and constant favorite with customers and, amazingly, fashion editors, the people most likely to blow with the fashion wind. This reinforces his original aim for clothes that always look interesting and last for many years. "You can only achieve quality if you eliminate what is superfluous," he declared.

—Kevin Almond; updated by Daryl F. Mallett

BAROCCO, Rocco

Italian designer

Born: Naples, Italy, 26 March 1944; christened Rocco Muscariello. **Education:** Attended Accademia delle Belle Arti, Rome, 1962 (Fine Arts). **Career:** Sketch artist, De Barentzen, 1963–65; joined group to form atelier producing high-fashion collections under Barocco label (disbanded 1974); independent designer using Barocco label, from 1977; Rocco Barocco ready-to-wear line added, 1978; knitwear and children's lines introduced 1982; produces ready-to-wear, jeans, knitwear, scarves, leather goods, accessories, perfume, porcelain tiles, and linens. **Exhibitions:** *Italian Fashion in Japan,* Daimaru Museum, Osaka, 1983; *Italian Fashion Design,* Italian-American Museum, San Francisco, and Pacific Design Center, Los Angeles, 1987; *La Sala Bianca,* Palazzo Pitti, Florence, 1992, and the Louvre Museum, Paris, 1993. **Awards:** Senior Singer Company award, New York, 1969. **Address:** Piazza di Spagna 81, 00187 Rome, Italy. **Websites:** "Rocco Barocco," FirstView Collections Online, spring 2001; "Rocco Barocco," Moda Online, fall 2000/2001; "Rocco Barocco," Quitidiano.net, fall/winter 2001.

PUBLICATIONS

On BAROCCO:

Books

Bottero, A., *Nostra Signora la Moda,* Milan, 1979.
Giordani Aragno, B., *40 Years of Italian Fashion,* Florence, 1983.
Italian Fashion in Japan, Osaka, 1983.
Giacomoni, S., *The Italian Look Reflected,* Milan, 1984.
McDowell, Colin, *Directory of Twentieth Century Fashion,* London, 1984.
Bianchino, G., and A. Quintaralle, *Fashion—From Fable to Design,* Parma, Italy, 1989.
La Sala Bianca, Milan, 1992.
Zito, Adele, *Italian Fashion: The Protagonists,* Italy, 1993.

Rocco Barocco, fall/winter 2001–02 collection: embroidered dress. © AP/Wide World Photos.

Rocco Barocco, fall/winter 2001–02 collection: coat with satin trim and collar, and satin pants. © AP/Wide World Photos.

Articles

Gargia, Massimo, "Barocco ou l'Amour des Passions Inutiles," in *L'Officiel* (Paris), September 1979.
Melendez, R., "Best of Italy," in *Women's Wear Daily,* 26 August 1989.
Lanza, S., "The A. W. Collections from Italy," in the *Sunday Times* (London), 2 September 1990.
"Italy's Passion for Fashion," in *Sunday Morning Post* (South China), 1 December 1991.
"La Botte Secrete de la Mode Romaine," in *Paris Capitale,* May 1994.
"Burani Buys Two Leather Firms," in *Women's Wear Daily,* 6 November 2000.

*

I started my career very young and so it is natural that I should have a certain leaning towards the avant-garde. My first creations were challenges to the styles of the period and very courageous. Technique and experience combined with my taste for the daring in fashion have led to the birth of a clearly defined style that can be recognized in my often repetitive choice of colors: black, black/white and optical effects.

In [one] collection a floral leitmotif (a rose in particular) appears, inserted into spotted or striped designs (leopards, zebras, tigers). The rigorousness of my cut can be recognized in the jackets and cloaks which in their different inspirations (oriental, African, military) always reveal a search for perfect construction. I have a predilection for soft and sumptuous materials, for embroidery and for gold in particular. If we want to define the Rocco Barocco style we must use words like rigor, humor, audacity, and poetic imagination.

—Rocco Barocco

* * *

Rocco Barocco, or Rocco Muscariello as he was christened, is an Italian ready-to-wear designer who creates collections for men, women, and children in a variety of ranges from jeans and knitwear to evening wear. Born in Naples in 1944, he moved to Rome in order to follow his chosen career path. After apprenticeship and training at the city's leading ateliers, he eventually opened his own in the Piazza di Spagna in 1968. Success was immediate, and his popularity with the

Roman jetset increased his fame throughout Europe. He was soon exporting clothes to France, the U.S., and Japan.

Rocco Barocco defines his style as being rigorous, humorous, impudent, and poetically imaginative. He has a taste for the daring and avant-garde in design and detailing, such as his bright red chiffon evening gowns with bold, asymmetrically draped necklines. He also enjoys working with embroidery and gold, in particular. A distinctive sequin and embroidered jacket from his spring/summer 1993 collection paid joint homage to the stars and stripes of the American flag and the daring circus performers from Elsa Schiaparelli's Circus Collection of the late 1930s. Barocco prefers to work in soft and sumptuous materials like paillettes and satins or cashmeres and crêpes. His favorite color combinations are black, black and white, or optical effects, combinations repeating themselves through numerous collections and which have helped define the Rocco Barocco style.

When he began designing, Barocco's intention was to challenge established silhouettes and shapes with a search for perfection in cut, construction, and symmetry. Examples of his cutting skills are displayed in his jackets and coats. His autumn/winter 1989 collection showed long, swinging, dove gray cashmere coats, perfect in balance and proportion and trimmed in fur. His fitted, shawl-collared jackets and suits hinted at masculine classics but exuded femininity in their curvaceous cut, proportion, and detailing. Barocco represents a unique Mediterranean flavor in contemporary fashion; he enjoys taking strong color and style combinations and mixing them in a diverse manner.

Barocco is also inspired by Hollywood, which he views as a fascinating land of unsettled heroes and heroines and a cornucopia of visual reference for high fashion. Hollywood movie stars and fashion in the movies have always been over the top—this undoubtedly contributes to Barocco's taste for the daring in fashion, exemplified in his newer, notorious swimwear-to-lingerie collection. The Rocco Barocco label is also found on ranges of leather goods, handbags, hosiery, jewelry, umbrellas, and shoes. His perfume and toiletry line, RoccoBarocco III, has had lasting success, and the designer branched out into designs for the home, including furniture, porcelain tiles, and refined ceramics. Barocco views his success as transitory, accompanied by inevitable changes. However, from an outsider's point of view, these changes only result in further expansion of the business, ultimately promoting the name of Rocco Barocco on a wider scale.

Probably best known outside Europe for his jeanswear and perfume lines, Barocco apparel ranges from shimmery fabrics such as silks and satins to houndstooth slacks paired with bright pink and lime green sweaters. In his fall 2000 women's collection, shown in Milan, Barocco reinterpreted styles of the 1950s with a postmodernist slant and a spirit of elegance, according to the website Moda Online. The reviewer compared the silhouettes in his spring/summer 2000 women's line to the creations of the French crystal company Lalique. In fall 2001, Barocco focused on a spiderweb theme, incorporating this design from nature into pants and tops that hugged the body yet remained free flowing.

Barocco's men's collection for fall/winter 2001 was described by Italian reviewers as typically British, a mix of the Rolling Stones and Prince William with a little Jimi Hendrix thrown in. Slacks were paired with long coats and no shirt, accessorized with long scarves, in a rock star-inspired style. The ever expanding Rocco Barocco collection includes licenses for leather goods, produced and distributed by the Italian firm Braccialini, and varied denim designs, manufactured and sold by Swinger International.

—Kevin Almond; updated by Karen Raugust

BARRIE, Scott

American designer

Born: Nelson Clyde Barr in Philadelphia, 16 January 1946. **Education:** Studied applied arts at Philadelphia Museum College of Art; fashion design at Mayer School of Fashion, New York, mid-1960s. **Career:** Designer, Allen Cole boutique, New York, 1966–69; cofounder, Barrie Sport, Ltd., New York, 1969–82; menswear collection and Barrie Plus collections introduced, 1974; also designed dresses for S.E.L., mid-1980s; loungewear for Barad, furs for Barlan; moved to Milan, 1982; formed Scott Barrie Italy SrL, in partnership with Kinshido Company, Ltd., of Japan, 1983; designer, Milan D'Or division for Kinshido, 1983–91; designer, signature line for Kinshido, 1983–91; freelance designer, Krizia, Milan, 1986–88. **Died:** 8 June 1993 in Alessandria, Italy.

Publications

On BARRIE:

Books

Morris, Bernadine, and Barbara Walz, *The Fashion Makers,* New York, 1978.

Milbank, Caroline Rennolds, *New York Fashion: The Evolution of American Style,* New York, 1989.

Articles

White, Constance C. R., "Scott Barrie: Back and Renewed," in *Women's Wear Daily* (New York), 20 November 1989.

———, "Scott Barrie Dies at 52; Made Mark on S.A. in 1970s," in *Women's Wear Daily,* 10 June 1993.

Schiro, Ann-Marie, "Scott Barrie is Dead; Designer, 52, Made Jersey Matte Dresses," in the *New York Times,* 11 June 1993.

"Fashion Designer Scott Barrie Dies," in *Jet* (Chicago), 28 June 1993.

* * *

Scott Barrie was one of a group of brassy and vibrant black designers and models to establish themselves on New York's Seventh Avenue in the late 1960s. Influenced by his godmother, who had designed and made clothes for sonorous and volatile jazz singers Dinah Washington and Sarah Vaughan, Barrie began designing in 1966. Although he graduated from the Philadelphia College of Art and the Mayer School in New York, his mother was not initially encouraging about his future in fashion designing for Seventh Avenue. "Blacks don't make it there," she warned her son—Barrie quickly proved her wrong.

Describing himself in the 1970s as being midway between the crazy extremes of Zandra Rhodes and Herbert Kasper, Barrie quickly established himself as a designer of sexy, often outrageous clothes. His eveningwear was particularly noteworthy: skinny gowns sprinkled with pailettes and dangerously high splits, or jersey slips that slid tantalizingly over the figure.

He began making clothes in his New York apartment, with a makeshift cutting table and domestic sewing machine. His first orders were from small independent boutiques but success came when prestigious stores Henri Bendel and Bloomingdale's in New York placed orders for his sparse and revealing jersey dresses. By 1969 he had christened his company Barrie Sport and moved into spacious workrooms at 530 Seventh Avenue.

Barrie's forté was the sensuous use of jersey, cut in inventive and unexpected ways, from which he created elegant and often risqué eveningwear. Popular devotees of the Barrie were extravagantly beautiful model Naomi Sims, who always ordered her clothes in white, and Lee Traub, wife of Bloomingdale's then-president.

Barrie also designed ranges of loungewear, furs, and accessories and was involved in costume design, creating clothes for films and the Joffrey Ballet's production of *Deuce Coupe.*

The intermingling of culture and race on New York's Seventh Avenue in the 1960s brought a new sort of creative energy that challenged accepted standards. Barrie's models did not parade the catwalk with elegance; instead they boogied wildly and arrogantly, with a streetwise brashness. It was a testimony to the changing times that the clothes were accepted at the higher end of the ready-to-wear market.

Barrie enjoyed being a fashion designer, but acknowledged the hard work and competitive nature of the business. In the early 1980s he ceased designing under his own name, taking a position with the dress firm S.E.L. as a designer. For the later years of the decade and the beginning of the 1990s, Barrie designed for the Italian design house Krizia and for the Japanese firm Kinshido. In 1993 Barrie died of brain cancer in Alessandria, Italy, he was 52.

—Kevin Almond

BARTLETT, John

American designer

Born: Cincinnati, Ohio, 1963. **Education:** Harvard University, B.A. in Sociology, 1985; graduated from Fashion Institute of Technology, 1988. **Career:** Interned with Willi Smith, Bill Robinson, and Ronaldus Shamask; men's designer for Williwear, 1988–89; design director, Ronaldus Shamask, 1989–91; own menswear line sold at Barneys, Bergdorf Goodman, and Charivari, 1992; partnership with Genny Spa and premiere of womenswear, 1997; creative director, Byblos menswear and womenswear collections sold at Saks and Neiman Marcus, own label sold at Henri Bendel, 1998. **Awards:** Fashion Institute of Technology Bill Robinson award, 1988; Woolmark "Cutting Edge" award, 1992; Fashion Institute of Technology Alumni award, 1994; Council of Fashion Designers of America Perry Ellis award for New Fashion Talent, 1994; Council of Fashion Designers of America award, 1997. **Address:** 450 West 15th Street, New York, NY, 10011, USA.

John Bartlett, spring 2001 collection: silk chiffon wrap blouse over crêpe satin ruched trouser. © Reuters NewMedia Inc./CORBIS.

Publications

On BARTLETT:

Books

Stegemeyer, Anne, *Who's Who in Fashion, Third Edition,* New York, 1996.

Articles

Spindler, Amy M., "Menswear Expands the Notion of Basics," in the *New York Times,* 3 August 1993.
Shaw, Daniel, "Rookie of the Year," in the *New York Times,* 5 December 1993.
Horyn, Cathy, "Crusoe for the Modern Man," in the *Washington Post,* 6 February 1994.
"Sharkskin Bites Bartlett," in the *DNR* (New York), 29 July 1994.

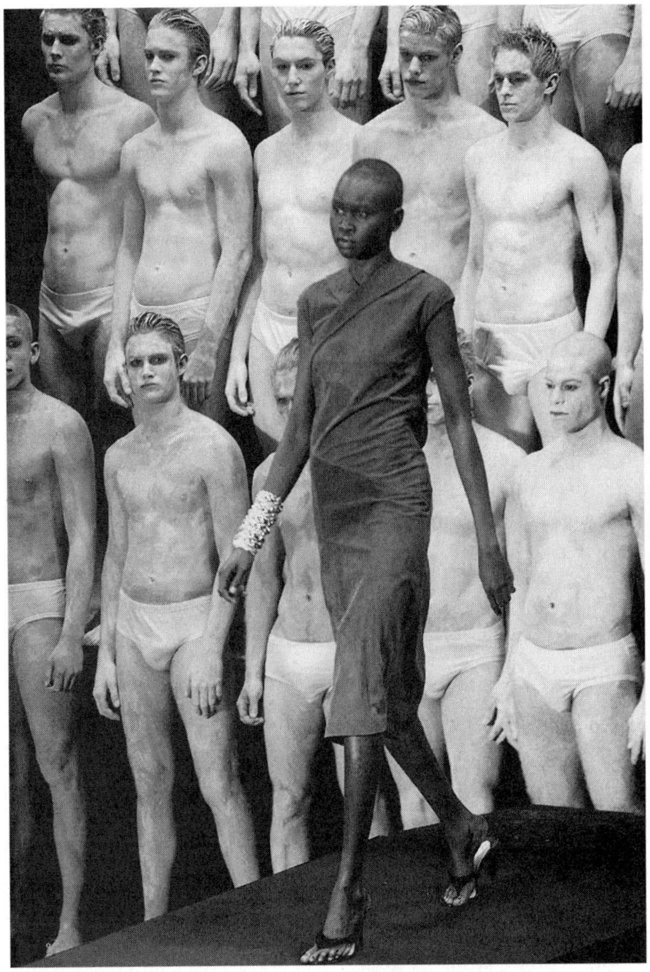

John Bartlett, spring 2001 collection: suede reverse kimono. © AP/ Wide World Photos.

Martin, Richard, "Style Is as Style Does: The 'Forest Gump' Look," in *Mondo Uomo* (Milan), November-December 1994.

Ezersky, Lauren, "Bringing Up Bartlett," in *Paper* (New York), December 1994.

DeCaro, Frank, "If You've Got It, Flaunt It," in *Newsweek,* 12 August 1996.

———, "Gender Bend: Hot Boys to Haute Girls," in *Newsweek,* 21 April 1997.

Tien, Ellen and Patti O'Brien, "From the Hip," in *Rolling Stone,* 30 October 1997.

Gliatto, Tom and Sue Miller, "Cincinnati Kid," in *People,* 8 December 1997.

Luscombe, Belinda, "The Anti-Calvin is Here," in *Time,* 24 August 1998.

Solomon, Andrew, "Balancing Act," in the *New York Times Magazine,* 21 March 1999.

Orecklin, Michele and Stacy Perman, "What Will We Wear?" in *Time,* 21 February 2000.

Bellafante, Ginia, "Men's Wear: Talking Revolution and Showing Suits," in the *New York Times,* 12 February 2001.

"John Bartlett," at FashionLive website (www.fashionlive.com/itv/designers/bartlett), 19 March 2001

Bressler, Karen, "Interview with John Bartlett," at FashionWindow website (www.fashionwindow.com/fashionwire), 22 March 2001.

Mui, Nelson, "John Bartlett Fall 2001," at FashionWindow website (www.fashionwindow.com/fashion_designers/john_bartlett), 22 March 2001.

* * *

When asked "What Will We Wear?" in a February 2000 *Time* magazine article about the future of fashion design after the dawn of the new millennium, John Bartlett answered, "The future will reference the past, drawing on everything from the Napoleonic era to the 1950s." This eclectic style of new and old, haute design and simple street clothes, ethos and pathos, personifies Bartlett and his clothes.

Bartlett's fashion is driven by ideas—astute ideas—about men and about clothes. For example, his spring/summer 1994 collection was for a man, as Bartlett said to the *New York Times*' Amy Spindler, "day-dreaming about cashing in his Gucci loafers for a lean-to on Easter Island." Bartlett's volitional Robinson Crusoe would have assembled an elegant mix of tribal tattoos, gauze tunics, and rough silk-twine jackets. As Spindler noted, "It's an ambitious designer who will take on Jean-Jacques Rousseau, but Mr. Bartlett did it with fervor." Bartlett never lacks fervor: he is determined—with a missionary's zeal—to make clothing meaningful.

Bartlett is a designer of convictions and of compellingly suggestive and allusive menswear. His spring/summer 1995 collection demonstrated the designer's learned and connected awareness of culture. A runway show that began with clothing inspired by the 1994 summer movie *Forrest Gump* in its nerdish normalcy, in distinctive mint greens, continued into navy-and-white evocations out of Jean Genêt (Edmund White's biography had just been published), sharp sharkskin two-button suits, and tour de force cross-dressing. Bartlett is a reader, observer, assimilator of contemporary culture in the best sense, bringing his acute sensitivity into his design. His shapeless structures were being updated into piquant reinterpretations of earlier silhouettes with trousers either cigarette-thin or perfectly tubular and shown on models as high-water pants. The *Daily News Record* (29 July 1994) enthused about the 1995 collection, "In just four short seasons, this glamor-boy designer has established himself as the *enfant terrible*—the Gaultier, if you will—of American men's wear." If there is a fault to Bartlett's work, it is that he is the best and consummate stylist of his own clothing. Few menswear customers will actually carry off the clothing with the full styling and intellectual jolt Bartlett imparts. But, of course, one might say the same of the ever-influential and beguiling Gaultier. One could easily imagine Bartlett fully assuming the Gaultier role of polite *provocateur,* a function woefully absent from American fashion.

Bartlett's designing capacity exploded in 1997 with the premiere of his first womenswear collection. "Designing for men is about subtlety; but women want fantasy. And I don't want to follow someone else's lead," Bartlett told *Newsweek* writer Frank DeCaro in April 1997. This aptly-named "Butch-Femme" collection mixed men's tailoring and sexual femininity featuring fitted leather shirts, cashmere Shaker-knit sweaters and slender Chesterfield coats. Very few menswear designers have been as successful as Ralph Lauren or Giorgio Armani in the leap across gender lines, but Bartlett's entry into the womenswear industry received rave reviews and left women wanting more of his flattering fashions. "A star is born," applauded *Allure* magazine's Polly Allen Mellen.

"My clothes are not for the woman who's shy...She's very self-confident," Bartlett told *People* magazine in December 1997, after his spring 1998 line was introduced. Inspired by the alluring charm of 1950s film noir, this naughty line matched sling-tops with leather pencil skirts and taffeta police pants with crystal-studded muscle t-shirts. Subsequently self-confidence presided over his 1999 collection when both men and women models presented his first-ever unisex showing, which Andrew Soloman of the *New York Times Magazine* found "to indicate the coherence of [Bartlett's] vision. It's a balancing act, sexual though ungendered, and balancing is his greatest strength."

Balance, sexuality, and drama united into a spectacular exposition of his spring 2001 line. Framed by a tower of white-powdered, body-building, Adonis-like men, Bartlett's Japanese-inspired silks and chiffons sailed down the runway metaphorically tied together by a strand of rope. "There are chiffon dresses within the rope theme featuring twisted pieces of fabric and graphic rope prints," described Bartlett for the FashionWindow website in March 2000. "There were chiffon pieces with floaty kimono sleeves worn with strict, sexy leather pants, as well as matte jersey dresses which are perfect to travel with." When author Karen Bressler asked him of the future, Bartlett answered, "The most heralded collections are individualistic."

Bartlett's distinct eccentricity and individuality came full-circle when he returned to his roots for the fall 2001 show and displayed his militaristic men's collection with emotion and meaning. Visitors entered his showroom and viewed models lying lifeless on army cots and wearing long, sexy military coats and fatigue jackets. A tribute to the struggle and survival of World War II German soldier and artist Joseph Beuys, this presentation, according to Nelson Mui of the FashionWindow website, followed in "perfect lockstep with the military beat fashion has been following once again."

John Bartlett, more than any other American designer of menswear, examines the basic tenets of men's bodies and their identity in dress. His "become yourself" philosophy is inexhaustibly optimistic. His clothing is so idiosyncratically shrewd and seductive, one could wish many more would choose either to become themselves or, perhaps even better, to realize the ideal thinking men and women Bartlett creates.

—Richard Martin; updated by Jodi Essey-Stapleton

BARTON, Germain "Alix"

See GRÈS, Madame

BASTILLE, Franck Joseph

French designer

Born: circa 1964. **Career:** Known for whimsical designs and embroidered motifs; clothing sold at Galeries Lafayette, New York, among other places. **Exhibitions:** *Fashion and Surrealism,* New York, 1987. **Address:** 13 rue de la Roquette, 75011 Paris.

Publications

On BASTILLE:

Articles

"Bastille's Day," in *Elle* (New York), July 1989.
Petkanas, Christopher, "Nouvelle Chic," in *Harper's Bazaar,* December 1991.

* * *

Irreverent is the word for the designs of Franck Joseph Bastille. In the best tradition of Elsa Schiaparelli, whose whimsical and dream-like designs shocked and delighted earlier fashion audiences, Bastille's witty collections launched him into the limelight as one of Paris' rising young stars. The presentation of his new ideas each season, often shown in an offbeat, trendy venue, invariably spurred fashion headlines, due in no small part to the ironic flourishes which have become his trademark.

Embroidered quotes from the animal kingdom have figured largely in Bastille's *oeuvre.* Lizards and lobsters, ants and rats, fish and cats—all have found their way onto his clothes. A thigh-high skirt might sport a creature snaking along the hem, or a plain vinyl shift may be stitched all over with a bright menagerie. Never one to be limited by convention, Bastille has been known to embroider frogs on a black vinyl coat and then upholster a chair with the same material.

Like his young Parisian peers he finds inspiration in a multitude of sources, sifting through a postmodern melange of ideas and adapting some directly, borrowing from others quite loosely. One fashion show had as its theme the permutations of water, from the beauty of the shimmering sea to the murky mystery of the subterranean underworld. Bastille showed a range of clever, bold clothes, including seaweed-hued frocks decorated with plastic fish, and his own kitschy interpretation of the sort of studded denim resort clothes worn on the Riviera. Other visual puns have included a black suit appliqued with silver guns, and a simple shift dress with a cut-out heart over the chest. And he is not above the sly tongue-in-cheek gesture, as in his wedding gown embroidered all over with the word *oui.*

Like many young designers, Bastille has rummaged about in the past for ideas, and references to different style periods can be discerned in his clothes. He became identified with 1950s–60s trapeze shapes and princess cuts for a time, but has also toyed with the body-revealing, sexy clothing of the 1980s and the decade's preoccupation with physical fitness. A collection that included clingy little body suits, short shorts, wispy slips, and satin bustiers showed that his clothes were not for the conservative customer, nor for one of advancing age. Pieces such as these demonstrate that Bastille is designing for a young, daring, and fashion-forward buyer who considers clothing a form of provocative personal expression.

Bastille has been called "fearless, with a touch of elegance." He has been known to turn a simple suit into an arch statement with the use of riotous color, as in his peacock-feather printed suit. In addition to appliqués and cut-outs he has experimented with "out of context" fabrics, using slippery synthetics, shiny satins, and crushed velvets for daytime wear, home-furnishing fabrics for clothing designs, and vice versa. Bastille might cover a blazer with sequins or fashion a strappy shift out of black vinyl, making a bold statement about the allure of "bad taste" while erasing demarcations between clothes for different events or times of day.

Bastille has crafted separates out of multihued patchwork fabric comprised of satin, floral print, and sequined squares, giving literal form to the bricolage cultural trend so prevalent in the late-20th century. In short, the imaginative, playful Franck Joseph Bastille (whose name is borrowed from the famous French prison destroyed during the French Revolution) aims to startle and amuse with his designs, asserting that fashion does not have to be such serious business.

—Kathleen Paton

BEENE, Geoffrey

American designer

Born: Haynesville, Louisiana, 30 August 1927. **Education:** Studied medicine, Tulane University, New Orleans, 1943–46, University of Southern California, Los Angeles, 1946; studied fashion, Traphagen School, New York, 1947–48, Chambre Syndicale d'Haute Couture and Académie Julien, Paris, 1948. **Career:** Display assistant, I. Magnin, Los Angeles, 1946; apprentice tailor, Molyneux, 1948–50; assistant to Mildred O'Quinn, Samuel Winston, Harmay, and other New York fashion houses, 1950–51; assistant designer, Harmony ready-to-wear, New York, 1951–58; designer, Teal Traina, New York, 1958–62; founder/director, Geoffrey Beene Inc., beginning 1962; showed first collection, 1963; first menswear collection, 1970; introduced Beenebag sportswear collection, 1971; established Cofil SpA, 1976, to manufacture for Europe and the Far East; opened first boutique, New York, 1989; introduced home furnishings collection, 1993; designed costumes for ballet *Diabelli,* 1999. Fragrances include *Gray Flannel,* 1975; *Bowling Green,* 1987. **Exhibitions:** *Geoffrey Beene: 25 Years of Discovery,* Los Angeles, Western Reserve Historical Society, Cleveland, Ohio, National Academy of Design, New York, and Musashino Museum, Tokyo, all 1988; *Geoffrey Beene Unbound,* Fashion Institute of Technology, New York, 1994; *Geoffrey Beene,* Toledo Museum of Art, Toledo, Ohio, 1997; China International Clothing and Accessories Fair, Beijing, 1998; *Zippers and Harnesses,* New York, 1999. **Awards:** Coty American Fashion Critics award, 1964, 1966, 1968, 1974, 1975, 1977, 1981, 1982; National Cotton Council award, 1964, 1969; Neiman Marcus award, 1965; Ethel Traphagen award, New York, 1966; Council of Fashion Designers of America award, 1986, 1987, 1989, special award, 1988; CFDA Lifetime Achievement award, 1997; Dallas Historical Society Fashion Collectors Stanley award, 1998; Marymount University (WA) Designer of the Year award, 2000; Fashion Walk of Fame, New York, initial inductee, 2000; Dallas Market Center Fashion Excellence award, 2001. **Address:** 550 Seventh Avenue, New York, NY 10018, USA.

Design by Geoffrey Beene, 1965. © Bettmann/CORBIS.

Publications

On BEENE:

Books

Morris, Bernadine, and Barbara Walz, *The Fashion Makers,* New York, 1978.

Milbank, Caroline Rennolds, *Couture: The Great Designers,* New York, 1985.

Diamonstein, Barbaralee, *Fashion: The Inside Story,* New York, 1985.

Coleridge, Nicholas, *The Fashion Conspiracy,* London, 1988.

National Academy of Design, New York, *Geoffrey Beene: The First 25 Years* [exhibition catalogue], Tokyo, 1988.

Milbank, Caroline Rennolds, *New York Fashion: The Evolution of American Style,* New York, 1989.

Martin, Richard, *Beene: Thirty Years,* New York, 1993.

Fashion Institute of Technology, *Geoffrey Beene Unbound* [exhibition catalogue], New York, 1994.

Cullerton, Brenda, *Geoffrey Beene: The Anatomy of His Work,* New York, 1995.

Jacobs, Laura, *Beauty and the Beene, a Modern Legend,* New York, 1999.

Articles

Bowles, J., "It's a Beene," in *Vogue,* January 1977.

"Geoffrey Beene: Maître incontesté de la couture," in *L'Officiel* (Paris), September 1985.

"Modern Attitude: The Essence of Geoffrey Beene," in *Vogue,* February 1986.

Hyde, Nina, "Geoffrey Beene, Simply Elegant: The Designer and His Lifetime Devotion to Fabric," in the *Washington Post,* 19 April 1987.

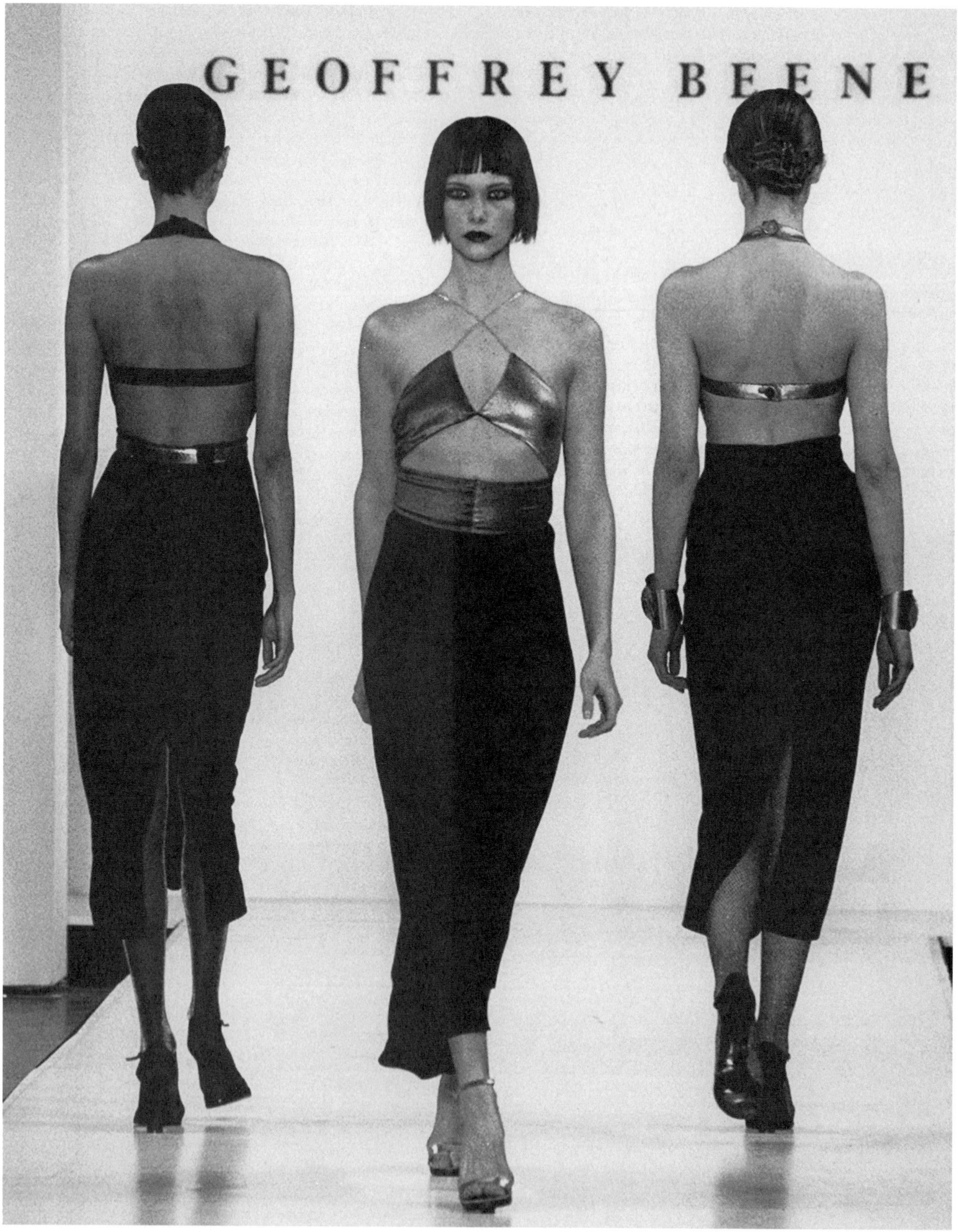

Geoffrey Beene, fall 1999 collection. © AP/Wide World Photos.

Bryant, Gay, "Living for Fashion," in *Connoisseur* (New York), May 1987.
Monget, K., "Designer Profiles: 1988 Marks 25th Year in American Fashion for Geoffrey Beene," in *New York Apparel News,* May 1987.
"The World of Geoffrey Beene," in *Vogue,* September 1987.
"Vogue's Spy: Geoffrey Beene," in *Vogue* (London), October 1987.
Morrisroe, Patricia, "American Beauty: The World of Geoffrey Beene," in *New York Magazine,* 30 May 1988.
Buck, Joan Juliet, "The Eye of Geoffrey Beene," in *Vogue,* September 1988.
Blane, Mark, "Mr. Beene: The First 25 Years," in *Harper's Bazaar* (New York), October 1988.
Armstrong, Lisa, "The Thoroughly Modern Mr. Beene," in *Vogue* (London), April 1990.
Betts, Katherine, "Showstopper," in *Vogue,* September 1991.
Donovan, Carrie, "Geoffrey Beene," in the *New York Times,* 9 May 1993.
Beard, Patricia, "Beene There, Done That," in *Town & Country,* July 1993.
Hirst, Arlene, "Mr. Beene: America's New Homebody," in *Metropolitan Home* (New York), July/August 1993.
Morris, Bernadine, "Beene: If Ever a Wiz There Was," in the *New York Times,* 5 November 1993.
Livingstone, David, "Beene Unbound, Grace Regained," in the *Globe and Mail* (Toronto), 5 May 1994.
Trittoléno, Martine, "L'Elégance Radicale," *Vogue* (Paris), June/July 1994.
Beckett, Kathleen, "Runway Report—In-Kleined to Wow Fans: Geoffrey Beene," in the *New York Post,* 1 November 1994.
Spindler, Amy M., "Beene: Innovative and, Yes, Intellectual," in the *New York Times,* 8 April 1995.
Menkes, Suzy, "A Crisis in Confidence: Reinventing the American Dream," in the *International Herald Tribune,* 11 April 1995.
Jacobs, Laura, "Beene There," in the *New Republic,* 20 November 1995.
Gash, Barbara, "Geoffrey Beene Elevates Clothing to an Art Form," in the *Detroit Free Press,* 18 January 1998.
Harris, Joyce Saenz, "A Cut Above," in the *Dallas Morning News,* 22 April 1998.
Luther, Marylou, "Fashion Twain Geoffrey Beene Addresses East-West Link with China," in the *Rocky Mountain News* (Denver, CO), 24 December 1998.
Donnally, Trish, "Anatomy of a Designer," in the *San Francisco Chronicle,* 8 June 1999.
Blanchard, Tamsin, "Agenda Two: Mr. Beene," in the *Observer* (London), 13 June 1999.
Wilson, Eric, "No More Runways for Beene," in *Women's Wear Daily,* 15 February 2000.
———, "Beene Walks Walk and Talks Some Talk," in *Women's Wear Daily,* 7 June 2000.
Moss, Meredith, "Fabric is Key to Geoffrey Beene Designs," in the *Dayton Daily News* (Ohio), 8 July 2001.

* * *

"Among the fashion *cognoscenti,* [Geoffrey] Beene has long been acknowledged as an artist who chooses to work in cloth," reported Carrie Donovan in the *New York Times* in May 1993. "Every season his work astounds as he ingeniously shapes the most modern and wearable of clothes." For some, the designation of fashion as art is simply a way of saying "the best," and Geoffrey Beene is certainly one of the best designers of the 20th century and still around in the 21st century. His art resides in certain principles and preoccupations—reversibility, superbly clean cutting, and a fluidity of cloth to body in the manner of Vionnet; an origami-like three-dimensionality that approaches sculpture; a propensity for cubism, piecing the garment from regular forms in a new tangency and relationship one to another; and a modernist indulgence in the medium, relishing the textiles of both tradition and of advanced technology.

Such abiding elements of art in his work do not mitigate other elements. History may be seized, as in a remarkable Confederate dress inspired by the gray uniform of the Southern army in the American Civil War. Sensuous appreciation of the body is ever present in Beene's work (he initially went to medical school and always demonstrates his interest in the body and ergonomics). His lace dresses expose the body in underwear—defying gyres of inset lace, a tour de force of the body's exposure and of the security of the wearer in the dress's perfect and stable proportions. He shifts, conceals, and maneuvers the waist as no other designer has since Balenciaga.

Born in the South, Beene's personal style is of utmost charm, and his clothes betray his sense of good taste, though often with gentility's piquant notes. His 1967 long sequined football jersey was sportswear with a new goal in the evening and played with the anomaly of simple style with liquid elegance. Sweatshirt fabric and denim would be carried into eveningwear by Beene, upsetting convention. A brash gentility combined leather and lace; a charming wit provided for circus motifs. In particular, Beene loved the genteel impropriety of stealing from menswear textiles (shirting fabrics and gray flannel) for women's clothing.

The designer has been careful to surprise, rather than shock, the viewer when dressing the female form. He attributes his respect for women to his Southern upbringing and aims for the sensuous rather than the sexy in his creations. Clothing from Beene is made for movement and never restricts or binds the wearer. He uses color well but sparingly and believed too much color overwhelmed the individual.

Beene had a profound affinity with his contemporary Southerner Jasper Johns, who practiced consummate good taste in art but with the startling possibilities of popular-culture appropriations, new dispositions to familiar elements, and a strong sense of modern cultural pastiche. Like Johns, Beene was fascinated by trompe l'oeil and played with illusion. Specific illusions of a tie and collar on a dress were the most obvious, but other wondrous tricks of illusion in clothing were found in three-dimensional patterns replicated in textile and vice versa. His bolero jackets so effectively complemented the simplicity of his dresses that jacket and dress became an indistinguishable ensemble. Even his preoccupation with double-faced fabrics and reversible abstract designs were sophisticated illusionism.

Optically, Beene demands both near-sightedness and far-sightedness. Even before his most fluid forms emerged in the 1970s and 1980s, he had been influenced by op art to create graphically striking apparel. His frequent use of black and white was a treatment that could be read across a room and acted as sign. But one can approach a Beene composition in black and white close up with the same scrutiny of a Frank Stella black painting: there is a fascination up close even more gratifying than the sign from afar. In Beene's case, texture is an important element, and the distant reading of graphic clarity became far more complex when disparate textures were mingled. Like reversibility, the near-far dialectic in Beene was provocative: utter simplicity from a distance became infinite technicality up close. Since the 1990s, Beene has often eschewed the catwalk showing of new collections, preferring to display garments on static dress forms, allowing viewers to examine the garment attentively and immediately, as one might appreciate painting or sculpture.

Contributing to the aura of Beene is his unapologetic individuality. He has never cared to please the critics or celebrities, preferring instead to dress the average person. Beene also dislikes runway shows; in 1993, he replaced his supermodels with dancers, highlighting the fluidity of his designs. In 2000 he announced he would no longer be presenting his clothing via runway shows but would instead look to presentation through film, television, or the Internet.

But despite, or perhaps in part because of Beene's eccentricities, he continues to draw acclaim from those in the fashion world who best know great design. He was one of only four living designers to be included in the initial induction of New York City's Fashion Center Walk of Fame (à la Hollywood's Walk of Fame) in 2000. His plaque reads, "A designer's designer, Geoffrey Beene is one of the most artistic and individual of fashion's creators. He is known for his surgically clean cutting and his fluid use of materials. His designs display a sensuous appreciation of the body and always permit movement. Beene blends masterful construction techniques with seemingly disparate elements, such as whimsically patterned fabrics. The end results are spirited garments, like his famous sequined football jersey evening gown."

Art, to describe Beene's clothing, is not vacuous or striving to compliment. Rather, art recognizes a process and suite of objectives inherent in the work. In a discipline of commercial fulfillment, Beene displays the artist's absolute primacy and self-confidence of design exploration.

—Richard Martin; updated by Carrie Snyder

BELLVILLE SASSOON-LORCAN MULLANY

British couture and ready-to-wear firm, Bellville Sassoon & Bellville Sassoon-Lorcan Mullany, respectively.

Founded: Belinda Bellville founded own company, 1953, joined by designer David Sassoon to form Bellville Sassoon, 1958; Bellville retired from company, 1983; Bellville Sassoon-Lorcan Mullany founded, 1987. *David Sassoon* born in London, 5 October 1932; attended Chelsea College of Art, 1954–56, and Royal College of Art, London, 1956–58; served in the Royal Air Force, 1950–53. *Lorcan Mullany* born 3 August 1953; trained at Grafton Academy, Dublin; worked for Bill Gibb, Hardy Amies, and Ronald Joyce in London before producing collection under his own name in 1983; joined Bellville Sassoon in 1987. **Company History:** Ready-to-wear collection sold in, among others, Saks Fifth Avenue, Bloomingdale's, and Henri Bendel, all in New York, and Harrods and Harvey Nichols, both in London; flagship store in Chelsea, London. **Exhibitions:** *Fashion: An Anthology,* Victoria & Albert Museum, London, 1971. **Company Address:** 18 Culford Gardens, London SW3 2ST, England.

Publications

On BELLVILLE SASSOON-LORCAN MULLANY:

Books

O'Hara, Georgina, *The Enyclopedia of Fashion,* New York, 1986.
The Cutting Edge: Fifty Years of Fashion, New York, n.d.

Articles

Thomas, Jacqueline H., "Profile," in *Vogue Pattern Book* (New York & London), 1984.
Holder, Margaret, "That Sassoon Touch," in *Royalty* (London), 1989.
Griffiths, Sally, "Well-Dressed Surroundings," in *House & Garden* (London), 1991.
Polan, Brenda, "Vital Sassoon," in the *Tatler* (London), September 1992.
Watson, Ines, "Sassoon Assesses South African Talent," in the *Dispatch Online,* 13 November 1998.

*

I like clothes that flatter a woman and are sexy; if a woman feels good in the clothes I design, she looks good. I enjoy designing cocktail and eveningwear with my codesigners Lorcan Mullany and George Sharp. We work together as a team to produce ready-to-wear dresses, sometimes in a romantic mood, sometimes whimsical or sexy… I love colour and beautiful fabrics. Each season we try to do something different, but always with a distinct Bellville Sassoon-Lorcan Mullany handwriting, which our buyers always look for. Our collection is sold internationally and each country looks for a different fashion concept, so our collections are always varied, never sticking to one theme. I do not like to philosophize about clothes; they are, after all, only garments to be worn and discarded as the mood of fashion changes.

—David Sassoon

* * *

The company of Bellville Sassoon-Lorcan Mullany has been jointly run by David Sassoon (who owned the company and designed the couture), and Lorcan Mullany who joined in 1987 and was responsible for the ready-to-wear. Together they provide a very English version of glamorous occasion dressing and eveningwear, uncomplicated, clear, and immensely flattering clothes worn by society ladies and the international jet set, which included the late Princess of Wales, Ivana Trump, Shakira Caine, Dame Kiri Te Kanawa, and the Countess von Bismarck, to name but a few. The company has also been renowned for its romantic wedding dresses, designed to order, and the selection of designs available in the *Vogue Pattern Book*'s designer section, which sell internationally.

"You have to find your own niche," declared David Sassoon to the *Tatler* in September 1992, when questioned about his approach to design. "You cannot be all things to all markets. My philosophy of fashion is that I like to make the kind of clothes that flatter. I am not interested in fashion for its own sake. If you make a woman feel good, she looks good automatically." On leaving the Royal College of Art fashion school in the late 1950s Sassoon was recruited as Belinda Bellville's design assistant. She recognized in him a designer who had a strong, distinctive signature and a simple approach that was romantic in style but dramatic and very feminine.

Together Bellville and Sassoon became business partners, naming the company Bellville et Cie, to capitalize on the prevalent conception that all smart clothes were French. From the start it attracted vast attention from press and buyers. "We gave our first show in my grandmother's house in Manchester Square and the next day there was a queue outside the shop, with Bentleys blocking the street," declared Belinda Bellville.

Sassoon identified the peak of his career as being the period between the late 1960s and 1970s when he believed the taste for high romanticism and fantasy clothes endorsed his style. The company was constantly featured in the pages of glossy magazines, sharing the stage with contemporaries such as Zandra Rhodes, Gina Fratini, and Bill Gibb. Sassoon regrets that the British fashion press often flippantly discarded designers as no longer newsworthy, comparing this with the American press who always acknowledged good design. Bill Blass and Oscar de la Renta, he declared, may no longer be in the forefront of fashion but the press still regards them as newsworthy.

In the 1970s emphasis on couture was dwindling and the company realized that in order to survive, the ready-to-wear line had to be built up. The decision proved correct as the firm's business grew immensely in America and was promoted with fashion shows across the U.S. and at trade fairs in London, Paris, New York, Munich, and Dusseldorf. Their agents had little problem building a strong and impressive clientèle.

Lorcan Mullany, who joined the company upon Bellville's retirement, had a strong background in occasion and eveningwear. He trained at the Grafton Academy in Dublin and before joining David Sassoon, worked for Bill Gibb, Ronald Joyce, and Hardy Amies. The label soon bore the joint name Bellville Sassoon-Lorcan Mullany, justifiably crediting all designers for the product. By the mid- and late 1990s the company's clothes represented the top end of British occasion dressing, from sumptuous ballgowns to flirty cocktail dresses. Frills, sinuous draping, streamlined side splits, and plunging backs evoked memories of Hollywood in its glamorous heyday. Tulle, encrusted embroideries, taffetas, duchesse satin, mink, and double silk crepes were characteristic of the luxurious fabrics used. Unlike some eveningwear, the clothes were never gaudy or overstated; their success was reliant on a streamlined sense of style.

In 1998, after more than 40 years in the design business, David Sassoon was selected as the secret "international judge" of J&B's Rare Designers award. Sassoon traveled to Johannesburg, South Africa, for the competition and enjoyed the experience. He told Ines Watson of the *Dispatch Online* (13 November 1998), "It's been an interesting experience because I arrived with no preconceived idea of the South African fashion industry." He did, however, see "two huge differences between European and South African design—the latter is more individualistic but the former has the advantage of the enormous resources of textiles on offer."

In the 21st century, Bellville Sassoon-Lorcan Mullany continues to clothe a discerning clientèle, creating an annual ready-to-wear collection sold to the best of stores worldwide, including Harrods, Harvey Nichols, Saks Fifth Avenue, and Nieman Marcus to name a few. Additionally, vintage designs remain popular Vogue patterns, available in sewing stores and at various international websites.

—Kevin Almond; updated by Owen James

BENETTON SPA

Italian sportswear firm

Founded: by Giuliana (1938—), Luciano (1935—), Gilberto (1941—), and Carlo (1943—) Benetton, in Treviso, in 1965 as Maglificio di Ponzano Veneto dei Fratelli Benetton. **Company History:** First Benetton outlet opened in Belluno, Italy, 1968; first shop outside Italy, in Paris, 1969; launched major European expansion campaign, from 1978; first U.S. store, New York, 1979; first Eastern European shop, Prague, 1985; went public in Milan, 1986; formed Benetton Sportsystem SpA, 1989; opened huge stores in Paris, London, Barcelona, Lisbon, Frankfurt, Vienna, Prague, and Sarajevo, 1994; opened 50 shops in China and factory in Egypt, 1995; opened London megastore and New York flagship, 1996; bought sports group from parent company, 1997; formed Benetton USA with Sears, 1998; introduced Playlife stores, 1998–99; dumped by Sears, 2000; concentrated expansion in U.S., 2001. **Company Address:** Via Chiesa Ponzano 24, 31050 Ponzano Veneto, Treviso, Italy. **Company Website:** www.benetton.com.

PUBLICATIONS

On BENETTON:

Books

Baker, Caroline, *Benetton Colour Style File,* London, 1987.

Belussi, Fiorenza, *Benetton: Information Technology in Production & Distribution,* Brighton, 1987.

Aragno, Bonizza Giordani, *Moda Italia: Creativity and Technology in the Italian Fashion System,* Milan, 1988.

Mantle, Jonathan, *Benetton—The Family, the Business, and the Brand,* New York, 1999.

Articles

Bentley, Logan, "The Tightknit Benetton," in *People,* 15 October 1984.

Lee, Andrea, "Being Everywhere: Luciano Benetton," in the *New Yorker,* 10 November 1986.

Coleman, Alix, "A Colourful Career," in the *Sunday Express Magazine* (London), 20 September 1987.

Fierman, Jaclyn, "Dominating an Economy, Family-Style: The Italians," in *Fortune,* 12 October 1987.

Finnerty, Anne, "The Internationalisation of Benetton," in *Textile Outlook International* (London), November 1987.

"Alessandro Benetton," in *Interview,* April 1988.

Fuhrman, Peter, "Benetton Learns to Darn," in *Forbes,* 3 October 1988.

Griggs, Barbara, "The Benetton Fratelli," in *Vogue* (London), October 1988.

Tornier, François, "Les 25 ans de Benetton," in *Elle* (Paris), 1 October 1990.

Baker, Lindsay, "Taking Advertising to Its Limits," in *The Guardian* (London), 22 July 1991.

Kanner, Bernice, "Shock Value," in *New York,* 24 September 1992.

Waxman, Sharon, "The True Colors of Luciano Benetton," in the *Washington Post,* 17 February 1993.

Rossant, John, "The Faded Colors of Benetton," in *Business Week,* 10 April 1995.

Forden, Sara Gay, "Luciano Benetton Sees a Rosy Future Despite Cloudy Days," in *Women's Wear Daily,* 20 April 1995.
Levine, Joshua, "Even When You Fail, You Learn a Lot," in *Forbes,* 11 March 1996.
Rossant, John, "A Cozy Deal at Benetton," in *Business Week,* 28 July 1997.
Edelson, Sharon, "Benetton's U.N. Mission," in *Women's Wear Daily,* 3 April 1998.
Sansoni, Silvia, "The Odd Couple," in *Forbes,* 19 October 1998.
Seckler, Valerie, "Benetton's Global Game Plan," in *Women's Wear Daily,* 1 July 1999.
Garfield, Bob, "The Colors of Exploitation: Benetton on Death Row," in *Advertising Age,* 10 January 2000.
"Sears Drops Benetton," in *Women's Wear Daily,* 17 February 2000.
Gallagher, Leigh, "About Face," in *Forbes,* 19 March 2001.
Moin, David, "Megastore Buildup: Benetton's Game Plan for U.S. Recovery," in *Women's Wear Daily,* 20 March 2001.

* * *

In recent years the Benetton Group of Italy has become better known for controversial advertising campaigns than for the brightly-colored knitted sweaters with which the company was founded in 1965. As part of a well defined global strategy to make the Benetton name as well known as McDonald's or Coca-Cola, the sibling members of the Benetton family—Giuliana, Luciano, Gilberto, and Carlo Benetton—created a multibillion-lire business with an ever growing cadre of shops in 120 countries worldwide. The company is a leading producer and retailer of casual apparel and sports-related goods, as well as licensed accessories such as cosmetics, toys, swimwear, eyeglasses, watches, stationery, underwear, shoes, and household items.

Benetton collections are aimed at young people and children, but over the years have been adopted by consumers of all ages. United Colors of Benetton attempts to transcend gender, social class, and nationality by manufacturing knitwear that exemplifies a philosophy of life. This was explicitly reflected in longtime creative director Oliviero Toscani's 1983 advertising campaign "Benetton—All the Colors of the World." The campaign depicted groups of children representing all walks of life wearing colorful Benetton garments. Subsequent campaigns commented on political and social issues including religion, sex, terrorism, race, AIDS, and capital punishment, without depicting actual Benetton garments. A number of controversial campaigns were banned by advertising authorities, fueling unprecedented media coverage.

Similar in attitude to the California-based Esprit company, Benetton epitomizes the values of a generation of young, socially aware consumers. Garments are designed to be fun, casual with an easy-to-wear cut. Inspiration is often drawn from past sentiments but produced with a contemporary twist, like 1950s ski fashions in high-tech synthetic ice-pastel fabrics, 1960s tailored suits in herringbone, 1970s disco garments with sequins and leather combined. Other collections have been based on themes such as the Nordic for little girls, designed in new fabrics like fleece, and Riding Star, drawn from the world of horseback riding. In keeping with the company's cosmopolitan attitude, collections have also been drawn from Benetton family travels.

In the beginning, Benetton sweaters were hand-knit by Giuliana in bright colors which distinguished them from existing English-made wool sweaters. The first collection consisted of 18 pieces, the most popular item being a violet pullover made from cashmere, wool, and angora. Today's apparel, of course, is produced on a much grander scale, using high-tech manufacturing and innovative marketing strategies. Benetton is certainly one of the most progressive clothing manufacturers in the world; yet its rapid rise has not come without a price. Profits fell off sharply after a lower-price initiative backfired in 1994; the European recession forced the closure of nearly 600 stores; its cosmetics division produced dismal results; then came family squabbles, and court battles with a group of German retailers who refused to pay for merchandise after another of Benetton's controversial ad campaigns (eventually resolved in Benetton's favor).

By 1995 a seemingly wiser Benetton had toned down its often offensive ads, belatedly realizing the shockwaves cost the firm time and money in having to defend its position. Instead, the firm concentrated on making money and much of it came from the expansion of sister firm, Benetton Sportsystem SpA, which unabashedly pursued its intention of becoming the world's largest sports equipment and accessory company. While Sportsystem was busy acquiring Rollerblade, Nordica, Langert, Prince, and others, Benetton was fielding major losses in the U.S. market.

By the end of the century, Benetton had opened a factory in Egypt and built megastores in London, New York, San Francisco, Moscow, Riyadh, Berlin, Hong Kong, and elsewhere. In a slick move, Benetton purchased a majorty stake in its sibling, Sportsystem, effectively segueing into the sporting goods and activewear industry, then introduced and stocked a chain of sporty stores called Playlife. To bolster its U.S. presence, the firm formed a joint venture with Sears (Benetton USA) and saw that alliance collapse after another provocative ad campaign ("We, on Death Row") enraged everyone from consumers to politicians in 2000.

Benetton had finally gone too far with its "shockvertising"—not only did it lose the lucrative contract with Sears and part ways with creative director Toscani after 18 years, but was forced to issue a formal apology to the families of those murdered by its poster-boy Death Row inmates. Ironically, a newer, gentler Benetton arose in 2001, surprising everyone with its low-key ads similar to those made popular by Gap. Generally panned, Benetton, as usual, ignored its critics and set about doing what it did best—selling Benetton. With new stores planned for a multitude of high profile cities in the U.S., Carlo Tunioli, executive vice president for Benetton USA, promised a bit of the old-style advertising in the near future. "Benetton will always be loyal to its brand DNA, which means social statement," Tunioli explained to *Women's Wear Daily* (20 March 2001). "Benetton will keep working in that direction, but much will be focused on product. It may be controversial, but we're not going to be controversial in the way you used to see Benetton." Time will tell if that holds true.

—Teal Triggs and Sydonie Benét

BENTZ, John

See CATALINA SPORTSWEAR

BERTELLI, Patirizio

See PRADA

BET, Xüly

See KOUYATÉ, Lamine

BIAGIOTTI, Laura

Italian designer

Born: Rome, Italy, 4 August 1943. **Education:** Degree in archaeology, Rome University. **Family:** Married Gianni Cigna, 1992; children: Lavinia. **Career:** Worked in Biagiotti family ready-to-wear firm, Rome, 1962–65; freelance designer for Schuberth, Barocco, Cappucci, Heinz Riva, Licitro, and others, 1965–72; founder/designer, Laura Biagiotti Fashions, Rome, from 1972; took over MacPherson Knitwear, Pisa, 1974; established headquarters in Guidonia, 1980; introduced Rispeste collection, 1981; introduced Laurapiu collection, 1984; launched diffusion knitwear collection for Biagiotti Uomo, 1985; Biagiotti jeans collection debuted, 1986; Biagiotti Uomo collection, 1987; created perfumes *Laura,* 1982, *Night,* 1986, *Roma,* 1988, and *Venezia,* 1992; signed licensing agreement for Biagiotti shops in China, 1993; opened LB shop in Beijing, Bangkok, and Moscow, 1994; expanded cashmere collection in the Kremlin fashion show, 1995; fragrance *Laura Biagiotti Roma* released, 2001. **Awards:** Golden Lion award for achievement in linen, Venice, 1987; named Commendatore of the Italian Republic, 1987; Marco Polo award for high achievement in diffusing Italian style worldwide, 1993; Frenio Fragene for fashion achievements, 1994. **Address:** Biagiotti Export SpA, via Palombarese Km, 17.300, 00012 Guidonia, Rome, Italy.

Laura Biagiotti, fall/winter 2001–02 collection: transparent chiffon top with leaf motif over satin pants. © AP/Wide World Photos.

Publications

On BIAGIOTTI:

Books

Mulassano, Adriana, *The Who's Who of Italian Fashion,* Florence, 1979.

Alfonsi, Maria-Vittoria, *Leaders in Fashion: I Grandi Personaggi Della Moda,* Bologna, 1983.

"Laura Biagiotti," in Bonizza Giordani Aragno, ed., *Moda Italia* (Milan), 1988.

Skellenger, Gillion, "Laura Biagiotti," in *Contemporary Designers,* London, 1990.

Steele, Valerie, *Women of Fashion,* New York, 1991.

Stegemeyer, Anne, *Who's Who in Fashion, Third Edition,* New York, 1996.

Articles

Gargia, Massimo, "Laura Biagiotti, Stylish et Italienne," in *Vogue* (Paris), August 1978.

Petroff, Daniela, "Women Designers," in the *International Herald Tribune,* 3 October 1981.

"Laura Biagiotti: Bianco per Tutte le Mode," in *Vogue* (Milan), October 1984.

"The House of Biagiotti," in *House & Garden,* December 1986.

"I Cashmere Ricamati di Laura Biagiotti," in *Donna* (Milan), October 1987.

"Laura Biagiotti: I Piaceri Naturali," in *Donna* (Milan), February 1988.

Menkes, Suzy, "Couture's Grand Ladies," in *Illustrated London News,* Spring 1990.

Lender, Heidi, "Biagiotti's U.S. Invasion," in *Women's Wear Daily,* 12 February 1992.

Costin, Glynis, "Laura Biagiotti's China Syndrome," in *Women's Wear Daily,* 21 May 1993.

Cover story on Biagiotti, in *Fashion Magazine,* September 1994.

Schiro, Anne-Marie, "Fashion: Russia, Women at Work and Elegance," in the *New York Times,* 8 March 1995.

Barone, Amy B., "Fragrance Launch Fever," in *Drug & Cosmetic Industry* (New York), March 1997.

Ball, Deborah, "In Fashion, Grasping English is as Relevant as Last Year's Handbag," in the *Wall Street Journal,* 17 October 2000.

Davis, Don, "New Lines," in *Global Cosmetic Industry* (New York), May 2001.

* * *

Indisputably Italian, trained by her tailor mother to admire the couture of France but also witness to the quality of her mother's work and employed early on in Schuberth's elegant Italian ready-to-wear, Laura Biagiotti might seem the quintessential European. She is firmly devoted to fine materials, especially Italian, and has been called the

Laura Biagiotti, fall/winter 2001–02 collection. © AP/Wide World Photos.

Queen of Cashmere. Close family ties reinforce the image, and Biagiotti's selection of Isabella d'Este as her ideal seemed to substantiate the nationalism of this designer's spirit. One of her fragrances is aptly named *Venezia.*

Looking at Biagiotti's clothes, however, one cannot help but think of America. Like Giorgio Armani, Biagiotti bespeaks Italian fashion but was redefining Italian fashion in the last quarter of the 20th century in a sense of sportswear, separates, menswear influences, and quality materials for the standardizing templates of clothing. Biagiotti tells the story that at the time of her first show in 1972, she had so few pieces that she showed one white jacket three times, once with a skirt for morning, once with a day dress, and finally with a shiny skirt for evening. "Unintentionally I had invented the use of only one item for morning to evening," she said.

If Biagiotti was, as she professes, initially inadvertent, her concept has become canny and global; her invention is necessarily as smart as it is coy. Her collections in the 1980s and 1990s sustained a sense of the marketably traditional, always freshened with insights and style inflections to become one of the most effective designers of the era.

Biagiotti's spring-summer 1990 collection, built around navy, red, and white (admittedly with other pieces as well but carefully constructed around the red, white, and blue core), not only anticipated 1993 merchandising of Carolyne Roehm but offered its clothes as wardrobe builders as well as dramatic outfits. Talking about her work to Valerie Steele for *Women of Fashion: Twentieth-Century Designers* (New York, 1991), Biagiotti said, "Elegance, taste, and creativity have belonged to the Italian tradition and character for centuries and I share this privilege with all other Italian designers."

Biagiotti has studied archaeology and is much engaged with the arts and architecture through generous support of archaeology and conservation. Yet again, her work is as much divorced from the historical past as one could imagine. It is as if she chose to restore the edifice (and she does live and work in what Gillian Skellenger, in *Contemporary Designers,* rightly calls the factory-castle of Marco Simone near Rome, a Romanesque-era edifice), but her decision is a gutted rehabilitation, putting everything new inside. There are no marks of historicism in her clothing, even in the fall-winter 1985–86 collection, when her monastics seem as much about Claire McCardell as about medievalism. Her abiding preference for white is symbolic, clean and notably modern in style, while her sensible knits address manifold uses for contemporary working women. As Skellenger noted, "Biagiotti reveals a mania for research," committed to new fabric study.

Biagiotti has spoken of her work as a personal projection, fit for a modern, self-confident, and business-aware woman. If she is considered the ideal client for her own clothing, her personal sensibility is toward simple almost reductive shape carried in luxury materials, an ethos sounding like three generations of American sportswear-to-evening designers. The women's clothing can be slightly flirtatious in the American mode, whereas her evening looks express her Roman sophistication, always with a reserve and sense of good taste. Biagiotti has come to represent decorum and fashion nuance unerring in its mainstream elegance, again a characterization she would share with Armani. What she does not share with Armani is his intense interest in menswear per se—while Biagiotti has designed menswear for many years, it seems even safer than her women's clothing and the epitome of conservative good taste.

Following the opening a Biagiotti boutique in Moscow, the Italian designer was invited to do a fashion show in the Kremlin. Featuring opera, ballet, and Biagiotti's fall collection, the 1995 show, not surprisingly, incorporated a taste of Russian elegance. Almost every piece of clothing—from evening dresses to pocket flaps—consisted of cashmere, thus reconfirming the designer's acclaimed title, Queen of Cashmere. In addition to cashmere, Biagiotti reintroduced beaded-flower, embroidered dresses in her Milan fashion show.

As 1997 neared and perfume launch activity began to slow, Italian perfumers released high-profile fragrances, including Biagiotti's *Sotto Voce.* Alone, the perfume did not, nor was it expected to, drive holiday sales. Even with the help of classics such as *Tresor, Chanel No. 5,* and *Eau Sauvage,* perfumes did not win over consumers' attention as they had in the past. With a new fragrance line, *Laura Biagiotti Roma,* launched in fall 2001, Biagiotti hoped to attract customers the perfume industry had not seen in years. As the fragrance is geared toward the younger generation, it was less expensive and more accommodating to a youthful market's budget. *Laura Biagiotti Roma* was available for both men and women, and had a seven-year licensing agreement with Singer International.

—Richard Martin; updated by Diana Idzelis

BIANCHINI-FÉRIER

French textile manufacturer

Founded: circa 1880 by Charles Bianchini and partners; changed name to Bianchini-Férier after partnership with Férier, around 1900. **Company History:** Signed Raoul Dufy, 1912; opened New York mill, 1921; teamed up with Vogue Patterns, 1949; merged with Tissage-Baumann, then acquired by Mayor-MDTA. **Company Address:** 4 rue Vaucanson, 69283 Lyon Cedex 01, France.

Publications:

On BIANCHINI-FÉRIER:

Books

Crawford, M.D.C., *The Ways of Fashion,* New York, 1948.
Musée de L'Impression sur Étoffes, *Raoul Dufy* [exhibition catalogue], Mulhouse, 1973.
Musée Historique des Tissus, *Les folles années de la soie* [exhibition catalogue], Lyon, 1975.
Arts Council of Great Britain, *Raoul Dufy* [exhibition catalogue], London, 1983.
Galeria Marcel Bernheim, *Raoul Dufy et la mode: ancienne collection, Bianchini-Férier* [exhibition catalogue], Paris, 1985.
Deslandres, Yvonne, and Dorothee Laianne, *Paul Poiret: 1874–1944,* London, 1987.
Mackrell, Alice, *Paul Poiret,* New York, 1990.
Schoesser, Mary, and Kathleen Dejardin, *French Textiles from 1760 to the Present,* London, 1991.

Articles

Dufy, Raoul, "Les tissues imprimés," in *Amour de L'Art,* No. 1, 1920.
Vallotaire, Michel, "New Textiles from France," in *Studio,* December 1928.
"Bianchini-Férier ou la créative continue," in *Vogue* (Paris), November 1988.
Weisman, Katherine, "Lyon Regaining Its Lost Cachet (Lyon, France, Silk Fabric Industry)," in *Women's Wear Daily,* 12 July 1994.
D'Aulnay, Sophie, "SEHM—A World View of Diversity," in *DNR,* 22 January 1996.
Maycumber, S. Gray, "European Rabrics to Preview This Week," in *DNR,* 15 January 2001.
Gilbert, Daniela, "Preview: Staple Looks Rule Spring 2002," in *Women's Wear Daily,* 23 January 2001.

* * *

From its beginnings in the 1880s the House of Bianchini-Férier has been associated with the world's most luxurious silks. The Lyonnais firm first achieved widespread recognition for a collection of silk velvets and brocades shown at the Paris Exposition of 1889. A few years later Charles Bianchini and his partners opened a sales office in Paris. Offices in London, Geneva, Brussels, Montreal, Toronto, New York, Los Angeles, Chicago, and Buenos Aires quickly followed.

Working in close association with the leading couturiers of the day, Bianchini-Férier created fabrics which are considered standards today, but for which the company held the original copyright. Among them are *charmeuse georgette,* and the semisheer crêpe Romaine. Undoubtedly one of the best known collaborations between an artist and a manufacturer was between Raoul Dufy and Bianchini-Férier. Dufy first designed textiles for Paul Poiret in 1911. Failing to imitate his bold hand wood-blocked patterns, Bianchini went to the source and in 1912 signed Dufy to an exclusive contract, then renewed it annually until the late 1920s. For Bianchini, Dufy created brilliant florals in the palette of the Fauve painters. He designed geometrics using blocks of opposing colors—the design created equally by the object and by the negative space enclosing it— and he continued to execute the large scale block-prints originally produced for Poiret.

Poiret continued to use Dufy's designs for Bianchini in his collections; his summer 1920 collection employed Dufy's fabrics exclusively and Dufy himself sketched part of the collection for the May issue of the *Gazette du Bon Ton.* Theirs was surely one of the most significant collaborations between artist, couturier, and manufacturer of the period. While many establishments geared to the luxury market were forced to close or reorganize during the Depression, Bianchini not only survived but continued to experiment with new fibers and weave structures. Consequently, when silk became unobtainable during World War II, Bianchini had the technology in place to increase its production of rayon. And because the firm had opened a mill in Port Jervis, New York, back in 1921 to replicate patterns and textiles originating from Lyons, they did not wholly lose their overseas market during the war.

Within the industry, Bianchini was known especially for silk velvets and silk and metal brocades for haute couture. After the war the firm increased its efforts to reach the discerning home sewer who could provide an expanded market for their collections of silk and rayon prints. A 1949 collaboration with Vogue Patterns paired a collection of garments designed especially for Bianchini with a group of specific hand-screened prints. The March *Vogue* claimed these private edition prints were available in no more than 20 dress lengths each, to be distributed to select stores around the country. The advertising copy read "For the Woman Who Wants to Be Exclusive—A Couture Plan for Your Personal Dressmaking." The patterns allowed women who could not attend fashion shows to dress in high style like their wealthier counterparts.

For more than 100 years Bianchini-Férier set the standard for fine fabrics, used the world over. After its centennial, however, the firm faced dwindling sales and competition in the late 1980s and 1990s from Italian textile firms, as well as not having the kinds of fabrics appropriate for the growing ready-to-wear sportswear markets. Bianchini and other Lyonnais fabric producers were forced to adapt; not only did they have to create a wider range of fabrics but had to work with designers in developing their collections. Gone were most of old guard designers who knew instinctively what they wanted; a newer, younger group of designers had come to the fore often without the intimate knowledge of textiles their predecessors possessed.

Bianchini reached the 21st century having weathered the difficult years and adapted to the new standards for textiles. In 2000 the firm was showing acetate and rayon fabric mixes, as well as updating its famous silk with iridescent denim-twill in 2001. hailed as the longest continuously-running mill in Europe, Bianchini is now renowed for much more than silk, though it has remained the silk manufacturer of choice, combining invention and artistry in equal measure.

—Whitney Blausen; updated by Sydonie Benét

BIKKEMBERGS, Dirk

Belgian designer

Born: Flamersheim, Germany, 3 January 1962. **Education:** Studied fashion at the Royal Academy of Arts, Antwerp. **Military Service:** Served with Royal Belgian Army, in Germany. **Career:** Freelance designer for Nero, Bassetti, Gruno and Chardin, Tiktiner, Gaffa, K, and Jaco Petti, 1982–87; launched Dirk Bikkembergs-Homme Co., with DB shoe line for men, 1985; introduced knitwear, 1986; first complete menswear collection, 1988; presented first womenswear line, Dirk Bikkembergs-Homme Pour La Femme, in Paris, 1993; moved to more luxe styling, 1998; participated in Mode 2001 Landed-Geland, Antwerp, 2001. **Awards:** For menswear collection, winter 1985–86, several Belgian fashion industry awards, including Golden Spindle. **Address:** Kidporp 21, 2000 Antwerp, Belgium.

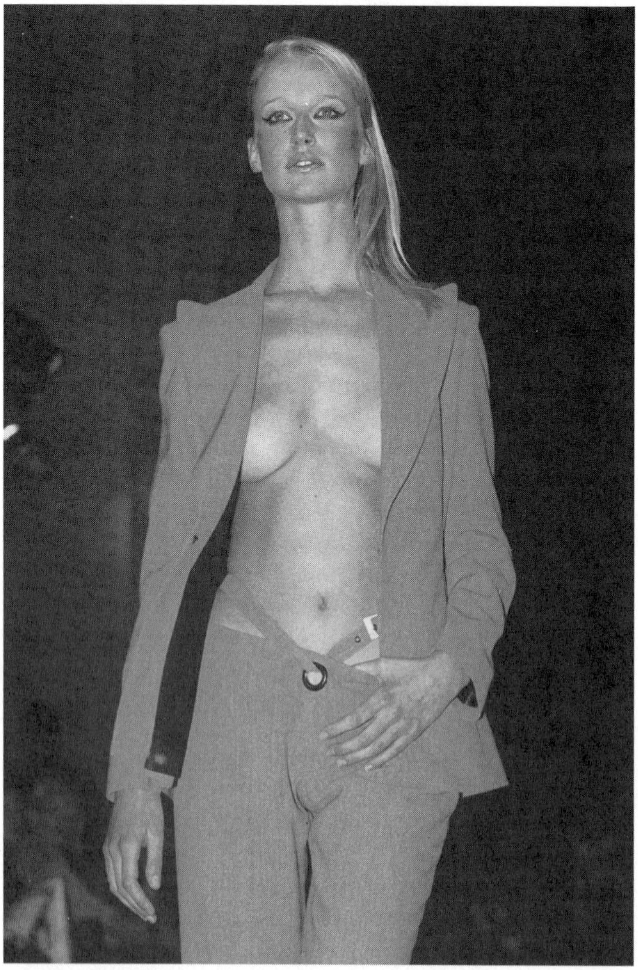

Dirk Bikkembergs, spring/summer 1997 collection. © AP/Wide World Photos.

Publications

On BIKKEMBERGS:

Articles

"Foreign Affairs—Antwerp," in *Blitz* (London), February 1987.
Mower, Sarah, "Six Romp," in *The Guardian* (London), 12 February 1987.
"Fashion," in *Interview* (New York), July 1987.
Ankone, Frans, "De Trots Van Vlaanderen," in *Avenue* (Antwerp), September 1987.
Tredre, Roger, "Belgians Go Branche," in *Fashion Weekly* (London), 10 September 1987.
Grauman, Brigid, "The Belgian Connection," in *Elle* (London), October 1987.
Lobrano, Alexander, "The Young Belgian," in *DNR* (New York), October 1987.
Fierce, Brad, "Il Menestrello Della Moda," in *Vanity* (Milan), February 1988.
"Nouvel Homme: Dirk Bikkembergs," in *Profession Textile* (Paris), 24 June 1988.
Grauman, Brigid, "Seam Stress," in *The Face* (London), August 1988.
Cocks, Jay, "A Look on the Wild Side: Two Young Designers Liven Up a Group Fashion Scene," in *Time,* 16 January 1989.
LaChapelle, David, "Dirk Bikkembergs," in *Interview* (New York), October 1989.
Rumbold, Judy, "Dirk Bikkembergs: Clean Cuts," in *Arena* (London), November 1990.
Valli, Jacopo, "The Antwerp Five," in *Donna* (Milan), January 1991.
Summers, Beth, "Obsession," in *i-D* (London), February 1991.
Tredre, Roger, "From Belgium but Far from Boring," in the *Independent* (London), 2 July 1992.
"Dirk Bikkembergs," in *L'Uomo Vogue* (Milan), September 1992.
Menkes, Suzy, "Cut, Color and Class: Male 'Haute Couture' Hits the High Cs," in the *International Herald Tribune,* 30 January 1996.
Daly, Steven, "Belgique: C'est Chique," in *Rolling Stone,* 17 September 1998.
Menkes, Suzy. "Chinese Dior Makes a Splash," in the *International Herald Tribune,* 12 March 1997.
———, "At Dior, Galliano Fluffs It—Gorgeously," in the *International Herald Tribune,* 15 October 1997.
———, "From Gucci, a Flash of Optimism," in the *International Herald Tribune,* 2 July 1998.
———, "At Dior, a Victory for the People," in the *International Herald Tribune,* 14 October 1998.
"Dirk Bikkembergs," available online at Fashion Live, www.fashionlive.com, 19 March 2001.
Lowthorpe, Rebecca, "Big in Belgium: Fashion," in the *Independent on Sunday,* 17 June 2001.
Menkes, Suzy, "A New Season That's Fit for Knits: Sweater Boys," in the *International Herald Tribune,* 17 July 2001.

*

I design clothes for men and women that have a special, strong attitude; for a younger, future-minded generation for whom fashion

Dirk Bikkembergs, fall/winter 1996–97 collection: knitted sweater and wool shorts. © AP/Wide World Photos.

has become a way to express themselves; to give shelter and strength and the feeling of looking good; a generation that has risen above the question of fashion, sure about its quality and style and their own; celebrating life.

I design collections that give one whole strong look, a vision of life, men and women with items that are nonchalant and easy to mix, give freedom and don't restrict the wearer; but there are always special pieces that are stronger and more defined, marking a certain period of time and setting a sign.

My clothes are never retro. I hate the idea of looking back. I don't have any idols from the past. I do strongly believe in tomorrow and the future of the human race. To achieve this I devote a lot of attention to the cut and fabric that I use. Yes, I tend to think about my clothes as fashion and I'm not afraid of that, nor are my clients.

I design strong clothes for strong individuals rather than wrapping up pretentious nerds in sophisticated cashmere. Nothing is so boring as a "nice and neat" look. Life is just too good and too short for that.

—Dirk Bikkembergs

* * *

Dirk Bikkembergs is one of the so-called Group of Six designers who have dominated the Belgian fashion scene in the last two decades in a country not previously known as a fashion mecca. Bikkembergs and several other graduates of the Royal Academy of the Arts at Antwerp—Ann Demuelemeester, Dries Van Noten, Dirk Van Saene, Walter Von Beirendonck, and Martin Margiela—have brought new attention to avant-garde fashion in Belgium. Deconstructionist in their designs, they have added such innovations as exposed seams, loose-fitting garments, and ragged edges.

Heavyweight fabrics and macho imagery quite literally dominate Bikkembergs' work. His best designs convey a solidity through their layering of leather and thick knitwear while still retaining the feeling of minimalist restraint that has come to be associated with Belgian fashion. Bikkembergs, although not the most prominent of the designers who formed the Belgian avant-garde of the later 1980s, is nonetheless a significant purveyor of their ideals. His clothing consists of dark and muted-toned separates that provide strong images of modern living, although his own work does not so frequently contain the deconstructed edge of his counterparts.

Bikkembergs first came to prominence with his treatment of footwear. A specialist in the field, he brought together the traditions of well-made, hard-wearing shoes made up for him by Flanders craftspeople with the late 1980s and early 1990s who epitomized the era's obsession with workwear. His designs were inspired by classic functional styles; he reworked the clearly defined shapes of 1930s' football boots, making them into neat, round-toed, lace-up urban footwear in 1987. In 1993, he tampered with the weighty infantryman's boot, stripping it of its utilitarian status when, with a deconstructivist flourish, he removed the eyelets that normally punctuated the boot and accommodated the distinctive high lacing. Instead, a hole was drilled into the sole through which the laces had to be threaded and then wrapped around the boot's leather upper to secure it to the foot. The style soon became de rigueur for both men and women in fashion circles, with copies being sold in High Street chains. Like all his other work, they were based on familiar designs that conveyed traditional notions of masculinity, conjuring up images of sporting and military heroics. Such ideals have also pervaded his menswear.

His carefully styled shows send muscle-bound models down the catwalk clad in the obligatory biker boots and black leather that become a staple of the late 20th-century male wardrobe. This machismo continued in his signature knitwear range. Heavy-ribbed V necks were worn with lightweight jogging bottoms or matching woolen leggings. His work may not show the more slim-line feminine notes that have been gradually breaking through the previously limited spectrum of menswear designs, but they still have influence. Bikkembergs helped widen the scope of knitwear with witty takes on classic Aran jumpers and cardigans and by using decorative detailing to add interest to simple designs: in 1992 with bright blue zips on either side of burnt orange sweaters, while back in 1987 by adding them to the high-necked jumpers popular at the time.

Although he works best with winter-weight fabrics, Bikkembergs still adds twists to his summer collections. In 1988, he produced collared linen waistcoats that could be layered over long-sleeved shirts or worn alone to give interest to plain suits. It was in the late 1980s that his designs were most attuned to the zeitgeist. He provided the overblown masculine imagery so popular then; this was encapsulated in his distinctive marketing, which demonstrated the same eye for detail. The catalogues produced for each collection show in grainy black and white his tough masculine ideals with his commandeering of popular stereotypes like the biker.

Despite this concentration on menswear, his work has extended to a womenswear range. In 1993, his first collection was warmly received, bringing together both his love of strong silhouettes and a deconstructed minimalism to provide a twist to basic shapes. The natural counterpart to his masculine lines, it carried through his use of sturdy footwear and accessories that had always been popular with women as well.

As part of the rise in status of Belgian fashion since in the later years of the 20th century, Bikkembergs' work appeals to the fashion cognoscenti. The overt masculinity of his designs is combined with a knowledge and exploitation of traditional styles to provide stark, modern imagery. If not as well known as contemporaries like Van Noten, he had still carved a niche for his work and heralded a fresh slant to his output with a divergence into womenswear.

In the late 1990s, Bikkembergs departed from his characteristic masculine style to enter the couture market with elegant tailored pantsuits. They still included his customary metallic effects, however, such as silver necktie knots and metal fox heads on fur boas. He also experimented with a lattice look, creating trellises of woven leather or knits, and he offered other knitwear with metallic accessories. His womenswear lines have included unadorned, tailored capes, long skirts, and reefer jackets.

In 1998 at a Milan fashion show, Bikkembergs returned to showy, strong masculine themes in such menswear pieces as form-hugging sweaters or coats with Velcro fastenings. In Paris, he stayed with virile themes and strong graphics. A typical outfit was a singlet with an asymmetrical scooped neckline and a torso crossed with compass twirls, with matching pants. He continued to produce knits with strong geometric patterns as well. Bikkembergs seemed to move more toward luxury at the end of the decade with couture items like a cashmere cat suit for men. His sportswear line has been compared to that of American designers, with items like hooded, zippered tops.

Bikkembergs and the other Group of Six designers participated in the Mode 2001 Landed-Geland, an important fashion festival in Antwerp that firmly established the city as cutting edge in the world of fashion. According to Rebecca Lowthorpe, writing in the *Independent on Sunday,* these designers offered looks that were "avant-garde, yet for the most part, eminently wearable," with "uncompromisingly hip visions."

—Rebecca Arnold; updated by Sally A. Myers

BLACK, Sandy

British knitwear designer

Born: Leeds, Yorkshire, England, 17 October 1951. **Education:** Educated in Leeds; B.S. (Honors), Mathematics, University College, London, 1973; M.A., Design Studies, Central St. Martins, London, 1994. **Career:** Freelance knitwear designer, 1973–79; designer/director, Sandy Black Original Knits Ltd., selling fashion knitwear collections worldwide, 1979–85; designed and published Sandy Black Knitting Patterns and Sandy Black Knitting Kits and Yarns, sold in prestigious stores in London, Japan, United States, Sweden, Germany, Australia, and Canada; introduced knitting kits for *Woman* magazine (London), 1983; started Sandy Black Studio Knitting Kits mail order business; freelance knitwear designer for, among others, Rowan, Jaeger, and BBC television, beginning in 1985; principal lecturer and course leader, University of Brighton, Sussex, England, from 1990. **Exhibitions:** *Much Ado About Knitting,* ICA, London, 1981; *One-off Wearables,* British Crafts Centre, London, 1982; the *Knitwear Review* British Crafts Centre, London, 1983; *Knitting—A Common Art,* Crafts Council Touring Exhibition, 1986; *Fashion in the '80s,* British Council touring exhibition, 1989; knitwear exhibition, Hove Museum, Sussex, 1990; *Contemporary Knitwear,* Pier Arts Centre, Orkney, 1994. **Address:** Flat 3, 15 Davigdor Road, Hove, East Sussex BN3 1QB, England.

Publications

By BLACK:

Books

The Numeracy Pack, with D. Cohen, London, 1984.
Sandy Black Original Knitting, London, 1988.

On BLACK:

Books

Sutton, Ann, *British Craft Textiles,* London, 1985.

Articles

Phillips, Pearson, "The Hills are Alive With the Sound of Knitting," in the *Telegraph Sunday Magazine,* 7 September 1980.
Lynam, Ruth, "Cast on a New Look," in the *Telegraph Sunday Magazine,* 7 September 1980.
"An Individual Approach to Fashion," in *Fashion & Craft,* November 1980.
Knitwear profile in *Ons Volk* (Belgium), 29 December 1981.
Jeffs, Angela, "Exclusively Sandy Black," in *Fashioncraft,* February, 1984.
Polan, Brenda, "Looping the Loop," in *The Guardian Women,* 19 July 1984.
Sherrill Daily, Martha, "Sew, You Want to Learn to Knit?" in the *Washington Post,* 6 September 1987.
Rumbold, Judy, "The Wonder of Creation," in *The Guardian Style,* 20 June 1988.
Samuel, Kathryn, "Those Who Can—Teach," in the *Daily Telegraph,* 20 June 1994.

*

Although I learned to knit and crochet as a child, it was while at university studying math that my interest in knitting really developed, and I started to design and make unusual and interesting clothes. At first, these were hand-knitted or crocheted, but I soon bought my first knitting machine, and by the time I finished my degree, I had decided to make knitting a full-time career, though I wasn't sure how. Being self-taught, I was not restricted by any boundaries and felt I could translate any idea into knitting by working out a logical way of doing it. This approach clearly owed something to my mathematical background, and for me, there was a natural relationship between the two. I often put many ideas and techniques together to create complex designs. I only became aware of their complexity when I had to train other people to knit them for me.

My work covers a wide range of designs, from casual sweaters to glamorous angora evening coats. *Original Knitting* shows some of this variety and gives an insight into the thinking behind the designs. One of the most important factors is the blending of color, shape, texture, and pattern to create each individual design, whether it's a bold geometric, a pretty floral, or an intricate stitch pattern.

Fashion buyers talk of designers' "handwriting" by which they identify their work. I have often thought that I must have several different signatures. I have always enjoyed working in a great variety of themes, colors, and yarns, inspired by anything which catches my eye or simply the pleasure of combining wonderful materials and textures. I like my designs to be nonrepetitive, and view the body as a canvas to be adorned with beautiful stitches and patterns, sometimes subtle, sometimes bold, but always with an underlying logic which combines color, texture, and form so completely that the result should appear totally natural.

Knitting continues to be, for me, the perfect blend of creative and technical skills, which my education seemed to want to separate. It used to be the poor relation of the textile crafts but has now grown to be properly recognized, and has a vital part to play in fashion. I know I shall continue to design as long as I can still be excited by a ball of yarn or inspired to develop a new stitch pattern from some unlikely detail I have seen—a mosaic shop front, a stone carving, or a wallpaper pattern, for example. I am equally happy designing for hand-knitting, machine knitting, or industrial production. One of the greatest attractions of knitting is the fact that the fabric is created from nothing but a length of yarn; everything is within the designer's control.

In my workshops and lecturing, I try to convey my own enthusiasm and enjoyment in creating fabrics, garment designs, and structures, and their realization in three dimensions around the body. I am particularly interested in the sculptural potential of knitting; a unique medium with endless possibilities.

—Sandy Black

* * *

Sandy Black helped lead the knitwear revolution of the 1970s. Out went the cozy image of old ladies making socks around the fire, in came fashion knitwear, and a craft was turned into an art. For Black, it was a logical development of a childhood love of old needlework shops where she bought 1940s knitting patterns, buttons, and yarns to knit and crochet. Using skills learned from her mother and grandmother, she produced traditional hand knits. Black received her B.S. degree in Mathematics from University College in London. Having studied mathematics, knitting proved an ideal way of combining her creative and logical instincts.

Black was able to chart out pictorial knits and to originate the landscape sweaters that became so popular in the mid-1970s. A natural wit emerged. Leopard skin-look sweaters and a knitted armadillo wrap illustrated an appealing sense of humor. Patterned angora jackets, stunning to the eye and to the touch, showed the luxuriance hand-knitting could achieve. Designer knitwear had arrived, and Black's career as a freelance knitwear designer was launched. In 1979 she created her own company, Sandy Black Original Knits Ltd. Major international fashion retailers, including Browns and Harrods in London, Isetan in Tokyo, and Saks Fifth Avenue and Bloomingdale's in New York, bought Sandy Black Original Knits for their upscale stores.

But the quality and details of Black's designs put them beyond the purse of most shoppers, including the designer herself. To make her designs more widely available to the less affluent shopper, Black employed her math training to create her own knitting patterns. By using larger needles and straightforward instructions, she tried to make her patterns as accessible as possible. They were complex but not too difficult for the determined knitter; the results more than justified the effort involved. Black's hand knits were distinctive and unique, and Sandy Black Knitting Patterns were created for the world to enjoy.

Another breakthrough came in 1983, when she designed a knitting kit as an editorial offer for *Woman* magazine. Its success stimulated the Sandy Black Knitting Kits, which were retailed in Liberty, Harrods, and John Lewis in London, and in Sweden, Germany, and Canada. She controlled the whole process, creating the patterns, supervising the dyeing of the yarns, and designing the packaging. She also produced her own range of yarns. Each step meant she was able to have greater responsibility over the whole process, from the idea to the finished garment.

Black took the process one step further with the publication in 1988 of her first book of patterns, *Sandy Black Original Knitting*. The tome is an excellent testament to her originality and creativity and provides insight into her inspiration. Whatever the design, a bold geometric, a pretty floral, or something understated, the consistent factor is the blending of color, texture, and pattern to create an individual design. Variety is a mark of her creativity. By seeing "the body as a canvas to be decorated and adorned with beautiful patterns, sometimes subtle, sometimes bold," she extended the existing boundaries of knitwear.

Black had gone back to designing freelance for companies such as Rowan, Jaeger, and BBC Television, among many others in 1985. She also began lecturing and teaching more, serving as principal lecturer and course leader for the University of Brighton at Sussex, from 1990. Black has been able to convey her obvious enthusiasm to others. Television shows, international lecture tours, workshops, and consultancies have all helped to promote her ideas. She has become increasingly involved in instructing, which is an ideal, if exhausting, means of continuing what she started decades ago. In her workshops and as a lecturer to textile and fashion students, she teaches about the dual importance of design and technique. Experimentation is an important way of building ideas and encouraging originality. She gives others the confidence to follow her example, to break down boundaries, and to cast aside preconceptions. Sandy Black has helped to take knitting from the fireside into the artist's studio.

—Hazel Clark; updated by Daryl F. Mallett

BLAHNIK, Manolo

Spanish footwear designer

Born: Santa Cruz, Canary Islands, Spain, 27 November 1942. **Education:** Educated at home, University of Geneva, degree in literature, 1965; studied art in Paris, 1965–70. **Career:** Jeans buyer for Feathers Boutique, London, early 1970s; encouraged to design shoes by Diana Vreeland; first collections for Zapata Boutique, London, and for Ossie Clark, early 1970s; opened London shop, 1973, opened New York boutique, 1981; subsequent shops in Hong Kong, Tokyo; designed shoes for Anne Klein, 1994–95; opened five-story Manhattan headquarters for Blahnik USA, 1998; online boutique at NeimanMarcus.com, 2000; teamed with Estée Lauder to create nail lacquer for Golden Globes, 2001. **Awards:** Fashion Council of America award, 1988, 1991; British Fashion Council award, 1991; Balenciaga award, 1991; American Leather award, New York, 1991; Hispanic Institute Antonio Lopez award, Washington, D.C., 1991; *Footwear News* Designer of the Year, 1992; Stiletto award, Council of Fashion Designers of America, 1998; Named "Fifth Star" of HBO series *Sex and the City,* 2000; Designer of the Year, QVC/FFANY, 2001. **Address:** 49–51 Old Church St., London SW3, England.

Publications

On BLAHNIK:

Books

Trasko, Mary, *Heavenly Soles,* New York, 1989.
McDowell, Colin, *Shoes, Fashion and Fantasy,* London, 1989.
Stegemeyer, Anne, *Who's Who in Fashion, Third Edition,* New York, 1996.
Steele, Valerie, *Shoes: A Lexicon of Style,* New York, 1999.
McDowell, Colin, *Manolo Blahnik,* New York, 2000.

Articles

Lester, P., "Manolo Blahnik," in *Interview,* July 1974.
Brampton, Sally, "Well-Heeled," in the *Observer* (London), 2 September 1984.
Burnie, Joan, "Upon My Sole: Best Feet Forward," in *You* (London), 5 January 1986.
Infantino, Vivian, "The Gift of Avant-Garde," in *Footwear News,* July 1987.
Simpson, Helen, "Manolo Blahnik's London Lobby," in *Vogue* (London), August 1987.
Campbell, Liza, "World at His Feet," in *Vogue* (London), September 1987.
Picasso-Lopez, Paloma, "Manolo Blahnik," in *Vogue* (Paris), April 1988.
Fallon, James, "Blahnik Keeps Moving," in *Footwear News,* February 1991.
Roberts, Michael, "Manolo," in *Interview,* September 1991.
"Feets of Brilliance," in *Vogue,* March 1992.
Baber, Bonnie, "The Design Masters," in *Footwear News,* 17 April 1995.
Kerwin, Jessica, "Manolo Contendre," in *Women's Wear Daily,* 13 March 1997.
"Manolo Blahnik, " in *In Style,* 8 May 1998.
"High Heel Heaven," in the *New Yorker,* 20 March 2000.
"Blahnik Walks Among His Faithful," in *Women's Wear Daily,* 23 October 2000.
Keogh, Pamela Clarke, "The Greatest Shoes on Earth: Manolo Blahnik," in *Town & Country,* January 2001.
"24-Karat Golden Globes," in *Footwear News,* 8 January 2001.

* * *

Established in the 1970s, Manolo Blahnik has become world famous. His beautiful shoes exude a level of craftsmanship rare in today's age of mass production, and he has a wonderful sense of line and silhouette. These talents, combined with the other footwear sense he displays and exploits, have ensured his rightful position as a true genius in his field, worthy of sharing the mantle worn by the other brilliant shoe designers of the 20th century, Yanturni, Vionnet, Perugia, Ferragamo, and the one he most admires—Roger Vivier.

Blahnik was born in 1942 in Santa Cruz, in the Canary Islands, to a Czech father and Spanish mother. This slightly exotic and romantic start to his life possibly determined the pattern his future was to assume. His awareness of shoes was an early memory. His mother, who had a fondness for satin and brocade fabrics, had her footwear made by Don Christino, the island's leading shoemaker. Blahnik inherited her love of the unconventional and remembers seeing a trunk containing shoes by Yanturni, the Russian designer and one-time curator of the Cluny Museum in Paris. The shoes, in brocades, silks, and antique lace, trimmed with buckles, were elegant and light, attributes Blahnik later sought to achieve in his own creations.

Blahnik studied law, literature, and Renaissance art in Europe before settling in London in 1970. His portfolio of theatrical designs was seen by the photographer Cecil Beaton and Diana Vreeland of American *Vogue,* who particularly admired his shoe designs and encouraged him to concentrate on this aspect of his work. His subsequent footwear collections were to prove how astute their instincts had been for this extraordinary talent.

The mood of the 1970s was lively, adventurous, and colorful. The advent of the miniskirt had focused attention on the legs and consequently on original interpretations of footwear. Creative thought produced new materials for footwear and a climate in which fresh ideas could flourish, and Blahnik dramatically interpreted these

A display of Manolo Blahnik shoes, 2000. © AP/Wide World Photos.

trends. Flowers appeared at the ankles, and there were cutout shapes and appliqués. Purple was the "in" color; ankle boots, lace-ups with small, chunky heels in stacked leather or shiny veneer, crêpe soles and a new craze for "wet-look" leather, all appeared in his collections. Footwear was zany, feet were in fashion, and it required endless imagination to stay in front.

Blahnik chose Zapata as the name of his first shop, opened in London in 1973. He now uses his own name, but from the beginning, his tiny, personalized salon was a mecca for devotees from all over the world. Blahnik has a deep understanding of contemporary trends and a genuine feeling for his clientèle and what they seek in a shoe. Constantly featured in the world's most prestigious fashion magazines, it is easy to see why his imagination and ability to translate fantasy into delectable and desirable foot coverings have won him such acclaim. His designs are always complementary to the feet; he believes fashion should be fun and his ebullient and energetic designs have always reflected this philosphy. He considers shape, material, and decoration with great care and combines handcraftsmanship with modern techniques. A master of materials, he handles leather, suede, velvets, silks, and the unconventional and unexpected with equal flair and panache, paying exact attention to detail and creating fine, elegant footwear with glamor and refinement. His shoes have a weightless quality, and a seemingly ethereal atmosphere often pervades his collections.

Many Blahnik styles are deliberately kept exclusive, with only small quantities produced, and his instantly recognized style remains constant, regardless of the fashion climate. Over the years, he has designed collections to enhance the work of, among others, Yves Saint Laurent, Emmanuel Ungaro, Calvin Klein, Perry Ellis, Bill Blass, Fiorucci, Zandra Rhodes, Jean Muir, Jasper Conran, and Rifat Ozbek. One of his most famous individual clients is fashion eccentric Anna Piaggi. She invariably selects a pair of Blahnik's shoes to complement the other unusual items in her wardrobe. The following is a typical description of her appearance: "Black velvet coat by Lanvin, circa 1925; t-shirt in cotton jersey by Missoni, circa 1975; Harem trousers made out of a silk kimono; grey suede shoes trimmed with mink by Blahnik; the jewel, a crystal iceberg with an orange bead by Fouquet."

Wherever they are featured, Blahnik's shoes are a copywriter's dream. Frequently executed in vivid colors, magenta, deep purple, bright scarlet, orange, emerald green, or saffron yellow, they retain a certain theatrical fantasy—"red mules with high, knotted vamps," or "jeweled satin shoes for the summer collection," or "ribbon-wrapped ankles for watered silk dancing shoes," or perhaps "the Siamese twin shoe"—completely original combinations of wit, sex, and allure. With their reference to history, they nevertheless remain entirely contemporary while catching the spirit of both.

Blahnik is a distinctive personality, much traveled, intelligent, and well educated, in demand for his opinions, wit, energy, and style. Like many true originators, he could probably have been a successful designer in another field. His distinctive sketches, for example, transmit a real feeling for his shoes and are used for his company publicity. They serve to underline how very individual his work is, and he clothes some of the world's best dressed feet; he produces shoes for all occasions. His creations are worn, and adored, by film stars, celebrities, socialites, and those who just love what he offers. He has an intrinsic feeling for the moment and a foresight into what will come next. His shoes are provocative and dashingly extroverted; almost—but not quite—too beautiful and desirable to be worn.

The exclusivity, handcraftsmanship, high style, and wild popularity of Blahnik's shoes have raised the Spanish-born, London-based cobbler to mythic proportions. The evolution of shoe design from protection to status took hundreds of years; yet the evolution of Blahnik design from status to icon took only decades. Even early in his career, the fashions—coats, dresses, and elaborate eveningwear—of his contemporaries in couture sought to complement the latest Blahnik creations and every fad.

By the close of the 20th century, Blahnik's taste appeared to rule the design world of the most fashionable women. Blahnik was honored with an extended profile in the *New Yorker* in 1998, where his shoes were described as objects not simply of desire but of worship. Cynthia Marcus, vice president of Neiman Marcus described to *Women's Wear Daily* an "annual pilgrimage" that Blahnik customers make to the Dallas store or to Beverly Hills or to White Plains when he visits each year. She explains that for Neiman Marcus, Blahnik shoes are an emblem: "The timing now is about sexy, beautiful shoes and luxury and if there's anything Manolo stands for its all those things."

Blahnik himself agrees that the relationship between shoes and sex is so important it cannot be underestimated: "When you put [on heels], most women walk differently… It makes you immediately sexy." And sex sells. The "erotic" stilettos that exemplify Blahnik design—he is said to have invented "toe cleavage"—produce a taller, thinner leg line and a shapely calf, which every woman understands as profoundly attractive and every man finds irresistible. The cost of such a chic pair of shoes is very high, but does not prevent women around the world from acquiring them in dozens or hundreds. "Manolo Blahnik shoes are ubiquitous at all Hollywood events," explained Aerin Lauder, creative marketing director for Estée Lauder, who commissioned Blahnik to devise a 24-karat gold nail polish in a limited edition bottle in honor of the Golden Globe awards.

Blahnik's shoes are legendary, recognized everywhere, and capable of making even the most ordinary apparel into a spectacular fashion statement.

—Angela Pattison; updated by Kathleen Bonann Marshall

BLAIR, Alistair

British designer

Born: Scotland, 5 February 1956. **Education:** Graduated from St. Martin's School of Art, London, 1978. **Career:** Assistant to Marc Bohan, Dior, Paris, 1977; design assistant, Givenchy, Paris, 1978–80; assistant to Karl Lagerfeld, Chloé, Paris, 1980–83; designer, Karl Lagerfeld, New York, 1983–84; designer, Alistair Blair, 1985–89; freelance designer and design consultant to Jaeger, Balmain, Complice, Turnbull and Asser, beginning in 1989; knitwear designer, McGeorge, beginning in 1988; designer, Ivoire ready-to-wear collection, Balmain, Paris, 1990–91; designer, Ballantine, beginning in 1989; creative director, Balmain, Paris, 1991; design consultant, Cerruti, Paris, beginning in 1991; design consultant to Valentino, Rome, beginning in 1993. **Address:** 4 Belmont Court, Pembroke Mews, London W8 6ES, England.

Publications

On BLAIR:

Articles

Kellett, Caroline, "Cue: The Return of Alistair Blair," in *Vogue* (London), June 1986.

Irvine, Susan, "British Style, the Designer Star: Alistair Blair," in *Vogue* (London), February 1987.

"Solid Talent (British Too) Pendrix," in *Connoisseur,* February 1987.

Hume, Marlon, "Backstage with Blair," in *Fashion Weekly* (London), 16 October 1987.

"Alistair Blair to Design for McGeorge," in *Fashion Weekly,* 29 October 1987.

Hillpot, Maureen, "Alistair Blair: Going for It!," in *Taxi* (New York), May 1988.

"Blair Quits Beleaguered Bertelsen as Hamnett Sues," in the *Independent* (London), 8 July 1988.

"Blair, with Backer, Plans Spring Relaunch," in *Women's Wear Daily,* 29 September 1988.

"Backing for Blair," in *Options* (London), December 1988.

Du Cann, Charlotte, "Return of the Pragmatic Professional," in the *Independent,* 18 March 1989.

* * *

When Alistair Blair showed his first collection in London in 1986, he was testing very tepid water. At that time, British designer fashion was recognized for its youth and eccentricity, fun and witty clothes, often unwearable and badly produced. Blair, complete with impeccable fashion credentials (a first class degree from St. Martin's School of Art in London, followed by training at Dior and Givenchy in Paris, then as design assistant to Karl Lagerfeld), seemed to pose little threat to this established reputation in terms of making a valid fashion statement. Blair, however, realized there was a gap in the British fashion market for continental couture at ready-to-wear prices, a gap that became the philosophy for his company.

This singular marketing notion met with immediate fashion applause at the first season's launch. "Blair has arrived as quite simply the most stylish designer in London," raved *Fashion Weekly* (16 October 1987). Things very quickly went from strength to strength; support came from top international stores such as Saks Fifth Avenue and Henri Bendel in New York, Harrods in London, and Seibu in Tokyo were quick to place orders. Possibly the greatest publicity came when the Duchess of York ordered her engagement outfit from him.

Blair's backer was Peder Bertelsen, the Danish oil millionaire. Blair, who was considering an offer to work for Royal couturier Norman Hartnell, was advised by a friend to discuss the move with Bertelsen. "Before I knew where I was he was suggesting that he would back me and I was agreeing," he was quoted as saying. Bertelsen was perhaps British fashion's most important asset in the mid-1980s. He injected a great deal of money into his creation of a fashion empire, buying several prestigious stores including Ungaro, Valentino, and Krizia, and backing John Galliano. In his analysis of British designer fashion he concluded that it fell into two categories—old and new money; old money was the Establishment, including the landowners; new money was in the city or in oil and each identified with its own dress designers. Blair was categorized as Bertelsen's designer for the Establishment.

There was certainly something chic yet traditional about Blair's clothes, even in his luxurious choice of fabrics: alpaca, cashmere and lambswool mixes, duchesse satin and satin backed crêpe, expensive soft suedes and kid leather, even sumptuous embroidery from the Royal embroiderer's Lock Ltd. Dog-tooth check wool coats, flannel jackets, and wool crêpe evening dresses in sharp, florid colors always incorporated a section in Blair's signature colors of orange and black.

Each collection evoked a grown-up sensuality, with obvious visual references to the soigné looks of French film stars like Michele Morgan or Catherine Deneuve, prompting Andrée Walmsley from Fortnum and Mason to enthuse, "He has a very French handwriting, which I adore." The catwalk shows enlivened British Fashion Weeks with their no-expense-spared glamor. A coterie of international models, from Linda Evangelista to Cindy Crawford, was flown in to promote the clothes as the *paparazzi* enthused that Paris had firmly established itself in London.

Even though Blair edited the collections with business-like alacrity, the Bertelsen empire was losing money. Bertelsen admitted to *Business Magazine* in December 1987 that he had lost a million on his first set of accounts. This nonaccumulation of profit eventually led to Bertelsen pulling out as Blair's backer. Even though Blair subsequently found alternative backing, it was not enough to keep the company afloat and it eventually folded. Despite the hype and publicity behind the name, this perhaps exemplifies a problem experienced by many British fashion companies—without the backing of huge textile conglomerates as happens in France, and the vast income earned from licensed goods such as perfume or cosmetics, sole clothing companies often struggle to survive.

As Blair has said, "It's a business. At the end of the day you have to make money for a lot of other people as well." Fortunately for Alistair Blair, his designing was a much respected commodity and led him to design consultancies with a host of firms, including Jaeger, Pierre Balmain, and Complice.

—Kevin Almond

BLASS, Bill

American designer

Born: William Ralph Blass in Fort Wayne, Indiana, 22 June 1922. **Education:** Attended Fort Wayne High School, 1936–39; studied fashion design, Parsons School of Design, 1939. **Military Service:** Served as a sergeant in the U.S. Army, 1941–44. **Career:** Sketch artist, David Crystal Sportswear, New York, 1940–41; designer, Anna Miller and Company Ltd., New York, 1945; designer, 1959–70, and vice-president, 1961–70, Maurice Rentner Ltd., New York; purchased Rentner company, renamed Bill Blass Ltd., 1970; introduced Blassport sportswear division, 1972; introduced signature perfume, 1978; began licensing products, including menswear, womenswear, furs, swimwear, jeans, bed linens, shoes, perfumes, etc.; donated $10 million to New York Public Library, 1994; suffered mild stroke, 1998; farewell gala, 1999; business sold to Haresh Harani and Michael Groveman, 1999; last collection, spring/summer 2000; Lars Nilsson named new Blass designer, 2001. **Awards:** Coty American Fashion Critics "Winnie" award, 1961, 1963, 1970, Menswear award, 1968, Hall of Fame award, 1970, and special citations, 1971, 1982, 1983; Gold Coast Fashion award, Chicago, 1965; National Cotton Council award, New York, 1966; Neiman Marcus award, Dallas, 1969; Print Council award, 1971; Martha award, New York, 1974; Ayres Look award, 1978; *Gentlemen's Quarterly* Manstyle award, New York, 1979; Cutty Sark Hall of Fame award, 1979; Honorary Doctorate, Rhode Island School of Design, 1977; Council of Fashion Designers of America award, 1986. **Address:** 550 Seventh Avenue, New York, NY 10018, USA.

Publications

On BLASS:

Books

Bender, Marilyn, *The Beautiful People,* New York, 1967.

Bill Blass, fall 1998 collection. © Fashion Syndicate Press.

Morris, Bernadine, and Barbara Walz, *The Fashion Makers,* New York, 1978.
Diamonstein, Barbaralee, *Fashion: The Inside Story,* New York, 1985.
Milbank, Caroline Rennolds, *Couture: The Great Designers,* New York, 1985.
Perschetz, Lois, ed., *W: The Designing Life,* New York, 1987.
Coleridge, Nicholas, *The Fashion Conspiracy,* London, 1988.
Milbank, Caroline Rennolds, *New York Fashion: The Evolution of American Style,* New York, 1989.
Daria, Irene, *The Fashion Cycle: A Behind-the-Scenes Look at a Year with Bill Blass, Liz Claiborne, Donna Karan, Arnold Scaasi, and Adrienne Vittadini,* New York, 1990.
Stegemeyer, Anne, *Who's Who in Fashion, Third Edition,* New York, 1996.
American Decades, Gale Research CD-ROM, 1998.
Lagasse, Paul, ed., *The Columbia Encyclopedia,* 6th edition, Farmington Hills, MI, 2000.

Articles

"Dialogue with Bill Blass," in *Interior Design,* June 1973.
"Bill Blass: Real American Class," in *American Fabrics and Fashions* (New York), Fall 1974.
"A Different Glamor at Bill Blass," in *Vogue,* September 1985.
Prisant, Carol, "Top Blass," in *World of Interiors* (London), October 1990.
Morris, Bernadine, "With Blass, Spontaneity Has Returned to Style," in the *New York Times,* 30 March 1993.
Orlean, Susan, "King of the Road," in the *New Yorker,* 20 December 1993.
Schiro, Anne-Marie, "Tasteful Comes in Many Colors," in the *New York Times,* 4 November 1994.
DeCaro, Frank, "Hairy Situations and Hula Baloos: Bill Blass," in *New York Newsday,* 4 November 1994.
Beckett, Kathleen, "Runway Report: My One and Only Hue: Bill Blass," in the *New York Post,* 4 November 1994.
"New York: Bill Blass," in *Women's Wear Daily,* 4 November 1994.
Schiro, Anne-Marie, "Chic and Quality from Bill Blass," in the *New York Times,* 7 April 1995.
"New York: Bill Blass," in *Women's Wear Daily,* 7 April 1995.
Geran, Monica, "Bill Blass Revisited," in *Interior Design,* May 1996.
Schiro, Anne-Marie, "Two Vanishing Breeds (Fashion Designers Bill Blass, Oscar de la Renta)," in the *New York Times,* 1 November 1996.
Geran, Monica, "Cut From the Same Cloth," in *Interior Design,* April 1997.
Interview, "Home at Blass," in *In Style,* March 1998.
Schiro, Anne-Marie, "Blass as Blass, Even Damp," in the *Wall Street Journal,* 22 December 1998.
"Simple But Not Too Sweet is Bill Blass for Spring," online at CNN.com, 1 March 1999.
Gandee, Charles, "The 1950s: Designer Bill Blass Remembers the Years of Cocktails, Café Society, and Cool American Chic," in *Vogue,* November 1999.
"Bill Blass Ltd. Sold to Haresh Tharani, Largest Licensee & Michael Groveman, Blass' CFO," in *Business Wire,* 8 November 1999.
"SOLD! Bill Blass Empire Goes to CFO, Licensee," in *Apparel Industry Magazine,* December 1999.
"Blass Bids Farewell with Signature Collection," online at CNN.com, 8 December 1999.
Wilson, Eric, "Slowik Said to Get Blass Design Job," in *Women's Wear Daily,* 27 January 2000.
"The Blass Menagerie," in *Women's Wear Daily,* 11 February 2000.
Hayt, Elizabeth, "A Blass Evening, Elegant and Understated," in the *New York Times,* 20 February 2000.
Wilson, Eric, "Bill Blass Receives a Retrospective," in *Women's Wear Daily,* 16 May 2000.
Cannon, Michael, "Parties," *Town & Country,* June 2000.
Bellafante, Ginia, "Those Who Defy, and Those Who Don't," in the *New York Times,* 22 September 2000.
"Braillard Denies Blass Move," in *Women's Wear Daily,* 2 February 2001.
"New York: A Delicate Balance," in *Women's Wear Daily,* 16 February 2001.
"Bill Blass," in *Biography Resource Center,* online at www.galenet.gale.com, 17 July 2001.

* * *

"Like most people who seem to be most typically New York, Bill Blass comes from Indiana," wrote native Midwesterner Eleanor

Bill Blass, fall 1998 collection. © Fashion Syndicate Press.

Lambert in an early press release for Blass when he worked at Maurice Rentner. Blass reigns as an American classic, the man who abidingly exemplifies high style because his work plays on the sharp edge of glamor but never falls into the abyss of indecency. Likewise, it defines sophisticated style because it has elements of the naive and the crude in impeccable balance. Blass is the perfect example of fashion's deconstructivist internal oppositions of real, hyper-glamor, and style synthesis.

Although Blass believes in eliminating the superfluous and stressing the essentials of clothing, he is no Yankee skinflint or reductive modernist and aims to beguile and flatter, adding perhaps a flyaway panel, not necessary for structure, that would never appeal to a Halston or a Zoran. He aims to create a fanciful chic, a sense of glamor and luxury. It may be that these desires are fashion's game, but it is undeniable that Blass is the expert player. Everything he does is suffused with style, and he creates evening gowns that would stagger Scarlett O'Hara. His shimmering Matisse collection, embroidered in India, transformed the wearer into a conveyor of masterpiece paintings.

Blass has always been an indisputable enchanter, a man who loves being with the ladies he dresses. Correspondingly, they love being with him, but the relationship is not merely indicative of the elevation of fashion designer from dressmaker to social presence. Blass learns from his clients and, in learning, addresses their needs and wishes. In designing separates, he describes what he likes with a certain top, admits that one of his clients prefers to wear it otherwise and acknowledges it looks better as she wears it.

There are essential leitmotifs in Blass' work. Recalling Mainbocher, he invents from the sweater and brings insights of daywear into the most elegant nighttime presentations. Blass imports menswear practicality and fabrics to womenswear. His evening gowns are dreamlike in their self-conscious extravagance and flattery to the wearer. He can evoke Schiaparelli in the concise elegance of a simulated wood embroidered jacket; but there is also something definably Blass about the garment. In a very old-fashioned way, he celebrates life without the cynicism of other designers. He can be audacious in mixing pattern and texture, though generally with the subtlety of his preferred palette of muted color. Texture is equally important—a red wool cardigan resonant to a red silk dress or the complement of gray flannel trousers to fractured, shimmering surfaces for day and evening. Layering is essential to Blass: whether it is a cardigan teamed with a blouse or sweater or gauzy one-sleeve wraps for evening, Blass flourishes in layers.

Blass evolved into a superb licensing genius and dean of American fashion designers. His is an intensely pictorial imagination, one that conjures up the most romantic possibilities of fashion. He maintains an ideal of glamor and personal aura, redolent of socialites and stars of screen and stage. Yet though there is little in Blass' work that is truly unique to him and not practiced by any other designer, one would never mistake a Blass for a Mainbocher or a Schiaparelli nor for any of his contemporaries.

In December 1998 the legendary designer suffered a mild stroke in Houston, Texas, at age 76. His last showing was the spring-summer collection of 2000. He appeared at a grand farewell, hosted by Manhattan society to honor his lengthy career in design, in fall 1999. From middle-class beginnings as the son of a dressmaker and hardware dealer, he had dressed the likes of Nancy Reagan, Barbara Bush, Nancy Kissinger, Candice Bergen, Barbara Walters, and the fashionable elite.

Of Blass' retirement party, Patrick McCarthy, chairperson of *Women's Wear Daily,* noted, "There are not many standing ovations in fashion. Bill just gave a little wave, barely perceptible, but it was a wave good-bye." On 5 November 1999, he signed over his $700 million design and licensing complex to Haresh T. Harani, chairperson of the Resource Club Ltd., the Blass licensing agency, and Michael Groveman, CFO of the Blass empire.

Retired to a historic 22-acre estate and colonial home in New Preston, Connecticut, a month after selling his fashion house, Blass has kept one foot in Manhattan at his in-town Sutton Place apartment. Of his departure from sketch pads and runways he declared, "I thought the end of the year, beginning of the new century, was the perfect time. After all, I'd been doing it for 60 years… God knows you're not immortal."

—Richard Martin; updated by Mary Ellen Snodgrass

BLUMARINE

Italian fashion design company

Founded: in Carpi, Italy, in 1977, by Anna Molinari, chief designer and artistic director, with husband Gianpaolo Tarabini. **Company**

Blumarine, fall/winter 2001–02 collection: chiffon ensemble with a fur hat. © AP/Wide World Photos.

History: First catwalk show in Milan, 1981; Anna Molinari line presented twice a year in Milano Collezioni shows, from 1986; added two lines, Blumarine Folies and Miss Blumarine, 1987; Blumarine licensing deals for perfume, glasses, leather goods, swimwear, jewelry, and home furnishings, 1987; opened flagship store in Via Spiga, Milan, 1990.**Awards:** Best Designer of the Year, Modit Milan, 1980; Griffo d'Oro award, Imola, Italy, 1981; Rotary Club Gold award, 1991; Lions Club Carpione d'Oro award, 1992. **Company Address:** Via Don Milani, 6–47814, Bellaria, Italy.

Publications

On BLUMARINE:

Books

Gastel, M., *Designers,* Milan, 1994.
The Best in Catalogue Design, London, 1994.

Articles

Pardo, D., "Modelle d'Italia," in *L'Espresso* (Rome), January 1993.
Mari, L., "Helmut Newton 1993," in *Vogue* (Milan), March 1993.
Staples, K., "Italy's Newest Line," in *Mademoiselle,* March 1993.
Cavaglione, P., "Il Mio Profeta," in *Amica,* August 1993.
Szlezynger, T., "Stilisti e Designer," in *Vogue Sposa* (Milan), March 1994.
Gagliardo, P., "Vogue Erfolg," in *Vogue* (Munich), August 1994.
"Fashion Notebook I: Copy Cats," in *Observer Magazine,* 15 June 1997.
"Rosella at the Helm," in *Women's Wear Daily,* 1 January 1998.
"Tales of Milano," in *Women's Wear Daily,* 3 March 1998.
"Material Science," in *Leather,* 1 June 1998.
"Milan: Fall/Winter Collections," in the *San Francisco Chronicle,* 2 March 1999.
Givhan, Robin, "Fear and Clothing Triumph in Milan," in the *Washington Post,* 29 September 1999.
Wilson, Jennifer, "Shop Appeal," in the *Los Angeles Magazine,* March 2000.
Edwards, Pamela, "Runway Report," in *Essence,* April 2000.
"Pikenz Evolves Fashion Classic," in *Duty-Free News International,* 1 June 2000.
"Milan Fashion Shows Start Upbeat," from *Reuters,* 9 September 2000.
"From Ralph Lauren to Chanel—Crystals Line the Runways," from the *PR Newswire,* 18 September 2000.
Menkes, Suzy, "A Few Vivacious Voices Hit the High Notes in Milan," in the *International Herald Tribune,* 7 October 2000.
"Designers Lose Their Common Tongue," in the *Irish Times,* 10 October 2000.
"Fling with the Wild Frontier," in the *Washington Post,* 9 March 2001.
"Fashion: Frock 'n' Roll Prom Queens Get a Dressing Down," in the *Independent* (London), 19 May 2001.
"Anna Molinari," available online at www.modaonline.it, 17 July 2001.
"Blumarine," online at *FirstView,* www.firstview.com, 17 July 2001.
"Blumarine," online at *Elle* online, www.Elle.com, 17 July 2001.
"La Semana del Moda en Milán," online at www.el-mundo.es, 17 July 2001.
"Personal Profile: Blumarine," online at *Virtual Runway,* www.virtualrunway.com, 17 July 2001.

*

The stylistic concept of Anna Molinari is very simple: fantasy, passion, curiosity, fascination, and romanticism. It's easy to describe the typical Blumarine woman: one has only to look to Anna Molinari, her intelligence, vivacity, creativity, femininity and passion: a vibration between angel and femme fatale. Helmut Newton, one of the world's greatest fashion photographers, has perceived this essence and, guided by the modernity of Anna Molinari, has created a new concept of feminine power.

—Blumarine

* * *

Blumarine collections are designed by the company's founder and owner, Anna Molinari. Based in Carpi in Italy, collections are shown seasonally, twice a year in Milan. Since its 1977 inception, the company has built up a steady international following that includes recent openings in the United Kingdom and the United States.

Blumarine collections are young, fun, and throwaway. Kitsch and naughty, sexy yet prudish, the clothes always represent an appealing

Blumarine, spring/summer 2002 ready-to-wear collection. © AFP/CORBIS.

ambiguity. A Blumarine promotional piece, for example, gives a peek-a-boo glimpse at a little girl plundering her elder sister's wardrobe and emerging half innocent, half saucy, into the sophisticated world. There is also a hard-edged defiance about the clothes, designed by a woman who combines her intelligence with the feminine powers of seduction.

Fashion photographer Helmut Newton has created a strong image for Blumarine since he began styling and photographing the company's promotional material. Whether it's set in the seedy world of a back street hotel, complete with tacky 1970s decor, or on the shores of a trashy Mediterranean seaside resort, there are always strong sexual connotations in the imagery. Clothes are styled with revealing accessories—suspender belts, the spiked patent stilettos of the dominatrix, or dog collars as chokers. The poses of the models, particularly Nadja Auerman, who resembles an early 1980s Debbie Harry, tantalize. The images, Molinari's and Newton's, are always provocative.

Molinari likes to emphasize the female figure, which is often achieved by exaggerated feminine styles. Very popular is her tutu miniskirt, which features a tiny cinched waist that suddenly explodes into a full bell skirt, and layer upon layer of net and lace petticoats. The line also featured delicate black lace baby doll dresses cut dangerously short, laced bustiers, short, striped milkmaid dresses, tiny cardigans, and figure-hugging sweaters, always worn in a way to reveal a lacy bra top or satin-trimmed slip.

Popular fabrics have included lace, brocade, chiffon, and fake fur either as a trim or made into a figure-hugging jacket. Accessories are important—bo-peep caps worn with schoolgirl pigtails, large feather boas, or top hats. Ruffles often reoccur in collections, on shirts or as flounced cuffs and necklines. Color mixes are always refreshing and unexpected: ice blues mixed with burgundy, peach, and cream, or chocolate brown mixed with sky blue and tangerine; dominating, though, is black, always sexy and suggestive.

Blumarine has also explored many directional fashion themes in collections. For spring/summer 1995, Molinari exploited the most accurate depiction of that season's "disco diva" look, with short, pleated-on-the-knee pencil skirts in sherbet satin, combined with fitted jackets, good-time hot pants, and kitsch-print Lurex t-shirts. Other collections exploit what Anna Molinari believes to be the dual personality in every woman: coyness combined with passion, or the little girl combined with the temptress. The company has steadily increased its influence and is now recognized as one of the more directional, risk-taking fashion labels in the world, with showrooms in Milan, New York, and Paris, and a steadily increasing coterie of boutiques in Hong Kong, Milan, and London.

The company's courtship of the moneyed, under-30 buyer brought a sharp turnaround in both style and taste. The arrival of Molinari and Tarabini's daughter Rosella into the design studio in 1998 splashed an obviously youthful élan over the Blumarine high-fashion severity. Long past its days in knitwear, Blumarine's theatrical reds, purples, torrid pinks, and turquoises teamed with cigarette skirts in satin, leather, and crocodile and body-hugging suits collared in mink and topped with fox stoles and full-length fur. In March 1998, Molinari presented satin and pointelle slip dresses, fur-collar velvet coats, and sweater sets for fall, a nostalgic return to the sweater girls of the 1950s and 1960s with a touch of the flapper. For dress-up, she stressed beaded evening wear for a head-turning party entrance.

In her second season, designing daughter Rosella toned down her ebullience with less exhibitionism, more control of her gala florals, sequined slip dresses, tailored pantsuits, and polka dot organza with ruffled hems and poufy sleeves. Balancing a mother's boldness with mother-knows-best, Molinari designs drew West Coast fans to Heaven 27, Sofia Coppola's Los Angeles boutique which debuted in 1999. In consecutive spring showings, Blumarine kept up the pressure with flirty flair and a sprinkling of Rosella's heart prints, a come-hither for the youngest fashion follower.

New lines bolstered the house image for tarty chic with embroidered and jeweled mules for 2000. Fall/winter 2000 also sought past glow and sparkle with black frocks from the 1980s and dress-up attire in beads and sequins, embroidery, ethereal lace, and silks with daring slit skirts, scalloped hems, chiffon blouses, and touches of Swarovski crystal mesh, a motif that continued into 2001.

—Kevin Almond; updated by Mary Ellen Snodgrass

BODYMAP

British design team

Founded: in 1982 by Stevie Stewart and David Holah. *Stewart* born in London, 1958; studied at Barnet College. *Holah* born in London, 1958; studied at North Oxfordshire College of Art. Both studied fashion at Middlesex Polytechnic, 1979–82; graduation collection purchased by Browns, London. **Company History:** Company expanded in 1985 to include Bodymap men's and women's collection, B-Basic junior line, Bodymap Red Label, and Bodymap swimwear; designed costumes for Michael Clark's *No Fire Escape in Hell* ballet, 1986; fell on hard times and closed, late 1980s. **Awards:** Martini Young Fashion award, 1983; Bath Museum of Costume Dress of the Year award, 1984.

Publications

By BODYMAP:

Articles

Stewart, Stevie, "Mapping the Future: Talking 'Bout My Generation," in *Fashion '86,* London 1985.

On BODYMAP:

Books

McDermott, Catherine, *Street Style: British Design in the 1980s,* London 1987.

Coleridge, Nicholas, *The Fashion Conspiracy,* London 1988.

Evans, Caroline, and Minna Thornton, *Women and Fashion: A New Look,* London 1989.

Articles

Warner, Marina, "Counter-Couture," in *Connoisseur* (London), May 1984.

"Bodymap: British BCBG Version B.D.," in *Elle* (London), September 1984.

Jones, Mark, "Followers of Fashion," in *Creative Review* (London), December 1984.

Cleave, Maureen, "Leading Them a Dance," in the *Observer* (London), 18 May 1986.

Mower, Sarah, "Off the Map," in *The Guardian* (London), 5 June 1986.

Jeal, Nicola, "Bodymap," in the *Observer,* 12 June 1986.

Tredre, Roger, "Body Style," in *Fashion Weekly* (London), 28 September 1989.

Elliot, Tom, and Robin Duff, "Rise and Fall," in *Blitz* (London), November 1989.

McRobbie, Angela, "Falling Off the Catwalk," in *New Statesman & Society,* 7 June 1996.

Fallon, James, "Shop Spawns Shopgirl Tops," in *Women's Wear Daily,* 25 November 1998.

Birns, Amanda, et al., "What's Hot...Shopgirl Hooks Up with Playboy," in *Women's Wear Daily,* 19 June 2000.

* * *

"Barbie Takes a Trip,"or "Querelle Meets Olive Oil," or even "The Cat in the Hat Takes a Rumble with the Techno Fish," are just some of the bizarre titles of Bodymap collections. The company, a male-female partnership between Middlesex Polytechnic graduates David Holah and Stevie Stewart, was one of the brightest design teams to emerge during the 1980s. By the middle of the decade London was being promoted by the media as a trendy hothouse of bright young things. Bodymap was regarded as being amongst the brightest of all, turning the Establishment upside-down with wild, young, and unconventional clothes. Fashion editors were clamoring for more, declaring Bodymap to be the hottest fashion label of the decade.

Founded in 1982, the name of the company was inspired by Italian artist Enrico Job, who took over a thousand photographs of every part of his anatomy, then collaged them together, creating a two-dimensional version of a three-dimensional object—in other words, a body map. A similar philosophy was adapted in Stewart and Holah's approach to pattern making and garment construction. Prints, knits, silhouettes, and shapes were restructured and reinvented to map the body. Stretch clothes had holes in unexpected places, so the emphasis was transferred from one place to another. Pieces of flesh were amalgamated with pieces of fabric in an effort to explore new areas of the body, previously considered unflattering.

Awarded the Individual Clothes Show prize as the "Most Exciting and Innovative Young Designers of 1983," Bodymap clothes were always for the young, avant-garde, and daring. Working predominantly in black, white, and cream, a familiar theme involved the layering of prints and textures on top of one another, to create an unstructured look, redefining traditional body shapes, overemphasizing shapeliness or shapelessness so both the overweight and underweight, plain or beautiful, could wear and be comfortable in an outfit.

Bodymap described itself in the 1980s as being a young company employing other young people to mix creativity with commerce. They worked very closely with textile designer Hilde Smith, who created many Bodymap prints and helped bridge gaps between fashion and textile design. Film and videographer John Maybury was responsible for Bodymap's outrageous fashion show videos, featuring dancer Michael Clark, singers Boy George and Helen Terry, and performance artist Leigh Bowery. Photographer David La Chappelle was responsible for many of the visual stills used in magazines.

While still at Middlesex Polytechnic, Bodymap recognized the importance of moving in a circle of talented, creative people. Holah and Stewart were part of the young 1980s generation attracting worldwide attention for London as a vibrant center for creative energy and ideas, not only in fashion but music, painting, video, and dance. Unfortunately for Bodymap, the end of the 1980s proved the end of the road of the once-hipster design house. Tough times and tougher competition brought the firm down, at a time when smaller British fashion design companies failed more often than not.

After Bodymap's demise, Stevie Stewart consulted for several companies then went on to design a new line of chic tops called Shopgirl for Max Kyrie and Pippa Brooks, owner of the Shop boutique on Brewer Street in London. The new collection debuted in 1998, alongside a Shopgirl jewelry line. By 2000 the Stewart-designed Shopgirl line was sold not only at Shop but at Harvey Nichols and Bloomingdale's in New York City. The Shopgirl collection expanded to include cardigans and lingerie, then teamed up with Playboy International to put the famous bunny logo on its hip leisurewear. Shop owners Brooks and Kyrie were in talks with Babycham in 2001 to put the popular fawn logo on Shopgirl threads and jewelry.

—Kevin Almond; updated by Nelly Rhodes

BOGNER, Willy, (Jr.)

German sportswear designer

Born: Munich, 23 January 1942, son of Maria and Willy Bogner Sr. **Family:** Married Sonia Ribeiro, 1973. **Career:** Willy Bogner GmbH established by Willy Sr., 1936; company began outfitting West German ski teams, from 1936; mother Maria designed revolutionary ski pants, dubbed "Bogners," 1948; skiied in Olympics, 1960 and 1964; took over family business, 1970s; U.S. subsidiary, Bogner of America, formed, 1976; began opening stores in U.S., 1985; launched fragrance, *Bogner Man* and bath and body lines; began extensive licensing program for leather accessories, eyewear, jeans, socks, shoes, gloves, jewelry, and bikewear, from 1990s; new licensing agreement with Cosmopolitan Cosmetics, 1999; also performed ski stunts in Bond films and others; then filmmaker with over two dozen films to his credit. **Address:** Willy Bogner GmbH & Co. KG, Postfach 80–02–80 Sankt-Veit Strasse 4, 8000 Munich 80, Germany.

Publications

On BOGNER:

Books

Lambert, Eleanor, *World of Fashion: People, Places, Resources,* New York & London, 1976.

Articles

Conant, Jennet, "Flash on the Slopes: Designer-Director Bogner Heats Up the Ski Scene," in *Newsweek,* 23 December 1985.
"Big Bucks Bogner," in *Forbes,* 13 January 1986.
Brooks, Hollis, "Designing Skiers," in *Skiing,* October 1994.
Feitelberg, Rosemary, "Jump-Starting Bogner Shop," in *Women's Wear Daily,* 26 October 1995.
"Cosmopolitan Continues Product Offensive (License Agreement with Willy Bogner)," in *Soap Perfumery & Cosmetics,* May 1999.
Drier, Melissa, "Bogner Licensing Plan: $80 Million in Three Years," in *Women's Wear Daily,* 22 November 2000.

* * *

The Bogner ski and sportswear company has been run by the Bogner family since its founding by Willy Bogner Sr. in 1936. Bogner Sr. was called the "Dior of ski fashion" while his wife Maria was considered the "Coco Chanel of sports fashion." Both Bogner Sr. and Bogner Jr.'s status as producers of the most stylish skiwear available is practically unrivaled, and the company bearing their name is just as well known for the unparalleled fit and quality workmanship of its activewear. The successful combination of design, cut, and technically-advanced fabrics has earned the Bogner company loyal customers throughout Europe, Asia, and North America.

The Bogner name has stood for innovation in the skiwear field since the introduction of Maria's stretch trousers design in 1948. The trousers were immediately popular owing to their feminine look, as compared to previous women's skiwear which was decidedly masculine and unflattering. Devotees of the new "Bogners,"as they were known at the time, included internationally recognized women such as Marilyn Monroe and Ingrid Bergman. The Bogner company also pioneered the development of the one-piece ski suit and the use of stretch fabrics. Their first one-piece racing suits were worn by the 1960 West German Olympic ski team; the team was subsequently outfitted and sponsored by the Bogner company for decades.

Willy Bogner Jr. joined the company in the early 1970s and continued the tradition of design innovation. The U.S. subsidiary, Bogner of America, was formed in 1976 and over the next three decades the variety of Bogner products grew to include cross-country skiwear, tennis and golf ensembles, swimwear, general sportswear, the Fire & Ice snowboarding line for younger enthusiasts, and an ever-growing range of accessories. In the middle and late 1990s, Bogner went on a licensing spree to spearhead expansion. While the Bogner name had already appeared on sports-related accessories available in its stores, licensing agreements brought Bogner products from shoes, boots, and socks, to bath and body products, jeans, gloves, and jewelry to worldwide markets.

Although the company had expanded into varied lines of sports- and actionwear, its skiwear remained the foremost vehicle for creative expression by its design team, headed by Willy Bogner Jr. His high energy personality encompassed multiple interests, from his own skiing career as a member of the West German Olympic ski team in 1960 and 1964, to films (the ski chase scenes from four James Bond films were filmed under his direction). Bogner's energy and skills have been evident in the creative motifs decorating his skiwear. Some collections have included Egyptian designs with detachable feathers; exotic embossed designs and turban-like headgear; suits with music-playing appartus; and younger-themed combinations of contrasting designs for the Fire & Ice line debuted in the early 1990s.

In the middle and later 1990s, Bogner incorporated snowboarding garb (considered by some as merely "street fashion"on the slopes) into the vocabulary of mainstream ski fashion. Bogner Jr.'s wife Sonia joined the design team to help inspire and create a more classic and feminine part of the collection bearing her name. Her styles were for the more subdued and sophisticated female customer, with such design details as cashmere linings and fur trims.

Despite the often outrageous decorative themes, the purpose of Bogner activewear has never been forgotten. A fabric may be printed to look like a silk brocade or embroidered with an intricate design, but it is still wind- and water-resistant. It is this attention to the practical needs of the wearer, coupled with a desire for style, that has kept Bogner an enduring leader in the world of activewear. Bogner élan is to the slopes what haute couture is to fashion.

—Melinda L. Watt; updated by Nelly Rhodes

BOHAN, Marc

French designer

Born: Marc Roger Maurice Louis Bohan in Paris, 22 August 1926. **Education:** Studied at the Lycée Lakanal, Sceaux, 1940–44. **Family:** Married Dominique Gaborit in 1950 (died, 1962); married Huguette Rinjonneau (died); daughter: Marie-Anne. **Career:** Assistant designer in Paris to Robert Piguet, 1945–49, and to Molyneux, 1949–51; designer, Madeleine de Rauch, Paris, 1952; briefly opened own Paris salon, produced one collection, 1953; head designer for couture, Maison Patou, Paris, 1954–58; designer, Dior, London, 1958–60; head designer and art director, Dior, Paris, 1960–89; fashion director, Norman Hartnell, London, 1990–92. **Awards:** *Sports Illustrated* Designer of the Year award, 1963; Schiffli Lace and Embroidery Institute award, 1963; named Chevalier de la Legion d'Honneur, 1979; Ordre de Saint Charles, Monaco.

Marc Bohan, designed for the house of Christian Dior's spring 1964 collection: gold-embroidered tulle gown. © Bettmann/CORBIS.

Publications

On BOHAN:

Books

Stegemeyer, Anne, *Who's Who in Fashion, Third Edition,* New York, 1996.

Articles

Devlin, Polly, "The Perfectionists," in *Vogue* (London), September 1974.

Kellett, Caroline, "A Celebrated Stylist: Marc Bohan Commemorates 25 Years at Christian Dior," in *Vogue* (London), June 1983.

Verdier, Rosy, "Marc Bohan: j'aime vivre dans l'ambre," in *L'Officiel* (Paris), August 1986.

"A Dior Original," in the *Observer Magazine* (London), 29 March 1987.

McColl, Pat, "Bohan: The Power Behind Dior," in *Harper's Bazaar* (New York), September 1987.

Michals, Debra, "Bohan Speaks Out: 27 Years of Fashion," in *Women's Wear Daily,* 12 November 1987.

"Bye-bye Bohan," in *Time* (New York), 22 May 1989.

Mulvagh, Jane, "Hartnell's New Marc," in *Illustrated London News,* No. 1098, 1990.

Wheeler, Karen, "Marc Bohan: New Heart to Hartnell," in *DR: The Fashion Business* (London), 7 July 1990.

Friedman, Arthur, "Hartnell's Silverman: Building on Bohan," in *Women's Wear Daily,* 18 September 1990.

Reed, Paula, "New Look for the Royals," in the *Sunday Times Magazine* (London), 27 January 1991.

Miller, Jeffrey, "House of Hartnell," in *Interview* (New York), January 1991.
Armstrong, Lisa, "Making His Marc," in *Vogue* (London), February 1991.
Grice, Elizabeth, "Designing for the Young at Hartnell," in the *Sunday Express Magazine* (London), 17 February 1991.
Smith, Liz, "Hartnell Goes High Street," in *The Times* (London), 21 January 1992.
Fallon, James, "Bohan Talks with Hartnell on Early End to His Career," in *Women's Wear Daily,* 16 September 1992.
Aillard, Charlotte, "Consolidating Households in Burgundy," in *Architectural Digest,* October 1994.

* * *

"N'oubliez pas la femme," Marc Bohan's much quoted comment in *Vogue* magazine in 1963, is the tenet which underscored all his work. It brought him success throughout his lengthy couture career, his design always based on the adult female form and a recognition of his customers' needs rather than an overriding desire to shock and provoke headlines in his name. From his early days at Molyneux he learned a sense of practicality, as well as an appreciation of the flattering potential of luxurious fabrics and good fit. His perfectionist zeal and attention to detail, and especially in the 1960s and 1970s at Christian Dior, a good fashion sense, were always at the foundations of his reputation.

It was at Dior that Bohan's talents were established, winning him international acclaim. He enabled the house to remain at the forefront of fashion while still producing wearable, elegant clothes. To achieve this end, Bohan combined innovation with repeated classic shapes and styles, reworked to express the current mood. In 1961 Dior included some of the briefest skirts of the couture collections, but the neat black-and-white tweed fabric of these little suits enabled Bohan to please the established clientèle, as well as attracting new customers with wit and modernity. His suiting always showed the most directional styles and cut, which others soon followed.

This ability to ease normally cautious clients towards new, more radical styles by carefully balancing all the elements of a design was seen again in his 1966 collection, when he showed the by then *de rigueur* mini with longer coats, promoting a shift in hemlines gradually rather than dictating a change. It was this desire to coax and flatter which distinguished his couture work. His sensitivity to the needs of women prevented him from trying to mold them into ever-altering silhouettes, or forget their desire to look grown up and elegant even when fashion promoted girlish styles in the 1960s. His use of decoration was equally discreet; he prefered the demure wit of pussycat bows on simple silk blouses and shirtwaist dresses or naturalistic floral prints to add interest to his creations, rather than any overblown gestures that might render the garments less easy to wear, making the client self-conscious.

Bohan was unafraid to tell his customers what was most flattering for them and they appreciated his honesty; his rich and famous client list remained faithful even when he switched from one house to the next. His eveningwear, with his clever suiting styles, was his greatest strength—with an understated sense of style allowing the luxurious fabrics and subtle detailing to shine through the simple forms he preferred.

In his work for Dior and his later creations for Norman Hartnell, Bohan's love of simplicity was continually evident. At the former he presented stark modernist shapes, like the angular ivory silk evening

Marc Bohan, designed for the house of Christian Dior's 1965 collection: gazar cocktail dress with an embroidered underskirt. © Bettmann/CORBIS.

tunic and matching cigarette trousers (1965), with rich red floral design creeping over its surface. At Hartnell he again excelled at reviving the spirits of an established couture name. He developed his pared-down style to fulfill the house's design brief, attracting a younger audience with his first collection, combining flirtatious shaping with classic styles. In 1991 he showed the sophisticated chic of black sheath dresses with diamanté buttons next to witty fuchsia silk scoop-necked dresses with short, very full skirts—harking back to the bubble dresses that had reinvigorated his work for Dior in the late 1970s. Again he provided choice for his customers and commercial designs which were well received by the press.

Bohan's time at Hartnell was brief, curtailed by the recession of the early 1990s, which caused a decline of interest in couture and precipitated the demise of several smaller houses. His sense of elegance, however, remained undiminished. In an October 1994 interview and pictorial featuring his newly-renovated, 18th-century country home in Burgundy, France, for *Architectural Digest,* Bohan declared, "For me, elegance is a yardstick, [it is] the art of knowing how much free rein one can allow one's imagination without overstepping the boundaries of classicism." If his suits were the most innovative area of his work, he balanced their fashionable cut with well-constructed feminine separates and striking eveningwear, which had the lasting appeal characteristic of all elegant design.

—Rebecca Arnold; updated by Jodi Essey-Stapleton

BRIGANCE, Tom

American designer

Born: Thomas Franklin Brigance in Waco, Texas, 4 February 1913. **Education:** Attended Waco Junior College; studied in New York at the Parsons School of Design, 1931–34, and the National Academy of Art; studied in Paris at the Sorbonne and at the Academie de la Grande Chaumière, Paris. **Military Service:** Served in the U.S. Air Corps Intelligence Service, South Pacific, 1941–44, decorated for bravery. **Career:** Worked in Europe as a freelance fashion designer, designed in London for Jaeger and for Simpson's of Piccadilly, late 1930s; designer, Lord & Taylor, New York, 1939–41 and 1944–49; opened own firm, 1949; also designed in New York for Frank Gallant, and freelanced for Fonde, Sportsmarket, and designed swimwear for Sinclair and Gabar, Water Clothes, 1950s; retired, late 1970s. **Awards:** Coty American Fashion Critics award, 1953; International Silk citation, 1954; National Cotton award, 1955; Internazionale delle Arti award, Italy, 1956. **Died:** 14 October 1990, in New York City.

Publications

On BRIGANCE:

Books

New York and Hollywood Fashion: Costume Designs from the Brooklyn Museum Collection, New York, 1986.

Milbank, Caroline Rennolds, *New York Fashion: The Evolution of American Style,* New York, 1989.

Stegemeyer, Anne, *Who's Who in Fashion, Third Edition,* New York, 1996.

Articles

Sheppard, Eugenia, "What's Coming Next?" in the *Herald Tribune,* 28 October 1947.

"Designer Brigance Speaks to a Mill," in *American Fabrics and Fashions* (New York), No. 25, 1953.

Schiro, Anne-Marie, "Thomas F. Brigance Dies at 70: Designed Sophisticated Swimwear," in the *New York Times,* 18 October 1990.

* * *

Eleanor Lambert's 1951 press release for Tom Brigance quotes the young designer: "Good American clothes should be able to go anywhere. They should not be designed with a single town or section in mind. They should be appropriate for the American woman's mode of living, expressive of her individual personality, and suitable for the climate she lives in." Brigance spoke and designed with the plain common sense of Will Rogers and the utmost simplicity of the American ethos. No one could more readily have epitomized the Main Street ideal of an American fashion designer than Brigance. From Waco, Texas, slim, dark, and charming, Brigance became a recognized designer in 1939, while still in his twenties, as part of Dorothy Shaver's campaign to create American designer identities at Lord & Taylor.

His first success was in active sportswear and beachwear. In an advertisement in *Vogue* (15 May 1939), Lord & Taylor boasted of its new American hero, "When you come to the World's Fair be sure to visit our Beach Shop on the fifth floor, home of creations by Brigance, one of our own designers, whose ideas enchant even the blasé Riviera." Anne-Marie Schiro reported in Brigance's obituary in the *New York Times* (18 October 1990) that the Duchess of Windsor bought half a dozen outfits from his first beachwear collection in 1939, a formidable endorsement for any young designer. Brigance remained a designer at Lord & Taylor until 1949. Although he later designed a full spectrum of clothing, including eveningwear, his forte through his retirement in the late 1970s was sportswear, especially playsuits, beach- and swimwear. At Brigance's death in 1990 Schiro reported: "He retired in the late 1970s after a two-year stint with Gabar whose owner, Gabriel Colasante, said this week that a Brigance-designed skirted swimsuit is still one of his company's bestselling styles. Colasante decreed that regardless of the print, the Brigance-designed suits still sell consistently."

Brigance was at his best when at his most simple. His employer Lord & Taylor boasted of Brigance in a 1947 advertising in the *Herald Tribune*: "His suits and coats have the distinctively American lines that inspire individuality with accessories." Like Claire McCardell, Brigance used fabric ties and sashes to shape waists and create form; his coats and suits were uniformly unadorned, but inflected with relatively large buttons in interesting placement.

By the late 1940s, he was acknowledging the New Look, not in its extreme forms, but in a modified version in which the skirt or peplum flared with pockets, adding practicality to the gesture of the wider skirt. His play clothes were his most imaginative, suggesting the spectrum of leisure from beach pajamas through halter tops and playsuits with shorts and skirts. For summer, his preference was generally for colorful cottons, often with dots. His swimwear presaged the American idiom of dressing in warm climates in clothes as suitable for the street as for the beach and swimming.

Distinctively, Brigance enjoyed pattern mixes more than most of his contemporaries. Today his surprising combinations of florals, geometrics, and exotics are strikingly bold and seem more advanced as textile fusions than others of his generation. While his ideological interest was reductive, his style was always to supply plenty of material and ample coverage. He kept a loyal, even aging, clientèle because he flattered the body with informal exposure that was never scanty, even in swimwear and playsuits. One could be unfailingly modest and self-assured in Brigance. His design sensibility for minimalism was also aided by his interest in fabric technology—his nylon swimsuit of 1960 exploited the fast-drying material. In 1955 he was the only man among seven American designers, including Anne Fogarty, Pauline Trigère, and Claire McCardell, to style interiors for Chrysler Corporation cars.

Eugenia Sheppard, writing in the *Herald Tribune* in October 1947, claimed that Brigance had Aristotle's phrase "nothing is permanent but change" set over the mirror in his design workroom at Lord & Taylor. Change for Brigance was ever modest; sportswear was also a credo, believing in the practical aspects of clothing. Less adventurous than McCardell or Cashin, Brigance (along with John Weitz) anticipated the emergence of great male designers in the 1970s and 1980s era of American sportswear. Like them, he was his own best salesperson and a kind of native hero, the man who not only dressed the

American ideal woman of suburban chic, but also the man for whom she dressed. His 1949 dinner separates in pleated jersey exemplify Brigance's contribution to design: a quintessentially American look—informal, sporty, innovative, open, and yet demure.

—Richard Martin

BRIONI

Italian fashion house

Founded: by tailor Nazareno Fonticoli and entrepreneur Gaetano Savini in via Barberini, Rome, in 1945. **Company History:** First men's tailored clothing show, Palazzo Pitti, Florence, 1952; launched accessory line, 1952; first men's runway show in New York, 1954; first show in Britain, 1959; manufacturing company, Brioni Roman Style, launched in Penne, Italy, with 45 workers, 1960; neckwear collection launched, 1979; Penne factory established tailoring school, 1980; first American freestanding Brioni store opened, Park Avenue, New York, 1982; company acquired Burini of Bergamo, 1991, and controlling interest in Sforza of Bologna, leather creator, 1994; ready-to-wear line, Brioni Roman Style, produced in Penne, Italy; first sportswear-only freestanding store opened, Aspen (CO), 2000. **Awards:** *Esquire* (New York) award for valued contribution to menswear, 1959; International Fashion Council award, 1962. **Company Address:** via Barberini 79–81, Rome, Italy. **Company Website:** www.brioni.com.

Publications

On BRIONI:

Books

Schoeffler, O. E., and William Gale, *Esquire's Encyclopedia of 20th Century Men's Fashion*, New York, 1973.

Chenoune, Farid, *Brioni*, New York, 1998.

Articles

Gellers, Stan, "Brioni Goes Beyond Its Sartorial Suits," in *Daily News Record (DNR),* 21 May 1997.

———, "Brioni to Open First Free-Standing Sportswear Store," in *DNR,* 10 April 2000.

Courtney Colavita, "Brioni's Luxuriant Express on Global Track," *DNR,* 1 January 2001.

* * *

Brioni was the definitive Roman tailoring establishment of the "Continental look" of the 1950s. The silhouette was immediately identifiable, with its pitched shoulders, tapered waist, and narrow hips and trousers, suggesting the architectural purity and astringency of the postwar Italian aesthetic. Brioni's sensitive tailoring was also one of the first postwar softenings of men's tailored clothing, bringing immediate pliability in slim silhouette and delicate drapery. The fabrics advocated by Fonticoli and Savini were borrowed from womenswear for a beautiful hand and lush suppleness which also brought color to the sober traditions of men's tailoring.

American film stars such as Clark Gable, Henry Fonda, John Wayne, Kirk Douglas, and others had suits custom-made by Brioni—these avatars of masculinity were important in introducing American men in particular to the comfort of Brioni's labor-intensive and meticulous tailoring. America was very important to Brioni's image and business: the American tendency to men of big frame and naïve awkwardness was superbly civilized by the sophistication of Brioni tailoring. Moreover, American masculinity's embrace of the lean Italian style created an alliance powerful enough to serve as an alternative to Savile Row, softening the structure of the suit and allowing the heretical interventions of style and fashion to come into men's tailored clothing. Brioni is said to be the first men's tailor to employ raw silks and rich brocades in men's tailoring and these innovations in men's tailoring may seem less than radical today, but in the 1950s Brioni was a thorough innovator in the stolid world of tailoring.

The slim modesty of the Brioni "continental" silhouette encouraged the experimental play of textiles, and the suit's clean modernism allowed for color as eye-opening as color-field paintings. Even today, Brioni tailoring is among the most tactile and luxurious in the world. One line of suits, known as Vaticano, employs the dense but silky fabrics traditionally used for priests' robes. Brioni and Sorelle Fontana often showed together in fashion shows, so pronounced was the affinity between the most extravagant style of Roman fashion for women and Brioni's ideal tailoring for men. Brioni suits have had the discernible difference of labor and quality, from handmade buttonholes to the composition of a suit as a perfect harmonics of proportion. Production of a Brioni suit required 10 hours of handsewing, 18 hours of fine craftsmanship, 42 pressing stages, and 186 manufacturing phases.

After a difficult period in the early 1990s when the company did not have a clear brand or retail strategy and essentially marketed one product, Brioni is back on track, with revenues increasing fivefold over the 1990s. It has opened stores throughout the world and expects a total of 35 in upscale locations by 2005, all featuring VIP rooms for the customized suits that remain at the company's core. Brioni's Aspen store, opened in 2000, is its first sportswear-only unit; the Milan flagship offers only the most exclusive collections, at a price 15-percent above the company's other outlets.

Brioni expanded outside tailored suits, introducing not only high-end sportswear for men under the Brioni Sport label, but women's clothing as well. The women's line, initially designed by Fabio Piras and introduced in 2000, featured the same classic styling and attention to fabric and detail as the men's line, but with a softer, more feminine silhouette.

Accessories and sportswear, formerly a minimal part of Brioni's business, accounted for 40 percent of turnover in the new century. The company's sportswear line includes tailored sportscoats, cashmere and wool sweaters, and unconstructed silk and leather jackets. As in the 1950s, the company enhanced its visibility by associating movie stars with its clothing, including Pierce Brosnan in the James Bond films and Richard Gere in *Dr. T and the Women* in 2000.

Although Brioni has diversified into other product categories, it continues to maintain its focus on customers it calls "luxuriants," defined as those apparel-buyers who are able to interpret and appreciate luxury. The company employed this strategy to become a $100-million international brand, with the U.S. representing its most important market, accounting for 35 percent of export sales. (American tourists are estimated to account for 45 percent of sales in Europe as well.)

As part of Brioni's commitment to quality and detail, the company continues to eschew licensing and manufacture all of its products in-house, except shoes, which are made in Italy by small workshops. And, despite all of its recent diversification, tailored suits remain Brioni's focus. As one executive emphasized in the *Daily News Record,* "A man wears a suit."

—Richard Martin; updated by Karen Raugust

BROOKS, Donald

American designer

Born: New York City, 10 January 1928. **Education:** Studied art, Syracuse University, New York, 1947–49, fashion design and illustration, Parsons School of Design, New York, 1949–50. **Career:** Designed for a series of New York ready-to-wear firms, circa 1950–56; designer for Darbury, 1956; partner/designer, Hedges of New York, 1957–59; designer, own label for Townley Frocks, 1958–64; designer, custom apparel, Henri Bendel department store, 1961; owner/designer, Donald Brooks, Inc., 1964–73; designed sweaters for Jane Irwill, 1965; shoes for Newton Elkin, 1966; furs for Coopchik-Forrest, Inc., 1967; furs for Bonwit Teller department store, 1969; robes and sleepwear for Maidenform, shoes for Palizzio; launched Boutique Donald Brooks line, 1969; designed drapery fabrics and bedlinens for Burlington, 1971; DB II line introduced, about 1980; Donald Brooks ready-to-wear, 1986; consultant for fabric and color design, Ann Taylor stores, from 1990; joined Tony awards nominating committee; also designed for theater, film, television, as well as custom clothing, from 1961. **Awards:** Coty American Fashion Critics award, 1958, 1962, 1967, 1974; National Cotton award, 1962; New York Drama Critics award, 1963; Parsons Medal for Distinguished Achievement, 1974; Emmy award, 1982. **Address:** c/o Parson's School of Design, 66 Fifth Avenue, New York NY 10011, U.S.A.

Publications

On BROOKS:

Books

Maeder, Edward, et al., *Hollywood and History: Costume Design in Film,* New York, 1987.

Owen, Bobbie, *Costume Designers on Broadway: Designers and Their Credits 1915–1985,* Westport, Connecticut, 1987.

Milbank, Caroline Rennolds, *New York Fashion: The Evolution of American Style,* New York, 1989.

Leese, Elizabeth, *Costume Design in the Movies,* New York, 1991.

Stegemeyer, Anne, *Who's Who in Fashion, Third Edition,* New York, 1996.

Articles

"Designers Who are Making News," in *American Fashions & Fabrics* (New York), No. 37, 1956.

Morris, Bernadine, "A Return to Fashion Staged with Flair by Donald Brooks," in the *New York Times,* 14 May 1986.

"Parsons Students Strut Theit Stuff," in *Women's Wear Daily,* 4 May 1998.

McBride, Murdoch, "Gotham Gothics Nurture Nightmares on and Off Broadway," in *Back Stage,* 30 October 1998.

Wilson, Eric, "The Sixties—Seizing the Moment, a Band of American Upstarts Lays the Groundwork for a New World Order," in *Women's Wear Daily,* 13 June 2000.

* * *

Staying power characterized Donald Brooks every bit as much as the simply cut, easy fitting dresses in distinctive fabrics for which he is best known. A summer job in the advertising and display department at Lord & Taylor led him into ready-to-wear, first as a sketch artist and subsequently as designer for a series of undistinguished manufacturers. After a stint as designer at Darbury and Hedges of New York, where his work was admired by the fashion press, Brooks moved to Townley Frocks as successor to Claire McCardell. There, Brooks was given his own label as well as the chance to develop his own prize-winning printed fabrics.

By the mid-1960s, Brooks was one of the few American designers to have financial control of his own business. From that base he diversified along the usual lines, designing sweaters, shoes, swimsuits, furnishing fabrics, and other items under a multitude of licensing agreements. At the same time he built a secure base for his custom-made clothes that stood him in good stead throughout the recession years of the 1970s and 1980s. Brooks also developed a parallel career, interpreting the contemporary scene for television, film, and the theater, beginning in 1961. His many stage credits include the musical *No Strings,* which earned him a New York Drama Critics award in 1963, and a nomination for the Antoinette Perry, or Tony award. For his film design Brooks has received four Oscar nominations. The parallel careers often supported one another, as when Brooks' clothes for the film *Star,* set in the 1920s and 1930s, provided the direction for his 1968 ready-to-wear collection.

Brooks' clothes were known for their clean lines, often surprising colors, and for their distinctive fabrics, most of which he himself designed. There is a boldness about a Brooks design that makes an impact and makes his contemporary dresses for the stage particularly successful. The Parsons Medal for Distinguished Achievement has been awarded less than half a dozen times in almost as many decades. Brooks received it in 1974, to join a roster that singled out Adrian, Norman Norell, and Claire McCardell as especially noteworthy American designers.

In the 1990s Brooks enjoyed a myriad of activities related to the many facets of fashion design. He had returned to the theatre as one of the annual Tony awards nominating committee; mentored students at the Parsons School of Design, and participated in the annual Parsons Fashion Critics awards; and designed for the Theater for the New City's Annual Village Halloween Costume Ball.

—Whitney Blausen

BROOKS BROTHERS

American clothier

Established: in New York as Brooks Clothing Company by Henry Sands Brooks, 1818; renamed Brooks Brothers, 1854. **Company History:** First American firm to market such staples as the button-down collar shirt and polo coat; has also sold womenswear from

1940s; opened womenswear department in own New York store, 1976; sold to Marks & Spencer, Plc. by the Campeau Corporation, 1988; expanded into textiles, 1994; opened third New York City store, 1995; revitalized image with new design director, 1996; began work on new flagship store in New York, 1998 (opened, 1999); sustained damage to New York stores during World Trade Center terrorist attack, 2001; sold to Alliance SA, December 2001. **Company Address:** 346 Madison Avenue, New York, NY 10017, U.S.A. **Company Website:** www.brooksbrothers.com.

Publications

By BROOKS BROTHERS:

Books

The Development of Male Apparel, New York, 1901.
Big Game and Little Game: A Brief Survey of the Hunting Fields of the World, New York, 1914.
International Trophies, New York, 1914.
A Catalogue of Clothing and Many Other Things for Men and Boys, New York, 1915.
Brooks Brothers Centenary, New York, 1918.
Brooks' Miscellany & Gentlemen's Intelligencer [several volume set], New York, 1926.
A Chronicle Recording 125 Years...of Brooks Brothers Business, New York, 1943.
Christmas 1988, Our 170th Year—Gift Selections for Men and Boys, New York, 1988.

On BROOKS BROTHERS:

Books

Roscho, Bernard, *The Rag Race,* New York, 1963.
Fucini, Joseph, and Suzy Fucini, *Entrepreneurs,* Boston, 1965.
Boyer, G. Bruce, *Elegance,* New York, 1985.
Milbank, Caroline Rennolds, *New York Fashion: The Evolution of American Style,* New York, 1989.

Articles

Millstein, Gilbert, "The Suits on the Brooks Brothers Men," in the *New York Times Magazine,* 15 August 1976.
Attanasio, Paul, "Summer of Size 42," in *Esquire,* June 1986.
"Taking Over an American Tradition," in *Management Today,* May 1988.
Graham, Judith, "Brooks Bros. Spiffs Up Its Image," in *Advertising Age,* 30 October 1989.
Barron, James, "Pleats? Cardigan Cuddling? Brooks Brothers Unbuttons," in the *New York Times,* 11 November 1989.
Barmash, Isadore, "Brooks Brothers Stays the Course," in the *New York Times,* 23 November 1990.
Better, Nancy Marx, "Unbuttoning Brooks Brothers," in *M Inc.,* March 1991.
Palmieri, Jean E., "When Brooks Put Fashion on the Front," in *DNR,* 11 March 1991.
Guzman, "He Ain't Stuffy, He's Brooks Brothers," in *Esquire,* September 1991.
Palmieri, Jean E., "An American Icon Celebrated a Milestone; Brooks Brothers Still Spry at 175," in *DNR,* 31 May 1993.
Plimpton, George, "Under the Golden Fleece," in *American Heritage,* November 1993.
"Brooks Bros. Goes into the Textile Biz," in *DNR,* 13 October 1994.
Palmieri, Jean E., "Brooks Brothers Finds Its Colorful Past," in *DNR,* 15 July 1996.
Fallon, James, "Brooks Bros. Plans Opening of 24 Stores," in *Women's Wear Daily,* 24 February 1999.
Palmieri, Jean E., "Brooks Brothers: The Inside Story," in *DNR,* 25 June 2001.
Edgecliffe-Johnson, Andrew, "Buyers Line Up for Brooks Brothers," in the *Financial Times,* 30 June 2001.
Curan, Catherine, "Downtown Retailers Rocked But Unbowed—Brooks Brothers...Hopes to Press on in Area," in *Crain's New York Business,* 17 September 2001.
Anderson, Katie, "Marks & Spencer Postpones Brooks Sale," in the *Daily Deal,* 18 September 2001.

* * *

Brooks Brothers is one of the oldest clothiers in America; a company with a distinctive image of quiet good taste. Henry Sands Brooks first opened the store under his own name in 1818. His sons Henry, Daniel, John, Elisha, and Edward, officially changed the name to Brooks Brothers in 1854.

Since the beginning, Brooks Brothers has been innovative. When Henry Sr. first opened his doors in New York, he offered ready-to-wear clothing for sailors who were in port for short periods of time and who had no time to have their clothing custom tailored. Henry Sr. also offered or custom-tailored clothing for the gentry, professionals, and the well-to-do. For more than 100 years Brooks made military uniforms, including those for Civil War Generals Lee, Sheridan, Grant, and Custer. George Bush was one of the many U.S. presidents who wore Brooks Brothers clothes, while President Abraham Lincoln was wearing a Brooks' frock coat the night he was shot.

Brooks Brothers introduced many new styles to men's fashion. The firm adapted the button-down collar from shirts the English wore playing polo; introduced the so-called sack suit, which had as little padding as possible and became a staple of businessmen's wardrobes with its understated design. In 1890 they introduced madras clothing, in 1904 Shetland wool sweaters, in 1910 the camel hair polo coat, in 1930 the lightweight summer suit, and in 1953 came the wash-and-wear shirt. Mainstays in the Brooks line have included the foulard tie, khakis, and the navy blazer. These are all part of the so-called Ivy League styles associated with the Ivy League schools of America. People who wear Brooks Brothers clothes are generally not concerned with fashion, but with stylish good looks. Lawrence Wortzel summed up the look in *Forbes,* by saying "if Brooks dressed you, no one would laugh."

The Brooks image is so distinctive American authors have used it in their work: Mary McCarthy wrote a short story called, "Man in the Brooks Brothers Suit." F. Scott Fitzgerald dressed his characters in Brooks clothes, just as they were worn by John O'Hara's good guys.

While Brooks has always been a clothier for men and boys, surreptitiously women also bought their clothes for themselves, often resorting to purchasing their goods in the boys' department for sizing. They, too, wanted good quality and exceptional design. Brooks Brothers did provide clothing for women as early as the mid-1940s, introducing Shetland wool sweaters. In 1949 *Vogue* magazine showed a model wearing a pink Brooks Brothers button-down collar shirt. It was not until 1976, however, that Brooks officially opened a small women's department at the back of their store in New York.

Known throughout the world, Brooks Brothers was bought by the English firm of Marks & Spencer, with stores in Tokyo as well as throughout the United States. No matter where the label is found, the style is Brooks Brothers, and no adjustments are made for regional or national differences. In a *New York Times* article, Lawrence Van Gelder called Brooks Brothers a "bastion of sartorial conservatism." It would be easy to classify Brooks as stodgy, old-fashioned, and showing little concern for fashion, but this would be erroneous. Brooks Brothers clothes were not revolutionary when it comes to design, but evolutionary. While not at the forefront of fashion, Brooks' style has quietly maintained a classic style evolving to meet the needs of the times. In the 1918 centenary, Brooks Brothers advised that one "be not the first by whom the new is tried, nor yet the last to lay the old aside."

At the dawn of its second century, Brooks remained a steadfast leader in beautifully tailored, conservative style—though the firm made a few concessions to keep abreast of the times. With the advent of casual dressing in the corporate world, Brooks Brothers reluctantly relaxed some of its clothing to reflect the growing workplace trend. Additionally, new stand-alone womenswear stores were planned for the next several years, as were more traditional Brooks Brothers shops in the U.S. and worldwide. Yet a downturn in the menswear market and falling sales took their toll, and rumors swirled for two years before the firm's parent announced its intention to sell the retailer. Among the high profile contenders was Tommy Hilfiger Corp., Polo Ralph Lauren, Men's Warehouse, Claudio Del Vecchio, May Department Stores, and Dickson North America.

Plans by Marks & Spencer to sell the company were abruptly put on hold in fall 2001. Retailing and dealmaking were stopped cold by the devastation in New York City on 11 September 2001. A newly-renovated store at Liberty Plaza, near the World Trade Center, was destroyed by debris when terrorists leveled the center, while another in the area was used as makeshift morgue. In December of that year, Marks & Spencer found its buyer, Alliance SA, and Brooks Brothers was sold.

—Nancy House; updated by Nelly Rhodes

BRUCE, Liza

American designer working in London

Born: New York City, 21 September 1954. **Family:** Married Nicholas Barker (divorced); married Nicholas Alvis-Vega.**Career:** Designed high-end bathing suits, from 1982; began designing ready-to-wear, 1988; launched outerwear designs, 1989. **Address:** 37 Warple Way, London W3, England.

Publications

On BRUCE:

Books

Stegemeyer, Anne, *Who's Who in Fashion, Third Edition,* New York, 1996.

Articles

Polan, Brenda, "So Long as the Octopus Giggles," in *The Guardian* (London), 6 June 1985.

"Designs Do Swimmingly," in *Chicago Tribune,* 4 December 1985.

"Creative Collaborators," in *Harper's Bazaar,* June 1989.

Starzinger, Page Hill, "Out of the Water, Onto the Street" in *Vogue,* June 1990.

Jeal, Nicola, "Truly, Madly, Modern," in *Elle* (London), May 1993.

Baker, Lindsay, "A Room of My Own," in *The Observer* (London), 10 June 1993.

Spindler, Amy M., "Color It with Silver and Spice," in the *New York Times,* 4 November 1993.

D'Innocenzio, Anne, "Bruce's New Moves," *Women's Wear Daily,* 4 May 1995.

Fallon, James, "Liza With a Z," *Women's Wear Daily,* 26 February 1998.

Aldersley-Williams, Hugh, "The Swimsuit Issue: Liza Bruce Opens Swimsuit Store," in the *New Statesman,* 27 February 1998.

D'Innocenzio, Anne, "Liza Bruce Opens Soho Store," in *Women's Wear Daily,* 10 February 2000.

* * *

Lean, pared-down shapes, devoid of decoration or unnecessary seams, dominate Liza Bruce's work. Shaped with Lycra, her clothes cling to the body. She has removed tight clothing from its conventional daring context and defined notion of simple stretch garments as the basis for the modern wardrobe in the mid-1980s. Her designs are founded on the flattering silhouette they produce, emphasizing shape while narrowing the frame.

Her background in swimwear design, which continues in her collections, has given her a confidence in working with the female form. Although at first her stretch luster crêpe leggings made some women feel too self-conscious and underdressed, they became the ultimate example of 1980s innovation and were soon a staple in the fashion world, taken up by the 1984 revival interest in synthetics.

Minimalist shape was one of the early examples of her highly recognizable style. She has built on the garments that supplement her streamlined swimwear range, originally modeled on bodybuilder Lisa Lyons, who embodied the toned strength of Bruce's design. Her swimsuits and closely related bodices produce the characteristic smooth line that pervades her work, some in stark black and white with scooped-out necklines (in 1989), others more delicate and decorative. In 1992, soft peach bodies were sprinkled with self-colored beads across the breast area.

Bruce's detailing maintains the aerodynamic line of her clothes while adding definition and interest to their usual matte simplicity. In 1992 she also produced columnlike sheath dresses and skirts that clung to the ankle like a second skin, punctuated by beads at regular intervals down their sides, which were quickly copied throughout London. The subtle sophistication of such tubular styles avoided the pervasive retro fashion of the year; indeed, Bruce's work, based as it is on easy-to-wear, timeless separates, pays only lip service to current trends. In 1990 this took the form of catsuits made of a black crêpe and Lycra-mix with fake fur collars, and her 1993 collection nodded toward deconstructionist styles, with shrunken mohair jumpers, crumpled silk shifts, and narrow coats with external seams. It was perhaps inevitable that her work incorporated such touches as her outerwear range, begun back in 1989, and further expanded.

Bruce's signature is most strongly stamped on the lean, sculptured stretchwear she consistently produces. It presents an ideal of modernity in its streamlined design, confident shape, and essential minimalism. She was able to build on these basic garments as her confidence as a designer of outerwear grew, enabling her to incorporate contemporary fashion preoccupations into more tailored pieces which complement and expand upon the postmodernist tenets of her style. Her popularity in the fashion world has been firmly established and her appeal to confident, independent women—who appreciate simple yet sexy clothes bereft of unnecessary detail—continues to grow.

During the mid-1990s, Bruce expanded her product line in the U.S. while maintaining her large showroom and studio in London. She opened a large showroom in New York offering more affordable swimwear and activewear, and introduced a fragrance. Bruce wanted to have a home base in the U.S. to better serve her American clients, who include Barneys, Marks & Spencer, Charivari, and Saks Fifth Avenue. Yet in 1996 Bruce went into a voluntary liquidation of her wholesale business due to several financial factors, including a long copyright dispute with Marks & Spencer and the bankruptcy of her biggest account, Barneys New York. After a few years of regrouping, Bruce opened a small retail shop in London, selling to only a few selective American clients such as Bergdorf Goodman, Neiman Marcus, Saks Fifth Avenue, and Harvey Nichols. Her new business once again features her popular swimwear, lingerie, and sportswear, and she planned to add jewelry and footwear.

The new London retail business was successful, and in 1999 Bruce returned to the U.S. and opened a store on Melrose Avenue in Los Angeles. The following year she opened a small, 350-square-foot shop in Manhattan's Soho district. Of the new shop, Bruce told *Women's Wear Daily,* "It has a closet-like effect. I'm into how clothes interact with the interior."

Bruce's new approach of opening smaller, more intimate stores appeals to her desire to veer away from commercialism. Her new sportswear collections feature the same wearable and functional fabrics as she has used for her swimwear—modern fabrics that travel well. She has added Velcro closures to her clingy and stretchy pieces, and on some of her pieces she has haphazardly sewn in a label that reads, "Luscious Bitch."

—Rebecca Arnold; updated by Christine Miner Minderovic

BRUNO MAGLI

Italian footwear and accessories firm

Founded: in 1936 by designer Bruno Magli and siblings Marino and Maria; **Company History:** Moved out of basement and into factory, 1947; opened first retail store, 1967; U.S. operations formed by Rolf Grueterich, mid-1970s; began franchising retail locations, 1980s; gained notoriety and increased sales during the O.J. Simpson trial, 1996; Magli by Monica launched, designed by Bruno's granddaughter, Monica, 2000; controlling share purchased by investment firm Opera, 2001. **Company Address:** Via Larga 33, 40138 Bologna, Italy. **Company Website:** www.brunomagli.it.

Publications

On BRUNO MAGLI:

Articles

Schiro, Anne-Marie, "New Paths for Bruno Magli," in the *New York Times,* 11 August 1992.

Newman, Jill, "Bruno Magli Goes for It All," in *WWD,* 21 August 1992.

Ilari, Alessandra, "A Bruno Magli Comeback in the Cards?" in *Footwear News,* 1 August 1994.

Zargoni, Luisa, "Decorating Rita," in *Footwear News,* 7 August 1995.

Corwin, Miles, "Brush With Infamy Makes Products Shine," in the *Los Angeles Times,* 8 April 1997.

Schneider-Levy, Barbara, "Burgeoning Bruno," in *Footwear News,* 2 August 1999.

DeMartini, Marilyn, "Modern Appeal," in *Footwear News,* 8 May 2000.

Lenetz, Dana, "Opera Out to Build Bruno Magli into Powerhouse," in *Footwear News,* 3 September 2001.

* * *

Italian manufacturer Bruno Magli is known for its high-end, well-crafted, classically styled shoes. Launched as a women's footwear manufacturer in 1936, the company expanded into men's shoes and later into accessories and select apparel. By the 21st century it was an $83-million manufacturer and retailer of shoes, leather and fabric accessories, and leather clothing.

Designer Bruno Magli, son of a cobbler, founded the company along with his sister, Maria, who sewed the uppers, and brother, Marino, who was responsible for the soles. The firm grew quickly and, over the next six decades or so became a huge industrial concern in Italy, always remaining (until 2001) under family control. In 1947, the firm moved out of the family basement into its first factory, expanding into men's shoes during the same decade.

In 1967 the company opened its first retail store (it moved into franchising as a means of expanding its retail operations in the 1980s) and two years later, in 1969, moved to a larger, more modern factory, which it continues to occupy today. Despite the use of the latest in modern technology, much of the craftsmanship in Bruno Magli footwear continues to be done by hand; 30 people touch each shoe during the course of its manufacture.

In the early 1990s the company began to take a new direction in its women's business both in Italy and abroad, branching out from its classic styles such as slingbacks and pumps (which remained an important part of the line) into zebra stripes and polka dot sandals and boots. At the same time, the firm expanded into apparel and accessories in denim, leather, and animal prints. Many of these changes were credited to Rolf Grueterich, who had handled the men's shoe business in the U.S. for 14 years and had recently taken over the women's side in America as well. As women's footwear was trending toward the contemporary during this period, the men's styles were taking a turn back to the classic.

Company sales in U.S. skyrocketed in 1996, thanks to the Bruno Magli brand's role in the O.J. Simpson murder trial, in which its shoes took center stage as evidence. The increased brand recognition, albeit with a certain amount of infamy, caused U.S. sales to rise by 50 percent in early 1997, after a rise of 35 percent in 1996, both attributed to the Simpson connection. Although the company welcomed the added sales, it discontinued the Lorenzo model, of which Simpson reportedly owned a pair and referred to them during the trial as "ugly-ass shoes," despite the fact he was seen wearing them in many photos.

Starting in the mid-1990s and continuing through the early 2000s, Bruno Magli began to update its image, under the direction of Rita Magli. Stores and shoe designs were updated for a consistent global look. Previously, designs had been tailored to each country, and retail outlets placed more focus on the product and less on store décor. Since 2000, Bruno Magli concentrated on its worldwide image, with new store designs, advertising, styles, materials and colors. Bruno Magli U.S. president Peter Grueterich (Rolf's son) told *Footwear News* (8 May 2000) the company was "making a transition from classic to modern."

The goal was to create an entire collection for men and women that was fashion forward yet maintained the quality always associated with the company. One facet of the firm's new direction was to hire Bruno Magli's granddaughter, Monica, to design a label called Magli by Monica, which was targeted to a more youthful market than for which it had historically aimed. Bruno Magli also added high-end custom footwear for men and its first men's sportswear line. The apparel mirrored its three men's footwear tiers, Platinum, Modern, and Sport.

In 2001, the Luxembourg-based investment fund Opera, half owned by Bulgari, acquired a controlling interest in Bruno Magli, representing the first time the founding family lost majority ownership. The firm planned to use the cash to expand its international presence; as part of the deal, Bruno Magli and Opera also acquired Bruno Magli's U.S. operations which managed many franchising and licensing agreements. At the time of the acquisition, Bruno Magli had 60 stores around the world, five of which were wholly-owned, and generated the vast majority of its sales from outside Italy.

Bruno Magli manufactures more than a million pairs of shoes and 60,000 handbags (always coordinated with the footwear) per year. From the beginning, the firm's shoes were purchased by many celebrities; current customers range from Hillary Clinton to Queen Elizabeth II of England. The company retains its dedication to quality—its designs are sometimes likened to architecture—and boasts several products on display at New York's Museum of Modern Art.

—Karen Raugust

BURBERRY

British clothiers

Founded: in 1856. Originally a draper's shop in Basingstoke, Hampshire, founded by Thomas Burberry (1835–1926), and specializing in waterproof overcoats. **Company History:** Opened London store in the Haymarket, 1891; trenchcoat introduced, 1901; Burberry established as a trademark, 1909; women's clothing lines added, and Paris branch opened, 1910; bought by Great Universal Stores, 1955; New York branch opened, 1978; toiletries line introduced, 1981; fragrances introduced, 1991; Christy Turlington ads make plaid trench chic again, 1993; Anne Marie Bravo hired as chief executive, 1997; Roberto Menichetti hired as head designer, 1998; Menichetti departs, replaced by Christopher Bailey, 2001; New York store refurbished and expanded, 2001; public offering of shares planned, 2002. **Exhibitions:** Victoria and Albert Museum, London, 1989. **Company Address:** 29–53 Chatham Place, Hackney, London E9 6LP, England. **Company Website:** www.gusplc.co.uk/burberry/html.

Burberry, spring 2001 collection. © AP/Wide World Photos/Fashion Wire Daily.

Publications

By BURBERRYS:

Books

Burberrys: An Elementary History of a Great Tradition, London.
The Story of the Trenchcoat, London, 1993.

On BURBERRYS:

Books

Garrulus, Coracias, ed., *Open Spaces,* London.
Coatts, Margot, *The Burberry Story* [exhibition catalogue], London, 1989.

Articles

Brady, James, "Going Back to the Trenches," in the *New York Post*, 10 October 1978.

Morris, Bernadine, "Coat Maker Marks 125 Years in the Rain," in the *New York Times*, 21 January 1981.

Gleizes, Serge, "Burberry's Story," in *L'Officiel* (Paris), October 1986.

Britton, Noelle, "Burberry Brightens Its Image," in *Marketing,* 11 February 1988.

Kanner, Bernice, "Scents of Accomplishment," in *New York,* 18 March 1991.

White, Constance C.R., "Excitement at Burberry," in the *New York Times,* 31 December 1996.

Goldstein, Lauren, "Dressing Up an Old Brand," in *Fortune,* 9 November 1998.

Schiro, Anne-Marie, "Burberry Modernizes and Reinvents Itself," in the *New York Times,* 5 January 1999.

Menkes, Suzy, "Durable Chic: A Century of the Trench," in the *International Herald Tribune,* 4 April 2000.

Heller, Richard, "A British Gucci," in *Forbes,* 3 April 2000.

Profile, "Stretching the Plaid: Face Value," in the *Economist,* 3 February 2001.

Voyle, Susanna, "Burberry Nets Gucci Designer," in the *Financial Times,* 4 May 2001.

Kapner, Suzanne, "Suddenly Less Plaid is More for Burberry's Chief," in the *New York Times,* 24 June 2001.

* * *

Burberry was founded by Thomas Burberry (1835–1926), the inventor of the Burberry waterproof coat. The origin of the term "Burberry" to describe the famous waterproof garments is thought to have derived from the fact that Edward VII was in the habit of commanding, "Give me my Burberry," although Burberry himself had christened his invention "Gabardinee."

The original shooting and fishing garments were produced in response to the perceived need for the ideal waterproof—one that would withstand wind and rain to a reasonable degree and yet allow air to reach the body. From Thomas Burberry's original drapery shop in Basingstoke, Hampshire, in 1856 to the opening of its prestigious premises in London's Haymarket in 1891, Burberrys has employed what the trade journal *Men's Wear* of June 1904 termed "splendid advertising media" to promote their clothing. Some of the earliest advertising read, "T. Burberry's Gabardinee—for India and the Colonies is the most suitable of materials. It resists hot and cold winds, rain or thorns, and forms a splendid top garment for the coldest climates."

Endorsement was given at the beginning of the century by both Roald Amundsen, on his expedition to the South Pole, who wrote from Hobart on 18 March 1912: "Heartiest thanks. Burberry overalls were made extensive use of during the sledge journey to the Pole and proved real good friends indeed," and Captain Scott, whose Burberry gabardine tent used on his sledge journey "Furthest South" was exhibited at the Bruton Galleries in that same year. Burberry also produced menswear and womenswear for motoring from the earliest appearance of the motor car, or as their illustrated catalogues put it, "Burberry adapts itself to the exigencies of travel in either closed or open cars…and at the same time satisfies every ideal of good taste and distinction."

Burberry, spring 2001 collection. © AP/Wide World Photos/Fashion Wire Daily.

The turn-of-the-century appeal to the ideal of "taste and distinction" always proved a potent force in the appeal of Burberry designs. The traditional Burberry Check and the New House Checks are protected as part of the UK trademark registration and are now used in a wide range of Burberry designs, from the traditional use as a lining for weathercoats to men's, women's, and children's outerwear, a range of accessories and luggage, toiletries, and several collections of Swiss-made watches featuring the Burberry Check and the trademark Prorsum Horse.

In the 1980s such distinctive goods satisfied the desire for label clothes in their appeal to young consumers as well as to traditional buyers both in Britain and abroad. In the 1990s the diversity of goods designed by Burberry, from a countrywide home shopping and visiting tailor service in Great Britain, to an internationally available range of Fine Foods proved the efficacy of the Burberry tradition. The company's power as an international household name signifying an instantly identifiable traditional Englishness is attested by the fact that "Burberry" and the logo of the equestrian knight in armor are registered trademarks.

Near the end of the 20th century, Rose Marie Bravo, who was credited with the turnaround of Saks Fifth Avenue, was brought in to revitalize the company and its image. With Asia, its biggest market, rocked by economic woes and flooding the market with grey goods, Bravo set about rebuilding the Burberry brand in the UK and Europe, and to control licensing by selling only to select luxury retailers. She also hired Italian-American Roberto Menichetti as her new head designer in 1998, who quickly made Burberry's Prorsum brand fashion's hottest ticket for women. Then, with the recognizable Burberry plaid on everything in sight, from swimwear and baby clothes to shoes and dog accessories, Bravo scaled back to avoid overexposure, cleverly hiding the trademarked pattern in a wide range of nonplaid garments.

Burberry took a hit when designer Menichetti left the company. Replaced with the virtually unknown Christopher Bailey from Gucci in 2001, Bravo hoped Bailey could bring a cohesive style to all of the Burberry clothing, though he would be responsible only for the Prorsum line.

Parent company Great Universal Stores was planning a public offering of Burberrys shares sometime in 2002, and continued an aggressive expansion to increase its presence in France, Italy, and the United States. In the U.S., which accounted for only a fifth of the retailer's worldwide sales, several new Burberry stores were slated to open in smaller upscale malls while the New York City flagship store on East 57th Street underwent extensive renovation and expansion. Burberrys also planned to open its first store in Beverly Hills.

With the Burberry name once again firmly entrenched as a fashion must-have, the 145-year old company has proven that its plaid will never go out of style. Looking back at her odyssey of pulling Burberry back from the brink of extinction, Bravo told *Forbes* in April 2000, "Coming in, I had studied Hermès and Gucci and other great brands, and it struck me that even during the periods when they had dipped a bit, they never lost the essence of whatever made those brands sing." With Bravo on board, Burberry has once again hit a high note.

—Doreen Ehrlich; updated by Owen James

BURROWS, Stephen

American designer

Born: Newark, New Jersey, 15 September 1943. **Education:** Philadelphia Museum College of Art, 1961–62; fashion design, Fashion Institute of Technology, New York, 1964–66. **Career:** Designer, Weber Originals, New York, 1966–67; supplier to Allen & Cole, circa 1967–68; manager (with Roz Rubenstein), O Boutique, 1968–69; owner, Stephen Burrows' World Boutique, Henri Bendel store, New York, 1970–73; founder/director, Burrows, Inc., New York, 1973–76; designer, Henri Bendel, 1977–82, 1993; returned to ready-to-wear design, 1989, and to custom design, 1990; designed knitwear line for Tony Lambert Company, 1991. **Exhibitions:** Versailles Palace, 1973. **Awards:** Coty American Fashion Critics special award (lingerie), 1974; "Winnie," 1977; Council of American Fashion Critics award, 1975; Knitted Textile Association Crystal Ball award, 1975.

Publications

On BURROWS:

Books

Morris, Bernadine, and Barbara Walz, *The Fashion Makers,* New York, 1978.

Milbank, Caroline Rennolds, *New York Fashion: The Evolution of American Style,* New York, 1989.

Stegemeyer, Anne, *Who's Who in Fashion, Third Edition,* New York, 1996.

Articles

Morris, Bernadine, "The Look of Fashions for the Seventies—In Colors that Can Dazzle," in the *New York Times,* 12 August 1970.

Fulman, Ricki, "Designer Has Last Laugh on His Critics," in the *New York Daily News,* 4 October 1971.

Klensch, Elsa, "Burrows: I Am Growing More," in *Women's Wear Daily,* 6 April 1972.

Carter, M. R., "The Story of Stephen Burrows," in *Mademoiselle,* March 1975.

Butler, J., "Burrows is Back—With a Little Help from His Friends," in the *New York Times Magazine,* 5 June 1977.

Talley, Andre Leon, "Black Designers Surviving in Style," in *Ebony,* November 1980.

Hunter, Norman L., "The Drama of Femininity for Evening and Cocktail," in *Ebony,* March 1981.

Schiro, Anne-Marie, "Stephen Burrows, Sportswear Designer," in the *New York Times,* 3 September 1989.

Morris, Bernadine, "Color and Curves from Burrows," in the *New York Times,* 9 January 1990.

———, "The Rebirth of New York Couture," in the *New York Times,* 1 May 1990.

———, "The Return of an American Original," in the *New York Times,* 10 August 1993.

"Black Designers," in *Jet,* 17 May 1999.

* * *

Phoenix and firebird of the New York fashion world, Stephen Burrows is one of the most audacious and auspicious talents in contemporary fashion. "Pure genius," said Roz Rubenstein Johnson of Burrows in a telephone interview in 2001. As Bernadine Morris said of Burrows, he is "incapable of making banal clothes." When creating custom-made clothes in the 1990s, Burrows insisted he would make only one dress of a kind. He told Morris, "Why not? I have plenty of ideas—I don't have to repeat myself."

There were relatively few African American designers at all in 1970 and certainly none who had achieved any kind of stature. Pauline Trigère was one of the first to begin using dark-skinned models, which set the fashion world abuzz with shock. Then came Ann Lowe and Burrows, the first African Americans to achieve stature as designers. Today, there are numerous African American designers, ranging from Bonga Bhengu and Bongiwe Walaza to Heather Jones and Patrick Robinson.

Burrows worked as a designer for Weber Originals in New York and supplied feathered vests he made to Allen & Cole in the mid-1960s before becoming the co-manager, with Rubenstein, of James Valkus' boutique in New York, called O, in 1968. When the boutique closed in 1969, Burrows was given his own boutique in the Henri Bendel department store by its president, Geraldine Stutz. Rubenstein, meanwhile, was hired to be the jewelry buyer there and eventually went on to found her own public relations company in California, with clients such as John Paul Mitchell Systems in her portfolio.

With the 1970 launch of Stephen Burrows' World Boutique within the Henri Bendel store, Burrows was catapulted into the limelight, being recognized for his remarkable color block, fluid, flirting with the *nonfinito,* sexy separates that typified the assertive woman of the 1970s. Spectacularly successful during that decade, Burrows has enjoyed alternating periods of triumph and quiescence in the subsequent years, with forays into sportswear in the early 1990s, custom-made clothing in the 1980s, and evening wear in 1993, again for Henri Bendel. He has come and gone and come again in the public gaze, partly for business reasons, but his design sensibility has been consistent. He sees bold color fields and tests color dissonance to achieve remarkable new harmony. His great mentor, Geraldine Stutz, erstwhile president of Bendel's, commented that he "stretches a rainbow over the body." But Burrows' rainbow has never sought a Peter Max popularity; his rainbow is extraordinary and unexpected, juxtaposing the strongest colors.

Serviceable separates have always been a large part of Burrows' look. Even his flirtatious dresses of the 1970s, often with his characteristic lettuce edging, seem to be parts when broken by color blocks and zones. As a result, his clothing always seems unaffected and young in the tradition of American sportswear. Clinging jersey, curving lines, and offsetting of easy drape by tight cling make Burrows' clothing both comfortable and very sexy. Of his 1990 collections, the designer himself said, "The dresses are sexy. Women should have an escort when they wear them."

Like Giorgio di Sant'Angelo and, to a lesser degree, Halston, Burrows was the quintessential fashion expression of the 1970s in a disestablishment sensibility, young nonchalance, and unfailing insistence on looking beautiful. Native American themes (also explored by Sant'Angelo in 1969 and 1970), bold color fields in jersey with exposed seams as edges, and the unfinished appearance of puckered lettuce edging seemed almost careless in 1969 and 1970 when invented by Burrows, but they can also be recognized as hallmarks of a truthful, youthful culture demanding no deceit in dress and a return to basics. If Burrows never yielded the sensuality of the body, he again prefigured the last quarter of the century as the body becomes the inevitable discourse of a society freed of Victorianism only at its end. His honesty in technique is an "infra-apparel" trait, betokening a strong feeling for clothing's process, not merely a superficial result. Ricki Fulman, of the *New York Daily News* suggested that "you've got to have a sense of humor to understand Stephen Burrows' clothes."

If the clothing offers an immediacy and vivacity, Burrows himself and the recognition received in his twenties were a comparable phenomenon. Emerging from among the Bendel's designers in 1969, Burrows was a world-class Coty award-winning talent in the early to mid-1970s and was one of the five designers selected to represent American fashion in the epochal showing at Versailles in November 1973.

Although Burrows may have offered fresh ideas in palette and color combination, he was also sustaining a sportswear idea. Even his laced cords and snaps have affinity with Claire McCardell's germinal work. Many designers after Burrows have looked to African American, African, and Latin styles for inspiration and especially to the sexy zest he found there for his designs. Elsa Klensch argued that the name "Stephen Burrows' World" was more than a store sign. "It is his own world—a philosophy, a lifestyle, an environment," one composed of astute street observation, a lively sense of contemporary living and its impatience with rules and convention, and of a nonverbal self-communication through clothing. As much as Halston and Sant'Angelo, Burrows was the avatar of new styles accorded to a cultural transfiguration in the 1970s. Perhaps he so personified the early 1970s that his later erratic career was inevitable: we have sacrificed our fullest appreciation of him to another sexy lady he dressed, Clio.

Burrows did design work for Tony Lambert Company in 1991 and Bendel in 1993, but with the departure of Stutz from Bendel's (she went on to work for Gump's in San Francisco), his visibility faded. His designer clothing, however, is considered collectible and can still be found for sale at such places as Keni Valenti Retro-Couture in New York. He currently resides in New York, and as Rubenstein said, "Whenever he has a pencil in his hand, he is always drawing," so there may be more innovations forthcoming from this fashion mogul.

—Richard Martin; updated by Daryl F. Mallett

BYBLOS

Italian fashion house

Founded: in 1973 as a division of Genny SpA. **Company History:** Independent company formed, circa 1983; designers have included Versace and Guy Paulin; principal designers, since 1981, Alan Cleaver and Keith Varty; collections include Byblos Uomo, 1983, Byblos USA, and Options Donna, 1985, Vis à Vis Byblos, 1986, and

Byblos, fall/winter 2001–02 collection. © AP/Wide World Photos.

Options Uomo, 1988; Cleaver and Varty dismissed, 1996; Richard Tyler debuts first collection for Byblos, 1997; Tyler and Byblos end relationship, Richard Barlett takes over as creative director, 1998; Barlett leaves Byblos, 2000; Martine Sitbon hired as women's creative director and Sandy Dalal as men's creative director, 2001. **Company Address:** Via Maggini 126, 60127 Ancona, Italy.

Publications

On BYBLOS:

Articles

Buckley, Richard, "Byblos: The Boys' Own Story," in *DNR: The Magazine* (New York), January 1985.

Haynes, Kevin, "Leave It to Byblos," in *Women's Wear Daily,* 5 June 1985.

Elms, Robert, "Italian Fashion: The British Connection," in the *Sunday Express Magazine* (London), 9 February 1986.

Frey, Nadine, "Varty and Cleaver: Revitalizing Byblos," in *Women's Wear Daily,* 28 April 1987.

Harris, Lara, "La Sera di Byblos," in *Donna* (Milan), October 1987.

Phillips, Kathy, "Men of the Cloth," in *You,* magazine of the *Mail on Sunday* (London), 8 November 1987.

Lomas, Jane, "Byblos Brits," in the *Observer* (London), 24 April 1988.

Cook, Cathy, "Boys Just Wanna Have Fun," in *Taxi* (New York), March 1989.

Racht, Tione, "Der Byblos Stil," in *Vogue* (Munich), March 1989.

Lobrano, Alexander, "Both Sides of Byblos," in *DNR,* 19 June 1989.

Ozzard, Janet, "Byblos Boys Out After 15 Years, as Milan Firm Appoints Richard Tyler," in *Women's Wear Daily,* 12 November 1996.

Conti, Samantha, "Behind the Purge at Byblos," in *DNR,* 4 December 1996.

Forden, Sara Gay, "Cleaver and Varty Seeking Compensation From Byblos," in *Women's Wear Daily,* 31 July 1997.

Conti, Samantha, and Miles Socha, "Bartlett Already Sketching for Byblos," in *Women's Wear Daily,* 9 April 1998.

Ilari, Alessandra, "Bartlett Paring Down His Steamy Side for Byblos Collection," in *DNR,* 26 June 1998.

Ozzard, Janet, "Bartlett, Byblos Part Company," in *Women's Wear Daily,* 21 March 2000.

Dodd, Annmarie, et al., "Bartlett to Take Front Row Seat at Byblos," in *DNR,* 26 June 2000.

"Byblos Appoints Martine Sitbon as Women's Creative Director," in *Women's Wear Daily,* 19 March 2001.

Brown, Wendell, "Byblos Names Sandy Dalal Creative Director," in *DNR,* 21 March 2001.

* * *

Byblos takes its name from a hotel in St. Tropez, France. Since its inception in 1973, it has been a kind of international grand hotel of design, starting with a group of stylists, then engaging the Milanese Gianni Versace as designer from 1975 to 1976, then Frenchman Guy Paulin, and finally Keith Varty from the Royal College of Art in London via a period in Paris at Dorothée Bis with Alan Cleaver. Varty and Cleaver became the personification of Byblos objectives: a young line, international, with panache, and a carefree, optimistic nonchalance. In the 1980s, the market-acute colorful palettes and relaxed resort-influenced informality of Cleaver and Varty for Byblos became a young lingua franca in fashion for the twentysomething and thirtysomething generations.

Byblos, autumn/winter 2000–01 ready-to-wear collection: dress with embroidered black pearls. © AFP/CORBIS.

What Varty and Cleaver lacked was any sense of the sinister or cynical: they were intent upon making clothes that were fun and exuberant. Varty described their design challenge to *Women's Wear Daily* in 1987: "Our product has to be salable, in the right fabrics with this young image and it's got to be fresh every season." The crux of the Cleaver-Varty achievement was color—they brought Matisse colors to clothing, captured aubergines and gingers with a grocer's discrimination and knew the earth colors of every part of the globe with a geologist's imagination. The *Daily News Record* (11 January 1989) rightly described the menswear: "Gold at the end of the rainbow. If anyone can make color successfully commercial, it's Keith Varty and Alan Cleaver for Byblos." They were to contemporary fashion what David Hockney is to contemporary art: British travel, observation, effervescence, and childlike delight in the world's bright colors.

Travel and exoticism was an important theme in Cleaver and Varty's work, reflecting their vacationing in Marrakech, Hawaii, and the South Pacific; a recurring spirit of the American West (especially in their menswear); old-Havana machismo; and their love of tropical colors and refreshing prints inspired by Southeast Asia and South America. In 1987 resort collections, the voyage was specific, with big skirts featuring postcards from the Bahamas and maps of islands. Fiesta brights were almost invariably featured in the spring and resort collections, with options for khaki, chocolates, mud, and tobacco brown. If the spring 1987 collections seemed like the British in India, their colonialism was mellowed by supple shapes, fluid lines, and khaki silk poplin. In 1988, the trek was to Russia in a savagely romantic display of fake fur, folkloric embroidery and motifs, and grand silhouettes that *Women's Wear Daily* (29 February 1988) called "Anna Karenina comes to Milan."

It seemed unlikely that the sun would ever set on these two brilliant adventurers who had done so much to establish the Byblos style. Yet Byblos experienced turmoil and turnover beginning in the mid-1990s and in 1996 Varty and Cleaver were dismissed after 15 years with the company. Sales had been in decline, and the two were accused of a lack of innovation; while the remainder of the fashion industry was moving on to more sophisticated, elegant creations, they continued with the fun, colorful fashions they had been known for since the early 1980s.

Varty and Cleaver's replacement was Richard Tyler, who debuted his first Byblos collection in Milan for fall 1997. Tyler's emphasis on simplicity in his designs, along with his popularity in the U.S., where Byblos generated 10 percent of its sales at the time were two of the factors that encouraged Byblos' parent company, Genny, to hire him. Tyler, who continued to design his own label concurrently with his work for Byblos, lasted only a year and a half with the house, being replaced by John Bartlett in 1998.

Bartlett, whose first collection was for spring/summer 1999, recognized the need to stay true what he characterized as the Byblos tradition of "young, light, colorful, and thematic" clothing (*Women's Wear Daily,* 9 April 1998), while moving forward to embrace current design trends. Color was something the brand had gotten away from under Tyler's oversight, when minimal and monochromatic were the rule of the day. Bartlett set out "to reinvigorate and revitalize the Byblos brand without completely changing it beyond recognition," as he told *Women's Wear Daily.* At the same time, Bartlett had to tone down the sexiness typical of his own line, in a bow to Byblos' commercial direction.

Bartlett's short reign lasted just over a year, when he stepped down after completing the fall 2000 collections. (Byblos and Barlett simultaneously discontinued a licensing deal that had allowed Byblos to manufacture and distribute Bartlett's signature line.) Bartlett stayed on as a consultant on fashion trends for two seasons but did no hands-on designing at Byblos. An in-house design team took over, garnering lukewarm reviews for the homogeneity of their early collections. As *Women's Wear Daily* pointed out in October 2000, Bartlett had creative highs and lows during his tenure, but his signature style always showed through. The subsequent line, on the other hand, "lacked the singular focus that would distinguish it from a sea of others."

In March 2001, Byblos announced two new creative directors, Martine Sitbon for women and Sandy Dalal for men. Paris-based Sitbon was recognized for her use of graphic prints and according to *Women's Wear Daily,* "a style that blends rock 'n' roll with romance." The 24-year-old Milan-based Dalal, who planned to continue his own signature collection in addition to his work for Byblos, told *DNR* (21 March 2001) that he looked forward "to reinterpreting the essence of the roots from which Byblos began: playful, sexy, colorful clothes." Debut collections were expected from the designers for spring 2002.

—Richard Martin; updated by Karen Raugust

C

CACHAREL, Jean

French designer

Born: Jean Louis Henri Bousquet in Nïmes, 30 March 1932. **Education:** Studied at École Technique, Nïmes, 1951–54. **Family:** Married Dominique Sarrut, 1956; children: Guillaume, Jessica. **Career:** Cutter/stylist, Jean Jourdan, Paris, 1955–57; founder/director, Société Jean Cacharel, women's ready-to-wear, from 1964; children's line added, early 1970s; introduced perfume and jeans lines, 1978; cosmetics range introduced, 1991; menswear debuted, 1994; elected mayor of Nïmes; convicted on multiple corruption charges while serving as mayor, 1995–96; Cacharel headquarters moved from Nïmes to Paris, 1999; Clements Ribeiro design team signed to produce womenswear, 2000; accessories line launched, 2000; opened first "blue" décor store, Marseilles, 2001; fragrances (licensed to L'Oreal) include: *Anaïs Anaïs,* 1978; *Cacharel pour Homme,* 1981; *Loulou,* 1987; *Eden,* 1994; *Loulou Blue,* 1995; *Eau d'Eden,* 1996; *Noa,* 1998; *Nemo,* 1999. **Awards:** Export Trade Oscar, Paris, 1969; FiFi "Star of the Year" award for both Best New Fragrance and Best Fragrance Launch (for *Noa,*), 1998. **Address:** 3 Rue du Colisée, 30931 Nïmes, France. **Website:** www.cacharel.com.

Jean Cacharel, fall 2001 collection. © AP/Wide World Photos/ Fashion Wire Daily.

Publications

On CACHAREL:

Books

Lynam, Ruth, *Paris Fashion: The Great Designers and Their Creations,* London, 1972.

Articles

Manser, José, "Cacharel's Rag Trade Riches," in *Design* (London), October 1969.

Raper, Sarah, "Cacharel to Sell Temptation with Eden," in *Women's Wear Daily,* 7 January 1994.

Aktar, Alev, "Loulou Blue Looks to Youth to Color Sales," in *Women's Wear Daily,* 10 March 1995.

Lewis, Madeleine, "Profiles of Jean Cacharel, Gerard Pasquier and Zannier," in *Textile Outlook International,* May 1995.

Cooney-Curran, Joyceann, "Noa's Mystique: With a Message and Vision in Hand, Noa Takes on the U.S. Fragrance Market," in *Global Cosmetics Industry,* April 2000.

Weisman, Katherine, and James Fallon, "Clements Ribeiro to Do Cacharel Line," in *Women's Wear Daily,* 18 May 2000.

Murphy, Robert, "Catching Up with the New Cacharel," in *Women's Wear Daily,* 9 August 2000.

Deeny, Godfrey, "Cacharel Cashes in on Couture," available online at Fashion Windows, www.fashionwindows.com, 10 March 2001.

Murphy, Robert, "Cacharel's New Blue Horizon," in *Women's Wear Daily,* 15 May 2001.

Nelson, Karin, "Cacharel: Colorful & Spirited," available online at Fashion Windows, www.fashionwindows.com, 6 October 2001.

* * *

Jean Cacharel became an established designer name in the mid-1960s when his fitted, printed, and striped shirts for women became fashion "must haves"—so much so that by the end of the decade French women went into stores not asking for a shirt, but for a

Jean Cacharel in ca. 1980–97. © Frédéric Huijbregts/CORBIS.

"Cacharel." The designer had finally done for women what others had not—created a shirt that was flattering, comfortable and easy to wear.

Cacharel, Jean Bousquet, came to Paris from Nïmes in the mid-1950s, where he had apprenticed in men's tailoring. Adopting the name of Cacharel, which was taken from the Camargue's native wild duck, he moved into womenswear as a designer/cutter for Jean Jourdan in Paris. At the time womenswear was dominated by Parisian haute couture and mass market took a dim second place. Cacharel was one of the first designers to foresee a fashion future beyond the old-monied clientèle and catered to an emerging nouvelle riche and fashion-conscious mass market. The strong emergence of youth culture in the 1950s and 1960s strengthened his vision.

Cacharel opened his own business at the end of the 1950s and employed Emmanuelle Khanh as a stylist and designer. Together they created a company image that was very French, young, and sporty in fresh matching separates that were colorful, pretty and wearable. Success was sealed in 1965 when Cacharel began working with Liberty of London. He rescaled and recolored traditional floral prints so they became softer and more flattering. Prints previously scorned as frumpy and homely were transformed by Cacharel's cut and taste into snappy, feminine, wearable clothes. Liberty of London subsequently stocked and sold the Cacharel label for decades.

Further developments at Cacharel included moves into licensing and distribution agreements. Cacharel's sister-in-law, Corinne Grandval, joined the firm and helped introduce a successful mini couture line for children, which was widely copied and adapted in the industry. Cacharel's children, Guillaume and Jessica, also joined the family business in the 1990s. Yet by the turn of the century, the Cacharel name needed a boost. Though it still represented stylish ready-to-wear for women in France and throughout Europe and Latin America, the name was recognizable only in fragrances in the United States. Setting out to crack the American market and spruce up its image, Cacharel decided to launch new versions of two if its earlier fragrances.

Cacharel's *Loulou* and *Eden* came out in 1987 and 1994 respectively; their younger, hipper counterparts, *Loulou Blue* and *Eau d'Eden* debuted in 1995 and 1996. The introductions, however, came at difficult time for the company, as its namesake was on trial for misdeeds while the mayor of Nïmes, where the business was based. Subsequently convicted, Jean Cacharel was fined and sentenced to a year in jail, followed by a year of probation. Cacharel, the business, continued during its founder's confinement. In 1998 came the launch of *Noa,* an exciting fragrance and body products line symbolizing female empowerment and spiritual harmony. Its mate, the first Cacharal men's fragrance in almost two decades, *Nemo,* came out the following year.

The complementary scents, like all of Cacharel's later fragrances, were directed at a youthful crowd complete with flashy packaging and aggressive advertising campaigns. Boldly going against the unisex fragrance trend, Cacharel's distinctly male and female scents were a welcome hit in the U.S., which had proven resistant to earlier Cacharel fragrances (with the exception of *Anaïs Anaïs* which had been an enduring success). While *Noa* brought the Cacharel name to the forefront of the fragrance industry, with mega sales worldwide, Cacharel's womenswear was bolstered with arrival of the Clements Ribeiro design team in 2000. Husband-and-wife team Suzanne Clements and Inacio Ribeiro's ready-to-wear collections in 2000 and 2001 were warmly received. While the duo continued to design under their own label as well as at Cacharel, Clements commented to *Women's Wear Daily* in August 2000, "Now we can be more whimsical and extreme with Clements Ribeiro. Cacharel, on the other hand, is more grounded in reality. It is more simple and has pieces, like suits, that we wouldn't do for our own line, but that are important for Cacharel because it is a full collection with an economic reality."

Under the artistic direction of Clements and Ribeiro, the 40-year-old house of Cacharel was in good hands. The company's founder, Jean Cacharel said, "Clements and Ribeiro have tapped into the true Cacharel spirit. The line is about creative pieces that can be easily mixed and matched—all at an affordable price." In addition to reinvigorating its ready-to-wear and other clothing collections, Cacharel introduced matching accessories and opened a new store in Marseilles in 2001. The new décor, almost completely outfitted in various shades of blue, was another step in redefining Cacharal worldwide, with the remainder of firm's shops slated for renovation in 2001 and 2002.

—Kevin Almond; updated by Owen James

CALUGI E GIANNELLI

Italian design house

Founded: in Florence, 1982, by Mauro Calugi (born 1941) and Danilo Giannelli (1957–1987). **Company History:** Incorporated, 1984; renamed Danilo Giannelli, SpA, circa 1987; principal designer, Mauro Calugi. **Exhibitions:** *Pitti Immagine Uoma,* Fortezza da Basso, Florence, 1985; *A Dress Beyond Fashion,* Palazzo Fortuny, Venice, 1991. **Awards:** Ecco L'Italia (New York), 1985. **Company Address:** Via Catalani 28—Zona Industriale Bassa, 50050 Cerreto Guidi, Florence, Italy.

Publications

On CALUGI E GIANNELLI:

Articles

Macchia, Susanna, "Calugi e Giannelli—Look Lunare All'insegna della Comodita,"available online at Moda Online, www.moda online.it, November 2001.

* * *

Since beginning in 1982, Calugi e Giannelli has invented and reinvented clothing—menswear in particular—as if it were conceptual art. Arguably, Calugi e Giannelli clothing is an advanced art of the idea, often conveying avant-garde principles, frequently invoking and investing language and word play, and always bringing an edge to clothing. Formal properties matter, especially as they are developed from the properties of fabrics and fabric technology, most notably stretch, but the essence of a Calugi e Giannelli garment is its idea, or what 1993 press materials described as "ironic temperament, a strong core and decisive taste."

As playful as the Milanese Franco Moschino and as avant-gardist at the Parisian Jean-Paul Gaultier, Calugi e Giannelli's erudite conceptualism is accompanied by an equally strong sense of sensuality. Transparency applied to textiles and the body becomes a tour de force of ideas, but it also serves as a grand tour of erogenous zones. Pop Art is remembered, especially in the spring/summer 1991 collection, but when labels end up on tight swimwear and biker shorts, the equation of sex and consumption is only heightened. Both the Church and masculinity are special targets of Calugi e Giannelli satire and wit. A leitmotif of the collections is an interest in clerical dress subverted to secular clothing, with crosses and vestment details appearing again and again with schoolboy irreverence. Studded leather jackets are an over-the-top machismo that can only be interpreted as tongue-in-cheek. Calugi e Giannelli's work is always winning and not subject to the tiresome jokes of some sportswear—it is a fashion animated by fresh ideas and interpretive energy.

Learned and yet fun referencing to both dollar signs and the hammer and sickle (spring/summer 1989), Arab motifs and script (spring/summer 1991), mocking motifs of ecclesiastical hats (fall/winter 1988–89), Tahiti and tattoos (spring/summer 1993), and tough biker leathers (fall/winter 1993–94) establish clothing as a widely referential, all-encompassing art. Singularly characteristic of the design's sartorial surrealism is the fall/winter 1988–89 anamorphic jacket with two lapels in which the exterior and interior, jacket and waistcoat, shell and marrow are purposely confused with resulting asymmetry and winsome disorder. A spring/summer 1988 double-collared shirt plays with the same uncertainties of the doppelganger. Art-like in its proposition, knowledgeable in its deliberate discords (snakeskin and lace together in spring/summer 1989), supremely sexy in its orientation, Calugi e Giannelli clothing sets a distinctive style in menswear.

While partner Danilo Giannelli died in 1987, the sensibility continued by Mauro Calugi was seamless with the design duo's original objectives. Clothing is subject to aesthetic consideration. The fall/winter 1988–89 collection included a series of jackets with barbed wire motifs, introducing faux barbed wire at the shoulders or around the waist. In the seeming disparity of soft clothing and the fictive brutalism of barbed wire, Calugi e Giannelli displayed characteristic wit and irrepressible irony. In the same season, the "Violent Angels" leather jacket set metal plates with letters in continuous reading on a leather jacket: its diction is the continuous language of computer input; its effect is to put language onto the supposedly inarticulate form of the leather jacket. By such paradox, Calugi e Giannelli offers contradiction and incongruity about clothing, but also with an ideal of harmony and reconciliation. Even the language of the "Violent Angels" title, suggests the combination of the ferocious and the chaste.

Despite heady artistic purpose, Calugi e Giannelli clothing is well made and is never wearable art or craft. The interest in the basic templates of clothing arises in part from the preference in silhouettes for standard types, perfectly executed, and the knits and performance sportswear have the integrity of quality clothing. Detailing of embroidered suits, knit jackets with representational scenes, and sweaters with a range of illustration and image are consummately made; the lace t-shirts and jackets, and the tailored clothing with sudden apertures, have been copied in expensive and inferior versions, but the Calugi e Giannelli originals are beautifully made. The spring/summer 1988 block cutouts with sheer panels are a body peek-a-boo inflected with the design language of Piet Mondrian or Mark Rothko.

Menswear is the forum for Calugi e Giannelli ideas, though womenswear has also been produced. In the later 1990s the firm produced collections harking back to the 1970s with long woolen coats, funky midriff-baring tees, mohair or black acetate shirts, and long jackets. The style was at once derivative and new, mod and hip yet only for a particularly daring male. Perhaps menswear's accustomed reserve from fashion controversy and aggressive aesthetics lends itself to Calugi e Giannelli's definitive work. Mauro Calugi's insistence that fashion is an art of compelling dissent and dissonance is a significant social and personal statement.

—Richard Martin

CAPELLINO, Ally

See ALLY CAPELLINO

CAPUCCI, Roberto

Italian designer

Born: Rome, 2 December 1930. **Education:** Attended Liceo Artistico and Accademia di Belle Arti, Rome, 1947–50. **Career:** Assisted designer Emilio Schuberth before opening first studio, Via Sistina, in Rome, 1950; opened Paris studio, rue Cambon, 1962–68; launched first fragrance, for men, *Capucci,* 1965; returned to Rome and opened Via Gregoriana studio, 1968; designed costumes for Pasolini's film *Teorema,* 1970; first fragrance for women, *Yendi de Capucci,* 1974; designed costimes for opera *Norma,* 1976, in Verona; designed occasional fashion collections, from 1982; second women's fragrance, *Capucci de Capucci,* 1987. **Exhibitions:** *Variété de la Mode 1786–1986,* Münchener Stadtmuseum, Munich, July 1986; *60 Years of Italian Cultural Life,* Columbia University, New York and Palazzo Venezia, Rome, 1986–87; *Fashion and Surrealism,* Victoria & Albert Museum, London, 1988; *Roberto Capucci: Art in Fashion—Volume, Colour and Method,* Palazzo Strozzi, Florence and Stadtmuseum, Munich, 1990 and at the Palazzo delle Esposizioni in Rome, late 1990s; *Roben wie Rüstungen,* Kunsthistorisches Museum, Vienna,

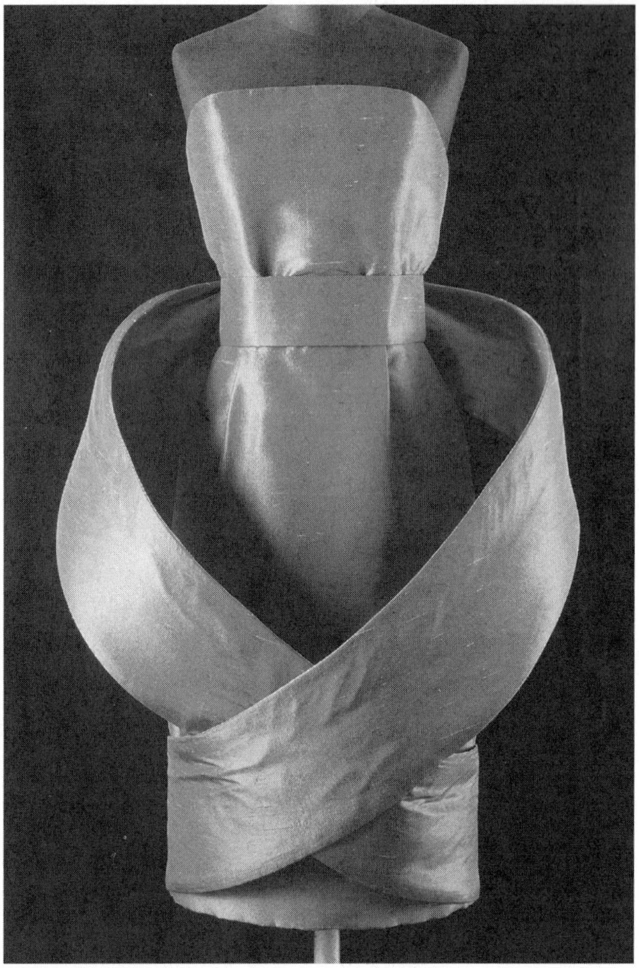

Design by Roberto Capucci, ca. 1980–97. © Massimo Listri/ CORBIS.

1991; *La Biennale di Venezia, Centenary 1895–1995,* Venice, 1995; *In difesa della bellezza,* Palazzo della Pilotta, Parma, 1996; *L'elogio della bellezza—Roberto Capucci alla Galleria di Palazzo Colonna,* Rome, 2000. **Awards:** Medaglione d'Oro, Venice, 1956; Filene's Fashion Oscar, Boston, 1958; honoured by the Austrian Minister of Culture 1990. **Address:** Via Gregoriana 56, Rome, Italy.

PUBLICATIONS

By CAPUCCI:

Books

Roberto Capucci: L'arte nella moda—colore, volume, metodo [exhibition catalogue], Fabbri Editore, 1990.
Roberto Capucci: Roben wie Rüstungen [exhibition catalogue], Vienna, 1991.
Roberto Capucci: Testo Italiano = Texte Français = English Text, with Patrick Mauriès and Massimo Listri, Milan, 1993.
Roberto Capucci: I percorsi della creatività [exhibition catalogue], with Massimo Ferretti, Rome, 1994.
Roberto Capucci al Teatro Farnese [exhibition catalogue], with Lucia Fornari Schianchi, Rome, 1996.
L'elogio della bellezza—Roberto Capucci alla Galleria di Palazzo Colonna [exhibition catalogue], Rome, 2000.

On CAPUCCI:

Books

Lambert, Eleanor, *World of Fashion: People, Places, Resources,* New York & London, 1976.
Alfonsi, Maria-Vittoria, *Leaders in Fashion: i grandi personaggi della moda,* Bologna, 1983.
Relang, Regina, *30 anni di moda,* Milan, 1983.
Milbank, Caroline Rennolds, *Couture: The Great Designers,* New York, 1985.
Buiazzi, Graziella, *La moda italiana,* Milan, 1987.
Stegemeyer, Anne, *Who's Who in Fashion, Third Edition,* New York, 1996.
Bauzano, Gianluca, *Roberto Capucci: Timeless Creativity,* Milan & London, 2001.

Articles

Pivano, Fernanda, "Roma alta moda: Roberto Capucci," in *Vogue* (Milan), September 1985.
"Roberto Capucci: Sontuose magie di un grande alchimista," in *Vogue* (Milan), March 1987.
Hume, Marion, "In Love with the Frill of It All," in the *Sunday Times* (London), 14 January 1990.
Gastell, Minnie, "A Solitary Artist," in *Donna* (Milan), March 1990.
Battaglia, Paolo, "Lo scenario per gli abiti scultura," in *Abitare con Arte* (Italy), May 1990.
Mölter, Veit, "Die Kunst der Mode," in *Parnassus* (Germany), July/ August 1990.
Bertelli, B., "Quando la moda è arte," in *F.M.R.* (Italy), September 1990.
Celant, Germano, and Massimo Listri, "Roberto Capucci," in *Interview* (New York), September 1990.
Vergani, Guido, "Il sofà delle muse," in *Il Venerdì di Repubblica* (Rome), September 1990.
Hilderbrandt, Heike, "Florenze: Art and Fashion," in *Contemporanea* (Vienna), November 1990.
Plener, Doris, "Roben wie Rüstungen für Groâe Festlichkeiten," in *Die Presse* (Vienna), November 1990.
Kruntorad, Paul, "Drei Wiener Schaustücke Zur Gegenwart Von Harnischen," in *Der Standard* (Vienna), December 1990.
Morteo, Enrico, "Il lusso come ricerca," in *Domus* (Milan), February 1991.
Celant, Roberto, "Capucci," in *Interview,* September 1991.
Wagner, Steven, "A Cut Above [Capucci]," in *Town & Country,* July 1994.
"Fashion Scoops," in *Women's Wear Daily,* 11 July 2001.

*

I first became curious about fashion as a child, when I observed, with a critical eye, the clothes worn by the women of my family. My talent for design and love of colour led me to art school, the Accademia delle Belle Arti, where I came into contact with art in its many forms.

Nature is my mentor. In my garden, quietly watching with a childlike sense of fantasy, has helped to instill in me a sense of balance and a constant search for perfection, proportion, harmony,

Eveningwear by Roberto Capucci, modeled on the Spanish Steps in Rome during the "Donna sotto le stelle" ("Women Under the Stars") fashion gala, 1999. © AP/Wide World Photos.

and colour. This has given me the strength to avoid being influenced by fashion trends. Following my belief has enabled me to be true to myself, but this has meant renunciation. If my work lacks a commercial aspect, it is due not only to my desire for truth. For me, creating is a great experience and, while I would not have refused to diversify in my designs, the moment is not yet right.

In this field, it is difficult to strike the right balance. To attempt a compromise between the will of the designer and that of the manufacturer inevitably leads to disappointment. On one side, industry takes a commercial stance; on the other the designer has an idealized view of fashion. Creating a design away from the reality of a woman, the dress has no form, it is merely a symbol.

In my continuing quest for beauty and purity, I concentrate initially on the basic form. During this phase I do not want to be influenced by outside factors, and I think in black and white. Next comes colour, in all its intensity, blending with the pencil lines and producing the effect that I am looking for—faithful to my concept and to the women I am addressing. Only today is my work understood and accepted.

Because it is a work of luxury, it may be enjoyed by a few, but by those few who have a sense for luxury rather than the desire for ostentation and opulence. Luxury does not necessarily mean money. One can, perhaps, say that luxury is an art, like painting or sculpture, with its own scheme. To be inspired by art does not mean to imitate it, nor to establish a recognizable connection with it, but almost to fall in love with it. This is the feeling of culture for clothes and fashion which, as I said before, is sadly lacking today. I am confident, nevertheless, that everyone wants to follow their own style rather than to conform.

—Roberto Capucci

* * *

One of Italy's most gifted and imaginative couturiers, Roberto Capucci has a select following of women who appreciate his architectural creations, and have the grand occasions on which to wear them. Having a Capucci wedding dress has long been the goal of fashionable brides looking for a special sense of shape and style. Capucci is an uncommon couturier who shows infrequently, and produces only a few extraordinary designs for his clients.

The retrospective held at the Palazzo Strozzi in Florence in 1990 highlighted the variety of his genius and the sources of his art. The elegance of the 1950s shaped his concept of haute couture as an art form, and he has rigorously practiced it in this tradition. He has approached design as a form of architecture, building structures the body can inhabit, and has rejected the arbitrary dictates of what might be momentarily fashionable. Instead he deals with elements of design such as line, color, texture, and volume in a more abstract sense but always as they relate to the human body.

Capucci's sense of line can be found in the geometric planes imposed upon the body and apparent both in his sketches and the finished garments. The sketches show strong relationships with the work of the Italian Futurists, and some of his work has also been considered surrealistic. His second major source of inspiration draws from natural forms, where curvilinear volumes might refer to floral shapes while the linear, planar qualities might refer to crystalline structures. There can be no question of his mastery of the use of textiles. Crisp, lustrous silks are pleated and manipulated into moving, fluted sculptural forms; wools are cut and inlaid like mosaics. The care with which he works his materials into his humanly habitable structures ensures that they are wearable and the finished garments are true to his original concepts. Many of the textiles are a combination of silk and wool, in fabrics with the weight and resilience needed to execute his complex volumes.

Capucci's sensitivity to color, or its absence, is equally impressive. In the black and white costumes, where the linear qualities are dominant, the absence of color is used for emphasis. One series of white silk crêpe dresses from 1980 had mask-like human faces sculpted into the structure of the sleeves, pockets, or bodice front. In combination, the use of black and white served to make the spatial relationships even more effective. Instances of Capucci's dramatic use of color are usually found in his evening dresses of pleated silk taffeta. The brilliant colors, often juxtaposed in close harmonies, give added dimension to the linear effects.

The strength of Capucci's personality and his determination to remain true to his chosen art are obvious in his designs. His interest in seeking a variety of forums in which to display his work, like the many exhibitions featuring his creations, demonstrates a creative approach to establishing a context for his work. Many such opportunities have arisen in the 1990s, like his participation in the Venice at La Biennale di Venezia Centenary celebration in 1995, where Capucci was an honored guest alongside a few of his treasures. The designer surprised many in 2001, however, when it was announced he had secured financial backing and would present a new collection in Paris later in the year. A renaissance for the Italian house of Capucci was on the horizon, and the designer's devoted clients awaited his newest works of art.

—Jean Druesedow; updated by Sydonie Benét

CARDIN, Pierre

French designer

Born: Son of French parents, born in San Andrea da Barbara, Italy, 2 July 1922. **Education:** Studied architecture, Saint-Etienne, France.

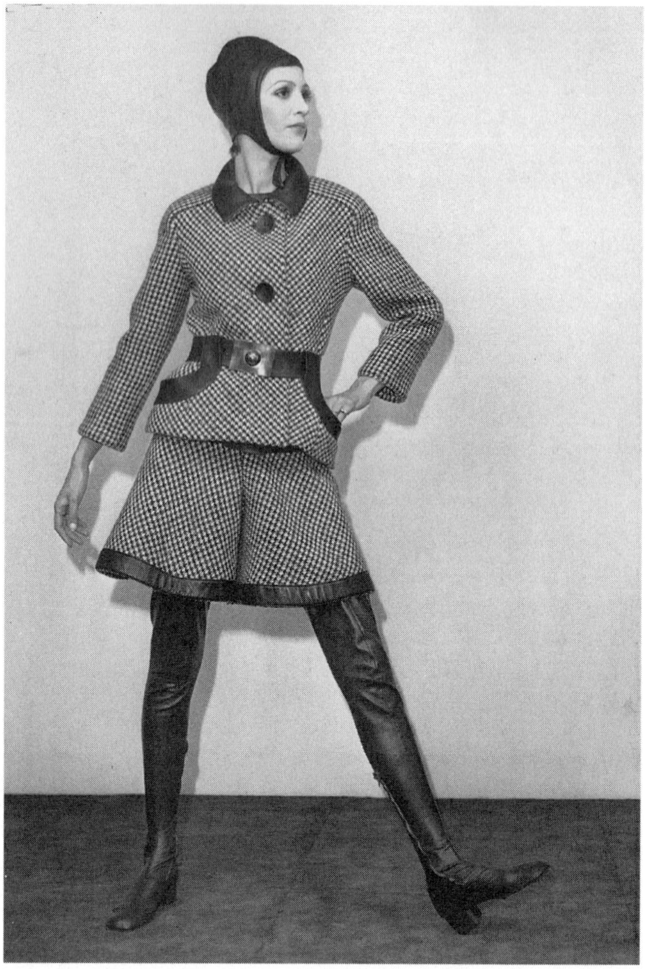

Pierre Cardin, fall/winter 1968 collection. © AP/Wide World Photos.

Military: Served in the Red Cross, World War II. **Career:** Worked as a bookkeeper and tailor's cutter, Vichy, 1936–40; Apprentice, Manby men's tailor, Vichy, 1939; design assistant, working for the Madame Paquin and Elsa Schiaparelli fashion houses, Paris, 1945–46; head of workrooms, Christian Dior fashion house, Paris, 1946–50, began costume designing for films, from 1946; helping to design "New Look" in 1947; founder/director and chief designer, Pierre Cardin fashion house, Paris, from 1950, presented first collection, 1951; opened up market in Japan, 1958; first ready-to-wear collection introduced, 1959; marketed own fabric, Cardine, 1968; children's collection introduced, 1969; created Espace Cardin, 1970; special Atlanta showing, pre-Olympic Games, 1996; launched *Orphee,* 1998; new cultural center named for Cardin, Saint-Ouen, France, 2000; decided to sell and sought buyer for firm. **Exhibitions:** *Pierre Cardin: Past, Present and Future,* Victoria & Albert Museum, London, October-January 1990–91. **Awards:** *Sunday Times* International Fashion award (London), 1963; Dé d'Or award, 1977, 1979, 1982; named Chevalier de la Légion d'Honneur, 1983; Fashion Oscar, Paris, 1985; Foundation for Garment and Apparel Advancement award, Tokyo, 1988; named Grand Officer, Order of Merit, Italy, 1988; named Honorary Ambassador to UNESCO, 1991. **Address:** 82 rue Faubourg Saint-Honoré, 75008 Paris, France. **Website:** www.pierrecardin.com.

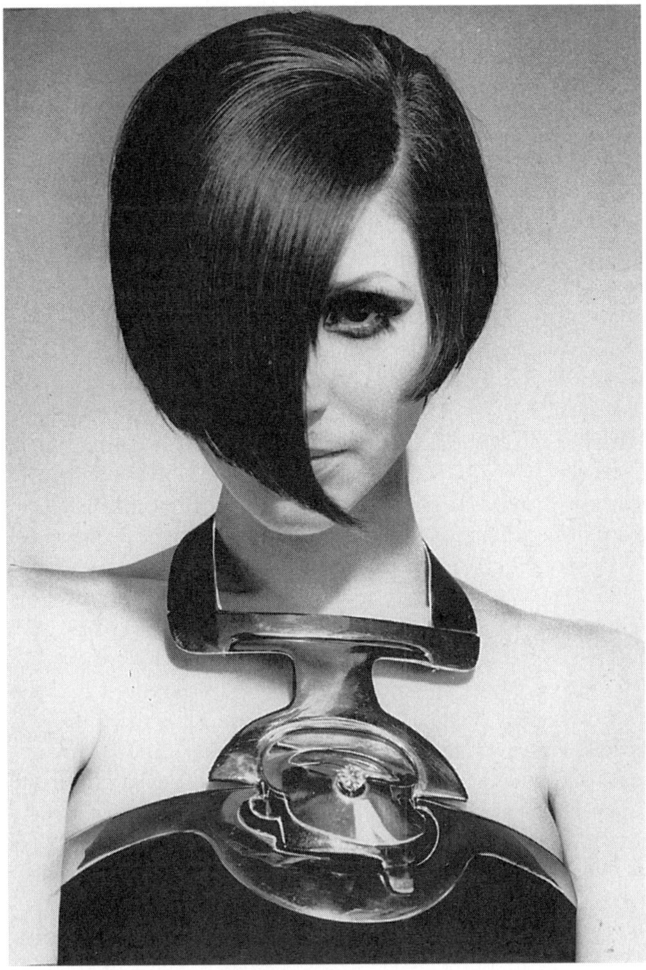

Pierre Cardin, spring 1968 collection: sculpted silver necklace with a $60,000 diamond built into the halter top of a crêpe evening gown. © AP/Wide World Photos.

Publications

On CARDIN:

Books

Picken, Mary Brooks, and Dora L. Miller, *Dressmakers of France,* New York, 1956.

Bender, Marylin, *The Beautiful People,* New York, 1967.

Lyman, Ruth, ed., *Couture: An Illustrated History of the Great Paris Designers and Their Creations,* New York, 1972.

Carter, Ernestine, *Magic Names of Fashion,* London, 1980.

Pierre Cardin [exhibition catalogue], Tokyo, 1982.

Milbank, Caroline Rennolds, *Couture: The Great Designers,* New York, 1985.

Guillen, Pierre-Yves, and Jacqueline Claude, *The Golden Thimble: French Haute Couture,* Paris, 1990.

Mendes, Valerie, *Pierre Cardin: Past, Present, Future,* London, 1990, 1991.

Morais, Richard, *Pierre Cardin: The Man Who Became a Label,* London, 1991.

Articles

Parinaud, A., "Cardin Interviewed," in *Arts* (Paris), 11 September 1981.

Corbett, Patricia, "All About Cardin," in *Connoisseur* (London), January 1986.

Beurdley, Laurence, "Pierre Cardin fête ses quarante ans de création," in *L'Officiel* (Paris), May 1990.

Milbank, Caroline Rennolds, "Pierre Cardin," in *Vogue,* September 1990.

Watt, Judith, "The World According to Pierre Cardin," in *The Guardian* (London), 24 September 1990.

Etherington-Smith, Meredith, "Pierre Pressure," in *Correpondent Magazine* (London), 30 September 1990.

Bowles, Hamish, "Pierre the Great," in *Harpers & Queen* (London), October 1990.

McDowell, Colin, "The Pierre Show," in the *Daily Telegraph* (London), 6 October 1990.

Rambali, Paul, "Pierre Cardin," in *Arena* (London), November 1990.

Niland, Seta, "Cardin Seeks to Widen Profile," in *Fashion Weekly* (London), 6 June 1991.

Pogoda, Dianne M., "Cardin Collection: Coming to America," in *Women's Wear Daily,* 24 March 1992.

"Pierre Cardin Shows Collection in Atlanta," in *Women's Wear Daily,* 16 July 1996.

Raper, Sarah, "Cardin Looks to Future of Firm," in *Women's Wear Daily,* 17 March 1999.

Menkes, Suzy, "Fifty Years a Futurist," in the *International Herald Tribune,* 18 April 2000.

"Pierre Cardin Denies Reports (to Split Up Business)," in *Women's Wear Daily,* 5 December 2000.

* * *

The shrewd entrepreneurial skills displayed by Pierre Cardin throughout his career have made him one of the world's wealthiest fashion designers and a household name. A global phenomenon, he was the first designer to open up markets in Japan in 1958, China in 1978, and more recently Russia and Romania, applying the Cardin name to hundreds of products, from ties and alarm clocks to linens and frying pans.

Cardin was the first designer to understand the potential of the business of fashion. His move into ready-to-wear in 1959 scandalized the Chambre Syndicale, the monitoring body of haute couture in Paris, and he was expelled from its ranks for what was essentially an attempt to make designer clothes more accessible, and also displaying an astute sense of where the real money to be made in fashion lay.

From his earliest work for the House of Dior up to the 1950s, Cardin displayed an interest in the sculptural qualities of cut and construction that are still his trademarks in the 1990s and into the 2000s. Cardin produces garments of a hard-edged minimalism, backed up by exquisite tailoring he manipulates to produce sparse, geometric garments offset by collars and bizarre accessories (such as the vinyl torso decoration he introduced in 1968). His designs resist the rounded curves of the traditional female body, aided by his use of materials such as heavyweight wool and jersey rib, creating clothing

Pierre Cardin, spring 2000 collection. © AFP/CORBIS.

that stands away from the body thereby produces its own structural outline. From the balloon dress of 1959 that delineated the body only at the pull of a drawstring at the hem, through the geometrically blocked shifts of the 1960s to his series of hooped dresses in the 1980s, Cardin obliquely describes the underlying form of the body, creating planes that intersect with, yet somehow remain disconnected from, the body itself.

Cardin's embrace of science and technology, together with the notion of progress was expressed in his 1964 Space Age Collection, which featured white knitted catsuits, tabards worn over leggings, tubular dresses, and his growing interest in manmade fibres. He created his own fabric, Cardine, in 1968, a bonded, uncrushable fiber incorporating raised geometric patterns.

Cardin's curiously asexual designs for women in the 1960s remained so even when making direct reference to the breast by the use of cones, outlines, cutouts, and molding. Similarly, the exposure of the legs afforded by his minis was desexed by the models wearing thick opaque or patterned tights and thigh-high boots. Experiments with the application of paper cutout techniques to fabric with which Cardin was preoccupied in the 1960s were replaced in the 1970s by more fluid materials such as single angora jersey and the techniques of sunray and accordion pleating. A spiraling rather than geometric line began to be more noticeable and Cardin became renowned for his frothy evening dresses of layered, printed chiffon while continuing his experimentation with a series of unusual sleevehead designs.

Cardin was the first postwar designer to challenge London's Savile Row in the production of menswear. The high buttoned collarless jackets worn by the Beatles became de rigueur for the fashionable man in the 1960s and provided a relaxed yet elegant look when combined with a turtleneck sweater. Cardin, by paring away collars and relinquishing pockets, broke with tradition to create a new look for men realizing that the male suit, once a bastion of tradition, could be high fashion too.

Although merchandising and licensing his name may have overshadowed his influence as a fashion designer in recent years, Cardin's inventiveness and technical flair have often been underestimated. In a speech to American College students in Atlanta in July 1996, he said, "I may design everything from chairs to chocolate, but fashion is still my first love. You may do something classic, something beautiful, but that is just good taste. True talent has a bit of shock element to it; I did black body stockings 30 years ago, and everyone thought they were ugly. Now, they have become classic."

Nearing the end of the year 2000, Cardin sought a buyer for his fashion empire. He rejected overtures from French luxury giant LVMH, as well as the Gucci Group, holding out for someone he believed would not only maintain the brand's integrity but would protect his many longtime employees. "I'm not getting any younger," he told *Women's Wear Daily* (5 December 2000). "I don't have any heirs and I want to assure my company will continue to exist in the future. I don't need to sell; I still get up and work every day. But if I want to insure my employees' job security, I have to start planning for the future."

—Caroline Cox; updated by Sydonie Benét

CARNEGIE, Hattie

American designer

Born: Henrietta Kanengeiser in Vienna, 1889. **Family:** Married third husband, John Zanft, in 1928. **Career:** Left school at age 11 and moved with parents to New York, 1900; established as Carnegie-Ladies Hatter, 1909; opened custom dressmaking salon, 1918; offered Paris models after first buying trip to Europe, 1919; opened East 49th Street building to sell own label, imports, and millinery, 1925; added ready-to-wear, 1928; Hattie Carnegie Originals carried in stores throughout the U.S. by 1934; custom salon closed, 1965. **Awards:** Neiman Marcus award, 1939; Coty American Fashion Critics award, 1948. **Died:** 22 February 1956, in New York.

Publications

On CARNEGIE:

Books

Epstein, Beryl Williams, *Fashion is Our Business,* Philadelphia and New York, 1945.

Design by Hattie Carnegie: sequined dinner ensemble. © AP/Wide World Photos/Fashion Wire Daily.

New York and Hollywood Fashion: Costume Designs from the Brooklyn Museum Collection, New York, 1986.

Milbank, Caroline Rennolds, *New York Fashion: The Evolution of American Style,* New York, 1989.

Steele, Valerie, *Women of Fashion: Twentieth Century Design,* New York, 1991.

Stegemeyer, Anne, *Who's Who in Fashion, Third Edition,* New York, 1996.

Articles

"Luxury, Inc.," in *Vogue* (New York), 15 April 1928.

"Profiles: Luxury, Inc.," in the *New Yorker,* 31 March 1934.

"Hattie Carnegie," in *Current Biography* (New York), October 1942.

Bauer, Hambla, "Hot Fashions by Hattie," in *Collier's* (Philadelphia), 16 April 1949.

"Hattie Carnegie" (obituary), in the *New York Times,* 23 February 1956.

* * *

For decades Hattie Carnegie's personal taste and fashion sense influenced the styles worn by countless American women. Whether they bought her imported Paris models, the custom designs, the ready-to-wear collections, or the mass market copies of her work, women welcomed Carnegie's discreet good taste as a guarantee of sophistication and propriety. Carnegie's business ability and fashion acumen enabled her to build a small millinery shop into a wholesale and retail clothing and accessory empire and made her name synonymous with American high fashion for almost half a century.

Carnegie's place in fashion history was assured not because of her own designs, but because of her talent for choosing or refining the designs of others. Between the World Wars, the list of couturiers whose models she imported included Lanvin, Vionnet, Molyneux, and Mainbocher—classic stylists—but also select creations for Chanel and Patou, Schiaparelli, and Charles James. In fact, Carnegie claimed in an April 1949 *Collier's* article to have had a three-year unauthorized exclusive on selling Vionnet models in the early 1920s, a few years before Vionnet started selling "to the trade."

The Custom Salon was generally considered to be the heart of the Hattie Carnegie operation, since it was with made-to-order fashion that Carnegie began. The focus of her business was to interpret European style for American consumers, but the sense of dress she chose to champion was not contained in the minutiae of design. It was instead an approach to fashion that emphasized consummate polish in every outfit. Norman Norell, who was with Carnegie from 1928 to 1940 (primarily as a ready-to-wear designer), remarked in *American Fashion* (New York, 1975) that he often worked from models that Miss Carnegie had brought back from Paris. He could legitimately claim, however, that he had imprinted his own signature on his designs for the firm, and it is often possible to make an informed attribution of Hattie Carnegie styles to her other designers. Certainly one gown featured in a 1939 magazine layout is recognizably the work of Claire McCardell, who spent two years with the firm. Others who worked for Carnegie were Emmett Joyce, Travis Banton, Pauline Trigère, Jean Louis, James Galanos, and Gustave Tassell.

Carnegie was already established as a taste-maker by the time she added the ready-to-wear division to her company in the 1920s. "Vogue points from Hattie Carnegie" contained her style tips and forecasts for *Vogue* readers. At the Hattie Carnegie salon, a customer could accessorize her day and evening ensembles with furs, hats, handbags, gloves, lingerie, jewelry, and even cosmetics and perfume—everything, in fact—but shoes.

The Carnegie customer, whatever her age, seems to have been neither girlish nor matronly, but possessed of a certain decorousness. Even the casual clothing in the Spectator Sportswear and Jeunes Filles ready-to-wear departments was elegant rather than playful. The Carnegie Suit, usually an ensemble with dressmaker details in luxury fabrics, traditionally opened her seasonal showings. She often stressed the importance of black as a wardrobe basic, both for day and evening, but was also famous for a shade known as "Carnegie blue." Perhaps Carnegie's preference for 18th-century furnishings in her home relates to the devotion of formality so clearly expressed in her business.

During World War II Carnegie was an impressive bearer of the standard of the haute couture. French style leadership was unavailable, and designs from her custom salon took pride of place in fashion magazines and on the stage, as in the original production of *State of the Union* by Lindsay and Crouse. Carnegie's leadership was also important to other fashion industries. She had always used fabrics from the best American textile companies, and continued to patronize

Design by Hattie Carnegie: sequined-studded rayon and cotton net dress and cape. © AP/Wide World Photos/Fashion Wire Daily.

specialty firms such as Hafner Associates and Onondaga Silks, which were not immersed in war work. She also used fabrics designed and hand-printed by Brook Cadwallader, and continued to do so after French materials again became available. Only after Carnegie's death did the company claim to use exclusively imported fabrics.

Hattie Carnegie died in 1956; the fashion empire she had built survived into the 1970s, but in 1965 the custom salon was closed and the company concentrated on wholesale businesses. The informal youth culture of the 1960s and 1970s was ill-suited to the type of clothing and client that had made Hattie Carnegie's reputation. The strength of her personal identification with the company made it difficult for it to succeed without her, and it quickly lost ground to the younger desginers who emerged in the 1960s.

—Madelyn Shaw

CARPENTIER, Suzie

See MAD CARPENTIER

CARVEN

French fashion house

Founded: Established by Mme. Carven Mallet in Paris, 1945; **Company History:** Launched Carven Scarves and Carven Junior lines, 1955; introduced Kinglenes and Kisslenes sweater collections, 1956; neckwear collection, 1957; swimwear, 1965; furs, 1966; jewelry, Ma Fille children's line, and blouse collection, 1968; opened Monsieur Carven boutique, Paris, 1985; also designed uniforms for Air India, SAS, Aerolineas Argentinas, and Air France; merged divisions in reorganization, 1995; hired Angelo Tarlazzi as artistic director, 1995; purchased by French perfume company Daniel Harlant, 1998; Edward Achour named artistic director and designer, 1998. Fragrances include *Ma Griffe,* 1948, *Robe d'un Soir,* 1948, *Chasse Gardée,* 1950, *Vetiver,* 1957, *Vert et Blanc,* 1958, *Madame,* 1980, *Guirlandes,* 1982, *Carven Homme,* 1990, and *Variations,* 2001. **Exhibitions:** *The Grog-Carven Collection,* consisting of cabinetry, Dutch and Flemish paintings, and other artwork collected by Madame Carven and her late husband, René Grog, on permanent display at the

Madame Carven in ca. 1989–99. © Photo B.D.V./CORBIS.

Louvre, since 1981; Retrospective, Paris, 1986. **Awards:** Chevalier de la Légion d'Honneur, 1964, Grande Medaille des Arts et Lettres, 1978; French Officer of the Legion of Honor to Madame Carven, 1996. **Company Address:** 6 rond-point des Champs-Elysées, 75008 Paris, France. **Company Website:** www.carven.fr.

PUBLICATIONS

On CARVEN:

Books

Perkins, Alice K., *Paris Couturiers and Milliners,* New York, 1949.
Bertin, Celia, *Paris à la Mode,* London, 1956.
Picken, Mary Brooks, *Dressmakers of France,* New York, 1959.
Black, J. Anderson, et al., *A History of Fashion,* London, 1980.
Guillen, Pierre-Yves, and Jacqueline Claude, *The Golden Thimble: French Haute Couture,* Paris, 1990.
Stegemeyer, Anne, *Who's Who in Fashion, Third Edition,* New York, 1996.

Articles

"Carven Stages RTW Comeback with a Collection for Spring," in *WWD,* 7 August 1989.
Aillaud, Charlotte, "Madame Carven: Eighteenth Century Splendor in Her Avenue Foch House," in *Architectural Digest,* September 1989.
"French Fashion Designer Honored," in the *Detroit News,* 28 June 1997.
"Top Notes: Harlant Buys Carven," in *WWD,* 17 July 1998.
Costello, Brid, "Carven Updates Image with Scent," in *WWD,* 15 December 2000.
"Carefree on the Riviera," available online at La Mode Française, www.lamodefrancaise.tm.fr, 2001.

* * *

In 1949 when Jacqueline François sang of "Les robes de chez Carven" in her immortal song "Mademoiselle de Paris," the clothes of Madame Carven embodied all the charm, gaiety, and beauty of the city of Paris and its fabled women in the magical period after the war. The 1950s are seen as the golden age of the haute couture in Paris, and Carven is regarded as having been one of its primary practitioners. She is still designing, and although Carven's vast array of licensed products, from perfume to golfwear, have been distributed throughout the world, her name is not immediately recognized in America. Perhaps this is because she has never sought to shock or create trends or to follow the whims of fashion.

The single conceptual basis for Carven's work has always been to create beautiful clothes for all women, but in particular women of petite size: "I felt that I was small, and the contemporary taste for tall mannequins combined with my own admiration for Hollywood stars ended up giving me a complex. At the age of 25 I was a *coquette.* France was learning to dance again after the war and I wanted to be slinky. This desire to be attractive inspired a few reflections. First I noticed that I wasn't the only petite woman I knew, and that the grand couturiers weren't very interested in us. But I had a feeling for proportion and volume. All that remained for me to do was to create, with the help of friends who were scarcely taller than I was, dresses that would allow us to be ourselves. I'd found an opening where there was no competition and a moment when Paris was overflowing with happiness."

Carven's designs from the late 1940s through the early 1960s, while conforming to the prevailing stylistic tendencies of the period, are distinguished by the delicate decorative detail that flatters the wearer without overwhelming her. Trims at collar and cuff are frequently executed in all variations of white lace and embroidery. Occasionally, coolly plain white linen collar and cuffs assert the propriety of the wearer while enhancing an image of chic self-assurance. White on white is a recurring theme in Carven's designs, as evident in an evening dress of 1950 in which an embroidery of white *fleurs de Mai* completely covers a white bustier and asymmetrical long skirt, supported by a white halter and pleated underskirt. A bouffant-skirted afternoon dress with a closely fitted top from 1954 is executed in white linen subtly embroidered with white flowers, almost as if the dress were created from a fine tablecloth. Another recurring design motif is the use of fabrics and embroideries which shade from light to dark, subtly enhancing the wearer's figure and stature.

Carven was one of the first designers to promote her clothes in foreign countries, presenting her collections in Brazil, Mexico, Egypt, Turkey, and Iran. These travels greatly influenced her designs. After a trip to Egypt, she introduced a tightly-gathered type of drapery to her evening designs mimicking ancient Egyptian gowns—a 1952 design shows a bodice of sinuous gathers closely outlining the body in white jersey that, under beaded fringe at the hip reminiscent of a belly dancer's jeweled belt, breaks loose into a long flowing skirt. Another dress of 1952 is covered with an all-over design of Aztec-inspired motifs. An entire collection in 1959 was inspired by the beauties of Spain, as seen in paintings by Velazquez.

Today the Carven label can be found throughout the world as a result of extensive distribution of licensed products and especially Carven's perfume *Ma Griffe,* in its familiar white and green packaging. Madame Carven always includes a signature white and green dress in her collections, which, to this day, stand for a tasteful style of charm and beauty that complements the wearer no matter her proportions.

The late 1990s were a period of change for the House of Carven. In 1995 the company was reorganized, with the perfume, couture and accessories divisions merged and Angelo Tarlazzi taking over as artistic director of couture. three years later, in 1998, the Daniel Harlant Group, a French perfume firm, acquired Carven, whose financial performance was marred by a large amount of debt. Although Harlant was thought to be mainly interested in Carven's fragrance line, it focused on the house's couture activities as well, hiring Edward Achour as artistic director the same year it purchased the company. The Harlant Group also expanded Carven's licensing activity, signing a large ready-to-wear partner almost immediately. Carven is operate independently from the Harlant Group's other businesses.

Achour has emphasized the house's reputation for luxury, utilizing fabrics such as organza, lambskin, and silk to create sumptuous collections. As the website La Mode Française described it, his summer 2000 collection featured everything from sequined bikinis to a long skirt, complete with train, paired with a bra top. The collection's color palette was typically broad, focusing on Mediterranean shades from periwinkle to coral and every soft pastel shade in between.

Carven has attempted to reverse its somewhat conservative image in the fragrance category, the area for which the company is probably best known on a global basis, especially in North America. Company executives told *Women's Wear Daily* in December 2000 that the perfume division hoped to emulate the changes that had occurred since Achour had taken over in couture. His creations appeal to a younger consumer than Carven has historically attracted. The fragrance division began to reposition itself in the late 1990s, introducing the men's fragrance *Carven Homme* to target male consumers in their 30s, an unfilled niche for the house. A new women's scent, *Variations,* launched in 2001, was aimed at the same age bracket among females.

In terms of marketing, Carven has long supported its image by sponsoring events appealing to its upscale clientèle, including book fairs, horse races, and sailing and golf competitions. It continues this tradition today and also gives back to the fashion industry by offering grants to assist young designers just getting started.

Even without the active participation of Madame Carven since the mid-1990s, Carven maintains its haute couture image around the world. This profile is not only furthered by its seasonal collections but, perhaps even more, by a wide range of licensed luxury products, including leather goods, fragrances, jewelry, watches, pens, cognac and champagne, carpets, porcelain, furniture, corporate gifts, and uniforms. All told, more than 60 licensees market Carven branded products worldwide.

—Alan E. Rosenberg; updated by Karen Raugust

CASAGRANDE, Adele

See FENDI

CASELY-HAYFORD, Joe

British designer

Born: Ghana, 24 May 1956. **Education:** Trained at Tailor and Cutter Academy, London, 1974–75, St. Martin's School of Art, 1975–79, graduated 1979; studied history of art at the Institute of Contemporary Arts, London, 1979–80. **Family:** Married Maria Casely-Hayford, 1 August 1980. **Career:** Worked on Saville Row, pre-1974; designed stage outfits for rock groups and stars, including Mica Paris, Tori Amos, Neneh Cherry, Liam Gallagher, Suede, Lou Reed, and U2, from 1984; created own company, Joe Casely-Hayford Fashion, 1984; designs appeared in Derek Jarman's film *Edward II,* 1991;

Joe Casely-Hayford, fall/winter 2001 "Supertramp" collection. © Reuters NewMedia Inc./CORBIS.

designed hosiery range for Sock Shop chain, London, 1991; commissioned to design clothes for ballet *Very,* by Jonathan Burrows, 1992; established diffusion line, Hayford, 1992; flagship boutique opened, London, 1993; freelance designer, Panchetti label, Italy, and Joseph and Top Shop chain, Britain. **Exhibitions:** *Street Style*, Victoria and Albert Museum, London, November 1994–February 1995. **Address:** 128 Shoreditch High Street, London E1 6JE England.

Publications

By CASELY-HAYFORD:

Articles

"Bovril Babes," in *Face* (London), June 1992.
"Year Review of Fashion," in *i-D* (London), January 1993.
"Fashion," in *Face* (London), December 1993.
"Urban Nomad," in *i-D* (London), The Urgent Issue.
"A Question of Culture," in *i-D* (London), The Strength Issue.

Joe Casely-Hayford, fall/winter 2001 "Supertramp" collection. © Reuters NewMedia Inc./CORBIS.

On CASELY-HAYFORD:

Books

Tulloch, Carol, "Rebel Without a Pause: Black Street Style and Black Designers," in Juliet Ash and Elizabeth Wilson (eds.), *Chic Thrills, A Fashion Reader,* Berkeley, CA, 1993.
De La Haye, Amy, editor, *The Cutting Edge: 50 Years of British Fashion, 1947–1997,* New York, 1997.

Articles

"New Talent," in *Harpers & Queens,* September 1985.
"Da Londra, Moda Come Provocazione: Eclectics," in *L'Uomo Vogue* (Milan), December 1985.
McCooey, Meriel, "East Side Story," in the *Sunday Times Magazine* (London), 27 April 1986.
DuCann, Charlotte, "Independent Style: Young British Design," in *Vogue* (London), November 1986.
"Shooting Stars," in *Women's Journal* (London), February 1988.
Bain, Sally, "The New Order of Nights," in *Elle* (London), December 1988.
Profile of Joe Casely-Hayford, in *Details,* February 1989.
Profile of Joe Casely-Hayford, in the *Observer,* 12 March 1989.
Hochswender, Woody, "Fashion Iconoclasts Rediscover Subtleties," in the *New York Times,* 2–3 April 1989.
Samuel, Kathryn, "Designer of the Year," in the *Sunday Telegraph,* 15 October 1989.
Griggs, Barbara, "The Italian Connection," in *Vogue,* May 1990.
"Joe Casely-Hayford," in *Clothes Show* (London), March 1991.
Rodgers, Toni, "Double Vision," in *Elle* (London), March 1991.
Clarke, Adrian, "Black Panther," in *Fashion Weekly* (London), 14 March 1991.
Profile of Joe Casely-Hayford, in the *Guardian,* 22 April 1991.
"Five Cut Loose (and Ties Will Not Be Worn)," in the *Independent* (London), 22 August 1991.
Profile of Joe Casely-Hayford, in the *Glasgow Herald,* 9 October 1991.
"Fashion Warriors Set Sights on Impact," in the *Independent* (London), 17 February 1992.
"Joe Casely's Costume Karma," in the *Weekly Journal* (London), 23 May 1992.
Plewka, Karl, "Spotlighting Joe Casely-Hayford," in *Interview,* January 1993.
Profile on Joe Casely-Hayford, in *Collezioni,* January/February 1993.
Tredre, Roger, "In the Black-White-Rock-Fashion World," in the *Independent Weekend* (London), 13 February 1993.
Schacknat, Karin, "Joe Casely-Hayford: Pure Vormals Ultieme Doel," in *Kunsten de!* (Arnhem), May 1993.
Rawlinson, Richard, "Top Shop Signs Up Joe Casely-Hayford," in *Fashion Weekly* (London), 22 July 1993.
Alford, Lucinda, "Hey, Joe!" in the *Observer Review* (London), 22 August 1993.
Profile of Joe Casely-Hayford, in the *Manchester Evening News,* October 1993.
Scott, Alexander, "Platform, Rusty New Ideas," in *Ticket* (London), June 1994.
Sims, Josh, "Cape Crusaders," in the *Guardian* (London), 3 November 2000.

* * *

The traditional design tenets of quality fabric, attention to detail, and excellent cut underpin all of Joe Casely-Hayford's work. This is not to deny the surprise of his designs, which often have unusual details of decoration or spicy color combinations to enliven them. His clothes are for the discerning customer who wants styles to retain their appeal for more than one season. The clothes are always very contemporary in feel, though rarely following fashion fads. Although he returns to his skillful pleating and cutting of traditional wool fabrics for classic suits each season, his influences are wide ranging. He can just as stylishly redefine 1970s wide collar coats as create American Indian-style soft leather jackets.

His menswear is perhaps his perennial tour de force. Always interesting and innovative, his collections are a combination of highly desirable good quality with witty detailing. His clean-cut wool suits are given a stylish twist through pleating or cut-out lapels with curling velvet inserts, making them more individual. His designs may reveal a certain amount of anarchic license in their cut, but he is never cultish or unwearable, carefully balancing the elements in his work with his original vision to make clothes with a long life span. Even his more experimental garments, like the all-in-one suit he created in the late 1980s that looked like a two-piece from the front but had a battle-dress back, still have a beauty in their fit and the refined finish that distinguishes all his work.

Casely-Hayford, like Stephen Burrows and Ozwald Boateng, was one of the few early black designers to attain prominence in the international fashion world, and he passes his knowledge along to the next generation; one of his protégés is Walé Adeyemi. Having arrived on the wave of the exciting new art school-trained British designers that included John Richmond and John Galliano, he has also remained dedicated to increasing Britain's fashion standing on the international market. To that end, he is active in teaching future designers, lending his time and expertise to programs like the Marymount London Fashion Program, which teaches students and gives them the opportunity to intern with working designers and get hands-on experience.

Although he is part of the 5th Circle, set up in August 1991 to showcase the menswear of five homegrown designers, he is equally committed to his womenswear collection. It has the same strength of cut and clarity of design, often initiating ideas that are later taken up by others. Examples are the bra tops of his early shows that were later to flood the market; the hot-colored patchwork suede wide collar jackets, long coats, and hot pants he used that heralded the 1970s revival of the early 1990s; and the beehive hairdos he brought back in his fall 2001 show.

His clothes for women have a sexy feel, with sculpted leather waistcoats and neatly fitted suits alongside funky knitwear and simple yet sophisticated dresses, each with the usual Casely-Hayford twist marking out their design. His designs are complemented by the seasonal addition of interesting and unusual footwear created for Shelly's, the London shoe chain.

Beginning in about 1984, Casely-Hayford entered the music world, dressing such stars as Tori Amos, Black Uhuru, Neneh Cherry, The Clash, Liam Gallagher, Glamma Kid, Lynden David Hall, Mica Paris, Lou Reed, Suede, and U2 (including their two-year world tour in 1991–93), and enjoying a popularity rivaled only by Gianni and Donatella Versace. He also served as a costume designer on Derek Jarman's film *Edward II* (1991).

Casely-Hayford has quietly built a niche for himself in British fashion as a master of cut, and his work has also just as quietly gained an international following, especially in Japan, where his work is very popular. His clothes have the appeal of longevity while at the same time maintaining style and well-balanced beauty through the combination of each element of design, providing carefully thought-out garments that flatter the wearer with their witty detail and consistently good fit.

He has remained very active, showing collections regularly from 1998 to 2001, not only in London but from Paris to Milan and from Rome to New York. His collections in 2000–01 featured an eclectic riot of colors and fabrics, from orange and green to white and black, from solid to tie-dye, from leather to tweed, from tulle to suede, from fake fur to wool. Described alternatingly as conservative, cutting edge, bold, and subliminal, Casely-Hayford's designs, while remaining experimental, are still very wearable.

—Rebecca Arnold; updated by Daryl F. Mallett

CASHIN, Bonnie

American designer

Born: Oakland, California, 1915. **Education:** Studied at the Art Students League, New York, and also in Paris. **Family:** Briefly married to Robert Sterner. **Career:** Costume designer, Roxy Theater, New York, 1934–37; designer, Adler and Adler sportswear, New

Bonnie Cashin, 1962 collection: suede and wool coat with a jersey dress. © Bettmann/CORBIS.

York, 1937–43 and 1949–52; costume designer, Twentieth Century Fox, Los Angeles, California, 1943–49; designer, Bonnie Cashin Designs (with partner Phillip Sills), New York, 1953–77; established The Knittery, 1972; founder, Innovative Design Fund, circa 1981. **Exhibitions:** Brooklyn Museum (retrospective), 1962; Metropolitan Museum of Art, 1997; Fashion Institute of Technology (retrospective, "Bonnie Cashin, Practical Dreamer"), September 2000. **Awards:** Neiman Marcus award, Dallas, Texas, 1950; Coty American Fashion Critics award, New York, 1950, 1960, 1961, 1968, 1972; Sporting Look award, 1958; Philadelphia Museum College of Art citation, 1959; Woolknit Associates Design award, 1959, 1961; Lighthouse award, 1961; Sports Illustrated award, 1963; Detroit Business Association, national award, 1963; the *Sunday Times* International Fashion award, London, 1964; Leather Industries American Handbag Designer award, 1968, 1976; Kaufmann Fashion award, Pittsburgh, 1968; Creator citation, Saks Fifth Avenue, 1969; Mary Mount College Golden Needle award, 1970; Hall of Fame, 1972; I. Magnin's Great American award, 1974; American Fashion award for furs, 1975; Drexel University citation, Philadelphia, 1976; inducted to Fashion Walk of Fame, Seventh Avenue, New York, 2001. **Died:** 3 February 2000.

Publications

On CASHIN:

Books

Levin, Phyllis Lee, *The Wheels of Fashion,* Garden City, New York, 1965.

Carter, Ernestine, *The Changing World of Fashion: 1900 to the Present,* London, 1977.

Milbank, Caroline R., *Couture: The Great Designers,* New York, 1985.

New York and Hollywood Fashion: Costume Designs from the Brooklyn Museum Collection, New York, 1986.

Maeder, Edward, et al., *Hollywood and History: Costume Design in Film,* New York, 1987.

Milbank, Caroline R., *New York Style: The Evolution of Fashion,* New York, 1989.

Leese, Elizabeth, *Costume Design in the Movies,* New York, 1991.

Steele, Valerie, *Women of Fashion,* New York, 1991.

Stegemeyer, Anne, *Who's Who in Fashion, Third Edition,* New York, 1996.

Articles

"Bonnie Cashin: Trail Blazer in Fashion," in *American Fabrics* (New York) 1956.

Reily, Robert, "Bonnie Cashin Retrospective," in *American Fabrics and Fashions* (New York), No. 60, 1963.

"Bonnie Cashin," in *Current Biography* (New York), May 1970.

"Round Table: Bonnie Cashin," in *American Fabrics and Fashions* (Columbia, South Carolina), No. 133, 1985.

Elliott, Mary C. "Bonnie Cashin: Design for Living," in *Threads* (Newtown, Connecticut), Oct./Nov. 1990.

Weir, June, "Natural History," in *Mirabella* (New York), January 1995.

Wilson, Eric and Janet Ozzard, "Designer Bonnie Cashin Dead at 84," in *Women's Wear Daily,* 7 February 2000.

Obituary, in the *Economist,* 12 February 2000.

Scully, James, "Cashin' In," in *Harper's Bazaar,* July 2000.

Wilson, Eric, "Bonnie Cashin's Inspiration," in *Women's Wear Daily,* 18 September 2000.

Spindler, Amy M., "Design for Living," in the *New York Times Magazine,*7 January 2001.

* * *

An awareness of the body in motion informs Bonnie Cashin's design style. Her earliest efforts were created for dancers: as a California high school student, Cashin costumed the local ballet troupe, Franchon & Marco. After graduating from high school, she became the company's costume designer and later, with the encouragement of the troupe's manager, moved to New York to study dance and take classes at the Art Students' League. Soon after moving, Cashin began making costumes for the Roxy Theater, which during the 1930s was a major competitor to Radio City Music Hall's Rockettes. An article in *Variety* described Cashin as the "youngest designer to hit Broadway." During her tenure as house costumer with the famed Roxy Theater, which she considered her "formal schooling in design,"she designed three sets of costumes a week for the Roxy's chorus of 24 dancing showgirls. With minimal budgets, Cashin used her ingenuity, a little paint, and knowledge learned from her mother, a custom dressmaker, to transform inexpensive fabrics into striking costumes that looked equally graceful in motion or in repose. Whether for stage or street, Cashin's work has always been styled for the active woman on the move, who prefers an easy, individual look with a minimum of fuss. The May 1970 issue of *Current Biography* quoted her as saying, "All I want is to speak simply in my designing; I don't want the gilt and the glamor."

A 1937 production number, in which the Roxy dancers emerged smartly dressed from between the pages of a fashion magazine, sent Cashin in a new direction. Louis Adler, co-owner of the sportswear firm Adler and Adler, saw Cashin's designs and recognized her potential importance to the fashion industry. Wary of the garment district's regimentation, Cashin initially played it safe. She stayed on in the familiar collegial world of the theater and freelanced for Adler. In 1938 Cashin left the theater to work for Adler, quickly earning a name in the ready-to-wear fashion circles. When the U.S. entered World War II, Cashin was appointed to a committee to design uniforms for the women in the armed forces. Her designs for the mass-produced uniforms were practical—they were protective, comfortable, and allowed for freedom of movement. The uniforms were made from long-lasting fabrics such as canvas and leather, featuring large pockets, toggle fastenings, and industrial-size zippers. Eventually she signed with the firm and designed for about 12 years before and after World War II.

After a brief marriage to art director Robert Sterner, and having become frustrated with the Seventh Avenue fashion scene, Cashin returned to California where she exercised her talents in a completely new arena—the motion picture industry. Cashin began working for Twentieth Century Fox in 1943, where she designed wardrobes for more than 60 films including such classics *Laura, Anna and the King of Siam* and *A Tree Grows in Brooklyn.* In 1949 Cashin returned to New York and began designing again for Adler and Adler, and the following year won both the Neiman Marcus award and the first of five Coty awards for a prototype of her signature *Noh* coat, an unlined, sleeved or sleeveless T-shaped coat with deeply cut armholes to wear singly, in combination, or under a poncho or cape. Despite this success, Cashin sensed she would never achieve her creative best working under contract in the profit-oriented canyons of Seventh Avenue. She began designing on a freelance basis in 1953, creating Bonnie Cashin Designs from her studio, which was located across from the Metropolitan Museum of Art. Unusual for the time, she worked on a royalty basis, creating complete coordinated wardrobes—accessories, knits, capes and coats, dresses, and separates—to be combined in layers to suit the climate or the event.

On a trip to Japan during the early 1950s, the practical aspects of the kimono, a garment consisting of a variable number of layers, was described to Cashin. In terms of the ever-changing weather, the kimono was especially appropriate for cooler temperatures or what the Japanese described as a "nine-layer day." Upon her return to New York, Cashin "introduced" the concept of layering garments into Western fashion. Of course, people around the world had been dressing in layers to accommodate the climate for centuries, but as an obituary in the *Economist* explained, "Fashion writers are ever grateful for something that looks new, and for a while layering was praised as the big new idea."

As Cashin had so aptly explained to one reporter, "fashion evolved from need." Cashin's unusual ideas were welcomed and she typically worked years ahead of the market, pioneering clothing concepts which today seem part of fashion's essential vocabulary. In the 1950s when most women's clothing was concerned with structure, the Cashin silhouette was based on the rectangle or the square and called for a minimum of darting and seaming. Cashin showed layered dressing long before the concept became a universal option; she brought canvas boots and raincoats out of the show ring and into the street in 1952 and she introduced jumpsuits as early as 1956.

Signature pieces included her *Noh* coats, funnel-necked sweaters whose neck doubles as a hood, classic ponchos, and such innovations as a bicycle sweater with roomy back pockets. Other Cashin hallmarks were her use of toggle closures, leather piping, and pairing various fabrics such as tweeds with tartan plaid or suede. Other notable Cashin "icons" were her leather coats and jackets made by leather manufacturer Phillip Sills. Cashin introduced handbags into her collections as far back as the 1930s, and in the early 1960s designed bags for Coach. She also created rainwear designs for Modelia and gloves for Crescendoe-Superb.

Very likely because of her early work in the theater, both color and especially texture played a starring role in Cashin's designs. An organza *Noh* coat could be trimmed with linen and shown over a sweater dress of cashmere. A jersey sheath could be paired with an apron-wrap skirt cut from a boisterous tweed. Her palette was both subtle and controlled—earth tones, sparked with vivid accents. Cashin has been recognized as one of the few women fashion designers who made an impact on American fashion during a time when Parisan designers were dominant on the runway

For several decades Cashin created a myriad of fashion items and has been identified as a pioneer of American sportswear design. In 1978 *New York Times* fashion writer Bernadine Morris called Cashin "an American fashion institution." She was recognized with some two dozen awards, was a featured designer for one of Lord & Taylor's "American Design Rooms,"and influenced fashion industry giants. Cashin professed a "profound distaste" for the fashion industry and retired in the mid-1980s. She died in February 2000 at the age of 84. Several months after her death, a retrospective of her work, entitled "Bonnie Cashin, Practical Dreamer," was organized at New York's Fashion Institute of Technology. The retrospective featured Cashin's most identifiable creations along with several personal artifacts from her apartment; where she was among the first to move her work space and living space into the United Nations Plaza during the 1960s. Even before her death, many of her fashion items came to attention of collectors and in 1997 some of her clothes were exhibited at Metropolitan Museum of Art in New York City. According to the exhibit catalogue, Cashin's designs reflected "democracy's magnitude and the consequence of independent and intrepid women."

Bonnie Cashin worked to her own brief, designing for women who were smart, active, self-aware, and, like herself, of independent mind.

—Whitney Blausen; updated by Christine Miner Minderovic

CASSINI, Oleg

American designer

Born: Oleg Loiewski in Paris of Russian parents, 11 April 1913. Raised in Florence; adopted mother's family name, Cassini, 1937. Immigrated to the U.S., 1936, naturalized, 1942. **Education:** Attended

Oleg Cassini, 1958 couture collection of the New York Dress Institute: crêpe sheath cocktail dress with a deep V decolletage in chiffon over chiffon. © Bettmann/CORBIS.

English Catholic School, Florence; studied at Accademia delle Belle Arti, Florence, 1931–34; political science, University of Florence, 1932–34. **Military Service:** Served five years with U.S. Army Cavalry during World War II. **Family:** Married Merry Fahrney, 1938 (divorced); married actress Gene Tierney, 1941 (divorced, 1952); daughters: Daria, Christina. **Career:** After working in his mother's Maison de Couture in Florence, opened his own Maison de Couture, Rome; sketch artist, Patou, Paris, 1935; design assistant to couturier Jo Copeland, New York, 1936; designer, William Bass, 1937, and James Rotherberg Inc., New York, 1938–39; New York salon, Oleg Inc., established, 1937–39; owner of Cassini fashion studio, New York, 1939–40; designer, Paramount Pictures, Los Angeles, 1939–42; designer under contract with Twentieth Century Fox, Los Angeles, 1940; owner, Cassini Dardick fashion firm, New York, 1947–50: established Oleg Cassini Inc., New York, 1950; appointed official designer to U.S. First Lady Jacqueline Kennedy, early 1960s; established ready-to-wear business, Milan, 1963; returned to New York, designed tennis clothes for Munsingwear and swimwear for Waterclothes under own label, 1974; introduced new fragrance line, *Cassini,* 1990; inked deal with Cascade International to develop specialty stores, 1991; launched fake fur collection, 1999. **Exhibitions:** *Jacqueline Kennedy: The White House Years* (featuring many of Cassini's designs), 2001. **Awards:** Numerous awards, including five first prizes, Mostra della Moda, Turin, 1934; Honorary Doctor of Fine Arts, International College of Fine Arts, Miami, 1989; American Society of Perfumers Living Legend award, 2001.

Oleg Cassini with his wife, actress Gene Tierney, who is modeling one of his designs, 1941. © Bettmann/CORBIS.

PUBLICATIONS

By CASSINI:

Books

Pay the Price, New York, 1983.
In My Own Fashion, New York, 1987, 1990.
One Thousand Days of Magic, New York, 1995.

On CASSINI:

Books

Bender, Marylin, *The Beautiful People,* New York, 1967.
Milbank, Caroline Rennolds, *New York Fashion: The Evolution of American Style,* New York, 1989.
Leese, Elizabeth, *Costume Design in the Movies,* New York, 1991.

Articles

"Oleg Cassini," in *Current Biography,* July 1961.
"Oleg Cassini, un couturier collectionneur de femmes," in *Elle* (Paris), 25 October 1987.
Tedeschi, Mark, "Cassini's Career—Straight Out of a Hemingway Novel," in *Footwear News,* 17 December 1990.
Buck, Geneviève, "You're Not Excused if You Sniff at the Idea of Mixing Fragrances and Fashion," in the *Chicago Tribune,* 19 December 1990.
"Cassini to Design for Cascade," in the *South Florida Business Journal,* 17 June 1991.
"Oleg Cassini Comes to Town," in *Clothes Show* (London), December 1991.
"The Charm of First Lady's Man Oleg Cassini Shines On," in *Vogue* (London), December 1991.
Witchell, Alex, "A Lifetime's Pursuit of Glamour, Grandeur and Women's Trust," in the *New York Times,* 16 November 1995.
"Oleg Cassini Bailout Plan Falls Through," in *Women's Wear Daily,* 22 July 1997.
Maxwell, Alison, "Oleg Cassini Launches Fake-Fur Line," in *Women's Wear Daily,* 9 November 1999.
Horyn, Cathy, "Fashion's Gadfly Tangos With A Legend," in the *New York Times,* 15 April 2001.

* * *

Oleg Cassini has had an extremely varied, glamorous, and exotic career but is perhaps best known for the personal style and clothing he developed when official designer for First Lady Jacqueline Kennedy in 1961. He worked closely with Mrs. Kennedy, a personal friend, and together they created many widely copied garments that became American fashion classics and firmly established Kennedy as a style leader.

The First Lady frequently wore a fawn wool two-piece outfit, a dress and a waist-length semifitted jacket or coat with a removable round neck collar of Russian sable, often topped by the famous pillbox hats created by Halston. Another popular outfit was a high-necked silk ottoman empire-line evening gown that gently flared in an A-line to the floor. Jacqueline Kennedy's vast public exposure proved a huge boost for Cassini's profile and brought worldwide attention to American fashion in general.

Cassini was born a count and was brought up by Italian/Russian parents in Florence, where his mother ran an exclusive dress shop. He began his career in 1934 by making small one-off designs sold through his mother's shop. He moved to New York in 1936 and worked for several Seventh Avenue manufacturers before joining Twentieth-Century Fox in Hollywood as a costume designer in 1940. He worked for several major film studios and created glamorous clothes for many film stars—eventually marrying one, Gene Tierney—against studio wishes.

In 1950 the designer opened Oleg Cassini Inc., his ready-to-wear dress firm in New York, with $100,000-worth of backing. Femininity quickly became the keyword in describing his work; he produced dresses made from soft, romantic fabrics like lace, taffeta, and chiffon. He popularized ladylike fashion innovations, such as the A-line, the smart little white-collared dress, the sheath, the knitted suit, and dresses with minute waistlines. Military details such as brass buttons and braid were also popular features. In the 1960s the Cassini look evolved to incorporate ease and simplicity. The straight, lined cocktail and evening dresses popularized by Jackie Kennedy were customer favorites, as were his plain, boxy jacket suits.

Retiring from his ready-to-wear and couture business in 1963, Cassini's next venture was a ready-to-wear business in partnership with his brother Igor. He presented a menswear collection for the first time, breaking tradition by introducing color to shirts that had always been white, and teaming them with traditional three-piece suits.

An author of several books, beginning with his autobiography *In My Own Fashion* back in 1987, Cassini published *One Thousand Days of Magic* in 1995 about his experiences dressing Jackie Kennedy during her White House years. The 217-page book sold well and Cassini toured the country making appearances in its behalf. Yet he was still equally active in fashion; in 1997 Cassini and an investment group prepared to acquire He-Ro Group Ltd., producer of the designer's Black Tie eveningwear collections. The new company was to be renamed Oleg Cassini Group International, but the deal fell through after the sudden death of a He-Ro chairman, William J. Carone. He-Ro was then bought and merged with Nah Nah Collections to form the Nahdree Group, and subsequently cut ties with Cassini.

The veteran designer bounced back in 1999 with a fake-fur collection, launched at a fundraiser for the Humane Society of America. Working with Monterey Fashions to produce the 100-piece faux fur line, Cassini commented to *Women's Wear Daily* in November 1999, "You won't be able to distinguish between the real and man-made."

At the turn of the century, Cassini was entering his 90s and still a man about town. He ran an extensive empire, exporting to over 20 countries through an ever expanding number of licensing agreements. The company produced womenwear, menswear, children's clothing, and innumerable accessories including ties, luggage, cosmetics, shoes, umbrellas, and fragrances.

In 2001, six years after the publication of Cassini's *One Thousand Days of Magic* and 40 years after he began designing for Jackie Kennedy, the Metropolitan Museum of Art mounted an exhibition called "Jacqueline Kennedy: The White House Years." The exhibit featured many of the designer's famed creations for the First Lady, and brought the Cassini name to the forefront of the industry once more.

—Kevin Almond; updated by Nelly Rhodes

CASTELBAJAC, Jean-Charles de

French designer

Born: Of French parents in Casablanca, Morocco, 28 November 1949. **Education:** Attended Catholic boarding schools in France, 1955–66; studied law, Faculté de Droit, Limoges, 1966–77. **Family:** Married Katherine Lee Chambers, 1979; children: Guillaume, Louis. **Career:** Founder and designer, with his mother Jeanne-Blanche de Castelbajac, of Ko & Co., ready-to-wear fashion company, Limoges, beginning in 1968; freelanced for Pierre d'Alby, Max Mara, Jesus Jeans, Etam, Gadgling, Julie Latour, Fusano, Amaraggi, Carel Shoes,

Jean-Charles de Castelbajac, fall/winter 2001 collection. © AP/ Wide World Photos.

Ellesse, Hilton, Levi Strauss, and Reynaud, beginning in 1968; director, Jean-Charles de Castelbajac label, Paris, 1970, and Sociétè Jean-Charles de Castelbajac SARL, Paris, 1978; established boutiques in Paris, New York, and Tokyo, 1975–76; also designed for film and music, including Elton John, Talking Heads, and Rod Stewart, from 1976; interior and furniture designs, from 1979; member, Didier Grumbach's Les Créateurs group of designers, Paris, 1974–77; designer for Courrèges, 1994–96; created outfits for the Pope and priests at World Youth Days, 1997; revamped label, 1998; introduced fragrance line with Parfums Lolita Lempicka, 2001. **Exhibitions:** Cêntre Georges Pompidou, Paris, 1978; Forum Design, Linz, Austria, 1980; Laforet Museum, Belgium, 1984. **Collections:** Musée du Costume, Paris; Fashion Institute of Technology, New York. **Address:** 15 rue Cassette, 75006 Paris, France.

PUBLICATIONS

By CASTELBAJAC:

Books

J.C. de Castelbajac, 1993.

On CASTELBAJAC:

Books

Carter, Ernestine, *The Changing World of Fashion,* London, 1977.

Who's Who in Fashion, Karl Strute and Theodor Doelken, ed., Zurich, 1982.

Delpais, Delbourg, *Le Chic et la Mode,* Paris, 1982.

McDowell, Colin, *McDowell's Directory of Twentieth Century Fashion,* London, 1984.

O'Hara, Georgina, *The Encyclopaedia of Fashion from 1940 to the 1980s,* London, 1986.

Stegemeyer, Anne, *Who's Who in Fashion, Third Edition,* New York, 1996.

Articles

"Un styliste bourree d'idees: Jean-Charles de Castelbajac," in *Gap* (Paris), October 1975.

"Jean-Charles de Castelbajac: French Revolutionary," in *GQ* (New York), April 1981.

Barrett, Amy, "Pope's Choice for Paris Vestments Doesn't Have Everyone's Blessing," in the *Wall Street Journal,* 19 August 1997.

Castro, Peter and Cathy Nolan, "Man of the Cloth," in *People,* 25 August 1997.

Ozzard, Janet, "Castelbajac Signs Deal for Perfume," in *Women's Wear Daily,* 3 February 1999.

"Short Circuits: Baccarat Falls in Love," in *Duty-Free News International,* 1 December 1999.

"Lempicka Enters Fresh Territory," in Duty-Free News International, 1 December 2000.

* * *

If color produces optimism, then Jean-Charles de Castelbajac is the most optimistic designer in existence. Void of lux rhinestones or glitz, his collection features color to luxuriate the world. The designer, who has been deemed "the space age Bonnie Cashin," not only clothes people in color but creates an environmental lifestyle, with everything from sofas to crystal to carpets.

Castelbajac is a man of passions—for form and function, for color, for comfort and protection—and therein lies the basis of this humanistic designer. Castelbajac began his obsession by cutting his first garment out of a blanket from boarding school. Because the material already existed, he was left to play only with the form. Many times each year he returns to this first gesture, cutting the cloth, so he remains close to its essence and function.

Having been titled Marquis, Castelbajac has erected the first monument to celebrate the living in Paris: 150,000 names of young people are inscribed on a steel totem pole to support Castelbajac's project to give inspiration and a sense of worth to generations used to growing up with war memorials celebrating the dead. Despite his interest in youth, he has always been involved with heroes and heritage, but he has never been archaic in his designs. Castelbajac is a man of the future, but he does not make futuristic clothing; his designs fulfill the need for practical and unassuming fashion of maximum quality. While favoring natural textures and fibers, Castelbajac creates designs that are innovative but respectful of the classics; he has been called a modern traditionalist.

Castelbajac's fondness for architecture is apparent in the harmonious, finely-drawn shapes that flow through every collection. He has a great affinity with painters, with whom he spends much time to strengthen his creative impulses. Having a strong revulsion to prints on garments, he humorously solved the predicament by using large scale motifs of Tom and Jerry, or phrases from Nerval or Barbey d'Aurevilly inscribed on silk, for very simply shaped dresses. At other times his garments are filled with angels, medieval and heraldic motifs, or childlike inscriptions drawn with the skill of an artistic adult but with the imagination of a child.

In 1994 when Castelbajac began designing the collections of André Courrèges, the futuristic designer of 1960s, Castelbajac managed to successfully to rejuvenate the original spirit of Courrèges clothes. Castelbajac had a somewhat similar style to Courrèges, but he added courageous touches along with his trademark sense of humor. Castelbajac worked with the house about two years, after which he went out on his own again. At this time in the mid- to late 1990s, however, minimalist fashions were in vogue, and Castelbajac's eccentric, fun-loving designs did not find as much acceptance.

In a surprise choice, Castelbajac was selected as the official designer for the 1997 Catholic celebration World Youth Days, held in Paris, for which he created the Pope's vestments and the apparel for the 5,000 priests at the event, as well as souvenirs such as t-shirts and baseball caps that helped subsidize attendees from poorer countries. Although his selection was controversial, Castelbajac pointed out that much of the inspiration for his designs had always come from the liturgical shapes and stained-glass window colors familiar from his Catholic upbringing. His design for the papal robe was inspired by the story of Noah's Ark.

Castelbajac revamped his label significantly in 1998, collaborating with young designers—including for his noted "Painting Dresses"—and opening several concept stores. He has also continued to expand into a variety of categories, notably home furnishings, where he has refreshed classic furnishings styles, such as the Chesterfield sofa, but with his own colorful flair. He has lent his name to a line of brightly colored paints, manufactured by Castorama, as well as porcelains, linens, carpets, light fixtures, and other home-related objects. His ideal for the home is warm and cozy but still luxurious.

Jean-Charles de Castelbajac and two of his designs following the presentation of his fall/winter 2001–02 collection. © AP/Wide World Photos.

Castelbajac's product lines, best-known in his home country, include his signature designer sportswear and jeanswear, as well as women's and men's deluxe ready-to-wear and accessories including bags, umbrellas, glasses, ties, and jewelry. He introduced a line of fragrances with Parfums Lolita Lempicka in 2001; an earlier line with another company dating from the early 1980s had been discontinued. Outside the world of products, Castelbajac has dipped into broadcast design, creating vignettes for the cable television network Muzzik.

Castelbajac's spring/summer 2001 collection was typical of his style. Using materials such as varnished leather, embroidered jersey, and camouflage, his clothes featured Op Art, depictions of action figures, huge comic book-style characters and words such as YAOOW! and KLINK! His traditional bright colors—evidenced in creations such as Day-Glo green and orange skirts of tulle—were accented with touches including brooches in the shape of marijuana leaves and giant fabric pins. His sense of fun and color were on display, as they are in all of his endeavors.

The inscription of Cervantes in Castelbajac's 1993 self-titled book reads: "Always hold the hand of the child you once were." His clothing and his art are identifiable by his manner of being true to himself; by being profoundly human and knowing something is not simply style.

—Andrea Arsenault; updated by Karen Raugust

CATALINA SPORTSWEAR

American swimwear and sportswear firm

Founded: in 1907 by John C. Bentz as Bentz Knitting Mills, manufacturing underwear and sweaters; renamed Pacific Knitting Mills (1912), Catalina Knitting Mills (1928), and Catalina, from 1955. **Company History:** knitted swimwear introduced, 1912; sponsor, Miss America pageant until 1951 dispute; originated and sponsored additional pageants, including Miss USA, Miss Teen USA, and Miss Universe, 1950s; company purchased by Kayser-Roth apparel division of Gulf & Western Company, 1975; bankruptcy, 1993; acquired by Authentic Fitness, 1997; combined with Cole of California to become Catalina Cole. **Awards:** Los Angeles Chamber of Commerce Golden 44 award, 1979.

Publications

On CATALINA:

Books

Lençek, Lina, and Gideon Bosker, *Making Waves: Swimsuits and the Undressing of America,* San Francisco, 1989.

Koda, Harold, and Richard Martin, *Splash! A History of Swimwear,* New York, 1990.

Articles

Ross, Adele, "Catalina: A Giant Need Not Be Inflexible," in *California Apparel News* (Los Angeles), 1 October 1976.

"Catalina," in *Apparel Industry Magazine* (Atlanta, Georgia), December 1984.

Shaffer, Gina, "Catalina Charts New Course," in *Man*, January 1985.

"Bathing Beauties at One Time,"*Chicago Tribune,* 18 February 1987.

Horton, Cleveland, "Russians Get Taste of U.S. Sun, Fun (Catalina Swimwear TV Ad Airing in the Former Soviet Union)," *Advertising Age,* 13 July 1992.

Ryan, Thomas J., "Authentic Fitness Net Gains 52.7-Percent" in *WWD,* 27 January 1995.

D'Innocenzio, Anne, "Swimwear Dives, Hopes to Surface," in *WWD,* 10 August 1995.

Conklin, Mike, "Miss America Timeline," *Chicago Tribune,* 27 October 2000.

* * *

Catalina Sportswear evolved from an obscure California knitting mill into a world-leading swimwear manufacturer, reigning from the 1930s through the early 1990s. The U.S. and Eastern Europe experienced a physical fitness and sports craze in the 1920s and 1930s. Catalina, along with Jantzen in Oregon, shrewdly and stylishly propelled West Coast fashion into prominence as they filled the growing need for active outdoor clothes, especially swimwear.

The early wool knit suits, patterned after a simple one-piece style introduced to the U.S. by Australian swim star Annette Kellerman, allowed women new freedom in the water. They also challenged and broke down the Edwardian modesty codes. In the 1920s, Catalina produced increasingly baring and fashionable as well as functional swimwear, notably, the boldly striped Chicken Suit, men's Speed Suit, and Ribstitch "S" suits.

Catalina incorporated new fabrics into its products as fast as technology developed them. When Lastex, the rubber-cored thread, appeared in the 1930s, Catalina advertised the LA or "Lastex Appeal" in men's swim trunks. Lastex and Spandex, and Vyrene Spandex in the 1960s, would provide the elasticity and shaping power under and in combination with knits, cotton, velour, Celanese Rayon, DuPont Antron, nylon, and Lycra fabrics.

Particularly in the 1930s and 1940s the company had a symbiotic relationship with Hollywood. Warner Bros. costume designer Orry Kelly and film color consultant and makeup man Perc Westmore designed for Catalina. Starlets and stars like Ginger Rogers, Joan Crawford, Ronald Reagan, and Marilyn Monroe were photographed in Catalina sportswear for advertising and publicity purposes. Such shots boosted the stars, the California mystique, pool and beach business, and Catalina sales. Catalina's influence was also intertwined with the myth and icon of the Miss America Beauty Pageant. When the company sponsored the contest in the 1940s, contestants wore essentially off-the-rack Catalina suits, except that pageant suits had the flying fish logo on both hips instead of one. Catalina dropped sponsorship of Miss America after 1951 winner Yolande Betbeze refused to wear a Catalina suit for the traiditonal swimsuit tour; the company then went on to found the Miss USA, Miss Teen USA, and Miss Universe pageants and cosponsored them for decades. Since 1960 television beamed contestants wearing Catalina styles with gold embroidered flying fish to worldwide audiences. Catalina's participation in these fashion and body-conscious fixtures in American culture exemplifies an underlying modus operandi to design suits that allowed women and men to show off their bodies in a fashionable, abbreviated, yet socially acceptable garment.

In its long history, Catalina experienced bursts of innovative flair and attracted high profile design talent: swimwear designer Elizabeth Stewart went on to found her own company, while Lee Hogan Cass specially commissioned patterns in European-inspired browns and innovative citrus batiks that delighted consumers. Jacquard knit suits and casual wear in bright colors were a hit in Italy, and bikini-clad Europeans sought the maker of an innovative Grecian pleated suit seen on the Riviera.

Fashion editors of the better magazines paid close attention to Gustave Tassell's swimwear and coverups. After the boned and corseted 1950s suits, his natural styles without bra cups were a hit with the New York *cognoscenti*, including Diana Vreeland, as were the soft cup designs by Edith Stenbeck. Frank Smith, who went on to head Evan Picone for Saks Fifth Avenue, had designed women's sportswear for Catalina, just as John Norman, later with Vogue and Butterick patterns, designed menswear. Menswear tended toward the country club look, at times showing influences of Pierre Cardin. The Sweethearts in Swimsuits line in the 1950s offered his and hers matching swimsuits and accessories.

Catalina successfully expanded its lines to appeal to the widest possible audience, offering knits, menswear, children's, Catalina Jr., sporting gear, and classic and trendy styles. The company had a knack of producing well-made mainstream fashions which sold in high volume and allowed average buyers to feel stylish and comfortable.

In recent decades many lines were conservative versions of revealing trendmakers. At times they went head-to-head with the competition, countering Body Glove's slick neons with Underwets while the slimming Contour Suit was the answer to Jantzen's Five-Pounds Under line. Considering its ability to adapt, especially through changes in ownership, perhaps its logo should have been the chameleon, rather than a fish.

Cataline went into bankruptcy in 1993 and languished for several years. It was purchased by Authentic Fitness, a subsidiary of the Warnaco companies in 1997 and paired with another legendary West Coast swimwear producer, Cole of California. The new unit was renamed Catalina Cole, and was highly successful as a part of Authenic Fitness' swimwear division, which also included the Anne Cole Collection and Speedo.

Catalina was and continues to be a keystone of the California swim and sportswear industry, with worldwide influence. It began as an early 20th-century swimwear pioneer and has remained an important player in the American fashion industry as Catalina Cole. The company's fashions significantly contributed to women's athletic liberation and the propagation of the Hollywood and California looks as well as molding and perpetuating beauty pageant culture.

—Debra Regan Cleveland; updated by Nelly Rhodes

CAUMONT, Jean Baptiste

French designer working in Italy

Born: Pau, France, 24 October 1932. **Education:** Studied fine arts in Paris. **Career:** Design assistant, Balmain, Paris, and freelance illustrator, *Vogue, Femina, Album du Figaro,* and *Marie-Claire,* late 1950s; textile consultant, Legler; design consultant La Rinascente stores, Italy; designer/coordinator, Apem, 1960–63; design consultancies in Italy and France, including Christian Dior boutique, and others; moved to Milan, 1963; designed for Rosier, 1963–66; designed own ready-to-wear with own label, from 1965, and for Confezioni Amica, Treviso; first show in Milan, then New York, in 1966; Caumont SrL founded with Paolo Russo in Treviso, Italy, 1968; knitwear line for men, then women, introduced, 1968–69; men's ready-to-wear collection, Monsieur Caumont introduced, 1970; signed contract with Gruppo Finanziario Tessile (GFT), producing exclusive menswear line for Canada and U.S., 1986; boutiques opened in Milan, Tokyo, and New York; introduced *Jib* fragrance line. **Awards:** Oscar from Rome fashion school; Oscar from Store Palacio de Ierro, Mexico. **Address:** Corso Venezia 44, 20121 Milan, Italy.

Publications

On CAUMONT:

Books

Mulassano, Adriana, *The Who's Who of Italian Fashion,* Florence, 1979.

Khornak, Lucille, *Fashion 2001,* New York, 1982.

Articles

de la Falaise, Maxime, "Right for the Moment: Jean Baptiste Caumont," in *Interview,* January 1980.

Moor, Jonathan, "Caumont: Classic Renegade," in *DNR: The Magazine,* 28 January 1980.

"Champion a l'étranger," in *Madame Figaro* (Paris), No. 12471.

Scio, Marie Louise, "Four Stars to Caumont and Missoni," in the *International Daily News,* 12 June 1990.

* * *

Throughout his long career, Jean Baptiste Caumont never wavered from his original vision: classic, sophisticated ready-to-wear clothing and accessories for men and women. Beginning with his first women's collection in 1966, Caumont consistently delivered stylish, refined sportswear, knits, leather, and evening clothes aimed at the well-bred customer who wanted a look of elegance and ease devoid of affectation.

A Frenchman originally from the Basque country, Caumont based his operations in Italy. He was one of the original group of designers (Walter Albini, Cadette, Krizia, Missoni, and Ken Scott) who broke with the Italian fashion industry in Florence and brought Milan into the limelight. His first foray into womenswear was quickly followed by men's knits and then a complete menswear collection. As his reputation as a tastemaker grew, his business continued to expand, including luggage, handbags, shoes, jewelry, and other goods. But Caumont continued to adhere strictly to his notion of line, form, craftsmanship, and control, creating clothing and accessories using rich fabrics, elegance of cut and richness of color, never sacrificing quality to mass production no matter how fast his fortunes grew.

Caumont often looked to the past for inspiration for his classic styles. He was particularly drawn to the styles worn by the wealthy during the early 20th century, clothes that might have been worn on Grand Tour holidays or at exclusive resorts. But these references were used only to conjure a mood—never for slavish revival. Some design sources, for example, were the glamor of luxury travel on the Orient Express, the prim uniforms of English schoolgirls, and the natty men's silk smoking jacket. But instead of degenerating into clichés, in Caumont's capable hands these sources were translated into great sweeping fur and leather coats, classy traditional sportswear separates, and oversized quilted evening coats for women.

In keeping with his taste for clothes that suggest patrician nonchalance, Caumont's trench coats, suits, blazers, and other sporty looks for men and women were frequently fashioned of richly-textured tweeds, houndstooth, and glen plaids. His daytime looks often featured layering, using wools and cashmere for pullovers and sweaterjackets for colder weather, linen and silk for summer/resort wear. For evening he favored unabashed luxury, with soft silks and crêpe de chine. Whatever the occasion, the telling Caumont signature was understatement—his clothes signaled their high quality with quiet restraint.

Caumont's devotion to subdued luxury also resulted in the use of a relatively pared-down palette. Early collections were nearly monochromatic, with black, gray, and white punctuated very occasionally by a dash of red. Otherwise, he has shown a predilection for earth tones, marrying various camels, beiges, and tans to create subtly harmonious variations on a theme. It was only after many seasons that he began to experiment with brighter hues, tropical tones, and bolder prints, as fashion dictates in the 1970s began to loosen the notion of proper palettes for men and women.

Caumont placed much more emphasis on style than fashion. "Fashion is a thing of the moment," he had remarked, "Fashion is a gimmick. Who can afford to pay for a gimmick?" During the 1980s his design philosophy paid off, as the trend toward elegance and glamor placed Caumont yet again at the forefront. His menswear—combining his hybrid talent for Italian tailoring, French lines, and English coloring—was especially well-received as being fresh, comfortable, and eminently wearable. The Caumont look, a worldly and sophisticated one, was considered at once timeless and yet essentially Milanese, embodying the urbane chic for which the Italian center of fashion became known.

Caumont designed for himself and others of his kind: well-traveled, well-heeled clients who believed in a refined and understated way of life. Not a true fashion innovator, he nonetheless found his niche as a designer—clothes spoke of elegance, gentility, and propriety, and never went out of style.

—Kathleen Paton

CERRUTI, Nino

Italian designer

Born: Biella, Italy, 1930. **Career:** General manager, family textile firm (founded 1881), Fratelli Cerruti (Cerruti Brothers), Biella, Italy, from 1950; introduced Hitman men's ready-to-wear line, 1957; introduced knitwear line, 1963; first menswear collection presented in Paris, opened Cerruti 1881 boutique, Paris, and launched unisex clothing line, 1967; added women's ready-to-wear, 1976; helped create fashion revolution on *Miami Vice* television show, 1980s; designed costumes for some 150 films, including *The Witches of Eastwick* (1987), *Philadelphia* (1993), and *Pretty Woman* (1990); appeared in *Cannes Man* (1996); sells controlling interest of company to Italian company Fin.part, 2000; Fin.part buys remaining interest and forces Cerruti out, 2001. Fragrances include *Nino Cerruti Pour Homme* (1978), *Cerruti Fair Play* (1984), *Nino Cerruti Pour Femme* (1987), and *1881* (1988). **Awards:** Bath Museum of Costume Dress of the Year award, England, 1978; Cutty Sark award, 1982, 1988; Pitti Uomo award, Italy, 1986. **Address:** 3 Place de la Madeleine, 75008 Paris, France. **Website:** www.cerruti.net.

PUBLICATIONS

On CERRUTI:

Books

Mulassano, Adriana, *The Who's Who of Italian Fashion,* Florence, 1979.

Articles

Crome, Erica, "Nino Cerruti: Designers of Influence No. 2," in *Vogue* (London), December 1978.

Hicks, Sheila, and Barbara Grib, "Nino Cerruti," in *American Fabrics and Fashions* (New York), 1982.

Boyer, G. Bruce, "The Return of the Double-Breasted Suit," in *Town and Country,* March 1983.

Menkes, Suzy, "King of the Supple Suit," in the *Times* (London), 11 November 1986.

"Buon Anniversario," in *Profession Textile,* 18 September 1987.

"Nino Cerruti Refined," in *Esquire,* September 1987.

Watt, Judith, "By Design," in *For Him* (London), Autumn 1989.

Tredre, Roger, "Nino, the Wardrobe Master," in the *Independent* (London), 9 August 1990.

"Biella," Supplement to *L'Uomo Vogue* (Milan), November 1990.

Fiedelholtz, Sara, "Escada Sees Good Year for Cerruti Collection," in *Women's Wear Daily,* 13 May 1993.

Morche, Pascal, "Eleganze der Hoflichkelit," in *Manner Vogue* (Wesseling, Germany), August 1993.

Aillaud, Charlotte, and Simon Upton, "Nino Cerruti: Tailoring an Italian Villa in Biella," in *Architectural Digest,* October 1994.

White, Constance C.R., "Hollywood Style, From Classic to Kitsch," in the *New York Times,* 18 October 1995.

Horyn, Cathy, "Cerruti's Soft Sell; Christine Ganeaux: Name Recognition; For Rhinestone Cowgirls and Boys," in the *New York Times,* 6 April 1999.

Interview with Giorgio Armani, in *Le Figaro,* January 2000.

Rubenstein, Hal, "The Look of Cerruti," in *InStyle,* 1 February 2000.

Menkes, Suzy, "Nino Cerruti Discreetly Exits the Fashion Stage," in the *International Herald Tribune,* 27 June 2001.

Nino Cerruti in ca. 1980–97. © Frédéric Huijbregts/CORBIS.

* * *

Nino Cerruti's life could be the most dramatic narrative of the post-World War II Italian renaissance. *L'Uomo Vogue* declared in November 1990: "Nino Cerruti, a name synonymous with modern restraint. Industrialist-designer, one of the founding fathers of Italian fashion." In 1950, at the young age of 20, Cerruti assumed control of his family's textile mills in Biella, Italy. He transformed the staid business that had been significant for generations in the textile-producing region of Biella. Cerruti saw the quiet revolutionary possibility of a vertical operation, a kind other Italian textiles companies would later pursue with astounding success, following Cerruti's model. His sensibility was for fashion rather than for the traditionalism of textiles manufacturing, and his fashion sense leaned to the streamlined, near-industrial tailoring design applied to richly textured fabrics.

Cerruti's first men's ready-to-wear line, Hitman, considered a revolution in menswear at the time, was launched in 1957, and he showed unisex clothing in 1967. He also opened his first Cerruti 1881 boutique in Paris on the Rue Royale, off the Place de la Madeleine, in 1967, in order to be closer to the fashion capital of the world. (Boutiques were later opened in London, Milan, Tokyo, Munich, and New York.) Lanificio Cerruti, however, the fabric production division of his enterprises, remained in Biella. Along the way, Cerruti taught young talent: Giorgio Armani began his career designing menswear for Cerruti in the 1960s; Narcisso Rodriguez and Peter Speliopoulous both crossed over the threshold of Cerruti's company as well.

His icons were distinguished dates and places; tradition abides in the stable factors of 1881 and Cerruti's elective association with Paris. Adriana Mulassano, writing in *The Who's Who of Italian Fashion,* (1979) noted that Cerruti was once known as "the madman of fashion" but considered the designer as a kind of vanguard genius: "Among those working for him (and perhaps even outside) there might be those who still think he's crazy. Perhaps it is the fate of the avant-garde, of those who know that the mind guides the hand, to be perennially misunderstood." It was Mulassano, however, who at times misunderstood Cerruti—he was always the businessman-designer, not the raw-talent creative, and he actively displayed the tempered intelligence of vertical operations and commercial acumen.

Cerruti, reflecting in September 1987, explained to *Esquire*: "I like to describe my operation as a modern version of the handcraft bodegas of centuries ago. It is important to know each link in the chain. I consider myself still very close to the theory of industrial design: using modern technology to reach the market. It's a very modern challenge: the continuous harmonization between the rational or scientific world and the emotional or artistic world." His involvement in fragrances and advertising was not been out of unremitting creativity but out of the controlling perspicacity of business. The raging revolutionary of the 1950s and 1960s mellowed into the judicious businessperson of the 1980s and 1990s and his model was fully copied by others, both in menswear and in women's clothing.

The Cerruti fall-winter 1993–94 menswear collections were shown in Paris with none of the histrionics of some menswear presentations. He kept to his simple principle in his tailored clothing: "A man should look important when he wears a suit," allowing for the unconstricted jackets of the period but rendering them with sufficient solidity to avoid being too limp for the office. He showed the prevailing elongated three-button single-breasted look of Giorgio Armani and others. One can always tell, however, that Cerruti was a man of cloth: his menswear fabrics were textural, in pebbled and oatmeal grains, and so luxurious in their handling.

Cerruti also experimented with dandies and even designed Jack Nicholson's costumes in the movie *The Witches of Eastwick* (1987), as well as those for Julia Roberts and Richard Gere in *Pretty Woman* (1990) and Tom Hanks and Denzel Washington in *Philadelphia* (1993). Cerruti himself even appeared in a cameo role in the film *Cannes Man* (1996). In addition, he used actors as models for his work; but anyone can experiment.

Nonetheless, Cerruti made his mark with the restraint of his clothes. His principal effort in menswear took advantage of the thriving operations he commanded from mills to clothing to advertising and promotion and related products. Mulassano did recognize Nino Cerruti as an enlightened businessman; and there was Cerruti's own 1987 statement in *Esquire,* "I think that innovation and fancy are essential to daily life. But my clothes are designed to be real. It's easy to indulge in decadence in fashion, but I don't think that's meaningful. The world has been full of enough of that."

Commenting to *In Style* magazine in 2000, as both a designer and a business professional, Cerruti said, "What I see today is a desire from the public for more than clothes to wear on the beach or at nightclubs. Men and women have a daily life, and they want us to help them take care of it. It is wonderful that women no longer need to use clothes to establish their place at work…and men are starting to understand the concept of wardrobe. So there is no reason any longer to deny one's personality [at] work. Besides, work should be where you experience some of the most interesting moments of your life. Not necessarily the most amusing, but certainly moments of interest. Is there a more appropriate place to dress with self-respect?"

If Cerruti exemplified postwar Italy, perhaps in his judiciousness, cautious good taste, or reversion to his own basic values, he further exemplified Everyman. He foresaw menswear's future in *L'Uomo Vogue* in 1990, "as a fashion that will be more refined and yet at the same time more everyday…" and had become the consummate businessman. He commanded an empire of numerous boutiques, franchise stores, some 1,500 vendors carrying Cerruti products, textile mills, and a holding company (Final Gastaldi Group) to control it all. And just as many of the independent fashion houses fell under the spell of globalization in the middle and late 1990s, Cerrruti, too, decided to sell a controlling interest in his firm to Italian industrial group Fin.part in 2000.

In 2001 Fin.part took over the remainder of Cerruti's business and forced the 71-year-old designer out. At his spring-summer 2002 showing in Milan, Cerruti took his final bow before a standing crowd, taking leave of the family business created more than 120 years before. As Cerruti embraced the two young designers hired to take his place, he assured the *International Herald Tribune*'s Suzy Menkes he was not retiring, but already researching a "new project" involving the family-owned textile company.

—Richard Martin; updated by Daryl F. Mallett

CESARANI, Sal

American designer

Born: 25 September 1939 in New York. **Education:** Studied design at the Fashion Institute of Technology, New York, 1959–61. **Family:** Married Nancy Cesarani, 1961; children: Lisa, Christopher. **Career:** Junior designer, Bobby Brooks, New York, 1961–63; fashion display coordinator, Paul Stuart menswear store, New York, 1964–69; merchandising director, Polo by Ralph Lauren, 1970–72; designed menswear and sportswear for Thomas Co. Inc., in Japan; Cesarani shops opened in Japanese retailers Matsuya, Seer, and Tobu, 1972; designer, Country Britches, New York, 1973–75; designer, Stanley Blacker, New York, 1975–76; formed Cesarani Ltd., New York, 1976; women's collection introduced, 1977; company closed then reorganized as Cesarani division for Jaymar Ruby; formed licensing agreements with Hartmarx, 1987–88, Corbin, 1989, Britches of Georgetowne, 1991, and Japan Toray Diplomode; launched leather bag collection for Ace Luggage, 1992; created eyeglass collection for Nanamua Co., 1992; designer/president, Cesarani and SJC Concepts Inc., from 1993; introduced childrenswear collection for Matsuta Co., 1993; designed menswear collection for Thomas Co. Inc., 1994; created men's clothing collection through Panther, a division of Maruben; teacher/critic, Fashion Institute of Technology. **Exhibitions:** Institute of the Metropolitan Museum of Art, 1995. **Awards:** Special Coty award for Menswear, 1974, 1975; Coty award for menswear, 1976; Fashion Group award of Boston, 1977; Coty Return award, 1982. **Member:** Advisory Board of the Fashion Crafts Educational Commission of the High School of Fashion Industries; founding member, New York Advisory Board of the Shannon Rodgers and Jerry Silverman School of Fashion Design and Merchandising, Kent State University, Ohio. **Address:** 201 East 79th Street, New York, NY, 10021, USA. **Website:** www.cesarani.com.

Sal Cesarani with one of his designs from his spring 1996 collection: basket weave sports coat, tattersall Cooper vest, twill pants, silk tie, and chambray shirt. © AP/Wide World Photos.

Publications

On CESARANI:

Books

Stegemeyer, Anne, *Who's Who in Fashion, Third Edition,* New York, 1996.

Articles

Guerin, Ann, "Spotlight on Sal Cesarani," in *Playbill,* November 1977.

"Sal Cesarani: Tradition Missing," in *GQ* (New York), January 1982.

Staetter, Suzanne, "Cesarani Collection is Just for Certain Women," in the *Houston Chronicle* (Texas), 12 December 1984.

Lane, Dotty, "Cesarani Designs for the International Man," in *Record-Courier,* 20 August 1993.

Boies, Elaine, "Clothes for the Well-Dressed Man," in *Staten Island Advance,* 3 June 1994.
Socha, Miles, "New York's Dean of Good Taste, Sal Cesarnai, is Applying his Spruce Esthetic to a New Range of Sportswear," in *Daily News Record (DNR),* 14 August 1996.
Goldstein, Lauren, "Redaelli Aims to Take Cesarani to the Majors," in *DNR,* 27 October 1997.
"Give Him a Hand," in *DNR,* 16 February 1998.

* * *

To the earthbound, Sal Cesarani's menswear might be traditional or even historic. For the dreamer, the wanderer, or the imaginer, Cesarani's evocative and romantic apparel epitomizes and condenses the perfect past. Like a Cindy Sherman portrait, Cesarani's work is seldom a precise equivalent, but gains its power from suggestive resemblance and its ultimate inability to be classified into the past, so powerful are its connections and so focused is its originality. Extracting a nonchalance from American style between the wars and an élan from English aristocracy in its palmier days, Cesarani possesses the power to transport one into a Merchant-Ivory film or to the revery of Golden Age Hollywood. Were Cesarani merely offering history and a wardrobe inventory that is of grandfathers and imagined heroes, we would be respectful, but not captivated. Cesarani's renderings enhance historic designs with subtle change.

Cesarani refuted the 20th-century predisposition to believe menswear was mundane. Rather, he gave sentimental spirit to the classic templates of the century's menswear. Having worked both as a designer for Polo/Ralph Lauren and Stanley Blacker, and for a while as a menswear coordinator at Paul Stuart, Cesarani has consistently emphasized styling and the adventuresome ensemble of clothing. Sportswear and tailored clothing, tennis separates, classic tuxedos with the debonair slouches of the 1930s and 1940s, and the looser cuts and drape of Hollywood chic evoking Gary Cooper and Cary Grant characterize Cesarani's style. True, not every man realizes the harmony of proportions of C.S. Bull or Hurrell heroes, but each Cesarani client is capable of some aspiration to such pictorial grace.

When he relaunched a tailored clothing line in 1993, Cesarani's Trans-Atlantic collection was not only Anglo-American, but as suggestive as a crossing on the *Normandie.* Redolent of the 1930s and 1940s, the collection employed separate vests with lapels, pattern mixes of herringbones, glen plaids, and other standard elements for the cool look of the era's styles. What is exceptional about Cesarani is his sense of the fashion composition and modification: the slight eccentricity of a peak lapel on a single-breasted jacket or tartan blazer paired with evening separates evokes memories, but also jostles them, making the clothing fresh again.

Key to Cesarani's sensibility, in addition to his Paul Stuart fashion styling, was his work as a design assistant to Ralph Lauren. If Lauren condenses nostalgia into an impacted sentiment more perfect than any real world that has ever existed, Cesarani creates a fictive, movie-star desire, the fantasy of men's clothing and nonchalant style. Like Lauren, his is a study in composition, offering some perfectly regular components as well as a few that suggest special flourish.

As a designer, Cesarani has displayed a unique gift for understanding the market: in the 1990s, both his ties and his later tailored clothing came at the right moment for a renewed classicism. The more understated ties then were composed into imaginative ensemble dressing with the grand patterns of vests, mixed slacks, and jackets. "I perceive," said the designer, "each piece of the collection as a component of man's personal style, to be worn and combined according to his own needs." Cesarani invents menswear that is never tedious and his penchant for vintage perfection and superb collection editing is akin to Ralph Lauren's, though Cesarani tends to greater fullness and drape as well as a greater informality and more congenial prices.

Cesarani's extensive knowledge of fabric and cut are at the heart of his devotion to expert craftsmanship. In 1997 Cesarani welcomed a partnership with Italian clothing manufacturer Redaelli. American-sold Cesarani clothing, formalwear, outerwear, and neckwear collections are now produced in Milan. In addition to designing clothing, Cesarni's astute sense of fashion trends makes him a sought-after special consultant for major fashion color forecasting companies and special projects, which even included designing ceremonial uniforms for the 1980 Winter Olympics.

"My passion is design," Cesarani has explained, to take "a vision, a dream, a fleeting image of the American spirit...and creating something real from it." The integrity of his creations reflect his unerring focus on versatility, elegance, and craftsmanship. Cesarani has continued to be heralded for his imaginative twists on classic styling. In his 1998 collection, he brought together a chestnut glen-plaid vested suit with a burnt-orange plaid cotton shirt and a foulard silk tie. His innovative combinations of pattern and color play together in his own collections but also open new possibilities in any man's existing wardrobe. The elegance in styling evident in clothes bearing the Cesarani label lends them the versatility to be important pieces in an evolving wardrobe for years.

—Richard Martin; updated by Janette Goff Dixon

CHALAYAN, Hussein

British designer

Born: Huseyin Caglayan in Nicosia, Cyprus, 1970. **Education:** Highgate School, London; St. Martin's School of Art, London, 1989–93. **Career:** Launched own company, Cartesia Ltd., in 1994; designer, Autograph at Marks & Spencer; designer, TSE Cashmere, New York, 1994–2001; designer, Topshop, London; company liquidated, 2000; relaunched own label under his name in 2001. **Collections:** Senior year collection, St. Martin's School of Design, displayed at Browns, London. **Awards:** Absolut Vodka's London Fashion Week award, 1995; Designer of the Year, British Fashion Awards, 1999, 2000; British Designer of the Year, 1999, 2000.

Publications

On CHALAYAN:

Articles

White, Constance C. R., "Hussein Chalayan's High-Wire Act," in the *New York Times,* 21 April 1998.
———, "Taking the Fad Out of Fashion," in the *New York Times,* 4 November 1998.
Goldstein, Lauren, "The Fashion Games: These Seven Up-and-Coming Designers are the Ones to Watch...," in *Time International,* 9 October 2000.
Craik, Laura, "The Designer Who Dared Not Do Sexy," in the *Evening Standard* (London), 10 January 2001.

Hussein Chalayan, winter 2000 collection: demonstration of how a table becomes a skirt. © AP/Wide World Photos.

Menkes, Suzy, "Hussein Chalayan Maps His Journey," in the *International Herald Tribune,* 13 March 2001.

Alexander, Hilary, "Chalayan Returns," in the *Daily Telegraph* (London), 15 March 2001.

Armstrong, Lisa, "A Clever Comeback," in the *Times* (London), 26 March 2001.

* * *

Among those fashion designers considered intellectual or avant garde, Hussein Chalayan has the distinction of having been dubbed both a genius and the mad professor of British fashion. A thoughtful designer of collections with purity of vision, integrity, and wearability, he is often counted in company with designers like Rei Kawakubo and Martin Margiela.

Chalayan's collections consistently challenge familiar notions of fashion while still succeeding in being elegant and beautiful. His work is inspired by the interfaces of technology, science, culture, and the human body. His more conceptual designs are often sculptural, with pieces like the aeroplane dress, molded of glass fiber with a remote-control panel, a tiered wooden skirt doubling as a table, and dresses of sugar-spun glass making their appearances in various shows. While in school, one of his professors suggested he switch to sculpture. If he had, the fashion world would have lost a unique voice whose work blurs the line between art and style with evocative and sometimes brilliant results.

Shortly after graduating, Chalayan started his own line, also doing collections for TSE of New York, Autograph at Marks & Spencer in London, and a line for Topshop of London. Although his clothes are available at high-end venues like Browns, Harvey Nichols, Harrods, and Liberty, he has worked in cross-media, designing an installation for London's Millennium Dome, doing collaborations with a variety of other artists and designers, and having his more sculptural designs exhibited in art galleries. He is reticent of the fashion scene and is not given to courting celebrity power.

A designer of ideas, Chalayan is also a designer of clothes to be worn. Though some critics judge his work as too eccentric and heady for actual people to wear, an examination of any given Chalayan collection belies this sentiment. Although several high-concept pieces will usually anchor one of his collections, they are accompanied by finely cut, deceptively simple, eminently wearable garments. This kind of commerciality with pure vision at its heart is not a common commodity in any field of design, including fashion; consequently, Chalayan's praises have been much sung by the press, his work well respected by other designers. As one fashion journalist put it, "Watching a Chalayan show is like listening to Mozart. It is moving and magical, always with a hidden meaning, which to detractors sound pretentious." A theme common to all of Chalayan's collections is the body itself, in relation to various aspects of the world we live in from space, religion, and cultural mores to technology and war.

His fall 2000 collection, which included the table skirt, was inspired by the designer's thinking on the wartime impermanence that finds homes raided and families forced to flee or be killed. At the end of the show, the living room set on the catwalk stage was turned into dresses and suitcases, and off the models went, with their homes on their backs. Also included in this collection were finely tailored coats with unexpected draping, highlighted in white piping, creating a sense of volume, depth, and luxury, as well as elegant dresses in lush colors, and full, layered skirts and tops, exposing a hidden layer of ruffles at cutouts in the hem—all extremely wearable garments. In another collection, underlining the constraints imposed on women by the Muslim religion, Chalayan created chadors of varying lengths and sent the models out wearing nothing beneath them, drawing attention, inescapably, to the fact that beneath the delimitations of the garment there are living, breathing women. Indeed, Chalayan's models almost always wear low- or flat-heeled shoes, and there is a decided emphasis on grace and dignity over the overt sexuality of high-heeled couture in his designs.

A unique and elegant futurism achieved through complex cutting and a clean architecturalism are the hallmarks of Chalayan's collections. One spring collection offered splashes of sweet color in crisp, off-the shoulder dresses and deceptively simple frocks with multiple gathers. Another delivered these features in starker shades with smock dresses of fine pleats, pieces made up of pleats within pleats, mesh overlays, and sharply tailored jackets. Other innovations and contributions that Chalayan's idea-driven design have produced include unrippable paper clothes, suits with illuminated flight-path patterns, long knitted dresses with built-in walking sticks, pleated "concertina" dresses, cone and cube headdresses, designs based on experiments, flight paths, abstractions of meteorological charts, and a host of exquisite, minimal, subtly draped works.

Hussein Chalayan, winter 2000 collection: skirt which transformed from a table. © AFP/CORBIS.

At the end of 2000, due to some mishaps with manufacturers and despite rising profits, Chalayan took his company into voluntary liquidation. The collection he designed in the interim between liquidation and the relaunch of his new label were described as "hugely desirable" and "timeless." The collection came from Chalayan's meditations on journeys and maps. Shirttails emerge briefly from under a skirt's hips, a white cotton shirt turns into a dress, meteor-streaked inserts distinguish tailored coats—all part of the designer's idea that "there's a progression that carries over from one piece to another." Taking the conceptualization further, into the consideration of personal journeys of identity, Chalayan addresses the subject of cultural assimilation with clothes like wool jackets inset with fragment of denim and leather.

Speaking about this "map reading" collection, the designer sums up the dichotomy that marks his collections, that fashion is both intellectual and relevant, "I'm fascinated by the idea of cultural assimilation, the way people transform their identities and how other people see that as a threat. Actually, in some ways, that's irrelevant. You don't need to know any of that stuff to wear these clothes. All you need to know is how to enjoy them."

—Jessica Reisman

CHAMPION PRODUCTS INC.

American sportswear manufacturer

Founded: as Knickerbocker Knitting Company by Abe and Bill Fainbloom, in 1919. **Company History:** Named changed to Champion Knitting Mills, Inc.; introduced reversible t-shirts for Navy training, 1940s; introduced the Jogbra, 1977; acquired by Sara Lee Corporation; official outfitter for U.S. Oylmpic basketball team, 1992; official sponsor and apparel licensee of WNBA, 1996; launched children's roller hockey line, 1997; debuted collection of backpacks and sports bags, 1999; introduced Fiberzone and Double Dry Bodywear lines, 2000; signed on as exclusive outfitter of the XFL, 2000; launched Tactel line of activewear and Champion Silver line, 2001. **Company Address:** 1000 E. Hanes Mill Road, Winston Salem, NC 27105, U.S.A. **Company Websites:** www.championusa.com; www.championjogbra.com.

Publications

On CHAMPION

Articles

Arlen, Jeffrey, "Champion Brands Overseas Markets," in *DNR,* 18 April 1985.

Murray, Kathy, "Thanks for the Advice," in *Forbes,* 2 May 1988.

Robb, Gregory A., "Champion Products Accepts Bid," in the *New York Times,* 14 February 1989.

Berger, Warren, "Champion Starts to Show Its True Colors Off the Field," in *Adweek's Marketing Week,* 23 April 1990.

Sterne, Hilary, "Honest Sweats: Champion's Cotton Shirts are the Real McCoy," in *Gentlemen's Quarterly,* May 1992.

Leibowitz, David S., "Two Cases Where Quality Will Out," in *Financial World,* 23 June 1992.

Phalon, Richard, "Walking Billboards," in *Forbes,* 7 December 1992.

Grish, Kristina, "Champion, Starter Test Mainstream Appeal in Youth Roller Hockey Apparel," in *Sporting Goods Business,* September 1997.

"Vendors Lead Charge with Women's Causes," in *Sporting Goods Business,* 15 October 1998.

Feitelberg, Rosemary, "Hoop Apparel: Not a Slam Dunk Yet," in *WWD,* 14 January 1999.

Grish, Kristina, "Sport Labels Have Accessory Additions in the Bag for Fall," in *Sporting Goods Business,* 8 March 1999.

Bronson, Cory, "The XFL Will Champion Its Uniforms at Retail This Fall," in *Sporting Goods Business,* 11 October 2000.

Cassidy, Hilary, "Champion Gives Retailers Online Hot Market Resource," in *Sporting Goods Business,* 10 November 2000.

"Champion Takes Seamless Approach to Active Apparel," in *Sporting Goods Business,* 19 January 2001.

Griffin, Tara, "Champion Silver Debuts," in *Sporting Goods Business,* 14 May 2001.

* * *

Champion Products Inc. has always catered to the customer who wants ease of movement from activewear. The company was formed in 1919 by brothers Abe and Bill Fainbloom, as the Knickerbocker Knitting Company to produce sturdy sweaters. The company pioneered a heavy-duty cotton, which it patented as Reverse-Weave, and manufactured sweatshirts primarily for athletes. Champion sweatshirts were only the earliest of several industry innovations—including the first cotton football jerseys, the first hooded sweatshirts (originally worn on the sidelines during games), the first reversible t-shirts (for the Navy during World War II), the first breathable mesh shirts and shorts, the first lined nylon-shell jackets, and the first comfortable, supportive jogging bra for women. This sports bra, which evolved into the Jogbra, was originally designed by two women joggers who sewed men's athletic supporters together to wear while running. The patented Jogbra went on sale in 1977 and has been a bestseller ever since.

Eight decades after its founding, Champion has diversified into all facets of the activewear market, supplying sweats, uniforms, and an ever-expanding line of women's workout apparel. Serious athletes are often the most loyal fans of Champion products, yet its myriad of products suits both active and casual lifestyles. Staples such as Champion jerseys and sweatshirts have been supplied to hundreds of intercollegiate and high school-level athletic programs to use as both practice and competition uniforms. Champion has long been an official outfitter to many professional sports teams, predominantly in football and basketball. Even the U.S. Olympic basketball team named Champion its official supplier for practice and game uniforms in 1992—the ultimate compliment to be worn by some of the world's top athletes.

Champion's sportswear has been unparalled for its durability and the longevity of its garments. For the rough and tumble world of professional sports, Champion more than held its own against the harsh conditions of long practices and games. "Vintage" Champion sweatshirts and trousers, time-worn with holes or frayed edges, frequently seemed as dear to consumers as new ones.

Over the years Champion has allied itself with nonprofit groups, and in 1998 joined the National Alliance of Breast Cancer Organizations (NABCO) to raise awareness of breast cancer. The company's commitment was twofold: first by placing NABCO's logo and a pink ribbon on all WNBA apparel, and secondly, donating a portion of licensed sales to NABCO. Yet by the end of the year, however, many activewear manufacturers were worried about sales—or lack thereof—in basketball apparel since the American Basketball League had folded, the WNBA's popularity waxed and waned, and the sport's top competitor, Michael Jordan, had retired. To pick up the slack Champion and other outfitters turned to accessories, creating extensive lines of backpacks and athletic bags customized for virtually every sport.

In 2000 Champion was put on the selling block by parent company Sara Lee Corporation, who was in the midst of a reorganization. Though Champion was securing the rights to provide apparel for several NFL teams, it had also signed on as the official outfitter of the XFL. In the XFL deal, Champion agreed to supply official uniforms and practicewear for the league's eight teams, as well as replica jerseys for retailers. Yet by 2001 the XFL had folded and Champion lost a lucrative contract.

To bolster its bottomline, Champion introduced a new Jogbra line called Champion Silver. The Silver collection was manufactured with Static-X, a new yarn comprised of silver-coated threads woven into the fabric, which inhibited the growth of bacteria and helped control odor. The new line consisted of sports bras, tanks, tops, and shorts made with the Static-X yarn. Next came women's seamless apparel made from Tactel, a technology-advanced nylon with superior wicking, comfort, and support.

In the 21st century, Champion remained the outfitter of choice for many collegiate and professional teams. With almost a dozen NBA teams, seven collegiate teams, and a number of sponsored events (Sail Boston 2000, the YMCA World's Largest Run), Champion's name is firmly emblazoned in activewear history. From its traditional sweatshirts and mesh jerseys, from socks and hats to watches and eyewear, athletes the world over have sought out Champion's reliable, comfortable apparel. Champion products continue live up to their name.

—Lisa Marsh and Nelly Rhodes

CHANEL, Gabrielle "Coco"

French fashion designer

Born: Saumur, France, 19 August 1883. **Education:** At convent orphanage, Aubazine, 1895–1900; convent school, Moulins, 1900–02. **Career:** Clerk, Au Sans Pareil hosiery shop, Moulins, 1902–04; café-concert singer, using nickname "Coco," in Moulins and Vichy, 1905–08; lived with Etienne Balsan, Château de Royalieu and in Paris, 1908–09; stage costume designer, 1912–37, established millinery and women's fashion house with sponsorship of Arthur "Boy" Cappel, in Paris, 1913, later on rue Cambon, Paris, 1928; established fashion shops in Deauville, 1913, Biarritz, 1916; fragrance, *No. 5,* marketed from 1921; film costume designer, 1931–62; headquarters closed during World War II; exiled to Lausanne for affair with Nazi officer, 1945–53; rue Cambon headquarters reopened and first post-war showing, 1954; Broadway musical *Coco,* starring Katherine Hepburn debuted on Broadway, 1969; company continued after Chanel's death, 1971; ready-to-wear introduced, 1977; Karl Lagerfeld brought in as designer for couture, 1983; Lagerfeld took over ready-to-wear, 1984; gun manufacturer Holland & Holland acquired, 1996; French beachwear company Eres pruchased, 1997; one licensing agreement with Luxxotica for eyewear. Other fragrances include *No. 22,* 1921, *Cuir de Russie,* 1924, *No. 19,* 1970, and from the House of Chanel, *Cristalle,* 1974, *Coco,* 1984, *Egoïste* for men, 1990, *Allure,* 1996, and *Allure Homme,* 1998; launch of *Precision* skincare line, 1999; introduced line of his-and-hers watches, 2000. **Exhibitions:** *Les Grands Couturiers Parisiens 1910–1939,* Musée du Costume, Paris, 1965; *Fashion: An Anthology,* Victoria & Albert Museum, London, 1971; *The Tens, Twenties & Thirties,* Metropolitan Museum of Art, New York, 1977; *Folies de dentelles: Balenciaga, Cardin, Chanel, Dior...Exposition du 24 juin au octobre 2000,* Musée des Beaux-Arts et de la dentelle, 2000. **Awards:** Neiman Marcus award, Dallas, 1957; *Sunday Times* International Fashion award, London, 1963. **Died:** 10 January 1971, in Paris. **Company Address:** 29–31 rue Cambon, 75001 Paris, France. **Company Website:** www.chanel.com.

Marlene Dietrich modeling a masculine-styled pant suit designed by Coco Chanel, 1933. © AP/Wide World Photos.

PUBLICATIONS

On CHANEL:

Books

Crawford, M.D.C., *The Ways of Fashion,* New York, 1948.

Baillen, Claude, *Chanel solitaire,* Paris, 1971, and London, 1973.

Haedrich, Michael, *Coco Chanel secrète,* Paris, 1971; published as *Coco Chanel: Her Life, Her Secrets,* Boston, 1972.

Galante, Pierre, *Les années Chanel,* Paris, 1972; published as *Mademoiselle Chanel,* Chicago, 1973.

Charles-Roux, Edmonde, *L'irrégulière, ou mon itinéraire Chanel,* Paris, 1974; published as *Chanel, Her Life, Her World,* New York, 1975, London, 1976.

Morand, Paul, *L'allure de Chanel,* Paris, 1976, 1996.

Charles-Roux, Edmonde, *Chanel and Her World,* Paris, 1979, London, 1981.

Delay, Claude, *Chanel solitaire,* Paris, 1983.

The Polytechnic, *Coco Chanel,* Brighton, 1984.

Milbank, Caroline Rennolds, *Couture: The Great Designers,* New York, 1985.

Haedrich, Marcel, *Coco Chanel,* Paris, 1987.

Leymarie, Jean, *Chanel,* New York, 1987.

Charles-Roux, Edmonde, *Chanel,* London, 1989.

Kennett, Frances, *Coco: The Life and Loves of Gabrielle Chanel,* London, 1989.

Grumbach, Lilian, *Chanel m'a dit,* Paris, 1990.

Madsen, Axel, *Chanel: A Woman of Her Own,* New York, 1990.

Guillen, Pierre-Yves, and Jacqueline Claude, *The Golden Thimble: French Haute Couture,* Paris, 1990.

Steele, Valerie, *Women of Fashion: Twentieth-Century Designers,* New York, 1991.

Mackrell, Alice, *Coco Chanel,* New York, 1992.

Ash, Juliet, and Elizabeth Wilson, eds., *Chic Thrills: A Fashion Reader,* Berkeley, California, 1993.

Lagerfeld, Karl, *Chanel,* Paris, 1995.

Baudot, François, *Chanel,* New York, 1996.

Musée des Beaux-Arts et de la dentelle, *Folies de dentelles: Balenciaga, Cardin, Chanel, Dior…,* [exhibition catalogue], Alençon, 2000.

Articles

"Gabrielle Chanel," [obituary] in the *Times* (London), 12 January 1971.

"Chanel No. 1," in *Time,* 25 January 1971.

Shaeffer, Claire, "The Comfortable Side of Couture," in *Threads* (Newtown, Connecticut), June/July 1989.

Kazanjian, Dodie, "Chanel Suit," in *Vogue,* August 1990.

Fedii, Daniela, "Coco la ribelle," in *Elle* (Milan), November 1990.

Steele, Valerie, "Chanel in Context," in Juliet Ash and Elizabeth Wilson, eds., *Chic Thrills, A Fashion Reader,* Berkeley, California 1993.

Collins, Amy Fine, "Haute Coco," in *Vanity Fair* (New York), June 1994.

Menkes, Suzy, "Strong Chanel Holds Up Couture's Falling Walls," in the *International Herald Tribune,* 21 March 1995.

Spindler, Amy M., "Lagerfeld Tones Down the Look at Chanel," in the *New York Times,* 21 March 1995.

"Chanel: The Naughty Professor," in *Women's Wear Daily,* 21 March 1995.

Sakamaki, Sachiko, "Chanel Surfing in Tokyo; Japan is Nuts About the French Brand Name," in the *Far Eastern Economic Review,* 11 January 1996.

Menkes, Suzy, "Magnificent Chanel Defines the Season," in the *International Herald Tribune,* 4 March 2000.

———, "Class and Classics at Chanel," in the *International Herald Tribune,* 24 January 2001.

———, "Chanel Goes to the Head of the Class," in the *International Herald Tribune,* 11 July 2001.

Coco Chanel in New York. © Underwood & Underwood/CORBIS.

* * *

A woman of ambition and determination, Gabrielle Chanel, nicknamed "Coco," rose from humble beginnings and an unhappy childhood to become one of the 20th century's most prominent couturiers, prevailing for nearly half a century. In contrast to the opulent elegance of the *belle époque,* Chanel's designs were based on simplicity and elegance. She introduced relaxed dressing, expressing the aspirations of the day's woman, replacing impractical clothing with functional styling.

Chanel's early years tended to be vague in detail, being full of inaccuracies and contradictions, due to her deliberate concealment of her deprived childhood. It is generally accepted that Chanel gained some dressmaking and millinery experience prior to working in a hat shop in Deauville, France. Using her skills as a milliner she opened shops in Paris, Deauville, and Biarritz with the financial assistance of a backer. Chanel was an astute businesswoman and skillful publicist, quickly expanding her work to include skirts, jerseys in stockinette jersey, and accessories.

Recognized as the designer of the 1920s, Chanel initiated an era of casual dressing, appropriate to the occasion, for relaxed outdoor clothing created to be worn in comfort and without constricting corsets, liberating women with loosely fitting garments. Her style was of uncluttered simplicity, incorporating practical details.

In 1916 Chanel introduced jersey, a soft elasticated knit previously only used for undergarments, as the new fashion fabric. Wool jersey produced softer, lighter clothing with uncluttered fluid lines. She made simple jersey dresses in navy and grey, cut to flatter the figure rather than to emphasize and distort the natural body shape. The demand for her new nonconformist designs by the wealthy was so great and the use of jersey so successful Chanel extended her range, creating her own jersey fabric designs, which were manufactured by Rodier.

Highly original in her concept of design, Chanel ceaselessly borrowed ideas from the male wardrobe, combining masculine tailoring with women's clothing. Her suits were precise but remain untailored, with flowing lines, retaining considerable individuality and simple elegance. Riding breeches, wide-legged trousers, blazers, and sweaters were all taken and adapted. A major force in introducing and establishing common sense and understated simplicity into womenswear, Chanel's coordination of the cardigan, worn with a classic straight skirt, became a standard combination of wearable separates.

Chanel produced her cardigans in tweed and jersey fabrics, initiating the perennially popular "Chanel suit," which usually consisted of two or three pieces: a cardigan-style jacket, weighted with her trademark gilt chain stitched around the inside hem, a simple easy-to-wear skirt, worn with a blouse (with blouse fabric coordinated with the jacket lining). Her work offered comfort and streamlined simplicity, creating clothes for the modern woman, whom she epitomized herself. The key to her design philosophy was construction, producing traditional classics outliving each season's new fashion trends and apparel. While other designers presented new looks for each new season, Chanel adapted the refined detailing and style lines.

Her colors were predominantly grey, navy, and beige, incorporating highlights of a richer and broader palette. Chanel introduced the ever popular "little black dress,"created for daywear, eveningwear, and cocktail dressing which became a firm fixture in the fashion world during her tenure, and is still popular today.

Attentive to detail, adding to day and eveningwear, Chanel established a reputation for extensive uses of costume jewelery, with innovative combinations of real and imitation gems, crystal clusters, strings of pearls, and ornate jewelled cuff links, adding brilliant contrast to the stark simplicity of her designs. The successful development of *Chanel No. 5* perfume in 1922 assisted in the financing of her couture empire during difficult years. An interesting aspect of Chanel's career was the reopening of her couture house, which was closed during World War II. After 15 years in exile for having an affair with Nazi officer Hans Gunther von Dincklage, Chanel relaunched her work in 1954 at the age of 71, reintroducing the Chanel suit, which formed the basis for many of her collections and become a hallmark. The look adopted shorter skirts and braid trimmed cardigan jackets.

Despite her work and individual style, Chanel craved personal and financial independence, and was ruthless in her search for success. She was unique in revolutionizing the fashion industry with dress reform and in promoting the emancipation of women. Her influence touched many American and European designers, who have continued to reinforce her concept of uncomplicated classics. Once such designer is Karl Lagerfeld who took over designing the Chanel couture line in 1983 and its ready-to-wear collections the following year. He is widely credited with bringing Chanel back to the forefront of fashion, by taking original Chanel designs and tweaking them to appeal to younger customers.

Throughout the 1990s and into the 2000s Lagerfeld kept the Chanel name alive and well. His collections receive high praise, season after season, and he is among the last of the great old-school designers. As Suzy Menkes of the *International Herald Tribune* so aptly put it in March 2000, "Lagerfeld will soon be the last of the fashion Mohicans, the tribe that came center stage in ready-to-wear in the 1960s but were schooled in the old couture ways of rigorous cut, perfect execution, invention in detail.... Who in the next generation can ever fill his seven-league boots?" Who indeed?

—Carol Mary Brown; updated by Sydonie Bénet

CHARLES, Caroline

British designer

Born: Cairo, Egypt, c. 1943. **Education:** Attended boarding school in Harrogate, England; studied fashion at the Art School in Swindon. **Career:** Worked for couturier Michael Sherrard, and for Mary Quant, Knightsbridge; assisted fashion photographer Tony Rawlinson; returned to Mary Quant; established own business, 1963; moved to Beauchamp Place, 1966; designed for a number of celebrities and musicians, 1960s; designed for British royalty, beginning in the 1980s; opened new store on Bond Street, London, 1990s. **Address:** 9, St. Johns Wood High Street, London NW8 7N6 England.

Publications

On CHARLES:

Articles

"Designs for the Princess of Wales," in the *Times,* 3 November 1981.

Brampton, Sally, "Showing the Rest of the World," in *The Observer,* 20 March 1983.

Kendall, Ena, "Caroline Charles: A Room of My Own," in *The Observer Magazine,* 16 August 1987.

Lomas, Jane, "Staying Power," in *The Observer,* 16 August 1987.

Samuel, Kathryn, "A Feel for the Fabric of the Times," in the *Daily Telegraph,* 16 May 1988.

Coleman, Alix, "Breaking New Ground," in *Sunday Express Magazine,* 22 October 1989.

Haggard, Claire, "The House that Caroline Built," in *Fashion Weekly* (London), 9 November 1989.

———, "Setting the Style," in *Country Life* (London), 18 January 1990.

Nesbit, Jenny, "A Perfect Fit," in the *Sunday Times Magazine,* 14 October 1990.

Bridgstock, Graham, "Me and My Health," in the *Evening Standard* (London), 19 July 1994.

Tyrrell, Rebecca, in the *Tattler* (London), November 1994.

Johnson, Sarah, "WestPoint Acquires Foothold in Europe," in *HFN,* 3 February 1997.

Morris, Belinda, "Fashion: Uphill, Down Dale and Upmarket," in the *Financial Times of London,* 14 June 1997.

Klensch, Else, "Deep Color, Easy Outlines Mark New Caroline Charles Collection," at *CNN Online,* 3 August 1998.

* * *

Caroline Charles has described herself "as a child of the 1960s" and certainly she could be said to have been in the right place at the right time. Born to an army family in Cairo, Charles was sent to a boarding school in Harrogate, England, where she claims to have "picked up a survival kit for life." She studied fashion at the Art School in Swindon, after which she worked for couturier Michael Sherrard and for Mary Quant at her Shop Bazaar in Knightsbridge. She then assisted fashion photographer Tony Rawlinson before returning to Mary Quant.

In 1963 she set out on her own and moved to Beauchamp Place in 1966. From there her business boomed, and with sound and sensible strategies she expanded from London to the rest of Europe, Japan, and America. She built an empire that takes in more than 40 top store accounts and licenses for wedding dresses, hosiery, bed linens, underwear, and menswear.

Armed with talent and ambition—"I do have tremendous drive," she has said—Charles admits to having in the early days a woeful lack of business acumen, a trait she was to acquire very quickly as the momentum of the "swinging" 1960s launched her onto the fashion scene. In 1965 she was jetting around the world and the subject of headlines in the U.S. as Americans loved her fresh, "kinder, London ladylike-look," and at the tender age of 22 she was fêted by trend-hungry New York audiences.

During these years she created Ringo Starr's wedding outfit, dressed Petula Clark, Madame George Pompidou, Barbra Streisand, Lulu, Marianne Faithfull, and Mick Jagger. "The 1960s were totally celebrity-driven," she said. "There was this mood and we got great press. The editors loved the mini-star designer who dressed the major-star pop singer." With singular inspiration she transformed a lace bedspread into a long empire-line dress and sold it to Cilla Black. When Cilla's record "Anyone Who Had a Heart" became a hit, the dress became a bestseller. Charles took this in stride and became one of London's "swinging set."

Quite a celebrity in her own right, she was a regular guest on *Juke Box Jury,* the popular "Teen Scene" program; was interviewed on the *Tonight Show* by Johnny Carson; was a guest writer for the teen press; and modeled her own trendy designs. She was one of a myriad of talented young designers in the 1960s who made the clothes she and her friends wanted, full of youthful energy and gaiety, invention and individuality. People seemed to want everyday clothing for the streets of London, Paris, or anywhere in Europe, a trend that turned out to be well marketed and exploited by the new young designers.

Charles is treated with reverence in the fashion industry as someone who "got it right." She is a business-like technician, straightforward, and in love with her craft. "I enjoy what I do now more than I ever have. Every day I do precisely what I want and I am not so anxious now." Despite more than 35 successful years in the industry, she admits to an irrational fear that she will not be able to design clothes.

After such an auspicious start in the 1960s, she reflects that the 1970s were "a terrible time for fashion." But the 1980s saw her in full swing again, attiring the newly married Prince of Wales in a tartan suit for the Braemar games and an oatmeal wraparound dressing-gown coat for a walkabout in Wales. She became one of the exclusive breed of "Royal Designers." The exuberance of the swinging 1960s had given way to a more classic, sensible look. Charles has an eye for lavish fabrics combined with easy wearability. Hers are beautifully-made clothes with simple accessories; she hopes her clients would wear them to the supermarket.

Caroline Charles, spring 1996 collection. © AP/Wide World Photos.

Her many illustrious clients, Lady Lloyd Webber and Dame Diana Rigg among them, have attested to the beguiling quality of her fabrics: perennial velvets, rich wool paisleys and elegant brocades, and, in the 1990s, black leather mixed with flippy lace skirts (a slightly vampy departure for the designer) toned down into wearable sexy party clothes. The 1990s have seen yet another phase of extremely successful, well-thought-out business expansions. A new flagship shop in Bond Street, and with it an entirely new Bond Street customer, opened up a whole new market for Charles.

Charles is that rare commodity who has survived the vicissitudes of the fashion industry while retaining her own personal signature. She continues to create practical clothing that can be worn by working men and women. Her style is considered quintessentially British, which explains why she was a favorite of the late Diana, Princess of Wales, yet her clothing is available for everyday, albeit somewhat upscale, British consumers as well. She sells through retail outlets, including her own stores, as well as the mail-order catalogue Kingshill's, for which she was one of three initial designers.

In the late 1990s, Charles expanded into accessories and home furnishings. Her high-end home collection includes manufacturers such as PJ Flower, which was acquired by WestPoint Stevens in 1997, extending Charles' international distribution. (The designer shows her apparel in Asian cities including Tokyo and Bangkok, as well as in New York.) Elsa Klensch of CNN described Charles' 1998 fall/winter collection as being a mix of deep jewel-like colors and neutrals, accented by spots of bright hues. The colors, which Klensch described as olives, umbers, ambers, golds and plums, were inspired by the painters Rosetti and Klimt.

The slouchy, comfortable line typified Charles' use of soft fabrics and her rejection of too much tailoring and padding. Throughout her more than three-decade career, this British designer's focus has been on clothes that are easy to wear.

—Elian McCready; updated by Karen Raugust

CHLOÉ

French deluxe ready-to-wear house

Founded: by Jacques Lenoir and Gaby Aghion, in 1952; **Company History:** Acquired by Dunhill Holdings, Plc., 1985, and by Vendome, 1993; Karl Lagerfeld, designer, 1965–83, and again from 1992–97; Martine Sitbon, designer, 1987–91; Stella McCartney, designer, 1997–2001; Phoebe Philo, hired as designer, 2001. Fragrances include *Narcisse,* 1992. **Company Address:** 54–56 rue du Faubourg St. Honoré, 75008 Paris, France.

Publications

On CHLOÉ:

Articles

Gross, Michael, "Paris Originals: Chloé in the Afternoon," in *New York,* 15 May 1989.

Friedman, Arthur, "Chloé Reshapes Its Identity," in *WWD,* 2 January 1991.

White, Constance C.R., "Chloe's New Chief Designer," in the *New York Times,* 15 April 1997.

Mower, Sarah, "Chloe's Girl," in *Harper's Bazaar,* June 1997.

McCartney, Stella, "My Chloé Diary," in *Harper's Bazaar,* January 1998.

"She Grooves; Will She Go? The Hottest Item at Chloe is Designer Stella McCartney," in *Newsweek,* 18 October 1999.

Singer, Sally, "Chloé's Choice," in *Vogue*, August 2001.

Chloé, spring/summer 2002 ready-to-wear collection designed by Phoebe Philo. © Reuters NewMedia Inc./CORBIS.

* * *

Style, modernity, and a strong sense of femininity have been the key elements of Chloé since its inception. Maintaining a quiet confidence among the Parisian ready-to-wear houses, Chloé has relyied on the abilities of various already-established designers to produce fresh and vibrant clothing which reflected and, in the high points of its history under Martine Sitbon, Karl Lagerfeld, and upstart Stella McCartney defined the *zeitgeist* of Chloé élan.

Riding the wave of prêt-à-porter companies set to challenge couture in the 1950s, Chloé was keen from the start to produce wearable clothes conveying the immediacy of modernism in clear, strong styles. The house's identity has remained true to the design tenets of its early days, producing simple garments made from fluid fabrics. These promote a sense of elegant movement, enlivened by the

Chloé, spring/summer 2001 ready-to-wear collection designed by Stella McCartney. © Reuters NewMedia Inc./CORBIS.

artistic sense of color distinguishing French fashion; a constant feature at Chloé, despite the varied nationalities of its designers.

Chloé and its peers provided a lively, frequently directional alternative to haute couture, whose dictatorial status had diminished. The company was able to headhunt inspirational designers with the talent to translate the Chloé design image into clothing which would remain distinct to the label, while consistently evolving to embrace contemporary styles. In the 1960s this meant keeping pace with the youth-orientated look in London, with clothes imbued with a futuristic vitality. In 1966 this sense of freedom through technology was assimilated by Jeanne Do into a slim, straight-falling Empire line dress in stark white decorated with metallic geometric shapes. This modern armor as eveningwear was a major fashion trend, picking up on the science fiction trend of the time. The dress also pinpointed the introduction that year of maxi skirts, reinforcing Chloé's place at the cutting edge of fashion.

Chloé's reliance on different names to pursue the design house's viability has given a chameleon-like adaptability to its contemporary fashion, calling upon such catalytic freelancers as Karl Lagerfeld who worked on and off for some 23 years. From the late 1960s until his departure in 1997, the Chloé name became synonymous with Lagerfeld. The house style remained pared-down sheath dresses, hovering around the figure, adorned with minimal decoration, which distilled the late 1960s fashion directive. Under his guidance, the label moved with ease into the pluralistic 1970s, absorbing and refining the myriad of reference points with which fashion toyed. Lagerfeld's strongly conceived and modernistic designs throughout his tenure never compromised the supple femininity for which Chloé was renowned. After Lagerfeld's exit to takeover Chanel in the early 1980s, Chloé languished until Martine Sitbon was chosen to reinject a sense of originality and verve in 1987.

Sitbon embodied facets of Chloé's style which had been established in the 1960s—uncluttered designs drawing on popular culture, with distinct themes for each collection, translated into classic shapes for women confident of their own identity. Sitbon toned down the more overtly 1970s rock-influenced styles of her own named line to produce masculine tailored suits. These were softened by a dandyish swing to their cut and by delicately coloured silk chiffon blouses which blossomed into curving frilled collars. She defined Chloé's look during the 1980s and in the early 1990s, rounding the edges of the decade's often over-extravagant silhouette with well placed decoration and rich fabrics.

Sitbon left the label in 1991, and a desire to remain at the forefront of design prompted the return of Lagerfeld in 1992. He then captured the mood for unstructured easy-to-wear styles with his fluid slip dresses—harking back to the heights of his Chloé collections of the 1970s—and tapped the nostalgia for the flower child look upon which they drew. Lagerfeld adorned the faded print slips with flair, throwing long strings of beads around the models' necks and silk blooms in their hair. Although the initial reaction was uncertain, Chloé had judged the fashion moment for change well, and Lagerfeld once again fit comfortably into the house's mold.

When Lagerfeld bid adieu again in 1997, upstart Stella McCartney took the reins and reinvigorated Chloé, as well as its sales. Though many believed her girlish, feminine designs would attracted only younger women, her Chloé collections proved more sensual and sophisticated than anticipated, and crossed age barriers. Chloé's hipper image led to the opening of a new Manhattan boutique at the turn of the century, yet the house's new muse was lured away by Gucci in early 2001. McCartney left Chloé to create her own global label, and her longtime assistant, Phoebe Philo was hired as her replacement.

Chloé's place in history has already been assured by the house's ability to allow designers to flourish under its auspices. Lagerfeld, Sitbon, and McCartney all proffered their ideals of femininity and sophistication in designs for Chloé, keeping the house contemporary while still maintaining its classic style.

—Rebecca Arnold; updated by Owen James

CHOO, Jimmy

Malaysian couture shoe designer

Born: Penang, Malaysia. **Education:** Entered Cordwainer's Technical College, London, 1980. **Career:** Began designing shoes in

Jimmy Choo, fall 2001 collection. © AP/Wide World Photos/Fashion Wire Daily.

London, 1984; established custom shoe business, 1988; debuted wholesale shoe line and opened London boutique and showroom, 1996; niece Sandra Choi named creative director; established Jimmy Choo USA; opened New York and Beverly Hills stores, 1998; opened in Las Vegas shop, 1999; scouted further U.S. locations and Asia for additional stores, from 2000; opened new London store, 2001. **Exhibitions:** *Fashion in Motion,* Victoria & Albert Museum, London, 1999. **Awards:** British Accessory Designer of the Year, 1999. **Address:** 6 Pont Street, London, England, SW1 X9EL. **Website:** www.jimmychoo.com.

PUBLICATIONS

On CHOO:

Books

O'Keefe, Linda, *Shoes,* New York, 1996.

Steele, Valerie, *The Fashion Book,* London, 1998.

———, *Shoes: A Lexicon of Style,* New York, 1999.

Articles

Gurevitch, Ruth, "Choo's New Shoes," in *Footwear News,* 5 August 1996.

Anniss, Elisa, "Designing Superstars," in *Footwear News,* 26 May 1997.

Hesson, Wendy, "Jimmy Choo Struts Across the Pond," in *WWD,* 16 January 1998.

"Choo Prepares for U.S. Olympic Tower Store," in *Footwear News,* 2 November 1998.

Ginsberg, Merle, "The Red Carpetbaggers," in *WWD,* 22 March 1999.

"Choo's Shoes," in the *New Straits Times,* 7 June 1999.

Parrott, Stuart, "The Girl From Uncle," in *Asia, Inc.,* August 1999.

Fallon, James, "Liberty Bets on Women's," in *WWD,* 22 September 1999.

Edelson, Sharon, et al., "Excess Evolution," in *WWD,* 11 February 2000.

De Courtney, Romy, "The Big Preen," in *WWD,* 27 March 2000.

Conway, Susan, "High Heal Factor is Feng Shui in Choo's New Shoes," in *The Guardian,* 14 September 2000.

Miller, Samantha, "Shoes? Choos! Jimmy Choo Footwear Designer Sandra Choi…," in *People Weekly,* 20 November 2000.

Seckler, Valerie, "Give 'Em Shell," in *W,* December 2000.

———, "Alter Egos," in *W,* January 2001.

———, "Last Look," in *Vogue,* January 2001.

Medina, Marcy, "New Best Friends," in *WWD,* 8 January 2001.

Seckler, Valerie, "Oscar Scoops," in *WWD,* 26 February 2001.

Greenberg, Julie, and Leonard McCants, "Concerns Aside, Fall Gets Going," in *WWD,* 27 February 2001.

Seckler, Valerie, "Net-a-Porter Adds Jimmy Choo," in *WWD,* 28 March 2001.

Jimmy Choo, fall 2001 collection. © AP/Wide World Photos/ Fashion Wire Daily.

McAlister, Maggie, "Fit for a Queen…," in *Footwear News,* 2 July 2001.

* * *

Had Jimmy Choo been a resident of Oz, Dorothy's slippers would likely have sported genuine rubies. No stranger to extravagance, Choo is legendary for elegant, imaginative shoes. The sandals he fabricated for a *Vogue* photo shoot displayed 30-carat diamonds and carried a price tag of $1 million, and Cate Blanchett's 1999 Academy Awards footwear featured diamond ankle straps and cost a mere $110,000.

Jimmy Choo is actually two distinct enterprises. Choo heads the exclusive couture company that produces only three or four handmade pairs of shoes per day. His customer list reads like a Who's Who of actresses, royalty, and the rich and famous. Wealthy feet from all over the world have found their way to this master craftsman. The late Princess Diana owned more than 30 pairs of his shoes, and the beauty and elegance of his footwear are believed to have helped create Diana's sexier image.

Born to a shoemaking family on the Malaysian island of Penang, Choo made his first pair of shoes at age 11. He attended Cordwainer's Technical College in London and is considered one of London's leading shoe designers. His excellence earned him the title of British Accessory Designer of the Year in 1999. Choo favors crystalline colors, aqua, fuchsia, and bright orange and applies them to luxury fabrics like silk satin and shantung. Python and fish skin are some of his favorite materials because of the way they accept dye, and mink and feathers grace some of his styles. He has used a wide variety of stones, from Swarovski crystals to natural crystals for their healing power. His stiletto heels have been described as "dainty and deadly." Choo's philosophy is that shoes can be both beautiful and comfortable, and his devotees prove the point by their nearly fanatical devotion to his footwear.

Fashion stylist Tamara Yeardye Mellon of British *Vogue* approached Choo about starting a ready-to-wear business, having realized the tremendous potential for mass-market high-end footwear. The company opened in 1996 on Oxford Street in London with Choo lending his name and becoming a silent partner while Mellon served as managing director. Choo's 26-year-old niece, Sandra Choi, joined the firm as creative director. Choi was raised in Hong Kong and spent a year at St. Martin's Art School while living and working with her uncle. The demands of his custom work were such that she chose the business over formal education and left school to devote all her energy to the new company. Choi has achieved tremendous success in her own right and a strong following that includes everyone from Madonna to the Bush twins.

Though not custom-made, the Jimmy Choo line is all fabricated in Italy with an eye toward top quality. The collections are shown twice a year to coincide with the designer fashion shows in Paris, Milan, London, and New York. The company also offers men's shoes, handbags, and small leather goods. Choo has freestanding stores in London, New York, Las Vegas, and Beverly Hills and is carried in luxury retailers such as Neiman Marcus, Liberty of London, Bergdorf Goodman, and Harrods. It has become one of the largest off-the-shelf luxury shoe companies in the world, with prices running from $300 to $1,600 per pair. In a very short length of time, Choo is selling almost as many pairs of shoes as his major competitor, 30-year-old Manolo Blahnik.

—Christina Lindholm

CLAIBORNE, Liz

American designer

Born: Elizabeth Claiborne in Brussels, Belgium, 31 March 1929, to American parents from New Orleans; moved to New Orleans, 1939. **Education:** Studied art at Fine Arts School and Painters Studio, Belgium, 1947, and at the Nice Academy, 1948; self-taught in design. **Family:** Married Ben Schultz, 1950 (divorced); married Arthur Ortenberg, 1957; children: Alexander. **Career:** Sketch artist and model, Tina Leser, 1950; design assistant, Omar Kiam for Ben Reig, New York; designer, Youth Guild division of Jonathan Logan, 1960–76; founder/partner with Art Ortenberg, Liz Claiborne Inc., 1976; went public, 1981; introduced petite sportswear line, 1981; formed dress division, 1982; introduced shoes, 1983; purchased

Liz Claiborne in 2000, at the Council of Fashion Designers of America awards. © AP/Wide World Photos.

Kaiser-Roth Corporation, 1985; introduced Lizwear label featuring jeans, 1985; introduced men's sportswear, Clairborne, 1985; inaugurated Dana Buchman and Claiborne Furnishings, 1987–88; introduced larger-size line, Elizabeth, 1988; launched First Issue, 1988, formed Liz & Co. knitwear division, 1989; Claiborne and Ortenberg retire, 1989; Elizabeth Dresses introduced, 1990, Sports Shoes and Suits, 1991, Sport Specific Activewear and Liz Sport Eyewear, 1992; purchased Russ and Crazy Horse labels from Russ Toggs, 1992; closed First Issue stores, 1995; launched swimwear label with Sirena Apparel Group, 1996; signed licensing deal with Candie's, 1998; acquired Laundry, and stakes in Segrets, Lucky Brand Dungarees, and Kenneth Cole, 1999; bought Monet Group, 2000; initiated children's clothing lines, 2000; fragrances include *Liz Claiborne,* 1986; *Claiborne,* 1989; *Vivid,* 1994; *Curve,* 1996; *Lizsport* and *Claiborne Sport,* 1997; *Lucky You,* 2000; *Mambo,* 2001. **Awards:** Winner, *Harper's Bazaar* Jacques Heim national design contest, 1949; Hecht & Company Young Designer award, Washington, D.C., 1967; Woolknit Association award, 1973; Entrepreneurial Woman of the Year, 1980; Council of Fashion Designers of America award, 1985; award from Barnard College, 1991; High School of Fashion Industries award, 1990; award from Marymount Manhattan College, 1989; the Council of Fashion Designers Humanitarian award, 2000. **Address:** 1441 Broadway, New York, NY 10018, USA. **Website:** www.lizclaiborne.com.

Publications

On CLAIBORNE:

Books

Milbank, Caroline Rennolds, *New York Fashion: The Evolution of American Style,* New York, 1989.

Daria, Irene, *The Fashion Cycle,* New York, 1990.

Stegemeyer, Anne, *Who's Who in Fashion, Third Edition,* New York, 1996.

Le Dortz, Laurent, and Béatrice Debosscher, *Stratégies des Leaders Américains de la Mode: Calvin Klein, Donna Karan, Liz Claiborne, Polo Ralph Lauren, et Tommy Hilfiger,* Paris, 2000.

Articles

Klensch, Elsa, "Dressing America: The Success of Liz Claiborne," in *Vogue,* August 1986.

Stan, Adele-Marie, "Four Designing Women," in *Ms.,* November 1986.

Sellers, Patricia, "The Rag Trade's Reluctant Revolutionary: Liz Claiborne," in *Fortune,* 5 January 1987.

Gannes, Stuart, "American's Fastest-Growing Companies," in *Fortune,* 23 May 1988.

Morris, Michele, "The Wizard of the Working Woman's Wardrobe," in *Working Woman,* June 1988.

Deveny, Kathleen, "Can Ms. Fashion Bounce Back?" in *Business Week,* 16 January 1989.

Graham, Judith, "Clairborne Opens Its Own Sites," in *Advertising Age,* 5 June 1989.

Armstrong, Lisa, "Working Woman's Ally," in *Vogue* (London), February 1991.

Hass, Nancy, "Like a Rock," in *Financial World,* 4 February 1992.

Agins, Teri, "Liz Claiborne Seems to Be Losing Its Invincible Armor," in the *Wall Street Journal,* July 1993.

Larson, Soren, "Claiborne to Try the Sporting Life," in *Women's Wear Daily,* 14 March 1997.

"Liz Claiborne Inc.," in *Industry Week,* 17 August 1998.

D'Innocenzio, Anne, and Zimmermann, Kim, "Liz Claiborne Gets Virtual," in *Women's Wear Daily,* 12 February 1999.

Mazzaraco, Margaret, "Liz Claiborne: Some Thoughts About the Future, Before Her Name Became an Empire," in *Women's Wear Daily,* 13 September 1999.

Agins Teri, "Claiborne Patches Together an Empire," in the *Wall Street Journal,* 2 February 2000.

Wilson, Eric, "Liz's Wildlife Lessons," in *Women's Wear Daily,* 14 June 2000.

Monget Monget, "Launching Liz Sleepwear," in *Women's Wear Daily,* 14 August 2000.

* * *

In 1976, after a 25-year career as a designer, Liz Claiborne founded her own company to provide innovative designs for professional women. By 1988 Liz Claiborne Inc. was competently filling the needs of the rapidly expanding women's workforce and its owner was among those profiled in *Working Woman* magazine's June 1988 series "Women Who Have Changed the World."

Claiborne preferred to view herself as one of her own down-to-earth clients, whom she called "the Liz Lady," one of the working women who had rapidly come to comprise nearly half of the U.S. workforce. Her original concept was, as she explained in a *Vogue* interview in August 1986, "to dress the women who didn't have to wear suits—the teachers, the doctors, the women working in Southern California and Florida, the women in the fashion industry itself."

In 1980 Claiborne's innovative designs were so successful she became the first woman in the U.S. fashion industry to be named Entrepreneurial Woman of the Year, and in the following year her firm went public, prospering financially to such a degree it was described by Merrill Lynch as "a case history of success." The phenomenal growth of Liz Claiborne Inc. was spurred on by diversification from the two original basic lines—active sportswear and a slightly dressier collection—to include a dress division in 1982 and a unit for shoes in 1983. In 1985 the company acquired the Kaiser-Roth Corporation, which had been a licensee producing accessories, including handbags, scarves, belts, and hats.

Also in 1985, a collection of men's sportswear, Clairborne, was introduced, and 1986 saw the launch of a perfume *Liz Claiborne,* described by its eponymous designer to *Vogue* in August 1986 as appealing "to a woman's idealistic version of herself.... She's active, whatever her age. It's the same feeling we try to give in the clothes."

Since Claiborne's resignation from her company in 1989, the company has pursued various strategies to offer a wide range of fashion apparel, accessories, and fragrances for men and women. The basic strategy was to meet consumer needs and wants on all levels by pursing a multibrand, multichannel diversification. Under the leadership of Paul R. Charron, chairman and CEO, the company grew into a fashion empire including 22 owned and licensed brands available at 22,000 different retail locations throughout the world.

The company's brands can be found throughout the world at upscale, mainstream, promotional, and chain department stores and mass merchandisers. A customer can purchase a suit by the brand Dana Buchman at an upscale department store such as Saks Fifth Avenue or a sweater by Russ available only at Wal-Mart stores. In 2000, Target Stores successfully sold women's apparel under the Niki Taylor name. It will be renamed Meg Allen and available to Target exclusively in 2001. Classifications include upscale brands, middle line, urban, hip, and the budget brand, offering a wide range of prices in varied retail outlets.

Liz Claiborne Inc. was actively testing e-commerce through to of its brands, luckybrandjeans.com and elisabeth.com. The sites proved moderately successful as of 2001 and the company also had its corporate website at www.lizclaiborne.com. Another area of growth was accessories, with a presence in the costume jewelry segment, under the Liz Claiborne name. In addition, the company had acquired the trademarks of the Monet Group in 2000, which enhanced its accessories line and increased market share.

Liz Claiborne also continued to expand internationally. Its first retail outlet on London's Regent Street was opened in 2000 to celebrate the 10th anniversary of the company's presence in Europe. Future growth leaned toward Europe and Canada but company executives were eyeing Latin America, especially Mexico, where sales had been strong.

Claiborne herself has been buying back shares of the company recently, and she and her husband run the Liz Claiborne and Arthur Ortenburg Foundation. They spend their time in St. Barts or Montana, active in environmental and social issues. Claiborne does not wear the clothes bearing her name; she claims she would rather wear DKNY or Ralph Lauren casual clothes than her namesake brand, which itself had fallen on hard times in the past few years and moved only when markdowned. More recently, the trendy Kenneth Cole label produced by the company proved quite successful in taking business from the Liz Claiborne label. CEO Charron commented to the *Wall Street Journal* in February 2000, "It is better to steal market share from yourself than to sit back and let somebody else do it."

In the 21st century Liz Claiborne Inc. was the number-one retailer of clothes and accessories for career women in the United States. As such the company was firmly committed to furthering its brand recognition and making its many products available to consumers wherever they chose to shop.

—Doreen Ehrlich; updated by Donna W. Reamy

CLARK, Ossie

British designer

Born: Raymond Clark in Oswaldtwistle, Lancashire, 2 June 1942. **Education:** Studied fashion design, Manchester College of Art,

Ali MacGraw in an Ossie Clark-designed ensemble, 1969. © Hulton-Deutsch Collection/CORBIS.

1957–61, and Royal College of Art, 1961–65. **Family:** Married Celia Birtwell, 1969 (divorced); children: Albert. **Career:** Freelance designer, selling to Quorum, London, and Henri Bendel, New York, 1964–74, and to Mendes, French ready-to-wear firm; designer, Quorum, 1965–74; designer, Radley, 1968 and 1983; business closed, 1981; business reorganized, 1983; signed contract with Evocative boutique for made-to-measure clothes, 1987; murdered, 1996; diaries published, 1999; homage by Decades retro shop, 2000. **Exhibitions:** Warrington, Cheshire, gallery and museum showing, 1999. **Awards:** Bath Museum of Costume Dress of the Year award, 1969. **Died:** 6 August 1996, of stab wounds.

PUBLICATIONS

On CLARK:

Books

Lambert, Eleanor, *World of Fashion: People, Places, Resources,* New York & London, 1976.
Howell, Georgina, *Sultans of Style: 30 Years of Fashion and Passion 1960–1990,* London, 1990.

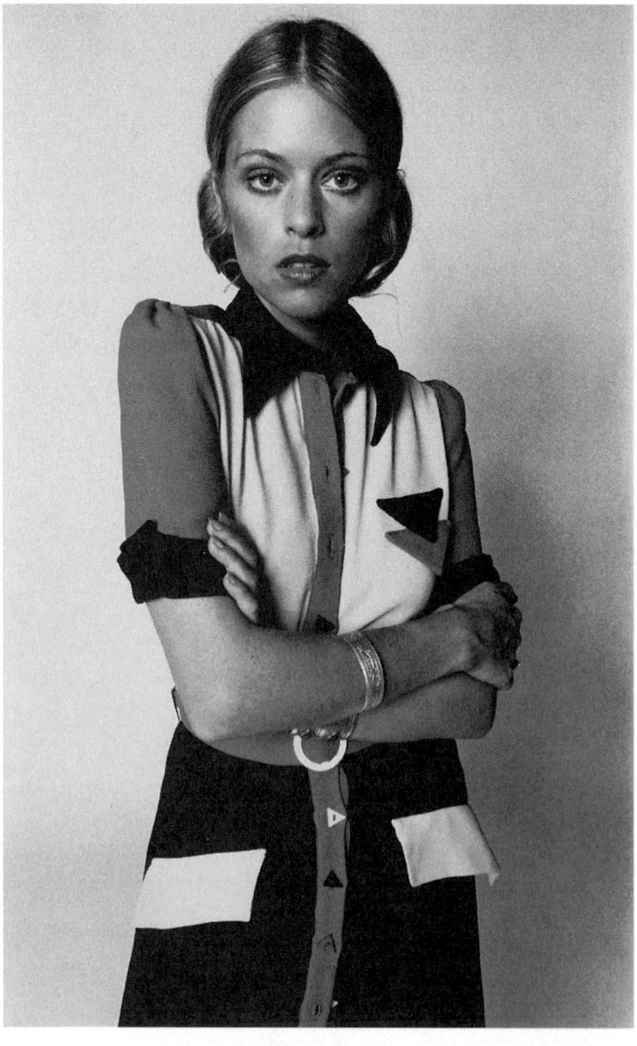

Design by Ossie Clark, 1970. © Hulton-Deutsch Collection/CORBIS.

Mulvagh, Jane, *Vivienne Westwood: An Unfashionable Life,* New York, 1999.
Rous, Lary Henrietta, ed., *The Ossie Clark Diaries,* London, 1999.

Articles

Peters, Pauline, "Ossie and Alice in Wonderland," in the *Sunday Times Magazine* (London), 11 January 1970.
Roberts, Michael, "Michael Roberts Talks to Ossie Clark," in the *Sunday Times* (London), 16 November 1975.
"Ossie Clark Designs," in the *Times* (London), 27 January 1976.
"Ossie Clark Special," in *Ritz* (London), No. 5, 1977.
"Ossie Clark Goes Out of Business," in the *Times* (London), 5 February 1981.
"Peace in Our Time: Summer of Love Revisited," in *Elle* (London), June 1987.
Howell, Georgina, "The Dressmaker," in the *Sunday Times Magazine* (London), 12 July 1987.
Flanagan, Kathryn Flett, "Darling I've Seen It All Before," in the *Observer,* 15 August 1996.
Thomas, Robert, "Ossie Clark...British Designer Defined Mood," [obituary] in the *New York Times,* 12 August 1996.
Bowles, Hamish, "Ossie Clark: 1942–1996," in *Vogue,* November 1996.
Bachrach, Judy, "Hooked on Glamor," in *Vanity Fair,* December 1996.
Leadbeater, Charles, "And This Was 1996," in the *New Statesman,* 20 December 1996.
Rouse, Antony, "The Other Clark Diaries," the *Spectator,* 28 November 1998.
Young, Elizabeth, "Vivienne Westwood: An Unfashionable Life," in the *New Statesman,* 1 January 1999.
———, "The Ossie Clark Diaries," in the *New Statesman,* 1 January 1999.
Frankel, Susannah, "Warrington Celebrates Ossie Clark, the Designer Who Dressed the Sixties," in the *Independent* (London), 30 October 1999.
Arbetter, Lisa, "News," in *In Style,* 1 February 2000.
Thomas, Dana, "Ossified," in the *New York Times Magazine,* 20 February 2000.
Lycett, Andrew, "Something Sensational," in the *New Statesman,* 11 December 2000.
"Ossie Clark," [profile], available online at Decades Inc., www.decadesinc.com, 17 July 2001.
"Ossie Clark," [profile], available online at The Fashion Page, www.ukfirst.com, 17 July 2001.
"Ossie Clark," [profile], available online at Fashion Avenue, www.geocities.com, 17 July 2001.

* * *

Ossie Clark, described as the King of King's Road, rose to prominence as a fashion designer during the swinging 1960s. Trained at the Manchester College of Art, then at the Royal College of Art, London, he graduated at a time when London was entering a period of international prominence for its designs for the youth market. In a pre-Green era, variety and the ability to produce a fast turnover of styles were desirable qualities in a designer. Clark provided a great variety of images for both daywear and eveningwear.

From 1966 Clark was designing for Quorum, a London-based wholesale and boutique business, in partnership with Alice Pollock. His wife, Celia Birtwell, also an RCA graduate, provided many of the pattern designs for the printed textiles used by Clark. He designed both daywear and eveningwear, often using sensuous fabrics such as satin, chiffon, crêpe, and clinging jersey. Although, since he was so versatile and prolific, it is hard to characterize his style, he was probably best known for clinging crêpe and jersey dresses with plunging necklines, figure-hugging waists, and swirling skirts, but he was equally capable of producing close-fitting crisp linen suits. Innovations in terms of cut included suits with elbow-length tight-fitting sleeves over full long-sleeved blouses. In the late 1960s, he used exotic materials such as snakeskin, feathers, and metallic prints.

Clark launched his menswear line in 1968, which reflected the period's more relaxed attitude to male dressing. Examples from his first menswear collection included a pink crêpe shirt with a fall of ruffles at the front, diminishing in size and edged in white silk braid. His clothes for Quorum were in the medium-to-expensive price range, comparing with other contemporary designers such as Zandra Rhodes and Jean Muir. Quorum produced garments for direct sale as well as more specialized outfits to order. The company sold through its own retail outlets, through department stores such as the Way In section of the Harrods chain, and through individual boutiques such as Image in Bath. Clark's clothes were sold in America and Europe, being stocked in Italy by Fiorucci. His clientèle in the 1960s and 1970s read like a catalogue of the trendy rich and famous and included Marianne Faithful, Mick and Bianca Jagger, Twiggy, Marie Helvin, Cathy McGowan, and Goldie Hawn. In 1972 Mick Jagger owned no less than 10 Clark jumpsuits. Jagger wore a blue sequined stretch velour jumpsuit that unzipped down the front for his performance at Madison Square Garden in 1972. Clark's clothes were regularly featured in the fashion press, and fashion editors reputedly fought for tickets for his shows in the early 1970s.

From 1970, Quorum was two-thirds funded by Rady Fashions and Textiles, which provided the business premises. Alice Pollock dealt with day-to-day practicalities such as organizing staff, buying cloth, and having it dyed. From 1977 Clark had his own company using the design label Ossie Clark Ltd. However, in 1981, Clark's company succumbed to the economic recession, despite having been taken over in 1980 by MAK Industries, which wished to gain control of the Ossie Clark label and attempted unsuccessfully to open an American branch. Ossie Clark Ltd. went into voluntary liquidation in 1981, and Clark was declared bankrupt in 1983. Clark lasted longer than most designers who began in the late 1960s youth boom, which was a tribute to the enduring quality of his design stamina and the range and flexibility of his ideas.

Bankruptcy, however, was not the end of Clark's fashion career. He taught at the Royal College of Art and designed evening dresses for Radley Fashions, and in 1986 he launched a lingerie company in partnership with Gina Fratini, trading under the name Rustle. He made use of his skills in employing the bias cut to produce clinging lingerie in silk satin with lace trimmings and insertions.

In 1987, Evocative, the newly opened Grosvenor Street boutique, ordered one-off made-to-measure dresses from Clark for individual clients, with ball dresses retailing for £3,000. Despite his still evident international fame, in 1987 Clark was reduced to living by a barter system, such as making a hat for dancer Wayne Sleep, who in exchange paid for Clark's sewing machine to be mended—an enterprising solution all too many young designers may identify with.

Clark died in his Notting Hill apartment on 6 August 1996 of stab wounds inflicted by his lover, Diego Cogolato. He left photos and a meager journal of his well-connected life and art, which Lady Henrietta Rous edited in 1999. Reviewer Andrew Lycett dismissed the text as "meanderings." In a less judgemental double review for the *New Statesman* of a Vivienne Westwood biography and of Clark's diaries, Elizabeth Young summarized: "Ossie Clark's name evokes a familiar pantheon of imagery-prettiness and privilege, spun-sugar rebellion, Mick 'n' Bianca, Twiggy and Bailey, white butterflies, Moroccan lamps, dim rooms swagged and draped with ethnic tassels and fabrics, a fog of incense, rose-coloured spectacles and those early cocksure, thundering chords of the Beatles-Stones-Who soundtrack."

After riding out the turmoil from drug problems, bankruptcy, and depression with noticeable grace, Clark received a posthumous renown honoring the chiffon, snakeskin, and op-art funware with which he decked the Beatles, Ali McGraw, Elizabeth Taylor, Faye Dunaway, and Sharon Tate. The town of Warrington, Cheshire, where Clark's family resides, celebrated his talent with a 1999 museum and art gallery showing. Late 20th-century postpunk collectors Sandra Bullock and Nicole Kidman were among those who snapped up Clark's crêpes and gauzes. In February 2000, Decades, a source of vintage chic in Los Angeles, featured a retro honorarium of 100 Clark originals. Shop owner Cameron Silver stated, "I hope to be the one to put Ossie back on the map."

—Linda Coleing; updated by Mary Ellen Snodgrass

CLEAVER, Alan

See BYBLOS

CLERGERIE, Robert

French footwear designer

Born: 18 July 1934, in Paris, France. **Education:** École Superieure de Commerce, Paris. **Career:** Manager, then designer, Xavier Danaud, of the Charles Jourdan factory, 1970s; purchased men's shoe company, Fenestrier, 1978; designed the first Robert Clergerie women's shoe line, 1981; established Clerma Company, for the opening of the first Robert Clergerie store, 1981; Lyon, Toulouse, and Paris Place des Victoires stores opened, 1982; J. Fenestrier men's store in Paris opened, 1983; franchise opened in Tokyo, 1986; New York store opened, 1987; Madrid and Brussels stores opened, 1988; London store opened, 1989; represented by 17 stores in France, six abroad, and three licensees in Japan, 1992; opened Los Angeles store, 1994; centenary of the firm, 1995; Clergerie sells majority of his shares, 1996; New York store transferred to Madison Avenue, 1996. **Awards:** *Footwear News* Designer of the Year, 1987, 1990.

PUBLICATIONS

On CLERGERIE:

Books

Stegemeyer, Anne, *Who's Who in Fashion, Third Edition,* New York, 1996.

Articles

"Bandals Galore," in *Newsweek,* 21 May 1984.
Infantino, Vivian, "Clergerie Hears the Pitter Patter of Sandals for the Winter Season," in *Footwear News,* 23 May 1994.
Baber, Bonnie, et al., "The Design Masters," in *Footwear News,* 17 April 1995.
"Clergerie, Furla Launch Units on Mad Avenue," in *WWD,* 18 June 1996.
"Clergerie Takes Madison," in *Footwear News,* 25 November 1996.
Weisman, Katherine, "The Romans Empire," in *Footwear News,* 1 September 1997.

* * *

Robert Clergerie's shoes exhibit a sense of style and class equivalent to the artistic impression of a painter's sculpture. But for Clergerie, shoes are not made solely for fashion; shoes are made for walking. While paying close attention to technique and detail, his designs stress purpose and comfort. The grace and practicality of Clergerie's shoes have led him to be named the "functionalist" of shoe fashion. With respect to practicality, many men and women are drawn to Clergerie's shoes because he successfully designs stunning, functional shoes that can be worn in today's career-oriented society.

Clergerie uses a three-part design crtieria when introducing a new line: first, each proposed item needs to be within the scope of the manufacturer's expertise; second, as a designer Clergerie must have the right idea at the right time—anticipating what his customers want, a year in advance; and third, he has to be the only designer creating within a particular area, to offer his clientèle unique, beautiful items. Clergerie believes his simplistic design technique is the only way to success and excellence in shoemaking. He has said that the stronger the idea, the simpler the design, and therefore, the less need for ornamentation. Clergerie's designs are not complicated with adornments, but are simple and chic. This has made him one of the most influential shoe designers of his time, and his designs have had a marked influence in the fashion arena.

In 1981, for example, Clergerie debuted his line with lace-up oxfords, a man's shoe made for a woman that has since become an essential item to wardrobes. He also designed the raffia sandal in 1992 and the parallelogram heel in 1984. Since then, cobblers have imitated the parallelogram heel and call it the Clergerie heel. In 1994, to be unconventional, he designed sandals for the winter season because, as he stated, he had a "feeling for sandals in the winter." To accommodate the cold weather, the sandals were designed to be worn with big, thick socks. Clergerie went on to design the horn-shaped heel in 1989 and his metal heel in 1993, which was the inspiration for the spike heel.

Clergerie is inspired by the world; it is where he receives his originality and the innovation of his designs. As he lives his life, he takes on the world and engulfs all aspects of it. He pays close attention to the details, such as architecture, food, and the breeze felt from a motorcycle ride. He encompasses all of life's joys and arranges them into his designs, giving Clergerie shoes their stylish beauty, individuality, and simplicity.

—Kimbally A. Medeiros

COLE, Kenneth

American designer

Born: 23 March 1954 in Brooklyn, New York. **Education:** Emory University, 1976. **Family:** Married Maria Cuomo in 1987; three children. **Career:** President, CEO, and designer for Kenneth Cole

Kenneth Cole, fall 2001 collection: twill denim satin lapel suit and satin shirt. © AFP/CORBIS.

Productions, Inc., since 1982. **Awards:** Creative Coalition Spotlight award; Devine Design's Humanitarian of the Year, 1996; CFDA's award for Humanitarian Excellence, 1996; Mothers' Voices Extraordinary Voice award; Council of Foundations Humanitarian Leadership award, 1996; Footwear News Person of the Year, 1996; FFANY's Fashion Medal of Honor award, 1997; Amnesty International Media Spotlight award, 1998; T. Kenyon Holly award, 2000. **Address:** 152 West 57th Street, New York, NY 10019, USA. **Websites:** www.kennethcole.com; www.reactiononline.com.

Publications

On COLE:

Articles

Critchell, Samantha, "Designer Combines Style, Activism," in *Associated Press Online,* 21 July 1999.
Gonzalez, Isabel, "In Style: For Kenneth Cole, Fashion, Activism Are Driving Forces," in *Atlanta Journal and Constitution,* 3 October 1999.
D'Innocenzio, Anne, "In the Zone," *WWD,* 22 March 2000.

Kenneth Cole, fall 2001 collection: napa leather shirt, pinstripe skirt, wide suede belt, and wrap choke collar. © AP/Wide World Photos.

Cunningham, Thomas, "Kenneth Cole: Firing on All Cylinders," *WWD,* 17 April 2000.
Sturrock, Staci, "Direct from Grand Central Casting: Kenneth Cole Mixes Politics and Pleasure With His Fresh Inaugural Collection," in *Palm Beach Post,* 21 September 2000.
Cole, Patrick, "Kenneth Cole Dives Into 'Shark Tank'," in *Newsday,* 31 October 2000.

*

I design products you can wear today and tomorrow from season to season. You want to look modern without being too edgy, and you always want value. I mean, you can buy a pair of shoes for a dollar, but if you never wear them you've paid too much.

—Kenneth Cole

* * *

To be aware is more important than what you wear.

—Kenneth Cole advertising tagline.

Kenneth Cole launched Kenneth Cole Productions with a trailer full of his women's shoe designs parked on Sixth Avenue during a 1982 shoe show. Eschewing the anonymity of being one among thousands in a room at the Hilton and unable to afford the grand midtown Manhattan showrooms preferred by the large companies, Cole changed his company's name from Kenneth Cole, Inc. to Kenneth Cole Productions, Inc. in order to obtain a film production permit (the only kind the city of New York would give) to park the truck. The name of the film listed on the permit was *Birth of a Shoe Company.* Within two and a half days, he and his crew sold 40,000 pairs of shoes. The Kenneth Cole name soon became synonymous with modishly hip urban footwear, followed by accessories. In 1998 Cole took on menswear, in which his collections quickly made a mark; he then debuted his first womenswear collection in a show at New York's Grand Central Station in 2000.

The term "hip-classic" has often been applied in describing Cole's designs. In both men's and women's collections, he utilizes a preponderance of leather and suede, along with silk shantung, cashmeres, wools, cottons, and synthetic fabric blends to create styles that manage to be both elegant and relaxed. Cole designs, in his own words, fashion for the "contemporary person who wants to have a sense of identity and personality, but also doesn't want to be the focal point of the crowd because of what he or she is wearing." His designs do not push the boundaries of comfort and wearability but court classic lines with imaginative twists and modern edges. In seeking a balancing point between fashionable élan and practical functionality, Cole's style blurs the lines between everyday casual and dresswear.

Cole's menswear collections have included everything from denims, quilted vests, and shirt jackets to narrow three- and four-button suits and techno-inspired outerwear in black with vivid linings. Black leather is generally in abundance for everything from streamlined coats to zippered vests to shirts worn under tailored pinstriped suits. Cole also uses a lot of metallic glazed or embossed leather. For women, collections range in these same areas, with a touch of whimsy in patchwork suedes in lime and tan, tie-dyed hot pants, hip-slung long pants, more metallics, and antiqued leathers. His colors tend toward the urban: black on black, navy, olive, gunmetal gray, bronze, though with his entry into womenswear the palette xpanded to include fresher and more vivid hues. His Fall 2001 collection, described as "his most sophisticated and luxe collection to date," joined menswear and womenswear into a harmonious whole on the runway.

A defining aspect of all of Cole's work has always been an active implementation of his social conscience through advertising campaigns, show themes, sales incentives, benefits, and a general dedication to consciousness-raising. His advertising campaigns typically feature taglines, such as "...sixty-two percent of society believes preferences other than their own are wrong. So much for seeing eye to eye," or "For every dollar a man makes, a woman earns seventy-six cents. Change please," and "The family gun stands a greater chance of killing you than a stranger." Cole writes much of this ad copy himself and grappling with such issues, he has stressed, is not just an advertising gimmick for the company but very much a part of its identity. Other examples of this commitment have been shows requiring attendees to donate a pair of shoes for the homeless, a traveling warehouse sale to benefit AIDS research, and sales incentives in the form of discounts in return for a donation of shoes or clothing. Preceding his shows have been films encouraging voting or talking about prejudice with, instead of the usual gifts found at fashions shows on attendees' seats, pamphlets or books underlining and informing on the issue in question.

As Cole says, "I'm trying to add value to the process of shopping. I'm trying to make what we do more relevant than it normally would be, because at the end of the day, I make shoes and pants, so sometimes it's hard to get totally motivated. You make what you do part of something bigger than it is. Then what you do becomes important and you can justify the compromises we all make." As well as being socially progressive, Cole is technologically forward, one of the first to engage in live webcasts of his runway shows. The live webcast of his Fall 2000 menswear show was designed to raise awareness about homelessness and benefit HELP USA.

Kenneth Cole Productions now oversees a retail empire spanning the U.S., with additional stores in Amsterdam, Hong Kong, Singapore, and Taiwan. Near the end of 2000, Cole opened an 18,000-square-foot flagship store on Fifth Avenue in New York at the entrance to Rockefeller Center. In addition to shoes, accessories, and men's and women's collections, the designer has ventured into jewelry, perfume, and a number of other licensing ventures. Future plans include expansion into children's clothing and home décor. It seems likely that both Cole's approach to style as a practical component of everyday life and his commitment to humanitarian causes will remain constant no matter how many areas of fashion and design he chooses to explore.

—Jessica Reisman

COLE HAAN

American footwear design house

Founded: in Chicago by Trafton Cole and Eddie Haan, 1928. **Company History:** Cole Haan sold to group of partners headed by George Denney, 1975; launched retail division, 1982; sold to Nike for $80 million, 1988; repositioned under Modern Artisan theme, late 1990s; redesigned retail stores, 2000; signed license with G-III for apparel, 2000; licensed Air technology from Nike for Cole Haan shoes, 2000. **Company Address:** 1 Cole Haan Drive, Yarmouth, ME 04096, USA. **Company Website:** www.colehaan.com.

Publications

On COLE HAAN:

Articles

"Alone by Design," in *Forbes,* 20 May 1996.
"Cole Haan Cuts Staff by 74, Prez Taylor Steps Down," in *Footwear News,* 6 April 1998.
Mullins, David Philip, "Stoking the Cole," in *Footwear News,* 8 November 1999.
"Cole Haan Licenses Apparel," in *Footwear News,* 21 February 2000.
LoRusso, Maryann, "New Cole Haan Lifestyle Line Injected with Nike Technology," in *Footwear News,* 6 March 2000.
Mui, Nelson, "Comfort is in the Air at Cole Haan," in *DNR,* 6 March 2000.
Brumback, Nancy, "Cole Haan Redesigns Flagship Stores in Line with the Brand's Updated Look," in *Footwear News,* 2 October 2000.

* * *

Cole Haan was formed in Chicago in 1928 by Trafton Cole and Eddie Haan, who built the company on a reputation of quality, craftsmanship, style, and service. Cole Haan—which began life as a men's footwear brand but expanded into women's and children's products as well—has sought to maintain this spirit throughout its more than 70-year history.

Cole Haan was sold to a group of partners headed by George Denney in 1975. These executives built upon the foundation established by Cole and Haan over the following decade, transforming the label into one of the leading U.S. footwear brands. They launched a retail division in 1982, which comprised 42 stores worldwide and cumulative annual sales of nearly $70 million by 1996.

Sports giant Nike purchased Cole Haan for $80 million in 1988, a move that represented Nike's first foray outside the athletic shoe business. Cole Haan's management—though based at the firm's international headquarters in Yarmouth, Maine, and its design headquarters in New York City—has continued to operate largely autonomously since the merger.

Many of Cole Haan's competitors have relied on licensed designer labels to increase their sales, but the company has preferred to focus on building its own brand. It has expanded the Cole Haan name into pumps, flats, sandals, and other casual and formal styles, and has since segued into leather accessories such as handbags, briefcases, belts, and wallets and into compatible products such as hosiery. During the mid-1990s Cole Haan worked to extend its presence internationally, especially in Europe. The company introduced a collection of driving shoes targeted at European customers in 1996; this style had long been one of Cole Haan's bestsellers on the Continent, but the relaunch made the line more fashion forward, with new colors, longer-lasting materials, and softer leathers. At the same time, as reported in *Footwear News,* Cole Haan introduced fashion leather and suede versions of its Anaconda chukka boots specifically for Europe. The company sold its European products through more than 300 retail doors in Italy alone.

The late 1990s represented a rough period for Cole Haan. Sales were lower than expected, which led to layoffs and the departure of the company president. Nike, too, was having financial and marketing problems at the same time, but Cole Haan's troubles were thought to be unrelated to those of its parent. Starting in 1998, several Nike executives began moving to the Cole Haan unit to help revitalize the brand. The next year Nike repositioned the Cole Haan label, introducing new footwear items with more modern styling while continuing to emphasize the high quality upon which the company was founded. The new positioning was referred to as "Modern Artisan" and supported by a lifestyle advertising campaign.

At the time of the repositioning, the company estimated that 60 to 80 percent of each year's product lines would be new styles, with the remainder comprised of carryovers of classic styles. The added items were intended to appeal to more market segments within the company's core target of affluent 30- to 50-year-olds. Cole Haan differentiated itself from its competitors by dividing its line into several unique lifestyle collections, each appealing to different customers and as well as different aspects of the customers' lives. Groupings have included Country, City, Studio, Resort, Evening, Home, and Bregano.

Cole Haan translated its new Modern Artisan positioning to stores starting in 2000, redesigning two prototypes, in Chicago and Boston, to be followed by others later in the year. Store designs reflected the company's new gray-green and red logo and afforded an opportunity to bring together all the Cole Haan-branded products under one lifestyle image. (The Chicago store is located next to the parent company's flagship Niketown outlet.) Additionally, Cole Haan also announced its intention to add more stores within its retail division.

At the front of each redesigned store, a new product line, Cole Haan with Nike Air Technology, was featured. This line formed the focal point of Nike's new Modern Artisan strategy, which included comfort among its primary attributes. Cole Haan licensed Nike's Air technology—made famous in its athletic footwear line endorsed by Michael Jordan—for use in several shoe stylings. The patented Air cushioning is integrated into the sole, with small windows on the bottom of each Cole Haan shoe show the technology at work.

Upon launch, Cole Haan executives explained that they expected this new line to ultimately account for 15 percent of the division's volume, which stood at $200 million in 2000. By devoting 25-percent of the Cole Haan advertising budget to the Air-branded products, the company intended to emphasize the technology itself rather than the Nike brand, though both companies' logos appear on the bottom of the shoes. Cole Haan also planned to eventually expand into other products, such as travel accessories, featuring Air technology. The company also expanded by granting its first license to an outside company, extending its brand further into the apparel category. G-III Apparel Group announced it would make leather and fabric outerwear, as well as other clothing under the Cole Haan label, to be sold in Cole Haan stores and at other retailers (mostly upscale department stores) carrying Cole Haan footwear.

Although the new Nike Air technology represents the "modern" in Cole Haan's positioning, the company continues to stress the quality and craftsmanship suggested by the word "artisan." Company literature points out that a single craftsperson is responsible for each pair of shoes, overseeing its progress from beginning to end with said craftsperson putting the pair of completed shoes into the Cole Haan box himself or herself. This personal touch, combined with technological and stylistic innovation, is what Modern Artisan means to Cole Haan.

—Karen Raugust

COLEMAN, Nick

British designer

Born: circa 1960. **Education:** Graduated from St. Martin's School of Art, London, mid-1980s. **Family:** Married Lucy Coleman. **Career:** Produced such collections as Kimota Returns; operated London night clubs, including Solaris; cofounder/owner, with Lucy Coleman, of Body Control Pilates, from 1997. **Addresses:** 202 New North Road, London N1 7BJ England; 66 Neal Street, London WC2H 9TA England.

Publications

On COLEMAN:

Articles

Buckley, Richard, "UK Designer Exhibition Has Promise," in *DNR,* 4 September 1986.

Flett, Kathryn, "Patsy Looks Perfect," in the *Sunday Times Magazine* (London), 12 April 1987.

"British Designers to Give AIDS Research Benefit," in *Daily News Record,* 14 September 1987.

Lobrano, Alexander, "British Designers Salvage a 'Lost Season' at SEHM," in *Daily News Record,* 14 September 1987.

"London Now," in *Women's Wear Daily,* 12 October 1987.

"Model Interiors," in the *Sunday Express Magazine* (London), 25 October 1987.

"Shooting Stars," in *Women's Journal* (London), February 1988.

Hume, Marion, "The Italian Connection," in the *Sunday Times* (London), 14 May 1989.

Rosenblum, Anne, "Kashiyama Will Distribute Todd Oldham Women's Line," in *Women's Wear Daily,* 17 May 1989.

Fallon, James, "Galliano to Show Fall-Winter Line in Paris, March 14," in *Women's Wear Daily,* 2 February 1990.

Collen, Matthew, "Nick Coleman," in *i-D* (London), April 1990.

Carter, Charles, and Charlotte Du Cann, "Europe 1990: Designers to Watch," in *Vogue,* August 1990.

Yusuf, Nilgin, "London Sport Deluxe," in *Elle* (New York), August 1990.

"London Shows: Wacky is Out and Safe is In," in *Women's Wear Daily,* 15 October 1990.

Rodgers, Toni, "Double Vision," in *Elle* (London), March 1991.

Leitch, Brian D., "Tales of London," in *Women's Wear Daily,* 8 March 1993.

d'Aulnay, Sophie, "The Top of the Tops," in *DNR,* 24 September 1993.

Fallon, James, "Alternative-Fashion Devotees Turn to Neal Street," in *Footwear News,* 18 October 1993.

Feitelberg, Rosemary, "Body Control to Hit U.S.," in *Women's Wear Daily,* 5 August 1999.

"India: British Airways Introduces Onboard Exercises," in *Hindu,* 15 June 2001.

* * *

Nick Coleman's work has reflected the shift in mood that has taken fashion from the sleek tailoring and obvious luxury of the mid- to late 1980s into the more casual-based sports influence of the early 1990s.

Among the rash of London-based talent heralding the designer boom, which included the likes of 31 Fevrier, Julien Anryon, Corinne Cobson, Claire Deve, Irie, Pascale Risbourg, and Zucca, Coleman produced consistently strong silhouettes for women. His earlier work had been based mainly on careful tailoring, dresses fitted to the body and then flared into little, full skirts, concentrating on charcoal and navy blue pinstripes for daywear and branching into warmer shades for sharply balanced modern evening designs.

In 1986 Coleman showed his Legion of the Lost collection at the First British Designer Menswear Trade Exhibition, a military and safari styled collection. A prime piece in this collection was described by Richard Buckley in the *Daily News Record* (4 September 1986) as "a long, body-conscious jacket featur[ing] a belted waist, military-style pockets, pockets at the chest for bullet storage and a double layered back with Y-cutout construction." In 1988, he showed a popular claret palazzo trouser all-in-one, which hugged the torso in gauzy georgette, with tucked silk forming a bustier section linked to the trousers by a strip of buttons that reached from the collar.

In the late 1980s Coleman clothes encapsulated the confidence and streamlined modernity that dominated fashion. His menswear was equally well adapted to the smart, tailored look that was aspired to, with, in 1986, black double-breasted trench coats and classic turn-up trousers. By the dawning of the 1990s, however, Coleman was immersed in the burgeoning rave scene with its more relaxed attitude to clothing. After taking a break from fashion to run his own nightclubs, his designs began to reflect the tribalism and body-conscious sports influence of the scene. The freer feel of young London clubbers led to the development of a more recognizable signature to his work.

The variations on the classic biker jackets he had designed in 1989, with fringing for sleeves and chain-trimmed bra tops, were obviously influenced by the music scene. Later versions were even teamed with punk-inspired tartans. These, however, were quickly surpassed by sexy, sporty, shaped separates that gave ease of movement and a recognizable image for the dance floor. Coleman's strong advertising campaigns followed this mood, with models daubed with body paint to represent the shield emblem adorning much of his diffusion range.

Coleman dressed ardent clubbers in the heavily padded puffa jackets that were obligatory at raves during the first two years of the decade, worn with his bodies, stretch skirts, and trousers with striped trim that referred to school sportswear in its detailing. Although it is this club wear that is most instantly recognizable, he continues to produce well-cut suiting (including, in the 1990s, velvet-collared slim-fitting Teddy Boy styles) for his main line, mixing classic shapes with more experimental elements. His involvement in the 5th Circle menswear collective underlines this dedication to innovative designs and the attention to detail echoed in his consistently strong leather and denim lines.

By 1989 Coleman had joined designers like Dolce & Gabbana, Bent Boys, Luciano Soprani, and Todd Oldham in being distributed by Onward Kashiyama. In 1997 he and his wife, Lucy, cofounded Body Control Pilates, a company manufacturing understated athletic-inspired apparel, featuring activewear as well as bags, blankets, slippers, robes, cosmetic bags, and pillows. The company brought in approximately $350,000 in its first few years.

Coleman's work has continued to fall under the influence of the London club scene, but his ability to produce interesting tailored designs widens his appeal and prevents his clothes from being too narrowly pigeon-holed. His popularity in London is based on his skill in producing clothing imbued with zeitgeist as well as more classic garments that prolong the longevity of his appeal.

—Rebecca Arnold; updated by Daryl F. Mallett

COLE OF CALIFORNIA

American swimwear company

Founded: Formed by Fred Cole from family knitwear firm in Los Angeles, 1923. **Company History:** Began collaborating with Hollywood costume designer Margit Fellegi, 1936; signed Esther Williams to represent the company, 1950; began producing swimwear from Christian Dior, 1955; purchased by Kayser-Roth, early 1960s; sold to the Wickes Company; launched Anne Cole Collection, 1982; signed licensing agreement with Adrienne Vittadini, 1983–93; company purchased by Taren Holdings, 1989; Juice junior line debuted, 1990; acquired by Authentic Fitness Corp., combined with Catalina to form Catalina Cole, 1993; Anne Cole introduced the "tankini," 1997; ultimate parent, Warnaco, filed for bankruptcy protection, 2001. **Awards:** Los Angeles Chamber of Commerce Golden 44 award, 1979. **Company Address:** Authentic Fitness, 6040 Bandini Boulevard, Los Angeles, CA 90040, U.S.A.

Publications

On COLE of CALIFORNIA:

Books

Lencek, Lena, and Gideon Bosker, *Making Waves: Swimsuits and the Undressing of America,* San Francisco, 1989.

Martin, Richard, and Harold Koda, *Splash! A History of Swimwear,* New York, 1990.

Articles

Sajbel, Maureen O., "Sea Notes: Anne Cole Takes the Plunge," in *WWD,* 28 July 1982.

Magiera, Marcy, "Swimwear Makers Aim for 'Older' Women," in *Advertising Age,* 21 April 1986.

Flint, Jerry, "Cover-Up: Cole of California," in *Forbes,* 2 May 1988.

Drizen, Ruth, "High Spirits at Cole," in *Apparel Industry Magazine,* (Atlanta, Georgia), August 1990.

D'Innocenzio, Anne, "Swimwear Dives, Hopes to Surface," in *WWD,* 10 August 1995.

Belgum, Deborah, "Swimming in a New Wave: Anne Cole," in *Los Angeles Business Journal,* 12 June 2000.

Robinson, Roxanne, and Rosemary Feitelberg, "Class of 75," in *WWD,* 10 August 2000.

* * *

The high-water mark of swimwear exposure was 1964: Rudi Gernreich showed a topless bathing suit that achieved awestruck attention, but sold very few copies. Then *Sports Illustrated,* the New York magazine, began its annual swimsuit edition. Cole of California, in the same year, produced the three-item "scandal suit" collection

Design by Cole of California, 1950. © Genevieve Naylor/CORBIS.

that likewise plunged to new exposure with an astonishing commercial success, typifying the long tradition of Cole's being the most provocative—yet commercial—swimwear manufacturer in America.

Ever since former silent film star Fred Cole had first hitched his company's wagon to the stars of Hollywood, Cole had been a trendsetter, P.T. Barnum style. Cole knew by unerring instinct, like his film producing *confrères,* how to be sensational and to sell to the American public without being overly salacious. As Lena Lencek and Gideon Bosker described in their book, *Making Waves: Swimsuits and the Undressing of America,* "Cut extremely conservatively by mid-1960s standards, the Scandal suits put everything under wraps, at least theoretically. In practice, however, the vast expanses of see-through netting turned their wearers into sizzling sex goddesses."

If black mesh only made a plunging décolletage or midriff seem more radical and seductive in the tantalizing peekaboo of exposure or coverage, Cole encouraged the sensation in dramatic public events and publicity. Hence this American company was in the vanguard of what was already being described as a 1960s sexual revolution and

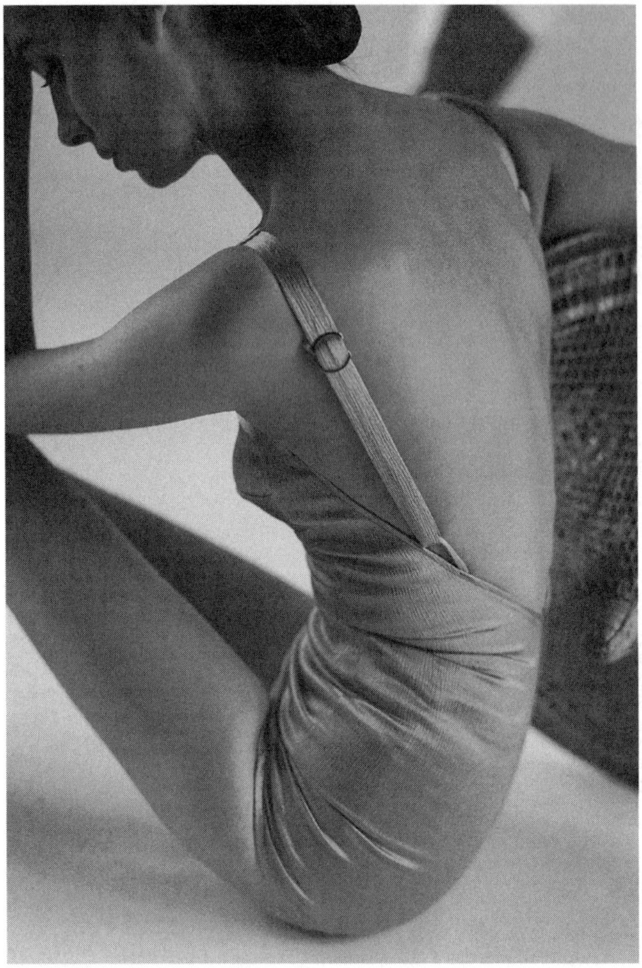

Cole of California, 1950: nylon satin swimsuit. © Genevieve Naylor/CORBIS.

seemed ready to bring all of its license to the beach. Fred Cole knew that going to the beach or pool was recreation, but that it was also a spectator sport.

Cole had three brilliant ideas, put into action step by step: first, he transformed the family's prosaic knit underwear firm into a swimsuit business; second, he seized upon California and Hollywood to bring glamor to the swimwear industry and specifically to the imagery of Cole of California; and third, he knew sex appeal would be determined in the middle and late years of the 20th century by public relations and popular opinion. The health and dress-reform issues of knitwear paled beside the excitement Cole brought to the swimwear industry. His conjunction to Hollywood, working with the ingenious designer Margit Fellegi, who was to the Hollywood swimsuit what Edith Head was to every other Hollywood film garment. It was a cunningly American ideal—sexy without being smarmy, a pin-up excused by the sun-drenched healthy lifestyle of California and linked to another persuasive product, the movies.

In the trio of great American swimwear manufacturers, Cole went to Hollywood while Jantzen emphasized family fun and healthy sport, and Catalina became associated with beauty pageants. More than any other American company, Cole connected fashion and swimwear. Fred Cole reshaped the wool knit swimsuit to define the bust and waist and introduced a sunny California palette of colors. With the popularity of tans in the 1930s, Cole progressively sheared away the bulk of the traditional swimsuit to provide more and more exposure.

Fellegi, the Hollywood costumer, began working with Cole in 1936 and, immediately utilizing rubberized and stretch possibilities of new fibers that could surpass the old wool knits, brought a body-clinging science to the sex appeal that Cole desired. When rubber was restricted in World War II, Cole created the "swoon suit," a two-piece suit that laced up the sides of the trunk and tied for the bra, still an enduring pin-up. After the war, Cole and Fellegi pursued fashion and Hollywood glamor with New Look-inspired dressmaker swimsuits and profligate details of sequins, gold-lamé jersey, and water-resistant velvets.

In 1950 Cole signed film/swimming star Esther Williams to a merchandising-design contract that created and promoted the most popular and glamorous swimwear of its time. In 1955, with the phenomenal success of Esther Williams secured in her film aquacades and romances, Cole entered into agreement to produce swimwear for Christian Dior, thus bringing the most famous fashion name of the moment to swimwear design. Throughout the 1960s and 1970s Cole produced a variety of lines addressed to the increasingly segmented (principally by age and body type) swimwear market. In the early 1980s, Anne Cole, daughter of founder Fred, began designing her own line of swimsuits.

The Anne Cole Collection sustained the designer swimwear ideal; the swimsuits were beautiful, feminine, and quietly sensual. Anne Cole's sensibility was traditional elegance, and her swimsuits often recalled the 1930s beach scene as well the most elegant sportswear of Patou. Yet while Cole of California's swimwear lines thrived, the company itself endured a succession of corporate parents. Kayser-Roth was bought by Gulf & Western, then sold to the Wickes group of companies, which in turn sold the firm to Taren Holdings, Inc. In 1993, Cole of California, the Anne Cole Collection, and fellow swimwear producer Catalina were all rescued from bankruptcy and acquired by Authentic Fitness Corporation, a subsidiary of Warnaco.

The swimwear division of Authentic Fitness proved a snug fit for Cole of California, which was paired with Catalina to create the Catalina Cole unit. In addition to Catalina Cole and Anne Cole, Speedo and Oscar de la Renta made up the Authentic Fitness swimwear division. While many swimwear producers had poor results in 1995, Catalina Cole and Anne Cole both experienced record growth and profits. Two years later, Anne Cole introduced the "tankini," an instant hit and the must-have swimsuit of the season and beyond.

In the 21st century, almost 70 years after its formation, the Cole name has come to represent both Catalina Cole and Anne Cole. While each prospered under the ownership of Authentic Fitness, their future was once again in peril when ultimate parent Warnaco Group filed for bankruptcy protection in 2001. The quest, however, of Cole swimwear will not change—these suits were never merely for the water, but to not only be on the crest of the wave but to define and enhance bathing beauty.

—Richard Martin; updated by Nelly Rhodes

COLONNA di CESARO, Simonetta

See SIMONETTA

COMME DES GARÇONS

See KAWAKUBO, Rei

CONNOLLY, Sybil

Irish designer

Born: Sybil Veronica Connolly in Swansea, Ireland, 21 January 1921. **Education:** Sisters of Mercy Convent. **Career:** Apprentice dress designer, Bradley's, London, 1938–40; apprentice to Jack Clarke at Richard Alan, 1940–43; director, Richard Alan, 1943–57; Designer, Sybil Connolly, Inc., 1957–98; consultant and designer for Tiffany's, New York, 1984–98; author and editor, 1986–98. **Awards:** Britain's Woman of the Year, 1958. **Died:** 6 May 1998, in Dublin, Ireland.

Publications

By CONNOLLY:

Books

Editor, *In An Irish Garden* with Helen Dillon, New York, 1986.
Editor, *In An Irish House,* New York, 1988.
Irish Hands: The Tradition of Beautiful Crafts, New York, 1994.

Lady Melissa and Lady Caroline Wyndham-Quinn modeling Sybil Connolly-designed evening gowns, 1954. © Norman Parkinson Limited/Fiona Cowan/CORBIS.

On CONNOLLY:

Books

Stegemeyer, Anne, *Who's Who in Fashion, Second Edition,* New York, 1980.
———, *Who's Who in Fashion, Third Edition,* New York, 1996.

Articles

Brenner, Douglas, "Eire Apparent," in *House & Garden,* September 1989.
Collins, Amy Fine, "Tribute to the Fashion Style of Jacqueline Kennedy Onassis," in *Harper's Bazaar,* 1 August 1994.
Greiner, Virginia, "Improving Old Skills and Finding New Ones," in the *Washington Times,* 19 March 1995.
Bryant, Kathy, "A Pattern of Success," in the *Los Angeles Times,* 15 June 1996.
"Sybil Connolly," in the *Daily Telegraph,* 9 May 1998.
"Sybil Connolly," in the *Economist,* 16 May 1998.
Smith, Liz, "Bring Back Madeline," in *Newsday,* 19 May 1998.
"Obituary: Sybil Connolly," in the *Independent,* 26 May 1998.

*

There comes a moment in everyone's life as a designer when you have to decide whether you want to create the beautiful or the merely fashionable. Sadly, there can be a conflict between the two.

—Sybil Connolly

* * *

In the course of her career, Sybil Connolly gave Irish fashion a name and designed gowns for American lights such as Merle Oberon, Elizabeth Taylor, Fred Astaire, and Jacqueline Kennedy while she was First Lady, as well as for many of Britain's peers. Connolly began her fashion apprenticeship while in her teens, going to work for a London dressmaker to study dress design. Her most notable experience during her two-year tenure there was holding pins for Queen Mary's fittings at Buckingham Palace and noting the immense care being taken to design dresses that softened and complemented the dowager Queen's advanced age. Her apprenticeship at Bradley's was cut short by the outbreak of war, and she returned to Ireland. In 1940, she continued her apprenticeship at Richard Alan, which was at the time Dublin's premiere fashion house. At the age of 22, Connolly became director at Richard Alan and proceeded to build the store's couture department. In 1950 she designed a small collection that sold quite well, and her career as a designer began.

One of Connolly's early patrons was Lady Dunsany, and her first major show took place at Dunsany Castle in 1953. There, her designs came to the notice of members of the American fashion press, and the same year she took a collection to the United States. Her singular designs and handsome Irish fabrics were well received. Over the next few years, she was profiled in *Time* magazine, and her designs appeared in *Vogue* and *Harper's Bazaar* and on the cover of *Life.* She left Richard Alan and set up Sybil Connolly, Inc. in 1957 at her Merrion Square house in Dublin, and her clothes were soon carried at specialty boutiques across the United States.

Connolly's design philosophy was in keeping with that of Hubert de Givenchy, whose work was a source of inspiration for her.

Elegance without sacrificing comfort, the finest craftsmanship, and attention to detail were the hallmarks of her work. She felt that a dress should show a woman's curves, saying, "I must see movement in a dress. A woman's body is inside. It breathes. It moves." Her other major sources of inspiration were nature and the traditional fabrics and everyday clothing of the Irish. Working in Donegal tweeds, Eliot's poplin, Carrickmacross lace, *bainin* (a thin, handwoven wool) and Irish linen, she created collections based on the simple slim lines of riding habits, and utilized the hooded cloaks, scarlet flannel petticoats, crocheted blouses, and black Connemars shawls of Irish traditional dress. She also designed evening dresses with ruffled tops, a coming-out gown made entirely of men's linen handkerchiefs, and handkerchief linen nightgowns embroidered with flowers and hand-sewn with tiny tucks, which were a favorite of Jacqueline Kennedy's.

Throughout her career, Connolly sought out and utilized the traditional crafts and artistry of her native land: Donegal embroidery, handwoven lace, and iridescent Donegal tweeds. She commissioned the nuns of Clones Convent to make lace for her and found inspiration in the simple lines of a Carmelite nun's habit. Connolly brought echoes of Irish daily life into vogue among the best dressed of the rich and famous. Indeed, Connolly was herself often included on American best-dressed lists.

The invention of a unique linen fabric is considered one of Connolly's greatest achievements. Using nine yards of handkerchief linen backed by taffeta to make one yard of hand-pleated dress material, she created an uncreasable, uncrushable linen, which she then custom-dyed in rich colors and fitted into lovely ball gowns. The gowns were so resistant to the ravishments of time that they were an investment lasting generations, handed down from mother to daughter to granddaughter. Jacqueline Kennedy wore a skirt of Connolly's pleated linen when she was painted by Aaron Shickler for a portrait that hangs in the White House.

Throughout the 1950s and early 1960s, Connolly enjoyed popularity on both sides of the Atlantic. In the 1970s she continued to bring small collections to New York. She would show them at the Fifth Avenue apartment of a friend, gather orders for custom designs, and take them back to be made up in her Dublin workshops. But the trends of fashion in those years were not to her taste, and she had no interest in following them. She was known to comment that she couldn't understand why the young people of the time were so set on making themselves look "awful." The skirts were too short, the lines were not right, and trousers were "only for riding."

Like her great inspiration Givenchy, Connolly's sense of style found expression in a full range of mediums beyond couture. She was a designer of lifestyle, not just clothing. She wrote books on garden design and interior decor—specifically Irish gardens and Irish homes—and restored a 1789 cottage in Cahair, County Tipperary. Connolly also designed crystal, china, and pottery for Tiffany & Company (New York), as well as wall coverings, clocks, and fabrics.

—Jessica Reisman

CONRAN, Jasper

British designer

Born: London, 12 December 1959. **Education:** Attended Bryanston School, Dorset; studied at Parsons School of Design, New York,

Jasper Conran, fall 2001 collection: sequined evening dress. © AP/ Wide World Photos.

1975–77. **Family:** Married Jeanne Spaziani. **Career:** Worked for Fiorucci, New York, 1977, then for ICI and Courtaulds, London; design consultant, Wallis Fashion Group, 1977; showed first womenswear collection, 1978; opened boutique, Beauchamp Place, London, 1986; showed menswear from 1988; has also designed for the theatre. **Awards:** Fil D'Or International Linen award, 1982, 1983; British Fashion Council Designer of the Year award, 1986; Fashion Group of America award, New York, 1987; Laurence Olivier award for Costume Designer of the Year, 1991. **Address:** 2 Berners Street, London W1P 4BA, England.

Publications

On CONRAN:

Books

Coleridge, Nicholas, *The Fashion Conspiracy,* London, 1988.
Stegemeyer, Anne, *Who's Who in Fashion, Third Edition,* New York, 1996.

Jasper Conran, fall 2001 collection. © AP/Wide World Photos.

Articles

"Lookout: A Guide to the Up and Coming," in *People,* 8 March 1982.
Search, Gay, "The Conran Clan: Jasper," in *Women's Journal* (London), April 1984.
Kendall, Ena, "Jasper Conran: A Room of My Own," in *The Observer* (London), 22 September 1985.
McDowell, Colin, "Jasper Conran," in *The Guardian* (London), 31 October 1985.
Powell, Fiona Russell, "Jasper Conran," in *Fashion '86* (London), 1985.
Soames, Emma, "British Style: The Impact of the Designer Star," in *Vogue* (London), February 1987.
Barron, Pattie, "24 Carat Jasper: Fashion's Brilliant Brat," in *Cosmopolitan* (London), April 1987.
Young, Russell, "Jasper," in *Blitz* (London), April 1987.
Nickson, Liz, "The Conrans: A Genuine Dynasty," in *Time,* 20 July 1987.
Allott, Serena, "Jasper Conran in Search of Something Perfectly Simple," in the *Sunday Telegraph Magazine* (London), 20 September 1987.
Menkes, Suzy, "Jasper and John," in *The Independent* (London), 9 October 1987.
Sinclair, Paul, and Lesley Jane Nonkin, "Designer, Client: The Modern Equation," in *Vogue* (New York), November 1987.
Nadelson, Regina, "Scion of the Times," in *Metropolitan Home* (New York), August 1988.
"Bon Magique," in *Elle* (London), November 1988.
"Jasper Conran Joins Bidermann Stable," in *DNR,* 10 August 1990.
"Jasper Conran," in *Fashion Weekly* (London), 16 August 1990.
Jeal, Nicola, "Conran's Comeback," in *The Observer Magazine* (London), 18 November 1990.
"Conran: the Gamut," from London Fashion Week, at the Vogue website (www.vogue.co.uk), 2001.

* * *

Dubbed the "Calvin Klein of London," Jasper Conran creates menswear and womenswear collections that epitomize urbane, classic lines. As the British Fashion Council's Fashion Designer of the Year in 1986, Conran has balanced British imagination with international chic. His designs are inspired by early garments of Coco Chanel and the American look of Claire McCardell's monastic and "popover" dresses but the outcome reflecting modern sophistication, not retro style. He is known for updated, yet elegant, versions of traditional British tweed suits.

Conran attended Parsons School of Design in New York, and his first collection was produced for Henri Bendel in the United States. He returned the the UK and worked briefly for the British company, Wallis, as design consultant, producing its Special Label. He introduced his first independent womenswear collection in 1978 showing black cashmere trousers, and coats and jackets lined with cream satin. This established his hallmark use of expensive fabrics such as silk, cashmere, taffeta, and lines with classic cuts. *Vogue* writer Emma Soames observed that British fashion editors discovered Conran early, as the refined simplicity of his work contrasted sharply with other British designers of the time (for example Vivienne Westwood, Katherine Hamnett, and Rifat Ozbek). Main pieces from his collections changed very little from season to season, allowing many of his garments to be regarded as long-term wardrobe investments. For two years running, 1982 and 1983, Conran won the Fil D'Or International Linen award.

Color has been an important factor in the overall look of Conran's collections: i.e., the brightly colored cashmere jackets in cerise, orange, chrome yellow, and mint green, produced for the 1992 collection, and earlier eveningwear in fuchsia, cobalt, and kelly green organza highlighting the clean lines of each garment. Silk separates have since been designed in ice blue, cocoa, bright red, and sorbet tints. As his designs moved into the new millennium, Conran, who continues to be considered one of the most successful designers in the UK, toned down his color pallette. His early 2001 womenswear collection featured baby blues, dusky pinks, white, beige, and black. Skinny tie-belts, diamond prints, and tube tops were reinvented, trousers were low-waisted, and A-line leather skirts and satin frocks were suggested for evening wear. His menswear collection was an updated version of the classic English gentleman look featuring double-breasted jackets, sleeveless pleated shirts, and pinstripes.

While in many collections Conran has produced undemanding and straightforward designs, he occasionally incorporated elements characteristic of what might be expected of British fashion fantasy—fur-trimmed suits and wedding dresses, trumpet-hem jersey skirts, bold plaid toppers over leather jacketed pantsuits, and brightly coloured chevron-patterned sweaters with white flannel pleated skirts. The 1950s nostalgia of Grace Kelly and *Breakfast at Tiffany's* inspired Conran to design enormous bell-shaped coats, boxy cropped jackets, and little flirtatious minis with stiff, standaway backs in white cotton poplin for his 1986 collection. The English seaside set the background for a 1920s classic approach with oversized three-quarter-length wool tailored jackets and palazzo pants in the early 1990s.

In 1988 Conran began his menswear line, maintaining the same classic designs as his women's collections. A black-and-white ticking stripe cotton jacket with matching high-buttoned waistcoat and tapered trousers depicted a quintessentially English style, while the importance of color was maintained in Conran's intense red suede blazer and waistcoat. Also in the late 1980s, Conran designed a less expensive, Jasper "J" Conran collection for the Debenhams department store and produced a collection of bridal wear for Caroline Castigliano.

Extending himself beyond the typical fashion scene, Conran organized the "Fashion Aid" charity evening for African famine relief in 1985 and ventured into costume design for Jean Anouith's ballet, *The Rehearsal* and subsequently to the theatre for a London revival of *My Fair Lady,* and David Brintley's *Edward II,* performed by the Birmingham Royal Ballet in 1997. His theatrical flair for color and defined style readily translated to the stage. In 1991 Conran received the Laurence Olivier award for Costume Designer of the Year. Conran also became very outspoken about governmental attempts to regulate the fashion industry; he went public with his personal battle with anorexia in an attempt to shed some light on the nature of this condition. He believes it is an oversimplification to assume that eating disorders are caused by subliminal messages from the fashion industry.

In 1990 Conran signed a ten-year licensing agreement with the Marchpole Group Plc, the UK subsidiary of Bidermanns S.A., to produce and market his men's clothing lines. Michael Reiney, managing director of Marchpole, described Conran (Bidermann's first British designer) as a "very talented guy who has not had the opportunity to expand himself to his fullest extent. We believe he has great potential." This arrangement would allow for Conran's menswear designs to penetrate the market in Continental Europe and the U.S., and to expand his men's collection to include coats and accessories. Conran would also be able to produce a more affordable line of menswear as well.

Conran's contribution to the British fashion scene is well recognized. He has a strong commercial sense positioning him solidly within the international arena, with clients who included Diana, the late Princess of Wales. The timeless quality of his classic designs has ensured him a place alongside Calvin Klein, Karl Lagerfeld, and Perry Ellis.

—Teal Triggs; updated by Christine Miner Minderovic

CORD, Barry Kieselstein

See KIESELSTEIN-CORD, Barry

CORNELIANI SPA

Italian menswear firm

Founded: in Mantova, Italy, 1930s. **Company History:** Modernized, 1958, by Carlalberto (born 1931) and Claudio Corneliani (born 1921), Sergio Corneliani (born 1959) became chief designer; lines include Via Ardigo, Styled by Corneliani, Corneliani, Corneliani Trend, and Corneliani Sportswear; trademarks include Nino Danieli, Browngreen, and Full Time; producers and manufacturers, beginning in 1984, for Daniel Hechter, Erreuno, Karl Lagerfeld, Krizia Uomo, Trussardi, and Renoma; costume designers for various films, including *Little Women*; Carlalberto Corneliani, president of Italy's fashion committee Comitato Moda, 1976 and president of Federtessile, Italian textile association, 1991; opened Milan flagship store, 1997; acquired Polo Ralph Lauren license for North America, 1998; expanded Polo distribution into Europe, 2000; signed license with Chinese company for manufacture and distribution of Corneliani-branded products in Asia, 2000; launched casual Trend line into U.S. market, 2001. **Awards:** Pitti Immagine prize, 1989; Carlalberto Corneliani named Cavaliere del Lavoro, 1991. **Company Address:** Via M. Panizza 5, 46100 Mantova, Italy.

Publications

On CORNELIANI:

Books

Alfonsi, M., *Figli d'Arte? No Grazie,* Trento, 1989.

Articles

Lobrano, Alexander, "Still Growing Corneliani," in *DNR: The Magazine* (New York), 4 January 1988.

"Dietro la Griffe," in *Vogue* (Milan), February 1991.

"I Corneliani Dell'Abital Agli States," in *L'Arena* (Verona), 24 February 1991.

"Vestiremo All'Americana," in *Il Mondo* (Milan), 29 April 1991.

"Corneliani," in *La Repubblica* (Rome), 12 June 1991.

"Corneliani—Hartmarx il Patto Atlantico," in *Harper's Bazaar* (Milan), 8 July 1991.

Gabbianio, M., "La Quinta di Corneliani," in *La Repubblica,* 6 March 1992.
"I Segreti di Corneliani," in *L'Arena* (Verona), 13 March 1992.
Perego, G., "Corneliani, 172 Miliardi di Vestiti," in *Italia Oggi* (Milan), 3 April 1992.
Forden, Sarah Gay, "The Cornelianis of Mantova: A Family, a Company, a Label," in *DNR,* 4 January 1993.
Bagnoli, D., "Fratelli Corneliani, Nuova Organizzazione in Germania," in *Textil-Wirtschaft,* 3 March 1994.
Conti, Samantha, "Corneliani Opens First Boutique in Milan," in *DNR,* 21 April 1997.
Gellers, Stan, "Viva Italia! Corneliani Gets Polo Blue Label Clothing License," in *DNR,* 4 May 1998.
———, "Corneliani Set to Launch Its Polo Ralph Lauren Clothing," in *DNR,* 25 November 1998.
Boye, Brian, "Technical Fabrics are the Talk of Cologne…," in *DNR,* 2 August 1999.
Gellers, Stan, and Samantha Conti, "Corneliani: A Family Affair," in *DNR,* 12 June 2000.
Deeny, Godfrey, "Milan: Seriously Elegant Corneliani," available online at Fashion Wire Daily, www.fashionavenue.com, 26 June 2001.

*

Corneliani: a designer label, a company, a family. An important blend which embodies the secret of the Corneliani success. The Corneliani company is run by the Corneliani family: quite different from the traditional stylist, and probably far superior, on today's scene.

Now that stylists work on an industrial level and the consumer is no longer prepared to accept something just because it carries a designer label, the winning card appears to be the entrepreneur stylist, capable of guaranteeing taste and creativity but first and foremost the quality of the product. This trend seems custom made for the Cornelianis, since this has always been our philosophy, the thinking that has made our company what it is today. Corporation styling, indicated by everyone as the true future of Italian fashion, has been practiced successfully for years at Corneliani by the Cornelianis.

Corneliani style interprets the Italian culture of fine clothing. Corneliani quality is the technological version of the great Italian tailoring tradition.

—Corneliani

* * *

Corneliani is a high-quality menswear design company based in Mantova, Italy. Seeking out the perfect balance between fashion content and classic style, the family company, now in its third generation, had its start in the tailoring business in the 1930s. By the late 1950s, the group had established itself as producers of fine men's clothing, a tradition it upholds today.

Corneliani constitutes a company, a family, and a designer label, a blend that seals their success. The group does not promote itself as an individual designer-led label but as "corporate styling." Opposed to the idea that the consumer only purchases clothes because they carry a designer label, Corneliani believes a group-led label guarantees not only creativity, taste, and style but also quality in the cut and manufacture of the product.

Elegance defines the look; styles tend to denote the relaxed, classic taste of Hollywood stars like Cary Grant or George Sanders. The customer is style-conscious, not necessarily fashion-conscious, and his clothes need to be dependable, functional, and highly durable yet also have a feeling of comfort and quality. Corneliani is also aware its customer can have moments of extravagance: a man can suddenly be taken with a striking detail, like an unusual color mix or an interesting fabric.

Corneliani develops most of its own fabrics from the initial selection of fibers, design, and color to the final approval of ideas from among hundreds of samples. Natural fibers predominate: linens, cottons, pure woolen tweeds and herringbones, wool crêpes, and wool venetians. Colors are simply and classically combined. Super-fine, madras checked jackets in navy, beige, and cream are teamed with a sky blue checked shirt, navy trousers, and distinctive navy, beige, and cream striped tie. Beige on beige is a recurrent effect—a crêpe beige suit with matching waistcoat is teamed with a brown checked tie and checked shirt. It's a tweedy English elegance, combined with slick Italian styling.

The company produces four main seasonal collections, all of which adhere to the style principle of relaxed classicism. The flagship collection is named Corneliani. Elegant and restrained, it is defined by the company as the point at which fashion and style meet. Corneliani Trend is a more fashion-oriented collection, designed for a customer who wants to follow fashion but retain a sense of good taste and intelligence. The Corneliani Sportswear collection is refined sportswear combining both comfort and function. Via Ardigo, Styled by Corneliani is a more upbeat, fashion-conscious sportswear line, easy to wear but adhering to the company's trademark respect for quality and elegance.

Corneliani produces a wide range of men's apparel, from jackets and trousers to car coats and overcoats. They rarely work to a design theme or make fashion trend statements; instead they produce an array of seasonal coordinates, within their four main seasonal collections, from which the customer can choose to put together his own look according to his own personal taste. The company's one aim and philosophy is to meet the clothing needs of contemporary, professional men who lead high-gear lives demanding a wardrobe to allow them comfort and freedom.

During the late 1990s and early 2000s, Corneliani focused on increasing its presence in territories outside Europe, particularly in the United States. It also has strived to broaden its customer base by adding more casual apparel to its traditional sartorial offerings. Two developments led Corneliani to launch its younger, more affordable Trend line and to move into sportswear. First, the rise of casual Fridays in both Europe and North America meant increased demand for casual and sporty clothing, an area where Corneliani had historically not been active. Second, a growing number of younger men—a market not actively targeted in the past by the company, whose primary customer was 45 to 60 years old in the U.S. and 10 years younger in Europe—desired fashionable suits priced below the top end of the market. Although Corneliani had been able, in the mid- to late 1990s, to expand in the U.S. by taking advantage of the popularity of Italian-made suits there, it recognized the need to expand further by targeting a wider range of customers.

The Trend brand, which was a success in Europe before being launched in the U.S. in 2001, consists of suits, sport coats, dress and sports shirts, neckwear, casual slacks, active sportswear, and outerwear. Executives reported to the *Daily News Record* (12 June 2000) that the line's canvas construction and technologically enhanced performance fabrics were expected to translate well into the U.S. market, whereas the lighter, sportier designs were a good fit with casual trends around the world.

As of 2000, *Daily News Record* reported the company sold its wares to stores in 45 countries. Its business in the U.S. had grown to encompass more than 10 upscale retail customers, including Saks Fifth Avenue and Nordstrom. Corneliani's market share in Italy remained strong and its presence was on the rise in countries such as Belgium and the Netherlands. Corneliani was also making inroads into Asia, signing a license with a Chinese company in 2000 to market its branded clothing throughout the region.

In addition to allowing Corneliani to enhance its revenues, the launch of Trend, as well as sportswear and men's furnishings, enabled the company to market its products as a collection rather than simply as a line of tailored suits (which accounted for two-thirds of the company's worldwide business in 2000). With the collection, Corneliani has been able to focus on expanding its retail presence, opening a flagship in Milan in 1997 and planning additional outlets in Paris, London, and New York.

Although casual and sporty styles are driving much of the company's growth, Corneliani is not ignoring the tailored suits on which it built its reputation. It introduced a new suit model in the late 1990s, Spencer, which had a more modern silhouette than the company's other suits but retained Corneliani's traditional concern with performance and luxurious fabrics. In addition to expanding its own brand, Corneliani has been focused on its licensed Ralph Lauren label. Corneliani acquired the rights for the U.S. market in 1998, at a time when many U.S. designers were looking to Italy for their men's licensees, and expanded into Europe in 2000. Corneliani produces and distributes Polo Ralph Lauren's blue-label products.

Although the Polo and Corneliani lines have distinct sensibilities and styles, the acquisition of the Polo license helped the Corneliani brand boost its status in the U.S. quickly, after more than a dozen years in the market with a relatively low profile. The company took advantage of this awareness to launch a print advertising campaign in the U.S. featuring trendsetting celebrities from politics, business and entertainment, and has continued to solidify its recognition among American consumers and retailers.

—Kevin Almond; updated by Karen Raugust

CORREGGIARI, Giorgio

Italian designer

Born: Pieve di Cento, Bologna, Italy, 5 September 1943. **Education:** Studied political science, University of Bologna. **Career:** Apprenticed in textile companies in Lyon, France, 1967, and in England and Germany; freelance designer with own boutique, Pam Pam, in Riccione, Italy, 1968; opened second boutique with brother Lamberto in Milan, 1969; designer for Fancy, New Delhi, 1972–73; designed UFO jeans for Gruppo Zanella, Italy, from 1974; designer for Daniel Hechter, Paris, 1975; formed Giorgio Correggiari SrL, 1975; designed Cadette collection, 1977; launched Giorgio Correggiari womenswear line, 1977; also in 1970s designed menswear for Herno, leatherwear for IGI of Perugia, Reporter line of menswear in USA, Cleo and Pat knitwear, furs for Pellegrini (1970–73), Trifurs (1976), and Bencini (until 1985); consultant to International Wool Secretariat, adviser to Cantoni on printed velvets, 1979; adviser to International Cotton Institute, Brussels, Lana Gatto wool mill, and Tessitura e Filature di Tollegno, Italy; designer for Divi, 1986; produced line of leather coats for Robrik and young jackets and raincoats for Coral; designer for SAHZA House of Fashion, Valencia, Italy. **Exhibitions:** Museum of Modern Art, New York, 1976. **Address:** Via San Lorenzo 21 20020 Lazzate, MI, Italy.

Publications

On CORREGGIARI:

Books

McDowell, Colin, *McDowell's Directory of Twentieth Century Fashion,* London, 1984.

Italian Fashion, Milan, 1986.

Articles

Buckley, Richard, "Byblos Gets Kudos for Playful Men's," in *DNR,* 13 July 1984.

Profile in *Donna* (Milan), April 1986.

"City of the Arts and Science's Hemispheric, Last Night," available online at *Valencia World,* www.cacsa.com, February 2001.

*

Giorgio Correggiari can be regarded as an intellectual critic of top fashion designers. His philosophy is to offer customers a high degree of fashion at highly competitive prices without sacrificing quality. His design is simple, unsophisticated, but unquestionably fashionable and very avant-garde. He uses few accessories and avoids printed materials. He is not strong on color and prefers to bring out the color of the person.

—Giorgio Correggiari

* * *

Giorgio Correggiari is a spontaneous designer who loves his work. There is a constant feeling of improvisation about his designs, and he thrives on the unexpected and the irregular. This open-minded approach keeps him on his toes, ready to face the uncertainties of the fashion business, and maintains his interest, essential for a man who has declared he would stop designing the moment it ceased to amuse him.

Born into a wealthy textile family (his father owned a textile mill near Bologna, Italy), Correggiari went on to study political science at the University of Bologna. He was 20 years old when a fire completely destroyed the textile mill, decimating the family fortunes. Correggiari then took off to travel through Germany, England, and France. An eight-month stint in a Lyon mill revived his interest in textiles, and on returning to Italy he ventured into business on his own. He opened a boutique in Riccione, christened Pam Pam, which he decorated in papier maché. He filled it with his own avant-garde designs, called Follies, which were made by a group of local outworkers. This first shop was successful, but shortly after opening a second in Milan, the designer declared himself disillusioned with his profession and left to travel around India.

The lure of fashion proved irresistible, however, and Correggiari was soon back designing in Italy. A contract with the leather firm Zanella, in 1974, was an instant success. He created a collection of 12 styles in leather and introduced a new style called UFO jeans. The success was justified, as the company took 1.5 billion lire in sales in the first season alone. At the same time, Correggiari was also commissioned to work for Daniel Hechter in Paris, designing menswear, womenswear, and childrenswear lines.

In 1976 he formed his own company, Giorgio Correggiari, to produce his own ready-to-wear collections. His frenzied, restless approach to his work rapidly made the company a success. His designs reflected his insatiable curiosity and thorough research into detail and themes. He has been known to pound the streets of Milan on foot trying to find someone who can replicate an original Liberty buckle, or stay up all night in his kitchen dyeing accessories to exactly the right shade to complement a collection. He also enjoys pillaging junk shops and second-hand stores for original buttons or old velvet fabrics that can be reproduced or incorporated into his designs.

The 1980s brought technically innovative clothing from Correggiari, including sweaters made of a cellulose yarn paper developed in Japan. He also created garments that could be stuffed into a suitcase but come out still looking fresh. The designer has not lost any steam since then: his work for spring 2001 included flattering black pantsuits for women with a high, angled neckline and knee-length wraparound dresses with wide collars and ties at the waist, harkening back to popular 1970s looks.

If one word could be used to describe Giorgio Correggiari it should be "prolific." Establishing his own company did not contain him; he also designs a knitwear line called Cleo and Pat; a men's line, Reporter; a leather collection for leather goods company IGI in Perugia; and a collection of velvets that returns him to his textile roots for Cantoni. In addition, he has ventured into licensing, designing belts, scarves, handbags, ties, and raincoats under his own label. The Parisian branch of the International Wool Secretariat also commissioned his services as a design consultant. Small wonder, therefore, that Correggiari declares a day has to be frenzied for him to feel alive.

—Kevin Almond; updated by Carrie Snyder

COSTA, Victor

American designer

Born: 17 December 1935, Houston, Texas, **Education:** Studied fashion design at Pratt Institute, Brooklyn, New York, University of Houston, and École d'Chambre Syndicale de la Haute Couture, Paris, 1954–58. **Family:** Married Terry Costa, 1958; children: Kevin, Adrienne. **Career:** Bridal designer for Murray Hamberger, New York, 1959–61; bridal designer, Pandora, 1962–65; joined Suzy Perette, and became known for "line for line" copies of European couture, 1965–73; partner, Anne Murray Company, Dallas, 1973; established Victor Costa, Inc., Dallas, Texas, 1975–85; established Victor Costa Bridal, Dallas, 1989; licensing agreement with Dior for American market, 1990; Victor Costa Boutique line, 1992; Romantica line for J.C. Penney, 1994–95; designer, A.S. Design Group, 1995–97; designer, eveningwear division of Nahdree Group, 1998–99; designer, Couture Fashions, maker of Rose Taft Couture, from 1999. Lives in Sherman, Connecticut and New York City. **Awards:** May Company American Design award, 1967; Stix, Baer & Fuller Golden Fashion award, 1975; Wild Basin award from the state of Texas, 1979, 1982; American Printed Fabrics Council Tommy award, 1983, 1984, 1988, 1989; Dallas Fashion award, 1980, 1987, 1991; University of Houston distinguished alumni award, 1990; Fashion Group of San Antonio, Night of Stars award, 1991; Northwood University's Outstanding Business Leader, 1991.

Publications

On COSTA:

Books

Fairchild, John, *Chic Savages,* New York, 1989.

Milbank, Caroline Rennolds, *New York Fashion: The Evolution of American Style,* New York, 1989.

Articles

Primeau, M., "Victor Costa," in the *Dallas Morning News* (Texas), 4 September 1983.

McCue, J., "Costa Lends Voice, Designs," in the *Cleveland Plain Dealer* (Ohio), 10 September 1987.

Swartz, Mimi, "The Fantasy World of Victor Costa: Texas' Most Famous Dress Designer Had a Dream: He Would Copy His Way to the Top," in *Texas Monthly,* September 1987.

Foote, Jennifer, "King of the Copycats: Costa Cashes in on the Highest Form of Flattery," in *Newsweek,* 4 April 1988.

Johnson, B., and L. Powell, "Copycat King Victor Costa Cuts the High Costa Designer Duds," in *People,* 22 August 1988.

Cohen, R., "Hot Costa," in the *Baltimore Jewish Times* (Maryland), Fall 1989.

Saenz, Harris J., "Victor Goes Legit," in the *Dallas Morning News,* 23 May 1990.

Paul, M., "Victor Costa Threads History Through High Fashion," in the *Dallas Morning News,* 25 March 1990.

Bischoff, R., "Victor(ious) Costa Calls the Shots," in *Trends,* June 1990.

Charles, D., "Not Dior by Ferré, but Dior by Costa," in the *New York Times,* 12 June 1990.

Haber, H., "Victor Costa on Life with Dior," in *Women's Wear Daily: Best of Group III* (New York), August 1990.

Williamson, Rusty, "Costa Files Chapter 7: Copycat Champ Shutters Operations," in *Women's Wear Daily,* 8 May 1995.

Wilson, Eric, "Costa Closes Nahdree Eveningwear," in *Women's Wear Daily,* 15 July 1999.

Haber, Holly, "Survivor: Victor Costa Knows How to Weather Hard Times," in *Women's Wear Daily,* 5 October 2000.

*

"The word 'fashion' would not exist if there were no copying," Costa said in the *Baltimore Jewish Times* in the fall of 1989. "The mirroring of the highest standard has been the basis of our society from Day One. There's a Rolls Royce, a Tiffany, a Beluga caviar—and there's a customer who knows and wants what is considered the ultimate. It takes talent to look at the world and see what is in the wind for his customer so that she always looks pretty and feels provoked to buy."

I am in the business of dressing ladies when they are seen socially in the latest fashions [which] basically has to do with social sameness. A lady goes to the same places and sees the same faces so she needs changes in social attire. Whether she is a career woman, housewife, or executive, each day she may go about her daily duties while her clothing is a secondary concern. When she is seen socially, she thinks about what she will wear and that is where I come into play. Social dressing has evolved into a "pay and play" occasion. Private parties have merged with charity events and new outfits are required frequently.

I have some customers that I have been dressing for 30 years and now I'm dressing their daughters and their granddaughters. So there are three generations of Victor Costa customers out there—it keeps you young because the younger girls, the granddaughters, have made a whole return to tradition. In the 1990s, with the AIDS epidemic, a return to traditional values has put a new emphasis on the wedding and all of its attendant parties, teas, fêtes, and receptions.

Special occasion dresses have always been the hallmark of my business. My quest for what is new sends me around the world. It is a sense of pride and fulfilment that some of the most noted and important women in the world are wearing my clothes. But also a young girl of 13 may get a Victor Costa dress which will have name recognition and make her feel special. Women adore how they look in their Victor Costa dresses.

—Victor Costa

* * *

Victor Costa has always loved fashion. Known as the "King of the Copycats," his status in the design world is unique. Costa designed dresses for childhood friends in Houston and was entranced by Hollywood film stars and their glamor. He went on to study at the Pratt Institute, New York, and later spent a year at the École of the Chambre Syndicale de la Haute Couture in Paris. This early contact with the Paris fashion world as it existed in the days when Christian Dior reigned and before changes were ushered in by the 1960s, had a great impact on Costa. His feeling for dressing women is based on a 1950s sense of style and formality.

New York's Seventh Avenue fashion business was built on copying Paris designs. Buyers and designers alike would flock to Paris to buy a model to "knock-off" or reinterpret. Hattie Carnegie built a respectable business doing this and nurtured several important designers, among them Norman Norell. The years after World War II saw an escalation of Paris couture show photographs being published in newspapers, but with a significant lag time. When Costa returned from Paris to New York in 1959 he was immediately charged with copying the latest Paris designs. Costa, who had a photographic memory and a quick hand at sketching, was able to translate what he saw on the Paris runways into successful designs for the Suzy Perette company during the 1960s.

Costa has parlayed his early training into a multimillion-dollar business. He travels to Europe frequently to attend the haute couture, prêt-à-porter fashion shows, and Premier Vision fabrics. His ability to comprehend couture and ready-to-wear fashions is a complex and masterful talent. He is not content with only a quick sketch or photography but often goes so far as to purchase the original couture design to study the construction and fabric. He chooses many fabrics in Europe and the U.S., but prefers to do construction where he can oversee it, as he did with his Dallas-based company.

Costa is openly doing what others often attempt to mask. In a rapidly changing fashion world where shopping has become a recreational hobby, Costa has at times delivered merchandise to five different markets a year. All of these dresses are not replicas but may represent a distillation of the most current fashion trends. Costa translates the essence of these trends in his work. Designers' reactions to his imitations of their work vary from being flattered to being irritated by his intrusion into their diminishing market. The voluminous designs of Arnold Scaasi are a Costa favorite, as are the silhouettes in Christian Lacroix's work. During the controversial tuxedo-dress dispute in 1994 between Ralph Lauren and Yves Saint Laurent, Costa asserted that he, in fact, had designed the dress in 1990 as a copy of a look by Parisian designer Bernard Perris. Fashion runways are not the only source for Costa. Recognizing the increasing influence of movie and television stars, Costa is quick to turn dresses seen at the Academy Awards into eveningwear available to women of all ages for a fraction of the originals' price.

Business problems, including a lawsuit by a former employee and embezzlement by an officer in the company, forced Costa to close his Dallas-based company in 1995. He has, however, continued to offer his designs with the backing of several companies. He updated his line of suits and dresses offered in 2000 by including bare dresses and glitzy evening pants, some with embellished fabrics. His attention to clothing construction now takes him to China to work with beaders and embroidery artisans. Costa welcomes the admiration of new, younger patrons but remains devoted to the mature women he has served for so many years. There are loyal customers to whom he personally caters with the loving attention of a couture designer. Costa, whose client list reads like a "Who's Who" of society and entertainment personalities, seeks to make all women feel beautiful.

—Myra Walker; updated by Janette Goff Dixon

COSTELLOE, Paul

Irish designer

Born: Dublin, Ireland, 27 June 1945. **Education:** Studied at the École d'Chambre Syndicale de la Haute Couture, Paris, 1968–69. **Family:** Married Anne Cooper, December 1981; children: Justin, Paul-Emmet, Gavin, Jessica, Robert, William, Nicholas. **Career:** Worked with Jacques Esterel, Paris, circa 1967, and for the Rinascente Group in Italy, 1970–73; moved to New York, worked on Seventh Avenue and for Anne Fogarty; moved back to Ireland, 1978; showed first collection, 1979; showed first men's collection 1981; introduced diffusion line, Dressage, 1989; launched Studio Line 1992; opened shop in Knightsbridge section of London, 2000; created uniforms for Sainsbury's supermarkets, 2000. **Exhibitions:** Featured in Victoria and Albert Museum's "50 Years of British Fashion" exhibit, 1997. **Address:** Main Road Moygashel, Dungannon, County Tyrone, BT71 7QR, Ireland; 7 Tunsgate Square, Guildford, Surrey, GU13QZ England.

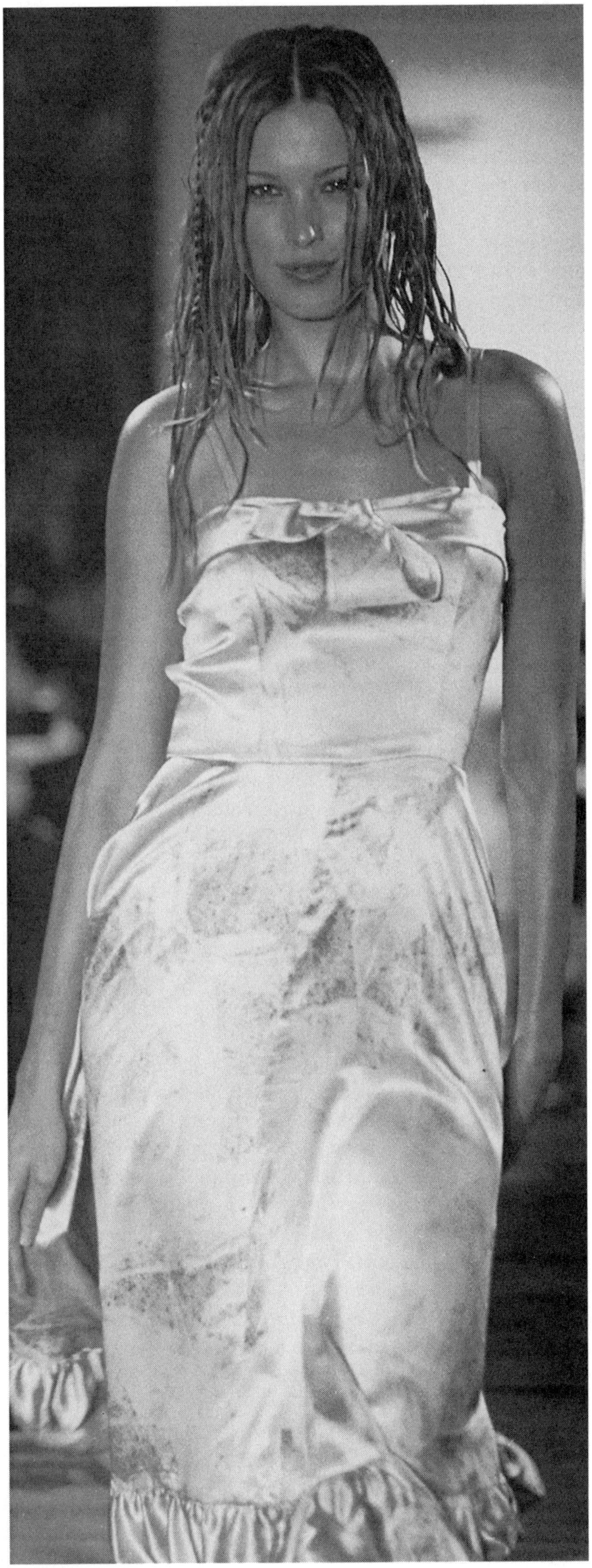

Paul Costelloe, spring/summer 2000 ready-to-wear collection. © AFP/ CORBIS.

Publications

On COSTELLOE:

Articles

"Paul Costelloe: Designer Profile," in *Vogue* (London), November 1981.

Buckley, Richard, "A Bit o'Costelloe," in *DNR: The Magazine* (New York), August 1984.

Eastoe, Jane, "The Tall Guy," in *Fashion Weekly* (London), 3 August 1989.

Jeal, Nicola, "A Profit in His Own Land," in *The Observer Magazine* (London), 17 September 1989.

Burgess, Robert, "Man of the Cloth," in *Country Living* (New York), May 1991.

McGowan, Cliodhna, "Oh Dear—Costelloe Gets Thumbs Down from Fashionable Galway Women," in the *Galway Advertiser,* 15 October 1997.

Brannigan, Tim, "Habit and Costelloe," in the *Irish Times,* 7 November 1998.

Fearon, Francesca, "London Doffs Hat at Irish Milliner's Show," in the *Irish Times,* 25 September 2000.

* * *

In its time, the fashion industry has been accused of being many things: flippant, bitchy, overly theatrical, or suffering from short-lived trends too wacky to sustain economic gain. Amid such hysteria and uncertainty, it is perhaps reassuring to find a designer like Paul Costelloe. Unpretentious and realistic, the Irish-born Costelloe is known as an ordinary man, level-headed, and calm. Attributing his drive, ambition, and success to his wife and family in Dublin, he has remained a popular figure in London fashion circles and is held in great affection by his employees.

Renowned for his use of natural fibers and fabrics, the best-quality wools and silks, and a particular bias toward traditional Irish linen, Costelloe clothes are one of the most subtle, understated, yet beautifully designed and manufactured collections available today. Acknowledging his love of Giorgio Armani's tailoring and the influence of Italian taste and style on the cut and flair of his collections, Costelloe always manages to fit an inspirational visit to Italy into his schedule before commencing the design of a new collection.

In general, three collections are produced each season under the Costelloe label, including the main line range (elegant, formal, and quietly sexy), the diffusion range called Dressage (country casual, timeless, and more suited to weekend dressing), and a third collection, the Studio Line, which was launched in 1992 and features what has been decribed as "investment tailoring," in neoclassic colors. The clothes are aimed at today's modern career woman who has a distinctive, quiet taste and understated sophistication.

Costelloe's spring-summer 1992 collection was an example of the designer at his peak. A series of sharp, sugary suits in pink, yellow, and green wool opened the collection. Teamed with short, flirty, polka dot skirts or blouses and oversize double crown hats, they were perfect for summer events like Ascot or garden parties. Ladylike check-cotton suits followed. Teamed with straw boaters and decorated with Costelloe's distinctive brass buttons, the look was demure

Paul Costelloe, spring 2000 collection: wrap top with a denim skirt. © AP/Wide World Photos.

and pristine, offset by soft kid gloves and gold jewelry. Like Armani, Costelloe loves beige, and this color, in various hues, features strongly in nearly all of his collections. For the Dressage spring-summer 1992 collection, long slim-line linen separates were shown teamed with an overscaled beige and cream lily print. The look was very Greta Scaachi in the film *White Mischief,* accessorized with round dark glasses and panama hats.

Before starting his own label, Costelloe had a varied and well-traveled fashion career. Born in Dublin, he was from an early age fascinated by women: the way they dressed, talked, and acted. This inspired him to pursue a career in fashion, and he enrolled at a local design college. He graduated in the early 1960s, and his sense of adventure directed him to Paris.

Armed with only a portfolio of design ideas, he followed the familiar route of knocking on fashion company doors, asking for work. The house of Jacques Esterel took him on, followed by work for an Italian manufacturer, then several positions in fashion houses on Seventh Avenue in New York. By this time, Costelloe had become experienced in fashion design, import, and export. Ever the opportunist entrepreneur, he realized he should use his talent and knowledge for his own benefit rather than someone else's, so he returned to Ireland to set up his own business.

He teamed up with Robert Eitel, a successful Irish businessman, to form the company Paul Costelloe and launched the first collection in 1979. The small fashion company has since grown into a multimillion-pound concern. Until recently, the collections were shown seasonally at the British Designer Show at Olympia in London, where Costelloe was always a popular figure. Yet following a trend established by several other London designers, he began showing at smaller, more distinctive venues.

Costelloe envisages the company expanding into other product areas and has ambitions to extend his love of cloth and color into the creation of a Paul Costelloe lifestyle. He wants to surround his customer with the subtle Costelloe touch, incorporating accessories and an interior collection for the home as well as a line of clothes for men and women. A keen member of the Chelsea Arts Club, where he stays in London, Costelloe retains his down-to-earth Irish charm and wit, as exemplified when he met Bruce Oldfield in Paris. Forgetting his name he quipped, good naturedly, "Ah, the King of Fashion."

Ireland's leading fashion designer, however, got himself into hot water in October 1997 for some comments in a British magazine suggesting Irish women were not fashion-forward. The comments were not taken lightly by female couture purchasers in Ireland, who were offended and said so in numerous follow-up articles in the Irish press. They went so far as to accuse his clothing of being well-tailored but uninspirational; to note that his apparel, made of natural fabrics such as linen, gets rumpled in the rainy Irish weather; and to call his women's suits drab and dowdy. Through it all, Costelloe maintained that his comments were misinterpreted.

The controversy did not impede Costelloe's success as a designer. He continued to find acclaim using natural materials such as lambswool, tweeds, and linens, and featuring low-key styling which melded both with his personality and with Irish tradition, as noted by Tim Brannigan in the *Irish News.* Brannigan explained that Costelloe considered clothing a frame and woman the picture within it; the frame should never take away from the picture. Although Costelloe sometimes introduces surprises into his collections, such as combining checks with floral prints in 1997, his designs remain elegant and unaffected by short-lived trends.

Costelloe was honored as one of the designers featured in the Victoria and Albert Museum's "50 Years of British Fashion" exhibit in 1997. In the mid- and late 1990s, he expanded outside of men's and women's apparel, designing cutlery for Newbridge, crystal for Cavan, earthenware for Wedgwood, and eyewear sold through the retailer Boots, all incorporating his well-known "fox" logo.

Costelloe's spring 2001 women's collection further solidified his long-established reputation for high-quality tailoring and classic designs. Following the theme of "A Parisian Afternoon," Costelloe drew on his experiences as a young designer in Paris to create a collection of European-styled, structured clothing featuring subdued colors and fur highlights, accessorized with scarves and hats.

Costelloe has long supported Irish charities, such as hosting an annual fashion show to support Northern Ireland Mother and Baby Appeal (NIMBA) in the late 1990s. He has heightened his profile within Europe by becoming a sponsor of a Formula One auto racing team. In addition, he designed 30 suites in the Star Court Hotel, the largest hotel convention center in Limerick, Ireland, and created uniforms of orange fleece, with baseball caps, for the floor staff of Sainsbury's supermarkets in Britain. In 2000, he opened a shop in the

Knightsbridge section of London and hoped to break into the U.S. market in the near future.

Costelloe's London show in September 2000 expanded upon the designer's interest in cultures around the world. It featured white and navy dresses and peasant blouses, accessorized with white socks, brown brogues, and scarves, all in an homage to the film *Pleasantville,* set in the middle America of the 1950s. Francesca Fearon of the *Irish Times,* in a review, termed the collection "optimistic." Costelloe's collection the following season, typically, was very tailored, emulating the style of the Parisian house of Chanel.

—Kevin Almond; updated by Karen Raugust

COURRÈGES, André

French designer

Born: Pau, Pyrenées Atlantiques, 9 March 1923. **Education:** Studied engineering at École des Pont et Chaussées; studied fashion in Pau and Paris. **Family:** Married Jacqueline (Coqueline) Barrière, 1967; children: Marie. **Career:** Cutter, Cristobal Balenciaga, Paris, 1945–61; independent fashion designer, Paris, 1960–61; founded Courrèges fashion house, boulevard Kléber, Paris, 1961–65; first haute couture collection, 1965; business sold to l'Oréal, 1965; resumed designing, 1967, with Prototype custom line, Couture Future high priced ready-to-wear line introduced 1969; designed own boutiques, from 1970; first fragrance line *Empreinte* introduced, 1971; men's ready-to-wear line and men's fragrance introduced, 1973; introduced accessories, leather goods, watches, belts, furniture, luggage, windsurfing equipment and more, from 1979; Hyperbole lower priced ready-to-wear line, 1980; company purchased by Itokin, 1983; fragrances bought by Swiss Burrus Group, 1992; produced collection with Jean-Charles de Castelbajac, 1994–95; bought back perfume business, 1997. **Awards:** Couture award, London, 1964. **Address:** 40 rue François Premier, 75008 Paris, France.

Publications

By COURRÈGES:

Books

La robe: essai psychanalytique sur le vêtement, with Eugénie Lemoine-Luccioni, Paris, 1983.

On COURRÈGES:

Books

Halliday, Leonard, *The Fashion Makers,* London, 1966.
Bender, Marylin, *The Beautiful People,* New York, 1967.
Lynam, Ruth, *Couture: An Illustrated History of the Great Paris Designers and Their Creations,* Garden City, New York, 1972.
Lambert, Eleanor, *World of Fashion: People, Places, Resources,* New York & London, 1976.
Milbank, Caroline Rennolds, *Couture: The Great Designers,* New York, 1985.
Stegemeyer, Anne, *Who's Who in Fashion, Third Edition,* New York, 1996.
Guillaume, Valérie, *Courrèges,* Paris & London, 1998.

Articles

Wolfe, David, "Courrèges," in *International Textiles* (London), April 1990.
Schneider, Karen, "Up, Up and Hooray! Designer André Courrèges Celebrates 25 Years of Miniskirt Fame," in *People,* 9 July 1990.
Betts, Katherine, "Courrèges: Back to the Future," in *Women's Wear Daily,* 22 January 1991.
Schiro, Anne-Marie, "Sixties Revival is Official: Courrèges is Back," in the *New York Times,* 19 February 1991.
Drake, Laurie, "Courrèges and Balenciaga: Some of the Best Spring Fashion Bears the Signature—or the Spirit—of Two Great Designers," in *Vogue,* March 1991.
"Back on the Block: With 1960s Fashions Back in Vogue, André Courrèges is Decades Ahead of the Trend," in *Chicago Tribune,* 6 March 1991.
Horyn, Cathy, "Men of Metal and Mod," in the *Washington Post,* 14 March 1991.
"Courrèges,"special supplement of *L'Officiel* (Paris), 1994.

André Courrèges, designed for Samuel Robert's 1964 collection: goatskin walking suit. © AP/Wide World Photos.

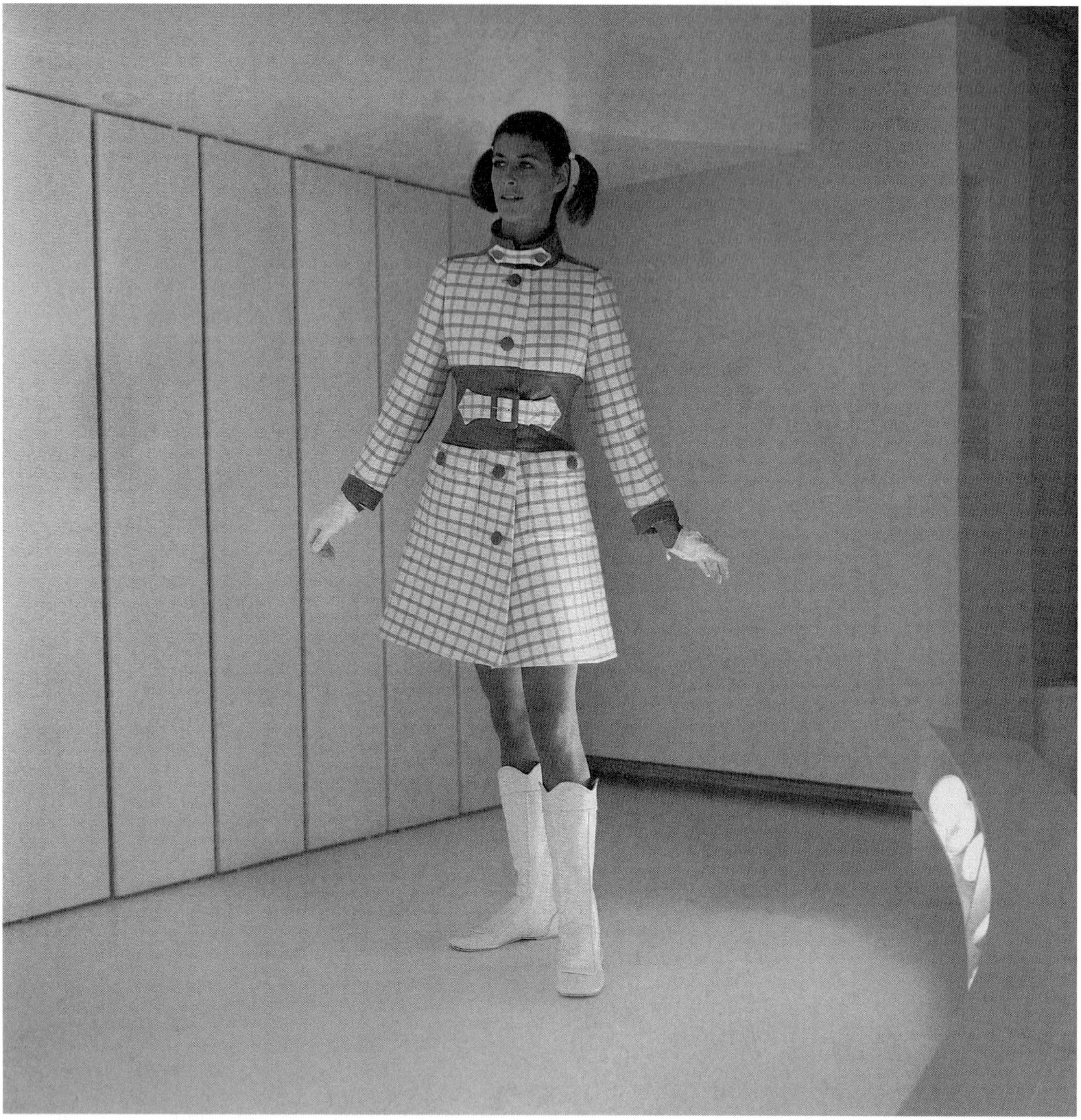

André Courrèges, fall 1968 collection: wool coat with leather inset band. © Bettmann/CORBIS.

White, Constance R., "Courrèges Encore," in the *New York Times,* 20 March 1995.
"Courrèges Buys Back Perfume," in the *Wall Street Journal,* 6 September 1996.

* * *

One of a generation of strikingly innovative designers working in Paris in the 1960s, André Courrèges was one of the first since Chanel to understand the potential in womenswear of using items from the male wardrobe. His goal became to provide the same simple range of garments for women, not by mere appropriation of male adornment, but inventing a totally new modernistic aesthetic.

Courrèges regarded the 1950s silhouette of a tightly boned and wasp-waisted mannequin, teetering on impossibly high stiletto heels, as completely alien to the needs of the modern woman of the 1960s, even though he had worked for Balenciaga for 11 years, from 1950 to 1961, as chief cutter. Courrèges subsequently left to set up his own business with his wife Coqueline. Their first collection, using tweeds and soft wools, had yet to shake off Balenciaga's influence.

Ultimately Courrèges saw the male wardrobe as more logical and practical than a woman's because of its unadorned and reductionist nature, resulting from its being pared down to the barest essentials over the passage of time. Yet he responded to the challenge as an engineer—one well-versed in functionalism and utilizing the skills he had learned and finely honed at Balenciaga—and with his own modernist tendencies conceived a new look of femininity entirely different from that of Balenciaga.

Cutting skills were used to free rather than contain the body, emphasized by short trapeze skirts for extra movement. By 1964 Courrèges was producing spare but not spirited ranges of clothing, such as his monochromatic pinafore dresses and suits with hemlines well above the knee, all in crisply tailored, squared-off shapes. Renouncing the stiletto as an item of clothing symbolizing women's subordination, Courrèges provided his models with flat-heeled white glacé boots and accessorized his honed-down clothes with extraordinary headgear such as futuristic helmets and strange baby bonnets.

Courrèges believed the foundation of successful design was in understanding function; correct form would automatically follow. Aesthetics was only the wrapping. The only decoration to be found on Courrèges clothes was either directly allied to its construction, as in the use of welt seaming, or was minor such as the small half belt on the back of his coats. One decorative device he reveled in and which was copied extensively within mass market fashion was his use of white daisies made out of every conceivable material such as sequins, lace, or used as patches.

It is still debated whether or not Courrèges invented the mini skirt, but he was indisputably responsible for making trousers and matching tunic tops *de rigueur* for every occasion, overturning the taboo of trouser wearing by women, creating versions slit at the seam to give an exaggerated elongation to the female body and emphasizing this clean streamlined look by using lean, well-muscled female models.

Courrèges displayed his love of construction in his use of chevron stitching, such as that used in 1965 at the hips of dresses and trousers, and his use of devices such as the bib yoke, keyhole neckline, and patch pocket. Hip yokes and welted seams with top stitching emphasized the lines of the garment, the stitching occasionally deployed in contrasting colors, such as orange on white, to exaggerate the details of assembly.

Courrèges collections were copied and disseminated worldwide, although the taut outline of the originals was lost when cheaper materials were used. Consequently he refused to stage shows for the press or retail buyers and would only sell to private clients, biding his time until he was ready to produce his own ready-to-wear collection, entitled Couture Future, in 1969. By this time, however, his hard-edged style had become dated in comparison with the hippie, ethnic style of the 1970s and his seminal structured A-line dresses with welt seams and square-cut coats on top seemed out of step with contemporary fashion.

By the early 1990s Courrèges was again designing successfully, spurred by a 1960s revival where his short trapeze dresses and metallic clothing were rediscovered by a new generation. He had his own boutique in Bloomingdale's New York flagship store, as well as in Bloomingdale's stores around the country. The Courrèges name was on everything from his well-known bodysuits and skirts to scooters, gourmet food, and home furnishings. Like fellow futuristic designer Paco Rabanne, Courrèges enjoyed this fashionable rebirth for several years, reveling in the limelight and a slew of new, younger clients. In 1992 Courrèges sold his fragrance division to the Swiss Burrus Group; five years later, still riding high and one of the few remaining independent designers in a time of mass consolidation (think LVMH), Courrèges was able to buy back his perfume business from Burrus for $7.5 million.

In the 21st century, the Courrèges name still carried clout—in and around in Paris and in New York. Dozens of shops ringed the globe, especially in Japan, where the Courrèges label was a favorite in department stores. Will the future be a bright and wonderful place for Courrèges fashion? As he explained to the *Chicago Tribune* in 1991, "It wasn't me who was ahead of my time, it was my time that was behind me." Has time caught up with André Courrèges? Only he knows for sure.

—Caroline Cox; updated by Sydonie Benét

COVERI, Enrico

Italian designer

Born: Prato, Italy, 26 February 1952. **Education:** Studied stage design, Accademia delle Belle Arti, Florence, 1971–74. **Career:** Freelance designer for Touché, Gentry, Tycos, Aquarius, Lux Sports, and Ilaria Knitwear, Milan, 1972–79; formed Enrico Coveri, SpA, 1978; formed Enrico Coveri France S.A.R.L., 1983; opened boutique in Milan, 1981, with subsequent shops in Genoa, Viareggio, Piacenza, Paris, Saint Tropez, Beirut, and New York; launched perfumes *Paillettes,* 1982, and *Dollars,* 1983; introduced home furnishing line, 1984. **Exhibitions:** *Consequenze impreviste,* Prato, 1982; *Italian Re-Evolution,* La Jolla Museum of Art, California, 1982. **Awards:** Uomo Europeo award, Rome, 1982; Fil d'Or award, Munich, 1982. **Died:** 6 December 1990, in Florence, Italy.

PUBLICATIONS

On COVERI:

Books

Mulassano, Adriana, *The Who's Who of Italian Fashion,* Florence, 1979.

Sartogo, Piero, ed., *Italian Re-Evolution: Design in Italian Society in the 1980s* (exhibition catalogue), La Jolla, California, 1982.

The Power of Paris, video, New York, 1991.

Articles

Baldacci, Luisa, "Enrico Coveri: lo stilista del colore," in *Arbiter* (Milan), No. 2, 1982.

"Enrico Coveri illustra il segreto della sua moda," in *La Nazione* (Milan), 14 June 1983.

"Enrico Coveri: graffiti che corrono e ballano," in *Vogue* (Milan), January 1985.

"Parigi: spot su Enrico Coveri. Enorme o incollato, la moda degli opposti," in *Vogue* (Milan), February 1985.

"Enrico Coveri: nuovi schemi per il classico," in *L'Uomo Vogue* (Milan), July/August 1985.

Enrico Coveri, fall/winter 2001 collection: sequined sweater with a fur collar and gold-tone pants. © AP/Wide World Photos.

Morera, Daniela, and Joe Dolce, "Enrico Coveri," in *Interview* (New York), February 1986.

"Enrico Coveri: uno stile all'inglese," in *Donna* (Milan), July/August 1987.

"Enrico Coveri: righe, quadri, forme base...," in *Vogue* (Milan), January 1988.

Obituary, "Enrico Coveri Dies in Italy of Stroke," in *Women's Wear Daily,* 10 December 1990.

Obituary, "Enrico Coveri, Italian Fashion Designer," in *Chicago Tribune,* 10 December 1990.

* * *

"You Young" is the name of one of the several seasonal Enrico Coveri collections. It is also perhaps the most succinct description for his bold, unpretentious, and fun-loving fashion: strong, vibrant colors and striking, witty designs that have always been clear and intelligible, with zany prints and knits often incorporating Pop Art designs and cartoon characters.

Enrico Coveri, spring/summer 2001 collection. © AP/Wide World Photos.

Enrico Coveri was born in Prato, near Florence, Italy and studied at the Accademie delle Belle Arti in the city. He began his career as a freelance designer, creating knitwear and sportswear lines for three collections, Touché, Gentry, and Tycos, making his mark by being one of the first designers to use soft pastel shades. After a brief move to Paris in 1978 to work for Espace Cardin, he returned to Italy and established his own namesake company. Each season the company produced a ready-to-wear women's line and several less expensive boutique collections for men, women, teenagers, and children, as well as a vast array of subsidiary Coveri accessory products such as shoes, bags, hats, scarves, and gloves.

Although he excelled at casual clothing, even his eveningwear exuded a young, sporty, wearable feel. Coveri enjoyed shocking and going out on a limb with design. "I love the unexpected to the point of traveling everywhere without set itineraries," he declared when, after three seasons pursuing his ultra casual look, he suddenly produced a collection of extremely feminine tight skirts and high heels. "That certainly shattered the common belief of Coveri only doing things for 16-year-olds," he recalled.

Asked for his design inspiration, he replied that he never really gave it any serious intellectual thought, preferring spontaneous incidents to spark ideas and feelings. His ideal woman, he declared, was as indistinct and volatile as he, living for the present and spurning retrospectives or fashion revivals. He studied the contemporary woman in the street, her attitude, her clothes, movements, and accessories.

Perhaps Coveri's strongest and most recurrent theme was in his use of *paillettes* or sequins. Each collection produced a new garment in the fabric, a bright red skin-tight all-in-one, for instance, or a full-length evening dress, or it promoted a new development in the fabric, such as stretch sequin or mixtures of matte and shine. Other favorite fabrics included Lycra and stretch satin, superfine linen, silk, and cotton poplin. The young, sporty Coveri woman's silhouette seemed to always fluctuate between cling or fluidity, with a recurrent ethnic theme interpreted in a fresh and contemporary way. This led journalist Hebe Dorsey to dub Coveri the "Italian Kenzo" in the *Herald Tribune.*

In a 1978 interview Coveri declared a disdain for the usual work methods of a fashion designer, adding that he hated to draw or do fittings. His approach was very immediate: ideas would come in torrents during long, sleepless nights and were sketched out rapidly the next day. Models were also dressed and styled at the last minute, the outcome on the catwalk being directed by his mood at the time. "I probably make and will continue to make dreadful mistakes," he explained. His mistakes, however, were obviously not serious enough to prevent his establishment as one of Italy's most famous and successful fashion names.

Although Enrico Coveri died of a stroke in 1990, at the age of 38, the business was continued by his family. Under the direction of his sister and a chosen design team, successive collections continued to evoke Coveri's acknowledged fashion legacy.

—Kevin Almond

COX, Patrick

Canadian footwear designer working in London

Born: Edmonton, Canada, 19 March 1963. **Education:** Studied at Cordwainers College, Hackney, London, 1983–85. **Career:** Established firm in London and designed collections for Bodymap, Vivienne Westwood, John Galliano, and others, from 1987; London shop opened, 1991; hired CEO from Hermès, 1995; ran controversial suicide-themed ad for footwear, 1999; introduced first signature fragrance, 2000. **Awards:** Accessory Designer of the Year, British Fashion awards, 1994 and 1995; British Marie Claire Accessory Designer of the Year, 1996; Fashion Medal of Honor by the Footwear Association of New York, 1996. **Address:** 30 Sloane Street, London SW1X 9NJ, England.

Publications

On COX:

Books

McDowell, Colin, *Shoes: Fashion and Fantasy,* New York, 1989.
Trasko, Mary, *Heavenly Soles: Extraordinary Twentieth Century Shoes,* New York, 1989.
Bloch, Phillip, *Elements of Style,* New York, 1998.
Callan, Georgina O'Hara, *Dictionary of Fashion and Fashion Designers* New York, 1998.
Doe, Tamasin, *Patrick Cox: Wit, Irony and Footwear,* New York, 1998.

Articles

"Shoe Shines," in *Elle* (London), March 1987.
Rumbold, Judy, "The Last Shall Be First," in *The Guardian* (London), 21 September 1987.
Thackara, John, "Put Your Foot in It," in *The Observer Magazine* (London), 22 November 1987.
Lender, Heidi, "Foot Fetish: Patrick Cox's Wild and Woolly Shoes Have Come to Paris," in *W,* August 1989.
"Best Foot Forward" in *The Guardian* (London), 10 June 1991.
"Patrick Cox," in *DR: The Fashion Business* (London), 2 November 1991.
"Shoe Shine Boy," in *Toronto Life Fashion,* December/January 1991–92.
"Shoe King," in *For Him* (London), April 1992.
"Taming of the Shoe," in the *Evening Standard* (London), 30 June 1992.
"ASA Blasts Patrick Cox for Tasteless 'Suicide' Shoe Ad," *Marketing Week,* 11 March 1999.
"Fall Fashion–Just One Word: Plastics," in the *Wall Street Journal,* 20 September 1999.
Johnson, Jo, "Getting A Sure Footing in Foreign Markets," in *Management Today,* November 1999.
"Getting High," in *European Cosmetic Markets,* September 2000.

* * *

"My early shoes stick in people's minds," Patrick Cox has said, "but things are getting more refined." Those who may remember him as the devoted nightclubber of the early 1980s might have been surprised to find him, a decade later, presiding over the salon atmosphere of his shoeshop-cum-antiques emporium in London. Patrick Cox grew up, but also went beyond the image of the shoemaker with "street credibility," designing for Vivienne Westwood, John Galliano, et al. He survived the designer decade of the 1980s and emerged in the early 1990s with his ability to wittily reinterpret traditional styling, still constantly in tune with contemporary fashion.

Cox's fascination with the British fashion scene brought him to London, rather than the obvious footwear design centers of Italy. He enrolled at Cordwainers College, Hackney, London to study, but soon found college life was less rewarding than meeting and making contacts within the London club world. His involvement with the music and fashion scene brought him the chance to design for Vivienne Westwood's first solo collection, whilst he was still at college. "I used to shop at Westwood's quite a lot and my flatmate David was her assistant," he recalled. "Six weeks before the show someone realized nothing had been done about shoes and David suggested that I could probably help.… My gold platform shoes with large knots went down a treat. Everyone noticed them—you couldn't miss them really—and my other commissions have followed from there."

Indeed they did: in no time at all he was designing shoes to accompany the collections of the young English designers who were then flavor of the month on the international fashion circuit. Cox shod the feet to fit the willful perversities of Bodymap, the calculated eccentricity of John Galliano, and the ladies-who-lunch chic of Alistair Blair.

Cox went on to design his own label collections with such delightfully named styles as Chain Reaction, Rasta, and Crucifix Court. These were typical, hard-edged classic women's silhouettes given the Cox treatment—chain mesh, silk fringes and crucifixes suspended from the heels. Witty and amusing as these styles were, they had limited appeal and Cox would not have attained his current prominence had he not sought a larger audience.

The launch of his own London shop in 1991 gave Cox the opportunity to show his collections as a whole, displaying the brash alongside the sophisticated. His audience soon came from both the devotees of the off-the-wall fashion experimentation of King's Road and the classic chic of the Sloane Square debutante. Cleverly, his shop was geographically situated between the two.

Selling shoes alongside antiques was a novelty that appealed to the press and boosted Cox's profile. There was something delightful in the presentation of shoes balanced on the arms of Louis XVI gilt chairs or popping out of the drawers of beautiful old dressers. The shoes gained an aura of respectability; a sense of belonging to some tradition, which perfectly complemented Cox's reinterpretation of classic themes. No longer was there a typical Cox customer; they were the young and not so young. Cox took great delight when elderly ladies appreciated his more subtle styling; his women's shoes even rivaled those of Manolo Blahnik in their sophistication—a calculated move.

In contrast, the development his men's footwear was less obvious. Cox has always loved traditional English styling, and commented: "I believe that British men's shoes are the best in the world, so mine are just an evolution from those classic ideas." This evolution kept him close to the spirit of British footwear, if not to the colorways. He reproduced the weight and proportions of the styles whilst exaggerating the soles and fastenings.

Cox is the shoe designer who admits there is little you can do with shoes. The very nature of footwear imposes constraints upon the designer, where there are fewer problems for the clothing designer. Cox sees shoes as more architectural than clothes; a free standing form with an inside and out. Yet these restrictions do not stop him producing fresh contemporary styles which still work within the perceived framework of what a classic silhouette should be.

During the second half of the 1990s, Cox was at a crossroads. He had lost some of the cachet associated with his Wannabe brand, but did not, as a self-financed company, have the resources to step to the next level and compete with other luxury goods brands. His margins were low compared to other companies and he spent a high nine percent of sales on advertising. He continued to enhance his footwear line; in spring/summer 1997, for example, he added a jelly boot to his colorful jelly wedges and sandals. Meanwhile, he entered the apparel market, introducing a small clothing line for men and women in 1995. By fall 1999 his London runway show featured items such as $363 neoprene pants and a $295 black cotton-and-rubber-ribbed sweater. His entry into apparel has been credited with moving men's clothing away from the staid elegance associated with French designers to a funkier tailored look. The women's apparel is brightly colored with a fun, comfortable sensibility.

The designer also extended distribution in the mid- to late 1990s by opening stores and boutiques throughout Europe, North America, and Asia, including an 800-square-foot section at the Tokyo department store Isetan that carried his whole line of footwear, apparel, and accessories. He also opened a Tokyo office to work more closely with his Japanese licensees, as well as a New York showroom. The latter closed; many observers believe he moved into the U.S. market too quickly.

As of 1999 the designer's wholly owned business, Patrick Cox International, had annual turnover of £19 million ($30 million), earned not only from his flagship footwear line but from apparel, jewelry, bags, and ties. (The Wannabe loafer is not the trendsetter it was, but still accounted for about half of Cox's shoe sales in the late 1990s.) That same year, Cox was widely criticized for a two-page spread in the glossy men's magazine *FHM,* showing the feet of a man who appeared to have hung himself. Critics called the suicide-themed depiction "tasteless."

Cox announced his first fragrance line for men and women, "High," in partnership with Paris-based IFF in 2000. It debuted at the upscale British department store Harvey Nichols before being introduced into Asian markets. The scent typifies the Cox image: fun, addictive, and "of the moment."

—Chris Hill; updated by Karen Raugust

C.P. COMPANY

Italian design house

Based in the Emilia-Romagna region of Italy, C.P. Company produces menswear fashions designed principally by Massimo Osti; **Company History:** Introduced women's line, mid-1990s; U.S. subsidiary called C.P. Company Sportswear Inc.; purchased by the Rivettis and their Sportswear Company of Italy, 1993; Moreno Ferrari took over as designer from Osti, mid-1990s; closed New York flagship store, 1996; introduced fabrics containing metals such as copper and titanium, 1998; opened London flagship, 2000; launched Transformables, jackets that inflate into furniture, 2001. **Exhibition:** *Uniform: Order and Disorder,* P.S.1/Museum of Modern Art, Pitti Immagine, 2001. **Company Address:** Via Confine 2161, 41017 Ravarino, Italy.

Publications

On C.P. COMPANY:

Books

Rinaldi, Paolo, ed., monograph on Carlo Rivetti, Milan, 2001.

Articles

Bober, Joanna, "C.P. Company's City of Women," in *WWD,* 29 September 1994.

Socha, Miles, "C.P. Company is Vacating Flatiron Location," in *DNR,* 22 August 1996.

Lohrer, Robert, "C.P. Relaunches Sportswear with a Twist," in *DNR,* 2 February 1998.

Fallon, James, "C.P. Company to Open Freestanding London Store," in *DNR,* 17 November 1999.

Ilari, Allessandra, "Italian Manufacturers Adjusting Product to Suit American Tastes," in *DNR,* 3 January 2000.

Smith, Claire, "Pret-a-Voyager: Novelty Travel Fashion," available online at Virgin.net, www.Virgin.net, 19 December 2000.

* * *

Massimo Osti, long synonymous with C.P. Company, represented what C.P. Company stood for. He chose to live and work in his native Bologna, Italy, a university town populated by a young, international set. C.P. Company's headquarters is situated in the Emilia-Romagna region of Italy, renowned for its cuisine and local produce. As such, it—and Massimo Osti—were far removed from the hustle and bustle of Milan.

While Italian fashion designers have a propensity for generating myths around their collections, Osti's approach was in stark contrast to this prevailing trend. Osti conjured up no myths and was proud of it. He fashioned his collection not only from an aesthetic point of view but, first and foremost, from a functional one. Osti stuck close to his roots, and lived an understated lifestyle. Unlike some of his better-known counterparts, he was never in the limelight. He did not hold fashion shows, and his catalogues highlighted only clothes, with no glamorous models or exotic locations and no fancy studio lighting.

Osti was against artifice in any form; he did not consider himself to be a true designer, simply occupied with mastering the technical challenge of his line—specifically, the fabrics and finishes. He showed a new line twice a year but never referred to his output as a collection; rather, they were "pieces." There was never any uniting theme or story in the C.P. Company line.

The designer's working uniform consisted of a navy C.P. silk shirt and a pair of navy Stone Island jeans, with perhaps a navy tie. Osti loved to sail and even had a soccer field on his property. Hence, as a sportsman, he understood the need for performance sportswear. All his woven fabrics for C.P. Company were garment-washed, and he started using this process long before it was the rage in the men's sportswear industry. He was also one of the first to use water-repellent coatings on his fabrics, a process now standard on outerwear.

What would otherwise be a delicate item—such as a burlap linen raincoat—would be coated with polyurethane to make it practically indestructible. An indigo denim shirt would be garment-bleached and enzyme-washed to have the feel of silk. Such was the essence of Osti's philosophy, if he were willing to articulate one: to take fine, even luxury fabrics, and to treat them in such a way that they could be worn nonchalantly—or to take common fabrics and give them a luxury finish.

C.P. Company has been the essence of casual elegance and rugged versatility. It is stylish, never trendy, ideal for the man with good taste, a modicum of style, and a love of the finer things in life. Men who wear C.P. Company are averse to displaying designer labels, preferring instead to appear well dressed in an unself-conscious way. They also have an intellectual bent and are not impressed with flashy things. In other words, C.P. Company's customers were very much like Osti, who chose the Flatiron Building as the location for the company's New York store not only because of its architectural and historical significance, but because it was slightly off the beaten path, setting C.P. Company apart from the pack.

For over 20 years, Osti did for men's sportswear what perhaps Balenciaga did for women's couture. He honed it almost to a science, becoming the standard against which many other sportswear firms measured themselves. There is a strong probability that any novelty in finishing or dyeing one may encounter in the men's market has been tested—and probably developed—first by Osti. He was as thorough as they come in the area of fabric research, having at his disposal an archive of tens of thousands of items of used clothing, what he referred to as his "inspirational muse," and the "conscience" of the past. He deeply respected the styles of the past and strove to perfect them for the future. Although his fabrics were novel, his silhouettes were consistently classic, with an appealing lived-in quality.

For many years, the C.P. Company label carried the slogan "Ideas from Massimo Osti," and that in itself spoke volumes about the pragmatic approach of the line's designer. Yet C.P. Company underwent major changes in both ownership and design leadership at the end of the 20th century. Both the company and its sister brand, Stone Island, formerly owned by the Italian apparel powerhouse GFT, were purchased in 1993 by Carlo and Christina Rivetti, who operated the brands through their Sportswear Company of Italy. By the mid-1990s, founder Massimo Osti had moved on to other endeavors, and the designer Moreno Ferrari was established in his place. Despite these changes, the C.P. Company brand retained its focus on technical innovation, especially in the development of new materials, and fashion designs followed the dictates of the fabric.

In the mid-1990s, the company publicized its plans for a broad retail expansion, spearheaded by its Flatiron district store in New York. Over the years, it honed its expectations, opening flagship stores only in its two leading markets, the UK (London) and Italy (Milan), along with a smaller store in St. Tropez, France. The brands were also featured in freestanding stores in countries such as Japan and Korea. The New York outlet was shuttered in 1996. Although C.P. Company has periodically talked of opening another store in New York, it had not yet come to pass as of 2001.

The firm's retail spaces feature both C.P. Company and Stone Island branded sportswear items for men as well as C.P.'s women's sportswear range. As of 2000, the company sold through a total of 420 retail doors worldwide, including Bloomingdale's and Barneys New York according to the *Daily News Record* in January 2000.

Ferrari became Osti's focus, emphasizing durability and utilitarianism over fashion fads. In his fall-winter 1998/1999 collection, he reinvigorated some of the characteristics that had helped boost the brand's sales in the 1980s, notably a series of blousons designed for wary urban consumers. As *DNR* described the line in February 1998, it included one item (called "Metropolis") with an antismog mask, computer, mobile phone, and pockets for documents; another ("Life") with a noiseproof headset; and a third ("Munch") with a personal safety alarm. The last was inspired by Edouard Munch's famous painting, *The Scream.*

The year 1998 also brought the introduction of fabrics composed of copper, steel, carbon, and titanium initially intended to give a futuristic slant to the garments. The Italian journal *Interni* noted in June 2001 that these materials also provided performance advantages and a distinctive look and feel (light-reflective, movement-highlighting, crumpled-casual vintage) making them an integral part of the collection today.

For the 2001 season, C.P. Company's reputation for innovation moved to the foreground with its Transformables line, consisting of inflatable items that change nearly instantaneously from wearable objects into furniture. Packaged with an air compressor that could be plugged into a car's lighter, the line included jackets that become armchairs, mattress-tent combinations, sleeping bags, hammocks, and inflatable seats, representing the ultimate in convenient and minimalist travel gear.

—Vicki Vasipoulos; updated by Karen Raugust

CRAHAY, Jules-François

French designer

Born: Liège, Belgium, 21 May 1917. **Education:** Studied fashion and art in Paris, 1934–35; worked in his mother's dressmaking salon, Liège, 1936–39; salesman, Jane Regny, Paris, circa 1939. **Military Service:** Performed military service, taken prisoner of war in Germany, 1940–44. **Career:** Opened own fashion house, Paris, 1951 (closed); designer, Nina Ricci, Paris, 1952–63; joined Lanvin, Paris, 1963; head designer, 1964–84; formed ready-to-wear company, Japan, 1985. **Awards:** Neiman Marcus award, Dallas, 1962; Maison Blanche award, New Orleans, 1963; Dé d'Or award, 1984. **Died:** 5 January 1988, in Monte Carlo.

Jules-François Crahay, designed for Nina Ricci's 1962 "Tomboy" collection. © Bettmann/CORBIS.

Publications

On CRAHAY:

Books

Stegemeyer, Anne, *Who's Who in Fashion, Third Edition,* New York, 1996.

Articles

"Le Dé d'Or à Jules-François Crahay: vingt ans de création," in *L'Officiel* (Paris), September 1984.
"Jules-François Crahay Dead at 70," in *WWD,* 7 January 1988.
Obituary, "Jules-François Crahay," in *The Observer* (London), 31 January 1988.

* * *

Jules-François Crahay made his name as a designer, not through the establishment of a label under his own name, but through his work for two of the more elegant Parisian haute couture houses, Nina Ricci and Lanvin. His polished, graceful eveningwear, young and unrestrained, was particularly sought out by many *soignée* French society ladies in the 1950s, 1960s, and 1970s.

Crahay is an interesting, well-known example of many designers who worked for fashion houses in virtual anonymity. It should be remembered that many couture and ready-to-wear fashion houses have been supported by a vast retinue of designers and assistant designers, whose talent and vision have elevated the established name of a house into the annals of fashion history.

Crahay was born in Liège, France, in 1917, to a dressmaker mother and industrialist father. After attending university and a fashion design school in Paris, from 1934 to 1935, he returned to Liège and a position in his mother's dressmaking business, remaining there until 1951 when he was offered a position as salesman at the house of Jane Regny in Paris.

In 1952 Nina Ricci employed Crahay as a dress designer. Initially, he assisted Ricci with the collections and reorganized and rejuvenated the workshops. He was eventually entrusted with the ready-to-wear and presented his first collection in 1959. The range proved a peak in Crahay's design career. It featured low plunging necklines that foresaw the gypsy styles of the early 1960s; it also highlighted Crahay's unique understanding of pattern cutting, cloth, and garment construction.

In October 1963 Crahay succeeded Antonio del Castillo as the designer at Lanvin in Paris. Jeanne Lanvin had created her Maison de Couture in 1889 and since then it had conveyed the prestige and traditional image of French elegance. Crahay did little to revolutionize this tradition; instead he emphasized and flattered it. His first collection for the house, spring/summer 1964, met with an enthusiastic response from both buyers and the international press, and verified his position as one of the top Parisian designers, though he did not work under his own name.

Crahay was one of the first designers to glamorize trousers for eveningwear. Elegant slacks, in sequined or pleated silk, proved bestsellers. He also innovated and reintroduced leg o' mutton sleeves in organdy, bejewelled leather gauchos, and alluring jumpsuits for evening. When it came to his studio work he established a reputation as a demanding taskmaster. He adhered to the best haute couture traditions, where nothing was left to chance and original, fine details were researched and executed with the greatest care. When asked about his work he replied simply, "Look at my dresses; they are what I have created and they are much more important than anything I can say."

Crahay's achievements have been recognized with several important fashion awards, including the Neiman Marcus award in 1962. In the early 1970s he succeeded in seeing his own name on a label, when Arkins of New York commissioned him to design a ready-to-wear collection for their department store. Jules-François Crahay died in January 1988, at the age of 70, in Monaco, Monte Carlo.

—Kevin Almond

CUMMINGS, Angela

American jewelry designer

Born: Klagenfurt, Austria, in 1944. **Education:** Art Academy, Perugia, Italy; Zeichenakademie, Hanau, West Germany. **Family:** Married Bruce Cummings, 1970. **Career:** Joined Tiffany & Co., 1967; designed first full jewelry collection under own name, 1975; started Angela Cummings, Inc., 1984; launched first branded in-store boutique, at Bergdorf Goodman, 1984; designed accents for Candie's shoes for charitable line, 1997; designed limited-edition compact for Estée Lauder exhibition, 2001. **Address:** 730 Fifth Avenue, New York, NY 10019 USA.

Publications

On CUMMINGS:

Books

Stegemeyer, Anne, *Who's Who in Fashion, Third Edition,* New York, 1996.

Loring, John, *Tiffany Jewels,* New York, 1999.

Kirkham, Pat and Wendy Kaplan, *Women Designers in the U.S.A., 1900–2000: Diversity and Difference,* New Haven (CT), 2000.

Loring, John, *Magnificent Tiffany Silver,* New York, 2001.

Articles

Cunningham, Billy and Wendy Murphy, "A Rural Setting for Jewelry Designer Angela Cummings," in *Architectural Digest,* April 1982.

Clurman, Shirley, "Look Out, Little Miss Muffet: Angela Cummings Jewelry May Have Designs on You," in *People,* 13 September 1982.

Duka, John, "An Angela Cummings Shop," in the *New York Times,* 21 February 1984.

Johnson, Sharon, "Breakfast At Tiffany's, Lunch at Bergdorf's," in *Working Woman,* May 1984.

"Angela Cummings's Dishes are a Feast for the Eyes: A Jewelry Designer Who Creates Gems for the Table, in *Chicago Tribune,* 26 October 1986.

Beard, Patricia, "Country Charm," in *Harper's Bazaar,* October 1990.

"Jewelry Designers Do Candie's," in *Women's Wear Daily,* 29 September 1997.

Klensch, Elsa, "Cummings' Jewelry Springs from Nature," on *CNN Interactive,* 11 December 1997.

———, "Comfortable and Beautiful: Cummings' New Jewelry Combines Abstract Design, Soft Finishes," on *CNN Interactive,* 21 February 1999.

Kampmann, Anne, "The Unique Style of Angela Cummings," online at LuxuryFinder.com, 2001.

* * *

Born in Klagenfurt, Austria, in 1944, Angela Cummings moved to the United States with her family at age three. She returned to Europe to study at the Art Academy in Perugia, Italy, and in 1967 earned degrees in goldsmithing and gemology from Zeichenakademie in Hanau, West Germany. Upon graduation at age 23, she moved to New York and immediately joined Tiffany & Company, where she remained until 1984. After creating her first full collection under her own name in 1975, she became one of a small group of well-known, innovative jewelry designers (along with Paloma Picasso, Jean Schlumberger, and Elsa Peretti) associated with Tiffany.

Several representative examples of Cummings' work for Tiffany were featured in a September 1982 *People* magazine article, including a $38,000 gold-and-diamond spiderweb necklace; $12,000 earrings made of gold and diamonds and shaped like elm leaves; $150-and-up brooches of 18-karat gold, inspired by seagulls; a $5,800 crocodile bracelet fashioned out of 18-karat gold; and a $1.5 million geometric emerald and diamond necklace. One of her bestselling jewlery pieces, a $3,875 petal necklace, was inspired when Cummings held a rose in her hand and accidently crushed it when surprised by a ringing telephone. According to *Working Woman* magazine, her line was bringing in $10 million in revenues by 1982.

Cummings was known mainly for working in 18-karat gold as well as platinum and sterling silver, highlighted with exquisite gems. But she often mixed these materials with unconventional counterpoints such as wood. She experimented with classic jewelry-making techniques, such as inlaying precious metals into iron, a process known as damascene, and broke the rules of high-end jewelry early in her career by using lots of color.

The inspiration for Cummings' work is rooted in nature. She incorporates forms such as ginkgo leaves, spiderwebs, vines, shells, feathers, sea foam, dragonflies, and orchids into her jewelry. Cummings is known for her innovation, trompe d'œil effects, intricate designs, attention to the surface of the metal, and her concern with the smallest of details. Her work has been praised by critics as well as loved by customers.

In 1984 Cummings left Tiffany to form her own business with her husband, Bruce Cummings, a former Tiffany gemologist whom she had married in 1970. One of the reasons Cummings decided to leave Tiffany was to have more control over her work. She wanted to expand into other categories such as tabletop accessories, leather goods, and flatware, and she hoped to expand her price range so her pieces would be more affordable. She opened her first boutique across the street from Tiffany at the upscale Bergdorf Goodman department store. The 500-square-foot space, a first for a jewelry designer at the Fifth Avenue retailer, was located in the middle of the first floor. Soon

Cummings had other boutiques in stores such as Bloomingdale's and Macy's San Francisco.

Cummings' first collection as an independent included a great deal of silver—she had not been allowed to sign her silver works at Tiffany—as well her trademark gold. A February 1984 article in the *New York Times* about her new boutique detailed several of her new, unique pieces: a linked necklace made of gold with an etched woodgrain surface; a matching cuff and collar of inlaid black opals; an inlaid black opal necklace of gold, with links shaped like orchids; gold and burnished silver pieces inlaid with a zebra pattern of black jade; and a necklace of South Sea pearls with a 4.5-carat (total) diamond clasp. Although the collection included many of the high-end pieces for which Cummings had long been known (the top price was $117,000), there were also items as low as $30. In addition, she mirrored some of the same designs in different media to appeal to a broad range of customers. Thirty percent of the items were nonjewelry pieces, including tableware and leather goods; she has since moved into other categories such as watches. Cummings also established international operations in Japan and elsewhere.

In 1997 Candie's shoe company partnered with several jewelry designers to create a line of footwear to benefit the American Cancer Society. Cummings designed metal accessories for four styles of shoes in the line, each pair of which retailed for $180 to $350. Her simple accents for the slip-ons included a single, squared gold button at the top of the shoe.

Style and fashion guru Elsa Klensch of CNN has noted that many Cummings pieces during the late 1990s featured movement, such as through stems that twisted and curving leaves. One necklace called Breakers (1997) was composed of a series of waves going around the neck. The slightly asymmetrical quality of many of Cummings' pieces is not only eye-catching but extends this illusion of movement. Some of her creations have been influenced by Asian motifs, such as gold bracelets, earrings, and necklaces with a cloud-like shape incorporating jade into the design. Cummings often designs around a particularly beautiful stone, whether an emerald or a semiprecious stone such as tourmaline or peridot.

Cummings' 1999 collection was described by Klench as more abstract than her organic designs of the past, although they retained their sculptural quality. Cummings combined semiprecious and precious stones with metals, such as peridot with diamonds and gold. Her sense of color was demonstrated in a piece mixing mauve-, brown- and gold-colored black pearls with diamonds that were also slightly tinted in mauve and brown. Cummings' sense of texture was illustrated in the brushed finishes; she has said that to achieve more light in a piece, she would rather use additional diamonds than a highly polished metal.

In 2001 Cummings designed a limited-edition compact called Beautiful Blossom to house an Estée Lauder perfume called aptly titled *Beautiful*. The work debuted at Estée Lauder's Solid Perfume Compact Exhibit in Washington, D.C., after which it was sold at Bergdorf Goodman and Neiman Marcus.

Although Cummings continues to favor organic designs, she sometimes surprises by adding geometric pieces to her collections. Yet one goal remains constant: the finished piece has to be comfortable. The beauty of an Angela Cummings jewelry design is undisputed, but the comfort it provides to the wearer is always a top priority.

—Karen Raugust

D

DACHÉ, Lilly

American millinery designer

Born: Bègles, France, circa 1904; immigrated to New York, 1924. **Education:** Left school at 13. **Family:** Married Jean Desprês, 1931; children: Suzanne. **Career:** In Paris, apprenticed with Reboux, later worked for Maison Talbot and Georgette; designer, Darlington's (Philadelphia); millinery saleswoman, Macy's, 1924; saleswoman, The Bonnet Shop, New York, 1924; purchased shop from owner and established own millinery business, 1924; expanded and moved business in 1925, 1928; built Lilly Daché Building, East 56th Street, New York, 1937; added dresses and accessories, introduced fragrances, *Drifting* and *Dashing,* 1946; launched own clothing line, 1949; added coats, stockings, cosmetics, early 1950s; ready-to-wear millinery collections Mlle. Lilly and Dachettes introduced, early 1950s; closed business, 1968. **Awards:** Neiman Marcus award, 1940; Coty American Fashion Critics award, 1943. **Died:** 31 December 1989, in Louvecienne, France.

Lilly Daché, spring 1940 collection: polka-dotted foulard hat with quill. © Bettmann/CORBIS.

Publications

By DACHÉ:

Books

Talking Through My Hats, New York & London, 1946.
Lilly Daché's Glamour Book, New York, 1956.

On DACHÉ:

Books

Morris, Bernadine, and Barbara Walz, *The Fashion Makers,* New York, 1978.
Milbank, Caroline Rennolds, *New York Fashion: The Evolution of American Style,* New York, 1989.
McDowell, Colin, *Hats: Status, Style, Glamour,* London, 1992.
Fashion for America! Designs in the Fashion Institute of Technology, New York, Haslemere, Surry, 1992.
Stegemeyer, Anne, *Who's Who in Fashion, Third Edition,* New York, 1996.

Articles

"Lilly Daché," in *Current Biography,* July 1941.
"Lilly Daché," [obituary] in the *New York Times,* 2 January 1990.
"Lilly Daché," in *Current Biography,* March 1990.

* * *

Lilly Daché was the archetypal flamboyant immigrant beloved of Americans and so often taken to their hearts. In approved rags-to-riches fashion, she arrived in New York with a few dollars in her pocket ($13, henceforth her lucky number) in the heady days of the mid-1920s. Twenty years later, her name was as much a household word as any milliner's could be.

Daché's heyday coincided with a period in fashion history, the mid-1930s to the mid-1940s, during which one's hat—one always wore a hat—was often more important than one's frock. Great heights of chic and absurdity were achieved by the milliners of the day: tiny doll's hats perched over one eye, two-tone "Persian" turbans stuck with jewelled daggers, pom-poms of mink or marabout; Daché's hats were amongst the most outrageous of all. Her "complexion veil" was tinted green across the eyes, and blush-rose across the cheeks. For Beatrice Lillie, she made a "hands-across-the-sea" hat, with two clasped hands on the front, for the actress to wear both in England and America.

Lilly Daché, 1945 collection: shantung day dress. © Genevieve Naylor/CORBIS.

Daché's verve and skills attracted a high-profile clientèle of stage and film stars: Marlene Dietrich, Carole Lombard, Joan Crawford, Marion Davies, Gertrude Lawrence—all the big names. She worked with Travis Banton on Hollywood films, providing the hats to top his costumes, as many as 50 for one star for one movie. Often it was she who stuck Carmen Miranda's towering turbans with birds and fruit, and yet more birds and more fruit.

At her New York headquarters, Daché created a setting for herself which now seems the essence of kitsch glamor. Her circular salon was lined with mirrors; she had a silver fitting-room for celebrity brunettes, and a golden one for blondes. For wholesale buyers, she had another circular room padded with tufted pink satin, where she reigned from a leopard-skin divan wearing a leopard-skin jacket and leopard-skin slippers with bells (to warn her girls of her approach, a job later undertaken by her armful of jingling bangles).

Not an early riser, Daché conducted her morning's business from her bed, in the style of an 18th-century *levée,* dictating letters, buying supplies, designing, and interviewing employees while wrapped in a leopard-skin rug (she also had a robe made from the skins of more of these unfortunate cats, lined with shocking-pink felt). Occasionally business would be conducted from the reasonably modest depths of a neck-high bubble-bath. But Daché, like so many fashionable New Yorkers of her day, professed herself never so happy as when digging around in the garden of her upstate Colonial home.

Daché was one of the so-called "Big Three" New York milliners of her day, the others being John Fredericks and Sally Victor, and as such exerted a powerful influence on the American millinery trade, designing for wholesale manufacturers as well as for personal clients. Her designs sold worldwide and she embarked enthusiastically on promotional tours, accompanied by mountainous luggage and concomitant publicity.

At the height of her fame, Lilly Daché had shops in Chicago and Miami Beach, and employed 150 milliners at her flagship building off Park Avenue in New York City. Daché was a great self-publicist and epitomized the kind of woman to whom her smart American customers aspired. She was chic and flamboyant, and presented herself with self-assured bravado—"I like beautiful shoes in gay colors, with thick platforms and high heels. I like splashy jewellery that clinks when I walk, and I like my earrings big. I am. . .Lilly Daché, milliner de luxe."

—Alan J. Flux

DAGWORTHY, Wendy

British designer

Born: Gravesend, Kent, England, 4 March 1950. **Education:** Northfleet Secondary School; studied at Medway College of Design, 1966–68, and at Hornsey College of Art (now Middlesex University), London, 1968–71; first-class honours. **Family:** Married Jonathan Prew in August 1973. **Career:** Designer, Radley, 1971–72; founder, designer, Wendy Dagworthy Ltd, 1972–88; joined London Designer Collections, 1975, director, 1982–90; lecturer in fashion from 1972, including Royal College of Art, London; course director on Fashion BA course at Central St Martin's College of Art and Design, London, 1989; freelance designer and consultant, Laura Ashley, 1992; exhibitor at Victoria and Albert Museum, London; member of British Fashion Council management committee; speaker at the Fashion Conference, Lagos, Nigeria, 1992; design consultant for Betty Jackson, Liberty Retail Ltd., and Liberty International, 1996–present; Professor of Fashion, the Royal College of Art, London, 1998–present; speaker at many industry functions. **Awards:** Fil D'Or International Linen award, Monte Carlo, 1985. **Address:** 18 Melrose Terrace, London W6, England.

Publications

On DAGWORTHY:

Articles

Polan, Brenda, "The Discreet Charms of a Dagworthy," in *The Guardian* (London), 12 November 1981.

"Influences: Wendy Dagworthy," in *Women's Journal* (London), April 1984.

Polan, Brenda, "British Open," in *The Guardian* (London), 21 March 1985.

———, "Natural Leaders," in *The Guardian* (London), 25 April 1986.

"Face to Face," in *Creative Review* (London), June 1986.

"Dagworthy Goes Under," in *Fashion Weekly* (London), 24 November 1988.

"The Learning Curve," in *Drapers Record,* 29 May 1993.

Duffy, Martha, "On the Cutting Edge," in *Time,* 11 November 1996.

Roux, Caroline, "How a Small London Art School Quietly Colonized the World," in *Metropolis (London),* October 1999.

* * *

For nearly 20 years Wendy Dagworthy produced bright, easy, wearable separates and established herself as one of the most successful British designers in the wacky world of 1980s fashion. Her style was always distinctive and colourful, incorporating cheerful mixtures of fabrics, patterns, textures and an attention to fine detail; "You wear them, they don't wear you," was Dagworthy's fashion philosophy.

She formed her company in 1972 after one year as a designer for the wholesale firm Radley and a year after graduating from the Hornsey College of Art fashion course, with a first-class honours degree. There was an immediate consumer demand for Dagworthy's designs, and prestigious international stores soon placed orders. Italy, in particular, proved a lucrative outlet for her very English look and during the early 1980s she was exporting nearly half of her total output to that country.

Dagworthy loved to use vibrant colours and prints, embroidered Caribbean style *batiks,* mixed with stripes or swirling floral designs in fuchsia, scarlet, and orange. Favourite fabrics were mohairs, strongly textured woven wools, and wool baratheas. Her most popular, signature garments were oversize wool coats, back buttoning smocks, circular skirts, and gathered skirts with boldly tied waists, teamed with easy cardigans or wide-cropped jackets. The menswear collections, introduced in the early 1980s adhered to the same lively, colourful themes and quickly emulated the success of the womenswear, being comfortable and easy to wear.

Dagworthy was always been a strong supporter of British fashion design. In 1975 she joined the London Designer Collections, a prestigious collaboration of British designers, supporting and promoting their industry, and became a director in 1982. She was active in British fashion education, both as a lecturer and assessor, participating in design competitions like the Royal Society of Arts awards and the British Fashion awards. She also appeared regularly as fashion consultant to television shows like *The Clothes Show, Frocks on the Box,* and *Good Morning America.*

Wendy Dagworthy Ltd. exhibited their seasonal collections at trade shows in London, Milan, New York, and Paris. Her international reputation strengthened each season and her work was recognized with several awards including the Fil d'Or International Linen award in 1985. The Victoria and Albert Museum in London even displays a Wendy Dagworthy outfit in their permanent costume collection.

Dagworthy closed her business in 1988 and in the following year became the course director for the BA fashion program at London's Central St. Martin's College of Art and Design, where she remained until 1998. During her tenure, she was instrumental in solidifying the reputation of one of the best-known and most brash fashion schools in the world. In 1998 she became the head professor of fashion at the Royal College of Art, the world's sole postgraduate-only university of art and design, where she has remained. Her impact on the fashion program was evident immediately; critics at the RCA's well-received fashion show in 1999 noted her influence.

—Kevin Almond; updated by Karen Raugust

DALLAS, Sarah

British knitwear designer

Born: Bristol, England, 1 August 1951. **Education:** Studied at Middlesex Polytechnic, 1971–74; Royal College of Art, London, 1974–76. **Career:** Designed and produced women's knitwear collections under the Sarah Davis label, 1976–88; introduced men's knitwear line, 1987; freelance design work, from 1980; began teaching and lecturing at various institutions; course leader, Royal College of Art, Fashion Knitwear, from 1990; Knitted Textiles, from 1992. **Awards:** British Design Council award, 1987.

Publications

On DALLAS:

Books

Menkes, Suzy, *The Knitwear Revolution,* 1983.

Sheard, Stephen, *Rowan: Designer Collection Summer and Winter Knitting,* 1987.

Sheard, S., *The Rowan/Brother Designer Machine Knitting Boor,* 1987.

Articles

Chubb, Ann, "Knitting it Together with the Skipton Factor," in the *Daily Telegraph,* August 1982.

"Designer Knits for You," in *Pins & Needles,* Fall 1982.

"Sarah Dallas Knitwear Collection," in *Design,* February 1987.

Dodd, Celia, "Knit Wit in Bold Strokes," in *Field,* April 1987.

*

I feel quite passionately that knitwear should have an identity of its own and be an intrinsic part of fashion rather than an accessory to woven garments. This is something I have always striven to achieve with my own knitwear collections.

Knitwear is incredibly versatile, and is an ideal way of producing your own exclusive fabric, often engineered to suit each garment.... Nothing satisfies me more than to see someone of twenty and someone of sixty wearing the same garment but probably styled in quite a different way.

—Sarah Dallas

* * *

Sarah Dallas is a prominent knitwear designer who ran her own company and now works as a consultant and an educator. It was while studying for a degree in woven textiles that she first became fascinated by the more spontaneous results made possible by hand-knitting. At London's Royal College of Art she studied in the Textile School, but challenged established boundaries to create fashion knitwear.

After graduation, fashion knitwear designers were still quite rare and the knitwear boom was yet to come. Many companies were very conservative in their approach and in order to get her designs into production, Dallas had to set up on her own. Initially she produced knitwear exclusively for the London-based, upmarket fashion shop Bombacha, creating designs made by outworkers on domestic knitting machines. This led to her first independent coordinated fabric and knitwear collection. Building up a market was very time consuming, particularly as it meant shattering preconceptions of the role and potential of knitted garments. Increasing demand for her work led to the decision to move away from hand-knitting to full factory production. The change enabled Dallas to extend her range and output, but also affected the appearance of the fabrics and the finished garments; she did not favor the chunky, earthy look which characterized some hand knits. She was more concerned with creating interesting fabrics suitable for a classic fashion look. For her, fashion knitwear has always been about style.

Dallas' fabrics were usually produced using natural yarns; pure wool for winter and cotton for summer. She had yarns specially spun and dyed in England to match her own specifications and to provide an exact color palette. The basics were the classic neutrals, navy and black, but her talent was in enlivening them with current fashion tones. Black and white were combined in geometric patterns to create simple crew-necked sweaters highlighted by a bright colored handkerchief in a breast pocket—a detail which became a signature of her work.

The Dallas look consisted of bold classic shapes with a feel for current fashion. A concentration on detail and an accent on splashes of bright color characterized each collection. Her ranges sold at the middle and upper ends of the market, with a broad customer profile covering ages 20 to 60. This extensive range was due to the versatility of the look and the uncomplicated styling. Described as "New Classics," her designs won a British Design Council award in 1987.

Since she ceased to work under her own label, Dallas undertook freelance consultancy for British based companies and for those in other manufacturing centres such as Italy, Hong Kong, and China. She designed hand- and machine knit patterns for books and magazines. Much of her work was for Rowan Yarns, of Holafirth, West Yorkshire, creating patterns for people to knit at home. Her emphasis was still on clean lines and interesting yarns; a minimalist approach concentrating on using every element, yarn, color, and shape to its fullest extent in each design.

Dallas became a course leader of the new M.A. course in Fashion Knitwear and Knitted Textiles at the Royal College of Art in the early 1990s. Her intention was to develop the potential of knitted fabrics and fashion, especially since the recession affected knitwear sales quite severely. The future, in Sarah Dallas' view, was in machine knitting and in the use of factory techniques. Hand-knitting became too expensive for a depressed market and machines were increasingly sophisticated. Dallas continued to influence the direction of fashion knitwear through her teaching and her consulting work; each enabled her to preserve high standards and to prepare the way for a revival in knitwear and knitted fabrics.

—Hazel Clark

DANSKIN

American dancewear, activewear, and hosiery manufacturer

Founded: in 1882 by Joel and Benson Goodman in New York City. **Company History:** Founded as a dry goods store; imported hosiery items introduced in 1923. Specialty dance items such as leotards and nylon tights offered in the 1950s; Danskin sold by Goodman family to International Playtex, Inc. (part of Esmark, Inc.), 1980; Esmark bought by Beatrice Companies, Inc., 1984; Beatrice bought by Kohlberg Kravis Roberts & Company for $6.2 billion, 1986; Beatrice sells Danskin and Pennaco Hosiery units (as Esmark Apparel, Inc.) to Eaglewood Partners, 1986; named changed back to Danskin, Inc.; Danskin goes public, 1992; SunAmerica, Inc. acquires a 33.7-percent stake in Danskin, 1996; stock delisted by NASDAQ, 1997; Packables and Zen Sport lines introduced, 1999; acquired licenses for Ellen Tracy and Evan Picone hosiery lines, 2000. **Awards:** Coty award, 1978. **Company Address:** 530 Seventh Avenue, New York, NY 10018, USA. **Company Website:** www.danskin.com.

Publications

On DANSKIN:

Books

McGill, Leonard, *Disco Dressing,* Englewood Cliffs, New Jersey, 1980.

Articles

de Ribere, Lisa, "Danskins Are For Dancers," in *Dancemagazine*, October 1983.

Grieves, Robert T., "Stretching the Image," in *Forbes*, 18 April 1988.

Moore, Lila, "Danskin Leaps Back from the Bunk," in *Apparel Industry Magazine*, January 1993.

* * *

After many years of financial struggle, it looks as if Danskin may have the opportunity to pull in more of the activewear market with its Packables and Zen Sport yoga lines, combined with newer designer name hosiery lines. Trying not to place all of its eggs in one basket, Danskin will need a strong consumer reaction to pull itself up to the barre and out of a financially troublesome slump.

Danskin began as a small dry goods store founded in 1882 by Joel and Benson Goodman in New York City. The store found a niche in the dance apparel market by selling imported European hosiery and tights to local dancers of the time. Seizing the opportunity this demand presented, the Goodmans began to manufacture items specifically targeted to dancers, and it was soon apparent the Goodman brothers' operation dominated the dance industry market in America. The Goodmans were the first to introduce knit tights, fishnet stockings, and leotards, standardizing the popular colors designated as "Ballet Pink"and "Theatrical Pink."

During the 19th century and into the 20th, Danskin governed the dancewear market in the U.S. but it wasn't until the 1950s that Danskin acquired its trademark name. At that time, nylon was first introduced into the manufacture of hosiery, calling more attention than ever to the wearer's skin. Hence the name Danskin, a simple combination of the words "dance" and "skin." In 1952 Danskin offered a waist-to-toe tight, made of a versatile two-way stretch nylon. Soon the Danskin name was synonymous with dancewear and became the favorite apparel for skaters and gymnasts as well.

By the last years of the 1950s and the early 1960s, Danskin's name and products had become more mainstream. The company made resourceful changes to its bodysuit line by adding snap closures for expedience and revising the overall look of the bodysuit to make it more appealingly stylish to the casual wearer. The company launched its first public advertising campaign in the fall of 1958, with huge success; Danskin's most profitable item was fast becoming the nylon waist-to-toe tight.

Peter Goodman, the grandson of the original Goodmans, kept the Danskin operation lucrative during the remainder of the 1960s and throughout the 1970s. With more and more leg showing in the fashion world, the fitness and disco craze, and swimwear taking on the look of the leotard, it was easy for Danskin to live up to its ads, stating that Danskins weren't just for dancers anymore. For marketability's sake, Danskin started hosting athletic events to try and boost sales of their products. Danskin supported everything from universal skills rating tests for gymnastics to the very popular triathlons of today. Coupled with advertising campaigns featuring popular athletic and Olympic personalities, sent scores of children to the balance beam and the ballet barre, and an equal number of adults to the workout room. Department stores began incorporating athletic wear and hosiery sections into their stores, and have since become commonplace markets for Danskin products.

Danskin lost its privately owned status when it was sold to International Playtex, Inc. in April 1980. Esmark, founded in 1972, was the parent company of International Playtex and was itself acquired four years later by Beatrice Companies, Inc. in 1984. Beatrice, however, was soon in financial turmoil and Danskin was put on the back burner. By 1985 Beatrice announced its intention to sell off all of its knitwear operations, including Danskin. In anticipation of this event, Beatrice paired Danskin with another Esmark apparel component, Pennaco Hosiery, to form Esmark Apparel, Inc. in February 1986. A few months later, Beatrice announced the successful sale of their knitwear division to the Eaglewood Partners investment group.

At the time of the sale, Esmark Apparel, Inc. (which included Danskin), maintained the greatest portion of the feminine exercise clothing business. In charge of Esmark was Byron A. Hero, who had grandiose plans for expanding the company. Hero's expansion banked on the names and reputations of Danskin and Pennaco Hosiery, and he was determined to infuse company proceeds into expanding operations and market infiltration. By the end of 1986, Esmark purchased Dance France Ltd. which was merged with Danskin's operations. With the aid of a huge ad campaign in 1987, Danskin unveiled its first line of plus-sized dancewear with Danskin-Plus, and promoted a line of short, tight-fitting dresses. Esmark's next move was the purchase of Repetto France, a specialty ballet shoe and tutu manufacturer, as well as the license to distribute Givenchy hosiery overseas. Business was profitable for a time, and Esmark Apparel changed its name back to Danskin in July 1992.

In order to raise capital for more expansion, the company went public with three million shares in 1992, to the tune of $13 a share. For the next couple years Danskin was able to turn a profit until the final quarter of 1994 when Hero took out a loan from SunAmerica, Inc. with the idea of broadening Danskin's athletic swimwear products. When plans fell apart, financial turmoil quickly followed. Hero stepped down from daily operations but retained the title of chairman, and was replaced by Howard D. Cooley, former president of International Jockey. When the SunAmerica loans came due and Danskin was unable to pay, SunAmerica took control of a 34-percent stake of the company and put it up for sale.

Incapacitated by overwhelming debt and several changes in leadership, Danskin finally fell under the control of an investment group led by Onyx Partners in 1997, which controlled about three-quarters of the company. In an effort to attract more consumers and boost sales in a declining hosiery market, Danskin acquired licenses for several top designer hosiery labels, including Ralph Lauren. Next the company initiated its "Packables" line in February of 1999, followed by the Zen Sport yoga line in August. By May 2000 *Brandweek* reported that Danskin had brought Barry Tartarkin aboard with a deal to license both the Ellen Tracy and Evan Picone hosiery lines. Despite questionable decisions and financial missteps, Danskin executives maintained hope that it wasn't too late for the dance and activewear pioneer.

—Sandra Schroeder

DAVIES, George

See NEXT PLC

de CASTELBAJAC, Jean-Charles

See CASTELBAJAC, Jean-Charles de

de GIVENCHY, Hubert

See GIVENCHY, Hubert de

de la RENTA, Oscar

Dominican designer working in New York

Born: Santo Domingo, Dominican Republic, 22 July 1932. **Education:** Studied art, National School of Art, Santo Domingo, 1950–52; Academia de San Fernando, Madrid, 1953–55. **Family:** Married Françoise de Langlade, 1967 (died, 1983); married Annette Reed, 1989; children: Moises. **Career:** Staff designer under Balenciaga, Madrid, from 1949; assistant designer to Antonio Castillo, Lanvin-Castillo, Paris, 1961–63; designer, Elizabeth Arden couture and ready-to-wear, New York, 1963–65; partner/designer, Jane Derby Inc., New York, 1965–69; designer/chief executive, Oscar de la Renta Couture, Oscar de la Renta II, de la Renta Furs and Jewelry, Oscar de la Renta Ltd., from 1973; introduced signature perfume, 1977, followed by *Ruffles,* 1983, and *Volupté,* 1991; owner, de la Renta specialty shop, Santo Domingo, from 1968; designer, couture collection for Balmain, from 1992. **Exhibitions:** *Versailles 1973: American Fashion on the World Stage,* Metropolitan Museum of

Oscar de la Renta, fall 2001 collection: shearling coat, cashmere halter dress, and feather beaded boots. © AFP/CORBIS.

Art, 1993. **Awards:** Coty American Fashion Critics award, 1967, 1973; Coty Return award, 1968; Neiman Marcus award, 1968; Golden Tiberius award, 1969; American Printed Fabrics Council "Tommy" award, 1971; Caballero of the Order of Juan Pablo Duarte, and Gran Comandante of the Order of Cristobal Colón, Dominican Republic, 1972; Fragrance Foundation award, 1978. **Address:** 550 Seventh Avenue, New York, NY 10018, U.S.A. **Website:** www.oscardelarenta.com.

Publications

On de la RENTA:

Books

Morris, Bernadine, and Barbara Walz, *The Fashion Makers,* New York, 1978.
Diamonstein, Barbaralee, *Fashion: The Inside Story,* New York, 1985.
Milbank, Caroline Rennolds, *Couture: The Great Designers,* New York, 1985.
Perschetz, Lois, ed., *W, The Designing Life,* New York, 1987.
Coleridge, Nicholas, *The Fashion Conspiracy,* London, 1988.

Oscar de la Renta, fall 2001 collection: feather and beaded slip dress. © AP/Wide World Photos.

Milbank, Caroline Rennolds, *New York Fashion: The Evolution of American Style,* New York, 1989.
Martin, Richard, and Harold Koda, *Orientalism: Visions of the East in Western Dress* [exhibition catalogue], New York, 1994.
Stegemeyer, Anne, *Who's Who in Fashion, Third Edition,* New York, 1996.
Carrillo, Louis, *Oscar de la Renta,* Austin, Texas, 1996.

Articles

Greenstein, S., "The Business of Being Oscar," in *Vogue,* May 1982.
"Françoise de la Renta," [obituary], in *Variety,* 22 June 1983.
Kornbluth, Jesse, "The Working Rich: The Real Slaves of New York," in *New York,* 24 November 1986.
Bentley, Vicci, "King of Ruffles," in *Woman's Journal* (London), November 1987.
Gross, Michael, "A Fitting with Oscar," in *New York,* 18 April 1988.
Howell, Georgina, "Charmed Circles," in *Vogue,* September 1989.
Hirshey, Gerri, "The Snooty Dame at the Block Party," in the *New York Times Magazine,* 24 October 1993.
Schiro, Anne-Marie, "Tasteful Comes in Many Colors," in the *New York Times,* 4 November 1994.
Beckett, Kathleen, "Runway Report: My One and Only Hue—Oscar de la Renta," in the *New York Post,* 4 November 1994.
"New York: Oscar de la Renta," in *WWD,* 4 November 1994.
"New York: Oscar de la Renta," in *WWD,* 7 April 1995.
Brown, Jeanette, "From Looking Good to Doing Good," in *Business Week,* 9 November 1998.
"The Look of Oscar de la Renta," in *InStyle,* 1 February 2001.
Horyn, Cathy, "Creating a Fantasy Life Beyond the Seams," in the *New York Times,* 14 February 2001.
Lockwood, Lisa, "Oscar's Evolutionary Theory," in *WWD,* 13 June 2001.
"Oscar's Winners," in *Town & Country,* July 2001.
"Casa de la Renta," in *InStyle,* 1 August 2001.
"Fashion of the Times," in the *New York Times,* Autumn 2001.
"Fall 2001 Ready to Wear," available online at Style.com, 28 October 2001.

* * *

Although he was born in the Dominican Republic and moved to New York at the age of 30, Oscar de la Renta has become a great ambassador for American fashion. His appointment as designer to the French couture house of Pierre Balmain in 1992 was a historic occasion—the first time an American designer had been commissioned by French haute couture. The choice in many ways reflected the growing eminence of New York as a fashion force and the international status of American designers.

As a designer, de la Renta has inspired many international trends. During the 1960s, his clothes were elaborate and witty parodies of experimental street fashion: jackets and coats of bandanna-printed denim, embroidered hot pants under silk minidresses, or caftans made out of silk chiffon and psychedelic silk saris. He was largely responsible for initiating the ethnic fashion of the 1970s with gypsy and

Russian fashion themes incorporating fringed shawls, boleros, peasant blouses, and full skirts. In the 1990s de la Renta was popular for his romantic evening clothes, glamorous, elegant, and made from richly opulent fabrics such as brocade, transparent chiffon, fox fur, ermine, and embroidered faille.

Throughout his career, de la Renta has concentrated on simple shapes and silhouettes to create dramatic and flashy statements. He has an inherent feeling for women's femininity and established fashion classics, such as variations of his portrait dresses in taffeta, chiffon, or velvet with ruffled necklines or cuffs, or his ornate luncheon suits, embroidered in costume jewelry and gold. Since founding his own company in 1967 to produce luxury women's ready-to-wear, de la Renta expanded to create jewelry, household linens, menswear, and perfumes. These products are marketed and sold all over Europe, Asia, and South and North America.

The designer had a well-traveled international fashion pedigree before establishing his own label business. He studied art at the Academia de San Fernando in Madrid and began sketching for leading Spanish fashion houses, leading to a job at Balenciaga's Madrid couture house, Eisa. A move to Paris in 1961 brought him work as an assistant to Antonio De Castillo at Lanvin-Castillo. He moved with Castillo to New York in 1963 to design at Elizabeth Arden. Joining Jane Derby Inc. as a partner in 1965, he began operating as Oscar de la Renta Ltd. in 1973.

His first marriage to the late Françoise de la Langlade, editor-in-chief of French *Vogue,* in 1967 was an undoubted asset to de la Renta's business. Together they created soirées that were the equivalent of 18th-century salons. The environment enhanced the wearing of an Oscar de la Renta creation and provided valuable publicity, with frequent mentions in society columns. He has not forgotten his Dominican associations though and has been honored as its best-known native son and one of its most distinguished citizens with the Order de Merito de Juan Pablo Duarte. He also helped build a much needed school and daycare center in the republic for over 350 children.

Still designing in New York today, de la Renta continued to redefine American elegance with his famous womenswear line, Signature; the couture line, Studio; his ready-to-wear, and a range of sophisticated dresses and suits known as Miss. When in 2001 a signature line of accessories by de la Renta made its debut on the New York fashion scene, the designer was asked once again to describe the forces that influenced his design and sensibility. He told the *New York Times*' "Fashion of the Times" column about the two places he lived as a child and young man, the Dominican Republic and Spain, and how they dramatically affected his work: "From my island side comes my love for the exotic, for color and light. From my Spanish side comes my love of gypsies and bullfighters," he said. And indeed, the new line of accessories—bags and shoes, boots and belts—repeats motifs familiar in de la Renta's earliest designs.

The drama and sexiness of high fashion is not ignored even in the simplest accessory. There is, after 36 years of design, a kind of rebirth for de la Renta in his accessories collection: "As clothes become more minimalist, you can tell who a woman really is by her accessories." And de la Renta's signature formula of casual, feminine, graceful, and comfortable yet elegant clothes prevails. If a design itself is very simple, then the materials used are luxurious. Utilitarian boots, for example, take on an entirely new status with heavy embroidery. If a particular design is complicated, then de la Renta edits the colors or the fabrics to produce a consistently wearable and classic line of clothing and accessories.

In 2001 de la Renta launched a fall collection for Balmain combining his love of the ethnic influence (Spanish-Russian) with hot colors and sleek sophisticated styling. Oscar de la Renta continues to be a major presence in the contemporary fashionable world.

—Kevin Almond; updated by Kathleen Bonann Marshall

DELL'OLIO, Louis

American fashion designer

Born: New York, 23 July 1948. **Education:** Graduated from Parsons School of Design, 1969. **Career:** Intern for Norman Norell, 1965; assistant at Teal Traina, 1969–71; designer for Originala's Giorgini

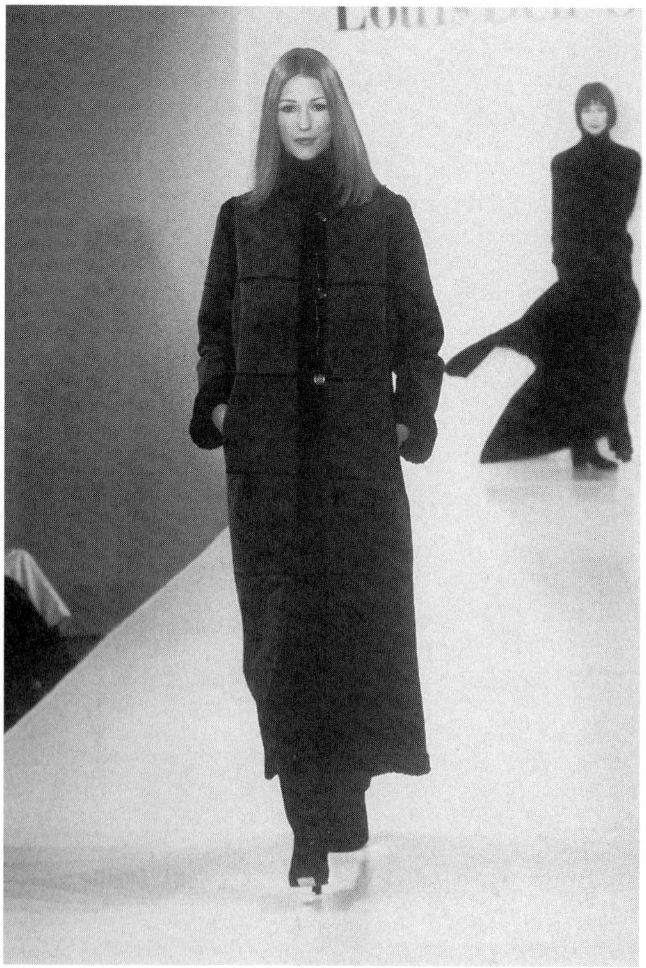

Louis Dell'Olio, fall 1999 fur collection. © Fashion Syndicate Press.

and Ginori divisions, 1971–74; joined Anne Klein as codesigner with Donna Karan, 1974; took over as sole designer for Anne Klein after Karan's departure, 1984; left Anne Klein, replaced by Richard Tyler, 1993; spent time working with CFDA's Fashion Targets Breast Cancer initiative, 1993–96; created Dei Tre collection for Bergdorf Goodman, Neiman Marcus, and Holt Renfrew, 1996; launched outerwear collection, 1997; introduced exclusive collection for QVC, 2000. **Awards:** Parsons Gold Thimble award, 1969; Coty American Fashion Critics awards (all with Donna Karan), 1977, 1982, and 1984. **Address:** 435 Ocean Drive, Stamford, CT 06902, U.S.A.

Publications

On DELL'OLIO:

Books

Stegemeyer, Anne, *Who's Who in Fashion, Third Edition,* New York, 1996.

Louis Dell'Olio, fall 1999 fur collection. © Fashion Syndicate Press.

Articles

Dougherty, Margot, "Making Anne Klein Click," in *Life,* November 1982.
Conant, Jennet, "The Man Behind Anne Klein," in *Newsweek,* 3 November 1986.
Gross, Michael, "Louis Who?" in *New York,* 17 October 1988.
Morris, Bernadine, "The Dell'Olio Formula: Start with the Classic, Then Add Aggression," in the *New York Times,* 15 November 1988.
———, "From Louis Dell'Olio, Clean Cuts and Colors," in the *New York Times,* 14 April 1989.
Capitain, Jenny, "Louis the First," in *Vogue,* February 1990.
Staples, Kate, "Louis Dell'Olio: Back in Form," in *WWD,* 26 June 1991.
Morris Bernadine, "Dell'Olio's Soft Spin Enlivens Sportswear," in the *New York Times,* 6 November 1992.
Rourke, Mary, "Made for the U.S.A. Designer," in the *Los Angeles Times,* 22 February 1993.
White, Constance C.R., "Easy Transition is Top Property at Anne Klein," in *WWD,* 5 May 1993.
Ozzard, Janet, "Accento Americano," in *WWD,* 9 August 1995.
———, "Dell'Olio's New Gig," in *WWD,* 10 July 1996.
Daria, Irene, "Dell'Olio: The Rush to Be Creative," in *WWD,* 5 January 1997.
Wilson, Eric, "Dell'Olio Unwraps Outerwear," in *WWD,* 9 April 1997.
Ozzard, Janet, "Dell'Olio Fashions Collections for QVC," in *WWD,* 2 May 2000.

* * *

Louis Dell'Olio is acknowledged as one of the leading American women's sportswear designers, creating wearable and commercial pieces that feature the classic lines typical of sportswear yet manage innovative twists to set them apart. Dell'Olio has achieved the rare distinction of being loved by critics and consumers alike.

Dell'Olio made his name first as codesigner (with Donna Karan) and then as lead designer at Anne Klein, the label launched by the legendary American sportswear designer. After Klein's death in 1974, Karan, who had been her assistant, asked longtime friend Dell'Olio—who had attended Parsons School of Design with her—to become her codesigner at Klein. The partners were just a few years out of Parsons when they took over the firm. Their first collections were not highly regarded; they designed initially by trying to emulate what they imagined Klein would do.

After a few years, the two designers broke away from traditional Klein wares and began to come into their own, designing a series of critically acclaimed collections. Consumers embraced the brand, and sales grew robustly. When Karan left in 1986 to launch her own label, Dell'Olio took over as the sole designer for Anne Klein. Although retailers and the fashion press wondered if the quiet designer would be able to maintain the company's high reputation and sales, their fears were put to rest after the first few collections. Critics proclaimed Dell'Olio's work became stronger over time, and customers must have agreed, because he ultimately took his place as the bestselling American designer. Anne Klein under Dell'Olio grew to a $200-million wholesale brand in sportswear alone, enhanced by another $250 million in sales of licensed products.

As the president of Bergdorf Goodman told the *New York Times* (15 November 1988), "[Dell'Olio] understands the needs of women in all walks of life. He makes clothes that are fashionably up to date but that a woman can feel she will be able to wear the next year. And his business is growing." Retailers have always appreciated Dell'Olio's penchant for listening to their needs. His interest extends to the business side of fashion as much as to the creative side.

Bernardine Morris, writing in the *New York Times* (6 November 1992), noted Dell'Olio's ability to create familiar and comfortable apparel, yet at the same time use innovative designs. "Serene and comforting as the show was to watch," she said of his spring 1993 collection (one of his last for Anne Klein), "the clothes still looked different from what women already have in their wardrobes. But they didn't look fussy or overdesigned. Just soft, basic shapes that could be combined in different ways, the basic premise of sportswear dressing."

Dell'Olio's designs are purposely American in sensibility; he is known for taking European designs and Americanizing them. Many of his collections have a certain masculine quality—such as boxy shoulders on his blazers, always a core item in his sportswear lines—and he has favored apparel that is flattering and make women feel sexy yet fully dressed. These clothes are targeted at upscale working women, with celebrities ranging from Oprah Winfrey to Cher (in her more serious moments). In addition to blazers, other core items include narrow pants, turtleneck sweaters, and wraparound skirts in black, ivory, and neutrals, set off by the occasional burst of color (such as an all-red series that stood out in one of his collections).

Dell'Olio left Anne Klein in 1993 to pursue his own collections, replaced by Richard Tyler, who the company hoped would take the brand into younger, more exciting directions. Dell'Olio had, some criticized, started to have an element of sameness in his clothes each season. Retailers were taken by surprise at the transition, which both Anne Klein executives and Dell'Olio stressed was his decision. Unfortunately for Klein, the departure of Dell'Olio marked a downward slide for the retailer, and Tyler was soon ousted. Dell'Olio, however, began to forge alliances with a range of companies through consulting and licensing agreements. He became a consultant for Italian sportswear manufacturer Marzotto, helping it hone its bridge line, Accento, especially for the U.S. market. He launched a collection called Dei Tre exclusively for Bergdorf Goodman, Neiman Marcus, and the Canadian chain Holt Renfrew, which he designed with the input of the retailers.

Dell'Olio also started to expand into categories outside sportswear. He created a licensed line of outerwear for the Tepper Collection (the contract transferred to Androu when Tepper shut down), in which he took sportswear looks and translated them into moderate-priced stadium jackets, bathrobe coats, and other items under the Louis Dell'Olio Luxe and LDO Studio labels. He also expanded into furs and shearlings with Legar. In 2000, Dell'Olio began an alliance with the television shopping network QVC for an exclusive line of moderate separates and dresses under the Linea by Louis Dell'Olio label. The partners planned four collections a year, with Dell'Olio appearing on QVC to help promote the line.

All of Dell'Olio's new ventures remained true to his desire to create wearable, consumer-friendly women's clothes, although they tended to show more of a focus on color than his previous work. His reputation for quality craftsmanship and good fit, built during his 18 years at Anne Klein, remains strong.

—Karen Raugust

DEMEULEMEESTER, Ann

Belgian designer

Born: Kortrijk, Belgium, 29 December 1959. **Education:** Studied at the Royal Academy of Fine Arts, Antwerp, 1978–81. **Family:** Married Patrick Robyn; son: Victor. **Career:** Showed first collection of women's ready-to-wear, 1981; freelance designer for international ready-to-wear men's and women's collections, 1981–87; founded B.V.B.A. "32" company with husband, 1985; has also designed shoes, handbags, sunglasses and accessories since 1987, outerwear since 1989, knitwear since 1991; opened Paris showroom, 1992; opened first store in Antwerp, 1999; one of initial labels in Galeries

Ann Demeulemeester, fall 2000 collection. © AP/Wide World Photos/Fashion Wire Daily.

Lafayette Vibre concept, 2000; introduced bold color into her spring collections, 2000. **Exhibitions:** *La bienale de venise avec Rodney Graham,* Anvers, 1993. **Awards:** Golden Spindle award, Belgium, 1983; Golden T award, Spain, 1992. **Address:** B.V.B.A. "32," Populeerenlaan 34, B-2020 Antwerp, Belgium.

PUBLICATIONS

On DEMEULEMEESTER:

Articles

Mower, Sarah, "Six Romp," in *The Guardian* (London), 12 February 1987.

Grauman, Brigid, "The Belgium Connection," in *Elle* (London), October 1987.

"Ann Demeulemeester en grande," in *Le Nouvel Observateur,* 15 November 1991.

Betts, Katherine, "La Nouvelle Vague," in *Vogue,* September 1992.

Sepulchre, Cécile, "Ann Demeulemeester," in *Journal du Textile,* 12 October 1992.

Dombrowicz, Laurent, and Pascale Renaux, "Ann Demeulemeester, belle et rebelle," in *Jardin des Modes,* November 1992.

Spindler, Amy M., "Three Designers Thrive on Fashion's Unraveled Edge," in *New York Times,* 15 March 1993.

Mair, Avril, "This is the New Vision," in *i-D* (London), 11 May 1993.

Spindler, Amy M., "Coming Apart," in *New York Times,* 25 July 1993.

"Trois créateurs: Ann Demeulemeester," in *Arte Magazine,* 27 November–3 December 1993.

"La Cote des Createurs: Les 'baroques' sont plébiscites par les boutiques," in *Journal du Textile,* 28 February 1994.

"The Paris Collections: The Ideas of March: Ann Demeulemeester," in *Women's Wear Daily,* 17 March 1995.

Spindler, Amy M., "A Mature Mugler, Demeulemeester and Lang," in the *New York Times,* 18 March 1995.

"Tales of Paris," in *Women's Wear Daily,* 16 October 1998.

Raper, Sarah, "Ann of Antwerp," in *Women's Wear Daily,* 4 October 1999.

"Tales of Paris,"*Women's Wear Daily,* 3 March 2000.

Ann Demeulemeester, fall 2000 collection. © AP/Wide World Photos/Fashion Wire Daily.

* * *

Linked to a group of designers to come out of Belgium in the mid-1980s, Ann Demeulemeester's deconstructed style has come into its own as the 1990s have progressed. Her work, with its monochromatic color schemes and matt layering onto the body of flowing columns of fabric, encapsulates the contemporary *Zeitgeist.*

The impact of this Belgian avant garde designer's pared-down structure, combining rough edges with more traditionally cut suiting, has been comparable to that of Japanese designers Kawakubo and Yamamoto a decade earlier. Both superseded more overtly designed fashions in favor of purer silhouettes combining references to antique clothing with the worn-in patina of their fabrics and a disregard for the more conventional notions of fit.

Demeulemeester's work represents (along with Margiela, Dries Van Noten, et al) a recognizable 1990s approach to clothing and designer style. It overtakes the often directionless attempts to integrate the sportswear styles of the late 1980s into a high-fashion context and the myriad of 1970s reworkings in the early 1990s. Dedicated to this more experimental strain of fashion, Demeulemeester, having won early accolades for her designs while still at college, pays great attention to detail. From the start she used local craftsmen to create her work. In the late 1980s her designs were more attuned to fashionable classic garments. In 1987 short, black, sunray-pleated skirts were shown with crossover braces and crisp white shirts, worn with stark gabardine coats. Even at this stage, however, she showed concern for proportion, constructing skirts and dresses with adjustable waistlines that could be worn high or low, altering the emphasis of the design to suit the figure of the wearer and give a different sense of balance to the overall outfit.

The appeal of designs which are at the cutting edge of fashion and yet ultimately still wearable has ensured Demeulemeester's success, and, as her work has grown in confidence, so have her sales. The strong lines of her signature long coats and dresses are punctuated by more deconstructed styles like the frayed-edged lacy knit top shoe showed in 1993. This, with its shrunken fit, married the resurgent punk ethos of rough, makeshift antifashion to the languorous swing of gothic-inspired floor-skimming coats.

Her autumn-winter collection for 1993 continued in this vein. Shroud-like white dresses with overlong cuffs and black velvet and brocade coats were set against fitted crêpe sheaths, their differing textures giving a sense of shade and light to provide interest and definition to each outfit. The trumpet cuffs and jet crucifixes with which these were teamed gave a religious aspect to the show which was echoed amongst her contemporaries.

Although there will inevitably be a backlash against such austerity, Demeulemeester's work is strong enough to outlive short-term trends and consolidate her name as a designer of avant-garde independent styles, incorporating an artistic use of fabric and texture and an attention to detail.

Demeulemeester's first dedicated store opened in her hometown of Antwerp in 1999 and features both her men's and women's collections. She wanted her first store to be close to home so she could be there as much as possible, rather than opening in a more high-profile location such as New York. The store, housed in a historic building, has an interior design that reflects the fabrics and draping typical of her clothing.

The designer's fashion-forward reputation has placed her in many retail locations specializing in cutting-edge designers. She was one of the initial labels, for example, in the Vibre concept shop launched in 2000 by Paris-based Galeries Lafayette.

Demeulemeester maintains total control over her business. Unlike many other labels, she does not license but rather oversees most production and all creation and distribution in-house. Her operation is self-financed and has grown slowly according to plan. She has been successful internationally, as well, especially in Asia, where Japan, Singapore, South Korea, and Hong Kong together represent one-fifth of total turnover.

Demeulemeester's clothes are often termed minimalist, yet they sometimes feature a certain amount of complexity. In the late 1990s, her twist tank tops and handkerchief-wrap dresses—which typify her love of twisting and asymmetrical silhouettes—came with instructions. She loves a variety of unusual fabrics, such as painter's canvas, parachute nylon, polished leather, washed denim and distressed suede. Her interest in unusual fabrics adds a surprising amount of diversity to all-white or all-black ensembles. She takes simple items such as a t-shirt or slacks and gives them an almost sculptural feel, often through the use of innovative surface treatments. Her accessories designs are also critically acclaimed.

Some critics have commented that Demeulemeester seemed out of sync with trends at the turn of the century, creating similar spiraling, draping, asymmetrically hanging, and often monochromatic clothing year after year. This was one concern with her spring 2000 collection, at which *Women's Wear Daily* pointed out that one of the few surprises was her bold and bright use of color.

Yet Demeulemeester remains true to her own vision, creating smart clothing independent of fashion trends. And her loyal cadre of customers, including rocker Patti Smith (who has influenced many of her designs), appreciate her simple, wearable, and relaxed apparel, which, despite its practicality, has an aura of cool.

—Rebecca Arnold; updated by Karen Raugust

de PRÉMONVILLE, Myrène

French designer

Born: Pays Basque region of France, 1949. **Career:** Assistant to Popy Moreni; freelance designer; designer, Prémonville et Dewavrin, from 1983; also freelance designer for Fiorucci; chose Michael Atchison & Associates, Inc. as the first American agency to represent her designs, 1989; opened first boutique in Paris, 1990; opened New York boutique, 1991; opened Munich boutique, 1992. **Address:** 52 Boulevard Richard Lenoir, 75001 Paris, France.

Publications

On de PRÉMONVILLE:

Books

Stegemeyer, Anne, *Who's Who in Fashion, Third Edition,* New York, 1996.

Articles

Bogart, Anne, and Leslie Cochran, "Paris: de Prémonville's Spare Chic Suits Stand Out," in *WWD,* 17 October 1985.

"The Young French Fashion Fever; in Paris, the Mood is All-Out Flair," in *Harper's Bazaar,* June 1986.

Joby, Liz, "Designing Women: Myrène de Prémonville," in *Vogue* (London), July 1987.

"Prémonville Tabs Exclusive Agent for U.S.," in *WWD,* 14 March 1989.

Voight, Rebecca, "Paris: Moving and Shaking," in *WWD,* 19 September 1989.

Edelson, Sharon, "Retailers Say Bridge Sales Keep Growing," in *WWD,* 18 September 1994.

Ozzard, Janet, "Showroom with a View," in *WWD,* 10 September 1997.

"Vintage Sewing Patterns—1960s to the Present," available online at the *Blue Gardenia,*www.thebluegardenia.com, 17 July 2001.

* * *

"Great feel, beautiful proportions, fantastic color," declared Myrène de Prémonville stockist Carole Cruvellier, whose Manchester, England, shop, de la Mode, stocks exclusively French designers. "I particularly remember a petrol blue trouser suit, with a wine cuff, that seemed to sum up her meticulous research and use of color," she said. Lucille Lewin of the Whistles shops in London, who backed the opening of Myrène de Prémonville's first British boutique in 1991, enthuses about her superb cut. She believes the clothes have a longevity that makes economic sense to the customer, always flattering, yet never trite; not classic, they are collectable for their quirky individuality.

Myrène de Prémonville began her company in the mid-1980s, with Giles Dewavrin as partner. Backed by a large finance group, the Union Normand Investissement, her first designs were a response to what she felt was not available to women at that time: effervescent, young, tailored suits in bright colors, often with witty contrasting color trims or bright check details; unexpected colored appliqués on bright white, translucent blouses; a huge, painted sunflower detail on a cream georgette mini tunic, teamed with black leggings. She even introduced her own stirrup trousers because, as she said at the time, "No one else's felt comfortable."

There is always a hint of 1950s couture in her work but never heavy or overly structured. She brings a younger, lighter, more modernistic feel to miniskirted frock coats in yellow wool, with Balenciaga-style gathered sleeves. Full skirted jackets with huge belts, reminiscent of Doris Day shirtwaists, and a pastel, deckchair-striped trouser suit looked perfect for a 1950s into 1990s St. Tropez. Very concerned with practicalities of the fashion business, de Prémonville's positions at Hermès, then at Fiorucci, strengthened her appreciation of vivid color and kitsch, both prominently combined in her designs today. She sees her customer as being practical yet artistically and intellectually aware, with a witty sense of fun, very much an extension of her own personality. This also explains why her designs are often a reaction to what she feels her wardrobe lacks.

She believes that a designer's work should evolve, rather than change radically, each season. Gradual alterations in detailing, proportion, and silhouette are the key to de Prémonville's appeal. She has looked to English eccentricity for inspiration, feeling that the French have become opposed to change and somewhat institutionalized in their dress sense. Conclusively it is the suit that emerges as the signature Myrène de Prémonville garment. Sharp, quirky, and geometric, it has been restyled and restructured for the 1980s and 1990s woman.

In March 1989, the de Prémonville firm chose designer and bridge showroom manager Michael Atchison & Associates, Inc. as the first American agency to represent its continental styles. Valued for its wide range of inventive shapes and elegant, feminine lines, the French house banked on Prémonville Studio, a restrained, fundamental suit collection, which debuted in a variety of fabrics. In 1997, Atchison spread the entire collection along with the clothing lines of youthful stylists Donald Deal, Eric Gasking, Eva Chun, and Sylvia Heisel. He anticipated that his appealing 24th-floor studio on Seventh Avenue South overlooking the Hudson River would draw $5 million worth of business from the metropolitan fashion savvy. Of his capture of a stable of young designers, Atchison exulted, "It's great. It means they're successful." He characterized customers for the Myrène de Prémonville look as "young, fashionable, Park Avenue day-into-evening."

The Vogue pattern company honored de Prémonville by including her designs in Vogue Attitudes, a selection of vintage fashions for seamstresses to sew at home. Featured along with Calvin Klein skirts and slacks, a Ralph Lauren skirt and blouse, and a Chloé dress was a de Prémonville jacket and pants outfit, pictured in op-art bold black-on-white structured jacket and understated dark pants. Vogue's Internet archive pictured de Prémonville's red and white hussar jacket as a facet of the 1987 military trend.

—Kevin Almond; updated by Mary Ellen Snodgrass

de RIBES, Jacqueline

French designer

Born: Jacqueline de Beaumont in Paris, 1931. **Education:** Studied architecture. **Family:** Married Comte Edouard de Ribes, 1947; children: Elizabeth, Jean. **Career:** Freelance fashion designer, Paris, from 1982; showed first collection, 1983; jewelry collection introduced, 1984; continued to show designs publicly and privately, 1990s; remained active in charity circuit. **Awards:** Rodeo Drive award, Los Angeles, 1985.

Publications

On de RIBES:

Books

Nars, François, and André Leon Talley, *X-Ray,* New York, 1999.
Seren, François-Xavier, *Noblesse Oblige: Intimate Portraits of European Nobility, 1985–2000,* New York, 2001.

Articles

"Parisienne," in *Holiday* (Philadelphia), January 1956.
Donovan, Carrie, "Social Graces," in the *New York Times Magazine,* 10 July 1983.
"Jacqueline de Ribes Style: Allure and Tradition," in *Vogue,* May 1984.
Morris, Bernadine, "Jacqueline de Ribes Had a Design Suited to Success," in the *New York Times,* 30 September 1985.
Shapiro, Harriet, "Going from Riches to Rags, Designing Vicomtesse Jacqueline de Ribes Reaps as She Sews: Handsomely," in *People Weekly,* 16 December 1985.
"Jacqueline de Ribes," in *Harper's Bazaar,* April 1986.
Connet, Jennet, "The Social Sewing Circle; Those Designing Blue Bloods Get Ever so Haute," in the *Newsweek,* 30 July 1986.
Morris, Bernadine, "Laurent: Classic Canon, Soberly Restated—Yves Saint Laurent, Patrick Kelly, and Jacqueline de Ribes," in the *New York Times,* 24 March 1988.
Dryansky, G.Y., "Jacqueline de Ribes Jewelry: Specially for the Upper Crust," in *Connoisseur,* April 1988.
Bogart, Anne, "Regal Air," in *Harper's Bazaar,* September 1989.
Menkes, Suzy, "Couture's Grand Ladies," in the *Illustrated London News,* Spring 1990.
"Jacqueline de Ribes," in *Town & Country,* September 1995.
Hollander, Anne, "Viva la Haute Couture! Reports of Its Demise Have Been Greatly Exaggerated," available online at Slate.com, www.slate.com, 10 Decemeber 1997.
Menkes, Suzy, "Couture in Euroland: A New Confidence in Gallic Chic," in the *International Herald Tribune,* 19 January 1999.
Glueck, Grace, "François-Xavier Seren—*Noblesse Oblige: Intimate Portraits of European Nobility, 1985–2000* [review], 13 July 2001.

* * *

When the January 1956 *Holiday* magazine featured Vicomtesse Jacqueline de Ribes in the series "The Most Fashionable Women" she was, at the age of 25, already recognized for her good taste in clothes. Even then she favored line and color over excessive detail. Growing up in privileged surroundings, she had worn couture all of her life, secretly harboring a desire to become a fashion designer herself, an occupation unsuitable for someone of her status.

Throughout her life de Ribes had been making suggestions to the couturiers who dressed her, bringing sketches, making changes, so when she took the plunge and produced a collection for fall 1983, she was using all of her years of exposure to haute couture, synthesizing with it her own carefully developed aesthetic taste. It helped that another society woman, Carolina Herrera, had successfully entered the fashion business two years before.

Known as a great beauty with an aristocratic profile and demeanor, possessed of a tall, long-necked, slender figure, de Ribes designed what she knew best: evening dresses and sophisticated daytime suits.

The gowns were long, slim, with shoulder interest consisting of dramatic ruffles, drapes, or simple bows. Tailored suits were detailed with black velvet. The clothes were expensive ready-to-wear, each suit or gown priced at thousands of dollars. Clearly de Ribes was designing for herself, and for women with her money and physical elegance. The clothes were well received in Paris and especially by American buyers. Critics did point out that de Ribes's work showed the clear influence of Saint Laurent, Dior, Cardin, and Valentino. She knew, nevertheless, how to create elements to focus on her own special "look."

Consistent with her emphasis on color and line, de Ribes continued to design plain, almost severe, dinner suits in bright pastel satins. Her gowns of unadorned bright or deep colors became the perfect background for her next venture—jewelry. To maintain her own less-is-more philosophy, de Ribes turned to designing jewelry deliberately made of nonprecious materials such as rhinestones, beads, fake pearls, even ceramics. Her clients had adequate supplies of real jewelry; de Ribes' designs were a chunky, modern, dramatic, perfect adornment for her clothes.

Even lace could find an eye-catching use in a slim black de Ribes gown featuring a V-shaped bodice and side insertions of see-through fabric. The highest of compliments was paid to the designer when Carolyne Roehm, another socialite designer of the late 1980s, created a long black evening gown featuring sections of sheer black georgette in a similar fashion. By 1990 de Ribes had softened her look, her evening gowns began to be made of gathered, draped bodices and yards of sherbet-hued chiffon. An even younger look evolved the next year with the introduction of above-the-knee cocktail dresses, with seductive side draping or flouncy layered organza.

In the late 1990s de Ribes traveled to show fashions at charity balls; she remained her own best advertisement. Though she had slowed her pace, she was always impeccably dressed and commanded attention. As a testament to her skills as a designer, former fashion wild child Jean-Paul Gaultier, who had harnessed his bad-boy energy into beautifully tailored collections, not only cited de Ribes as a major inspiration but dedicated his spring/summer 1999 show to her. "I was flattered that he dedicated the show to me," de Ribes told Suzy Menkes of the *International Herald Tribune* in January 1999. "It was fun, young, elegant, and modern all at the same time—and that's not easy."

Jacqueline de Ribes, as socialite and designer was prominently profiled in two recent books, *X-Ray,* by photographer François Nars and André Leon Talley (1999) and François-Xavier Seren's *Noblesse Oblige: Intimate Portraits of European Nobility, 1985–2000* (2001). Both featured a perfectly coiffed, bejeweled, and flawlessly dressed de Ribes, creating a striking and unforgettable image of the designer.

—Therese Duzinkiewicz Baker; updated by Nelly Rhodes

de SENNEVILLE, Elisabeth

French fashion designer

Born: Paris, 16 October 1946. **Education:** Studied at Notre Dame des Oiseaux school in Paris. **Family:** Children: Loup, Zoé. **Exhibitions:** *Elisabeth de Senneville,* Musée des Arts Décoratifs, Paris, 1986; *Elisabeth de Senneville: une mode hors mode,* Musée d'Art et d'Industrie, Roubaix, France; *Elisabeth de Senneville,* Musée de la Mode, Marseille, 1994. **Collections:** Musée Galliera, Paris; Musée de la Mode, Paris; Musée de Roubaix; Musée de la Mode de Marseille. **Address:** 3 rue de Turbego, Paris, France.

Publications

On de SENNEVILLE:

Books

Elisabeth de Senneville: une mode hors mode [monograph], Paris 1994.

Articles

Lafee, Scott, "Geek Chic," in *New Scientist,* 24 February 2001.

*

I like to see myself as a designer of futurism and technology. Since 1979 I have been designing all my prints with computers and I have introduced futuristic fabrics into fashion, such as holographic material. I always try to think that my clothes can still be worn after the year 2000. I also like to design for children; I make very modern prints and shapes for them. My clothes have often been compared to Chinese clothes because they have simplicity.

—Elisabeth de Senneville

* * *

While Elisabeth de Senneville has been active in French fashion since the 1960s, she came to prominence in the late 1970s and 1980s with her collections of avant-garde contemporary sportswear, defining her design signature, a combination of functionalist and futuristic sensibilities. Her look and inspirations have remained consistent since she founded her own line in 1975. Rather than following trends, de Senneville has been primarily interested in new technological developments and constantly seeks to apply nonapparel industrial processes and materials to her clothes.

Her vivid, often neon or fluorescent colored prints are derived from computer generated images, using video technology and images from the mass media or art history that she appropriates and applies to her clothes. Unconventional and industrial materials she has used include plastic, Tyvek (an extremely strong, nonwoven fireproof material), canvas, knitted copper threads, rubber, and wool mattress padding. Among her most unusual innovations were the creation, in 1981, of plastic clothes imprinted with holograms. While many of her materials have been unusual, the shapes of de Senneville's clothes are often basic and functional, inspired by athletic wear, work clothes such as jumpsuits, or the quilted clothes of the masses of China. Her signature Chinese inspired outerwear jacket is hip-length quilted canvas that snaps up to a bright plastic collar.

The de Senneville customer is young, adventurous, and intelligent. In her stores in Paris, customers can shop for avant-garde books as well as clothes and can see and hear the work of young artists and musicians. The designer has not only had an affinity for contemporary art but has also actively participated in the intellectual discourses of current art practice by adopting theoretical techniques such as appropriation and reinterpretation and recycling of images. Her work is not meant, however, for an intellectual élite. She has consistently sought new means of exposing her clothes to a wider audience, through licensing agreements, mail-order, and worldwide distribution arrangements.

In 1994 and 1995, de Senneville celebrated 20 years designing her own collection with an exhibition at the Musée de la Mode de Marseille. The exhibition title, *Une mode hors mode* (A Fashion Outside Fashion), aptly expressed de Senneville's design point of view which, though always stylish and contemporary, was a distinct manifestation of her individualistic concerns with materials and processes.

While de Senneville had hoped her clothes would have relevance in the 21st century, she was right on target. In 2001 the futuristic designer met the future head on and created clothing with New Age accoutrements. As Scott Lafee of *New Scientist* (24 February 2001) remarked, "Clothing of the future will be smart, so smart it will organize your day." The de Senneville take on such a proposition was designing dresses with built-in microcapsules with a variety of substances from heat-sensitive dyes (that vary color with body temperature), sunscreen or fragrance. In addition, according to Lafee, "She even has dresses with stripes of moisture-sensitive pigments that change color according to the weather. They turn blue when the sun's out, grey on cloudy days, and pink when it's raining." While such creations may not be everyone's cup of tea, de Senneville most definitely represents the future of fashion designing.

—Alan E. Rosenberg; updated by Nelly Rhodes

DESSÈS, Jean

French designer

Born: Jean Dimitre Verginie, in Alexandria, Egypt, 6 August 1904. **Education:** Studied law, then design, in Paris. **Career:** Designer, Mme. Jane in Paris, 1925–37; opened own house in Paris, 1937; launched Jean Dessès Diffusion line in America, 1950; in Paris, opened boutique Les Soeurs Hortenses, 1951, and made-to-measure dress shop, Bazaar, 1953; closed couture house, 1960; closed ready-to-wear house, 1965; freelance designer in Greece, to 1970. **Died:** 2 August 1970, in Athens, Greece.

Publications

On DESSÈS:

Books

Bertin, Célia, *Paris à la Mode,* London, 1956.

Carter, Ernestine, *With Tongue in Chic,* London, 1974.

Lambert, Eleanor, *World of Fashion: People, Places, Resources,* New York and London, 1976.

Carter, Ernestine, *The Changing World of Fashion: 1900 to the Present,* London, 1977.

Stegemeyer, Anne, *Who's Who in Fashion, Third Edition,* New York, 1996.

* * *

Jean Dessès belongs to the small group of couturiers, such as Vionnet, Balenciaga, and Grès, whose clothing combines technical skill with sculptural aesthetic. Although he began as a designer for a small couture house in Paris in the 1920s and opened his own house in 1937, it was not until the postwar years of the 1940s and 1950s that his work gained its greatest acclaim.

The hallmarks of his postwar fame are evident in his prewar work. Draped and twisted sashes and bodices, cape or kimono sleeves, a fondness for asymmetry, and ornament derived from the architecture of the garment rather than applied as surface decoration, were all elements of both his day and evening wear in the late 1930s. Magazine coverage during that period suggests that he favored jerseys and crêpes, with the jersey dresses in particular anticipating the draping skill which Dessès would use to such advantage after 1945.

Immediately after the war Dessès began to explore his own heritage for design themes which would best use his cutting expertise. He showed a collection inspired by ancient Egyptian costume in 1946 and returned to this theme in the mid-1950s, while the costume of ancient Greece provided a continuous thread through his work. His design legacy rests primarily on the pleated and draped silk chiffon evening dresses which notably expressed Dessès' historical interests.

Dessès' transition from jersey to chiffon may have been mandated by the fuller silhouettes of the 1940s, or perhaps by the fact that Madame Grès was the acknowledged master of the draped jersey column, but the change set him on a path which made his name. In September 1951 *Vogue* lauded Dessès' chiffon gowns as the "Fords" of his collection and "good for a lifetime." By 1958 they were termed "classic." The variations on the theme seemed endless, but there are several important common factors. Appearances notwithstanding, the dresses were not always simple Grecian draperies. The understructures were formal and the cuts were complex, with swags, sashes, bows, and scarves twisted and pleated into shapes that seem effortless and defy analysis; in lesser hands they might simply seem contrived. The dresses also show his sensitive, if somewhat conservative, color sense. Cream or ivory, always flattering, are constants, but Dessès often used two or three shades of one hue, or used three different hues, but of equal value, to maintain harmony. It is also worth noting that the garments are impeccably made; every yard of hem in the double- or triple-tiered chiffon skirts has a hand-rolled finish.

Dessès was equally deft with crisp silks, rough tweeds, and fine dress wools, and his most skilful and inventive draping and cutting techniques were often allied with these fabrics. Dropped shoulder lines, raglan or kimono sleeve variations, and draped collars softened voluminous mohair coats and tweed suit jackets. Tucks, godets, and intricate seaming molded crêpe and gabardine dresses to the contours of the figure. Skirt fullness was swept to the back, folded in at the side, or turned into tiers of flounces which spiraled from hem to hip—all through manipulation of the grain in one piece of cloth.

The most successful of his silhouettes, such as the Streamlined and Winged collections of 1949 and 1951, may not have set trends, but they interpreted the trend with elegance. He favored asymmetry and oblique lines, which gave the garments a sense of movement even in repose. Bold, architectural details such as stand-away pockets and cuffs were used like punctuation marks, adding drama and intensity to a silhouette. Dessès made complex but not fussy clothes, and, on occasion, did set the trend in 1950 when he introduced a one-sleeved stole.

Dessès made an easy transition to the 1960s. His stylistic talents were well suited to the cutting possibilities of the stiffer fabrics and simpler silhouettes in vogue at the time. He was also able to devote more of his attention to the ready-to-wear "Jean Dessès Diffusion" line he had started in 1949, and licensed to two U.S. manufacturers—one for suits and one for evening clothes. Dessès closed his couture operation in 1965, apparently due to poor health, and lived in Greece, occasionally designing on a freelance basis until his death in 1970. His influence on fashion has outlived him, however, figuring into the work of Valentino, who was with the Dessès house for several years in the 1950s.

—Madelyn Shaw

DIOR, Christian

French designer

Born: Granville, France, 21 January 1905. **Education:** Studied political science at École des Sciences Politiques, Paris, 1920–25. **Military Service:** Served in the French Army, 1927–28, mobilized, 1939–40. **Career:** Art dealer, 1928–31; freelance designer and sketch artist, 1934–37; assistant designer, Piguet, 1937–39; lived in Provence, 1940–42; designer, Lelong, 1941–46; Maison Dior opened, 1947; Christian Dior-New York opened, 1948; firm continued after death, Yves Saint Laurent took over designs, 1957–60; Marc Bohan signed as designer, 1960–89; Miss Dior boutique opened, 1967; fragrances and cosmetics sold to Moët-Hennessey, 1972; acquired by Agache-Willot; acquired by Bernard Arnault, 1984; went public as Christian Dior SA, 1988; Gianfranco Ferré became head designer, 1989; brought most licensing in-house by 1995; hired John Galliano, 1996; began opening new stores, 1999–2000; owns majority stake in LVMH; fragrances include: *Miss Dior,* 1947; *Diorama,* 1949; *Diorissima,* 1956; *Diorling,* 1963; *Tendre Poison,* 1994; *Dolce Vita,* 1995; *Hypnotic Poison,* 1998; *Higher Dior,* 2001. **Exhibitions:** *Christian Dior et le Cinéma,* Cinémathèque Francaise, Paris, 1983; *Dessins de Dior,* Musée des Arts de la Mode, Paris, 1987; *Gruau: Modes et publicité,* Musée de la Mode et du costume, 1989; *Réne Gruau pour Christian Dior,* Musee des Beaux Arts, 1990; *Christian Dior: The Magic of the Fashion,* Powerhouse Museum, 1994; Metropolitan Museum of Art, [retrospective], 1996; *John Galliano at Dior,* [retrospective], Design Museum of London, 2001–02. **Awards:** Neiman Marcus award, Dallas, 1947; Remise de la legion d'honneur a Christian Dior, 1950; Parsons School of Design Distinguished Achievement award, New York, 1956; Fashion Industry Foundation award, to the House of Dior, New York, 1990. **Died:** 24 October 1957, in Montecatini, Italy. **Company Address:** 30 avenue Montaigne, 75008 Paris, France. **Company Website:** www.dior.com.

Publications

By DIOR:

Books

Talking About Fashion, with Alice Chavane and Elie Rabourdin, London, 1954.
Dior by Dior, London, 1957.

On DIOR:

Books

Lyman, Ruth, ed., *Couture: An Illustrated History of the Great Paris Designers and Their Creations,* New York, 1972.
Keenan, Brigid, *Dior in Vogue,* London, 1981.
Milbank, Caroline Rennolds, *Couture: The Great Designers,* New York, 1985.
Musée des Arts de la Mode, *Homage à Christian Dior* [exhibition catalogue], Paris, 1986.
Giroud, Françoise, *Dior: Christian Dior 1905–1957,* London, 1987.
Pochna, Marie-France, *Christian Dior,* Paris, 1994.
———, *Christian Dior: The Man Who Made the World Look New,* London, 1994, 1996.
Christian Dior: The Magic of Fashion, Sydney, 1994; London, 2000.
Cawthorne, Nigel, *The New Look: The Dior Revolution,* London, 1996.
———, *Key Moments in Fashion,* London, 1998.
Drosson, Monique, and Lidia Popielska, *Christian Dior, Marcel Boussac, 1947–1978,* Alsace, 1998.

Christian Dior, fall/winter 2001 ready-to-wear collection designed by John Galliano. © AP/Wide World Photos.

Christian Dior, 1968 collection: wedding gown and long cape with a fur lined hood. © AP/Wide World Photos.

de Réthy, Esmeralda, and Jean-Louis Perreau, *Christian Dior and the Founding of His House,* London, 2001.

Articles

McCooey, Meriel, "The New Look," in the *Sunday Times Magazine* (London), 11 August 1968.

"Dior is Dior is Dior," in *American Fabrics & Fashions,* No. 114 (New York), 1978.

McDowell, Colin, "Dior: The Myth, the Legend and Tragedy," in *The Guardian,* 12 February 1987.

Buck, Joan Juliet, "Dior's New Look, Then and Now," in *Vogue,* March 1987.

Bricker, Charles, "Looking Back at the New Look," in *Connoisseur* (New York), April 1987.

Harbrecht, Ursula, "Hommage à Christian Dior," in *Textiles Suisses* (Lausanne), May 1987.

Snow, Carmel, "It's Quite a Revolution, Dear Christian; Your Dresses Have Such a New Look," in the *Independent,* 23 October 1987.
Ingrassia, Michele, with Meggan Dissly, "Dior Meets Disney World," in *Newsweek,* 26 December 1994.
Schiro, Anne-Marie, "Color-Filled Chloé and Rarefied Dior," in the *New York Times,* 17 March 1995.
"Designing Dior—Who's Next?" in *WWD,* 16 July 1996.
Mehle, Aileen, "Dior New York Look," in *WWD,* 11 December 1996.
Duffy, Martha, "The Pope of Fashion: Bernard Arnault…," in *Time,* 21 April 1997.
Weil, Jennifer, et al., "Arnault's New Agenda for LVMH, Dior Puts Emphasis on Retailing," in *WWD,* 10 June 1998.
Weisman, Katherine, "Galliano's Open-Dior Policy," in *WWD,* 3 December 1999.
Rubenstein, Hal, "The Look of Christian Dior," in *InStyle,* 1 November 2000.
Socha, Miles, "The Galliano Factor: Dior Lays Groundwork for 'Exceptional' 2001," in *WWD,* 16 January 2001.
"Born Again Christians," in *Time International,* 19 February 2001.
"Dior Income Rises, Galliano Sales Cited," in *WWD,* 12 March 2001.
Deeny, Godfrey, "Christian Dior: Too Many Clothes, Not Enough Models," at Fashion Windows, www.fashionwindows.com, 7 July 2001.
Davis, Boyd, "Christian Dior à la America," at Fashion Windows, www.fashionwindows.com, 9 October 2001.

* * *

Although Christian Dior died in 1957, he is perhaps one of the most famous fashion designers of both the 20th and 21st centuries. In the years after the debut of his first collection in 1947 he was a legendary figure and the world press developed an extraordinary love affair with him, increasing their enthusiasm with each new collection. Dior never disappointed them, constantly creating clothes that were newsworthy as well as beautiful.

Dior was middle-aged when he achieved fame. A sensitive and gentle personality, he had previously worked as a fashion illustrator, then as a design assistant for both Robert Piguet and Lucien Lélong in Paris. In 1946 the French textile magnate Marcel Boussac offered to finance the opening of Dior's own couture house and secured the lease on 30 avenue Montaigne, Paris. The first collection was revolutionary, heralded as the "New Look" by the fashion press—Dior himself had christened it the "Corolle Line." It was a composition of rounded shoulders, shapely emphasis of the bust, cinched waist, and curvaceous bell-shaped skirt in luxurious fabric.

The concept of the collection was not new, bearing a striking resemblance to French fashions of the 1860s. Dior himself attributed his inspiration to the pretty, elegant clothes he had remembered his mother wearing to the Deauville races in the 1900s. Even though several other designers had experimented with or predicted the new silhouette, Dior's luxurious version reawakened the world to the importance of Parisian couture. At a standstill during World War II, Paris had lost its way as the world's fashion capital. Dior reestablished it as a center of excellence, creating what Janey Ironside of the Royal College of Art in London described as "a new chance in life, a new love affair."

There were many criticisms of the New Look; feminists have argued it was an attempt to return women to an oppressed, decorative role with its emphasis on the restrictive padding, corset, and crinoline.

Christian Dior, fall/winter 2001 collection designed by Hedi Slimane. © AP/Wide World Photos.

Others were shocked by the extravagant use of ornament and fabric when clothes were still being rationed. The New Look, however, rapidly became a postwar cultural symbol for what Dior himself described as "Youth, hope, and the future." After creating a furor with his first collection, Dior established himself as a cautious, methodical designer. Subsequent collections were a continuation of the New Look theme of highly constructed clothes. They were christened with names that described their silhouettes, the Zig Zag Line, A Line, Y Line, Arrow Line, etc. All the collections were realized with the finest tailoring and the most sumptuous fabrics: satins, traditional suiting, fine wools, taffetas, and lavish embroideries.

Throughout Dior's ten years of fame, none of his collections failed, either critically or commercially. The only threat to his run of success occurred when Chanel made a fashion comeback in 1954 at the age of 71. Chanel's philosophy—clothes should be relaxed, ageless, dateless, and easy to wear—completely opposed Dior's philosophy. "Fifties Horrors," was how she described male couturiers, deploring them for torturing bodies into ridiculous shapes. Dior's reaction was to introduce his most unstructured collection, the "Lily of the Valley" line was young, fresh, and unsophisticated. Relaxed, casual jackets with pleated skirts and sailor-collared blouses, these Dior clothes were easy and beautiful.

By the time Dior died his name had become synonymous with taste and luxury. The business had an estimated turnover of $20-million annually, a phenomenal figure in those days, thanks in part to Dior's own shrewdness. Dior organized licence agreements to manufacture accessories internationally, and at the time of his death, perfume, furs, scarves, corsetry, knitwear, lingerie, costume jewelry, and shoes were being produced.

Many of Dior's associates have said that his death was timely and that his work and fashion philosophy were entirely suited to his period. It would be interesting to speculate how Dior would have adapted to the excesses of fashion in the 1960s, 1970s and 1980s, because, as his former personal assistant, Madame Raymonde, once said, "If Dior had lived, fashion would not be in the state it is in now." Nor would his business have gone through multiple owners, or his name become so overlicensed its cachet was nearly lost. After years of struggle, the Dior reclaimed its licenses and rebuilt an empire in the capable hands of Bernard Arnault who bought the firm in 1984 from its bankrupt owner, Agache-Willot.

Many top designers have had stints at Dior, including Yves Saint Laurent who took over after Christian's death, followed by Marc Bohan, Gianfranco Ferré, and John Galliano. Galliano's bad-boy image brought much attention to Dior, but his designs have reinvigorated the house and once again brought renown to the Dior name.

—Kevin Almond; updated by Sydonie Benét

DKNY

See KARAN, Donna

DOLCE & GABBANA

Italian ready-to-wear firm

Established: by Domenico Dolce and Stefano Gabbana, 1982. *Dolce* born in Palermo, Italy, 13 August 1958; *Gabbana* born in Venice, Italy, 14 November 1962. Both designed in Milan, 1980–82. **Company History:** First major women's collection, 1985; knitwear collection first shown, 1987; opened showrooms in Milan, 1987, and New York, 1990; introduced lingerie and beachwear, 1989; Dolce & Gabbana Monogriffe shops opened in Tokyo, 1989, Milan, 1990, Hong Kong, 1991, and Milan shop for menswear, 1991; menswear collection first showing, 1990; launched signature fragrance line, 1992; introduced lower-priced D&G line, 1993; consultants to Genny for Complice line, 1990; opened Dolce & Gabbana and D&G stores in New York, 1997; signed licensing deal with Onward Kashiyama to distribute designs in Japan, 1998; opened Dolce and Gabbana nightclub, Postgarage, in Legnano, Italy, 1998; company assumed ownership stakes in two licensees, Dolce Saverio and Marcolin, 1999; split signature line into White Label and Black Label, 1999; launched complementary male and female fragrances, 1999; opened West Coast flagship store in Beverly Hills, California, 2000; launched *Light Blue* fragrance, 2001. **Awards:** Woolmark award, 1991. **Company Address:** Via Santa Cecilia, 7, 20122 Milan, Italy.

Dolce & Gabbana, fall/winter 2001–02 collection. © AP/Wide World Photos.

Publications

By DOLCE & GABBANA:

Books

10 Years of Dolce & Gabbana, New York, 1996.
Dolce & Gabbana: Wildness, Milan, 1997, New York, 1998.

On DOLCE & GABBANA:

Books

Stegemeyer, Anne, *Who's Who in Fashion, Third Edition,* New York, 1996.
Rossellini, Isabella, *Ten Years of Dolce & Gabbana,* Munich & New York, 1996.
Sozzani, Franca, *Dolce & Gabbana,* New York, 1998, London, 1999.
Baudot, François, *Fashion: The Twentieth Century,* New York, 1999.

Articles

Hume, Marion, "La Dolce Vita," in the *Sunday Times* (London), 4 March 1990.

Dolce & Gabbana, fall/winter 2001–02 collection. © AP/Wide World Photos.

Spindler, Amy M., "Dolce & Gabbana: Salt-of-the-Earth Chic," in *DNR,* 26 September 1990.
Hume, Marion, "The Sicilian Connection," in *Elle* (London), March 1991.
"Italy Now: Dolce & Gabbana," in *DNR,* (New York), 14 January 1992.
"Day of the Dolce," in *WWD,* 9 March 1992.
"La Dolce Vita and the Top Gabbana," in *WWD,* 13 March 1992.
Costin, Glynis, "Dolce & Gabbana," in *W,* 14 May 1992.
Broome, Geoff, "Dynamic Duo," in *International Collections,* Spring/Summer 1992.
Orlean, Susan, "Breaking Away," in *Vogue,* September 1992.
Koski, Lorna, "The Mod Couple," in *WWD,* 16 November 1994.
Forden, Sara Gay, "Dolce and Gabbana Present Dolce & Gabbana," in *DNR,* 2 January 1995.
Menkes, Suzy, "A Manhattan Melody in Italian Shows," in the *International Herald Tribune,* 7 March 1995.
"Distinctly Dolce," in *Elle* (London), April 1995.
Anniss, Elisa, "Dolce & Gabbana Deliver," in *Footwear News,* 26 May 1997.
Kaplan, Don, "New York's Double Dose of Dolce & Gabbana," in *DNR,* 3 September 1997.
Ilari, Alessandra, "Animal Instinct," in *Footwear News,* 15 December 1997.
Conti, Samantha, "Dolce & Gabbana Acquires Holdings in Two Licensees," in *WWD,* 10 May 1999.
Cooperman, Jackie, "D&G Makes Beauty Its Business," in *WWD,* 30 July 1999.
Murphy, Robert, "Dolce & Gabbana: Ready to Rise to the Next Level," in *DNR,* 12 June 2000.
Young, Kristen, "Dolce & Gabbana's Hollywood Dream Comes True," in *DNR,* 19 July 2000.
Rubenstein, Hal, "The Look of Dolce & Gabbana," in *In Style,* 1 April 2001.
Jones, Rose Apodoca, "Dolce Hits Hollywood, Solo," in *WWD,* 1 June 2001.
Naughton, Julie, "Dolce & Gabbana: Targeting the Young at Heart with Light Blue," in *WWD,* 6 July 2001.
Brodie, Honor, "Love Dolce Vita," in *In Style,* 1 August 2001.

* * *

Since their first womenswear collection in 1985, Dolce & Gabbana have evolved into perhaps the definitive purveyors of sexy clothes for women who want to revel in their voluptuous femininity. They have taken items like satin corset bodies, black hold-up stockings, fishnets, and maribou-trimmed baby dolls out of their previous demimonde existence and put them together in such a way that they have become classy outfits for the new glamorous image of the 1990s, an escape from the pervasive unisex sporty styles.

Loved by fashion magazines and film stars alike, the partnership of Domenico Dolce and Stefano Gabbana revives the Southern Italian sex bomb look, inspired by the films of Roberto Rossellini, Luchino Visconti, and Federico Fellini the pair grew up on, coupled with an adoration of the strongly romantic Mediterranean ideals of Sicily. They can take a large amount of credit for the rise in images of the fashionable woman empowering herself by reclaiming sexual stereotypes and using them to her own benefit.

They brush aside the preoccupations of other Milan-based designers with mix-and-match separates and revamp potent images previously deemed degrading to women—the geisha, the baby doll, the scantily clad starlet—and give them a new lease on life. Confidence and irony are key for Dolce & Gabbana: their women are very much in control, whether in one of their glittering rhinestone-covered bodices—notably chosen by postfeminist icon Madonna to make an impact at the 1991 Cannes Film Festival and subsequently filtered down into every High Street chain—or a slightly more sober but nonetheless sexy stretch velvet Empire cut jacket and leggings.

Although originating from opposite ends of Italy, Dolce and Gabbana's shared interests and influences give a sense of unity to their collections and an instantly recognizable look. Their use of film imagery and obvious love of the fiery beauty of stars like Sophia Loren and Gina Lollobrigida has imbued their advertising with an unforgettably glamorous style of its own. They combine supermodels with screen stars to create images that ooze an earthy sexuality.

The same key elements of sexiness mixed with traditional elements are applied to the menswear range, first shown in January 1990 and designed to complement Dolce & Gabbana's women. Skilled Sicilian craftswomen and tailors, supervised by Dolce's father, are employed to produce the internationally acclaimed menswear collections espousing a more laid-back, witty approach to the 1990s, after the brasher, more rigid styles of the previous decade. Muted shades of earthy browns are used alongside blacks with flashes of scarlet to produce modern-day versions of Sicilian bandits, with bandannas around their necks, and bikers in tattoo-covered leather jackets, lightened by the leggings used so widely by Dolce & Gabbana. Current fashion influences are often absorbed, the tie-dyed 1970s feel of their 1992 summer collection being a prime example, but there is always a more timeless selection of unstructured suits, often based on a 19th-century high-buttoning tighter-cut style, and knitwear that explores all its textural possibilities to give it a very tactile appeal.

Both Dolce & Gabbana's menswear and womenswear lines have been international bestsellers. Influential and innovative, the clothes express a confident, sexy glamor that, however potent, never overpowers the wearer's personality, making them one of the most important design forces to emerge from Italy in recent years. The partners have been working to expand their business outside of Italy and the rest of Europe, which together account for 70 percent of the company's business as of 2001. In 1998 Dolce & Gabanna signed a deal with Onward Kashiyama to distribute their designs in Japan, and in 2001, they held their first showing outside Milan. Naturally, given the pair's longtime ties to Hollywood, they chose the Los Angeles area as their venue.

The company's retail operations are growing worldwide, with owned and franchised boutiques in place for both the lower-priced D&G and signature Dolce & Gabbana lines throughout Asia, North America, and Europe, as well as in-house boutiques in upscale retail outlets worldwide. About half the company's approximately 50 stores are under the Dolce & Gabbana banner, with the remainder as D&G boutiques. The company entered New York's retail scene in 1997, opening both a flagship Dolce & Gabbana store on the Upper East Side and a D&G shop in SoHo, as well as debuting a West Coast flagship store in Beverly Hills in 2000.

Dolce & Gabbana has also expanded its licensing activity for both the Dolce & Gabbana and D&G brands, having moved into fragrances, eyewear, beachwear, innerwear, home furnishings, and teen collections. In 1999 Dolce & Gabbana took increased control over some of its licensed lines by maintaining a 51-percent ownership position in its signature collection licensee, Dolce Saverio (owned by Dolce's father) and six percent of its eyewear licensee Marcolin.

The company's footwear collection is one of its licensed success stories. Popular especially in the U.S., the Dolce & Gabbana shoe line includes more than 40 designs each year, along with 20 more under the D&G label. The partners believe footwear is not just an accessory but an art object on its own. They advocate free expression in footwear choices, such as wearing a chiffon evening dress with combat boots, as Gabbana told *Footwear News* in May 1997.

Fragrances are another significant category; the designers added new scents in the late 1990s to appeal to younger consumers, enhancing their already successful fragrance line. *D&G Feminine* and *D&G Masculine* were launched in 1999, first in Italy and then in the United States. *Light Blue,* for 25- to 40-year-olds, debuted in 2001.

Dolce & Gabbana split its signature line into Black and White labels in 1999. The former incorporated the duo's more cutting-edge work, whereas the latter was more basic and casual. The movement toward more casual dressing in the late 1990s favored Dolce & Gabbana's designs at all price points, since no matter how upscale, their clothing has always retained a certain degree of comfort and casualness. Combining luxury and comfort is an ongoing hallmark of Dolce & Gabbana collections.

Dolce & Gabbana has continued, as throughout its history, to be influenced by Hollywood and to spread the word about its line by outfitting Hollywood celebrities. In addition to maintaining their longtime relationship with Madonna (for whom they created costumes and sets for performances and albums in 2000), the duo has outfitted the likes of Mary J. Blige and Whitney Houston for appearances and performances. In some cases, Dolce & Gabbana designs for musicians and actors influence their direction in subsequent collections, when they incorporate some of the pieces and themes from music tours with which they have been involved.

Throughout the late 1990s and early 2000s, the designers maintained their focus on fun, sexy clothes for men and women, featuring animal prints, vibrant colors, high-tech and experimental fabrics, and innerwear-inspired items. They favor unusual combinations of styles and materials, dubbed "the corsets-and-pinstripes look" by *Time International* in March 1999. Dolce and Gabbana told *Women's Wear Daily* in the fall of 1999 that their goal was to achieve a mood of "comfortable elegance," an apt description of the sensibility typical of a Dolce & Gabbana collection.

—Rebecca Arnold; updated by Karen Raugust

DOLCI, Flora

See MANDELLI, Mariuccia

DOMÍNGUEZ, Adolfo

Spanish designer

Born: Orense, Spain, 1950. **Education:** Graduated with degree in philosophy, Universidad Santiago de Compostela, 1968; studied cinematography and aesthetics in Paris and London. **Career:** Formed men's ready-to-wear company, early 1970s; first presentation of work, Madrid, 1981; added women's line, opened first Domínguez shops, 1980s; with Jesús, Javier, María-José, Kerme, and Ada Domínguez, established Adolfo Domínguez, S.A., Vigo; introduced first womenswear collection, 1983; designed jewelry, accessories, shoes, handbags; introduced Domínguez Basico bridge line, 1987; introduced perfume, 1990s; also designs Jeans line of casual sportswear; licensing and distribution agreement in Japan with company Taka-Q; company went public, 1997. **Address:** Poligono San Ciprian de Vinas, Apartado 1160, 32080 Orense, Spain. **Website:** www.adolfo-dominguez.com.

Publications

On DOMÍNGUEZ:

Articles

Coad, Emma Dent, "Flamenco, Fabrics and Fun," in *Design* (London), January 1988.

Burns, Tom, "Europe: Bolsa to Try On Domínguez," in the *Financial Times,* 4 March 1997.

Burns, Tom, "Europe: Domínguez Sets Bolsa Record," in the *Financial Times,* 13 March 1997.
McColl, Pat, "Ready-to-Wear Labels from Spain Quietly Infiltrate Paris," in the *International Herald Tribune,* 17 October 1997.
Dam, Julie K. L., and A. Coruna, "Simply Galician," in *Time,* 17 November 1997.
Nash, Elizabeth, "Forget Paris and Milan—Fashion's Cutting Edge is in Rural Spain," in the *Independent Sunday* (London), 12 April 1998.
"Spanish Retailers Aim to Increase Presence on British High Street," from the *London Evening Standard* in *Knight-Ridder/Tribune Business News,* 19 October 1999.
Burns, Tom, "Cortfiel Bids for Spanish Rival," in the *Financial Times,* 15 March 2001.
Vitzthum, Carlta, "Cortfiel Launches Takeover Bid for Rival Firm Adolfo Domínguez," in the *Wall Street Journal,* 15 March 2001.
"Spaniards for the 21st Century: Adolfo Domínguez," available online at *Freelance Spain,* www.spainview.com, 23 July 2001.

* * *

Working from his native Galicia, Adolfo Domínguez represents the new wave of post-Franco Spanish design. His international corporation has helped to widen the influence of Spanish fashion around the world. The Domínguez family business grew in 30 years from a small manufacturer of ready-to-wear men's clothing to a fashion house with more than 140 owned and franchised outlets in 11 countries worldwide, including shops in Spain, London, Paris, and Hong Kong. The rapid expansion of the business from the early 1970s was founded on the decision to emphasize design and image for the wealthy, urban consumers of the new Spain and also for a sophisticated international clientèle.

The opening of the first Domínguez shop in Madrid marked the beginning in Spain of such chic establishments, presenting an appropriate ambience to support the image of the clothes on sale. The Madrid shop was quickly followed by another in Barcelona, and eight more opened from the home market. With Spain's entry into the European Union, shops were established in London and Paris. The appearance of Domínguez's women's collections in the early 1980s helped to ensure his status in the international fashion world, and markets were consolidated in the U.S. and Japan, where a manufacturing operation was subsequently established. The company went public in 1997 on the Spanish stock market Bolsa with thrilling results. The initial public offering of stocks, representing 70 percent of the company's holdings, set a record for the Bolsa with demand for the shares at more than 50 times the supply.

The success on the stock market, at least in the short run, prompted strong growth in the Domínguez chain, but the surge could not be sustained. The *Wall Street Journal* concluded that operating costs skyrocketed when "Mr. Domínguez embarked on an expansion spree, opening up stores in Asia and Europe without building up the proper industrial and logistic support to underpin the move." Troubles on the business front, however, did not affect Domínguez's fashion sense.

His intellectual and cosmopolitan approach to design reflects Domínguez's Parisian education in literature and philosophy. He likens fashion to industrial design, describing it as a response to need. Similarly, he rejects the willfulness of much designer clothing and couture, asserting instead the designer's responsibility to the user. Domínguez's clothing is purposeful in the modernist idiom, providing a solution to a particular problem, and a solution that will stand the test of time. He has little use for originality for its own sake, preferring to create quality, classic pieces.

Domínguez's Apollonian view of design as an activity also extends to his sense of the human figure and his treatment of the form through tailoring. He concentrates on elegant contour rather than overt body consciousness; he accentuates stature and elegance of proportion to allure, rather than revealing flesh or emphasizing obvious sexual characteristics. He makes use of classic drapery patterns in his garments for women. His unstructured cuts emphasize the drape of fine materials and the traditional Spanish skill of soft tailoring.

Through his ranges of high-quality menswear and womenswear, a lower-cost Basico line and Jeans, a casual line, Domínguez has developed a reputation for producing unpretentious and comfortable-looking garments of the highest quality in materials and construction. A characteristic of Domínguez designs is the elimination of superfluous detail. His clothes are not ornamented by applied decoration, and surface patterning is rare, yet austerity is relieved by soft drapery and the subtlety of colors. Domínguez's rich, earthy palette of colors is reminiscent of the landscape of his native Galicia.

The Domínguez shops designed by Santiago Seara and Alfredo Freixedo, like the clothes sold in them, reflect a classic, modern simplicity, discreetly detailed and finished in high-quality materials. Both the shops and the fashions mirror the elegant minimalism that has proven so successful for the designer. Domínguez's work presented the sophisticated face of the new Spanish design to both a recently liberated and affluent home market and to an increasingly appreciative world market. His name is synonymous with minimalist perfection of form, material, and construction.

—Gregory Votolato; updated by Carrie Snyder

DOROTHÉE BIS

French fashion house

Founded: by Jacqueline (designer) and Elie (manufacturer) Jacobson in 1962. **Company History:** Became known for casual knitwear; opened first Dorothée boutique in Paris, 1958; first Jacqueline Jacobson collection shown and opening of Dorothée Bis boutique, 1962; boutiques found in Henri Bendel and Bloomingdale's, New York; Jacqueline served as set designer for film *The Weekend,* 2000. **Exhibition:** *VizonShow,* Istanbul, 1994. **Company Address:** 17 rue de Sevres, 75006 Paris, France.

Publications

On DOROTHÉE BIS:

Articles

Snead, Elizabeth, "In Paris, Short Cuts to the '60s," in *USA Today,* 18 October 1990.
"Paris Now," in *Women's Wear Daily,* 19 October 1990.
Parola, Robert, "Sportscast," in *DNR,* 25 August 1993.
Parola, Robert, and Catherine Salfino, "Reports," in *DNR,* 25 August 1993.
Israel, Betsy, "Flash: The Return of Disco Style," in *Elle,* February 1995.

* * *

Dorothée Bis, the Paris ready-to-wear house, was founded in 1962 by Jacqueline and Elie Jacobson and quickly and firmly established its now long-standing reputation for unusually stylish and wearable contemporary sportswear, particularly for knits of every variety and description. The jargon of a 1978 Macy's New York advertisement for the firm's clothes sums up the Dorothée Bis look: "Easy fashion with all-over chic appeal. The kind of clothes that you know look right. Anytime, anyplace."

The original boutique, Dorothée, was opened in 1958 by Elie Jacobson. Four years later, along with wife Jacqueline, they opened Dorothée Bis, a new concept in clothing boutiques that catered to young people and employed young people who wore the same clothes as the shoppers. Since then, the firm has been presenting clothes that manifest contemporary trends in a sophisticated and wearable way. Dorothée Bis was among the first houses to present styles such as the long and skinny maxi look in knit coats and vests in the late 1960s, the peasant look in the early 1970s, the layered look in the mid-1970s, and the graphic color block look of the late 1970s and early 1980s. Generally, these looks were presented in a particularly Parisian way, as total ensembles (as opposed to the American idea of mix-and-match), with coordinating accessories—such as a knit dress and coat shown with a hand-knit shawl and beret in the same yarn with matching belt, bag, and fashion jewelry. Materials came from as far away as Nepal, India, and China.

Bernardine Morris, writing for the *New York Times,* described Dorothée Bis as one of "the quintessential Paris ready-to-wear houses aiming at the young swinging crowd who prefer to change their style every season if not oftener." Indeed, in 1969 and 1970, while the hemline debate was fought by other designers, Jacobson satisfied her customers' shifting desires by giving them the mini, the midi, and the maxi, all in the same collection. By 1972, those debating skirt lengths had reached a momentary consensus at mid-knee, leaving the design agenda open for a new focus on silhouette.

Freed from the hemline discourse, with its implied bourgeois conflict between "appropriateness" and fashion, Jacobson continued enthusaistically to develop her concept of dressing in layers, a look that reflected women's growing liberation and consciousness. The feminist theory of the day proposed that as women entered the workforce in rapidly expanding numbers, and in a wide variety of career options, they would no longer need to seduce men to obtain financial support and would therefore no longer be compelled to wear seductive, figure-revealing clothes. Dorothée Bis' layered look evolved from the skinny knits of 1972–73 to the ethnic layers of the mid-1970s and culminated in the extreme and voluminous layers of 1976–77, in which a typical outfit might consist of a boldly patterned cardigan coat over a belted, striped tunic dress, over a full gathered skirt, over wide-legged or sweat-style trousers, with a knit scarf and hat to match. Although seemingly cumbersome, the look's appeal lay in its ease and comfort and in Jacobson's ability to give it all a Parisian stylishness.

In the 1980s, with the rise of conservatism in culture and politics, there was a return to conventionally body-revealing fashions. Many women began to feel that in their adherence to orthodox feminism, they had abdicated the power inherent in their sexuality, and sought to regain that sense of power through their dress. Dorothée Bis was right in step with this trend with a new focus on dresses, especially in the firm's signature knits. A typical Dorothée Bis outfit of the period, a navy-and-white striped wool knit two-piece dress with deep V-neckline and padded shoulders, was described in a Macy's 1986 advertisement as evidence of "a new body emphasis…curve conscious and deserving of its stripes."

Also during the 1980s, the company created a sports line called Dorotennis, and Christophe Lemaire, who served his apprenticeship under the tutelage of Thierry Mugler and worked later for Yves Saint Laurent and Michel Klein, joined the company as a collaborative designer. He eventually would move on to Jean Patou, where he worked with Christian Lacroix. Klein himself also spent 17 years working with the Dorothée Bis firm. Others who worked with the French firm included K. Jacques, who created models and window designs in the 1950s, and Agnès B., who served as a designer, press attaché, and buyer before 1965.

The company has numerous boutiques throughout France, each with a life-sized rag doll sitting in a chair somewhere on the premises. With the firm's emphasis on its highly adaptable and appealing signature knits, Dorothée Bis has been able to remain at the forefront of stylish and realistic fashion for nearly 40 years.

—Alan E. Rosenberg; updated by Daryl F. Mallett

DUKE, Randolph

American designer

Born: Las Vegas, Nevada.**Education:** Scholarship to study music, University of Southern California, turned to theatre and making costumes; graduated from the Fashion Institute of Design and Merchandising, Los Angeles. **Career:** Began designing swimwear, 1978; worked for Jantzen, then became swimwear designer for Anne Cole, California, 1982; left Anne Cole, 1984; designed the Viewpoint by Gottex swimwear line, 1984; opened Randolph Duke, Inc., and unveiled his first collection, 1986; developed a sportswear line under his own name, New York, 1987–92; debuted his first men's line, Duke Men, 1990; dissolved his company, 1990; signed a contract with 168, Inc. for a swimwear line, 1990; launched first jewelry collection, 1991; reorganized sportswear line under the name Randolph Duke, 1993–95; named creative designer, Halston International under the Signature Collection and Halston Lifestyle, 1996; began designing formal wear, 1996; debuted his formal evening wear, 1997; left Halston, 1998; opened store and began designing in Los Angeles, 1999; debuted the Randolph Duke Resort Collection, 2000. **Address:** 260 West 39th Street, New York, NY 10018, USA.

Publications

On DUKE:

Books

Stegemeyer, Anne, *Who's Who in Fashion, Third Edition,* New York, 1996.

Randolph Duke, spring 2001 collection: jet-beaded chiffon evening gown. © AP/Wide World Photos.

Articles

Green, Wendy, and Melissa Fedor, "New York: Coming Attractions," in *WWD,* 11 May 1987.
"Noms de Bloom: Five Designers Ripe for Recognition," in *Chicago Tribune,* 10 September 1989.
"Designers Travel from Las Vegas to Old Pompeii," in *WWD,* 3 November 1989.
"One Part Bach, Two Parts Vegas," in *People,* Spring 1990.
"Randolph Duke," in *DNR,* 6 April 1990.
Lockwood, Lisa, "Duke Dissolves Firm, Gets New Backer," in *WWD,* 30 May 1990.
Hartlein, Robert, "New Laps for Randolph Duke," in *WWD,* 11 July 1990.
Newman, Jill, "Randolph Duke Takes on Jewelry," in *WWD,* 1 March 1991.
"WWD Quizzes Designers on the Upcoming Collections," in *WWD,* 4 April 1991.
"Great Expectations," in *WWD,* 12 June 1991.
Lockwood, Lisa, "Randolph Duke's Designer Sportswear Business Closed," in *WWD,* 17 November 1992.
White, Constance, "Randolph Duke's Triple Play," in *WWD,* 7 July 1993.
Fiedelholtz, Sara, "Duke Introducing Signature Beach, Swim Line," in *WWD,* 18 August 1993.
Levine, Lisbeth, "Everything Old is New Again," in *Chicago Tribune,* 15 April 1997.
Dominguez, Juliette, "Urbane Renewal," in *People,* 4 May 1998.
D'Innocenzio, Anne, "Duke Said Poised to Leave Halston," *WWD,* 7 July 1998.
"Duke Rejoining Anne Cole," in *WWD,* 19 October 1998.
"Finishing Touches," in *WWD,* 22 February 1999.
"Duke to Bring Celebrity Flair to Symphony League Show," in *Journal Sentinel,* 2 June 2000.
Young, Kristin, "Trunk Show Hits," in *WWD,* 5 July 2000.
"Much Ado About Dazzle," in *WWD,* 21 September 2000.
McCants, Leonard, "Halston Sets Designer for Fall," in *WWD,* 14 November 2000.
Davis, Boyd, "Randolph Duke," online at FashionWindows.com, Inc., 27 January 2001.

Randolph Duke, 2001: leather paillette evening gown with fox cuff designed as an option for an Academy Award® nominee. (Jewelry designed by Tony Duquette.) © AP/Wide World Photos.

* * *

Randolph Duke came to realize the fame of being "the Duke of Stars" after he made his formal eveningwear debut during fall 1997. Hollywood embraced his styles and designs with marked enthusiasm and admiration; among the likes of his Hollywood followers are Sharon Stone and Celine Dion. Duke progressed from swimwear to sportswear to evening wear, a progression that came naturally for a designer who has claimed that change itself is his inspiration; this particular need is what made him Hollywood's designer of choice in the late 1990s and the beginning of the 21st century.

Duke began his career designing simple yet stylish swimwear. He worked as swimwear designer for Anne Cole in 1982 and stayed until he ventured off on his own, creating for his own label from 1987 to 1992. His designs were vibrant, young, colorful, and full of innovative fabric use. Though he had shifted from swimwear to clothing design, Duke returned to swimwear in from 1993 to 1995, again giving the garments fresh, lively looks.

The transition from swimwear to sportswear seemed a natural step for Duke. When he joined Halston International in 1996, he continued his fashion style from his years of producing collections for his own label. The aim was to reach working women with a fashion sense who were also functioning on a limited budget. In 1997, he enlivened the Halston show at the New York Historical Society with a collection of cashmere tube tops and sexy, fitted evening dresses. Jackets for spring came in either a fitted, cropped style or a multipocketed safari design, along with four or five colors with coordinating prints.

During his years of creating sportswear collections under his own name, Duke's designs were bold, simple, tailored in contrasting stitching, and included supple knit pieces to round out his line. Almost all fabrics were domestic and the result was a charming, trendy sportswear collection full of life. Included in a hip 1989 line was a bright yellow motorcycle jacket, sharp suits, and an array of wet-weather wear including raincoats.

In 1998 Duke opened a store in Los Angeles and successfully began creating his own line of formal eveningwear. He introduced the future of fashion with circular shapes and red snapper-skin sandals. His gowns made a bold statement in 1999, starting with a dark velvet dress with braided shoulder straps and a long slip in mohair over beaded tulle. Moving back into sportswear in 2000, Duke presented a resort collection with a selection of blouses, including one in taffeta with two drawstrings down the center that, when pulled, rose up to show the midriff. The collection also introduced a t-shirt emblazoned with rhinestones, sequined ombre pants in lavender, sequined ombre short skirts with matching cashmere twinsets, and a beaded sarong skirt.

Being the Duke of Stars, Randolph Duke found himself increasingly catering to Hollywood clientèle. His spring 2001 collection was composed predominantly of elegant eveningwear. His designs have become highly visible at awards ceremonies, such as the Academy Awards®, with award-winners Hilary Swank (in a bronze ball gown) and Marcia Gay Harden (in ruby silk satin) in 2000 and 2001 respectively. Duke's designs, whether for high profile clients or not, continue to be bold, direct, elegant, and of star quality.

—Kimbally A. Medeiros

E

EDDIE BAUER

American sportswear and lifestyle company

Founded: in 1920 by Eddie Bauer, in Seattle, WA. **Company History:** Patented quilted goose down jacket, 1936; developed B-9 Flight Parka, 1942; Bauer sold company to partner William Niemi, 1968; company sold to General Mills, 1971; Ford produced first Eddie Bauer Edition vehicle, 1983; Spiegel purchases company, 1988; 100th store opening, 1989; formed partnerships with Lane Company for furniture, 1997; Giant Bicycle, Signature Eyewear, and Cosco, Inc., all 1998; stores in all 50 states, 2000. **Company Address:** 15010 NE 36th Street, Redman, WA 98052, USA. **Company Website:** www.eddiebauer.com.

PUBLICATIONS

On EDDIE BAUER:

Books

Spector, Robert, *The Legend of Eddie Bauer,* New York, 1995.

Articles

"Eddie Bauer Makes Employees' Health Its Business," in *Hospitals & Health Networks* (Chicago) 70, 1996.

Faust, Leslie, "At Eddie Bauer You Can Work and Have a Life," in *Personnel Journal* (Costa Mesa, CA) 76, 1997.

Van Yoder, Steven, "Retailers Target Hidden Costs of On-the-Job Injuries," in *Stores* (New York), December 1999.

Cuneo, Alice Z, "Eddie Bauer Gets Update to Battle Dwindling Sales," in *Advertising Age*, 14 August 2000.

"Eddie Bauer Launches Website," in *Home Textiles Today,* 11 September 2000.

Cole, Wendy, "SUV Strollers," in *Time,* 29 January 2001.

Sloane, Carole, "Eddie Bauer Home Plans New Stores, Catalogue Growth" in *Home Textiles Today,* 12 March 2001.

*

The Eddie Bauer Creed: To give you such outstanding quality, value, service and guarantee that we may be worthy of your high esteem.

The Eddie Bauer Guarantee: Every item we sell will give you complete satisfaction or you may return it for a full refund.

—Eddie Bauer, 1920

* * *

It is possible to live an entirely Eddie Bauer existence. Whether dressing for work or leisure, Eddie Bauer has you covered. Literally. With few exceptions, nearly everything in a casual or business casual wardrobe is available for men, women, and children. The company's Lifestyle division offers selections from the sheets on your bed (and the bed itself) to bathroom shower curtains, towels, and accessories; furnishings (even wallpaper) for your living room, home office, and children's rooms, to the outdoor furniture on the deck. Parents might purchase a stroller, car seat, or a full line of camping gear, including tents, sleeping bags, packs, as well as outdoor and beach furniture.

Eddie Bauer luggage allows you to travel in style while visiting an Eddie Bauer store in every state of the U.S., and in Germany and Japan. A collaboration with Signature Eyewear offers sunglasses for driving your Eddie Bauer Edition Ford Explorer or Expedition or cycling away on an Eddie Bauer bike. Eddie Bauer corrective glasses might be in order when sitting down in front of your Eddie Bauer Special Edition Compaq Presario notebook computer. All the better for shopping online at, you guessed it, www.eddiebauer.com. Eddie Bauer will help you match an outfit, figure out your size, and remind you of your anniversary. While doing all this, Eddie Bauer supports education, gives to the community, empowers women, sponsors the U.S. Canoe and Kayak Team, PGA and LPGA players, an Iditarod musher, and Eddie Bauer/Global ReLeaf, the Eddie Bauer Tree Project.

Unlike companies named for fictitious characters, Eddie Bauer was the founding father of the successful company bearing his name. Established in 1920 in Seattle, Washington, 21-year-old Bauer opened Eddie Bauer's Sport Shop in the back of a local hunting and fishing store. A great lover of the outdoors, Bauer offered high-quality gear at good prices. His commitment to his customers evolved into the creed and guarantee still honored today. While hunting in the 1930s, an unexpected winter rainstorm waterlogged his woolen clothing and led him to develop a protective outerwear garment. The Skyliner, the first American quilted goose down-insulated jacket, was patented in 1936. It was so successful that Bauer was commissioned in 1942 by the U.S. Army Air Corps to develop the B-9 flight parka. More than 50,000 jackets were manufactured for World War II airmen flying at high altitudes.

Astute at business, Bauer added women's clothing about the same time as the Skyliner. He issued a mail order catalogue in 1945 and began to outfit scientific and exploratory expeditions in the 1950s. Bauer retired in 1968, selling the business to his partner, William Niemi, who sold it to General Mills in 1971. The company shifted its focus from expedition gear and apparel to casual clothing and expanded to 61 stores and $250 million in sales between 1971 and 1988.

Spiegel purchased Eddie Bauer in 1988 and continued the aggressive growth and product development that would result in a huge variety of Eddie Bauer merchandise. The first Eddie Bauer Ford was manufactured in 1984, and in 1997 and 1998, the Lane Company signed on to produce Eddie Bauer Home; Giant Bicycle to produce bikes; Signature Eyewear for eyewear; and the company partnered with Cosco, Inc. to expand Baby by Bauer. An additional 300 stores opened by 1996, catalogues and stores were introduced in both Germany and Japan, size ranges were expanded, and a Web presence was introduced.

As a company, Eddie Bauer has a corporate conscience. Its employees' health and well-being are of genuine concern, and proactive health measures are embraced. The company offers many philanthropic opportunities, from education to community volunteerism. In 1995, Eddie Bauer joined with American Forest to establish the Eddie Bauer/Global ReLeaf project to help restore fire-ravaged forestlands. The project is more than halfway toward completing its goal of planting 2.5 million trees.

The success of Eddie Bauer lies in its ability to provide dependably comfortable, affordable, well-made clothing. Shopping is a pleasant experience, whether in the store, by catalogue, or online, and customer service is alive and well. The casual styles are reflective of an ever relaxing American lifestyle, with a nod toward the company's rugged roots.

—Christina Lindholm

EISEN, Mark

South African fashion designer

Born: Cape Town, South Africa, 27 September 1958. **Education:** Attended University of Southern California, B.S., 1982. **Career:** Founded own design firm in Los Angeles, 1982; moved to New York, 1993; launched Urchin and Urchin Knits apparel lines (later combined and renamed Urchin Mark Eisen), 1996; signed licensing pact with World Gym for uniforms, 1996; designed interior of GM car for charity, 1997; signed licensing agreements for Mark Eisen Studio, 1997; moved headquarters from Los Angeles to New York, 1998; launched bridge knitwear line, Eisen, 1999; formed partnership with Italian firm Sportswear Company SpA for Mark Eisen Collection, 2000; footwear licensing deal with Lerre, 2000. **Awards:** Alumni of the Year, University of Southern California Business School, 1988.

Mark Eisen, fall 1997 collection. © AP/Wide World Photos.

Publications

On EISEN:

Articles

McNamara, Michael, "Synthetic Chic," in *WWD,* 30 August 1994.
"Mark Eisen Sets Launch of Contemporary Label," in *WWD,* 9 February 1996.
"New York: On the Runways," in *WWD,* 1 April 1996.
Socha, Miles, "World Gym," in *DNR,* 2 October 1996.
"Eisen Works Out," in *WWD,* 10 October 1996.
D'Innocenzio, Anne, "Brand Strategies are Paying Off," in *WWD,* 4 December 1996.
Muir, Lucie, "Fibers Mix it Up at Prato," in *WWD,* 11 March 1997.
Monget, Karen, "Committment's in Fashion," in *WWD,* 6 October 1997.
"Up & Down the Fashion Food Chain," in *WWD,* 5 November 1997.
D'Innocenzio, Anne, "Eisen's New Moves," in *WWD,* 8 October 1997.
Winter, Drew, "Interiors Become Extroverts," in the *Ward's Auto World,* November 1997.
D'Innocenzio, Anne, "Young, Contemporary Styles Take Center Stage," in *WWD,* 25 February 1998.
"And the Beat Goes On," in *WWD,* 31 March 1998.
Lee, Georgia, "Urchin Betting on Knits Line," in the *WWD,* 22 April 1998.
"Eisen Plans Bridge Line for Fall 1999," in *WWD,* 2 November 1998.
Socha, Miles, "Mark Eisen Merges with Italian Producer," in *WWD,* 31 January 2000.
Daswani, Kavita, "Seventh on Sixth Gets New Global Groups," in *WWD,* 9 April 2000.
Socha, Miles, "Face of Africa Showcases Africa," in *Africa News Service,* 25 April 2000.
Bressler, Karen, "Mark Eisen: Making His Mark," available online at Fashion Windows, www.fashionwindows.com, 2000.

* * *

Mark Eisen began his illustrious design career at the University of Southern California, where he was earning a degree in business. He

Mark Eisen, fall 1997 collection: stretch jacket with a faux fur collar and wide leg pants. © AP/Wide World Photos.

designed a stylish gold-and-red helmet celebrating the school's famed Trojans football team and was soon selling them by the thousands. His first press coverage was a brief mention in *Newsweek* praising his entrepreneurial spirit. The fledgling designer went on to create a name for himself, first as the purveryor of spare, elegant minimalism then as the king of high-tech chic.

Despite his evident success, Eisen is never complacent. He admitted to Karen Bressler, of the Fashion Live website, he has a superstitious routine he follows before each major showing. "The night before a show," he says, "I eat in the same restaurant with the same people at the same table in the same seat and order the same thing, crab meat and thin pasta. I used to carry a friend's pearls in my pocket on the runway, but then I heard that pearls could be bad luck." From his success, however, it appears he has little to be concerned about. High-profile celebrities have turned into diehard fans, and his creations continue to garner positive press from fashion critics and fellow designers alike.

Womenswear in the hands of Eisen is elegant and well cut, made from the finest fabrics. Eisen is unabashedly smitten with textiles and has enjoyed combining opposites for surprising results. He likes mixing Lycra in with more delicate fabrics for its ability to retain its shape, and has used a myriad of luxurious fabrics like silk, sateen wool, cashmere, mohair, alpaca, angora, and suede in his designs. His collections in 1994 and 1995 featured what became an early trademark—minimalist chic—with tailored suits and simple dresses in dark hues of black, charcoal, and chocolate browns, while throwing in a few splashy neon separates to brighten the range. After several minimal collections, Eisen turned to synthetics, such as resortwear collections using acetate, rayon, and even polyurethane. Eisen's fascination with textiles is always evident, concocting high-tech fabrications as laminated chiffon, linen coated with resin, rayon crêpe, and nylon blends.

In early 1996 the designer launched two new labels, Urchin and Urchin Knits (later combined and renamed Urchin Mark Eisen). Eisen declared to *Women's Wear Daily* (9 February 1996) that Urchin, a sporty ready-to-wear collection, would "be affordable, fun and functional, as opposed to trendy." Colors were deep earth tones, with brown, beige, and black, as well several variations in blue: navy, indigo, turquoise, and sky blue. The Urchin Knits line, comprised of cardigans, tunics, twinsets, and trousers, used silks, cashmere, crêpe, lambswool, and cotton, with Lycra mixed in for fit and flexibility.

Eisen segued into designing uniforms through a licensing agreement with the famed the Santa Monica-based World Gym in fall 1996. Both trainers and staff at the health club operator's New York City locations were given stylish and sporty activewear separates, with the range eventually reaching all of World Gym's 400 sports complexes worldwide. Additionally, the activewear, under the Mark Eisen for World Gym label, was sold in World Gym clubs around the world, beginning in 1997.

To help combat breast cancer, Eisen and fellow designers Nicole Miller, Todd Oldham, Anna Sui, and Richard Tyler joined General Motors and the Council of Fashion Designers of America (CFDA) for the ConceptCure program. The designers teamed up to work on the interior of GM cars, which were then auctioned off to raise funds for the Nina Hyde Center for breast cancer awareness. Richard Ruzzin, director of interior character for Chevrolet told *Ward's Auto World* (November 1997), "These fashion designers used color, texture, and material in ways we never dreamed possible with our products." Like the famed Eddie Bauer designer Fords, the vehicles had plenty of style and raised over $700,000 for the cause.

In an effort to take his name and designs global, Eisen hired Brad Saltzman, formerly of Adrienne Vittadini, to become president and CEO of his firm. Eisen remained chairman and still handled all design responsibilities. Commenting to *Women's Wear Daily* (8 October 1997) on the arrival Saltzman, Eisen said, "I have searched for over three years for a partner who shared my same vision and goals. I am most excited to be able to hand the business side of the company to Brad and to have my primary focus on design. We are now poised to explode the business both domestically and internationally through multiple categories."

Licensing agreements reflecting the global plan included Nissho Iwai Corporation and Ichida Company to produce and distribute the Mark Eisen Studio collection, which had ceased production in the U.S. for some time. The Mark Eisen Collection, the firm's strongest line, was poised for licensing in Europe and throughout Asia in 1998. The newer line, Urchin Mark Eisen, had experienced swift growth and was already in 350 U.S. high-end department stores such as Bloomingdale's, Barneys, Bergdorf Goodman, and Henri Bendel. Eisen and Saltzman hoped to increase U.S. retail locations to more than 500, and to find a new licensing partner for the better Mark Eisen Collection.

For fall 1999 came a new bridge knitwear line, simply titled Eisen. Targeted to women, aged 30 to 50, the range was intended to offer a stylish and less expensive alternative to misses. Next, in 2000, came a new suitor for the Mark Eisen Collection, a partnership with Sportswear Company SpA, once a unit of GFT and backer behind the C.P. Company, to manufacture and distribute the range internationally. Eisen also entered into a licensing deal with Lerre, a Naples-based footwear manufacturer, for an upscale footwear collection.

Returning to his roots, the South African-born Eisen helped sponsor the African Designs Fashion Competition in 2000, a contest for new African designers to win a three-month internship with Eisen and a chance to show their designs at New York's Fashion Week for the summer 2002 season. Eisen also served as a juror at the Seventh on Sixth global design forum, which brought in design teams from Hong Kong, Africa, and Portugal. While Mark Eisen's creations firmly reflect American design sensibilities, he has not forgotten the difficulties of his countrymen and women. With designers of all ethnic origins blooming in South Africa, Eisen is well positioned to bring what he calls the "cross-global reality" of African designs to America and beyond.

—Owen James

ELBAZ, Alber

Israeli American fashion designer

Born: Casablanca, Morocco, 1961. **Education:** Graduated from Shenkar College of Textile Technology and Fashion, Tel Aviv, Israel, circa 1988; studied with Geoffrey Beene, New York, circa 1989–96. **Career:** Creative director, Guy Laroche, 1996–98; designer, Yves Saint Laurent Couture, Rive Gauche collections, Gucci Group N.V., 1998–2000; designed for Krizia SpA, 2000; signed on as creative director/designer, Lanvin, 2001. **Awards:** American Committee for Shenkar College, Israel, Alumni award, 2001.

Publications

On ELBAZ:

Articles

Phelps, Nicole, "The New Guy at Laroche," in *WWD,* 2 July 1997.

Klensch, Elsa, "New Designer Modernizes Laroche Line," available online at CNN.com, 18 August 1997.

Bellafante, Ginia, "Tired of Chic Simple? Welcome to the New Romance," in *Time,* 6 April 1998.

Menkes, Suzy, "A New Generation in Ready-to-Wear: Alber Elbaz Gets Aboard at YSL," in the *International Herald Tribune,* 9 June 1998.

Yanowitch, Lee, "Israeli Designer to Produce Yves Saint Laurent Line," in *Jewish Bulletin of Northern California,* 17 July 1998.

Silva, Horacio, "Chic Happens," in *Hint Fashion Magazine,* 7 October 1998.

Patterson, Suzy, "Spring is Abloom on Paris Runways, and the View is Beautiful, Elegant," in *SouthCoast Today,* 21 October 1998.

Steifel-Kristensen, Tom, "Individuality Rules in Paris," available online at Furs.com, fall 1999/2000.

Raper, Sarah, and Samantha Conti, "Gucci Takeover of YSL May Have hit a Snag," in *WWD,* 11 October 1999.

Conti, Samantha, et al, "Gucci Acquires YSL," in *WWD,* 16 November 1999.

Menkes, Suzy, "His Last Collection for Saint Laurent is a Smash," in the *International Herald Tribune,* 29 February 2000.

Deeny, Godfrey, "Krizia Top: Alber Elbaz Ravishes in His Third Act," in *Fashion Wire Daily,* 5 October 2000.

Menkes, Suzy, "A Few Vivacious Voices Hit the High Notes in Milan," in the *International Herald Tribune,* 7 October 2000.

O'Brian, Heather, "A Bitter Parting Between Alber Elbaz and Krizia," in *Fashion Wire Daily,* 30 November 2000.

"Shenkar College Honors Three Prestigious Alumni," in *WWD,* 17 April 2001.

"Fashion Scoops (Alber Elbaz)," in *WWD,* 11 October 2001.

* * *

Alber Elbaz was born in 1961 in Casablanca, Morocco, to a Jewish family. He was raised in Israel, where he graduated from the Shenkar College of Textile Technology and Fashion. Later he moved to New York, where he spent seven years training with Geoffrey Beene, described by critics and other designers as "one of the few American designers who follows the rules and tenets of true couture."

In June 1996 Elbaz was hired by the venerable French design house, Guy Laroche. Although a graduate of a top-rate fashion school and a protégé of Beene's, Elbaz was still an unknown in the couture world at the time when Laroche's president, Ralph Toledano, hired him. Toledano had been duly impressed by Elbaz's sketches, drawn while on a recent vacation. Toledano found the designs breathtakingly feminine, and liked the designer's personal style as well. "When he came to see me," Toledano told *Arts/Fashion* magazine (6 April 1998), "he had on red shoes and a red jacket. The guy knew how to capture your attention."

Elbaz brought luxurious skirt suits, pink-and-white dresses of layered tulle, billowy-sleeved jackets, and Capri pantsuits, all accented in strips of fur, lines of sequins, or wild pink and pink-toned colors to Laroche at a time when the fashion industry had spent a decade slowing down and moving away from loud outrageousness and toward austere, sensible, classy clothes. "Maybe, if we can find it in our hearts, we should reserve a small 'Thank You' to *Titanic* for making women so hungry to look feminine right now. The era depicted in the movie was, after all, the era of languid dress," Richard Martin, curator at the Metropolitan Museum of Art's Costume Institute, wrote in *Arts/Fashion,* in April 1998.

In 1998 Elbaz was spirited away from Laroche with an offer from Yves Saint Laurent Couture. The legendary Saint Laurent, after 32 years of designing, had decided it was time for a change. At his direction, Pierre Berge, president of YSL Couture, hired the 37-year-old Elbaz to take over for the Rive Gauche ready-to-wear line. "For me, this isn't a career move, but the realization of my life's dream," Elbaz said in a press release from YSL. But it was not an easy move for the young designer; he was anguished over his departure from

Laroche and Toledano, who was proud of Elbaz's success yet sorry to see him go.

Bringing Elbaz on board had been the second big change at YSL in as many years. Berge had already hired Hedi Slimane as YSL's menswear designer in 1996, a move that had bolstered sales in that arena. The appointment left many in the fashion world wondering how it would all work out. Saint Laurent had been designing blazers, pantsuits, shorts, lady's suits, and the safari look for more matronly clients, searching for elegant businesswear and streamlined eveningwear. Elbaz, on the other hand, designed silk-pouch dresses, halter tops with droopy, hanging necklines, riots of deep green, light yellow, blue, gray, red, and purple colors, featuring fabrics like taffeta, jerseys, tulle, tweed, and fox fur-lined sleeves.

Yet buyers and critics at Elbaz's first show for YSL in early 1999 responded enthusiastically to this new look in a venerable couture house. "Alber Elbaz is...the spirit of YSL; but the technique of Elbaz...is bringing the house into the new millennium," said Kal Ruttenstein of Bloomingdale's after Elbaz's opening show for YSL. Glowing reviews aside, corporate shenanigans came into play in 2000 after YSL was acquired by the Gucci Group. The fall YSL women's ready-to-wear showing in Paris would be Elbaz's final collection for the firm. "Alber Elbaz has made an important contribution to the history of Yves Saint Laurent Rive Gauche," Domenico DeSole, president and CEO of Gucci, said in a press release. Gucci Group's creative director and chief designer, Tom Ford, was assuming all design responsibilities for the burgeoning fashion empire.

Elbaz moved on to Krizia, where he designed a beautiful, well received African-influenced collection for their Krizia Top line, featuring feathers, chunky jewelry, sporty tailoring, wrapped satin blouses, and suede skirts, in rich African colors such as earth brown, clay red, and tan, with tribal markings as patterns. But his tenure there would only last a scant three months before a bitter parting over artistic differences between Elbaz and Mariuccia Mandelli. He was replaced there by Belgian designer Jean-Paul Knott.

Elbaz, however, landed on his feet. In 2001 he signed with Lanvin (recently bought from Revlon by Harmonie SA) as creative director for its women's ready-to-wear and accessories lines. His first collection debuted in March for fall 2002.

—Daryl F. Mallett

Perry Ellis, spring 2001 collection: wool/viscose crepe jacket and pants with a cotton dress shirt. © Reuters NewMedia Inc./CORBIS.

ELLIS, Perry

American designer

Born: Perry Edwin Ellis in Portsmouth, Virginia, 30 March 1940. **Education:** Bachelor of Arts, business, College of William and Mary, Williamsburg, Virginia, 1961; Master of Arts, retailing, New York University, New York City, 1963. **Family:** Had child with Barbara Gallagher, Tyler Alexandra. **Military Service:** Served in the U.S. Coast Guard, 1961–62. **Career:** Sportswear buyer, Miller & Rhodes department stores, Virginia, 1963–67; design director, John Meyer of Norwich, 1967–74; vice-president, sportswear division, 1974, and designer, Vera sportswear for Manhattan Industries, 1975–76; designer with own Portfolio label, Manhattan Industries, 1976–78; president/designer, Perry Ellis Sportswear, Inc., 1978–86; Perry Ellis International menswear line launched, 1980; Portfolio label, lower priced sportswear revived, 1984; fragrance collection launched, 1985; company went public, 1993; womenswear discontinued, 1993; Perry Ellis America for men line introduced, 1996; announced new bridge line, 1998; firm acquired by Supreme International, 1999; reintroduced womenswear, 2000; discontinued women's sportswear, 2001; acquired Bugle Boy, 2001. **Exhibitions:** Fashion Institute of Technology, 2000. **Awards:** Coty American Fashion Critics award, 1979, 1980, 1981, 1983, 1984; Neiman Marcus award, Dallas, 1979; Council of Fashion Designers of America award, 1981, 1982, 1983; Cutty Sark award, 1983, 1984; Council of Fashion Designers of America Perry Ellis award established in memoriam, 1986; California Men's Apparel Guild Hall of Fame award, 1993. **Died:** 30 May

1986, in New York City. **Company Address:** 575 Seventh Avenue, New York, New York 10018, USA. **Company Website:** www.perry-ellis.com.

Publications

On ELLIS:

Books

Morris, Bernadine, and Barbara Walz, *The Fashion Makers,* New York, 1978.
Diamonstein, Barbaralee, *Fashion: The Inside Story,* New York, 1985.
Milbank, Caroline Rennolds, *Couture: The Great Designers,* New York, 1985.
Perschetz, Lois, ed., *W, The Designing Life,* New York, 1987.
Moor, Johnathan, *Perry Ellis,* New York, 1988.
Milbank, Caroline Rennolds, *New York Fashion: The Evolution of American Style,* New York, 1989.

Perry Ellis, spring 2001 collection: cotton double-faced top coat, cotton ribbed sweater and wrinkled cotton flat front pants. © Reuters NewMedia Inc./CORBIS.

Stegemeyer, Anne, *Who's Who in Fashion, Third Edition,* New York, 1996.

Articles

Morrisoe, Patricia, "The Death and Life of Perry Ellis," in *New York,* 11 August 1986.
Fressola, Peter, "Perry Ellis," in *DNR,* 13 April 1987.
Parola, Robert, "At Ellis: Discord on Design and Direction," in *DNR,* 24 July 1992.
Larson, Soren, "Parlux Set to Chase American Dream," in *WWD,* 2 February 1996.
Williams, Stan, "Perry's Parry," in *DNR,* 31 January 1997.
———, "Keeping Perry's Image Positive," in *WWD,* 23 February 1998.
Lohrer, Robert, "Supreme to Acquire Perry Ellis," in *WWD,* 29 January 1999.
D'Innocenzio, Anne, "A Perry Ellis Revival," in *WWD,* 23 December 1999.
"In Miami, Perry Ellis Reigns Supreme," in *DNR,* 4 February 2000.
"Perry Ellis to Acquire Bugle Boy," in *WWD,* 9 February 2001.
Wilson, Eric, and Antonia Sardone, "After One Season, Perry Ellis Yanks Women's Sportswear Line," in *WWD,* 6 April 2001.

* * *

The house of Perry Ellis has seen more than its share of tumultuous times. From the early days things had never been particularly easy, with Ellis continuously battling over finances with his parent company, Manhattan Industries. Problems with stability continued after Ellis' death in 1986, when Robert McDonald assumed the helm of Perry Ellis International, only to die four years later.

Then came Salant's $100-million takeover of Manhattan Industries and its subsequent bankruptcy filing. Obstacles with direction, especially within the menswear divisions, to the disjointed running of Perry Ellis International (PEI) in the mid-1990s, continued the company's disarray. After several top management changes, PEI finally seemed to stabilize, and once again received notice for the fashions bearing the Ellis label, including the launch of a new bridge line for 1999. Yet before plans were finalized on the bridge line, Salant went bankrupt again, and Supreme International came forward to buy the beleaguered Ellis kingdom. Supreme then took the Ellis moniker, establishing the Perry Ellis International Corporation.

Perry Ellis was known as a flirtatious, fun-loving man with a great sense of humor. According to Claudia Thomas, former chair of Perry Ellis International, it is hard to characterize Ellis, except to describe him as whimsical. There was, however, an air of seriousness about him when it came to creating and fulfilling his objectives, as reflected in his personal philosophy of "never enough." Yet it was the playful side of his personality most reflected in his fashions. When his company arrived on the scene in the 1970s, it was a time of increasing emphasis on American designers and designer name merchandise. Ellis did his best to create a mystique about himself and his lifestyle that would attract fans.

The Perry Ellis look began as a casual, relaxed style exclusively American in feeling and sportswear-like in its practicality. It was so playful and comfortable, in fact, models at his shows would skip down the catwalk. As Ellis matured as a designer, his clothing occasionally took on a more serious tone, but even his most formidable collections were considered easy-dressing by fashion industry standards.

Inspiration came in many forms—California, artist Sonia Delaunay, movies or Broadway shows (like *Chariots of Fire* or *Dream Girls*—all retained the casual ease for which Americans are known internationally and the sense of proportion and freedom from fashion conformity which became the hallmark of Perry Ellis. The company's subsequent womenswear designer, Marc Jacobs, and menswear design director, Andrew Corrigan, appeared to create their collections with the feeling Ellis had tried to instill into a consumer's mind when buying clothing.

Ellis once said, "Always provide the clothes needed for daily life. Never be afraid to take risks and, most importantly, never take the clothes you wear too seriously." Through all the transitions and the fickle nature of fashion, Perry Ellis menswear—and at times its womenswear—remained relatively consistent and true to the tenets and goals espoused by Ellis himself.

—Lisa Marsh; updated by Owen James

EMANUEL, David and Elizabeth

British designers

Born: *David*—Bridgend, Wales, 17 November 1952; *Elizabeth*—born Elizabeth Weiner in London, 5 July 1953. **Education:** *David*—Attended Cardiff School of Art, Wales, 1972–75, and Harrow School of Art, Middlesex, 1974–75. *Elizabeth*— Attended Harrow School of Art, 1974–75. Both David and Elizabeth studied fashion in postgraduate courses at the Royal College of Art, 1976–77. **Family:** Married in 1976 (divorced 1990); children: Oliver and Eloise. **Joint Career:** Partners and directors of Emanuel, in London, 1977–90; created ready-to-wear line 1977–79; designed custom clothing only, 1979–90; fellows, Chartered Society of Designers, London, 1984; ballet and stage production designers, from 1985; established The Emanuel Shop, Beauchamp Place, London, 1987–90; collections also sold at Harrods and Harvey Nichols, London, and Bergdorf Goodman, Henri Bendell, and Neiman Marcus, New York; partnership dissolved, 1990. **Individual Careers:** *David*—Formed David Emanuel Couture, autumn 1990; fellow, the Society of Industrial Artists and Designers; designed wedding dress for actress Catherine Zeta-Jones, 2000; began monthly fashion column in *Nurse2Nurse* magazine, 2001. *Elizabeth*—Launched Elizabeth Emanuel Couture fashion label, 1991; designed complete range of Virgin Airways uniforms and accessories, 1991; established Sew Forth Productions, 1993; launched wedding dress line for Bridal Fashions, London, 1994; designed costumes for Ballet Rambert, London Contemporary Dance Theatre, and Royal Ballet productions, London, 1990–94, and for musical theatre production of *Jean de Florette,* London, 1994–95; designed costumes for films, television, music videos, ad campaigns, and dance productions, mid- to late 1990s; designed flight attendant uniforms for Brittania Airlines, 1999. **Addresses:** David Emanuel Couture, Lanesborough Hotel, Lanesborough Place, London, SW 1X 7TA, England; Elizabeth Emanuel, Sew Forth Productions, 26 Chiltern Street, London, W1M 1PF, England.

Publications

By the EMANUELS:

Books

Style for All Seasons, London, 1983, 1984.

Articles

"Getting Going: David and Elizabeth Emanuel," in *Designer,* July 1981.
"Eyewitness in Manchester," in *Manchester Online,* 1 February 1999.
David—*Nurse2Nurse* magazine, August 2001 and forward.

On the EMANUELS:

Books

Stegemeyer, Anne, *Who's Who in Fashion, Third Edition,* New York, 1996.

Articles

Morris, B., "Couple's Design: Fit for a Queen," in the *New York Times Biographical Service,* November 1981.
Lynn, Frances, "The Amazing Emanuels," in *Women's Journal* (London), October 1983.
"New London Look: Lush, Plush," in *Chicago Tribune,* 20 March 1985.
Staniland, Kay, "The Wedding Dresses of H.R.H. the Princess of Wales and H.R.H. the Duchess of York," in *Costume* (London), 1987.
"Royal Treatment: Some of Britain's Top Designers have Taken Up Residence in London's Beauchamp Place," in *Chicago Tribune,* 10 February 1988.
Fairley, Josephine, "The 10-Year Stitch," in the *Sunday Express Magazine* (London), 27 November 1988.
"The Emanuel Gallery," in *Vogue* (London), December 1988.
Dutt, Robin, "The Emanuels," in *Clothes Show* (London), April 1989.
Fernand, Deirdre, "Framing a Fashion Career Move," in the *Sunday Times* (London), 7 January 1990.
Lee, Vinny, "Cream Sequence," in *Sunday Express Magazine* (London), 31 March 1991.

* * *

The romantic renaissance revival came to life in the early 1980s in the music world and in films. Nowhere, however, was it more apparent than in certain fashion circles. The announcement of the engagement of Charles, Prince of Wales, to Lady Diana Spencer made this an even bigger trend than it would normally have been. Lady Diana's penchant for ruffles created a need for this type of apparel, as she was already becoming a woman many wanted to emulate fashionwise.

It is appropriate the future princess chose the design team of David and Elizabeth Emanuel to create her wedding dress, because romance was the underlying theme to all of their clothing. Ruffles were the rule for the Emanuels, used on everything from gowns to pant suits and even swimwear. The duo, the only married couple to be accepted at the Royal College of Art, had operated their dressmaking shop in London since 1977, and in 1979 they took the unusual step of closing their ready-to-wear business to concentrate on the made-to-order business.

Although it was the ivory silk taffeta and tulle wedding dress worn by Diana in 1981 that brought the Emanuels international fame, they had a firmly entrenched business catering to what Americans would call the "carriage trade." It also enabled the Emanuels to enter into licensing agreements for items such as linens, sunglasses, and perfume.

Princess Anne and Princess Michael of Kent have both worn Emanuel designs for portraits. Her Royal Highness the Duchess of Kent joined these women and the Princess of Wales in their love of the Emanuels' work. Each dress was created specifically for the intended client, taking into account the ocassion where it would be worn, and the style of the wearer. Then a suitable reference in art was determined, and work progressed from there. Creations by artists from Botticelli to Renoir and Degas were used as influences, as were photographs of some of the more romantic women in history. The garments seen on Greta Garbo in *Camille,* Vivien Leigh in *Gone with the Wind,* and Marlene Dietrich in *The Scarlet Empress* were all recreated to some degree.

In this respect, David and Elizabeth were more stylists than designers, recreating a mood or image. They usually reinterpreted a design, however, rather than copied it—adding a fresh dimension through fabric or hidden detail. A wedding dress, for example, had subtly glittering mother-of-pearl sequins for a woman who was marrying in a dark church. The sequins picked up the light, allowing the bride to glow luminously. The veil for the Princess of Wales incorporated just such a sequin design, drawing attention to the bride. David and Elizabeth Emanuel were nothing if not retrospectively romantic, and all of their creations consciously reflected this trend.

Though Elizabeth and David divorced both personally and professionally in 1990, each continued in the couture businesses since their split. Both outfit numerous celebrities and are celebrities in their own right, particularly in the United Kingdom. They continue to separately design the wedding dresses for which they were best known during their partnership. Elizabeth has designed costumes for several ballet and dance companies, as well as for plays, movies, television series, music videos, and advertising campaigns. In 1997, she held a trunk show of her wedding dresses at Saks Fifth Avenue in New York, with her trip to the U.S. coinciding with the auction of the Princess of Wales' belongings at Christie's. As a result of this timing and the heightened interest in Princess Diana—Elizabeth appeared on many U.S. television programs, expanding her international reputation.

At the same time she was receiving such acclaim as the creator of Princess Diana's wedding gown, Elizabeth designed the wedding dress worn by actress Elizabeth Hurley in Estée Lauder's advertising campaign for the fragrance Beautiful. Elizabeth also designed the uniforms for Britannia Charter Airlines' flight attendants, which debuted in 1999. Additionally, Elizabeth's couture designs were embraced by celebrities including Joan Collins, Faye Dunaway, Twiggy, Drew Barrymore, and many other actresses, as well as members of the royal family.

As for David, his most highly publicized fashion design in recent years, at least in terms of worldwide renown, was the wedding gown worn by actress Catherine Zeta-Jones in her marriage to Michael Douglas in a ceremony at New York's Plaza Hotel in 2001. Zeta-Jones hails from David's native Wales.

In addition to his couture work, David has been active in a number of other endeavors. He writes a monthly column on fashion for the UK monthly trade magazine *Nurse2Nurse* and appeared on numerous television shows, including a program called *OOPS!* on which he was part of a celebrity panel discussing topics such as raising teenagers. He has also experimented in interior design, creating the honeymoon suite at the small Sheene Mill Hotel in the United Kingdom.

—Lisa Marsh; updated by Karen Raugust

EMARY, John

See AQUASCUTUM, LTD.

EMILIA, Reggie

See MARINA RINALDI, SrL

ENGLISH ECCENTRICS

British textile design and fashion company

Founded: by Helen and Judy Littman, 1982; *Helen Littman* born in Brighton, Sussex, 1955; studied at Brighton and Hove High School for Girls, 1966–72; Eastbourne College of Art and Design, 1972–74; Camberwell School of Arts and Crafts, 1974–77; founded Personal Items design company with Judy Littman, 1979. **Company History:** Began printing under name English Eccentrics, 1982; English Eccentrics made a limited company, 1984; opened Fulham Road, London, shop, 1987; first catwalk show, London, 1985; designed scarves for Royal Academy, London, 1989; Royal Pavilion, Harvey Nichols, and Girl Guides Association, 1990; designed scarf and clothing for Joseph, London, 1990; **Exhibitions:** *Mad Dogs and Englishmen,* Young Designer Show, London, October 1983; *London Goes to Tokyo,* Hanae Mori Building, Tokyo, November 1984; *Innovators in Fashion,* Pitti Palace, Florence, October 1985; *British Design,* Vienna, 1986; *British Scarves,* London, 1987; *British Design, New Traditions,* Boymans Museum, Rotterdam, 1989; *British Design,* Tokyo, 1990; *British Design 1790–1990,* Costa Mesa, California, 1990; *Collecting* *for the Future,* Victoria & Albert Museum, London 1990. **Awards:** Avant Garde Designer Preis, Munich, 1986. **Company Address:** 9/10 Charlotte Road, London EC2A 3DH, England.

PUBLICATIONS

On ENGLISH ECCENTRICS:

Books

Johnson, L., ed., *The Fashion Year,* London 1985.
McDermott, Catherine, ed., *English Eccentrics: The Textile Designs of Helen Littman,* San Francisco, 1993.

Articles

"Fabricated Fashion," in *You* magazine of the *Mail on Sunday* (London), 10 July 1983.
Brampton, Sally, "Still Crazy," in the *Observer* (London), 24 March 1985.
"English Eccentrics," in *DNR,* 25 March 1985.
Polan, Brenda, "Eccentric Fantasy," in *The Guardian,* 20 June 1985.
Thorpe, Brendan, "English Eccentrics in Retail Adventure," in *Design Week* (London), 7 August 1987.
Bain, Sally, "British Designers Preview," in *Draper's Record* (London), 5 March 1988.
Weibe, Susanne, "Beyond the Louvre," in *WWD,* 8 October 1991.
Fitzmaurice, Arabella, "Appearing in Print," in the *Sunday Times* (London), March 1992.
Gattemayer, Michela, "English Eccentrics: Moda Souvenir," in *Elle* (Italy), March 1992.
Menkes, Suzy, "From Cultural Symbols to Fabric Designs," in the *International Herald Tribune,* March 1992.
McHugh, Fionnuala, "Material Success," in the *Telegraph Magazine* (London), 14 March 1992.
Feron, Francesca, "The Eclectic Eccentrics Whose Designs Got to Your Head," in the *Glasgow Herald,* May 1992.
Davis, Maggie, "Fashion Notebook One," in the *Observer,* 9 November 1997.
Moin, David, "Saks Showcases British Style," in *WWD,* 26 August 1998.
"English Eccentrics," in *Footwear News,* 3 January 2000.
"From Ralph Lauren to Chanel: Crystals Line the Runways," in *PR Newswire,* 18 September 2000.
"Final Word on Fall, available online at Fashion Planet, www.fashion-planet.com, 29 September 2001.

*

I believe that all women have their own beauty and that striving to look like the stereotyped images in our media can undermine this. However, I feel there is no reason why we should not enjoy using beauty products and I think dressing well is a great pleasure. We dress to enhance our appearance, and my aim in designing is that the clothes and accessories we produce are fun to wear and help to make any woman look wonderful be she overweight, over eighty, or a fashion model. I am always conscious of the body as the final showplace for my designs.

—Helen Littman

* * *

Named after Edith Sitwell's book of the same title, English Eccentrics established an international reputation for its distinct printed textiles since they were first sold at a stall in London's Kensington Market in 1984. The company was founded in 1982 by sisters Helen and Judy Littman when they began printing their designs onto fabric on the floor of their studio in Wapping. Helen Littman, the creative inspiration behind the company, trained as a textile designer at Camberwell School of Art, while Judy, who studied painting, controlled the business and promotions side.

The Littman sisters and their quirky company name were timed perfectly with the emergence of London as the most happening fashion center during the early 1980s, when the likes of John Galliano, Katharine Hamnett, and Vivienne Westwood were beginning to make their mark in international fashion. English Eccentrics was also mentioned in the famous article published by *Women's Wear Daily* (New York), when it announced in 1983 that "London Swings Again."

English Eccentrics is recognized for its use of extravagantly rich combinations of color and unusual trompe l'oeil designs inspired by a myriad of subjects, including travel, ecology, architecture, costume, and nature, which are translated onto the highest quality silks. Helen credits much of her inspiration from what she calls her own "Grand Tour," which was in fact a series of short trips abroad during which she used a sketchbook and a camera to record ideas for future designs. It is, however, the way in which Littman uses the ideas that is the key to her success as a designer.

Littman acknowledges "obvious cultural piracy is boring" and thus reworks each idea in a thoroughly modern way. Littman's treatment of her inspiration is clearly illustrated by what has become one of English Eccentric's best-known designs, called Hands. On a visit to Manhattan, Littman was surprised by the number of palmistry parlors she saw, which she found completely at odds with her personal image of the powerful city. For the design, Littman combined a handprint with elements taken from New York graffiti and palmistry diagrams. Its spiral border pattern was inspired by Gustav Klimt's painting the *Tree of Life.* The result is an abstract pattern printed in five colorways for scarf squares and which was also adapted for giftwrap paper as well as designs for hosiery.

The special qualities of silk have proved to be the ideal fabric medium for English Eccentrics because it enables very intense, vibrant colors as well as softer muted shades to be printed in accurate detail. Another feature of Littman's designs is that all printing is done by hand with acid dyes rather than pigment colors, which do not have the same qualities of clarity. Between 1984 and 1988, English Eccentrics also produced 10 clothing collections and translated their designs onto stationery, furnishing fabrics, and packaging.

The ensuing financial climate of the late 1980s, however, forced the company to tailor these activities, and the Littmans began to concentrate solely upon producing the silk scarf squares for which they were best recognized. These designs were also used to create a small range of classic garments such as shirts and waistcoats that incorporated the square scarf into their design. The company introduced *devore* velvet into their collection for winter 1993 with great success—their *devore* tunic became one of the season's key garments, worn by fashion editors, buyers, and film stars alike. The same season, English Eccentrics also enlarged the scarf range to include more than 60 colors, fabrics, and styles.

In 1991, Catherine McDermott, author of definitive works on Gianni Versace and Vivienne Westwood, edited *English Eccentrics: The Textile Designs of Helen Littman,* a lavishly illustrated, richly colored compendium of Helen and Judy Littman's prints reprising myth-based designs over the past decade. The vibrant patterns suit ties, shirts, jackets, shawls, dresses, and silk scarves, have appealed to a wide range of buyers, including Mick Jagger, Paul McCartney, and Prince. For the book blurb, Littman explained the importance of travel, the women's peace movement, and environmental issues to her creativity, with which the design group Carroll, Dempsey & Thirkell permeated the text.

To Susan Weibe of *Women's Wear Daily,* Helen Littman elaborated on her label's individualism, "Our signature is our color sense and our imagery, which is unusual." For spring 1991, English Eccentrics showcased Elements of the Portman Vase at the British Museum for a tapestry appeal reflecting the painted imagery and abstractions of Cy Twombly, the Virginia-born contemporary artist. On exhibition in the Quai Branly tent at Paris sur Mode near the Eiffel Tower rather than the standard location at the Louvre, the English Eccentrics collection featured prices ranging from $30 to $400. Buyers from the U.S. could find Littman prints at Barneys, Henri Bendel, and Bergdorf Goodman.

For spring-summer 1994, English Eccentrics introduced its first ready-to-wear collection since 1988, which included sarong skirts, trousers, shirts, and jackets in plain linens, silks, and *devore* velvet combined with pieces featuring the season's new print designs on silk. Unlike many of their designer counterparts who achieved notoriety during the early years of the 1980s, English Eccentrics has managed to build upon its success while remaining firmly based in Britain. They export all over the world from England, which is, after all, the only proper base for a company of that name.

On-target choices have kept English Eccentrics current and hot. In fall 1998, Littman was showing clingy little-girl looks in button-up cardigans with scoop necks and circlets of glitter at above-the-wrist sleeves. For fall 2000, the design group incorporated a sprinkling of Swarovski crystals. Of the ideas that impact her work, Littman commented that she likes the hobo look for hand-printed dresses and chooses simple designs because—simply—she can't sew.

—Catherine Woram; updated by Mary Ellen Snodgrass

ERMENEGILDO ZEGNA GROUP

Italian design firm and retailer

Founded: in 1910 by Ermenegildo Zegna (1892–1966) in Trivero, Biellese Alps, Italy. **Company History:** Business turned over to sons, Aldo and Angelo, who expanded into ready-to-wear clothing, menswear line, 1960s; opened branches in Spain, France, Germany, Austria, U.S., Japan, and United Kingdom; group-controlled production units opened in Spain and Switzerland, 1968; specializes in men's ready-to-wear; first U.S. boutique, 1989; fragrance, *Zegna;* opened Beijing flagship, 1991; E.Z. line, designed by Kim Herring, launched 1993; Oasi Zegna, land recovery program, Trivero, 1993; opened first outlet store, New York, 1997; opened first store in India, 1999; acquired Angora womenswear, launched Zegna Sport, and began online selling, 1999; formed partnership with Armani, 2000. **Exhibitions:** *Made in Italy,* Pier 84, New York, 1988; *Wool Bicentennial,* Barcelona, 1990; *The Meandering Pattern in Brocades and Silk,* Milan, 1990–91; and at the Fashion Institute of Technology, New York, 1992. **Collections:** The Power House Museum, Sydney; Museo della Scienza e della Tecnica, Milan. **Awards:** Cavaliere del Lavoro (to Ermenegildo Zegna), 1930. **Company Address:** 5 Via Forcella, 20144 Milan, Italy. **Company Website:** www.zegnaermenegildo.com.

Publications

On ERMENEGILDO ZEGNA GROUP:

Books

Storie e favole di moda, Italy, 1982.
Giacomoni, Silvia, *The Italian Look Reflected,* Italy, 1984.
Canali, Renato, *La Panoramica Zegna,* Italy, 1985.
Enciclopedia della moda, Milan, 1989.
Villarosa, R., and Angeli, G., *Homo elegans,* Milan, 1990.
The Meandering Pattern in Brocaded Silks, 1745–1775, [exhibition catalogue], Milan, 1990.
Chaille, F., *La grande histoire de la cravatte,* France, 1994.
Martin, Richard, and Harold Koda, *Two by Two: Metropolitan Museum of Art,* New York, 1996.

Articles

"Fuori la stoffa, ragazzi," in *Panorama* (Milan), 24 May 1992.
"Der Kaschmir-Clan," in *Stern* (Germany), September 1992.
"Zegna alla Conquista della Cina," in *La Stampa* (Turin), 7 July 1993.
"La seconda conquista dell'America," in *L'indipendente,* 26 November 1993.
Siow, Doreen, "High Price Can be a Strong Suit," in the *Sunday Times* (London), 13 December 1993.
"Ecology: The Best Strategy," in *Newsweek,* 31 January 1994.
"La ricerca Zegna sui materiali," in *Il Sole 24 Ore* (Italy), 15 March 1994.
Dubini, Laura, "La géneration verte," in *Jardin des Modes* (Paris), April 1994.
Gellers, Stan, "There's Hard Business Sense Behind the Soft Suit," in *DNR,* 25 April 1994.
Bow, Jospehine J., "China Acquires a Small Taste of Italy," in *DNR,* 16 May 1994.
"Zegna quota 500 miliardi nel 1994," in *Il Sole 24 Ore* (Italy), 17 May 1994.
Levine, Joshua, "Armani's Counterpart," in *Forbes,* 4 July 1994.
Gellars, Stan, "Zegna Built its $85M U.S. Business by Using Americana Marketing," in *DNR,* 20 December 1995.

Palmieri, Jean E., "Zegna Sets Florida, Hawaii Stores," in *DNR,* 3 June 1996.
Gellars, Stan, "Zegna Finds a New Outlet for Its Fashion," in *DNR,* 14 April 1997.
Kline, Maureen, "Chic Executives Go for Zegna," in the *Wall Street Journal,* 27 August 1998.
Betts, Paul, "A Range of Ties for All Occasions," in the *Financial Times,* 23 September 1998.
Conti, Samantha, "Zegna to Buy Lanerie Agnona," in *WWD,* 14 January 1999.
Sman, Katherine, "Zegna Licensed to Make Ungaro Signature Collection," in *DNR,* 15 January 1999.
Zargani, Luisa, "Armani and Zegna Form Joint Venture," in *WWD,* 25 July 2000.
Daswani, Kavita, "Indian Men Beginning to Embrace High Fashion...Zegna Stores Appeal to Newly Fashion-Conscious Customer," in *DNR,* 21 February 2001.
"Zegna Vision Lives On," in the *New Straits Times,* 2 April 2001.

*

Ermenegildo Zegna was founded in 1910 as a company which created and produced woolen fabrics. Our philosophy has always been based on quality and the search for excellence.

What makes Zegna unique is that it is the only company of its type in the world specialized in the direct purchase of natural raw materials on their markets of origin, with a totally verticalized creative and production cycle going from raw materials to cloths, clothing and accessories, which are internationally distributed through Zegna's salespoints and other selected menswear shops.

Finally, Zegna is also characterized by its sensitivity and respect for the environment. As early as 1930, Ermenegildo Zegna established and financed a vast project for the reclamation of the mountain overlooking Trivero, the village in the Alpine foothills of Biella where Zegna's headquarters are located. Following in the footsteps of the company's founder, the younger generations of the family have created "Oasi Zegna,"a project designed to protect nature over an area of about 100 square kilometres.

—Ermenegildo Zegna Group

* * *

"Our typical client believes in understated classic styles," says Gildo Zegna, grandson of the family firm's founder. "That's why they like Ermenegildo Zegna." Ermenegildo Zegna Group is not a brand of radical fashion statements; on the contrary, very classic tailoring, rich and supple fabrics, and obsessive attention to detail make Zegna the Rolls Royce of menswear, an image the firm is quick to reinforce.

The company's marketing and advertising copy describes wool spun into strands so fine one kilo stretches 150,000 metres, hand-sewn buttons, and the hand-pressing of each jacket before leaving the factory. The latter, it was said, took 45 minutes, but then suit prices are high. Zegna built a reputation on catering only to the richest of businessmen, well-established celebrities, and the world's royalty; only near the end of the 20th century did the firm expand into less exclusive apparel.

Zegna clothes are quintessentially English, from the suits of a world-class banker to the casualwear of a world-beating yachtsman or horsemaster. The fabrics are Italian, made for lightweight softness and presoaked in the waters of the Italian Alps, whose mineral-free quality has been sought after by Italian cloth merchants since the Middle Ages. The craftsmanship is Swiss—accurate, precise, always correct, while colors change year on year. Winter 1993 was brick, brown, tobacco, evergreen, billiard green, emerald; winter 1994 was eye-blue, cobalt, stone grey, tobacco, some red, more browns. Raw materials come from the world over—wool from Australia, cashmere from China, mohair from South Africa. Although most upmarket menswear producers use similar resources and methods, Zegna takes its selection a few steps further—for example, the firm's preferred cashmere is that of a Chinese goat, aged between three and five years. It then becomes understood the creators at Zegna are not just professionals but inspired visionaries of men's clothing.

Much of Zegna's strength lies in its manufacturing process. The company is vertically integrated, buying its own raw materials, making its own fabrics, designing its clothes, and running its own boutiques. The firm has always been forward-looking, yet steeped in tradition; it uses the most advanced databases to maintain and update customer measurements, purchases, and personal details, and uses CAD (computer-aided design) programs to adjust patterns. Wool fabrics, however, were still handwashed and suits still finished by hand.

Zegna is, however, successful in a highly competitive sector. The 1994 market for men's suits costing over $1,000 was considered one million units per year; Zegna sold 300,000 such suits during the year, capturing 30-percent of the market. To maintain and grow in this sector, their marketing has been subtle—like sponsoring a yacht race in Portofino, Italy, with no loud banners or posters, just models walking through the crowd wearing Zegna blazers with the small white EZ logo. Then there are the seat covers for Saab 9000 cars, where Saab salesmen were drilled in the virtues and qualities of Zegna fabrics so they would pass the information on to buyers. Zegna has also mailed sample swatches and possible combinations of jackets, ties, and shirts to their best customers.

In the middle and later 1990s, Zegna expanded into new markets with soft suits, the casual cut, and mix-and-match coordinates which were popular in the U.S., France, and Italy. Specifically for the U.S. market, Zegna designed sportswear to compete with Hugo Boss, Giorgio Armani, and Calvin Klein—shirts, slacks, and sports and outerwear jackets aimed at the 35-plus market. To complete a man's wardrobe, Zegna also makes natural cotton undergarments, high quality corporate gifts, and a signature fragrance.

Perhaps Zegna's most important strength is the tightknit family behind the company; the children of founder Ermenegildo Zegna as well as many of his grandchildren and great-grandchildren have roles within the firm. There was no indication such a reliance on home-grown talent led to stagnation, although outsiders also played major roles in the firm, especially in America. By 1996 there were five freestanding Zegna stores in the U.S., with the latest shops opening in Hawaii and Florida. Zegna also ventured into lower-priced goods with its first outlet store, in a large mall in Central Valley, New York, in 1997. Surrounded by such high-end designers as Christian Dior, Tommy Hilfiger, Ralph Lauren, Brooks Brothers, and Barneys, the firm was in exceedingly good company.

Ermenegildo Zegna menswear is internationally known for its high quality and exquisite fabrics. Rapidly approaching its centennial, the firm has kept abreast of the times, from launching a website and introducing sportswear, to forging alliances with other menswear leaders like Armani and Ungaro. The family-run empire has a growing global presence in Europe, as well as two dozen shops in China, and its second store opening in the virtually untapped menswear market in India.

—Sally Anne Melia; updated by Sydonie Benét

ERREUNO SCM SPA

Italian ready-to-wear firm

Founded: by Ermanno Ronchi (born 28 May 1947) and Graziella Ronchi Pezzutto (born 24 November 1945) in Milan, 1971. **Company History:** Added Donnaerre line of women's clothes, 1981; Erreuno Uomo line, 1985; Erreuno Jeans collection, 1986; Graziella Ronchi Cocktail line, 1986; Erreuno Golf lines, 1989; Erreuno J line, designed by Michael Kors, introduced in U.S, 1990; launched first fragrance, 1994; signed with Guaber Group to license fragrances, 1995; second fragrance launched with fall ready-to-wear line, 1996; Guglielmo Capone hired as stylist. **Company Address:** Via Bensi 6, 20152 Milan, Italy.

Publications

On ERREUNO:

Articles

Haber, Holly, "Erreuno J Makes U.S. Debut in Dallas," in *WWD,* 15 August 1990.
"Cosmoprof Exhibit Fragrance Launches," in *Cosmetics International,* 10 May 1994.
Barone, Amy B., "Eurocosmesi's Worldwide Plan," in *WWD,* 9 June 1995.

Erreuno SCM SpA, fall/winter 2001–02 collection: suit with fox fur sleeves. © AP/Wide World Photos.

Erreuno SCM SpA, fall/winter 2001–02 collection. © AP/Wide World Photos.

Muir, Lucie, "Italian Designers Bring Body Conscious Looks Center Stage for Spring/Summer 1997 with High-Tech Fabrics," in *WWD,* 18 September 1996.

Dichter, Peter, "Vegetable, Mineral, Celebrity: Is Name Alone Enough to Sell a Fragrance?" in *Global Cosmetic Industry,* October 2000.

* * *

Erreuno is the brainchild of Ermanno and Graziella Ronchi, who established the company in Milan in 1971. The company name is a combination of the pronunciation of the first letter of the Ronchi name R (Erre) and Uno, the Italian word for one, chosen because it was the couple's first business venture.

The Ronchis wanted to create something influential and significant in the Italian fashion world, to establish a company that provided top quality ready-to-wear designs for the smart, modern, and discerning woman. Extremely positive in their approach, their success has been the result of hard work, commitment, and teamwork. Ermanno handles all the administrative and financial side of the business while Graziella oversees design and marketing.

Fabric is of prime importance in any Erreuno collection. Designing often appears to be a grouping together of expensive fibers, textures, plaids, prints, mattes, and shines, then coordinating these into wearable, sporty, classic clothes. Graziella Ronchi places great emphasis on fabric research and over two-thirds of the fabrics are developed in the firm's Milan studios. Great care is given to the choice of fabrics used in each collection to ensure that, when made into garments and styled together, they give a strong visual impact and provide versatility of choice for a wide variety of women.

Never at the cutting edge of designer fashion, Erreuno instead evolves its own particular style each season. A feeling for softness combined with architectural design is reflected in each individual garment and, when incorporated as part of an outfit, adds its own contribution to the finished look. Erreuno's initial success was in the design and manufacture of skirts. The range expanded and developed to include complete womenswear outfits and in 1975 led to a seasonal ready-to-wear collection, shown twice a year in Milan. Since then the company has steadily evolved to incorporate many other goods: leathers, wallets, foulards, key pouches, bags, hats, and gloves. Sold in worldwide boutiques, the products give customers the opportunity to coordinate an Erreuno outfit with top quality accessories, adding greater credence to the company's marketing strategy.

Erreuno collections provide a refreshing presence on the Milan catwalks. Perched midway between the extremes of Dolce & Gabbana's expensive vamps and Giorgio Armani's exquisite classicism, the Erreuno look is one of neutrality. A softly tailored tiny-check suit is teamed with a belted, collarless blouson, an oversize ankle-length, belted mackintosh is teamed with shorts, subtly playing on long and short, or an understated mix of stripes in an outfit comprised of four different types of stripe. Color for Erreuno is soft and discerning; the beiges, browns, creams, lilacs, off-whites, or warm greys are never loud or unflattering.

In the mid-1990s the Ronchis segued into fragrance, with their first scent for women aptly named *Erreuno.* Although many fashion firms were producing fragrances, Erreuno differed in that the floral scent was not licensed but created in-house under the supervision of Graziella. The Ronchis decided to pursue further fragrances, however, forming Erreuno Parfums and signed a licensing agreement with the Guaber Group in 1995. A second women's fragrance debuted with the firm's ready-to-wear collection in the fall of 1996.

The expression and imagination of Ermanno and Graziella Ronchi, combined with their flair for design, marketing, and manufacturing, have found the perfect complement in their company. Erreuno and its major lines, Erreuno, Donna Erre and Miss Erreuno, play a pivotal role in Italian fashion, whether through strong showings in Milan or the special identity the firm's clothes create for women.

—Kevin Almond

ESCADA

German fashion house

Founded: by Wolfgang and Margarethe Ley (died 1992) in Munich, 1976. **Company History:** Expanded throughout Germany, then into U.S., 1982; company went public, 1986; began opening retail stores

Escada, spring/summer 2001 collection. © AP/Wide World Photos.

in Europe and U.S., from 1987; granted license for Nino Cerruti womenswear, 1989; Escada leather goods, from 1990, and Apriori bridge line, from 1991; purchased U.S.-based St. John Knits, 1991; formed cosmetics division, Escada Beauté, 1991; Michael Stolzenburg succeeded Ley as designer, 1992–94; St. John Knits sold, 1993; Todd Oldham named creative consultant, 1995; debut of first Escada Couture collection, 1995; Escada Sport formed, 1996; acquired Parfums Gres, 1998; Escada Golf line launched, 1999; company reorganized, 2000; Dinh Vang Co. Ltd. named exclusive distributor for brand in Vietnam, 2001; partnered with SECON Group to buy Louis Féraud, 2001; fragrances include *Escada Margaretha Ley* introduced in U.S., 1990, in Germany and UK, 1991; *Escada Pour Homme,* 1993; *Chiffon Sorbet* (seasonal scent—summer), 1993; *En Fleur,* 1997; *Grain de Folie,* 1998; *Collection* (seasonal—winter) and *Sunny Frutti* (seasonal—summer), 1998; *Casual Friday* for men, 1999; *Loving Bouquet* (summer), 1999; *Lily Chic* (summer) 2000; *Tropical Punch* (summer) 2001; *Sentiment,* 2001; lines include Laurèl, Primera, and Kemper/Cerruti brands. **Awards:** Dallas Fashion award, Best Designer Sportswear, 1986; Fragrance Foundation award, 1990; Dallas Fashion award, for Fashion Excellence, 1998; Wolfgang Ley awarded the Officer's Cross of the Order of Merit (1st Class), Federal Republic of Germany, 1999. **Company Address:** Margaretha-Ley-Ring 1 D-85609 Aschheim bei München, Germany. **Company Website:** www.escada.com.

Publications

On ESCADA:

Articles

Shiro, Anne-Marie, "Black Ties Come Out to Herald a New Boutique (Escada in New York)," in the *New York Times,* 24 November 1991.

Agins, Teri, "Despite the Recession, High Fashion Escada Expands World-Wide," in the *Wall Street Journal,* 15 April 1992.

"Swede Success," in *Woman's Journal* (London), May 1992.

"Margarethe Ley, Cofounder of Escada AG Dead at 56," in *WWD,* 8 June 1992.

Shiro, Anne-Marie, "Margaretha Ley, Sportswear Designer and Merchant, Dies," in the *New York Times,* 9 June 1992.

Geran, Monica, "Escada (Design of New York Flagship Store)," in *Interior Design,* July 1992.

White, Constance C.R., "Escada Evolves," in *WWD,* 4 November 1992.

Drier, Melissa, "Escada Sport: Going Casual," in *WWD,* 2 March 1994.

Lender, Heidi, "Escada's New Era," in *WWD,* 21 December 1994.

Spindler, Amy, "Eyes on Escada," in the *New York Times,* 10 January 1995.

Aykroyd, Bettina, "Escada Beauté: Growth Through Acquisition and Innovation," in *Soap & Cosmetics Specialties,* January 1998.

Manan, Dazman, "Escada Finds Sweet Success," in the *New Straits Times,* 6 May 1999.

Rubenstein, Hal, "The Look of Escada," in *In Style,* 1 January 2001.

"Fascinating Escada," in *Siagon Times Magazine,* 30 September 2001.

Escada, spring/summer 2001 collection. © AP/Wide World Photos.

* * *

The Escada group was founded in 1976 near Munich, Germany, by Wolfgang and Margarethe Ley. The company took its name from an Irish thoroughbred racehorse and both Leys were betting on their enterprise to win. The group designs, produces, and distributes high quality women's fashion, marketed worldwide to leading fashion stores and proprietary boutiques. Apart from Escada by Margarethe Ley, which included apparel, luggage, fragrance, and accessories, the group's other labels have included Cerruti 1881, Crisca, Kemper, Laurel, Apriori, Seasons, Natalie Acatrini, Marie Gray, Schneberger, and St. John (sold in 1993).

Margarethe Ley was the chief designer for the group until her death in 1992. She strongly adhered to the belief that a designer must never rely solely on creative talent to be a success; creativity must be balanced by a strong market appeal. Ley created a highly distinctive identity for Escada—clean, slick, and sophisticated. She also pioneered the development of exiciting new fabric combinations and color schemes when so many other designers were solidly into black.

When Ley died, she was succeeded by Michael Stolzenburg who brought a younger, more modern perspective to the company. Taking his influence from daily life, he believed the balance of a collection relied on the mix of tried and true design and fresh new ideas. He was backed by a strong team of designers, chiefly from British and German fashion schools. During this time Escada also spearheaded an unusual fragrance turn, producing the company's first "seasonal" scent. The earliest concoction, *Chiffon Sorbet,* was a summer fragrance and had been marketed only through the summer months in 1993. The seasonal gambit garnered attention, yet 1994 brought the untimely death of Stolzenburg. The firm turned to Todd Oldham to serve as the company's creative consultant in 1994, the same year Escada Sport was launched. Oldham's creations were enthusiastically received, and in 1995 both Escada Knit and Classic Elements became available in the company's wide spectrum of colors and fabrics.

In the late 1990s Escada launched an eyewear collection with Airess, its first major licensing deal, then followed with a slew of accessories including jewelry, lingerie, shoes, scarves, and ties. New fragrances, both traditional and the experimental seasonal scents, were also introduced including the Escada Sport trio (*Sport Spirit, Feeling Free,* and *Country Weekend,* 1997), *En Fleur* (1997, and later brought out in a compact design in 1999), *Casual Friday* (1999), *Loving Bouquet* (a seasonal installment, 1999), and *Sentiment* (2001).

In the early 2000s Escada had over 375 boutiques worldwide, including new boutiques in Paris and Kuala Lumpur, and was relocating its New York flagship store to larger digs on Fifth Avenue. The luxury retailer was considered the world's largest ready-to-wear producer with some 1,500 different styles available each year, and to increase its marketshare further, Escada entered into a joint venture in the summer of 2001 with the SECON Group, each buying a 45-percent stake in Louis Féraud. The entrepreneurial spirit of founders Wolfgang and Margarethe Ley is alive and well in the enduring success of Escada.

—Kevin Almond; updated by Nelly Rhodes

ESPRIT HOLDINGS, INC.

American fashion design company

Cofounded: as Plain Jane Dress Company by Susie and Doug Tompkins and Jane Tise in San Francisco, 1968; the Tompkins became sole owners, 1975; couple divorced, 1989; shares sold to Susie Tompkins, 1990; company incorporated and name changed to Esprit de Corp., 1970; **Company History:** Worldwide sales reached more than $1 billion by 1987; Esprit Men designed in Dusseldorf and launched in Europe, 1989; Ecollection, environmentally friendly line using organic fabrics and low impact fibers, launched, 1992; ready-to-wear in Japan, 1993; 240 retail stores worldwide by 1994; Susie Tompkins line discontinued, 1995; creditors take over, Tompkins replaced by Jay Margolis, 1996; joint venture with China Resources Enterprises, 1997; celebrated 30th anniversary and launched DKNY toddler and infant line, 1998; lost DKNY children's license to Oxford Industries, 2000; Margolis departed and Joe Hein took the reins, 2000; debuted *Esprit Scents and Senses* line of fragrances, 2001; signed licensing deals for sleepwear, outerwearm and swimsuits, 2001. **Company Address:** 900 Minnesota Street, San Francisco, CA 94107, U.S.A. **Company Website:** www.esprit.com.

Publications

On ESPRIT:

Articles

Sudjic, Deyan, "Esprit: The Singular Multiple," in *Blueprint* (London), June 1987.
Benson, Heidi, "Reinventing Esprit," in the *San Francisco Focus,* February 1991.
McGrath, Ellie, "Esprit, the Sequel," in *Working Woman,* September 1991.
White, Constance C.R., "Tompkins Gets Her Line," in *WWD,* 2 March 1992.
Zinn, Laura, "Will Politically Correct Sell Sweaters?" in *Business Week,* 16 March 1992.
Lawson, Skippy, "Esprit and the Rain Forests," in *WWD,* 29 April 1992.
White, Constance C.R., "Susie Tompkins: Crossing a New Bridge," *WWD,* 10 March 1993.
"Susie's New Spirit," in *W,* 10 May 1993.
Stodder, Gayle Sato, "A Perfect Fit," in *Entrepreneurial Woman* (New York), Summer 1993.
Ozzard, Janet, "Jay Margolis Heading Esprit, Opting Out of Deal on Tracy, in *WWD,* 9 January 1996.
Underwood, Elaine, "Reinventing Esprit's Core," in *Brandweek,* 13 May 1996.
White, Constance C.R., "Esprit Shifts Its Focus," in the *New York Times,* 4 February 1997.
"Esprit Slates DKNY Line for Infants," in *WWD,* 11 June 1998.
Hofman, Mike, "Susie and Doug Tompkins," in *Inc.,* September 1998.
Lockwood, Lisa, "Margolis to Exit Esprit," in *WWD,* 9 September 1999.
Carlsen, Clifford, "Revlon Exec to Lead the Troops at Esprit de Corp.," in the *San Francisco Business Times,* 3 December 1999.
"Karan Switches License for DKNY Kids to Oxford," in *WWD,* 7 March 2000.
Drier, Melissa, "Lancaster Launches Esprit Scent Sextet," in *WWD,* 20 October 2000.
"Esprit Set for Return to UK," in *UK Retail Report,* December 2000.
"Hochman's Esprit Deal," in *WWD,* 16 July 2001.

*

When we started the Plain Jane Dress Company in 1968, we never dreamed it would develop into the worldwide organization now known as Esprit, with operations in [dozens of] countries. "Esprit de Corp.," our official corporate name, was intended to inspire the spirit of the organization and evoke a sense of cooperation, camaraderie, and community.

When we started Esprit we had no previous experience whatsoever in the fashion business...what business skills we might have possessed came from being in the mountain climbing equipment industry for a brief time, where any reference to fashion was an anathema. The idea of fashion, image, and image-making was far from our minds. It was not, in fact, until 12 years after the founding of the company that any attempt to form an image and create a context for the product was made. In 1980 a radical shift in direction was undertaken. A mixed bag of seven different trade names was consolidated under one name, Esprit, and a new logo along with new labels, tags, packaging, and strong fashion photography was created.

As in all things that start modestly and by amateurs, progress, growth, expansion, and refinements come in steps and stages. Experience is gathered on the job and a process begins and evolves. Likewise, success leads to more opportunities, mistakes, improvements, and avoidance of repeating past errors, or hopefully so!

Today, Esprit designs, manufacturers, and distributes product lines four seasons per year, including infant, toddler, kids, womenswear, menswear, footwear, accessories, bath and bed, eyewear, and watches. Because clothing is one of our most basic means of self expression, the fashion industry lends itself toward the communication of values, and offers us the challenge and opportunity to interpret the ongoing changes throughout the world. Our corporate mission statement is: "Be informed. Be involved. Make a difference." It may seem like an idealistic and unusual guiding philosophy for an international fashion company, but Esprit has never been "business as usual."

—Esprit

* * *

The Esprit label graces clothing, shoes, accessories—anything a woman can wear with comfort both at work and at play. As *W* magazine put it, Esprit is "part of that huge, growing category of well-priced clothes that range from the street-smart style of DKNY and CK Calvin Klein to the career-oriented mood of Ellen Tracy and Anne Klein II." Perhaps the most distinguishing features of Esprit fashions are what the clothing are not—Esprit labels may never appear on the clingy cocktail dress, the stifling "power suit," or the crippling high-heeled pump. Instead, a typical Esprit outfit shows a looser-fitting rayon vest or tunic over wide-legged pants or perhaps a flowing, calf-length skirt made of soft cotton.

According to the journal *View on Colour,* Esprit "has come to epitomize the Northern California lifestyle, an informative mix of a sunny climate, bold colors, outdoor sports, eternal youth, and social values. Esprit's saucy sportswear…encouraged (if not triggered) the worldwide sportswear boom." This success was the result of the personal vision of Esprit de Corp. cofounder Susie Tompkins, who got her start, along with partner Jane Tise, in her native San Francisco selling homemade frocks under the name Plain Jane in 1968. For its first several years, the line was especially popular with teenagers. Eventually, however, the clothing represented both youthful style and career-minded fashion that might be found in grown-up settings, such as the casual office.

In the early 1980s, a poor business decision over shopping venues nearly caused the downfall of Esprit de Corp. Though it had its best success as a subsection of other retail outlets the company attempted to expand its base into individual outlets. This put Esprit into direct competition with such names as Gap and The Limited. By the time Esprit had extricated itself from this marketing notion, the fashion line had, according to industry expert Allan Millstein, "missed the market for five years. They missed 20 seasons…[meaning] they lost half a generation of kids."

Between 1975 and 1987, Esprit's worldwide sales approached $1 billion. But by 1987, after Tompkins and her husband/business partner Doug Tompkins disagreed on the company's direction, sales dropped. Doug offered to buy the company from under Susie; she considered the proposal until a meeting with another fashion entrepreneur, Bruce Katz of Rockport Shoes, persuaded her to stay with the company she had founded. So the designer elected to buy out Doug instead, enlisting the financial support of Katz and several others. The estranged Doug and Susie met to work out the future of Esprit. They came to the decision that Susie would buy back the company, and Doug would bow out to the tune of $125 million.

Under Tompkins' direction, the company initiated the Ecollection line of clothing in the spring of 1992—"a big step, even for trendsetting Esprit," according to *View on Colour.* The Ecollection fashions were notable for being produced in the most environmentally friendly way possible. Ecollection wasn't the only Esprit subsection, however, since the 1970s the company has initiated several product lines. Besides the regular Esprit-branded products, there are Esprit Footwear and Accessories, Esprit Kids, and the Susie Tompkins signature line which was considered more sophisticated and aimed at working women older than 25 (line discontinued in 1995).

In the field of marketing, Esprit worked hard to keep its brand name in chain department stores like T.J. Maxx and in various company-owned venues. Franchises ranged in location from Hawaii to Puerto Rico, and Esprit maintained outlet stores throughout the United States. In March of 1993 Tompkins outlined Esprit's future for *Women's Wear Daily,* stating that the firm wanted to "Develop business with existing customers as well as with existing stores…Esprit, like the entire junior market, is in the process of reevaluating the customer today, and I'm continuing to pursue this marketplace with consideration of the roots and culture of this company."

Tompkins also stressed Esprit wasn't "trendy," as she stated in a *San Francisco Focus* article. "We don't have to be doing what everybody else is doing. We just have to do our style, which is a kind of eclecticness and an integrity of design. Mixing old things with new things; having a really nice way of presenting color." Unfortunately for Tompkins and Esprit, however, was the company's slide into trouble in the mid- and late 1990s. Tompkins left the company after creditors took control, and Jay Margolis, formerly of Tommy Hilfiger, was brought in to save the ailing retailer in 1996.

Margolis succeeded in revitalizing Esprit's image and bringing the firm back to profitablility through a slew of shrewd marketing deals. Declining to renew his contract, he left in late 1999 was replaced by Joe Heid, a former Revlon executive. Heid focused less on licenses and more on Esprit's own brands, telling Clifford Carlsen of the *San Francisco Business Times* (3 December 1999), "We need to grow Esprit, and the avenues are limitless." Heid reintroduced the company in the UK by opening two large stores in 2000, even though only two years earlier nine Esprit outlets had been shuttered. Additionally, Heid initiated a $10-million advertising campaign in home base San Francisco, signed licensing deals for sleepwear, outerwear, and swimsuits for women and girls, and launched a line of bath and body products, called *Esprit Scents and Senses,* in its two biggest markets, Germany and Hong Kong.

—Susan Salter; updated by Owen James

ESTEREL, Jacques

French designer

Born: Charles Martin, 1918. **Education:** Studied engineering. **Career:** Writer and composer; couture house, Creations Jacques Esterel established, 1953, filed suit against Yves Saint Laurent, 1979; suit resolved in his favor, 1985. **Died:** 1974.

Publications

On ESTEREL:

Articles

"L'univers de Jacques Esterel," in *Jardin des Arts* (Paris) May/June 1973.

"YSL is Fined for Being a Copycat," in the *Chicago Tribune,* 17 July 1985.

* * *

Couturier Jacques Esterel liked to refer to himself as a "Parisian craftsman of dresses and songs." And in fact he was an entertainer as well as a designer, writing several plays and songs for the guitar in addition to running his many boutiques in France and throughout Europe. He brought his theatrical side into his clothing design, creating amusing novelties and employing outrageous styles and props, so much so that many of his admirers and critics considered him more of a showman than a serious couturier.

Jacques Esterel, 1966 collection: "Playtime 1," a beachshift ensemble with "Happy Glasses." © AP/Wide World Photos.

Esterel, whose real name was Charles Martin, was the son of a French industrialist and was originally educated as an engineer. He established his couture house, Jacques Esterel, in 1953. The first years were especially successful as Esterel contributed to a playful fashion spirit, illustrated by the "Vichy" bridal gown which he designed for French actress Brigitte Bardot. Esterel built up an international reputation for his couture house, traveling the world to promote his collections, even appearing behind the Iron Curtain when the Soviet Union was off-limits to Westerners. But Esterel always remained true to his love of the stage and his background as an engineer, claiming that the 72 patents he held on machine tools allowed him to support his fashion design career.

There was something of the carnival performer in Esterel's attitude toward fashion. His designs were often extremely fanciful—and often ridiculed by the fashion press. It was as if couture for Esterel was more about exploring his own sense of whimsical creativity rather than about designing clothes. In 1963 his show included tweed hats with small black veils and umbrellas with built-in lights. Prior to the 1964 show he declared that several of his top models would appear with shaved heads "to give a new importance to a woman's face." His 1965 collection was called "confused and complicated," and included striped bathing suits with long skintight legs described as looking like "something out of a Mack Sennett movie."

Esterel was not simply a jester at the court of fashion, however, he was often in the forefront of fashion trends in the 1960s and 1970s, taking *au courant* looks from stylish young "Mods and Rockers" on the streets and translating them into haute couture. His 1965 designs for men included a plaid suit with a kilt and a salmon-colored Nehru jacket in corduroy, worn over high yoked pants with zippers on front and back. For women he created dramatic evening wear, including an ensemble of overblouse, floor-length skirt and great hooded evening cape of matching velour.

Esterel's lively intelligence saw no creative boundaries, whether he was designing a garment, writing a song, making his own store fixtures, or sharing his vision with other designers. In the early 1970s Esterel created his most well-known and talked-about collection, the "unisex" line, presenting clothes designed for both men and women. Ever the iconoclast, his first foray into the U.S. found him opening a couture shop in the New York suburbs, far from the fashion industry center in New York City. And the high-spirited, uninhibited house of Esterel attracted and fostered young talents, including future stars Anne Marie Beretta and Jean-Paul Gaultier.

Esterel's unfortunate and sudden death in 1974 did not signal the end of the house of Esterel. His widow and daughter strove to continue his spirit of fashion adventure, overseeing Creations Jacques Esterel. Throughout the 1980s the company was involved in several highly-publicized lawsuits in regard to trademark infringement against Yves Saint Laurent (for a design Esterel called the Petit Marquis and YSL called the Toreador) and also over the disputed purchase of the venerable house of Madame Alix Grés. The trademark suit, originally dismissed from criminal court, was refiled in civil court and resolved

Jacques Esterel, 1966 collections: "Mironton" (left), a Scottish-style plaid kilt ensemble, and "False Brother" (right), a vinyl pantsuit with zipped jacket ensemble. © AP/Wide World Photos.

in favor of the Esterels in 1985. Yves Saint Laurent, roundly considered the most respected house in Paris haute couture, was fined $11,000 and required to pay a $1,100 fine for every suit made from the plagarized Petit Marquis design. Because of the messy legal wranglings, Creations Jacques Esterel was dropped from the Fashion Creators Union and banned from showing collections as a grand couturier in Paris for several years.

—Kathleen Paton; updated by Nelly Rhodes

ESTÉVEZ, Luis

Cuban/American designer

Born: Luis Estévez de Galvez in Havana, Cuba, 5 December 1930. **Education:** Studied architecture, University of Havana, and fashion design, Traphagen School, New York. **Career:** Window display designer, Lord & Taylor; design assistant, House of Patou, Paris,

1953–55; began designing menswear, 1967; founder/designer, Grenelle, 1955–68; designer, Radley Furs, 1959–68; swimwear designer, Estévez for Sea Darlings and Resort Sports, 1960s–1977; menswear designer, St. Joseph Knitting Mills, France, 1967–73, moved to California, 1968; designer, Somper Furs, 1968–72; menswear designer, JayMar Ruby, 1972–73; designer, Universal Studios, 1969–1970s; designer, Eva Gabor collections, 1972–74, and Luis Estévez International line for Gabor, 1974–77; designer, Estévez for Neal and other freelance work; founder/designer, Estévez Enterprises, 1977–present; operated Estévez boutique on Melrose Avenue in Los Angelos, 1986–92; relocated to Florida, 1992–95; Estévez design studio/boutique, Santa Barbara, 1996–97; LEG Bridge line, from 1997. **Exhibitions:** Showcased collection during theater productions of *Hello Dolly,* 1964 and *Hair,* Los Angeles, 1969; gowns displayed in the Smithsonian Institute, Washington, D.C., and Gerald R. Ford Museum in Grand Rapids, Michigan. **Awards:** Coty American Fashion Critics award, 1956; Burdines Sunshine award (FL), 1957; Chicago Gold Coast award; Bambergers Golden Scissors award, 1962; Tommy award, 1988; Hispanic Designers, Inc. lifetime achievement award, 1990.

PUBLICATIONS

On ESTÉVEZ:

Books

Morris, Bernadine, and Barbara Walz, *The Fashion Makers,* New York, 1978.

Milbank, Caroline Rennolds, *New York Fashion: The Evolution of American Style,* New York, 1989.

Articles

"A Success Story in Necklines: Luis Estévez is a One-Year Wonder," in *Life,* 2 April 1956.

"A Cuban Way of Styles," in *Life,* 5 May 1958.

"Return of the Leg," in *Newsweek,* 21 June 1965.

Ginsberg, Steve, "Another Comeback for Luis Estévez," in *WWD,* 17 October 1989.

Romano-Benner, Norma, "Shaping the 1990s," in *America,* September/October 1990.

Vannett, Kasey, "He Likes Black Velvet," in *Hispanic,* January/February 1991.

Farr, Louise, "LEG Man," in *WWD,* 8 July 1997.

*

I'm most grateful to God for the gift of an energetic talent and my parents for exposing me to significant style—living life to the fullest and showing me the living discipline that helped me do all I've done.

—Luis Estévez

* * *

Throughout his career, Luis Estévez has produced elegant and restrained eveningwear for prestigious Californian clients, including Merle Oberon and Betty Ford. His style has been well suited to the Californian lifestyle, with its emphasis on wealth, luxury, and success.

Born to a privileged background in Cuba in 1930, Estévez studied architecture in Havana but switched to fashion after spending a summer job as a window dresser for Lord & Taylor department store in New York. After study at the Traphagen School of Fashion, New York, he left for Paris and found work at the house of Jean Patou for two years. This experience in Parisian couture was to influence his creative approach to design for the rest of his life.

By 1955, Estévez was designing under his own name, for a company called Grenelle-Estévez. Specializing in evening and cocktailwear, with occasional forays into daywear, Estévez was an immediate success. Sales reached $3 million in his first year of business alone, and *Life* magazine dubbed him "The One-Year Wonder." In 1956, he was the youngest designer honored with the Coty American Fashion Critics award. Estévez's clothes had an exclusive, individual look but were made from reasonably priced fabrics, selling well in the higher brackets of the mass market. He attributed much of his inspiration to his wife, who liked to dress in sexy but tasteful clothes with sharp and uncluttered silhouettes.

In the 1950s and 1960s Estévez clothes were distinguished by dramatic, theatrical showings, usually along a set theme. The Night and Day collection and gala, at the Waldorf Astoria, was dedicated to Cole Porter; the Broadway cast of *Hello Dolly* was featured prominently in his 1964 collection; and Estévez took over the Great Hall of the Met for his 1965 Fly Me to the Moon collection. His clothing was further distinguished by individual craftmanship as well: cutout neck designs, unusual angles like Os or Vs or in the shape of daisy petals, the edges of the fabric appearing jagged.

Frequent use was made of stark black and white and of full, rustling skirts, or narrow lines with floating back panels. He also introduced less fitting clothes in the form of barrel-shaped ottoman coats and dresses in two versions; one with a narrow skirt, the other with a puffball skirt. Evening jumpsuits were late 1960s innovations, as was a foray into menswear which featured horizontally tucked evening shirts. He was fond of designing around a strong theme, as in his ethnic-African inspired collection of 1959, featuring oversize tiger and zebra stripe prints. Estévez was also know for his imagainative use of accessories and designed swimwear and furs on a freelance basis for other companies.

After moving to California in 1968, Estévez became well established in West Coast fashion and society. He developed a clientèle of well-known women, including Lana Turner, Rosalind Russell, and Nancy Reagan. Actress Eva Gabor commissioned his talents as a glamorous eveningwear designer for her own label Eva Gabor Collections. This venture was so successful that in 1974 he signed a contract with her parent firm to design a line called Luis Estévez International. In 1977 he formed his own company to concentrate on the couture market. He served this loyal clients at his successful Melrose Avenue boutique in Los Angeles and later his design studio/boutique in Montecito. Although less celebrated than in the 1950s and 1960s, his reliability and expertise were well respected by clients, who eagerly poured themselves into his sensual black velvet dresses and embroidered sheaths. Estévez retired from fashion design in 1997, but he remains active in community affairs and is writing a book about his life. Estévez has received many awards and tributes for contributions to fashion as well as his civic activities.

Throughout his career, Luis Estévez's designs celebrated the glamor he cultivated in his personal life. The 1950s remain his favorite period of fashion because women looked feminine and life was beautiful. He believed, and still does, that clothing should flatter the person wearing it—otherwise fashion is more like a costume and not worth designing.

In February 2001, in commenting on his life in fashion design, Estévez said: "As I review my career, the first thing that comes to mind are my many fashion firsts and my talent's built-in drive and dedication to doing things as they had never been done before—all without fear of failure." Indeed, Estévez did go where designers had never gone before—heralding the future of fashion shows with bold, dramatic extravaganzas, the likes of which are rarely seen today. Though new, hip designers like Viktor & Rolf could be considered heirs to Estévez's lavish style, his dedication and singular designs remain unique.

—Kevin Almond; updated by Janette Goff Dixon and Sydonie Benét

ETTEDGUI, Joseph

British retailer and fashion entrepreneur

Born: in Casablanca, 1938; immigrated to England, 1965. **Family:** Married twice; two children. **Career:** Hairdresser, Joseph Salon 33, London, 1969–72; proprietor, Coco boutique, 1974; established chain of shops including Joseph, from 1977, Joseph Tricot and Joseph pour la Maison, from 1985; Joseph pour la Ville, from 1986; and Joseph Bis; Joseph *Parfum de Jour* introduced, 1985; opened Joe's Café restaurant, 1985; launched Joseph Denim; opened Paris boutique, 1993; celebrated 25th anniversary in retailing, 1996; redesigned all stores, 1997; sold majority interest in Joseph to Albert Frere and LVMH, 1999; opened new Paris store, 2001. **Awards:** *Woman* magazine award, London, 1985; Knitwear Designer of the Year award, 1990, 1992; Contemporary Collection award, Rover British Fashion Awards, 2000. **Address:** 88 Peterborough Road, London SW6 3HH, England. **Website:** www.Joseph.co.uk.

Joseph Ettedgui, fall 1998 collection. © Fashion Syndicate Press.

PUBLICATIONS

On ETTEDGUI:

Books

Roberts, Michael, *Joseph Tricot,* London, 1986.
Coleridge, Nicholas, *The Fashion Conspiracy,* London, 1988.
Manser, José, Eva Jiricna, and Joseph Ettedgui, *The Joseph Shop: London, 1983–1989,* New York & London, 1991.
Hoppen, Kelly, with foreword by Joseph Ettedgui, *In Touch: Texture in Design,* San Diego, 2000.

Articles

Cleave, Maureen, "Makers of Modern Fashion: Joseph," in the *Observer Magazine* (London), 5 October 1980.
Miller, Sarah, "Joseph: Where Fashion Meets Design," in *Blueprint* (London), June 1984.
White, Lesley, "Saint Joseph," in *The Face* (London), June 1984.
Brampton, Sally, "Still Crazy," in the *Observer,* 24 March 1985.
Miller, Sarah, "Stainless Reputation," in *Elle* (London), 29 September 1985.
Appleyard, Bryan, "Coordinated Style of a Clone Prince," in the *Times* (London), 4 June 1986.
Verdier, Rosy, "Joseph: Un homme de mode," in *L'Officiel* (Paris), August 1986.
Jaffe, Michele, "Ragtrade to Riches: My First Million: Joseph," in the *Observer Magazine,* 25 October 1987.
"Joe's Public," in *Fashion Weekly* (London), 7 January 1988.
De Gramont, Laurie, "Joseph le lutin," in *Vogue* (Paris), September 1988.
Filmer, Denny, "The Story of Joseph," in *Cosmopolitan* (London), December 1988.
Gandee, Charles, "The Merchant of Style," in *House & Garden* (New York), April 1989.
Brampton, Sally, "Joe Cool," in *Elle* (London), October 1989.
Fallon, James, "Driving Fashion His Own Way (Joseph Ettedgui)," in *WWD,* 29 January 1997.
McColl, Pat, "Tracing Avenue Montaigne's Slow Evolution to a Must Mecca for the Elite," in the *International Herald Tribune,* 15 March 1997.
Fallon, James, "Ettedgui's New Store…," in *DNR,* 31 March 1997.
———, "Heeere's Joseph," in *DNR,* 8 December 1997.
"Transforming Tradition," in *WWD,* 23 February 1999.
Fallon, James, and Katherine Weisman, "LVMH's Joseph Connection," in *WWD,* 23 September 1999.
Menkes, Suzy, "Offstage Action Steals the Show," in the *International Herald Tribune,* 28 September 1999.
"Designer Wins Fashion Accolade," available online at BBC News, www.bbc.co.uk, 19 February 2000.

Trocme, Suzanne, "Joseph's Technicolor Dream Shop," in *Interior Design,* April 2001.

* * *

A love of precision and a good eye for detail underpin Joseph Ettedgui's skills as an entrepreneur, enabling him to build up a group of shops which bring together a selection of the best and most innovative contemporary designer fashions alongside his own strong self-named lines, all aimed at a modern and confident clientèle.

The endless black and chrome of his London stores defined the stark monochromatic obsession of the 1980s and spawned endless concrete-floored imitators, eager to espouse the same sense of sophisticated style but unable to match his unfaltering mix of carefully chosen labels. Wise enough not to buy entire collections, he selected only the most streamlined and well designed pieces. His constant search for perfection, combined with convincingly structured in-store and window displays, brought many designers to the fore. So influential is Ettedgui's choice of names that his favor can raise a designer's status overnight. Having overseen the careers of many, including Kenzo, Katharine Hamnett, Franco Moschino, John Galliano, and Bodymap, he continues to purvey a mixture of new and established names.

The omnipresent black Ettedgui favored during the 1980s spread throughout the fashion world, as endless stretch-fit Azzedine Alaïa dresses hung from his rails, mingling with the bold suiting that ruled the decade. His power as a buyer is huge, backing avant-garde designers and hand-picking new talents who often found such support or retail space difficult to secure. The slick image of the Joseph emporia was underlined by the stark black and white minimalism of the shops; yet in 1997 the designer completely rehauled his stores to make them less sterile, more comfortable, and even fun. Fun? As Ettedgui explained to *Women's Wear Daily* (29 January 1997), "Stores provide too much stability today. You have to give customers the element of surprise, because shops should be like a stage that changes every three months."

Ettedgui's own Joseph lines, which slowly gained in popularity, have always complemented the other labels he sells. They provide classic garments to be mixed with other designer wear, or constitute carefully designed and coordinated outfits themselves. Joseph pour la Ville provides smart suiting and witty, easy to wear casuals. Alongside the bright, bold, striped trouser suits with shiny gilt buttons he produced in 1989 were more relaxed and feminine sheer georgette skirts and multicolored waistcoats, the subtle shades of which added a twist to the more pervasive dark hues. His ranges always contain clothes for every occasion, directed at the sophisticated metropolitan. The silhouette is usually well defined, to enhance the wearer with its simple chic, like the matte violet and beige column dresses side split to the waist for the evening in 1991, with three buttons at the top of each slash adding definition to the plain line.

Running alongside these classic garments is the Joseph Tricot collection, filled with thick rib woolens to layer with softer leggings and strikingly patterned cardigans and tube skirts, as well as subtle-toned wrap tops and fine jersey t-shirts. In 1987 chunky cream cardigans with little gold buttons were given bold black decoration, one of his perennial basic designs. These complemented more fashion-led shapes and yarns, like the claret chenille belted jackets of 1992 and the huge rose off-the-shoulder jumper with wide foldover collar shown in 1991.

In 1996 and 1997 new Joseph stores opened in New York (bringing the total to three) along with a second London store. The new London shop was Ettedgui's first freestanding menswear shop; additional men's-only stores were slated to follow in major U.S. cities like Boston, Chicago, and Miami. Then in early 1999 Ettedgui bought a controlling interest in Connolly Luxury Goods, which specialized in custom leather. His wife, Isabella, was the firm's designer. Ettedgui commented on the Connolly acquisition to *Women's Wear Daily* (23 February 1999), stating, "I've been retailing for a long time, and the Connolly type of luxury is what interests me now.... Fashion today is about beautiful things, very understated."

In late 1999 Ettedgui and his brothers Franklin and Maurice surprised many by selling a 54-percent stake in the Joseph brand to Belgian financier Albert Frere, and a minority interest to luxury giant LVMH. A few months later, Cherie Blair, wife of British Prime Minister Tony Blair, presented Ettedgui with the Contemporary Collection award. The recognition and accolades were long overdue for the designer, who had been shaping fashion for nearly three decades.

Joseph Ettedgui, designer, retailer, and entrepreneur, is widely recognized in the fashion world for his profound contributions not only to apparel, but to the atmosphere in which apparel is bought and sold. His ability to act as a catalyst, bringing together the work of innovative designers as well as classic ensembles—many from his own designs—has provided a unique environment for both men and women seeking clothing and accessories for not only occasions for but for an entire lifestyle.

—Rebecca Arnold; updated by Brian Louwers and Nelly Rhodes

F

FABIANI, Alberto

Italian designer

Born: Tivoli, Italy, circa 1910. **Family:** Two marriages; second to Duchessa Simonetta Colonna di Cesaro, 1952. **Career:** Apprenticed to Paris tailor, circa 1930s; took over his parents' Italian couture house and thrived in the 1940s and 1950s; formed Simonetta et Fabiani, 1962; returned to solo designing, 1960s; retired, 1974.

PUBLICATIONS

On FABIANI:

Books

Fairchild's Dictionary of Fashion, New York, 1988.

20th Century Fashion: The Complete Sourcebook, London, 1993.

Stegemeyer, Anne, *Who's Who in Fashion, Third Edition,* New York, 1996.

Callan, Georgina O'Hara, *The Thames and Hudson Dictionary of Fashion and Fashion Designers,* New York, 1998.

Articles

Robertson, Nan, "Happily Wed Pair Compete for Rome's Fashion Trade," in the *New York Times,* 19 October 1955.

Emerson, Gloria, "Husband-and-Wife Team," in the *New York Times,* 21 July 1961.

Morris, Bernadine, "Despite Dire Predictions, the Couture Carries On," in the *New York Times,* 19 July 1973.

* * *

Alberto Fabiani, born around 1910 in Tivoli, Italy, was the son of couturiers. His parents had launched a fashion house in Rome in 1909. Fabiani was further exposed to fashion through an apprenticeship with an Italian tailor, a family friend, in Paris, where he worked from age 18 to 21. He returned to Italy and, five years later, took over his parents' business, renaming it under his own label. His quickly became one of the top couture houses in Italy.

Fabiani is best known for his uncluttered tailoring and conservative designs, whether creating one of his famed chemises, a sheath dress, poncho coat, long tunic top, or even a fur. Over the years, he became known as "the surgeon of suits and coats," a term coined by Nan Robertson in the *New York Times* in 1955. Several years later, in July 1961, Gloria Emreson of the *New York Times* pointed out that fashion editors had called Fabiani's designs "a quiet marvel of architecture."

Fabiani was among the designers who led something of an Italian renaissance during the 1950s. Italian designers, including his parents, had previously looked to Paris for inspiration, but during the 1950s, they began to trust their own Italian sensibility. Fabiani was emblematic of this movement and became one of the best-known Italian designer labels, recognized not only in Italy but increasingly throughout Europe and the United States.

In North America, however, Fabiani was outshone, at least in terms of publicity, by his second wife, the Duchessa Simonetta Colonna di Cesaro, later Simonetta Visconti, known professionally as Simonetta. They met at a fashion show in 1949, after both were well established as designers—Simonetta had risen to the top tier of Italian designers during the 1940s—and were married in 1952. The two had a child together, as well as one each from previous marriages.

Alberto Fabiani, spring/summer 1963 collection: two-piece evening dress with the top embroidered in rhinestones and gold, and silver-colored fringe. © AP/Wide World Photos.

Fabiani and Simonetta were often the subject of fashion industry gossip over what they discussed at home, since they were two of the top fashion houses in Italy and fierce competitors. They always maintained that they did not discuss the particulars of their lines with each other but simply reviewed trends together before beginning each collection, taking a look at each other's work for the first time during runway show dress rehearsals each season.

Fabiani became known in the U.S. and around the world for his clean lines, his quality tailoring, and his conservative yet imaginative women's clothes, whereas Simonetta's reputation was established through the creation of highly feminine sportswear and cocktail dresses intended for a young female customer. The two had contrasting personalities as well: Fabiani was reserved while Simonetta was very outgoing.

Although they adamantly denied they would ever combine their two houses, the couple did try to do so briefly in 1962, forming Simonetta et Fabiani in Paris. The effort was a success at first but failed quickly, and Fabiani returned to Italy without Simonetta. (Two years later, she retired from designing and established a leper colony in India.) He returned to designing alone, regaining his status as one of the leading couturiers in his home country. He created not only apparel, specializing in suits and dresses, but accessories as well.

Fabiani's designs were timeless. He was in touch with the current trends each season, but his pieces were classics that always came back into fashion. And despite his conservatism, he was also an innovator, creating new trends—especially during the 1950s—such as the cocoon silhouette (fitted in front, loose in back) and pleated column dresses. His tent coats, introduced in 1960, made a particular splash. Many of these innovations were disliked at first but were eventually embraced by consumers, retail buyers, and critics alike. In fact, Fabiani's designs were some of the couture pieces most emulated by American retailers in the 1950s and 1960s. Fabiani retired in 1974.

—Karen Raugust

FABRICE

American fashion designer

Born: Fabrice Simon in Port au Prince, Haiti, 29 January 1951; moved to the U.S., 1964. **Education:** Studied textile design and fashion illustration, Fashion Institute of Technology, New York, 1969–70. **Career:** Freelance textile designer, 1971–76; formed own company producing hand-painted and beaded gowns, 1976; menswear line introduced, 1985; abandoned designing for painting, 1990s; abstract paintings exhibited in New York and Palm Beach, 1997. **Awards:** Coty American Fashion Critics award, 1981. **Died:** 29 July 1998, in New York.

Publications

On FABRICE:

Books

Milbank, Caroline Rennolds, *New York Fashion: The Evolution of American Style,* New York, 1989.

Articles

Wihlborg, Lee Wohlfers, "Style," in *People* (New York), 25 April 1983.

Milbank, Caroline Rennolds, "Fabrice," in *Interview* (New York), December 1986.

"Famed Fashion Designer Fabrice, 47, Succumbs in New York," in *Jet,* 24 August 1998.

"Fashion Designer Fabrice Simon Dies at the Age of 47," in *People Weekly,* 24 August 1998.

* * *

Since founding his company in 1976, Haitian-born Fabrice was known primarily for eveningwear targeted to the high end of the custom and ready-to-wear markets. He trained as a textile designer. When he turned from textile to fashion design in 1975, not surprisingly he began to work in hand-painted fabrics. His first significant sale was a small number of gowns purchased by the New York specialty shop Henri Bendel. Bendel's was instrumental in establishing the career of many young designers. This was the heyday of Bendel's "open house," where the store's buyers set aside a weekly time to view, sometimes to purchase, work from unknown artists. Typically, these unknowns lacked major financial backing and production resources. More than a few of them were also producing hand-painted silks in limited quantity. It was a labor intensive but otherwise relatively inexpensive way to enter the world of fashion.

Fabrice sought to distinguish his product from others and to expand his market. He found the way when he discovered a selection of beaded motifs originating in Haiti. Fabrice commissioned Haitian beaders and embroiderers to execute his designs, beginning in 1979. Although he still worked with hand-painted fabrics throughout his short career, he is best remembered for his distinctive beaded gowns.

Fabrice's work reflected a contemporary approach to the ancient craft of beading. His gowns were imbued with a modern sensibility, designed from within a frame of reference suggesting a response and asking for a second look. His beaded squiggles invite comparison with the paintings of Joan Miró and with the graffiti found on public buildings. On a dark ground, his abstract designs seem suspended in space, like the lights of a far off bridge at night. More easily read patterns also startle and amuse when worked in bugle beads. Imagine, for example, a beaded gown patterned like an argyle sock, or one inspired by a woven *ikat.* Fabrice's references included cobwebs and comic strips; he acknowledged trendy street styles without ignoring past traditions.

In his formal menswear collections, Fabrice offered alternatives to the traditional black tie ensemble. He showed silk t-shirts for evening, pairing them with houndstooth or floral damask dinner jackets, or with unstructured smoking jackets for an even more relaxed look. Acknowledging the street influence on his work, Fabrice introduced a bridge collection in 1992 called Graffiti. His nylon, rayon, and Lycra Spandex dresses in stinging colors with contrasting insets or appliqués were sleek and colorful wearable graphics. In his ready-to-wear and in his custom clothes, Fabrice's wit always complemented his artistry.

The extent of Fabrice's fashion reign was brief; he made a major splash and then gave up dressmaking for painting. Though his boldly colorful abstracts received some critical praise, he will be remembered for the flashy beaded gowns wore by a bevy of celebrities, including Iman, Madonna, Natalie Cole, Whitney Houston, Ivana Trump, Shirley MacLaine, and Kathleen Turner. In July of 1998, at the age of 47, Fabrice succumbed to AIDS in New York City.

—Whitney Blausen; updated by Nelly Rhodes

FAINBLOOM, Abe and Bill

See CHAMPION

FARHI, Nicole

British designer

Born: France, 25 July 1946. **Education:** Studied fashion illustration at Studio Bercot, Paris. **Family:** Longtime companion of Stephen Marks, daughter: Candice; married David Hare, 1993. **Career:** Freelance designer for Pierre D'Alby, Bianchini-Férier, *Elle, Marie-Claire,* 1966–circa 1973; designer, French Connection, from 1973; introduced own label to coincide with first Nicole Farhi boutique, 1983; opened freestanding shops, London and New York, 1984, Norway, 1987; menswear collection introduced, 1989; opened flagship new York City store, complete with restaurant and bar, 1999. **Awards:** British Fashion award, 1989; British Design Council award, 1991. **Address:** 16 Fouberts Place, London W1V 1HH, England.

Nicole Farhi, winter 2001 collection: beaded evening dress. © AFP/CORBIS.

PUBLICATIONS

On FARHI:

Books

Stegemeyer, Anne, *Who's Who in Fashion, Third Edition,* New York, 1996.

Articles

Bloomfield, Judy, "Nicole Farhi Strengthens U.S. Connection," in *WWD,* 28 September 1988.
"Din Adds Spice to French Dressing," in *Design Weekly* (London), 14 July 1989.
Martin, Rosie, "So Farhi, So Good," in *Vogue* (London), April 1991.
Honan, Corinna, "Why Do So Many British Women Dress Like Tarts? Top Designer Nicole Farhi Reveals Her Contempt for Modern Fashions," in the *Daily Mail* (London), 2 October 1992.
Fearon, Francesca, "Goodbye to the Changing Seasons," in the *Herald* (Glasgow), 11 November 1992.
Dempster, Nigel, "Farhi's New Hare-Style," in the *Daily Mail* (London), 9 February 1993.
Young, Lucie, "Design Notebook: Who's the Coolest of Them All?" in the *New York Times,* 19 August 1999.
Deegan, Carol, "Five Questions: Nicole Farhi," in the *Associated Press,* 4 February 2000.

*

My clothes are for women like me who are active, either because they work or simply live life to the fullest. The designs are understated but with tremendous style…never boring…and even when it is a fun garment, I like to keep the shape very simple.

—Nicole Farhi

* * *

Nicole Farhi was born in France of Turkish parents and trained in Paris to be a fashion illustrator, working first for Parisian fashion magazines illustrating the haute couture collections in Paris. When she was 20, she made the transition to fashion design because she was asked to design dresses by such magazines as *Marie-Claire* and *Elle,* which were sold as patterns for their readers. She then met Stephen

Nicole Farhi, autumn/winter 2001 collection. © Reuters NewMedia Inc./CORBIS.

Marks and began designing for the company that soon became French Connection. "We went to India," she relates, "sourcing fabrics and designing textiles. This was 1973–74 and there was a demand for Eastern fabrics and embroidery." By 1983, when French Connection was floated on the London Stock Exchange, Farhi launched a company under her own name, backed by the now considerable resources of the larger label. In 1984, she wrote, "The clothes I was designing for French Connection were too constricting for me. They were very successful, but I wanted to design unstructured clothes for women."

Unstructured design is a distinctive feature of Farhi's work, as is the importance of understatement, attention to detail, and subtle colors and textures: "My collections over the years have become more and more feminine…altogether softer, using layers of color and texture. I think a woman should express her sexuality…not in a blatant way, but subtly—perhaps just by using fabric that is pleasing to the touch." In winter 1989, Farhi launched her first collection for men, a move welcomed as a new development in British menswear. As Farhi explained at the time, "Many of the fabrics and shapes I had used for women in the past had been quite simple and 'masculine,' so it was not too difficult to make the transition."

Both women's and men's collections express Farhi's Europe-based design philosophy. "Nowadays the way we live means less of a partition between day and evening clothes.… They need to be relaxed in the day yet sophisticated enough for the evening. We must mix them to suit ourselves. At last there is no dictation."

There are a total of eight London Nicole Farhi shops, including those in Covent Garden, Knightsbridge, Hampstead, and the original at St. Christopher's Place, as well as concessionary outlets in many major stores throughout the UK, Europe, Japan, and Hong Kong. In 1989, Farhi won the British Classics category at the British Fashion awards and in 1991 was awarded the British Design Council award for Design Excellence for her spring/summer 1991 collection, the first time in five years the award had been given to a fashion designer.

Business boomed for Farhi in the 1990s. In September 1999, she launched a 20,000-square-foot flagship store in New York City, showcasing her signature clothing plus antique furniture and flea market treasures from Europe, South America, and Madagascar. The 1901 building, once the Copa Cabana nightclub, is home not only to Farhi's menwear and womenswear, but home collection and to Nicole's Restaurant and Bar.

Farhi ended a long romantic relationship, which produced daughter Candice, with business partner Stephen Marks in the late 1980s, although the two have continued to work together. In February 1993, Farhi married playwright David Hare, who wrote the film *Damage* and has directed at Britain's National Theatre.

Even as she reigned as one of Britain's most successful designers, collecting an estimated £50 million ($80 million) in 1998 and dressing movie stars such as Judi Dench, Jeremy Northam, and Mary Elizabeth Mastrantonio, Farhi has remained low key, driving a 25-year-old Volkswagen Beetle and attending high-brow events wearing jeans. Her attitude toward the fashion industry is similarly practical: "I want to stop this nonsense of people saying there is a 'revolution' in hemlines or whatever," she told Corinna Honan of London's *Daily Mail.* "My advice is—ignore what the fashion magazines are saying. I wear jackets and sweaters that are 10 years old; I'm not worried about what people think. There are pieces in my collection that have been the same for five years."

—Doreen Ehrlich; updated by Lisa Groshong

FASSETT, Kaffe

American knitwear designer working in London

Born: San Francisco, California, 7 December 1937. **Education:** Museum of Fine Arts School, Boston. **Career:** Moved to Britain, 1964; created knitting patterns for Women's Home Industries, Browns of London, and Rowan Yarns of Yorkshire; knitting stores opened, mid-1980s; television series *Glorious Colour,* for British Channel 4, 1988; flowing coats and shawls showcased in Stockhold ballet, 1990; produced video, *Kaffe's Colour Quest,* 1998; queue opened in Liberty's Department store, London, 1999; radio series, *A Stitch in Time,* for Britain's Radio 4, 1999. **Awards:** Chelsea Flower Show, for garden design for Hilliers Garden Centres, 1998. **Exhibitions:** *Kaffe Fassett at the V&A,* Victoria and Albert Museum, London, 1988; Art and Industry Museum, Stockholm, 1990; paintings, Catto Gallery,

London, 1997, 1999; quilt exhibit, Japan World Quilt Fair, 1998; needlepoints, wall hangings, rugs, displayed at the Luise Ross Gallery, 1999. **Address:** c/o Ebury Press, 20 Vaux-Hall Bridge Road, London, SW1V 2SA, England. **Website:** www.kaffefassett.com.

Publications

By FASSETT:

Books

Glorious Knitting, London, 1985.
Glorious Needlepoint, London, 1987.
Kaffe Fassett at the V&A (exhibition catalogue), London, 1988; published as *Glorious Colour,* New York.
Family Album, with Zoë Hunt, London, 1989.
Glorious Inspiration, London, 1991.
Kaffe's Classics, London, 1993.
Glorious Interiors: Needlepoint, Knitting and Decorative Design Projects for Your Home, Boston, 1995.
Glorious Patchwork: More Than 25 Glorious Quilt Designs, New York, 1997.
Welcome Home: Kaffe Fassett, Bothell, WA, 1999.
Mosaics, Inspiration and Original Projects for Interiors and Exteriors, with Candace Bahouth, Newtown, CT, 1999.
Kaffe Fassett's Glorious Inspiration for Needlepoint and Knitting, New York, 2000.
Kaffe Fassett's Glorious Color for Needlepoint and Knitting, New York, 2000.
Passionate Patchwork, Newtown, CT, 2001.

On FASSETT:

Books

Sutton, Alan, *British Craft Textiles,* London, 1985.
Mably, Brandon, *Brilliant Knits: 25 Colorful Contemporary Designs from the Kaffe Fassett Studio,* Boston, 2001.

Articles

Coleman, Marigold, in *Crafts* (London), March/April 1975.
"Craftsmen of Quality," Crafts Advisory Committee, 1976.
Green, William, "Kaffe Fassett, the Colour Man," in *Vogue* (London), April 1980.
Innes, Jocasta, in *Cosmopolitan* (London), January 1984.
Polan, Brenda, in *The Guardian* (London), 21 March 1985.
Schneebeli, Heini, "Observatory," in the *Observer* (London), 9 November 1986.
Roberts, Glenys, in the *Sunday Telegraph Magazine* (London), 15 February 1987.
Kendall, Ena, "A Room of My Own," in the *Observer Magazine* (London), January 1988.
Interview, in *New Pins and Needles* (London), May 1988.
Hilliard, Elizabeth, "A ***** in the Life of Kaffe Fassett," in the *Evening Standard* (London), 16 November 1988.
Campbell, Sylvia, "Kaffe Fassett: Fiber Artist," in *Needlepoint Plus* (California), May/June 1989.
Molesworth, Melanie, "Table Manners," in *Woman's Journal* (London), January 1990.
Smith, Roberta, "Art in Review: Kaffe Fassett and Steve Lovi—'Two About Color,'" in the *New York Times,* 17 December 1999.
Koplos, Janet, "Kaffe Fassett and Steve Lovi and Luise Ross," in *Art in America,* June 2000.

* * *

Kaffe Fassett was born in 1937 in San Francisco. His family moved to the former home of the Aga Khan and Rita Hayworth in the wild and rocky Big Sur region of California. An unconventional childhood in an artistic household fostered a creative talent in the young Fassett, and days spent at a school run by followers of the Indian guru Krishnamurti were also to be a lasting influence. A scholarship took him to study at the Museum of Fine Arts School in Boston, but Fassett stayed only briefly and left to make his way as a society painter. Arriving in Britain in this capacity on a three-month vacation in 1964, he met the newly graduated fashion student Bill Gibb. He accompanied Gibb on a trip to Scotland and fell in love with the colors of the landscape and the Shetland wools. A woman on the train home taught him how to knit, and he says, "that is all I've done in 20 years."

His first waistcoat sold for £100 in 1969 and earned a full page in *Vogue.* Thus began "a wonderful obsession," which was to ensure him a place in fashion history. "I think knitting is just mysteriously, incredibly magic. I mean who would ever think that you could just take two sticks and rub them together with a bit of thread in between and out would come this incredible tapestry of colour?"

Abandoning his paints but still with the painter's eye, he set about using yarns to explore the world of color. He designs organically, learning techniques when necessary. He has never been interested in rules or in a variety of stitches and claims to have arrived at nonangst knitting. He abhors the hard-and-fast rules that have kept hand-knitters enslaved for so long. Fassett uses only stocking stitch and rib. "I wanted to make it elegant so there was no point in trying anything fancy which immediately goes wrong when you drop a stitch. If you make a mistake according to my method, it can be a positive benefit." He works with as many as 150 colors in a garment—"anything worth doing is worth overdoing," he claims. After a brief spell working in machine knits with dress designers—notably Bill Gibb—Fassett turned his back on the machine. The intricacy of pattern he sought was incompatible with the industrial process.

Fassett works impulsively and intuitively and at an astonishing pace. Using circular needles he sits cross-legged, barefoot, on his bed, the design emerging line by line. He seldom uses a graph. For him, color and pattern are paramount, styling very much secondary. "The colouring is totally instinctive, a gut thing." He worships color, uses it with great abandon and total assurance, seeing it everywhere, even in the most inauspicious surroundings. He advocates "if in doubt, add twenty more."

His inspiration comes from the world of ethnic decorative arts: Turkish kilims, Islamic tiles, Chinese pots, Spanish brocades. For him, knitting garments is about patterns, not pictures. He doesn't feel that large pictorial sweaters are really flattering to wear. Repeats and stylization render the figurative more appropriate for knitwear. Decoration follows through the entire garment, often using a contrasting tartan or stripe on the back. Favorite themes—circles, spots, squares—recur, transformed by a change in scale or color.

As well as individual commissions, he began to design for Women's Home Industries and for Browns, who made up the patterns and sent them out to home knitters. His early work used mainly small repeat geometric motifs inspired by oriental rugs. Next there were grand romantic coats like the Romeo and Juliet coat inspired by the Nureyev ballet, with extravagant gathered shoulders and floor-sweeping skirts in stripes of mohair and bouclé with a tight jewelled bodice. A commission from the Aberdeen Art Gallery produced the huge "map coat," a landscape extravaganza.

Of enduring appeal have been his ballooning coats: large, simply cut, T-shaped garments gathered at mid-calf into horizontally striped ribs—loose, enveloping shapes sized to fit anyone. They are vast canvases for oversize geometric patterns or stylized Chinese pots or autumn leaves—more than garments, more three-dimensional works of art, but very much intended to be worn, to swirl, to drape, to cling around the figure. He makes giant triangular shawls resplendent with a dazzling variety of dots and spots inspired by the Roman glass at the Victoria and Albert Museum, London. In October 1988, the ultimate accolade in craft circles came with his exhibition at the Victoria and Albert Museum. It was the first by a contemporary textile designer.

High fashion has been influenced by Kaffe Fassett. At the London Fashion Week in 1985, in collaboration with Bill Gibb, he produced "simply-cut, richly-coloured, knitted suits and throws," and closed "with a series of fairy-tale exercises in the baroque, the beaded and the burnished"—all in "the glowing richness of Kaffe Fassett's colours." Bill Gibb's huge American Indian style coat-sweaters came from Fassett's American past.

Missoni, the renowned Italian designers, invited Fassett to Milan to design knitwear for them. Fassett generously left the Italian fashion house with years of ideas. In 1990 in Stockholm, a ballet featuring flowing Fassett coats and shawls was staged at the Art and Industry Museum for the opening of his exhibition there. The queues were so long that the opening had to be restaged three times, and 107,000 people attended. A 1998 exhibit of quilts from Fassett's book *Patchwork* at Tokyo's Japan World Quilt Fair drew 120,000 spectators. In 1997 and 1999, Fassett exhibited his paintings at London's Catto Gallery. He mounted a New York City show at the Luise Ross Gallery in 1999, displaying needlepoints, wall hangings, lampshades, rugs, waistcoats, and other designs. "For many of us, any one of these creations would be more than enough," noted Roberta Smith of the *New York Times.* "But to see them massed together is to glimpse a grand obsession expressed with consummate exquisite control, hedonistic flair and historic sophistication." Collectors of Fassett's work include such luminaries as Barbra Streisand, Lauren Bacall, Ali McGraw, Helen Frankenthaler, and Princess Michael of Kent.

Extensive lecture tours and workshops have brought Fassett's message to millions of people the world over. Students have described these talks as "electrifying." He also starred in a series on color on British television in 1988. Ten years later, he released a video called *Kaffe's Colour Quest,* which explored the influence of travel on Fassett's design and color inspiration. In 1999, he recorded a radio series entitled *A Stitch in Time* for Britain's Radio 4.

Fassett freely shares all he knows with the hand-knitting public and has tirelessly campaigned to awaken the unexplored potential he believes lies in everyone. To that end, he was asked by the international charity Oxfam to give marketing and design advice to weaving villages in India and Guatemala. He performed similar work in South Africa.

His first book, *Glorious Knitting* (London, 1985), sold 180,000 copies, and a string of knitting shops opened in its wake. London's Liberty's Department Store opened a concession featuring Fassett's one-of-a-kind designs and products in 1999. Fassett's eleventh book, *Passionate Patchwork,* was published in 2001.

In recent years, Fassett has turned some of his attention to more unusual projects. In 1998, he won a medal in the Chelsea Flower Show for a garden design for Hilliers Garden Centres. Several performance groups have commissioned Fassett's designs, including Britain's Northern Ballet Theatre and the Royal Shakespeare Company.

—Elian McCready; updated by Lisa Groshong

FATH, Jacques

French designer

Born: Lafitte, France, 12 September 1912. **Education:** Studied bookkeeping and law, Commercial Institute, Vincennes, France. **Family:** Married Geneviève Boucher de la Bruyère, 1939; son: Philippe. **Military Service:** Completed required military service and served again in the artillery during World War II. **Career:** Bookkeeper, then trader at the Paris Bourse, 1930–32; showed first collection, Paris, 1937; reopened salon, 1940; designed ready-to-wear collection for American manufacturer Joseph Halpert, 1948; formed own company in the U.S., 1951; developed ready-to-wear collection in Paris, 1954, including Fath scarves and hosiery; business sold, 1957; fragrance license bought back from L'Oreal, 1992; Tom Van Lingen hired as designer, 1992; relaunched several fragrances, from 1993; company bought by Groupe Emanuelle Khanh, 1997; Elena Nazarhoff replaced Van Lingen as artistic director, 1997; Nazarhoff fired and Octavio Pizarro hired, 1998; fragrances include: *Green Water,* reissued 1993; *Fath de Fath,* 1957 and 1995; *Yin* and *Yang,* 2000. **Exhibitions:** *Jacques Fath Création-Couture des Années 50* (retrospective), Palais Galleria, Paris, 1993. **Awards:** Neiman Marcus award, Dallas, 1949. **Died:** 13 November 1954, in Paris.

Publications

On FATH:

Books

Bertin, Célia, *Paris à la Mode,* London, 1956.
Ballard, Bettina, *In My Fashion,* New York, 1960.
Oster, André, "Jacques Fath Recalled," in Ruth Lynam, ed., *Couture: An Illustrated History of the Great Paris Designers and Their Creations,* New York, 1972.
Milbank, Caroline Rennolds, *Couture: The Great Designers,* New York, 1985.
Veillon, Dominique, *La mode sous l'occupation,* Paris, 1990.
Guillaume, Valérie, *Jacques Fath* (exhibition catalogue), Paris, 1993.
Stegemeyer, Anne, *Who's Who in Fashion, Third Edition,* New York, 1996.

Jacques Fath adjusting one of his ball gowns, 1951. © Genevieve Naylor/CORBIS.

Articles

Coughlan, Robert, "Designer for Americans: Jacques Fath of Paris Sells U.S. Women Wearable Glamour," in *Life Magazine* (New York), October 1949.

"Jacques Fath," in *Current Biography* (New York), April 1951.

Roberts, Eleanor, "Fath Brings Paris Chi-Chi to Boston," in the *Boston Post,* 18 December 1953.

Obituary, in the *New York Times,* 14 November 1954.

"Page After Page of the Good and the Controversial in the World of Fashion," in the *Chicago Tribune,* 11 December 1991.

Deeny, Godfrey, "A Revival of the House that Jacques Built," in *WWD,* 26 February 1992.

Stern, Suzanne Pierrette, "Memories of a Parisian Seamstress: Tales and Techniques from the Workrooms of Couturier Jacques Fath," in *Threads* (Newtown, Connecticut), April/May 1992.

Milbank, Caroline Rennolds, "Jacques Fath: The Mercurial Host at Corbeville and Paris," in *Architectural Digest,* October 1994.

Jacques Fath, fall/winter 1954 collection: "s"-line suit in wool with an ermine cape collar and velvet ribbons. © Bettmann/CORBIS.

Weisman, Katherine, "The Renewal of Jacques Fath," in *WWD,* 25 May 1995.

Larson, Soren, "Giving the Jacques Fath Fragrances a New Life," in *WWD,* 8 September 1995.

"Khanh Acquires House of Fath," in *WWD,* 17 March 1997.

Wilson, Eric, "Fath Dismisses RTW Designer Elena Nazar," in *WWD,* 24 November 1997.

"Opposites Attract," in *Soap Perfumery & Cosmetics,* January 2000.

* * *

Jacques Fath had a short career—from 1937 until his death in 1954—and after he died his name fell into obscurity. In contrast to his great contemporaries, Christian Dior and Cristobal Balenciaga, Fath has been largely forgotten, but he deserves to be rediscovered as a talented creator.

Fath was born in 1912 into a Protestant family of Flemish and Alsatian origin. His great-grandmother had been a dressmaker to the empress Eugène and, from an early age, he showed an interest in designing clothes. He also toyed with the idea of becoming an actor, a craving he later indulged in private theatricals and costume parties.

Fath had "the showy elegance of a character from a Cocteau play and the charm of an *enfant terrible,*" recalled Célia Bertin in *Paris à la Mode,* in London, in 1956. But fashion editors like Bettina Ballard and Carmel Snow (of *Harper's Bazaar*) tended to dismiss Fath as "a good-looking child prodigy…with slightly theatrical fashion ideas not worthy of the hallowed pages of *Vogue* or *Harper's Bazaar.*"

Fath's career was interrupted by the outbreak of World War II. Taken prisoner in 1940, he was, however, soon back in Paris, where he reopened his couture house with his wife Geneviève. A book on fashion during the Nazi Occupation noted that scruples of conscience did not embarrass Fath, who was closely associated with various Franco-German groups and whose clientèle consisted heavily of Germans, wealthy collaborators, and black marketeers. Unlike Chanel, however, whose reputation as a Nazi sympathizer temporarily injured her postwar career, Fath's image emerged intact, and after the war, his international career took off.

His glove-fitted dresses glorified the female form, and some have said Fath even inspired Dior's New Look. Certainly, Fath designed some of the sexiest and most glamorous dresses to come out of Paris. The typical Fath dress featured a fitted bodice that molded a slender waistline and emphasized the swelling curves of bosom and hips. Sleeve and collar treatments were important to Fath, and he favored irregular necklines that drew attention to the breasts. Skirts were either very slim or very full, characterized perhaps by a whirlpool of pleats or interesting draped effects.

If Dior and Balenciaga were known for the architectural beauty of their designs, Fath's style was praised for its glamor and vivacity. He often used diagonal lines, asymmetrical drapery, and floating panels to give a sense of movement. Nor was he afraid of color, even using such daring combinations as bright blue and green. (He himself liked to wear a red tartan jacket.) Whereas Dior's career was characterized by striking shifts of silhouette (the A-line, the H-line, etc.), Fath maintained an unswerving fidelity to the female form divine, focusing on sexy lines and novel decorative details, such as rows of nonfunctional buttons. Fath's style of wearable glamor had a wide appeal, and in 1948 he signed an agreement with the American manufacturer, Joseph Halpert. Henceforth, in addition to his own couture collections, Fath produced a low-priced American line as well.

Fath was increasingly regarded as the "heir apparent to Dior's throne." As *Life Magazine* said in 1949: "Dior is still generally acknowledged to be the head man, so to speak, of the fashion world, but Fath has recently had a spectacular rise in prestige, and it now seems likely that the next look to confront and impoverish the U.S. male will be the Fath look." Carmel Snow, editor of *Harper's Bazaar,* revised her earlier opinion of Fath, declaring, "He makes you look like you have sex appeal—and believe me, that's important."

Fath himself had tremendous personal appeal, with his blond wavy hair and slender physique (a 28-inch waist, claimed one source). He was also very much a social personality; he and his pretty wife loved throwing lavish and imaginative parties, which had the pleasant side-effect of providing excellent publicity. "An atmosphere of glitter, chic, and perfumed excitement permeates both his personal and business affairs," observed *Life* magazine in October 1949. Yet behind the scenes, Fath was struggling with illness. Only a year before his death in 1954, the American press had hailed him as the "fabulous young French designer who…is out to make every woman look like a great beauty." This promise was tragically cut short; Fath died of leukemia at the age of 42.

Though the Fath house languished for some time, the firm was revived by new designer Tom Van Lingen, who came aboard in 1992, and the relaunch of several of the firm's early fragrances. In 1997, Groupe Emanuelle Khanh and its subsidiary, Jean-Louis Scherrer, bought the fashion house and installed Elena Nazaroff as its ready-to-wear designer, replacing Van Lingen. Yet Nazaroff was fired after one season and Fath hired Octavio Pizarro, who had designed his own label in Chile before working at Jean-Louis Scherrer with Bernard Perris. Two new complementary fragrances, his-and-hers fragrances, *Yin* and *Yang* were released in 2000.

—Valerie Steele

FENDI

Italian design firm

Established: as a leather and fur workshop by Adele Casagrande (1897–1978), Rome, 1918; renamed Fendi with her marriage to Edoardo Fendi, 1925 (died, 1954); current principals include daughters Paola, Anna, Franca, Carla, Alda, their husbands, and children.

Fendi, autumn/winter 2001–02 ready-to-wear collection. © AFP/ CORBIS.

Company History: Firm designs leather and fur clothing, accessories, ready-to-wear, knitwear, beachwear, eyewear, watches, and more; Selleria handbags and accessories launched, 1925; Karl Lagerfeld began collaborating on designs, 1962; introduced first fragrance, 1988; launched bridge line, 1990; licensed jewelry line, 1991; signed licensing deal with Japan's Naigai Co. Ltd., 1994; Selleria accessories line reintroduced, 1996; buyout from Prada and LVMH, 1999; flagship store opened in Paris, 2001; initial public offering planned, 2002; fragrances include *Fendi Uomo,* 1988; *Fendi Classic,* reissued; *Theorema* and *Life Essence,* 1998. **Awards:** National Italian American Foundation award to Paola Fendi, 1990. **Company Address:** Fendi Paola e S.lle S.A.S., Via Borgognona 7, 00187 Rome, Italy.

Publications

On FENDI:

Books

Mulassano, Adriana, *Moda e Modi,* Milan, 1980.

Alfonsi, Maria-Vittoria, *Leaders in Fashion: I Grandi Personaggi Della Moda,* Bologna, 1983.

Giocomoni, Silvia, *The Italian Look Reflected,* Milan, 1984.

Soli, Pia, *Il Geno Antipatico,* Venice, 1984.

Stegemeyer, Anne, *Who's Who in Fashion, Third Edition,* New York, 1996.

Articles

Schiavi, Maria, "Che Cosa Di Chi: Fendi," in *Vogue* (Milan), October 1984.

"Da Fendi: Lusso, Classe e Successo," in *Linea Italiana* (Milan), No. 157, 1985.

Acquarone, Lele, "Le Incredibili Pellicce Fendi," in *Vogue* (Milan), September 1985.

"La Grande Moda di Fendi," in *Vogue* (Milan), September 1986.

"Fendi: Stupore Nel Lusso," in *Donna* (Milan), July/August 1987.

Bachrach, Judy, "The Roman Empire," in *Savvy,* December 1987.

Barron, Pattie, "La Famiglia Fendi," in *Cosmopolitan* (London), September 1988.

"Fendi Furs: Karl Goes on a Tear," in *WWD,* 17 March 1992.

Forden, Sara Gay, "Fast Forward at Fendi," in *WWD,* 24 January 1994.

"Some Russians in New York Meet Winter in All-Out Style," in the *New York Times,* 26 February 1995.

Taliabue, John, "Gucci's Shares Rise on a Report of Progress in Its Bid for Fendi," in the *New York Times,* 10 September 1999.

Kamm, Thomas, and Deborah Ball, "LVMH, Prada Ready Joint Bid to Win Control of Designer Fendi," in the *Wall Street Journal,* 30 September 1999.

Tagliabue, John, "Fendi Gets Better Offer," in the *New York Times,* 1 October 1999.

Kamm, Thomas, and Deborah Ball, "LVMH, Prada Open Purse Strings to Bag Fendi," in the *Wall Street Journal,* 13 October 1999.

Taliabue, John, "French-Italian Alliance Takes Controlling Stake in Fendi," in the *New York Times,* 13 October 1999.

Agins, Teri, "All the Trimmings," in the *Wall Street Journal,* 23 November 1999.

"Offering Seen for Fendi," in the *New York Times,* 24 November 1999.

Socha, Miles, "Fendi Family," in *W,* February 2000.

Conti, Samantha, "Prada, LVMH Said Mulling a Jil Sander-Fendi Trade," in *WWD,* 28 February 2000.
"Bag-ettes," in *Ladies Home Journal,* May 2000.
Scrambles, Mary Tannen, "Follow That Fur!" in *Harper's Bazaar,* September 2000.
Murphy, Robert, "Retail Reignites in the City of Light," in *WWD,* 2 October 2000.
"The Unclutchables," in *Entertainment Weekly,* 12 January 2001.
"Fendi Opens Paris Flagship With Focus on Accessories," in *WWD,* 7 March 2001.
Colavita, Courtney, "Luigi Formilli, Executive, Husband of Franca Fendi," [obituary] in *WWD,* 27 August 2001.

* * *

Like many Italian firms producing luxury goods, the Fendi company is a family dynasty owing a great deal of its success to the strong blood links comprising an intrinsic part of the business. Fendi is unique in that it has been run not by male members of the family (of which there are none, except by marriage) but by five sisters, daughters of Adele and Edoardo Fendi, who became involved in the business after the death of their father in 1954. Fendi originally specialized in producing high-quality furs and leather goods on the Via del Plebiscito in Rome in 1925. It was at this point that the firm moved toward a more high-fashion profile, with the first Fendi fashion show staged in 1955.

Fendi, autumn/winter 2001–02 collection: broadtail shift under a knitted fur jacket designed by Karl Lagerfeld. © AP/Wide World Photos.

Although Fendi produces a ready-to-wear sports line, the name is probably best known in the fashion arena for its dramatic fur collections, which have been designed by Karl Lagerfeld since 1962. It has been the company's relationship with Lagerfeld that brought the Fendi name to the attention of the fashion press, where it has since remained. Lagerfeld was also responsible for designing the double-F griffe that is almost as well recognized among the fashion cognoscenti as the double-C and double-G symbols of Chanel and Gucci.

Lagerfeld's innovative treatment of fur was both witty and, at times, shocking and has kept the Fendi company at the forefront of this particular field. In Lagerfeld's capable hands, real fur took on the appearance of fake fur; having been perforated with thousands of tiny holes to make the coats lighter to wear and printed to look like damask and other similar fabrics. Denim coats have been lined with mink by Lagerfeld, who also employed unorthodox animal skins such as squirrel and ferret in his creations. More recently, Lagerfeld covered an entire fur coat with woven mesh and created completely reversible fur coats as his stand against the antifur movement, which created great problems for the trade. Another design he produced for autumn-winter 1993–94 consisted of a small zipped bag that unfolded into a calf-length fur coat.

Whatever one's personal beliefs regarding the wearing of animal furs, the partnership of Karl Lagerfeld and Fendi undoubtedly broke barriers in the field of fur design. In Italy, fur sales have continued to constitute a major part of the company's business—where the Fendi sisters claim to have changed the age-old tradition of fur as being a status symbol to being a covetable high-fashion garment.

Like many luxury goods companies, Fendi has capitalized upon its name with the usual plethora of accessories, gloves, lighters, pens, glasses, and fragances that have become a natural progression for a well-recognized label. The new millennium found Fendi at the forefront of fashion buzz after the 1999 buyout by Prada-LVMH. A year later, insider undercurrent predicted a shift of Jil Sander from Prada to Fendi following the resignation of Prada chief Patrizio Bertelli in January. The extended Fendi family posed for photos in Rome in February to announce plans to go public by 2002.

Amid money talk, collectors of chicery clutched Fendi's next-to-nothing baguette purse, which found its way under the elbows of the glitterati and started an avalanche of knockoffs. Showrooms were filled with women ogling Fendi's sheared mink, a new breath of luxury. In August 2000, the death of Luigi Formilli, husband of Franca Fendi, shook the Fendi fashion house. He had dedicated himself for four decades to production and distribution of the company's fashion and leather goods. His energetic promotion helped establish Fendi at Bergdorf Goodman, Henri Bendel, Neiman Marcus, and Saks Fifth Avenue. At the time, two of his and Franca's three sons, Guido and Andrea, were working at Fendi, while daughter Federica directed the Fendissime line.

Fendi moved steadily into challenging opportunities, including Japan, near-virgin territory for Italian luxe. In March 2001 the company opened its first freestanding store, a 6,000-square-foot Paris headquarters at 24 Rue François Premier. While reestablishing Paris as fashion's luxury capital, the new store bolstered brand recognition with a full line of accessories, shoes, luggage, ready-to-wear, and a fur line heavily tinged with mink. To *Women's Wear Daily,* president Carla Fendi confided, "This first store is a very significant step for Fendi. Paris is a very important place. Its creativity is very stimulating because it is home to fashion labels from all over the word with a well-informed public."

—Catherine Woram; updated by Mary Ellen Snodgrass

FENG, Han

Chinese designer

Born: Hangzhou, China. **Education:** Graduated from Zhejiang Art Academy, Southeast China. **Career:** Began career designing scarves in the U.S., in the 1980s; first full-line collection, 1995; created costumes for performance pieces "Helix" and "Gandhara," 1995–98; moved into home furnishings, mid-1990s. **Awards:** Honored by the Asian American Federation of New York, 1995. **Address:** 333 West 39th Street, New York, NY, 10018, USA.

Han Feng, fall/winter 2000 collection. © AFP/CORBIS.

Publications

On FENG:

Books

Gumpert, Lynn and Richard Martin, *Material Dreams* (exhibition catalogue), New York, 1995.

Articles

Goodman, Wendy, "Living with Style: Hang Feng Comes Round the World to Spin Heavenly Tales in Silk," in *House and Garden* (New York), June 1993.

Enfield, Susan, "Meditative Pose," in *Avenue* (New York), September 1993.

Spindler, Amy M., "Bringing New Life (and Bamboo Bra Tops) to the Party," in the *New York Times,* 3 November 1993.

Staples, Kate, "Feng's Fashion: Smooth as Silk," in *Departures* (New York), March/April 1994.

"New York: Han Feng," in *WWD,* 7 November 1994.

Schiro, Anne-Marie, "Designed for Retailers and Real Women," in the *New York Times,* 5 April 1995.

Louie, Elaine, "Cool, Summery and in the City," in the *New York Times,* 31 July 1997.

Schiro, Anne-Marie, "Finding Motifs On Other Shores," in the *New York Times,* 6 November 1997.

Klensch, Elsa, "Exotic Cross-Continent Clothes Cover Feng For Fall," on CNN, 30 November 1998.

Ma, Fiona, and Heather Harlan, "Fusion Fashion," in *Asian Week,* 25 March 1999.

Klensch, Elsa, "Feng Lets Fashion Flow," on CNN, 18 June 1999.

Givhan, Robin, "N.Y. Collections Sway Their Hips to a Latin Beat," in the *Washington Post,* 14 September 1999.

* * *

Amy Spindler, writing in the *New York Times,* compared Han Feng's clothing to her contemporaries, stating, "she offers a few lines of the poetry of Romeo Gigli and Issey Miyake, but for much lower prices." Spindler rightly perceives the affinities of the gossamer-pleated yet practical clothing and accessories Feng designs, but it may be that a touch of poetry is just the levitating apparition we need in the midst of practical clothing. Feng creates unremittingly real clothing, wearable and practical, but with a concise, haiku-like hint of the historicist romance conveyed by Gigli and of the Cubist authority suggested by Miyake. There is something about Feng's inventiveness that is so radical a disposition for clothing that, like Miyake's pleats, it will either be a significant historical interlude in reform dress (for an avant-garde margin of the population) or a revolution in the way in which all people dress.

One wonders, however if clothing is the ultimate or exclusive goal of a designer who, growing up in Hangzhou, China, a great silk city, has become a devotee of the extraordinary organic materials that yield even more possibilities of organic shapes. A graduate of the Zhejiang Art Academy, Feng approaches her work as an artist. She began her work in the U.S. in the 1980s creating scarves, and the effect of the clothing is still a wondrous wrapping and veiling uncommon in the

Han Feng, fall/winter 2000 collection. © AFP/CORBIS.

tailored West. Her clothing wraps the body as the clouds enclose a mountain; her "smoke rings" are wraps of the kind made by Charles James and Halston, allowing a gentle helix of cloth to fit from hand to hand and sheathe the shoulders in an arch out of nature.

In as much as Feng is using materials Wendy Goodman described as, "magic out of silk' (*House and Garden* New York, June 1993) the organic compositions are only reinforced by the pliant materials, diaphanous delicacy, and classic shapes, often defying clothing as ceremony. She all but ignores tailoring and, in fact, uses many of the same experiments in textiles for her home furnishings. Not bothering with tailoring and instead assembling the garment as a light sculpture on the body, Feng fulfills the most predicted expectations in the West of design from the East. Spindler notes, "Her most beautiful dresses were of organza, which was gathered in little puffs, as if filled with helium. Han Feng's vision is so romantic that the clothes look dreamily feminine even when draped over the tattooed form of the auto mechanic-cum-model Jenny Shimizu." Feng offers soft shells of body wrap and comfort that return us to the most primitive, pretailored sensibility for dress.

In delving into clothing at the fundamental principle of wrapping, Feng is offering an alternative to the evolved forms of Western dress. It was unlikely that a relatively young, unknown designer had the opportunity to transform so thoroughly and effectively the principles of fashion, yet Feng's work has the visionary impact to cast a wide and important influence. Even in apparel, pleated, weightless ringlets do not seem to be the stuff of insurrection, but in this case they were an anticipation of clothing for the 21st century. It is not surprising that Feng's work was prominently featured in the Museum of Modern Art's Christmas catalogue in 1994.

Critics considered 1995 to be a breakthrough year for Feng. She presented her first true full-line collection, consisting of fitted items such as tailored suits, coats, and furs, as well as her trademark accordion-pleated scarves and dresses. She continued to play with shape and texture, integrating curves into seams, collars, and backs. In terms of fabric, her eye was still set on silk, whether silk velvet, silk and wool blends, silk satin, or silk organza. With her broader line, Feng was able to attract a more diverse roster of buyers than before. Retailers such as Dayton-Hudson, Brown's in London, and Isetan in Malaysia and Singapore joined the upscale department stores and boutiques already carrying her designs.

In the mid- and late 1990s, Feng expanded into items for the home, including table linens, bed covers, pillows, and other soft goods. She also moved beyond the realm of products, creating costumes for the performance pieces "Helix" (1995) and "Gandhara" (1998), commissioned by the Kennedy Center for the Performing Arts. The pieces' theme of East meets West was perfectly suited to Feng's style.

Each season, Feng's runway shows illustrate an evolving sophistication. In her fall/winter 1998 collection, she was inspired by the story of a love affair between a fabric trader and a young women along the silk road to China. Woolen coats, strapless dresses, fox shawls, and velvet jackets incorporated reds and burgundies, sometimes combined with pinks and greens, and accessorized by iridescent pleated scarves. In 1999 her focus was on the neckline; one item was a high-collared Chairman Mao jacket accented with a chinchilla scarf. Roses and rosette patterns were a theme throughout the collection, carrying from a rose-patterned long gray chiffon skirt with a pleated ruffle to evening wear featuring velvet pants, skirts, and coats with rosette smocking.

Feng's spring/summer 2001 collection highlighted her signature accordion-pleated skirts and crinkled silk blouses, printed with Impressionistic floral patterns. An asymmetrical, sculptural silk tube dress was pleated into a single sleeve and seemed to show the influence of Miyake. Despite Feng's evolution as a designer, the scarves for which she originally became known remain a central element; in this collection, pleated scarves featured woven ribbon inserts in blue, yellow, turquoise, and lilac.

In all her collections, Feng's designs are about fabrics and textures, pairing an American sensibility with Chinese and Japanese textiles and silhouettes. Her narrow skirts, wide pants, column dresses, and asymmetrical sweaters highlight her own distinctive style, dependent on light and balance but not on changing trends. Uneven hems and asymmetric cuts are her signature, as much as her pleating and origami-styled folds. Her palette combines colors in subtle ways, highlighted in items mixing burgundy with fuchsia or combining several shades of light green, enhanced by printed patterns. Her main focus is often reds, from geranium to cerise, with a secondary love of greens and blues from chartreuse and lime to lapis and turquoise. Han Feng keeps her customer at the forefront, always designing for the career woman who wants to be comfortable yet beautiful.

—Richard Martin; updated by Karen Raugust

FENN WRIGHT MANSON

British fashion house

Founded: by Trevor Wright, Colin Fenn, and Glynn Manson in London, 1974. **Company History:** American subsidiary formed in New York, 1977; Glynn Manson departed, 1984; acquired by Cygne Designs, 1994; branded UK unit sold to Colin Fenn, 1995. **Company Addresses:** Moray House, 23–31 Great Tichfield St., London W1P 7FE, England; 500 Seventh Avenue, New York, NY 10018, U.S.A. **Company Website:** www.fwm.co.uk or www.fennwrightmanson.com.

Publications

On FENN WRIGHT MANSON:

Articles

"Cygne Inks Deal to Buy Fenn Wright and Manson," in *DNR,* 14 December 1993.

"Cygne Designs Buys Fenn Wright and Manson," in *WWD,* 8 April 1994.

Green, Roy E., "Cygne Designs, Inc. Announces Record Fourth Quarter and Year-End Results," in *Business Wire,* 14 April 1994.

"Cygne to Buy Hong Kong Intimate Apparel Maker," in *WWD,* 5 August 1994.

Furman, Phyllis, "Apparel Maker's Star Waxing with Purchase," in *Crain's New York Business,* 8 August 1994.

"Cygne Designs Inc. Agrees to Sell UK Subsidiary of its Fenn, Wright & Manson Unit," in the *Wall Street Journal,* 30 March 1995.

"Cygne Sued by Holder on Fenn Buy," in *WWD,* 20 December 1995.

"Cygne, Holders Settle Suit," in *WWD,* 15 January 1997.

Alexander, Hilary, "Soft, Slinky and Back in Style," available online at the Telegraph Network, www.portal.telegraph.co.uk, 2001.

* * *

The Fenn Wright Manson (FWM) Group was founded in 1974 by Trevor Wright, Colin Fenn, and Glynn Manson, as a British-based company operating from London. Initially, all sales were to the UK market, and production was wholly in Hong Kong. The company designs, manufactures, and sells both women's and men's clothing, with by far the largest part of the business generated through the women's divisions.

An international market has been established since 1976, in which year the company also formed a buying office to oversee and control its production requirements in the Far East. The firm established its own American subsidiary in 1977, and began trading in the U.S. in 1978. The firm sells to the high-end department stores internationally, the better specialty chains, and independent specialty stores. Sales in the U.S. accounted for most of FWMs volume, and a large proportion of these sales were made through the operation of retail outlets, situated in outlet malls on the East Coast. The company also had a showroom at the Dallas Mart which operated only during show weeks.

Fenn Wright Manson womenswear draws on the themes of timeless classics, stylish and functional sportswear, and refined tailoring. The combination of styles creates a feeling of warmth, comfort, and easy dressing. Collections in the 1990s featured longer lines, with softer tailoring, uncluttered shapes, and clean layers in soft and earthy colors: cream, mushroom, camel, tobacco, and chocolate. A variety of fabrics and knits include lambswool, angora, wool, cotton, as well as leather and Lycra. In addition, there were sandwashed silk shirts available in 30 different colors, and silk twill, as well as needlecord and cotton poplin shirts taking on the guise of the classic denim shirt, with top stitching detail and billow pockets.

The middle and later 1990s ushered in a host of problems for FWM. In April 1994 the firm was acquired by Cygne Designs, Inc., a producer of womenswear sold mostly to the Ann Taylor and Limited chains. Within months of the buy, Cygne bought GJM International Ltd., the Hong Kong-based intimate apparel manufacturer founded by Glynn Manson (who left FWM in 1984). It was an odd coupling of past and present, and Cygne executives believed the three firms represented all major segments of women's apparel, from GJM's lingerie to FWM's sportswear and classic separates. The marriage of brands, however, was not a happy one; poor sales in womenswear in 1995, especially FWM's mainstay silk, turned the union sour. Cygne spun off Fenn Wright Manson's UK branded unit back to founder Colin Fenn, slashed jobs at FWM's Hong Kong and U.S. divisions, and sold GJM to Warnaco in 1996.

Despite the corporate imbroglios, FWM survived and will always be known for its wearable fashion with an emphasis on quality and value. Its sweaters, silks, and sportswear are a hallmark of British fashion sensibility, and available not only from well known retailers Nicholsons and Gray & Osbourn, but from several new Fenn Wright Manson stores as well.

—Doreen Ehrlich; updated by Owen James

FÉRAUD, Louis

French designer, painter, and author

Born: Arles, France, 13 February 1920. **Family:** Married Zizi (Alice) Boivin, 1947 (divorced, 1963); married Mia Fonssagrièves, 1964 (divorced, 1972); children: Dominique (also known as Kiki). **Military Service:** Served as lieutenant in the French Resistance. **Career:** Opened first couture boutique in Cannes, 1955; moved to Paris, entered ready-to-wear, 1956; first menswear line launched, 1975; costumer designer for films and television; perfumes *Justine,* introduced, 1965, *Corrida,* 1975; *Fantasque* introduced (and later licensed to Avon Products), 1980, *Fer* (also licensed to Avon, but under the name *Féraud pour Homme*), 1982; *Jour de Féraud/Vivage,* introduced, 1984; sportswear line introduced, 1989; New York flagship store opened, 1990; accessories line introduced, 1992; retired, giving control of business to daughter Kiki and former wife Zizi, 1995; ready-to-wear division sold to Secon; remaining business units sold to Secon, 1999; Yvan Mispelaere hired as designer, 2000. **Exhibitions:** Exhibition of paintings in Paris, 1988, 1989, 1992, 1993, 1994, and in Japan, 1989; Gallery Urban, New York, 1990. **Awards:** Légion d'Honneur; Golden Thimble Award, 1984; Dé d'Or Award, 1978, 1984. **Died:** 28 December 1999, in Paris. **Company Address:** 88, Frabourg Saint-Honoré, 75008, Paris, France.

Louis Féraud, autumn/winter 1999–2000 haute couture collection. © AFP/CORBIS.

PUBLICATIONS

By FÉRAUD:

Books

"L'éte du pingouin (The Penguin's Summer), Paris, 1978.
Louis Féraud, Paris, 1985.
Memoir, *L'hiver des fous (The Winter of Fools),* Paris, 1986.

On FÉRAUD:

Articles

Hunter, Catherine Ellis, "Avon Embraces the Designer Fragrance," in *Drug & Cosmetic Industry,* September 1984.
"Louis Féraud l'atout coeur," in *L'Officiel* (Paris), September 1984.
"Louis Féraud, mille facettes," unpaginated feature in *L'Officiel* (Paris), September 1985.
"Louis Féraud: le chic," in *Vogue* (New York), April 1986.

Smithers, T. S., "Fast Times with Louis Féraud," in *WWD,* 20 October 1986.
"Louis Féraud: pour fêter l'Espagne," in *L'Officiel* (Paris), March 1987.
Guernsey, Diane, "The Other Féraud," in *Town and Country* (New York), October 1990.
Petkanas, Christopher, "French Accents," in *Harper's Bazaar* (New York), February 1991.
Bowles, Hamish, "Louis the Fun King," *Harpers & Queen,* December 1991.
"Feraud, Bardot's Discoverer, Dies in Paris at Age of 79," in the *Chicago Tribune,* 28 December 1999.
Riding, Alan, "Louis Feraud is Dead at 79; Prominent Fashion Designer," in the *New York Times,* 29 December 1999.
Brady, James, "The Designer Who Loved Women," in *Crain's New York Business*, 10 January 2000.

* * *

It has been said of Louis Féraud that he was a man who loves women. Indeed, he described himself as "Louis Féraud who adores women, Louis Féraud who admires women." This devotion no doubt inspired the former French Resistance lieutenant to pursue a career in the rarefied worlds of French haute couture and ready-to-wear.

Féraud designed for a seductive woman who lived in harmony with life and herself, a woman looking for comfort and freedom. He was fascinated by the different personalities of women and how this inspired him to create different moods and themes. For women, he said, "Fashion is an opportunity to be chic, to conspire between reality and desire."

Féraud created glamorous, luxurious clothes at ready-to-wear prices; he also designed for couture. Among his celebrity clients were Joan Collins, for whom he designed some of the clothes worn in the television series *Dynasty* and Madame Mitterand, wife of the former French President. His collections were divided between the prêt-à-porter Louis Féraud Paris collections and the less expensive Louis Féraud set.

A strong team backed up the Féraud business, originally led by Féraud himself and consisting of nearly a dozen international designers, color specialists, and stylists who worked together to form what he described as a weather forecast that predicts trends. In addition to the suits and dresses for *Dynasty,* Féraud designed for the television series *Dallas,* for film, and for starlets Brigitte Bardot, Paulette Goddard, Kim Novak, Catherine Deneuve, Mireille Mathieu, and Sabina Anzema. Yet when asked if given the chance to design clothes for women from another era, and which era that would be, Féraud declared: "Tomorrow. I am often seriously asked what fashion will be doing next year. I am like an art medium for these people, who has the ability to look into the future."

Féraud listed painting as being amongst his passions; it inspired him to develop color in his work. "Colors are fantasies of light," he claimed. "However, all colors are diffused in black, memories of the sun, the indispensable, and the perfect that is beauty." He selected specific color ranges each season, but declared himself unaffected by fashion trends. "The only thing that we must know in our business is what doesn't exist as yet." Color specs were developed within the design team, which also created new ideas for fabric trims.

When asked how, out of the French Resistance in World War II, he emerged one of the leading fashion designers of the world, Féraud replied: "Fashion does not separate people but holds them together. One can also describe fashion as the meeting place out of love."

In the mid-1990s Féraud turned the business over to his daughter, Dominique (known as Kiki), and his former wife, Zizi, who had remained his partner after their divorce. Kiki, like her father, was a designer, though the younger Féraud favored more detailed and ornate designs than the elder. In 1997 the Féraud ready-to-wear division was sold to Dutch textile group Secon. Three years later, in the fall of 1999, Secon acquired the remaining Féraud assets. Louie Féraud, designer, painter, and author, died in December 1999 at the age of 79.

—Kevin Almond; updated by Nelly Rhodes

FÉRIER, M.

See BIANCHINI-FÉRIER

FERRAGAMO, Salvatore

Italian footwear designer

Born: Bonito, near Naples, Italy, June 1898; immigrated to the U.S., 1914. **Family:** Married Wanda Miletti, 1949; children: Fiamma (died, 1998), Giovanna, Ferruccio, Fulvia, Leonardo, Massimo. **Career:** Apprentice shoemaker, Bonito, 1907–12; with brothers, opened shoemaking and shoe repair shop, Santa Barbara, California and also created footwear for the American Film Company, 1914–23; relocated to Hollywood, 1923–27; returned to Italy, established business in Florence, from 1929; bankrupted in 1933; back in business by late 1930s; firm continued after this death, with each child overseeing a slice of the firm; Fiamma took over shoe designing and showed her first collection, 1961; built new stores in Beverly Hills, New York, Paris, Chicago, Las Vegas, San Francisco, 1995–2000; bought Emanuel Ungaro, 1996; first fragrance, *Salvatore Ferragamo Pour Femme,* 1998; *Salvatore Ferragamo Pour Homme,* 1999; redesigned SoHo store, 2001. **Exhibitions:** *Salvatore Ferragamo 1898–1960* [retrospective], Palazzo Strozzi, Florence, 1985; *The Art of the Shoe* [retrospective], Los Angeles County Museum, 1992; established the Salvatore Ferragamo Museum, Florence, Italy, 1995. **Awards:** Neiman Marcus award, 1947; *Footwear News* Hall of Fame award, 1988 [Fiamma Ferragamo]. **Died:** 7 August 1960, in Fiumetto, Italy. **Company Address:** Salvatore Ferragamo SpA, Palazzo Feroni, Via Tornabuoni 2, 50123 Florence, Italy. **Company Website:** www.salvatoreferragamo.it.

PUBLICATIONS

By FERRAGAMO:

Books

Shoemaker of Dreams: The Autobiography of Salvatore Ferragamo, London, 1957.

Salvatore Ferragamo, spring/summer 2001 ready-to-wear collection: leather ensemble. © Reuters NewMedia Inc./CORBIS.

On FERRAGAMO:

Books

Swann, June, *Shoes,* London, 1982.

Alfonsi, Maria-Vittoria, *Leaders in Fashion: I grandi personaggi della moda,* Bologna, 1983.

Palazzo Strozzi, *I protagonisti della moda: Salvatore Ferragamo (1898–1960)* [exhibition catalogue], Florence, 1985.

McDowell, Colin, *Shoes: Fashion and Fantasy,* New York, 1989.

Almansi, Guido, et al., *Salvatore Ferragamo,* Milan, 1990.

Ricci, Stefania, Edward Maeder, et al., eds., *Salvatore Ferragamo: The Art of the Shoe,* New York, 1992.

Ricci, Stefania, *Salvatore Ferragamo Museum,* Milan, 1995.

———, *Cinderella: The Shoe Rediscovered,* Milan, 1998.

Baudot, François, *Ferragamo,* New York & Paris, 2001.

Articles

Infantino, Vivian, "Salvatore Ferragamo (1898–1960): A Retrospective," in *Footwear News* (New York), July 1985.

"The Flourishing Fashions of the Ferragamo Family of Florence," in *Vogue* (Paris), October 1985.

Harlow, Vanessa, "Sole Obsession," in the *Observer* (London), 27 September 1987.

Morrison, Patricia, "Feet Were Ferragamo's World," in the *Daily Telegraph* (London), 2 November 1987.

McDowell, Colin, "Wanda Ferragamo: A Woman of Destiny," in *Women's Journal* (London), December 1987.

Hope, Emma, "Designed to Last," in *Design* (London), January 1988.

"Salvatore Ferragamo: The Art of the Shoe, 1927–1960," in the *Arts Review* (London), 15 January 1988.

McKenzie, Janet, "Shoemaker of Dreams," in *Studio International* (London), No. 1020, 1988.

Horovitz, Bruce, "Well-heeled Controversy," in the *Los Angeles Times,* 24 April 1992.

Stengel, Richard, "The Shoes of the Master," in *Time,* 4 May 1992.

Baber, Bonnie, et al., "The Design Masters," in *Footwear News,* 17 April 1995.

"Ferragamo Acquires the House of Ungaro," in *WWD,* 3 July 1996.

Barret, Amy, "Ferragamo's Growth Tests Family Values," in the *Wall Street Journal,* 10 July 1997.

Zargani, Luisa, "Fiamma Ferragamo Dies at 57," in *WWD,* 1 October 1998.

"Fiamma Ferragamo," [obituary] in the *Economist,* 10 October 1998.

Moin, David, "Reinvented Ferragamo Rides Luxe Boom," in *WWD,* 11 April 2000.

Edelson, Sharon, "Ferragamo's New Attitude," in *WWD,* 25 May 2000.

Moin, David, "Ferragamo, Refined," in *WWD,* 10 October 2001.

* * *

A master craftsman, Salvatore Ferragamo was known as one of the world's most innovative shoe designers, transforming the look and fit of the shoe. He broke away from conventional footwear designs, exploring not only innovative design, but also the technical structure of the shoe.

Ferragamo acquired the basic skills of shoe production while apprenticed to the local village cobbler in Bonito. Ambitious for success, he emigrated from his home town in Naples to America, where he studied mass production in shoe design. The years in the U.S. assisted him in fully understanding the technical procedures implemented in manufacturing his unique design. Owing to his excellent grounding in shoe design exploration and study, Ferragamo fully understood all the technical aspects of shoe production, the anatomy, and the balance of the foot. Eventually he set up in business in Santa Barbara, California, where his original, inventive designs caught the regard of many famous customers. Private commissions came from celebrities including Sophia Loren, Gloria Swanson, the Duchess of Windsor, and Audrey Hepburn.

Initially a designer and creator of handmade one-off shoes for individual customers, Ferragamo introduced the possibility of creating shoes that were exotic and beautiful, yet supportive to the foot and

Salvatore Ferragamo, spring/summer 2001 collection. © AP/Wide World Photos.

ankle. Function and comfort, together with an understanding of good design, were the essential elements behind his success. The Ferragamo name is synonymous with style, glamour, ingenuity, and quality. Ferragamo diverged from the restrictions of conventional shoe design and manufacture, exploring the realms of fantasy and creating footwear well advanced of contemporary classic designs. He produced shoes for every occasion; ankle boots, moccasins, laced shoes, Oxford brogues, stilettoes, shoes for evening and daywear, including classic traditional styles.

The shortage of leather and quality skins during the war years encouraged Ferragamo to explore new materials, continually searching beyond the realms of traditional materials for aesthetically attractive alternatives. Cork, crochet, crocheted cellophane, plaited raffia, rubber, fish skins, felt, and hemp were successful if unconventional alternatives. His designs were brilliant in concept and craftsmanship, creating many unique and outrageous styles. He was inspired by past fashions, cultures, Hollywood, oriental clothing and classical styling. He created over 20,000 styles in his lifetime and registered 350 patents, including oriental mules with a unique pointed toe, patented by Ferragamo at the end of the 1930s. From the late 1930s his amusing, ambitious, and extreme designs involved the use of perforated leathers, raffia checks, elasticated silk yarns, appliqué motifs, needlepoint lace, sequined fabrics and patchwork.

In 1938 he launched the platform shoe which reemerged in varying forms ever since. His "invisible shoe," created in 1947, was produced with clear nylon uppers and a black suede heel and Ferragamo produced many variations on this design. His innate sense of color extended from traditional browns and beiges to vivid contrasting colors of ornate richness. The technical knowledge attained while developing new dyeing techniques assisted him in combining technical knowledge with his creative color flair.

In 1927 Ferragamo returned to Italy, setting up a workshop in Florence, a city which was to become the fashion center of Italy. He continued to produce custom-made shoes, many of his customers' individual lasts still being in existence today, maintained in collections in Feroni. Using modern production methods his made-to-measure shoes had quality, durability, and style. He was modern in his approach to design, taking advantage of new technology to improve his output, without jeopardizing standards. Through ambition and ingenuity his productivity and creativity improved greatly, leading to the industrialization of his work for mass production yet Ferragamo maintained high standards by overseeing all aspects of production. The mass produced shoes were manufactured under the label Ferrina Shoes, produced in England.

After his death in 1960 his family continued to the firm and in addition to producing quality shoes branched out into accessories and designer apparel. Wife Wanda ran the firm; daughter Fiamma, who had worked by her father's side from when she was a teenager, took over designing and producing the shoes; Giovanna initiated women's ready-to-wear; Ferruccio was at his mother's side and helped run the company; Fulvia handled all accessories bearing the firm's name; Leonardo oversaw marketing and introduced Ferragamo to Asia; Massimo headed the burgeoning North American operations. Despite its successful expansion, the Ferragammo name remains world renowned for its shoes. Fiamma's creations, as beautiful and unique as those of her father, are still the Ferragamo's principal selling point in boutiques in the U.S. and throughout Europe and the Far East.

In 1998 the Ferragamos were bowed by the loss of 57-year-old Fiamma after a lenghty battle with breast cancer. Widely credited with ensuring the family firm's future with her shoe designs, she claimed to have learned everything from her father. In an interview in *Footwear News* (17 April 1995), she discussed how far the family business had come since Salvatore's death. "I'm sure he would be very pleased, not only for the success, development, and growth of the company.... I think he would be very happy to see his dreams fulfilled, but also that we are keeping shoes the main part of his business."

The Ferragamo clan persevered after Fiamma's untimely death, a year in which they ventured into fragrance with the firm's first fragrance, *Salvatore Ferragamo Pour Femme,* in 1998 which was followed by a complementary male scent, *Salvatore Ferragamo Pour Homme,* in 1999. Several new flagship Ferragamo stores had also opened during the last several years in pivotal markets such as New York, Beverly Hills, Chicago, and Las Vegas.

The legacy of Salvatore Ferragamo is alive and well in Italy, and the rest of the world—where "Ferragamo" means innovation, beauty, and quality.

—Carol Mary Brown; updated by Owen James

FERRÉ, Gianfranco

Italian designer

Born: Legnano, Italy, 15 August 1944. **Education:** Graduated in architecture from Politecnico, Milan, 1969. **Career:** Freelance jewelry and accessory designer, Milan, 1969–73; designer, Baila, Milan, 1974; launched own label for womenwear with partner Franco Mattioli, Milan, 1978; introduced secondary Oaks by Ferré line, 1978; debut of menwear collection, 1982; fragrances introduced, 1984; watches, 1985, eyewear and bath line (men), 1986; launched haute couture collection, 1986–88; introduced furs, 1987; signed agreement with Marzotto for the Studio 000.1 by Ferré lines for men and women, 1987; named artistic director, House of Dior, 1989; feminine fragrance, *Ferré by Ferré,* 1991; introduced household linens collection, 1992; took 000.1 diffusion line to the U.S., 1995; Gieffeffe bridge line and men's jeans collection debuted, 1996; *Gieffeffe* unisex fragrance launched, 1996; women's jeans line introduced, 1997; opened two London stores and new HQ in Milan, 1998; firm sold to Gruppo Tonino Perna, 2000; began custom tailoring, 2000; opened first U.S. Ferré Jeans store, Miami, 2001; new atelier and Ferré couture collection, 2002; initial public offering planned, 2003. **Exhibitions:** *Italian Re-Evolution,* La Jolla Museum of Art, California, 1982; *Intimate Architecture: Contemporary Clothing Design,* Massachusetts Institute of Technology, Cambridge, 1982; *Design Italian Society in the Eighties,* La Jolla Museum of Contemporary Art, 1982; *Creators of Italian Fashion 1920–80,* Osaka and Tokyo, 1983; *Il Genio Antipatico: Creatività e tecnologia della Moda Italiana 1951–1983* (*The Unpleasant Genius: Creativity and Technology of Italian Fashion 1951–1983*), Rome, 1984; *Tartan: A Grand Celebration of the Tradition of Tartan,* Fashion Institute of Technology, 1988; *Momenti del design italiano nell'industria e nella moda,* Seoul, 1990; *Japonism in Fashion,* National Museum of Modern Art, 1994. **Awards:** Tiberio d'Oro award, 1976; Best Stylist of the Year award by *Asahi Shimbun* and *Women's Wear Daily,* 1983; Modepreis for women's fashions, Monaco, 1985; Cutty Sark Men's Fashion award, New York, 1985; Medal of Civic Merit, Milan, 1985; named Commendatore dell'Ordine al Merito della Repubblica Italiana, 1986; Dé d'Or prize for first haute couture collection for Dior, 1989; named "Milanese of the Year" by the Famiglia Meneghina, 1989; I Grandi Protagonisti prize from the Italian Furs Association, 1990; Lorenzo il Magnifico award from the Medicean Academy, Florence, 1990; Occhio d'Oro prize, 1983, 1983/84, 1985, 1986/87, 1987/88, 1989; Il Fiorino d'Oro award, 1991; Pitti Immagine Uomo award, 1993. **Address:** Via della Spiga 19a, 20121 Milan, Italy.

Gianfranco Ferré, fall/winter 2001–02 collection: silver sequined top and mini skirt under a fur-trimmed leather coat. © AP/Wide World Photos.

Publications

By FERRÉ:

Books

Lettres à un jeune couturier, Paris, 1995.

Articles

"Le ragioni del sentimento," in *L'Uomo Vogue* (Milan), October 1987.

On FERRÉ:

Books

Mulassano, Adriana, *I mass-moda: Fatti e personaggi dell'Italian Look,* Florence, 1979.

Sartogo, Piero, ed., *Italian Re-Evolution* [exhibition catalogue], La Jolla, California, 1982.

Alfonsi, Maria-Vittoria, *Leaders in Fashion: I grandi personaggi della moda,* Bologna, 1983.

Giacomoni, Silvia, *The Italian Look Reflected,* Milan, 1984.

Soli, Pia, ed., *Il genio antipatico* [exhibition catalogue], Milan, 1984.

Perschetz, Lois, ed., *W, The Designing Life,* New York, 1987.

Aragno Giordani, ed., *Moda Italia* [exhibition catalogue], Milan, 1988.

Howell, Georgina, *Sultans of Style: Thirty Years of Fashion and Passion 1960–90,* London, 1990.

———, *In Vogue,* London, 1992.

Ferri, Edgarda, *Ferrè,* Milan, 1995.

Stegemeyer, Anne, *Who's Who in Fashion, Third Edition,* New York, 1996.

Ferré, Giusi, *Gianfranco Ferré: Itinerario,* Milan, 1998, 1999.

Ferré, Giusi, and Samuele Mazza, *Gianfranco Ferré,* Corte Madera, CA, 1998.

Articles

"The New Architectural Approach to Fashion," in *Vogue,* June 1982.
"Gianfranco Ferré: Expanding His Research," in *WWD,* 5 April 1986.
"Roma alta moda: Gianfranco Ferré," in *Vogue* (Milan), September 1987.
Smith, Liz, "Architect of New Classics," in the *Times* (London), 8 December 1987.
"Gianfranco Ferré: Dà alla donna forma e slancio," in *Vogue* (Milan), January 1988.
Howell, Georgina, "Gianfranco Ferré, the Nonconformist," in *Vogue,* July 1988.
"Ferré and Gigli, Architects of Modern Style," in *Elle* (London), October 1988.
"Gianfranco Ferré," in *Donna* (Milan), March 1989.
Menkes, Suzy, "The Italian Connection," in the *Sunday Express Magazine* (London), 11 June 1989.
Smith, Liz, "My Fair Ferré," in the *Times* (London), 25 July 1989.
Baudet, François, "Gianfranco Ferré," in *Vogue* (Paris), August 1989.
Menkes, Suzy, "Ferré Strikes Gold," in the *Illustrated London News* (London), Autumn 1989.
Kleers, Paul, "Ferré in Focus," in *GQ,* March 1990.
Mayle, Peter, "Ferré's a Jolly Good Fellow," in *GQ,* September 1990.
Boriou, Gisella, "Gianfranco Ferré: I Am a Mix of Sensitivity and Concreteness," in *Donna,* November 1990.
Forden, Sara Gay, "Frankly Ferré," in *DNR,* 21 June 1993.
Aspesi, Natalia, "Le Donne di Ferre," in *Il Venerdi' di Repubblica,* April 1994.
Carloni, Maria Vittoria, "Bello & Brutto: Lo Stile Secondo Ferré," in *Panorama,* June 1994.
Blanchard, Tamsin, "New-Look Dior Fails to Suit 1990s Woman," in the *Independent* 11 October 1994.
Forden, Sara Gay, "It's Time (Italian Fashion Designer Gianfranco Ferré)," in *DNR,* 31 January 1995.
Spindler, Amy M., "Armani and Ferré: A Study in Contrast, in the *New York Times,* 11 March 1995.
Forden, Sara Gay, "Ferré's New Jeans Line...," in *DNR,* 17 July 1996.
Socha, Miles, "Ferré Plans Multitiered Line of Men's Accessories," in *DNR,* 6 September 1996.
"Ferré Sets Up U.S. Division, Names a Head," in *WWD,* 5 June 1997.
Forden, Sara Gay, "Gianfranco Ferré Joins Ranks of Designers with Itch for an IPO," in *WWD,* 15 September 1997.
"Gianfranco Ferré," in *WWD,* 24 February 1998.
Conti, Samantha, "Mattioli Sells Part of His Ferré Stake," in *WWD,* 23 December 1999.
———, "Ferré Tries His Hand at Sartorial Line," in *DNR,* 22 March 2000.
———, "GTP Acquires Ferré," in *WWD,* 22 December 2000.
"Ferré New Owners Consider Stock Listing," in *WWD,* 15 March 2001.

*

Fashion is a reality connected with the changes of our society, of which it is an attentive interpreter. Artistic trends, new expressive languages, individualistic or mass behaviour and any other event which marks our society or determines its choices also determines trends or, at least, [change in] fashion. A fashion designer has to be an attentive interpreter of these events; has to be able to prophecy, without forgetting the realities of industry and commerce.

My role as a fashion designer comes from a complex process, where creativity and imagination play an important role, but are supported by a firm rational analysis.

—Gianfranco Ferré

Gianfranco Ferré, fall/winter 2001–02 collection. © AP/Wide World Photos.

* * *

Gianfranco Ferré has been dubbed by *Women's Wear Daily* as the "Frank Lloyd Wright of Italian Fashion." Trained initially as an architect, his work bears many references to this early discipline. He draws up a plan for each collection based on a philosophy that his customer wants functional, classic yet powerful clothes, constructed in the highest quality materials. The clothes are then created with a distinct eye for dramatic proportion and purity of line.

There is nothing understated about Ferré womenswear. His minimalist approach has often made opulent, theatrical statements on the catwalk, recalling the film star glamor projected by Anita Ekberg in the film *La Dolce Vita.* The clothes reflect a glamorous, fantasy dressing, combined with architectural symmetry. Ferré often exaggerates proportions in tailoring and dressmaking; classic shirt shapes often have extreme cuffs or collars, coats and jackets are defined by silhouette. An extravagant use of luxury fabrics like fur on dresses or long evening coats, leather, and taffeta often in the distinctive, stark colors of red, black, white or gold reinforce this definition of modern elegance.

Ferré menswear collections are less extravagant, based on tradition but designed with his characteristic modernist approach. He sees his customer as a man who appreciates traditional cloth and a classic line. Ferré has developed new tailoring techniques to create a more relaxed, expansive shape for men, a reaction to the hard-edged lines so prevalent in 1980s power dressing. Ferré often looks to London for inspiration, believing the British capital is a key point in the world of fashion. As he explained to journalist Liz Smith, "There is an in-bred eccentricity in London which allows clothes to be worn in original and completely modern proportions."

Ferré has a reputation for being a realist, with a practical approach to projects—working with everything in his head from market requirements, manufacturing schedules, financial limitations, and development of themes, to advertising. Brought up in a secure family environment, his mother instilled him with an obsessive sense of duty and responsibility; she was strict when it came to homework and passing exams. This level-headed approach even caused him to react with economic sense to Diana Vreeland's famous fashion quote, "Pink is the navy blue of India," made during the course of a conversation with Ferré. He replied judiciously, "Naturally pink is the navy blue of India because it's the cheapest of all dyes."

In 1989 Ferré was appointed designer for Dior, to supply the house with an image for the 1990s. His first collection introduced a refined, sober, and strict collection inspired by Cecil Beaton's black-and-white Ascot scene from the film *My Fair Lady,* a theme revisited in 1996 with the launch of a men's jeans collection. The new Ferré Jeans line, all in black and white, came in casual separates of three styles—basic, athletic, and beach wear. Ferré commented to Sara Gay Forden of the *Daily News Record* (17 July 1996), "This is not your standard, classic jeans line... This is a forward-looking collection for the future generation."

Ferré further forged ahead in 1996 with the debut of the *Gieffeffe* unisex fragrance, along with the Gieffeffe bridge collection priced to battle DKNY and Calvin Klein's CK for the hearts and dollars of hipster youth. The first Gieffeffe store opened as well, in Florence, Italy, with a second shop planned for Milan in 1997 and several more elsewhere in Europe. The Ferré Jeans line for women was also introduced in 1997, along with the formation of the Gianfranco Ferré USA to oversee the firm's increasing interests in America. Additionally, Ferré signed an agreement with Japanese conglomerate Mitzuno to open over a dozen shops in Japan, and to segue into producing golf apparel and equipment.

In 1998 the Ferré empire celebrated its 20th anniversary, considered going public, and tweaked its image. Stores in New York and Rome were renovated, two London shops opened, a new Milan headquarters was unveiled, and offices and showroom for its recently-created U.S. subsidiary opened on Fifth Avenue in New York. Yet the year proved far from jubilant when Ferré's longtime partner Franco Mattioli decided to retire and sell his 49-percent stake in the company. The news caused a contentious rift between the partners, and in 1999 Mattioli sold 21-percent of his holdings to Gruppo Tonino Perna (GTP), corporate parent of the IT Holding fashion group.

Gianfranco Ferré, after much negotiation, finally decided to sell all but 10-percent of the company bearing his name. Under the December 2000 agreement, GTP received 90-percent of the firm, and Ferré not only maintained creative control, but gained an atelier in Milan and a new couture line set to debut in 2002. The couture collection was a natural extension for Ferré, who had begun creating custom-made suits for a limited number of clients earlier in the year. Like Ferré a few years before them, the executives of GTP announced plans for an initial public offering scheduled for sometime in 2003.

Gianfranco Ferré is easily identifiable as an Italian designer; his clothes are well-shaped, confident, and powerfully feminine or masculine. Through his own label collections, he has developed such hallmarks as the crisp white shirt with stand-up collar or in his signature color, red. The Ferré product, whether it be prêt-à-porter or leather goods, glasses, furs, or shoes, has become synonymous with precision and elegance, an identity which he believes has greatly increased the cachet of "made in Italy."

—Kevin Almond; updated by Owen James

FERRETTI, Alberta

Italian designer

Born: Cattolica, Italy. **Family:** Two sons from an earlier marriage; companion, Giuseppe Campanella. **Career:** Opened own boutique at the age of 18, established the company Aeffe with her brother, Massimo Ferretti, opened Palazzo Viviani, a four-star hotel, 1994; signed fragrance deal with Proctor and Gamble, 2000. **Address:** Aeffe, Via delle Querce, 51, 47842 S. Giovanni In Marignano, Italy. **Website:** www.aeffe.com.

PUBLICATIONS

On FERRETTI:

Articles

"Stepping Out: Ferretti at BG," in *WWD,* 17 September 1997.
Castro, Peter, "Italian Dressing" in *People,* 26 January 1998.
Sischy, Ingrid, "Ferretti-to-Wear," in *Interview Magazine,* October 1998.
Schiro, Anne-Marie, "In Italy, Alluring Ideas Are Blossoming," in the *New York Times,* 5 March 1999.
Lavin, Cheryl, "A Vision in White," in the *Chicago Tribune,* 16 May 1999.
Tien, Ellen, "For Brides Who Stroll a Sandy Aisle," in the *New York Times,* 4 June 2000.
"Whatever Gets You Through the Day and Night," in *WWD,* 10 October 2000.
"Ferretti Signs with P&G," in *WWD,* 27 October 2000.
Norwich, William, "The Latest Temptations of Uma," in the *New York Times Magazine,* Fall 2000.
"The Philosophy of Philosophy," available online at www.philosphy.it, 6 June 2001.

Alberta Ferretti, spring/summer 2002 ready-to-wear collection: chiffon dress. © AFP/CORBIS.

* * *

In the town of Montegridolfo, Italy, sits a 23-room castle 20 miles inland from the Adriatic Sea. It is here that designer Alberta Ferretti has tried her hand at the hotel business. She has turned this medieval structure into Palazzo Viviania, a modern four-star hotel that opened to the public in 1994. The castle exudes a medieval charm combined with a modern feel, the embodiment of which can also be found in Ferretti's clothing design. Soft, romantic allure, combined with clean, structured lines, impart a composed, subtly sexy feel to her work.

Growing up along the coast of the Adriatic Sea in the small hamlet of Cattolica, Italy, Ferretti spent her girlhood among a myriad of fabrics and clothing designs displayed throughout her mother's dress shop. Perhaps inspired by her mother's work, and certainly her surroundings, 18-year-old Ferretti dropped out of high school and opened her own boutique. Offering mainly other designers in the beginning, she went on to carry Versace, Krizia, and Armani clothing within a few years. The grand scale launch of her own design collection stemmed from an auspicious beginning. When a salesman entered Ferretti's boutique, he noticed some of her pieces hanging throughout the store. Commenting that the designs should be offered in more locations, he inadvertently started Ferretti down a more promising career path. By taking the sage advice of the salesman, the Ferretti name was officially launched into the design world.

Today, the apparel of Alberta Ferretti can be seen on several of Hollywood's comeliest personalities. Nicole Kidman, Uma Thurman, Julia Roberts, and Andie MacDowell are all subscribers of Ferretti's whimsical yet sleekly contrived raiments. *People* (October 1998) reported actress Andie MacDowell as saying, "Alberta's clothes are feminine, soft and romantic, but at the same time chic and elegant." With such a winning combination, Ferretti has come a long way in a short time. No longer the youthful entrepreneur of a small boutique, Alberta, together with her brother, Massimo Ferretti, now own the design company Aeffe.

Catering to the diversity of women's tastes and trends, Aeffe produces and distributes designwear not only of the Ferretti name but others as well, including Rifat Ozbek, Narciso Rodriguez, and Jean Paul Gaultier. Cheryl Lavin of *Fashion Magazine* (16 May 1999) said of Ferretti, "The Alberta Ferretti dress, a slim sheath with folded pleats, separated by rows of tucking, is as stylized as a column at the Parthenon." Ferretti's trademark, the little dress, has as many possibilities as a blank sheet of paper. Seizing an opportunity, she has succeeded in capturing everything from a soft allure or subtle romanticism to a quietly arousing feel in a continuously impressive array of proffered dresses. She seizes a feminine, womanly appeal without being too girlish in design.

Of Ferretti, the 10 October 2000 issue of *Women's Wear Daily* stated, "Softly, ever so softly, that's Alberta Ferretti's motto for spring. She showed full skirts, boxy jackets and simple belted knits, all in china blue, tan and tangerine, and let the colors speak for themselves. The shapes brought a hint of Courrèges classics to mind, while top stitching gave lightweight coats in suede and in cotton a quiet charm of their own... Ferretti didn't skimp on the filmy dresses she does so well...they came tucked, knotted, appliqued with flowers, decorated with tiny strips of fluttering chiffon or bands of ruffles, inset with sheer chiffon and layered." Season after season, Ferretti has managed to stay on top of the growing demand for something new, without losing her hallmark touch.

Anne-Marie Schiro of the *New York Times* (5 March 1999) also reported on Ferretti's dresses: "Pretty, rather than glamorous, is the word for Alberta Ferretti's evening dresses, in colors like rose, wine, yellow, cream or brown velvet forming geometric or mazelike patterns on tulle. With high waistlines and uneven hems, the clothes have a youthful femininity that was more ingenue than movie star.... She is one of the Italian designers who snuggle comfortably and tastefully into fashion's current decorative mood." Expanding upon her gown creations, Ferretti has also succeeded in the realm of matrimonial vogue. Ellen Tien of the *New York Times,* writing in June 2000 reported that "at Intermix, whimsical brides have all but bought out Alberta Ferretti's freeform white taffeta strapless dress with space-age silver bugle beads, square rhinestones and oversize white sequins."

Stressing individuality, one of Ferretti's successful clothing lines, "Philosophy," actually has an Alberta Ferretti philosophy to go with it: "You are you. Free in a world taking shape in harmony with the New Age. Universal symbols of Conscience, Peace, Love energize and transform the traditional concepts of Earth, Sex, Money. An interior being that must be immediately visible throughout the total style, from clothes to accessories to interior décor. Whoever encounters you must grasp your spirit on the spot. No mediation. Immediacy calls the shots; it sparks your personal uniqueness."

Alberta Ferretti, spring/summer 2001 ready-to-wear collection: from the "Philosophy" line. © Reuters NewMedia Inc./CORBIS.

Although Ferretti seems to have a definite flair for fashion, she also has an eye for business. According to *Women's Wear Daily* in October 2000, Ferretti will be launching a Ferretti fragrance line with the fragrance division of Proctor & Gamble. Capturing her own imagination and dreams, combined with dedication and hard work, Ferretti reached great heights from modest beginnings.

—Sandra Schroeder

FEZZA, Andrew

American designer

Born: New Haven, Connecticut, 1955. **Education:** Graduated from Boston College, 1976; traveled in Europe, summer, 1976; studied at the Fashion Institute of Technology, New York, 1976–77. **Family:** Married Marilyn Cousa, 1985; two children. **Career:** Assistant designer for womenswear, Schrader Sport, New York, 1977–78; freelance designer, selling to Camouflage and other New York menswear stores, 1977–78; formed own company, Andrew Fezza Ltd., 1979; designer, Firma by Andrew Fezza for Gruppo GFT from 1986; designer, Andrew Fezza Company, joint venture with Gruppo GFT, from 1990; maintained Assets by Andrew Fezza boutique to 1991; launched leather collection, 1996; formed joint venture with George Weintraub & Sons, New York, 1997; signed license agreement with Supreme International for sportswear line, 1998; new licensing deal for neckware and belts with Aron Group, 2000; signed with Farash & Robbins for watches, 2001; also licenses hosiery, outerwear, other smaller accessories and produces tuxedos. **Awards:** Chrysler Stargazer award, 1981; Cutty Sark award, 1982, 1984, 1985; Coty American Fashion Critics award, 1984. **Address:** 300 Park Avenue, New York, NY 10022 USA. **Website:** www.andrewfezzatux.com.

Publications

On FEZZA:

Articles

Buckley, Richard, "Andrew Fezza," in *DNR,* 27 December 1982.

Fressola, Peter, "Andrew Fezza," in *DNR,* 25 November 1987.

Trachtenberg, Jeffrey A., "Designers are Made as Well as Born," in *Forbes,* 11 July 1988.

Morrisroe, Patricia, "Almost Famous: Turning Andrew Fezza into the 'American Armani,'" in *New York,* 24 October 1988.

Sterne, H., "Fezza's New Point of Hue," in *GQ,* September 1989.

"Something Wild," in *GQ,* July 1990.

"What's Coming Up: Men's Style," in the *New York Times Magazine,* 29 December 1991.

Parola, Robert, "Andrew Fezza," in *DNR,* 25 March 1992.

Rubiner, Michael, and Patti O'Brien, "Out of the Shadows...Into the Night," in *Rolling Stone,* 29 October 1992.

Aquino, John, and Thomas Iannaconne, "The Collections," in *DNR,* 28 January 1994.

"Combos: Getting it Together," in *DNR,* 31 March 1994.

"Assets by Andrew Fezza," in *DNR,* 13 July 1994.

"New York Collections," in *DNR,* 10 February 1995.

Walsh, Peter, and Catherine Salfino, "Sportscast," in *DNR,* 15 March 1995.

MacIntosh, Jeanne, "State of the Union Ad-Dress," in *DNR,* 27 March 1995.

Gellers, Stan, "The Suit Strikes Back," in *DNR,* 10 April 1995.

———, "Designers Put Muscle Behind Power Suits," in *DNR,* 27 April 1995.

"Assets by Andrew Fezza," in *DNR,* 19 July 1995.

"Knot Options," in *DNR,* 27 October 1995.

Socha, Miles, "Sportscast," in *DNR,* 13 March 1996.

Gellers, Stan, "Sartorial Suits Hit Executive Row," in *DNR,* 22 July 1996.

———, "Weintraub Gets Master License for Andrew Fezza," in *DNR,* 24 September 1997.

———, "Fezza Seeks to Fly in the Fast Lane...," in *DNR,* 10 December 1997.

Marlow, Michael, "Licensing Drives Business at Vegas Show—Supreme Does Deals with Fezza...," in *DNR,* 23 February 1998.

Gellers, Stan, "George Wintraub's Specialty Designers at a Price (Andrew Fezza)," in *DNR,* 16 December 1998.

"Fezza Licenses Belts and Ties to Aron," in *DNR,* 30 June 2000.

Askin, Ellen, "Licensing Deals," in *DNR,* 4 June 2001.

* * *

Andrew Fezza's designs are based around unchanging elements that have characterized his men's clothing throughout changing labels and businesses. Relaxed drape, soft silhouette in all garments, but never at a loss of proportion, are combined with an interest in unusual materials, whether in leather or fabric, luxurious richness in fabric more often associated with womenswear, and mellifluous color harmony in individual collections, always including neutrals and earthbound tones. Respect for American sportswear is challenged and complemented by a sensibility that is not provincially American or traditional, often with influences from Italy.

In such intensity of conviction and integrity of sensibility, Fezza is unusual in menswear (although he trained for and has designed womenswear, he is traditionally a menswear designer) and has inevitably been called an American Armani, so sincere and sustained are his design objectives. Menswear is seldom thought of as a profession for purists with distinct aesthetic marks, given the market-driven practicality of the field, but Fezza has flourished with an uncompromising crusade for male attire. He suffers, however, from the Armani characterization. So reminiscent is his style of the Milanese master that some have chosen, especially after he entered into production agreements in 1990 with Gruppo GFT, to call Fezza a "poor man's Armani."

Almost all advanced menswear designers in the 1990s were displacing collars, mutating jackets into longer and softer shapes, and watching the textile industry for both innovation and the most sumptuous materials. Similarly, Fezza created tailored clothing with the unconstructed effects of the Armani-inspired contemporary jacket, for casual living as well as the conventional office, but so have almost all other menswear designers of the past decade. But looking at Fezza's tuxedos, one is definitely reminded of Armani's style.

Fezza's aesthetic, however close at times to Armani's, is nonetheless his own. That he began in knitwear and leather, as Armani had some five or six years earlier, is partly a matter of how designers can get started in small-scale production and partly an example of parallelism, but not of derivativeness. Points of differentiation include Fezza's deep colors, consistent in his collections, his reliance on sportswear, and a keen sense of comfort for the American male body, large and athletic.

Fezza brings his own style to each achievement, beginning with his first sweaters, made freelance and delivered by hand to Camouflage when still working in womenswear at Schrader Sport, soon after graduating from the Fashion Institute of Technology in New York. Subsequently, his leathers, of which the *Daily News Record* wrote in 1981, "Andrew Fezza is a leather innovator. In his approach to color, silhouette, and texture, Fezza has consistently broadened the scope of American leather design, which is rapidly catching up with the European market," generated excitement and esteem for their directional colors, embossed treatments, and knowledgeable shapings; unconventional for leather, but not extreme.

Fezza likewise brought a lifetime interest in luxurious textiles and the traditional designs of textiles into menswear, often making a garment seem even softer and more costly by virtue of the fabric. Even his earliest collections, in the early 1980s, brought together linens, cotton, silk-wool blends, and knits with leather and suede. Arguably, Fezza brings elements of womenswear sensibility to menswear with such emphases as proportion and luxury in textiles. In such a characteristic, he indicated the great shift in menswear in the 1980s and 1990s.

Few menswear designers possess Fezza's unity and clarity of vision. Business shifts, which might have diverted or deflected most other designers in the big business climate of menswear, have not deterred him. In his second decade as a still-young designer, Fezza pursued the relaxed new look, acknowledging Europe but affirming America. When he says he entered the menswear business because he was uninspired when looking for clothing for himself, he anticipates some characteristics of his designs: so purposeful they are elegant, so unassuming they become the nonchalance of high style in menswear, and so luxuriously casual they fit the lifestyles of men in the 1980s, 1990s and beyond.

Fezza deliberately avoided, with one or two exceptions in the early 1980s (with some justice, Melissa Drier in *Daily News Record* attacked his spring 1984 collection as overworked), any of the excesses of menswear, with extraneous detailing or extreme proportions, but he has insisted upon clothing with texture and an interest in color and shape. A 1983 press kit for Fezza reported, "Andrew's unique hand with fabric, shape, and color reflects a designing mind that is both thoughtful and provocative, without surrendering to fashion 'trends,' either here or in Europe. But from the beginning, Andrew Fezza's trademark has been his individuality." In this instance, a press kit is true. In the fixed and fascinating domain of menswear, Andrew Fezza has offered a highly consistent and individual aesthetic in the last decades of the 20th century, dressing such stars as Del Amitri guitarist Iain Harvie.

In the mid-1990s, Fezza joined Donna Karan, Joseph Abboud, and Ralph Lauren designing power suits for businessmen, as well as working in the sportswear segment, going so far as to hire Ceppos Consultants to represent him in his worldwide marketing efforts. He also designed specialty wear such as a wool houndstooth sport coat, and Perry Ellis International licensed the Andrew Fezza name for its line of sportswear in the 1990s, adding it to their already existing Perry Ellis and Mondo di Marco lines. In 1996 Fezza segued into leather, the next year he created the Andrew Fezza New York line of sportswear and dress shirts for sale in the U.S., Canada, and Mexico.

Fezza's nod to the 21st century is a website, in which the designer and his work are described. "During his almost twenty-year career as a menswear designer, Fezza has artfully combined a European sensibility toward style and quality with an unerring understanding of the active and casual lifestyles of the American sportswear customer. The sportswear and dress shirts reflect Andrew's unique talent, his recognizable way with color and fabric, and his ability to create complete, impactful collections. Without surrendering to trends, the designs convey a modern sensibility that stakes out its own distinctive territory in the marketplace." With all of his work throughout the last two-plus decades, Andrew Fezza has become synonymous with sophisticated yet affordable design.

—Richard Martin; updated by Daryl F. Mallett and Owen James

FIELDEN, David

British fashion designer

Career: Studied theatre design, then choreographer, Ballet Rambert, in France; choreographed for Ballet Theatre Contemporain; returned to London, specialized in fashion, concentrating on bridalwear and eveningwear. **Address:** 15 Lots Road, London SW10 0QD, UK.

Publications

On FIELDEN:

Articles

"Fielden's Body English," in *WWD,* 12 June 1991.

Fallon, James, "British Waiting for the Rebound (Women's Clothing Industry Emerges Slowly from Recession)," in *WWD,* 16 February 1994.

"It's Show Time," in *WWD,* 23 February 1999.

* * *

David Fielden is a small British fashion company producing ladies' eveningwear and bridalwear, mainly ready-to-wear, although some pieces are made to measure. Fielden's designs are similar to those produced by Catherine Walker or Caroline Charles in London, but are perhaps less understated and sophisticated, more brash, bold, and glitzy.

Fielden uses a lot of traditional eveningwear fabrics in his collections, such as crêpe, velvet, chiffon, and georgette. Embroidered fabrics, fabrics using bugle beads, sequins, and fake stones are popular as is lace, especially imported from France. For a small company the collections are unusually large; the winter collection for 1993, for instance, contained over 130 pieces. This is advantageous from a selling point because many different themes and styles can be covered, catering to various different customers. Smart navy and white ballgowns head straight for Saks Fifth Avenue, while short, brightly colored halter neck dresses with net petticoats head for Italy.

Fielden built up a loyal band of followers when he had a shop on London's King's Road in the 1980s. After the shop closed, the clothes were sold through a number of distinctive stores throughout Britain such as Harrods in London, À La Mode, and Pollyanna with an international clientèle. Boutiques from Italy, Germany, the U.S., Hong Kong, and Saudi Arabia all place orders.

A typical Fielden customer is a woman who needs a large amount of occasion wear in her wardrobe. She is not particularly fashion-conscious but is involved in county or society events and an avid reader of society style bibles like *Harper's & Queen* and *The Tatler.* She probably aspires to buying a Valentino or an Yves Saint Laurent, but cannot quite afford it.

Fielden is often nominated for a glamour award by the British Fashion Council, acknowledging his undoubted contribution to this area of fashion. Popular styles include long, simple and elegant vest top dresses in velvet, enhanced by beaded belts; sharply tailored double-breasted coat dresses with satin lapels or velvet tuxedo-style jackets; short, sexy cocktail dresses with revealing back and side slits, and the romantic glamor evoked by embroidered, full-skirted, tulle and taffeta ball dresses with matching stoles. Fielden is also noted for the recurrent use of brightly colored satins in his eveningwear.

Fielden himself is the sole owner of his company. He oversees the production and design and is at the end of the day financially responsible. This is probably one reason why the company is so small and has not expanded into lucrative licensing areas like perfume and accessories. Fielden's decisions affect the entire business and a wrong move by him could close the company. Fielden has a definitive niche within British fashion, producing distinctive clothes that often compete with the best of Italian and French eveningwear. The irony is the clothes emerge from a culture that is still similar to a cottage industry. Teams of outworker specialists work on production, while the company itself is streamlined to be a small, cost effective unit. This is probably one of the strengths of British fashion and companies like David Fielden can acknowledge credit for this strength, from the 1980s through the remainder of the 20th century.

Fielden designs have continued to be classic, understated, and elegant. American buyers, too, became more aware of Fielden's eveningwear, some from visiting his London shop, others from viewing his collections, like the dresses shown in Milan in 1999. Though not as world-renowned as many designers, David Fielden may be the best-kept secret of British occasionwear.

—Kevin Almond; updated by Nelly Rhodes

FIORUCCI, Elio

Italian designer and manufacturer

Born: Milan, 10 June 1935. **Career:** Founder, Fiorucci shoes, Milan, 1962–67; director, Fiorucci fashion shop, Galleria Passerella, Milan, selling clothes by Ossie Clark, Zandra Rhodes, and others, from 1967; began wholesale production of jeans, fashion, and home accessories, 1970; founder, Fiorucci SpA, 1974, and Fiorucci Inc., New York, 1976; opened first American boutique, New York, 1976; founder, Technical Design School, Milan, 1977; opened boutiques in Boston and Los Angeles, 1978; opened stores throughout Europe, U.S., Japan, and Southeast Asia, from 1978; management of label ceded to Carrera, 1989; signed eyewear license with Swan International Optical, 1995; brand relaunched in U.S. with Bennini, Inc., 1997; contributor to *Donna* magazine, Milan. **Exhibition:** *Italian Re-Evolution,* La Jolla Museum of Art, California, 1982. **Address:** Fiorucci SpA, Galleria Passerella 2, 20122 Milan, Italy. **Website:** www.fiorucci.com.

Publications

On FIORUCCI:

Books

Mulassano, Adriana, *I Mass-moda: Fatti e Personaggi dell'Italian Look,* Florence, 1979.

Babitz, Eve, *Fiorucci: The Book,* Milan, 1980.

Malossi, Giannino, *Liberi Tutti: 20 Anni di Moda Spettacolo,* Milan, 1987.

Connikie, Yvonne, *Fashions of a Decade: The 1960s,* London, 1990.

Articles

Neustatter, Angela, "Clown Prince," in the *Guardian* (London), 9 August 1978.

Besemer, H. C., "Fiorucci," in *Novum Gebrauchsgraphik* (Munich), No. 7, 1981.

Jones, Terry, "Mr. Fiorucci: 20 Years of Global Pollution," in *I-D* (London), September 1987.

Mills, Simon, "Elio Fiorucci, 52, Comes of Age," in the *Observer* (London), 3 January 1988.

Alden, Tim, "The Key to the Door," in *Fashion Weekly* (London), 19 May 1988.

Tredre, Roger, "Fiorucci: Going Places Again," in *Fashion Weekly* (London), 28 July 1988.
Morozzi, Cristina, "Orfani di un Mito," in *Moda* (Milan), August/September 1988.
"Carrera to Get Control of Fiorucci Biz," in the *DNR,* 14 April 1989.
"Elio Fiorucci Jail Sentence is Suspended," in *WWD,* 23 January 1996.
D'Innocenzio, Anne, "Cashing in on the 1970s Retro Rage," in *WWD,* 20 November 1997.
Redecker, Cynthia, "Fiorucci's Foray into the Mall," in *WWD,* 29 April 1999.
Cardona, Mercedes, "Fiorucci Dances Back onto Scene," in *Advertising Age,* 31 May 1999.
Haber, Holly, and Rusty Williamson, "Seventies Brands Seeking a New Groove," in *WWD,* 24 June 1999.
Johnston, Robert, "Fiorucci: Where Have They Gone?" in the *Sunday Times* (London), 19 September 1999.
Kletter, Melanie, "Fiorucci's New Forays," in *WWD,* 6 July 2000.
"Elio Fiorucci," available online at www.designboom.com, 6 June 2001.
"Fiorucci is Coming to New York," available online at www.fiorucci.com, 6 June 2001.
"Vogue: The Fashion Designer Database—Fiorucci, Elio," online at handbag.com, 6 June 2001.
"Fashion Houses: Fiorucci," online at www.made-in-italy.com, 6 June 2001.

* * *

Visitors to Milan, Italy, during the late 1960s could not fail to notice a constant crowd trying to enter a narrow-fronted shop in the center of the city. The birth of Elio Fiorucci's boutique caused consternation among the elders and delight among their offspring. Those who traveled the European city circuit in pursuit of fashion and footwear inspiration now ensured that this was one retailer who could not be missed.

Visiting manufacturers and designers fought over the limited stock with local customers. Italy, the accepted home of stylish clothing, had seen nothing like it. It was Fiorucci, more than any other single entrepreneur of the time, who possibly created a worldwide market for the youth culture that first expressed itself in music, then in clothing. In the mid-1960s young people were creating and dictating the fashions they wanted to wear. The skill of Fiorucci, who had his finger on the pulse and brought it into reality, created the visual dreams and recognized the aspirations of this new and hitherto untapped market.

Fiorucci had inherited a shoe store from his father. In 1967, at the age of 32, he added miniskirts brought from what was then "swinging" London. Designs by Ossie Clark, Zandra Rhodes, and other young English talents soon followed, and the store was gradually enlarged to accommodate a vast range of assorted items. From this embryonic beginning grew a world-famous chain of boutiques, culminating in outlets in New York, Boston, Beverly Hills, Rio de Janeiro, Tokyo, Hong Kong, Zurich, and London. Conceived for the youth culture, the stores were constantly filled with new ideas and exciting styles. The atmosphere was unique and the presentation always witty and original. Shopping for clothes was suddenly a different and stimulating experience. The sales assistants were teenagers, too, who helped customers put together the latest looks in fashion clothing, accessories, and even makeup.

Fiorucci was a constant traveler, collecting ideas from around the world, including the original hippie woven bags from Morocco that became so synonymous with the spirit of flower power. A team of designers translated ideas, always seeming to capture the moment—recycling the themes of the 1950s with plastic shoes in riotous colors, fluorescent socks, or graffiti t-shirts. Possibly best remembered of all were the tightly cut, streamlined jeans, which established Fiorucci as a label in the marketplace for many years. At one time, they even replaced Levi's as the most desirable and fashionable shape of the moment.

After this huge success, however, the company fell on hard times in the late 1980s. By 1989 profits had fizzled, and Fiorucci filed for bankruptcy and handed over the management of the label to Carrera, an Italian sportswear manufacturer. Further troubles came when he and five others who had been on the board were accused of bankruptcy fraud and falsifying company reports, to which he pleaded guilty to avoid a long and expensive trial. He has maintained his innocence, however, and stated he was not in control of the company when the alleged abuses took place. Despite the difficulties, Fiorucci stayed involved with clothing design as the company's creative director.

The Fiorucci brand has changed hands multiple times, but was poised to make a comeback in the U.S. in the late 1990s. Bennini Inc., which operated the brand in the U.S., made several unsuccessful attempts to market the clothing through large department store chains and in mall outlets. The company then opened its own megastore on Broadway in New York City with approximately 20 percent of its clothing being Fiorucci, and the remainder coming from other designers.

The company's mark on Italy, on the other hand, has continued to be impressive. Its most popular store, a 1,600-square-meter building sprawled over three levels in Piazza San Babila in Milan opened in 1993 and claimed 7,000 customers daily, with more on holidays. A primary factor in the overwhelming traffic is Fiorucci's uncommon publicity campaigns, such as the 1995 live Wonderbra display or the 1999 live filming of an MTV show on the premises.

Elio Fiorucci, meanwhile, has tried his hand in communications since 1980, producing with Rizzoli USA the film *New York Beat* and in 1981 cofounding the magazine *I-D (Instant Design).*

One of the Fiorucci brand's greatest strengths and the reason for its place in fashion history was its ability to control all aspects of advertising, packaging, store design, and merchandising in a clever and original way. It should not be forgotten that Elio Fiorucci was the first to establish what has subsequently become an indispensable part of so many success stories, a Total Concept. His designs strike a balance between nostalgia and the future, transforming the ordinary into hot new fashions with just a few tweaks to the look. He is able to observe a group of teenagers, extract the latest trend, and emerge with a bestselling accessory or item of clothing in the price range of young buyers.

—Angela Pattison; updated by Carrie Snyder

FISHER, Donald and Doris

See THE GAP

FLETT, John

British designer

Born: 28 September 1963. **Education:** Received diploma in fashion, Worthing Polytechnic, West Sussex; graduated from St Martin's College of Art, 1985. **Career:** Formed own business, selling to Joseph Ettedgui, London, and Bergdorf Goodman, New York, 1985–89; assistant designer, Claude Montana, Paris, and Enrico Coveri, Florence, 1989–91. **Died:** 18 January 1991, in Florence, Italy.

Publications

On FLETT:

Articles

"Alright John?," in the *Sunday Express Magazine* (London), 3 August 1986.

"Flett in Business Split," in *Fashion Weekly* (London), 16 February 1989.

Obituary, "John Flett," in the *Daily Telegraph* (London), 28 January 1991.

"Style Victim," in *The Independent on Sunday* (London), 3 February 1991.

* * *

The story of John Flett is a short and sad one; an extreme example of the good and bad aspects of the British fashion industry. Flett graduated in 1985 from St Martin's College of Art, London, in a blaze of glory. His first collection was bought by Joseph Ettedgui for his Joseph shops in London and there was a prestigious order from Bergdorf Goodman in New York. By 1988 he was showing on the international catwalk at the British Designer Show, in company with John Galliano (a friend from St Martin's), Jasper Conran, and Betty Jackson. By 1989 money had run out and Flett parted company with his backer, Miles Gill. Short-lived positions followed, first as assistant to Claude Montana at Lanvin in Paris, then in the studio of the Enrico Coveri house in Florence, Italy. While at Coveri, Flett was approached by Zuccoli who proposed to sign him as their rainwear and knitwear designer, with the promise of his own label to come. Before signing, John Flett was found dead of a heart attack in his hotel room in Florence. He was but 27 years old.

Many of Flett's friends and contemporaries attributed his premature death to the strain of dealing with Britain's inadequate fashion system. Renowned for having the best fashion schools in the world, excellent breeding grounds for creative talent, British industry, at the ground level of production and mass market manufacture, is at a loss to know how to capitalize on this talent, employing merchandisers and selectors, who copy designs in the shops, rather than a designer to originate. As a result, many British fashion graduates have left to find work abroad. The Italian and French fashion industry are subsidized by governments who understand how to direct creativity towards financial gain.

Described as "wickedly talented" by Galliano, much of Flett's skill was in his cutting, intricate and inventive, with which he developed clothes that seemed to cling to the body. In fact, many of his garments were difficult to understand on the hanger and needed to be worn to be appreciated. Galliano declared that Flett could run up the "sexiest frocks in town," but this seems to generalize his often complex and avant-garde approach.

In his critically successful autumn/winter 1988–89 show, Flett presented sophisticated, opulent fabrics cut into lean, elongated shapes. Another success was a white transparent pleat dress that seemed to coil itself around the body like an asymmetric floral display. He wanted to redefine the much abused fashion adjective "chic" to designate an updated modernity.

Flett was an avid socialite during his time in London and participated in the thriving avant-garde club scene. Contemporaries like the designers of Bodymap and performance artists Leigh Bowery and Trojan combined to create a flourishing atmosphere for designers, models, photographers, and artists to meet and relax, at their Thursday night club Taboo. Flett quickly gained a reputation as a wild boy who partied every night. He worked as hard as he played, however, recalled a friend who described his energy capacity as "enormous."

In an interview with fashion journalist Sally Brampton, Galliano recalled how Flett seldom allowed his creative temperament to affect his sound business acumen. "He had a passion for the business side of fashion as well as the creative," Galliano stated. This, perhaps, makes an even more tragic symbol of Flett, an original design talent whom fate and circumstances did not allow to realize his potential.

—Kevin Almond

FLUSSER, Alan

American designer

Education: Studied at the University of Pennsylvania, Fashion Institute of Technology, and Parsons School of Design, New York. **Family:** Married Marilese Flusser; children: Morgan, Kaitlin. **Career:** Head designer, Pierre Cardin Relax Sportwear (six years); designer, Van Heusen Company, New York; formed own company; hosiery line introduced 1980; women's sweater collection introduced, 1983; custom tailored collection introduced, 1985; East 52nd Street shop opened, New York, 1987; Wall Street shop opened, New York, and Washington, D.C., shop opened, 1989; company reorganized, sold to Copley of Canada, 1993. **Awards:** Coty American Fashion Critics award, 1983; Cutty Sark award.

Publications

By FLUSSER:

Books

Making the Man, the Insider's Guide to Buying and Wearing Men's Clothes, New York, 1981.

Clothes and the Man: The Principals of Fine Men's Dress, New York, 1985, 1987, 1989.

Style and the Man, New York, 1996.

Permanent Fashion: The Art of Fine Men's Dress, New York, forthcoming.

Articles

"Hints on Hats," in the *New York Times Magazine,* 16 September 1990.

On FLUSSER:

Articles

"Men Will Find a Fashion Coup at Penneys," in *Chicago Tribune,* 28 August 1985.

Boyer, G. Bruce, "The Compleat Outfitter," in *Town and Country* (New York), November 1989.

Sterba, James P., "Style: Father of the [ED] Look," in the *Wall Street Journal* (New York), 18 May 1990.

"Mr. Right: If He's Good-Looking, Elegantly Dressed and Socially Sensitive, He Must Be an Alan Flusser Man, in *Chicago Tribune,* 22 April 1992.

Levine, Lisbeth, "To Dress Well…Designer Alan Flusser [Says] Just Follow Some Basic Rules," in *Chicago Tribune,* 24 October 1996.

"At Home with: Alan Flusser, Where 'Bespoke' is Spoken Fluently," in the *New York Times,* 30 January 1997.

Swanson, James L., "Impeccable Fit Custom Tailored or Made to Measure: The Ultimate Suit Makes a Comeback," in *Chicago Tribune,* 12 September 1999.

* * *

There is a certain relaxed elegance about the way Alan Flusser designs and styles his tailored clothing. His sartorial skill is best known to those outside the fashion industry through his costuming work for Michael Douglas in the movie *Wall Street.* Flusser's Gordon Gekko dressed with the excessiveness of the 1980s. His wide, bead-striped single-breasted suits with peak lapels and turned-back roll-back cuffs showed that he was a man of style, yet not one to follow the rules. Shirts continued the look with bold, heavy, and wide stripes, extra long spread white collars, French cuffs, braces, and ties. To flaunt oneself in this fashion was pure arrogance, not unlike the character Douglas played (remember, Gekko was the originator of the tenet "greed is good").

The commonly known Flusser style, however, is a more understated elegance. His influences run the gamut from the Duke of Windsor to the glamorous gentlemen of film in the 1930s and 1940s—including Douglas Fairbanks Jr. and Cary Grant—and stemmed from Flusser's own father, a successful industrial realtor in northern New Jersey, who had suits custom made by Brooks Brothers and shoes and shirts made in London.

Flusser's career as a fashion influence started when he was still in college at the University of Pennsylvania in Philadelphia. He was following his father's lead, already having his clothing custom-made at Brooks Brothers, and friends, recognizing the style Flusser refers to as "relaxed elegance," would come to him for wardrobe advice. Advising his friends on what was appropriate was not enough for Flusser—he wanted to influence the direction of style and elegance as well.

The archetypal Flusser suit comes from his custom-made business. The environment of his shop is not unlike that of an old-world gentleman's club, and it is from there that the relaxed elegance is derived. A man coming in for a suit can choose between a ready-to-wear suit or one custom made to his size and specifications. It is the latter choice that allows Flusser to create what he is known for. The customer chooses a fabric from a finely edited group of swatches, followed by the style of the suit. Flusser generally tries to be on the scene, supervising and offering helpful suggestions, almost as if he were still advising his college friends.

Then begins the lengthy process of sewing and fitting the garment. More often than not, by the time a Flusser suit is finished, the customer has decided that he must also be fully outfitted with Flusser accoutrements. Flusser ties, shirts, braces, and pocket squares are as exquisitely made and as stylish as the suits they will accessorize.

It is unfortunate that Flusser's attempt to introduce a line of sportswear, in fall 1992, failed. The offerings included tweed sports coats and trousers, rich cashmere sweaters, roomy car coats, and field jackets worthy of any gentleman farmer. The styling of the collection evoked weekends at the country estate. A victim of the economic climate, it offered the wearer of Flusser's formal suits a more casual alternative.

A brush with bankruptcy in 1993 resulted in the consolidation of Flusser's three custom shops into one location at Saks Fifth Avenue in New York. Along with Copley Apparel of Canada, Flusser operates a wholesale men's business retailed in 50 stores in the United States. Several Japanese companies currently hold licenses to produce and market products under the Alan Flusser label.

Flusser continues to advocate for his traditionalist style. His designs were again in the public eye when he provided a wardrobe for television host Bob Costas during the 1992 and 1996 summer Olympics, and he regularly contributed a fashion column to *Men's Health Magazine.* The successful publication of several books of sartorial advice have firmly established Flusser as a respected authority on not only menswear but also on the civilized manner the man wearing the clothing must possess. The man wearing Flusser's traditionalist designs chooses much more than the cut of his collars and lapels, he chooses a lifestyle.

—Lisa Marsh; updated by Megan Stacy

FOGARTY, Anne

American designer

Born: Anne Whitney in Pittsburgh, Pennsylvania, 2 February 1919. **Education:** Attended Allegheny College, Meadville, Pennsylvania, 1936–37; studied drama at Carnegie Institute of Technology, Pittsburgh, 1937–38; studied design at East Hartman School of Design, 1939. **Family:** Married Thomas E. Fogarty, 1940 (divorced); married Richard Kollmar (widowed, 1971); married Wade O'Hara (divorced); children: Taf, Missy. **Career:** Worked as a fit model and copywriter in New York; designer for Sheila Lynn, New York; fashion stylist, Dorland International, New York, 1947–48; fashion designer, Youth Guild, New York, 1948–50, and with Margot Dresses Inc., New

Anne Fogarty, spring 1967: linen culotte ensemble. © AP/Wide World Photos.

York, 1950–57; designer, Saks Fifth Avenue, 1957–62; managed own business, Anne Fogarty, Inc., New York, 1962–74; lines included Anne Fogarty Boutique, Clothes Circuit, Collector's Items; closed business, circa 1974; freelance designer to 1980; final collection designed for Shariella Fashion, 1980. **Awards:** Coty American Fashion Critics award, 1951; Neiman Marcus award, 1952; Philadelphia Fashion Group citation, 1953; International Silk Association award, 1955; National Cotton Fashion award, 1957. **Died:** 15 January 1980, in New York.

Publications

By FOGARTY:

Books

Wife Dressing: The Fine Art of Being a Well-Dressed Wife, New York, 1959.

On FOGARTY:

Books

Williams, Beryl, *Young Faces in Fashion,* Philadelphia, 1956.
Roshco, Bernard, *The Rag Race,* New York, 1963.
Milbank, Caroline Rennolds, *New York Fashion: The Evolution of American Style,* New York, 1989.
Stegemeyer, Anne, *Who's Who in Fashion, Third Edition,* New York, 1996.

Articles

"Fogarty Was Ahead of Dior," in *Life,* 31 August 1953.
"Anne Fogarty," in *Current Biography* (New York), October 1958.
"Anne Fogarty," [obituary] in the *New York Times,* 16 January 1980.
"Anne Fogarty," [obituary] in *Current Biography* (New York), March 1980.
Buck, Genevieve, "All Dressed Up and a Place to Go: Film Costumer's Lincoln Avenue Store Brings Back a Trendy Time," in *Chicago Tribune,* 15 December 1994.

* * *

Anne Whitney Fogarty designed the American look, creating clothes that were youthful, simple and stylish. Although Fogarty studied drama at the Carnegie Institute of Technology in Pittsburgh, Pennsylvania, her real love was for the costumes she wore. Moving to New York she worked as a fitting-model for Harvey Berin while looking for acting parts. When she received an acting job, Berin encouraged her to think about becoming a stylist instead, and in 1948 Fogarty began designing clothes for the Youth Guild. Youth Guild's market was teenagers, who were perfect for the narrow waist and full skirts of the "New Look," a style Fogarty used.

In 1950 Fogarty began designing junior-sized clothing for Margot, Inc. She still favored the "paper-doll" silhouette for both day and evening wear, with its full skirt, narrow waist, and fitted bodice. To help create the shape, she adopted the idea of crinoline skirts from the Edwardian age. These stiffened petticoats made of nylon net, frilled or trimmed in lace, helped hold out the skirt and Fogarty encouraged wearing two at a time to enhance the silhouette. She herself had an 18-inch waist.

Fogarty wrote a book called *Wife Dressing* in 1959, a guide for "the fine art of being a well-dressed wife with provocative notes for the patient husband who pays the bills." In the book she recognized that women led varied lives working, as students, wives, and mothers, and encouraged women to find their own style and color—recommending an understated, natural look that did not slavishly follow the fashion of the day.

Fogarty continued to design for Margot, Inc., and eventually for Saks Fifth Avenue. In 1962 she opened her own business, Anne Fogarty, Inc., and added misses' sizes to her line of clothes. Although she began with full skirts, and fitted bodices, she adapted her designs to suit the times. After the paper-doll silhouette came the tea cozy dress in which the full skirt fell from a dropped, rather than natural waist. She used a narrow silhouette without fullness, the Empire line, with its emphasis on the bust line, and she introduced the "camise," a chemise which fell from a high yoke. Fogarty designed separates and long dresses, quilted skirts over hot pants, and mini skirts. She produced designs in a peasant style, blouses with ruffles, long skirts with ruffled hems, and ethnic styling. Whatever the silhouette or fashion type, her interpretation was youthful, with details like puffed sleeves and round collars.

Fogarty produced different design collections under the names of A.F. Boutique, Clothes Circuit, and Collector's Items. In 1950 she

Anne Fogarty, fall 1964 collection: wool dress with a satin pull-through bow under a raccoon fur cape coat. © AP/Wide World Photos.

was selected as one of the Young Women of the Year by *Mademoiselle* magazine. In 1951 she received a Coty award for dresses and in 1952 the Neiman Marcus award.

Although she closed her own business in the 1970s, Fogarty continued to design. She finished a collection for Shariella Fashion in 1981, just months before her death in January 1981. During her career Fogarty worked with a variety of silhouettes and fabrics, in a broad range of sizes. She was a prolific designer who was able to adjust to a changing market, responding with designs that typified the all-American look.

—Nancy House

FOLEY, Brigid

British knitwear designer

Born: Yorkshire, England, 9 December 1948. **Education:** Studied at Sheffield College of Art, 1967–68; Nottingham College of Art, BA with Honors, Fashion and Design, 1968–71. **Family:** Married Kevin Keegan, photographer, 1973; children: Shelley, Peter, Jennifer. **Career:** While at art college began knitting and supplying shops with own designs; part-time lecturer, Plymouth College of Art, specializing in knitwear, 1971; designed, manufactured, and supplied shops with knitwear; joined Carr Jones designer group, London, 1973; first showed at London collections, 1975; went on to exhibit at international prêt-à-porter shows, including Milan, Paris, New York; introduced first hand-knits into collection, 1980; first Brigid Foley shop opened, Tavistock, Devon, 1991; second shop opened, Exeter, 1994. **Address:** Greenway, Harrowbeer Lane, Yelverton PL20 6DY, Devon, England.

*

I like women to look elegant and feminine. From classic simple shapes, my clothes are often adorned in some way to make them special for the woman who wears them. One of my specialities is luxurious handknitted sweaters and jackets. Texture and colour play a large part in the intricate hand embroidery applied. My work has a typically English look about it, many of my designs are inspired from nature—flowers, wildlife, poppy fields, the Devon countryside where I live and work in. Other sources of inspiration are paintings, tapestries and Persian carpets.

I chose knitwear as my medium because it is such a challenge, creating the entire article deciding on the colours, the texture, the weight and softness of the fibres, choosing the embroidery threads, seeing the sweater or jacket emerge stage by stage, after such a lot of painstaking handwork. I take great pride in endeavouring to reproduce each design as closely to the original as possible. I am very proud of the people who work for me—such skill, patience and dedication.

Fashion today is gloriously diverse with no direct style imposed; such a variety of shapes, lengths, colours are available. Women can choose a style for themselves. Of my designs I would say they are classic, timeless, wearable, comfortable and appealing. I like to think they are clothes to enjoy and treasure.

—Brigid Foley

* * *

Brigid Foley's first designs were mainly for sweaters for a young age group. She experimented with knitting machines, mixing geometric patterns with stripes and plains. After joining the Carr Jones designer group in 1973, a more feminine style emerged, with calf-length flowing skirts, fitted to the hips and swirling around the hemline with inset panels of different texture or color matched to sweaters with soft cowl necklines, and accompanied by plaited knitted belts in tones of the suit. These suits were among the first of their kind, attractive, feminine, comfortable, and easy to wear.

In 1975 Foley was invited to join the London Collections and exhibited at the London fashion shows each season, building on her growing success by exhibiting later at the Paris Prêt-à-Porter, and in New York, Dusseldorf, and Copenhagen. The colors of the collections at this time were mainly soft, and often marled as several different fine yarns would be used through the machine at once. A distinctive feature was the gored skirt, where the swing of the skirt was emphasized by the different shades used in the gores. The ranges varied from heavier, sometimes tweedier suits for autumn, fine knits with a sheen and hints of gold for cocktail wear, and fine lacy knits for the spring. Commenting on her work, Foley explained, "fully fashioned knitwear is a very exciting medium. You start with nothing but cones of yarn, and mix textures, colour, and mathematical skill to shape into lovely flattering outfits. These can suit many different shapes, ages, and types of women."

By 1980 Foley had brought a selection of hand-knits into the collection. Finding mohair a good medium, she introduced a range of soft fluffy sweaters highlighted with hand embroidery. Most notable were the designs featuring wildlife—one called "Hedgehog" was still selling decades later. Other designs featured wild flowers and landscapes, some of which were beautifully embroidered with a wide range of textured yarns and silks, bringing them to life.

Foley lives in a village in the middle of Dartmoor, Devon, and considers the distinctive Dartmoor landscape to be a constant source of inspiration for her designs. Recurring hand-knit designs included a range of landscape-inspired themes such as cornfields and meadows, as well as other wildlife scenes drawn from the countryside, including rabbits and hedgehogs. Her designs are considered to be very English and stocked by retailers worldwide, as well as at Brigid Foley shops in Devon, one in the traditional market town of Tavistock, opened in the early 1990s and another which opened three years later in the cathedral city of Exeter.

—Doreen Ehrlich

FONTANA

Italian fashion house

Founded: in Rome, 1944, by sisters Zoë (1911–78), Micol (born 1913), and Giovanna (born 1915) Fontana. **Company History:** Sisters began working in their mother's tailoring business; Zoë and Micol worked in Milan, early 1930s; Zoë moved to Paris after her marriage, returning to Italy, to work for Zecca in Rome, 1937; created accessories division, Valextra, 1937; Micol and Giovanna moved to Rome, 1940; Zoë, Micol, and Giovanna opened Fontana studio in Palazzo Orsini, Rome, 1943, designing and producing gowns for the Roman aristocracy and many film stars; first catwalk presentation of Italian Alta Moda, Florence 1951; studio moved to present address, 1957; designed first ready-to-wear collection, 1960; incorporated as Sorelle Fontana Alta Moda SrL by Micol Fontana, Rome, 1985; sold Valextra to French firm Andrelux, 1985; designed for films, from 1950s to 1995. **Exhibitions:** retrospective, University of Parma, 1984; evening dresses, Venice, 1985; Castel Sant'Angelo Museum, Rome, 1985; Munich, March 1986. **Collections:** Metropolitan Museum of New York; Metropolitan Museum of San Francisco; Museo Fortuny, Venice. **Awards:** Silver Scissors award, Pittsburgh Fashion Group, 1956; Silver Mask award, Rome, 1960; Fontana sisters named Cavaliere della Repubblica, Rome, 1965; Fashion Oscar award, St Vincent, 1968; Stella di Michelangelo award, Rome, 1985; Polifemo prize, Sperlonga, Italy, 1985; Minerva prize, Rome, 1985; Attraction 1986 prize, Italy; Europe Plate, 1987; Europe Gold Plate, 1988. **Company Address:** Via San Sebastianello 6, 00187 Rome, Italy.

Publications

By FONTANA:

Books

Fontana, Micol, *Specchio a tre luci,* Rome, 1992.

Fontana, spring/summer 1968 collection: wool plaid waistcoat over matching Bermuda wool shorts and a crêpe silk blouse. © AP/Wide World Photos.

On FONTANA:

Books

Bianchino, Gloria and Rossana Bossaglia, *Sorelle Fontana,* Parma, 1984.
Alta Moda: grandi abiti da sera anni cinquanta-sessanta, Venice, 1984.
Cinquant'anni di moda: Sorelle Fontana, [exhibition catalogue], Parma, 1985.
Villa, Nora, *Le regine della moda,* Milan, 1985.
Steele, Valerie, *Women of Fashion,* New York, 1991.
Stegemeyer, Anne, *Who's Who in Fashion, Third Edition,* New York, 1996.

Articles

Da Riz, Oscar, "La via della seta parte da Roma e arriva in Cina," in *Paese Sera* (Rome), 20 June 1980.
"Le Sorelle Fontana hanno aperto la via alle grandi griffe," in *Sole 24 Ore* (Milan), 17 May 1988.

Mendia, Fabiana, "Via Zoe Fontana: Una strada da indossare," in *Il Messaggero* (Rome), 12 July 1988.
Pilolli, Carla, "Il matrimonia torna di moda," in *Il Messaggero* (Rome), 5 December 1990.
Pertica, Domenico, "Bianco vince: Micol Fontana, la regina dell'abito da sposa," in *Paese Sera* (Rome), 4 July 1991.
Tiezzi, Monica, "Quel successo appeso a un filo," in *Gazzetta di Parma* (Parma, Italy), 12 February 1992.
Conti, Samantha, "The Italian Conquerors," in *WWD,* 28 September 1998.
———, "Fifty Years of Fashion," in *WWD,* 22 February 2000.
———, "Lights, Camera, Fashion—The Marriage of Fashion and Films…," in *WWD,* 22 February 2000.
———, "First and Always—The Italians See Themselves as Pioneers at Luxury Branding…,"in *WWD,* 30 May 2000.
Colavita, Courtney, "Italy's Golden Moment," in *WWD,* 2 March 2001.

* * *

Fontana created fantasy dresses, wedding gowns, ball gowns, and possessed an aura of glamor. In the 1950s, in particular, the Fontana style was a rich excess and ideal of the sumptuous dress. For the client, these were the most flattering kinds of party dresses cognizant of the New Look, buoyant in full skirts, and attentive to the bust. To the observer, theatrical high-style 1950s style was crystallized in the internationally known clientèle including Linda Christian (her wedding dress to marry Tyrone Power), Audrey Hepburn, and preeminently Ava Gardner.

Gardner was the perfect Fontana client and model—unabashedly and voluptuously sexy and known for alluring and elegant dressing. Gardner wore Fontana for film roles in *The Barefoot Contessa* (1954), *The Sun Also Rises* (1957), and *On the Beach* (1959). While American film had its own specialty costume designers such as Edith Head and Travis Banton, postwar Rome reignited its status as a glamor capital by the conflation of life and film. Sisters Zoë, Micol, and Giovanna Fontana had begun their business in 1936, but seized the public imagination when American films were made on location in Italy using their designs and, to a lesser degree, with the Italian film industry. The popular international appeal of the Power/Christian wedding and Ava Gardner's paparazzi-trailing fame brought vast worldwide visibility and recognition.

If waning Hollywood found its ideal Trevi Fountain wardrobe in Fontana, Fontana came to America with the demure but unequivocally rich lace wedding dress designed for the 1956 wedding of Margaret Truman, daughter of the ex-President of the United States, and Clifton Daniel, *New York Times* journalist and editor. Longtime celebrity Margaret Truman Daniel, famous as the apple of her father's eye and as a television performer, put the good-girl seal of approval on Fontana for America that Gardner's sultry looks, Elizabeth Taylor's buxom beauty, or Loretta Young's dream-girl radiance had been unable to provide. For Americans, Roman grace and opulence were, in many ways, more accessible than the couture of Paris.

By the late 1950s, the strong silhouettes of Balenciaga and Dior (under Yves Saint Laurent) were so immediately and carelessly processed into American clothing that Roman dress, with its conspicuous extravagance of lace and taffeta and luxuriance, seemed ineffably richer than Paris design. The preference of the Fontana sisters for wedding dresses, eveningwear, and full-skirted cocktail dresses through the 1950s and 1960s, made their style seem especially colorful, a kind of pre-*La Dolce Vita* for Americans covetous of Italian flair.

The Fontana sisters were so much a part of the Italian postwar renaissance that Rome designated a street Via Zoë Fontana. Later works by Fontana assumed the more tubular silhouettes of the 1960s and 1970s and some similarity to Princess Irene Galitzine, but the definitive work of the Fontana sisters remained the bust-enhanced, narrow-waisted, full-skirted resplendence of their style in the 1950s. Their extravagance walked a fine line between vulgarity and richness, one to which Americans felt a keen affinity. The Fontanas created a Roman Empire of postwar fashion; they enjoyed an influential and unforgettable decade of style sovereignty.

While the glory days of the Fontana sisters ended decades ago (Zoë died in 1978), Sorelle Fontana has remained a fixture of Italian fashion. In an article chronicling the rise and fall and rise of Italian style, Micol reminisced to *Women's Wear Daily* (28 September 1998) about the firm's precarious 1944 startup, "We could still hear the bombs going off on the beaches when we moved into our first atelier in Rome. But that didn't matter, it was our dream to own an atelier."

The Fontanas, along with several other Italian firms, brought their own sensibility to fashion. In a 2000 profile of Italian couture and ready-to-wear, Micol commented to *Women's Wear Daily* (22 February 2000) about why Italian clothing caught on: "We broke away from the French—we were more informal, our fashion was more linear and more practical…. The Americans," she further explained, "were instrumental in shaping our attitude toward fashion. They were practical and needed clothing they could live in, and we were ready to deliver."

—Richard Martin and Nelly Rhodes

FONTICOLI, Nazareno

See BRIONI

FORD, Tom

American designer

Born: Austin, Texas, 27 August 1961. **Education:** Studied at New York University, Parsons School of Design both in New York and Paris. **Career:** Started working on the creative staff of Cathy Hardwick, 1986; joined Chloé for a brief period, then Perry Ellis as a design director, 1988; went to Gucci, 1990; named creative director, 1994; resigned with Gucci for five years, 1998; Gucci buys Yves Saint Laurent, 1999; named creative director, Yves Saint Laurent Couture and Yves St. Laurent perfumes, 2000; wowed critics with second YSL collection, 2001. **Awards:** VH-1 Fashion and Music Awards, Future Best New Designer, 1995; Council of Fashion Designers of America, International Designer of the Year, 1996; International Designer of the Year, Fashion Editors Club Japan, 1996; VH-1 Fashion and Music Awards, Menswear and Womenswear Designer of the Year, 1996; *People* magazine, among Most Beautiful People, 1997; VH-1 Fashion and Music Awards Womenswear Designer of the Year, 1999; VH-1 Fashion and Music Awards Elle Style Icon award, 1999; Council of Fashion Designers of America (CFDA), Designer of the Year award, 2000; nominated, CFDA Womenswear

Tom Ford, designed for Gucci's fall/winter 2001 collection. © AP/ Wide World Photos.

Designer of the Year, 2001; Commitment to Life award, AIDS Project Los Angeles. **Address:** Gucci Group N.V., Rembrandt Tower, 1 Amstelplein, 1096 HA Amsterdam, Netherlands.

Publications

On FORD:

Books

Forden, Sara Gay, *The House of Gucci,* New York, 2000.

Articles

Infantino, Vivian, "Ford Drives Gucci into Faster Fashion Lane," in *Footwear News,* 14 November 1994.

———, "Tom Ford: The Driving Force Behind Gucci's Revved-Up Performance," in *Footwear News,* 4 December 1995.

Middleton, William, "Ford Mulls Addition of Own Line, But Says He's Staying at Gucci," in *WWD,* 14 March 1996.

Hirschberg, Lynn, "Next. Next. Next? Tom Ford Has Made Gucci Chic Again…," in the *New York Times Magazine,* 7 April 1996.

"Ford Signs for Five More Years at Gucci," in *WWD,* 29 September 1998.

Wilson, Jennifer, "What Drives Gucci's Tom Ford?" in *Los Angeles Magazine,* 1999.

Gordon, Maryellen, "Tom Ford: Before Gucci Was a Glimmer in His Eye," in *WWD,* 13 September 1999.

"Ford's Design Galaxy," in *WWD,* 18 January 2000.

Socha, Miles, "Ford's YSL: Full Steam Ahead," *WWD,* 12 January 2001.

Fallon, James, "Tom Ford," in *WWD,* 5 June 2001.

Luscombe, Belinda, "Tom Ford: An American in Paris and London…," in *Time,* 9 July 2001.

* * *

Tom Ford has earned a reputation for his strong, sexy designs. "Sex is something I think about all the time," he commented to *Los Angeles Magazine.* "Is that sexy? Is she sexy? Sex is not a new thing but everything comes down to interaction with other people." Since 1995, his clothes and accessories have been on the pretentious fashion wave; his sensuous styles are in demand around the world.

As an American designer who works and designs for the Gucci empire in Europe, Ford visualizes the moment of fashion over and over again. Each time he is more successful than the last. He sleeps for only four or five hours a night and turns out two collections per season, Gucci and YSL. Very few people can keep up with his frantic pace and maintain a fashion following, yet Ford won't be nailed down to one look or one couture house. He has the vision to change just as moment changes and is one of the few designers who understands the ambiguous mind of the consumer. With each passing collection, Ford seems to grow and understand not only the fashion industry but the fashion consumer who embraces his fashions.

Ford moved to New York when he was a teenager. He started his postsecondary education at New York University studying art history, later he studied architecture at Parsons School of Design in New York and then completed his studies at the Parsons School of Design in Paris. He began his career as part of the creative staff with designer Cathy Hardwick in 1986. Two years later, he moved to Perry Ellis, then in 1990 joined the Gucci Group N.V. as a womenswear designer in Milan. Gucci originally wanted to fire him because he was too trendy; two years passed and Ford was promoted to design director. His foresight into fashion trends helped him become the creative director of Gucci in 1994.

Ford became responsible for the design of all Gucci product lines, from clothing to fragrance, advertising campaigns, store design, and the Group's corporate image. At the time Gucci was a struggling brand as a result of family disputes, yet Ford built Gucci into a megabrand producing and distributing high-quality goods throughout the world in company-owned stores, franchises, boutiques, department stores, and specialty stores. In the early 2000s, there were approximately 180 Gucci stores worldwide.

Gucci acquired Yves Saint Laurent and Sergio Rossi at the beginning of 2000. As if being design director wasn't enough, Ford took on the role of creative director of Yves Saint Laurent Couture. He works with the overall image of YSL, helping to position the brand in the marketplace. As a designer, he has set a certain standard for modern style and is beloved by the press, who dubbed him the "King of Cool." In his 1999 collection, Ford used Las Vegas and Cher as sources of inspiration for his clothes. In a 1999 article in *Los Angeles* magazine,

Tom Ford, designed for the house of Yves Saint Laurent's spring/summer 2001 ready-to-wear collection. © AFP/CORBIS.

Ford was quoted as saying, "I like to make [my designs] a little tacky. Push them so they're a little too much. When things are too perfect, they're kind of dull."

Ford has been viewed by some in the fashion industry as too commercial. His reply is "Commercial is a compliment. It means people will buy it." He was further quoted in a July 2001 *Time* magazine profile as saying, "I'm always perplexed by people wanting to divide this into business and fashion. My job is to create something amazing that sells; I don't think you can divorce the two." Ford is a designer with vision of what people want and what they will buy. He is truly one of the most exciting and successful designers of the last decade, dressing such famous people as Sting, Tom Hanks, and Jennifer Lopez. He designs for urban men and women, and in his Gucci runway show for fall 2001, he was one of the few designers who sent models out wearing clothes most clients would actually wear—like cargo pants and olive-colored suits. As he told *Time,* for him, "Fashion doesn't stop at clothes; fashion is everything—art, music, furniture design, graphic design, hair, makeup, architecture, the way cars look—all those things go together to make a moment in time, and that's what excites me."

—Donna W. Reamy

FORTUNY (Y MADRAZO), Mariano

Spanish designer

Born: Granada, Spain, 1871. **Family:** Married Henriette Negrin, 1918. **Career:** Produced Knossos printed scarves from 1906; produced Delphos gowns, 1907–52; Delphos robe patented, 1909; method for pleating and undulating fabric patented, 1909; methods for printing fabrics patented, 1909, 1910; 18 other patents received, 1901–33; opened showroom for sale of textiles and clothing, Venice, 1909; established Società Anonima Fortuny, factory for printed textiles, 1919; opened shops in Paris and Milan, 1920; also an inventor, stage designer, painter, and photographer. **Exhibitions:** *Mariano Fortuny y Madrazo* [drawings and paintings], Galeria Dedalo, Milan, 1935, Galerie Hector Brame, Paris, 1934; *Exposition Fortuny y Marsal y Fortuny y Madrazo* [etchings], Biblioteca Nacional, Madrid, 1952; *A Remembrance of Mariano Fortuny,* Los Angeles County Museum, 1967–68; *Mariano Fortuny (1871–1949),* Musée Historique des Tissus, Lyons, and Brighton Museum, 1980, Fashion Institute of Technology, New York, 1981, and Art Institute of Chicago, 1982; Chicago International Antiques Show (featuring Fortuny gowns from the Martin Kamer Ltd. collection of New York), 1988. **Died:** 2 May 1949, in Venice.

Publications

By FORTUNY:

Books

Éclairage scénique: Système Fortuny, Paris, 1904.
Fortuny 1838–1874, Bologna, 1933.

On FORTUNY:

Books

Deschodt, Anne Marie, *Mariano Fortuny: Un magicien de Venise,* Paris, 1979.

Brighton Museum, *Mariano Fortuny (1871–1949)* [exhibition catalogue], Brighton, 1980.

de Osma, Guillermo, *Mariano Fortuny: His Life and Work,* London, 1980, 1994.

Fashion Institute of Technology, *Fortuny* [exhibition catalogue], New York, 1981.

Milbank, Caroline Rennolds, *Couture: The Great Designers,* New York, 1985.

Mint Museum of Art, *Fortuny: Robed in Riches,* [exhibition catalogue], Charlotte, N.C., 1992.

Skrebneski, Victor, and Laura Jacobs, *The Art of Haute Couture,* New York, 1995.

Stegemeyer, Anne, *Who's Who in Fashion, Third Edition,* New York, 1996.

Desveaux, Delphine, *Mariano Fortuny, 1871–1949,* London, 1998.

Deschodt, Anne Marie, and Doretta Davanzo Poli, *Fortuny,* New York, 2001.

Articles

"The Beauty of Fortuny is Brought to America," in *Vogue,* 15 May 1923.

"Mariano Fortuny," in *La renaissance de l'art Français et des industries de luxe,* June 1924.
Malaguzzi Valeri, Francesco, "Le stoffe Fortuny," in *Cronache d'arte,* Volume 4, 1925.
"Fortuny of Venice," in the *Nomad,* April 1928.
de Cardona, Maria, "Mariano Fortuny y Madrazo," in *Arte Español,* Spring 1950.
Sheppard, Eugenia, "The Fortuny Dress," in the New York *Herald Tribune,* 10 September 1962.
Hale, Sheila, "Fragments from the Fortuny Rainbow," in the *Daily Telegraph Magazine* (London), 27 October 1972.
Quennell, J.M., "Precious Stuff: Fortuny," in *Vogue* (London), December 1972.
Minola de Gallotti, Mariana, "El Museo Fortuny de Venecia," in *Goya,* September/October 1975.
Deschodt, Anne Marie, "Seeking Your Fortuny," in the *Sunday Times Magazine* (London), 23 July 1978.
Blasi, Bruno, "Con la firma di Fortuny," in *Panorama* (Italy), 22 August 1978.
Abercrombie, Stanley, "Palazzo Fortuny: A Venetian Palace, Now the Museum of the Work of Master Textile Designer Mariano Fortuny," in *Architectural Digest,* October 1984.
"Fame and Fortuny at Navy Pier Show," in *Chicago Tribune,* 2 October 1988.
Tosca, Marco, "Fortuny," in *Vogue* (Milan), July/August 1989.
Lydon, Mary, "Pli selon pli: Proust and Fortuny," in the *Romantic Review,* November 1990.
Collier, Peter, "Le Manteau de Fortuny," in *French Studies,* January 1991.
Farrell, Sarah, "In the Footsteps of Fortuny, Rich Venetian Fabrics," in the *New York Times,* 28 July 1991.
Smith, Roberta, "An Eye for Art to Dress a Room," in the *New York Times,* 18 August 2000.

* * *

Mariano Fortuny was an artistic genius with an insatiable curiosity; this led him to pursue a variety of disciplines, which evolved through an interesting series of interconnections. Always a painter, he turned to etching, sculpture, photography, lighting design, theatre direction, set design, architecture, and costume design, ultimately to be a creator of magnificent fabrics and clothing.

Through painting Fortuny learned the subtle uses of color that enabled him to produce unequalled silks and velvets from which he made exquisite gowns. Fortuny's work as a fabric and dress designer was determined by a combination of external and internal influences: externally by Modernism and the English Aesthetic movement, during the early part of the 1900s, as well as Greek and Venetian antiquity; internally by a love inherited from his father of everything Arabic and Asian. During all these creative experiences he maintained a keen artistic sense and the mind of an inventor.

Fashion, as we know it, did not interest Fortuny and he rejected commercial fashion and couture houses. First and foremost a painter who happened to create stage scenery and lighting effects, as well as clothes, Fortuny's initiation with fabrics and fashion was through costumes for the theatre designed in conjunction with his revolutionary lighting techniques. His first textile creations, known as the "Knossos scarves," were silk veils, printed with geometric motifs (inspired by Cycladic art) which were made in any number of variations until the 1930s. These scarves were, essentially, a type of clothing—rectangular pieces of cloth that could be wrapped, tied, and used in a variety of ways—always allowing for freedom of individual expression and movement. His sole interest was the woman herself and her personal attributes, to which he had no wish to add any ornamentation. These simple scarves allowed Fortuny to combine form and fabric as they adapted easily into every kind of shape, from jackets to skirts, and tunics.

Fortuny's most famous garment was the Delphos gown. It was a revolution for the corseted woman of 1907 in that it was of pleated silk, simply cut, and hung loosely from the shoulders. Fortuny regarded his new concept of dress as an invention, and patented it in 1909. The dress was modern and original and numerous variations were produced—some with short sleeves, some with long, wide sleeves tied at the wrist, and others that were sleeveless.

The original Delphos gowns had batwing sleeves and usually had wide *bateau* necklines and always, no matter what the shape, a cord to allow for shoulder adjustments. They were invariably finished with small Venetian glass beads with a dual purpose: not only did the beads serve as ornamentation, they also weighed the dress down, allowing it to cling to the contours of the body rather than float. The pleats of the Delphos were achieved through Fortuny's secret, patented invention. However unconventional for the time, these dresses were extremely popular for at-home women entertaining and considered primarily tea dresses. It was not until the 1920s that women dared to popularize them as clothing acceptable to be worn outside the home. Fortuny's techniques were simple but effective. Today the Delphos dress has pleats that are as tight and crisp as when they were new. Storing them as rolled and twisted balls makes them convenient for travel and eliminates the need for ironing.

In addition to his work in silk, Fortuny began printing on velvet, first with block prints followed by the development of a stencil method that was a precursor of the rotary silk screen. The velvet found its use in dresses, jackets, capes, and cloaks to cover the Delphos gowns, as well as home furnishing fabrics, still available today. Since his work in silk and velvet never radically changed into anything different, it is almost impossible to establish a chronology of his garments.

To Mariano Fortuny fashion was art, an unchanging fashion outside the world of fashion. Although many of his contemporaries were innovative designers, their designs were created for a specific time and season with built-in obsolescence. By contrast, Fortuny's clothes are timeless. The elegant simplicity, perfection of cut, and unusual sensuality of color is where their beauty lies. Perfectly integrating these elements and placing them on the female figure makes a Fortuny garment a work of art—and as such they are in demand by museums and private collectors alike, often fetching as much as $40,000 per gown at auctions.

—Roberta H. Gruber; updated by Owen James

FOWLER, Grahame

See TIMNEY FOWLER LTD.

FRASER, Graham

See WORKERS FOR FREEDOM

FREIS, Diane

American fashion designer

Born: Los Angeles, California. **Education:** Studied Fine Arts at the University of California at Los Angeles. **Career:** Opened first boutique, Hong Kong, 1978; established own design and manufacturing studio, 1982; launched diffusion line, Freis Spirit, 1994; signed licensing agreement with Guryich International for distribution of imported line throughout North America, 1999. **Awards:** Governor's award for industry for export, Hong Kong, 1993. **Address:**12/F, World Interests Building, 8 Tsun Yip Lane, Kwun Tong, Hong Kong, China. **Website:** www.dianefreis.com.

Publications

On FREIS:

Articles

Block, Elizabeth J., "After a Rough Start, Designer Diane Freis Hopped Aboard the Orient Express to Success," in *People,* 18 July 1983.

Rourke, Mary, "Designer Diane Freis Oriented to Pace of Hong Kong," in the *Los Angeles Times,* 19 June 1987.

Wallace, Charles P., "A Rags and Riches Tale in Hong Kong," in the *Los Angeles Times,* 5 February 1991.

"Diane Freis, Designer and Company Profile," online at the company website (see above).

Lee, Georgia, Julia Fellers, and Rebecca Kleinman, "New Lines," in *WWD,* 11 August 1999.

* * *

Diane Freis is one of the few Hong Kong-based designers to have gained an international reputation. Hers is a typical Hong Kong success story, based on hard work and determination. Since arriving in the territory in 1973, she built a commercially successful brand name that became a role model for Hong Kong manufacturing.

The Freis signature is represented by multicolored prints applied to one-size, easy-care dresses, primarily designed in polyester georgette. Noncrushable and easy-to-pack, they have presented a travel solution for higher income, more mature women in search of a glamorous and feminine look. The fashion philosophy is pragmatic: Freis stresses the importance "of making a one-size dress that allows the freedom of fit in our daily schedules of health programmes one day and over-indulgence the next." With their hallmark elasticated waists and shirring, the dresses covered imperfections but would never be called dowdy. The prints were usually exotic, the designs included pretty florals, dramatic geometrics, bold stripes, and plaids,with embroidery and beading as particular features of the look. Besides her traditional georgette, Freis has used silk, cotton, and wool coordinates, hand-knits for casual daywear, and chiffon and taffeta for grand evening ensembles.

Freis' eye for color and design can be attributed to her fine arts education at the University of California in her native Los Angeles. While a student, her sideline was to create elaborately beaded jackets, which she sold to celebrities such as Diana Ross. It was a search for new, exotic materials and skilled embroiderers that first attracted her to the Far East. In Hong Kong she found the fabrics and workmanship that contributed to her distinctive fashion identity.

In 1978 Freis opened her first fashion boutique in Hong Kong; by 1986 she had six more. But her influence did not remain in the local market. International buyers from Europe and the United States soon took her work overseas. In the U.S., her dresses came to adorn the bodies of society women who shopped at the likes of Neiman Marcus in Dallas or Bergdorf Goodman in New York. Suited more to the European figure than to the Asian, today the label can be found in over 20 countries. Her success has been based on locating a market niche, not by following international fashion trends. Falling somewhere between haute couture and prêt-à-porter, the designs have been produced in limited editions: no more than 10 of any one design are distributed around the world. Basic shapes remain consistent; the variety is provided by new fabric designs and combinations. To retain exclusivity, the company set up its own print design studio and manufacturing base in 1982. In recognition of her commercial achievement for Hong Kong, Freis was awarded the Governor's award for Industry for Export in 1993.

Despite its established success, the company continued to develop new ranges and to target new markets. Freis' easy-flowing garments have gradually gained some structure via shoulder pads, more tucking, and fitted pleat detail. In recognition of changing lifestyles, Freis Spirit was launched in spring 1994 as a diffusion line aimed mainly in the Southeast Asian market. Featuring a pared-down silhouette and more subdued designs, the collection offered mix-and-match coordinates in quality fabrics to a younger market.

Headquartered in Hong Kong, Freis continues to focus on her trademark polyester georgette dresses in bright patterns and solids. She has expanded from a focus on dresses and skirts to a broader line comprising suits and eveningwear. She is now able to clothe a woman during her workday career, at night in formal attire, or in casual situations, although she remains best known for her flexible, easy-fit, all-over-printed dresses. The designer's daywear business is divided into knitwear, classic polyester silk dresses and blouses, basic coordinates, and printed stretch tops, and her eveningwear line consists of beaded gowns, special occasion wear, beaded and embroidered jackets, camisoles, and scarves.

Freis has traditionally appealed to a more mature consumer but has extended her market into more youthful customers with her "young classics" line, consisting of tanks, chemise-and-jacket combinations and coverups, which *Women's Wear Daily* described as "sleek" in August 1999. A line of all-black polyester and silk tanks, dresses, and pants coordinate with all the products in her daywear and eveningwear lines, from beaded jackets to printed skirts.

Freis has also expanded geographically from her roots in the Asian market. She maintains a distribution network not only in Hong Kong, Taiwan, Malaysia, and Australia, but in the U.S., South Africa, and the Middle East. In 1999 Freis signed a licensing agreement with Guryich International, a Canadian company, for distribution in North America of a broad collection imported from Hong Kong. The line incorporates the one-size-fits-all polyester print dresses for which she is still best known but also includes 50 items from all facets of her line.

—Hazel Clark; updated by Karen Raugust.

FRENCH CONNECTION

British fashion house

Founded: in London by Stephen Marks, 1969. **Company History:** Introduced French Connection label, 1972; launched menswear collection, 1976; hired Nicole Farhi as designer, from 1978; introduced Nicole Farhi label, 1983; launched "fcuk" marketing campaign in Britain, 1997; debuted same campaign in U.S., 1999; expanded into lifestyle products through licensing, late 1990s and early 2000s; created first television/cinema advertising, 2000; acquired mail order company, Toast, 2000; opened San Francisco-based U.S. flagship, its 50th U.S. store, 2001; purchased all of its U.S. operations, 2001. **Company Address:** 60 Great Portland Street, London W1N 5AJ, England. **Company Website:** www.fcukinkybugger.com.

Publications

On FRENCH CONNECTION:

Articles

Bloomfield, Judy, "Nicole Farhi Strengthens U.S. Connection," in *WWD,* 28 September 1988.

Gordon, Maryellen, "French Connection's Broadway Debut," in *WWD,* 14 April 1993.

Fallon, James, "French Connection Clicks in U.S.," in *WWD,* 8 January 1997.

———, "French Connection Profits Climb…," in *DNR,* 5 April 1999.

Cowen, Matthew, "TBWA Plans to Promote fcuk to a Wider Audience," in *Campaign* (UK), 1 September 2000.

Fallon, James, "French Connection to Buy Entire U.S. Business," in *DNR,* 21 February 2001.

Benady, David, "FCUK America," in *Marketing Week,* 22 March 2001.

Jardine, Alexandra, "Style Offensive," in *Marketing* (UK), 5 April 2001.

Young, Kristin, "French Connection United Kingdom Opening Flagship in San Francisco," in *WWD,* 16 July 2001.

* * *

French Connection was founded in 1969 by Stephen Marks with a range of tailored upmarket womenswear in traditional materials marketed under his own name. Marks recognized the need for a less expensive but carefully conceived womenswear collection for a broader market. Marks introduced the French Connection label in 1972 and four years later showed its first menswear collection.

The firm was one of the first British companies to address the market for well-designed, accessible men's casualwear, and soon expanded into both formal and informal clothes for men, women, and children. The childrenswear range, for children aged six to 16, began as a scaled-down version of the primary French Connection womenswear and menswear collections, using the same designs, fabrics, and sources of manufacture and including everything from t-shirts to tailored clothing. The lion's share of revenue, however, remained the menswear division which grew exponentially since its origination.

French Connection design studios were based at the company's headquarters at Bow, East London, and led by Nicole Farhi, who trained in Paris and worked for many major French and Italian companies before joining the firm in 1978. She was the designer in charge of the company's entire range, as well as having her own label. French Connection's design philosophy, in its own words, was to "always give its product that extra fashion content and value," for clothes "remarkable for their comfort and reliability, their continuing anticipation of fashion trends in fabrics, shape, lengths, and styles and their attention to detail."

Womenswear and menswear collections were produced in several annual collections, for summer and winter as well as mid-season ranges in between. These collections represented some 1,000 new designs each year, in a wide variety of fabrics, cuts, and styles from formal clothes to leisurewear. A summer collection for women, for example, might include the extremes of straps and Lycra in a salute to minimalism, while also featuring elegantly classic navy and white prints. A winter menswear collection "translates a look of understated distinction," while including "untraditional fabrics, colorful cables, and crunchy winter whites with primitive embroidery."

After nearly failing in the late 1980s, French Connection was once again one of the hottest and fastest growing brands in Britain during the late 1990s and early 2000s, thanks in large part to its controversial and suggestive marketing campaign, and subsequent rebranding under the "fcuk" logo. Thought the letters did represent the firm's initials (French Connection UK), it was controversial due to its use by porn purveyors on the Internet to get around censors.

Although the company creates apparel and accessories loved by young consumers, its growth was attributed to an aggressive marketing campaign, launched in 1997 using posters, print ads, and publicity to reach young consumers with slogans based on the new logo. The ads, as well as the company's website, attracted the notice of the UK's Advertising Standards Authority, resulting in some censorship, but more than enough publicity to make up for it. The campaign was so successful French Connection decided to rebrand itself under the "fcuk" name, creating packaging, hangtags, and store designs reflecting the logo and minimizing the French Connection name. As of 2001, the company had 60 stores in the England as well as 2,000 other outlets in the UK; its Oxford Street store in London boasted a banner with the words "the world's biggest fcuk."

French Connection has expanded through licensing into a wide variety of accessories and apparel as well as into other products such as home furnishings, footwear, health and beauty products, condoms, and alcoholic drinks. All are closely tied to the risqué corporate image, marketed under subbrands such as fcuk spirit, fcuk at home, fcuk spa, and fcuk vision. The goal is to become a lifestyle brand rather than simply a fashion retailer, as executives told *In-Store Marketing* in November 2000.

French Connection maintains its highest profile in the UK but has expanded across the world, especially into the U.S. market. It had been present in America for nearly 20 years, but its recognition factor was raised significantly when the "fcuk" advertising campaign came to the country in 1999. The advertising generated similar controversy in the U.S. as it did in the UK—albeit to a lesser extent—such as when New York cabbies refused to drive with the posters on their roofs and Mayor Rudolph Giuliani vocally protested the slogans.

French Connection launched a flagship store in San Francisco, patterned after its London flagship, in 2001, bringing the total number of stores to 50 in the U.S. and 150 around the world. After less-than-rosy results in its U.S. operations in the late 1990s and early 2000s, the firm purchased the remainder of its U.S. business (it had previously owned half) in February 2001, and prepared for a major expansion effort. In 2001, fcuk began its first nonprint advertising campaign, with its controversial positioning maintained, but in a slightly more subliminal way. According to *Marketing* (21 June 2001), the ads showed a couple kissing and whispering to each other with words beginning in "f, c, u" and "k." The woman's head then moves down the man's chest until it is invisible under the frame of the screen, and the man says, "FC you kinky bugger." The ad ends with a fcuk-logoed condom. The ad ran in cinemas in the UK because it was rejected for television; in the U.S., it ran on cable networks such as MTV.

The company's controversy-based strategy seemed to be working, as sales and earnings rose at a pace of 20 percent annually for several years, despite a lagging retail marketplace. The Nicole Farhi label also continues to be strong and the firm segued into mail order by purchasing a direct response company, Toast, which focused on home furnishings and women's apparel. Although marketing spurred French Connection's growth, its apparel and other products have kept customers coming back.

—Doreen Ehrlich; updated by Karen Raugust

FREUD, Bella

British designer

Born: London, 17 April 1961. **Education:** Attended Michael Hall School, Forest Row, East Sussex. Left school at 16 to work as shop assistant to Vivienne Westwood, London, 1977. Studied at Accademia di Costume e di Moda, Rome, and tailoring at the Istituto Mariotti, Rome. **Career:** Design assistant to Vivienne Westwood, circa 1980–83; launched own label, 1989; showed collection for first time at London Designer Show, October 1991; capsule collection for Stirling Cooper, Bella Freud for Stirling Cooper, 1994; consultant designer to Dewhirst, manufacturers for Marks and Spencer Plc, 1994. **Exhibitions:** Court Couture exhibition, Kensington Palace, London, 1991. **Collections:** Victoria and Albert Museum, London. **Awards:** British Fashion Council Innovative Design New Generation award, 1991. **Address:** 21 St. Charles Square, London W10 6EF, England.

Bella Freud in ca. 1980–90. © Mike Laye/CORBIS.

Publications

On FREUD:

Articles

Casadio, Mariuccia, "Bella Freud," in *Interview* (New York), August 1991.
Baker, Lindsay, "Freud's World of Dreams," in *The Guardian* (London), 16 September 1991.
Tredre, Roger, "The Fears and Dreams of Bella Freud," in *The Independent* (London), 10 October 1991.
Brampton, Sally, "Joined by the Hip," in the *Times Magazine* (London), 28 December 1991.
Lender, Heidi, "A Freudian Clip," in *Women's Wear Daily* (New York), 8 January 1992.
Ferguson, Stephanie, "Living with Labels," in the *Sunday Times Magazine* (London), 5 April 1992.
Woram, Catherine, "Freudian Analysis," in *Australian Collections Magazine,* Autumn/Winter 1992.
Harris, Martyn, "The Art of Not Coming Apart at the Seams," in the *Daily Telegraph* (London), 8 October 1992.
Kay, Karen, "Me and My Style by Bella Freud," in the *Daily Mirror* (London), 20 October 1993.
Armstrong, Lisa, "Safe Sex," in *Vogue* (London), February 1994.
Watson, Shane, "Freud's Kinky Years in Morocco," 31 January 1999, from the website (www.kwfc.com).
"Ring My Bella," from the Vogue Daily website, (www.vogue.co.uk).

* * *

Bella Freud is known for her whimsical designs which include somewhat kitschy elements, colorful knitwear, and modern tailoring. Essentially, her designs are recognizably British, but as one of Freud's friends described, "Chanel gone kinky." Bella, the great-granddaughter of psychoanalyst Sigmund Freud and the daughter of painter Lucien Freud (who designed her logo), is now part of the London fashion establishment.

Freud's involvement with British fashion began in 1977 when, at the age of 16, she was offered a job by Vivienne Westwood at her World's End shop, then called Seditionaries. Freud decided to study fashion in Rome and left Westwood's shop for Italy where for the next three years she studied fashion at the Accademia di Costume e di Moda, tailoring at the Istituto Mariotti, and designed shoes for private clients in her spare time. Freud completed her fashion training under Vivienne Westwood (who is held in high regard for her tailoring technique) where she worked as an assistant in the Westwood design studio for four years.

It was in 1989 that Freud decided the time was right to launch her own label—a move many thought was foolhardy—with Britain in the midst of recession. Freud presented her first collection for fall/winter 1991 in March 1990, which consisted of tailored knitwear and accessories. Her "violin case" bags, typical of her slightly quirky style, were photographed by *Vogue* magazine in New York. The following season the designer added tailored pieces to the collection which were manufactured for her in Italy. Knitwear continued to play an important role in Freud's collections and became a Freudian hallmark, along with the bags and shoes which made up the total Freud look. Success and recognition came in October 1991, when she launched a collection at the London Designer Show exhibition for the first time, the very same month she was named Young Innovative Fashion Designer of the Year at the British Fashion Awards ceremony.

Freud's designs are an interesting combination of tailored pieces which have a somewhat prim air about them, teamed with short skirts and ultra-high-heeled shoes—blending an air of innocence with provocative appeal. The designer cites the Edwardian period as being a major source of inspiration, with its formal silhouette and what Freud describes as its "suppressed-looking" style. Other important influences include designers Coco Chanel and Yves Saint Laurent and, not surprisingly, her mentor Vivienne Westwood. Westwood's influence is evident in Freud's decidedly English-styled tailoring, although it is somewhat less structured, which Freud admits she owes to the Italian influence during her fashion training: "Their tailoring is much more extravagant—and sexy—whereas English tailoring is much plainer." Eveningwear by Freud is more glamorous and has included floor-length satin sheaths and crêpe gowns with maribou cuffs in a distinctive 1940s-style air. Freud's little day dresses, which come in both stretch fabrics and as more tailored shapes, also possess the same balance of formality and quietly provocative sex appeal.

For spring/summer 1993 Freud introduced a range of denim pieces which included a jeans-style dress, jacket, and trousers, and these soon became an established part of each collection, produced in different designs and colored denims. Freud also works closely with milliner Philip Treacy who has designed the hats for her collections. Fashion journalist Lisa Armstrong, writing for the February 1994 issue of London *Vogue*, succinctly described Freud's style as being "...a bit like Sharon Stone wearing a St. Trinian's uniform designed by a Paris couturier."

Freud is typical of the new breed of young British designers who emerged during the 1990s; they concentrated upon building their businesses at a slower, more carefully-planned rate than their predecessors who, in the early 1980s, came and went at an alarming rate. Freud set up her business in what she described as a "humble way" and gradually built up a reputation that established her as a recognized name in British fashion.

In 2000 Freud became the fashion designer for Jaeger, a century-old label known for its reliably traditional clothing often associated with wealthy countrywomen and school teachers. Jaeger hired Freud to update its image and since Freud has always relied on traditional English fabrics and tailoring, the outcome should be interesting. Imagine Jaeger hiring a designer whose clients have included Madonna, Jerry Hall, and Courtney Love! According to Pat Burnett, Jaeger's chief executive, "Freud will add a bit of wit, fun and frippery."

In addition to using traditional British styles, Freud has also relied on the elements and style of dress that she was accustomed to while growing up in Morocco. As a child, she was "mad about uniforms" and even wanted her mother to dress in a kaftan with a veil "like all the other mothers." She became aware of the importance of clothes and wanted her own clothes "to be like armor," to make her feel like she could "forget about myself." Yet as an adult, in dealing with fashion, Frued contends that "when you look fantastic then you can stop worrying." Fans of Freud can learn more about her childhood in the video *Hideous Kinky,* a film based on her sister Esther Freud's fictionalized account of their early life in Marrakesh.

—Catherine Woram; updated by Christine Miner Minderovic

FUJIWARA, Giuliano

Japanese designer working in Italy

Education: Studied law and oriental literature at Chuo University, and design at Bunka College of Fashion, Tokyo. **Career:** Designer, Van Jacket, Japan; immigrated to Italy, 1976; designer, Barbas, beginning 1976; designer, Giuliano Fujiwara, Srl, from 1986; women's collection introduced, 1988. **Address:** Via della Spiga 2, 20121 Milan, Italy.

Giuliano Fujiwara, spring/summer 2001 collection. © AP/Wide World Photos.

Publications

On FUJIWARA:

Articles

Lobrano, Alexander, "East Meets West in Giuliano Fujiwara," magazine supplement to the *Daily News Record (DNR),* 29 June 1987.
Fressola, Peter, and Alexander Lobrano, "Italian Collections Fall/Winter 1988," in *DNR,* 20 January 1988.
"Italian Collections Spring/Summer 1989," in *DNR,* 13 July 1988.
Lobrano, Alexander, "Milan Sets Stage for 1990s Code," in *DNR,* 7 July 1989.
"Giuliano Fujiwaro," online at FirstView, www.firstview.com, 9 June 2001.

* * *

It is paradoxical for Giuliano Fujiwara to be based in Milan, working as a part of the Italian fashion design community. Characteristically Japanese, Fujiwara seems antithetical to everything Italian. He is introverted while Italians are generally extroverted. He understates while Italians exaggerate. He is reserved while Italians are expressive. Nevertheless, he seems comfortable in Milan where he has lived and worked since 1976, first as a designer for Barbas and then creating his own line of menswear. "If I stayed in Japan," Fujiwara muses, "my work might have followed the direction of Comme des Garçons and Yohji Yamamoto." Presumably he is talking about the Japanese fashion environment, which encourages avant-garde approaches to menswear.

The Fujiwara style is a curious mixture of American Ivy League, Japanese stark simplicity, and Italian sensitivity in fabrication and workmanship. Take a typical Fujiwara jacket: it has many similarities to the traditional American style—a straight-cut body, the high button stance, small lapels, the jacket length shorter that the Savile Row prototype. "The Ivy League style was my first love. I loved the way JFK looked," he says, remembering his college days when he organized a group to study the manner of dressing. His first job was with a company called Van Jacket. Although it has long been defunct, Van was a catalyst in propagating the Ivy League look in post-World War II Japan, and its influence is felt even today, as in Fujiwara's case.

"Traditional menswear is restricted with numerous rules. My clothes are based on the classic look, but I have eliminated inflexible rules," says Fujiwara. Such a method, however, is not Fujiwara's monopoly. Rather, it is the basic principle for most Milanese designers, with Giorgio Armani being the most notable example. What distinguishes the Fujiwara look from the others is its stoic cleanliness and serene simplicity. To paraphrase, his clothes are disciplined and refined, but lack carnal sexiness. Fujiwara readily agrees; he hates macho images, such as exposed hairy chests and brash exhibition of the male body. When he shows coarsely knit sweaters or open-neck shirts, his models always wear t-shirts under them. Nor does he like slouchy looks: his trousers are always cut at the top of the shoes, or above. He is quite definite about the choice of colors, too, eschewing dayglo brights or ice cream pastels.

These likes and dislikes reflect his concept of masculinity which derives from his nostalgia for old Japan. "I like the image of men from the *Meiji* and *Taisho* periods (1862–1926)," says Fujiwara. "They ware slightly rough around the edges and gutsy and robust inside." These men, however, were taught not to show inner feelings and weaknesses, and excessive concern for one's appearance was looked down upon as a sign of shallowness or femininity. "At the same time," Fujiwara continues, "I also like the certain roguish charm of Italian men."

Since he launched his own business in 1986, Fujiwara's silhouette has changed little, but his clothes are refreshed each season with innovative details. Intricate inlays and patchwork, oddly placed extra pockets, decorative stitching and pipings, and many other clever ideas are delights for Fujiwara fans who are rather limited in number at this writing. "It takes much longer to build business on your convictions than on trendy fashions. But unless you stick to your guns, I see no reason to be in this business," he says, and he counts stubbornness as one of the essential qualities of a designer.

In January 1988, Fujiwara began experimenting with three- and four-button sport and suit coats cut full for the athletic build and military posture, but overplayed styling with hoods, toggles, and bows. For spring/summer 1989, he caught the pacesetter's eye with unusual details for Europe—tweed and pleated center vents on suit coats, precisely tailored cutaway jackets, bell bottoms, and decorative belts, lapels, plackets, and yokes. Long on variation, his focus on boxy short jackets as well as trim and longer styles took the yawn out of menswear. Full-chested topcoats reaching to the knee brought kudos from the out-of-the-ordinary buyer. He made the greatest hit with a three-button suit in straw-toned lined, a red-laced suit lapel, body defining back seams, and jersey motorcycle jackets.

Fujiwara's 1990s nostalgia brought back the wide-wale seersucker jackets, but failed to dim his Eurasian charm after twelve years's residency in Italy. His Ivy League sack suits in male monochrome beige, sage, charcoal, and navy stuck to the plain-Jane American lines of the Kennedy years marked by a few quirks, notably, tab-waist short-sleeve shirts and a jacket with lapel zipper. Still looking to the past in 2001, he let black set an ascetic tone and mood in sleek leather and structured basics. For a change, he tied a scarf at the waist of his waterproof Transylvanian cloak. His choice for winter 2002 was a body-conscious layered look with glossy leather gloves and belts to define waistbands.

—Yoko Hamada; updated by Mary Ellen Snodgrass

FURSTENBERG, Diane Von

See VON FURSTENBERG, Diane

G

GABBANA, Stefano

See DOLCE & GABBANA

GALANOS, James

American designer

Born: Philadelphia, Pennsylvania, 20 September 1924. **Education:** Studied at the Traphagen School of Fashion, New York, 1942–43.

James Galanos, 1964 collection: brocade evening dress with a gold mesh top and matching brocade coat. © AP/Wide World Photos.

Career: General assistant, Hattie Carnegie, New York, 1944–45; sketch artist for Jean Louis, Columbia Pictures, Hollywood, 1946–47; apprentice designer, Robert Piguet, Paris, 1947–48; designer, Davidow, New York, 1948–49; designer, Galanos Originals, from 1951; first showing, New York, 1952; licenses include Parfums Galanos, 1980, and Galanos Furs, introduced in 1984; retired, late 1990s. **Exhibitions:** *Galanos Retrospective, 1952–74,* Costume Council of the Los Angeles County Museum of Art, 1975; *Galanos—25 Years,* Fashion Institute of Technology, New York, 1976; Los Angeles County Museum of Art, 1997 (retrospective); Smithsonian Institution; Metropolitan Museum; Brooklyn Museum; Philadelphia Museum; Ohio State University; Dallas Museum of Art. **Awards:** Coty American Fashion Critics award, 1954, 1956; Neiman Marcus award, Dallas, 1954; Filene's Young Talent Design award, Boston, 1958; Cotton Fashion award, 1958; Coty American Hall of Fame award, 1959; *Sunday Times* International Fashion award, London, 1965; Council of Fashion Designers of America Lifetime Achievement award, 1985; Stanley award, 1986; inducted, Fashion Walk of Fame, Seventh Avenue, New York, 2001. **Address:** 2254 South Sepulveda Boulevard, Los Angeles, CA 90064, USA.

Publications

On GALANOS:

Books

Bender, Marylin, *The Beautiful People,* New York, 1967.

Waltz, Barbara, and Bernadine Morris, *The Fashion Makers,* New York, 1978.

Diamonstein, Barbaralee, *Fashion: The Inside Story,* New York, 1985.

Milbank, Caroline Rennolds, *Couture: The Great Designers,* New York, 1985.

———, *New York Fashion: The Evolution of American Style,* New York, 1989.

Stegemeyer, Anne, *Who's Who in Fashion, Third Edition,* New York, 1996.

Articles

Donovan, Carrie, "Good as Gold Clothes," in the *New York Times,* 23 November 1980.

Morrow, Suzanne Stark, "The World of James Galanos," in *Architectural Digest,* October 1981.

Talley, André Leon, "A Certain Quality: Galanos," in *Vogue* (New York), April 1985.

Batterberry, Ariane and Michael, "The Loner," in *Connoisseur* (New York), May 1985.

Milbank, Caroline Rennolds, "James Galanos: Disciplined Elegance in the Hollywood Hills," in *Architectural Digest,* September 1988.

Morris, Bernadine, "By Galanos, the Simplest of Splendors," in the *New York Times,* 27 February 1990.
"A Galanos...Why is It Worth It?" in *Harper's Bazaar,* June 1991.
Morris, Bernadine, "Galanos Has the Last Word for Fall," in the *New York Times,* 24 August 1993.
Hainey, Bruce, "James Galanos: Art Exhibit," in *Artforum,* September 1997.
Givhan, Robin, "Saluting Fashion's Ageless Wonders," in the *Washington Post,* 20 July 2001.

* * *

Dedication to excellence, in craftsmanship and design, was the foundation of James Galanos' career. The quality of workmanship found in his clothing is unsurpassed in America today. It may seem a contradiction that his sophisticated, mature, and elegant clothing was designed and produced in southern California, traditionally the land of sportswear. But Galanos was satisfied to remain where he began his business in 1951, a continent away from New York and the center of the American fashion industry.

Galanos knew what he wanted to do early in life and pursued his dream to design school, an internship in Paris, and several design positions with companies in New York. When the opportunity arose for him to open his own company, he created a small collection, which was immediately ordered by Saks Fifth Avenue. From this first collection his clothing has been admired for its particularly high quality, especially considering it was ready-to-wear, not custom-made. His chiffon dresses in particular made his reputation in the early 1950s, with their yards of meticulously hand-rolled edges.

Galanos gathered some of the most talented craftspersons available in his workrooms; many were trained in Europe or in the costume studios of Hollywood. If his work is compared to that of anyone else, it is compared to French haute couture. His business was more comparable to a couture house than a ready-to-wear manufacturer; there was an astonishing amount of hand work in each garment and all of his famous beadwork and embroidery is done by his staff. Galanos always chose fabrics and trimmings personally during trips to Europe. He lined dresses with silks that other designers used for dresses themselves; and was always a firm believer in the importance of hidden details, such as exquisite silk linings. These details made a difference in the feel of the clothes on the body and the hang of the fabric, and his clients all over the world were happy to pay for them.

Many of the world's most socially prominent women were Galanos customers. In the 1980s, he made national headlines as one of First Lady Nancy Reagan's favorite designers. The fact that Mrs. Reagan wore a 14-year-old Galanos to her first state dinner at the White House attests to the timelessness and durability not only of his workmanship, but more importantly, of his design. This type of occurrence was commonplace among his faithful customers.

His silhouette remained narrow with a fluid ease and Galanos continued to refine his shapes until his retirement in the late 1990s. If his design stylings changed in 50 years of business, they became more simple and refined. Not one to be satisfied with past success, Galanos relished the challenge of creating the perfect black dress. But despite his fondness for black in design, he was also known for his brilliant and unusual combinations of darker shades. His masterful handling of chiffon and lace tended toward the softly tailored, staying away from excess fullness of any kind. Galanos was not necessarily synchronized with the rest of the fashion world; if the themes of his collections bore similarities to others from year to year, it was coincidental.

Galanos preferred to work somewhat in isolation, both geographically and ideologically. His goal was to make the most elegant clothing possible for a select group of the world's most sophisticated women. The number of women who he considers truly elegant became smaller than it was when his career began, but he certainly succeeded in his goal of providing the clothing they required. Even before his retirement, Galanos designs were collected by his customers like other objects of artistic value, and have been well represented in museum collections around the United States.

In the 21st century, James Galanos and his contributions to fashion continue to be revered. He was inducted into Seventh Avenue's Fashion Walk of Fame in New York City in July of 2001. The plaques, embedded in Seventh Avenue, like Hollywood's tribute to the stars, were awarded to Galanos, Donna Karan, Oscar de la Renta, and Pauline Trigère. Bonnie Cashin, Giorgio di Sant'Angelo, Anne Klein, and Charles James were also honored with Seventh Avenue plaques, posthumously.

—Melinda L. Watt; updated by Owen James

GALITZINE, Irene

Russian designer working in Rome

Born: Tiflis, Russia, 1916. **Education:** Studied art and design in Rome. **Family:** Married Silvio Medici. **Career:** Assistant, Fontana, circa 1945–48; established own import business, Rome, 1949; first collection, 1959; business closed 1968; worked as freelance designer, 1968–70; designer for own business, reopened as Princess Galitzine, from 1970. **Awards:** Filene award for new talent, Boston, 1959; Designer of the Year award, Italy, 1962; *Sunday Times* International Fashion award, 1965; Isabella d'Este award, Italy, 1965.

Publications

On GALITZINE:

Books

Lambert, Eleanor, *World of Fashion: People, Places, Resources,* New York & London, 1976.
Soli, Pia, *Il genio antipatico* (exhibition catalogue), Venice, 1984.
Villa, Nora, *Le regine della moda,* Milan, 1985.
Stegemeyer, Anne, *Who's Who in Fashion, Third Edition,* New York, 1996.

Irene Galitzine, spring 1962 collection: silk gown with a chiffon cape in a pattern designed by her. © Bettmann/CORBIS.

Articles

"Galitzine seta e lustrine: tutto scivola," in *Vogue* (Milan), September 1984.

"Roma Alta Moda: Irene Galitzine," in *Vogue* (Milan), September 1985.

Colen, Bruce, and Massimo Listri, "Princess Irene Galitzine: Rich Patterns in the Heart of Rome," in *Architectural Digest* (Los Angeles), September 1988.

* * *

Nathaniel Hawthorne and Henry James were Americans who dreamed of Italy; after World War II, the dream was a film, *Three Coins in a Fountain,* eventually superseded by the Italian-made *La Dolce Vita.* Italian freedom and innate style held romance; Italian nobility in the fashion and beauty industries such as Emilio Pucci, Princess Marcella Borghese, and Princess Irene Galitzine were fairytale heroes.

In the 1950s and 1960s (launching her business in 1949), Princess Irene Galitzine exemplified Roman high style and the princely life. Diana Vreeland, then of *Harper's Bazaar,* dubbed Galitzine's full, liquid trousers for at-home leisure (introduced to a standing ovation at the Palazzo Pitti fashion showing in 1960) "palazzo pajamas" and every aura of Renaissance and romantic (and erotic) Italy flooded the American imagination. Galitzine's palazzo pajamas were, in fact, not wholly an invention, but they became in Galitzine's countless versions of uncompromising luxury a silken reverie.

The silks of Italy were a factor, but Galitzine was especially inventive in the elaboration of the palazzo pajamas, bringing to the leisure trousers expressions of *alta moda* embellishment. She treated the drapey silks as a scrim for attached necklaces in the manner of Mainbocher and created other illusions of encrusted ornament and articulated hems and sleeves with beads in a manner reminiscent of Fortuny's Murano bead edges, but even more of Renaissance paintings. Even with the comfort and casualness of palazzo pajamas, the

Irene Galitzine, spring/summer 1969 ready-to-wear collection: organdy minidress. © AP/Wide World Photos.

wearer seemed to step out of a lustrous, bejewelled world of Renaissance art. Similarly, her decoration of hems, collars, and cuffs articulated countless Pierrots (often with long tops over either palazzo trousers or narrow trousers).

Galitzine used applied effects not only to establish the grandeur of what might otherwise lapse into a too casual mode, but also to apply a countervailing weight to the almost fly-away big cutting of her styles. Weight and the illusion of weight was an effective punctuation of the clothing. Likewise, in her signature toga top over trousers, the elaborate fibula at the shoulder not only secures, but gives a solid balance to the loose drape.

Roman grandeur led rather dramatically, in the 1960s, to the Cardin-like futurism in Galitzine's work. A quilted vinyl jumpsuit with matching helmet on the cover of the May 1966 *Harper's Bazaar* is of *Brave New World* anticipation, but continues to observe Galitzine's dress rationalism. In the same era, she was converting her palazzo pajamas into ensembles with Empire-waisted tops and boxy jackets in reinforcement of the new geometry. In fact, her clothing had always understood lifestyle and the reductivism of the 1960s. After a brief hiatus in the late 1960s, Galitzine reopened to show for spring/summer 1970. In this collection, she used bold graphics for trousers and dresses to be worn with sleeveless tunics, again a device that could seem to step out of a Renaissance painting or step forward into fantasies of outer space.

For a fashion designer able to trace her Russian ancestry back to Catherine the Great and insistent on her Russian style even as much as her Roman, Galitzine became the epitome of Roman style. "I've always tried to design new outlines that feel good on the body.... I don't care for clothes that you have to think about after you've put them on. No elegant woman ever looks ill at ease." Galitzine's formula for easy and comfortable dressing managed to combine the avowed comfort of the clothing with an unmistakable pomp of Roman refinement and the abiding presence of Italian Renaissance luster.

Always adding to the aura of Galitzine's design was her remarkable client list, the best of Italy and an international clientèle who discovered Italian clothing in the 1950s and 1960s. *Architectural Digest,* in a September 1988 article, remembered Eleanor Lambert remarking of a Galitzine show, "The audience is snob, not mob." Yet, the supreme evidence is Galitzine's clothing: luxurious, inventive, high-style casualness with grace.

—Richard Martin

GALLIANO, John

British designer

Born: Gibraltar, Spain, 1960. **Education:** Studied design at St. Martin's School of Art, London. **Career:** Graduation collection, Les Incroyables, sold to Brown's; freelance designer, establishing John Galliano fashion house, London, from 1984; designer for haute couture and ready-to-wear at Givenchy 1995–96; designer for haute couture and ready-to-wear at Christian Dior, from 1996; opened own shop in Bergdorf Goodman store, 1997; licensed fur line, 1998; opened shop in Saks Fifth Avenue, 2000; launched watch collection, 2001. **Exhibitions:** *John Galliano at Dior,* [retrospective], Design Museum of London, 2001–02. **Awards:** British Designer of Year award 1986, 1994, 1995; Bath Costume Museum Dress of the Year award, 1987; Telva award, Spain, 1995; International Fashion Group, Master of Fashion, 1997; Designer of the Year, Council of Fashion of America, 1998. **Address:** 60 Rue d'Avron, 75020 Paris, France. **Website:** www.dior.com.

Publications

On GALLIANO:

Books

Coleridge, Nicholas, *The Fashion Conspiracy,* London, 1988.
McDowell, Colin, *Galliano,* New York, 1997.
Watson, Linda, *Vogue Twentieth Century Fashion: 100 Years of Style by Decade and Designer,* London, 1999.

Articles

Brampton, Sally, "Capital Collections: John Galliano," in *Elle* (London), March 1987.

John Galliano, designed for the house of Christian Dior's fall/winter 2000–01 haute couture collection. © AFP/CORBIS.

Menkes, Suzy, "Jasper and John," in the *Independent* (London), 9 October 1987.
Rumbold, Judy, "A Steal for Galliano," in *The Guardian* (London), 14 October 1987.
Mower, Sarah, "London Follows Galliano," in *The Observer* (London), 18 October 1987.
Coleman, Alix, "Viva Galliano!" in the *Sunday Express Magazine* (London), 8 November 1987.
Filmer, Deny, "Designer Focus: John Galliano," in *Cosmopolitan* (London), February 1988.
Jobey, Liz, "John Galliano: Romantic Hero," in *Vogue* (London), February 1988.
Brampton, Sally, "The Great Galliano," in *Elle* (London), March 1988.
Irvine, Susan, "Galliano and Co.," in *Harrods Magazine,* Spring 1988.
Gasperini, Nicoletta, "John Galliano's Golden Year," in *Donna* (Milan), April 1988.
Collin, Matthew, "The Boy Wonder: An Interview with John Galliano," in *i-D* (London), November 1989.
Rumbold, Judy, "Galliano Leaps onto Centre Stage," in *The Guardian,* 26 February 1990.
Dickson, Elizabeth, "A Life in the Day of John Galliano," in the *Sunday Times Magazine,* 1 March 1992.
Billen, Andrew, "Galliano: Can He Really Cut It?" in *The Observer Magazine,* 28 February 1993.
Reed, Julia, "Incurable Romantic," in *Vogue,* March 1993.
Ingrassia, Michele, with Meggan Dissly, "Dior Meets Disney World," in *Newsweek,* 26 December 1994.
Mauriès, Patrick, "Ma Poulette, Quel Style," in *Vogue* (Paris), February 1995.
"Sei Grande, Grande, Grande.../Nobody Does It Better," in *Moda In* (Modena), January–March 1995.
Spindler, Amy M., "Four Who Have No Use for Trends," in the *New York Times,* 20 March 1995.
Menkes, Suzy, "Show, Not Clothes, Becomes the Message," in the *International Herald Tribune,* 20 March 1995.
Kerwin, Jessica, "Galliano in Gotham," in *WWD,* 23 May 1995.
Weisman, Katherine, and Janet Ozzard, "The Galloping Galliano," in *WWD,* 9 September 1996.
"Galliano Shop Bows with Bergdorf Gala," in *WWD,* 11 December 1997.
"Galliano Sets Fur Line Debut," in *WWD,* 4 May 1998.
Weisman, Katherine, "Galliano's Open-Dior Policy," in *WWD,* 3 December 1999.
Dowd, Maureen, "Haute Homeless," in the *New York Times,* 23 January 2000.
Givhan, Robin, "In Paris, Clothes Aren't Everything," in the *Washington Post,* 14 October 2000.
Rubenstein, Hal, "The Look of Christian Dior," in *In Style,* 1 November 2000.
Socha, Miles, "The Galliano Factor: Dior Lays Groundwork for 'Exceptional' 2001," in *WWD,* 16 January 2001.
"Born Again Christians," in *Time International,* 19 February 2001.
Sischy, Ingrid, "Inside Paris Fashion: John Galliano," in *Interview,* October 2001.

* * *

Experimental and innovative, John Galliano has become internationally renowned as one of Britain's most exciting designers, acclaimed from the start for his brilliance in cut and magpie-like ability to take inspiration from diverse sources to create a completely new look. Although his clothes are often difficult to understand when on the hanger—with collars that seem to be bows or halter necks that actually fit over the shoulders—they are frequently ahead of the current fashion trends and eventually filter down the clothing chain to the High Street, as well as being picked up by other designers. A favorite among fashion aficionados, Galliano was spotted as soon as his first student collection was completed and has continued to develop since, despite repeated problems with backers who have hampered his career.

As part of a new breed of avant-garde British designers, Galliano led the way in the mid-1980s with his historically influenced designs. This fascination for period detail and adaptation of traditional styles into highly contemporary pieces has continued throughout his work. Studying surviving garments in museums to learn about construction methods and different ways to cut and drape fabric to create new shapes inspired his innovative 18th-century Incroyables collection for his degree showing. He suffused this knowledge with other diverse influences to produce collections always exciting and different. His

John Galliano, designed for the house of Christian Dior's spring/summer 2001 haute couture collection. © AFP/CORBIS.

great belief in the necessity to push fashion forward by learning from the past—coupled with his skill at balancing his designs with modern ideals—has earned him the reputation of a prodigy.

Every outfit is thought out to the last detail, producing a series of completely accessorized looks as Galliano constantly strives for perfection. His love of bias cut gives added fluidity to the asymmetrical hemlines of many of his designs, with a taste of 18th-century dandyism thrown in, always with a surprise twist—often in his use of fabric, another area where Galliano loves to experiment and challenge. In one collection, he presented Napoleon-style jackets in bright neoprene, in another, *devoré* velvet bias-cut dresses clinging to the body, giving the element of sexiness that pervades his work. His love of shock gave us the camped-up glamour of his "underwear as outerwear," with satin knickers worn with feathered bras and leather caps, tapping the trend for drag in the London clubs.

With Galliano's Girl and, perhaps to an even greater extent, the largely denim and Lycra-based line Galliano Genes, the designer demonstrated his ability to redefine existing subcultures to develop clothes for the younger, funkier sisters of his mainline buyers. Produced at a cheaper cost by using less exclusive fabrics, these designs are nonetheless inventive. Three-way jackets can be worn with attached waistcoats outside or inside, and there are other basic items more commercially viable, confronting occasional claims from his critics that his work is too avant-garde and less popular than other European names.

The sheer breadth of vision in Galliano's designs, which frequently rethink form and shape, and the great inventiveness of his cut have surely ensured his reputation as one of the best of British designers. The research he does before forming a collection—bringing together influences and details from the French Revolution to Afghan bankers to Paul Poiret—and his experimentation with fabrics demonstrate his dedication to pushing fashion and dress forward, yielding excitement and surprise in every collection.

Galliano stunned the fashion world in 1995 when he was named designer for Givenchy and became the first British designer appointed to lead an established French fashion house. In addition to designing for both haute couture and ready-to-wear at Givenchy, Galliano continued to show designs under his own label. By October 1996, the LVMH group moved Galliano to its crown jewel and appointed Galliano designer for haute couture and ready-to-wear collections at Christian Dior. Critics questioned whether Galliano's maverick reputation would appeal to Dior's established clientèle, but the designer arrived with the energy to shake up the haute couture world, which was showing signs of losing the interest, and sales, of its customers. In his spring/summer 1997 collection, Galliano took classic Dior themes and spun them together with exotic African Masai tribal forms to create silk evening dresses accented with colorful beaded choker necklaces. The collection presented a younger image yet remained glamorous and refined, definitely worthy of the Dior name.

Galliano's collections have never failed to enchant, or shock, audiences. Each has expressed a theme complete with historic personalities and forces that have inspired Galliano's creations for the season. Edwardian elegance, the surrealist movement, the Soviet or Red Guard, the movie *The Matrix,* or classic English sportsmen have all been at play in Galliano collections. His push for a more contemporary, sexier image has proven at times to be a difficult and frightening change at Dior.

In addition to his extravagant romanticism and love of the bias-cut gown, Galliano still retained much of his British bad boy flair. He drew public ire when the homeless theme in his spring 2000 collection included models in newspapers carrying empty liquor bottles and, in the following year's spring collection, when runway models were accompanied by blared vulgar lyrics offering women for sale. Even his critics acknowledge Galliano has brought excitement and fun to haute couture, and customer interest may be his best vindication—by 2001 Dior sales had doubled since the arrival of Galliano four years earlier. The ever-inventive Galliano will continue to hold the fashion world's attention and certainly keep it guessing for years to come.

—Rebecca Arnold; updated by Janette Goff Dixon

THE GAP

American apparel and accessories company

Founded: by Donald and Doris Fisher as a jeans retailer in San Francisco in 1969. **Company History:** Company expanded into

Display window from a Gap store, fall 1998. © Fashion Syndicate Press.

separates for men and women, and added propietary brands, throughout the 1970s; went public on NYSE, 1976; added retail stores throughout the U.S. and abroad; purchased Banana Republic chain, 1983; GapKids introduced, 1986; BabyGap, 1989; GapShoes, 1993; Old Navy Clothing Company launched, 1994; bath and body products introduced, 1994; BodyGap established, 1998; reached 2,600 stores and sales of $9 billion, 1999; flagship Paris store opened, 1999; flagship London store, opened 2001; added sizing for larger women, 2001. **Awards:** *Sales and Marketing Management* Marketing Achievement award, 1991; American Choreography awards, Governor's award (for the support of dance), 2000. **Company Address:** 1 Harrison Street, San Francisco, California, 94105, USA. **Company Website:** www.gap.com.

Publications

On THE GAP:

Books

Hoover, Gary, et al., *Hoover's Handbook of American Business 1994,* Austin, TX, 1993.

Pederson, Jay P. (ed.), *International Directory of Company Histories,* Detroit, MI, 1996.

Articles

Forman, Ellen, "Widening The Gap," in *DNR,* 26 May 1987.

Conant, Jennet, "The Age of McFashion: Specialty Stores are Selling Prepackaged Style for Busy Shoppers," in *Newsweek,* 28 September 1987.

Callagher, Sue, and Ros Ormiston, "Filling The Gap," in *Fashion Weekly* (London), 16 November 1989.

Van Meter, Jonathan, "Fast Fashion," in *Vogue,* June 1990.

Kantrowitz, Barbara, "Now You Can Crawl into The Gap," in *Newsweek,* 29 October 1990.

"Ready, Set, Gap!" in *Harper's Bazaar,* February 1991.

Pogoda, Dianne M., and Thomas Ciampi, "Growing The Gap," in *WWD,* 6 January 1992.

Kahn, Alice, "Filling Every Gap...," in the *New York Times* 23 August 1992.

Tyrer, Kathy, "Back to Basics: Gap Too Hip for Its Britches in the Value-Oriented 1990s," in *Adweek Western Advertising News,* 9 November 1992.

Ozzard, Janet, "Is The Gap Losing Its Fashion Edge?" in *WWD,* 9 June 1993.

The Gap store on Sixth Avenue, New York City, winter 2000. © AP/Wide World Photos.

Mitchell, Russel, "The Gap Dolls Itself Up," in *Business Week,* 21 March 1994.

Strom, Stephanie, "How Gap Inc. Spells Revenge," in the *New York Times,* 24 April 1994.

"Who's Who in the American Sportswear Market 1995," in *Sportswear International* (New York), Vol. 13, May 1994.

Duff, Christina, "'Bobby Short Wore Khakis'—Who is He and Who Cares?" in the *Wall Street Journal,* 16 February 1995.

Caminiti, Susan, "Will Old Navy Fill The Gap?" in *Fortune,* 18 March 1996.

Bensimon, Giles, "How They Learned to Stop Worrying and Love The Gap," in *Elle,* April 1996.

Barboza, David, "The Gap Brings Wall Street a Casual Friday," in the *New York Times,* 27 September 1997.

Moomey, Kelly, "Banana Republic vs. The Gap vs. Old Navy," in *Consumer Reports,* May 1998.

"The Jean Pool," in *Forbes,* 11 October 1999.

"Mend that Gap," in *Time,* 14 February 2000.

Kaufman, Leslie, "Sales at Gap and Limited Spur Fears of Slow Season," in the *New York Times,* 30 November 2000.

"Gap Goes After Larger-Size Women," in *Marketing to Women: Addressing Women and Women's Sensibilities,* May 2001.

* * *

At a time when the disenfranchised youth of America threatened much of the status quo, a new store aptly name "The Gap" opened in San Francisco. It was 1969 and Donald Fisher, a successful real estate developer, had an idea to capitalize on the growing "generation gap," by offering young people what they wanted—blue jeans and music. While jeans made by the venerable Levi Strauss & Company could be found in local department stores, size and availability were restricted and the antiestablishment youth was unlikey to shop there. Fisher, along with his wife Doris, decided to fill this void in a hip, fully-stocked atmosphere.

The Fishers parlayed cool tunes and low-priced Levi's jeans into a chain of stores in California, then the remainder of the U.S. and eventually abroad. By continually changing its clothing (which had grown from just Levi's to shirts, skirts, shorts, jackets, and other casual separates) to keep up with the evolving trends of baby boomers, The Gap became a hip hangout for jeans lovers from 18 to 49 years of age. By the early 1970s Gap introduced its own labeled apparel and the company went public in 1976. Despite ups and downs in the ensuing years, The Gap remained a firm purveyor of style for the casually dressed crowd.

In the late 1980s Millard "Mickey" Drexler, formerly of Ann Taylor, revamped the Gap organization. From the ground up, Drexler recreated the company, ridding stores of all nonproprietary brands, bringing in a team of designers to produce casual apparel from natural fibers for men and women, then children (GapKids debuted in 1986, BabyGap in 1989). The Gap had begun print and media advertising in earnest, not only attracting new customers, but changing its image along the way. The Fishers had also acquired another California-based company, Banana Republic, and opened the first international Gap store in London.

In the 1990s BabyGap grew into a major retailer, Banana Republic experienced a welcome resurgence in popularity, and a new lower-priced franchise called Old Navy Clothing Company became an immediate success. In 1996 several titans of fashion, including Giorgio Armani, Nino Cerruti, Carolina Herrera, Todd Oldham, and Cynthia Rowley, paid tribute to the clothier in the April issue of Elle magazine, all wearing Gap apparel. There were now hundreds of Gap stores dotting Europe and increasingly renowned print and television advertising for both Gap and Old Navy. As the 20th century closed and the 21st arrived, the Fishers had retired but retained a healthy stake in the now-legendary clothing empire. The second generation of Fishers, three sons, worked in some capacity in the family business, while Mickey Drexler continued to reign in the executive suite. In nearly every metropolitan area was a Gap, GapKids, BabyGap, Banana Republic, or Old Navy store, or a combination storefront featuring both adult and children's clothing.

Shrewd marketing, tight control, exceptional quality, and consistency in an ever-evolving and inconsistent marketplace has kept The Gap, Inc. at the forefront of the apparel and accessories industry. There's Banana Republic for the higher-end market, Gap for the middle road, and Old Navy for lower-priced dressing with style and panache. With sales topping $11 billion by 2000, the Gap's empire seemed boundless; further evidence of the company's continuing acuity was its expansion into cyberspace, with a very popular website.

—Nelly Rhodes

GARAVANI, Valentino

See VALENTINO

GARRATT, Sandra

American designer

Born: Sandra Harrower in Milwaukee, Wisconsin, 16 December 1951, to British parents. **Education:** Graduated from Fashion Institute of Design and Merchandising, Los Angeles, 1975. **Family:** Married Michael Garratt in 1977; one son: Wesley. **Career:** Design assistant to Ossie Clark, London, 1971–73; design assistant to Bob Mackie, Los Angeles, 1974–75; textile research/design assistant, Holly Harp, San Francisco, 1975; first design assistant, Dinallo, Beverly Hills, California, 1975; textile designer, Mary McFadden, New York, 1976; window and showroom display designer, Halston, New York, 1976; first design assistant, Zoran, New York, 1976; illustrator, Giorgio di Sant'Angelo, New York, 1976–77; textile design, CMS Spectrum, New York, 1976–77; director, Texas Developmental Group, Dallas, 1978–80; director and designer, Units, Dallas, 1981–86, sold to JCPenney, 1986; artistic/creative director responsible for all aspects of design including textile, packaging, marketing, fashion shows and videos, Multiples, Dallas, Texas 1987–89; designer, New Gotham and Moda Vida collections, Greaten Corporation, Los Angeles, 1990; director and designer, New Tee, Inc., original line of 100-percent organic materials 1992–98; director and designer, Sandra Garratt Design 1994–98; head designer for new divisions, Spiegel Catalogue, 2000—. **Exhibitions:** Scott Theatre, Ft. Worth, Texas, 1980; 500X Gallery, Dallas, Texas, 1981; Milam St. Gallery, Houston, Texas, 1982; Wadsworth Atheneum Museum, Hartford, Connecticut, 1989; Musée des Arts décoratifs, Paris, 1990; Natural History Museum, Los Angeles, 1990. **Awards:** Bob Mackie award for Outstanding Achievement in Design, Los Angeles, 1976; Female Entrepreneur of the Year, 1988. **Address:** 4501 Broadway, Suite 2G, New York City, New York, 10040, USA.

Publications

On GARRATT:

Books

Milbank, Caroline R., *New York Fashion: The Evolution of American Style,* New York, 1989.

Articles

"Sandra Garratt Jumps into the Dallas Designer Game," in the *Dallas Morning News* (Texas), 4 April 1979.

Anderson, K., "Close to the Edge," in the *Dallas Morning News* (Texas), 31 October 1979.

Brobston, Tracy, "Five Easy Pieces," in the *Dallas Morning News* (Texas), 28 July 1982.

Ennis, M., "The Empress' New Clothes," in *Texas Monthly* (Texas), September 1982.

Zimmerman, A., "Bits and Pieces," in *Dallas City Magazine,* (Texas), 11 May 1986.

Herold, L., "Picking Up the Pieces," in the *Dallas Morning News* (Texas), 1 February 1987.

———, "A Designer Is Reborn," in the *Dallas Morning News* (Texas), 6 January 1988.

"Sandra Garratt," in *Detour* (Texas), April 1988.

Herold, L., "No Hang-Ups," in *Texas Business* (Texas), June 1988.

Shapiro, H., "Style: Success Comes in Many Forms for Mix and Match Designer Sandra Garratt," in *People* (New York), 20 June 1988.

Mangelsdorf, M., "Dressed for Success," in *Inc.* (Boston), August 1988.

Hockswender, Woody, "Modular Clothes: Count the Ways," in the *New York Times,* 18 October 1988.

Mitchell, C., "Riches from Rags," in the *Wall Street Journal,* 20 March 1989.

Haber, Holly, "New Tee Shop Aims to Reap Budding 'Green' Awareness," in *Women's Wear Daily,* 2 July 1992.

———, "Garratt Reinvents Herself," in *Women's Wear Daily,* 11 January 1994.
———, "Sandra Garratt Ready to Go Nationwide," in *Women's Wear Daily,* 19 October 1994.

*

I see my original modular concept as a classic—like Levi's 501 jeans. The empty-canvas-like appearance begs for personal touches. I'm taking a flat, square architectural design in a soft, knit fabric, which makes it pliable, then putting it on a three-dimensional form so there are contradictions. It stirs up dynamics. Stiff clothes lack body awareness. Through my designs, I offer people a tiny opportunity at self-expression which everyone craves.

Both Jean Muir and Zandra Rhodes have influenced me throughout my career but my favourite designer of all times is Paul Poiret. He really created a new approach for all of 20th-century fashion. Other inspirations that can be seen in my work come from Rudi Gernreich, who was also trained as a dancer, and Giorgio di Sant'Angelo. Working with Halston in the 1970s gave me a new direction. Halston offered a basic way of dressing that seemed suited to Americans. His clothes were realistic in the sense that they worked for you instead of your having to adopt the characteristics of the clothes.

I think people relate to jeans and simple t-shirts because they are functional and authentic. The challenge is to offer good design in an average price range for people. It is easy to work with beautiful, fancy fabrics but not easy to create things that work out of simple, pure materials. This is why working with organically produced fabrics is a great challenge for me and is where I want to focus my designer energies for the rest of my career.

—Sandra Garratt

* * *

Sandra Garratt's career evolved from an early interest in dance and costume design. Forced to abandon the ballet studies that took her to Canada and Europe, Garratt ended up in London as a design assistant to Ossie Clark during the early 1970s. Returning to the U.S. in 1973, Garratt worked on elaborate clothing out of luxury fabrics as a design student at the Fashion Institute of Design and Merchandising in Los Angeles. As a senior, she was asked to design a line contrary to her then-baroque interest in costume dressing. She created a collection of slim skirts and bright tunics out of silk, which became the basis for her career.

After a series of design positions in New York, where she was influenced by Halston and Giorgio di Sant'Angelo, Garratt moved to Dallas, Texas. In 1978 her lifestyle as a busy working mother made her realize millions of women like herself were struggling with increasing demands on their time and resources. Most available clothing failed to address these issues so she began to cultivate ideas based on her senior show. Garratt pioneered the concept of modular one-size-fits-all cotton knits in basic shapes: t-shirts, leggings, tunics, bandeaux, and bikinis. The interchangeable, mix-and-match pieces were eventually called Units. Garratt marketed Units as "modular clothing for the masses expressing individuality through apparent uniformity."

Units were affordable, could be worn alone or layered, and made customers feel both casual and fashionable. The early 1980s were swept by an aerobics and jogging craze and Units offered an appealing, comfortable alternative to sweatsuits and workout clothes. Garratt's early interest in dance contributed to her ability to respond to a woman's need for comfort and flexibility in her wardrobe. She eventually sold her interest in Units in 1987 after a dispute with her financial partners. Units, which was later purchased by JC Penney, operated as a chain of stores in shopping malls.

Another company, called Multiples, was launched in 1987 with Garratt at the design helm. Described as a "system of dressing," Multiples was a collection of 20 knit separates sold in more than 350 department stores nationwide. Garratt monitored the production by the Jerrell company and helped market and promote the line vigorously. Multiples were more sophisticated shapes than previous forms designed by Garratt; cut out of square pattern pieces, the knit jackets often echoed the Japanese design concepts pervasive in fashion of the late 1980s. Multiples offered a versatile group of tunics, skirts, jumpsuits, leggings, and tubular accessories that could be worn as a scarf, cowl, belt, etc. The boxy shapes were sold folded in practical plastic bags at a low price to a huge cross-section of women.

Multiples could be casual or sophisticated depending on the mood of the wearer. Claire McCardell, an American designer during the 1940s and early 1950s, designed comfortable jersey knits similar to Multiples but her timing was unfortunate. Garratt, who also formulated her own ideas ahead of the market, was fortunate enough to be in step throughout the 1980s. Since 1989 Garratt discontinued her relationship with the Jerrell company and Multiples.

Garratt also took time to explore her other love: romantic dressing. She introduced a line of one-of-a-kind, hand-sewn original confections of lace, tulle, and taffeta referred to as "Viennese pastry" dresses during the early 1980s. While not sold specifically as a separate line, these designs were carried by specialist stores and had a devoted following.

Garratt opened a New Tee store in Dallas in 1992. Organic cotton t-shirts with a variety of silk-screened graphics and nontoxic dyes were a favorite of her customers. When the store closed in 1993, she continued to sell her 45-piece collection of simple, comfortable styles in specialty stores and to serve her private customers from a shop adjoining her studio. In 1994 she introduced two collections she called "lifestyle dressing" because the clothing could dress women for the office, an evening out, or a cruise. Her new signature label, Sandra Garratt Design, featured softly-tailored cotton and linen separates, cotton gauze pieces, and bias-cut dresses in silk charmeuse and silk shantung.

The newer label, Sandra Garratt Design, continued to reflect Garratt's concern for the environment, but was not strictly organic. She did, however, introduce an expansion of her New Tee business, which was lower priced and offered organic cotton styles in body-hugging dresses and leggings, big jackets, blouses, and pajama pants. Garratt closed both companies in late 1998 when her financial partners abruptly left the company. She designed on a freelance basis and did consulting work until she joined Spiegel Catalogue in August 2000. As head designer for new divisions, she is guiding the direction of new design for the company. The first of her collections, called

"Transforming the Body," is scheduled for an August 2001 launch. Other lines will include casual clothing with the dressier feel of a Californian boutique.

—Myra Walker; updated by Janette Goff Dixon

GAULTIER, Jean-Paul

French designer

Born: Arcueil, France, 24 April 1952. **Education:** Educated at the École Communale, the College d'Enseignement, and at the Lycée d'Arcueil, to 1969. **Career:** Design assistant, Pierre Cardin, 1972–74; also worked for Esterel and Patou; designer, Cardin (U.S.) Collection, working in the Philippines, 1974–75; designer, Majago, Paris, 1976–78; founder, Jean Paul Gaultier S.A., from 1978; menswear line introduced, 1984; Junior Gaultier line introduced, 1987; furniture line introduced, 1992; licenses include jewelry, from 1988, perfumes, from 1991, and jeans, from 1992; created controversy with line inspired by male Hasidic Jewish apparel, 1993; opened his own couture house, 1997; created costumes for several films, 1980s and 1990s; stake in his company acquired by Hermès, 1999; renewed fragrance license, 2000. **Awards:** Fashion Oscar award, Paris, 1987. **Address:** 70 Galerie Vivienne, 75002 Paris, France. **Website:** www.jpgaultier.fr.

Jean-Paul Gaultier, spring/summer 2001 haute couture collection: satin bustier. © AFP/CORBIS.

PUBLICATIONS

By GAULTIER:

Books

À nous deux la mode, Paris 1990.

On GAULTIER:

Articles

"An Audience with Jean-Paul," in *Fashion Weekly* (London), 11 December 1986.
Drier, Deborah, "The Defiant Ones," in *Art in America* (New York), September 1987.
Arroyuelo, Janvier, "Gaultier: Tongue in Chic," in *Vogue* (New York), August 1988.
"Alaia e Gaultier, due stilisti a confronto," in *Vogue* (Milan), October 1988.
Duka, John, "Gaultier," in *Vogue* (New York), January 1989.
Martin, Richard, "An Oxymoranic Jacket by Jean-Paul Gaultier," *Textile and Text,* 13 March 1990.
Mower, Sarah, "Gaultier, Comic Genius," in *Metropolitan Home,* February 1991.
Howell, Georgina, "The Maestro of Mayhem," in *Vogue* (New York), March 1991.
Spindler, Amy, "Jean-Paul Gaultier: France's Homeboy," in the *Daily News Record* (New York), 22 July 1991.
Martin, Richard, "Machismo in Trapunto: Jean-Paul Gaultier's 1991 Physique Sweater," *Textile and Text,* 14 March 1992.
Yarbrough, Jeff, "Jean-Paul Gaultier: Fashion's Main Man," in *The Advocate* (USA), 17 November 1992.
Weldon, Fay, "Jean Paul the First," in *Tatler* (London), March 1995.
Spindler, Amy M., "Four Who Have No Use for Trends," in the *New York Times,* 20 March 1995.
Menkes Suzy, "Show, Not Clothes, Becomes the Message," in *International Herald Tribune* (Paris), 20 March 1995.
Thomas, Dana, "The French Connection," in *New York Times Magazine,* 25 October 1998.
"Jean-Paul Gaultier," in *Current Biography Yearbook,* 1999.
Murphy, Robert, "Gaultier Goes Global," in *Daily News Record,* 10 January 1999.
"A Man for All Seasons," in *Travel Retailer International,* January 2000.
Naughton, Julie, "Gaultier: Bridging the Gender Gap," in *Women's Wear Daily,* 17 January 2000.

* * *

By injecting kitsch into couture, Jean-Paul Gaultier has redefined the traditionally elegant trappings of Paris fashion. He is a playful, good-natured iconoclast, glamorizing street style and cleaning it up for haute couture. By turns surreal but never completely bizarre,

Jean-Paul Gaultier, fall/winter 2001 collection. © AP/Wide World Photos.

rebellious but always wearable, he has produced seductive, witty clothes which redefine notions of taste and elegance in dress.

Gaultier's eclectic source material, inherited from punk via the fleamarket, and an astute sense of the origins of style mean his clothes make constant historic and literary references, as opposed to the cool modernism of contemporaries such as Issey Miyake, displayed in his use of heraldic motifs in the late 1980s or a collection based on Toulouse-Lautrec in 1991.

Gaultier challenges orthodox notions of the presentation of gender through both male and female dress and ignores the stereotypical femininity normally paraded on the catwalks of traditional Parisian haute couture. During his employment at Jean Patou, Gaultier recognized how most couturiers ignored the female form at the expense of the construction of a particular line. He was, on one occasion, horrified to see a model having to wear heavy bandages to suppress her breasts in order for the dress she was modelling to hang properly. This impulse eventually culminated in a controversial series of negotiations of the corset, stemming from his interest in the exaggerated definition of the female form it produced. In the 1980s he redefined this usually private, hidden garment, whose traditional function is to provide a structure from which to hang the more important outerwear, by recreating it as outerwear itself. One of these, the Corset Dress of 1982, commented astutely on femininity, constructing the breast less as a soft malleable object of passive attraction and more as an object of power, a female weapon, whilst at the same time alluding to the conically stitched bras of the 1950s sweater girl—a particularly tacky glamor. These ideas achieved mass attention when Gaultier designed the costumes for Madonna's Blonde Ambition tour in 1990.

By 1984 Gaultier had decided to move more directly into menswear. Through personal experience he could find nothing he really wanted, particularly in terms of sizing, and even unstructured Armani jackets seemed too small. He noticed that men had been buying his women's jackets because of the unusual fabrics and cut, so he began his seminal reworking of the pinstriped suit for both men and women. He displayed a traditional male wardrobe by redesigning such classics as the navy blazer and Fair Isle jumper and dismantling clichés of masculine styling by producing skirts, corsets, and tutus for men. During one notorious catwalk show, female models smoked pipes and men paraded in transparent lace skirts. This acknowledgement of male narcissism and interest in the creation of erotic clothing for men, as shown in the Man-Object Collection of 1982, influenced designers such as Gianni Versace into the early and mid-1990s.

Gaultier is perhaps best associated with the rise of popular interest in designer clothing in the mid-1980s. His redefinitions of traditional male tailoring made his clothes instantly recognizable amongst so-called fashion victims in most of the major European capitals, using details such as metal tips on collars and extended shoulder lines. Structured, fitted garments like jackets were reworked, being cut long and slim over the hips to mid-thigh to give an hourglass shape to the wearer's physique.

Gaultier has always been interested in new developments in fabric and intrigued by the design possibilities of modern artificial fibers, and is known for using unconventional fibers like neoprene. He uses fabrics outside of their usual context, such as chiffon for dungarees, resulting in a utilitarian garment being produced out of a delicate material traditionally associated with eveningwear. This juggling with expected practice directs him to produce items such as a willow-patterned printed textile incorporating the head of Mickey Mouse, and Aran sweaters elongated into dresses with the woollen bobbles taking the place of nipples.

Gaultier rebels against the old school of Parisian couture but, because of his years of training within its system under Pierre Cardin, Jacques Esterel, and Jean Patou, he is a master craftsman. However avant-garde his collections may seem, they are always founded in a technical brilliance-based inventive tailoring and are able to convince because of the technique. While his kitschy designs in the late 1980s and early 1990s gave Gaultier a reputation as the enfant terrible of fashion, his fall 1998 collection–which featured beaded fisherman's sweaters and formal tartan skirts—was one of many that wowed critics by being innovative yet wearable and elegant. Gaultier has noted that the 1990 AIDS death of his lover and business partner influenced his designs by making them simpler and more sober, with less aggression and toughness. After a time, however, he decided his designs were becoming too classic and he went back to making the sexy, irreverent clothing he had been known for.

Gaultier's interest in pulling together diverse cultures has continued, with his fall 1993 line being one of the most controversial examples, inspired by the traditional apparel of male Hasidic Jews.

Other collections in the 1990s were influenced by the dress of Mongolia, the punk subculture of London, and Eskimo culture, among others. Mixed in were departures such as a 1996 tribute to Pierre Cardin and a 2000 line inspired by the 1970s television series *The Love Boat.* Gaultier admits he watches television constantly, sometimes several programs at a time, to gain inspiration.

Gaultier's profile has been raised by his work as a costume designer for films such as Peter Greenaway's *The Cook, the Thief, His Wife and Her Lover* (1989), Pedro Almodovar's *Kika* (1993) and Luc Besson's *The Fifth Element* (1997). He has also hosted a comedy series, *EuroTrash,* on British television and created a line of furniture which included a two-person chair on wheels and a dresser constructed from luggage.

Gaultier opened his own couture house in 1997, becoming just the second designer in three decades to create couture under his own label. Some of his most creative and praised collections have occurred since that time. From a strapless, feather-enhanced denim ball gown to a seashell- bodiced dress with a feather-covered skirt, he has won a reputation for apparel combining outrageous features with high-quality tailoring and detailing.

French classic luxury goods company Hermès purchased a 35 percent stake in Gaultier's operation for $23.1 million in 1999, a seemingly odd-couple pairing that caught the industry by surprise. The infusion of cash will help Gaultier expand his retail operation, take control of some of his licensing operations, such as jewelry, expand into new categories such as timepieces and footwear, and boost his international business

In 2000 Gaultier renewed his fragrance and cosmetics license with Shiseido and Beauté Prestige International, a longtime alliance known for its daring packaging. BPI launched Gaultier's *Fragile* fragrance in 2000 with a highly publicized snow globe package featuring a tiny figure dressed in Gaultier couture. Meanwhile, the designer expanded his licensee list with the additions of companies such as Wolford, an Austrian luxury hosiery firm.

Despite positive critical reviews and a high profile, Gaultier's revenues have been lower than many other couture labels; the Hermés stake may cause this to change. But what will not change is Gaultier's attention to hand-crafting and singular details, his gender- and culture-crossing designs, and his sense of fun.

—Caroline Cox; updated by Karen Raugust

GENNY HOLDING SPA

Italian ready-to-wear manufacturer

Founded: in Ancona by Arnoldo and Donatella Girombelli in 1961. **Company History:** Lines include Genny Moda, Complice, Byblos (introduced 1973, became independent company, 1983), Malisy (to 1993), Montana Donna and Montana Uomo (to early 1990s); underwent restructuring, 1992–94; Genny Ono eveningwear line launched, 1994; Richard Tyler replaced Byblos longtime designers Cleaver and Varty, 1997; signed John Bartlett to produce his menswear line and a new women's collection, 1997; Martine Sitbon and Sandy Dalal signed to take over Byblos designs, 2001; other designers have

Genny Holding SpA, fall/winter 2001–02 collection: leather halter ensemble. © AP/Wide World Photos.

included Gianni Versace, Claude Montana, Dolce & Gabbana, Guy Paulin, and Rebecca Moses. **Company Address:** Via della Spiga 30, Milan, Italy. **Company Website:** www.gennymoda.com.

Publications

On GENNY:

Articles

"Armonie a confronto," in *Linea Italiana,* October 1984.

Griggs, Barbara, "Lo stile Donatella," in *Vogue* (Milan), October 1988.

Rolfe, Gail, "The Winning Genny," in the *Daily Mail* (London), 6 March 1991.

Smith, Liz, "Polished Touch to Milan Line," in the *Times* (London), 6 March 1991.

"Snappy Dressing Italian-Style," in the *Daily Mail,* 12 March 1992.

Gordon, MaryEllen, "Varty, Cleaver in New York: High Spirits," in *WWD,* 16 September 1992.

Levine, Joshua, "Italy's First Lady of the Factory," in *Forbes,* 28 September 1992.

Forden, Sara Gay, "Versace, Genny, to End 19 Years Together with Spring Collection," in *WWD,* 23 July 1993.
Gordon, Maryellen, "Genny's New Look a Hit at Saks," in *WWD,* 25 May 1994.
Weaver, William, et al., "Donatella Girombelli: Romantic Rooms on the Italian Coast," in *Architectural Digest,* October 1994.
Ozzard, Janet, "Byblos Boys Out After 15 Years, as Milan Firm Appoints Richard Tyler," in *WWD,* 12 November 1996.
"Genny to Make Bartlett Line," in *WWD,* 13 January 1997.
"Byblos Appoints Martine Sitbon as Women's Creative Director," in *WWD,* 19 March 2001.
Brown, Wendell, "Byblos Names Sandy Dalal Creative Director," in *DNR,* 21 March 2001.
"Genny, Steele Talking," in *WWD,* 26 March 2001.

* * *

Named after their first-born child, Genny was the brainchild of Arnoldo and Donatella Girombelli, who founded the company in 1961. Genny Holding SpA then became one of Italy's foremost fashion companies, designing, manufacturing, and distributing its own ranges including Genny, Genny Due, Complice, Byblos, and others. From relatively humble origins as a small clothing factory based in Ancona, Italy, the company was operating at an industrial scale by 1968. During the 1970s it experienced rapid growth when its founder made radical changes in the company structure, steering it towards a more fashionable product in terms of garment styling. These changes did not, however, alter the company's original commitment to the production of high quality, predominantly tailored garments. As an early protagonist of the "Made in Italy" label, Genny assumed a leading role during the 1970s when the Italian fashion industry took its first steps toward becoming a serious competitor with French ready-to-wear fashion.

Genny is typical of a number of Italian fashion companies manufacturing high fashion lines designed for them by leading names in the industry, yet launched under the company's own label. Fashion writer Colin McDowell has described this very successful, as well as lucrative, format as a form of "moonlighting." Considerable financial reward, coupled with the high quality of the Italian ready-to-wear product, has meant there was no shortage of well-known designers willing to supply their creative talent for such companies. Genny's earliest working relationship with an outside designer was with the young, virtually unknown Gianni Versace who designed his first collection for Genny in 1974. Versace was also responsible for designing the early Byblos collections, a younger range introduced in 1973 to complement the classic Genny image.

After the death of Arnoldo Girombelli in 1980, his wife, Donatella, assumed a leading role in the company and chaired its board of directors. Described by fashion retail entrepreneur Roberto Devorik as "a rare catalyst for design talent," Donatella Girombelli continued her husband's policy of employing top designers to create lines for the Genny labels, and have included a who's who of top designers like Stefano Dolce, Domenico Gabbana, Alan Cleaver, and Keith Varty.

The position of Genny and its other labels were not quite cutting edge, nor dramatically avant-garde or barrier-breaking, but rather top quality ready-to-wear clothing with a strong design element. This style was what led to the company's widespread success in the

Satin evening gown by Genny Holding SpA, modeled on the Spanish Steps in Rome during the "Donna sotto le stelle" ("Women Under the Stars") fashion gala, 1999. © AP/Wide World Photos.

international market. By the mid-1990s Genny produced over two million items under its different labels, which were distributed worldwide through the company's nearly two dozen freestanding boutiques and in better department stores in the U.S., Middle East, Europe, and Japan. A growing number of carefully controlled licensing agreements encompassed such products as eyewear, fragrances, bridalwear, leather handbags, belts, and shoes sold worldwide.

Heading into the later 1990s, Genny had undergone restructuring from top to bottom. New designers were brought in and others let go; among the new faces were Americans Rebecca Moses and Richard Tyler, the longtime Byblos design team of Cleaver and Varty was gone, and Donatella Girombelli focused on a more American feel for Genny's womenwear. Commenting to *Women's Wear Daily,* Girombelli said she aimed for a "succinct combination of straightforward American sportswear and Italian flair." Next came John Bartlett, who signed with the Italian firm in 1997 to produce his existing menswear designs as well as to create a new womenswear line.

In the new century, Genny and its varied holdings seemed to have a revolving door with designers. The latest were Martine Sitbon and

Sandy Dalal at Byblos, and Girombelli had approached Lawrence Steele to sign on as a consultant to freshen the Genny labels. Yet despite Genny Holding's frequent overhauls and team changes, it continues to be a well known and widely respected Italian fashion firm.

—Catherine Woram; updated by Nelly Rhodes

GEORGES RECH

French design company

Company History: Georges Rech designer collection established in Paris, 1960; Synonyme separates division established, 1973; Unanyme division of coordinated knitwear and woven separates established, 1981; Georges Rech Group accessories division founded, 1983; licensing department established, 1983; Georges Rech Homme men's ready-to-wear established, 1987; joined Courtaulds as part of textile division, London, 1989; renamed Courtaulds Textiles Plc., 1990; initiated licensing agreement in Thailand, 1993; turnaround after several years of low sales, 1997; Courtaulds acquired by Sara Lee Corp., 2000; franchised or wholly-owned Georges Rech boutiques around the world, including Paris, London, Brussels, Montreal, and Hong Kong; Unanyme distributed through 45 stores in France; group lines also found in many multibrand retailers throughout the world. **Company Address:** 112 rue Reaumur, 75002 Paris, France.

Publications

On GEORGES RECH:

Articles

Mower, Sara, "Anglo-French Mix of Aggression and Chic," in *The Independent* (London), 23 November 1989.

Nicholson, Kathleen, "Private Labels Finding a Welcome in Areas Where Designers Live," in *WWD,* 14 August 1997.

Kibazo, Joel, "Courtaulds Soars on U.S. Bid," in the *Financial Times,* 15 February 2000.

Fallon, James, "Sara Lee Will Buy Courtaulds for $237.8 Million," in *WWD,* 27 March 2000.

"So Rech, So Global: The Georges Rech Spring-Summer Collection Goes Down Well," in the *Bangkok Post,* 11 April 2001.

"Fiercely Feminine Rech," in the *New Straits Times,* 14 May 2001.

* * *

When asked once to sum up his style philosophy, French ready-to-wear designer Georges Rech replied with a single word, "Balance." His fashion house aimed to create a synthesis of ideas, designing not for any one woman or type of person, but for an ever-changing, contemporary ideal. His simple, relaxed, well-made, and affordable coats, suits, dresses, and separates projected an easy-going accessibility, without compromising on creativity or style, and his name became synonymous with casual chic. As Rech put it early in his career, "Sportswear corresponds to the way people live. I don't like to shut a woman up in fabric."

Rech first emerged in the 1960s as one of the pioneers of Parisian ready-to-wear for women. He became known as a leading French manufacturer of tailored coats and suits, before branching out into raincoats. The early coat and suit collections were rather structured and masculine in feeling, but into the 1970s his styles broadened and loosened, with easy jackets over trousers, bloused windbreakers, billowing dresses, and both short and long skirts. Rech was interested in bringing the comfort of leisure wear and sportswear into focus at a time when the fashion majority still upheld notions of clothing propriety, whether it was dressing for city/country, or day/evening. He looked to the youth movements of his day for inspiration, noticing how the young defied adult conventions in their clothing, and he began to experiment with work and leisure fabrics for daytime. He declared denim was the "perfect" fabric, and transformed the humble, working class cloth into several sophisticated and urbane looks, such as a short, black-and-white striped denim pantsuit with witty elbow patches.

In 1973 Rech created Synonyme, a collection of coordinating basic separates. The line was an immediate success, gaining special notice for an elegant black panne velvet sweatshirt over black crepe flare-leg pants. Rech also designed a bestselling "sweatshirt dress"for day, and adapted other sportswear styles in his loosely-draped Qiana top and skirt for evening. One observer referred to these dressing up/dressing down crossover ideas in fabric and cut as "le Style Americaine," and the designer's clever takes on casual sportswear were indeed well-received in the U.S. when he opened a boutique there in 1978.

The Unanyme junior line, combining knitwear with woven and tailored pieces was premiered in 1981, emphasizing lower-priced compatible separates that could be freely mixed and matched. The next expansion was into a line of accessories, and then came the establishment of Georges Rech Homme, creating for men the clean-cut yet stylish look for which Rech's womenswear had become known. The fourth arm of the house remained the high-end Georges Rech designer line offering structured sophisticated coats, suits, and dresses for women, with a timeless style independent of ephemeral fashion trends. Though each group had a separate identity, the pieces designed for each division continued to embody the basic Rech philosophy of creativity mitigated by realism and wearability.

The company was bought out in 1989 by Courtaulds Textiles of London, and Georges Rech relinquished his personal interest in the house. Since then Daniele Jagot, who worked for the company for over 20 years, took over designing the Georges Rech top-range label, while Fumihiko Harada designed the Synonyme line. By the mid-1990s the label had little flash and sales were far from robust, in part due to a depressed market. The brand made a comeback in 1996 when designer clothing sales rallied in Europe and stayed in the black for several years, prompting expansion. The Georges Rech name became more prevalent in France, with 40 stores in the country (more than a dozen new outlets opened in 1998 alone), the same year parent company Courtauld bought Claremont Garments to augment its apparel division.

By the new century Courtauld was locked in battle with the U.S.-based Sara Lee Corporation over a hostile takeover attempt. To bolster its funds, Courtauld sold several units and put Georges Rech up for sale as well. Despite its efforts, however, Courtauld succumbed and became part of Sara Lee's Branded Apparel Group, which consisted of a slew of apparel, undergarment, and hosiery companies worldwide. Given the similarities in the two firm's business segments, industry analysts believed the acquisition was a good fit for both sides.

The Georges Rech brand for women in 2001 remained feminine and beautiful, still designed by the founder's one-time assistant Jagot. Covering the label's growing success in the the Far East, the *New Straits Times* characterized a recent Jagot collection as "Masculine styles in unforgettably female forms with a strong and sexy mood, animal stripes look wild on rock-chic suits while ribbon corset dresses flirt with naughty-but-nice eveningwear theme." The *Bangkok Post* (11 April 2001) similarly enthused, "Suits—the brand's field of unrivalled expertise and its springboard to fame—were offered in a variety of forms, from the classic, impeccable male costume to the feminine low-neckline and skirt ensemble to trouser suits. Splendid materials and prints, as well as sophisticated details, were the leitmotif of the show."

—Kathleen Paton; updated by Sydonie Benét

GERNREICH, Rudi

American designer

Born: Vienna, 8 August 1922. Immigrated to the United States, 1938, naturalized, 1943. **Education:** Studied at Los Angeles City College, 1938–41; Los Angeles Art Center School, 1941–42. **Career:** Dancer, costume designer, Lester Horton Company, 1942–48; fabric salesman, Hoffman company, and freelance clothing designer, Los Angeles and New York, 1948–51; designer, William Bass Inc., Beverly Hills, 1951–59; swimwear designer, Westwood Knitting Mills, Los Angeles, 1953–59; shoe designer, Genesco Corp., 1958–60; founder, GR Designs, Los Angeles, 1960–64; designer, Rudi Gernreich Inc., 1964–68; designs featured in first fashion videotape, *Basic Black,* 1966; designed furnishings for Fortress and Knoll International, 1970–71; lingerie for Lily of France, 1975; cosmetics for Redken, 1976; also designed knitwear for Harmon Knitwear, kitchen accessories, ceramic bathroom accessories, and costumes for Bella Lewitzky Dance Company. **Exhibitions:** *Two Modern Artists of Dress: Elizabeth Hawes and Rudi Gernreich,* Fashion Institute of Technology, New York, 1967; *Fashion Will Go Out of Fashion,* retrospective, Kunstlerhaus Graz, Austria, 2000. **Awards:** *Sports Illustrated* Designer of the Year award, 1956; Wool Knit Association award, 1960; Coty American Fashion Critics award, 1960, 1963, 1966, 1967; Neiman Marcus award, Dallas, 1961; Sporting Look award, 1963; *Sunday Times* International Fashion award, London, 1965; Filene's Design award, Boston, 1966; inducted to Coty American Fashion Critics Hall of Fame, 1967; Knitted Textile Association award, 1975; Council of Fashion Designers of America Special Tribute, 1985. **Died:** 21 April 1985, in Los Angeles.

Rudi Gernreich, 1966 collection: ensemble in a cheetah print that includes coat, blouse, skirt, stockings, shoes, underwear, and helmet. © AP/Wide World Photos.

Publications

On GERNREICH:

Books

Bender, Marylin, *The Beautiful People,* New York, 1967.
Morris, Bernadine, and Barbara Walz, *The Fashion Makers,* New York, 1978.
Faure, Jacques, editor, *Rudi Gernreich: A Retrospective, 1922–1985,* Los Angeles, 1985.
Milbank, Caroline Rennolds, *New York Fashion: The Evolution of American Style,* New York, 1989.
Loebenthal, Joel, *Radical Rags: Fashions of the Sixties,* New York, 1990.
Moffitt, Peggy, and William Claxton, *The Rudi Gernreich Book,* New York, 1991, 1999; London, 1992.
Stegemeyer, Anne, *Who's Who in Fashion, Third Edition,* New York, 1996.
Moffitt, Peggy, *Rudi Gernreich,* New York, 1999.

Articles

Steinem, G., "Gernreich's Progress; or, Eve Unbound," in the *New York Times Magazine,* 31 January 1965.
"Rudi Gernreich," in *Current Biography* (New York), December 1968.
"Fashion Will Go Out of Fashion," interview, in *Forbes* (New York), 15 September 1970.
Guerin, T., "Rudi Gernreich," in *Interview* (New York), May 1973.
"Head on Fashion," interview, in *Holiday* (New York), June 1975.
Lockwood, C., "The World of Rudi Gernreich," in *Architectural Digest* (Los Angeles), October 1980.
Kalter, S., "Remember Those Topless Swimsuits?" in *People Weekly,* 25 May 1981.
Obituary in *Newsweek,* 6 May 1985.

Rudi Gernreich, 1966 collection: jersey shifts with matching tights and feathered helmets in peacock (left) and a pheasant (right) patterns. (Mule shoes by Capezio.) © AP/Wide World Photos.

"Rudi Gernreich," obituary, in *Current Biography* (New York), June 1985.
Timmons, Stuart, "Designer Rudi Gernreich Stayed in the Fashion Closet," in *The Advocate,* 25 September 1990.
Shields, Jody, "Rudi Gernreich was a Designer Ahead of His Time," in *Vogue,* December 1991.
Armstrong, Lisa, "Peggy and Rudi Go Topless," in *The Independent on Sunday Review* (London), 2 February 1992.
O'Brien, Glenn, "Back to the Future," in *Artforum,* September 2000.

* * *

Son of a hosiery manufacturer, born into an intellectual Viennese family in the 1920s, Rudi Gernreich was to become one of the most revolutionary designers of the 20th century. After fleeing the Nazis in the late 1930s he settled in Los Angeles, becoming an American citizen in 1943. Perhaps because of this geographic detachment from the centers of fashion and the fact that he refused to show in Paris, Gernreich is a name not spoken in the same breath as Balenciaga, Dior, or even Courrèges, although Gernreich had just as much influence on women's appearance, especially during the 1960s and 1970s.

Gernreich studied dance before entering the world of fashion and, using as inspiration the practice clothes of dancers, particularly leotards and tights, he produced pared down body-clothes in the 1960s, aimed at what seemed to be the new woman of the era. To cater to this popular construction of femininity, Gernreich attempted to produce a new version of women's clothing, freed of all constraints.

Influenced by Bauhaus functionalism, Gernreich conceived a body-based dressing with coordinated underwear, celebrating the unfettered movement of the body based on his early involvement with Lester Horton's modern dance troupe. This interest in liberating the body from the limitations of clothing surfaced in his early swimwear designs of 1952 in which he eliminated the complicated boned and underpinned interior construction that had been obligatory in the 1950s. He revived the knitted swimsuit or "maillot" of the 1920s, which he elasticized to follow the shape of the body. These experiments were continued in his knitted tube dresses of 1953.

Gernreich was interested less in the details and decorations of clothes and more in how they looked in motion. In the 1950s he was designing relaxed, comfortable clothes fabricated out of wool, jersey, and other malleable materials, usually in solid colors or geometric shapes and checks. During the next decade he went on to use unusual fabrics and bold color disharmonies such as orange and blue or red and purple.

In the early 1960s Gernreich opened a Seventh Avenue showroom in New York where he showed his popular designs for Harmon knitwear and his own more expensive line of experimental garments. During the decade he acquired a reputation for being the most radical designer in America; his designs included the jacket with one notched and one rounded lapel, tuxedos made of white satin, and the topless bathing suit of 1964, which reflected the new vogue for topless sunbathing.

Gernreich's freeing of the breasts was a social statement, somehow part of the emancipation of women, and a portent of the unfettering of the breast by the women's movement in the 1970s. Gernreich invented the "no bra" bra in 1964, a soft nylon bra with no padding or boning in which breasts assumed their natural shape, rather than being molded into an aesthetic ideal. He went on to overtly display his sympathy for women's liberation with his 1971 collection of military safari clothes accessorized with dogtags and machine guns.

Gernreich was also responsible for developing the concept of unisex, believing that as women achieved more freedom in the 1960s, male dress would emerge from the aesthetic exile into which it had been cast in the 19th century. He conceived interchangeable clothes for men and women such as floor-length kaftans or white knit bell-bottomed trousers and matching black and white midriff tops, and even, in 1975, Y-front underwear for women. Other designs included the first chiffon t-shirt dress, see-through blouses, coordinated outfits of dresses, handbags, hats, and stockings, mini dresses inset with clear vinyl stripes, and the thong bathing suit, cut high to expose the buttocks. He experimented constantly with the potentials of different materials using cutouts, vinyl, and plastic, and mixing patterns such as checks with dots.

His clothing was part of a whole design philosophy which encompassed the designing of furniture, kitchen accessories, rugs, and quilts—even, in 1982, gourmet soups. His notion of freeing the body was taken to its logical extreme in his last design statement, the pubikini, which appeared in 1982, revealing the model's dyed and shaped pubic hair.

—Caroline Cox

GHOST

British fashion house

Founded: in 1984 by Tanya Sarne. **Company History:** Opened London shop, 1994; opened flagship London store, 1997; launched G2 collection, 1997; opened boutiques in Paris, Los Angeles, and Amsterdam, 1998; signed licensing agreement with Oliver Goldsmith for eyewear, 1998; introduced shoe and knitwear lines, 1999; launched signature fragrance *Ghost,* 2000; planned second women's fragrance, 2001–02. **Awards:** British Apparel Export award, 1992. **Company Address:** The Chapel, 263 Kensal Rd., London W10 5DB, England.

Ghost, fall 2001 collection. © AP/Wide World Photos/Fashion Wire Daily.

Publications

On GHOST:

Books

Stegemeyer, Anne, *Who's Who in Fashion, Third Edition,* New York, 1996.

Articles

Fallon, James, "Ghost: Getting the U.S. Spirit," in *WWD,* 11 January 1993.
Spindler, Amy M., "Color It with Silver and Spice," in the *New York Times,* 4 November 1993.
"New York Update—Ghost," in *WWD,* 11 April 1994.
Orlean, Susan, "The Talk of the Town: Fashion Designers Uptown and Downtown Get Ready for This Week's Shows in Bryant Park," in the *New Yorker,* 7 November 1994.
Fallon, James, "Ghost readies Trendy G2 for Spring-Summer 1997," in *WWD,* 20 August 1996.
———, "Ghost Focuses on Growth," in *WWD,* 18 June 1998.
Hammond, Teena, "L.A.'s a Ghost Town," in *WWD,* 24 June 1998.

"Ghost—Fashion Designer Tanya Sarne," in *WWD,* 29 September 1998.
Watson, Shane, "Tanya Boards the Ghost Train," from London Life, available online at www.thisislondon.co.uk, 1999.
"Ghost Story," in *Soap, Perfumery & Cosmetics,* February 2000.
"Fashion Marches On," in *WWD,* 23 February 2001.

* * *

The British label Ghost was founded in 1984 by Tanya Sarne and has since become a firmly established name in the fashion industry. The company's signature use of flowing fabric, with its softly crinkled look cut in loose, flowing shapes, forms the basis of each collection. Ghost designs are not usually viewed as the cutting edge of fashion; this was particularly true during the power-dressing period of the 1980s, when strict tailoring and padded shoulders were a major element in fashion. A label such as Ghost offered an individual and alternative way of dressing.

Fabrics are the hallmark of each Ghost collection and almost all of them are woven from viscose yarns derived from specially-grown soft wools with a fluid, crêpe-like texture. An intricate process of washing, shrinking, and dyeing is applied to each garment, which is constructed from the unfinished material or "grey cloth" and dyed at the final stage. These "grey cloth" garments are cut several sizes bigger to allow for the ensuing process of shrinking that occurs when the viscose is boiled to the consistency of vintage crêpe fabric.

The traditional dyeing and shrinking process employed by Ghost is rarely used in production today, due to its cost and the fact that it is extremely time-consuming. Another feature of Ghost design is its richly varied use of color, which can achieve great depth on the viscose fabric and changes each season from softest pastels and pale powdery shades to rich autumnal and spicy tones. The signature fabric is also treated with surface decoration such as embroidery, cutwork, and *broderie anglaise* lace effects. Due to the soft, fluid nature of the fabric, Ghost was initially perceived as being primarily summerwear. Over the years, however, new fabrics have been introduced, such as in the autumn-winter collections which have included quilted satin, velours, and mohair wool mixes.

Like many of its British counterparts, the vast majority of Ghost's business is export, of which America and Japan represent around half of its sales volume (Europe, Australia, the Caribbean, and the Middle East make up the rest). Sarne began selling her designs in New York through high-end department and specialty stores in 1987, and Ghost' winning of the British Apparel Export award in 1992 gave the company a much higher profile. The following year, 1993, Sarne began showing her collections in New York.

According to Sarne, her philosophy of creating clothes (which she describes as "by women, for women,") is the key to the considerable success of the Ghost label and its appeal to a wide-ranging age group. The revolutionary nature of each Ghost collection, which means existing pieces can be added to each season, is another appealing feature of the company's designs and may be the key to dressing in the 1990s. "It's a unique product and very feminine," says Sarne of the Ghost label. "It also has a very 'antipower dressing' stance—a look I believe will only increase in importance as the decade progresses."

Sarne and Ghost were very busy in the mid- and late 1990s. A London store was opened in 1994, followed by a 3,500-foot flagship store three years later. Sarne expanded her design range to include

Ghost, fall 2001 collection. © AP/Wide World Photos/Fashion Wire Daily.

knitwear, eyewear (through a license with Oliver Goldsmith), and shoes. In 1998 came new boutiques in Paris, Amersterdam, and Los Angeles, with future plans for a New York store.

Sarne's lovely, hardly-there viscose dresses have remained a favorite for women around the world, but especially in California. To mark the opening of her Los Angeles shop, Sarne threw a festive bash well attended by the area's glitterati. Though the company's roots are still firmly planted in the UK, Sarne much admires her American clientèle. "Our clothing is perfect for the L.A. climate and the L.A. mentality," Sarne told *Women's Wear Daily* in June 1998. In New York, stores like Neiman Marcus, Henri Bendel, and Barneys do a brisk business selling Ghost designs, but as Sarne explained, "People in New York think they're trendier and sharper, but our best sales have always been in L.A."

So just who wears Ghost designs? As Sarne told Shane Watson of London Life, from the This is London website in 1999, "I can find any woman a Ghost outfit that will make her look wonderful. Guaranteed, any shape, any size, any age." In 2000 Sarne admirers had a new way to wear Ghost, with the debut of a signature fragrance, with another women's scent planned for the next year or so. Back in London, Sarne and her new head designer, Amy Roberts, showed a winning collection of dresses and separates in February 2001. *Women's Wear Daily* commented (23 February 2001), "This collection should definitely give the label a boost."

—Catherine Woram; updated by Nelly Rhodes

GIANNELLI, Danilo

See CALUGI E GIANNELLI

GIBB, Bill

British designer

Born: William Elphinstone Gibb in Fraserburgh, Scotland, 23 January 1943. **Education:** Studied in Fraserburgh until 1960; studied at St. Martin's School of Art, London, 1962–66, Royal College of Art, London, 1966–68. **Career:** Founder/partner, Alice Paul clothing boutique, London, 1967–69; freelance designer, working for Baccarat, London, 1969–72; founder/chairman Bill Gibb Fashion Group, London, 1972–88; opened first shop, in Bond Street, London, 1975. **Exhibitions:** *British Design,* Musée du Louvre, Paris, 1971; *Fashion: An Anthology,* Victoria and Albert Museum, London, 1971; *Bill Gibb: Ten Years,* Albert Hall, London, 1977. **Collections:** Bath Costume Museum, Avon; Leeds Museum, Yorkshire; Victoria and Albert Museum, London; Royal Ontario Museum, Toronto. **Awards:** *Vogue* Designer of the Year, 1970; ITV Best Fashion Show award, London, 1979. Fellow, Society of Industrial Artists and Designers, London, 1975. **Died:** 3 January 1988, in London.

Publications

By GIBB:

Articles

"Getting Going Again," in *The Designer* (London), May 1981.

On GIBB:

Books

Howell, Georgina, editor, *In Vogue, Sixty Years of Celebrities and Fashion,* London, 1975; New York, 1976.

Carter, Ernestine, *The Changing World of Fashion,* London, 1977.

Bond, David, *The Guinness Guide to 20th Century Fashion,* Enfield, Middlesex, 1981.

Glynn, Prudence, *Sixty Years of Faces and Fashion,* London, 1983.

Sparke, Penny, et al., *Design Source Book,* London, 1986.

Bill Gibb: A Tribute to the Fashion Designer of the '70s, Aberdeen, Scotland, 1990.

Articles

"Top of the Bill," in the *Sunday Times Magazine* (London), 8 May 1977.

Ebbetts, L., "The Fall and Rise of Bill Gibb," in the *Daily Mirror* (London), 12 October 1978.

Boyd, Ann, "Gibb's Comeback," in the *Observer* (London), 22 October 1978.

"Bill Gibb Comes Back with Flowers," in *Art & Design* (London), November 1985.

"Obituary: Bill Gibb," in the *Daily Telegraph* (London), 4 January 1988.

"Bill Gibb, 44, Fashion Designer for the Famous," in *Chicago Tribune,* 7 January 1988.

O'Dwyer, Tom, "Bill Gibb—An Appreciation," in *Fashion Weekly* (London), 14 January 1988.

Rancer, Katherine, "Bill Gibb: 1943–1988," in *Vogue* (London), March 1988.

* * *

Arriving in London at the age of 19 from northern Scotland, Bill Gibb was already obsessed with the dream of a career in fashion. He trained at St. Martin's School of Art, then at the Royal College under the aegis of Professor Janey Ironside. An unprecedented flow of new talent was to emerge from the college in the early 1960s. For the next three years Gibb worked for Baccarat, the prestigious London fashion house, before setting up his own company in 1972 with a complete team, including designers, cutter, and business manager. By 1975 he was in retail.

In the early 1970s unconventionality was the order of the day and Gibb was one of several young designers in the British wholesale market whose work reflected this trend. He responded to the new predilection for romantic and ethnic clothes, inspired by the folk costumes of Europe or the Near East and displaying, too, a feeling of nostalgia for the dress of an earlier historical age, with his full-length skirts and billowing slashed sleeves.

Gibb's was a career of considerable variety and change, "I strove for the top and achieved it within ten years," he said. He believed consummately in his "rare gift...to design beautiful clothes" which would appeal to the sensuality of women. This talent led him through a series of outlets from the personal customer to department stores, from boutiques to newspaper and magazine fashion features, to the opening of his first shop in London's Bond Street in 1975, and was to earn him an international reputation for unique special occasion clothes.

Always an individualist, Gibb was faithful to his own design principles, which relied on the enterprising and ingenious use of textures, weaves, and patterns in fabrics and knitting. Boldly inventive to the point of abandon at times, he mixed and matched materials and colors. His mood was romantic and far out: the effects often larger than life and always unmistakably his own. "I feel," he had said, "rather than dictate. I create a mood." Gibb wanted to create coordinates that gave women choice and pleasure to assemble in the "Gibb style," and with homage to the ethnic feeling of the day, he mixed florals with geometrics, tartans with checks, and produced sunray pleated, beaded and fringed separates, all of which became very popular.

Gibb's output during the 1970s was of such a consistently high standard, it verged on couture. He was probably best known for his evening gowns, fabulous concoctions in floaty and exotic fabrics embellished with appliqués or heavily embroidered nets and lace, silks, brocades, and chiffon panels. In this vein was his 1976 hooded cape, a favorite shape, and voluminous smocks, and kimonos with colored braid trims.

Gibb confessed to a strong feeling for knitwear, which he attributed to his Celtic roots, and he certainly produced some very fine knitted garments, reflecting an interest in soft, thinner fabrics, layered upon themselves, which originated with the Italian school of designers, notably the Missoni family. He also made some beautifully elaborate outfits in printed wool, often Liberty fabrics. By the mid-1970s Gibb was creating stunning leather clothes, using the softest of skins for coats and jackets with wide collars and peplums.

Throughout most of the 1970s Gibb ran a small wholesale business, but was forced into liquidation. A brief period of financial support followed, but it is doubtful whether he enjoyed the restrictions and deadlines implicit in such an arrangement. The mid-1980s saw a brief recovery and, with a renewed collaboration with the knitwear designer Kaffe Fassett, Gibb showed a collection at the London Fashion Week in 1985. His clothing was roundly applauded, with critics dubbing him the "the master of the decorative," praising his "simply cut, richly colored knitted suits and throws," and what was characterized as his "fairytale exercises in the baroque, the beaded, and the burnished."

Gibb will best be remembered for his flights of fancy, and his unique contribution to 20th-century fashion. As *Vogue* said in 1962, in a feature called "Fresh Air in the Rag Trade," for "the first time the young people who work in the rag trade are making clothes which are relevant to the way they live…ours is the first generation that can express itself on its own terms." Bill Gibb was very much a product of his time, a free spirit. He died at the very young age of 44, in January 1988, from bowel cancer.

—Elian McCready

GIGLI, Romeo

Italian designer

Born: Castelbolognese, Faenza, Italy, 12 December 1949. **Education:** Studied architecture; has traveled the world extensively. **Family:** Married; children: Diletta. **Career:** First collection for Quickstep by Luciano Papini; small collection of handknits, 1972; designer, Dimitri Couture, New York, 1979; Romeo Gigli label, from 1981; first showing, 1982; designer, Romeo Gigli for Zamasport, from 1984; distribution agreement with Takashimaya, 1987; opened Corso Como boutique, Milan, 1988; collaboration with Ermenegildo Zegna Group, from 1989; *Romeo di Romeo Gigli,* women's fragrance launched and Paris store opened, 1989; lower-priced G. Gigli sportswear line introduced and New York store opened, 1990; formation of NUNO to distribute G. Gigli line, 1992; made limited edition handmade rugs for Christopher Farr, 1993; signature line of jeans, 1996; **Awards:** Accademia del Profumo award [for fragrance packaging], 1990; Woolmark award, 1990; American Fragrance Foundation award [fragrance packaging], 1991. **Address:** Via Fumagalli, 6–20143 Milan, Italy. **Website:** www.romeogigli.it.

Publications

On GIGLI:

Books

Martin, Richard, and Harold Koda, *Orientalism: Visions of the East in Western Dress* (exhibition catalogue), New York 1994.

Romeo Gigli, fall/winter 2001 collection: wool suit. © AP/Wide World Photos.

Stegemeyer, Anne, *Who's Who in Fashion, Third Edition,* New York, 1996.

Articles

Kellett, Caroline, "Cue: New Talent, Take Two: Romeo Gigli," in *Vogue* (London), March 1986.

"Ferre and Gigli: Architects of a Modern Style," in *Elle* (London), October 1986.

Cocks, Jay, "The Color of New Blood: Some Snazzy Duds from Three Upstarts," in *Time,* 10 November 1986.

Morena, Daniela, "The Solitary Chic of Romeo Gigli," in *Interview* (New York), December 1987.

"In diretta da Milano: I virtuosi difetti di Gigli," in *Donna* (Milan), February 1988.

Brubach, Holly, "The Master of Understatement," in *Vogue,* May 1988.

"Designer Focus: Romeo Gigli," in *Cosmopolitan* (London), August 1988.

"Opinions: Romeo Gigli," in *Donna,* September 1988.

Gross, Michael, "Romeo, Romeo: The Monk of Milan," in *New York,* 5 December 1988.
Thim, Dennis, "Romeo and Paris: A New Love Story," in *WWD,* 22 March 1989.
"Gigli's Genius," in *International Textiles* (London), May 1989.
Rafferty, Diane, "The Empress' New Clothes," in *Connoisseur* (New York), July 1989.
Petkanas, Christopher, "Romeo, Romeo," in *Harper's Bazaar,* August 1989.
Pringle, Colombe, "Au pays de Romeo," in *Vogue* (Paris), August 1989.
Alexander, Hilary, "Romeo's Affairs," in *Women's Journal* (London), October 1989.
"The Designers Talk Passion, Whimsy, and Picassos," in *ARTnews* (New York), September 1990.
Lesser, Guy, "Milan: One Night Art Extravaganzas," in *ARTnews,* September 1990.
Gerrie, Anthea, "Designer Profile: Romeo Gigli," in *Clothes Show* (London), March 1992.
Buckley, Richard, "Romeo's Imbroglio," in *Mirabella* (New York), March 1992.
Spindler, Amy M., "Lagerfeld Tones Down the Look at Chanel," in the *New York Times,* 21 March 1995.
Menkes, Suzy, "Gender-Bending: Milan Shows Reopen Familiar Debate," in the *International Herald Tribune,* 11 March 1997.
Allen, Derek, "Romeo Gigli: Alchemist Par Excellence," available online at Yes Please, www.yesplease.it, January 1999.
"Romeo Gigli," [profile], available online at Moda Online, www.modaonline.it, 7 September 2001.

* * *

Romeo Gigli produces clothes that are always subtle and sophisticated. He blends a spectrum of muted colors with a fluid sense of cut and drape to give a feeling of balance and harmony to all his designs, perhaps as a result of his architectural training. His prime influences are fine art and travel, both apparent in the Renaissance luxury of the fabrics he uses and the mix of cultural influences discernible in their shaping and decoration. A soft sculptural beauty pervades both his day and eveningwear, with a talent for shaping clothes to the body in an elegantly flattering way without ever clinging too tightly or restrictively.

His womenswear encapsulates these qualities and has been very influential, having taken its cue from the elastic fluidity of dancewear to produce garments that are soft and feminine. Although Gigli's clothes are obviously designed for the busy modern woman, they are never merely a series of mix-and-match separates, nor indeed are they as ostentatious as the work of some of his Italian counterparts. His use of stretch fabrics and rich warm woollen suiting have inspired many imitators with their purity of cut and sensuous, body-skimming fit. The classical virtues of the body which pervade Gigli's work give a feeling of an evolutionary process to fashion, rather than a slavish following of seasonal dictates, and it is perhaps this innate classicism that gives his clothes a timeless air.

Some Gigli garments, like his richly enveloping embroidered coats, seem destined to become treasured collectors' items, passed on like heirlooms rather than falling victim to the fickleness often

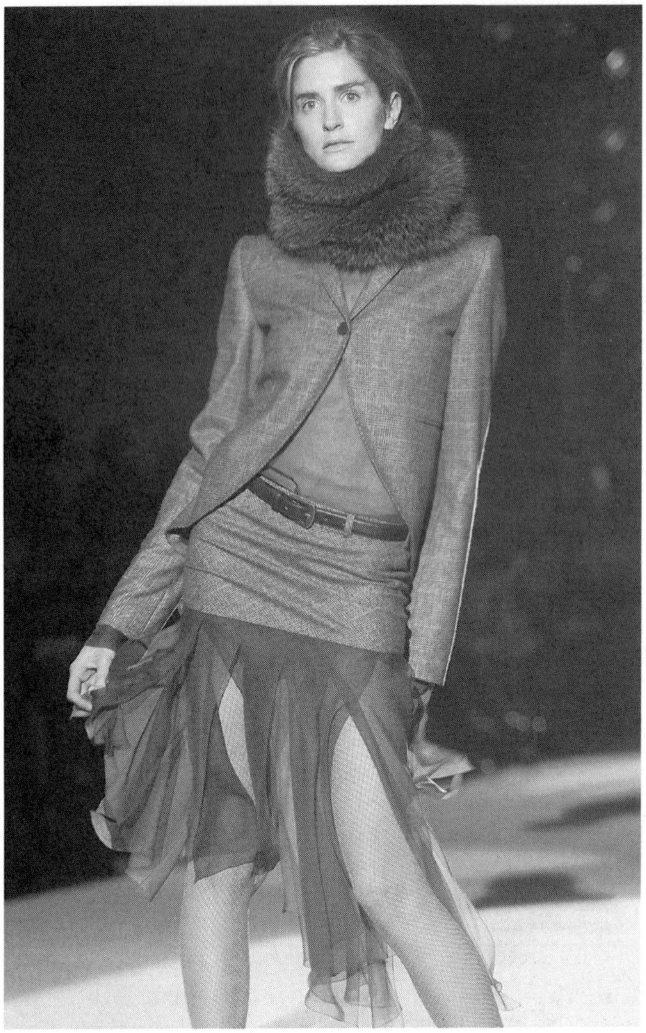

Romeo Gigli, fall/winter 2001 ready-to-wear collection. © AP/ Wide World Photos.

associated with fashion. His use of detailing is subtle and uncluttered, as in the minimal silhouette of the Empire line dresses and ballet-styled wrap tops introduced and popularized during the mid-1980s. When decoration is used it follows his restrained ideals of iridescent beauty—golden thread embroidered around the edge of a soft bolero jacket, evoking a feeling of the East, dull amber gold beads making a shimmering glow of fringing from waist to floor, or thousands of glittering gunmetal blue beads on a cocoon-like evening dress.

If Gigli's strength is perhaps his gently romantic womenswear, his menswear is nonetheless notable for the same kind of muted colours and sinuous cut, giving it a feeling of luxury without any obvious show of wealth. Suiting is again unstructured, working with the shape of the body rather than against it. His jackets are often high-buttoned, with an extra sense of depth and texture given to their rich wools by the subtle range of mossy greens, dull aubergine and bitter chocolate browns used to stripe the fabric. It is this kind of color sense which, combined with clever mixing of shiny and matte fabrics, marks all his work. Even his most formal menswear has an effortless elegance and a fluidity of cut, which have made it unfailingly popular with discerning male customers.

Gigli has followed the increasingly popular notion of the diffusion range with the more practical daywear basics of his G. Gigli line, launched in 1990. Here the silhouette is bulkier, with rich berry chenilles and sage and golden corduroys being used to produce a collection of classic zip-style cardigans, hooded tops, trousers, and soft leggings for men and women. Although less ethereally beautiful than much of his main collection, there is still the same signature use of contrasting fabrics and muted colors to produce a very tactile appeal through texture and shade.

An intelligent balance of all elements of design and choice of textiles makes Gigli's work uniquely sophisticated and beautiful. His subtlety of touch and soft sculptural forms have influenced all levels of design from the High Street up, and his work has continued to develop along his self-assigned tenets of harmony and balance, always retaining a feeling of sensuous luxury.

While Gigli continued to debut collections in Paris, he returned to the Milan catwalk in 1997 after an absence of seven years. Critics approved of his women's line featuring three-piece pantsuits, skirts, and knit dresses and his men's collection of retooled jackets, shoes and ties. As always, his use of fabric and texture drew the most praise. Suzy Menkes, who had sung Gigli's praises after his first Paris showing years before, enthused, "But the joy of the show was in its opening coats in fabrics that seemed to draw their rich colors and lattice or tapestry textures from the artistic soul of Italy."

By the 21st century the Gigli name could be found on an increasing number of products, from ties, shoes, and eyewear to fabrics and handmade rugs for Christopher Farr. The limited edition *kilims* featured wool from Kurdish sheep, and were handmade on looms in Turkey. Gigli continues to be propelled by his beliefs in intrinsic beauty; as he told Derek Allen in a 1999 interview for the Italian website Yes Please, "All the pieces I create must be beautiful in character, and that means they must possess beauty outside the context of the overall project. If I remove a piece from the collection and it doesn't fuction in alternative contexts, then it lacks the necessary sense of balance." For Gigli, balance and beauty go hand in hand.

—Rebecca Arnold; updated by Nelly Rhodes

GIRBAUD, Marithé & François

French designer team

Born: *Marithé Bachellerie*—Lyon, France, 1942; *François Girbaud*—Mazamet, France, 1945. **Joint Career:** Business formed in 1965; showed first collection, 1968, first boutique selling Girbaud-designed jeans opened, Paris, 1969; Halles Capone boutique opened in Paris, from 1972; first U.S. shop, Nantucket Island, Massachusetts, 1984; Jeaneration 21 line introduced, 1993; HiTech/HiTouch line developed, 1993; other lines included Complements for women, Closed for men, Reproductions for children, Complete Look accessories, Kelian-Girbaud shoes, Maillaparty, Compagnie des Montagnes et des Forêts, 11342, and Millesimes; launched promotional campaign for X-yoke shorts called the Cool Front featuring in-store refrigerator displays, 1996; moved men's jeanswear license from V.F. Corporation to I.C.

Marithé & François Girbaud, fall 2000 collection. © AP/Wide World Photos/Fashion Wire Daily.

Isaacs & Company, 1997; added women's jeanswear license to Isaacs line, 1998; introduced Freedom Jeans for women, a variant on cargo pants, 1998; introduced Denim Tool Belts, 1999; sponsored College Rock Tour 2001, a fashion show and concert series, 2001. **Address:** 8 rue Babylone, Paris 75007, France.

Publications

On the GIRBAUDS:

Books

Stegemeyer, Anne, *Who's Who in Fashion, Third Edition,* New York, 1996.

Articles

La Ferla, Ruth, "François & Marithé Girbaud: Beyond Fashion," in the *Daily News Record,* 20 September 1982.

Daria, Irene, "After the Switch: The Girbauds," in *WWD,* 21 December 1984.

Walsleben, Elizabeth C., "The Girbauds' Design is in Their Jeans," in *California Apparel News* (Los Angeles), 11–17 July 1986.

Daily News Record (New York), 11 February 1987.

Bloomfield, Judy, "Girbaud: Keeping It Simple," in *WWD,* 3 February 1988.
Martin, Richard, "Wordrobe: The Messages of Word and Image in Textile and Apparel Design of the 1980s," *Textile and Text,* 12 January–February 1989.
———, "The Eleventh Little Middle Ages: Signs and Chivalry in the Reconstitution of Medieval Dress in the 1980s," *Textile and Text,* 12 March 1990.
Vasilopoulos, Vicki, "The World According to Marithé and François," in the *Daily News Record* 3 May 1993.
Spevack, Rachel, "A Cold Front Moving In," in the *Daily News Record,* 8 April 1996.
Socha, Miles, "Girbauds' Freedom," in *WWD,* 26 March 1998.
Curan, Catherine, "I.C. Isaacs Hopes Girbaud License Can Stem Flow of Red Ink," in the *Daily News Record,* 7 December 1998.
Socha, Miles, "Gladstone's Plan for a New Girbaud," in *WWD,* 4 February 1999.
Malone, Scott, "Girbaud Jeans: On the Rise," in *WWD,* 3 February 2000.
Cunningham, Thomas, "I.C. Isaacs Breathes New Life into Girbaud," in the *Daily News Record,* 5 June 2000.

* * *

Marithé and François Girbaud have created fashion that emanates from the street; reveling in design problems of cylinders, mutation, and reversibility; and bringing high-style aspirations to casual materials and effects. Their proclivity to oversizing seems akin to Japanese design and Middle Eastern and East Asian peasant garb, as their futurist vocabulary of tubes and metamorphosis can seem a highly conceptual eventuality worthy of Marinetti or Balla, but also functions as fluid streetwear. Their deconstructivist bent, exposing the elements of garment manufacture, parallels Karl Lagerfeld at Chanel, but their medium is a more accessible casual wear—almost hip-hop homeboy style in New York or the carefree flair of a weekend in Paris. In the casual jeans-based look the Girbauds have created and recreated, they have consistently been the most innovative, experimental, concept-driven designers.

The Girbauds have, in fact, commanded the avant-garde position in casualwear, customarily characterized by stasis, in the manner of high-fashion designers such as Jean-Paul Gaultier or Issey Miyake, thriving on conceptual development and change yet never failing to represent the irrefutable leadership position in the field. Ruth La Ferla, of the *Daily News Record,* called François Girbaud "three parts fashion technician, one part theoretician," yet the Girbauds have also been savvy interpreters, bringing out Ninja-inspired pantaloons with ankle snaps, rugged survival wear, and sophisticated 1940s and 1950s revival-wear. Beginning in retailing, the Girbauds were as street smart as they were conceptually witty and ingenious. François Girbaud told Irene Daria of *Women's Wear Daily,* in December 1984, "We design from the streets. We start at the bottom and move up."

Their streets are global. Roomy drawstring trousers, loose shirts worn over the waist, and other styles evade traditional European and American notions of fit. The Amerasian collection for summer 1984—featuring Moudjahadin outfits with drawstring jackets and wide tubular trousers inspired by the Middle East and Afghanistan as well as boxy jackets inspired by China—typifies the eclectic, globetrotting ethos of the Girbauds' design. For summer 1985, the Jet Laggers collection showed no straggling or fatigue: trousers called

Marithé & François Girbaud, fall 2000 collection. © AP/Wide World Photos/Fashion Wire Daily.

Kaboul/Champs Elysées could be worn in the Middle East or in Paris in their amplitude, cargo pockets adding to the engorged size, with a rustic combination of buttons and drawstrings. For fall 1986, big dhoti trousers and exotic cumberbunds and kilto-pants with voluminous tops and tapered legs combined East and West, exercise and boudoir. Yet the virtuoso accomplishment of the Girbauds is their repertory of trouser options for men and women, international in possibilities and strikingly original and inventive in realization.

The Girbauds have also been aware of the history of Western dress. In menswear, their high-waisted Hollywood style for fall 1987 evoked the glamor era of movies in the 1940s. Their interest has also been in materials, from quilting and fabric-backed leather to a soft, stone-washed denim. Another conceptual element of the Girbaud style is the didactic display of the garment's construction, one Momento Due jacket revealing its pattern components, other garments inscribed with all their wearing options. In addition to the language of clothing, the Girbauds have played with language itself, vocabulary, hieroglyphs, and alphabets appearing again and again in the collection.

When interviewed, the designers like to suggest their work is a perfect synthesis of their childhood preoccupations, she with creating doll clothes, he with American pop culture, films, and military outfits.

There is truth to this proposition, yet it also is unlikely that these two designers who began as retailers are only pursuing personal desires. The casual clothing they have created is imbued with heritage, even if this legacy is working clothing, brought to the present in technical and even futuristic ways. In the evident conceptualism of their clothing (and in their bridge lines), they have expanded the market of casual clothing beyond the young, so their clothes are as appropriate to the market for persons in their 30s and 40s as they are to the primary market for jeans of teens or in their 20s.

The Girbauds face many competitors in stylish casual wear for the young; they command the market for an abiding casual style for an older market, which has been increasing. In a July 1986 article, the *California Apparel News* reported, "In an industry where fashion changes with each season, the Girbauds' clothes have kept the image of comfort while growing in style and versatility to become 'concept dressing'."

Innovation has remained a keystone of the Girbauds' line each season. Their fall 2001 collection combined futuristic and prairie touches, which, according to *Women's Wear Daily (WWD),* unexpectedly worked well together. Although both *WWD* and the *Daily News Record* commented on the Girbauds' relative conservatism and simplicity in this collection, they noted the inclusion of items more typical of their work, such as down-filled shirts and navy boiled-wool jackets with exposed seams in orange. These nicely complemented the simpler direction in their jeanswear, critics said.

François Girbaud expressed his frustration with the retro trends in jeanswear design at the turn of the century. He told *WWD* in a December 2000 interview, "I do not believe in that 1970s look. It is like opening up a book about the '70s and taking something from it—we already did that when we were there."

Fabric innovation, of which the Girbauds were always proponents, has continued with projects such as Blue Eternal, a treated denim that holds its color after multiple trips to the laundry, as well as the development of a detergent to revive denim. In their designs, the Girbauds have often used synthetic fibers to emulate natural fibers—sometimes in combination with actual natural fibers—resulting in more flexibility of design. Synthetics, for example, can be fused or heated and not just saddle-stitched.

In the late 1990s and early 2000s, the Girbauds' designs were emblematic of "utilitarian chic." Shirts and jeans featured many pockets and were made of wrinkle-resistant fabrics or were permanently wrinkled. An example of the latter was a vest twisted to look like a Sharpei's skin, as described by the Philippine publication *Business World* in November 2000. The Freedom cargo pant featured pockets for cell phones, personal digital assistants (PDAs), and pagers; an anorak had a front zipper allowing for a baby carrier; a utility bag with pockets was sold under the Denim Tool Belt brand.

According to the *Daily News Record* in June 2000, one of the Girbauds' bestsellers is the shuttle, a carpenter pant with Velcro straps. Popular basic items include Brand X jeans with crisscross hip stitching and the Cowboy, which features a twist at the top of the front pocket, making it easier to insert and remove items. Complementing these basics are the Girbauds' newer, more experimental items, which include a stretch gabardine and nylon "climbing" pant with a belt buckle that the wearer can lock with a plastic key. Additionally, their European Sporcity brand serves as their couture sportwear line on the Continent.

From a business point of view, the Girbaud jeanswear line has suffered ups and downs in the U.S. market. With its first licensee, V.F. Corporation, the Girbaud brand reached an estimated $250 million in annual volume in 1992, but after a too-quick expansion and overexposure, sales fell to less than a tenth of its previous high. In 1997 the men's license was transferred to a new manufacturer, I.C. Isaacs & Company, which added the women's license a year later. Isaacs struggled financially in the late 1990s and early 2000s, leading it to shed some of its brands, but the Girbaud line has remained a bright spot.

Women's clothing is seen as a business segment with significant growth potential in the U.S., where it accounts for between 15 percent and 20 percent of sales volume for the Girbaud lines, compared to about 70 percent in Europe. In general, Isaacs is working to limit distribution in order to prevent the too-fast growth that occurred in the early and mid-1990s.

The Girbauds enjoy breaking away from what other designers are doing in an attempt to create, rather than follow, fashion trends. Their designs always emphasize utility but can be far out of the mainstream in terms of style. As François told *Women's Wear Daily* (14 December 2000), "Our work is sometimes a little crazy—sometimes we are on the bull's-eye of fashion and sometimes we are not."

—Richard Martin; updated by Karen Raugust

GIROMBELLI, Arnoldo and Donatella

See GENNY SpA

GIVENCHY, Hubert de

French designer

Born: Hubert James Marcel Taffin de Givenchy, in Beauvais, 21 February 1927. **Education:** Studied at the Collège Felix-Fauré, Beauvais and Montalembert; École Nationale Supérieure des Beaux Arts, Paris; Faculty of Law, University of Paris. **Career:** Worked in Paris for Lucien Lelong, 1945–46; for Piguet, 1946–48; for Jacques Fath, 1948–49; for Schiaparelli, 1949–51; established Maison Givenchy, 1952; president, Société Givenchy Couture and Société des Parfums Givenchy, from 1954; sold company to LVMH, 1988; presented last show and retired, 1995; John Galliano hired as house designer, 1995; replaced by Alexander McQueen, 1996; Hong Kong flagship opened, 1999; opened new Paris showroom, 2000; Julien Macdonald signed as artistic director, 2001; fragrances include *De,* 1957; *L'Interdit,* 1957; *Givenchy III,* 1970; *L'Eau de Givenchy,* 1980; *Vetyver*; *Ysatis,* 1984; *Xeryus,* 1986; *Amarige,* 1991; *Fleur d'Interdit,* 1994; *Organza,* 1996; *Amarige Extravagance,* 1998; *Hot Couture,* 2000. **Exhibitions:** *Givenchy: 30 Years,* Fashion Institute of Technology, New York, 1982; *Givenchy: 40 Years of Creation,* Palais Galliera, Paris, 1991. **Address:** 3 avenue George V, 75008 Paris, France. **Website:** www.givenchy.com.

Publications

On GIVENCHY:

Books

Lynam, Ruth, ed., *Paris Fashion: The Great Designers and Their Creations,* London, 1972.

Hubert de Givenchy, fall/winter 2000–01 haute couture collection: spangled decollete dress designed by Alexander McQueen. © AFP/CORBIS.

Fashion Institute of Technology, *Givenchy: 30 Years* [exhibition catalogue], New York, 1982.
Milbank, Caroline Rennolds, *Couture: The Great Designers,* New York, 1985.
Leese, Elizabeth, *Costume Design in the Movies,* New York, 1991.
Givenchy: 40 Years of Creation [exhibition catalogue], with texts by Catherine Join-Dieterle, Susan Train and Marie-Jose Lepicard, Paris, 1991.
Martin, Richard, and Harold Koda, *Bloom,* New York, 1995.
Mainiece, Violeta, *Apropos Givenchy,* Paris, 1998.
Mohry, Françoise, *The Givenchy Style,* Paris, 1998.

Articles

"Givenchy: 30 ans de couture," in *Textile Suisses* (Lausanne), April 1982.
"Givenchy Bucol," in *Vogue* (Paris), February 1985.
Arroyuelo, Javier, "La haute couture: Givenchy," in *Vogue* (Paris), March 1985.
"Le point sur les collections: Givenchy," in *L'Officiel* (Paris), September 1986.
Menkes, Suzy, "Strong Chanel Holds Up Couture's Falling Walls," in the *International Herald Tribune* (Paris), 21 March 1995.
Denbigh, Dorie, "The Muse and the Master (Audrey Hepburn and Fashion Designer Hubert de Givenchy)," in *Time,* 17 April 1995.
"Moving Day in Paris: It Was an Emotional Farewell to Givenchy...," in *WWD,* 12 July 1995.
Laushway, Esther, "Givenchy to Galliano," in *Europe,* October 1995.
Min, Janet, "A Cut Above," in *People,* 15 January 1996.
"Givenchy: The Lady and the Tramp," in *WWD,* 13 March 1997.
Singer, Natasha, "Comrade McQueen Takes Moscow," in *WWD,* 10 December 1997.
Daswani, Khavita, "Givenchy Continues to Conquer Asia," in *DNR,* 24 November 1999.
Weisman, Katherine, "Shaking Things Up at Givenchy," in *WWD,* 10 January 2000.
Naughton, Julie, "Givenchy: The Fashion of Fragrance," in *WWD,* 22 September 2000.
Givhan, Robin, "Givenchy's Loss, Gucci's Gain; Designer Alexander McQueen Leaves LVMH," in the *Washington Post,* 5 December 2000.
Socha, Miles, "Givenchy Cancels Big Show," in *WWD,* 19 January 2001.
Menkes, Suzy, "Welsh Wizard Julien Macdonald Takes Over at Givenchy," in the *International Hearld Tribune,* 15 March 2001.
Socha, Miles, "Julien de Givenchy," in *WWD,* 16 March 2001.
"Grace Note, Club Gear and Futurism—Alexander McQueen Said a Graceful Farewell to Givenchy," in *WWD,* 19 March 2001.
Socha, Miles, "Givenchy's Clean Slate: Restoring the Elegance to a Venerable House," in *WWD,* 5 July 2001.
Frankel, Susannah, "In the Shadow of Greatness," in the *Indepedent,* 15 August 2001.

* * *

In 1992 Hubert de Givenchy celebrated his 40th anniversary as a couturier. Givenchy chose his vocation at the age of ten, and as a youngster admired the designs of Elsa Schiaparelli and Madame Grès. Later, after stints with Jacques Fath, Robert Piguet, and Lucien Lelong, he spent four years working for Schiaparelli, during which he designed the clothes sold in her boutique, many of them separates, an American idea new to Paris in the early 1950s, for which Givenchy gained a following.

Although he is now appropriately acclaimed as a classicist and traditionalist, it was as an *enfant terrible* of sorts that Givenchy burst upon the couture scene in 1952, just weeks before his 25th birthday. He had a novel collection based on separates, in which even eveningwear was conceptualized as a series of interchangeable pieces. Also noteworthy in this first collection was his generous use of white cotton shirting, which had an economic as well as an aesthetic rationale: the shirting was as inexpensive as it was fresh-looking. The Bettina blouse Givenchy used in later years as his signature was part of this cotton group, and it has reappeared on and off in more simplified and refined incarnations.

Again and again in Givenchy's early years as a couturier, his designs appealed to young women, and the most famous of them was Audrey Hepburn, the actress whose rise to fame paralleled his own. Givenchy created the clothes worn by Hepburn in several of her most beloved roles, starting with *Sabrina* (1954) for which Edith Head won the Oscar for costume design and Givenchy received no credit at all. Although Head designed some of Hepburn's *Sabrina* wardrobe, the

Audrey Hepburn, with William Holden, in a publicity still from the film *Sabrina* (1954) wearing a gown designed by Hubert de Givenchy. © Bettmann/CORBIS.

Hubert de Givenchy being applauded by his models at the last show before his retirement, the spring/summer 1996 ready-to-wear collection. © AP/Wide World Photos.

very soigné black tailleur and hat in which Sabrina returned from Paris, and the strapless white organdie gown embroidered with black and white flowers (which was the envy of every young woman who saw the film), were both from Givenchy's collection.

Givenchy's designs were the clothes that transformed Hepburn from charming gamine to paragon of chic sophistication. Similar transformations were at the heart of *Love in the Afternoon* (1957), *Funny Face* (1957), and *Breakfast at Tiffany's* (1961). By 1963, when *Charade* appeared, the gamine had finally grown into the sophisticate, and "the world's youngest couturier" had become the most elegant of classical couturiers. Hepburn remained Givenchy's muse for almost 40 years, the quintessential Givenchy client, even flying into Paris from Switzerland to sit in the front row for his collections until shortly before her death.

Givenchy shared the ideal of creating a perfect, simple dress from a single line with his idol, Balenciaga. When the two men finally met by accident in 1953, they developed a relationship that was perhaps unique in the annals of couture, with Balenciaga giving Givenchy unprecedented access not only to his sketches, but also to his fittings and his workrooms. Starting in 1959, after Givenchy moved to Avenue George V, almost across the street from Balenciaga, they conferred daily, critiquing each other's sketches and collections. Their aesthetic affinity was such that when Balenciaga closed his couture salon, he referred his most valued clients to Givenchy.

Because of the emphasis on line rather than decoration, Givenchy's designs were easy to adapt, endearing him to the many American manufacturers who interpreted them. Givenchy himself helped to make his clothes accessible to a much wider market in the early prelicensing years, designing junior sportswear to be made by American manufacturers with American fabrics, for *Seventeen* and *Glamour* magazines. The caption for *Glamour*'s December 1955 cover, featuring a Givenchy sweater, spoke directly to the appeal of his designs: "The Givenchy marks young chic...meant for long, lean people in pipestem skirts...for when they want to look casual in a worldly way."

In the 1990s Givenchy continued designing fashions that make a woman look beautiful; his œuvre bespeaks restraint and refinement, with gradual transitions from one season and style to the next. Although Givenchy still produced cotton separates, including some with Matisse-inspired patterns in his 40th anniversary collection, his designs have matured along with his original clientèle. Givenchy's creations begin with the fabric; his forte is choosing or developing Europe's most luxurious yet tasteful fabrics and embroideries in an expansive range of colors. From these he creates exquisite couture clothes complementing the lifestyles of a clientèle which has included several of the world's most elegant women. He is known for deceptively simple day dresses, superbly tailored suits, coats that are marvels of line and volume, sumptuous cocktail dresses or suits, extravagant evening dresses that are nevertheless eminently wearable, and hats revealing his sense of whimsy and fantasy.

Givenchy showed his last couture collection in July 1995, amid a crowd of fashion's most respected and well-known designers, all present to pay homage to the departing master. Nudged out of his own empire by LVMH, who brought in wild-child John Galliano, Givenchy was not bowed. "You have to know when to stop," he was quoted in *People* magazine, "that's wisdom." After leaving his design house, Givenchy worked on an exhibit about Balenciaga, and had been commissioned to help restore the magnificent gardens of Versailles.

Givenchy by Galliano was not a success, and the British badboy was abruptly replaced by Alexander McQueen. Though McQueen managed to last five years, until late 2000, he was unhappy and his designs often did not fit Givenchy any better than Galliano's had. McQueen's last hurrah with Givenchy, however, was a brilliant success. *Women's Wear Daily* (19 March 2001) commented, "McQueen passed on his final chance to throw a fashion tantrum chez Givenchy. Instead, he showed beautiful, elegant clothes… McQueen's work is ultimately about tailoring, and he showed one great look after another…."

Welshman Julien Macdonald was the next to come through Givenchy's revolving door, hired in 2001 as McQueen took up with LVMH rival Gucci, who had invested in McQueen's independent design label. Macdonald, a professed admirer of Givenchy, poured over archival designs as inspiration for his first showing in July 2001. Macdonald described his collection to *Women's Wear Daily* (5 July 2001) as "Victorian dressing interpreted through the eyes of Helmut Newton." More importantly perhaps for the venerable house was Macdonald's stance as pupil, "I'm listening to everybody… people have been here for 20 years. I can listen to them and I can learn. Givenchy has huge potential; if it's handled right, it could be one of the biggest fashion brands."

—Arlene C. Cooper; updated by Nelly Rhodes

GODLEY, Georgina

British designer

Born: London, 11 April 1955. **Education:** Putney High School, London; Thames Valley Grammar School, London; Wimbledon School of Art; Brighton Polytechnic; Chelsea School of Art. **Family:** Married Sebastian Conran, 1988; sons: Samuel, Maximillian. **Career:** Worked as art restorer, illustrator, mannequin maker, freelance designer, late 1970s; designer, Brown's, London and Paris, 1979–80; designer/partner, with Scott Crolla, Crolla menswear boutique, London, 1980–85; women's collection added, 1984; director/sole designer, Georgina Godley Ltd., with own label collections, from 1986; presently lecturer, St. Martin's School of Art and School of Fashion and Textiles; member, British Fashion Council Designer Committee. **Collections:** Victoria and Albert Museum, London; Bath Costume Museum, Bath, England. **Address:** 42 Bassett Road, London W10 6JL, England.

Publications

On GODLEY:

Books

McDermott, Catherine, *Street Style: British Design in the 1980s* (exhibition catalogue), London 1987.

De La Haye, Amy, *The Cutting Edge: Fifty Years of British Fashion, 1947–1997,* New York, 1997.

Debrett's People of Today, London, 2001.

Articles

"Cue: Talking to New Designers," in *Vogue* (London), November 1981.

"Scott Crolla & Georgina Godley of Crolla," in *Vogue* (London), November 1982.

Buckley, Richard, "Crolla's Counter Couture," in the magazine supplement to *DNR,* January 1985.

Brampton, Sally, "Fashion Wallahs," in *Vanity Fair* (London), April 1985.

Reed, Paula, "Spirit of Godleyness," in the *Sunday Correspondent* (London), 8 October 1989.

Sharkey, Alix, "On the Trail of the Elusive 'X' Factor," in *The Guardian* (London), 30 April 1990.

Stead, Deborah, "Georgina Godley," in the *New York Times,* 2 July 1990.

MacSweeney, Eve, "London After Dark," in *Harper's Bazaar* (New York), November 1990.

"Architecture: A New Twist in Fashion," in the *Independent,* 27 November 1998.

"Is Fashion Art?" in the *Irish Times,* 8 July 1999.

"Dark, Sexy & Cool," in *ART 4D,* September 2000.

"Reaching the Other Side," in *Cabinet Maker,* 20 October 2000.

"Georgina Godley" online at the Fashion Page, www.fashionz.co.uk, 9 June 2001.

* * *

High-minded, serious, and intellectual in her approach to fashion design, Georgina Godley began her fashion career in the early 1980s in partnership with designer Scott Crolla. They emerged in a period when most of the important designers were making unisex, androgynous clothing. Gender barriers were being broken down, as the difference between clothing for men and women seemed old-fashioned and no longer relevant. The media had latched on to this trend with its enthusiastic hyping of role swapping pop stars like Annie Lennox and trendy male/female design partnerships like Bodymap and Richmond/Cornejo, who were making clothes that anybody could wear. In opposition Georgina Godley returned to the idea of womanliness and the female form. She used floral-patterned chintz or sections of transparent gauze over breasts and referred to female fertility symbols in her advertising, such as a bridal figure gazing adoringly at the male phallus. She also plundered a traditional female submissiveness and medieval imagery in her research.

In many ways Godley has worked against fashion but, rather than taking an aggressively feminist antifashion stance, she has been aesthetic in her reaction. Her first collection without Crolla was entitled Body and Soul. Featuring a body dress, a soul dress, and a muscle dress, the collection celebrated the female form by exaggerating its proportions. Using fabric to drape, pad, pull, and stretch over the body, the results were often distortive and faintly erotic. The aim was simply to exemplify the beauty of a woman's body.

Never a commercial designer, Godley is primitive yet sophisticated: primitive in that she emphasizes and magnifies the primary female form; sophisticated in the fact that the result is often desexed by a high seriousness. The clothing is usually impractical, designed to be collected rather than worn: a clinging, thin white cotton jersey dress inset with organza panels for maximum bodily exposure and a curved wire hem; shaped underwear dresses in which elements of corsetry distort curvaceousness; a pregnancy dress, padded to make the wearer look pregnant; a pair of hoof-bottomed trousers; and an infamous wedding dress with cutouts for the breasts.

Godley is similar in context to her contemporary, Azzedine Alaïa, but whereas Alaïa's clothes are erotic and sexy in their contouring of the body, Godley's clothes are womanly. Alaïa's clothes create a curvaceous shape by reacting with the body; Godley's often have their exaggerated shapes constructed onto the clothes.

Whether Godley can be termed a fashion designer is arguable because her clothes have often reacted against contemporary trends. Her work is designed for the connoisseur of specialist clothing, rather than mass public acceptance.

When Tom Dixon began directing design at Habitat, a retail chain, in 1998, he formed a team of hot new stylists, including Mathew Hillon, Ross Menuez, and Godley. Their immediate focus was the "Dark & Sexy Home,"an application of art to domestics. Early in 2000, Staffordshire University reported on Godley's switch from fashion design for the likes of Paul Smith and Jasper and Joseph Conran to ceramics. As head of home accessories for Habitat, she critiqued crafts and design at the MA Ceramics Show 2000 in terms of contribution to a style-driven, label-conscious market. In her opinion, "Today's buying public is hungry for quality and design, they now want to invest in something that's good and special."

Key to her career shift is the challenge of British excellence and its global impact on design. Godley noted that she and other artisans were influenced by Jonathan Ive's transformation of Apple computers with a unique blend of function and innovation. She lauded student efforts with the comment that "Almost every item I've seen could go straight into production."

—Kevin Almond; updated by Mary Ellen Snodgrass

GRÈS, Madame

French designer

Born: Germain "Alix" Barton in Paris, 30 November 1903. **Education:** Studied painting and sculpture, Paris. **Family:** Married Serge Czerefkov, late 1930s; daughter: Anne. **Career:** Served three-month apprenticeship with Premet, Paris, 1930; made and sold *toiles* using the name Alix Barton, Paris, 1930s; designer, Maison Alix (not her own house), 1934–40; sold rights to the name Alix and adopted Grès, from husband's surname, 1940; director, Grès Couture, from 1942; accessory line introduced, 1976; ready-to-wear line introduced, 1980; retired, 1988; perfumes include *Cabochard,* 1959, *Grès pour Homme,* 1965, *Qui Pro Quo,* 1976, *Eau de Grès,* 1980, *Alix,* 1981, *Grès Nonsieu,* 1982, and *Cabotine de Grès,* 1990. **Exhibition:** Madame Grès, Metropolitan Museum of Art, New York, 1994. **Awards:** Named Chevalier de la Légion d'Honneur, 1947; Dé d'Or award, 1976; New York University Creative Leadership in the Arts award, 1978. **Died:** 24 November 1993, in the South of France (not made public until December 1994).

Publications

On GRÈS:

Books

Perkins, Alice K., *Paris Couturiers and Milliners,* New York, 1949.

Lynam, Ruth, editor, *Couture: An Illustrated History of the Great Paris Designers and Their Creations,* New York, 1972.

Milbank, Caroline Rennolds, *Couture: The Great Designers,* New York, 1985.

Guillen, Pierre-Yves, and Claude, Jacqueline, *The Golden Thimble: French Haute Couture,* Paris, 1990.

Steele, Valerie, *Women of Fashion: Twentieth-Century Designers,* New York, 1991.

Petit Précis de Mode: Collections du Musée de la Mode, Marseilles, 1992.

Martin, Richard, and Harold Koda, *Madame Grès,* Metropolitan Museum of Art (exhibition catalogue), New York, 1994.

Stegemeyer, Anne, *Who's Who in Fashion, Third Edition,* New York, 1996.

Articles

"Grès Grey Eminence," in *Realities* (San José, California), July 1965.

"Mme. Grès," in *Current Biography* (New York), January 1980.

"Mme. Grès, Hélène de Paris," in *Jardin des Modes* (Paris), December/January 1980–81.

Villiers le Moy, Pascale, "The Timeless Fashions of Madame Grès," in *Connoisseur,* August 1982.

Sciaky, Françoise, "Lovely Grès," in *American Fabrics and Fashions* (New York), No. 128, 1983.

"Mme. Grès for the People," in *Connoisseur,* January 1985.

Cooper, Arlene, "How Madame Grès Sculpts with Fabric," in *Threads* (Newtown, Connecticut), April/May 1987.

Aillaud, Charlotte, "Timeless Style of the Parisian Couturiere," in *Architectural Digest,* September 1988.

Bernasconi, Silvana, "Madame Grès," in *Vogue* (Italy), March 1994.

"The Ionic Woman," in *Harper's Bazaar* (New York), September 1994.

Auchincloss, Eve, "Eminence Grès," in *Town & Country* (New York), September 1994.

"New York: Grès Gardens," in *WWD,* 1 November 1994.

Benaim, Laurence, "La Mort confisquée de Madame Grès," in *Le Monde* (Paris), 13 December 1994.

Deeny, Godfrey, "The Strange, Secret Death of Madame Grès," in *WWD,* 14 December 1994.

Spindler, Amy M., "Surprising the Fashion World, to the Last," in the *New York Times,* 14 December 1994.

Mulvagh, Jane, "Grès Eminence," in *Vogue* (London), May 1995.

* * *

According to many who attended, the Madame Grès showings were exquisite anguish. With alterations up to the last minute by the

Design by Madame Grès, 1946. © Genevieve Naylor/CORBIS.

designer, models would be delayed, garments could appear trailing strings, and long intervals might occur between the display of individual garments. At the very end, a flurry of models in flowing draped jersey evening dresses would come out on the runway in rapid succession, an abrupt finale to a halting presentation. Known for designing with the immediacy of draping with cloth, Grès was the self-committed and consummate artist, never the agreeable couturière. Her white salon bespoke her austerity in engineering and her clarity in grace.

Grès shunned the promotional grace and personal identification of many fashion designers, insisting instead on rigorous attention to the clothing. First a sculptor, Grès depended upon sculptural insight even as she, in her most famous and signature form, brought the Louvre's statue of the *Nike of Samothrace* to life in clothing form. Grès' draped and pleated silk jerseys flattered the body with the minimalist and rationalist radicalism of 1930s design, but provided a classical serenity as well. The real achievement of the draped dresses was not their idyllic evocation, but their integrity. They were a unified construction, composed of joined fabric panels continuously top to bottom, fullest in the swirling flutes of the skirt, tucked at the waist, elegantly pinched through the bodice, and surmounted at the neckline—often one-shouldered—with the same materials resolved into three-dimensional twists. Grès was creating no mere lookalike to classical statuary, but a characteristically modern enterprise to impart the body within clothing.

Grès, however, was never a one-dress designer. Her 1934 black Cellophane dress with a black-seal-lined cape (photographed by Hoyningen-Heuné) is, as *Vogue* described, a scarab, but with the cling of bias cut. Following a trip to the Far East in 1936, Grès created a brocaded "Temple of Heaven" dress, inspired by Javanese dancing costumes. Throughout the 1930s, she took inspiration from North Africa and Egypt; in the 1940s, after managing to keep her business alive through most of the war, Grès became interested in tailoring and created some of the most disciplined suit tailoring for daywear in the 1940s and 1950s.

By the 1960s and 1970s, Grès was translating the planarity of regional costume into a simplified *origami* of flat planes, ingeniously manipulated on the body to achieve a minimalism akin to sportswear. Ironically, she who exemplified the persistence of couture treated the great dress with the modernist lightness of sportswear, and she who held out so long against ready-to-wear turned with a convert's passion to its possibilities in the 1980s, when she was in her late 80s. The personalizing finesse of a plait or wrap to close or shape a garment was as characteristic of Grès as of Halston or McCardell; her ergodynamics brought fullness to the chest simply by canting sleeves backward so the wearer inevitably created a swelling fullness in the front as arms forced the sleeves forward, creating a pouch of air at the chest.

For evening, Grès practiced a continuous antithesis of body disclosure and hiding the body within cloth. Even the Grecian "slave" dress, as some of the clients called it, seemed to be as bare as possible with alarming apertures to flesh. But the Grès draped dress, despite its fluid exterior, was securely corseted and structured within, allowing for apertures of skins to seem revealing while at the same time giving the wearer the assurance that the dress would not shift on the body. Conversely, more or less unstructured caftans, clinging geometries of cloth, could cover the wearer so completely as to resemble dress of the Islamic world, but in these instances the softness of structure complemented the apparent suppleness.

Never was a Grès garment, whether revealing or concealing, less than enchanting. The slight asymmetry of a wrap determined by one dart, the fall of a suit button to a seaming line, or the wrap of a draped dress to a torque of shaping through the torso, was an invention and an enchantment in Grès' inventive sculptural vocabulary. History, most notably through photographers such as Hoyningen-Heuné and Willy Maywald, recorded the sensuous skills of Madame Grès chiefly in memorable black-and-white images, but the truth of her achievement came in garden and painterly colors of aubergine, magenta, cerise, and royal blue, along with a spectrum of fertile browns. Her draped Grecian slaves and goddesses were often in a white of neoclassicism, but an optical white that tended, with exposure to light, to yellow over time. Grès' streamlined architecture of clothing was the pure white of dreaming, of languorous physical beauty, and apparel perfect in comfort and image.

—Richard Martin

GRIFFE, Jacques

French designer

Born: Near Carcassonne, France, in 1917. **Education:** Apprenticed with local tailor at age 16, later with the dressmaker Mirra, in Toulouse. **Military Service:** Completed required military service, 1936; served in World War II and was imprisoned for 18 months. **Career:** Employed at the house of Vionnet, 1936–39; opened own salon in rue Gaillon, 1941; with backing from Robert Perrier, opened Jacques Griffe Evaluation, in rue du Faubourg Saint-Honoré, 1947; contributed styles to Vogue Patterns, 1950–68. Fragrances: *Enthusiasme, Griffonnage,* and *Mistigri.* Retired in 1968. **Exhibitions:** *Elégance and Création: 1945–1977,* Musée de la Mode et du Costume, Palais Galliera, Paris, 1977. **Collections:** Fashion Institute of Technology, New York; Costume Institute of the Metropolitan Museum of Art, New York; Musée de la Mode et du Costume, Palais Galliera, Paris.

Publications

On GRIFFE:

Books

Perkins, Alice K., *Paris Couturiers and Milliners,* New York, 1949.

Bertin, Célia, *Haute Couture,* Paris, 1956; as *Paris à la Mode,* New York & London, 1956.

Pickens, Mary Brooks, and Dora Loues Miller, *Dressmakers of France,* New York, 1956.

Delpierre, Madeleine, *Elegance and Creation: 1945–77* (exhibition catalogue), Paris, 1977.

Milbank, Caroline Rennolds, *Couture: The Great Designers,* New York, 1985.

Articles

Martin, Richard, "Zeitgeist Becomes Form," in *Artforum,* March 1997.

* * *

One of the few designers capable of taking an idea from concept to realization, Jacques Griffe sketched, draped, cut, and sewed. He was taught sewing and encouraged towards haute couture by his mother, who placed him with the local tailor. Although he found the work tedious, he later recognized it as the foundation for perfecting his craft. His skills were expanded when he learned dressmaking at the house of Mirra, and he came to Paris with the proficiency needed for haute couture. His placement at the house of Vionnet exposed him to unique ways of cutting, and the belief that draping cloth would relate to and enhance the female body. He would adapt this philosophy for his own creativity. Temporarily delayed by World War II, during which time he served his country and was taken prisoner, he was prepared to open his own house at war's end.

Vionnet gave him one of her dolls as encouragement solely to drape new models. Since he was equally able to sketch, he did both. Unlike his mentor, he was more of a colorist. He chose conservative colors—grey, brown, black, and checks in alpaca, wool jersey, crêpe, and broadcloth for suits and coats. Seen in them is the hand of a creative tailor—he was the first to introduce the boxy jacket, tunic, and cone-shaped coat of the 1950s. Aesthetically pleasing lines were imposed by his cut onto darts and seams used for fitting between the waist and shoulders. Decorative curved welt seams ending in an arrow were often used.

His day and afternoon dresses were softer than his suits. Sleeves were often kimono cut; bodices often blouson. Asymmetrical clothing ended in drapes, scarves, or bows at neck or hips. Pleating was used for insets of sunburst panels or for entire dresses. Polka dots were his favorite print. Evening dresses were also soft, supple, and feminine. Colors were pink, mauve, apricot, chartreuse, yellow, bright blue, navy, or black in chiffon, lamé, moiré, faille, satin, tulle, lace, taffeta, velvet, or brocade. High-waisted or camisole bodices had halter, strapless, or shepherdess necklines. Gowns were sheaths, or had extremely elaborate full skirts, floor or ballet length that ended in harem or flounced hems. Skirt decorations were either shirred, bands graduated in size, repeated swirled ruffles, or petal-like panels of pleating.

Griffe retired in 1968, and though his skill as a designer was second to none, he has, unfortunately, been largely fogotten in the 21st century.

—Betty Kirke; updated by Sydonie Benét

GRUPPO GFT

Italian fashion manufacturer

Founded: Established in Turin, 1887, as Donato Levi e Figli for production of men's off-the-rack clothing. **Company History:** Company purchased in 1925 by the Rivetti family who formed Gruppo Finanziario Tessile in 1930; GFT USA established, 1971; GFT Mode Canada established; 1983; manufacturers for Abboud, Armani, Dior, Fezza, Montana, Ungaro, Valentino, and others; also publisher of *Il libro del sarto*, 1987; *L'abito della rivoluzione*, 1987; *Giornale delle nuove mode di Francia e d'Inghilterra*, 1988; *Apparel Arts*, 1989; *Ready-Made Fashion: An Historical Profile of the Clothing Industry in Great Britain, France and Germany*, 1990; *Women and Modernity: Fashions, Images, Female Strategies in Germany from the Beginning of the Century to the 1930s*, 1991; *Pagine e tavole del costume antico e moderno*, 1992; company sold to Giovanni Agnelli's Gemina, 1994; Gemina restructured, Holding di Partecipazioni Industriali (HDI) becomes new parent of GFT, 1997; acquired Valentino house, 1998; bought Joseph Abboud, 2000. **Company Address:** Corso Emilia 6, 10152 Turin, Italy.

Publications

On GRUPPO GFT:

Articles

"Protectionism Ill Fits Apparel," in *Chicago Tribune,* 13 December 1986.

Trachtenberg, Jeffrey A., "Designers Are Made as Well as Born," in *Forbes,* 11 July 1988.

Rosenbaum, Andrew, "Italy's Fashion Trillionaire," in *Avenue* (New York), September 1988.

Nardoza, Edward, "GFT Gets Set for the 1990s," in the *Daily News Record* (New York), 31 May 1991.

Howard, Robert, "The Designer Organization: Italy's GFT Goes Global," in the *Harvard Business Review* (Massachusetts) September/October 1991.

Bannon, Lisa, "Apparel Maker for Top Labels to Sell Big Stake," in the *Wall Street Journal* (New York), 6 April 1993.

Profile, "Holding di Partecipazioni Industriali SpA," online at Hoover's Online, www.hoovers.com, 11 January 2001.

* * *

Before being sold in 1994 to Gemina, one of several companies owned by the legendary Giovanni Agnelli, Gruppo GFT (Gruppo Finanziario Tessile, or Textile Financial Group) was the world's largest manufacturer of designer clothing, competing at the highest end of the fashion business with ready-to-wear designer collections, one step below made-to-order haute couture. Its success is rooted in its unparalleled history, cutting edge technologies, well-organized labor practices and thorough understanding of fashion as an expression of contemporary culture. Innovative and flexible in an ever changing market, GFT single-handedly revolutionized the way artistic clothing was conceived, manufactured, marketed, and distributed. Its heart was on the pulse of social trends and needs, keeping it way ahead of its competitors.

GFT's involvement in contemporary fashion went way beyond the business world. The company was deeply committed to publishing rare treatises on the history of costume, organizing exhibitions with accompanying catalogues, and working with major contemporary artists. The exhibitions organized by Gruppo GFT, usually in conjunction with international events such as the Florentine Pitti Uomo shows, have been a symbolic expression of this world and of GFT's relationship with contemporary creativity. Exhibitions have featured the work of Frank O. Gehry (1986); Arata Isozaki (1986–87); and Giulio Paolini (1988); GFT sponsored major exhibitions of the work of Claes Oldenburg, Coosje van Bruggen, and Aldo Rossi, who also designed corporate headquarters in Turin, Italy. And in the 1990s, GFT helped to support the Rebecca Horn show at the Guggenheim Museum in New York.

Before 1887, most clothing was produced by cottage industry tailors who produced a small range of styles for local clients. In that year, however, in the Piedmont region of Italy, Donato Levi e Figli produced one of the first prototypes of a suit made to standardized measurements. In 1925 the Rivetti family purchased Donato Levi and Sons and created Finanziario Tessile (Fites), and by 1930 Gruppo Finanziario Tessile (GFT) was established as an organization to produce and market ready-made clothing. The company flourished in the period after World War II; while the rest of the world was still producing clothes in small cottage industry workshops, GFT laid the foundations for mass-produced clothing and created a vast new market for this ready-made clothes.

The democratic, mass-market and homogeneous styles of the 1960s gave way in the 1970s to a new era of increased individualization to which GFT responded immediately. It entered the more upscale market by catering to a stable of looks and added exclusive prêt-à-porter collections by some of Europe's leading fashion designers to its mass production activities. GFT's core group has consisted of Valentino, Armani, Ungaro, Fezza, and Claude Montana. GFT grew intellectually in their craft through their exchanges with its designers. Marco Rivetti, chief executive officer of GFT until 1994, commented that the company learned much from its fashion artists: "From Armani, a great deal about the construction of jackets, from Valentino, the design of shirts and the use of silk." These designers were, in turn, drawn to GFT's commitment to quality workmanship, openness to new systems of production, and superb distribution system.

GFT's ability to operate in a global market immensely benefitted the designers. Armani's classicism was less classic and more sporty for the GFT-USA lines; Giorgio Armani, Mani by Giorgio Armani, Valentino Boutique, Valentino Night, Valentino Uomo, and others were all adaptations of the European lines produced and marketed by the American division.

Since 1987 GFT collaborated with American designer Joseph Abboud, recognizing his world market appeal. In the following years, the company signed Andrew Fezza, Joan Helpern, and Calvin Klein, designers who were truly representative of our time, with the artistic sensibility of understated elegance accessible to a variety of markets.

In 1993 GFT had 46 companies worldwide, 18 manufacturing plants, and some 10,000 employees. The following year the company was acquired by Gemina, one of a stable of companies owned by the Agnelli family, due in part to financial problems from mismanagement. Ironically, another scandal somewhat tarnished GFT's struggling image in 1995, this time involving a number of its parent company Gemina's top executives. GFT weathered the storm and sought to regain its standing as the leading manufacturer of designer clothing in Italy.

In 1997 Gemina announced it would divide its industrial, apparel, and publishing businesses. GFT's corporate parent was christened Holding di Partecipazioni Industriali SpA (HDI) and the new holding company would concentrate more fully on fashion, in an attempt to regain GFT's supremacy and to challenge its closest rival in the luxury market, LVMH (Moët Hennessey Louis Vuitton SA). True to its word, HDI bought the Valentino couture business in 1998 as its founders considered retirement, adding a new brand to the company's fold. GFT, however, suffered two major setbacks: first, the loss of Ungaro's contracts in 1998, and second, all of Armani's licensing and production in 2000.

As Armani moved to control its own manufacturing and licensing, GFT and HDI countered by buying another leading design house, Joseph Abboud, for $65 million. Though GFT already licensed much of Abboud's product line—at a time when LVMH was buying Celine, Gucci, Pucci, and entering a joint venture with Prada to buy Fendi—buying Abboud's label and licensing rights outright was a sound investment.

GFT's mandate and goals have remained the same as they were in 1887—to create fashion for the truly contemporary world, to pay attention to detail, to produce efficiently, and to create the market and deliver the goods on time. The company met its goals by immersing itself in the history of the fashion arts and in the interrelation of the genre and other contemporary artforms. GFT's vision changed the way designers worked, without disturbing the integrity or soul of their creations.

—Marianne T. Carlano; updated by Nelly Rhodes

GUCCI

Italian fashion and accessories house

Founded: in Florence, Italy, as saddlery shop by Guccio Gucci (1881–1953), 1906, after family millinery business failed. **Company History:** Became retailer of accessories, 1923; Gucci shops opened in Florence, 1923; boutiques open in Rome, 1938; firm renamed Società Anonima Guccio Gucci, 1939; stores opened in Milan, 1951; renamed Guccio Gucci Srl, 1945; New York boutique opened, 1953; opened in Paris, 1963; shop opened in Hong Kong and Gucci Parfums formed, 1975 (renamed Gucci Parfums SpA, 1982); company renamed Guccio Gucci SpA, 1982; appointed Dawn Mello creative director, 1989; Tom Ford joined company, 1990; acquired by Investcorp, 1993; Mello departed and Ford named creative director, 1994; deaths of Mauritzio and Paolo Gucci, 1995; listed on the NYSE, 1995; rival Prada bought stake, 1998; sold stake to LVMH, 1999; Pinault Printemps Redoute acquired major stake and fought off LVMH, 1999; Alexander McQueen defected from LVMH to Gucci, 2000; hired Stella McCartney to create her own line, 2000; designer Nicolas Ghesquière came to firm with acquisition of Balenciaga, 2001. **Exhibitions:** Costume Archive, Metropolitan Museum, New

Gucci, autumn/winter 2001–02 ready-to-wear collection designed by Tom Ford. © AFP/CORBIS.

York. **Awards:** National Italian-American Foundation Special Achievement award, 2001 [de Sole]. **Company Address:** 73 Via Tornabuoni 50100, Florence, Italy. **Company Website:** www.gucci.com.

PUBLICATIONS

On GUCCI:

Books

Swann, June, *Shoes,* London, 1982.

Alfonsi, Maria-Vittoria, *Leaders in Fashion: I grandi personaggi della moda,* Bologna, 1983.

McKnight, Gerald, *Gucci: A House Divided,* New York, 1987.

Forden, Sara Gay, *The House of Gucci,* New York, 2000.

Articles

Crittendon, Ann, "Knock-Offs Aside, Gucci's Blooming," in the *New York Times,* 25 June 1978.

"Artisans & Art: Gucci," in *Fortune,* 23 July 1984.

"Gucci, Taking Control," in *WWD,* 9 January 1987.

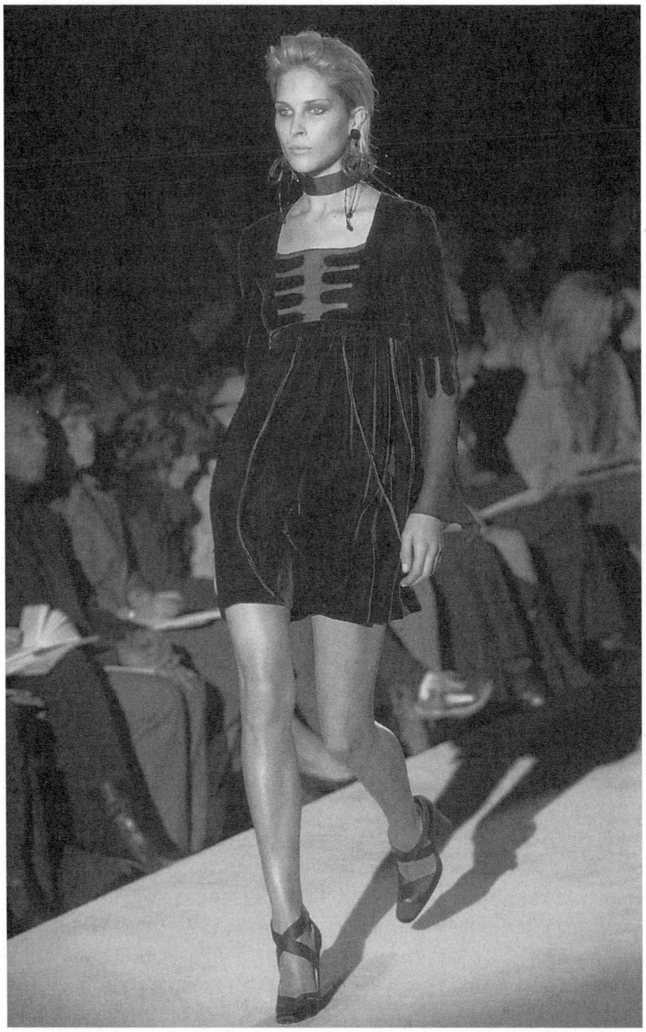

Gucci, fall/winter 2001–02 collection: velvet baby doll dress. © AP/ Wide World Photos.

McKnight, Gerald, "Gucci: Hell for Leather," in the *Sunday Times Magazine,* (London), 6 September 1987.

Wolman, Karen, "Can an Outsider Fill Aldo Gucci's Loafers?," in *Business Week,* 30 November 1987.

"Gucci's Empire Splits a Seam," in *Time,* 20 June 1988.

"Aldo Gucci," in the *New York Times,* 21 January 1989.

McKnight, Gerald, "Aldo Gucci," [obituary] in *The Independent,* 23 January 1990.

Rossant, John, "Can Maurizio Gucci Bring the Glamor Back?" in *Business Week,* 5 February 1990.

Jereski, Laura, "Watch Your Step, Cousin Paolo," in *Forbes,* 15 October 1990.

Howell, Georgina, "Gucci Again," in *Vogue,* December 1990.

Dudar, Helen, "Reversal of Fortune: Dawn Mello Gets Gucci Back on Its Feet," in *Working Woman,* April 1991.

Friedman, Arthur, "Aldo Gucci Dies at 84," in *WWD,* 29 May 1992.

Costin, Glyn, "Dawn Mello Revamping Gucci," in *WWD,* 29 May 1992.

Infantino, Vivian, "Ford Drives Gucci into Faster Fashion Lane," in *Footwear News,* 14 November 1994.

Spindler, Amy M., "A Retreat from Retro Glamor," in the *New York Times,* 7 March 1995.

"Paolo Gucci," [obituary] in the *Economist,* 28 October 1995.

Infantino, Vivian, "Tom Ford: The Driving Force Behind Gucci's Revved-Up Performance," in *Footwear News,* 4 December 1995.

Min, Janice, "Couture de Force: Gucci is Once Again Chichi Thanks to the Savvy Designs of Tom Ford," in *People,* 4 March 1996.

Conti, Samantha, "Prada Buys Five-Percent Gucci Stake," in *WWD,* 8 June 1998.

Luscombe, Belinda, "Catfight on the Catwalk," in *Time,* 22 June 1998.

Rawsthorn, Alice, "Prada Move Puts Gucci on Defensive," in the *Financial Times,* 7 July 1998.

Weisman, Katherine, "It's Getting Serious: LVMH Buys Prada's 9.5-Percent Stake in Gucci," in *WWD,* 13 January 1999.

Menkes, Suzy, "Gucci Buys House of YSL for $1-Billion," in the *International Herald Tribune,* 16 November 1999.

Givhan, Robin, "Givenchy's Loss, Gucci's Gain—Designer Alexander McQueen Leaves LVMH," in the *Washington Post,* 5 December 2000.

"At Yves Saint Laurent, Tom's Triumph," in *WWD,* 15 March 2001.

Menkes, Suzy, "Gucci Gets Europe's Hottest New Designer," in the *International Herald Tribune,* 7 July 2001.

* * *

The illustrious name of Gucci began as a mark on leather goods produced in Florentine workshops for the young Guccio Gucci. Inspired by the grandiose luggage transported by wealthy guests to the Ritz Hotel in London, where Gucci worked in the kitchens, the young Italian returned to his native country where he began making leather luggage.

The characteristic double-G motif printed on the canvas was introduced after World War II due to a shortage of leather. Its bold red and green bands on suitcases, bags, satchels, wallets, and purses have become one of the most copied trademarks in the world, along with France's Louis Vuitton. The Florence-based company grew to international proportions in the postwar period, expanding its range to include clothing, fragrances, household items such as decanters and glasses painted with the distinctive red and green bands, scarves, and a slew of other accessories. It was this indiscriminate expansion that ultimately proved to be detrimental to the name of Gucci for, as Yves Saint Laurent's director Pierre Bergé once said, "A name is like a cigarette—the more you puff on it the less you have left."

Added to this overexposure was the proliferation of Gucci imitations which reputedly cost the company a fortune in legal fees, along with infamous conflicts between the volatile members of the Gucci clan. All were detrimental to the high profile image the company needed to maintain. There were, however, many Gucci items that became status symbols in their own right—such as the Gucci loafer with its unmistakeable gilt snaffle trim which, according to the *New York Times* was what carried the company to fortune. Biographer Gerald McKnight notes in his book *Gucci: A House Divided,* (New York, 1987) that the loafer even became the subject of well-worn jokes in the 1970s when the name Gucci became as well known as household items such as the Hoover and cellophane tape.

Having lost a great deal of the prestigious aura that is a vital element to the success of a luxury brand, the house of Gucci suffered bad press during the 1980s, as journalists hungered after stories of bitter rivalry between family members and their legal battles. It was an American woman, Dawn Mello, who restored the luxurious image of Gucci when, in 1989, she was appointed executive vice-president and creative director of the company. Under her control, the existing Gucci lines were edited and refined, and fewer, more select new items introduced.

Gucci, spring/summer 2002 ready-to-wear collection. © Reuters NewMedia Inc./CORBIS.

Mello provided a clever combination of just the right balance of historical relevance and a real sense of modernity which restored Gucci to its former glory as a "must have" name. She was helped by designer Tom Ford who came to Gucci in 1990. Three years later, in 1993, the Gucci clog was a sell-out item among the fashion *cognoscenti* and became the most copied shoe style of the season. Gucci was once again established as a purveyor of luxury goods but also as a serious contender in the high fashion stakes. This same year, the firm was acquired by Investcorp, and the following year relocated its headquarters from Milan to Florence. Mello however, left to rejoin Bergdorf Gordman in New York, and Ford was named Gucci's creative director.

Ford proved a good fit for Gucci, his collections took the house back to its must-have status. Along the way came corporate intrigue, when rival Prada suddenly acquired a chunk of Gucci in 1998, only to turn around and sell to archrival LVMH in 1999. The events sparked a takeover attempt, with Gucci narrowly escaping due to white knight François Pinault, whose Pinault Printemps Redoute bought in to Gucci. Pinault and Gucci CEO Domenico de Sole soon gave LVMH a run for its money in the bid to become the world's largest luxury firm. Though LVMH was ahead, Gucci was a force to be reckoned with and pursued the same targets as LVMH, such as Fendi in 1999. LVMH, partnered with Prada, prevailed; with Prada eventually selling its stake to LVMH. Gucci itself then went on a buying spree, acquiring stakes in Boucheron, Sergio Rossi, and Bottega Veneta.

By the end of the 20th century, Gucci had become a global competitor and flexed its muscle with the acquisition of Yves Saint Laurent and Balenciaga. Tom Ford, widely considered Europe's top designer by this time, took the design reins at YSL in addition to his Gucci responsibilities, and the Balenciaga buy brought hot new designer, Nicolas Ghesquière into the fold. Alexander McQuuen, who had defected from LVMH, and Stella McCartney, another sensation, had also joined Gucci. With four of the fashion world's most acclaimed designers under its roof, Gucci was sure to take the catwalk by storm.

—Catherine Woram; updated by Owen James

GUESS, INC.

American fashion house

Founded: by Georges, Maurice, Armand, and Paul Marciano, 1981. **Company History:** Signed license for knitwear, 1982; sold half ownership to Jordache, 1983; brothers regained ownership, 1988; signed license with Revlon for signature fragrance, 1990; Rodeo Drive store opened and eyewear line added, 1992; Georges sold his stake to brothers, 1993; launched golf apparel line and entered home furnishings, 1994–95; went public, 1996; brought apparel licensing back in-house, 1999; opened Baby Guess, Guess Kids, and Guess Home stores, 2000; launched G Brand line, 2001. **Company Address:** 1444 S. Alameda Street, Los Angeles, CA 90021, U.S.A. **Company Website:** www.guess.com.

Publications

On GUESS, INC.:

Books

Byron, Christopher, *Skin Tight: The Bizarre Story of Guess v. Jordache—Glamour, Greed, and Dirty Tricks in the Fashion Industry,* New York, 1992.

Articles

Behar, Richard, "Does Guess Have a Friend in the IRS?" in *Forbes,* 16 November 1987.

Byron, Christopher, "The Great Jeans War," in *New York,* 24 July 1989.

Welles, Chris, "A 'Blood War' in the Jeans Trade," in *Business Week,* 13 November 1989.

"Blue Jeans," in *Consumer Reports,* July 1991.

Marlow, Michael, "Guess at 10: $550 Million and Growing," in *WWD,* 20 December 1991.

Appelbaum, Cara, "Recession Killers," in *Adweek's Marketing Week,* 10 February 1992.

Marlow, Michael, "Guess on Rodeo: The Beverly Hills Cowboy," in *WWD,* 24 November 1992.

Wilson, Marianne, "Guess Ranch Lassos Rodeo Drive," in *Chain Store Age Executive,* January 1993.

"Guess? Solving Fashion Formula," in *Sporting Goods Business,* March 1993.

Ryan, Thomas J., "Marchianos Buy a Piece of Gitano," in *WWD,* 17 March 1993.

Strom, Stephanie, "Guess Names Specialty Store Chief to Lead its Retail Unit," in the *New York Times,* 31 August 1993.

Foley, Bridget, "The Thrill is Back—A Voracious Appetite for Fashion Emerges," in *WWD,* 12 August 1996.

Davidson, Kirk, "Guess Ads Cross Line from Fashion Art to Pornography," in *Marketing News,* 21 October 1996.

Ozzard, Janet, "Thoroughly modern mega brands," in *WWD,* 31 October 1996.

Malone, Soctt, "Under New Owner, Guess Sport to Push Fashion," in *Footwear News,* 13 April 1998.

Cunningham, Thomas, "Guess Losses Hit $13.1M in Fourth Quarter," in *DNR,* 9 March 2001.

Caplan, David Grant, "Guess' New Fashion Plate," in *WWD,* 24 May 2001.

* * *

It is sometimes hard to see beyond the sexy image projected by Guess, Inc., created by Paul Marciano, one of the four Marciano brothers who founded the Guess empire in 1981. Guess fashions, which began with jeans for men and women, have expanded to include denim-driven collections for all ages, including Baby Guess and Guess Kids.

Criticized for being demeaning to women, the controversial Guess advertisements have created such response that most American men or women can name at least one Guess "girl." Supermodels Claudia Schiffer, Naomi Campbell, and Shana Zadrick were among the small group of Guess models who vaulted to celebrity status. The line evokes a playful, body-conscious attitude. When Guess appeared on the scene in the early 1980s, the designer jeans craze was all but over. The Marciano brothers, however, created enough of a stir through their powerful advertising to induce a new trend in designer denims.

There is usually a seasonal theme to the Guess collections from year to year, but a longrunning Western tone has permeated the line in some shape or form. Yet it took more than a simple image and basic denim line to make this company so successful; Guess works hard to develop innovative treatments and washes for denim, all the while experimenting with colors other than indigo. It pioneered the use of acid and enzyme washes in its textiles, abrading and brushing denims and twills and using different types of denims, such as ring-spun.

Businesswise, Guess went through a bit of a shake-up in the mid-1980s, when the Nakash brothers of Jordache Enterprises challenged the Marciano brothers in a long legal battle over ownership of Guess. A stronger Guess, Inc. emerged from the fight, larger and more successful than ever before, with forceful entries into the men's and children's areas as well as a foray into a more sophisticated category for women, the Georges Marciano signature line. The Marciano line offers more tailored dressing in the form of skirts, trousers, jackets, and related coordinates. Again, however, this is no ordinary power dressing line—the clothes were cut and fitted closer to the figure of a woman's body. Although the clothes can be worn in the more casual work environment, wearers must be supremely confident women—confident in their sensuality and in their position.

The Guess suffered growing pains in 1993 when Georges wanted to take the mass marketing route and his siblings insisted the label stay more exclusive. Unable to compromise, Georges sold his 38-percent stake in the firm and struck on his own, founding rival Yes brand in 1994. After Georges departure the remaining Marcianos continued to expand the Guess empire, producing golf apparel and home furnishings, in addition to its other licensing agreements for footwear, watches, handbags, eyewear, and fragrances. Guess stores opened throughout the U.S., including shops in vast outlet malls as well.

In 1996 the Marcianos took Guess public and used funds to take the brand into Europe. Yet the debut of designer duds from Tommy Hilfiger, DKNY, and Clavin Klein's CK denim collections gave chase and Guess found itself foundering. Initiating a major restructuring, the firm brought its licensing in-house, refurbished existing stores, and planned new retailers for its Baby Guess, Guess Kids, and Guess Home lines in 1999 and 2000.

Guess suffered losses in late 2000, due to soft department store sales, costs related to revamping its image, and its expansion. Guess bounced back, however, announcing the launch of a new line, G Brand, in 2001 which the firm characterized as "more sophisticated and more detailed" than its other denim collections.

—Lisa Marsh; updated by Owen James

GUILLEMIN, Olivier

French fashion designer

Born: Paris, France, 10 July 1961. **Education:** Studied art history at the Sorbonne, Paris, 1978–80, and Studio Bercot, 1979–80. **Career:** Assistant to Thierry Mugler, 1981; assistant to Azzedine Alaïa, 1982; consultant and freelance designer for Woolmark, Claude Montana menswear, 1987–88; launched own line, P.A.P. for women, 1987; label produced under Paco Rabanne, 1991; specializes in ready-to-wear, accessories, fibers and yarns, and fabrics; Président du Comité Français de la Couleur, 1994. **Exhibitions:** *Fashion and Surrealism,*

Fashion Institute of Technology, New York, and Victoria and Albert Museum, London, 1984; *La Fée Electricité,* Musée d'Art Moderne, Paris, 1985; *Les Créateurs,* Villa Noaille, Hyères, France, 1992; *Mode et Liberty,* Musée des Arts Decoratifs, Paris, 1993; *CONTREX,* Musée des Arts Decoratifs, Paris, 1994; *Mode et Gitane,* Carousel du Louvre, Paris, 1994; *Voyage dans la Matière,* Grand Palais, Paris, 1994. **Collections:** Union Francaise des Arts du Costume, Paris; Musée de la Mode à Marseille, France. **Awards:** Bourse pour la Création, Ministère de la Culture, 1990; 1er prix de la Création Woolmark, 1990. **Address:** 177 rue du Temple, 75003 Paris, France.

Publications

On GUILLEMIN:

Articles

Voight, Rebecca, "Vanity Fairs," in *Paris Passion* (Paris), October 1990.

Hepple, Keith, "The Young and the Fun," in *DR: The Fashion Business* (London), 1 December 1990.

"Guillemin to design RTW for Paco Rabanne," in *WWD,* 17 October 1991.

Hood, Frederique, "Fantastic Meteor," in *Elle* (New York), March 1992.

Valmont, Martine, "Les fils de l'été 1995," in *Journal du Textile,* 29 November 1993.

Molin Corvo, Roberta, "Vive la recherche!" in *Trends: Collezioni* (Modena, Italy), Spring/Summer 1995.

"*Yes Minister* Meets *Ab Fab:* The F.O. Has Designs on EU," in *M2 Communications,* 24 February 1998.

"China Hosts International Young Designers Contest," in the *Xinhua News Agency,* 27 March 1999.

"The Best Deal for Young Fashion," available online at Guillemin, www.scalaire.com/fashion, 9 June 2001.

"Fashion Cultures Exhibition," online at Intersélection, www.interselection.com, 9 June 2001.

*

I chose the profession of fashion designer because it was the catalyst for my various creative aspirations—commercial, sociological, and technical. I consider myself an experimentalist and it is this reason my path is very varied. The way my career is developing leads me increasingly towards a more forward way of looking at clothes, in unusual fibers, threads, and fabrics, but also at the process of distribution and consumption. I think we are at a turning point in our Western society and that in future years other codes of fashion are going to appear. It is with this in mind that I see my collections, which were elitist at the beginning of my career, becoming increasingly creatively democratic.

—Olivier Guillemin

* * *

Olivier Guillemin designs wearable art for the fashion follower who is looking ahead to the next century. One of a group of hot young Parisian stars, including Sophie Sitbon and Corinne Cobson, Guillemin frequently uses unusual and novel fabrics to surprising effect. His modern, futuristic designs often appear to signal a world where high technology will triumph over nature and the human body. Not unlike the 1960s science fiction looks of Paco Rabanne, with whom Guillemin is associated, these designs address today's postindustrial, satellite-linked global society head-on.

Guillemin demonstrated his stubborn individuality from the beginning by premiering his collections in odd and diverse places, from a gloomy medieval church to an old-fashioned hotel ballroom, or the French Institute of Fashion. In accord with the spirit of his times, he has been allied with other fashion deconstructivists; his designs have been called "absurd and enchanting." He has created garments which seem to have been literally torn apart and then patched back together, or merely draped over the figure, or left ragged and unfinished.

One collection included a frock made from pieces of a dress pattern secured haphazardly with strips of black tape, exposing bits of the model's skin. Others appeared to be exploding, as in his dress of woven paper fabric covered with forbidding spiky cones radiating from the bodice. A backless, gathered, knee-length shift looked like a paint-spattered drop cloth picked up off an atelier floor and draped around an artist's model. He created a jumpsuit with one leg missing; other garments have been shorn into bandage-like strips. As these examples show, Guillemin is not timid about exploiting the limits of what constitutes "clothing" within the fashion arena.

Unusual shapes, materials, and accessories are a Guillemin trademark, such as his black plastic jewelry designs coiling in arabesques around the model's face and body. One collection was comprised mainly of metallic fabrics, including metallic indigo toile suits and long, metallic toile coats. He has toyed with neon-colored fake fur, transparent plastics, and stretch Lycra. His fascination with industrial materials has resulted in long, rubberized apron dresses and black plastic luggage closures used as jacket fasteners. His clothes often seem to refer to a nonspecific, postapocalyptic era, where body covering will be cobbled together from the remains of urban destruction. But his fantastic designs have also been prescient; his use of neon colored fabrics easily predated the trend for those materials by several seasons.

When Guillemin was named ready-to-wear designer for Paco Rabanne in 1991, he expressed the desire to continue working on his own line and to keep the two collections separate. His own lines continued to display the inventiveness, unusual fabrics, and devotion to experimental fiber technologies for which he was already known. And, lest the impression be given that he is only a provocateur, he has also made quite wearable, (though still playful) clothing. Guillemin has demonstrated that both before and during his association with Paco Rabanne, he has not been entirely unwilling to create realistic styles.

Like many of his contemporaries, Guillemin revels in the exposure of the human form. The body is to be peeked at through a red plastic raincoat, peered at through slashed fabric, or simply left starkly nude. His penchant for peekaboo styles was protrayed in a most surrealistic selection of garments resembling hedges in a topiary garden. Models paraded in clingy dresses and bodysuits covered with tightly-cut net and tulle patches, giving the impression of a group of cartoonish, mobile shrubbery. In the same show, ruffs of stiff tulle were positioned around the figure like fur, with bare portions of the midriff showing through, creating a look somewhat akin to an oversized poodle. (The finale to this event was a bare-breasted stilt-walker.)

For Paco Rabanne, Guillemin has drawn upon the famous looks of the 1960s with their references to space travel and their use of metallic stretch fabrics. He has even revived Rabanne's famed silvery plastic and metal disk garments. But Guillemin is not simply paying homage to the past; he brought his unique vision to Rabanne with dramatic, well-cut modern garments utilizing the latest advances in microfiber technology. Whether creating his own phantasmagorical styles or updating the venerable but forward-looking designs of Paco Rabanne, Guillemin has remained on the cutting edge.

In February 1998, Guillemin was one of four designers to join 23 of Europe's up-and-coming designers in a 45-minute catwalk showing for London Fashion Week, held at the Natural History Museum to support the UK's presidency of the European Union. The spring/summer collection touted the distinct flair of native design displayed by what Doug Henderson, Minister of Europe, called the "brightest young fashion stars." It was a busy year for Guillemin—in fall of the same year, 1998, he was a feature designer at the Prêt à Porter Paris fair; the next spring, he took part in China's International Young Designers Contest.

In mid-May 2000, Guillemin spoke for the environment by addressing the Fashion Cultures Exhibition in Clichy, France, on "Well-Being Through Today's and Tomorrow's Colors." He earned respect for his choice of clean, organic cotton uncontaminated by fertilizers or pesticides and updated viscose manufactured by a non-polluting method.

—Kathleen Paton; updated by Mary Ellen Snodgrass

H

HALSTON

American designer

Born: Roy Halston Frowick in Des Moines, Iowa, 23 April 1932. **Education:** Studied at Indiana University, Bloomington, and at the Art Institute of Chicago to 1953. **Career:** Freelance milliner, Chicago, 1952–53; window dresser, Carson Pirie Scott, Chicago, 1954–57; designer and hats division manager, Lilly Daché, New York, 1958–59; millinery and clothing designer, Bergdorf Goodman, New York, 1959–68; founder/designer, Halston Ltd. couture, New York, 1962–73; with Henry Pollack Inc., established Halston International, ready-to-wear, 1970; established Halston Originals with Ben Shaw, 1972; Halston Ltd. renamed Halston Enterprises, 1973, and company, design services and trademark sold to Norton Simon; menswear and signature fragrance introduced 1975; launched *Halston I-12* and *Halston Z-14* (for men), 1976; company sold to Esmark, Inc., and Halston III collection initiated for J.C. Penney Company, 1983; company sold to Revlon, 1986; introduced *Halston Couture* (for women), 1988; acquired by Saudis and renamed Halston Borghese Inc., from 1991; *Catalyst,* fragrance (for women) launched, 1993; *Catalyst for Men,* 1994; fragrances sold to French Fragrances Inc., 1996; womenswear licenses bought by Tropic Tex and Randolph Duke signed as designer/creative director, 1996–98; launched bed and bath lines for fall 1997; firm sold to Catterton Group and Kevan Hall named designer, 1998; licensed Halston Signature, 1999; firm sold to Neema Clothing Ltd., 1999; Craig Natiello hired as design director, 1999; fragrances acquired by Elizabeth Arden; new fragrance, *Halson Unbound,* 2001. **Exhibitions:** Fashion Institute of Technology, New York, 1991 (retrospective). **Awards:** Coty American Fashion Critics award, 1962, 1969, 1971, 1972, 1974; placed on Fashion Walk of Fame, New York, 2000. **Died:** 26 March 1990, in San Francisco. **Company Address:** Halston International, 530 Seventh Avenue, New York, NY 10018, U.S.A.

Halston, spring/summer 1978 made-to-order collection. © Bettmann/CORBIS.

Publications

On HALSTON:

Books

Milbank, Caroline Rennolds, *Couture: The Great Designers,* New York, 1985.

Gaines, Steven, *Simply Halston: The Untold Story,* New York, 1991, 1993.

Rottman, Fred and Elaine Gross, *Halston: An American Original,* New York & London, 1999.

Bluttal, Steven, and Patricia, *Halston,* London, 2001.

Articles

"The Private World of Halston," in *Harper's Bazaar* (New York), February 1973.

Bowles, J., "Will Halston Take Over the World?" in *Esquire,* August 1975.

Lemann, N., "The Halstonization of America," in *Washington Monthly* (Washington, D.C.), July 1978.

Belkin, Lisa, "The Prisoner of Seventh Avenue," in the *New York Times Magazine,* 15 March 1987.

Halston (center) in 1979, surrounded left to right by Martha Graham, Betty Ford, Elizabeth Taylor, and Liza Minnelli, all wearing gowns designed by him. (At the Third Annual Martha Graham Award, New York.) © Bettmann/CORBIS.

Darnton, Nina, "The Inimitable Halston: The Legendary Designer Breaks the Silence on his Current Dilemma," in *Newsweek,* 7 August 1989.
Morris, Bernadine, "Halston, Symbol of Fashion in America in the 1970s," [obituary] in the *New York Times,* 28 March 1990.
"Halston: An American Original," [obituary] in *WWD,* 28 March 1990.
Mulvagh, Jane, "Halston," [obituary] in the *Independent* (London), 29 March 1990.
"Hat Man: Halston," [obituary] in *U.S. News & World Report,* 9 April 1990.
Sporkin, Elizabeth, "The Great Halston," [obituary] in *People,* 9 April 1990.
Brady, James, "A Prince of the Captivity," in *Advertising Age,* 16 April 1990.
"Halston," [obituary] in *Current Biography,* May 1990.
Minnelli, Liza, and Polly Mellen, "Halston: 1932–1990," in *Vogue,* July 1990.
Gaines, Steven, "The Man Who Sold His Name," in *Vanity Fair,* September 1991.
"Halston: Modernist Master," in *Connoisseur* (New York), November 1991.
Hoppe, Karen, "Halston Borghese: Revamping, Retrenching, Revitalized," in *Drug & Cosmetic Industry,* December 1994.
Born, Pete, "Halston Borghese Seeks a Partner," in *WWD,* 14 July 1995.
Fine, Jenny B., "Halston Borghese being Sold," in *WWD,* 19 January 1996.
"French Fragrances Purchasing Four Halston Borghese Scent Brands," in *WWD,* 13 February 1996.
Lockwood, Lisa, "Halston: Classic Comeback," in *WWD,* 30 August 1996.
Pagoda, Dianne M., "Halston Taps Duke for Top Design Post," in *WWD,* 24 September 1996.
D'Innocenzio, Anne, "The Halston Blitz," in *WWD,* 26 March 1997.
Gault, Ylonda, "...Halston's Back and Trying to Convert Men," in *Crain's New York Business,* 19 January 1998.
D'Innocenzio, Anne, "Catterton Signs Deal for Halston," in *WWD,* 28 April 1998.
Gault, Ylonda, "Halston's New Owner Tries to Re-Revive Brand," in *Crain's New York Business,* 25 May 1998.
Young, Vicki M., "Duke Sues Halston for Breach of Contract," in *WWD,* 15 July 1998.

D'Innocenzio, Anne, "Halston in Deal with Sinolink to Produce Its Signature Line," in *WWD,* 14 May 1999.
———, "Halston Rehires Kevan Hall," in *WWD,* 17 July 1999.
———, "Halston Assets Acquired by Neema," in *WWD,* 6 December 1999.
McCants, Leonard, "Halston Sets Designer Line for Fall," in *WWD,* 14 November 2000.
"Guise and Dolls," in *WWD,* 24 September 2001.
Braunstein, Peter, "Obsessed with Halston," in *WWD,* 12 October 2001.

* * *

The life of Roy Halston Frowick was marked by deeply American directness. He was known internationally, and in a nonchalant elegance that stripped away all that was superfluous in his life and art, Halston was the creation of his own obsessive, workaholic achievements. In the 1970s and early 1980s Halston was not only the supreme American fashion designer, but the quintessential one.

Again and again, Halston would say to the press, as he told Eugenia Sheppard in the *New York Post* (7 February 1973), "Women make fashion. Designers suggest, but it's what women do with the clothes that does the trick." While this modest disavowal was in part canny public relations, granting to the client or potential client the creativity of dress, Halston believed his statement. He recognized and accounted for the women who would wear the clothing as much as for his own creation and acknowledged a partnership between designer and wearer. One aspect of the partnership was Halston's continuous synergy with important clients, beginning with his millinery work which, after all, started from the top to reconcile personal attitude and physiognomy with apparel.

Later in his career, as he strove to be the "total designer," Halston's personal affection for and connections to clients in show business, design, dance, and public life gave him an intimate and abiding affiliation with the wearer. And when he sought to dress every woman, there was a grounded, natural aspect to Halston that readily reminded the wearer this cryptically simple designer was born in Des Moines, Iowa and raised in Evansville, Indiana.

If Halston ascribed the social function to the wearer, he himself was the consummate creator of the garment in formal terms and his work corresponded to the minimalism in American arts. His geometry of design, employing bias as the three-dimensional element causing the geometry to drape splendidly on the body, was as conceptual as that of Vionnet. Some design problems were played out in paper origami, as he created twisted forms in white paper on a black lacquer tray. Discovering such form, Halston projected it onto the body with absolute integrity, cutting as little as possible, and allowing the simplicity of the two-dimensional design to be felt, even as it assumed form on the body.

Likewise Halston's colors were as selective as Mondrian's, preferring ivory, black, and red, but knowing that fuchsia, electric blue, or deep burgundy could provide accent and emphasis. Of textiles, he worked with cashmere, silk and rayon jerseys, double-faced wools, and Ultrasuede. His machine-washable Ultrasuede shirtwaist, which sold 60,000 copies, was one of the most popular dresses in America in the 1970s—in its utmost simplicity, the same dress could be worn in a multitude of ways to allow each woman to wear it in her own personal style. His rich double-faced wool coats were the luxury of color fields, an art brought to apparel; his athletic looks in bodysuits and sports-inspired dressing were as much an ancipation of the late 1980s American fashion as they were renewals of 1940s and 1950s Claire McCardell. He could dress a Martha Graham dancer as readily as he could create a mass-market dress.

Halston's eveningwear was acclaimed for its glittery, gossamer shimmer, but often unacknowledged for the same principles of simplicity. Working on the bias, Halston caressed the body with spiralling scarfs of form. His one-piece, held-at-the-shoulder "orange-peel" dress was the product of a deft hand, like that of the fruit peeler. His evening jackets were often nothing more than rings of material twisted into cocoon fantasies. As Liza Minnelli has said of Halston, he made one feel comfortable and feel beautiful.

Merging the special chic of a custom business and a vast ambition to dress everyone in the world was Halston's high goal, briefly achieved in the late 1970s and early 1980s. But business changes ignited the American Icarus' wings and he plummeted to earth, having lost most his empire and the ability to do what was most precious to him—designing. His company was bought and sold numerous times before his death in 1990, and in 1992 was acquired by Saudi businessmen who combined it with the Borghese fragrances to become Halston Borghese Inc.

New fragrances bearing the Halston name were introduced in 1994 and 1995, but the name and its legacy languished until the company was dismantled in 1996. French Fragrances Inc. bought the Halston scents; Tropic Tex Apparel bought the remainder of the Halston's products. "We wanted to bring Halston to the next millennium," Carmine Porcelli, Halson's new director of licensing, told *WWD* (30 August 1996). To support the reintroduction of the Halston brand and image, Tropic Tex launched a major advertising campaign and brought Randolph Duke on board as creative director.

Over the next few years, the Halston name was licensed for beds and linens, scarves, belts, handbags, hosiery, sunglasses, jewelry, timepieces, leather apparel, sleepwear, and foundations. In the capable hands of Duke, Halston Signature womenswear regained much of its cachet—trunk shows at Bergdorf Goodman and Saks Fifth Avenue sold over $200,000-worth of couture in a few days in 1997. A menswear launch, however, was not as successful and the overexposure in licensing caught up with Tropic Tex. After experiencing financial difficulties, Tropic Tex agreed to sell Halston International to the Connecticut-based Catterton Group in April 1998.

Halston's new owners fired Duke and hired Kevan Hall, who had worked there briefly earlier in the year and abruptly left. Yet by 1999 Catterton had sold Halston's assets to Neema Clothing Ltd., which then hired Craig Natiello as design director. A new Halston Signature menswear line debuted in 2001 after a series of delays, and Natiello had settled in with his womenswear designs. *Women's Wear Daily* (24 September 2001) commented, "After some rough going, designer Craig Natiello seems to be refining his vision at Halston. While still sexy and amply embellished, his spring collection has a newly controlled feeling, expressed in short, delicately beaded layered dresses, printed chiffon gowns and long skirts."

While the Halston brand spun out of control during the designer's lifetime, it was nothing compared to after his death. In the 21st century, however, the name Halston was again conjured up images of elegance and luxury in womenswear was emerging in menswear as well.

—Richard Martin and Sydonie Benét

HAMNETT, Katharine

British designer

Born: Gravesend, 1948. **Education:** Studied at Cheltenham Ladies College and at St Martin's School of Art, London, 1965–69. **Family:** Children: Samuel and William. **Career:** Cofounder, Tuttabanken Sportswear, London, 1970; freelance designer, London, Paris, Rome and Hong Kong, 1970–79; Katharine Hamnett, Ltd. founded, London, 1979; menswear line introduced, 1982; launched "Choose Life" shirts, 1983; flagship London shop and three others opened, 1986; showed spring/summer womenswear collection at the Natural History Museum, 1995; men's business suit collections—the "body" suit, 1996. **Awards:** International Institute for Cotton Designer of the Year award, 1982; British Fashion Industry Designer of the Year award, 1984; Bath Museum of Costume Dress of the Year award, 1984; Menswear Designer of the Year award, 1984; British Knitting and Clothing Export Council award, 1988. **Address:** 202 New North Road, London N1 7BJ, England.

Publications

On HAMNETT:

Books

Coleridge, Nicholas, *The Fashion Conspiracy,* London, 1988.
Stegemeyer, Anne, *Who's Who in Fashion, Third Edition,* New York, 1996.

Articles

Hall, Dinah, "Streets Ahead," in *You,* magazine of the *Mail on Sunday* (London), 21 August 1983.
Warner, Marina, "Counter-Couture," in *Connoisseur* (London), May 1984.
"Katharine Hamnett: La mode pour sauver le monde," in *Elle* (Paris), September 1984.
Etharington-Smith, Meredith, "New Guard/Old Guard: Fashion Designers Katharine Hamnett and Jean Muir," in *Ultra,* December 1984.
Buckley, Richard, "Katharine the Great: Miss Hamnett Talks," in *DNR: The Magazine* (New York), February 1985.
Polan, Brenda, "Under the Hamnett Influence: 12 Pages of Key Looks for Summer," in *Cosmopolitan* (London), March 1985.
Roberts, Yvonne, "The Queen of Radical Chic," in the *Sunday Express Magazine* (London), 9 March 1986.
"Designer Reports. Summer 87. London: Katharine Hamnett," in *International Textiles* (London), December 1986.
Stan, Adelle-Marie, "Four Designing Women: Donna Karan, Liz Claiborne, Diane von Furstenberg, Katherine Hamnett," in *Ms. Magazine* (New York), November 1986.
"Katharine Hamnett Interview," in *Art and Design* (London), December 1986.
"Be Bardot Says Hamnett," in the *Sunday Times Magazine* (London), 1 February 1987.
Mower, Sarah, "British Style: The Designer Star Katharine Hamnett," in *Vogue* (London), February 1987.
Cocks, Jay, "Been There, Seen That, Done That: London's Katherine Hamnett Has a Deft Hand for Funk, *Time,* 16 March 1987.
Cottam, Francis, "Katharine Hamnett," in *Unique* (Bridgeview, Illinois), No. 3, 1987.
Rowe, Gillian, "Katharine Hamnett," in *The Observer* (London), 31 January 1988.
"Katharine Hamnett Goes It Alone in London," in *Fashion Weekly* (London), 24 March 1988.
"Hamnett: Retailing Push for 1989," in *Fashion Weekly* (London), 5 May 1988.
Filmer, Deny, "Katharine Hamnett," in *Cosmopolitan* (London), July 1988.
Cottam, Francis, "Katharine Hamnett," in *Clothes Show* (London), November 1988.
"Perspectives," in *Blueprint* (London), November 1988.
Manser, José, "Nigel's Fishing Trip," in *Designers' Journal* (London), January 1989.
Hume, Marion, "Hamnett Soars to Designer Stardom," in the *Sunday Times* (London), 5 March 1989.
"Euro Hamnett," in *Cosmopolitan* (London), October 1989.
"Sex, Money, and Golden Oldies: Katharine Hamnett, Fashion's Fireball," in *The Independent* (London), 14 October 1989.
Mathur, Paul, "Hamnett," in *Blitz* (London), November 1989.
Mills, Simon, "Katharine Hamnett," in *Sky* (London), February 1990.
Polan, Brenda, "Katharine's Cutting Edge," in *The Independent* (London), 10 March 1991.
Goodkin, Judy, "Fashion Rebel with a Cause," in the *Sunday Times* (London), 5 May 1991.
Hochswender, Woody, "Turn-of-the-Century Chic," in *Esquire* (New York), October 1995.

* * *

A British designer as much recognized for her political and environmental beliefs as she is for her catwalk collections, Katharine Hamnett designed some of the most plagiarized fashion ideas in the 1980s. Hamnett set up her own company in 1979 after freelancing for various European companies for ten years. Although the designer claims she never intended to become involved in the manufacturing side of the fashion industry, preferring to concentrate solely on design, she was often, as a freelancer, treated badly. In 1979 she produced her own collection under the Katharine Hamnett Ltd. label, of which six jackets were taken by the London fashion retailer, Joseph Ettedgui, and subsequently sold out. Hamnett's early collections utilized parachute silk, cotton jersey, and drill, which she cut as functional unisex styles, based on traditional workwear that became her hallmark and, like many of her designs, spawned a thousand imitations.

Her nomination as British Fashion Industry Designer of the Year in 1984 testified to her influence in the early years of that decade. One of Hamnett's most influential designs was the idea of the slogan t-shirt bearing statements about political and environmental issues in bold print on plain white backgrounds. Perhaps the most famous read "58% Don't Want Pershing," which Hamnett wore when she met Margaret Thatcher at a Downing Street reception in 1984. Like Coco Chanel before her, Hamnett sees imitation as a form of flattery—particularly in the case of her slogan t-shirts which, she says, were meant to be copied to help promote her cause. Another example of Hamnett's obsession with politics was seen in the launch of her own magazine, *Tomorrow,* in 1985, where the designer attempted to parlay both fashion trends and political views. Unfortunately this combination was not a great success and the magazine folded after the first issue.

By 1986 a change was evident in Hamnett's design as she embraced the theme of sex as power with her Power Dressing collection aimed at postfeminist women. Since then her collections have become decidedly less workwear-oriented, to which critical reactions have been somewhat mixed.

Although the slogan t-shirts are no longer part of her collection, Hamnett's devotion to environmental issues continues to play an important role in her approach to fashion design. One project in which Hamnett became involved is the Green Cotton 2000 campaign, launched in conjunction with the Pesticides Trust in 1990, which aimed to reduce the harmful waste and discharged effluent produced by the textile industry. The power of the media is seen by Hamnett as a vital instrument in her personal campaign for the protection of the environment, and her fashion has provided an ideal vehicle. Hamnett admits she has more publicity than she needs to sell the clothes themselves, and can afford to use her influence as a designer to promote her own causes. However, while undoubtedly a major force in British fashion during the 1980s, along with John Galliano and Vivienne Westwood, her influence as a designer declined somewhat in recent years.

Hamnett's latest commitment, men's fashion, is yet another controversial career move that has not only brought her fame and fortune, but heated debate. Where styles for women were typically form-fitting and revealing to the body, men's styles were always baggy, oversized, and even shapeless. Men's bodies were not the focus; they had fewer options in their wardrobes, and fewer options for what was acceptable. It was Hamnett who changed this trend.

The highly opinionated and edgy British designer expanded her collection to focus primarily on the workplace. Slim suits, tight-fitting sport shirts, body-hugging knits, and chunky loafers—to be worn without socks—were just some of the prime examples from Hamnett's more recent collections. Ties, shoes, eyewear, and accessories also played a big part in her lines. Some say these styles resembled those of the early 1960s, and some say that's where they should have stayed. Although most of what Hamnett designed included pantsuits and jackets, they seemed to lack the professionalism most workplaces required. Allowing a male employee to show up to work in an iridescent, single-breasted slim suit with Lycra was certainly not the standard dress code of many companies.

In 1997, Hamnett escaped the runway scene and had an unforgettable show in Milan. It was a performance of two male models in shiny silk suits, lounge-lizard hats and pointy shoes. To many critic's surprise, the show was a success. Women absolutely loved it; as for the men however, well, that may take some getting used to.

Hamnett's most important contribution to fashion, and the one for which she will best be remembered, was her use of clothing as a vehicle for political and environmental change. Her success as a fashion designer enabled her to ultimately pursue her commitment to these issues.

—Catherine Woram; updated by Diana Idzelis

HARDWICK, Cathy

American designer

Born: Cathaline Kaesuk Sur, in Seoul, Korea, 30 December 1933; immigrated to the U.S., 1952; naturalized, 1959. **Education:** Studied music in Korea and Japan. **Family:** Married Anthony Hardwick, 1966 (divorced); four children. **Career:** Freelance designer and boutique owner, San Francisco, circa 1966–70; knitwear designer, Alvin Duskin, San Francisco, 1960s, and Dranella, Copenhagen; moved to New York, 1960s; sportswear designer, Pranx, New York; designer, Cathy Hardwick 'n' Friends, New York, 1972; president/designer, Cathy Hardwick Ltd., New York, 1975–81, and Cathy Hardwick Design Studio, New York, from 1977; company reorganized, 1988; additionally, sportswear designer for Sears Roebuck and Co., from 1990. **Awards:** Coty American Fashion Critics award, 1975. **Address:** 215 West 40th Street, New York, NY 10018, USA.

Publications

On HARDWICK:

Books

Morris, Bernadine, and Barbara Walz, *The Fashion Makers,* New York, 1978.

Milbank, Caroline Rennolds, *New York Fashion: The Evolution of American Style,* New York, 1989.

Stegemeyer, Anne, *Who's Who in Fashion, Third Edition,* New York, 1996.

Articles

O'Sullivan, Joan, "She's a Natural," in *Living Today* (Wheaton, Illinois), 16 September 1977.

Colborn, Marge, "East Village with Seoul: A Hands On Approach to Fall," in the *Detroit News* (Michigan), 4 May 1986.

Daria, Irene, "Cathy Hardwick: Craft, Compromise and Creation," in *WWD,* 3 August 1987.

Klensch, Elsa, "Cathy Harwick—Success with Style," in *Vogue* (New York), June 1988.

News brief, "Cathy Hardwick Designs Clothes for Sears," *Chicago Tribune,* 19 December 1990.

Kornbluth, Jesse, "Manhattan Romance," in *Architectural Digest,* February 1997.

Klensch, Elsa, "Mario Buatta: Fluid Interiors," in *Style* on CNN (New York), 25 September 1997.

* * *

Cathy Hardwick has designed ready-to-wear for the audience she knows best—the modern career woman with an active lifestyle. There is a certain spirit and success about Hardwick's designs that come from this defining relationship to the clothing and its purpose. Hardwick's collections consistently offer women clothing with ease and simplicity, appealing to the young and young-minded spirit of the confident, self-assured businesswoman. Her clothing is not merely a somber uniform, but rather has an air of wit and sophistication that makes it fun, worn by the stylish young woman who is secure with her life and is moving in a positive direction. "Know your physical type and personal style, and be true to it. Any current look can be adapted in silhouette, scale, and color so it's right for you. You have to feel comfortable. The most fabulous clothes won't work if you're self-conscious," Hardwick said in a February 1978 *Harper's Bazaar,* article.

Recognized early in her career as a talented young designer involved in creating simplistic, modern clothing, Hardwick began designing knitwear for Alvin Duskin in San Francisco in the late 1960s. The designs were well-received and commercially successful. Soon after, she developed her own company and continued to design knitwear as a part of her collections throughout the 1970s and 1980s. She continued to design under her own label in New York, using almost exclusively natural fibers.

Hardwick's design success has been a result of the masterful execution of her pure and basic principles—neutral colors and simplicity of form. By centering her collections around neutral colors and relating the colors of current collections to previous ones, the wearer can develop a wardrobe of pieces that work together. Her designs recognize fashion trends but always retain a clean, simplistic style that is distinctly her own. Hardwick's clothing is associated with the modern woman's ability to go from an effective day at work to an evening out with minimal changes.

A 1980 advertisement for B. Altman and Co. portrayed a Hardwick collection coordinated in different ways to suit the style of the potential wearer. The ad copy read, "Hardwick's…forward-looking collection lets you choose the new length you like, a little or a whole lot shorter. Another fine fashion point you should notice: these separates are all cut and colored (in magenta and black) so you can build your own new-decade pants-set." Such a philosophy of personal style and selection has been apparent in Hardwick's collections throughout her career.

Based on strong, simple shapes reminiscent of traditional Korean clothing, Hardwick's collections hard back to her childhood. She was born to a Korean family of diplomats and financiers including her grandfather, who was an ambassador to France. Her clothing reflects her lifelong exposure to and depth of understanding of the fusion of Eastern and Western styles. The *chinoiserie* elements in the designs seem to be a part of the total vision and philosophy she has about clothing rather than a motif simply applied to Western fashion. In her first formal show in New York in 1974, Hardwick showed *obi* style wrapping in the closures of her skirts and trousers along with Oriental prints and accessories. In 1975, she showed the effectiveness of shaping a "Big Dress" with an *obi*-inspired tie. Earlier Hardwick incorporated frog closures in her mandarin collared jacket for a more direct use of the Eastern look. The mandarin collar and frog closures were used again in her spring 1994 collection on light and easy shaped tops.

Hardwick's style hasn't stopped at fashion. The freelance designer is as true to her passion for individualism in clothing design as she is to individualism within the home. Inspired by interior decorator Mario Buatta, Hardwick transformed her home into a modern masterpiece, which seems to have somehow maintained the simplicity and quaintness of English country living. Convention dominates the five-star apartment, with its 18th-century twist to modern conveniences. What was once a 2,000-square-foot loft became a traditional apartment with rooms overlooking Park Avenue.

Keeping up with the American designer's style of living, however, is the greatest challenge any Hardwick admirer would endure, not to mention Hardwick herself. The apartment is nowhere near being finished, nor will it ever be finished. "Rooms and houses are never finished," Buatta claims, "It's all a work in progress. You always buy new things. You always travel. You always change. After all, it's a living room, not a dead room." And for Hardwick, this means allowing herself to sit back while Buatta takes charge (with Hardwick's permission, of course).

While Hardwick's interest in home furnishings seem to have taken center stage in her life at the moment, fashion design, she says, is still her greatest love. There is no word, however, as to when she plans to continue with her career.

—Dennita Sewell; updated by Diana Idzelis

HARP, Holly

American designer

Born: Buffalo, New York, 24 October 1939. **Education:** Attended Radcliffe College; studied art and fashion design, North Texas State University. **Family:** Married Jim Harp, 1965 (divorced, 1975); son: Tommy. **Career:** Opened first boutique on Sunset Strip, Los Angeles, 1968; opened in-store boutique, Henri Bendel, New York, 1972; developed wholesale collection, 1973. Also designed for Simplicity Patterns, Fieldcrest Linens, and Hollywood films including *Cabaret, Sleeper,* and *She Devil.* **Died:** 24 April 1995.

Publications

On HARP:

Books

Milinaire, C., and C. Troy, *Cheap Chic,* New York, 1975.
Morris, Bernadine, and Barbara Walz, *The Fashion Makers,* New York, 1978.
Lobenthal, Joel, *Radical Rags: Fashions of the Sixties,* New York, 1990.
Stegemeyer, Anne, *Who's Who in Fashion, Third Edition*, New York, 1996.

Articles

"Holly's Harp," in *WWD,* 7 November 1974.
"Rainy Day Women?" in *People,* 21 February 1977.
Sajbel, Maureen, "The Unsinkable Holly Harp," in *WWD,* 6 January 1987.
"Holly Harp," obituary, in *WWD,* 26 April 1995.
Lynn, Alison, "Passages," obituary, *People,* 25 May 1995.

*

I've been designing clothes since the late 1960s. I always try to remind myself that I am dressing a woman's soul as well as her body. Souls and bodies do best when they are relaxed, fluid, and comfortable. They love to play "dress-up." They love a good laugh as well as perfect quiet and softness. I hope my clothes reflect a woman's soul.

—Holly Harp

* * *

Many students are torn between the glamor of stage or film design and high fashion. Holly Harp was able to merge both her love of costume and fashion into a successful professional career that lasted more than 25 years. Harp went with an early instinct after designing sandals on a whim, and returned to college with her sights set on becoming a designer. She studied in the theatre department and worked on her fashion degree. Her style was dramatic, feminine, and refined.

Harp moved to the West Coast during the height of hippiedom in 1966. San Francisco hippies tended to borrow street styles and recycle clothing salvaged from the local Goodwill, while Los Angeles, where Harp set up shop, was more interested in marketing styles and trends in the form of new designs. The latter was more of a "rich hippie" look. Harp was inspired by the youthful street fashions and was referred to by the *Los Angeles Times* as the city's "doyenne of feathers and fringe." Her rock star clients had included Janis Joplin and Grace Slick, who loved Harp's wonderful batiks, feathers, and hand-dyed fabrics. Harp's clothes suited the tastes of the youthful population who loved psychedelic colors and melodramatic effects.

It was more than being in the right place at the right time. Harp began to distill her designs into her own personal expression. During the 1970s there was more emphasis on the body. The soft matte jersey Harp experimented with became a signature fabric along with chiffon. There was a continuation of using beadwork, flowers, feathers, and airbrushed designs but with a softer, refined touch. Harp used complicated draping techniques to emphasize feminine qualities rather than the prevailing minimal approach.

Harp became known for making fabulous dresses that attracted the attention of the Hollywood élite. Her customer list reads like a Who's Who: Liza Minelli, Jane Seymour, Lauren Hutton, Bette Midler, Diana Ross, Jane Pauley, and Sally Field were just a few. Her clients also included a long list of famous male customers such as Ryan O'Neal, Jon Voight, and Jack Nicholson, who selected Harp's clothing for the women in their lives. Some Harp originals have appeared in Hollywood films as well. She successfully challenged the glitzy Hollywood image with nostalgically beautiful designs.

The ability to create clothing with both romantic and classic qualities carried Harp through the 1980s into the 1990s; by limiting her production and not overextending herself, Harp maintained the integrity of her designs. Whatever bright and trend-setting clothes were in her future, however, were cut short: Holly Harp died of cancer in April of 1995. She was 55.

—Myra Walker; updated by Nelly Rhodes

HARTNELL, Norman

British designer

Born: London, 12 June 1901. **Education:** Studied at Magdalen College, Cambridge, 1921–23. **Career:** Assistant to Court Dressmaker, Mme. Désiré, 1923; opened own dressmaking studio, London, 1923; first Paris showing, 1927; appointed dressmaker to the Royal Family, 1938; designed women's uniforms for the Royal Army Corps and the Red Cross; introduced ready-to-wear lines, from 1942; also designed for Berkertex, from the late 1940s, for *Women's Illustrated* magazine, 1950–60s, and lingerie line for Saks Fifth Avenue, 1950s; theatrical designer, 1923–60s. **Exhibitions:** *Norman Hartnell, 1901–1979* (retrospective), London, 1985; *Norman Hartnell* (retrospective), Brighton, 1985; *Hartnell: Clothes by the Royal Couturier, 1930s–1960s* (retrospective), Bath, 1985–86. **Awards:** Officier d'Academie, France, 1939; first Royal Warrant received, 1940; Neiman Marcus award, 1947; appointed Member of

Norman Hartnell, ca. 1945. © Hulton-Deutsch Collection/CORBIS.

the Royal Victorian Order, 1953; appointed Knight Commander of the Royal Victorian Order, 1977. **Died** 8 June 1979, in Windsor, Berkshire, England.

Publications

By HARTNELL:

Books

Silver and Gold, London, 1955.
Royal Courts of Fashion, London, 1971.

On HARTNELL:

Books

Brighton Art Gallery, *Norman Hartnell* (exhibition catalogue), Brighton, 1985.
Kennett, Frances, et al., *Norman Hartnell, 1901–1979* (exhibition catalogue), London, 1985.
McDowell, Colin, *A Hundred Years of Royal Style,* London, 1985.
Milbank, Caroline Rennolds, *Couture: The Great Designers,* New York, 1985.
Stegemeyer, Anne, *Who's Who in Fashion, Third Edition,* New York, 1996.

Articles

Wyndham, Francis, "The Pearly King," in *Vogue* (London), September 1960.
Glynn, Prudence, "Hartnell: The Norman Conquest," in *The Times* (London), 6 January 1977.
Sinclair, Serena, "For Sir Norman, At Last, a Royal Reward," in the *Daily Telegraph* (London), 10 January 1977.

Hassian, Nicky, "Sir Norman Hartnell," in *Ritz* (London), No. 3, 1977.
Laurance, Robin, "But Will Sir Norman Arise?" in *The Guardian* (London), 2 March 1977.
Scroggle, Jean, "The Norman Conquests," in *Homes and Gardens* (London), June 1985.
Hoare, Sarajane, "Relaunch of Ready-to-Wear at Hartnell," in *The Observer* (London), 9 March 1986.
McDowell, Colin, "The Rise of the House of Hartnell," in *The Guardian* (London), 13 March 1986.
Williams, Antonia, "Hartnell Then and Now," in *Vogue* (London), August 1986.
Hume, Marion, "Heart to Hartnell," in *Fashion Weekly* (London), 15 January 1987.
Brown, Malcolm, "Trading Places: Peter Moss, Moss Brothers; Manny Silverman, Norman Hartnell," *Marketing,* 3 December 1987.

* * *

Norman Hartnell began his fashion career working as an assistant to extravagant society couturière Lucile. Through his exposure to this rarefied world of fashion, gossip, decoration, and illicit romance, he was inspired to open his own dressmaking business in 1923, establishing what became one of the best-known and longest-running couture houses in Britain. Situated in the heart of London's Mayfair, the house on Bruton Street always had an air of splendor. A graceful staircase, panelled with mirrors, led up to the splendid salon where gilt mirrors and two giant crystal chandeliers created an air of tranquillity. Seated on their gilt-encrusted chairs, society hostesses, actresses, film stars, debutantes, and royalty watched countless collections float elegantly by.

The early collections shown in both London and Paris quickly established Hartnell's reputation for lavishly embroidered ballgowns in satin and tulle, fur-trimmed suits, and elegantly tailored tweed day ensembles. His first wedding dress fashioned from silver and gold net was a showstopping finale to an early collection and was described as "the eighth wonder of the world" when worn by the bride of Lord Weymouth. Other early commissions included a 1927 wedding dress for romantic novelist and socialite Barbara Cartland, and informal clothes for actress Tallulah Bankhead who scandalized 1920s London with performances both on and off-stage.

Hartnell's clothes often stood apart from fashion, owing a greater allegiance to costume; this was no doubt fueled by his early experience designing theatrical productions while at Cambridge University. He drew inspiration from the saucy French paintings of Watteau and Boucher, purity of line from Italian masters like Botticelli and painters such as Renoir and Tissot for what he described as a touch of "chi chi." Summoned to Buckingham Palace on the succession of King George VI to discuss designs for the coronation dresses of the maids of honor, the King led Hartnell through the hall of Winterhalter portraits. This gave him the inspiration for the crinoline dresses that later become a symbolic royal look for the two monarchs—Queen Elizabeth the Queen Mother and Queen Elizabeth II. The dresses also influenced the silhouette of Dior's New Look of 1947, a line that came to epitomize a postwar return to femininity.

Hartnell was officially appointed dressmaker to the royal family in 1938 and subsequently designed for various royal occasions, eventually being acknowledged for creating a stylistic royal image that remains today. He was responsible for both the wedding dresses of Queen Elizabeth II and Princess Margaret. In 1953 he created the Queen's historic coronation dress, embroidered with the emblems of Great Britain and the Commonwealth. In the late 1990s and early 21st century, the House of Hartnell was still responsible for the personal wardrobe of the Queen Mother.

It could be argued that Hartnell limited himself as a designer by his work for British royalty and aristocracy. He created to promote and protect an establishment, encasing it in a grandiose aura of ornament and glamor, a service honored by a knighthood in 1977. It should be remembered, however, that Hartnell also produced ready-to-wear collections, sold through department stores from 1942 onwards. He also designed for Berkertex and created the uniforms of the British Red Cross and the Women's Royal Army Corps during World War II.

Although Norman Hartnell died in 1979 his legacy was continued in the early 1990s by French couturier Marc Bohan. Bohan designed haute couture and ready-to-wear collections and successfully maintained the Hartnell name for a few years, but the recession of the early 1990s soon took its toll. Norman Hartnell closed its doors in 1992.

—Kevin Almond

HAWES, Elizabeth

American designer

Born: Ridgewood, New Jersey, 16 December 1903. **Education:** Studied at Vassar College, Poughkeepsie, New York, 1921–25. **Family:** Married Ralph Jester in 1930 (divorced, 1934); married Joseph Losey in 1937 (divorced, 1944), son: Gavrik Losey. **Career:** Worked in Paris as fashion copyist, stylist, journalist, then designed for Nicole Groult, 1925–28; designer and partner, Hawes-Harden, New York, 1928–30; designer, Hawes, Inc., New York, 1930–40; designer, Elizabeth Hawes, Inc., New York, 1948–49; occasional freelance designer, New York and California, 1950–68. Additionally an author, union organizer, and political activist. **Exhibitions:** *Two Modern Artists of Dress: Elizabeth Hawes and Rudi Gernreich,* Fashion Institute of Technology, New York, 1967; Brooklyn Museum (retrospective), 1985. **Died:** 6 September 1971, in New York.

Publications

By HAWES:

Books

Fashion is Spinach, New York, 1938.
Men Can Take It, New York, 1939.
Why is a Dress?, New York, 1942.
Good Grooming, Boston, 1942.
Why Women Cry, or Wenches with Wrenches, New York, 1943.
Hurry Up Please, It's Time, New York, 1946.
Anything But Love, New York, 1948.
But Say It Politely, Boston, 1954.
It's Still Spinach, Boston, 1954.

Articles

Writing as "Parasite," fashion items in the *New Yorker,* 1927–28.
Columns in *PM* magazine, 1940–42.

On HAWES:

Books

New York and Hollywood Fashion: Costume Designs from the Brooklyn Museum Collection, New York, 1986.
Berch, Bettina, *Radical by Design: The Life and Style of Elizabeth Hawes,* New York, 1988.
Milbank, Caroline Rennolds, *New York Fashion: The Evolution of American Style,* New York, 1989.
Steele, Valerie, *Women of Fashion,* New York, 1991.

Articles

Obituary, in the *New York Times,* 8 September 1971.
Mahoney, Patrick R., "Elizabeth Hawes," in *Notable American Women,* New York, 1980.
———, "In and Out of Style," in *Vassar Quarterly* (New York), Spring 1986.
Berch, Bettina, "Early Feminist Fashion," in *Ms. Magazine,* March 1987.
Jones, Barbara, "Radical by Design (book review)," in *The Nation,* 6 February 1989.

* * *

Brainy and articulate, Elizabeth Hawes challenged the fashion industry's dictum that stylish clothing must originate only in the salons of a handful of French couturiers, to be worn by a privileged few. Hawes was trained in the French system and from 1928 to 1940 her studio in New York provided custom-made clothing and accessories for a distinguished clientèle. A gifted publicist with a knack for self-promotion, Hawes successfully debunked the myth that beautiful clothes could only be created in Paris and became one of the first American designers to achieve national recognition. She saw no reason, however, why mass-produced clothing should not be equally as distinctive and she became increasingly interested in designing for the wholesale market. It was an unhappy collaboration: Hawes' clothes were both too simple and too forward-looking for most manufacturers. She found her ideas compromised time and time again in the finished product.

In her bestselling 1938 autobiography *Fashion is Spinach,* Hawes called fashion and the fashion industry parasites on true style. Style, she said, gives the feeling of the period, and changes only as there is a real change in point of view. Fashion, by contrast, changes not in response to events or to public taste or need, but because industry payrolls must be met, magazines published, a myth perpetuated.

Hawes despaired that most men and women were clothing conformists; in her view, clothes should be the expression of personality, of fantasy, and above all of individuality. If a woman occasionally wanted trousers to wear, or a man ruffles, she argued provocatively, why shouldn't they have them? The important thing was to dress to please yourself.

Hawes' iconoclastic theories about clothing were supported by solid academic and practical training. As an undergraduate she studied anatomy and economics before apprenticing herself to the workrooms of Bergdorf Goodman and Nicole Groult, among others. Her fluid bias-cut clothes moved with the body, revealing its natural curves. She believed a successful dress must fuse with the wearer, that line, in relationship to anatomy, was the basis for a beautiful dress. Not surprisingly, the designer Hawes most admired was Madeleine Vionnet.

Those who might not have been familiar with Hawes as a designer knew her as an author and journalist, a witty and astute critic of the fashion system. In her writing Hawes incited men and women to rebel against the status quo to speak up for clothing that suited the way they lived. She explained how the system worked against the consumer, producing shabbily made clothes that fit poorly and which were certainly not intended to last beyond a single season. Hawes disliked seeing women in unbecoming, uncomfortable clothes which cost more than they were worth, all in the name of fashion.

In 1940 Hawes turned her business over to her staff in order to concentrate on applying her theories about design to mass production. In her 1942 treatise, *Why is a Dress?,* Hawes said that she had come to regret the Paris training which prepared her for the past when the future clearly lay in ready-to-wear. Hawes once again found herself at moral and philosophical odds, however, with the wholesale garment manufacturers. She did not return to designing until 1948, and then only briefly.

Elizabeth Hawes was a visionary and an iconoclast. She was a designer of inventive clothing and a fashion writer whose analytic prose still illuminates the world of Seventh Avenue.

—Whitney Blausen

HEAD, Edith

American film costume designer

Born: Edith Claire Poesner in San Bernadino, California, 28 October 1897. **Education:** University of California at Los Angeles, B.A.; Stanford University, Palo Alto, California, M.A.; also studied at the Otis Art Institute and Chouinard School, Los Angeles. **Family:** Married Charles Head in 1923 (divorced, 1923); married Wiard Ihnen in 1940 (died 1979). **Career:** Instructor in French, Spanish, and art, The Bishop School for Girls (La Jolla, California) and at Hollywood School for Girls, 1923; sketch artist, Paramount Pictures, 1924–27; assistant to Travis Banton, Paramount, 1927–38; Head of Design, Paramount Studios, Hollywood, 1938–66; chief costume designer, Universal Studios, Hollywood, 1967–81. Also author, editor, radio and television commentator. Designed uniforms for the Coast Guard and Pan American Airlines; lecturer, University of Southern California and University of California at Los Angeles. **Exhibitions:** *Romantic and Glamorous Hollywood Design,* Metropolitan Museum of Art, New York, 1974; *Hollywood Film Costume,* Whitworth Art Gallery, Manchester, 1977; *Edith Head: A Retrospectacular,* presented by Chivas Regal benefitting the Design Industries Foundation Fighting AIDS and the Motion Picture & Television Fund Foundation, 1998. **Awards:** Academy® award, 1949, 1950, 1951, 1953, 1954, 1960, 1973; Film Designer of the Year award, Mannequins Association, Los Angeles, 1962; Costume Designers Guild award,

Lana Turner modeling an Edith Head-designed silk pants outfit from the film *Love Has Many Faces* (1965). Overblouse is covered with crystal beads. © AP/Wide World Photos.

1967. **Died:** 26 October 1981, in Los Angeles, California. **Website:** www.edithhead.com (A Retrospectacular Tribute).

Publications

By HEAD:

Books

The Dress Doctor, with Jane Ardmore, Boston, 1959.
How to Dress for Success, with Joe Hyams, New York, 1967.
Edith Head's Hollywood, with Paddy Calistro, New York, 1983.

Articles

in *Silver Screen* (New York), September 1946, January 1948.
in *Hollywood Quarterly* (Los Angeles), October 1946.
in *Photoplay* (New York), October 1948.
in *Good Housekeeping* (New York), March 1959.
in *Holiday* (New York), January and July 1973, September and November 1974, January, March and September 1975, March 1976.
in *Inter/View* (New York), January 1974.
in *Take One* (Montreal), October 1976.
in *American Film* (Washington, D.C.), May 1978.
in *Cine Revue* (Paris), 19 April 1979.

On HEAD:

Books

Epstein, Beryl Williams, *Fashion Is Our Business,* Philadelphia, 1945, London, 1947.
Steen, Mike, *Hollywood Speaks: An Oral History,* New York, 1974.
Vreeland, Diana, *Romantic and Glamorous Hollywood Design* (exhibition catalogue), New York, 1974.
Chierichetti, David, *Hollywood Costume Design,* New York and London, 1976.
McConathy, Dale, *Hollywood Costume,* New York, 1976.
Regan, Michael, *Hollywood Film Costume* (exhibition catalogue), Manchester, 1977.
Morris, Bernadine, and Barbara Walz, *The Fashion Makers,* New York, 1978.
La Vine, W. Robert, *In a Glamorous Fashion: The Fabulous Years of Costume Design,* New York, 1980, Boston and London, 1981.
Pritchard, Susan, *Film Costume: An Annotated Bibliography,* New Jersey and London, 1981.
New York and Hollywood Fashion: Costume Designs from the Brooklyn Museum Collection, New York, 1986.
Acker, Ally, *Reel Women: Pioneers of the Cinema,* New York, 1991.
Stegemeyer, Anne, *Who's Who in Fashion, Third Edition,* New York, 1996.

Articles

Hollywood, Molly, "Film Colony, New York Battle to Set Styles," in the *Los Angeles Examiner,* 21 September 1941.
Scallion, Virginia, "Meet the Woman Who Dresses the Stars," in the *California Stylist,* July 1954.
"Dialogue on Film: Edith Head," in *American Film,* May 1978.
"Edith Head, Designer of Hollywood Glamor," in the *Los Angeles Times,* 27 October 1981.
McCarthy, Todd, "Edith Head Dies at 82; Costumes Subordinate to Story, Character," *Variety,* 28 October 1981.
Dolan, Judith, "A Head for Design," in *Stanford Magazine* (Stanford, California), 1991.
Locayo, Richard, "Inside Hollywood! Women, Sex, & Power," *People,* Spring 1991.
Spoto, Donald, "Edith Head," *Architectural Digest,* April 1992.

* * *

As head of design for Paramount Pictures, Edith Head was the last great designer to work under contract to a major film studio. Head's first significant assignment was to create the wardrobe for silent film star Clara Bow in *Wings* (1927). Her last was costuming Steve Martin in the 1940ish mock noir film, *Dead Men Don't Wear Plaid* (1982). In a career spanning 60 years, Head was responsible for the on-screen persona of such stars as Mae West, Dorothy Lamour, Bob Hope, Barbara Stanwyck, Ginger Rogers, Olivia de Haviland, Gloria Swanson, Grace Kelly, and Elizabeth Taylor.

Head had no formal training in design and she took care to work within what she saw as her limitations. She might never be considered a couturier, but she could—and did—become a taste-maker. Thus while contemporaries Erté and Adrian came to be known for gowns

Edith Head surrounded by some of the 700 costumes she designed during her career, 1967. © AP/Wide World Photos.

which epitomized fantasy and glamor, Edith Head made herself known for designing beautiful and flattering clothes which the movie-going public could easily imagine wearing.

Head's wardrobe for Barbara Stanwyck in *The Lady Eve* (1941) advanced her growing reputation as a designer particularly attuned to the psyche of the average woman. Stanwyck had most often been cast in roles which required she look plain. Her on-screen transformation to a woman of style thrilled audiences as much as it thrilled Stanwyck herself. The star had Edith Head written into her contract, and the studio publicity department saw to it that the name Edith Head became synonymous with home-grown American fashion.

Beginning in 1945, Head had a featured spot on Art Linkletter's radio program "House Party," giving advice on matters of dress to the listening audience. When the show moved to television in 1952, Head moved with it. On live television, she would perform an impromptu verbal and visual makeover on members of the studio audience, sometimes using some element of her own clothing to suggest a more effective personal presentation. Head had a keen intellect, and when she brought her gift of analysis to the human figure, she created a look to flatter the wearer and fit the occasion. This was one of her great strengths as a costumier and it was a skill which could benefit anyone.

In her film work, Head was known as a "director's designer" whose interpretation of a character became the visual embodiment of the directorial thought process. Olivia de Haviland's subtly ill-fitting costumes for the opening scenes of *The Heiress,* or Gloria Swanson's clothes for *Sunset Boulevard,* with their simultaneous references to the 1920s and the 1950s, remain superb examples of characterization. Head often said that even without a soundtrack the story of *The Heiress* could be understood through its costumes.

One of the most challenging problems for any theatrical designer is so-called "modern dress." A motion picture may be shot up to two years before it is shown to the public but clothing must not betray this fact by seeming dated. If so versatile a designer may be said to have a trademark, Head's would be a clean and simple line with a minimum of detail, in a subdued palette. Head produced timeless classics which never competed with the performer and never took focus from the storyline. It was all, she said, "a matter of camouflage and magic."

—Whitney Blausen; updated by Nelly Rhodes

HECHTER, Daniel

French designer

Born: Paris, 30 July 1938. **Education:** Completed trade school education, 1956. **Family:** Married Marika Hechter; married Jennifer Chambon, 1980; children: Carinne. **Military Service:** Served in the French Army, 1958–60. **Career:** Delivery boy, Paris ready-to-wear firm, 1956; formed own design studio, 1956; salesman, then designer, Pierre d'Alby, Paris, 1960–62; founder and designer, the Hechter Group, from 1962; added children's line, 1965; introduced menswear, 1968; active sportswear and home furnishings lines introduced, 1970; added accessory range, 1976; launched furniture collection, 1983; offered first men's fragrance, 1989; created DH 621 men's line, 1994; added second men's fragrance, 1996. **Address:** 4 Ter, Avenue Hoche, 75008 Paris, France. **Website:** www.hechtermontres.com.

Publications

By HECHTER:

Books

Le Boss, Paris, 2000.

On HECHTER:

Books

Stegemeyer, Anne, *Who's Who in Fashion, Third Edition,* New York, 1996.

Articles

Moor, Johnathan, "The Americanization of Daniel Hechter," in *DNR,* 21 January 1980.

———, "Daniel Hechter: Taking it Easy...With Enthusiasm," in *DNR,* 18 August 1980.

Wood, Mary Ann, "Daniel Hechter: Bringing High Fashion Down to Earth," in *Fashion Retailer N.E.,* November 1980.

Highe, Jackie, "Decision Makers: The Fashion Dictators," in *Living* (London), 13 July 1983.

"Court Orders Removal of Anti-Hechter Posters," in *WWD,* 4 December 1988.

D'Aulnay, Sophie, "Daniel Hechter: Coming to America—Again," in *DNR,* 12 July 1993.

———, "The Directional Daniel Hechter," in *DNR,* 25 January 1996.

"Lapidus: Fantasy Becomes Fragrance" in *European Cosmetic Markets,* 1 April 1997.

"Celebrities in Switzerland: Daniel Hechter," available online at switzerland.isyours.com, Micheloud & Co., 6 June 2001.

"Daniel Hechter," available online at www.hechtermontres.com, 6 June 2001.

* * *

Daniel Hechter was one of the first designers to recognize the commercial viability of lifestyle dressing and has marketed the concept with enormous success, today exporting to some 47 countries and licensing goods in the U.S., South America, Europe, Australia, and Canada. In many ways, he provided the inspiration for the 1980s' explosion of lifestyle concepts in retailing.

Hechter identified his particular market as including the young, sometimes married with children, upwardly mobile 20- to 30-somethings, who may not have the income to finance the designer lifestyle and fashionable appearance to which they aspire. As a mass market designer, it is essential to be able to perceive what is right for the moment, particularly when dealing with the fickle youth-oriented market. Hechter's taste and style have often been directed by the unpredictable forces of pop, club, and street culture, and his business rapidly prospered because of his adaptability and speed.

Born into a family who owned a ready-to-wear company, Hechter was brought up in an environment sympathetic to fashion. He worked for designer Pierre d'Alby from 1958 before opening his own house in 1962 with friend Armand Orustein. The company opened with a womenswear collection that captured the developing need of the 1960s—young, fun, and sometimes throwaway. He produced sweaters, maxi coats, trouser suits, smoking jackets, gabardine raincoats, and boot top-length divided skirts. His casual jersey and ribbed duffle coats and greatcoats emphasized his skills for sophisticated unisex outerwear, sporty yet wearable and stylish.

The business grew to incorporate many areas of fashion and clothing design, producing shoes, sunglasses, school uniforms, corporate wear, and tennis and ski clothes. He also moved into designing for the home, broadening his lifestyle concepts by producing household linens furniture, crystal stemware, and patterns for china place settings. Other additions to the Hechter line were men's fragrances: *Caractére* in 1989, promoted as a simple, warm scent, and *XXL* in 1996, said to have a woodsy, energetic character.

The company has been a regular employer of fashion design graduates from all over the world. Hechter believes this inserts a continual flow of fresh ideas and invigorates the Daniel Hechter image. The company exports goods and has numerous licensing contracts throughout the world, as well as operating its own boutiques in nearly every Western European country, one in Russia, fourteen in Asia or the Middle East, three in Africa, two in South America, and two in the United States. The company is looking toward Eastern Europe for further expansion. The success of the business has sparked Hechter's creative flow—he developed a new line of clothing using natural fabrics called DH 621. The products were first launched in Israel in 1994 and spread to Asia from there. Hechter says the clothing falls between casual and sportswear and costs a bit less than his other lines.

Hechter attributes his success to his practical, matter-of-fact approach to design. He displays none of the airs or temperament associated with the stereotypical fashion designer. In fact, Hechter has allowed his personal interests to shape and extend the direction of the company. Sports have been a lifelong passion, and in 1972 he cofounded the Paris Saint-Germain Football Club. Years later, in 1998, he designed the streetwear for the French Soccer World Cup team. His support of tennis with over 20 years of annual parties during the French Open led to a request from the French Tennis Federation for him to create the umpires' outfits in 1993.

Hechter has also dabbled in politics, sitting on the Marseilles Regional Council since 1992. In 1997 he moved to Geneva, Switzerland, and wrote a novel entitled *Le Boss,* published in 2000. Daniel Hechter has used his personal experiences to perceive and fill voids left by others in the fashion world.

—Kevin Almond; updated by Carrie Snyder

HEIM, Jacques

French designer

Born: Paris, 8 May 1899. **Family:** Married; one son: Philippe. **Career:** Manager, Isadore and Jeanne Heim fur fashion house, from about 1920; initiated couture department for coats, suits, and gowns, circa 1925; opened own couture house, 1930; Heim Jeunes Filles collection introduced, 1936; Heim sportswear boutiques established in Biarritz and Cannes, from 1937; Heim-Actualité girlswear collection introduced, 1950; fragrances included *Alambie,* 1947, *J'Aime,* 1958, *Shandoah,* 1966; house closed, 1969; president, Chambre Syndicale de la Couture Parisienne, 1958–62. Also owner and publisher, *Revue Heim,* 1950s. **Died:** 8 January 1967, in Paris.

Publications

On HEIM:

Books

Milbank, Caroline Rennolds, *Couture: The Great Designers,* New York, 1985.

Stegemeyer, Anne, *Who's Who in Fashion, Third Edition,* New York, 1996.

Jacques Heim, fall 1963 collection. © Bettmann/CORBIS.

Articles

Peterson, Patricia, "Heim Drops Hemline and Ban on Photographs," in the *New York Times,* 23 July 1962.

Obituary, in the *New York Times,* 9 January 1967.

* * *

Caroline Rennolds Milbank called Jacques Heim an "innovator by nature," in her 1985 book, *Couture: The Great Designers*. Few would agree. Heim's *New York Times* obituary (9 January 1967) read: "Mr. Heim's fashion house designed and made clothes of a modest style. He was never in the front ranks of the big houses that radically changed the looks of women by offering new silhouettes in the manner of Balenciaga, Chanel, or Saint Laurent." Perhaps the median truth was expressed in *Women's Wear Daily*'s obituary: "Heim was basically an innovator in business. He didn't want to be called a designer, but rather an editor of clothes." He aggressively conceived of ways in which couture might be vital to new audiences (his Heim Jeunes Filles brought garments to a young audience long before other couture designers, and engendered early client loyalty) and was an impeccable spokesman for the fashion industry of France (until he broke with the couture schedule for delayed photographs in summer 1962). He was an editor of many design ideas, beginning with the possibilities of fur, continuing through beach and play outfits, even the two-piece swimsuit, and the plane and planar simplifications of design in the youth-conscious 1960s.

If he was not driven by the market, he was at least keenly sensitive to it. Heim was a smart, eclectic designer of many styles; through consistent sales sensitivity he transformed the fur business of his parents Isadore and Jeanne Heim, founded in 1898, and persevered and prospered as a designer for nearly four decades. Heim's fashion breakthrough was to realize that fur could be worked as a fabric. Wool and fur combinations, geometries of fur and textiles, and fur accents became hallmarks of the Heim fashion in the 1930s. At the same time, along with Chanel and Patou and others, Heim was alert to the possibilities of elegant sportswear and observed bathing and sports costumes as inspiration. According to Milbank, Heim was inspired by the Tahitian exhibits in the Paris colonial exhibition of 1931 to create *pareos* and sarongs. Later, his 1950 two-piece swimsuit Atome came considerably after the bikini incident and invention, but addressed a broader public.

Through the 1950s, Heim addressed American needs for sportswear in innovative and utilitarian fabrics, while still remaining, in the vocabulary of the day, very ladylike. Moreover, his Heim *Actualité* diffusion line, launched in 1950, extended his influence into ready-to-wear along with the young styles of Heim Jeunes Filles. From 1958 to 1962 he was president of the Chambre Syndicale de la Couture Parisienne, and was "probably the last effective president of the couture's professional body," according to *Women's Wear Daily.* When, however, he permitted immediate release of collection photographs to the press in July 1962, in advance of the agreed-upon delayed release, he precipitated a furor among designers to preserve the design's secret until their slow dissemination. Heim was steadfastly modern and business-oriented. In this decision, he anticipated the couture's gradual détente in the 1960s, but did it so abruptly that he lost the confidence of his colleagues. Patricia Peterson, writing for the *New York Times,* in July 1962, reported, "Photographs were not to have been published in the United States until August 26, for Europe the release date was to have been August 27. When Heim allowed

Design by Jacques Heim, 1954. © Genevieve Naylor/CORBIS.

photographs to run even before the opening, the chase was on to find photographers. Men used to shooting wars, riots, and dignitaries were suddenly faced with swirling models. Other couture houses were besieged with queries." Perhaps it always takes an insider to bring the certain news of change, but Heim was as wounded as any messenger with the apparent bad tidings that couture's control was over and the camera and the press held sway.

Favored by Mme. Charles de Gaulle and a designer for Mrs. Dwight D. Eisenhower, Heim understood the expression "old soldiers never die." He never married a style or became one form's advocate; instead, he had insisted on the business principle that fashion would thrive in change and adaptation. "The life of a couturier is a magnificent and continuous torture," Heim said. But he was probably only expressing a businessman's shrewd romanticism and a leader's quixotic belief in fashion's anguish. His commerce was clearly his passion and his métier, not the design itself. As the *New York Times* commented in his obituary, "Jacques Heim, a tall good-looking man with a cheery disposition, seemed more like a businessman or banker than a couturier. He exhibited none of the flamboyance or temperament of competitors like Yves Saint Laurent or Christian Dior." But, of course, design is made by acumen as well as by inspiration.

—Richard Martin

HEISEL, Sylvia

American fashion designer

Born: Princeton, New Jersey, 22 June 1962. **Education:** Barnard College, New York, 1980–81. **Career:** Designed and sold costume jewelry, 1981–82; designed collection of coats for Henri Bendel, New York, 1982, and exclusive line of womenswear for Barneys New York, 1987; film costume designer, mid-1980s; first full catwalk collection shown, 1988; introduced first line of lingerie, 1999; opened first retail store, in New York's SoHo neighborhood, 1999; participated in auction of designer Halloween outfits for DISHES Project to battle pediatric AIDS, 1999. **Awards:** Chicago Gold Coast award, 1993. **Address:** 230 West 39th Street, New York, NY 10018, USA.

Publications

On HEISEL:

Books

Stegemeyer, Anne, *Who's Who in Fashion, Third Edition,* New York, 1996.

Articles

"Fashion," in *Interview* (New York), July 1987.
Washington, Roxanne, "Designer Heisel Guided by the Feel, Not the Look," in the *Ann Arbor News,* 10 September 1991.
Pandiscio, Richard, "Sylvia Heisel: Gun Control Fashion," in *Interview,* January 1993.
Siroto, Janet, "Evening Star," in *Vogue,* February 1993.
"Autumn in New York," in *Women's Wear Daily,* 2 April 1998.
Monget, Karyn, "Style, Substance Lead the Way," in *WWD,* 17 May 1999.
Gilbert, Daniela, "Fright for a Cause," in *WWD,* 2 November 1999.
Fass, Allison, "Retail Renaissance on Thompson Street," in the *New York Times,* 21 November 1999.
"The Last Hurrah," in *WWD,* 15 February 2000.
Doonan, Simon, "Get Pushy with a Dressmaker; Cram Your Closet with 'Originals,'" in the *New York Observer,* 5 February 2001.

*

I think fashion is about who you are right now. What you're wearing says who you are at that moment in time. It's the first thing you communicate to another person.

My favorite clothes are easy, comfortable, creative, and beautiful because that's what I'm attracted to in people. What we wear is a combination of reality and what is in our minds. The reality is where we have to go, what we have to do, and what we can afford. The dream is who we want to be, what's beautiful and exciting to us, and what we desire. I try to design clothes with a combination of these qualities: wearability in the real world with an aesthetic of dreams.

Inspiration comes from everything in the world, more often from the zeitgeist than from other pieces of clothing or designed items. Historically, fashion is interesting because of what it says about any particular moment in history. What looks good, new, and exciting one day looks old and tired the next. It is the most transient of art and design fields. The clothes I design combine skills of construction and manufacturing with the communication of my ideas.

—Sylvia Heisel

* * *

Sophisticated elegance is perhaps the most distinguishing characteristic of Sylvia Heisel's collections. Her use of exquisite fabrics, colors and the simplicity of cuts have ensured her favorable recognition by fashion buyers and critics alike. As one of New York's young contemporary fashion designers, Heisel has instinctively avoided catering to recent trends. Her approach to fashion combines an "aesthetic of dreams" with the reality of modern wearability and affordability.

Heisel studied art history briefly at Barnard, leaving college eventually to pursue a freelance career designing costume jewelry, theatre costuming, and fashion display. With no formal training in fashion design, Heisel launched her first coat collection for Henri Bendel in New York, followed by an exclusive line for Barneys first women's store in New York in 1987. Her first independent collection appeared in the spring of 1988.

Heisel is interested in communicating ideas intrinsic to particular moments in history. The 1980s' emphasis on body consciousness led Heisel to embrace the notion of executing a controlled draping of her now signature slip and tank dresses. Constructed in fabrics such as jersey, mesh, and silk, these dresses are contoured, accentuating the body with deep-cut backs and high slits. They are simultaneously wearable and feminine.

The growth of professional American women in the job market highlighted fashion designers' need to accommodate this new status with garments both practical and timeless. Heisel addressed these needs with small, tightly-edited collections, including "sportswear-inspired suits, separates for day and sophisticated dresses and coats for evening." Her jackets range from waist length to sleek over-the-hip styles. The selected fabrics, such as silk and wool crêpe, are comfortable and travel well. Her garments are architectural, employing both bodyfitting silhouettes and a boxy construction in her coats and jackets. Heisel's color selection is based on instinct rather than forecasts, and she often uses black for balance. The use of solids highlights the minimalist cut, drape, and texture of each garment. At the same time, simplicity allows for a variety of ways of wearing each piece.

Heisel's awareness of contemporary culture was successfully transferred into costume designs for the 1985 film *Parting Glances.* In 1985, Heisel was included in the *New York Times* list of young designers—including Carol Horn, Cathy Hardwick, and Mary Jane Marcasiano—who were "currying favors with American women and retailers." Heisel has on several occasions deviated from collections based on minimalist constructions—fake pony-fur coats, lizard prints, and McFaddenesque dresses. She still maintains a consistent approach, stressing that how a woman feels in her clothes is as much a part as how the clothes look.

Though known for her elegant, classic eveningwear designs, Heisel has expanded into other areas, notably lingerie, which she launched in 1999, and sportswear, of which she has been designing a growing number of pieces. While ensuring that her clothes maintain a classic appeal, Heisel injects a sense of humor into much of her work, especially her lingerie and sportswear items. In her fall 2000 sportswear collection, for example, she combined tartan plaid dresses with plaid-lined gold metallic nylon tops and created a strapless dress and jacket from plum tweed cashmere. *Women's Wear Daily* (15 February 2000) described the collection as combining "a dressed-up sensibility with a schoolgirl approach."

Heisel's lingerie line, which includes camisoles, slips, tank tops, and crop pants, is meant to be worn either under clothing or as clothing. As Heisel told *Women's Wear Daily* back in May 1999, "We're leaving it up to the woman to decide how she wants to wear it. It's not lingerie you try to hide." For evening, Heisel tends to stick with the bias-cut silk dresses for which she is known. They appeal to all types of customers, not only in their flattering, elegant fit, but because they are available in 100 colors. Similarly, her lingerie designs come in 50 hues, ranging from bright neons to subtle pales.

Heisel opened her first retail store in 1999 on Thompson Street in New York's SoHo neighborhood. There she showcases what *Women's Wear Daily* describes as her pretty, well-cut apparel, ranging from long skirts, tailored taffeta shirts, sheaths, and boleros to tweed cashmere coats, colored scarves, velvet tank dresses, and printed pants. Most of her pieces are classics that can be worn from season to season, simply updated with a new accessory.

In the store, Heisel is able to highlight some of her fun fantasies, such as boleros of organdy flowers or cocktail dresses featuring two-foot-long gold chains as trim. In a February 2001 article, the *New York Observer* termed the store's overall sensibility, however, as one of "affordable, hip restraint," a phrase that could be used to describe much of Heisel's work.

—Teal Triggs; updated by Karen Raugust

HELPERN, Joan and David

See JOAN & DAVID

HEMINGWAY, Wayne and Geraldine

See RED OR DEAD

HENDERSON, Gordon

American designer

Born: Berkeley, California, 19 March 1957. **Education:** Studied medicine, University of California; studied fashion design, Parsons School of Design, New York, 1981–83. **Career:** Assistant designer, Calvin Klein, 1984; formed own company, 1985; launched lower priced "But, Gordon" line, 1990; signed exclusive contract with Saks Fifth Avenue, 1992; designed wedding suit for John F. Kennedy Jr., 1996; design critic at student fashion shows, from late 1990s. **Awards:** Council of Fashion Designers of America Perry Ellis award, 1989.

Publications

On HENDERSON:

Books

Stegemeyer, Anne, *Who's Who in Fashion, Third Edition,* New York, 1996.

Articles

Darnton, Nina, "At What Price Young Success?" in *Newsweek* (New York), 20 November 1989.

Haynes, Kevin, "Gordon Henderson: All the Rage," in *WWD,* 22 November 1989.

Hochswender, Woody, "Realism Takes Henderson to Top," in the *New York Times,* 28 November 1989.

Duffy, Martha, "But Gordon, I Want It All," in *Time,* 26 February 1990.

"Flash! Gordon Has Designs on You," in *Mademoiselle* (New York), March 1990.

Shapiro, Harriet, "Gordon Henderson's Affordable Designs are Making Him Fashion's Man for the Woman Who Works," in *People,* 19 March 1990.

———, "Designer Clothes at a Lower Price," in the *New York Times,* 16 September 1990.

Agins, Teri, "In Fashion, the Talent and His Money Man Make Promising Team," in the *Wall Street Journal,* 18 September 1990.

Washington, Elsie B., "Now: Brothers on Seventh Avenue," in *Essence,* November 1991.

* * *

Versatile separates. Dressing with ease. These American sportswear tenets are the meat and potatoes of Gordon Henderson's fashion. Although young, he has shown the discipline of engaging in no design that is superfluous and of giving the customer what she wants—garments that can be multipurpose and mixable in a wardrobe, favoring fashion that is neither flamboyant nor expensive. Henderson is anomalous among designers making a mark in the late 1980s in adhering so intensely to the sportswear ethos, never succumbing to the glamour of high-priced fashion. His penchant for vegetable and earth colors seems even politically correct in the ecology-aware 1990s.

He is, as Woody Hochswender of the *New York Times,* "a realist." Such sportswear orthodoxy and awareness to design's realization in sales made Henderson the "hottest new designer" on Seventh Avenue, New York, according to the *Wall Street Journal* on September 1990. As there is a pragmatism to Henderson's view of fashion, there is a corresponding restraint in the designer. Photogenic enough to pose for a Gap advertisement (wearing denim) and for selection as one of *People* magazine's beautiful people, Henderson provides a beguiling and handsome personal accompaniment to his plain message of fashion modesty. For Hochswender, Henderson is "a designer many are calling the first important new talent of the 1990s." Henderson told Kevin Haynes, "People identify me as doing classics with a twist—it sounds like a drink to me. But there's beauty in using relatively inexpensive fabrics and treating them like they're very expensive. I don't like people getting uptight with clothes."

The ideal Henderson client would be a woman who shops for other labels and perhaps even buys basics at the Gap or other retailers, allowing the Henderson separates to work as accent pieces. "You can take the clothes and put them together for career women," Henderson told Nina Darnton, "or combine them for weekend or evening. That's what the 1990s are about—servicing your customer in the way she needs." Even beyond his eponymous line, Henderson created "But, Gordon," an even more responsive, inexpensive line with its name coming from stores who liked certain garments, but wanted them at lesser prices, whining, "but, Gordon..." again and again until the designer acquiesced with a secondary line.

When one examines Henderson's work, one realizes its appeal as fashion basics, from simple dresses to halter tops, beautifully cut trousers, and other wardrobe-building elements. Inevitably, one designer he acknowledges as a favorite is Claire McCardell, whose ingenuity with materials and basic sportswear elements is recapitulated in Henderson's imagination with materials and flair for a simple, uncluttered style. Henderson's lyrical summer dresses, bandeaux, and capelet jackets reflect the spirit of McCardell. His slightly off-beat colors (occasioned in part by necessity and in part by a commitment to the earth) and his love of plaids and checks also align Henderson with McCardell. But Henderson also admires Chanel, an admiration evident in his very serviceable boxy jackets.

McCardell, however, works better as a Henderson muse since she realized the sensibility of suburbs and country (Henderson was brought up in California.) There is something so unabashedly price-conscious and trend-avoiding about Henderson's clothing that it becomes almost antiurban. And it may be precisely the gleeful suburban, campus, low-pressure calm that makes his work so attractive to a broad audience. After all, the working woman is no longer an exclusive phenomenon of the big city, but a staple of suburban lifestyle as well. Henderson also says of his work at Calvin Klein, "I learned everything there. He gives you consistency, and he's so clean and precise it's almost ridiculous. He can take a good idea and go on with it forever."

Henderson has produced a promising prospect of his own "forever" in a consistent and compelling vision of sportswear separates kept at a reasonable price for both American and international customers. Fashion, which has a tendency to drift upward, even among designers who start out with the intention of serving the broadest public, has not corrupted Henderson. He continues to give every sign of being different: reaching the top of his field by adamantly and effectively staying at the bottom of the price ranges, and in giving something back to the industry. In the late 1990s he acted as a design critic for student fashion shows at institutions such as the Parsons School of Design and Marist College. He also gained notice, in September 1996, as the designer of the blue suit worn by the late John F. Kennedy Jr. during his wedding to the late Carolyn Bessette Kennedy, a former Calvin Klein publicist and a friend of Henderson's.

As of July 2000, Henderson was reported by the website Urbangoods.com as planning to open a New York City gift and home furnishings store in partnership with artist Conan Hayes. His loyal clients, no doubt, are looking forward to this next endeavor.

—Richard Martin; updated by Karen Raugust

HERMÈS

French design house

Founded: in Paris by Thierry Hermès in 1837 to manufacture bridles, saddles, and riding boots for the carriage trade. **Company History:** Company moved to rue de Faubourg in Paris, 1879; began accessories, including silk scarves, 1926; founder's grandson, Emile Hermès, established luggage and couture clothing in 1930s; Hermès scarf introduced, 1937; silk ties first sold, 1949; first fragrances, 1950 (later including *Caleche,* 1961; *24, Faubourg,* 1995, and *Hermès Rouge,* 2001); glassware, tableware introduced, 1980s; initial public offering, 1993; Martin Margiela appointed ready-to-wear designer, 1997; purchases 35-percent stake in Jean-Paul Gaultier's design business, 1999; opened Madison Avenue store, New York, 2000. **Company Address:** 24 rue du Faubourg Saint-Honoré, 75008 Paris, France.

Hermès, fall 2001 collection. © AP/Wide World Photos/Fashion Wire Daily.

Hermès, fall 2001 collection. © AP/Wide World Photos/Fashion Wire Daily.

Publications

By HERMÈS:

Books

Hermès Handbook, New York, n.d.
How to Wear Your Hermès Scarf, Paris, 1986, 1988, 1994.
Baseman, Andrew, *The Scarf,* New York, 1989.
Hermès: Le Monde d'Hermès 1992, Paris, 1991.

On HERMÈS:

Books

Hermès Handbook, New York n.d.
Keller-Krische, Christiane, *The Book of Scarves: Scarves, Shawls, and Ties Dressed with Imagination,* 2000.

Articles

"A Boutique Where You Don't Just Buy—You Invest," in *Vogue,* October 1974.
Van Dyke, Grace, "Hermès: Old World Luxury in the New World," in *USA Today,* July 1984.
Dryansky, G.Y., "Hermès: Quality with a Kick," in *Harper's Bazaar,* April 1986.
"Scarves Everywhere," in the *New Yorker,* 30 January 1989.
Aillaud, Charlotte, "The Hermès Museum: Inspiration for the Celebrated Family Firm," in *Architectural Digest,* January 1989.
Beckett-Young, Kathleen, "Signature in the Social Register," in *Connoisseur,* June 1989.
Tompkins, Mimi, "Sweatshop of the Stars," in *U.S. News & World Report,* 12 February 1990.
Gandee, Charles, "Jean-Louis Dumas—Hermès is Flying High," in *House & Garden,* August 1990.
Hornblower, Margaret, "As Luxe as It Gets," in *Time,* 6 August 1990.
"Hermès: Still in the Saddle," in *WWD,* 25 September 1991.
"Hermès of Paris, Inc.," in the *New York Times,* 5 October 1991.
Andrieu, Frederic, "European Accents: A Gold Brooch Here, a Quilted Bag There, and Hermès Scarves Everywhere...," in *Lear's* (New York), January 1992.
Slesin, Susan, "Ah, the Horse: Hermès Introduces New Porcelain Pattern," in the *New York Times,* 21 May 1992.
Rotenier, Nancy, "Tie Man Meets Queen of England," in *Forbes,* 13 September 1993.
Morris, Bernadine, "Five Designers Reveal a Sense of Calm in Paris," in the *New York Times,* 10 March 1994.
White, Constance C.R., "Hermès Seeks a New Image," in the *New York Times,* 20 March 1995.
Mead, Rebecca, "The Crazy Professor: Why was Paris Persuaded that the Radical Martin Margiela was Right for the Venerable House of Hermès?" in the *New Yorker,* 30 March 1998.
Strom, Stephanie, "Luxury in Recession Land; the Hermès of the World Find New Ways to Prosper in Japan's Weak Economy," in the *New York Times,* 29 October 1998.
Thomas, Dana, "Gaultier Goes for Growth," in the *Newsweek International,* 19 July 1999.
"Time and Again: Hermès Opens Boutique on Madison Avenue...," in *Elle,* December 2000.
Taber, Andrew, "Hermès," [profile] available online at Fashion Live, www.fashionlive.com, 19 March 2001.

* * *

Emile-Maurice Hermès, grandson of founder Thierry Hermès, summed up the philosophy of his family's celebrated firm in the 1920s as "Leather, sport, and a tradition of refined elegance." Passed down over generations, the House of Hermès has been committed to quality in design and production for more than 160 years. At the dawn of the 21th century, the name Hermès continues to represent the ultimate in French luxury.

Hermès began as a Parisian leather goods shop in 1837, making finely wrought harnesses, bridles, and riding boots for the carriage trade. As early as 1855 Hermès was earning accolades, winning first prize in its class at the 1855 Paris Exposition. Thierry's son Emile-Charles established the current flagship store at 24 rue du Faubourg Saint-Honoré, where he introduced saddlery and began retail sales. Emile-Charles sold his stake in the company to his brother, Emile-Maurice, who in turn was the true visionary of the Hermès family.

With the advent of the automobile, the firm adapted its careful saddle stitching techniques to the production of wallets, luggage, handbags, watchbands, and accessories for golfing, hunting, and polo playing, and began to design couture sportswear. All were made with the same fine materials and attention to detail as the original leather wares, and the firm continued to build on its reputation for quality. Hermès made fashion news in the 1920s by designing one of the first leather garments of the 20th century, a zippered golfing jacket, for the Prince of Wales. For a time the zipper was called the *fermature Hermès,* because of its European impact (Emile-Maurice had bought a two-year patent on the unusual Canadian invention).

The fourth generation of proprietors were two sons-in-law, Jean Guerrand and Robert Dumas. Guerrand and Dumas added scarves and perfume to the line, while the leather artisans remained loyal, often staying on for decades. Into the 1960s the company continued to expand, with the introduction of new styles and fragrances. Jean-Louis Dumas, the son of Robert Dumas, became président-directeur général in 1978.

The 1980s were a period of unprecedented growth for the firm. Hermès benefitted from the revival of status dressing. Women sported the crocodile-skin Kelly bag (named for Grace Kelly), the Constance clutch, brightly colored leathers, sensuous cashmeres, bold jewelry, tricolored spectator shoes, and silk ballet slippers. For men, Hermès made leather jackets with sherpa lining and trim, gabardine blazers and dashing greatcoats, and richly patterned silk ties. Dumas introduced new materials like porcelain and crystal, expanding the line to some 30,000 items. It is to the firm's credit that they have never licensed any of their products, but keep tight control over the design and manufacture of this vast range of goods. Thus every leather-bound datebook, porcelain teapot, silk waistcoat, scarf, and handbag is made under a watchful Hermès eye.

One of the most visible and bestselling items in the Hermès line is the scarf, or *carré* as they are called. The carefully printed, heavy silk scarves are coveted for the air of Parisian style they impart. Many of the *carrés* feature equestrian motifs, as well as other symbols of prestige, like coats of arms, banners, and military insignia. Women boast of how many they own, and hand them down through generations; some of the scarves end up as framed wall-hangings or are made into pillows. The firm corresponds regularly with Hermès addicts trying to collect every scarf on the books, and reports that during the holiday season in the Paris store, a scarf is sold every 20 seconds. Queen Elizabeth II was pictured on an English postage stamp with an Hermès scarf wrapped around her royal head. Each scarf could be considered a small symbol of all of the carefully made luxury goods Hermès has produced for generations.

Hermès, rarely one to keep pace with trends, astonished the fashion world with the appointment of decontructionist Martin Margiela as its ready-to-wear designer in 1997. The Dutch eccentric, known for his savage avant-garde designs—often literally ripping the seams of garments and haphazardly stitching them back together—proved an excellent albeit bizarre fit. The first Margiela collection debuted in March 1998 and was well received. Andrew Taber, writing for Fashion Live, found the collection "quietly subversive" and further commented, "Margiela's sweeping camel coats and unstructured layers of cashmere and deerskin were timeless, serene, and utterly luxurious in their lack of ostentation."

Though many had their doubts when Jean-Louis Dumas brought Margiela into the Hermès fold, the designer brought a hint of radicalism into the lap of conservative luxury. Another move into the fashion left came with the purchase in 1999 of a 35-percent stake in Gaultier Couture, the company of fashion bad boy Jean-Paul Gaultier. Gaultier got funds for expansion; Hermès extended its empire to keep up with luxe conglomerates like LVMH. Yet the recent additions of Gaultier and Margiela far from tarnished the Hermès name; the company's clothing and accessories have continued to transcend fashion. The Hermès look relies not on trends but on the finest materials, exquisite construction, and the instinctively casual chic of French style.

Over the course of the 20th century and into the 21st, the cut of the clothing and the palettes may have changed, but the classic quality of Hermès designs have remained constant. Beyond mere status symbols, the firm's goods are the embodiment of simplicity and elegance in extremely well made and durable products. Whether it be a jacket of meltingly soft leather, a paisley silk dressing gown, a Kelly bag, a valise, or a *carré,* an Hermès purchase comes with the assurance that it will be stylish and appropriate for a lifetime. With more than 215 Hermès stores around the world and countless boutiques in high-end department stores in Europe, Asia, and the U.S., the Hermès name has certainly gained more prominence, but its goods land not in the hands of the masses but in the chosen few.

—Kathleen Paton; updated by Nelly Rhodes

HERRERA, Carolina

Venezuelan designer working in New York

Born: Maria Carolina Josefina Pacanins y Nino in Caracas, Venezuela, 8 January 1939. **Education:** El Carmen School, Venezuela. **Family:** Married Reinaldo Herrera, 1957; children: Mercedes, Ana Luisa, Carolina, Patricia. **Career:** Showed first couture collection, 1981; introduced fur collection for Revillion, 1984; launched CH diffusion line, 1986, Couture Bridal collection, 1987, Carolina Herrera Collection II sportswear line, 1989, Herrera for Men, Herrera Studio bridge line, and W by Carolina Herrera, 1992; introduced Carolina Herrera fragrances, 1988; introduced jewelry collections, 1990, 1991; moved toward more youthful styles influenced by her daughters, late 1990s; signed deal with STL of Spain for men's and women's gold-range apparel and retail stores in Europe, 2000; opened first free-standing boutique on Madison Avenue in New York, 2000. **Awards:** Pratt Institute award, 1990; Dallas Fashion Excellence award. **Address:** 48 West 38th Street, New York, NY 10018, USA.

Publications

On HERRERA:

Books

Diamonstein, Barbaralee, *Fashion: The Inside Story,* New York, 1985.

Steele, Valerie, *Women of Fashion: Twentieth-Century Designers,* New York, 1991.

Riehecky, Janet, *Carolina Hererra: International Fahsion Designer,* Chicago, 1991.

Navarette Talavera, Ela, *Perfiles latinoamericanos de los 1990s,* Panama, 1992.

Stegemeyer, Anne, *Who's Who in Fashion, Third Edition,* New York, 1996.

Telgen, Diane, and Jim Kamp, *Latinas! Women of Achievement,* Detroit, 1996.

Morey, Janet, and Wendy Dunn, *Famous Hispanic Americans,* New York, 1996.

Carolina Herrera, fall 2001 collection: sheared mink top and black pants. © Reuters NewMedia Inc./CORBIS.

Articles

Shapiro, Harriet, "From Venezuela to Seventh Avenue, Carolina Herrera's Fashions Cast a Long Shadow," in *People,* 3 May 1982.

Rayner, William, and Chesbrough Rayner, "An Evening with Carolina and Reinaldo Herrera: Strong Opinions, European Style," in *Vogue,* March 1987.

Daria, Irene, "Carolina Herrera: A Personal Evolution," in *WWD,* 2 March 1987.

———, "Designers on Designing: Carolina Herrera," in *WWD,* 2 March 1987.

Estrada, Mary Batts, "Carolina Herrera Talks About Fashion," in *Hispanic,* March 1989.

Reed, Julia, "Talking Fashion: Carolina Herrera is the Undisputed Queen of Seventh Avenue," in *Vogue,* June 1990.

Koski, Lorna, "Carolina's Prime Time," in *WWD,* 18 June 1991.

Struensee, Chuck, "Carolina Herrera's New Horizons," in *WWD,* 20 October 1992.

"New York: Carolina Herrera," in *WWD,* 1 November 1994.

"New York: Carolina Herrera," in *WWD,* 4 April 1995.

"Carolina Herrera," in *Current Biography Yearbook,* 1996.

Schiro, Anne Marie, "Designers Who Know Their Customer," in the *New York Times,* 10 April 1997.

Tapert, Annette, "Women of Style: Carolina Herrera," *Town & Country,* September 1997.

Horyn, Cathy, "And Now, a Gentle Nudge from Herrera and de la Renta," in the *New York Times,* 15 September 1999.

Wilson, Eric, "Herrera Mines for Spanish Gold," in *WWD,* 23 March 2000.

Givhan, Robin, "The Lady Flourishes: Herrera's Work Blossoms with Understated Femininity," in the *Washington Post,* 8 December 2000.

"WWD Luxury" Special Supplement, in *WWD,* February 2001.

* * *

When Carolina Herrera introduced her first fashion collection in 1981, *Women's Wear Daily* dubbed her "Our Lady of the Sleeve." Her early interest in the shoulder area has remained constant throughout her many lines and seasons. The Herrera look is characterized by strong fitted shoulders, tight bodices, straight lines, and slightly pushed-up sleeves.

Though she has often been referred to as a socialite turned designer, her contributions to the industry are many. Prior to beginning her career as a designer, Herrera was on the International Best Dressed List for over 10 years and was then nominated to the Best Dressed Hall of Fame. Her personal style influenced how women dressed around the world. Her affluent, South American background exposed her to the work of the best couturiers and dressmakers in the world; she cites Balenciaga as her greatest influence. It was a natural transition from socialite to fashion designer, as Herrera is a member of the world for which she designs. She understands her customers' lifestyles and needs because she is one of them. Her friends, impressed with her design quality, fabric selection, attention to detail, construction and drape, soon became her clients.

Herrera's designs have been described as being for the "quintessential woman of the 1980s who has consummate style and taste as well as an active lifestyle." Her clothes have a couture element, feminine detail, and genuine ease. Herrera herself believes her clothes are feminine, elegant, and most important, comfortable. Though she loves to mix and match expensive Italian and French fabrics, she maintains the importance of the cut of the clothes. Herrera states, "You don't have to buy very expensive materials if the clothes are well cut." In terms of color, Herrera favors the combination of black and white or black and brown.

Becoming a designer seemed a logical evolution in Herrera's life. She was married, had four children, and came to symbolize the upper-class South American lifestyle. When her children were grown she decided, with the financial backing of a wealthy South American publisher, to open a design house in New York.

Like many designers, Herrera expanded her business to include other lines. The CH Collections, introduced in 1986, are less expensive versions of her high-fashion lines, similar silhouettes in cut and finish but made of different fabrics. Herrera also launched a successful bridal line in 1987 after designing Caroline Kennedy's wedding gown. A perfume for both women (1988) and men (1991) also followed.

In the early collections, Herrera's strengths were in her day dresses and luncheon suits. They expressed femininity through their beautifully tailored hourglass design. In more recent collections, she has ventured into the downtown New York scene for inspiration, showing chiffon split skirts topped with satin motorcycle jackets, thus illustrating her ability to interpret and combine the surrounding culture with her own design sense. Most important, her clothes are about style and

Carolina Herrera, spring 2001 collection. © AP/Wide World Photos.

elegance achieved by her trademark of shoulders, sleeves, line, and construction.

Herrera has continued to design for women like herself who are wealthy and sophisticated. As Anne-Marie Schiro pointed out in the *New York Times,* Herrera's customers desire tasteful, flattering clothing, fashionable yet not cutting-edge, incorporating a few surprises yet wearable. Her fall/winter 1997 collection offered some challenges in the form of snakeskin print and black glossy leathers, leopard pattern chiffons, and tiger print velvets. All of these, according to Schiro, were fashioned into the sorts of jackets, coats, and shifts that feel comfortable to Herrera's customers.

Cathy Horyn, also writing in the *New York Times,* compared Herrera's spring/summer 2000 collection to the designer's personality: both practical and lavish. Most ensembles were comprised of basic pants and a top, but the pants were made of materials such as shantung and the tops of fabrics such as peony-pink fitted suede. A new wrinkle were younger, sexier designs than Herrera had shown in the past, including a lemon-colored bikini and a ball gown with a skirt starting two inches below the waist.

Robin Givhan in the *Washington Post* also noted Herrera's skew toward the youthful at the end of the millennium, pointing out that the transformation earned her new customers, such as young Hollywood actresses, as well as a wider distribution in specialty stores. Her two daughters, a filmmaker and a fashion editor, were cited as influences. They encouraged her, for example, to create more mix-and-match pieces rather than full ensembles. At the same time, Herrera has kept her traditional customers in mind, moving toward more youthful styles but not shocking them or turning them away. Givhan called Herrera's spring 2000 collection an example of well-groomed, genteel femininity.

In 2000 Herrera signed a licensing agreement with the Spanish apparel company STL to develop a women's and men's gold-range line called CH Carolina Herrera. The deal was expected to lead to the establishment of 40 stores throughout Europe—where her signature and *212* perfume lines have a high profile—within a few years. Herrera had experimented with two bridge lines in the mid-1990s, both of which were discontinued quickly. The new CH line is priced about a third lower than her signature apparel and includes women's sportswear for day and evening as well as men's tailored clothing and sportswear. The deal marked Herrera's first foray into men's apparel, although she had previously produced accessories and scents for men.

The deal paved the way for stores in the U.S.; Herrera opened her first freestanding boutique on New York's Madison Avenue in 2000. In the past, her signature line had been available in only about 100 stores worldwide.

—Margo Seaman; updated by Karen Raugust

HILFIGER, Tommy

American designer

Born: 1952. **Career:** Owner/designer, People's Places, New York, until 1979; founder/designer, and vice chairman, Tommy Hilfiger Corporation, New York; company floated on NYSE, 1992; member, Council of Fashion Designers of America; introduced women's sportswear and Tommy Girl fragrance, 1996; opened 20,000-square-foot U.S. flagship on Rodeo Drive in Beverly Hills, 1997 (later scheduled for closure); launched first European products, 1997; introduced athletic footwear and apparel collection, licensed to Stride Rite, 1997; acquired jeanswear, womenswear, and Canadian businesses from licensees, 1998; opened flagship stores in London (closed in 2000) and Mexico City, 1999; launched women's line in Europe, 1999; introduced unisex fragrance, *Freedom,* 1999; sponsored rock tours for the likes of Britney Spears and Rolling Stores during its Year of Music, 1999; attempted but failed to acquire Calvin Klein, 2000; switched men's accessories licensee from Ghurka to Swank, 2000; announced first quarterly loss since going public, 2000; introduced watch line with Movado, 2001; created first full women's swimwear collection with Jantzen, 2001; menswear lines dropped from most Bloomingdale's stores, 2001; effected turnaround women's and junior's businesses, 2001. **Awards:** Council of Fashion Designers of America Designer of the Year, 1995; VH1's From the Catwalk to the Sidewalk award, 1995; Parsons School of Design Designer of the Year, 1998; GQ Designer of the Year, 1998; several fragrance industry FiFi awards. **Address:** 25 West 39th Street, New York, NY 10018, USA. **Website:** www.tommy.com.

Tommy Hilfiger (foreground) posing with designs from his fall 2001 collection. © AP/Wide World Photos.

Publications

By HILFIGER:

Books

Hilfiger, Tommy, with David A. Keeps, *All-American: A Style Book,* New York, 1997.

Hilfiger, Tommy, with Anthony DeCurtis, *Rock Style: How Fashion Moves to Music,* New York, 1999.

On HILFIGER:

Books

Mandle, Jay, "In a Word, Hilfiger: Fragrances, Film, Books on Fashion Titan's Runway," in Sora, Joseph, editor, *Corporate Power in the United States,* New York, 1998.

Le Dortz, Laurent, and Béatrice Debosscher, *Stratégies des leaders américains de la mode: Calvin Klein, Donna Karan, Liz Clairborne, Polo Ralph Lauren, et Tommy Hilfinger*, Paris, 2000.

Articles

La Ferla, Ruth, "Hilfiger Re-Emerges," in the *New York Times,* 31 July 1990.

Younger, Joseph D., "The Man Makes the Clothes," in *Amtrak Express* (Washington, D.C.), September/October 1993.

"Throwing Down the Trousers," in *Newsweek,* 11 July 1994.

Mather, John, "Tommy Hilfiger's Great Leap," in *Esquire,* August 1994.

Duffy, Martha, "H Stands for Hilfiger: The Former Menswear Laughingstock Expands into the Women's Market," in *Time,* 16 September 1996.

Brown, Ed, "The Street Likes Hilfiger's Style," in *Fortune,* 16 March 1998.

Dodd, Annmarie, "From Hip-Hop to the Top: Tommy Tells How He Pushes the Envelope," in *Daily News Record,* 2 November 1998.

Jenkins, Maureen, "Tommy Hilfiger Success Rooted in Music Tie-Ins, Multiple Niches," in *Knight-Ridder/Tribune Business News,* 6 August 1999.

Lockwood, Lisa, "Crossing Over: Hilfiger Charts His Course in Women's Wear," in *WWD,* 13 September 1999.

Curran, Catherine, "Tommy's Swoon; Designer Lost Touch with Core Audience; Overexpansion Diluted Brand's Cachet," in *Crain's New York Business,* 4 September 2000.

Young, Vicki M., "Bloomingdale's to Drop Tommy Men's From Branches," in *Daily News Record,* 26 March 2001.

Fallon, James, "Hilfiger is Soaring in Europe; Designer's European Business is Over $100M," in *Daily News Record,* 30 March 2001.

Tommy Hilfiger, fall 2001 collection. © AP/Wide World Photos.

* * *

In an article titled "Throwing Down the Trousers" (*Newsweek,* 11 July 1994), Calvin Klein and Tommy Hilfiger are rendered in a showdown over men's underwear, the former having long occupied Times Square billboard space with provocative underwear ads. Hilfiger, seen standing on Broadway and 44th Street with his boxer-clad male models, meekly states, "My image is all about good, clean fun. I think Calvin's image is about maybe something different." Hilfiger is smart. He juxtaposes his hunky models in flag-and-stripe-designed boxers at surfer jam length with the implied enemy in bawdy, black, sopping promiscuity. Hilfiger has been right—in design and business—in promising "good, clean fun" in an unabashed American style that has achieved phenomenal success. America has wanted a menswear mainstream, neither aristocratic nor licentious. Emerging first in the 1980s with a clever campaign announcing himself among established designers, he has come to fulfill his own declaration to become one of the leading names in American design, certainly in menswear.

Acknowledging "I'm both a designer and a businessman" in the September-October 1993 issue of *Amtrak Express,* Hilfiger divides his own successful role into its two components that he himself has rendered indivisible. Hilfiger has most certainly learned from American designers Ralph Lauren and Calvin Klein that fashion is a synergy of business, aspiration, and classic design—with the image and craving constituting aspiration as perhaps the most important element. Hilfiger has shrewdly chosen a particular place for himself in American menswear imagery.

Whereas Lauren has preempted old-money WASP styles and Klein has successfully created a sexy vivacity, Hilfiger has come closer to Main Street, a colorful Americana that still waves flags, still loves button-down collars, that appreciates classics, and adores his "good, clean fun" along with family values. His customers may even abhor pretense or promiscuity, and may strive for collegiate looks but would never rebel too much—dressing a little more modestly and traditionally than those who prefer his designer-commerce confreres. His closest kinship (or competitor) in the market is David Chu's similarly brilliant work for Nautica, likewise reaching into the smalltown, cautious American sensibility for roots and imagination.

The "real people" effectiveness of Hilfiger is, of course, both real and illusory: he is stirring the deep-felt American conservative sensibilities of the late 20th century at the very time when culture is annulling any vestige of *Our Town* sentimentalities. The "feel good" ethos of Hilfiger's design is not image alone, for his intense commitment to value-for-price and quality materials confirms the joy in his design. His colorful, sporty, comfortable clothing appealed preeminently in the 1980s to the middle class in America. In 1988 Hilfiger said in his own advertising, "The clothes I design are relaxed, comfortable, somewhat traditional, affordable and...simple. They are the classic American clothes we've always worn, but I've reinterpreted them so that they fit more easily into the lives we live today." By the 1990s, Hilfiger was a clothing symbol of African American and Hispanic urban youth, engendering immense street-smart urban loyalty along with his classic Main Street constituency. Hilfiger's clothing is readily identified, with logos clearly visible on his ever-expanding clothing collections.

Hilfiger has associated himself with two other popular American images, both with special appeal to youth: sports teams and rock music. He has captured 30-something clients who are aging into their 40s, and yet Hilfiger is also building his young following. His great success has defied much élitist fashion skepticism. Ruth La Ferla, writing for the *New York Times* in July 1990, reported unforgivingly, "As a 'name' designer Mr. Hilfiger sprang full grown from the mind of his sponsor, Mohan Murjani, in the mid-1980s. Explicitly promoted as a successor to Perry Ellis or Calvin Klein or Ralph Lauren, Mr. Hilfiger achieved a degree of fame, or notoriety. But the stunt never came off; Mr. Hilfiger's fashions and image did not gel."

Of course, American enterprise is full of "stunts," from P.T. Barnum to Henry Ford to Dr. Kellogg, all with origins in harmless chicanery and old-fashioned chutzpah. Despite detractors, Hilfiger has consistently created his own dynamic and vigorous vision. After Murjani's backing, Hilfiger took his business public on the New York Stock Exchange in 1992, a rare instance of a designer-name business trading with success.

Hilfiger's sensitivity to casualwear can be brought to the business side of the male wardrobe, especially as it is already inflected by casual and sports-influenced notes. In 1994 he added tailored clothing to his line, confident the men who had already associated him with comfort and clean-cut exuberance would carry those same ideals to a full-cut American suit or jacket for business. Part of his business acumen and pragmatism is expressed a statement to Joseph Younger that he wanted to dress men from head to toe before dressing women and children—which was exactly what he did (though many of his men's shirts, shorts, and trousers were worn by women and teens).

Hilfiger's business experienced ups and downs during the late 1990s and early 2000s, going from being Wall Street's fashion-industry darling for eight years (starting in 1992) to suffering lowered profits and stock prices in 2000. Many of the company's troubles were attributed to overexpansion, both in customer base and retail presence. During the late 1990s, Hilfiger entered several new business segments, including fragrance (Tommy, Tommy Girl, Freedom); a cosmetics line, Tommy Hilfiger Color; women's sportswear; a watch collection (licensed to Movado); a full line of women's swimwear (licensed to Jantzen), athletic apparel and shoes (licensed to Stride Rite), and the Hilfiger Home collection, which like the apparel, was influenced by the designer's preppy and patriotic sensibilities. This aggressive strategy led the brand to lose some of its cachet, especially in the eyes of its loyal consumers. Stores began to discount Hilfiger merchandise, and retailers were quoted in publications such as *Crain's New York Business* as saying its core designs were a season or two behind the trends.

Hilfiger's marketing direction in 1999—called the Year of Music—did not help matters. Sponsorship of tours by mainstream musicians such as the Rolling Stones and Britney Spears alienated the hip-hop youth who had been the company's loyal customers since 1994. Some of the designer's problems were beyond his control, however; email rumors circulated, suggesting Hilfiger was a racist (unfounded), which had ramifications on sales. All of this led the Tommy Hilfiger company to announce a loss in the quarter ending March 2000, the first ever since it went public eight years earlier. The design firm now found itself in the position of explaining to the financial community how it would turn itself around.

Although the company's retail operation grew quickly in the late 1990s, with 15,000- to 20,000-square-foot flagship stores opened in London, Mexico City, and Beverly Hills, many of these large stores were closed within a few years. Hilfiger refocused its retail strategy on smaller stores, such as a planned outlet in New York's SoHo neighborhood. In addition, the designer's expansion into womenswear did not meet expectations, and as of 2001, the company was in the midst of turning this segment around.

Other setbacks included Bloomingdale's decision, as part of a restructuring, to eliminate the Tommy men's brand from all its stores except the 59th Street New York flagship—women's and children's apparel were unaffected—and Hilfiger's failed attempt in 2000 to acquire rival Calvin Klein. One bright area of Hilfiger's business in the early 2000s, however, was Europe, launched through a license with Pepe Jeans London in 1997. The business began with men's sportswear and segued into other men's categories, as well as women's and children's apparel and licensed fragrances. Europe was Hilfiger's largest market outside North America, with products sold in upscale department stores such as House of Fraser, Harrods, Galeries Lafayette, El Corte Ingles, and Brown Thomas.

To get its domestic business back on track in 2001, Hilfiger concentrated on returning to what company executives (quoted in *Crain's*) termed "traditional Tommy Hilfiger styling—classics with a twist." Hilfiger continues to oversee a youthful, purely American look with ties to music and pop culture; part of his fall 2001 collection was inspired by auto racing and featured sleek leather pieces. The challenge for Hilfiger now is to continue his appeal to a broad range of demographic groups yet not lose sight of the fashion-forward urban consumers who put him on the map.

—Richard Martin; updated by Karen Raugust

HOBBS LTD.

British fashion company

Founded: in 1981 by Marilyn and Yoram Anselm. **Company History:** Marilyn studied sculpture at the Central School of Art, London; married Yoram and they had two children (Kate, Amy). The Anselms, along with Yoram's brother Ronnie, began retailing to English design labels before turning to shoe and clothing design; developed idea of "capsule wardrobes," coordinated clothes, shoe, and accessory design for women, 1980s; brothers Yoram began feuding, 1990s; case settled against Ronnie Yoram, 2000; **Company Address:** 122 Gloucester Ave, London NW1 8HX, England.

Publications

On HOBBS LTD.:

Articles

Garrett, Pat, "Hobb's Choice," in *Homes & Antiques,* n.d.

Quick, Harriet, "Cold Shoe Shuffle," in *The Guardian,* 6 December 1995.

Mendick, Robert, "Hobbs Brothers Settle Feud in Own Fashion," in *The Independent Sunday,* 19 March 2000.

* * *

A family business based in London, Hobbs Ltd. is a successful clothing and footwear chain owned by designer Marilyn Anselm, with her husband Yoram in charge of finance, daughter Kate Anselm as footwear designer, and daughter Amy Anselm as the merchandise director in charge of shoes, clothes, and accessories. The targeted customer is perceived as an average woman between the ages of 20 and 40 interested in clothing "designed by mothers and daughters for mothers and daughters," displaying an understated yet unmistakably English sense of style.

The origins of the business were in clothing, although footwear made the company's name. This success is possibly due to the fact that Marilyn Anselm has a background in sculpture, having studied at London's Central School of Art, and has rendered three-dimensional forms in a convincing manner. "A shoe designer should be a sculptor rather than a painter," she points out. Her fine arts training has certainly come into use in the company's designs.

The popularity of Hobbs footwear can be explained by Marilyn Anselm's goal—to produce shoes of the same quality, style, and above all—with the comfort usually found in men's shoes. In women's footwear design, the emphasis is often put on fashion, above all other considerations, the traditional idea being that the shoes are meant to be quickly phased out owing to rapidly changing trends in the women's retail market. Hobbs, however, produces classic, albeit slightly quirky designs that attempt to provide quality and style at an affordable price. An emphasis on good craftsmanship has led to the majority of Anselm's shoe and knitwear designs being manufactured in Italy, which achieves the desired quality of finish unavailable in Britain for the same manufacturing costs.

Originally based in Hampstead in the early 1970s, the business concentrated on the retailing of leading English design labels until Anselm visited a shoe fair in Italy and was bowled over by what she saw. She began designing her own collection of shoes and clothes, which led in turn to the setting up of the company and its first shop in South Molton Street, London. Yoram Anselm and his brother Ronnie, both born in Israel, added business acumen to the company. The three of them, and later Marilyn and Yoram's two daughters, built the company to the brand of choice for well-off Englishwomen by the early 1990s. The family, particularly the brothers, remained very private in spite of their great success. In 2000, however, a long-running feud between the brothers became public when it went to court for settlement. Ronnie Anselm, the financial head of the business, was accused of skimming funds from the company. Despite these difficulties, however, the company remains extremely successful.

Hobbs' success is ultimately due to an emphasis on redesigning traditional British styles, using luxury natural fibers alongside newly developed fabrics such as Lycra for stretch or drape and the notion of the capsule wardrobe, a coordinated approach to women's fashionwear. Anselm believes in designing a top-to-toe look, with every garment following a specific theme or fashion story, an idea later popularized on a massive scale by the lifestyle marketing campaigns of companies such as Next.

The name Hobbs makes direct reference to a particular kind of British living, as created and espoused by magazines such as *Country Living.* The name itself was filched from an advertisement in *Horse & Hound,* for George Hobb's Horseboxes. The imagery Hobbs has played on in its numerous shops—from their fruitwood shelves and wardrobes, wrought iron brackets, and tapestry-woven stools to the classic court shoes, cashmere reefers, jodhpurs, and linen trousers—is one of an ineffable and timeless Englishness, reflective of country houses, horses, and herbaceous borders. All this mediated through the gaze of a 21st-century businesswoman trading on the type of associations Paul Smith so successfully conjured up for men.

—Caroline Cox; updated by Carrie Snyder

HOGG, Pam

British fashion designer

Born: Paisley, Scotland; grew up in Glasgow. **Education:** Studied Fine Art at Glasgow School of Art; switched to printed textiles course, winning two medals and two scholarships; MA in Textiles at Royal College of Art, London. **Career:** Lectured in Derby, England, and Glasgow while selling paper designs to New York and Paris; first collection Psychedelic Jungle, 1981; singer in rock band, from 1987; current band Doll, from 1993. **Exhibitions:** Art Gallery Museum, Glasgow, June-August 1991.

Pam Hogg, spring/summer 2000 collection. © AFP/CORBIS.

Publications

On HOGG:

Articles

Franklin, Caryn, "Hogg in the Limelight," in *Clothes Show* (London), April 1989.

Godfrey, John, "Warrior Queen," in *i-D* (London), August 1989.

Niland, Seta, "Hogging the Spotlight," in *Fashion Weekly* (London), 22 March 1990.

Rodgers, Toni, "Double Vision," in *Elle* (London), March 1991.

Godfrey, John, "Pam Hogg," in *Elle,* June 1994.

McRobbie, Angela, "Falling Off the Catwalk," in the *New Statesman & Society,* 7 June 1996.

* * *

Drawing on influences as diverse as sportswear, S&M rubberwear and 15th-century armor, Pam Hogg produced distinctive clubwear with a punk feel. Exploring similar routes to those charted by Vivienne Westwood, she developed her own niche in the London fashion scene, while vehemently retaining elements of her native Scotland in her designs.

Riding the wave of British talent which swept to the forefront in the mid-1980s, Hogg, in common with John Richmond, represented the coming together of popular culture and fashion. She used rock music as a constant source of visual ideas, to create strong images for womenswear in PVC and studded leather. In a sense her clothes reflected her own lifestyle, her aspirations to pop stardom, which sometimes took precedence over her designing, and her enthusiastic involvement in London clubland. This close contact with street life enabled her work to remain in tune with shifts in focus among the generation of clubbers and popstars she dressed.

Hogg's work was infused with the desire to create fashion as a series of costumes, first for the early 1980s New Romantic nightlife, with heady silver-printed velvets which drew upon her training in textiles, and later, as she began to establish a more coherent and distinctive look, in sporty stretch jersey with leather. Her clothes promoted strong, often provocative images for women that dabbled in the confrontational sexual and tribal motifs of punk, and responded to her own uncompromising personality.

In 1990 this interest in raw sexual statements was crystallized in a collection that included shiny black rubber front-laced catsuits and thigh-high spike-heeled platform boots, which toyed with fetishism. The stark, anarchic personae created by such clothes was tempered by a sense of humor and frequent references to another strong look from the 1970s—glam rock. Hogg often used sparkling gold lurex for leggings or bell bottoms flouting convention, fake cowhide chaps, and red tartan panels and fringing.

Her silver leather minikilts and studded biker jackets equally exemplified her mixing of imagery. In characteristic style, in the autumn-winter of 1989–90, she combined references to Joan of Arc with Hell's Angels and go-go dancers, dubbed the "Warrior Queen" collection. It was typical of her work; shiny corsets were worn with jersey separates with puffed shoulder and elbow sections that referred to slashed 15th-century styles and seemingly castellated cutout hems, and leather crowns-cum-helmets providing a nocturnal urban armor. Her work ran parallel with Westwood's, yet Hogg was more concerned with exploring subcultures and historical inspirations for strong imagery than for overriding philosophies.

The ability to combine shock tactics with wearable clothes continued in Hogg's menswear, which derived its distinctive style from similar sources, with punkish overtones and an overblown humor, combining macho leather with lace, gold trimmings, and the obligatory tartan. It challenged notions of what is acceptable as menswear and set Hogg within the movement from the late 1980s to broaden the horizons of this area of design. Her own line was developed in response to the success of unisex garments within her women's range, with male customers keen to adopt Hogg's upbeat style and sport her flaming heart logo.

Despite having shifted her interest from clothing to music in 1992, her last collection continued to sell well, having become as close to a classic style as clubwear could. Her encapsulation of the traits of British city street life—music, sex, rebellion, and a perverse sense of its own heritage—ensured its continued popularity. Hogg's success in Britain was complemented by the appeal of such witty, indigenous imagery to foreign buyers, who quickly recognized her cult status.

—Rebecca Arnold

HOLAH, David

See BODYMAP

HOPE, Emma

British footwear designer

Born: Portsmouth, England, 11 July 1962. **Education:** Studied at Cordwainers College, Hackney, London, 1981–84. **Career:** Established business in London, 1984, first collection sold to Whistles, Joseph & Jones, London; designed and manufactured six collections for Laura Ashley, 1985–87; designed for, among others, the Chelsea Design Co., Betty Jackson, Jean Muir, English Eccentrics, 1985–87; opened first London store, 1987; designed for Harel, Paris, 1988, for Arabella Pollen, 1989, and for Nicole Farhi, from 1989; footwear fashion critic, from 1988; opened second London store, 1997; expanded line to include handbags and leather goods, 1997; opened third London store, 1999. **Awards:** Five Design Council awards, 1987–88; Martini Style award, 1988; *Harpers and Queen* award, 1989. **Address:** 53 Sloan Square, London SW1, England.

Publications

By HOPE:

Articles

"Shoe Design: Tiptoeing into Industry," in *Design* (London), November 1988.

"Emma Hope, Shoe Designer," in the *Independent* (London), 12 June 1998.

On HOPE:

Books

Debrett's *People of Today,* London, 1991.

Articles

Callen, Kerena, and Liz Freemantle, "Bit Parts," in *Elle* (London), May 1987.

Lott, Jane, and Charity Durant, "Hoofers to the Nation," in the *Observer* (London), 30 August 1987.

Rumbold, Judy, "The Last Shall Be First," in *The Guardian* (London), 21 September 1987.

"Brave New Heels," in *Connoisseur* (London), October 1987.

Thackara, John, "Put Your Foot in It," in the *Observer Magazine* (London), 22 November 1987.

Allott, Serena, "A Foot in Every Door," in the *Daily Telegraph,* 20 November 1989.

Schneider-Levy, Barbara, "U.K.'s Emma Hope Bolsters Men's Line," in *Footwear News,* 25 November 1991.

"A Life in the Day of Emma Hope," in the *Sunday Times* (London), November 1991.

Sharpe, Antonia, "Frivolity with Discipline," in the *Financial Times* Saturday edition (London), June 1992.

Baber, Bonnie, "On the Verge of a Nervous Breakdown," in *Footwear News,* 30 January 1995.

Williams, Sally, "Hot on the Heels of the Hackney Mafia," in the *Independent* (London), 25 May 1996.

Cook, Emma, "How We Met; Raffaella Barker and Emma Hope," in the *Independent Sunday* (London), 14 July 1996.

Fallon, James, "Hoping for Success," in *Footwear News,* 3 February 1997.

Blanchard, Tamsin, "Made to Pleasure," in the *Independent* (London), 28 October 1998.

Fox, Imogen, "Shopping with...Emma Hope—Emma's Box of Tricks," in the *Independent Sunday* (London), 3 January 1999.

O'Riordain, Aoife, "The Evidence: The Shoe Designer's Work Table," in the *Independent* (London), 6 March 1999.

Lewis, Henny, "Fashion & Lifestyle: Emma Hope," available online at *My Village: Notting Hill,* (www.portowebbo.co.uk/nottinghilltv), October 2000.

"Emma Hope's Shoes," online at *Create Britain,* (www.create-britain.co.uk), 6 June 2001.

* * *

Emma Hope was part of the flowering of talent in British shoe design in the late 1980s. She trained at Cordwainers Technical College in London's Hackney along with successful contemporaries Christine Ahrens, Elizabeth Stuart-Smith, and Patrick Cox. There she received a thorough technical grounding that enabled her to design free, fanciful shoes that are also practical and comfortable to wear. Her first collection was sold to shops in London and America in 1984. She produced shoes for leading fashion designers such as Jean Muir, Bill Gibb, John Flett, Betty Jackson, and Joe Casely-Hayford. From 1987 Hope began exhibiting collections under her own name; in the same year, her work was featured in the 22 different styles of boots and shoes accepted by the Design Council for their footwear selection.

The opening of Hope's own shop in London in 1987 marked a new phase. She acknowledged it caused her to produce designs that were more straightforward and wearable and has described her shoes as "regalia for feet," decorative and distinctive but with comfort being an important feature. Inspiration comes from historical sources studied in the collections of the Victoria and Albert Museum in London and the Shoe Museum in Northampton. Paintings and Greek and Roman statues have been explored for source material as well. Louis heels and elongated toes were often seen in her work. Hope's shoes have been featured in the style pages of fashionable magazines such as *Vogue, Cosmopolitan,* and *Harpers and Queen*. The regular appearance of her shoes in more specialized publications such as *Wedding and Home* reflects her prominence in the field of decorative special occasion shoes, particularly for brides.

When Hope started her business, her shoes were made to her specifications in London by skilled craftspeople, but this method became increasingly difficult and in 1995 she moved production of all her shoes to Italy. According to Hope's statement in *Footwear News* (1997), the change was a wonderful success: wholesale sales increased by a third in the first season and had doubled by 1997. About two-thirds of Hope's business has come through the wholesale market, while the remaining third sells through her stores.

Hope has become one of the most well-known shoe designers in Britain, and her shoes are easily found in the U.S., Europe, Hong Kong, Japan, and Australia. She has also added a handbag collection to match her shoes, using the same materials—suede, silk, velvet, nappa, brocade, and the like. Her incredible success can in part be attributed to the combination of practicality and luxury that she pairs for each shoe she designs. Hope always has a mind toward where the shoes might be worn and how they will make the wearer feel; in other words, she puts herself in their shoes.

—Linda Coleing; updated by Carrie Snyder

HORN, Carol

American sportswear and knitwear designer

Born: New York City, 12 June 1936. **Education:** Columbia University, New York, and Boston University, Boston, MA. **Career:** Began designing sportswear for juniors, Bryant 9; designer, Benson & Partners and Outlander Sweater Company, 1968; designer/director, Carol Horn line for Malcolm Starr International; established her own company, Carol Horn's Habitat, 1974; launched Carol Horn Sportswear, 1983. **Awards:** Coty award, 1975; May Company award for Best Designer of the Year, 1976; Neiman Marcus Best Designer of the Year, 1977; Macy's Best Taste award, 1983; Knitwear Association's Knitwear Designer award, 1984. **Address:** 215 West 40th Street, New York, New York 10018, USA.

Publications

On HORN:

Books

Stegemeyer, Anne, *Who's Who in Fashion, Third Edition,* New York, 1996.

Articles

"Carol Horn Back in April with Lowered Price Tags," in *WWD,* 28 February 1983.

"Fall on SA Still in a Fashion Fog," in *WWD,* 21 April 1983.

Lockwood, Lisa, "Carol Horn Exclusive Set for Limited," in*WWD,* 14 February 1986.

———, "Christine Thomson Signs Up for a Flagship Line," in *WWD,* 19 February 1986.

Hartlein, Robert, "Carol Horn Reorganizes Firm," in *WWD,* 12 October 1987.

———, "Horn Won't Ship Spring, Zeroing in on Backer," in *WWD,* 9 December 1987.

Chua, Lawrence, "Carol Horn Enters Licensed Leather Pact (with Marquette Ltd.)," in *WWD,* 6 April 1988.

White, Constance C. R., "Carol Horn's New American Indian Bent," in *WWD,* 12 July 1989.

Friedman, Arthur, "Carol Horn Comes to Saril," in *WWD,* 11 September 1990.

"Carol Horn's Kids," in *WWD,* 6 May 1991.

"Seventh Avenue Continues March into Kids," in*Children's Business,* June 1991.

Lockwood, Lisa, "Carol Horn's Comeback Collection," in *WWD,* 29 September 1993.

* * *

Bringing cultures and traditions of the past and present into her designs, Carol Horn uniquely creates a style that is both stylish and comfortable. She was the first to implement the essence of the 1960s, with collections of separates that carried over from season to season. Further, Horn blended such disparate looks as British nomad and the ultra structured lines of formal Japanese attire into her collections. Her fringed suede clothing, inspired by the Micmac Indians of Massachusetts, led to a 21-piece collection called Carol Horn's American Indian Collectibles.

To create fashionable designs from various cultures and traditions, Horn has used travel as a source of inspiration throughout her career. She made her first trip to India in 1969, in collaboration with the Indian Government's Department of Handicrafts. While on her trip, she examined and admired the gauzy sheer fabrics, in bright and vibrant colors, made and worn by the country's people. The clothing made an everlasting impression on Horn, which in turn led to what became her signature style. In addition to the color combinations of the Indian fabric, Horn also found the simplicity, function, and comfort of the clothing of lasting value and encouraging to her designs. After her India trip, Horn traveled extensively to find inspiration for her designs, including visits through Europe, Asia, the Middle East, and the Far East.

Newer collections featured knitwear created from multidyed yarns in rich colors, with each garment meticulously produced on a hand-loom. Her designs are never mass produced, and are all one of kind originals. Horn's knitwear line is just a small part of her business, however, her sweaters, leathers, fake furs, and sportswear have also well received by critics and customers. A recent sportswear collection, developed exclusively for The Limited's flagship store on Madison Avenue, was a great success.

Never leaving any target group ignored, Horn developed an interest in children's clothes in the beginning of the 1990s. The new line offered girls' sportswear in sizes 4 to 14. The designs were body-conscious and paralleled Horn's popular sportswear collections for women. Styles were offered in velour and stretch Lycra and featured several themes, including a harlequin or houndstooth prints, and ribbed velour.

Carol Horn's style of function and comfort, in vibrant mostly natural fabrics, is the key to her success as a fashion designer. She knows her customers want clothing that is both fashionable and simple, and she creates moderately priced collections to meet these needs. The traditions and cultures that her designs mimic are creatively integrated, producing unique, noticeable, and stylish designs.

—Kimbally A. Medeiros

HORSTING, Viktor

See VIKTOR & ROLF

HOWELL, Margaret

British fashion designer

Born: Tadworth, Surrey, 5 September 1946. **Education:** Studied Fine Art at Goldsmiths' College, London. **Family:** Divorced; children: two. **Collections:** Museum of Costume, Bath; Victoria and Albert Museum, London. **Address:** 5 Garden House, 8 Battersea Park Road, London SW8 4BG, UK.

Margaret Howell, fall 2001 collection. © AFP/CORBIS.

Publications

On HOWELL:

Books

Mulvagh, Jane, *Vogue History of 20th Century Fashion,* London, 1988.
Rothstein, Natalie, *400 Years of Fashion,* London, 1984.

Articles

Rubold, Judy, "A Howell of Triumph," in *The Guardian* (London), 26 October 1987.
"Designs on Men," in *Elle* (London), February 1990.
Armstrong, Lisa, "Fashioned for Life as Women Live It," in the *Independent* (London), 2 April 1992.
Reed, Paula, "Out of the Woods," in the *Sunday Times* (London), 13 September 1992.
"Suits You," in *New Business,* Winter 1999.
Barron, Susannah, "Always and Forever," in *The Guardian* (London), 7 January 2000.

Margaret Howell, fall 2001 collection. © AFP/CORBIS.

*

From an early age I remember having an awareness of clothes and a response to those of my parents; the softness of my Father's well-worn cotton shirts and raincoat, the slim hang of a pleated chiffon dress my Mother used for ballroom dancing. She made her children's clothes; I loved the smell of new cotton as it was cut. I had fun making my school uniform stylish in the early 1960s. We wore our skirts long with ankle socks. We bought men's cardigans from Marks and Spencer. I enjoyed the androgynous character of the white shirt, the duffle coat and the double-breasted gabardine raincoats. In fact, I was styling the basics which I think is what I do now. I take a classic and reinterpret it by cut, detailing and the choice of fabric to make it modern and enjoyable to wear.

I am interested in the selection and then the editing process that goes on in design and in the grouping of things together to make a statement as a result of their selection. I am more interested in styling, quality, and workmanship than in the impact of fashion, but the styling has to run parallel with a current fashion that is determined by lifestyle and the needs of today.

—Margaret Howell

* * *

An established name in British fashion design, Margaret Howell originally trained as a fine artist at Goldsmiths' College of Art in London in the 1960s. Although having no formal training in fashion, in 1971 she produced her first range of accessories, the success of which led to the creation of a small business, printing and selling scarves to boutiques. Later she began designing men's shirts, which were sold in South Molton Street by Joseph.

Her clothes for both men and women, designed from the early 1970s onwards, are based on a typically English look, using vernacular materials such as Melton cloth, tweed, and wool. The clothing makes references to what are considered to be traditional approaches to dressing—the British traditions of cashmere and tweeds but twisted into a more relaxed image which is particularly appealing to Americans.

Howell has operated a shop in New York, and her reinterpretations of classic English clothes—a style dubbed "preppy" in the U.S. and equally successfully interpreted in Ralph Lauren's Polo range—negotiate a series of experiments around standard garments such as the striped cotton shirt, box pleated skirt, Fair Isle sweater, or archetypal cardigan as in the 1994 cashmere version with tiny pearl buttons worn with silk pajama bottoms. The clothes themselves seem hardly to alter from season to season, and it seems ironic that Howell, a designer noted for timeless classics, is involved in the fashion world, which operates on the notion of novelty for novelty's sake rather than being allied to any improved functionality.

"Timelessness" and "classic," however, are a staple part of fashion terminology used to describe and market looks connoting notions of wealth and taste through good tailoring and the use of traditional materials. The classic look signifies affluence through the wearing of clothes that fit within the parameters of understated elegance and sophisticated taste; an emphasis on the texture of the materials used and the expertise of tailoring rather than more obviously conceptual ideas like grunge or punk. This concept has been successfully utilized in the design and marketing of Armani, say, or Hermès.

Howell's clothes also operate successfully on the notion of nostalgia. Past eras such as the 1930s are referenced in women's eveningwear, particularly the 1950s in daywear, an evocation of an Enid Blyton world where boys wear cricket flannels or knee-length shorts and girls wear cotton frocks, short socks, and cardies. In the early 1980s, British style guru Peter York dubbed Howell the designer for Babytimers, those who wore archaic children's clothes particularly from their own childhoods, clothes with a children's book feel as worn by the Famous Five or Just William. Striped blazers, Fair Isle slipovers, macintoshes, and flannel trousers in archaic cuts are all staples of Howell's collections. With the demise of the Babytime era, however, and the assertion of the tougher 1980s power look, Howell's clothes were later bought for their comfort and "classic" qualities by the more "aesthetically aware" consumer who considered yarns, dyes, and reworkings of conventional clothing forms before the vagaries of high fashion.

The contemporary Howell look is praised for its pared-down line and simple silhouettes, the controlled restraint of shape and color, the workmanship and quality of cloth and cut. By the mid-1990s, she was concentrating on women's clothing, particularly trouser suits, which have always been an integral part of her collections. The 1994 autumn/winter version featured masculine suiting feminized with soft chiffon scarves. Her designs for jackets, eveningwear, and nightwear still have a feel for styles of the past—such as her 1994 white handkerchief linen pajamas. These styles evoke memories of her own childhood, such as her father's gardening raincoat that hung on the back door, her mother's cotton dresses, and an English sporting look popularized by designers from Chanel onward and seen in Howell's nautical navy cotton cardigans with brass buttons and linen jodhpurs, worn with a white linen shawl-collared shirt.

By the beginning of 2000, Howell's empire had grown to employ 300 people worldwide, with global sales of £30 million. She has capitalized on the popularity of British design in Japan, designing under license for the Japanese company Anglobal and has 70 shops and concessions there, in contrast to only 10 in her home country. "Today Margaret Howell is the second biggest-selling British designer in Japan after Paul Smith," reported *New Business* magazine. "The Japanese love her linens, denims, and floral cottons for summer which are as English as cricket or cream teas. In winter, Howell's Far Eastern customers clamor for her tweeds, knitwear and stylish raincoats which have been adapted to their sophisticated demands."

Managing director Richard Craig was hired to help save Howell's company from a near collapse after the fashion industry shrank in the late 1980s at the same time Howell overexpanded. He has continued to guide the company, hoping to add to his successes in Britain and Japan by developing American and Western European markets. "But we want to build slowly, carefully and profitably," he told *New Business.*

Allowing a pro to handle the books while maintaining design freedom seems to work for Howell, who is entering her fourth decade at the cutting edge of a notoriously fickle business. She has become as much of a fashion classic as the clothing she favors. "Some things come back and have an appeal in a new era," she told Susannah Barron of *The Guardian.* "They are the real classics."

—Caroline Cox; updated by Lisa Groshong

HUGO BOSS AG

German menswear fashion house

Founded: in Metzingen, Germany, by Hugo Boss in 1923, to manufacture work clothes and uniforms. **Company History:** Bought U.S.-based Joseph & Feiss, 1966; subsequently taken over by Siegfried Boss and son-in-law Eugen Holly (1948–72) and in 1972 by grandsons Jochen Holly and Uwe Holly; introduced men's and children's lines, 1948; began export to Belgium and Netherlands, 1973; Scandinavia and England, 1975; formed Paris subsidiary and began exporting to U.S., 1977; added men's shirts, 1981; exported to Canada, 1982; introduced sportswear and cosmetics line, 1984; added Italy, Japan, and Spain to export countries, 1985–86; created U.S. subsidiary in New York, 1986; Portugal, Taiwan, and Korea, 1987–88; launched eyewear collection, 1989; firm acquired by Japanese investment group Leyton House, Ltd., 1989; womenswear collection debuted and discontinued, 1990–91; bought by Italian manufacturer Marzotto & Figli, SpA (which became Gruppo Industriale Marzotto), 1991; formed units in Milan and Japan, 1991; Hugo and Baldessarini lines for men introduced, 1994; opened new stores in Prague and Shanghai, 1994; major media blitz and image rehaul, 1995; opened shop inside Saks Fifth Avenue, New York, 1996; sold Joseph & Feiss, 1996; launched Hugo womenswear, 1998; second womenswear line, under Boss label, announced 1999; Boss womenswear debuted, 2000; fragrances include *Boss Sport, Boss Spirit, Boss Elements,* 1994; *Hugo,* 1995; and *Hugo Woman,* 1997. **Company Address:** Dieselstrasse 12, 72555 Metzingen, Germany. **Company Website:** www.hugoboss.com.

Hugo Boss AG, fall/winter 2001–02 collection. © AP/Wide World Photos.

PUBLICATIONS

On HUGO BOSS:

Articles

Syedain, Hashi, "What Suits Boss," in *Management Today* (London), June 1989.
"Modest Boss," in *DNR,* 25 January 1991.
Deeny, Godfrey, "The World According to Boss," in *DNR,* 1 April 1991.
Protzman, Ferdinand, "Hugo Boss: A Fading Status Symbol," in the *New York Times,* 23 June 1991.
Deeny, Godfrey, "Redirecting the Empire: Hugo Boss Adjusts to the 'Values' of the 1990s," in *DNR,* 5 August 1993.
Levine, Joshua, "I Am the Boss," in *Forbes,* 25 October 1993.

Hugo Boss AG, fall/winter 2001 ready-to-wear collection. © AFP/ CORBIS.

Laws, Malcolm, "Boss Cuts its Cloth to Suit the Modern Man," in the *European,* 22 December 1994.
"No Question Who's Boss," in *DNR,* 6 February 1995.
Gellers, Stan, "He's the Design Boss at Boss; Lothar Reiff is Busy Redesigning Boss Fashions and Image," in *DNR,* 13 March 1995.
Drier, Melissa, "Hugo to Start Chasing Generation X in October," in *Women's Wear Daily,* 26 May 1995.
Fisher, Andrew, "Hugo Boss Man Fashions Strategy for Expansion," in the *Financial Times,* 9 January 1996.
Palmieri, Jean E., "Brave New Boss Shop at Saks Flagship," in *DNR,* 15 August 1996.
"Hugo Boss USA Unveils Big Retail Expansion," in *DNR,* 26 September 1996.
Ozzard, Janet, "Men's Star Hugo Boss Planning Major Entry into Womenswear in 1998," in *Women's Wear Daily,* 7 April 1997.
Palmieri, Jean E., "Hugo Boss USA Building Retail Empire," in *DNR,* 1 August 1997.
Bow, Josephine, "In Huge China Market, Early Arrivals Zegna and Hugo Boss Make Gains," in *DNR,* 4 January 1999.
Weisman, Katherine, "Hugo Boss: Big Plans in Womenswear," in *Women's Wear Daily,* 31 March 1999.

* * *

A company originally producing workwear in the 1920s, Hugo Boss segued successfully into suits for aspiring executives. In the 1960s Uwe and Jochem Holy, grandchildren of the company's founder, saw a place in the market for a mid-range version of the kind of fashionable clothes they enjoyed wearing from Pierre Cardin. Since then the continuing success of the company and the incursion of similar middle-market concerns into the European clothing industry has resulted in top German designers and fashion groups like Jil Sander, Mondi and Hugo Boss becoming international brand names.

Using new technology and the strategy of subcontracting, together with high quality materials, stringent quality control, and the business acumen of the company directors, Hugo Boss became a household name; acknowledging the powers of advertising, particularly the use of product placement, the company created an indelible image in the power dressing of the 1980s. Early in the decade, Boss became associated with the hard metropolitan chic of the ubiquitous yuppie, through male characters sporting a variety of Boss garments on television's *Miami Vice* and *L.A. Law* series.

The popular conception of the Filofax-toting, mobile-phone wielding entrepreneur living in a warehouse apartment, surrounded by matte black accoutrements, was conflated by the young(ish) European man with Hugo Boss suits, although in reality if the yuppie existed in great numbers he was far more likely to frequent Paul Smith or Armani. Nevertheless the sharp Boss suit, styled by businessmen rather than tailors, became symbolic of materialism and power for large numbers of European men, as increasing sales figures throughout the 1980s proved.

The Boss look, based on a traditionally masculine 20th-century silhouette, revolved around variations on the wide-shouldered suit, usually double-breasted with front pleated trousers; the Euroman added his own styling by rolling up the sleeves of the jacket à la Don Johnson. In the 1990s the Boss logo began appearing at prestigious sporting events, not so much because the company was interested in producing a line of sportswear to rival those of the German firms Puma and Adidas, but because of the glamorous image and athletic machismo associated with Formula One racing and Davis Cup tennis. This was subsequently reflected in the marketing of *Boss Sport*—"fragrance and bodycare for the confident man leading an active lifestyle."

The company responded well to the 1990s; export success remained constant, although for a time the name Boss was seen in Germany as somewhat downmarket due to overexposure. Rather than concentrating on export and weathering the storm, Boss responded by quickly withdrawing deliveries from a number of German retailers who no longer fit its standards, prepared to accept a loss of revenue rather than downgrading—a strategy which appeared to work as the firm very successfully went public. As for the image which seemed to be so squarely rooted in the 1980s? The suits gained more rounded shoulders but the advertising and brandnaming gave more of a clue—Europeans were introduced to a Boss man with "a new attitude and vision," seemingly encapsulated in a new fragrance and marketing angle, *Boss Spirit.*

Part of the "Boss Spirit" had to do with new chief executive Dr. Peter Littman, who took the reins in 1993. A shrewd businessman, Littman initiated a reorganization of the firm and its image. The old logo was tossed in favor of three new ones, each representing one of the menswear lines: Boss, the high-end sophisticated collection; Hugo, with the younger, trendier male in mind; and Baldessarini, for more luxurious, handmade menswear. By 1996 several new in-store boutiques were opening in high-end department stores; the first and largest, measuring in at 1,000 square feet, was built inside Saks Fifth Avenue's New York flagship store. Boss announced it would build 25 freestanding Boss stores along with another 50 in-store boutiques within the next five years. Handsome furnished stores opened in Los Angeles, Washington D.C., and Las Vegas in quick succession.

Surprisingly, Boss revisited womenswear in the late 1990s despite a dismal attempt back in 1990. The first collections, under the Hugo label for women aged 20 to 40, featured ready-to-wear and sportswear and followed on the heels of the latest fragrance launch, *Hugo Woman,* which had debuted in the U.S. in fall 1997. Another collection under the more exclusive Boss label was announced in 1999 along with the formation of a new subsidiary, Hugo Boss SpA, to deal solely with the Boss womenswear line, based in Milan. Additionally, the company had continued to expand its licensing program, with the Hugo Boss label on innerwear, loungewear, watches, footwear, and a major push into golf apparel.

While Hugo Boss had been an enduring and successful brand in Germany and Europe, the company's push for dominance in the U.S. through numerous retail outlets and aggressive advertising was paying off by 1998 and 1999. The same was true for China, where the firm had five stores at a time when there was little competition from fashion's leading menswear labels. Other than Ermenegildo Zegna, which had been in China since the early 1990s, and newcomer Giorgio Armani, few menswear producers had ventured to the country.

—Caroline Cox; updated by Nelly Rhodes

HULANICKI, Barbara

British designer

Born: Warsaw, Poland, 8 December 1936; raised in Palestine, immigrated to England in 1948. **Education:** Studied fashion and fashion illustration at Brighton College, 1954–56; winner in the *Evening Standard* Design Competition, beachwear division, 1955. **Family:** Married Stephen Fitz-Simon, 1961 (deceased); children: Witwold. **Career:** Illustrator for Helen Jardine Artists, London, circa 1956–59; freelance fashion illustrator, 1961–64; opened Biba's Postal Boutique, 1963; established first Biba emporium, Abingdon Road, London, 1964; moved and expanded to Church Street, London, 1965; opened branch location in Brighton, 1966; launched mail order catalogue, 1968; moved Biba to High Street, Kensington, London, 1969; introduced line of Biba cosmetics, 1969; cosmetics distributed nationally through Dorothy Perkins shops, 1969; introduced line of footwear, 1969; majority stake in company sold to consortium of investors, 1969; Biba boutique established at Bergdorf Goodman, New York, 1970; purchased Derry and Toms Department Store for "Big Biba," 1972; control of firm passed to British Land, 1972; Big Biba opened, 1973 (closed, 1975); firm declared bankruptcy, 1976; designed in Brazil, 1976–80; relocated to Miami Beach, Florida, 1987; designer of hotel and club interiors, videos, ready-to-wear children's clothes, theatre costumes, from 1988. **Exhibitions:** Retrospective, Newarke Houses Museum, Leicester, England, 1993. **Awards:** Bath Museum of Costume Dress of the Year award, 1972; Miami Design Preservation League award, for her redesign of the Marlin Hotel, Miami, Florida. **Address:** 1300 Collins Avenue, Suite 205, Miami Beach, FL 35139, USA.

Publications

By HULANICKI:

Books

From A to Biba, London, 1983.
Disgrace, London, 1990.

Articles

"The Dedicated Modeller of Fashion," in the *Times* (London), 15 August 1983.
"When Big Becomes Beautiful," in the *Times* (London), 16 August 1983.
"The Shattering of a Dream," in the *Times* (London), 17 August 1983.

On HULANICKI:

Books

Bernard, Barbara, *Fashion in the Sixties,* London, 1978.
Harris, Jennifer, Sarah Hyde, and Greg Smith, *1966 and All That: Design and the Consumer in Britain, 1960–1969,* London, 1986.
Whiteley, Nigel, *Pop Design: Modernism to Mod,* London, 1987.
Loebenthal, Joel, *Radical Rags: Fashions of the Sixties,* New York, 1990.

Articles

"Twiggy in Bibaland," in *Vogue* (London), December 1973.
"Biba: What Went Wrong?" in *Drapers Record* (London), 30 August 1975.
"Biba," in the *Times* (London), 1 April 1976.
"Biba is Back: A 'Paradise' in London," in *Drapers Record* (London), 2 December 1978.
"Bye-Bye Biba—Hello Hulanicki," in *Women's Journal* (London), March 1981.
Brampton, Sally, "Bringing Up Baby," in the *Observer* (London), 4 September 1983.
Neustatter, Angela, "Biba and Son," in the *Sunday Times Magazine* (London), 18 May 1986.
Samuel, Kathryn, "Biba Goes Back to the Drawing Board," in the *Daily Telegraph* (London), 19 June 1986.
Neustatter, Angela, "Life No. 3 for the Biba Girl," in the *Daily Telegraph* (London), 21 January 1987.
Cuccio, Angela, "Mini Rock Rolls," in *WWD,* 10 October 1988.
Brampton, Sally, "Barbara Hulanicki and *Disgrace,"* in the *Correspondent Magazine* (London), 25 March 1990.
McRobbie, Angela, *"Disgrace,"* [book review] in the *New Statesman and Society,* 30 March 1990.
Fallon, James, "Barbara Hulanicki, Biba and Beyond," in *WWD,* 14 May 1990.
Gandee, Charles, "Barbara Hulanicki is Hot for Miami," in *House & Garden,* June 1992.

Webb, Michael, "Island Fantasy," in *Hospitality Design,* July/August 1992.
Wilson, Kennedy, "Gone But Not Forgotten: A Success Story of the Swinging Sixties," in the *Herald* (Glasgow), 5 January 1993.
Tredre, Roger, "Heaven Was a Place Called Biba," in the *Independent* (London), 12 February 1993.
Godley, Georgina, "The Importance of Biba," in *Blueprint* (London), No. 96, April 1993.
Young, Lucie, "At Home with Barbara Hulanicki: Color So Bright You Need Shades," in the *New York Times,* 31 December 1998.

* * *

In the decade from 1964 to 1974, Barbara Hulanicki's design and entrepreneurial skills contributed to the development of an entirely new ethos in British fashion that responded to ideas generated by the rising youth culture of the period. Hulanicki and her husband, Stephen Fitz-Simon, created a series of fashion businesses, under the name of Biba, perfectly suited to the spirit of change and adventure characterizing the Mod movement originating in London during the early 1960s. Unlike the English establishment rag trade, Hulanicki understood that fashion ideas would, henceforth, originate in the streets of British cities, rather than in couture houses across the Channel. She styled her shop as a meeting spot and a place of entertainment for those interested in a lifestyle represented by the clothes and other goods designed by Hulanicki.

Following a year at art school, Hulanicki set up Biba's Postal Boutique in the early 1960s, with herself as designer and Fitz-Simon as business manager. The success of their business was ensured when an early design for a simple smock dress was worn by Cathy McGowan, "Queen of the Mods," on the popular television program *Ready, Steady, Go.* The first Biba shop was opened in 1964 in a small, old-fashioned chemist's shop on a corner of Abingdon Road, Kensington, London. Hulanicki concentrated on generating a unique atmosphere through décor, music, and the glamor of the young shop assistants—all of which turned her shop into an instant "scene," a gathering place for a hip, young clientèle who knew where to go for the latest ideas in clothing, without even the benefit of a sign over the shop-front.

Hulanicki's early clothes were short, simple dresses, the "Biba smock," which became the uniform for an era. Her little girl look was given a major boost when Julie Christie selected her wardrobe for the film *Darling* from the Biba shop. Other early customers included Sonny and Cher, Twiggy, and Mick Jagger. The typical Biba dolly girl would have a slim, boyish figure, huge eyes and a childlike pout, updating the Audrey Hepburn gamine look of the 1950s. She would wear a simple mini dress selected from a wide range of muted colors—blueberry, rust, plum—which Hulanicki called Auntie colors, as they had previously been associated with the wardrobes of old ladies. At this time, she also introduced the first fashion t-shirts, distinguished from their ordinary equivalent by the range of Auntie colors in which they were dyed. The t-shirts initiated the unisex appeal of Biba goods.

In 1966 the shop moved to larger premises in Kensington Church Street. The new boutique sported a black and gold art nouveau logo and was decorated in an eclectic mix of late 19th-century decadent motifs, Victoriana, and art deco. Hulanicki expanded her range of clothing to include fashion accessories, including bangles and feather boas displayed on old-fashioned bentwood hatstands, cosmetics, menswear, and household accessories. The Church Street Biba became an internationally known symbol of swinging London in the mid-1960s.

In the early 1970s, the Biba style developed in the direction of retro glamor and glitter. Hulanicki introduced a line of children's clothing that followed the styles and colors of the adult ranges. She featured items such as straw hats with veils and artificial flowers, velvet, and lace, all enhanced by a new element of innocent eroticism and unchildlike glamor. Her cosmetics had, by the late 1960s, become big business, the range of colors corresponding to the Auntie colors of her clothing and including bizarre hues such as blue, green, purple, and black lipstick, eye shadow and powder.

Rapidly increasing sales forced Biba to move again, in 1969, to a larger shop in Kensington High Street, where art nouveau and art deco fused into a single style that became Biba's own. During the early 1970s, Hulanicki and Fitz-Simon expanded their operations to the U.S. through New York's Bergdorf Goodman, which set up a Biba boutique in its flagship store. The final phase of expansion came in 1973, when Hulanicki opened the Biba department store in the former Derry and Toms premises in Kensington High Street, London. This enormous art deco building housed a huge enterprise that provided a complete setting, including an all-day restaurant and nightly entertainment in the glamorous Rainbow Room, exotic roof gardens, and a kasbah for the elegant and exotic retro style clothes, all designed by Hulanicki.

The Biba store was, for a short time, a mecca for fashionable young Londoners looking for a setting in which to parade the elegant and eclectic clothing of the period. Management difficulties forced Hulanicki to leave Biba in the mid-1970s. She eventually moved to Brazil and thence to Florida, where she began to design under the Hulanicki name. Her groundbreaking designs in the 1960s and 1970s were showcased in an exhibition entitled "Biba, the Label, the Lifestyle, the Look," which opened in 1993 at the Laing Gallery in Newcastle and later traveled to the Aberdeen Art Gallery.

In the 1990s, Hulanicki turned to interior design, using bold colors to revitalize hotels in Miami's South Beach and the Caribbean. She drew both praise and criticism for her wild combinations that splashed together dozens of hues in buildings, including the Pink Sands Hotel and Compass Point in the Bahamas and the Leslie in Miami. She won an award from the Miami Design Preservation League for her redesign of the Marlin Hotel. Later, the same group blasted her color choices for other projects. "Barbara was at the forefront of changing the local colors from pastel to bright," Michael D. Kinerk, chairman of the Miami Design Preservation League, told Lucie Young of the *New York Times.* "It is the position of the league that the Art Deco district's colors should now swing back to more historically appropriate ones."

Young quoted Miami photographer Steven Brooke as observing that "the colors [Hulanicki] uses might be legal but they are egregiously ugly." Hulanicki took the criticisms in stride, noting that similar critiques had been leveled at her early fashions, which in the end revolutionized fashion. "It's about energy," she told Young. "It has the same effect on babies and adults: it makes our minds tick."

—Gregory Votolato; updated by Lisa Groshong

I

I. MAGNIN

American department store chain

Founded: by Mary Ann Magnin in San Francisco, 1876. **Company History:** First branch opened in Santa Barbara, 1912; Los Angeles store opened, 1938, flagship San Francisco store opened, 1948; sold to Bullock's, 1943; to Federated Department Stores, 1964, which was acquired by Campeau Corporation (after an attempted merger with R.H. Macy Corporation); R.H. Macy Corporation purchases I. Magnin stores, 1988; Federated and R.H. Macy merge, announcing closure of I. Magnin chain, 1994; several stores bought by Saks Fifth Avenue and others, 1994–95; remaining Magnin stores renamed as other Federated retailers.

Publications

On I. MAGNIN:

Books

Crawford, M.D.C., *The Ways of Fashion,* New York, 1948.

Riley, Robert, *Fashion Makers,* New York, 1968.

Birmingham, Nan Tillson, *Store,* New York, 1978.

Hendrickson, Robert, *The Grand Emporiums,* Briarcliff Manor, New York, 1979.

Dresner, Susan, *Shopping on the Inside Track,* Salt Lake City, Utah, 1988.

Frick, Devin Thomas, *I. Magnin & Company: A California Legacy,* Garden Groce, California, 2000.

Articles

Stabiner, Karen, "Store Wars," in *Savvy* (New York), July 1988.

Ginsberg, Steve, "I. Magnin: Seeking Solutions in the 1990s," in *WWD,* 9 October 1990.

Adelson, Andrea, "Retail Dinosaur Tries to Put Off Extinction," in the *New York Times,* 10 April 1993.

Schmeltzer, John, "A Merger on 34th Street," in the *Chicago Tribune,* 15 July 1994.

Adelson, Andrea, "R.H. Macy Planning to Close I. Magnin Specialty Stores," in the *New York Times,* 19 November 1994.

* * *

Founded by Mary Ann Magnin in 1876, I. Magnin & Company has always stood for beautiful designs of a high quality. They were responsible for making women in San Francisco, California, among the best dressed in the world.

Mary Ann and Isaac Magnin were married in London, England, though both were originally from Holland. They moved to San Francisco in the 1870s, traveling by boat around Cape Horn. They had eight children. Mary Ann did not want her husband working on ceilings as a wood carver, because he might fall and be crippled, leaving her with a large family to support. As a result she used her skills as an accomplished seamstress to make baby clothes which Isaac sold, carrying the items in a pack on his back. Before long they were able to open the first I. Magnin in San Francisco, selling needles, thread, and notions.

The store expanded to include the fashions Mary Ann made, including trousseau, and exquisite lingerie which she made for the fashion-starved ladies of Nob Hill, San Francisco. She made nightgowns, chemises and drawers, bridal gowns, and baby clothes, ordering her lace and linen from Europe. Owing to transportation costs, these items were expensive. Nevertheless, the orders increased and she was able to hire helpers. Her four sons—John, Grover, Joseph, and Sam—were encouraged to learn about fabrics and, most importantly, quality.

Magnin's moved to a larger store, but the 1906 earthquake destroyed it. Mary Ann and Isaac operated their business from their own home until they could rebuild. San Francisco was a thriving community of people who had money to spend and was an excellent market for the luxury goods available at I. Magnin. Eventually one son, John, moved to New York where he opened a buying office. While on a visit there, Mary Ann was so impressed with a marble floor she saw at B. Altman's store that she had one put into her own store. Magnin's store was elegant and designed as a stage for their fashions. Marble, crystal, and gold leaf were used extensively throughout; just as Mary Ann emphasized the best quality in fashion, she also demanded the best for the setting.

I. Magnin showcased the work of the major designers of the times, Jeanne Lanvin, Hattie Carnegie, and Christian Dior, where they introduced their new designs to the West Coast and the United States. The customers were wealthy—the Magnin woman purchased the best of everything, and price was no consideration. Magnin's was noted for fine apparel and having fashion firsts sometimes a year before they reached other stores. Quality, as Mary Ann impressed on her sons at an early age, was always an important ingredient in the operation of I. Magnin.

In her book *Store* (New York, 1978) Nan Tillson Birmingham described I. Magnin's doorman who would greet the car as customers arrived to shop for their school clothes. Clothing was selected by a personal shopper who would have them hanging in the dressing rooms, waiting for the approval of the shoppers. Service to the customer was another aspect of the Magnin shopping experience.

Throughout the 1980s and 1990s, the ownership of I. Magnin changed hands many times. In 1988 when R.H. Macy Corporation bought the luxury chain, the future still seemed bright. By 1993 R.H. Macy was struggling and attempted to revitalize the I. Magnin stores, to no avail. The following year, overwhelmed by debt, Macy closed its first Magnin store, located on Chicago's famed Miracle Mile. Federated Department Stores then stepped in and proposed a merger with the stricken R.H. Macy; in the deal all remaining I. Magnin stores were slated for closure. Several individual stores were bought by Saks Fifth Avenue and other upscale retailers, and the once world renowned I. Magnin name ceased to exist.

—Nancy House; updated by Owen James

IRIÉ, Sueo

Japanese designer working in Paris

Born: Osaka, Japan, 23 December 1946. **Education:** Graduated from Osaka Sogo Fukoso Gakium, 1970. **Career:** Assistant to Hiroko Koshino, 1968; moved to Paris, 1970; assistant designer, Kenzo, 1970–79; presented first collection as designer for Studio V, 1980; set up own shop, 1983. **Exhibitions:** *Technology and Design,* Victoria & Albert Museum, London; *Mode et Japonisme,* Paris. **Address:** 8 rue du Pre-aux-Clercs, 75008 Paris, France.

Publications

On IRIÉ:

Books

The Tokyo Collection, Tokyo, 1986.

Articles

de L'Homme, F., "Irié Ou L'art de la Simplicity," in *Dépèche Mode* (Paris), March 1987.

Betts, K., "The Next Wave," in *WWD,* April 1990.

Carter, Charles, "Europe 1990: Designers to Watch," in *Vogue,* August 1990.

Risbourg, P., "View: European Designers to Watch," in *Vogue,* August 1990.

Hochswender, Woody, "Clothes of Irié: Stylish, But Not Stuffy," in the *New York Times,* September 1990.

Bailhache, P., "Créateurs: Leur monde secret," in *Marie-Claire* (Paris), October 1992.

Menkes, Suzy, "On Paris' Left Bank," in the *International Herald Tribune,* May 1993.

Coppet, A., "Irié, le Succès Merité," in *Marie-Claire Bis* (Paris), Autumn 1993.

Zamelly, C., "Irié a l'affiche de St Germain-des-Pres," in *Elle* (Paris), Autumn 1993.

Ronaldson, F., "Designer Inspiration Focus: Irié," in *Joyce* (Hong Kong), Autumn 1993.

"AngloFiles, No. 13," available online at www.iway.fr/AngloFiles, 22 May, 1996.

Godoy, Tiffany, "Tiffany's Paris Fashion Week Diary," in *Composite* (Tokyo), December 2000.

"Japan/U.S.—Branding Operation Between Ariel and Irié," in *Usine Nouvelle,* 25 January 2001.

"Paris Shopping: Designer Directions," available online at Timeout.com (www.timeout.com/paris), 23 June 2001.

*

I wish to continue creating, inspired by the air of the present.

—Sueo Irié

* * *

Sueo Irié is the name of a Japanese-born designer who first traveled to Europe in the 1970s. Over the last 30 years, he has built a life and career in fashion based in St. Germain des Prés, Paris. With his clothes available from boutiques across France and outlets in Munich and Milan, Irié is a craftsman-artist of contemporary fashion.

Arriving in Paris on the Trans-Siberian Express with little money and no firm plans, Irié worked for Japanese designer Kenzo before opening his own shop and launching his own collection in 1983. Irié claims the opening of his first outlet would never have happened except that on the spur of the moment, he bought a Corinthian column from a Paris flea market and decided he needed a boutique in which to house it. The company has remained small, with Irié overseeing everything himself: stock, manufacturing, sales, and customer satisfaction. And for three weeks every August, the store shuts down so the designer can enjoy a vacation.

The style of Irié's collections has been simplicity paired with casual chic. Irié likes to design for women, all women, across the spectrum of age and profession. He keeps his clothes simple and believes they form a base upon which women can build; his are the raw components of a wardrobe from which a woman can add personal touches as required. The clothes adapt to let the wearer's identity shine through. Irié's early innovations included the use of Lycra to increase comfort of short skirts. He also designed colorful leotards as underclothes long before they became an established and popular fashion.

Irié excludes no colors from his designs. He also makes extensive use of patterned fabrics, some of which he designs himself. Patterns range from romantic florals to wild fantasy, and here we find the one recurring theme of his collections: animal skin prints. The materials and fabrics he uses are dictated by his professed preference for comfort and convenience: natural cotton, wool, silk, synthetics, polyester, vinyl, and fake fur. He uses stretch fabrics everywhere. His later collections paired the usual jeans, suits, and dresses with unusual details like sequins, hologram prints, and plastic coatings.

Irié's essential idea is cheap chic. His ideal woman would wear a Chanel jacket with cheap trainers. He defines elegance as an expensive shirt worn with old jeans and Tiffany earrings to a black-tie dinner. He has said he is motivated to create clothes that allow a woman to share lunch with her banker in *Paris 16e,* then drink a *café noisette* with some friends on the Rive Gauche.

Irié's influences are all French: café lifestyles and black-and-white French films. There is nothing of the Far East in his clothes, no hint of Asian heritage; champagne or Coca Cola, Irié is Westernized through and through. His originality is his presentation. For a small design company, he has big designer pretensions. His Paris boutique, all chrome and mirrors, houses a stuffed zebra, a grand piano, and the enduring Corinthian column. Another stuffed lion is kept in his flat. Though he may head a small-scale company, he does not act like a small player. The clothes he sells are the best quality at affordable prices.

The Irié collection is really too small to influence a larger fashion world, apart from one essential way: his influence is his choice to live in a small flat, two minutes from his shop, to keep his business small, and to enjoy a full life in Paris. He has neither the great fame nor the associated wealth and power problems of the large designers. During the day, he creates fabrics, designs, and sells clothes to pay his bills and fuel his moped. At night, he loses himself in a Parisian nightlife that might be a concert by Vanessa Paradis or a long night of philosophical conversation over pastis.

—Sally Ann Melia; updated by Carrie Snyder

ISANI

Korean design team; currently restaurant owners

Founded: by Jun Kim and Soyon Kim. *Jun Kim* was born in Korea, 1966; went on to study marketing at Pace University in New York (B.A., 1988), and fashion design at Parsons School of Design. *Soyon Kim* was born in Korea, 1968; studied fashion design at Parsons School of Design (B.F.A., 1989). Both trained in their family's Sao Paulo, Brazil, clothing firm, Anderson, Ltd. **Company History:** First designer sportswear line shown, 1988–93; introduced Isani Studio bridge line; introduced Christina line, 1990; introduced Isani Shirts blouse collection, 1992; Isani designer collection closed, 1993; Temple restaurant launched, 2000.

Publications

On ISANI:

Articles

"Great Expectations," in *WWD,* 12 June 1991.

White, Constance C. R., "Isani's Busy Signals: A Hot Line," in *WWD,* 4 September 1991.

———, "Isani: Facing Reality," in *WWD,* 2 June 1993.

Pettera, Angela, "Rearranging the Furniture, and Making Some Alterations," *Los Angeles Times,* 7 December, 2000.

Harper, Rebecca, "Fashion Plates," available online at One: Design Matters, onemedia.com, 17 June 2001.

* * *

Cosmopolitan, discreet, stylish clothing created by Jun and Soyon Kim for Isani emanated a worldly grace and a reserved, sensible approach to clothing rarely associated with young designers. But the Kim pair (brother Jun and sister Soyon) purposefully spared themselves the excesses more commonly seen in young designers to create clothes in the scrupulous heritage of Mainbocher and Halston as an American tailoring for a sophisticated client.

The design propensity of the Kims was modernist, but there was often a picturesque charm to the garments, whether in their Jackie O dresses in suave 1960s revival in 1991 or the fall-winter 1992 accommodations of menswear to the most delicate details and accentuated femininity of fit. Jun Kim avered, "Our clothes are directed at American women, but they're not typical American sportswear. They reflect an approach to fashion that looks right anywhere in the world." Isani represented the possibility of clothing in the 1990s to surpass a parochial sense of nationality and even global regionalism—to seek a style that would be right and reasonable in any major city of the world. The designers, who were born in Korea but grew up chiefly in Brazil, followed by higher education and the launch of their professional careers in New York, chose Isani as the firm's name from the Italian for "healthy."

There was a secure sense of anachronism about Isani. It eschewed the aggressiveness of much young design, and its bashful and absolute discretion was a predilection for exquisite refinement that were the hallmarks of fashion design before World War II. No such historicism actually existed in the work, but there was an ethos, a point of view distinctly and positively old-fashioned in its elegance and subtlety. Although Isani clothing was directed toward a middle-class consumer, the design recalls couture in its suppressed, cultivated aplomb.

Isani achieved a distinction in the marketplace even in its first collections, so refined was the sensibility and so subtle were the plays in the fabrication and proportions. But in early 1993, Isani decided to discontinue its designer collection and focus on lower-cost individual pieces. Later in the 1990s, the team chose to change careers, ending all Isani operations and opening a restaurant in Beverly Hills, California. The Kims have embarked on their new venture with much of the same fresh attitude they brought to the clothing industry. Called Temple, the restaurant showcases a modern Korean fare with hints of the Brazilian influence on the Kims' upbringing.

The Kims proposed that the most important aspect of fashion design was for clothes to be real, with the prospective client able to associate with the designer's vision. Their challenge then became to take this same vision and apply it to the culinary world, finding the subtle blend of tastes that will keep customers coming back for more.

—Richard Martin; updated by Carrie Snyder

J

JACKSON, Betty

British designer

Born: Bacup, Lancashire, 24 June 1949. **Education:** Studied at Birmingham College of Art, 1968–71. **Family:** Married David Cohen, 1985; children: Pascale, Oliver. **Career:** Freelance fashion illustrator, London, 1971–73; design assistant to Wendy Dagworthy, London, 1973–75; chief designer, Quorum, London, 1975–81; director/chief designer, Betty Jackson Ltd., London, from 1981; introduced Betty Jackson for Men collection, 1986; opened flagship shop in the Brompton Road, London, 1991; began designing and selling accessories, including jewelry, gloves, belts, bags, and scarves. **Awards:** *Woman* Magazine Separates Designer of the Year award, London, 1981, 1983; Cotton Institute Cotton Designer of the Year award, 1983; Bath Museum of Costume Dress of the Year award, 1984; British Designer of the Year award, 1985; Harvey Nichols award, 1985; International Linen Council Fil d'Or award, 1985, 1989; Viyella award, 1987; Member of the British Empire, 1987; Honorary Fellow, Royal College of Art, London, 1989; Fellow, Birmingham Polytechnic, 1989; Honorary Fellow, University of Central Lancashire, 1992; Designer of the Year, 1999. **Address:** 311 Brompton Road, London, England.

Betty Jackson, fall/winter 2001 collection: fur wrap over a leather top. © AP/Wide World Photos.

Publications

On JACKSON:

Books

Stegemeyer, Anne, *Who's Who in Fashion, Third Edition,* New York, 1996.

Articles

Spankie, Sarah, "First Sight: The Chiller Thriller from the Jackson File," in the *Sunday Times Magazine* (London), 6 May 1984.

Dodd, C., "Betty Jackson: Seeing Through to the Street," in *Design* (London), November 1984.

"Influences: Betty Jackson," in *Woman's Journal* (London), April 1985.

Brampton, Sally, "The Elle-Shaped Room: A Fine Collection," in *Elle* (London), April 1986.

"Designer Reports, Summer '87: London, Betty Jackson," in *International Textiles* (London), December 1986.

Rumbold, Judy, "Jackson Heights," in *The Guardian* (London), 28 September 1987.

Fremantle, Liz, "Designer Focus: Betty Jackson," in *Cosmopolitan* (London), November 1988.

"Betty Jackson," in *DR: The Fashion Business* (London), 3 December 1988.

Klensch, Elsa, "Getting Comfortable with Betty Jackson," CNN.com, www.cnn.com, 30 October 1997.

"Jackson, Betty," in *Chambers Biographical Dictionary 1997,* available online at Wilson Web, www.hwwilson.com, 10 July 2001.

Davis, Boyd, "Tryst at the Rose Garden," online at Fashion Windows, www.fashionwindows.com, 18 July 2001.

Betty Jackson, spring/summer 2002 collection. © Reuters NewMedia Inc./CORBIS.

*

My work is understated and easy. I do not like formal dressing and I always try to achieve a relaxed and casual look. The mix of texture and pattern is very important and we work with many textile designers to have specialness and exclusivity on fabrics. Unexpected fabrics are often used in simple, classic shapes.

—Betty Jackson

* * *

"What makes you most depressed?" Betty Jackson was once asked by a fashion editor. Her reply was that it was only when work was going badly, and that in such situations, strength of character and conviction became important assets. It comes as no surprise, therefore, to find that she admires strong women, "bold and casual like Lauren Bacall." A stoic, no-nonsense fashion approach underpins a business that Jackson declares began in a recession, only to find itself in another one when the company celebrated its 10th anniversary in 1991. As she celebrates her 20th anniversary, Jackson has diversified into home furnishings, accessories, and knits. She continues to be an important name in the international fashion industry.

Jackson began her career at Birmingham College of Art in 1968, working in London as a freelance fashion illustrator until 1973, when she joined Wendy Dagworthy as her design assistant. She moved to further positions at Quorum, then Coopers, before setting up her own design company with husband David Cohen in 1981. Success was quick to come, culminating in several awards, including the Cotton Institute Designer of the Year in 1983 and the Fil d'or award from the International Linen Council in 1985, the year she was also named British Designer of the Year; two years later she was awarded the MBE in the Queen's Birthday Honours list for services to British industry and export as well as becoming an elected member of the British Fashion Council.

Betty Jackson has gained an international reputation as a designer of young, up-to-the-minute clothes. "I've never liked prettiness much," she has said, and this is reflected in her designs. She rescales separates into larger, unstructured proportions; loose, uncomplicated shapes with no awkward cuts are often made up in boldly colored and patterned fabrics. Jackson loves bright prints and knits, often working in conjunction with the textile designers Timney Fowler in colors complementing the warm, smoky, and earthy base colors of the collections. The oversized printed shirts and hand-knit sweaters are always popular and usually the first garments to sell out. Her previous print and knit themes were inspired by Sonia Delauney, oversized paisleys or abstract painterly shapes and textures reminiscent of Matisse or Braque.

The rescaled sporty shapes give the clothes an androgynous feeling reflected when the menswear collection was launched in 1986. However, Jackson never uses androgyny to shock or alienate her established customer or to make a fashion statement. Instead, her themes evolve each season, incorporating the newest shapes, lengths, and fabrics. She tends to favor expensive, supple fabrics like linen, suede, or viscose mixes, crêpes, chenilles, and soft jerseys.

Jackson has said she prefers not to follow trends set by other designers or predictions from fashion forecasters. She prefers to source her own ideas for inspiration, ideas that are relevant to her and her own design philosophies. "There's nothing like taking a color you love, making something wonderful, and seeing a beautiful girl wearing it. I think if you ever tire of that feeling, then it's time to think again," she says.

An important development at Betty Jackson Ltd. was the opening of a shop that she describes as her greatest extravagance. She was quick, however, to deny this extravagance implied recklessness, "and it's certainly not reckless as it is part of a well laid plan." She has also turned her talents to accessories: chunky jewelry in bright colors encased in bronze and silver, soft suede gloves, belts, bags, and printed scarves.

Elsa Klensch on CNN in 1997 said that Jackson's spring-summer collection was "streamlined" and reminiscent of the 1940s' Bloomsbury period, with a mixture of fabrics, such as sheer with opaque or shiny with matte. "It's streamlined, I think, rather than tailored," Jackson told Klensch. "My collection has nothing to do with revisiting the

1980s or anything like that. I really think modern women want that choice of softness or fluidity or versatility in clothes, and it has to do with how you put different fabrics together, and is much more simple, I think, than before." Klensch noted that Jackson's color palette included suggestions of herbs such as rosemary, coriander, and sage.

The British Fashion Council has called Jackson a "directional classicist." Her designs are not "tailored" but are easygoing, with great fluidity. Her spring and fall collections in 2001 were noteworthy for their emphasis on freedom of body movement. According to Boyd Davis, online editor for the Fashion Windows website, Jackson's fall show "presented a contemporary romantic show straight from Mills & Boon and Barbara Cartland." She emphasized soft colors of beige and green, with brighter colors as highlights. The fluidity of the garments was complemented by harder leather accessories. Outerwear included fur coats and stoles and Pashmina, and skirt lengths varied from just above the knee to below the knee.

Jackson declares the single thing that would most improve the quality of her life would be more time. "I organize myself badly and never have enough time to do anything." It is the dilemma of many creative people, forced to sacrifice precious creative time to the day-to-day practicalities of running a business. Lack of time, however, has not halted Jackson's achievements. Her business is thriving and she was made honorary fellow of both the Royal College of Art, London, and the University of Central Lancashire.

—Kevin Almond; updated by Sally A. Myers

JACOBS, Marc

American designer

Born: New York City, New York, 1964. **Education:** Graduated from Parsons School of Design, New York, 1984. **Career:** Designer, Sketchbook label, for Ruben Thomas Inc., New York, 1984–85; managed own firm, 1986–88; named vice president for womenswear, Perry Ellis, 1988; head designer, Perry Ellis, New York, 1989–93, Marc Jacobs, from 1994; Marc Jacobs Look, distributed by Mitsubishi and Renown Look, 1996; opened Marc Jacobs Boutique in SoHo, New York, 1997; artistic director, Louis Vuitton, from 1997; designed Stain Boy t-shirt to benefit Elizabeth Glaser Pediatric AIDS Foundation, 2000; introduced Marc, line of mid-priced sportswear, 2001. **Awards:** Parsons School of Design Perry Ellis Golden Thimble award, 1984; Council of Fashion Designers of America Perry Ellis award, 1988; Womenswear Designer of the Year award, 1992, 1998. **Address:** 163 Mercer Street, New York, NY 10012, USA. **Website:** www.marcjacobs.com.

Publications

On JACOBS:

Books

Stegemeyer, Anne, *Who's Who in Fashion, Third Edition,* New York, 1996.

"Marc Jacobs," in *Current Biography Yearbook,* New York, 1998.

Marc Jacobs, fall 2001 collection. © AP/Wide World Photos.

Articles

Badum, John, and Kurt Kilgus, "So Good They Named It Twice: A Second Bite at the Big Apple," in *Fashion '86* (London), 1985.

Boyes, Kathleen, "Marc Jacobs: Getting Focused, Staying Passionate," in *WWD,* 4 April 1988.

Allis, Tim, "At 25, Whimsy-Loving Designer Marc Jacobs Has Been Up, Down, and Everywhere in Between," in *People* 2 May 1988.

Young, Lucie, "Corporate Greed: A Fashionable Vice," in *Design* (London), August 1988.

Lockwood, Lisa, "Jacobs is In, Pastor is Out at Perry Ellis," in *WWD,* 23 November 1988.

DeCaro, Frank, "A Very-Perry New Boss," in *Newsday,* 6 December 1988.

Edersheim, Peggy, "The Comeback Kid," in *Manhattan, Inc.,* February 1989.

Gooch, Brad, "Jacobs Makes His Mark," in *Vanity Fair,* April 1989.

Wayne, George, "Verry Jacobs," in *Paper,* May 1989.

Worthington, Christa, "The Three Choicest Dudes in the USA," in the *Sunday Times Magazine* (London), 26 August 1990.

Martin, Richard, "Double Entendres: Art, Decorative Arts, and Fashion Discourse in Marc Jacobs for Perry Ellis, 1991," in *Textile & Text* (New York), 13/4, 1991.

Marc Jacobs, fall 2001 collection: peplum dress. © AP/Wide World Photos.

Postner, Caryl, "Jacobs Ladder: Climbing to the Top," in *Footwear News* (New York), 3 June 1991.
Orlean, Susan, "Breaking Away," in *Vogue,* September 1992.
Boehlert, Bart, "Twelve Minutes: Marc Jacobs," in *QW* (New York), 8 November 1992.
James, Laurie, "On the Marc," in *Harper's Bazaar* January 1993.
"Designer Dish," in *WWD,* 29 March 1993.
Norwich, William, "As Retail Shrinks, Jacobs Thinks," in the *New York Observer,* 24 January 1994.
Berman, Phyllis, "Grunge is Out, Licensing is In," in *Forbes,* 23 May 1994.
Foley, Bridget, "Hard Acts to Follow: Marc Jacobs," in *WWD,* 24 October 1994.
Spindler, Amy M., "Lots of Sugar, With Some Pinches of Spice," in the *New York Times,* 31 October 1994.
"New York: Marc Jacobs," in *WWD,* 31 October 1994.
Menkes, Suzy, "Amid the Trashy Glamour, the Ladies Have Their Day," in the *International Herald Tribune,* 1 November 1994.
Davis, Peter, "Men à la Mode," in *Genre* (Hollywood), March 1995.
Spindler, Amy M., "Mod Look Returns, à la Jacobs," in the *New York Times,* 5 April 1995.
"New York: Marc Jacobs," in *WWD,* 5 April 1995.
Spindler, Amy, "Jacobs and Tyler Seize the Moment," in the *New York Times,* 1 November 1995.
White, Constance C.R., "New Designers Bestow a Fresh Elegance on Fur," in the *New York Times,* 28 May 1996.
———, "Young American Designers Make Inroads in Japan," in the *New York Times,* 31 December 1996.
Spindler, Amy, "Vuitton and Jacobs Seen in Ready-to-Wear Deal," in the *New York Times,* 7 January 1997.
Wayne, George, "Marc Jacobs," in *Vogue,* February 1997.
Spindler, Amy, "Two Take the Money and Produce," in the *New York Times,* 9 April 1997.
White, Constance C.R., "A Delicate Partnership," in the *New York Times,* 8 July 1997.
Klensch, Elsa, "Jacobs Collection: Urban, Unpretentious," available online at CNN.com, 25 August 1997.
White, Constance C.R., "New Wave of Designers Opening Stores in SoHo," in the *New York Times,* 2 September 1997.
Heller, Zoe, "Jacobs' Ladder," in the *New Yorker,* 22 September 1997.
White, Constance C.R., "Why Coy Can Sizzle Hotter than Brazen," in the *New York Times,* 5 November 1997.
"Marc Jacobs," in *Current Biography,* February 1998.
Barrett, Amy, "House of New Style," in the *Wall Street Journal,* 10 March 1998.
White, Constance C.R., "Taking the Fad out of Fashion," in the *New York Times,* 4 November 1998.
Luscombe, Belinda, "Spring/Summer Ready-to-Wear Marc Jacobs," in *Time,* 16 November 1998.
Schiro, Anne-Marie, "Warmth and Wearability, but Where's the Surprise?" in the *New York Times,* 17 February 1999.
Singer, Sally, "Paris Match," in *Vogue,* February 2000.
Foxman, Ariel, "It's a Bird, It's a Stain," in *In Style,* 1 February 2000.
Parr, Karen, "On the Marc: Fall Fashion Week's Peak," in *In Style,* 1 April 2000.
"A New Look for Louis Vuitton," in *Esquire,* September 2000.
Kirschbaum, Susan, "San Francisco Treat: Designer Jacobs Leaves His Mark on the City by the Bay," in *In Style,* 1 October 2000.
Bellafante, Gina, "Repressed Anguish as a Virtue," in the *New York Times,* 13 October 2000.
Deeny, Godfrey, "Louis Vuitton: Marc Jacobs Dresses the Neo-Romantic Gentleman," in Fashion Wire Daily, available online at fashionwindows.com, 26 January 2001.
Limnander, Armand, "Marc Jacobs," available online at style.com, 12 February 2001.
Deeny, Godfrey, "Marc Jacobs Fall 2001," in Fashion Wire Daily, online at fashionwindows.com, 13 February 2001.
Mui, Nelson, "Marc's Modern-Rock Schoolgirls," in Fashion Wire Daily, at fashionwindows.com, 13 February 2001.
Bellafante, Gina, "At Marc Jacobs, Dressing for Life as a Perpetual Child," in the *New York Times,* 14 February 2001.
Thomas, Dana, "Louis Vuitton's Return to Camelot," in Fashion Wire Daily, at fashionwindows.com, 12 March 2001.
Robinovitz, Karen, "When 200 Women Are Happily Crammed into a Boutique," in the *New York Times,* 15 April 2001.
Deeny, Godfrey, "Louis Vuitton Menswear by Marc Jacobs," in Fashion Wire Daily, at fashionwindows.com, 2 July 2001.

Lenander, Johanna, "Marc Jacobs," available online at fashionlive.com, 24 July 2001.

* * *

Marc Jacobs was from the start a fashion legend, a prodigy of mythical talent, tribulation, and triumph who attained unequivocal success and authority. The legend is indisputably true, but the clothing tells a similar and instructive story in which a special genius is realized—encyclopedic in its sources, poignantly romantic, remarkably sophisticated, and yet impudent and joyous. Through a succession of labels and collections, Jacobs has consistently demonstrated a strong personal sensibility and has altered the history of clothing forever.

Jacobs' first collection was hand-knit sweaters produced by Charivari, the New York clothing store where he worked as stock boy. Fatefully, those sweaters earned him the Perry Ellis Golden Thimble award at Parsons. Upon graduation in 1984, he designed Sketchbook for Ruben Thomas through the fall of 1985. There he created a memorable collection based on the film *Amadeus.* In 1986 he began designing his own label, first with backing from Jack Atkins and later from Onward Kashiyama.

In late 1988, Jacobs was named vice president for womenswear at Perry Ellis, succeeding Patricia Pastor, who had worked with and succeeded Ellis. Along the way, there were Homeric afflictions and distress, ranging from a major theft at the Ruben Thomas showroom to a fire that gutted his Kashiyama studio and destroyed his fall 1988 collection and fabrics two months before showings. The appointment at Perry Ellis was, of course, only another trial for the 25-year-old designer. As Peggy Edersheim wrote in *Manhattan, Inc.,* "Instead of staying one step ahead of the bill collector, he now has to worry about keeping up with Calvin Klein," a prodigious challenge in leadership for one of the principal sportswear houses in America. Jacobs, however, made a great critical success of Perry Ellis, reinstilling the firm with the bountiful energy and excitement of its founder.

Significantly, Jacobs' works reflected the design skills of Ellis before him. Jacobs did not perpetuate Ellis, but expanded on fundamental traits. For example, Ellis' imaginative palette was hauntingly revived in Jacobs' work, including extraordinary colors of fall in ocher, pumpkin, plum, camel, and rust, renewing the vitality of the Ellis spectrum. In fall 1991, Jacobs showed a grape princess coat over a brown cardigan, and a tangerine car coat with a butterscotch sweater and trousers with complete coloristic self-confidence. Ellis' sensuous fabrics were transmuted into Jacobs' hallmark sophistication: cashmere, camel, wool and angora, and mohair were soft, sumptuous materials.

Jacobs returns again and again to a basic vocabulary of design, treating each new interpretation of stripes, American flag, tartan, or gingham with a renewing luxury. His tailoring is also refined, returning to such classics as a Norfolk jacket or the eight-button double-breasted camel wool flannel suit for fall 1990 that appeared on the front page of *Women's Wear Daily.*

Jacobs' special interests include homages to other designers he admires in addition to Ellis. His "hugs" sequined dress of 1985 remembered Schiaparelli, and his spring 1990 English sycamore sequined short sheath "for Perry Ellis" was a touching tribute of the workroom and showroom environment of Perry Ellis, with its silver accents on blond sycamore. Jacobs has long loved the 1960s and returned not only in the early sweaters with happy faces but also in his voluminous mohair balloon sweaters for fall 1989. Suzy Menkes, reviewing his first collection at Perry Ellis, noted, "Jacobs' own-label collections have also been all-American, but much less innocent—celebrations of Miami Beach kitsch, sendups of the 1960s hippies and wacky versions of patchwork and down-home gingham."

New York-bred and street-smart, Jacobs is nimbly, naturally witty with a sliver of cynicism blended into his clothing. A spring 1990 red-and-white tablecloth cotton shirt and jacket was accompanied by embroidered and beaded black ants; his early "Freudian slip" was a simple dress imprinted with the face of the Viennese master; fall 1991 showed sweaters with aphorisms borrowed from the tart embroideries of Elsie de Wolfe. Language, too, cropped up even in Jacobs' fall 1990 "fresh berries and cream" collection that included blueberry herringbone patterns on a cream field in wool jackets and the same design in short chiffon flirt skirts. His spring 1992 collection, focused on the Wild West and Southern California, was a smart synthesis of Hollywood glamor (including an Oscar® dress with the Academy Award® statue) and boot-stomping country-and-western cowgirls, a perfect combination of rodeo and Rodeo Drive.

For spring 1993 Jacobs introduced his now legendary "grunge" collection with flowered silk little-girl dresses paired with combat boots and $300 silk shirts printed to look like flannel. Though the sensational collection never made it into retail stores, it was highly regarded for its trendsetting individualism by the fashion press. But Perry Ellis executives discontinued their designer clothing lines shortly thereafter, trying to maintain their more tailored reputation rather than embracing Jacobs' more unconventional designs. This transition helped launch Marc Jacobs International, guided by long-time business partner Robert Duffy, and ultimately paved the way for Jacobs to take a position as artistic director for Louis Vuitton.

Prior to taking the prestigious post, however, Jacobs' designs gradually progressed from unconventional cool to urban couture. "His early work was characterized by a certain amount of high-concept whimsy but his designs in recent years have grown sleeker and subtler," wrote Zoe Heller of the *New Yorker* in 1997. Well-tailored striped pantsuits, knee-length skirts, and calf-length double-breasted satin coats were featured in his 1970s-inspired spring 1994 collection. A fitted wool jacket topped a silk floral dress, and jeweled cashmere cardigans framed taffeta slip dresses in his successful spring 1996 collection. Then in 1997, when 146-year-old luggage and handbag company Louis Vuitton decided to expand, luxury-goods conglomerate LVMH (which includes Christian Dior, Givenchy, Kenzo, Christian Lacroix, and Louis Vuitton) chose Jacobs as its artistic director. His mission was to design a full line of ready-to-wear fashions for the first time.

Jacobs' designs for Louis Vuitton began with secret LV logos hidden beneath buttons, hems, and soles of shoes. Then came Damier-print pony-skin slingbacks, patent leather-embossed Bernis bags in Crayola hues, and stiff raincoats and trenches splattered with tiny LVs. "Jacobs has taken the house's signature and gone native," wrote Sally Singer in *Vogue* (February 2000). For spring 2000, Jacobs offered simple pleated trousers in lightweight wool adorned with bead-lined pockets and "fabulous swirly prints in 1960s colors that transform a low-key office dress into a sexy diva frock," according to Singer.

His fall 2001 menswear collection for Louis Vuitton broke through trends once again when Jacobs snubbed the widespread military theme. Instead he dressed the "neo-romantic gentleman" in black leather pea coats with red trimmed buttonholes and bold stripy shirts worn under high-necked sweatshirts. His fall/winter 2001–2002 womenswear collection was "sheer perfection," according to Dana Thomas of the Fashion Windows website, writing in August 2001. Reminiscent of Jacqueline Kennedy during her White House years, small fitted jackets had cropped sleeves and there were bell skirts, princess coats, and soft empire-waist dresses. Fabrics included cotton flannel, silk twill, denim, jersey, and sealskin. Striking details like mink-covered buttons and sexy leather lace-up boots finished off the collection.

For Jacobs' own line, the fall 2001 season portrayed girlish innocence dressed in elegance and sophistication. The crowdpleasers were cashmere coats using oversized, childlike buttons, colorful trompe l'oeil lapels, yellow mohair and sequin coats, and edgy jersey dresses. And as if four lines of clothing weren't enough, Jacobs debuted his Marc collection in 2001, creating a lineup for his creased front, hip-hugging jeans. For fall, the Marc line included heavily-buttoned military coats mixed with multiple tiered skirts, pink and yellow striped jeans, and graffiti sweatshirts.

"Talents like Mr. Jacobs have become exceptional," wrote Amy Spindler of the *New York Times.* "He has become the most consistently strong, individualistic, real, live, kicking designer in New York." The legend of fashion prodigy is probably inseparably attached to Jacobs; that he has performed prodigiously as a leading master of American style in an immediate and seamless transition is indeed a marvel.

—Richard Martin; updated by Jodi Essey-Stapleton

JACOBSON, Jacqueline and Elie

See DOROTHÉE BIS

JAEGER

British fashion house

Founded: in London in 1884 by Lewis Tomalin, based on the principles of Dr. Gustav Jaeger. **Company History:** Lewis Tomalin was the sole purveyor of Dr. Jaeger's Sanitary Woollens, to the 1920s. Tomalin obtained the rights, patents, and Jaeger name; began manufacturing undergarments, 1884; added cardigans, dressing gowns, jumpers, shawls, and, by the early 1900s, coats, skirts, suits, etc. Jaeger London launched, 1993; began renovating New York flagship store, 1994–95; hired designer Jeanette Todd and introduced Sport line, 1996; announced plans for new London store, 1997; hired Bella Freud, 2001; other designers associated with the firm have included Jean Muir, Sheridan Barnett, and Alistair Blair. **Company Address:** 57 Broadwick Street, London W1, England.

Publications

On JAEGER:

Books

Wilson, E., and L. Taylor, *Through the Looking Glass,* London, 1989.

Articles

"The Jaeger Story," in *American Fabrics & Fashion* (New York), No. 100, Spring 1974.
"Quiet, Classic Jaeger," in the *Sunday Times* (London), 25 May 1980.
Alexander, Hilary, "Mrs Roache (and Jaeger) Go to Court," in the *Daily Telegraph* (London), 2 November 1991.
"Suits Are Getting a Kinder Cut," in the *Eastern Daily Press* (Norwich, Norfolk), 22 April 1992.
"Jaeger Variation," in the *Watford Free Observer* (Watford, Hertfordshire), 28 May 1992.
Fallon, James, "Jaeger Rolls Out London, Drives for a Younger Crowd," in *WWD,* 29 September 1994.
Edelson, Sharon, "Jaeger Gives Contemporary Twist to Clothes, Madison Ave. Flagship," in *WWD,* 18 July 1996.
Manning, Clinton, "Top Fashion Chain Takes a Clobbering," in the *Mirror* (London), 12 September 1996.
Wheeler, Karen, "Jaeger's Collection Puts a Spring in Your Step," in the *Financial Times,* 8 February 1997.
Rice, Ann, "Ease Into Fashion Elegance," the *Birmingham Post* (England), 18 November 1998.
Clapp, Susannah, "Meet the New Jaeger Meister: Bella Freud," in the *Observer,* 30 July 2000.
Findlay, Jane, "Check Out Jaeger's Sexy Look," in the *Sunday Mail* (Glasgow, Scotland), 8 April 2001.
Watson, Linda, "Back to the Future," in the *Sunday Times,* 29 July 2001.
"Jaeger Tries to Throw Off Its Mrs. T Image," in *The Independent* (London), 10 August 2001.
Polan, Brenda, "How Jaeger Got Younger," in the *Daily Mail,* 16 August 2001.

* * *

Jaeger is a British retail fashion company producing distinctive clothes for both men and women. Its origins lie in Germany over a century ago—a period when theories of rational dress abounded throughout Europe and the United States. In 1880 Dr. Gustav Jaeger of Stuttgart, a zoologist and physiologist, expounded his belief that only clothes made of animal fibers (principally wool) were conducive to one's health.

Jaeger's theories were translated into English by Lewis Tomalin and taken up by the *Times,* which devoted a leading article to Dr. Jaeger's ideas on 4 October 1884, on the occasion of the London International Health Exhibition in South Kensington. Tomalin obtained Dr. Jaeger's permission to use his name and opened a shop to sell the "Sanitary Woollen System" of clothing on Fore Street, in London, where two of the earliest and most famous customers were Oscar Wilde and George Bernard Shaw. The latter heartily endorsed the product and wore Jaeger clothing for much of his long life.

Jaeger clothes were remarkable not only for their material—extraordinarily fine machine-knit wool jersey, cashmere, alpaca, and vicuna ("the woollen stuffs which are microscopically tested for adulteration with vegetable fibre can be supplied by the yard," ran an advertisement of 1884)—but also for their unrestrictive construction. This made both underwear and outerwear particularly suitable for traveling. "Day and night—prevents chill—a necessity to all who value health," claimed an 1898 advertisement for "lovely and luxurious dressing gowns."

Famous British expeditions were fitted out in Jaeger, from Scott and Shackleton in the Arctic to Stanley on his search for Dr. Livingstone in Africa and later. Before World War I, Jaeger's functional, mobile approach gave the firm much of its impetus in what was to prove a rapidly expanding market from its new purpose-built shops, such as those in Regent Street, London, and Edinburgh, and its wholesale company supplying agents as far afield as Shanghai. By the 1930s, however, Jaeger had greatly extended its range from the early emphasis on "sanitary wear" as exemplified in turn-of-the-century exhortations to "Wear wool to South Africa—khaki drill spells chill." Under the founder's son, H.F. Tomalin, the emphasis turned from functionalism to fashionability, all a woman (or man) needed for work and leisure, from country tweeds, twinsets, and stylish coats to swimsuits and slacks.

Jaeger exported its goods to such diverse locales as Beirut and Buenos Aires, upholding Tomalin's now-dated dictum, "Wherever you go among white people you will find that Jaeger is known." Jaeger's continuing attention to the actual fabric of their clothes gave them an honored place in the British postwar export market, but the emphasis on durability continues to the present. The original ethos of health clothing, however, has long been superseded by one of cool, timeless elegance, albeit still in fine materials—an image aided by the high caliber of Jaeger design.

After some difficult years during the 1990s when sales slumped, Jaeger began revamping its image and designs. The company successfully blended its traditional look with updated takes: tweeds were replaced with cashmere, suede, leather, and newer, high-performance fabrics. The firm's intention was to draw in younger buyers without alienating established clients. Shops emphasized service, and employees were specifically trained to assist customers in incorporating new pieces with items they already owned. In 2001 Jaeger hired well-known and highly respected designer Bella Freud to add some pizzazz to the mix. In addition to Jaeger's traditional lines, Freud brought in miniskirts, bomber jackets, a little black dress, and a "Juliette Greco resistance coat" inspired by Jaeger's 1930s and 1940s designs. Regardless of these design changes, the company remains committed to quality fabrics and tailoring at reasonable prices.

Jaeger is one of the few fashion companies able to produce a complete package, from sourcing exclusive fabrics and producing original designs through to manufacturing extensive ranges of tailoring and knitwear. These ranges are sold throughout the world, as exporting the Jaeger product has always been a prime part of the business. Jaeger Ladieswear and Jaeger Man are as distinctive as the firm's witty "straw" logo; Jaeger designs in the 21st century reach markets undreamed of by Dr. Jaeger and his English translator.

—Doreen Ehrlich; updated by Carrie Snyder

JAMES, Charles

American designer

Born: Camberley, England, of Anglo-American parentage, 18 July 1906. **Education:** Self-taught in design. **Family:** Married Nancy Lee Gregory in 1954 (separated, 1961); children: Charles, Louise. **Career:** Moved to U.S., established as Charles Boucheron, milliner, Chicago, 1924–28; milliner and custom dressmaker, New York, 1928–29; custom dressmaker, using the name E. Haweis James, London and Paris, 1929–circa 1939; also sold designs to wholesale manufacturers in New York, 1930s; relocated to New York, 1939; established as Charles James, Inc., primarily for custom designs, from 1940; became permanent resident of the United States, 1942; designer, couture collection, Elizabeth Arden salon, New York, 1943–45; worked as independent designer, 1945–78; Charles James Services, Inc., licensing company established, 1949; Charles James Associates, limited partnership for manufacture of custom clothes, established, 1954, then merged with Charles James Services; Charles James Manufacturers Company established, 1955. **Exhibitions:** *A Decade of Design,* Brooklyn Museum, 1948; *A Total Life Involvement* (retrospective), Everson Museum, Syracuse, New York, 1975; *The Genius of Charles James* (retrospective), Brooklyn Museum and Art Institute of Chicago, 1982–83; *Charles James, Architect of Fashion,* Fashion Institute of Technology, New York, 1993. **Awards:** Coty American Fashion Critics award, 1950, 1954; Neiman Marcus award, Dallas, 1953; Woolens and Worsteds of America Industry award, 1962; John Simon Guggenheim fellowship, 1975; inducted to Fashion Walk of Fame, Seventh Avenue, New York, 2001. **Died:** 23 September 1978, in New York.

Publications

By JAMES:

Articles

"Portrait of a Genius by a Genius," in *Nova* (London), July 1974.

On JAMES:

Books

Morris, Bernadine, and Barbara Walz, *The Fashion Makers,* New York, 1978.

Coleman, Elizabeth A., *The Genius of Charles James,* New York, 1982.

Milbank, Caroline Rennolds, *Couture: The Great Designers,* New York, 1985.

New York and Hollywood Fashion: Costume Designs from the Brooklyn Museum Collection, New York, 1986.

Stegemeyer, Anne, *Who's Who in Fashion, Third Edition,* New York, 1996.

Articles

Bosworth, Patricia, "Who Killed High Fashion?" in *Esquire* (New York), May 1973.

"Charles James, the Majority of One," in *American Fabrics and Fashions* (New York), No. 98, 1973.

Cunningham, Bill, "Is the New Subculture Getting You Down?" in the *New York Daily News,* 3 February 1975.

Barr, Jeffrey, "Charles James, Master of Couture," in *Fashion World Daily,* August 1978.

Duka, John, "Ghost of Seventh Avenue," in *New York,* 16 October 1978.

Bryant, Gay, "Charles James, 1906–1978," in *Harper's & Queen* (London), September 1979.

Taki, "Arbiter of Chic," in *Esquire* (New York), May 1981.

Coleman, Elizabeth A., "Abstracting the 'Abstract Gown'," in *Dress* (Earleville, Maryland), 1982.

Cocks, Jay, "Puttin' on the Ritz in Gotham (Metropolitan Museum of Art and the Brooklyn Museum, New York)," in *Time,* 10 January 1983.

Campbell, Lawrence, "Fashion Shapes by Charles James," in *Art in America* (New York), May 1983.
Turner, Florence, "Remembering Charles," in *Vogue* (London), May 1983.
Coleman, Elizabeth A., "Charles James at the Brooklyn Museum," in *American Fabrics and Fashions* (New York), No. 128, November 1983.
Lawford, Valentine, "Encounters with Chanel, Mainbocher, Schiaparelli, Valentina, and Charles James," in *Architectural Digest,* September 1988.
Tobias, Tobi, "A Man of the Cloth," in *Dance Ink* (New York), Winter 1994–95.
Als, Hilton, "The Insider's Outsider (The Life and Career of Fashion Designer Charles James)," in the *New Yorker,* 21 September 1998.

* * *

"Charles James is not only the greatest American couturier, but the world's best and only dressmaker who has raised it from an applied art form to a pure art form." From anyone other than their author, and James' closest professional equal, Cristobal Balenciaga, these words would seem potentially pretentious and inflated. Instead they constitute a balanced and deserved evaluation.

Charles Wilson Brega James was of Anglo-American parentage and possessed an incredibly sharp mind. He could have excelled in any number of fields but a foray into millinery in Chicago of the 1920s led to a career devising intellectually refined and devastatingly beautiful women's garments. James' lifetime career was devoted not to producing quantities of either designs or products but rather to refining and evolving concepts. His clientèle in Britain, France, and the U.S. was dedicated: they put up with his unpredictability and his inflated costs. When they ordered a garment there was no guarantee of its delivery or its permanence in their wardrobe as the designer would freely play roulette with his clients' clothes.

Why did clients remain loyal? Why is the word "genius" applied so frequently in describing James? Because James saw the female form as an armature on which to fashion sculpture, not just cover with clothes. He did not just sketch or drape a model. He approached the craft of dressmaking with the science of an engineer, often studying the weight distribution of a garment. Like an artist he analyzed the interacting elements of proportion, line, color, and texture. Construction details were not merely important, they were an obsession. He spent a vast sum on perfecting a sleeve. He turned a four-leaf clover hat into the hemline of a ballgown which he then built up into the garment he designated as his thesis in dressmaking.

A cruciform became a circular skirt; an evening dress (with matching cape of antique ribbons) which made its debut in 1937 was still offered 20 years later, the finesse of the ribbon replaced by other yardgoods of silk, but the detailing to infinity remaining. James was such a perfectionist that clients never banked on wearing either a new or old James to a function. Even his well-known quilted jacket designed in 1937, and now in the London's Victoria and Albert Museum, bears witness to his challenge to perfect. One can follow his tortured, ghost-like tracts of stitching and restitching.

As brilliant as his design sense was James' subtle sensibility of color. Open a coat or jacket of subdued hues and be confronted with a lining of an unexpected range. Follow his curvilinear pattern configurations and note that inset sleeves and darts are not part of either his design or construction vocabulary. His lines are seductive and intellectually intriguing. Rarely did he employ patterned materials, relying rather on the most revealing, unforgiving plain goods. While he is perhaps best remembered for his spectacular eveningwear, his tailored daywear was equally original. It was with his coats that he attempted to enter what he perceived to be the more lucrative ready-to-wear market. This, however, didn't suit his temperament or methods of working.

James dressed many of America's best-dressed women of the generation. They patronized the couture salons of Paris and could easily have been dressed abroad. Instead they had the courage and determination to support a unique creator of fashion: Charles James.

—Elizabeth A. Coleman

JANSEN, Jan

Dutch footwear designer

Born: circa 1945. **Family:** Married to Tonny Jansen. **Career:** Worked originally under the Jeannot label; became known for his original and often extreme footwear designs, 1960s; eventually designed under his own label; opened first shop in Amsterdam, 1968; subsequent boutiques opened in Heusden and Antwerpt; sold North American licensing for footwear to Meno Vos and Thoan Kho; opened first U.S. store near San Francisco, 2000.

Publications

On JANSEN:

Books

De Schoenen van Jan Jansen 1964–1974, [exhibition catalogue], Stedelijk Museum, Amsterdam, 1974.
McDowell, Colin, *Shoes, Fashion and Fantasy,* London, 1989.

Articles

Anniss, Elisa, "Going Dutch: Avant-Garde Footwear Artistry Blooms in the Netherlands, in *Footwear News,* 7 August 1995.
"Hide & Seek," in *Footwear News,* 10 May 1999.
Saeks, Diane Dorrans, "Go Dutch: The Netherlands Meets Northern California with Jan Jansen's First U.S. Footwear Boutique," in *Footwear News,* 4 December 2000.

* * *

Little known to the public but highly regarded by fellow professionals, Jan Jansen, the Dutch shoe designer, is one of the most inventive and original translators in his chosen field. Unlike designers who produce cosmetic updates of existing styles, Jansen conceives the item in a truly unique and conceptual way. An original and gifted man, his work inspires great admiration from those who recognize his quite individual style. His footwear is different, often extreme, unexpected with verve and daring. It can visually arrest you in a way the work of few other shoe designers can—and seems to push the boundaries of one's expectations of what a shoe should be.

Jansen worked originally under the Jeannot label, pouring out thousands of highly successful designs. His ability to translate his prototypes into commercially acceptable shoes is legendary. He kept many footwear retailers and factories on their feet through very tough economic times, despite the fact that his designs were widely copied and infiltrated lesser stores. He soon began, anonymously, to design for well-known companies like Charles Jourdan. When he finally decided to dedicate himself to his own line, his took his original wares to European trade fairs. When his footwear was eagerly anticipated by a growing number of devotees, the designer opened a tiny shop in Amsterdam in 1968. Two subsequent shops, in Heusden and Antwerpt, followed.

Liberated in his thinking, and a true entertainer, Jansen's ideas are visually stunning at times, and quite beautiful. His great affection for suede, whether of the finest quality or rougher and more casual, and his dramatic use of color have ensured that brilliant red, peacock blue, saffron yellow, or even black would be an integral part of each season's handwriting. No matter how extreme, the shoes are always wearable, but only by a courageous client. Jansen's creations are seldom understated in shape, and he has used unusual textures and modern materials (plexiglass, bamboo, cork, etc.) to augment his designs. His skills cover a wide range of disciplines; he still handcrafts his lasts and is able to translate his many inventive styles for quantity production to satisfy the mass market. Jansen easily stands alongside the familiar and respected names in the trade.

By the 1990s the Dutch had moved into the realm of fashion influence with a number of fashion forward designers. Jansen, Dries van Noten, and the design team of Viktor & Rolf brought mounting recognition to the Netherlands for their original fashion interpretations. As Elisa Anniss, writing for *Footwear News* (7 August 1995) explained, "In-the-know buyers were discovering that Holland offered some interesting looks, such as the sculptural designs by eclectic Dutch designer Jan Jansen, and an abundance of shoes that manage to fuse comfort features and athletic details with an edgy fashion sensibility."

In the 21st century, Jansen brought his one-of-kind creations to America, opening his fourth boutique (and first in the U.S.) in Mill Valley, California. Near San Francisco, the eponymously named store was made possible by a Dutch couple, Meno Vos and Thoan Kho, who also acquired the licensing rights to manufacture and distribute Jansen's footwear in North America. Vos is a longtime Jansen fan, having fell in love with the designer's shoes back in the early 1980s. The new Mill Valley store was a dream come true for Jansen, as well as Vos and Kho.

"Jan Jansen is a rare person in the shoe business," Vos told *Footwear News* (4 December 2000), "He works like an artist, designs every piece in his line, and doesn't follow fashions or care what other shoe design companies are producing. His shoe collections have a sense of humor and a carefree sense of style. And Jansen is one of the few true designers with enough diversity and creativity to fill a whole shop." For his part, Jansen simply says, "I want to make feet feel at home," something he has been doing with fantastically original style for well over three decades.

—Angela Pattison and Owen James

JANTZEN, INC.

American knitwear company

Founded: in Portland, Oregon, as the Portland Knitting Company by John A. Zentbauer, C. Ray Zentbauer, and Carl C. Jantzen, 1910; renamed Jantzen Knitting Mills, 1916, and Jantzen, Inc., beginning in 1949. **Company History:** Introduced first rib stitch swimsuit, 1913; North American sales extended to Mexico and Canada, beginning 1920; company went public, 1921; introduced diving girl logo, 1923; added knitwear and foundation lines, 1938; established separate men's and women's divisions, mid-1960s; company became a wholly owned subsidiary of Blue Bell, Inc., Greensboro, N.C., 1979–86, then a division of VF Corporation, 1986; opened first retail store, Portland, 1992; began designing and manufacturing Nike brand swimwear, 1995; added SwimFit Website to assist women in finding desired swimsuit styles, 1997; discontinued sportswear collection, 1999. **Awards:** Six Woolknit awards for men's sweater design, 1965–80. **Company Address:** P.O. Box 3001, Portland, OR 97208–3001. **Company Website:** www.jantzen.com.

Publications

On JANTZEN:

Books

Wallace, Don, *Shaping America's Products,* New York, 1956.
Wallis, Dorothy, *The Jantzen Story,* New York, 1959.
Cleary, David P., *Great American Brands,* New York, 1981.
Morgan, Hal, *Symbols of America,* New York, 1986.
Lencek, Lena, and Gideon Bosker, *Making Waves: Swimsuits and the Undressing of America,* San Francisco, 1989.
Martin, Richard, and Harold Koda, *Splash! A History of Swimwear,* New York, 1990.
Jantzen: A Brief History, Portland, Oregon, 1992.

Articles

Magiera, Marcy, "Swimwear Makers Aim for 'Older' Women," in *Advertising Age,* 21 April 1986.
Bloomfield, Judy, "Jantzen Turning the Tide," in *WWD,* 19 September 1990.
Smith, Matthew, "Jantzen Slimming Down to Fit Into New Corporate Suit," in *Business Journal,* 23 September 1991.
Parola, Robert, "Keep the Environment in Fashion," in *DNR,* 20 April 1992.
Van Dang, Kim, "Vintage Power," in *WWD,* 10 February 1992.
Hartlein, Robert, "On the Comeback Trail," in *WWD* (swimwear supplement), July 1992.
Walsh, Peter, "Jantzen Aims for Bigger Chunk of Sweater Biz," in *DNR,* 16 March 1993.
Halvorsen, Donna, "Jantzen Puts Swimsuit Fittings on the Internet," in the *Star Tribune* (Minneapolis, Minnesota), 12 March 1997.
"Seattle Gear and Jantzen Announce Cuts in Work Force," in the *Seattle Post-Intelligencer,* 18 February 1998.
Manning, Jeff, "Portland, Oregon-Based Sportswear-Maker Jantzen to Cut 140 jobs," in *Knight-Ridder/Tribune Business News,* 13 June 1999.

* * *

Eight decades ago, the struggling Portland Knitting Company developed "the suit that changed bathing to swimming." Due to a burgeoning fitness craze, their new knit swimwear found a ready audience. The renamed Jantzen Company quickly became an international name and gained a commanding position in the leisurewear industry by expanding its markets and manufacturing sites overseas.

Jantzen's success story and long-term fashion influence spring from its innovative merchandising and promotional programs as well as its appealing apparel. The firm led the way in creative, comprehensive marketing campaigns aimed at the mainstream market. The initial springboard product was a one-piece wool bathing suit in an elasticized rib stitch, made on knitting equipment used to make sweater cuffs. Like the improvised suit Australian swimming celebrity Annette Kellerman wore in 1907, the Jantzen suit eliminated the encumbering yardage of the standard bathing costume of the late Edwardian era. Men and women who wanted to swim, not just dunk and splash, embraced it.

Jantzen's subsequent designs combined fashion and function; new cutting and patented assembly methods achieved a better fit for ease of swimming movement and figure enhancement. The basic style—the so-called California style—of long shorts attached to a sleeveless clinging skirted top came in vibrant colors with accent stripes for all members of the family. Jantzen soon offered new styles, colors, and novelty knits. The company fostered swimming (and swimsuit sales) with its "Learn to Swim" campaigns.

Jantzen's clinging and increasingly abbreviated swimwear at first outraged local moral authorities and helped crumble recreational dress restrictions. This coincided with the evolving corsetless streetwear of the 1920s. Jantzen's swimwear lines tended toward the sporty, athletic look while adapting to technological and sociological changes. An advertising campaign with catchy phrases heralded each new style.

The eight-ounce "Molded-Fit" swimming suits knitted from "Miracle Yarn" elastic were akin to "nude bathing." Famed illustrator George Petty's 1940 "Pretty Girl" suit was made in "new superb-fitting Sea-Ripple with live all-way elasticity." Lastex fabric of rubber-cored thread made possible suits "with the figure control qualities of a foundation garment." French designer Fernald Lafitte designed textured knits "with a Paris flavor."

In the annals of fashion, Jantzen's Red Diving Girl symbol is notable as one of America's first pin-up girls and first memorable apparel logo. She leapt from the cover of a 1920 catalogue to make a sensational splash on groundbreaking billboard advertisements and as a sometimes-banned decal on millions of car windshields. Jantzen hired artists like Alberto Varga to update her figure periodically. The Red Diving Girl graced all advertising and countless advertising giveaways and gadgets. She was embroidered or sewn on Jantzen swimsuits for over 60 years.

Like the other major West Coast sportswear companies, Catalina and Cole of California, Jantzen created advertising featuring Hollywood celebrities. Collaborative promotions with First National and Warner Brothers included Loretta Young as Miss Jantzen in 1931. In 1947 independent campaigns used a teenage "Mr. Jantzen," actor James Garner, to model swim trunks, and a young Marilyn Monroe modeled the "Double-Dare" two-piece suit with peek-a-boo cutouts on the hips.

Jantzen often emphasized color coordination in their ads and in-store merchandising. For a smart fashion-conscious beach look, in 1928 customers turned to authority Hazel Adler's "Jantzen Color Harmony Guide." In the 1950s, Jantzen went in with Revlon for a "Love that Red" campaign and based a swimwear collection on a bright red line of lipstick and nail polish. Jantzen expanded its lines to include bras and foundation garments as well as a wide range of men's and women's leisurewear in interchangeable parts of coordinating and contrasting colors and fabrics. The "Darlings from Jantzen," traveling fashion consultants, prepared personalized color charts to encourage customers to buy flattering color-coded Jantzen wardrobes.

At times, Jantzen provided suits and sponsorship of both the Miss America and Miss Universe beauty pageants. Two modified suits gained mystique as lucky "supersuits," because whoever wore them won the swimsuit competition and often the Miss America crown or runner-up status. Jantzen's pioneering merchandising programs as well as fashion innovations put it into the forefront of influential American apparel manufacturers. Through its overseas operations it exported American West Coast- and Hollywood-inspired fashions to a worldwide audience. The Red Diving Girl logo, involvement in major beauty pageants, and Learn to Swim and recent Clean Water Campaign programs significantly contributed to American recreational and popular culture. The company was also quick to harness the power of the Internet—by the spring of 1997, it had created the SwimFit Website to allow women to experiment with swimwear styles before ever setting foot in a store to reduce frustration when purchasing a suit.

Today, Jantzen is the leading brand of swimwear in over 100 countries, although a tough business climate forced the company to lay off workers, move some production operations to Latin America and the Caribbean, and discontinue its sportswear lines. In the 21st century Jantzen focused on expanding its swimwear business, in part by designing and manufacturing swimsuits for major fashion labels like Nike.

—Debra Regan Cleveland; updated by Carrie Snyder

JAVITS, Eric

American milliner

Born: New York, 24 May 1956. **Education:** Choate School, 1970–74; graduated from Rhode Island School of Design, 1978. **Career:** Cofounder, Whittall and Javits, Inc., 1978, creating women's hats and later separates and t-shirts; sold out to partner, 1985; founded Eric Javits, Inc., specializing in women's hats and occasionally hair accessories, 1985; licenses included Maximilian Furs, 1991–93, and Kato International, Japan; also designed hats for films, including *Bonfire of the Vanities,* for television shows, including *Dynasty* and *Dallas,* for many advertising campaigns, and runway collections of other designers, including Carolina Herrera, Caroline Roehm, Mary McFadden, Pauline Trigère, Adolfo, Louis Féraud, and Donna Karan. **Exhibitions:** *Mad Hatters,* Women's Guild of the New Orleans Opera Association, 1989; *Current Trends in Millinery,* Fashion Institute of Technology, New York, 1990; *The Art of Millinery—20th Century Hat Design,* Philadelphia Museum of Art, 1993. **Collections:** Metropolitan Museum of Art Costume Institute, Fashion Institute of Technology, New York. **Awards:** "Millie" award, Hat Designer of the Year, 1991, 1992; Martin Birnbaum award for Excellence in Drawing and Painting; National Spanish Examination award, three years in a row at Choate. **Member:** Millinery Institute of America and Council of Fashion Designers of America. **Address:** 433 Fifth Avenue, Suite 200, New York, NY 10016, USA. **Email:** ejavitsinc@aol.com.

Design by Eric Javits. © Haig/Artlightning Productions NYC.

PUBLICATIONS

On JAVITS:

Articles

Berman, Phyllis, "Wearable Art," in *Forbes,* 19 October 1987.
Howard, Tammi, "Eric Javits: Changing the Shape of Millinery," in *WWD,* 18 March 1988.
Hochswender, Woody, "Designers Find Fashionable Ways of Talking through Their Hats," in the *New York Times,* 14 June 1988.
Stevenson, Peter M., "Crown Prince," in *Manhattan, Inc.* (New York), August 1989.
Newman, Jill, "The Many Hats of Eric Javits," *WWD,* 2 March 1990.
Sherman, Jean, "Top Hatter," *New York Magazine,* 16 September 1991.
"Hats are Back," in the *Kansas City Star,* 4 April 1993.
Kramer, Carol, "The Drape of the Locks," in the *New York Times,* 4 July 1993.
Carter, Reon, "The Proper Topper," in the *Cincinnati Enquirer,* 10 March 1997.
Barrett, Janet, "Eric Javits ('74) Designing Hats That Women Love," in *Choate Rosemary Hall Bulletin,* Winter/Spring 1999.
Wright, Jason Ashley, "Hat Designer Eric Javits to Visit Friday," in *Tulsa World,* 15 April 1999.
Homan, Becky, "Style with Squish: Eric Javits Makes Hats to Flatter and to Fold," in the *St. Louis Post-Dispatch,* 16 October 1999.
Robins, Cynthia, "Sun Screens," in the *San Francisco Chronicle,* 6 May 2001.
"Eric Javits, Inc.," available online at the Key West Madhatter, www.kw-madhatter.com, 9 June 2001.

*

My design work is only one aspect of involvement with owning my own hat company, and it remains the only part where I am not relying on the team's abilities but on my own.

Whenever an inspiration hits me, I make a note of the idea by sketching a small diagram. This provides a springboard from which many things can later develop. Using this method, I can have the concepts for an entire collection outlined within a few days. Sometime later in the process, when the designs are actually being fabricated, I will consider them from a production and marketing viewpoint. Those issues are quite complex given the varied needs of today's woman, and the ever-changing nature of the fashion business.

Many of my ideas are the result of an evolution, synthesizing and reworking bits and pieces of my most effective ideas and occasionally going off to test a completely new direction which, if successful, could eventually become part of the line's core. When a design arrives successfully, most of my developmental energy is not evident. What remains, seemingly, is an object which has its own logic and which appears to have been plucked effortlessly from our collective subconscious.

—Eric Javits

* * *

Style-consciousness began in Eric Javits' family in the 1920s, during which his grandmother, artist Lily Javits, made hats for the Shubert Organization and counted actress Mae West among her fans. Of his fascination with his grandmother's paintings, he commented, "I was the only grandchild who was permitted in her studio, because she knew I wouldn't touch anything. Then she saw how interested I was and bought me my own paints. That was when I was about five years old."A versatile, involved student, he directed the literary magazine, managed the campus radio station, sang with the chorus, and played soccer, squash, and tennis.

By September 1991, the skill of Eric Javits was touted in *New York Magazine*, as "quite simply, tops." In an era in which the hat is a style anachronism and a definite statement of individuality, if not idiosyncrasy and exhibitionism, Javits has created hats of distinct and discreet identity, both the designer's and that of the potential wearer.

Upon graduation as a painter and sculptor from the Rhode Island School of Design in 1978, Javits began his millinery career as a sculptural improvisation. Javits has created a wide range of hats: United Airlines flight attendant caps, private-label millinery for many American department stores and specialty chains, Louis Féraud hats, his own label, and its diffusion line, Lily J., named for his grandmother. But even though he is dubbed "crown prince" by Peter Stevenson in *Manhattan, Inc.* in August 1989, Javits is not making hats for grandmothers. He is almost Spartan in millinery adornment

Design by Eric Javits. © Haig/Artlightning Productions NYC.

and has concentrated on hats that are not agglomerations and concoctions, but are modest one-statement sculptures for the head. Javits' restraint is his focus on one important statement in each hat, seldom adding secondary elements.

Often the interest is, in fact, in the shape and he has searched the past for a wondrous array of traditional shapes to frame the face. Yet, even as shape is of critical importance to Javits, one millinery myth has he, or the archetypal hat designer, whipping a perfect hat out of his pocket—as Javits is said to have done for Carolina Herrera. The legerdemain of the hat in his pocket notwithstanding, Javits plays with a softening of shape so that even his military inspirations and his menswear derivations work as softer versions of the source, though never collapsing into Oldenburg flaccidity.

Defending his decision to enter millinery, as he did somewhat serendipitously, Javits describes the early hat-making as a relief from painting and sculpture. "Hatmaking was playful, there was no pressure. A weight was taken off, and it snowballed into something more serious." His play is quite serious, though, a *Bauhausian* caprice rather than Carmen Miranda theatrics. While some of Javits' hats are for a day at the races, his most important contributions are hats that can serve for day and cocktail hours. He makes one of the most convincing arguments for the possible return of millinery to daily attire in dealing with classic shapes, such as a velour beret or the most refined form of the basic derby. His red tophat with poinsettia photographed on the cover of *Town & Country,* (New York, December 1990) is Dickensian tradition manifested in a time-honored silhouette, but made fresh with a feminine and flattering red as well as the single note of the white poinsettia adornment. Javits excels in such distilled grace notes, projecting the hat as a deliberate statement for and upon the wearer.

Fred Miller Robinson argues for the bowler hat as a salient sign of the modern spirit (*The Man in the Bowler Hat,* Chapel Hill, 1993). He points out that it is ever and increasingly filled with the semantics of its origin. What happens in an Eric Javits hat? Customarily, saving most of the over-the-top extravagance for the Louis Féraud line, the Javits hats have the snappy stateliness of a wonderful tradition fittingly renewed. Without succumbing either to arid art or to a conceptual base alone, Javits' fundamentals of hatmaking likewise give the hat its historical function and purpose and offer it as a basic vessel adaptable to modern lives. Few milliners have been as conscientious as Javits in reconfiguring the hat in accordance with its historical templates and modern comforts. Few milliners have taken a modernist sculptural responsibility and talent in honing in one element of the hat to make it converse with the apparel to give presence to the face of its wearer.

Into the 21st century, Javits, the grandnephew of the late New York Senator Jacob Javits, earns a place among the creators of beautiful things. Some of his chicery, like the hats with wigs attached, he crafts especially to the tastes of the Big Apple to celebrate women, from the everday impulse shopper at Bergdorf's to Katie Couric, Whitney Houston, Hillary Clinton, and Madeline Albright. In his words, "What career woman cares about price? As long as career women care what they look like, I'm in business."

Javits has stayed in demand in a fickle, style-driven market by keeping abreast of what the youngest hat-wearers want and by knowing where and how people display head coverings. Consequently, he has maintained a steady fine-tuning of his classic, elegant, sensible, and fantasy models sold in the millinery salons of Bonwit Teller, Bergdorf Goodman, Saks Fifth Avenue, Bloomingdale's, Macy's, Chicago's Marshall Fields, and specialty shops. In the fall of 2000, LuxuryFinder.com, a top online retailer of luxury goods, touted its selection of Javits hats. Tops in the era were his Stetson in natural python and matching hat and hobo bag in cheetah, giraffe, leopard, and wildcat patterns. Of these whimsical models, he comments, "I like to see women have fun in hats. You wear them for all different reasons, but I think the main thing is that it's another way to express yourself. Marry that with function, and then you really need them."

—Richard Martin; updated by Mary Ellen Snodgrass

JEAN PATOU

French design company

Founded: by Jean Patou (1887–1936), who worked in a small dressmaking business, Parry, before World War I. **Company History:** Patou produced first collection, 1914; Captain of Zouaves during World War I; returned to fashion, launching first couture collection, 1919; moved to rue St. Florentin, Paris, 1922; visited U.S., brought back six American models, 1924; created perfume house,

Skiwear design by Jean Patou, ca. 1930. © Hulton-Deutsch Collection/CORBIS.

1925; introduced Princess line, 1929; brother-in-law, Raymond Barbas, took over business on death of Patou, 1936; Parfums Patou established in London, Milan, Geneva, Hong Kong, and Australia, by 1982; designers for the house have included Bohan (1954–56), Lagerfeld (1960–63), Gaultier (1971–73), Goma (1963–73), Tarlazzi (1973–77), Gonzalès (1977–82), and Lacroix (1982–87); signed licensing deal with Yohji Yamamoto for fragances, 1994; fragrances include: *Amour Amour, que sais-je, Adieu Sagesse*, 1925; *Chaldée,* 1927; *Moment Suprême,* 1929; *Joy,* 1930; *Divine Folie,* 1933; *Normandie,* 1935; *Vacances,* 1936; *Colony,* 1938; *l'Heure Attendue,* 1946; *Caline,* 1964; *1000 de Jean Patou,* 1972; *Eau de Patou,* 1976; *Patou pour Homme,* 1980; *Sublime,* 1992; *Prive,* 1994; *Quasar,* 1995; *Yohji,* 1996; *Yohji Essential* and *Patou for Ever,* 1998; *Yohji Homme,* 1999; *Nacre,* 2001. **Awards:** Scent of the Century (*Joy*), 2000. **Company Address:** 7 rue St. Florentin, Paris, 75008 France.

Publications

On JEAN PATOU:

Books

Etherington-Smith, Meredith, *Patou,* London, 1983.
McDowell, Colin, *McDowell's Directory of Twentieth Century Fashion,* Englewood Cliffs, NJ, 1985.
Milbank, Caroline Rennolds, *Couture: The Great Designers,* New York, 1985.
Ewing, Elizabeth, *History of Twentieth Century Fashion,* Totowa, NJ, 1986.
Milbank, Caroline Rennolds, *New York Fashion: The Evolution of American Style,* New York, 1989.
Steele, Valerie, *Women of Fashion: Twentieth-Century Designers,* New York, 1991.
Stegemeyer, Anne, *Who's Who in Fashion, Third Edition,* New York, 1996.

Articles

"Patou with a New Spirit," in *Vogue,* May 1985.
Donovan, Carrie, "The Two Sides of Paris Couture," in the *New York Times Magazine,* 23 February 1986.
Everett, Patty, "After Half a Century, Joy Adds Bath, Body Line," in *WWD,* 9 January 1987.
Koselka, Rita, "Affordable Luxury," in *Forbes,* 4 May 1987.
"Yohji Yamamoto in Deal to Develop Fragrance," in *WWD,* 5 July 1994.
"Patou Judgement Goes Against Gaultier," in *WWD,* 30 November 1994.
Aktar, Alev, "Yohji Readies Scent," in *WWD,* 12 July 1996.
"Vive l'Amour," in *WWD,* 13 March 1998.
Ozzard, Janet, "May Debut for *Yohji Homme* (Patou's New Men's Fragrance)," in *WWD,* 2 April 1999.
"Great Joy for Patou—*Joy,* Scent of the Century," in *Soap Perfumery & Cosmetics,* September 2000.
Born, Pete, "Newest Pearl in Patou's Crown," in *WWD,* 23 February 2001.

*

Since its origin, the House of Jean Patou has always associated fashion (1919) and perfumery (1925) activities. I think there are numerous similarities in the care given to these two industries, notably in the domaine of know-how, innovation, the constant research for quality and in the intervention of a highly qualified workforce.

Forever the forerunner, Jean Patou has always understood the tastes and aspirations of his contemporaries. Whilst he was the primary influence in women's sportswear and creator of the first knitted bathing-suits, he was also the first couturier to use his monogram as a design feature. For Jean Patou, "the modern woman leads an active life, and the creator must therefore dress her accordingly, in the most simple way, whilst maintaining her charm and femininity."

It is in this sense that the stylists that have succeeded Jean Patou have worked. They have created original and striking collections, with no limits, maintaining the label's prestigious aura, its liberty and quality. I think that fashion should reflect a woman's desires, should not constrain her but allow her to live with her epoch.

—Jean de Moüy

* * *

Fashion history records that Jean Patou is best known for *Joy,* the world's most expensive perfume, and for his famous cubist sweaters.

His contributions to fashion were, however, much more substantial and far reaching. His genius was his ability to interpret the times in which he lived and translate the ideals of that era into fashion. In Paris during the 1920s, couture was evolving from serving a few wealthy clients into a huge autonomous industry and Patou recognized couture's tremendous potential, both in France and in the United States. Patou helped expand the industry by introducing sportswear, expanding his business into the American market, emphasizing accessories and, like Paul Poiret, offering his customers a signature perfume.

The 1920s ideal woman was youthful, physically fit, and healthy looking. The truly athletic woman was realized in Suzanne Lenglen, the 1921 Wimbledon tennis star, who wore Patou clothes both on and off the court. The benefits gained by the sports stars and other celebrities publicizing Patou's designs were many. Patou also provided a complete wardrobe for American female aviator, Ruth Elder, as well as many well-known stage stars. Patou customers, most of whom did not play sports, sought to emulate this new look. Patou recognized the need for clothes for the sports participant, the spectator, and for those wishing to appear athletic, both in the U.S. and in Europe.

In 1925 he opened a Paris boutique called Le Coin des Sports where he devoted a series of rooms each to an individual sport. Complete accessorized outfits were available for aviation, riding, fishing, tennis, golf, and yachting, among others. Also recognizing the importance of leisure and travel to his customers, Patou opened salons in the resort areas, Deauville and Biarritz, where off-the-rack items such as sweater sets, swimsuits, and accessories were available.

After expanding his business in France, Patou realized the potential for the fashion industry in the U.S. and admired the long, lean lines of the American silhouette. In 1925 he traveled to New York and hired six women to return to Paris with him and work as mannequins. This well-publicized action made the couture more accessible to Americans, improving his overall market share and profits. The French sought to emulate this silhouette as well, making Patou one of the best-known names in fashion.

Patou's design philosophy was influenced by sportswear, continuing the theme of casual elegance into day and evening ensembles. He believed in beautiful but functional clothes which reflected the personality of the wearer. Patou never felt fashion should dictate; the cut of the clothes was simple, often accented with architectural seam lines, embroidery detail, and attention to fabric, trims, and finishings. By collaborating with textile mills on design and color, Patou was able to create exclusive colors through thread-dyeing methods, eliminating exact copies by lesser competitors. Patou also developed a swimsuit fabric which resisted shrinkage and fading, pleasing both swimmer and sun worshipper. Design inspirations included Russian embroideries, antique textiles, and modern art.

By interpreting the surrounding art movements and cultural ideas into his designs, Patou created such classics as "cubist" sweaters, which figured prominently in his business. By adding coordinating skirts, scarves, hats, and other accessories, he increased his overall sales. Patou revolutionized the knitting industry with machine production, which meant greater productivity and greater profits. The casual fit of sweater and sportswear, in general, was financially beneficial as it required fewer fittings and less overall production time. Patou also applied his own monogram to his sportswear designs—the first visible designer label (and over which the company later went to court with Jean-Paul Gaultier, suing the former in-house designer for a logo too closely resembling Patou's renowned initials).

The legendary rivalry between Patou and Chanel was intense and perhaps fueled both of their successful careers. Their visions for the modern woman were quite similar, and although it is Chanel that fashion history has credited with many of the silhouette and conceptual changes of 1920s fashions, it was Patou who, in 1929, dropped the hemline and raised the waistline—Chanel quickly followed suit.

The House of Patou prospered during the Depression but Patou himself was unable to interpret the 1930s as he had so successfully captured the 1920s. He died in 1936, a relatively young man. While Patou had demonstrated a brilliant business sense, ultimately undermined by his destructive gambling tendencies, the company stayed in family hands and remains world renowned today. Just as it had in the later years of the 20th century, Jean Patou in the 21st century revolved around an increasing stable of fragrances for men and women. Unlike many firms who contracted out, Jean Patou had not one but two full-time perfumers on its premises as of 1998. In addition to creating its own fragrances, licensing deals to distribute Hubigant's *Quelques Fleurs,* and to develop and sell Yohji Yamamoto's fragrance line have kept Jean Patou at the forefront of the industry.

The new millenium brought further exposure and accolades for Jean Patou. Yamamoto's first two fragrances had proven successful enough for a third, and perennial bestseller *Joy* was named the "Scent of the Century" in 2000, beating out longtime rivals such as *Chanel No. 5* and *Anaïs Anaïs* for the honor, which was sponsored by the UK's Fifi awards. Capitalizing on its higher profile, Jean Patou launched two new women's fragrances, *Lacoste* in 2000 and *Nacre* in 2001. The first was unveiled in Azerbaijan, and second, meaning mother of pearl in French, harked back to a dress called the "Fleur de Nacre," which debuted in spring 1922.

—Margo Seaman; updated by Nelly Rhodes

JOAN & DAVID

American footwear and fashion firm

Founded: by Joan and David Helpern in Cambridge, Massachusetts, 1967. **Company History:** Joan & David label introduced, 1977; David & Joan menswear division launched, 1982; Joan & David Too, lower priced line of shoes and accessories introduced, 1987; first women's apparel collection produced by Sir for Her, 1983–85; second women's ready-to-wear collection produced by Gruppo GFT, from 1988; licensing agreement with Ann Taylor chain of fashion shops, 1967–92; producer and distributor, Calvin Klein Footwear, from 1990, and Calvin Klein accessories, 1990–91; New York flagship shop opened, 1985; in-store boutiques opened at Harvey Nichols, London, and Ogilvey's, Montreal, 1987; freestanding Paris and Hong Kong boutiques opened, 1988; filed for Chapter 11 and sold Joan Helpern Designs, Inc. to Maxwell Shoe Company, 2000. **Awards:** American Fashion Critics Coty award, 1978; *Footwear News* Designer of the Year award, 1986; Cutty Sark award, 1986; Golden Slipper award, 1988; Golden Shoe award, 1989; Fashion Footwear Association of New York award, 1990; Silver Trophy, 1992; Michelangelo award, 1993; *Joan:* Girl Scouts of America Woman of the Year, 1995. **Member:** *Joan:* Council of Fashion Designers of America; Committee of 200. **Company Address:** 4 West 58th Street, New York, NY 10019, USA.

Joan Helpern in a Joan & David showroom, 1999. © AP/Wide World Photos.

PUBLICATIONS

On JOAN & DAVID:

Books

McDowell, Colin, *Shoes: Fashion and Fantasy,* New York, 1989.
Trasko, Mary, *Heavenly Soles,* New York, 1989.
Stegemeyer, Anne, *Who's Who in Fashion, Third Edition,* New York, 1996.

Articles

Bethany, Marilyn, "Sole Sister," in *New York,* 10 March 1986.
"Joan and David: Less is More," in *Vogue* (Paris), October 1986.
Infantino, Vivian, "Designer of the Year: Joan Helpern," in *Footwear News,* December 1986.
Williams, Lisa, "Uniquely Joan & David," in *Footwear News,* March 1989.
Huffman, Frances, "Role Model," in *Entrepreneurial Woman* (Irvine, California), March 1992.

Furman, Phyllis, "Putting New Foot Forward: Joan and David Rebuilds After Ann Taylor Rift," in *Crain's New York Business,* 23 March 1992.

Quinn, Colleen, "The Many Dimensions of Joan Helpern," in *Footwear News,* 1 June 1992.

Infantino, Vivian, "World Class Performances: Joan & David—It Ain't Just Shoes," in *Footwear News,* November 1992.

Moin, David, "Joan's New Platforms: Not Just Shoes," in *WWD,* 23 August 1993.

Barnett, Amy DuBois, "The Interview: Joan & David Matriarch," in *Fashion Planet,* Spring 1997.

* * *

Joan & David, Inc. is responsible for making flat shoes for women fashionable. The company developed because Joan Helpern wanted a comfortable, stylish shoe that would not become dated through its design. When Joan married David Helpern in the 1960s, she was a student in child psychology working on her Ph.D. at Harvard University. In her multiple roles of wife, mother, teacher, and student, Joan wanted a shoe that was not a gym shoe, loafer, or stiletto, the only readily available styles for women at the time. She needed a shoe that would look stylish yet allow her to get about the city in comfort. The solution was to design the shoe herself, an oxford style still available in a modified form today.

While editing academic manuscripts, Joan created footwear designs for department stores and private labels, including Harvard Square and Foreign Affairs. She began designing under the name of Joan & David in 1977. Joan served as president and designer, while David was chairman of the company.

Joan & David designs are found throughout the world. The shoes are manufactured in Italy, because it was there that Joan found craftspeople willing to produce limited editions of her designs, numbering from 12 to 120, to her specifications. Joan & David, Inc. produces shoes specifically for women under the name Joan & David, Joan & David Too, and Joan & David Couture. Men's footwear is designed under the names David & Joan and David & Joan Couture. Through the years, the product line has expanded to include purses, belts, scarves, socks, sunglasses, and other accessories as well as women's ready-to-wear.

Joan's entry into the design field was not planned, and she had no formal design training. She knew, however, what she wanted in a shoe, so she researched the market and technology involved in their manufacture. She was able to produce footwear to meet the needs of active women like herself, who race through the day serving in many different roles, who are not self-consciously fashionable but value good quality and style. Joan has a less-is-more philosophy when it comes to design; she concentrates on classic, usable styles such as oxfords and patent pumps with designs evolving from year to year. The colors she uses are subtle with the emphasis on interesting textures, and comfort is essential. Neither flat shoes nor shoes with low heels have extraneous details or extreme designs. In 1978 she was given the Coty award for her designs.

Joan has been influential in the field of shoe design. By successfully creating both comfortable and stylish shoes, she helped open up a new way of thinking about shoe design for women. Professional women wanted what Joan herself originally searched for—a fashionably comfortable shoe that would not be an obsolete design the next season—something more stylish than sneakers but more comfortable than stilettos. By providing herself with such shoes, Joan, along with her husband David, were able to fill this need and develop the successful business named Joan & David.

The Helperns have long been known for their philanthropy. "We try to support the major worldwide concerns like AIDS and breast and prostate cancer research," Joan told Amy DuBois Barnett of *Fashion Planet.* "But it's also a matter of where David and I feel most involved." In 1995, New York City's Columbia-Presbyterian Medical Center used a donation from the couple to open the Joan and David Helpern Clinical Noninvasive Vascular Diagnostic Laboratory. The Helperns have also been interested in vision care, providing glasses and medical treatment for needy children.

At the turn of the century, the Helperns' shoe business took a turn for the worse. In March 2000 Joan & David filed for chapter 11 bankruptcy protection. Later that year, Joan Helpern Designs, Inc. was purchased by the Maxwell Shoe Company for $16.8 million. The sale included most of the company's assets, including its 7,000-square-foot New York office, as well as trademarks for all Helpern designs. Footwear giant Maxwell Shoe, in business since 1949, also owns brands including Mootsies Tootsies, Dockers Footwear for Women, Anne Klein 2, and Sam & Libby shoes. The company planned to relaunch the Joan & David line in 2001, bringing down their customary prices in a long-term effort to increase sales to $40 million or $50 million.

—Nancy House; updated by Lisa Groshong

JOHN, John P.

American milliner

Born: John Pico Harberger in Munich, 14 March 1906; immigrated to the U.S., 1919. **Education:** Studied medicine, University of Lucerne, and art at the Sorbonne and l'École des Beaux Arts, Paris. **Career:** Milliner, Mme Laurel, dressmaker, New York, 1926; partner (with Fred Fredericks), John-Fredericks, milliners, 1929–48, with shops in New York, Hollywood, Miami, and Palm Beach; formed independent company, Mr. John, Inc., New York, 1948–70; designed for private clients, from 1970. **Awards:** Coty American Fashion Critics award, 1943; Neiman Marcus award, 1950; Millinery Institute of America award, 1956. **Died:** 25 June 1993, in New York.

Publications

By JOHN:

Articles

"It Had to Be Hats," with Nanette Kutner, in *Good Housekeeping* (New York), June 1957.

On JOHN:

Books

Lambert, Eleanor, *World of Fashion: People, Places, Resources,* New York and London, 1976.

Morris, Bernadine, and Barbara Walz, *The Fashion Makers,* New York, 1978.

McDowell, Colin, *Hats: Status, Style, Glamour,* London, 1992.

Stegemeyer, Anne, *Who's Who in Fashion, Third Edition,* New York, 1996.

Articles

Fredericks, Pierce G., "Mad Hatter," in *Cosmopolitan* (New York), April 1951.

"John P(ico) John," in *Current Biography* (New York), October 1956.

Morris, Bernadine, "Fashion's Mad Hatter Turns Conservative for Spring," in the *New York Times,* 7 January 1966.

Schiro, Anne-Marie, "Mr. John, 91, Hat Designer for Stars and Society," [obituary] in the *New York Times,* 29 June 1993.

"John P. John," [obituary] in *Current Biography* (New York), September 1993.

* * *

"My business," John P. John told *Good Housekeeping* in June 1957, "is strictly an individual business. When I go, there will be no more Mr John. I have only one worry: when I do go, should I reach heaven, what will I do? I know I cannot improve on the halo." Ironically, John, who had made almost every kind of head covering other than a halo, saw the demise of his kind of milliner on earth; by the time of his death in 1993, perhaps even the halo was obsolete. As early as 1957, he was already on the defensive, arguing, "A hat cannot actually give one golden curls if the hair is mouse-colored and stringy; it cannot lift a face, pay overdue bills, subtract ten years from one's age, or transform a plain soul into a reigning princess. But it *can* lend practically any woman a temporary out-of-herself feeling. For *the right hat creates a desired mood,* and that isn't fiction or fancy, but fact, fact, fact."

Like his contemporaries Lilly Daché and Halston who would follow later (translating the concept to apparel, but retaining John's contradictory modes of shape reductivism and theatrical sparkle), John successfully combined the glamor of a custom business with a wide-reaching appeal. He could create extraordinary hats for exceptional women. At the same time, he was a hero to countless middle-class women who copied his styles or had them copied by local milliners. John's hats adorned the cover of *Vogue* many times, in issues hitting newstands in 1943, 1944, 1946, and 1953.

From the opening of his own business in the 1920s, after apprenticing with his mother through the 1960s, John was an important milliner, never fixed in one style but producing eclectic variations of romantic picture hats, snoods, subdued cloches, and other forms. It was form indeed that was essential to John: his hats were sculptural, shaped to flatter the face, outfit, and presence. His historicist pieces, in particular, could use surface decoration, but the effect of a Mr. John hat nonetheless always resided in the shape. As Anne-Marie Schiro of the *New York Times* described in June 1993, "In the 1940s and 1950s, the name Mr. John was as famous in the world of hats as Christian Dior was in the realm of haute couture. At a time when other milliners were piling on flowers, feathers, and tulle, Mr. John was stripping hats naked, relying on pure shape for effect." Turbans, berets, and snoods—a specialty—were supple shapes in favor with John and were often shown in the style magazines with American fashion. He could, however, also cut crisp shapes and bow a brim to flatter the face and forehead to accompany Dior, Schiaparelli, and Balenciaga. For all the flamboyance of his own life and all the drama that he could vest in a suite of picture hats that ever seemed to belong at Tara, John could also create what *Vogue* characterized as a "strict" black hat of utmost simplicity in 1951. Even at their most whimsical and wild, John's hats were flattering to the wearer and to the ensemble of dress.

Eugenia Sheppard of the New York *Herald Tribune* called him "the artist among milliners" in July 1956 and he self-consciously courted the rubric of art, including collections with the themes of modern art and style history, and a sense of the avant-garde. It was one piece of historical recreation, however, that made John most famous: his millinery for Vivien Leigh in *Gone with the Wind.* Widely copied, the *Gone with the Wind* hats confirmed John's longtime association with Hollywood and women of style, including Mary Pickford, Greta Garbo, Gloria Vanderbilt, Gloria Swanson, Jacqueline Kennedy Onassis, and the Duchess of Windsor. His hats were also worn in films by Marilyn Monroe in *Gentlemen Prefer Blondes* and Marlene Dietrich in *Shanghai Express.* By the time Mr. John closed in 1970, hats were largely *démodé.*

Custom-made millinery is a matter of extreme codependency between client and milliner. If it is the purpose of the hat to flatter, the milliner, too, must practice a psychology of intervention and flattery. When Pierce Fredericks dubbed John the "Mad Hatter" in *Cosmopolitan* in April 1951, the madness was only of energy; rather, clients enjoyed John's "diplomatic manner." John used only one house model, a Miss Lynn, for many years; she was his type for countless hats, many of which he made directly on her head. He was also famous for his miniature hat collection, prototypes for his own hats and historical recreations based upon his study in museums and historical references. John lived in and defined the golden age of millinery.

—Richard Martin

JOHNSON, Betsey

American designer

Born: Weathersfield, Connecticut, 10 August 1942. **Education:** Studied at Pratt Institute, Brooklyn, New York, 1960–61; B.A., Phi Beta Kappa, Syracuse University, Syracuse, New York, 1964. **Family:** Married John Cale, 1966 (divorced); married Jeffrey Oliviere, 1981 (divorced); married Brian Reynolds, 1997 (separated); daughter: Lulu. **Career:** Guest Editor, *Mademoiselle,* New York, 1964–65; designer, Paraphernalia boutiques, New York, 1965–69; partner in boutique Betsey, Bunky & Nini, New York, from 1969; designer, Alvin Duskin Co., San Francisco, 1970; designer, Alley Cat, 1970–74; Butterick patterns, 1971 and 1975; Jeanette Maternities, 1974–75; Gant, 1974–75; Betsey Johnson's Kidswear division of Shutterbug, 1974–77; Tric-Trac by Betsey Johnson, 1974–76; Star Ferry by Betsey Johnson and Michael Miles, 1975–77; head designer, president, treasurer, B. J. Vines, from 1978; owner, Betsey Johnson stores, from 1979. **Awards:** *Mademoiselle* Merit award, 1970; Coty American Fashion Critics award, 1971; American Printed Fabrics Council Tommy award, 1971, 1990; Council of Fashion Designers of America Timeless Talent award, 1999. **Address:** 498 Seventh Avenue, New York, New York 10018, USA. **Website:** www.betseyjohnson.com.

Betsey Johnson, fall 2001 collection: lurex knit cardigan and chiffon mini skirt. © AP/Wide World Photos.

Publications

On JOHNSON:

Books

Milinaire, Caterine, and Carol Troy, *Cheap Chic,* New York, 1975.
Morris, Bernadine, and Barbara Walz, *The Fashion Makers,* New York, 1978.
Milbank, Caroline Rennolds, *New York Fashion: The Evolution of American Style,* New York, 1989.
Lobenthal, Joel, *Radical Rags: Fashions of the Sixties,* New York, 1990.
Steele, Valerie, *Women of Fashion,* New York, 1991.
Stegemeyer, Anne, *Who's Who in Fashion, Third Edition,* New York, 1996.

Articles

"We Orbit Around...Betsey Johnson," in *Mademoiselle,* August 1966.
Fraser, Kennedy, "On and Off the Avenue: Feminine Fashions," in the*New Yorker,* 1 April 1972.
Comer, Nancy, "Betsey Johnson," in *Mademoiselle,* August 1972.
Kaiser, Diane, "Profile on People," in *Fashion Accessories Magazine,* March 1979.
Burggraf, Helen, "Betsey Johnson: Alive and Well and Designing in New York," in *Apparel News,* 1981.
"Sweet and Tough," in *Soho News* (New York), 23 February 1982.
Bloomfield, Judy, "Happy Partners: Bacon and Johnson," in *WWD,* 7 September 1988.
Haistreiter, Kim, "Earth to Betsey," in *Paper* (New York), April 1989.
Benatar, Giselle, "Betsey Johnson," in *Mademoiselle,* February 1993.
"Betsey Johnson," in *Current Biography,* January 1994.
Loukin, Andrea, "Betsey Johnson and Tarik Currimbhoy," in *Interior Design,* May 1996.
Schiro, Anne-Marie, "Betsey Johnson: Honor for a Life of Celebrating Youth," in the *New York Times,* 18 May 1999.
D'Innocenzio, Anne, "Betsey Johnson's New Chapter," in *WWD,* 3 May 2000.
Shanahan, Laura, "Designated Shopper," in *Brandweek,* 13 November 2000.

* * *

For the youthquake generation, the names Betsey Johnson and Paraphernalia symbolized the hip, young fashions of mid-1960s America just as Mary Quant and Biba did for the equivalent age group in Great Britain. In the early 1970s, a second wave of young women with a taste for affordable style discovered the flippant body-conscious clothes Johnson designed for the ready-to-wear firm Alley Cat. Throughout the 1980s and into the 1990s, Johnson's clothes have been characterized by her sense of humor and an innocent, tongue-in-cheek sexiness. Wearing a Betsey Johnson dress is like putting on a good mood.

After graduating Phi Beta Kappa and magna cum laude from Syracuse University, Johnson won a guest editorship at *Mademoiselle* magazine. There, colleagues put her name forward to Paul Young, who was scouting out fresh new design talent to launch his Paraphernalia boutiques. It was a good match: Young encouraged experimentation and Johnson began to develop what was to be a long-standing interest in such unorthodox materials as vinyl, sequin sheeting, and the then-new stretch fabrics. Her "kit" dress, for example, was of clear vinyl with a trim-it-yourself package of stars, dots, and ellipses cut from reflective adhesive foil. The "noise" dress had a hem fringed with loose grommets.

Johnson's approach to clothing is very much influenced by her early days as a dancer. "I am basically about a ballerina torso and a full skirt," she told a reporter for the *Soho News* in 1982, "a dancing school dress-up craziness." Johnson's emphasis on tight, stretch bodices also grew out of her dancing school background. Not surprisingly, the shift in the 1970s to a subdued, tailored look was incompatible with Johnson's style as a designer. She continued to have her own label with a variety of manufacturers, but it was not until the end of that decade that Johnson's real *joie de vivre* emerged again, this time for her own company.

Johnson's company and her girlish, bohemian style have continued to endure, despite the economic downturns of the late 1980s and the

Betsey Johnson, fall 2001 collection. © AP/Wide World Photos.

androgynous "grunge" trends of the early 1990s. In the final years of the century, Johnson's flirty and whimsical designs were again at the forefront of fashion trends. As of 2001, almost 40 Betsey Johnson stores were open worldwide, with further expansion planned. Her label is available in several upper-end department stores and specialty stores, together with Johnson's designer-price brand, Ultra. Throughout the 1990s, Betsey Johnson, Inc. continued to broaden its offerings, developing a line of accessories, jewelry, footwear, children's clothing, bath and beauty products, and fragrance. Johnson's imaginative runway fashion shows are eagerly anticipated each year, opened by the designer's trademark cartwheel down the catwalk.

The youthful spirit of the company is kept alive through Johnson's own playful personality and the design talents of a young staff, including her daughter, Lulu Johnson. Betsey Johnson is the first to admit that her designs have changed little conceptually over her long career, but she is able to manipulate this basic style to suit a contemporary mood. Johnson's loyalty to her own vision has been crucial to her success and appeal. Kal Ruttenstein, Bloomingdale's fashion director, recognizes Johnson's enduring style: "Betsey reinvents herself," Ruttenstein says. "If she keeps doing what she does, fashion comes around to her every few years."

—Whitney Blausen; updated by Megan Stacy

JONES, Stephen

British milliner

Born: West Kirby, Cheshire, England, 31 May 1957. **Education:** Studied at High Wycombe School of Art, 1975–76; B.A. (with honors) in fashion from St. Martin's School of Art, London, 1979. **Military Service:** Served as chief petty officer in the Royal Navy, 1974–76. **Career:** Chairman/designer, Stephen Jones Millinery, from 1981; S.J. Scarves and Miss Jones lines introduced, from 1988; color creator, Shiseido Cosmetics, 1988; Jonesboy and S.J. Handkerchiefs, from 1990; S.J. Kimonos, from 1991; handbag line introduced, 1993; Jonesgirl, Stephen Jones Japan; license for gloves, scarves, and eyewear; opened shop in Covent Garden, 1995; hat featured on British postage stamp, 2001. **Exhibitions:** *Headspace by Stephen Jones,* Isetan Museum, Tokyo, 1984; *Fashion and Surrealism,* Victoria and Albert Museum, London and Fashion Institute of Technology, New York, 1988; *Mad Hatter,* Australian National Gallery, Canberra, Sydney, 1992; *Hats: Status, Style, Glamour,* The Collection, London, 1993; *Rococo Futura,* Ginza Artspace, Tokyo, 1994; *Blah, Blah, Blah,* London Fashion Week, 2000. **Address:** 36 Great Queen Street, Covent Garden, London WC2B 5AA, England.

Publications

By JONES:

Articles

"Heads You Win," in *You* magazine of the *Mail on Sunday* (London), 29 May 1983.

"England's Leading Milliner—The Collection," available online at www.eodel.com/events/milliner.shtml, 18 June 2001.

On JONES:

Books

Polan, Brenda, *The Fashion Year,* London, 1983.

McDowell, Colin, *Twentieth Century Fashion,* London, 1984.

Damase, Jacques, *L'histoire du chapeaux,* Paris, 1987.

Martin, Richard, *Fashion and Surrealism,* New York, 1987.

Mulvagh, Jane, *The Vogue History of Twentieth Century Fashion,* London, 1988.

Ginsburg, Madeleine, *The Hat,* London, 1990.

McDowell, Colin, *Hats: Status, Style, Glamour,* London, 1992.

Stegemeyer, Anne, *Who's Who in Fashion, Third Edition,* New York, 1996.

Articles

Jagger, Harriett, "Making Up is Art to Do," in the *Observer Magazine* (London), 11 December 1983.

"Stephen Jones: Un toque de chapeaux," in *Elle* (Paris), September 1984.

Smith, Liz, "Mad as a Hatter," in the *Standard* (London), 23 October 1984.

"Jones the Hat," in *You* magazine of the *Mail on Sunday,* 2 December 1984.

Grieve, Amanda, "Hat Check Job," in *Harpers & Queen* (London), December 1984.

"Hats to Turn Heads," in the *Observer* (London), 2 June 1985.

"Stephen Jones: Un Idea per Cappello," in *L'Uomo Vogue* (Milan), December 1985.

Gessner, Liz, "Thoroughly Modern Millinery," in *WWD,* 26 June 1987.

DuCann, Charlotte, "Keeping Ahead of Jones," in *Elle* (London), September 1987.

Barron, Patti, "Thoroughly Modern Millinery," in the *Standard* (London), 6 October 1987.

Ranson, Geraldine, "The Hatter Who Flatters," in the *Sunday Telegraph* (London), 24 April 1988.

Brampton, Sally, "Just a Trifle Over the Top," in the *Observer* (London), 3 October 1992.

McDowell, Colin, "Crown Jewels," in the *Sunday Telegraph* (London), 8 November 1992.

Davidson, John, "Crowning Glory," in the *Scotsman* (Edinburgh), 11 May 1994.

Rickey, Melanie, "The Milliner's Tale," in the *Independent Sunday* (London), 7 April 1996.

Menkes, Suzy, "Luxury and Fantasy: The Feel-Good Factor in Menswear," in the *International Herald Tribune* (France), 28 January 1997.

"How U2 Can Look Like This," in the *Sunday Telegraph,* August 1997.

Donnally, Trish, "Fall/Winter French Collections: Galliano Takes Dior on a Trip to Mexico," in the *San Francisco Chronicle,* 11 March 1998.

"Behind the Seams," in *American Cinematheque,* 30 November 2000.

"Jones, Stephen," in *Vogue: The Fashion Designer Database,* available online at handbag.com, 18 June 2001.

Hayes, David, and Harriet Arkell, "Milliners Stamp Their Designs on Ascot as Horses Go to Post," in the *Evening Standard* (London), 19 June 2001.

*

Hats for me are an expression of the spirit. They can parallel the whole range of human emotions and may exaggerate them to dramatic effect. The expression of an eye can be enhanced by the particular line of a brim, a Roman profile concealed or enhanced by twists of fabric, or the wearer can be veiled with mystery. Whatever effect my hats achieve, they must have, as Diana Vreeland would have said, "Pizazz." Therefore the balance between them and the wearer is all-important; too much emotion in the curl of a feather or the glint of a paillette is vulgar and dominating, too little and the exercise is pointless.

Unlike clothing, novelty is the raison d'être of millinery. I must rewrite the score in every hat I make. Making a hat should be like dancing; as one's body follows the beat, so must one's hands be in rhythm with the tempo of the particular hat. Hats make themselves, I merely help them along.

—Stephen Jones

* * *

When Stephen Jones left St. Martin's School of Art in London in 1979, hats were yet to become high fashion news for the young. Ethnic styles had spread from the mid-1970s onward, drably cloaking the fashion-buying public with serious good taste and leaving little room for wit or fantasy.

The late 1970s, however, brought a glimmer of change. Waists, hips, and padded shoulders were beginning to emerge from shapeless chemises and sloppy knits. What better to complete this new silhouette than an amusing and frivolous piece of headgear? Many of London's young clubgoers had first appeared on the scene wearing the spikely aggressive trappings of punk. They were new to this glamour born of Hollywood retro-kitsch and embraced it wholeheartedly, and Jones entered right on cue.

Jones was a champion of the eccentric, the stylish, and the innovative. He could be seen emerging from the morning train at Paddington, dressed like the other commuters in smart pinstriped suiting but with black patent stilettos emerging from his immaculate turnups. He was a great ornament to the clubs and parties of the era, usually wearing one of his own asymmetric and intriguing hats perched on his bald head. An enthusiastic self-publicist, his charm and good humor endeared him to many.

Jones' salons—the first in Covent Garden's P.X.—were unique environments, swathed in lush fabric and dripping with gilt cupids, where one might gaze leisurely at his always astonishing and delightful creations. He reinterpreted the chic and quirky styles of the past, cleverly draping, molding, and trimming his hats in a way so personal as to be entirely of its own time. Moreover, Jones' hats are well crafted—a reflection of early work at the traditional couture house of Lachasse.

Jones was soon a fast-rising star in the heady London galaxy of the early 1980s. His talent and that of his peers—Bodymap, Stephen Linard—burst on the scene like a vivid fireworks display, drawing the world's fashion buyers and press as moths to the British flame. During the following decades, Jones' esoterically titled collections—Sunset on Suburbia, Ole' Steamy, Passport to Pleasure—continued to delight and inspire, and he must take due credit for the current popularity of hats among the young. His designs have even attracted the attention and heads of such musical stars as Madonna and U2, and were featured in multiple films including Steven Spielberg's *Jurassic Park* (1993) and Disney's *101 Dalmations* (1996). Further proof of his influence and fame came in 2001 when one of his hats was featured on a British postage stamp.

Millinery remains a popular subject on fashion course timetables, whereas two decades ago it was fast becoming an endangered species. Jones himself, in fact, admits to hardly keeping up with demand during the show season. He begins meeting with designers in early winter, when he collects ideas and forms a general impression of the designers' moods. The process continues through the next two months as designers choose from sketches, view prototypes, and make a final selection mere days before a show is to begin. The grueling routine is repeated through spring and summer, only to begin again in the fall. Yet Jones thrives on the excitement and stress, using it to draw out his creative energies. More recent work was from the school of maximalism: three-foot plastic Stetsons, Christmas trees, full body-length Indian headdresses, even hats made from painted macaroni noodles and cardboard.

Jones' talents have naturally taken him abroad; he continuously designs for top French fashion houses—Gaultier, Montana, Mugler, Christian Dior—and enjoys much success in Japan with a line called Jonesgirls, in which genuinely innovative design skills allied with

Western charisma are justly lauded. American designer Jeremy Scott has also called upon Jones to complete his "king of kitsch" look. Other young milliners have arisen, some to stay and some to go, but Stephen Jones was the first of this new breed, and has remained one of its most influential and quixotic practitioners.

—Alan J. Flux; updated by Carrie Snyder

JONES NEW YORK

American retailer and design firm

Incorporated: by Sidney Kimmel as Jones New York, 1975. **Company History:** Acquired several licenses and became America's fastest-growing apparel company, 1980s; sales fell and company approached bankruptcy, 1987; went public, 1990; launched Rena Rowan for Saville label, 1991; purchased Evan-Picone brand, 1992; surpassed $1 billion in sales, 1996; licensed Lauren by Ralph Lauren, 1996, and Ralph by Ralph Lauren, 1998; launched Jones New York menswear program and purchased Sun Apparel, 1998; purchased Nine West Group and Todd Oldham, 1999; acquired Canadian Ralph Lauren licenses, repositioned Evan-Picone, and acquired Victoria & Company, 2000; designer Rena Rowan retired after 25 years with company, 2000. **Company Address:** 250 Rittenhouse Circle, Bristol, PA 19007, USA. **Company Website:** www.jonesnewyork.com.

Publications

On JONES NEW YORK:

Books

Derdak, Thomas, ed., *International Directory of Company Histories,* Chicago, 1988.

Articles

Lockwood, Lisa, "Jones: Keeping Up with the Laurens," in *WWD,* 17 July 1998.

"Jones New York Offers First Watch Line for Men," in *DNR,* 8 January 1999.

"Jones New York," in *Women's Wear Daily's Fairchild 100 Supplement,* November 1999.

Solnik, Claude, "Jones Buys Back Bags," in *Footwear News* (New York), 15 November 1999.

"G-III Gets License for Jones New York Outerwear," in *DNR,* 17 March 2000.

"Jones Apparel Acquires Polo's Canadian Licenses," in *DNR,* 7 April 2000.

D'Innocenzio, Anne, "Jones to Swing Some NWG Lines Into Fast-Track Mass Market," in *Footwear News* (New York) 29 May 2000.

Cunningham, Thomas, "Jones Men's Facing Uncertain Future," in *DNR,* 20 November 2000.

Wilson, Eric, "Polo-Jones New Deal, in *WWD,* 16 November 2000.

* * *

Jones Apparel Group, U.S.-based marketer of moderate women's suits, dresses, and sportswear under the Jones New York trademark, was incorporated in 1975 by Sidney Kimmel, an executive with two decades of apparel industry experience. His goal was to create clothes similar in style and quality to expensive designer fashions but at an affordable price.

Kimmel's fashion career began at a knitting mill, after which he became president of Villager, Inc., the women's sportswear firm. He remained there until 1969, when W. R. Grace & Company, which wanted to increase its presence in women's apparel, hired Kimmel as head of its new women's clothing division. Villager knitwear designer Rena Rowan joined him.

In 1975, W. R. Grace spun off the division to Kimmel and Gerard Rubin. They renamed the business Jones Apparel Group and went after the inexpensive designer lookalike market. The company's first five years were difficult, marked by debt and low cash reserves. All the same, management adhered to an aggressive growth strategy, launching new labels and acquiring rights to others. Its most successful brand was its Jones New York $100 to $300 careerwear line.

Jones New York generated steady demand in an era when women were entering the workforce and wanted affordable yet fashionable clothing. The company's practice of outsourcing manufacturing while concentrating on marketing, distribution, and design was sound. It achieved profitability at the beginning of the 1980s and, within a few years, became one of the fastest-growing U.S. apparel companies.

By the mid-1980s, the company boasted sales of $250 million, making it the leading supplier of moderate women's apparel. But Jones' fast growth and heavy debt, combined with poor acquisitions—including Murjani's Gloria Vanderbilt Jeans, for which Jones had purchased marketing but not manufacturing, pricing, inventory, or delivery rights and lost $20 million—left the company near bankruptcy. In 1987 creditors demanded a reorganization that required the firm to divest many of its licensed labels (although it kept some, such as Christian Dior), lay off employees, and close divisions and warehouses. The reorganization helped almost immediately, with the company showing a profit, albeit a small one, in 1988, after two years of declining sales and earnings.

The Jones New York label led the way for a growth spurt that continued into the mid-1990s. Consumers fought tight budgets during the era's economic recession by buying Jones New York rather than pricey designer apparel. In 1990 management took the firm public, with Kimmel retaining 45 percent ownership. The following year, 1991, Jones Apparel launched Rena Rowan for Saville, priced slightly below Jones New York. Two years later, Rena Rowan was the firm's fastest-growing label and accounted for 15 percent of company sales. Jones New York continued to expand, with its Sport line accounting for about 20 percent of sales; other related labels included Jones & Company, Jones New York Dress, and Jones New York Suits.

Jones Apparel Group purchased the Evan-Picone brand for $105 million in 1992. It also began to extend distribution from its base of department stores (which continued to dominate sales) and catalogues, adding 100 high-margin factory outlet stores across the U.S. (as of 2000, the company operated 970 specialty and 590 outlet stores.) By 1994, revenues were up to $600 million, and in 1996, they passed the $1-billion mark.

The success of the Lauren lines resulted in some changes for Jones New York. The company launched the first Jones New York advertising campaign in 15 years. While its labels, which now included Jones

Jeans and Jones New York Country, dominated moderate apparel in department stores, Jones New York's competitors had created recognized lifestyle images through advertising, something Jones New York had not done. In 1996, Jones Apparel Group launched the licensed Lauren by Ralph Lauren line, which, with heavy advertising, grew to $350 million in sales in 1998, when Jones added the Ralph by Ralph Lauren label. Lauren has continued to play a significant role in the company's fortunes. In 2000, Jones acquired the Canadian licenses for several Polo brands and forged a deal to export its licensed Lauren and Ralph brands overseas, its initial foray into foreign markets.

Jones also extended the label into other categories, including jewelry, swimwear, footwear, watches, and handbags through licensing. All products were advertised and cross-promoted with the core Jones New York line. By the late 1990s, the company had retaken control of some of those licenses, bringing footwear and handbags in-house.

In fall 1998, Jones launched a Jones New York menswear program, which it expanded further by signing several licensing agreements, such as for men's leather, outerwear, and tailored clothing. Menswear turned out to be a tough business, however. Despite repositioning the line from collection to main-floor pricing, Jones failed to receive orders from some of its key customers for spring 2001, leading it to consider closing down the division.

On the acquisition front, Jones purchased Sun Apparel, a jeanswear and sportswear company and Polo Jeans licensee, in 1998; Todd Oldham in 1999; and Victoria & Company, a designer and marketer of Givenchy, Tommy Hilfiger, Napier, Richelieu, and Nine West costume jewelry, in 2000. Another major purchase was the Nine West Group in 1999, the footwear marketer's brands included Nine West, Amalfi, Bandolino, Luca B. for Calico, cK/Calvin Klein, 9 & Company, Pappagallo, Pied à Terre, and Selby. In 2000, Jones began repositioning several of those brands, along with Evan-Picone, into the mass market.

Acquisitions boosted total company volume to more than $4.5 billion in 2000. Designer and cofounder Rena Rowan announced her retirement that year, but Sidney Kimmel remained chairman. Over the past two and a half decades, the two partners supplemented their flagship Jones New York career collections by moving into new brands, markets, customer bases, price points, and distribution channels—expansion that promises to continue.

—Karen Raugust

JOOP, Wolfgang

German designer

Born: Potsdam, Germany, 18 November 1944. **Family:** Married Karin Bernatzky; children: Henriette, Florentine. **Career:** Journalist, *Neue Mode;* freelance designer for Christian Aujard, Brecco, and others; showed first fur collection under own label, 1978; added Joop! ready-to-wear line, 1981; added menswear line, 1985; opened Joop! boutiques, Hamburg and Munich, 1986; introduced fragrances, 1987; added Joop jeans, 1989; introduced ready-to-wear fur collection, 1990; menswear introduced in the U.S., 1994; reintroduced leather, 1996; fragrances include *Joop! Berlin, Joop! Femme,* and

Wolfgang Joop, fall 2001 collection. © AP/Wide World Photos/ Fashion Wire Daily.

Joop! Homme. **Address:** Harvestehuder Weg 22, 2000 Hamburg 13, Germany.

Publications

On JOOP:

Books

Stegemeyer, Anne, *Who's Who in Fashion, Third Edition,* New York, 1996.

Articles

Morais, Richard, "Who is First in the Market, Sells," in *Forbes,* 16 September 1991.

Morris, Belinda, "Talking Fashion," in *FHM* (London), September 1993.

Drier, Melissa, "Joop Files 2 Suits Against CEO Frommen," *WWD,* 4 March 1997.

Larsen, Soren, "Joop Adds Scent to Garden Party," *WWD,* 18 July 1997.

Knight, Molly, "There's Hope for Joop," online at Fashion.com, www.fashion.com, July 2001.

Wolfgang Joop, fall 2001 collection. © AP/Wide World Photos/ Fashion Wire Daily.

* * *

Photogenic Wolfgang Joop is at least as recognizable as his fashion and fragrance products. Along with Jil Sander, one of the major figures of German fashion in the 1990s, Joop is as much a national anomaly as he is an international celebrity. Until Sander and Joop, Germany had few designers of sexy clothing achieving world-class status: suddenly, after years in Germany, both came into international recognition in the early 1990s.

Joop, the design identity with an exclamation point, is the hyperreal, hyperbolic badge of the designer. He has brought the American concept of the designer to Germany, with its strong sense of personal identification and the projection of style. Again and again, he appears charismatically, if a little too prominently, in his own imagery. Further, as he describes in a 1993 press release, "When it comes to designing the men's collection, the man I have in mind for the clothes is myself."

When Joop bought an apartment in New York in 1993, it was the former apartment of Bill Blass, for Joop has cleverly understood the impulse of contemporary fashion marketing to personification and projection. He has expressed his admiration for the work of American minimalists and marketing prodigies Donna Karan and Calvin Klein. Like Blass, Joop projects utmost self-confidence in style, an aplomb that allows him the polymath aptitude to design for menswear, women's apparel, and fragrance. In examining himself, he gives some surety in the ambiguous realms of style.

In telling his own story in a 1993 press release, with a merchant's beguiling fluency, Joop cites as an important influence growing up on a farm near Potsdam: "As the city of Philip the Great it was one of the poorest of the European courts, but the one with the most style," thus enjoying both a simple life and a proximity to high style. His statements on fashion lean to the populist, though his clothing is always on the well-mannered side of democracy (he called a fragrance *Joop! Berlin* after the fall of the Berlin Wall in 1989). He avers: "Fashion should not just be a blatant expression of money. It should be humorous and give dignity to the individual wearing the clothes."

Among his greatest successes have been jeanswear, likewise in the optimistic spirit of American style and ready-to-wear populism. But the Joop denim collections are not standard: fit, size, and style distinctions bring to the lowly subject of jeans at least a rudiment of tailoring and individuation. Joop's principle is that the ready-to-wear client, even in denim, must be served with a kind of customized distinction and satisfaction, again very much in the ethos of traditional American sportswear. Joop contends that "jeans are fashion's alter ego," and it is his conviction that jeans are part of daily life. His collections work for both casual dress and contemporary high style.

Essentially, Joop thinks fashion is about suspense and surprise and fantasy, not about rules. Flirting with incongruity, he mixes traditional clothing with new fashion, throwing a kimono over a little shift dress, pairing bobby socks with high heels, or mixing military styles with classic schoolgirl/schoolboy fashion items. He also designs his own prints. Having seen countless trends in the fashion industry, he has merged archived print designs with current trends, imparting a contemporary retro look.

At one time a leather clothing designer in Italy, Joop reintroduced leather into his collection in 1996, taking advantage of the new treatments that revolutionized the leather industry. Much lighter and easier to manipulate, the new leather allowed color possibilities beyond the traditional blacks and browns. Yet this collection and subsequent ones featured traditional leather jackets, pants, and dresses in neutral shades.

Joop in the 21st century featured fur-trimmed articles inspired by screen legends Greta Garbo and Marlene Dietrich. In an interview with Molly Knight, a fashion writer for www.fashion.com, Joop declared, "Dietrich was the best designer ever. She combined day and evening wear as well as men's and women's—it was the old glamor."

—Richard Martin; updated by Christine Miner Minderovic

JOSEPH

See ETTEDGUI, Joseph

JOURDAN, Charles

French footwear designer

Born: 1883. **Career:** Foreman at Établissements Grenier, shoe leather cutters, 1917; independent shoe manufacturer, 1919; Seducta, a luxury range, introduced in Romans sur Isère, France, 1921; extended distribution to all of France, in the 1930s; after World War II, sons Rene, Charles, and Roland took over factory, adding shoe lines in the mid-1940s; first Charles Jourdan women's boutique in Paris, 1957, and London, 1959; Dior contract with international distribution of shoes under Dior label, 1959; Perugia began designing for Jourdan in early 1960s; first New York boutique, 1968; created bags and ready-to-wear clothing line, 1970s; 21 franchises by 1975; firm continued after Jourdan's death, sons launched menswear and *Un Homme* fragrance in early 1980s; company bought by Portland Cement Werke in 1981, chief designer: Bernard Sucheras, outside designers commissioned including Hervé Leger for accessories, company specializes in shoes, leather goods, accessories, jewelry, scarves. **Exhibitions:** *Charles Jourdan: 70 Years,* Galeries Lafayette, Paris and The Space, Tokyo, both 1991. **Collections:** Musée de la Chaussure, Romans sur Isère, France; Charles Jourdan Museum, Paris, including 2000 creations by André Perugia. **Died:** 1976. **Company Address:** 28, Avenue de New York, 75116 Paris, France. **Company Website:** www.charles-jourdan.com.

Publications

On JOURDAN:

Books

Swann, June, *Shoes,* London, 1982.
Benaim, L., *L'année de la mode,* Paris, 1987.
McDowell, Colin, *Shoes, Fashion and Fantasy,* London, 1989.
Grumbach, D., *Histoires de la mode,* Paris, 1994.
Wilson, Eunice, *A History of Shoe Fashions,* Theatre Arts Books, n.d.

Articles

"Dateline Paris," *Footwear News* (New York), 15 April 1985.
Cohen, Edie Lee, "Charles Jourdan Monsieur," in *Interior Design,* September 1986.
"The Added Essence of Elegance: Charles Jourdan," *Elle* (London), September 1987.
"Flirtations of a High-Heeled Pump," *Vogue* (London), September 1987.
Pringle, C., "Quoi de neuf?," *Vogue* (Paris), October 1987.
"La couture a quatre mains," *Vogue* (Paris), August 1992.
Anniss, Elisa, "French Connection," *Shoe and Leather News,* November 1992.
"Le jeux de la métière," *Liberation* (Paris), March 1993.

* * *

Charles Jourdan, a shoe manufacturer, made the name Jourdan synonymous with couture by licensing and diversifying in the manner of the Paris haute couture houses. No other footwear company has so successfully marketed its image, and eight decades later Jourdan still symbolizes luxury, international fashion, and the best of couture.

The founder of the company, Charles Jourdan, was both a skilled craftsman and creative businessman. His aim was to produce shoes of quality, made with the best materials and the traditional skills of a *bottier.* He also recognized that many of these skills could be translated into the much larger ready-to-wear market, producing affordable luxury shoes. Jourdan believed in the power of advertising. As his business expanded during the 1930s he used a network of commercial travelers to introduce his brands across the whole of France, backing up this sales force with advertisement in popular magazines—a new concept at the time.

His styles were not trendsetting but their classic luxurious look succeeded. He produced perfectly handcrafted ladies shoes that could be worn in harmony with elegant outfits; not that these first simple styles were influenced by the direction of Parisian fashion. The only thing Jourdan had in common with his contemporaries Poiret, Schiaparelli, and Chanel, was that he also used only the finest materials. He did, however, benefit from the new higher hemline which raised the visibility of shoes, making them a much more important accessory in the modern woman's wardrobe.

The economic crisis of the 1930s, followed by the war, drastically affected the couture market, which could not cheapen its products. Jourdan, ever ready to diversify, recognized price was an important selling factor at all levels of the market, and he introduced new lines at lower prices. He sold to the newly emerging chain stores, and the Jourdan empire grew.

In the 1950s Jourdan's three sons began managing the business. The youngest son, Roland Jourdan, who was responsible for design and development, has been described as "the most able man in the shoe industry." He was fully aware that it was simplicity and quality, not wild innovation, that sold Jourdan shoes. When Jourdan's first boutique opened in Paris in 1957, Roland Jourdan only offered a small range of styles. But each style was available in 20 colors, all sizes, and three widths. At Jourdan, not only would the shoe fit, but it would also perfectly accessorize any shade of outfit.

The ultimate connection of the luxury shoe brand to haute couture came with the contract between Jourdan and the house of Christian Dior in 1959. Jourdan created, manufactured, and distributed shoe models for Dior worldwide; it was the ultimate seal of approval. The next two decades saw Jourdan at its most successful and creative—the company launched a series of seminal advertising campaigns that profoundly influenced both fashion and advertising. In the 1960s they commissioned Guy Bourdin, a young Parisian photographer, who produced a series of surreal, witty, and often visually stunning advertising photographs. The images usually had nothing to do with shoes, and the name "Charles Jourdan" appeared as a small caption in one corner. It is difficult now to imagine the impact of this campaign, but its success was such that for a time the brand became associated with a sense of innovation and modernity that the shoes themselves, perfect creations though they were, did not really possess.

The Jourdan boutique design helped perpetuate the company's innovative image. The ultra modern interiors and striking window displays of the first Paris boutique became a blueprint for a chain in every fashion capital of the world. It was the environment which created the Jourdan look, one extended at its peak in 1979 from neckties to sunglasses, allowing the dedicated customer to be completely Jourdan accessorized.

Jourdan achieved a level of product diversification unsurpassed in the footwear industry. Borrowing the haute couture strategies of licensing and franchising, and creating a global presence, Charles Jourdan became the couture accessory. This success attracted competition: new names such as Bruno Magli and Robert Clergerie were concentrating solely on footwear. The diversity that had made Jourdan so big suddenly threatened to dilute the brand name's exclusivity. Finally, the loyal customer base was growing older, and a new generation of women found alternative designers outside the classic couture mold.

In 1981 the family's dynastic control of the empire ended with the retirement of Roland Jourdan. The name and company survived and thrived, as true luxury would never be out of fashion. The continuing success of Jourdan, however, was also due to prescience—like bringing menswear into the fold in the early 1980s, and building a flagship store in New York City. In 1986, the town of Romans, France, paid tribute to the company and its founder through the dedication of a street, rue de Charles Jourdan.

In the 1990s, newer and younger lines were introduced yet still evincing the sleek, elegant style for which the Jourdan name is famous. The company went online with the Charles Jourdan website in 1997, one of the earliest couture houses to do so, and opened new boutiques in Australia, France, Germany, Israel, the Middle East, Russia, and the U.S. over the next two years. In 1999, the company redesigned its image and brand, creating an updated "visual identity" befitting the coming millennium. Charles Jourdan remains an important name in the fashion world, because its enduring strength is the recognition that what any man or woman really wants in shoewear or clothing, is the simply the perfect fit.

—Chris Hill; updated by Nelly Rhodes

JULIAN, Alexander

American designer

Born: Chapel Hill, North Carolina, 8 February 1948. **Education:** Graduated from the University of North Carolina, Chapel Hill, North Carolina, 1969; self-taught in design. **Family:** Married Lynn (divorced); married Meagan, 1987: children: Alystyre, Will. **Career:** Worked in his father's Chapel Hill menswear store to 1969; menswear designer/retailer with own store, Alexander's Ambition, Chapel Hill, 1969–75; founder/designer, Alexander Julian Company, New York, from 1975; showed first collection, 1975; introduced popular priced Colours by Alexander Julian line, 1981; launched womenswear line, 1983; Colours by Alexander Julian for Boys, and Watercolours simwear line, 1984; Colours girlswear and hosiery collection, 1984; introduced home furnishing line, 1985; Alexander Julian Enterprises men's couture line and Colours luggage collection, 1988; created fragrance for women, 1991; designed uniforms for the Charlotte (North Carolina) Hornets professional basketball team, 1988, and the Charlotte Knights semiprofessional baseball team, 1990; designed the Knights Stadium, 1990; licensed Windsong for sportswear worldwide and American Trouser for bottoms, 1996; expanded home furnishings, mid- to late 1990s; signed Couristan for rugs, 1997; signed tailored menswear license with PBM, 1998; rebranded main floor collection as Alexander Julian, removing "Colours" from the identity, 1999; rebranded home collection under Alexander Julian at Home, 2000; signed home décor deal with retailer Lowe's, 2000. **Awards:** Coty American Fashion Critics award, 1977, 1979, 1981, 1983, 1984; Cutty Sark award, 1980, 1985, 1988; Men's Woolknit Design award, 1981; Council of Fashion Designers of America award, 1981; Color Marketing Group's Forrest L. Dimmick award for Excellence in Color Marketing, 1998. **Address:** 63 Copps Hill Road, Ridgefield, CT 06877, USA.

PUBLICATIONS

On JULIAN:

Books

Stegemeyer, Anne, *Who's Who in Fashion, Third Edition,* New York, 1996.

Articles

Burggraf, Helen, "Profile: Alexander Julian," in *Men's Apparel News,* 6 January 1981.
Boyagian, Paula, "Alexander Julian," in *Fashion Retailer,* October 1983.
Schwatz, Tony, "Coats of Many Colors," in *New York,* 24 September 1984.
Fressola, Peter, "Alexander Julian," in *DNR,* 1 March 1988.
Barol, Bill, "Pastels on the Hardwood," in *Newsweek,* 3 October 1988.
"The Americans: Alexander Julian," in *DNR,* 15 August 1989.
Cameron, Victoria Pearson, "Why So Blue? (Men's Fashions)" in *Esquire,* March 1991.
Spevack, Rachel, "Julian's Colours Label Making a Comeback," in *DNR,* 6 February 1996.
Wyman, Lissa, "Julian for Couristan: Complete Home," in *HFN,* 14 July 1997.
"Big and Brights: A Designer and His Wife Play with Color and Scale in Their Hardworking Kitchen," in *Country Living,* November 1997.
Gellers, Stan, "Alexander Julian Now Colours PBM's Clothing World," in *DNR,* 23 November 1998.
Howell, Debbie, "Lowe's Signs Alexander Julian, Gives Home Décor Biz Big Push," in *Discount Store News,* 20 March 2000.

* * *

Alexander Julian stated his philosophy in his Colours collection, first launched in 1981: "I believe in men who want to dress in their own image and not according to any singular vision that would have all men appear alike."

Julian was born in Chapel Hill, North Carolina, and grew up in the retail environment of his father's shop, which Alexander managed from the age of 16. He moved to New York in 1975, winning the prestigious Coty Men's Wear award for the first time in 1977, and became the youngest designer to be included in the Coty Hall of Fame. Julian had citations on the U.S. International Best Dressed List for nine consecutive years and has won nearly all the most prestigious fashion design awards in the United States.

Julian was one of the first U.S. men's clothing designers to create his own exclusive fabrics by working with European mills and exploring a broad range of color with a special eye for innovative and unusual color effects. Since the launch of Colours by Alexander Julian in 1981, a well-priced collection reflecting the use of color and texture that had become Julian's signature on his couture menswear collection, the Colours range has expanded beyond menswear in the U.S. to include outerwear, furnishings, sleepwear, leather goods, belts, bed linens, eyewear, and women's and men's fragrances. Today the collections are a worldwide multimillion-dollar business, with licensees in Japan, Mexico, Canada, and the U.K., where the imaginative color palette, changing each season, is a novelty in British menswear.

Julian has designed uniforms for sports teams such as the Charlotte Hornets and North Carolina University Tar Heels basketball teams, and the uniforms, car colors, and crew clothes for the Newman Haas racing team, which is co-owned by Paul Newman. His clothes are worn by entertainment personalities such as Bill Cosby, Paul Newman, Tim Robbins, and jazz singer Harry Connick, Jr.

In 1992 Julian designed the clothes for all the male leads in Robert Altman's critically acclaimed movie *The Player,* creating a complex series of variations on the dress codes prevalent in the film industry. "What exists with most movie studios is that everyone tries to emulate the boss," states Julian, "and that's exactly what we did here." The personality of each character is played out in the color of his clothes: the style of jacket worn by all the male executives is identical, and as the narrative becomes more complex, the colors of the clothing worn by the main protagonist, played by Tim Robbins, change from green and gold to darker and darker colors as his situation changes. Additonally, Julian believes creative thinking in education should play a more significant role in children's learning development, and to this end he has set up the Alexander Julian Foundation for Aesthetic Understanding and Appreciation, which is helping to pioneer an experimental learning center in the United States.

Julian is one of the few menswear designers to successfully make the jump into home furnishings. Products for the home, from rugs and wallpaper to lamps and upholstered furniture, are marketed under the Alexander Julian at Home banner. Home décor has been his fast-growing business segment through the mid- to late 1990s and into the early 2000s, accounting for about 40 percent of revenues at the turn of the century. In 2000, Julian signed a deal for a range of home decorating products, including paint, carpeting, window treatments, countertops, and flooring, to be sold in the Lowe's do-it-yourself retail chain. Many of the products were available in other retail channels as well.

Julian favors a comfortable and casual style in the home, and his designs and color palette reflect the "modern traditional" identity of his menswear. In both areas of his business, he focuses on vibrant, mix-and-match colors and patterns and employs highly textured fabrics. The look of his upholstery mirrors the stripes, ties, and polka dots familiar from his ties and shirts; while his rugs are in the plaids and paisleys his customers know from his jackets and accessories. Julian's interior designs can also be viewed in public places, such as a baseball stadium he designed in Charlotte, North Carolina, and a restaurant in Westport, Connecticut.

In menswear and at home, Julian advocates flexibility, such as designing suits with jackets that can double as sports coats. The designer's menswear business underwent some changes in the late 1990s and early 2000s; he reassigned his tailored clothing license to Pincus Bros.-Maxwell (PBM) and simplified his main floor collection under the Alexander Julian name, deemphasizing the "Colours" label in that sector. He also continues to sign new licensees; the Alexander Julian brand encompasses all price tiers and customer segments within his core home furnishings and menswear markets. In addition to tailored apparel and home furnishings, others in his group of manufacturers market casual clothing, neckwear, fragrances, eyewear, and accessories.

Julian's strategy has been to bring a high-quality product to market at a fair price. He has been able to successfully walk the line between offering a creative, differentiated product and one that is commercially viable.

—Doreen Ehrlich; updated by Karen Raugust

K

KAHNG, Gemma

American designer

Born: Masan, Korea, 21 May 1954; immigrated to the U.S., 1969. **Education:** Graduated from the Art Institute of Chicago, 1979. **Family:** Married Charles Chang-Lima in 1984 (divorced, 1994). **Career:** Design assistant, Cathy Hardwick, New York, 1981–84; designed freelance before establishing own business, 1989. **Address:** 224 Centre Street, New York, NY 0013, USA.

Gemma Kahng, fall 1997 collection. © Fashion Syndicate Press.

Publications

On KAHNG:

Articles

Bizer, Karen, "A Designing Couple," in *WWD,* 22 July 1988.

Hartlein, Robert, "Gemma Kahng Emerges on Her Own," in *WWD,* 23 August 1989.

Staples, Kate, "The Kahng Formation," in *WWD,* 1 April 1991.

Darnton, Nina, "The New York Brat Pack: Their Clothes Are Coming Soon to a Closet Near You," in *Newsweek,* 29 April 1991.

Schiro, Anne-Marie, "With Help, Gemma Kahng's Star Soars," in the *New York Times,* 5 May 1991.

Saeks, Diane Dorrans, "Gemma's Jewels," in *West,* 16 June 1991.

Phillips, Barbara D., "Gemma Kahng: Paper Dolls to Haute Couture," in the *Wall Street Journal,* 6 August 1991.

Servin, James, "How I Got That Look: The Exotic Route," in *Allure,* June 1993.

"New York: Gemma Kahng," in *WWD,* 4 November 1994.

"Kahng Sets Secondary Line of Sportswear for Nordstrom," in *WWD,* 24 May 1996.

White, Constance C. R., "Patterns: Gemma Kahng Retrenches," in the *New York Times,* 30 December 1997.

"Hot Copy: Kid Luxe Update: Gemma Kahng," in *Children's Business,* April 1999.

*

The inspiration for each of my collections comes from my desire to create clothing that is sexy, witty, glamorous, comfortable, and most importantly, practical. I reflect on my own personality and lifestyle and think of things I would like to wear and what I need to expand my wardrobe.

Each of my collections begins with high-quality fabrics, an important tool for good design. Mostly I choose wools, silks, cottons, and linens that are luxurious yet basic, so that my design aesthetic becomes more prominent than the fabric itself. The details of clothing from the historical past are a good influence for my ideas. I am fascinated by the cultures of different time periods, especially the Victorian era, and find it challenging to combine them with the look of today.

This design sensibility appeals to my customer, a consistently busy woman who doesn't have the time to experiment with her image. She is a person who has enough confidence to incorporate a sense of humor in her style and can rely on my clothing and accessories for a complete look. Over the past five years, my image has become recognizable throughout the United States and is rapidly growing in foreign markets, especially in Hong Kong and Taipei where I have freestanding boutiques.

Gemma Kahng, fall 1997 collection. © Fashion Syndicate Press.

My goal is to perfect upon what it is that my customers like about my clothing and create something new. Design is a growing process and each season I experiment further by bringing more of my self-expression to a collection. What makes it exciting for me is the challenge and risk involved in taking the next step. No one can tell me what to bring to the future. I just have to be aware of the everyday world we live in.

—Gemma Kahng

* * *

"She's a lot like her designs," wrote Barbara Phillips of the *Wall Street Journal* in August 1991 of Gemma Kahng, "a winning mix of playfulness and practicality, forthrightness, and charm." Kahng's fashion design is practical, but at the same time, the chief trait of her work is to render a classic idea slightly askew or fresh with a theme of whimsy, exaggeration, or notice. The charm of the work is its perturbed normality: it is all just right but for that one eccentricity or detail that seems gloriously juvenile or marvelously anomalous in the template of a traditional garment.

Kahng's clothing is undeniably serious, addressed paramountly to an American working woman of some means, but always with a note of self-expression. Buttons can be almost as whimsical as those of Schiaparelli; pockets are unexpectedly given colorful flaps in accent colors; and pockets bounce with asymmetry. Schiaparelli is Kahng's soulmate in fashion history, not for the flamboyant garment but rather for those most restrained tailored suits that Schiaparelli created with nuanced absurdities and minor amazements. Kahng's identifying style resides in such quirky twists on classics, attention inevitably being drawn to the garment by an outstanding detail, but restrained in every other aspect of the composition.

Kahng works closely with her former husband, Charles Chang-Lima, who helms his own well-respected design line. For many years, Kahng worked out of Manhattan's Seventh Avenue garment district in New York, keeping production within the neighborhood rather than seeking large-scale production elsewhere. It is a matter for Kahng of quality and control; by keeping production local, she is attempting to guarantee production standards by watching the process, an old tradition of the garment industry now abandoned by many bigger companies. It is a working philosophy she has continued, even after her office moved to SoHo. Of course, there may be a reason for a designer not born in the U.S. to appraise American traditions and Western dress with a reasoning, potentially ironic eye. Kahng recalls that in her Korean childhood there were no store-bought dolls and that she had to fantasize and create clothing for her paper dolls.

"Classic with a twist" is a conventional goal of many young designers who take a minimal risk in construction and allow one lovely or bizarre note to make a memorable difference. The concept, however, is difficult to carry out, as one disturbance from the norm can seem to be an unwelcome aberration, especially in clothing that depends upon our sense of recognition of formality. Kahng has demonstrated an unusually sure and decisive sense of distorting or contributing enough in the gesture of discrepancy but without destroying the practical validity of the garment. When a tweed jacket is trimmed with red, the effect is at first of the most diabolically arresting house-painting on the block, but the combination settles into a rather winsome palette of clothing for the hunt. A pea jacket modified by horses on the pockets and jeweled buttons on the front ensures it will not be worn by Popeye, but deliberately softens the military regimen into a feminine and whimsical jacket. The anomaly for Kahng is never mere kitsch or cuteness: it is a feature that alters our perception (whether color or content) of the entire garment, an abnormality making us see the normal in a wholly new way.

Kahng departed somewhat from her established style in the late 1990s as she began to refocus both her design and her business strategy. While retaining her signature decorative accents, Kahng's designs and fabrics became softer and more delicate. Aside from moving her office to SoHo, she scaled down her staff and reduced the number of pieces in her new collections. Kahng also placed her couture line as well as her more affordably priced clothing in several high-end department stores under various labels. The designer ventured into the children's market in 1999 and also helped design the costumes and sets for fellow Korean American Margaret Cho's acclaimed one-woman performance piece.

From her emergence in the late 1980s, Kahng has stayed true to her proven and effective design statement; never unduly impulsive, the design is nonetheless different and enchantingly whimsical: Kahng honors the great traditions in dress and yet gives a happy surprise with each garment.

—Richard Martin; updated by Megan Stacy

KAISERMAN, Bill

American designer

Born: Brooklyn, New York, 8 September 1942. **Education:** Studied drama; no formal training in design. **Family:** Married Millie, 1971. **Career:** Millinery designer under the label Rafael; formed joint venture with Onward Kashiyama Co., 1989–92; launched independent label, WJK, to show menswear collection, 1992. **Awards:** Coty American Fashion Critics award, 1974, 1975, 1976, 1978; elected to Coty Hall of Fame, 1976; Hall of Fame citation, 1978. **Address:** Via Manzoni 43, Milan, Italy.

Publications

On KAISERMAN:

Books

Lambert, Eleanor, *The World of Fashion,* New York, 1976.

Morris, Bernadine, and Barbara Walz, *The Fashion Makers,* New York, 1978.

Khornak, Lucille, *Fashion 2001,* New York, 1982.

Articles

Hyde, Nina, "Bill Kaiserman, Putting His Shoulder to the Wheel," in the *Washington Post,* 7 December 1986.

"Tanned Blond and Dresses to the Hilt: We Must be in Milan," in the *Chicago Tribune,* 14 March 1990.

Marisa Fox, "Designers Sing a Soprano Tune for Fall," in the *Chicago Tribune,* 7 February 2000.

* * *

Bill Kaiserman has had success in the fields of menswear and womenswear. With no formal design training, he began his career as a salesperson in a men's clothing shop. While there, he started designing hats and sold them under the label Rafael. He was soon producing suede and leatherwear to complement the millinery. Cashmere sweaters and silk shirts were added, together with the safari suit—a revolutionary new shape in menswear establishing the concept of the leisure suit and leisure dressing for men.

Kaiserman's menswear success led him to produce ranges of womenswear, still under the label of Rafael. Beginning with tailored clothes, his look gradually became softer and more casual, evolving into a sophisticated daywear look, made to high standards in luxurious, discerning fabrics and colors. Produced in Italy, his clothes came to represent the best standards in American fashion.

Kaiserman cited his customers as being between 30 and 45, who wanted to look young and well dressed without resorting to the extremes of teenage fashion. As a menswear and womenswear designer, he has noted the marked difference in designing for both sexes. With womenswear, the approach is more creative and free. An idea can often be realized to its full potential, whereas with menswear, an imaginative idea often has to be restrained: "There are just a few shapes that are acceptable, there is less room for fantasy," he has said. He believes men should not look too formal, styled, or contrived. Women, on the other hand, look fabulous when the body shape is emphasized and exaggerated.

Amply recognized for his contribution to American fashion, Kaiserman has received several Coty awards and a Hall of Fame citation for his contribution to menswear. He and his wife Millie both declared themselves fitness and health fanatics. Kaiserman confessed he often gets design ideas when lifting weights and has joked that if he never made it as the world's biggest international designer, he would certainly be the strongest.

It is ultimately his menswear concept that was Kaiserman's greatest contribution to fashion. His leisurewear opened up greater boundaries for menswear design as a whole, and his leisure suit became a liberated classic for many men. He chose the name Rafael because he thought it would look better in print than his own; ironically, his name as a designer eclipsed the label he chose to represent his product.

In the 1980s, Kaiserman disappeared from the fashion industry, closing Rafael and moving to Italy. "My business had gotten too big for me to handle," he told Nina Hyde of the *Washington Post.* "I was spending 90 percent of my time trying to run a business and 10 percent designing, if that." He told Hyde that fashion's social scene, including parties and drugs, were "choking me to death." After about five years on hiatus from the business, Kaiserman eased his way back into designing by producing lines for other companies. In 1985 he signed an agreement to design womenswear for the upscale label Cache, founded in 1975. "His talent is superb," said Cache president Mitchell Rubinson. "His style is certainly compatible with the typical Cache client who is sophisticated and fashion-aware."

Kaiserman told Hyde that his ideal garment structure had changed a bit over the years. "What I care about is enough structure in the clothes to enhance the shape of the body," he said. "No one has a perfect body without a little help."

Returning to the Milan fashion scene with the backing of clothing conglomerate Kashiyama & Company, a licensee of menswear from Ralph Lauren and Calvin Klein, the new Kaiserman menswear was not always as well received as his Rafael clothing. Suits and jackets were looser and proportioned differently; critics and clients alike seemed to yearn for Kaiserman designs from decades ago. A former assistant, however, Michael Savoia, turned heads with his debut menswear collection in New York in 2000. The well-tailored suits harked back to Kaiserman's crisp and classic Rafael clothing so popular in the 1970s and 1980s.

—Kevin Almond; updated by Lisa Groshong

KAMALI, Norma

American designer

Born: Norma Arraes in New York City, 27 June 1945. **Education:** Studied fashion illustration at Fashion Institute of Technology, New York, 1961–64. **Family:** Married Mohammed (Eddie) Houssein Kamali in 1967 (divorced, 1972). **Career:** Freelance fashion illustrator, New York, 1965–66; airline reservation clerk, 1966–67; freelance fashion designer and partner, with Eddie Kamali, Kamali Fashion Imports, New York, 1967–78; opened first retail store, Kamali, in New York, 1968; established OMO (On My Own) Norma Kamali boutiques in New York, from 1978; ready-to-wear line introduced,

Norma Kamali standing in her Manhatten showroom with part of her spring 1997 line, featuring silkscreens of Mahatma Ghandi. © AP/Wide World Photos.

1981; produced sportswear for Jones Apparel Group, 1981; children's sportswear for Empire Shield Group, 1982; sportswear for Renown Corporation, Japan, 1983; costume designer for the Emerald City in *The Wiz,* 1983; designed and opened Norma Kamali Building, New York, 1983; bags and footwear for Vittorio Ricci, 1983–84, headwear for Stetson, 1983, and belts for Raymon Ridless, 1985; signature fragrance collection introduced, 1985; OMO home collection introduced, 1988; (800) 8-KAMALI line of casual wear introduced, 1993; cosmetics line introduced, 1994; produced and directed *Fall Fantasy* video; costume designer for three Twyla Tharp dance performances *(The Upper Room, Sweet Fields, Route 66),* 1995–96; commencement speaker for Fiftieth Anniversary of the Fashion Institute of Technology, 1995; Kamali website created, 1996; broadcasted Fall 1996 collection as virtual reality experience over the Internet, 1996; Internet shopping service "Shop Like a Celebrity" introduced, 1998; created New York Public Schools website (www.nycpublicschoolart4U2c.com) to exhibit student artwork, fashion, and poetry, 1998; Living Rubber collection introduced, 1999; website evolved into a directory of seven linked sites, 2000; business opportunity for local representatives of NK Jersey line introduced, 2000. **Exhibitions:** Parachute designs displayed at Metropolitan Museum of Art, New York, 1977. **Awards:** Coty American Fashion Critics award, 1981, 1982, 1983; Council of Fashion Designers of America award, 1982, 1985; Fashion Institute of Design and Merchandising award, Los Angeles, 1984; Fashion Group award, 1986; Distinguished Architecture award from New York Chapter of American Institute of Architects; Outstanding Graduate award from the Public Education Association of New York; award of merit, Video Culture International Competition; American Success award from the Fashion Institute of Technology in New York, 1989; Washington Irving High School's Hall of Fame for distinguished alumni, 1997; Youth Friends award, 1997; Pencil award, 1999; Willow award from Lower East Side Girls' Club, 1999; Fashion Outreach Style award, 1999. **Address:** Norma Kamali Building, 11 West 56th Street, New York, New York 10019, USA. **Website:** www.OMO-norma-kamali.com.

Publications

By KAMALI:

Articles

"Fashion," in the *New York Times,* 1 January 1989.

Norma Kamali, spring 1998 collection: wedding gown made of parachute nylon. © AP/Wide World Photos.

On KAMALI:

Books

Diamonstein, Barbaralee, *Fashion: The Inside Story,* New York, 1985.
Milbank, Caroline Rennolds, *Couture: The Great Designers,* New York, 1985.
Perschetz, Lois, ed., *W, The Designing Life,* New York, 1987.
Milbank, Caroline Rennolds, *New York Fashion: The Evolution of American Style,* New York, 1989.
Stegemeyer, Anne, *Who's Who in Fashion, Third Edition,* New York, 1996.

Articles

"Norma Kamali Talks to Sarah Montague," in *Ritz* (London), No. 25, 1978.
"The Kamali Effect," in *Vogue,* June 1982.
Krupp, C. "Reluctant Fashion Guru," in *Glamour,* September 1982.
"Working Seventh Avenue Has Been No Sweat for Fashion's Greta Garbo," in *People,* 27 December 1982.
Radakovich, Anka, "Hot Kamali's 'Kicky' Clothes," in *Apparel News* (New York), April 1984.
Talley, André Leon, "True Wit: The Zany World of Norma Kamali," in *Vogue,* November 1984.
"Norma Kamali: An Interview with the Fashion Video Pioneer," in *Back Stage,* 14 November 1986.
"Shirting the Issue: Norma Kamali," in *Self* (New York), November 1988.
Hamilton, William L., "The State of the Shape: Va-va-voom," in *Metropolitan Home* (New York), April 1989.
Schiro, Anne-Marie, "Pastels at the Plaza, Cowgirls in the Park," in the *New York Times,* 31 October 1989.
"The Designers Talk Passion, Whimsy, and Picassos," in *ARTnews* (New York), September 1990.
Schiro, Anne-Marie, "A Spectrum for Spring, Hot to Cool," in the *New York Times,* 31 October 1990.
Brubach, Holly, "In Fashion: On the Beach," in the *New Yorker,* 2 September 1991.
Schiro, Anne-Marie, "Patterns," in the *New York Times,* 4 August 1992.
———, "For Evening Wear, Various Degrees of Retro," in the *New York Times,* 31 March 1993.
"That Vargas Vamp," in *American Photo* (New York), March/April 1993.
Gandee, Charles, "Hot Kamali," in *Vogue,* April 1993.
La Ferla, Ruth, "Mode: Norma Kamali," in *Elle* (Paris), July 1993.
White, Constance, "Some Age Gracefully," in the *New York Times,* 31 October 1995.
Colman, David, "Norma Kamali Cleans House," in the *New York Times,* 22 February 1996.
Schiro, Anne-Marie, "Three Clear Signatures," in the *New York Times,* 28 March 1996.
White, Constance, "Norma Kamali Aids Students," in the *New York Times,* 11 February 1997.
———, "Eccentricity is the Key to Invention," in the *New York Times,* 9 April 1997.
———, "Definitive Lauren, Ingenious Kamali," in the *New York Times,* 2 April 1998.
"Norma Kamali," in *Current Biography Yearbook,* November 1998.
Luther, Marylou, "Kamali Meets Fans on Line," in the *New York Times,* 5 January 1999.
Crow, Kelly, "Mere Bits of Skimpy Plastic are Hits at Sample Sale Day," in the *New York Times,* 2 July 2000.
Bellafante, Ginia, "Kamali, Inspired by Kamali," in the *New York Times,* 14 November 2000.

* * *

In a highly original way, Norma Kamali has been designing with uncanny foresight for the modern woman's multifaceted lifestyle. The sensational success of her sweatshirt-fleece fabric line in 1981 brought Kamali clothes into the mainstream, while she continued to design experimental, one-of-a-kind fashions for wealthier clients. The mass produced sweats offered good design in comfortable clothes, with a touch of the eye-catching elements that have distinguished Kamali. Inspired by the late 1960s British clothes she brought back from England to sell in the New York Norma Kamali boutique—the retro Biba clothing of Barbara Hulanicki in particular—Kamali began offering her own designs to keep up with the demand. When she opened her New York OMO (On My Own) boutique in 1978 after her divorce, Kamali symbolized all newly independent women.

As early as 1972 Kamali designed bathing suits according to her own vision: gold lamé maillots, structured or spare bikinis, decorated or plain, introducing the then-startling high-thigh styles with cutouts to show off a well-toned body–beach fashions that became mainstream as the 1980s progressed. In the late 1960s Kamali was credited with the hot pants craze. A sense of playfulness combined rhinestones with stretch leotard material, pleasing the celebrities who patronized the Madison Avenue store. In 1974 Kamali changed to a more refined look, lacy and delicate, specializing in well-made suits and dresses.

It was in the West Side OMO store that Kamali came into her own. Cozy down-filled coats became popular after she introduced them, spurred by the necessity of sleeping in a sleeping bag after her divorce. Drawstringed jumpsuits made of colorful parachute material resulted in her inclusion in the *Vanity Fair* Exhibition at the Costume Institute of the Metropolitan Museum of Art. She showed draped 1930s-styled jerseys, and exaggerated broad shoulders on garments from coats to sweatshirt dresses to evening gowns, always a little before her time. She also utilized suede in bright colors before it became trendy. Kamali 1950s-style "Ethel Mertz" dresses were fabricated in plaid flannel, certainly different than anything else on the streets in the early 1980s. Her short cheerleader skirts were the first popular miniskirts in a decade. Dramatic lamé accents appeared on special occasion sweats and she designed sweatshirting for children.

Kamali epitomized the shy person who allowed her clothes to speak for her, yet there has always been an inner strength leading to her successful business enterprises and the willingness to take risks. Using her boutique as an atelier, Kamali has been producing one-of-a-kind garments from unusual fabrics in versatile shapes to be worn in a number of ways. She was one of the first to present unitards or bodysuits as serious fashion staples. As in French couture, Kamali listens to her customers, on whom she has waited in person in her boutique, to get their honest opinions. She has described herself as relying upon intuition, taking inspiration from the street, but making it her own as if in a creative trance. Her credo has been to make the functional aspects of clothing attractive, taking inspiration from the unique qualities of each fabric, always designing for the woman who will wear the clothes.

Kamali launched a modern collection of interchangeable pieces that blended as quickly as the modern woman's lifestyle in 1995. The collection featured a wardrobe made from a revolutionary polyester jersey fabric Kamali described as "soft as silk but strong as steel jersey." Highly suitable for travel, the collection, the NK Jersey Line, emphasized wrinkle-free and machine-washable comfort in black, red, or white. This line kicked off a wave of practicality and a less-is-more attitude. In 1996 Kamali purged many of her personal belongings and furniture in an auction, banned black from her new collection and wardrobe, and looked forward to the new millennium. The star ensemble of the fall collection featured a dark-brown velvet jacket over a yellow chiffon shirt and gunmetal leather pants. Improvements and ingenuity defined her designs for the remainder of the 21st century. Her ever-faithful 1970s silk parachute coat was modernized in a more practical nylon in colors reminiscent of military gear, and she maintained a standard of ensuring even her most luxurious European-styled designs remained wearable and unique.

Throughout her career Kamali has inspired other designers, and has been considered one of the most original designers in New York. She has brought the inventiveness that used to be allowed only in couture salons to versions affordable to working women, although many of her more exclusive designs remain high-priced. Kamali has also introduced revolutionary marketing techniques to fashion merchandising. Twenty-four hours a day, fashion videos play in the windows of OMO. Unlike ordinary catwalk videotapes, Kamali videos are actually minimovies, often as long as 30 minutes, with storylines and character development, showing various situations in which Kamali fashions might be worn. Kamali also advertised through the use of billboards and by staging fashion shows in New York's Central Park. By 1993 she was offering a toll-free number for ordering her new lower-priced label, while retaining the OMO Norma Kamali label for her expensive line.

But it was in 1996 marketing embarked on a high-tech journey to move OMO into the new millennium. The Internet became the runway for a virtual-reality simultaneous-broadcast of Kamali's fall 1996 collection. Later in the year the company website (www.omo-norma-kamali.com) was created, featuring Kamali's (800) 8-KAMALI collection, a direct marketing service called "Shop Like a Celebrity" which provides clients with a personal shopper and purchasing ease, and a business opportunity for individuals interested in becoming a local representative of the NK Jersey Line.

As OMO evolved into a 21st century marketplace, Norma Kamali continues to inspire. She has adopted the role of mentor and educator. Since 1997 Kamali has organized art students from her alma mater, Washington Irving High School, to develop a business for teaching art and commerce. She also set up an avenue for New York Public School students to exhibit their artwork, fashion, and poetry on a website (www.nycpublicschoolart4u2c.com).

Kamali clothes remain timeless in evoking past fashion eras while representing a modern outlook in interpretation, use of new materials, and technology. Back in 1991 Kamali presented bell-bottomed trousers, then scoffed at by the fashion press, which became standard in the revival of the 1970s. She herself revived her own fake leopard print coats to combine in the eclectic individualistic mood of the late 1990s with other garments having vintage and ethnic overtones. Soft flowing floral tunics, Edwardian and 1930s detailing, hip-huggers, lace dresses all in spirit with the times denote the experimentation that has always been the hallmark of Kamali's style and has at last caught up with her fashion forward attitude. Shiny Lurex bathing suits feature underwire cups and a direction toward a more covered-up look in response to the new consciousness about the dangers of sunlight. Her own best model, Kamali epitomizes the 1940s vamp, a characteristically classic expression of her aesthetic: she has made self-expression seductive.

—Therese Duzinkiewicz Baker; updated by Jody Essey-Stapleton

KAPLAN, Jacques

French fur designer

Born: Paris, 1924. **Career:** Joined father's furrier business (founded in Paris, 1889) on its move to New York, 1942; company bought by the Kenton Corporation, and Kaplan retired, 1971.

Jacques Kaplan, 1968 collection: calfskin jacket with initials stenciled on it. © AP/Wide World Photos.

PUBLICATIONS

On KAPLAN:

Articles

Richardson, John, "Fauve Country," in *House & Garden,* February 1992.

* * *

"One of the few means of self expression left today is fashion," Jacques Kaplan told Grace Glueck of the *New York Times* in the 1960s, and in many ways Kaplan used fashion as a canvas to express many innovative new ideas.

Kaplan's business had originated with his grandparents who founded a fur business in Paris in 1889. The business moved to New York in 1942 and Kaplan eventually became the chairman and chief designer

Jacques Kaplan, 1968 collection: fox parka. © AP/Wide World Photos.

for the house. His exuberant, lively personality soon elevated the company to its status as the biggest volume fur business in the United States.

Fur coats had long established themselves as a luxury item in fashion. Stylistically their image was somewhat stately, grand, and status conscious. Kaplan pioneered the concept of "fun furs" in unusual pelts, or fake fur, fur dresses, skirts, boots and hoods, all of which helped attract a younger, more fashion-conscious clientèle. He introduced stenciled and colored furs, and for a 1963 promotional campaign, he commissioned five avant-garde artists to paint fur coats. Marisol painted a pink nude, whilst Richard Auszkiewicz did an Op Art arrangement on calfskin.

Kaplan's philosophy was that bizarre or arty antics help to promote and sell furs. With his ranch mink coats retailing at a highly profitable $4,500 in the mid-1960s this entrepreneurial attitude certainly helped. He also found ways, however, to bring down the price of fur: in 1961 he produced a cheaper version of a black-dyed ranch mink, made famous by Jackie Kennedy. In a similar stylish, yet spare silhouette, with horizontally worked pelts, made from Japanese mink, the coats sold for $1,000 each. Kaplan was also known to stage fun fur shows in art galleries and was the first to admit he drove to work on a Honda motor scooter and underwent psychoanalysis that helped him come to terms with the idiosyncrasies of the fashion business.

In acknowledgement of the growing antifur movements in the socially aware 1960s, the company was one of the first to take a stand against the use of fur from endangered species. Kaplan himself said, "Twenty years ago I used to hate to be a furrier, I thought it was the lowest degree socially." He had learned to love the trade, though, and acquired a great deal of creative fulfillment from his role.

In the late 1960s the company was bought by the Kenton Corporation, and when they wished to sell it in the 1970s Kaplan decided to leave fashion and pursue his interests in art and painting.

—Kevin Almond

KARAN, Donna

American designer

Born: Donna Faske in Forest Hills, New York, 2 October 1948. **Education:** Studied at Parsons School of Design, New York. **Family:** Married Mark Karan, 1973 (divorced); married Stephan Weiss, 1977 (died 2001); children: Gabrielle, Lisa, Cory. **Career:** Assistant designer, Anne Klein & Co., and Addenda Company, New York, 1967–68; designer, Anne Klein, 1968–71; designer and director of design in association with Louis Dell'Olio, Anne Klein & Co., 1974–84; launched Anne Klein II diffusion line, 1982; designer, Donna Karan New York (DKNY), from 1985; added swimwear line, 1986; introduced hosiery collection, 1987; established DKNY bridge line, 1988; introduced DKNY menswear collection, 1991; founded Donna Karan Beauty Company, fragrance and cosmetic division, New York, 1992; introduced lingerie and children's line, DKNY Kids, from 1992; took company public, 1996; introduced new fragrance, *Chaos,* 1996; opened stores in Berlin, 1997; licensed DKNY Kids to Esprit, 1998; licensed timepieces collection and debuted fragrances *DKNY Men, DKNY Women*, 1999; introduced DKNY swimwear and Donna Karan Home, 2000; opened 10,000-square-foot DKNY store on Madison Avenue, 2001. **Awards:** Coty American Fashion Critics award, 1977, 1981, 1984, 1985; Fashion Footwear Association of New York award, 1988; Council of Fashion Designers of America award, 1985, 1986, 1990, 1992, 1996; Honorary Degree, Bachelor of Fine Arts, Parsons School of Design, 1987; named to Fashion Designer Walk of Fame, I. Magnin, 1991; Woolmark award, 1992. **Address:** 550 Seventh Avenue, New York, NY 10018, U.S.A.

Publications

On KARAN:

Books

Morris, Bernadine, and Barbara Walz, *The Fashion Makers,* New York, 1978.

Diamonstein, Barbaralee, *Fashion: The Inside Story,* New York, 1985.

Perschetz, Lois, ed., *W, The Designing Life,* New York, 1987.

Coleridge, Nicholas, *The Fashion Conspiracy,* London, 1988.

Steele, Valerie, *Women of Fashion: Twentieth-Century Designers,* New York, 1991.

Stegemeyer, Anne, *Who's Who in Fashion, Third Edition,* New York, 1996.

Donna Karan, fall 2001 collection. © Reuters NewMedia Inc./ CORBIS.

Le Dortz, Laurent, and Béatrice Debosscher, *Stratégies des leaders américains de la mode: Calvin Klein, Donna Karan, Liz Clairborne, Polo Ralph Lauren, et Tommy Hilfiger,* Paris, 2000.

Articles

"Cue: Designing Women—Donna Karan," in *Vogue* (London), September 1985.

Infantino, Vivian, "Interview: Donna Karan," in *Footwear News,* July 1986.

Gottfried, Carolyn, "In Conversation: Donna Karan and Joan Burstein...," in *Vogue* (London), October 1986.

Jobey, Liz, "Designing Women," in *Vogue* (London), July 1987.

Mansfield, Stephanie, "Prima Donna," in *Vogue* (New York), August 1989.

Conant, Jennet, "The New Queen of New York," in *Manhattan, Inc.,* October 1989.

Chubb, Ann, "Donna Karan," in *Options* (London), August 1990.

Weisman, Katherine, "Designing Woman," in *Forbes,* 1 October 1990.

Cihlar, Kimberly, "Donna's Man," in *DNR,* 12 April 1991.

White, Constance C.R., "Donna Karan: Talking Bridge," in *WWD,* 11 September 1991.

———, "DKNY: A Home of Its Own," in *WWD,* 12 February 1992.

Born, Pete, "Karan Fashions a Fragrance," in *WWD,* 1 May 1992.

Howell, Georgina, "Donna's Prime Time," in *Vogue,* August 1992.

Ducas, June, "Prima Donna," in *Women's Journal* (London), November 1992.

Rudolph, Barbara, "Donna Inc.," in *Time,* 21 December 1992.

Myerson, Allen R., "Partners at Odds, Donna Karan to Go Public," in the *New York Times,* 14 August 1993.

Cosgrave, Bronwyn, "Donna Karan Crosses the Atlantic," in *Élan* magazine of the *European* (London), 12–14 August 1994.

Beckett, Kathleen, "Slip-Sliding to a Close: Donna Karan," in the *New York Post,* 5 November 1994.

Spindler, Amy M., "Klein and Karan: Clothes That Do the Job," in the *New York Times,* 5 November 1994.

———, "Luxurious Armor by Karan, Klein, Mizrahi," in the *New York Times,* 8 April 1995.

"Donna Krishna," in *WWD,* 10 April 1995.

Rutberg, Sidney, "Donna Does It for Fall and Prepares an IPO for Imminent Delivery," in *WWD,* 3 April 1996.

"Donna Does It Today, Making Wall St. Bow with Stock Set at $24," in *WWD,* 28 June 1996.

Drier, Melissa, "Donna Karan: Global Retailer," in *WWD,* 24 April 1997.

Socha, Miles, "Esprit de Corp., Donna Karan Ink DKNY Kids License Deal," in *WWD,* 26 Feburary 1998.

Slott, Mira, "Retailers Ready for Donna Karan Home," in *Home Textiles Today,* 2 October 2000.

"Donna Karan: A Recent History," in *WWD,* 19 December 2000.

Deeny, Godfrey, "Post-Nuclear Donna," in *Fashion Wire Daily,* 16 February 2001.

Limnander, Armand, "Donna Karan," in *Style.com* (New York), 16 February 2001.

Singer, Sally, "Love Story," in *Vogue,* August 2001.

"Donna's Passion Play," in *DNR,* 27 August 2001.

"Donna Karan," in *Interview,* September 2001.

* * *

Donna Karan can be considered the designer who has made it fashionable to be voluptuous. She has based her corporate philosophy on clothes designed to hug a woman but also hide bodily imperfections. "You've gotta accent your positive, delete your negative," she declared in a press release, emphasizing the fact that if you're pulled together underneath, you can build on top of that. Karan firmly relates designing to herself and her role as a woman. She sees design as a personal expression of the many roles she has had to balance, being a wife, mother, friend, and businessperson. She believes her sex has given her greater insight into solving problems women have with fashion, fulfilling their needs, simplifying dress to make life easier and to add comfort, luxury, and durability.

Originating as a womenswear label, the Karan company also produces menswear, childrenswear, accessories, beauty products, and a fragrance that perpetrate the lifestyle and philosophy instigated by the womenswear line. Donna Karan stresses that she has not drawn the line there. "There's so much to be done. DKNY underwear,

Donna Karan, fall 2001 collection: savage shearling wrap jacket with a jersey wrap skirt. © AP/Wide World Photos.

swimwear, home furnishings…the designs are already in my head, it's just a matter of getting them executed."

Karan was born and raised on Long Island, New York. Both her mother and father were involved in fashion careers, so it seemed inevitable she should follow in their footsteps. After two years studying fashion at Parsons School of Design in New York, she was hired by Anne Klein for a summer job. She later became an associate designer until Klein died in 1974. Her next lucky break was to shape the rest of her career. She was named successor to Anne Klein and together with Louis Dell'Olio, who joined the company a year later, designed the Klein collection.

Shortly after the launch of the diffusion line, Anne Klein II, in 1982, Karan felt ready to go it alone. Together with her husband, Stephen Weiss, she launched the first Donna Karan collection in 1985 and since then the company has grown at a dizzying pace. Karan is inspired by New York; she believes its energy, pace, and vibrance attracts the most sophisticated and artistic people in the world, the type of people and lifestyle for whom she has always designed. Her principle is that clothes should be interchangeable and flexible enough to go from day to evening, summer to winter. Fashion should be a multicultural language, easy, sensuous, and functional, a modern security blanket. Perhaps this explains why her fundamental trademark items, the bodysuits, unitards, black cashmere and stretch fabrics and sensuous bodywrap styles owe great allegiance to the innate style and taste of the artist.

There is a great sense of urgency about Donna Karan; to say there are not enough hours in a day would be an understatement. Her interviews are always frenetic, emotionally charged yet human and blatantly honest. When asked by journalist Sally Brampton to describe her life, she replied, "It's chaos, C.H.A.O.S." Karan's magic touch is a combination of creative flair and marketing know-how. She designs for human needs, people who live, work, and play. She conceptualizes a customer and wardrobe and can then merchandise a line, applying her designer's eye for color, proportion, and fit. In many ways she is like a contemporary American Chanel in that she analyses women's needs with a question to herself: "What do I need? How can I make life easier? How can dressing be simplified so I can get on with my own life?"

In 2000 and 2001 the life of Donna Karan, as a designer and as a woman, changed dramatically. Negotiations with LVMH to acquire a controlling share of DKI (the conglomerate that includes DKNY, Donna Karan, and her widely popular brand of sportswear and jeans) brought immense scrutiny from the entire fashion universe. At the same time, Stephan Weiss—the sculptor, mentor, husband, and friend with whom Karan launched her own design company in 1985—was dying of lung cancer. His death in June 2001 seemed to have galvanized Karan into her finest and most spectacular display of creativity. A new space on Madison Avenue, which had been under construction for three years, was opened to extended accolades from architectural critics as well as the fashion press.

The new store, a three-story brownstone built in 1852, provides over 10,000-square-feet of retail space for Karan designs, which has come to include home accessories. Karan never hesitates to acknowledge her debt to and her admiration for other designers. The first floor of her new Madison Avenue shop is a domestic paradise where DK designs for the home are discreetly arranged among shawls and scented candles and dozens of one-of-a-kind items she has discovered and offers to her customers. She explains that "the first thing I hope people see when they walk in is objects of passion, objects of desire."

Karan has moved from designing the feminine, comfortable clothes that have defined and improved the life of her clients to designs for these customers' homes, and finally to suggesting possessions that appeal to their souls. All the Karan lines, whether for the woman or for the home, respect the busy and chaotic nature of contemporary life. She has never been interested in quantity but now even more emphasizes the choice to live with and dress only in those things of the highest quality that make one utterly happy. Karan's clothing designs (supplemented by accessories, fragrance, and makeup collections) reflect the image of a New York woman; her home furnishings provide a glimpse into a New York lifestyle.

—Kevin Almond; updated by Kathleen Bonann Marshall

KASPER, Herbert

American designer

Born: New York City, 12 December 1926. **Education:** Studied English at New York University, 1949–53; studied fashion at Parsons

School of Design, New York, 1951–53, and l'École de la Chambre Syndicale de la Couture Parisienne, 1953. **Family:** Married Betsey Pickering, 1955 (divorced, 1958); married Jondar Conning, 1979. **Military Service:** Served in the U.S. Army. **Career:** Spent two years in Paris working for Fath, Rochas, and at *Elle* magazine; designer, Arnold and Fox, New York, 1954–64; designer, Kasper for Joan Leslie division of Leslie Fay, New York, 1964–85; designer, J.L. Sport, and Kasper for Weatherscope, 1970–85; vice president, Leslie Fay; designer, Kasper for ASL, from 1980. **Awards:** Coty American Fashion Critics award, 1955, 1970, 1976; Cotton Fashion award, 1972; Maas Brothers Pavilion design award, 1983; Cystic Fibrosis Foundation, Governor of Alabama award, 1984; Ronald MacDonald House award, 1984. **Address:** 32 East 64th Street, New York, New York 10021, USA.

PUBLICATIONS

On KASPER:

Books

Morris, Bernadine, and Barbara Walz, *The Fashion Makers,* New York,1978.

Diamonstein, Barbaralee, *Fashion: The Inside Story,* New York,1985.

Milbank, Caroline Rennolds, *New York Fashion: The Evolution of American Style,* New York, 1989.

Stegemeyer, Anne, *Who's Who in Fashion, Third Edition,* New York, 1996.

*

Over a lifetime of designing I've evolved a philosophy that comes from creating clothes for a particular kind of American woman. (Who, by the way, I very much admire.) This woman is adventurous and vital with a lifestyle that demands she play many different roles throughout the day. It's the confident spirit of this kind of woman that inspires me most.

Whatever she's doing, running a home, a career, entertaining, mothering, traveling, I deeply believe this woman remains an individual. No one is going to tell her exactly what she has to wear, no matter what's currently in style. She wants and needs high style, high quality, fashion-conscious clothes that can last for more than one season.... And because I think I have an exceptional ability to anticipate trends, my clothes always have a "today" spirit. I'm constantly refining, improving, interpreting...trying to capture the essence of the times without being trendy. But from whatever source my ideas come from, I always keep in mind that lively, energetic, smart looking woman who is my customer. She's my motivation and my ultimate inspiration.

—Herbert Kasper

* * *

Herbert Kasper has made his name as a designer by working predominantly for one company, Joan Leslie in New York, whom he joined in 1963. In 1980 he became vice president of the company as well as designer, creating high fashion looks that reflected trends but were commercial and wearable. A private customer, Joanne Carson (then the wife of talk-show host Johnny) described his clothes as being both feminine and sexy: "He's got a totally female concept," she enthused, adding that he knew how to put together the perfect interchangeable wardrobe for her various excursions abroad.

Kasper is a designer who really cares about his customer. He wants the person who buys a dress to enjoy it and return for more. His satisfaction comes from seeing a woman look and feel good in his clothes. His reputation has always been that of a respectable craftsman who honors all levels of production involved in creating fashion, from design to manufacture.

After military service in World War II, where he designed costumes for the troupe shows in which he took part as a chorus boy, Kasper enrolled at Parsons School of Design in New York. He then spent two years in Paris perfecting his skills, with a short period at l'École de la Chambre Syndicale de la Couture, Paris, and positions at Jacques Fath and Marcel Rochas. Returning to the U.S., he worked for the milliner Mr. Fred, where his reputation grew. In his next position as dress designer for a company called Penart, Lord & Taylor in New York—which was promoting American designers—said they wanted to feature his work. Kasper's designs were then featured as Kasper of Penart. His talent was for making inexpensive clothes look exquisite and expensive, which endeared him to several other Seventh Avenue manufacturers in the 1950s.

Kasper's forte has always been dresses, but a designer's job involves adapting to the demands of the market and in the early 1970s he opened a sportswear division for Joan Leslie, J.L. Sport. Part of his fashion philosophy has been that clothes should always work together, so he often found it difficult to differentiate between these two lines when designing. A coat for Joan Leslie Dresses, he once declared, could work equally well with the less expensive separates line for J.L. Sport.

While working in Paris, Kasper noted that women spent a great deal of money on custom-made clothes, ordering several outfits for different occasions. He formed a philosophy based on these observations that individual garments should be mixed and matched with many others to create several outfits, a sportswear concept that has become a way of life in the U.S. and elsewhere.

Kasper has always been a great socialite. His social life inspired his work because it gave him an insight into how people live, their attitudes, and changing tastes. As a designer he is happy with his work, regarding each creation as one of his own children, which in a way justifies his devotion to his craft.

—Kevin Almond

KAWAKUBO, Rei

Japanese designer

Born: Tokyo, Japan, 1942. **Education:** Graduated in fine arts, Keio University, Tokyo, 1964. **Career:** Worked in advertising department, Asahi Kasei textile firm, 1964–66; freelance designer, 1967–69; founder/designer, Comme des Garçons, 1969, firm incorporated, 1973; introduced Homme menswear line, 1978; introduced tricot knitwear and Robe de Chambre lines, 1981; opened first Paris boutique, 1981; formed Comme des Garçons, S.A. ready-to-wear subsidiary, 1982, formed New York subsidiary, 1986; launched furniture collection, 1983; introduced Homme Plus collection, 1984;

opened men's Paris boutique, 1986; introduced Homme Deux and Noir collections, 1987; published Comme des Garçons *Six* magazine, from 1988; opened Tokyo flagship store, 1989; introduced, then removed men's pajama line, 1995; unveiled "padded" clothing, 1996; presented fused collection, 1998; opened Comme des Garçons shop in Chelsea, 1999; opened Comme des Garçons Two in Tokyo, 1999. **Exhibitions:** *A New Wave in Fashion: Three Japanese Designers,* Phoenix, Arizona, Art Museum, 1983; *Mode et Photo, Comme des Garçons,* Centre Georges Pompidou, Paris, 1986; *Three Women: Madeleine Vionnet, Claire McCardell, and Rei Kawakubo,* Fashion Institute of Technology, New York, 1987; *Essence of Quality,* Kyoto Costume Institute, Tokyo, 1993. **Awards:** Mainichi Newspaper Fashion award, 1983, 1988; Fashion Group Night of the Stars award, New York, 1986; Chevalier de L'Ordre des Arts et des Lettres, Paris, 1993; Harvard Graduate School of Design Excellence in Design award, 2000. **Address:** Comme des Garçons, 5–11–5 Minamiaoyama, Minato-ku Tokyo 107, Japan.

Publications

On KAWAKUBO:

Books

A New Wave in Fashion: Three Japanese Designers, [exhibition catalogue], Phoenix, AZ, 1983.

Koren, Leonard, *New Fashion Japan,* Tokyo, 1984.

Comme des Garçons, [exhibition catalogue], Tokyo, 1986.

Koda, Harold, et al., *Three Women: Madeleine Vionnet, Claire McCardell, and Rei Kawakubo,* [exhibition catalogue], New York, 1987.

Sparke, Penny, *Japanese Design,* London, 1987.

Sudjic, Deyan, *Rei Kawakubo and Comme des Garçons,* New York, 1990.

Steele, Valerie, *Women of Fashion: Twentieth-Century Designers,* New York, 1991.

Hiesinger, Kathryn B., and Felice Fischer, *Japanese Design: A Survey Since 1950,* New York, 1995.

Stegemeyer, Anne, *Who's Who in Fashion, Third Edition,* New York, 1996.

Articles

Cocks, Jay, "Into the Soul of the Fabric," in *Time,* 1 August 1983.

Saint-Leon, Rhoda Marcus de, "Comme des Garçons: Rei Kawakubo Makes Magic," in *American Fabrics and Fashions* (Newtown, CT), Fall 1983.

Koda, Harold, "Rei Kawakubo and the Aesthetic of Poverty," in *Dress* (Earlville, MD), No. 11, 1985.

Mower, Sarah, "The Kimono with Added Cut and Thrust," in *The Guardian* (London), 6 March 1986.

Sudjic, Deyan, "All the Way Back to Zero," in the *Sunday Times* (London), 20 April 1986.

Stetser, Maggie, "Future Shock, with the Brilliant Innovators of Japanese Fashion," in *Connoisseur* (London), September 1986.

Conant, Jennet, "The Monk and the Nun: The Shock Value of Two Japanese Designers," in *Newsweek,* 2 February 1987.

Martin, Richard, "Aesthetic Dress: The Art of Rei Kawakubo," in *Arts Magazine* (New York), March 1987.

Withers, Jane, "Black: The Zero Option," in the *Face* (London), March 1987.

Morris, Bernadine, "A New York Exhibition Traces the Evolution of Modern Fashion in the Designs of Vionnet, McCardell and Kawakubo," in the *Chicago Tribune,* 11 March 1987.

Weinstein, Jeff, "Vionnet, McCardell, Kawakubo: Why There Are Three Great Women Artists," in the *Village Voice* (New York), 31 March 1987.

Drier, Deborah, "Designing Women," in *Art in America* (New York), May 1987.

Klensch, Elsa, "Another World of Style...Rei Kawakubo," in *Vogue* (New York), August 1987.

Delmar, Michael, "Avec Rei Kawakubo," in *Jardin des Modes,* September 1987.

Filmer, Deny, "Designer Focus: Rei Kawakubo," in *Cosmopolitan* (London), May 1988.

Popham, Peter, "Modern Art by the Yard," in the *Sunday Times* (London), 16 April 1989.

Jeal, Nicola, "Mistress of Monochrome," in the *Observer* (London), 22 October 1989.

Livingston, David, "New Decade for Kawakubo," in the *Globe and Mail,* 26 October 1989.

"Back from Zero," in *Blueprint* (London), November 1990.

Morozzi, Christina, "Partire da Zero," in *Moda* (Milan), April 1991.

Yusuf, Nilgin, "My Criterion is Beauty: Rei Kawakubo of Comme des Garçons," in *Marie Claire* (London), April 1992.

Bowles, Hamish, "Fashion's Visionary," in *Vogue,* March 1993.

Menkes, Suzy, "'Auschwitz' Fashions Draw Jewish Rebuke," in the *International Herald Tribune,* 4 February 1995.

Martin, Richard, "The Shock(ing) Value at Fashion's Cutting Edge," in the *Los Angeles Times,* 19 February 1995.

Spindler, Amy M., "Beyond Sweet, Beyond Black, Beyond 2001," in the *New York Times,* 17 March 1995.

Brubach, Holly, "Witness for the Defense," in the *New York Times,* 2 April 1995.

Posnick, Phyllis, "The Rei Way," in *Vogue* (New York), October 1995.

Spindler, Amy M., "Avant-Gardist Comes into Bloom," in the *New York Times,* 14 March 1996.

———, "Three Revolutionaries Decide to Play It Safe," in the *New York Times,* 9 July 1996.

Als, Hilton, "Bump and Mind," in *Artforum International* (New York), December 1996.

"Venus Envy," in *Vogue* (New York), March 1997.

Schiro, Anne-Marie, "The Deconstructivists: Summing Up the Parts," in the *New York Times,* 13 March 1998.

White, Constance C.R., "Getting Personal in Paris with Romantic Visions," in the *New York Times,* 7 July 1998.

Viladas, Pilar, "Up from SoHo," in the *New York Times Magazine,* 14 March 1999.

Bussel, Abby, "The Mod Pod," in *Interior Design,* April 1999.

Szabo, Julia, "Comme des Garçons Christmas Pillow," in the *International Design Magazine* (New York), July/August 1999.

Larson, Soren, "A Futuristic Comme des Garçons Store in Tokyo Beckons Shoppers down its Meandering Paths," in *Architectural Record* (New York), September 1999.

McGuire, Penny, "Garçons a la Mode," in the *Architectural Review* (London), October 1999.

Cramer, Ned, "Unfashionable Fashion," in *Architecture* (Washington), May 2000.

Rapp, Alan E., "Star Studded," in the *International Design Magazine* (New York), June 2000.

Bellafante, Gina, "Paris Query: Just What is a Woman?" in the *New York Times,* 10 October 2000.

Profile, "Comme des Garçons," available online at Fashion Live, www.fashionlive.com, 19 March 2001.

Beals, Gregory, "Recession Rags: Japan's Young New Designers are Creating Functional Clothes with Conscience," in *Newsweek,* 9 July 2001.

*

My approach to fashion design is influenced by my daily life…my search for new means of expression. I feel that recently there has been a little more of an interest towards those who look for new ideas and who are searching for a new sense of values. My wish is to be able to continue my search for the new.

—Rei Kawakubo

* * *

Rei Kawakubo's work is both paradox and ideological imperative. Minimal, monochromatic, and modernist, her approach to fashion design challenges conventional beauty without forgoing stylish cloth, cut, and color. Her clothing is not so much about the body as the space around the body and the metaphor of self. Architectural in conception and decidedly abstract, the clothing nevertheless derives from Japanese traditional wear.

Kawakubo emerged as a clothing designer by an indirect route, from both a training in fine arts at Keio University in Tokyo and work in advertising for Asahi Kasei, a major chemical company that produced acrylic fibers—promoted through fashionable clothing. In 1967 she became a freelance stylist, a rarity in Japan at the time. Her dissatisfaction with available clothes for the fashion shoots provided the impetus for designing her own garments. She launched the Comme des Garçons women's collection in Tokyo in 1975 with her first shop in Minami-Aoyama and her first catalogue the same year. It was an especially fertile period for Japanese fashion design, with the concurrent rise of Issey Miyake and Yohji Yamamoto.

Kawakubo's themes combine the essence of Japanese traditional work-end streetwear, its simplicity of style, fabric, and color, with an admiration for modern architecture, especially the purism of Le Corbusier and Tadao Ando. Translated into clothing's rational construction, these affinities emphasize the idea of garment—the garment as a construction in space, essentially a structure to live in. The tradition of the kimono, with its architectural silhouette off the body and its many-layered complexity of body wrappings, combines with a graphic approach that is flat and abstract. It is a disarming look that requires a cognitive leap in wearability and social function.

The building block of Kawakubo's design is the fabric, the thread that produces the clothing structure. Her long-standing collaboration with specialty weaver Hiroshi Matsushita has allowed her to reformulate the actual fabric on the loom, the complexities of the weave, the imperfections, the texture of the fabric. Her 1981 launch of the Comme des Garçons line in Paris marked her first international exposure and the introduction of her loom-distressed weaves. What have been referred to as "rag-picker" clothes, an homage to the spontaneity and inventiveness of street people, was based on fabric innovation—cloth that crumpled and wrapped, that draped coarsely as layers, folded and buttoned at random. Most notable of these was her so-called "lace" knitwear of 1982, in which sweaters were purposely knitted to incorporate various-sized holes that appeared as rips and tears or intentionally intricate webs. This was an attack on lingering Victorianism in fashion, on the conventional, the precise, and the tight-laced. It offered a rational argument for antiform at a time when minimalism had lapsed into decorativeness.

Kawakubo's use of monochromatic black as her signature is analytical and subtle rather than sensual and brash. Black, which is often perceived as flattering, assumes the status of a noncolor—an absence rather than a presence. Her intent is to reject clothes as mere decoration for the body. Even with the later introduction of saturated color in the late 1980s lines, in which her clothes became slimmer, black was still a basic—evident in the Noir line as well as in Homme and Homme Plus, her menswear collections.

Her control of the presentation of Comme des Garçons in photography, catwalk shows, the design of store interiors, catalogues, and most recently a magazine is integral to the design concept that extends from the clothing. Kawakubo was the first to use nonprofessional models, art world personalities, and film celebrities, both in photography for catalogues and in catwalk shows. Her early catalogues from the 1970s featured noted figures from Japanese art and literature.

The 1988 introduction of the quarto-sized biannual magazine *Six* (for sixth sense) replaced the Comme des Garçons catalogues and pushed Kawakubo's antifashion ideas to extreme. These photographic essays became enigmatic vehicles for stream-of-consciousness, surrealism, exoticism, and Zen, which informs Kawakubo's sensibility and, ultimately, in a semiotic way, is imbued in her fashion designs. Kawakubo's ideas have explored the realm of possibilities associated with the production and selling of clothing. Her control of the environment of her stores—including the sparse design of the interiors (on which she collaborates with architect Takao Kawasaki), the industrial racks and shelves, the way the salespeople act and dress, and even the furnishings (which she designs and sells)—is total and defining. Her art is one of extending the boundaries of self-presentation and self-awareness into an environment of multivalent signs. It is an extension of fashion design into the realism of metaphysic, of "self in landscape," of which the clothing is a bare trace.

Controversy, for which the inventive icon was often criticized, sparked again when the "anti" designer introduced "Sleep," her Comme des Garçons men's pajama collection. Striped and available in layers, the pajamas came as a reminder of the Nazi death camps, for the show occurred on the 50th anniversary of the Holocaust. The line, described as being stamped with "identification numbers" displayed by "emaciated" models with "shaved heads," soon was removed by Kawakubo herself.

With her disputed pajama line behind her and experimental style still much a part of her work, Kawakubo continued to present obscure designs in her connoisseur show. This time floral prints took to the stage and, contrary to popular belief, screamed success—exactly the recognition the Japanese designer needed to regain her renowned reputation.

Nearing the end of 1996, Kawakubo introduced the concept that "body meets dress, dress meets body and becomes one." Experimenting with new forms and new bodies, the creator inserted basketball-sized pads into her clothing. These deformities, according to Kawakubo, exemplify the "actual" rather than the 'natural.' Critics claim the effect depends on the eye—to some, the eye adjusts and the look becomes real; to others, it is merely "strange."

Kawakubo's fashion is based on the event, not the clothes themselves. No music, no theatrics, and not even an audience are typical of the designer's shows. In 1998, the unpredictable artist designed outfits of unfinished patterns. The collection, as Kawakubo put it, was based on releasing energy through fusion. More recent, however, was the addition of her Comme des Garçons shop in the Chelsea district of New York City. The intimate, space-age interior occupies a bold, futuristic setting. The look is supposed to offer a highly personal experience of discovery. Described as mysterious, like its sculptor, the entranceway is hidden to imply exclusivity and says, "If you aren't in the know, then don't bother."

Next came Comme des Garçons Two, which opened in Tokyo, Kawakubo's first shop devoted strictly to clothing. This renovated boutique was inviting to outsiders, focusing on movement and interaction. A Paris shop followed, with "anti" perfumes as its focus. Kawakubo designed the new shops with Takao Kawasaki and Future Systems. Kawakubo's contemporary art and complex fashion trends later earned her the third recipient of the Harvard Graduate School of Design's annual Excellence in Design award.

—Sarah Bodine; updated by Diana Idzelis

KELLY, Patrick

American designer working in Paris

Born: Vicksburg, Mississippi, 24 September 1954. **Education:** Studied art history and black history at Jackson State University, Jackson, Mississippi, and fashion design at Parsons School of Design, New York. **Career:** Held various jobs in Atlanta, Georgia, including window dresser, Rive Gauche boutique; instructor, Barbizon School of Modeling; vintage clothing store proprietor, mid-1970s; moved to Paris, 1980; costume designer, Le Palais club, early 1980s; also freelance designer, 1980–90; Patrick Kelly, Paris, formed, and first ready-to-wear collection introduced, 1985; freelance sportswear designer, Benetton, 1986; opened first boutique in Paris, produced first couture collection, sold worldwide rights to ready-to-wear collections, 1987. **Died:** 1 January 1990, in Paris.

Publication

On KELLY:

Books

Stegemeyer, Anne, *Who's Who in Fashion, Third Edition*, New York, 1996.

Articles

Cocks, Jay, "The Color of New Blood: Some Snazzy Duds from Three Upstarts," *Time,* 10 November 1986.
Bain, Sally, "The King of Cling," in the *Drapers Record* (London), 16 May 1987.
Johnson, Bonnie, "In Paris, His Slinky Dresses Have Made Mississippi-born Designer Patrick Kelly the New King of Cling," in *People,* 15 June 1987.
George, Leslie, "Patrick Kelly: An American in Paris," in *WWD,* 15 January 1988.
Whitaker, Charles, "Black Designer Dazzles Paris," *Ebony,* February 1988.
Gross, Michael, "Kelly's Blackout," in *New York,* 23 May 1988.
Conant, Jennet, "Buttons and Billiard Balls: A Designer from the Deep South Captures Paris," in *Newsweek* (New York), 27 June 1988.
"Meet Patrick Kelly," in *Vogue Patterns* (New York and London), July 1988.
Dissly, Megan, in *Christian Science Monitor,* 25 August 1988.
Hornblower, Margot, "An Original American in Paris," in *Time,* 3 April 1989.
Goodwin, Betty, "Maverick and Mastermind," in the *Los Angeles Times,* 7 April 1989.
Johnson, Pamela, "Patrick Kelly: Prince of Paris," in *Essence,* May 1989.
"Glitz Tips: Do-it-Yourself Ideas from Glitzmeister Patrick Kelly," in *Chatelaine* (Toronto), September 1989.
Gross, Michael, "Patrick Kelly: Exuberant Style Animates the American Designer's Paris Atelier," in *Architectural Digest* (Los Angeles), September 1989.
"Patrick Kelly" (obituary), in the *New York Times,* 2 January 1990.
Moore, Jackie, "Patrick Kelly" (obituary), in *The Independent* (London), 11 January 1990.
"Designer Dies," in *DR: The Fashion Business* (London), 13 January 1990.
"Mississippi Couturier," in *U.S. News and World Report* (Washington), 15 January 1990.
"Designer Patrick Kelly Dies of Bone Marrow Disease," in *Jet* (New York), 22 January 1990.
"Patrick Kelly," in *Current Biography* (New York), March 1990.
Articles also in *Women's Wear Daily* (New York), 3 January 1990 and 2 April 1990.

* * *

According to a "Love List" published in *Women's Wear Daily* in March 1990, designer Patrick Kelly adored fried chicken, foie gras, and pearls. Kelly's designs celebrated pride in his spiritual upbringing in the American South and a tourist-like adoration of Paris. Not for the faint-hearted, his specialty was form-fitting knits irreverently decorated with oversized and mismatched buttons, watermelons, black baby dolls, and huge rhinestones densely silhouetting the Eiffel Tower.

Wearing too-big overalls and a biker's cap emblazoned "Paris," Kelly engendered folklore as important as the clothing he designed. Growing up in Mississippi where he was taught sewing by his grandmother, Kelly later sold vintage clothing in Atlanta, and failed to be hired on New York's Seventh Avenue. He bought a one-way ticket to Paris from a model/friend and the trip resulted in his being discovered while selling his own designs in a Paris flea market.

Kelly was exotic and different. He and his clothing charmed the French and the rest of the world, and he was the first American ever admitted to the elite Chambre Syndicale de la Couture Parisienne, the group of Paris-based designers permitted to show collections in the Louvre. Exuberantly witty, his first show at the Louvre began with Kelly spray painting a large red heart on a white canvas, and included dresses entitled "Jungle Lisa Loves Tarzan," a spoof of Mona Lisa featuring leopard-print gowns.

Kelly's designs remained unpretentious yet sexy, affordable while glamorous. Dresses were fun and uncontrived, yet Kelly paid great attention to design details. Bold, theatrical details such as white topstitching on black, low necklines, and dice buttons on a pin-striped business dress, silver fringe on a western skirt, and vibrant color combinations make one want to shimmy just looking at them. Kelly's art was in embellishment of women, young and old. Trims become jewelry; collars and hemlines become frames. Frills are exaggerated, enlarged, unexpected, and rethought, saucily decorating what would otherwise be rather simple designs.

A love-in atmosphere prevailed at an April 1989 show and lecture for students at New York's Fashion Institute of Technology. A standing-room-only crowd screamed, laughed, and applauded Kelly—his effervescence and his happiness were contagious. He showed a sassy and smart collection, including a tight black mini dress with shiny multicolored buttons outlining a perfect heart on the buttocks; wide, notched, off-the-shoulder collars; leopard-print trench coats and turtlenecked body suits; multicolored scarves suspended from the hip, swaying below abbreviated hemlines; and a *trompe l'oeil* bustier of buttons on a fitted mini dress. Kelly's models danced, even smiled, down the catwalk, delighted to be wearing his clothing (they modeled this show for free). The audience was delighted to be there: the clothing and designer seemed to be welcoming everyone to a good party, and everyone had a good time.

Kelly's personal attention to detail, his love of design, his spirit, sold his clothing. He stated "the ultimate goal is selling," but he did more than just sell. Wearing a Patrick Kelly dress meant embracing one's past, doing the best with what you have, triumphing over failure, and laughing at oneself. One could be part of Patrick Kelly's fairy tale and celebrate his *joie de vivre*. Kelly died too young, at age 35, of a brain tumor and bone-marrow disease, in Paris.

—Jane Burns

Kenzo, spring/summer 2002 ready-to-wear collection. © AFP/ CORBIS.

KENZO

Japanese designer working in Paris

Born: Kenzo Takada in Tokyo, Japan, 27 February 1939. **Education:** Bunka College of Fashion. **Career:** Designer for Sanai department store; pattern designer, *Soen* magazine, Tokyo, 1960–64; freelance designer, Paris, from 1965, selling to Féraud, Rodier, and several department stores; designer for Pisanti; established Jungle Jap boutique in Paris, 1970; opened Rue Cherche Midi Boutique, 1972; established Kenzo-Paris boutique, New York, 1983; launched menswear line, 1983; opened boutiques in Paris, Aix en Provence, Bordeaux, Lille, Lyon, Saint-Tropez, Copenhagen, London, Milan, and Tokyo, 1984–85; launched menswear and womenswear lines, Kenzo Jeans, and junior line, Kenzo Jungle, 1986; launched Kenzo Bed Linen and Bath Wear line, 1987; opened boutiques in Rome, New York, 1987; established childrenswear line, 1987; launched womenswear line, Kenzo City, 1988; opened boutique in Brussels, 1989, and Stockholm, 1990; launched line of bath products, Le Bain, 1990; opened boutique in Hong Kong, 1990, Bangkok, 1991, and Singapore, 1991; launched Kenzo Maison line, 1992; launched Bambou line, 1994. Perfumes: *Kenzo,* 1988; *Parfum d'été,* 1992; has also designed costumes for opera; film director. Company continued on after his retirement in 1999. **Awards:** Soen prize, 1960; Fashion Editors Club of Japan prize, 1972; Bath Museum of Costume Dress of the Year award, 1976, 1977; Chevalier de l'Ordre des Arts et des Lettres, 1984. **Address:** 3 Place des Victoires, 75002 Paris. **Website:** www.kenzo.com.

Publications

On KENZO:

Books

Milbank, Caroline Rennolds, *Couture: The Great Designers,* New York, 1985.
Sparke, Penny, *Japanese Design,* London, 1987.
Sainderichin, Ginette, *Kenzo,* Paris, 1989.
Stegemeyer, Anne, *Who's Who in Fashion, Third Edition,* New York, 1996.

Articles

"The JAP Designer," in *Newsweek,* 1 May 1972.
Morris, Bernadine, "Designer Does What He Likes—And It's Liked," in the *New York Times,* 12 July 1972.
———, "Kenzo Displays His Imagination," in the *New York Times,* 4 April 1973.

Kenzo, autumn/winter 1999–2000 ready-to-wear collection: wool knit ensemble. © AFP/CORBIS.

"Lively Influence on Dull Paris Scene," in the *Times* (London), 1 September 1976.
"Mini Redux," in *Newsweek,* 8 November 1976.
Dorsey, Hebe, "Kenzo Grows Up," in the *New York Times Magazine,* 14 November 1976.
Talley, André Leon, "Kenzo: One Needs Folly to Work in Fashion," in *WWD,* 17 February 1978.
Tucker, Priscilla, "Designer Becomes a Superstar: Kenzo Marches to Different Tunes; All of Them Are Hits," in the *New York Daily News,* 11 April 1978.
McEvoy, Marian, "Kenzo Barges Up the Nile," in *WWD,* 20 October 1978.
Cleave, Maureen, "Makers of Modern Fashion: Kenzo," in the *Observer Magazine* (London), 14 December 1980.
"L'oeil de Vogue: l'anniversaire de Kenzo," in *Vogue* (Paris) October 1985.
Salvy, Gerard-Julien, "L'art d'être soi l-même," in *Vogue* (Paris), February 1986.
Boyd, Ann, "Cap by Denny, So Why Buy Kenzo?" in the *Observer* (London), 8 January 1987.
"Kenzo: Créations Tous Azimuts," in *Profession Textile* (Paris), 5 February 1988.
Boriolli, Gisella, "Kenzo Back Home in Japan," in *Donna* (Milan), July/August 1989.
"Kenzo Modern Folklore," in *Elle* (New York), September 1989.
Baudot, Francois, "Le Pélerinage de Kenzo," in *Elle* (Paris), 5 September 1989.
Gwee, Elisabeth, "Kenzo Moves On," in the *Straits Times* (Singapore), November 9, 2000.
"Kenzo," in *Fashion Live,* March 2001.
"Kenzo Flirts with Red Poppy Flowers," in the *Jakarta Post,* February 18, 2001.
Gwee, Elisabeth, "Design on Kids: Brands 'R' Us," in the *Straits Times* (Singapore), June 14, 2001.

* * *

In 1986 Kenzo Takada called his menswear collection "Around the World in Eighty Days," but that expedition had long been underway in Kenzo's clothes for women and men. Significantly, for more than 20 years, Kenzo has been the most prominent traveler in fashion but also the most multicultural and the most syncretistic, insisting on the diversity and compatibility of ethnic styles and cultural options from all parts of the world. Kenzo has steadfastly mixed styles. This Japanese tourist has rightly perceived and selected from all cultures and styles. In February 1978 he told *Women's Wear Daily,* "I like to use African patterns and Japanese patterns together." Kenzo interprets style and specific costume elements of various parts of the world, assimilating them into a peaceful internationalism more radical than other designers.

Various collections have included Romanian peasant skirts as inspiration as well as Mexican rebozos and heavy Scandinavian sweaters (1973); a Chinese coolie look combined with Portuguese purses, Riviera awning-striped beach shirts, and t-shirt dresses for full cultural diversity (1975); Native American stylings in a highly textural, colorful, and feather-inflected collection (1976); Egyptian leanings and patterns (1979); North African inspiration, with elements of an excursion to India for a modified Nehru suit (1984); an homage to Al Capone (1988).

Considered a *Wunderkind* and celebrity in 1970s fashion, Kenzo never fixed on one look, but preferred to view fashion as a creative, continuous adventure. Shyly, Kenzo said in 1978, "It pleases me when people say I have influence. But I am influenced by the world that says I influence it. The world I live in is my influence." Other influences include American popular culture: Chinese tunics and wrappings, especially at the low-swung waist, batiks of East Asia, European peasant aprons and smocks, and Japanese woven textiles. For his 40th birthday, the designer became Minnie Mouse.

When asked by Joan Quinn about travels and ethnic clothing, Kenzo replied: "I prefer to travel only for vacations. I don't go around looking for influences. The energy arrives." In fact, Kenzo serves as "the prototype of the young designer, the designer with a sense of humor about fashion, culture, and life, as well as a lively curiosity about clothing itself," as Caroline Milbank described, precisely because his theme collections and almost volcanic change imply a continuous stream of ideas. Kenzo, after all, emerged first as a designer of poor-boy-style skinny sweaters. Like Elsa Schiaparelli, who likewise began with ingenious knits, he has become a prodigious continuing talent. His fashion references seem never to be imposed upon clothing but are reasonable as a consequence of his design exploration. Military and ecclesiastical looks in 1978 simply streamlined and simplified his style.

In addition, Kenzo has been fascinated by painting, drawing upon Wassily Kandinsky and David Hockney for inspiration, as well as calligraphy. His pallet has always been internationally vibrant, filled with ethnic eruptions, play of pattern, and unorthodox color combinations. Kenzo's work, in fact, argues strongly for the harmony of cultural influences, the most disparate and distinct expressions of dress coming together in the styles of a designer who has himself raised barbed issues of ethnicity by insisting upon "Jap" for his early collections, encouraging a racist pejorative to be converted into a positive identity.

Kenzo demonstrates a sustained aesthetic of absorption, assimilating many global influences into an integrated and wholly modern style of his own. The flamboyance of Kenzo's art and life captured the popular imagination of fashion in the 1970s, but his abiding and exemplary contribution is his ability to digest many style traits and to achieve a powerful composite. Kenzo told André Leon Tally, writing for *Women's Wear Daily* in February 1978, "One needs a lot of folly to work in fashion." It is this sense of exuberance, creative excitement, and caprice that has marked Kenzo's work for more than two decades. Claude Montana once commented, "Kenzo gives much more to fashion than all the couturiers lumped together." Kenzo epitomized fashion energy and imagination in the 1970s: his brilliant creative assimilation brought street initiative and global creativity to fashion.

By the early 1990s, Kenzo's company, which boasted 37 boutiques worldwide and 124 sales outlets, was acquired by the LVMH (Moët Hennessey Louis Vuitton) family, quickly becoming LVMH's second-largest fashion house after Louis Vuitton. LVMH also owns Loewe, Celine, and Christian Dior. Plans for the Kenzo brand included branching into home furnishings and launching a new sportswear line called Kenzo Ki (*Ki* is Kenji for "energy").

Kenzo announced his retirement in 1999 and celebrated his 30-year career with a stadium celebration that included a Kenzo retrospective and his final collection, spring-summer 2000. Kenzo was replaced by head designers Gilles Rosier for womenswear and Roy Krejberg for menswear. Suzy Menkes of the *International Herald Tribune* called Rosier's first show, for fall-winter 2000–2001, "one of the smoothest and successful transitions of recent seasons."

Even with its namesake in retirement, the Kenzo brand continues to grow. In 2001 the company added a new fragrance, *Flower by Kenzo* to its line, and the company sought a new generation of Kenzo devotees with the launch of Kenzo Kids. Marketing director Timothy Yoong told Singapore's *Straits Times* that "anyone willing to pay $1,000 for a suit won't mind buying three to four items from the same brand for their children."

—Richard Martin; updated by Lisa Groshong

KHANH, Emmanuelle

French designer

Born: Renée Mezière in Paris, 12 September 1937. **Family:** Married designer Quasar Khanh (Manh Khanh Nguyen), 1957; children: Othello, Atlantique-Venus. **Career:** Model for the Balenciaga and Givenchy fashion houses, Paris, 1957–63; began creating own designs and with Christiane Bailly, 1962; created collections for Belletête, Missoni, Dorothée Bis, Laura, Cacharel, Pierre d'Alby, Krizia, Max Mara, and Le Bistrot du Tricot, 1963–69; founder/director, Emmanuelle Khanh label and fashion garment and accessory company, from 1971; opened first Paris boutique, 1977; president, Emmanuelle Khanh International, from 1987. **Awards:** Chevalier des Arts et des Lettres, Paris, 1986. **Address:** Emmanuelle Khanh International, 45 Avenue Victor Hugo, 75116 Paris, France.

Publications

On KHANH:

Books

Lynam, Ruth, ed., *Paris Fashion: The Great Designers and Their Creations,* London, 1972.

Carter, Ernestine, *With Tongue in Chic,* London, 1974.

———, *The Changing World of Fashion: 1900 to the Present,* London, 1977.

Mulvagh, Jane, *Vogue History of 20th-Century Fashion,* London, 1988.

Loebenthal, Joel, *Radical Rags: Fashions of the Sixties,* New York, 1990.

Articles

"The Drop," in *Vogue* (London), February 1963.

Gabbey, Regine, "The Ready-to-Dare Designers," in *Réalités* (Paris), January 1969.

"Living in Heavenly Blue Blow-Up Space in Paris," in *Vogue* (London), February 1969.

Toll, Marie-Pierre, "Where Beauty is Not a Luxury," in *House & Garden* (New York), September 1984.

Witkin, Christian, "Options for the Office & After: Colors that Wake You Up for Work and Don't Fade After Five," in *Mademoiselle,* December 1995.

Zesiger, Carey, "One of a Kind," in *Far Eastern Economic Review,* December 1995.

*

Women inspire me—fashions bore me.

My strength is to make clothes which are timeless. To create clothes for me is a wonderful way to participate and belong to my era.

—Emmanuelle Khanh

* * *

While Mary Quant was revolutionizing fashion in England at the beginning of the 1960s, Emmanuelle Khanh was at the vanguard of the young French ready-to-wear movement. From the French pronunciation of the Beatles' "Yeah, yeah, yeah," the emerging clothes were known as yé yé fashion.

Khanh began as a model for Balenciaga and Givenchy. In 1959 she realized that haute couture was appealing only to a small portion of a larger potential audience. She believed the time was right for rebellion against the strictures of haute couture, and she was not alone in this thinking—during this time, Daniel Hechter created a style between comfort and sportswear, Cacharel redesigned its shirts, Michele Rosier began to create a cosmic line of windbreakers and anoraks, Chantal Thomass created her minidresses, Elie and Jacqueline Jacobson created Dorothée Bis, and Sonia Rykiel launched her knitwear line.

Khanh began to make attractive clothing for the masses. Her individuality quickly caught on in France, where she modeled and sold the clothes herself. In 1960 the magazine *IT* carried an article about Khanh and her work and her modern fashions soon reached the U.S. and were in demand in major department stores. The clothes Khanh had been making for herself, with the help of her husband, Quasar Khanh, were then noticed by *Elle* magazine. This exposure led to Khanh's collaboration with another ex-Balenciaga model, Christiane Bailly, to design their own groundbreaking Emmachristie collection in 1962.

Khanh criticized haute couture for hiding the beauty of the body. For her own designs, she emphasized femininity by cutting clothes along the body's curves, to follow the movement of the body, unlike Balenciaga's gowns, which could practically stand alone regardless of the woman's body within them. Khanh created an architecturally classic mode with a twist: careful seaming, narrow armholes, a slim, close to the body "droop" silhouette. Her suits had the surprise element of skirts that were actually culottes. Innovations included dog-eared collars, long fitted jackets with droopy collars, and blouses and dresses with collars consisting of overlapping petal-like shapes along a U-shaped opening.

Khanh also had a democratic approach to fabric. She used denim and tie-dyeing, chenille, and plastic. A characteristic evening top in 1965 was made of crèpe appliquéd with fluorescent plastic circles. Khanh often used Shetland wools and Harris tweeds long favored by middle-class French women. In the late 1960s, she introduced ready-to-wear furs and tulle and lace lingerie. In cooperation with the Missonis, Khanh made fashions from Italian knit fabrics. The results of her work for the Paris ready-to-wear house of Cacharel, and her work with designer Dorothée Bis, resulted in dresses with a long, slim, flowing 1930s feeling. The use of Romanian hand embroidery became a hallmark of the clothes Khanh produced under her own label.

Keeping pace with the ethnic trend of the 1970s, Khanh created short, loose, peasant-style dresses out of colorful Italian gauze fabrics. Feminine blouses were be trimmed with scalloped embroidered edges, short skirts were frilled, and lace was used to trim soft linen in her designs of the period. Khanh also joined the likes of Guy Paulin, Anne Marie Beretta, Karl Lagerfeld, Luciano Soprani, and Jean Charles de Castelbajac designing clothing for Max Mara. Later in the 1970s Khanh turned to designing knitwear and skiwear. A casual summer look consisted of a wide, striped cotton skirt, buttoned down the front, worn with a matching halter top and wedge-heeled shoes of matching fabric. The matching shoes were a couture touch for ready-to-wear.

During the next decade, Khanh continued to freelance, making soft, individualistic fashions, bouncing creative ideas off her engineer, inventor, and interior-designer husband. Her signature line of boldly-rimmed glasses (à la Drew Carey) is one such example. She often tells her favorite story about how her glasses line came about: "I had always refused to wear glasses because I thought it was ugly and, as a consequence of this whim, I have experienced quite a few annoyances…But most embarrassing…as I was waiting for a taxi to pick me up some place, I got inside the personal car of someone I never met before!" Ever since, Khanh—now never seen without her own pair of glasses—admitted glasses were an essential accessory to her daily life.

Khanh is well known for her original eyewear designs and especially in her innovative use of genuine lizard, snake, ostrich, crocodile, and shark skin on the frames of her handmade "EK"-initialed glasses. Khanh's clear plastic umbrellas have also been successfully marketed around the world.

In the 1980s, her clothes had a retro feeling about them, with extended shoulders and cinched waistlines that flattered the figure. One outfit featured a very long, very loose camel hair coat falling freely from the shoulders, caught about the waist by a narrow leather belt, worn over a soft, dark brown, wool jersey jumpsuit. In 1982 Khanh released a line of clothing under her own name and, in 1987, created Emmanuelle Khanh International. Some 150 boutiques around the world attest to her lasting popularity.

Khanh continued to be active in the 1990s. For Jet Lag Showroom in 1990, she designed a suit consisting of a waist-length, tightly fitting jacket, worn with a long, full flannel skirt. She continued throughout the decade to create comfortable simple jackets and coats for special orders from the firm. Indisputably, this successful woman was one of the pioneers of ready-to-wear fashion of the 1960s and hopefully will continue to amaze the fashion world in the future.

—Therese Duzinkiewicz Baker; updated by Daryl F. Mallett

KIESELSTEIN-CORD, Barry

American jewelry and accessories designer, and artist

Born: New York City, 6 November 1943. **Education:** Studied at Parsons School of Design, New York University, and the American Craft Institute. **Family:** Married Elizabeth Anne (CeCe) Eddy in 1974 (divorced); children: Elizabeth. **Career:** Worked as art director/producer for various advertising agencies, 1966–70; founded company, 1972; divisions include jewelry, belts, handbags (from 1991), gloves, and home furnishings and accessories; opened in-store boutiques at Bergdorf Goodman, New York, 1985, Neiman Marcus, Beverly Hills, 1990, and Mitsukishi, Tokyo, 1990; opened shops in Italy, Germany, and Switzerland; introduced black gold jewelry, 1995; transformed 1920s mansion into residence, 1998; also an artist; director, Council of Fashion Designers of America, 1987. **Collections:** Metropolitan Museum of Art, New York; Louisiana State Museum. **Awards:** Hollywood Radio & Television Society award, 1965; two Art Directors Club awards, New York, late 1960s; Illustrators Society of New York award, 1969; Coty American Fashion Critics award, 1979, 1984; Council of Fashion Designers of America award, 1981. **Address:** 119 West 40th Street, New York, NY 10018, USA. **Website:** www.kiestelstein-cord.com.

Publications

On KIESELSTEIN-CORD:

Books

Stegemeyer, Anne, *Who's Who in Fashion, Third Edition,* New York, 1996.

Articles

Talley, André Leon, "Double Jointed," in *WWD,* 14 November 1975.
Crowley, Susan, "Jewelry's New Dazzle," in *Newsweek,* 4 April 1977.
Grossman, Karen, "Barry Kieselstein-Cord, Artist and Designer," in *People,* September 1978.

Duka, John, "Postmodern Belt Buckles," in the *New York Times,* 11 October 1980.
Talley, André Leon, "Barry Kieselstein-Cord," in *Interview* (New York), November 1981.
Kingstone, Barbara, "New Status for Jewelry," in the *Toronto Globe and Mail,* March 1985.
Goodwin, Betty, "Designer Takes Artist's Tact with Buckles," in the *Los Angeles Times,* 10 May 1985.
Masse, Cheryl, "Moving Pieces," in *Beverly Hills 213,* 15 May 1985.
Tsutagawa, K., "The Sculptor as Jeweler: Interview with Barry Kieselstein-Cord," in *New York Style* (Japan), July 1985.
Allen, Jennifer, "Barry and CeCe Kieselstein-Cord," in *Architectural Digest,* September 1988.
"Creative Collaborators," in *Harper's Bazaar,* June 1989.
Ravel, Margo, "Barry Kieselstein-Cord: Pure Inspiration," in *Beverly Hills 213,* 20 September 1989.
Menkes, Suzy, "Kieselstein-Cord: Anthropomorphic Chic," in the *International Herald Tribune* (Neuilly, France), 14 November 1989.
Newman, Jill, "Kieselstein-Cord: Keeping It Tried and True," in *Women's Wear Daily Accessories Magazine,* January 1990.
———, "Kieselstein-Cord's Newest Luxury: Handbags," in *Women's Wear Daily Accessories Magazine,* 16 August 1991.
———, "A Bergdorf's Ace: Kieselstein-Cord," in *Women's Wear Daily,* 15 November 1991.
Beard, Patricia, "To Have and to Hold," in *Mirabella* (New York), April 1992.
Van Gelder, Lindsy, "Promenade Purse," in the *New York Times,* 7 June 1992.
Goodman, Wendy, "Challenging the Gold Standard," in *Harper's Bazaar,* January 1995.
Alhadeff, Gini, "House of Kieselstein-Cord," in *Architectural Digest,* July 1998.
Post, Tom, "Crafty," in *Forbes,* 11 January 1999.

*

My life as an artist started when I was about eight. My primary interest at that moment was directed toward North American Indian art. This was my first influence between the ages of 8 and 14. I produced large-scale carvings and effigies and interpretations. Between 14 and 22 my focus had switched to painting and metalwork. At 14 I had also started to bury objects and metal in the ground to observe color and patina changes.

From the earliest moments I can recall fascination with all past cultures and an intense attraction to art and architecture, not surprising, as in their youth my mother had been an illustrator and father an architect. I still hold these fascinations and occasionally some recall slips into my work. I have rarely ever looked at the ornamentation of other artists; my primary influences come from entire cultures and periods.

I am not influenced by fashion, preferring to be an influencer. Some of my most successful collections took three to five years to create the impact needed to make them commercially successful—really my most successful pieces I could not give away until people developed a new appreciation for my directions. Naturally this has produced my greatest reward (influencing direction) as an artist. My intent is to capture the illusive mental image—a single example is if you are riding in a car down a country road at a good speed, and think you see something wonderful. You stop your car and back up...only to find a jumble that your mind saw as a completed image. This is my creative process: to capture the illusive image that was the correlation between the speed, your mind's eye, and what you thought you'd seen; to make it three-dimensional; and to fill space with something new that was not there before this creation.

As to contemporary fashion, the present mode of "anything goes" is quite wonderful. One can live out one's fantasy, bring it out of the closet and, if in good taste, be really very chic. I do like black ties on men and sexy elegant evening gowns on beautiful women. It quickens the pulse.

—Barry Kieselstein-Cord

* * *

In his affirmation "I don't make jewelry; I do sculptures for the body," Barry Kieselstein-Cord has described the independence and the ambition of his work. Like Elsa Peretti and other contemporary designers of jewelry, Kieselstein-Cord has sought to define an art that is autonomous from fashion, boldly sculptural in a way that makes a clear distinction from the wondrous but miniaturized repertory of a designer like Miriam Haskell, and historically aware without being subservient to past styles. His scarab minaudière, for example, is indebted to ancient Egypt, as well as to the art deco Egyptian revival, but with the curtly reduced modernism that characterizes his work.

His landmark—in law as in art, as their copyright was legally upheld from accessories' pirates—belt buckles, the Vaquero, and the Winchester, are both of the Old West but transmitted through art nouveau curvilinear interpretation. It is hard not to call Kieselstein-Cord's work jewelry, even as he avoids the term with "bodywork" or "sculpture," but the feeling is undeniably different from that of most jewelry. The designer argues that it comes from all the sculpture having as its Platonic ideal some large, even monumental form, surpassing its role on the human body.

Kieselstein-Cord has been one of the critical designers who, from the 1970s, has offered a jewelry that aspires to the condition of sculpture, allowing shapes to reclaim their ancient expressive, even spiritual or prophylactic, aspect in allowing jewelry to become something more than trivial adornment. After expressing his admiration for Easter Island statues, Kieselstein-Cord told André Leon Talley, "I also like things which are sophisticated in an innately primitive way. Things that are transformed into a past and present that you can't identify. I like some of Miró's giant sculptures, some by Lipchitz, Noguchi, and Brancusi. The last thing I look at for inspiration is jewelry of any kind or period." Peretti, Robert Lee Morris, and Tina Chow would all probably adhere to the same spiritual striving and monumental desire for jewelry. Kieselstein-Cord had liberated jewelry from being paltry and precious in scale.

Similarly, Kieselstein-Cord disavows fashion as an influence, maintaining that jewelry must hold its separate aesthetic and power. While wife and partner CeCe also produced jewelry for Perry Ellis and was a model and muse for the fashion designer, Kieselstein-Cord's work has never bent to specific demands of fashion. "My accessories are not meant to be fashion," he told Jill Newman from *Women's Wear Daily Accessories Magazine* in January 1990. "They are designed to augment fashion. Things made of precious metal are meant to last forever and a day." Indeed, many of Kieselstein-Cord's designs have been of such enduring interest they continue to be produced, while some collectors wait for each new sculptural edition in the manner of collecting any other artistic production. In the early 1980s he produced accessories for the home, and later expanded into high-quality handbags.

If Kieselstein-Cord takes his art seriously enough to declare it sculpture and not jewelry, he is nonetheless playful enough to realize diverse properties of materials and to bring some elements of non-Western culture to the vocabulary of jewelry. In 1976, for example, a coiled choker of silk cord was accented with a gold orb; gold was used with tortoise shell hair combs. In the same year, he created a splendidly reeling art nouveau antelope minaudière, sandblasted onto the gold body to give the feeling of fur. A 1981 duck bandolier was a little Pancho Villa, a little nursery frieze for a fantastic equivocation in jewelry. John Duka declared his spring 1981 belt buckles "postmodern," perhaps the first time that appellation was used for accessories. Bold concha belts, Celtic interlace, and Gauguin-inspired shapes have been featured in his collections.

Kieselstein-Cord began his work in the 1970s, when American alternative culture might have convinced almost any marijuana-smoking hippie of the probity of body sculpture—and he even used cowboys and Indians to prove the point. What Kieselstein-Cord has done is more important and far-reaching: he has convinced all of us of the probity of body sculpture, spiritual and symbolic; he has enlarged the tradition of jewelry, giving it a chunky, palpable integrity; he has declared jewelry sovereign from fashion; and he has given jewelry and related accessories a standard of luxury along with a contemporary vocabulary.

With more than 3,000 pieces of jewelry behind him, Kieselstein-Cord passionately continues in his exploration to extend the limits of design. One of his most recent creations—black gold—expresses his love for historical beauty or the idea that things get better with time. He is, after all, said to be one of the most patient designers; it took the untraditional artist five years to sell his matte gold finish jewelry. "I like the look of objects that have been used," he explains. "There is a sense of humanity, a sense of affection."

Just as Kieselstein-Cord's jewelry goes back to his early school days, so does his passion for interior design. Using modern technology, industrial methods, and a sense of romanticism, the designer transformed a 1920 Manhattan mansion into a residence and showroom. Uninhabited for nearly 40 years, the building has 20-foot-tall ceilings, green oversized radiators, and eclectic paintings reminiscent of 1920 Italian architecture. Kieselstein-Cord's fondness for historic beauty held true in his innovations just as it did with jewelry. The original owners of his mansion told him they would remove certain items if they risked being destroyed in the renovation. They didn't have to worry with Kieselstein-Cord—the older the better.

Furnished with steel-framed black leather armchairs and square glass-and-steel low tables, Kieselstein-Cord's real masterpiece is the bedroom. Proud to describe it as an *Out of Africa* feeling, with its white linen curtains, tribal rugs, and kilim pillows, Kieselstein-Cord's elements of design can all be found implemented in some way throughout the Manhattan residence. Although Kieselstein-Cord is quick to state, "I've achieved everything I've ever wanted to," his dreams have always been advertising, design, and art. It's been two out of three for the persistent and even aggressive innovator, but Kieselstein-Cord says he's not worried about fulfilling his dream of one day becoming an artist. "I know I'm going to do it," he says matter-of-factly.

—Richard Martin; updated by Diana Idzelis

KIM, Jun and Soyon

See ISANI

KLEIN, Anne

American designer

Born: Hannah Golofsky in Brooklyn, New York, 7 June 1923. **Education:** Studied art at Girls' Commercial High School, New

Anne Klein, designed for Junior Sophisticates's 1964 collection. © AP/Wide World Photos.

York, and fashion at Traphagen School, New York, 1937–38. **Family:** Married Ben Klein (divorced, 1958); married Matthew Rubenstein, 1963. **Career:** Designer, Varden Petites, New York, 1938–40; designer, women's fashions for Maurice Rentner, 1940–47; founder/partner with Ben Klein, Junior Sophisticates, 1948–66; Anne Klein and Co., and Anne Klein Studio design firms established, 1968; firm bought by Takihyo Company after Klein's death, 1974; Donna Karan took over designing, 1973–85; Louis Dell'Olio, 1973–93; Richard Tyler, 1993–94; Patrick Robinson, 1995–98; Ken Kaufman and Isaac Franco, 1998–2001; sold by Takihyo to Kasper ASL Ltd., 1999; Charles Nolan hired as head designer, 2001. **Exhibitions:** Versailles, 1973; *American Fashion on the World Stage,* Metropolitan Museum of Art, New York, 1993. **Awards:** *Mademoiselle* Merit award, 1954; Coty American Fashion Critics award, 1955, 1969, 1971; Neiman Marcus award, 1959, 1969; Lord and Taylor award, 1964; National Cotton Council award, 1965. **Died:** 19 March 1974, in New York. **Company Address:** 205 West 39th St., New York, NY 10018, U.S.A.

Publications

On KLEIN:

Books

New York and Hollywood Fashion: Costume Designs from the Brooklyn Museum Collection, New York, 1986.
Milbank, Caroline Rennolds, *New York Fashion: The Evolution of American Style,* New York, 1989.
Stegemeyer, Anne, *Who's Who in Fashion, Third Edition,* New York, 1996.

Articles

Beckett, Kathleen, "Runway Report: In-Kleined to Wow Fans: Anne Klein," in the *New York Post,* 1 November 1994.
"New York: Anne Klein," in *WWD,* 1 November 1994.
Ozzard, Janet, "Anne Klein: The Next Act," in *WWD,* 1 March 1995.
Wadyka, Sally, "New Kid in Town," *Vogue* (New York), April 1995.
Schiro, Anne-Marie, "Ralph Lauren Does What He Does Best," in the *New York Times,* 6 April 1995.
"Anne Klein Said to Be Planning Revival of Designer Collection," in *WWD,* 18 December 1996.
Gault, Ylonda, "Redesigning Klein," in *Crain's New York Business,* 17 March 1997.
Parr, Karen, "Anne Klein's New Look," in *WWD,* 4 May 1998.
Carmichael, Celia, "A Suave Design Team...at Anne Klein," in *Footwear News,* 17 August 1998.
"Anne Klein's New Era: Kasper to Buy Name, Aims for Megabrand," in *WWD,* 17 March 1999.
D'Innocenzio, Anne, "Anne Klein: New Owners, New Era," in *WWD,* 27 January 2000.
McCants, Leonard, "Anne Klein: Bringing Back the Lion," in *WWD,* 6 June 2001.
Wilson, Eric, "Building Anne Klein to Bite Back," in *WWD,* 4 October 2001.

* * *

Known as an American designer, Anne Klein often bragged she had never seen a European collection. Klein's philosophy was "not with what clothes might be but what they must be." Klein's career spanned three decades and her contributions to the industry were many. Like Claire McCardell before her, Klein helped to establish casual but elegant sportswear as defining American fashion.

Most notably, Klein transformed the junior-sized market from little-girl clothes designed with buttons and bows to clothes with a more sophisticated adult look. She also recognized that clothes for juniors should be designed for size rather than age. By analyzing the lifestyles of young women, Klein realized the fashions offered to them did not reflect their needs. In 1948, Klein and her first husband, Ben Klein, opened Junior Sophisticates, a company dedicated to this market, thus expanding the industry. Her first collection for Junior Sophisticates featured the skimmer dress with jacket; full, longer skirts; small waists; and pleated plaid skirts with blazers.

During the mid-1960s Klein freelanced for Mallory Leathers, where she established leather as a reputable dress fabric in the ready-to-wear market. She designed leather separates in bright colors and smartly styled silhouettes. In 1968 Anne Klein and Company and Anne Klein Studio were opened by Klein and her second husband, Chip Rubenstein. Focusing on sportswear with elegant styling, Klein established the concept of separates dressing. In doing this, she was

Anne Klein, 2001: matte gold pailette wrap gown, designed as an option for an Academy Award® nominee. © AP/Wide World Photos.

teaching women a new way to dress. Klein proclaimed, "Do not buy haphazardly, but rather with a theme of coordination." In the showing of the collections as well as in the stores, Klein emphasized how interchangeable the clothes were. Her designs were sold in boutiques called Anne Klein Corners, which were in major department stores. This marked the beginnings of the individual designer shops within retail environments. Accessories also became an important part of the overall look; Klein designed belts, chains, shoes, and scarves which complemented her clothes.

Klein focused on the needs of the American business woman in many of her collections for Anne Klein & Company. She relied on her own instincts to understand the diverse needs of the 1960s woman. By simplifying clothing, and showing women how to coordinate separates and accessorize, Klein taught the American woman how to dress with a minimum amount of fuss. The result was a finished, sophisticated look. The classic blazer was the central garment with shirtdresses, long midis and trousers introduced as well.

Anne Klein died in 1974. Designers Donna Karan and Louis Dell'Olio made significant contributions to fashion in her name, but left to pursue separate careers. Richard Tyler briefly came on board but did not fit with the Anne Klein aestethic. Patrick Robinson, Ken Kaufman, and Isaac Franco designed over the next several years before Charles Nolan, formerly of Ellen Tracy, was hired as head designer in 2001. With Nolan at the helm, the Anne Klein name returned to the catwalk after an absence for several years. Jenny Bailly, writing for the Fashion Windows website (22 September 2001), commented on Nolan's second collection for Anne Klein, "Our favorite pieces...were the well-cut, slightly flared trousers, accented with side-stitching and two-inch slits at the bottom." Bailly also praised Nolan's cocktail dresses and a neon orange linen coat.

—Margo Seaman; updated by Owen James

KLEIN, Calvin

American designer

Born: Bronx, New York, 19 November 1942. **Education:** Studied at Fashion Institute of Technology, New York, 1959–62. **Family:** Married Jayne Centre, 1964 (divorced 1974); child: Marci; married Kelly Rector, 1986 (separated). **Career:** Assistant designer, Dan Millstein, New York, 1962–64; freelance designer, New York, 1964–68; Calvin Klein Co. formed in partnership with Barry Schwartz, 1968, daughter Marci kidnapped (released unharmed), 1978; Brooke Sheilds jeans commercial debuted, 1980; men's underwear introduced, 1982; purchased Puritan Jeans, 1983; Unilever secures fragrance license, 1989; company reorganized with help of music mogul David Geffen, 1992; debut of less expensive cK line, circa 1993; jeans and underwear businesses sold to Warnaco, 1994; flagship store opened on Madison Avenue, New York City, 1995; first freestanding cK store, Kent, 1999; second cK store, Manchester, 2000; trademark infringement suit filed against Warnaco, 2000; lawsuit against Warnaco settled, 2001; fragrances include *Obsession,* 1985, *Eternity,* 1988, *cK one,* 1994, *cK be,* 1996, also *Escape, Contradiction, Truth Calvin Klein.* **Awards:** Coty American Fashion Critics award, 1973, 1974, 1975; Bath Museum of Costume Dress of the Year award, 1980; Council of Fashion Designers of America award, 1993; named one of the "25 Most Influential Americans" by *Time,* 1996; Lifetime Achievement award, Council of Fashion Designers of America, 2001. **Address:** 654 Madison Avenue, New York, NY 10021, USA.

Publications

On KLEIN:

Books

Morris, Bernadine, and Barbara Walz, *The Fashion Makers,* New York, 1978.
Perschetz, Lois, ed., *W, The Designing Life,* New York, 1987.
Coleridge, Nicholas, *The Fashion Conspiracy,* London, 1988.
Milbank, Caroline Rennolds, *New York Fashion: The Evolution of American Style,* New York, 1989.
Howell, Georgina, *Sultans of Style: Thirty Years of Fashion and Passion 1960–1990,* London, 1990.
McDowell, Colin, *The Designer Scam,* London, 1994.
Gaines, Steven, and Sharon Churcher, *Obsession: The Lives and Times of Calvin Klein,* New York, 1995.
Stegemeyer, Anne, *Who's Who in Fashion, Third Edition,* New York, 1996.
Le Dortz, Laurent, and Béatrice Debosscher, *Stratégies des Leaders Américains de la Mode: Calvin Klein, Donna Karan, Liz Clairborne, Polo Ralph Lauren, et Tommy Hilfiger,* Paris, 2000.

Articles

Peer, Elizabeth, "Stylish Calvinism," in *Newsweek,* 3 November 1975.
Brown, Erica, "The Rag Trade to Riches Rise of Calvin Klein," in the *Sunday Times Magazine* (London), 29 April 1980.
Cleave, Maureen, "Calvin Klein," in the *Observer* (London), 7 December 1980.
Alter, Jonathan, and Ann Hughey, "Calvin and the Family Firm," in *Newsweek,* 12 December 1983.
Sherrid, Pamela, "Ragman," in *Forbes,* 15 February 1982.
Trachtenberg, Jeffrey A., "Between Me and My Calvins," in *Forbes,* 9 April 1984.
Morris, Bernadine, "Calvin Klein Keeps It Smart and Simple," in the *New York Times,* 1 May 1985.
Brady, James, "In Step with Calvin Klein," in *Parade* (New York), 26 October 1986.
Hume, Marion, "The Secret of My Success," in *Fashion Weekly* (London), 27 August 1987.
Brampton, Sally, "Drawing a Klein Line," in *Elle* (London), January 1988.
Gross, Michael, "The Latest Calvin: From the Bronx to Eternity," in *New York,* 8 August 1988.
Orth, Maureen, "A Star is Reborn," in *Vogue,* September 1988.
Howell, Georgina, "Mr. Klein Comes Clean," in the *Sunday Times Magazine* (London), 10 September 1989.
"Calvin Klein's Obsession," in *Cosmopolitan,* May 1991.

Calvin Klein, spring 2001 collection: plaster silk tissue radzimir dress. © AP/Wide World Photos.

"Calvin Klein's Bold Strategy in U.S., Europe," in *WWD,* 19 June 1991.

Behbehani, Mandy, "Nothing Between Success and Calvin," in the *San Francisco Examiner,* 30 January 1992.

Grant, Linda, "Can Calvin Klein Escape," in the *Los Angeles Times,* 23 February 1992.

Sloan, Pat, "I Don't Have Long-Term Plans. I Just Act Instinctively," in *Advertising Age,* 18 May 1992.

Mower, Sarah, "Calvin in Control," in *Harper's Bazaar,* 11 November 1992.

Hirshey, Gerri, "The Snooty Dame at the Block Party," in the *New York Times Magazine,* 24 October 1993.

Morris, Bernadine, "Master of Ease," in the *New York Times,* 6 February 1994.

Brampton, Sally, "Calvin Clean," in *Marie Claire* (London), August 1994.

Reed, Julia, "Calvin's Clean Sweep," in *Vogue,* August 1994.

Beckett, Kathleen, "Slip-sliding to a Close: Calvin Klein," in the *New York Post,* 5 November 1994.

Spindler, Amy M., "Klein and Karan: Clothes that Do the Job," in the *New York Times,* 5 November 1994.

"New York: Calvin's Minimal Magnetism," in *WWD,* 7 November 1994.

Spindler, Amy M., "Luxurious Armor by Karan, Klein, Mizrahi," in the *New York Times,* 8 April 1995.

"Calvin Cool Edge," in *WWD,* 10 April 1995.

Kaplan, James, "The Triumph of Calvinism," in *New York,* 18 September 1995.

Elliott, Stuart, "To Be or Not to Be? To Young People It's No Question, Klein Says," in the *New York Times,* 14 August 1996.

Young, Vicki, "Calvin Klein Jeanswear Suing Conway for Infringement," in *WWD,* 29 August 1996.

Lockwood, Lisa, "Calvin's Credo," in *WWD,* 22 July 1997.

Ryan, J., "With Quips and Kisses, Wachner Takes Over CK Jeans Business," in *WWD,* 15 December 1997.

Goldstein, Lauren, "Clever Clavin Sells Suits Like Socks," in *Fortune,* 23 November 1998.

Lockwood, Lisa, "Calvin's Model Moment," in *WWD,* 9 June 2000.

"Calvin Klein," in *Business Wire,* 13 June 2000.

"Calvin Klein's Truth is in the Scent," in *Cosmetics International Cosmetic Products Report,* August 2000.

Shiloh, Dina, "Calvin Klein Helps to Bring Jordan and Israel Together," in the *Times* (London), 22 August 2000.

Sellers, Patricia, "Seventh Avenue Smackdown: Calvin Klein and Linda Wachner are Going Toe-to-Toe in a Bitter Suit…," in *Fortune,* 4 September 2000.

Calvin Klein, fall 2001 collection: front and back view of a fluid matte silk dress. © AP/Wide World Photos.

Wilson, Eric, "Calvin Klein: After 33 Years in Businesses, the Designer Remains True to His Quest for Modernity While Searching for What's Next," in *WWD,* 5 June 2001.
Cojoucaru, Steven, "Behind the Seams," in *People,* 2 July 2001.

* * *

An indisputable genius in marketing, a recognized wizard in fashion financing, a charismatic image-maker and image himself, Calvin Klein is the quintessential American fashion expression of the last quarter of the 20th century and still world renowned in the 21st century. The energy of his identification with jeans in the late 1970s and early 1980s, his later frontiers of underwear, and his consistent edge for advertising image in print and media have rendered him a vivid figure in the landscape of American cultural life.

A sleazy, potboiler biography of Klein was published in 1995, titled *Obsession: The Lives and Times of Calvin Klein,* not only taking its title from his popular fragrance and beauty products line but

Klein's chameleon-like ability to be many things in the fashion industry. Years before, Michael Gross had already described Klein's life in *New York* magazine (8 August 1988) as "an extraordinary odyssey—a sort of one-man pilgrimage through the social history of modern America." Yet Klein is homegrown hero to young America, the elusive image of the creator as megapower and carnal charmer, the recurrent American worship of those few who achieve absolute power in a democracy. In his decades as a top designer, Klein has established himself as a veritable obsession. He has only intensified this stature in spiraling success that challenges, yet flourishes in, the very visible arenas of fashionable culture.

Is Klein a designer? Suffused with aura and surrounded by negotiation—commercial and social—Klein might seem to have sacrificed his essential métier as a designer. Significantly, he has not. His sensibility for minimalist aesthetics, in an active lifestyle with the ethos of sportswear, is as evident today as it ever was. Klein's clothing is as judicious as his marketing is advanced: streamlined clothes worn with ease prevail, with influences as far flung as Vionnet, Halston, di Sant'Angelo, and Armani. Klein's best eveningwear gives a first impression of delicacy and refinement, characteristically avoiding linings and complications, as the wearer enjoys an unexpected freedom and mobility.

Klein's fashion is the quintessence of American fashion expression and taste—his minimal construction promotes mass manufacturing; his ease allows comfortable dressing in all sizes and shapes; his penchant for quality wool, cashmere, cotton, and other feel-good textile luxuries affirms a sense of luxury in clothes otherwise so undistinguished in their simplicity as to pass unnoticed. Although in a 1994 press statement Klein avowed that "Everything begins with the cut," one does not think of cut and construction in the traditional fashion measure of Vionnet or Madame Grès. Klein's spare cut is not truly architectural; it is unobtrusive or, in the words of Bernadine Morris, writing in the *New York Times* in May of 1985, "without frills."

Klein's marketing of jeans, underwear, and fragrance were consistent in their aggressive even opportunistic address to gender and sexuality. Beginning with 1980 television advertising conceived by Richard Avedon and Klein using young model Brooke Shields, Klein steadily set and stretched the parameters of America's acceptance of overt sensuality in promotion of fashion and in public, with displays ranging from national television campaigns to Times Square billboards, and to print media. Klein's campaigns have been progressive, seeming in each instance to build upon and move beyond the first provocation and the inevitable acceptance of the prior campaign.

Defining the public protocols of the 1980s and 1990s, Klein made a distinct cultural contribution to advertising. He not only took the design of jeans and underwear to new heights, but brought gender into the fray as well. He was unerringly responsible for the surge of gender-sharing fragrances launched in the middle and late 1990s, as well as pushing the envelope with daringly sexual displays in adversitising.

James Brady wrote of Klein in *Parade* in October 1986: "His success is so enormous, his income so vast, his lifestyle so lavish, that we tend to forget that in life there are no free rides." And so controversy has often surrounded Klein as much as celebrity; but it is incontrovertible that Klein altered the landscape of modern American fashion and its perception as only a genius and a giant can—in an epoch of uncertainty and recriminations, Klein's imperfect but ever-upward course prompted dispute and jealousy. Yet he demonstrated, over and over, that his unerring fashion sense would prevail.

Klein's enduring success has been a balance of the no-nonsense fashion designer with the pretentious and unpredictable commercialism of the fashion industry. Since 1994 Calvin Klein Inc. has grown into a fashion empire producing everything—including menswear, womenswear, fragrances and skincare products, eyewear, socks, and pillowcases (Calvin Klein Home, a home fashion collection, was introduced in April 1995). Bearing the Calvin Klein name has grown into a lifestyle revered around the world; it is known in countries even where his products are not sold. Klein believes American clothes are an advantage in the global marketplace; nearly 90-percent of his business is through worldwide licensing agreements.

Klein has continued to receive notoriety from the publicity surrounding his advertisements. In 1995 his cK Jeans advertising campaign was pulled because of accusations of child pornography. New York Mayor Rudy Giuliani led the uproar in 1999 over a Times Square billboard showing seminaked youngsters. Even though Klein's advertisements are seen as inappropriate, his design philosophy has remained consistent—to keep the clothes modern, sophisticated, sexy, clean, and minimal. He once told *Time* magazine, "I've never been one to see women in ruffles and all kinds of fanciful apparel. To me it's just silly."

Klein confirmed in 1999 that he was looking ways to expand his business. He hired financial advisers to seek opportunities to develop his business through a merger, or by selling or developing other strategic options. Confirmed reports said Prada, Gucci, LMVH, and Ralph Lauren showed interest in purchasing Calvin Klein, Inc. Warnco, which owned the Calvin Klein underwear and jeans businesses, made an offer but the parties failed to agree on control of Calvin Klein trademark usage. In a statement, Klein said the "strongest path to growth lay in remaining an independent, privately held entity." As of 2001, both Klein and his company remained independent and private.

—Richard Martin; updated by Donna W. Reamy

KLOSS, John

American designer

Born: John Klosowski in Detroit, Michigan, 13 June 1937. **Education:** Studied architecture at Cass Technical High School, Detroit; studied fashion at Traphagen School of Fashion, New York. **Career:** Worked for couturier Bob Bugnand, Paris, 1957–58; established own business with signature boutique at Henri Bendel, New York, 1959; designer, Lily of France, New York, 1970s; designer, John Kloss for CIRA division of SLC Fashion Corporation, 1970s. **Awards:** Coty American Fashion Critics award, 1971, 1974; Knitted Textile Association Crystal Ball award, 1974. **Died:** 25 March 1987, in Stamford, Connecticut.

Publications

On KLOSS:

Books

Milbank, Caroline Rennolds, *New York Fashion: The Evolution of American Style,* New York, 1989.

Articles

Molli, Jeanne, "Designer Works in Loft Amid Art and Greenery," in the *New York Times,* 19 March 1962.

Taylor, Angela, "The Kloss Style: Modern Art and Jigsaw Puzzles," in the *New York Times,* 30 March 1966.

"Inspiration Comes from People," in *Intimate Apparel,* August/September 1971.

Shelton, P., "Fashion's Constant Nostalgia Kick Bores John Kloss," in *Biography News,* January 1974.

"John Kloss, Designer, Dies," in *WWD,* 30 March 1987.

* * *

Dress and lingerie designer John Kloss (John Klosowski) was born in Detroit, Michigan, where he studied architecture at Cass Technical High School. He moved to New York and worked for Irving Trust Company on Wall Street. Kloss ultimately gained his fashion training when he attended the Traphagen School of Fashion in New York. At age 20, he apprenticed with American-born couturier Bob Bugnand in Paris and went on to work for Serge Matta. In 1959 Kloss turned down an offer to work with Nina Ricci and instead began to design with Lisa Fonssagrives and later worked on his own, designing collections for wholesale manufacturers. Some of his designs were manufactured and distributed by Bendel's Studio, a part of Henri Bendel of New York, a store noted for discovering and supporting young fashion designers.

In the early 1960s, Kloss designed sculpturally-shaped dresses constructed from fabrics such as cotton brocades, that could be formed and molded to enclose the body. By the late 1960s he was using chiffon, matte jersey, and crêpe de chine; fluid materials which moved gracefully with the wearer. Simple dress shapes were formed without darts that did not fit tightly to the body, but flowed seductively over its curves.

Kloss used vivid colors like lemon yellows, greens, amethyst, and ruby in abstract shapes reminiscent of abstract expressionist paintings. Sophisticated, simple, clean designs were detailed with top stitching, tiny rows of buttons, simple edge trims, or tie closures. These nonstructured designs were adapted for lingerie and loungewear marketed by Lily of France and CIRA. Included were designs for nightgowns and bras, both seamless and underwired, again without superfluous lace trimmings.

The most revolutionary of Kloss' designs came about as a reaction to the "ban the bra" movement in the 1970s. He designed a bra that appeared not to exist in 1974 for Lily of France, called the "glossie," which was made from stretchy, sheer, glittery material. The design was seamless, unconstructed, but underwired, so it provided support for those women who needed it, yet wanted the braless look. The "glossie" came in solid colors such as amethyst, indigo, ruby, and mocha.

Kloss received two Coty awards, one in 1971 and another in 1974, for his lingerie designs. His nightgowns were cut from nylon in nonboudoir colors, in sophisticated, seductive cuts that emulated some of his eveningwear. In addition, Kloss also designed leotards, pajamas, swimwear, and sportswear. Under various licenses, he designed foundation garments, lingerie, loungewear, hosiery, tenniswear, and home sewing patterns. He was affiliated with the Kreisler Group of young designers under the management of Stuart Kreisler.

Whether designing dresses or loungewear, John Kloss was aware of the fashion trends, moving from sculptural, molded forms, to the free flowing more casual looks of the late 1960s and 1970s. He avoided unnecessary details, relying instead on the cut of the garment and the materials used to provide the design. The garments moved and flowed with the wearer. His designs were simple, clean, and seductive.

Kloss committed suicide in 1987.

—Nancy House

KNECHT, Gabriele

American designer

Born: Munich, Germany, 8 January 1938. **Education:** Studied fine arts, majoring in fashion design, Washington University, St. Louis, 1956–60; synergetics, cosmology, physics, New School for Social Research, New York, 1977–80; reflective theory, Hayden Planetarium, New York; insect kinematics, Museum of Natural History, New York. **Career:** Bra designer, Formfit Co., Chicago, 1959; dress designer, Carlye Dress Co., St. Louis, 1960–61; designer, boyswear, Hummelsheim, Murnau, West Germany, 1961–62; designer, junior dresses, Big Ben Modelle, West Berlin, 1962; childrenswear collection, Bill Atkinson, Glen of Michigan, New York, 1963–67; designer, Sally Forth childrenswear, Boe Jests Inc., 1967–68; designer, S.W.A.K. children and preteen sportswear, Villager, 1968–69; designer, women's sportswear, Boe Jests Inc., 1969–70; owner/designer, operating mail order hand-knit kits, I Did it Myself, Mother, 1970–73; designer, children's sportswear, Gabriele Knecht label, Suntoga, Miami, Florida, 1971–73; author/designer knitting booklets, 1973–77; freelance designer, junior and children's knitwear, 1977–82; designer/producer, G.K. Forward Inc., from 1982; U.S. patent awarded for garments constructed with forward sleeves, 1984; lecturer, Fashion Institute of Technology and Parsons School of Design, New York; Washington State University; North Carolina State University; University of Cincinnati School of Design; Fashion Group of St. Louis; American Association of University Women; Fashion's Inner Circle. **Collections:** Fashion Institute of Technology, New York. **Exhibitions:** *More Fashion Award Grand Prize-Winning Designs,* Henderson Gallery, Yellow Springs, Ohio, 1985; *Her Works Praise Her: Women as Inventors,* Goldstein Gallery, University of Minnesota, St. Paul, 1988; *A Woman's Place is in the Patent Office,* U.S. Patent and Trademark Office, Washington, D.C., 1990. **Awards:** Outstanding Women in America listing, 1966; Best New Designer in Women's Clothing Field, More Fashion award, New York, 1984; National Endowment for the Arts grant, 1986. **Address:** G.K. Forward Inc., 264 West 35th Street, New York, NY 10001, U.S.A.

Publications

By KNECHT:

Books

Learn to Crochet and *Learn to Knit* booklets for Columbia Minerva Corporation, New York, from 1973.

On KNECHT:

Articles

"Gabriele Knecht Receives First More Fashion Award," in *WWD,* 2 May 1984.

Peacock, Mary, "Gabriele Knecht's Patented Patterns and Other Fashion Breakthroughs," in *Ms.* (New York), March 1985.

Harte, Susan, "Patterned for Perfection," in the *Atlanta Journal & Constitution,* 4 August 1985.

Engelken, K., "Rethinking Sleeves," in *Washington University Alumni News,* March 1986.

Sayers, Donna, "Armed Revolution," in the *Cincinnati Enquirer,* October 1988.

Friedman, Arthur, "Knecht Steps Forward," in *WWD,* September 1991.

Van Horne, Gladys, "Maestra's New Suit Stitched Just in Time," in the *Wheeling News-Register,* September 1992.

*

I started my own company of designer sportswear and coats after spending several years developing an original clothing concept which relates the structure of clothing to the unique way the human body moves. The technology for this concept has been fully documented in a United States patent. Unlike clothing which fits a body at rest or standing still, I base my designs on an underlying construction which anticipates the forward direction the body takes in movement, producing new fashion shapes.

I achieve my designs from a pattern-making system based on squares, working out the technical construction in miniature first, then enlarging the squares for the life-size version. My "K" trademark illustrates the difference between conventional construction and my forward-sleeve construction: the left part of the logo showing the top view of the body with sleeve direction of conventional garments; the right part of the logo showing the top view of the body with sleeve direction of garments based on my patented forward sleeve.

—Gabriele Knecht

* * *

New York designer Gabriele Knecht believes that if you want to change fashion and achieve new shapes, you must change the underlying foundation. So she did. Conventional construction methods used in the making of garments were hundreds of years old and based on the T-shape, or kimono pattern. This method assumed our arms and legs had an equal range of movement around the anterior and posterior of the body.

Knecht states that although the arms have a large range of movement around the body, this freedom is not equal in all directions. "We can hug ourselves and move our legs forward, but there is a limited or different movement toward the back of the body." Knecht has, possibly for the first time in history, looked at the real differences between the body's front and back range of movement, studying kinematics, synergetics, physics, and cosmology in addition to fashion design and fine arts. Combining these drastically different areas of study, she looked at how the differences of movement of the body affected fashion design, pattern making, and garment construction. The result was her "forward-sleeve" design.

Knecht's one-piece and multipiece forward-sleeve pattern brought the axis of the sleeve substantially forward of the body's lateral plane and into the arm's center range of movement. This was accomplished by moving the low point of the armhole forward while leaving the high point in the lateral plane of the body. By doing this, Knecht put a larger degree of ease and mobility in the side front area of her garments, where it was needed, yet with a closer body fit. The forward-sleeve design was an evolution in pattern making and construction, a process developed over a 10-year period that earned Knecht a U.S. patent in 1984 and foreign patents in Canada and Japan.

Using the forward-sleeve orientation as the basis for all of her work, Knecht has designed a line of chic, well-cut, and excellently proportional sportswear. The range of movement achieved with her forward-sleeve design allowed for a fitted, even tailored garment to have the movement and comfort of a much less constructed piece. Knecht's work, like that of American sportswear designer Claire McCardell, is simplified, reductive, and appealing to our human nature. Using geometrical shapes and diagonals to break or eliminate side seams and, when possible, only one pattern piece, she has created a design aesthetic and spirit all her own.

Although Knecht will not bow to the mandates of changing trends, her innate ability to design and her integrity of cut and construction have been evident in every garment with the Gabriele Knecht label. The Gabriele Knecht line has been sold in a number of major retail and specialty stores, such as Saks Fifth Avenue (exclusively for one season), Bonwit Teller, Macy's, Bergdorf Goodman, and Neiman Marcus, as well as in smaller stores such as Joanie's of Memphis. Knecht's work can be found alongside that of Yeohlee, Lida Baday, Peter Cohen, Ronaldus Shamask, Gentry Portifino, and Ann McKenna.

Maestra Rachel Worby of the Wheeling Symphony in West Virginia states, "The best feature is that the sleeves are attached in such a way that when I move my arms up and down as I am conducting, the jacket does not hike up too."

In 1984 Knecht was awarded the first-ever More Fashion award in New York. The event, hosted by *Dynasty* star Joan Collins, was sponsored by R.J. Reynolds Tobacco Co., maker of More cigarettes. Knecht beat out finalists Hino and Malee, Frans Haers, Tamotsu, and Frederico and Alfredo Viloria to win the top prize. The trophy was a wisp of vermeil on an ebony base...which fell off during the ceremony; Knecht took it in stride.

Knecht's spirit and singularity of purpose are best expressed by Susan Harte in the *Atlanta Journal & Constitution* (4 August 1985): "There is unlimited direction open to her now that she has set her fundamental precepts. She will design human clothes, not necessarily 'with-it' ones, and will do it autonomously, not deferentially."

—Fred Dennis; updated by Daryl F. Mallett

KOBAYASHI, Yukio

Japanese designer

Career: Designer, menswear line, Monsieur Nicole line, for Matsuda; joined Matsuda, 1976; took over as designer of Matsuda's menswear collection (known as Nicole in Japan), 1983; showed collection in New York for the first time, 1983; initial showing of collection in Paris, 1987; named chief designer, Matsuda's menwear and womenswear lines, 1995; opened Kobayashi Design Office Company to develop signature brands, late 1990s. **Awards:** Art Director's Club of New York for photo collaboration with Nan Goldin, 1996; Kuwazawa award, 1997. **Address:** Kobayashi Design Office Co. Ltd., 103, 2–30–9, Jingumae, Shibuya-Ku, Tokyo.

PUBLICATIONS

On KOBAYASHI:

Books

Phaidon Press (ed.), *The Fashion Book,* London, 1998.

Articles

Fressola, Peter, in *DNR,* 5 November 1986.
DNR, 5 February 1992.
Klensch, Elsa, "Matsuda Paints a Second Skin for Spring '97," on CNN, 12 February 1997.
Ozzard, Janet, "Matsuda Out to Stake a Bigger Claim in U.S.," in *WWD,* 12 February 1997.

* * *

Memory, both in the collective and crystalline form of history and in the ether of personal recollection, is the primary concern of Yukio Kobayashi's menswear for Matsuda. Memory mingles in Kobayashi's work with a desire for literary expression. Language blurts out irrepressibly in the work in frequent words, letters, and numbers. A lapel, for instance, may vanish into linear design or letters may become a surrealist free fall of pattern. Literature abides in another way: the clothing is laden with an evocative knowledge of the literary past, as if costuming for a Merchant-Ivory film (Kobayashi's 1984 collections had reflected movie star elegance from the 1940s).

Kobayashi builds his clothing on the dandy's proposition that all clothing is to be seen in a self-conscious spectatorship. Tailored clothing explores a repertory of early 20th-century menswear; sportswear is supple and minimal, sometimes suggesting the Renaissance, Beau Brummel languor, or anticipating Utopia. Without contradiction to his historicism, Kobayashi is an apostle of advanced technology in synthetic fibers, often in startling juxtaposition with traditional materials and craft-domain handwork.

Kobayashi's aesthetic made Matsuda menswear favored apparel for artists and intellectuals; the boulevardier dandyism of the clothing is due to its intellectual edge. Peter Fressola characterized Kobayashi's work for Matsuda Men almost as an acquired, special taste in *DNR* (5 November 1986): "If you have never liked Matsuda, chances are good that you never will. But this designer has inspired the loyalty of a great many who willingly suspend judgement in favor of the rich, romantic, almost decadent aesthetic that is the world of his design." In literary traits and audacious style, Kobayashi created the most romantic menswear of the 20th century.

Kobayashi's aesthetic is invariably elegant, but he achieves his elegance not solely through refined materials but through the tactile satisfactions of fabric and pattern. A Norfolk jacket, a favorite template of Kobayashi's design, is transformed by blocks of pattern at differing scale; robust outerwear becomes luxurious by the swelled proportions of the collar; in the 1990s, trousers were transfigured by their uninflected plainness, flat front, and cropped just above the ankle. Kobayashi generally mediates between the inherent elegance of his style and a simple design sincerity—treating the basics of clothing, like allowing jackets to move with loose fit, or in his exploration of soft velvety and corduroy materials.

In February 1992 *DNR* called the Kobayashi fall menswear collection "a modern, down-to-earth, *very* Matsuda look," capturing its unpretentiousness. Even argyle-patterned Donegal tweeds, jackets with suppressed waists, seemed common, comfortable, and friendly. Thus Kobayashi achieves the dandy's grace with none of the dandy's disdain or arrogance: rugged materials, comfort, and vernacular borrowings are essential to his design. England and Scotland are the motherland of Kobayashi's historicist vision.

In brilliant command of menswear history, Kobayashi has favored early 20th-century clothing, the time of menswear codification. Nonetheless, he is capable of reflecting with bravura elegance on Victorian *tartanitis* and in creating revelers from a Venetian masked carnival in modern form. Responding to a question in *Details,* Kobayashi said: "The early part of the century was a time when the way people thought about clothes was radically changing. But the period I enjoy speculating about most is the future." Without such a sense of late-modern invention and adventure, the components of Kobayashi's style might seem to fall into clever but tiring eclecticism. Instead, he keeps a sharp analytical edge and an unremitting sense of the new and vanguard about his clothing. After all, almost all other menswear designers have recourse to the same body of Anglophilic and Edwardian styles that inspire Kobayashi, but his energy is quicker, more intellectual, and more transforming.

Kobayashi and Matsuda have a reputation for looking at fashion as art. As part of this belief, they have paired with a number of well-known photographers, many of them outside the fashion industry, to create advertising and art photos that have been exhibited around the world. They have included drug-culture photographer Nan Goldin (whose series "Goldin Meets Yukio Kobayashi," won an award from the Art Director's Club of New York), performance artist Laurie Anderson, Jan Saudek, and Bruce Weber.

Kobayashi often lets fabric lead when he creates a line. From wool tweed, sponge and quilting, to body-hugging synthetics and sheer fabrics that emulate tattoos on the body, Kobayashi looks to the material to inspire his designs, which always emphasize comfort. Much of his work is gender-bending and age-blind and incorporates a broad range of colors. The designer combines experimentation with an adherence to traditional, classic styles.

Kobayashi had been designing Matsuda's menswear lines since 1983 and, in 1995, took over the women's collection as well, working closely with Matsuhiro Matsuda on its direction. At the time, Matsuda had 500 stores in Japan and had $230 million in wholesale volume; just one percent of this figure was attributable to the U.S. market, according to *Women's Wear Daily.* The weekly publication further reported that Matsuda would focus on increasing its presence in the U.S. market in the late 1990s, using Kobayashi's expanding and favorable reputation as a launching point.

While the Matsuda label is solely for export, the company markets ten labels under the Nicole banner in Japan. Nicole is licensed for home furnishings, tabletop products, eyewear, luggage, and small leather goods in Japan and around Asia, and Matsuda planned to expand its licensing efforts in the U.S. as well. In the late 1990s, Kobayashi opened his own Tokyo-based studio, Kobayashi Design Office Company Ltd., to develop his own labels. His intention, as he told Hideki Iwauchi on the Internet publication Insite-Tokyo, was to create clothing that was fun and free, designed for wearability rather than to be viewed on models.

—Richard Martin; updated by Karen Raugust

KONISHI, Yoshiyuki

Japanese knitwear designer

Born: 1950 in Tsu, Japan. **Career:** Established Ficce Uomo Co. Ltd. and introduced Ficce Uomo menswear line, 1981; introduced Yoshiyuki Konishi menswear line, 1987; introduced Ficce Jeans menswear line, 1988; introduced Ficce Donna womenswear line and Ficce Sport ski wear line, 1993; first New York runway show, 1997. **Awards:** Mainichi Fashion grand prix, 1991. **Address:** Ficce Uomo Co. Ltd., 4–3–11 Minami Azabu, Minato-Ku, Tokyo 106, Japan.

Publications

On KONISHI:

Books

Tokyo Collection, Tokyo, 1986.
Yoshiyuki Konishi's Knits, Tokyo, 1986.
Takeshi Beat Wears Knits of Yoshiyuki Konishi, Tokyo, 1992.

Yoshiyuki Konishi, spring 1998 collection. © Fashion Syndicate Press.

Articles

Ozzard, Janet, "New York at Bat," in *WWD,* 7 April 1997.
Greene, Walter, "Sexy Spring Fashions," in *Black Elegance,* April 1998.

*

The yarns I design are the vital essences of my finished products and the finished products are the radiators of my energy. The clothes I design—the multicolored, multitextured products—are the results of numerous experiments and challenges made and built up in the years I have lived and worked. The productions—yarn making, dyeing, knitting and weaving, and construction of the final product—all need to attain a level of equilibrium that must be maintained throughout the entire process.

In order to sustain originality, my designs begin from the productions of the single yarns and I do not believe in rationalization. Most of my handmade products require time-consuming and complicated procedures, but when artisan and spirit unite, a new world is introduced. The finished product—well-designed wearable clothes that include fantastic colors, materials, silhouettes, and shapes—function as comfortable clothes with evidence of my identity in every aspect of the product.

I hope to establish and stablize my styles and at the same time I wish to analyze the world changes and affairs and translate them into my work.

—Yoshiyuki Konishi

* * *

Yoshiyuki Konishi is categorized as a men's sweater designer, but his sweater is not a sweater in the conventional sense. It may be called an objet d'art, an intricate tapestry, or a Jackson Pollock painting in three dimensions, but hardly an everyday variety of sweater. Not a few people see a similarity between Konishi's sweaters and Gaudi's architecture; a Japanese critic even had Konishi's sweaters photographed in front of Gaudi's buildings in Barcelona to prove the point.

"Until I saw those photos, I hadn't known anything about Gaudi. Later I looked at Gaudi's work and realized that some of my sweaters had a lot in common with Gaudi's baroque structures," says Konishi. He wonders if Gaudi shared his creative process. "I don't plan anything. I don't leaf through art books looking for an inspiration. An idea often comes to me while I stare vacantly at an empty wall," Konishi explains. "Once I get going, more ideas spring up, and I constantly add and change even after the production process has started. My production people think I am hopelessly disorganized."

Every aspect of a Konishi sweater is unusual and excessive. An average of 30 different colors are knit into a sweater, and he has used as many as 60 colors for a particularly elaborate one. He is obsessed with the quest for new materials, even experimenting with baling ropes, leather strips, vinyl tubes, and many other odd materials and still complains, "I wish I weren't making sweaters. The requirement for comfort prohibits the use of interesting materials." His staff processes and dyes raw materials such as silk, alpaca, and angora instead of buying already processed yarns. Konishi's knitting methods are as varied as his materials: machine knit, hand crochet, macramé, to name a few. Almost every season he comes up with new stitch patterns.

Yoshiyuki Konishi, spring 1998 collection. © Fashion Syndicate Press.

Obviously, Konishi is a black sheep in the fashion industry, albeit a cheerful and genial one. He does not mind being labeled a renegade or a rebel. "Actually," he confesses, "I feel embarrassed every time people call me a fashion designer. I am not sure if what I am making is fashion." But he was peeved when a French journalist called his work un-Japanese. "This person thought that black was a 'Japanese' color," he fumed. "But black is not traditionally Japanese. Look at kimonos and obis. Japanese have always loved a riot of radiant colors."

He should know, he grew up in Japan in an old feudal castle town called Tsu, where his maternal family had operated a kimono store for generations. "My childhood memories are all about kimonos," Konishi recalls. "A trip for me meant accompanying my mother on her buying trip, to Kyoto to select gorgeous obis, or to a trade show to look at hundreds of kimono fabrics." Konishi's penchant for color was probably nurtured by early experiences, but his design motifs are anything but traditionally Japanese, including such disparate inspirations as American cartoon characters, the Amazon jungle, or mythical ancient India. You cannot stay neutral about his sweaters; you either passionately love them or passionately hate them, which is fine with Konishi. He has a sizeable following among Japan's creative and professional circles. One ardent collector of Konishi sweaters asked Konishi to design his garden. Owning dozens of Konishi sweaters was not enough for him, he wanted even his house to enjoy a touch of Konishi. As long as he has such enthusiastic supporters, Konishi would happily consume his energies in pursuit of the perfect sweater.

In spring 1997, Konishi showed for the first time in New York, after a 25-year career as a designer in Japan, where, by the end of 1996 his wholesale business totaled $30 million in sales and he had developed a wide renown, according to *Women's Wear Daily.* His New York show reflected his use of lavish fabrics, from knits and brocade to mohair, crochet, and velvet, as well as his attention to details. *Women's Wear Daily* called his knits "elaborately detailed without becoming costumey."

His Asian-inspired looks—which were noted by the U.S. press even though many Japanese observers have long felt his designs did not reflect his heritage—attracted rave reviews from critics in the U.S., who commented on his elegant use of fabric and vibrant color palette. Noting that Konishi had never received the recognition in North America he deserved, critic Walter Greene wrote in *Black Elegance* (April 1998): "With a clear vision of the future, this designer moves into the 21st century with style and substance."

—Yoko Hamada; updated by Karen Raugust

KORS, Michael

American designer

Born: Long Island, New York, 9 August 1959. **Education:** Studied fashion design at Fashion Institute of Technology, New York, 1977. **Career:** Sales assistant at Lothar's boutique, New York, 1977–78 (while studying at FIT), then designer and display director, 1978–80; established own label for women's sportswear, 1981; designer, Lyle & Scott, 1989; introduced lower-priced Kors line and menswear collection, 1990; designer, womenswear collection, for Erreuno J, from 1990; bridge line discontinued, company reorganized, 1993; hired as creative director for Celine, 1997; reintroduced own menswear collection label, 1998; took over all design responsibilities at Celine, 1998; created costumes for film *The Thomas Crown Affair,* 1999; one-third of business purchased by LMVH (Moët Hennessy Louis Vuitton), 1999; opened Manhattan store for own labels, 2000; stake in business acquired by Onward Kashiyama USA, 2000; introduced first fragrance, 2000; debuted licensed handbags, footwear, and eyewear, 2001. **Awards:** Dupont American Original award, 1983; Council of Fashion Designers Womenswear Designer of the Year, 1999; Featured Designer at Neiman Marcus Crystal Charity Ball luncheon, 2000. **Address:** 550 Seventh Avenue, New York, NY 10018, USA.

Publications

On KORS:

Books

Stegemeyer, Anne, *Who's Who in Fashion, Third Edition,* New York, 1996.

Michael Kors, fall 2001 collection: wool ruana over a merino pullover and stretch flannel britches. © AP/Wide World Photos.

Articles

Sinclaire, Paul, and Lesley Jane Nonkin, "Designer, Client: The Modern Equation," in *Vogue* (New York), November 1987.

Boehlert, Bart, "On Kors," in *Connoisseur* (New York), August 1988.

Hochswender, Woody, "Designers on a Quiet Road to Success," in the *New York Times,* 1 November 1988.

Reiger, Nancy, "Michael Kors Keeps It Cool," in *Footwear News* (New York), 30 July 1990.

Worthington, Christa, "The Three Choicest Dudes in the USA," in the *Sunday Times Magazine* (London), 26 August 1990.

Hochswender, Woody, "Casual, for the Car Pool (or Whatever)," in the *New York Times,* 9 September 1990.

———, "Amid the Scramble of the Style Race, Individuality Lives," in the *New York Times,* 1 November 1990.

Darnton, Nina, "Acclaim for a New Mister Clean: Move Over, Calvin, and Make Room for Kors," in *Newsweek,* 3 December 1990.

Baker, Martha, "Of Kors," in *New York,* 17 December 1990.

Goodman, Wendy, "Upper-Deck Accommodations," in *HG* (New York), October 1991.

Rudolph, Barbara, "Why Chic Is Now Cheaper," in *Time,* 11 November 1991.

Smith, Liz, "Just the Way Mother Likes It," in the *Times* (London), 13 April 1992.

Morris, Bernadine, "The Evolution of Leather's Gentler Image," in the *New York Times,* 28 April 1992.

"New York: Michael Kors," in *WWD,* 7 November 1994.

Lockwood, Lisa, "Kors Designing Bridge Line for Onward Kashiyama," in *WWD,* 7 February 1995.

DeCaro, Frank, "Why Isn't He Calvin Klein? Michael Kors has Everything but Megastardom—So Far," in *Newsweek,* 29 July 1996.

Hanson, Holly, "Life and Business is Looking Up for Designer Michael Kors," from *Knight-Ridder/Tribune News Service,* 12 September 1996.

Weisman, Katherine, "Kors, Celine Confirm Post as Designer," in *WWD,* 24 November 1997.

White, Constance C.R., "Another Design Talent is Lured Away to France," in the *New York Times,* 25 November 1997.

"LMVH Buys 33-Percent Share in the Michael Kors Fashion House," in the *New York Times,* 17 February 1999.

Givhan, Robin, "Best Western: Michael Kors Breathes New Life Into a Dusty Genre," in the *Washington Post,* 18 February 1999.

Schiro, Anne-Marie, "An Ear for What Women Want," in the *New York Times,* 6 April 1999.

Meers, Erik, and Nancy Matsumoto, "Of Kors: After 18 Years, Designer Michael Kors Becomes Fashion's Man of the Moment," in *People,* 9 August 1999.

Edelson, Sharon, "Celine Plans Flagship for Madison Avenue," in *WWD,* 10 August 1999.

Boyes, Kathleen, "Michael Kors: A Young Designer Stays on the Sane Side of Fashion," in *WWD,* 13 September 1999.

"Michael Kors," in *Current Biography,* January 2000.

Horyn, Cathy, "For Kors and Lauren, a Fondness for the Paddock," in the *New York Times,* 15 February 2000.

Quintanilla, Michael, "Look, Ma! It's About More than Mutual Affection and Respect," in the *Los Angeles Times,* 12 May 2000.

Comita, Jenny, "Kors Scores," in *US Weekly,* 18 September 2000.

Haber, Holly, "Kors, Of Course," in *WWD,* 5 October 2000.

Givhan, Robin, "Flirting With the Feminine: Paris Spring Collections Follow the Curves," in the *Washington Post,* 12 October 2000.

Ozzard, Janet, "Kors Inks Deal with Kashiyama," in *WWD,* 13 November 2000.

Hessen, Wendy, "Michael Kors Cadre Grows, with Eyewear for Spring," in *WWD,* 5 March 2001.

Diamond, Kerry, "Michael Kors to Launch Men's Fragrance," in *WWD,* April 2001.

* * *

Perhaps the best summary of Michael Kors was offered by Woody Hochswender of the *New York Times* in November 1988 when he said, "Mr. Kors showed that simple doesn't have to be zero." Kors has been a minimalist working within a sportswear tradition. In this, he has perpetuated and advanced ideas of Halston, including strong sexuality. He particularly flattered the gym-toned body of the late 1980s and early 1990s in stretchy, simple dresses calling attention to the body within. Minimalists in art and architecture might seem to remove themselves from the figure and human proportion; the irony is that a fashion minimalist like Kors has drawn attention to the figure within.

Michael Kors, fall 2001 collection: "cashgora" ensemble. © AP/ Wide World Photos.

Although he has shown patterns, Kors prefers neutral color fields and emphasizes the apparel of the fabric with luxurious wools and cashmere for fall-winter and stretch and cotton for spring-summer. Leather in shirts, skirts, and jackets is essential for any Kors fall-winter collection; trousers are critical in all collections; and layering is important, even light layers in spring-summer collections. Kors spoke the language of separates in arguing with Bernadine Morris of the *New York Times* in April 1992 stating, "Store buyers are zeroing in on the idea that women will probably not be shopping for entire new wardrobes. A single piece or two that will enliven everything else is what they will be searching for. Leather fills the bill—suede for times they are in a softer mood, smooth leather when they feel more aggressive." Kors' distinctive position as a leading minimalist in late 20th-century sportswear was achieved by the precise harmony of color and fabric in separates.

There has been some affinity between Kors and Donna Karan, both creating innovative bodysuits, sensual stretch skirts and tops, and other sportswear elements, as well as borrowings from menswear. In fact, Karan and Kors are somewhat similar in their menswear collections as well. They shared the dubious distinction of both offering bodyshirts (underwear attached to shirts) in menswear collections for fall 1992. If anything, Kors' minimalism was a little more referential than Karan's—he deliberately evoked the glamor and sportiness of the 1930s, the "Belafonte" shirt of the 1950s, or vinyl clothing of the late 1960s. Despite his proclivity to the most simple in shapes, he has produced clothes that are undeniably romantic and Kors admits to loving the movies, telling *HG*'s Wendy Goodman in October 1991 that he believed he had only two choices in life: movie star or fashion designer.

Of Claire McCardell, Kors acknowledges his admiration of her clothes, seen in old magazines, "They were timeless. She was the first designer to look not to Paris for inspiration but to the needs of the American woman." A spring-summer silk shantung scarf blazer by Kors reminds one of the McCardell twists and ties but with all the sleek romance of a Noel Coward drawing room. Like the other sportswear designers, he learns from and responds to his clients and potential customers. He told Bart Boehlert of *Connoisseur* in August 1988 that he likes to talk with a variety of women from his office, customers, or his mother to ask what they most want in clothing.

His sportswear-based pragmatism has been particularly effective as a monitor to the sexuality of his clothing. A bare Kors dress or jumpsuit may be audaciously sexy, but tone it down with a neutral jacket or other cover-up and it can become suitable for the office. Conversely, Kors can take a simple skirt and blouse from the office setting into hot evening life with the addition of a leather jacket or a satin swing jacket. Only partly facetiously, he told Hochswender of the *New York Times* (September 1990) of his comfortable and chic Kors line, "In Texas they call it carpool couture. They all want to wear something pretty for the carpool." Kors creates the pretty, the sexy, and the highly practical, pure mastery in American sportswear.

Throughout Kors' decades as a designer, he has maintained the same casual-yet-luxurious sensibility he has been known for since launching his business in 1981. In the late 1990s and early 2000s, fashion trends caught up with his longtime focus on feminine, elegant simplicity, and he finally moved to the industry forefront. Whether taking inspiration from the equestrian world or from Native American culture, he has remained constant in his use of luxurious, often unique fabrics to create upscale yet wearable pieces.

Kors designs two lines simultaneously, his own labels and those of the French house Celine, for which he added design responsibilities in 1997. Both feature his identifiable signature look, yet each is distinct. As Kors told Jenny Comita in the *US Weekly* Style section (September 2000), Celine is slightly more indulgent, whereas Kors and the lower-priced Kors by Michael Kors are sharper and more efficient. The designer is credited with reviving the more than 50-year-old Celine brand. Additionally, his work for the French house has been cited as a key factor in a new freshness in his signature lines.

In 1999 LVMH (Moët Hennessy Louis Vuitton), owner of the Celine label, purchased a third of Kors' D5 signature business. Kors hoped the acquisition would boost his presence internationally as well as allow him to expand his licensing and advertising activity, neither of which he had pursued aggressively in the past. Wholesale sales for the Kors D5 signature labels in 1999 were $30 million, according to the *New York Times*, with sales growing 60 to 70 percent annually for two years.

Kors sold an additional tenth of his business in 2000 to Onward Kashiyama USA, a licensee for the Kors by Michael Kors bridge line (which was reintroduced in 1996 after having been discontinued several years earlier). The designer hoped the new relationship would support plans to expand further into Asia. Next came a Kors first—the introduction of a women's fragrance—launched in fall 2000 through licensee Parfums Givenchy. The debut was successful enough for

Kors to expand into men's scents the following year. He had also begun showing men's clothing again, after a hiatus, as part of his women's runway show in spring 1998.

In 2001, Kors—who considers fragrances one of his most personal creations—and Parfums Givenchy developed three new scents called *Notes from Michael* which could be worn in any combination or alone. In addition to fragrance, Kors has focused on expanding the rest of his licensed products since the turn of the century, including handbags, footwear, and eyewear, which all debuted in spring 2001.

Some observers have criticized Kors for being bland and predictable and for never departing from his focus on casual luxury, either in his work for Celine or for his own labels. Yet many praise his confidence in sticking with what he believes his customers want and remaining unaffected by short-lived trends. He always creates pieces that can be mixed and matched in unexpected ways—day with night, summer with winter, big and bulky with silky and slim. Kors is proud his clothes are bought by a customer base that ranges from 20-somethings to much more mature women.

—Richard Martin; updated by Karen Raugust

KOSHINO, Hiroko

Japanese designer

Born: 15 January 1937 in Osaka. **Education:** Graduated from the Department of Design of Bunka Fashion College, Tokyo, 1961. **Family:** Married, 1960 (divorced, 1976); children: Yuka, Yuma. **Career:** Designer, Komatsu Department Store, Tokyo, 1961–63; owner and designer, Hiroko Koshino haute-couture, textile, prêt-á-porter, children's clothing, nightie accessories and objects, boutique, Tokyo, from 1964; chairperson, Hiroko Koshino International corporation, Tokyo, from 1982; president, Hiroko Koshino Design Office, Tokyo, from 1988; created branch lines Hiroko Koshino Resort, Hiroko Koshino, Hiroko Bis, Hiroko Homme, Hiroko Koshino Golf; closed Paris store and stopped showing in Paris, late 1990s; designed uniforms for Kintetsu Buffalos baseball team, 1997; held joint collection with sisters Junko and Michiko, 2000; perfume line launch, 2002. **Exhibitions:** Roma Alta Moda Collection, 1978; *Three Sisters,* Osaka, 1982; Shanghai, 1984; exhibition with Borek Sípek and Bambi Uden, Prague, 1994. **Awards:** Osaka City award for Cultural Merit, 1989; highest honors at Mainichi Fashion grand prix, 1997. **Address:** 1–24–1, Sendagaya, Shibuya-ku, 151 Tokyo, Japan.

Publications

On KOSHINO:

Books

The Tokyo Collection, Tokyo, 1986.

Articles

"Japan's Master Strokes," in *The Guardian* (London), 28 April 1988.
"Architecture du Silence," in [special issue] of *Vogue,* September 1994.
Niwata, Manabu, "Designer Family Fueled by Competition," in *Mainichi Shimbun,* 16 October 2000.

Hiroko Koshino, spring/summer 2001 collection. © AP/Wide World Photos.

Saito, Mayumi, "Hiroko Koshino," available online at www.JapanToday.com, 6 April 2001.
Betros, Chris, with Maki Nibayashi, "Hiroko Koshino: Making the Right Cut," online at www.JapanToday.com, 27 April 2001.

*

I love Japan and have been attracted to traditional Japanese culture. I'm trying to express oriental sensitivities in a modern, Western framework. What I think, what I feel, my lifestyle—these are the starting points for my designs. They give me confidence in and a sense of identity with my creations.

—Hiroko Koshino

* * *

An established designer based in Japan, Hiroko Koshino first showed in Paris after the breakthrough of the more avant-garde Japanese group in 1983. A member of a very old and established

Japanese family that spawned two other successful designers, Junko and Michiko, Koshino was brought up to respect the past and grew to love traditional Kabuki theatre. Her designs are based on the traditional clothing idiom of the Japanese kimono, following its aesthetics of volume and layering, an area of focus for other designers such as Kenzo Takada.

Koshino's clothes explore the tension between Western influences and Japanese values—a notion that still has currency, as a Western conception of fashion has only been in existence in Japan since 1945. The encroaching influence of the West has meant that many traditional Japanese aesthetic concepts have been explored and brought into the present by designers attempting to unite the modern with a strong sense of their own cultural continuity and concerns. Tradition and Westernized ideas of progress were historically separated in Japanese culture; for example, in the 19th century, modern Japanese painting (*nihonga*) and modern painting displaying a Western influence (*yosa*) were shown in different rooms—the dualism made physically apparent. Yet since the Meiji period (1868–1912), Japan's former cultural isolation vanished and there were concerted efforts to overcome the dichotomy of East and West to achieve what was hoped to be a more unified cultural pattern.

Koshino's attempts to overcome cultural duality can be deduced in her endeavors to remove the kimono from its 20th-century function as formal wear for weddings and other ceremonial occasions and to introduce more current ideas of fashion terminology into its traditional form—a concerted effort to reintroduce the kimono as a form of everyday dress. The tradition of the kimono in which Koshino intervenes is essentially a rectilinear two-dimensional one, which could be considered shapeless in comparison with Western female clothing that tends to fit the body and emphasize its shape. In traditional Japanese clothing, padding and quilting are used to create a space between the body and the wearer, a concept clearly seen in the contemporary ready-to-wear explorations of Rei Kawakubo's Comme des Garçons designs.

The patterns of the kimono follow equally strict rules, being derived from nature, yet nature is then stylized and made graphic. These traditions can be discerned in the work of Koshino, who employs bird or bamboo prints to counteract the uniformity of her garment's more modular construction. Koshino's overlarge tops, dresses, and trousers of silk, cotton, and linen look back to the traditions of the Japanese court in which styles became so exaggerated that enormous amounts of material were used to signify status. Copious amounts of fabric and many layered undergarments led to a stiffened style in which the body all but disappeared. Koshino retains this volume but by the use of natural fibers brings this traditional styling into the 20th century, though her clothing is more fitted to the demands of contemporary women. Her modular units are more voluminous and asymmetrical than tradition allows, and she is renowned for utilizing bright colors for decoration though within traditional Japanese color symbolism, bright colors are reserved for the young.

With the fashion media's focus on the more obviously radical side of Japanese fashion—Miyake, Yamamoto et al—Hiroko Koshino's more understated experimentation has been somewhat ignored. Her popularity among European women in particular testifies to the wearability of her designs. Koshino, who celebrated 40 years in the fashion business in 1997, continues to combine East and West, melding the futuristic with the classic (as seen in her 2001 autumn/winter collection, themed "Timeless Vintage.") Further, she balances the feminine and the masculine and uses contrasting fabrics from elegant furs to modern metallics. Her pragmatic view of fashion is reflected in her frequent acceptance of commissions for uniforms, such as for the Chosi City Girls School and the Kintetsu Buffalos baseball team.

Koshino's overall business, as of 1997, was estimated to generate $100 million a year. Clothes under her label, distributed through 200 stores in Japan, sold more in that country than products marketed under many other well-known global designer names. Although she has long had global recognition—Koshino was one of the first Japanese designers to show her collections in Rome and in Shanghai, for example—she spent the late 1990s focusing on her native Japanese market. She closed her Paris-based shop and discontinued showing Paris collections after more than a decade as a fixture there while continuing to show in Japan, not only in Tokyo but in other Japanese cities such as Osaka. In 2002, Koshino expects to launch a new perfume line, which, since it is being developed in Paris, may lead the designer to reintroduce her collections in France.

Many of Koshino's designs have elements in common with those of her sisters, Junko and Michiko. Although the three (and their mother, Ayako, also a designer) have led entirely separate careers, in 2000 they held a joint collection, for the first time in 17 years, in their native city of Kishiwada. Hiroko Koshino's daughter Yuma is also studying design.

—Caroline Cox; updated by Karen Raugust

KOSHINO, Junko

Japanese designer

Born: Osaka, Japan, 1939. **Education:** Studied fashion design, Bunka Fashion College, Tokyo, to 1961. **Family:** Married Hiroyuki Suzuki; children: Yoriyuki. **Career:** Opened first boutique in Tokyo, 1966; opened Boutique Junko Koshino, Tokyo, 1970; showed first ready-to-wear collection, Paris, 1978; introduced couture collection, 1978; launched Mr. Junko menswear collection, 1980; introduced home furnishings line, 1988; opened boutiques in China, 1985 and 1987; opened Paris boutique, 1989; opened New York boutique, 1992; opened Singapore boutique, 1993; has also designed costumes for opera productions, uniforms for sports teams, and corporations; showed collection in Havana, Cuba, 1996; launched Opera Sauvage brand of office coordinates, 1997; launched Jeu de Junko line of wigs, 1998; held joint fashion shows with sisters, Michiko and Hiroko, late 1990s. **Exhibitions:** *Three Sisters,* Osaka, 1982; Metropolitan Museum of Art, New York, 1990; *Junko Koshino Design Exhibition,* National Museum of Chinese History, Beijing, 1992; *Modes Gitanes,* Carrousel du Louvre, Paris, 1994. **Awards:** Soen prize, Bunka College, Japan, 1960; Fashion Editors Club prize, Paris, 1978. **Address:** 6–5–36 Minami-Aoyama, Minato-Ku, Tokyo, Japan.

Publications

On KOSHINO:

Books

Tokyo Collection, Tokyo, 1986.
Modes Gitanes: Exposition de 50 Createurs, Paris, 1994.

Articles

Bernstein, Fred A., "Junko Koshino: Style that Translates," in *Metropolitan Home,* March 1990.

Berman, Phyllis, "Not for Everyone," in *Forbes,* 15 October 1990.

"'Art Futur' Designer Coming to Manila," in the *Manila Bulletin,* 12 January 1994.

"Japan's Junko Koshino: Imagining the 21st Century," in *Business World,* 14 March 1994.

Furukawa, Tsukasa, "Casual Friday's Getting Tokyo's Business," in *DNR,* 22 January 1996.

White, Renee Minus, "Junko Koshino Offers Feminine Geometric Shapes," in the *New York Amsterdam News,* 6 April 2000.

Niwata, Manabu, "Designer Family Fueled by Competition," in *Mainichi Shimbun,* 16 October 2000.

* * *

Sleek color-blocked sports uniforms, distinctive forward-looking corporate and exposition uniforms, costumes of opera fantasy and grandiloquence, and future-aimed clothing characterize the work of Junko Koshino. While producing a fashion and lifestyle line for men and women, Koshino's notable strength derives from her strong play between the individual and the group. Ironically—at least to a conventional view of fashion as self-expression—Koshino's best works are her uniforms, collective vestments, not the elective garments of individuals. Her sports samurai are elegant and reductive, almost a kind of refashioned nudity streamlined by fashion as a shell. In outfitting sports teams, she has excelled, noting the aerodynamics of sports and applying those principles to her technology-aware garments.

Koshino's sports uniforms realize Marinetti's visionary comparison toward "new beauty" in his 1909 Futurist Manifesto of the racing car and the Victory of Samothrace. But she has also sought the individual identity of futurism, a clothing inspired by the 20th-century dynamic of projecting oneself into an even more technologically intense outlook. Cocoons and spirals, concentric circles, ribbed construction, and materials from plastic to metal to cloth are typical of Koshino's exploring mind.

Graduating from the Bunka Fashion School in Tokyo in 1961, Koshino chose not to go abroad with Kenzo and Matsuda and other Japanese designers of her generation but to create design in Tokyo, where she opened her first boutique in 1966. Helmeted figures, sculptural forms, and biomorphic futurism suggest that Koshino is inspired in part by Cardin and the tradition of futurist design, though Koshino remains distinctive. Her uniforms for the 1990 Beijing Asian Games and Japanese 1992 Olympic volleyball team have a Flash Gordon futurism about them, but they are also serviceable, sport-specific outfits creating a flag and semaphore-like reading on the competitive field. Corporate uniforms for many clients include Asahi Brewing, Mitsubishi Chemical, and Seibu Department Stores. A paradox of humanity's future expectation is that often we dream of—or, conversely, fear—the role of the collective in the future; Koshino gives garb to that vision: her work fosters an easy and elegant collective character, one of utopia

Individual pieces are likewise utopian in vision. "Taikyoku" is the guiding philosophy of the work, signifying contrast and balance or harmony. Mystically and philosophically, the circle is most important to Koshino, who sees the form as complete and eternal, both ancient and futuristic. This symbolic approach to form animates not only Koshino's view of apparel but the outreach of her work to lifestyle and environmental design. As a designer, she has convened an Art-Futur Committee of various artists, designers, and thinkers, but she has also gone back into history to provide costumes for Mozart's *Magic Flute* and has shown her work in the Museum of History in Beijing. Moreover, Koshino has played a major role, in the late 1980s and 1990s, in introducing fashion ideas to China.

Each of her foreign headquarters is designated a gallery, and Koshino insists upon the identity of these establishments as more than mere boutiques or retail establishments. Koshino challenges almost every preconception about fashion from the materials available for clothing to the way in which clothing serves the commonwealth and the individual. Philosophically (and she requires such thought), she is cognizant of the past but straining with futurist and utopian vision. She brings fashion into fuller and more fulfilled discourse with the other arts of design. It is the area of attainment that gives Koshino a distinctive and enduring place in the history of design.

Koshino continues to design functional garments featuring geometric, sometimes asymmetrical shapes, bright and contrasting hues, varied lengths, and fabrics that range from alpaca to materials incorporating gold powder. She emphasizes the natural and places a focus on the feminine, yet she is not adverse to trying something new, such as creating clothes from metals, as she did in her winter 2000 collection.

Although she is best known in Asia, her reputation has expanded worldwide. In 1996 Koshino showed her collection in Havana, Cuba, and in the same year, she launched a line called Junko Koshino Homme in Korea. The following year, 1997, she launched a line of office-appropriate coordinates under the Opera Sauvage brand, marketed in conjunction with two Japanese trading companies, Mitsukoshi and Daimaru. In 1998, she introduced a line of wigs called Jeu de Junko in Paris, where she had long participated in the Paris Collections. In Japan and throughout Asia, where Koshino's name attracts nearly universal recognition, her garments range from kimonos and yukatas to casualwear for the workplace. Her designer fragrance label is also strong throughout Asia.

Koshino has stressed functionality, an attribute that is nowhere more in evidence than in the many uniforms she has designed. Recent projects range from outfits worn by vegetable growers at a grocers' conventions to garments for sumo wrestlers and J-League soccer uniforms for the team Kawasaki Verdy. One of Kawasaki Verdy's leading team members has appeared in advertising for Koshino's Mr. Junko line of men's apparel.

Koshino holds periodic joint fashion shows in Japan with her two designing sisters, Michiko and Hiroko, especially in their home town of Kishiwada. Aside from her design work, Junko Koshino has kept busy lecturing, serving on various governmental and municipal committees in Japan, and appearing on television shows and in commercials.

—Richard Martin; updated by Karen Raugust

KOSHINO, Michiko

Japanese designer working in London

Born: Osaka, Japan, 1950. **Education:** Graduated from Bunka Fashion College, Tokyo, 1974. **Career:** Showed first collection,

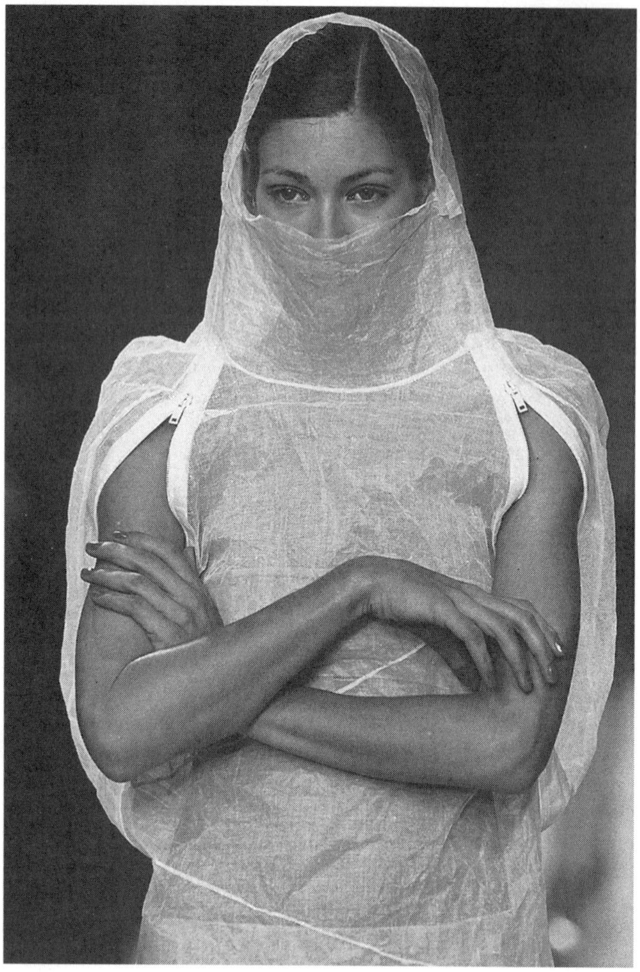

Michiko Koshino, spring/summer 2000 collection. © AFP/CORBIS.

London, 1976; opened flagship store in Neal Street, London, closed 1994; introduced knitwear, luggage, denim, children's clothes lines; signed licensing deal with Mitsubishi Rayon for line of casual apparel, 1997; created costumes for "The Art of Barbie" exhibit, part of the doll's 40th anniversary celebration, 1999; signed licensing deal with Chiyoda Bussan for footwear, 2001. **Exhibitions:** *Three Sisters*, Osaka, 1982. **Address:** 2E MacFarlane Road, Shepherd's Bush, London W12 7JZ, England.

PUBLICATIONS

On KOSHINO:

Articles

Hatfield, Julie, "The Bottom Line," in the *Boston Globe,* 14 May 1990.

"Take Five Designers," in *Clothes Show* (London), February 1991.

"New Textile Brand—Strategy," Mitsubishi Rayon press release, 10 February 1997.

Niwata, Manabu, "Designer Family Fueled by Competition," in *Mainichi Shimbun,* 16 October 2000.

"Michiko Koshino," available online at www.widemedia.com, London Fashion Week Fall/Winter 2000 coverage.

"Chiyoka Bussan Enters into Exclusive Manufacture and Sale Contract for Michiko London Koshino Shoes," Chiyoda Bussan press release, 18 January 2001.

"Michiko Koshino," online at www.widemedia.com, London Fashion Week Spring/Summer 2001 coverage.

Davis, Boyd, "Michiko Koshino's YWCA," available online at www.FashionWindows.com, London Fashion Week Fall 2001 coverage.

* * *

Michiko Koshino has come into her own since a switch in gear in the fashion world that began in the late 1980s. As sportswear became the major imperative of design, Koshino was one of the most successful in responding to customers' new needs, producing tightly thought-out collections that bridged the gap between sportswear and clubwear to appeal to a young streetwise consumer. Indeed, it seems to have been her aim to create a series of uniforms for the various London clubs with which she linked her name, and the logos she emblazoned them with had the same kind of recognizable impact as the established sports companies that were also increasingly popular.

Although Japanese by birth, Koshino eschews the more philosophical approach to fashion favored by her often more prominent counterparts, seeming to lean toward the quirkier modern side of the Japanese national character rather than its solemn traditions of harmony and balance. It was this that led Koshino to produce the infamous and much-copied inflatable rain jacket in the mid-1980s. This was itself based on the thickly quilted B-boy "goose" jackets so popular with clubbers at the time and clearly showed her ability to combine elements of both fun and functionalism.

In the 1990s, however, Koshino showed her design abilities could go much further than the witty garment for which she was most widely known. She consistently showed how closely attuned she was to the shifting sands of London's extensive club scene. Her past collections have responded to the growing wish for clothes reflecting a certain aspect of this scene, making the wearer an instant initiate. They give a kind of streetwise credibility that has as much to do with the tribalism of London's nightlife as with fashion itself. The need to feel and look good is enhanced by Koshino's use of stretch fabrics, comfortable to move in as well as being sexy, clingy but not restrictive.

Although she has embraced London culture as her own, she has not limited the appeal of her clothes. The very English Pukka Clobba tag she borrowed from the rave scene merely gave her designs a kind of brand-name authenticity that sells, albeit quietly, across the world and has enabled her to diversify. She produces funky accessories to complement each collection, from the sequin disco ball earrings to the ubiquitous ski hats so popular with ravers in the winter. There are also Koshino bags, umbrellas, shoes, and towels, all spreading her name by their very presence and adding to the brand-name feel of her very contemporary styles.

Koshino's collections also offer a selection of different types of clothes, to provide a whole wardrobe for her customers. Her flagship store in Covent Garden, London, with its DJ mixing tables providing a direct link with the clubs, always shows her full range, spanning the biker-inspired Motor King collection, its title often emblazoned on the stark contrast leathers, the designer name t-shirts and sweatshirts popular with tourists, the sharp, brightly colored suits, and the sexier, more overtly clubby Lycra, viscose, and leather of the Michiko London range.

Koshino's greatest talent is undoubtedly her ability to absorb changing emphasis in fashion and respond with sexy sports-based clothing targeted at the waiting customers of the club scene through marketing ploys like fashion shows in clubs and promotional wear for companies like Vidal Sassoon. Using her clever eye for striking designs and sexy styles, coupled with the kind of marketing skills that are anathema to many more traditional designers, she has developed an instantly recognizable style and loyal customer base among the often fickle younger fashion customer. And although Koshino has been described as "ultra-hip" and "cutting edge," she often incorporates classic fabrics such as tweed and denim (the latter a favorite) into her jackets, quilted coats, bags, and other items. At the same time, she does not ignore futuristic, high-tech fabrics such as silver reflectives. Her designs integrate her Eastern past with her Western surroundings, as she creates clothing that is oriental-inspired but with a sense of individualism associated more with the West.

Despite her long-time sojourn in London, she is a well-known name throughout Asia, both for her apparel and associated products such as cosmetics, sunglasses, watches, and underwear. Additionally, she claims to be the first designer to market condoms under her own brand name. Some of Koshino's licensees for her main brand umbrella, Michiko London, include Sudo for wool and acrylic scarves, Ta Feng for umbrellas, Shin Myung Mool San for lighters, Chiyoda Bussan for footwear, Mandom for cosmetics, Gunze for tights, and Mitsubishi Rayon for casual apparel.

Koshino's Motor King line of clothes were favored by participants in the London club scene of the early 1990s and are now collectors' items. In the 21st century she has a following among British and American musicians from David Bowie to Moby and is featured in not only fashion publications such as *Vogue* but in music and graphic design periodicals such as *Face, Mixmag, Scene* and *i-D.* In 1999 Koshino was one of the designers chosen to clothe the 40-year-old toy icon Barbie for the traveling exhibit "The Art of Barbie,"—she dressed the doll in one of her trademark puffa coats. She also created an environmentally friendly scooter for the Honda company in the late 1990s.

Koshino's focus in the 2000s has been on three lines: Main Collection, Yen Jeans, and her 100's line. For winter 2000/2001, she took her inspiration from the 1960s (Main Collection), Japanese workwear (100's), and Sumo culture (Yen Jeans); she was influenced by the 1970s' club scene in her fall 2001 men's line. Like much of her work, this collection appealed to both clubbers and aficionados of fashion.

—Rebecca Arnold; updated by Karen Raugust

KOUYATÉ, Lamine

Malian fashion designer working in Paris

Born: Bamako, Mali, circa 1963, son of a diplomat and a doctor; moved to Paris around 1986. **Education:** Studied architecture, Architecture School of Strasbourg, France, and at La Villette, Paris. **Career:** Designs under XULY.Bët label, based in Kouyaté's Funkin' Fashion Factory, Paris; became known for recycled, patched-together clothing; first New York runway show, 1997; opened store on New York's Orchard Street, 1997; changed New York store name to Fragile, 1999. **Address:** 8 Rouget-de-l'Isle, 93500 Pantin, Paris, France.

Publications

On KOUYATÉ:

Articles

Spindler, Amy M., "Prince of Pieces," in the *New York Times,* 2 May 1993.

Donovan, Carrie, "Paris Report," in the *New York Times Magazine,* 9 May 1993.

Hume, Marion, "Coming Unstitched, or Just a Stitch-up?," in the *Independent* (London), 30 September 1993.

Martin, Richard, "A Sweater as Quasi-Surreal Composition," in the *Independent* (London), 30 September 1993.

Talley, Andre Leon, "Piecing It Together," in *Vogue,* October 1993.

"The Last Word," in *WWD,* 14 March 1994.

Jacobs, Patricia, "Xüly Bet," in *Essence,* May 1994.

White, Constance, "Two European Lines Take on America," in the *New York Times,* 21 October 1997.

———, "Inspiration from the Compelling Land of the Visionaries," in the *New York Times,* 6 November 1997.

Greene, Walter, "Sexy Spring Fashions," in *Black Elegance,* April 1998.

White, Renee Minus, "A Fashionable Bet From Paris to New York," in *New York Amsterdam News,* 15 April 1999.

Colman, David, "After Pushcarts Comes a Catwalk," in the *New York Times,* 23 May 1999.

Barnett, Amy Du Bois, "Portfolio: Bet on It," in *Essence,* August 1999.

* * *

In a Paris collections report under the rubric "The Last Word," *Women's Wear Daily* (14 March 1994) recounted: "Deadly heat, a grating live band and groupies lounging on the floor.... But it wasn't a Grateful Dead concert—just XULY.Bët's *défilé* at La Samaritaine department store." Lamine Kouyaté, designing for his label XULY.Bët, has all the characteristics of an avant-garde and disestablishment fashion, but one that at least assumes a fashion system and even shows good likelihood of becoming a positive and lasting element of the fashion system.

Recycling, collage, rags to riches economics, exposed seams and construction, a profoundly African sensibility, and artistic temperament all seem at odds with establishment fashion but have, in fact, brought XULY.Bët to the mainstream and major recognition. Lauded as a fashion postmodernist and deconstructivist, Kouyaté's fashion coincides only with the intellectual postulation; his design creativity is more intuitive and personal, founded in his childhood in Mali, Africa, and the necessarily pastiched view of the world he perceived in a former French colony. The 1993 XULY.Bët collection was based on torn, dismembered, and reassembled surplus and flea market clothing, each a one-of-a-kind invention from the "given" of a distressed or discarded fashion object. Kouyaté's urban picturesque includes cropped jackets, bold African prints, graphics, and graffiti lacerated and reassembled, and long dresses that defy their own length in haphazard apertures, visible seaming, and a charming sense of coming apart. Kouyaté's dilapidated dresses and clothes are a romantic, enchanted vision.

As Kouyaté told Amy Spindler of the *New York Times* in May 1993, "At home, all the products come from foreign places. They're imported from everywhere, made for a different world, with another culture in mind. A sweater arrives in one of the hottest moments of the year. So you cut the sleeves off it to make it cooler. Or a woman will get a magazine with a Chanel suit in it, and she'll ask a tailor to make it out of African fabric. It completely redirects the look." Adaptation and alteration are paramount in XULY.Bët's work, beginning with the patchwork of distressed, repaired, and patched garments of 1993 and his 1994 compounds of cultures and fabrics.

Like the Futurist demand that sculpture relinquish its pedestal, material unity, and high-art status, Kouyaté's fashion demands that high fashion come to the streets and flea markets to renew itself. It is, of course, a demolition for the purpose of rejuvenation, but an extreme of ruin that some find difficult to accept. Yet few could deny the beauty of Kouyaté's vision: sensuous patching, often skin tight, gives dresses a sense of tattoo or body decoration more than of party dressing. His 1993 show sent African models out in Caucasian-colored "skin-tone" Band-Aids to reinforce the impression of scarification and the necessary politics of adornment.

If Kouyaté's œuvre shares principles with Martin Margiela's pensive and poetic deconstruction in fashion and both owe some debt to Rei Kawakubo's pioneering deconstructions of the early 1980s and again in the late 1980s, Kouyaté's African roots and sensibility set him apart, mingling rich pattern mix with the concept of collage. Kouyaté requires different eyes—the XULY.Bët name means the equivalent of "keep your eyes open," as with alertness and wonderment—and a Western willingness to accept an African aesthetic.

The reluctance to fully accept Kouyaté's innovative work resides less in its *épater les bourgeois* scorn for tradition and deliberate inversion of the economic order, for both of these are standard gambits of fashion novelty. The greater difficulty is probably in seeing improvised and aesthetically coarse (in Western terms and fashion's propensity to refinement) creation of fashion. But what Kouyaté proves is that the colonial disadvantage he might supposedly have begun with is an opportunity and offers its own aesthetic. The lesson to old imperialisms is obvious, and fashion must know better than to be one of the ruined empires. A few tatters, some exposed junctures, and disheveled first impressions may be tonic and certainly far more interesting than an inflexible and rarefied status for fashion. Like Jean-Michel Basquiat's brilliant and lasting impact on American art, Kouyaté is showing the "real thing" of an African taste rendered in his own meeting with Western terms, not merely rich peasants or tourist views of a Third-World pageantry. Kouyaté's aesthetic is irrefutably an eye-opener for fashion.

Kouyaté and XULY.Bët have made as much of an impression in the U.S. since their first New York runway show in 1997 as they did on their introduction to the Parisian fashion community in 1992. American fashion critics, musicians from INXS to Neneh Cherry, and more important, the youthful public, have embraced Kouyaté's multiethnic, flea market-driven style.

Kouyaté has continued to rely on bargain basement-found pieces as the basis for his designs, transforming them into colorful, fashionable items that have been described as sensual and glamorous, despite their origin as thrift shop underwear or crocheted blankets. His architecturally-driven visible seams, along with his large, outer labels, have become trademarks of his otherwise diverse work. As Constance White pointed out in the *New York Times* in November 1997, his skill and conviction—and his lack of reliance on fashion trends—are what make his work stand out.

Kouyaté's choice of New York's Orchard Street rather than SoHo for his first U.S. store, called XULY.Bët Funkin' Fashion, fit perfectly with his street-based sensibility. The store hosted graffiti contests and featured a changing roster of guest designers in addition to the XULY.Bët label. In 1999 the store, run by Damien Serrazin, changed its name to Fragile; it began featuring XULY.Bët as its lead line, along with other designers such as Punk Empire and Dexter Wong. It remains an off-the-beaten-track magnet for multicultural youth, always influenced by the active street culture surrounding it.

For the future, Kouyaté told *Essence* magazine in August 1999 that he hopes to expand into more department stores and shops—he has had success in Europe in retail chains such as Galeries Lafayette—as well as into other products such as footwear, accessories, and even housewares. Yet Kouyaté's primary focus will remain on what *Women's Wear Daily* called his "lively, mismatched patterned clothes" (1 April 1998), which appeal to both devotees of fashion and the street-smart customers who inspire him.

—Richard Martin; updated by Karen Raugust

KRIZIA

See MANDELLI, Mariuccia

L

LACHASSE

British fashion house

Founded: by Fred Singleton as couture sportswear branch of Gray, Paulette and Singleton, 1928; company incorporated as Lachasse Ltd., 1946. **Company History:** Chief designers include Digby Morton, 1928–33, Hardy Amies, 1934–39, Michael Donellan, 1941–52; Peter Lewis-Crown (born, 1930) joined Lachasse as apprentice, 1948; became director, 1964; later became designer and sole owner; Lachasse has also produced clothes for theatre, film and television productions. **Collections:** Victoria & Albert Museum, London; Costume Gallery, Castle Howard, York; Costume Museum, Bath, England. **Company Address:** 29 Thurloe Place, London SW7 2HQ, England.

Publications

On LACHASSE:

Books

Ewing, Elizabeth, *History of 20th Century Fashion,* London, 1974.

McDowell, Colin, *McDowell's Directory of 20th Century Fashion,* London, 1984.

* * *

Lachasse Ltd. was often referred to as London's tailoring stable and it saw a succession of British designers who completed their training there after Digby Morton established the couture house in 1928. The house of Lachasse was renowned primarily for its tailored suits which, in the tradition of British tailoring, were said to mature like vintage wine. Lachasse was representative of the distinctive type of British tailoring that evolved from the masculine style as opposed to the softer dressmaker tailoring employed in Paris.

The early success of Lachasse owed much to the popularity of sportswear during the 1920s, as advocated by Coco Chanel who also promoted the use of British wools and tweeds for these clothes. Certain other factors played a significant role in establishing Lachasse—Digby Morton presented his first collection there in 1929, the year of the Wall Street Crash, which saw a dramatic fall in the number of American buyers at the Paris couture houses. Many overseas buyers turned to London, attracted by the new generation of couturiers and the lower prices.

According to Peter Lewis-Crown, who joined Lachasse in 1949 and became the couture house's owner, its three main designers, all of whom left their mark, were Digby Morton, who popularized Donegal tweed for womenswear; Hardy Amies, who gave the tailored suit a geometrical approach by using the fabric selvedge around the body instead of downwards, and Michael Donellan, who made the tailored suit an acceptable mode of dress from morning through to evening.

Hardy Amies joined the house of Lachasse after Morton's departure in 1934, learning about the construction of tailored suits by examining copies of Morton's models. Michael Donellan followed Amies to Lachasse where he trained until he established his own house in 1953. Originally a milliner, Donellan was the only designer to have his name on the label, which read "Michael at Lachasse." The Irish-born designer was also likened to Balenciaga because of his strong, uncompromising signature. In the postwar period Lachasse enjoyed a sizeable export trade, particularly with America. The firm used to send a doll called Virginia around the world, dressed in the latest clothing by Lachasse, and took orders for her couture outfits. As a member of the Incorporated Society of London Fashion Designers (ISLFD), the house also partook in the export and publicity ventures organized by the ISLFD.

Lachasse was exclusively a couture house until 1981 when Peter Lewis-Crown opened a mini-boutique on the premises. He was also responsible for introducing more dresses and feminine clothes to the house, once famed principally for its tailored suits. Former attempts to introduce eveningwear had been unsuccessful. Hardy Amies describes Lachasse's La Soirée department as "un-epoch-making" and it was closed down, with many of the evening gowns unsold. While Lachasse can make no claims to breaking any fashion barriers, it is one of the longest-surviving couture houses and continues to attract an international clientèle to its Kensington premises.

—Catherine Woram

LACOSTE SPORTSWEAR

French sportswear company

Founded: in Paris, 1933, by René Lacoste (1904–96); son Bernard Lacoste (born 1931), chairman/managing director since 1963. **Company History:** Manufactures tennis, golf, and leisure clothing, technical products for tennis and golf; launched first Lacoste shirts, 1933; sent first exports to Italy and addition of color range to shirts, 1951; first exports to U.S., 1952; established first collection for children, 1959; René Lacoste invented first steel racket, 1963; first exports to Japan, 1964; licensed deal with Patou for *Lacoste Eau de Toilette,* 1968; licensed L'Amy S.A. for Lacoste sunglasses and frames, 1981; opened first Lacoste boutique, Paris, 1981; launched new line of men's toiletries with Patou, 1984; developed Lacoste tennis shoes, 1985; developed *Land* and *Eau de Sport* fragrances, with Patou license, 1991 and 1994, respectively; opened Lacoste boutiques in New Delhi, Madras, and Bombay, 1993; opened Lacoste corners at Saks and Barney's in New York, Neiman Marcus in Dallas, 1994;

opened first Lacoste freestanding boutique in U.S., 1995; launched men's Booster toiletries under Patou license, 1996; introduced *Lacoste 2000* for men and *Lacoste for Women,* 1999; signed license agreement with Samsonite for bags, travel items, and small leather goods, 2000; licensing deal with Procter & Gamble Prestige Beauté for Lacoste fragrance and beauty products, 2001; designer Christophe Lemaire's first collection, 2001; Lacoste includes, as manufacturer and sales partners, Jean Patou for toiletries, Dunlop France for tennis and golf equipment, Roventa-Henex and Vimont for watches. **Exhibitions:** *L'Art de Vivre en France*, Teien Museum, Tokyo, 1985, Haus der Kunst, Munich, 1987; *De Main de Maître,* Grand Palais, Paris, 1988; *Vraiment Faux,* Fondation Cartier, Paris, 1988; *Decorative Art and Design in France,* Cooper Hewitt Museum, New York, 1989; *Veramente Falso,* Rotonda di Via Besona, Milan, and Villa Stuck, Munich, 1991; designer renditions of Lacoste sportswear, Pompidou Center, Paris, 2001. **Collections:** Tennis Hall of Fame, Newport, Rhode Island; Museum of Modern Art, New York; Musée de la Mode, Paris; Musée du Sport, Paris. **Awards:** Design award, 1984; Innovation award, 1988; Global Recognition Trophy, the American Cotton Institute, 1995; Meryl award for sportswear, Venice, 1997; *René Lacoste:* Officier de la Legion d'Honneur, France; *Bernard Lacoste:* Chevalier de l'Ordre National de la Legion d'Honneur; Chevalier de l'Ordre National du Merité. **Company Address:** 8 rue de Castiglione, 75001 Paris, France. **Company Website:** www.lacoste.com.

Publications

By LACOSTE:

Books

Tennis, France, 1928.
Plaisir du Tennis, France, 1981.

On LACOSTE:

Books

Cornfeld, B., and O. Edwards, *Quintessence: The Quality of Having It,* New York, 1983.
Chapais, B., and E. Herscher, *Qualité, Objets d'en France,* Paris, 1989.
Koda, Harold, and Richard Martin, *Jocks and Nerds: Men's Style in the Twentieth Century,* New York, 1989.
Duhamel, J., *Grand Inventaire du Genie Français en 365 Objets,* Paris, 1993.
A Historic Look at Izod Lacoste Sportswear, Southport, CT, 1993.
The Story Behind Izod, Southport, CT, 1993.
Le Dictionnaire de la Mode au Vingtieme Siecle, France, 1994.
International Directory of Company Histories, London, 1994.

Articles

"Le 'Crocodile,' Dieu des Loisirs," in *Le Figaro* (Paris), 5 July 1991.
Hartlein, Robert, "Izod Women's Changes and Drops Croc," in *WWD,* 29 April 1992.
"Real Men, Real Style, René Lacoste," in *Esquire* (Japan), October 1992.
"Les Mousquetaires: Down to Two, Still Riding High," in the *International Herald Tribune,* 21 May 1993.
"Bon Anniversaire Monsieur Lacoste," in *Figaro Madame* (Paris), 5 June 1993.
"La Chemise Lacoste," in *Marie-France* (Paris), June 1993.
"Lacoste, Retour de Chine," in *Le Figaro* (Paris), 30 May 1994.
"Lacoste's Legacy," in the *Financial Times,* 14 October 1996.
"Lacoste Puts Teeth into Environmental Activism," in the *Los Angeles Times,* 20 November 1998.
Duffy, Tara Suilen, "Lacoste is Trying to Protect Its Crocodile in Hong Kong," in the *Commercial Appeal* (Memphis, TN), 14 October 1999.
Menkes, Suzy, "Lacoste: How Doth the Little Crocodile," in the *International Herald Tribune,* 3 July 2001.

*

The only way we consider fashion is color. Beyond fashion trends, because of our historic roots in tennis and golf, because we design activewear which must be comfortable, we try to provide the consumer with basics he can wear for many years as our products are durable. A brand remains powerful if it has a strong concept and adds on new lines of products solely when it has something new and worthwhile to offer to its existing consumers.

The quality of our products and the optimum price-to-quality ratio is the result of the quality of the men who create, manufacture, and sell and—moreover, the quality of teams prepared to work together in the same spirit. Quality is not controlling but manufacturing.

Even if I assume the final responsibility in the Company, I believe we form a true team, and it is this point which I am especially proud of, that allows us to be what we are today.

—Bernard Lacoste

* * *

Lacoste's seminal fashion impact rests on the cotton knit tennis shirt with alligator symbol developed in the 1920s by Jean René Lacoste. Lacoste, a popular French tennis player in a sports-mad and style-conscious era, was nicknamed "Le Crocodile" for his aggressive play and long nose. Back then, spectators and fashion editors eagerly noted what sports stars and celebrities wore to and from the matches. On the courts, players wore the unexciting standard tennis whites of flannel trousers and woven buttoned shirts with their long sleeves rolled up.

Lacoste challenged this traditional uniform by playing in short sleeveed knit shirts with a crocodile monogrammed on them. He designed his shirts for comfort and good looks during the rigors of the court. The short cuffed sleeve ended the problem of sleeves rolling down. The soft turned down collar loosened easily via the buttoned placket. The pullover cotton knit breathed, and the longer shirt tail prevented the shirt from pulling out.

Not content merely to introduce the style for his own use, Lacoste turned to producing and marketing them, following his retirement from tennis in the early 1930s. The shirts he commissioned from friends in the textile industry included an embroidered crocodile on the left breast at a time when few clothes had symbols. Lacoste's renown and photos of Riviera and Palm Beach notables in this type of shirt popularized the style for recreational wear, especially in the United States.

Although white remained traditional on tennis courts, the Lacoste shirt went technicolor on the American golf links in the 1950s. The same characteristics that made it comfortable for tennis, especially the longer shirt tail, made it the sought-after style. Licensed to American manufacturer David Crystal Inc., the crocodile swam on colored piqué knit versions of the original model. Munsingwear came out with a comparable style, dubbed the Grand Slam golf shirt.

As memories of René Lacoste faded, the crocodile trademark was increasingly referred to as an "alligator." The alligator symbol, like the country clubs at which it was seen, acquired an upscale reputation. David Crystal further enhanced this image by melding the Lacoste and Izod names. Izod derived from a British tailor who outfitted British royal family members. To update and increase its appeal in the late 1960s, Crystal made the shirt in double knit, easy-care Dacron polyester, but cotton had perennial appeal. The colors followed current fashion's whimsy, including the worn and faded look. As the shirt settled into an enduring style for sport and casual wear, other companies, including U.S. mass merchandiser Sears, Roebuck and Co., brought out their own variations with two- to four-button plackets and their own symbols. Ralph Lauren's polo shirt is a notable successful upscale rendition.

The preppy look of the 1970s ignited the alligator shirt's popularity and sales and gave it cachet among men, teenagers, and children. They wore the shirt differently—shirt tails were out and the ribbed collars open and flipped up. In the 1980s, collars went back down and all buttons were buttoned. Women sported feminine versions or wore their partner's. The alligator appeared on related garments with the name Izod Lacoste. At times, the symbol was revamped or removed. The shirt, or a facsimile, was a staple of the American middle class wardrobe. The phrase "Lacoste shirt" came to be a generic alternative term for a tennis or polo-style shirt.

Ultimately, the shirt and its trademark were hurt by overmarketing, copies, and caricature in the form of a satiric upside down "dead alligator" symbol. Lacoste began turning toward other items with the launching of numerous perfumes, men's toiletries, and even luggage and travel items through a contract with Samsonite in 1999 and 2000. The expansion marked the company's willingness to innovate and explore items outside the sportshirt in order to maintain and grow the prestige of its distinct symbol. Another move in this direction was the appointment of designer Christophe Lemaire, who showed his first collection in 2001. Lemaire, who believes in "affordable elegance," wowed Parisians with a limited edition black Lacoste shirt with a silver crocodile, which according to Suzy Menkes of the *International Herald Tribune* (3 July 2001), "sold up a storm."

—Debra Regan Cleveland; updated by Carrie Snyder

LACROIX, Christian

French fashion designer

Born: Christian Marie Marc Lacroix in Arles, France, 16 May 1951. **Education:** Studied art history at Paul Valéry University, Montpellier, and museum studies at the Sorbonne, Paris, 1973–76. **Family:** Married Françoise Rosensthiel, 1974. **Career:** Freelance fashion sketcher, 1976–78; assistant at Hermès, Paris, 1978–80; assistant to Guy Paulin, 1980; designer/artistic director, Jean Patou, 1981–87; opened own couture and ready-to-wear house, 1987; established

Christian Lacroix, fall/winter 2001–02 ready-to-wear collection. © AP/Wide World Photos.

Christian Lacroix haute couture and salons in Paris, 1987; developed cruise collection, 1988; designed ready-to-wear collection for Genny SpA, 1988, followed by menswear collection and boutique; introduced seven accessory lines, from 1989; line of ties and hosiery, 1992; launched *C'est la Vie!* perfume, 1990; designed costumes for American Ballet Theater's *Gaieté Parisienne,* New York, 1988; "Bazar" collection, 1994; launched Jeans Lacroix, 1994; introduced Christian Lacroix collection of fine china, 1997; created jewelry line, 2000; debuted "Enfants de Christian Lacroix," children's line, 2001. **Awards:** Dé d'Or award, 1986, 1988; Council of Fashion Designers of America award, 1987; Molière award (for costumes for *Phedre*), 1995. **Address:** 73 rue du Faubourg St Honoré, 75008 Paris, France. **Website:** www.christian-lacroix.fr.

PUBLICATIONS

By LACROIX:

Books

Pieces of a Pattern, Lacroix by Lacroix, with Patrick Mauries, London, 1992.

Lacroix, New York, 1992.

Christian Lacroix, spring/summer 2001 haute couture collection: silk evening dress. © AP/Wide World Photos.

Your World—and Welcome to It: A Rogue's Gallery of Interior Design, New York, 1998.

On LACROIX:

Books

Coleridge, Nicholas, *The Fashion Conspiracy,* London, 1988.
Mulvagh, Jane, *Vogue History of Twentieth Century Fashion,* London, 1988.
Wilson, Elizabeth, and Lou Taylor, *Through the Looking Glass,* London, 1988.
Howell, Georgina, *Sultans of Style: Thirty Years of Fashion and Passion, 1960–90,* London, 1990.
Guillen, Yves-Pierre, and Jacqueline Claude, *The Golden Thimble: French Haute Couture,* Paris, 1990.
Martin, Richard, and Harold Koda, *Bloom,* Metropolitan Museum of Art, 1995.
Mauries, Patrick, *Christian Lacroix: The Diary of a Collection,* New York, 1996.
Stegemeyer, Anne, *Who's Who in Fashion, Third Edition,* New York, 1996.
Baudot, François, *Christian Lacroix,* New York, 1997.

Articles

Verdier, Rosy, "Jean Patou et Christian Lacroix," in *L'Officiel* (Paris), November 1984.
"Lacroix: The New Paris Star," in *WWD,* 31 July 1986.
McEvoy, Marian, "Blithe Spirit," in *Connoisseur* (London), November 1986.
Harbrecht, Ursula, "Christian Lacroix: Nouvelle Étoile au Firmament de Paris," in *Textiles Suisses* (Lausanne), March 1987.
Baumgold, Julie, "Dancing on the Lip of the Volcano: Christian Lacroix's Crash Chic," in *New York,* 30 April 1987.
Baudet, François, "Christian Lacroix: La Nouvelle Couture," in *Elle* (Paris), August 1987.
Brampton, Sally, "Lacroix's Grand Entrance," in the *Sunday Express Magazine* (London), 30 August 1987.
Paquin, Paquita, and Francis Dorleans, "Christian Lacroix: Fièvre Inaugurale," in *L'Officiel* (Paris), September 1987.
Howell, Georgina, "How Lacroix Took Paris by Storm," in the *Sunday Times Magazine* (London), 4 October 1987.
Mestiri, Mohand, "Christian Lacroix: Portrait Chinois d'un Provincial Cosmopolite," in *Connaissance des Arts* (Paris), October 1987.
"Lacroix Designs for Us," in *Connoisseur,* October 1987.
Brubach, Holly, "Lacroix Goes to the Ballet," in *Vogue,* February 1988.
Garmaise, Freda, "Chic Frills," in *Ms.* (New York), February 1988.
"Christian Lacroix," in *Current Biography* (New York), April 1988.
"Les Trésors de Christian Lacroix," in *L'Officiel* (Paris), March 1989.
Grossman, Lloyd, "The Wider Side of Paris," in *Harpers & Queen* (London), May 1989.
Donovan, Carrie, "The Three Who are Key: Couture's Future," in the *New York Times Magazine,* 27 August 1989.
"A Day in the Life of Christian Lacroix," in the *Sunday Times Magazine* (London), 27 August 1989.
Gerrie, Anthea, "Lacroix's Business Scents," in the *Sunday Express Magazine* (London), 18 March 1990.
Rafferty, Diane, "Christian Lacroix: The Art of Sensuality," in *Connoisseur,* June 1990.
"Lacroix's Fan Club," in *WWD,* 18 December 1990.
Levin, Angela, "Christian Lacroix," in *You* magazine of the *Mail on Sunday* (London), 10 February 1991.
Rolf, Gail, "Racy and Lacy...A Perfect Paris Match from Lacroix," in the *Daily Mail* (London), 20 July 1993.
Menkes, Suzy, "Sweetness and Light by Lacroix," in the *International Herald Tribune* (Paris), 27 January 1995.
Spindler, Amy M., "Olé: Lacroix Conquers the Couture," in the *New York Times,* 27 January 1995.
Schiro, Anne-Marie, "Lacroix and Rykiel: Classics," in the *New York Times,* 18 March 1995.
Mirabella, Grace, "Grace Mirabella on the Lacroix Nanosecond," in the *Washington Post,* 10 September 1995.
Johnson, Eunice W., "Comfort With a Touch of Luxe," in *Ebony,* February 1999.
Kadri, Françoise "Christian Lacroix, a Twenty-Year Love Affair with Japan," in *Agence France Presse,* 24 June 2000.
Shard, Sarah, "Lacroix in Full Technicolor for Next Winter," in *Agence France Presse,* 11 March 2001.
Lowthorpe, Rebecca, "Excess All Areas," in the *Independent on Sunday,* 1 July 2001.

Alexander, Hilary, "Couture Tales Off on a Magic Carpet Ride," in the *Daily Telegraph,* 11 July 2001.

*

In a way I just love to mix everything for the sake of mixing. For many people fashion is being dressed as your neighbor, your best friend. But, for me, fashion is expressing your own deep individuality; that is why I have always done noticeable things.

—Christian Lacroix

* * *

There is a prevalent myth in French haute couture that only once every decade does a new star emerge. Writer Nicholas Coleridge traced this path of succession from Paul Poiret, to Chanel, to Balenciaga, to Saint Laurent, then Lagerfeld (*The Fashion Conspiracy,* London, 1988). Judging by the buzz and excitement that preceded the launch of his first collection in the Salon Impérial Suite of the Hotel Intercontinental in July 1987, there could be no doubt Christian Lacroix was a new star.

Quite why Lacroix became the new star of couture is debatable, but his timing was definitely right. There had been no opening of a couture house since 1961 with Saint Laurent (Lagerfeld had become a star by resuscitating the established house of Chanel.) As the chairperson and financial director of the new house, Paul Audrain was to declare, "We had a very strong presentiment that the climate was right for a new couture house." New social and cultural changes had reversed the values of the 1970s; the jeans and t-shirt dressing, so prevalent during that decade, had changed. A new sexual identity had emerged. The entrepreneurial spirit of the 1980s created new money, and Lacroix's debut was in time to capitalize on this trend.

Lacroix had begun his career with an aspiration to be a museum curator. After moving to Paris from Arles in the early 1970s, he met his future wife Françoise Rosensthiel, who encouraged his interest in fashion, which led to his taking positions at Hermès and Guy Paulin. He became the designer for Jean Patou in 1981, revitalizing the flagging couture house and upping sales from thirty dresses a season to 100. He seduced the fashion press with spectacular shows, reviving fashion staples such as the frou-frou petticoat and the puffball skirt. In 1987, with the backing of five million francs from the textile conglomerate Financière Agache, Lacroix opened his new couture house.

As a designer, Lacroix throws caution to the wind, providing the sort of luxurious product that, at first, justified the amount of "new money" spent on him. His collections are always an exotic, lavish cornucopia of influences, ranging from the primitive, rough naïveté of the paintings of the Cobra movement, to an homage to Lady Diana Cooper, to modern gypsies, travelers, and nomads. He uses the most luxurious fabrics in often unexpected mixes or even patchwork, embroidered brocades, fur, reembroidered lace, ethnic prints and embroideries, even gold embroidery. Nothing is considered too expensive or too outré to be included in the clothes.

An extravagant technicolor musical from the golden age of Hollywood would perhaps be an understatement when describing the impact of a Lacroix collection. As an artist, he is not afraid to plunder junk shops, museums, the theater and opera, or the glamor of the bullfight to create designs that astound yet are always stylish in their eclectic clutter. There are many strong retrospective references from the 1950s, 1960s, and 1970s in a Lacroix collection, like the detached hauteur or waiflike gestures of fashion models from the period. The unapproachable allure of movie stars like Tippi Hedren or Capucine, or real-life personalities who embody these qualities, all inspire his designs, often resulting in eccentric accessories, colors, and poses.

Lacroix recognizes that contemporary couture is often only a public relations exercise for money-spinning ventures such as perfume or licensing deals using a designer name to sell a product. Lacroix, however, is fully aware of the value couture has in pushing fashion, projecting a dream, and making dramatically important fashion statements. This is essential if fashion is to survive commercially, because the ready-to-wear and mass-market manufacturers always see designers as the inspirations that direct the movement of fashion. Before his first show, Lacroix seemed to synthesize this point of view when he said, "I want to get back to the position where the couture becomes a kind of laboratory of ideas, the way it was with Schiaparelli 40 years ago."

The minimalist 1990s saw not only a downturn in interest in Lacroix's over-the-top extravagance but also in couture itself. Fashion critics said the Lacroix moment had been the 1980s, and it was over. Lacroix continued to design, however, with a signature collection of tableware and homeware, eventually turning to costume and designing for theater, ballet, opera, and finally film, for all of which his creations have always been well suited. His work in costume has received many awards. Through the changing climes of the fashion world and his own fortunes, however, Lacroix's central interest has remained couture, and he has continued to create one-of-a-kind couture for a cadre of wealthy clients. And as is ever the case in fashion, his moment was destined to come again.

With collections skewed a little younger, less "heavy, outdated, obsolete," in Lacroix's words, and more casual, the designer's shows again became a hot ticket as the decade turned and the 1990s gave way to the 21st century. And whatever the changes, the collections are still everything one expects from Lacroix—an exuberant riot of color, ecstatic, nearly surreal details, and rich fabric upon rich fabric. Trompe-l'oeil collars, a lacquered chiffon dress with rhinestones, fluffy pom-poms in hot pink or lemon, and hems dangling fringes of pastel-colored mink tails show that the designer has not given up his delight in "the cross-fertilization of styles."

—Kevin Almond; updated by Jessica Reisman

LADICORBIC, Zoran

See ZORAN

LAGERFELD, Karl

German designer

Born: Hamburg, 10 September 1938; immigrated to Paris in 1952. **Career:** Design assistant at Balmain, 1955–58; art director, Patou, 1958–63; freelance designer for Chloé, Krizia, Ballantyne, Timwear, Charles Jourdan, Valentino, Fendi, Cadette, Max Mara and others, from 1964; launched Parfums Lagerfeld, 1975; director of collections and ready-to-wear, Chanel, from 1983; Karl Lagerfeld and KL ready-to-wear firms established in Paris and Germany, 1984; Karl Lagerfeld, S.A., acquired by Chloé parent company, Dunhill Plc., 1992; broke ties with Chloé and Dunhill (part of the Vendome Group), 1997;

Karl Lagerfeld, fall/winter 2001 ready-to-wear collection. © AP/ Wide World Photos.

bought back Karl Lagerfeld S.A., 1997; created fragrances *Lagerfeld,* for Elizabeth Arden, 1975, *Chloé-Lagerfeld,* 1978, *KL* for women, 1983, *KL* for men, 1984; *Lagerfeld Photo,* 1990; *Sun Moon Stars,* 1994; *Jako,* 1997; *Lagerfeld Femme,* 2001. **Exhibitions:** *Karl Lagerfeld: Fotografien,* Galerie Hans Mayer, Dusseldorf, 1989. **Awards:** Second prize, International Wool Secretariat design contest, 1954; Neiman Marcus award, 1980; Bath Museum of Costume Dress of the Year award, 1981; 20th Dé d'or, 1986; Council of Fashion Designers of America award, 1991; Fashion Footwear Association of New York award, 1991. **Address:** 14 Boulevard de la Madeleine, 75008 Paris, France.

PUBLICATIONS

By LAGERFELD:

Selected Books

Karl Lagerfeld: A Fashion Journal—A Visual Record of Anna Piaggi's Creative Dressing and Self-Editing, with Anna Piaggi, New York, London & Stuttgart, 1986.
Gilbert Poillerat, Maître Ferronnier, with François Baudot, Paris, 1992.
Karl Lagerfeld: Off the Record, Göttingen, Germany, 1994, 1995.
Chanel, Paris, 1995.
Karl Lagerfeld: Grunewald, Göttingen, 1995.
Claudia Schiffer, London, 1995.
Visionen, Göttingen, 1996.
Body Parts, Cologne, 1997.
Karl Lagerfeld: Parti Pris, Bonn, 1998.
The House in the Trees and *Casa Malaparte,* both with Eric Pfrunder and Gerhard Steidl, both Göttingen, 1998.
Aktstrakt, Göttingen, 2000.
*Escape From Circumstances,*Göttingen & London, 2000.
editor, *Iwao Yamawaki,* Göttingen & London, 2001.
Modern Italian Architecture, Göttingen & London, 2001.

On LAGERFELD:

Books

Milbank, Caroline Rennolds, *Couture: The Great Designers,* New York, 1985.
Piaggi, Anna, *Karl Lagerfeld: A Fashion Journal,* London, 1986.
Perschetz, Lois, ed., *W, The Designing Life,* New York, 1987.
Howell, Georgina, *Sultans of Style: Thirty Years of Fashion and Passion 1960–1990,* London, 1990.
Stegemeyer, Anne, *Who's Who in Fashion, Third Edition,* New York, 1996.

Articles

Buck, J., "How Karl Lagerfeld Changed Some Lives," in *Interview* (New York), March 1973.
"Great Designers of the World: Karl Lagerfeld," in *Vogue* (London), 1 March 1975.
Menkes, Suzy, "The Man Who Takes Over at Chanel," in the *Times* (London), 31 January 1983.
Shapiro, Harriet, "Tout Paris Applauds the Fashionable Vision of Karl Lagerfeld," in *People,* 11 June 1984.
"Karl Lagerfeld: The Many Faceted Man," in *Vogue* (Paris), October 1985.
Dryansky, G.Y. "Baroque to His Bones," in *Connoisseur,* December 1985.
Barron, Pattie, "Playing Court to Kaiser Karl," in *Cosmopolitan* (London), October 1986.
"A Life in the Day of Karl Lagerfeld," in the *Sunday Times Magazine* (London), 8 November 1987.
Barker, Rafaella, "Karlsberg," in *House & Garden,* December 1987.
Lobrany, Alexander, "Lagerfeld Logs On: At 50, King Karl Makes a Foray into Men's Wear," in *DNR,* 6 April 1988.
Brook, Danae, "King Karl," in the *Sunday Express Magazine* (London), 15 May 1988.
Talley, André Leon, "Petit Palais," in *Vogue,* April 1989.
Ciavarella, Michele, "Karl Lagerfeld: A Burst of Genius," in *Maglieria Italiana* (Modena), April/June 1989.
Bowles, Hamish, "Reviving the Past," in *Harpers & Queen* (London), September 1989.
"A Lagerfeld Extravagance," in the *Independent* (London), 28 September 1989.
Mynott, Lawrence, "Kaiser Karl: The Darling Dictator," in the *Independent,* 24 May 1990.

Etherington-Smith, Meredith, "He Came, He Drew, He Conquered," in *Harpers & Queen,* September 1990.
Mower, Sarah, "Karl Lagerfeld," in *Vogue* (London), April 1991.
Mayer, Margit, "King Karl," in *WWD,* 20 November 1991.
Orth, Maureen, "Kaiser Karl: Behind the Mask," in *Vanity Fair,* February 1992.
"The Kaiser's Empire," in *WWD,* 2 June 1992.
Lane, Anthony, "The Last Emperor," in the *New Yorker,* 7 November 1994.
Menkes, Suzy, "Chanel: Beauty Without Gimmicks," in the *International Herald Tribune,* 25 January 1995.
Spindler, Amy M., "Four Who Have No Use for Trends," in the *New York Times,* 20 March 1995.
White, Constance C.R., "Lagerfeld's Poetic License," in the *New York Times,* 24 June 1997.
Gabor, Lisa, "No Clothing, No Kidding," in *In Style,* March 1998.
White, Constance C.R., "Lagerfeld's Lesson for Younger Designers: Stay Relevant," in the *New York Times,* 16 March 1999.
Menkes, Suzy, "Magnificent Chanel Defines the Season," in the *International Herald Tribune,* 4 March 2000.
———, "Class and Classics at Chanel," in the *International Herald Tribune,* 24 January 2001.
Horyn, Cathy, "A Slimmer Karl Lagerfeld Makes his Concession to Fashion," in the *New York Times,* 19 June 2001.
Menkes, Suzy, "Chanel Goes to the Head of the Class," in the *International Herald Tribune,* 11 July 2001.

* * *

Universally recognized as one of the most prolific and high-profile designers of the last 20 years, Karl Lagerfeld has maintained his reputation through consistently strong work for the numerous lines he produces every year. Each label has its own distinct look, while clearly bearing the bold, uncompromising Lagerfeld signature that guarantees the success of everything he produces.

Moving between several main collections, Lagerfeld designs with consummate ease, displaying the skills he learned from his couture background in fine tailoring and flashes of surreal detailing. He has functioned best as a catalyst, reinvigorating labels and broadening their customer base. Since 1983 he most spectacularly demonstrated this capability at Chanel, where, despite some criticism, Lagerfeld brought the label back to the pinnacle of high fashion. He produced endless innovative variations on the signature tweed suits that often mix street style references, such as teaming the traditional Chanel jacket with denim miniskirts and the signature gilt buttons and chains.

Lagerfeld also stretched the Chanel look to embrace younger customers, with club-influenced black fishnet bodystockings, the traditional Chanel camellia placed cheekily over the breasts, and hefty lace-up boots set against flowing georgette skirts and leather jackets. This combination of wit with recognizable Chanel symbols rejuvenated the house, making Lagerfeld's fashion word an inspirational message to a new generation. His experiments have been at their most fantastic in the vibrant lines of the couture show, made more accessible in the ready-to-wear range. Only Lagerfeld could put the Chanel label on panties (1993) and camellia-trimmed cotton vests (1992) to make them the most talked-about elements of the Paris collections. Yet this quirkiness was underpinned by the quality of Lagerfeld's designs and the mix of classic separates that have always been an undercurrent in his work.

Karl Lagerfeld, spring/summer 2001 ready-to-wear collection. © AFP/CORBIS.

His own name label, KL, highlights these skills. Bold tailoring, easy-to-wear cardigan jackets in his favorite bright colors, combined with softly shaped knitwear, showed the breadth of his talents and ensured the longevity of his appeal. If his more outrageous combinations at Chanel have enabled him to outlive the excesses of the 1970s that trapped some of his contemporaries, then his clever manipulation of fabric and color has prolonged the life of his clothes still further.

During the 1970s Lagerfeld's work for Chloë was equally influential, his love of eveningwear coming to the fore, albeit in a more restrained form than at Chanel. The main look of this period was flowing pastel chiffon draped onto the body to give a highly feminine feel and trimmed with silk flowers. He recreated this style for his return to the label in spring-summer 1993, complete with models wearing Afro wigs. At first coolly received by the fashion press, it went on to inspire many with its floaty silhouette and flower-child air, reviving ethereal dresses with no linings, unnecessary seams, or extraneous detail.

While he continued to move from label to label, never quite losing the freelance mentality of his early days, it is only the occasional lack of editing in his collections betraying how widely his talents are spread. Idea follows idea, frequently inspired by his current model muse as he reinterprets garments to create very modern styles. At

Fendi this desire to continually push forward to greater modernity, absorbing the influences around him and seeking greater perfection in his work, led to his taking the furriers' trade a step further. The lightness of touch that had established his name as early as 1970 led him to strip the Fendi sisters' signature fur coats to the thinnest possible layer. He removed the need for heavy linings by treating the pelts to produce supple lightweight coats shown in 1973 with raglan sleeves and tie belts, which complemented the sporty feel of the knitwear he also produces for the company.

Lagerfeld has proven he is equally adept in his bold strokes at Chanel as in his delicate shaping at Fendi, or in the vibrant classics of his own lines. Though he severed his ties with Chloé and the Vendome Group in 1997 (and regained ownership of the company bearing his name), Lagerfeld had more than enough designing to keep him busy. He also continued to indulge in another passion, photography, producing a pictorial of nude celebrities for *Visionaire* magazine in 1998. He has published a growing collection of books on art, architecture, and photography, and collaborated with authors the likes of Helmut Lang, Peter Lindbergh, and Madonna.

Lagerfeld's consummate skills as a designer have enabled him to push the fashion beyond its constraints by combining the immediacy of ready-to-wear with the splendor and elegance of couture. Nearly two decades ago, in June 1984, Lagerfeld told *People* magazine's Harriet Shapiro, "I would like to be a one-man multinational fashion phenomenon." In both the 20th and 21st centuries, Karl Lagerfeld has more than achieved his goal.

—Rebecca Arnold; updated by Sydonie Bénet

LAM, Ragence

British fashion designer

Born: Lam Kwok Fai in Hong Kong, 24 January 1951. **Education:** Harrow School of Art, London, 1971–74, and at the Royal College of Art, London, 1974–76. **Career:** Designer for Fiorucci, Milan, 1976; designer/owner, Ragence Lam, London, 1977–83; Ragence, Hong Kong, 1980–83; Ragence Lam Ltd., Hong Kong, from 1983; founding member of Hong Kong Fashion Designers Association, 1984, chairman, 1985–88. **Exhibitions:** *Ragence Lam Fashion Design Exhibition,* Hong Kong Arts Center, 1985. **Awards:** Hong Kong Artist Guild Fashion Designer of the Year award, 1988; China Fashion Exhibition Competition gold prize, 1990. **Address:** 83085 Wongnei Chong Road, 17th Floor, Linden Court, Happy Valley, Hong Kong, China.

Publications

On LAM:

Articles

Kivestu, Pat, "Best of Hong Kong Fashions: The New Fashion Generation," in *WWD* (Hong Kong supplement), 1 December 1986.

Biography Resource Center, from the Gale Group, available online at www.galenet.galegroup.com, 4 October 2001.

Minghu, Gao, "Toward A Transnational Modernity: An Overview of the Exhibition: Inside Out," in *Chinese Type Online Magazine,* available online at www.chinese-art.com, 2001.

*

Growing up in a Chinese family in the British Colony of Hong Kong at the tip of south China, I have always felt the need to define my identity. Western culture was pervasive in my daily life. European art and history were part of my education and training, and so I had no difficulty adapting when I went to study at the Royal College of Art in London and then to work as a designer in Italy. But, paradoxically, it was when I was enjoying my first early success in the Western world, particularly in London where I had my own label, that I became keenly aware of my Chinese origins. I am not only modern and Western, but also Chinese, and I felt that unless my designs could capture my identity, they will never be entirely satisfying to me.

My work in the 1980s, when I returned to Hong Kong and opened my own shop with my own label, covered a wide diversity of styles. I frequently used unusual materials such as fishnet, or rattan mats. But in a way they were just random experiments, without my knowing exactly what I wanted. As designs they had merit and originality, but as self-expression they were to me lacking and uncertain. Then followed a period of contemplation and reassessment. I began to examine a tremendous amount of Chinese art forms—architecture, painting, sculpture, ceramics, textiles, furniture—whatever I could lay hands on, from all historical periods of China.

Not only did their immense richness astonish me, but I discovered I felt instinctively toward them an affinity, such as I never felt about Western art. It is as if I appreciate the Western sense of beauty only intellectually through my training, but the Chinese sense of beauty is in my blood. I also traveled to China. The vibrancy of the people and the often bold and witty way in which they seek expression in fashion struck me as entirely encouraging.

It became perfectly clear to me that what I wanted as a designer was to express the Chinese sense of beauty in contemporary and international fashion language. It must be contemporary; I want not historical revival but development, to carry…the great Chinese tradition of art and costume truncated by traumatic events in China's recent history. It must be international, because only then can it enter the mainstream and have real impact. Above all it must have depth and meaning, and not just superficial borrowings here and there from folk or court art or theatre or whatever. It must be truly new.

I see this as my life's work. In the exploration of the Chinese sense of beauty, I have an inexhaustible source of infinite variety, from the floating lines of elegant Sung-style robes to the elaborate bejeweled and embroidered Q'ing artefacts. Then there is something religious or ceremonial in this beauty—in Buddhist statues, in a monk's habit—an austerity and tranquility that deeply appeals to me. In addition, there are China's traditional fabrics and craftsmanship, the numerous techniques of embroidery, tapestry, ornamentation which could be put to exciting new use and create a totally new look.

My artistic aim, the identity I have sought to express, are all bound up with the history and the unique society of Hong Kong, and with its future. As Hong Kong's link with China grows in the coming years, I see my work growing with a strong sense of direction and inner purpose.

—Ragence Lam

* * *

In his native Hong Kong, Ragence Lam has been referred to as the Little Giant. He is one of the few local designers to have achieved an international reputation, and it is well deserved. For two decades, Lam has been developing his own lines and helping to promote the status of his fellow designers.

Lam's interest in fashion began as a child, but he never seriously considered it as a career. He became a fashion student at Harrow School of Art and the Royal College of Art, having never studied art. He went to London originally to study law, but became bored. At the Royal College of Art, his talent developed quickly and led to him winning a number of student competitions. After graduating he spent a short time in Milan, designing for Fiorucci, before setting up his own label in London and then in Hong Kong.

During the 1980s Lam evolved a look characterized by well-defined shapes and cut that revealed his passion for structure and three-dimensional forms. He highlighted his collections with quality fabrics, often from Italy or Japan, to provide an individual look. Frequently he experimented with unusual materials to create unique statements; he was never afraid of being experimental, even outrageous. Pure commercialism was not his goal, though, he was much more a provider of ideas. Lam became known, and loved by the press, as an innovator.

Toward the end of the 1980s, Lam began to change direction. The look became more minimal, with fewer dramatic details. The clothes were simpler but more versatile; customers appreciated the opportunity to be able to dress them up or down. He was moving away from the avant-garde to create something more stylish and lasting. For autumn-winter 1989–90, he featured knots and ties on simple silhouettes, interpreted in wool, Lycra, and jersey, using a subtle palette of textures and patterns. In the same collection, he created eveningwear and cocktail dresses in taffeta and lace. His designs have sold in Europe, Southeast Asia, and Japan. For a time, his collections, including both womenswear and menswear, were available in his own exclusive boutique in Hong Kong.

A testament to his achievement came in 1989 when he was invited to contribute to an international symposium as part of the World Fashion Fair in Japan. He formed part of a prestigious panel that included Issey Miyake, Sybilla, and Romeo Gigli. Lam has also acted as a consultant to fashion design education in Hong Kong. As a founder and one-time chairman of the Hong Kong Fashion Designers Association, he has helped to support and encourage young designers. He is not, however, a natural committee person; designing is his major interest and motivation.

At the beginning of the 1990s, Lam underwent a period of reassessment. Original though his work was, it did not provide the means of self-expression that he found he was seeking. To try and establish his fundamental identity, he began to examine his Chinese roots. He found a genuine affinity for Chinese art and culture and wanted to reflect this in his own work and a totally new direction began to evolve. This was not a mere pastiche of Chinese traditional dress but a more fundamental attempt to carry the great traditions of Chinese art into the late 20th century. Lam hoped to create an international fashion look reflecting his own Chinese identity and was committed to achieving this goal.

In the 21st century Lam was one of a coterie of painters, dramatists, dancers, and designers who enhanced Hong Kong's emerging Asian spirit. According to Gao Minghu's "Inside Out," an essay for *Chinese Type Online Magazine,* Lam commented, "I am beginning to feel a sense of belonging. I don't really have any roots, but now that we see more of the mainland Chinese I feel a need to identify."

—Hazel Clark; updated by Mary Ellen Snodgrass

LANE, Kenneth Jay

American jewelry and accessories designer

Born: Detroit, Michigan, 22 April 1932. **Education:** Studied at the University of Michigan, 1950–52, and at Rhode Island School of Design, Providence, 1953–54. **Family:** Married Nicola Samuel Waymouth, 1975 (divorced, 1977). **Career:** Art staff member, *Vogue* (New York), 1954–55; assistant designer, Delman Shoes, New York, 1956–58; associate designer, Christian Dior Shoes, New York, 1958–63; founder/designer, Kenneth Jay Lane, New York, from 1963; Kenneth Jay Lane shops located in the U.S., UK, France, and Austria. **Awards:** Coty American Fashion Critics special award, 1966; Tobé Coburn award, 1966; *Harper's Bazaar* International award, 1967; Maremodo di Capri-Tiberio d'Oro award, 1967; Neiman Marcus award, 1968; Swarovski award, 1969; *Brides* Magazine award, 1990. **Address:** 20 West 37th Street, New York, NY 10018, USA.

Publications

By LANE:

Books

Faking It, with Harrice Simons Miller, photographs by John Bigelow Taylor, New York, 1996.

On LANE:

Books

Bender, Marylin, *The Beautiful People,* New York, 1967.
Morris, Bernadine, and Barbara Walz, *The Fashion Makers,* New York, 1978.
Shields, Jody, *All That Glitters,* New York, 1987.
Becker, Vivienne, *Fabulous Fakes,* London, 1988.
Ball, Joanne Dubbs, *Costume Jewelry: The Golden Age of Design,* Schiffer, PA, 1990.
Stegemeyer, Anne, *Who's Who in Fashion, Third Edition,* New York, 1996.

Articles

Lynden, Patricia, "Kenneth Jay Lane: Faking It with Style," in *Northwestern,* November 1986.
Lane, Jane F., "Ballad of Kenny Lane," in *W,* August 1987.
Mehta, Gita, "The Fast Lane at Home," in *Vanity Fair,* November 1988.
Hawkins, Timothy, "Excellent Adventure," in *Egg,* March 1991.
Rubin, Robert H., "Kenneth Jay Lane," in *Night,* March 1991.

Shaw, Daniel, "Confessions of an Extra Man," in *Avenue* (New York), November 1991.
Nemy, Enid, "The King of Junque," in the *New York Times,* 27 June 1993.
Espen, Hal, "Portrait of a Dress," in the *New Yorker,* 7 November 1994.
Spindler, Amy M., "A Mature Mugler, Demeulemeester and Lang," in the *New York Times,* 18 March 1995.
Menkes, Suzy, "On the Road with Kenny Lane Jewels," in the *International Herald Tribune,* 10 June 1997.
Doran, Pat, "Kenneth Jay Lane at the Museum at FIT," in *Fashion Planet,* September 1998.
Menkes, Suzy, "Kenny Lane, Unreserved," in the *International Herald Tribune,* 3 April 2001.

* * *

Acclaimed by *Time* magazine as "the undisputed King of Costume jewelry" and called "one of the three great costume jewelers of the 20th century" by *Women's Wear Daily,* Kenneth Jay Lane transformed a previously undistinguished field into the height of fashion. "I believe that every woman has the right to be glamorous and have always believed that a woman can be just as glamorous in costume jewelry as million-dollar bangles and beads," Lane has said. "Style has little to do with money and expensive possessions; attitude and flair make all the difference."

Born in Detroit, Michigan, Lane attended the University of Michigan for two years, then went east to earn a degree in advertising design from the Rhode Island School of Design. After a brief stint in the art department at *Vogue* in New York, he went on to become the fashion coordinator at Delman Shoes, New York. Later, while working as an associate designer for Christian Dior Shoes, he spent part of each summer in Paris under the tutelage of the preeminent French shoe designer, Roger Vivier. He also designed a shoe collection for Arnold Scaasi in New York. In 1963 while adorning shoes with rhinestones and jeweled ornaments, he began to experiment with making jewelry.

"A whole new group of beautiful people began to exist," Lane said. "They started dressing up and costume jewelry was rather dull. I believed it didn't have to be." The thought that fake jewelry could be as beautiful as the real thing grew on Lane. He bought some plastic bangles at the dime store, covered them with rhinestones, crystals, leopard and zebra patterns and stripes, and a new era in costume jewelry was born.

In 1963, while still designing shoes, he worked nights and weekends creating jewelry. "I started moonlighting jewelry," he said. Since he was being paid by Genesco, Delman's parent firm, to design shoes, "I thought it would be in better taste to use my own initials and not my name for jewelry." His work was enthusiastically received, written about, and photographed by the fashion magazines. Neiman Marcus in Dallas and Bonwit Teller in New York placed orders for rhinestone earrings. Within a year, his jewelry was bringing in $2,000 a month wholesale and by June 1964 sales had risen to $10,000 a month wholesale. His part-time jewelry business became a full-time career. In 1969 Kenneth Jay Lane Inc. became part of Kenton Corporation, an organization that includes Cartier, Valentino, Mark Cross, and other well-known names in fashion. Lane repurchased the company in 1972.

Lane considers himself a fine jeweler and eschews the traditional methods of making costume jewelry. First, he fabricates his designs in wax by carving or twisting the metal. He often sets the designs with opulent stones highlighted by their cut and rich colors. Many of these stones, particularly the larger ones, he has created for himself. "I want to make real jewelry with not-real materials," he noted. He sees plastic as the modern medium: lightweight, available in every color, and perfect for simulating real gems. He likes to see his jewelry intermixed with the real gems worn by his international roster of celebrity customers. Lane is proud of the fidelity of his reproductions and claims some of his "faque" stones look better than the real ones.

"I work in less commercial ways than most manufacturers of costume jewelry," says Lane. He is realistic about the source of his designs. "My designs are all original—original from someone," he said. "There are original ideas, but a lot of good designing is editorial, choosing what is available idea-wise and applying these ideas practically. I think it's called 'having the eye'. It isn't necessarily reinventing the wheel."

Lane is as much a showman as a talented designer. In addition to receiving numerous fashion awards, his jewelry was regularly featured on several soap operas, including *Another World, Guiding Light,* and *Days of Our Lives.* He has also created jewelry for the Costume Institute exhibitions at the Metropolitan Museum of Art in New York.

In addition to being a fixture on the social circuit, Lane is frequently named on the International Best Dressed Men's List. "All you need is one person and you can meet the world," he said. Dinner partner and friend to some of the world's most fashionable women, his clients have included Jacqueline Kennedy Onassis, Princess Margaret, the Duchess of Windsor, Elizabeth Taylor, Audrey Hepburn, Nancy Reagan, Joan Collins, Babe Paley, Brooke Astor, and Lee Radziwill Ross. Former First Lady Barbara Bush wore his "pearls" to her husband's inauguration, and the triple-strand became an integral part of her signature style. He sent his $21 saxophone pin to another former First Lady, Hillary Rodham Clinton.

In 1993 Lane celebrated his 30th anniversary in business. The *New York Times* called him "the man who made costume jewelry chic and, more important to his bank account, readily available to what is loosely referred to as the masses. Chanel had done it earlier, but to a more affluent clientèle" (27 June 1993). Additionally, Lane is wildly popular on QVC, the cable television home-shopping network. In 1997 Lane took in about $1.5 million during each four-hour, bimonthly appearance.

Through his designing and socializing, Lane has achieved a level of fame comparable to the women he adorns. *Faking It* is Lane's 1996 memoir of his 30-plus years as faux jewelry master. Written with Harrice Simons Miller, the book is full of Lane's recollections of his many adventures and friendships with society women. The book includes photographs by John Bigelow Taylor. Lane followed the launch of the book with a European road show, celebrating with hundreds of fans in Rome, Madrid, London, and Paris.

Suzy Menkes asked Lane why he never made the switch to real jewels. He cited security, recalling the famous mock-up necklace he created for Jackie Kennedy Onassis so she could leave the original in the safe. With priceless gems, "You don't have the freedom," he told Menkes. "And I'm too lazy to pick up an emerald if it falls on the floor!"

Further proof of Lane's lasting influence on the fashion world came in 1998 when the Museum at New York's Fashion Institute of

Technology (FIT) presented an exhibition of the Lane collection, showcasing everything from his 1960s pieces to recent designs. The FIT museum contains the world's largest collection of costumes, textiles, and accessories.

—Janet Markarian; updated by Lisa Groshong

LANG, Helmut

Austrian designer

Born: Vienna, Austria, 10 March 1956. **Career:** Grew up in Austrian Alps and Vienna; became acquainted with Viennese art scene; established own fashion studio in Vienna, 1977; opened made-to-measure shop in Vienna, 1979; developed ready-to-wear collections, 1984–86; presented Helmut Lang womenswear, 1986, and Helmut Lang menswear, 1987, as part of Paris Fashion Week; established license business, 1988; moved several times between Paris and Vienna, 1988–93; professor of Fashion Masterclass, University of Applied Arts, Vienna, from 1993; other lines include underwear, 1994, eyewear, 1995, and jeans, 1997; sold 51-percent stake of company to Prada, 1999; introduced first fragrance, *Helmut Lang,* and Helmut Lang Parfums flagship store, 2000; launched bath and body lines, 2001. **Collections:** Museum of Applied Arts, Vienna. **Exhibitions:** "Vienne 1880–1939: L'Apocalypse Joyeuse," at the Pompidou, Vienna, 1986. **Awards:** *New York* Magazine New York award, 1998; CFDA's Menswear Designer of the Year, 2000. **Addresses:** Press Office, c/o Michele Montagne, 184 rue St. Maur, F-75010 Paris, France; Helmut Lang New York, 80 Greene Street, New York, NY 10012, USA. **Website:** www.helmutlang.com.

Helmut Lang, spring 2001 collection. © AP/Wide World Photos.

Publications

On LANG:

Articles

Cressole, Michel, "Une Lancinante Variation En Jersey Zippé," in *Libération* (Paris), 24 March 1986.

Kaupp, Katia D., "Une Manif Pour Helmut Lang," in *Le Nouvel Observateur* (Paris), 29 March 1990.

Blumenberg, H. C., "Der Retter des Einfachen," in *Zeit Magazin* (Hamburg), 1 March 1991.

Tredre, Roger, "The Maker's Culture: The Wearer's Imprint," in the *Independent* (London), 9 September 1993.

Mair, Avril, "Designs of the Times," in *i-D* (London), December 1993.

Mower, Sarah, "Brilliant," in *Harper's Bazaar,* February 1994.

Spindler, Amy M., "Lang Points the Way to a New Elegance," in the *New York Times,* 7 March 1994.

Brampton, Sally, "Langevity," in the *Guardian* (London), 20 August 1994.

Watson, Shane, "Cool Hand Lang," in *Elle* (London), September 1994.

Espen, Hal, "Portrait of a Dress," in the *New Yorker,* 7 November 1994.

Spindler, Amy M., "A Mature Mugler, Demeulemeester, and Lang," in the *New York Times,* 18 March 1995.

Teller, Jeurgen, "Langfroid," in *ArtForum International,* October 1995.

Hirschberg, Lynn, "The Little Rubber Dress, Among Others: The Fashion Desgins of Helmut Lang," in the *New York Times Magazine,* 2 February 1997.

"Helmut Lang," in *Current Biography,* April 1997.

Spindler, Amy M., "Three With the Touch to Inherit the Crown," in the *New York Times,* 18 October 1997.

Kaplan, James, "A New Yorker by Design: Helmut Lang…," in *New York,* 27 July 1998.

Horyn, Cathy, "New Wrinkles at Lang and Sui," in the *New York Times,* 11 February 2000.

Seabrook, John, "The Invisible Designer: Helmut Lang," in the *New Yorker,* 18 September 2000.

"A Delicate Balance: It's a Balancing Act," in *WWD,* 16 February 2001.

"Helmut Lang Creates First Body Line," in *Cosmetics International,* April 2001.

Deeny, Godfrey, "Helmut Lang: The Spark of a New Look," available online at Fashion Windows, www.fashionwindows.com.
"Interview with Helmut Lang," online at www.ocf.berkeley.edu.

*

At a moment of conflicting demands, people want modernity and identity, street style and savviness. Fashion now is fast, downbeat, and relentlessly urban. Because of that, I have been developing a particular vision, what I call a nonreferential view of fashion. It is all about today. It has to do with my personality, with my life, and with the idea that quality doesn't go out of style every six months.

Working effectively with fashion means adding pieces to a continuing story, evolving fluently year after year. The basis of really effortless style is found in minimal exaggeration. A perfect economy of cut and exacting attention to finish is sometimes lost to the careless eye, which gives it precisely the sort of anonymous status that the truly knowing admire. If you have to ask, you don't get it, in either sense. Downbeat elegance is founded in precise proportions and clean tailoring; balancing hi-tech fabrics with real clothing. The result is fashion put into a different context to become something known, unknown.

—Helmut Lang

Helmut Lang, fall/winter 2001 collection. © Reuters NewMedia Inc./CORBIS.

* * *

An attenuated, urban aesthetic, embodied by subtle mixes of luxury fabrics and post-punk synthetics, dominates Helmut Lang's confident designs. Both his menswear and womenswear are uncompromisingly modern: stark minimalist pieces in somber city shades are combined with harsh metallics and slippery transparent layers, questioning the restrictions of traditional tailored clothing.

Although Lang's work is avant-garde, he is not afraid to use sharply cut suiting, or have a punklike disregard for accepted fabric use, as cigarette trousers and three-buttoned jackets come in shiny PVC with clingy net t-shirts worn underneath. He enjoys the surprise of such cheap fabrics being lent a certain chic through their combination with their more luxurious counterparts, and often backs silk with nylon to give a liquid, shifting opacity to column dresses and spaghetti-strapped slips.

For all the deconstructed glamor of his clothes, they remain essentially understated, drawing their interest from the layering of opaques and transparents in sinuous strong lines, rather than unnecessary details that might dull their impact. Even the sexuality of his figure-hugging womenswear is tempered by a nonchalance and apparent disregard for the impact the clothes have. This parallels the growing sense of independence and confidence of women over the years Lang has been designing.

If his stylistic reference points originated touching the past, then his distillation of them is always utterly contemporary. In line with and often ahead of current trends, he honed his skills during the 1980s, contradicting the decade's often overblown characteristics and charming first the Parisian, then the international fashion scene, which was impressed by the modernity of his work. He remains a hero of the cognoscenti, influencing mainstream fashion.

The simplicity of the cut of a Lang garment is deceptive. The slim mannish-shaped trousers he favors for women may be timeless enough, but the surprise of rendering them in hot red stretch synthetic in 1992 and creating an urban warrior look with halter top and boned breastplate meant they appealed to the stylishly unconventional, who were not afraid to slip from day to night, informal to formal, disregarding the normal restrictions of what is appropriate to wear.

Lang's emphasis on the importance of innovative textiles is as prevalent in his menswear. He has been at the forefront of a shift in this area, which has gathered momentum during the 1990s. He has pushed for a crossover of fabrics from womenswear and a narrower line, shown in 19th-century cut, three-piece single-breasted suits, more attuned to the times than the big triangular silhouette of the 1980s. His deconstructed close-fit tops with visible seaming and layered angora tank tops over untucked shirts increased his popularity as fashion became tired of its own overpowering dogma in the early 1990s.

Lang's work continues to maintain a high profile in fashion magazines and the industry. The deceptive simplicity of his clothes, complicated by his constant comparisons of clear and opaque, matte and shiny, silky-smooth and plastic-hard, carried him successfully into the 1990s and enabled him to be part of a movement in fashion toward a redefinition of glamor and beauty in the early 2000s. For the 21st century, calling for a "new sensibility," Lang began to use classical natural fabrics such as satin and tweed while continuing with his characteristic shapes but changing his fabrics—such as rubberized lace replaced by real lace. Not wanting to confuse a subtle touch with sheer softness, Lang admitted that his change in fabric choice has something to do with romance and love, with "not being afraid, being able to live these different needs and different moods."

Not only did Lang shock the fashion world with his change of aesthetic, but he also moved up his spring 2000 show from November to September 1999, the same month he sold a 51-percent stake in his design firm to Prada. In essence, Lang continues to remain predictably cutting edge; he searches for hidden harmony and poetry in the multifarious, often dissonant, realms of everyday experience. Although still striving to merge and reconcile hard and fluid textures, he is now using cashmere, silk, and satin.

In 2000 and 2001 Lang ventured into fragrance and skincare products for both men (cologne, deodorant, shower gel, aftershave) and women (perfume, shower gel, body lotion). An eponymous fragrance was released in the fall of 2000, which coincided with the opening of a flagship perfumery, Helmut Lang Parfums, in New York City. After *Helmut Lang* came a complementary fragrance, *Velvonia,* which can be worn separately or along with other Lang body products. Helmut Lang fragrances and skincare products are available at Lang Parfumeries in Munich, Vienna, Hong Kong, and New York, as well as in high-end department stores worldwide.

—Rebecca Arnold; updated by Christine Miner Minderovic

LANVIN

French fashion house

Founded: in Paris in 1890 by Jeanne Lanvin (1867–1946). **Company History:** Began with offering custom children's clothing; offered women's clothing, 1909, introduced first fragrances, 1925; men's clothing, women's sportswear, furs, and accessories, from 1926; upon Lanvin's death, daughter Marie-Blanche de Polignac took reins of company, 1946–58; launched women's ready-to-wear, 1982; Jeanne Lanvin S.A. purchased by Orcofi and L'Oreal, 1989; couture collections discontinued, 1992; introduced bath and body lines, Ligne Deliceuse, 1994; designers have included Antonio del Castillo (1950–62), Jules-François Crahay (1963–85), Maryll Lanvin (from 1982), Claude Montana (1990), Dominique Morlotti (from 1992), Ocimar Versolate (1996–98), Cristina Ortiz, (from 1998); sold by L'Oreal to Harmonie SA, 2001; fragrances include *My Sin,* 1925, *Arpège,* 1927 (reintroduced 1994), *Scandal,* 1931, *Runeur,* 1934, *Pretexts,* 1937, *Crescendo,* 1960, *L'Homme,* 1997, *Oxygene,* 2001. **Exhibitions:** *Paris Couture—Années Trente,* Musée de la Mode et du Costume, Palais Galliera, Paris. **Collections:** Victoria & Albert Museum, London; Fashion Institute of Technology, New York; Costume Institute of the Metropolitan Museum of Art, New York; Musée de la Mode et du Costume, Paris; Musée des Arts de la Mode, Paris. **Awards:** *Jeanne Lanvin:* Chevalier de la Légion d'Honneur, 1926; Officier de la Légion d'Honneur, 1938. **Company Address:** 15 rue du Faubourg St.-Honoré, 75008 Paris, France.

Lanvin, fall/winter 2001–02 ready-to-wear collection designed by Cristina Ortiz. © AP/Wide World Photos.

Publications

On LANVIN:

Books

Bourdet, Denise, *Art et Style: Les Fées,* Paris, 1946.

Bertin, Celia, *Paris à la mode,* London, 1956.

Pickens, Mary Brooks, and Dora Loues Miller, *Dressmakers of France,* New York, 1956.

Contini, Mila, *Fashion From Ancient Egypt to the Present Day,* Milan, New York, 1965.

Lynam, Ruth, *Couture,* Garden City, New York, 1972.

Milbank, Caroline Rennolds, *Couture: The Great Designers,* New York, 1985.

Garnier, Guillaume, *Paris Couture—Années Trente* [exhibition catalogue], Paris, 1987.

Martin, Richard, and Harold Koda, *The Historical Mode: Fashion and Art in the 1980s,* New York, 1989.

Lanvin, spring/summer 1968 collection: "Charade," a shantung shirt under a waistcoat decorated with multi-colored beads and striped silk evening pants. © AP/Wide World Photos.

Stegemeyer, Anne, *Who's Who in Fashion, Third Edition,* New York, 1996.

Articles

"Living in Heavenly Blue Blow-Up Space in Paris," in *Vogue* (London), February 1969.

Toll, Marie-Pierre, "Where Beauty is Not a Luxury," in *House & Garden,* September 1984.

Bernier, O., "Art Deco Rooms at the Musée des Arts," in *Magazine Antiques,* October 1987.

Aillaud, C., "A Lanvin Legacy," in *Architectural Digest,* September 1988.

Penn, I., and C.C. de Dudzeele, "Rock 'n' Royalty," in *Vogue,* October 1990.

Johnson, E.W., and I. Hammond, "Cocktail Craze," in *Ebony,* January 1991.

Morris, B., "Saint Laurent Finds Beauty in a Perfect Cut," in the *New York Times,* 30 January 1992.

James, Laurie, "The State of Montana," in *Harper's Bazaar,* October 1992.

Deeny, Godfrey, "Lanvin Realigns Flagship to Include HQ and Staff," in *DNR,* 20 September 1993.

D'Aulnay, Sophie, "Their Man Armand," in *DNR,* 31 March 1994.

———, "Lanvin: There is a Doctor in the House," in *DNR,* 16 May 1994.

Testino, Mario, "The Skimp," in *Harper's Bazaar,* June 1994.

Larenaudie, Sarah R., "Asaria Gets Top Post at Lanvin," in *DNR,* 14 December 1994.

D'Aulnay, Sophie, "The Plan for Lanvin," in *DNR,* 13 February 1995.

———, "Men's Furnishings," in *DNR,* 21 April 1995.

Ehlert, Athena, "Arpège—The Gift of a Gifted Mother," in *Victoria,* May 1995.

Hoppe, Karen, "The Last Word," in *DCI,* November 1995.

White, Constance C.R., "Beautiful Flight or Dizzy Free Fall," in *Fashion,* March 1996.

———, "Patterns," in the *New York Times,* 14 October 1997.

Lennon, Christine, "Under the Influence," in *Harper's Bazaar,* December 1997.

Place, Jennifer, "1998 New Fragrance," in *Soap & Cosmetics Specialties,* March 1998.

Duncan, David Ewing, and Mark Connolly, "Something Old, Something New," in *Condé Nast Traveler,* March 1999.

Shea, Christine, "Fresh Air," in *Harper's Bazaar,* February 2001.

* * *

The youthful look identified with Lanvin came from Jeanne Lanvin's earliest couture, children's dresses; the many decorations were inspired by a trip to Spain during her childhood. The memory of the play on shadows and light would influence her choice of embroidery, such as multineedle sewing machine stitching and quilting. She had three embroidery ateliers. Beading and appliqué were also applied. With dyes she ombréed textiles. She had her own dye works—Lanvin Blue, inspired by stained glass was developed there. These decorations were applied to all categories, including millinery, couture, menswear, and accessories.

Lanvin did not drape or sketch but gave verbal instructions to the sketchers. Approved drawings were sent to ateliers for execution. Although Art Déco-style embroideries continued well into the 1930s, ideas came from all periods of art. She found inspiration everywhere—from her painting collection containing Vuillard, Renoir, Fantin-Latour, and Odilon Redon—as well as from from books, fruit, gardens, museums, travel, and costume collections. She had her own costume archives dating from 1848 to 1925. Nothing was taken literally, but interpreted.

The chemise as women's dress was introduced in 1913. Her best known innovation, the robe de style, was an adaptation of the 18th-century pannier. Introduced in the 1920s, it was repeated in a variety of fabrics: silk taffeta, velvet, metallic lace with organdy, chiffon, and net. New models were presented for two decades. She showed tea gowns, dinner pajamas, dolman wraps, hooded capes, and Zouave bloomer skirts that were either youthful, classic, or romantic. Her clear colors were subtle and feminine: begonia, fuchsia, cerise, almond green, periwinkle blue, cornflower blue. Silver was combined with black or white. Adjusting to World War II, Lanvin created the split coat for bicycling and bright-colored felt gas mask cases. During the Liberation, she presented showings for American soldiers.

Lanvin, fall/winter 2001 ready-to-wear collection designed by Dominique Morlotti. © AFP/CORBIS.

In 1927 Lanvin created a fragrance for her only child, Countess Marie-Blanche de Polignac, an opera singer. A heady mix of honeysuckle, jasmine, and patchouli, *Arpège* became a sensation, with fans including Rita Hayworth and Princess Diana. Relaunched in 1994, it continues to this day to be a bestselling classic.

Jeanne Lanvin died in 1946; her daughter continued the business after her death. Designer Antonio del Castillo, arriving in 1950, attempted to adapt to the house image. His Spanish background influenced his choice of brighter colors, light and heavy combinations of fabrics, and more severe, sophisticated styles. His successor, Jules-François Crahay, arriving in 1963, returned to the collections the youthful quality that remains today. Other major designers who have worked for Lanvin include Ocimar Versolato, Dominique Morlotti, Alberto Morillas, and most recently, Cristina Ortiz.

In 1989 Orcofi and L'Oreal, in a joint venture, together purchased Lanvin, one of the world's oldest fashion and fragrance houses. Over the years, L'Oreal—itself partially owned by Gesparal, which in turn was partly owned by Nestlé S.A.—slowly bought out Orcofi, and Lanvin became a part of the L'Oreal stable (until sold in 2001 to Harmonie SA), which includes such companies and brand names as Maybelline, Redken, Biotherm, Cacharel, Lancôme Paris, Le Club des Créatures de Beaut, and Vichy Labs.

In 2001 Lanvin introduced its 26th fragrance, called *Oxygene,* "the first," according to Christophe Toumit, general director of Lanvin Parfums, "since *Arpège* to come to America." So, more than half a century after her death, Jeanne Lanvin's legacy continues to grow.

—Betty Kirke; updated by Daryl F. Mallett

LAROCHE, Guy

French designer

Born: La Rochelle, France, 16 July 1921. **Career:** Began working as a milliner, Paris; began working for Jean Dessès, became his assistant, 1949; traveled to the U.S. to study ready-to-wear manufacturing, 1955; established first Paris salon, 1956; opened Guy Laroche couture house and introduced ready-to-wear collection, Paris, 1961; created first fragance, 1966; added menswear line, 1966; second boutique opened, 1973; launch of additional boutiques, in France and elsewhere, 1974; designed last collection, 1989. Fragrances include *Fidji,* 1966; *Eau Folle,* 1970; *J'ai Osé,* 1977; *Drakkar,* 1972; *Drakkar Noir,* 1982; *Clandestine,* 1986; fragrance division sold to L'Oréal, company sold to Sociètè Bic. **Awards:** Macy's outstanding creativity award, New York, 1959; Dé d'Or award, Paris, 1986, 1989; Chevalier de la Légion d'Honneur, 1987. **Died:** 17 February 1989, in Paris. **Company Address:** 29 Avenue Montaigne, Paris 75008, France. **Company Website:** www.guy-laroche.de.

Publications

On LAROCHE:

Books

Stegemeyer, Anne, *Who's Who in Fashion, Third Edition,* New York, 1996.

Articles

Parinaud, A. editor, "La Haute Couture intéresse-t-elle les peintres," in *Galerie des Arts,* March 1979.
"A chacon son Dé d'Or," in *Vogue* (Paris), February 1986.
"Guy Laroche à Bordeaux: le style de l'élégance," in *Vogue* (Paris), May 1987.
Obiturary, "France's Guy Laroche, Leading French Designer Dies," in *Chicago Tribune,* 18 February 1989.
Obituary, in the *Daily Telegraph* (London), 18 February 1989.
Obituary, in *The Independent* (London), 18 February 1989.
"Couturier Guy Laroche Dead at 67," in *WWD,* 21 February 1989.
"Un Dé d'Or au doigt de Guy Laroche," in *Vogue* (Paris), March 1989.
Benaim, Laurence, "Une griffe demeure: Guy Laroche un grand couturier," in *Elle* (Paris), 6 March 1989.
"Guy Laroche: l'album sur mesure," in *Vogue* (Paris), April 1989.
Premoli, Francesca, "The Realm of Illusion," in *Casa Vogue* (Milan), November 1989.
Beurdeley, Laurence, "Guy Laroche: l'esprit de la Renaissance," in *L'Officiel* (Paris), August 1990.
Givhan, Robin, "Nothing New Under the Paris Sun: Even the Best Doesn't Stand Out from the Rest," in the *Washington Post,* 12 March 1999.

Guy Laroche design, 1965: coq feather bonnet tied with a chiffon kerchief. © AP/Wide World Photos.

———, "In Paris, Runway of Gossip; Show Wrinkled by Talk of Change," in the *Washington Post,* 8 October 1999.

* * *

Before entering the industry in the 1940s, Guy Laroche had no formal training in fashion design. He soon, however, built up a varied portfolio of experience, beginning with styling and millinery in New York followed by work in fashion and merchandising on Seventh Avenue. Returning to Paris he was offered a job as design assistant at the fashion house of Jean Dessès. Dessès was famous for designing the stole and distinctive draped chiffon evening gowns in striking colors. He also designed one of the first diffusion lines in 1950 and this marked the beginning of ready-to-wear in French haute couture. Laroche was involved in these innovations and in 1955 traveled to the U.S. to study new fabrication methods for ready-to wear.

Larouche opened his own couture house in 1956 on Avenue Franklin Roosevelt in Paris, at the age of 37. His first collection, shown in his apartment, was one of subtle sophistication, reminiscent of Balenciaga's restrained elegance: simple tops that spread into huge bouffant skirts with baroque inspired, twisted drapes, or relaxed short evening dresses in black silk chiffon, with elegant capes bordered in satin ribbon. Later collections were more feminine, fun, and younger in feel: short puffed hems and schoolgirl dresses or delicate gathered drapes and scallop-effect necklines. Guy Laroche clothes were particularly noted for their skillful cutting and tailoring.

By the early 1960s Laroche had launched a ready-to-wear line and opened a boutique. His reputation as a creative but shrewd businessman grew as his company expanded. Capitalizing on his following amongst actresses and socialites, the company moved swiftly into licensing and perfumes. The major perfume, *Fidji,* was introduced in 1966 to immediate success and the men's aftershave *Drakkar Noir* was introduced in 1982, to complement the previously established men's ready-to-wear clothing.

Licensed goods promoted the reputation of the Guy Laroche name internationally, particularly in the lucrative Middle Eastern markets where the allure of Paris on a label sold goods. Lingerie, nightwear, hats, ties, bags, scarves, and jersey knits were exported and sold in 250 boutiques worldwide.

During the late 1960s, Laroche sold a large amount of shares in his business to Bernard Cornfeld and to L'Oréal, the hair and beauty product manufacturers. The perfume side of the business then became a division of the L'Oréal beauty company. Licensing deals throughout Europe, Asia, and South America helped maintain a high profile for Guy Laroche products, including intimate apparel, footwear, luggage, sunglasses, and outerwear, while the company itself was later bought by French pen and razor manufacturer, Socièté Bic.

Guy Laroche, the legendary designer, died in 1989, while his company struggled under successive designers, including Michael Klein, Elber Albaz, and Ronald van der Kemp. Albaz, widely credited with rejuvenating the company, left to head up Yves Saint Laurent in 1997. Dutch designer Ronald van der Kemp was hired to succeed Elbaz, but was fired after this first collection was panned by fashion critics. By 1999 Bic announced its intention of selling Guy Laroche, due to falling profits and currency rate fluctuations. After the departure of Albaz, the company lost much of its sheen; subsequent collections were the product of a design team and lacked the élan usually associated with the name Guy Laroche. Yet in 2001 the Guy Laroche name was still alive and well, and Bic had, apparently, decided to hold on to its investment for the foreseeable future.

—Kevin Almond; updated by Nelly Rhodes

LARS, Byron

American designer

Born: Oakland, California, 19 January 1965. **Education:** Studied at the Brooks Fashion Institute, Long Beach, 1983–85; Fashion Institute of Technology, 1986–87; selected to represent USA at the International Concours des Jeunes Créateurs de Mode, Paris, 1986, and at the Festival du Lin, Monte Carlo, 1989. **Career:** Freelance sketcher and pattern maker, Kevan Hall, Gary Gatyas, Ronaldus Shamask, Nancy Crystal Blouse Co., New York, 1986–91; showed first collection, 1991; first full-scale New York show, 1992; designer, En Vogue fashion collection, from 1993; signed licensing deal with San Siro for Shirttails collection, 1995 (agreement nullified in court, 1997); Cinnabar Sensation Barbie, 1996; signed with Mattel for new line of African American Barbies with designer clothes, 1997; backer pulled funds and firm closed, 1997; launched new collection, Green T, 1999. **Exhibitions:** *Byron Lars' Illustrations,* Ambassador Gallery, New

Byron Lars posing with one of his ensembles from his "Shirt Tales" show, spring 1996. © AP/Wide World Photos.

York, 1992. **Awards:** Vogue Cecil Beaton award for Illustration, London, 1990. **Address:** 202 West 40th Street, New York, NY 10018, U.S.A.

Publications

On LARS:

Books

Stegemeyer, Anne, *Who's Who in Fashion, Third Edition,* New York, 1996.

Articles

White, Constance C.R., "Rookie of the Year," in *WWD,* 24 April 1991.

Washington, Elsie B., "Now: Brothers on Seventh Avenue," in *Essence,* November 1991.

Gerber, Robert, "Byron Lars: Elmer Fudd Fab," in *Interview* (New York), December 1991.

"Byron Takes Off," in *WWD,* 15 April 1992.

Schiro, Anne-Marie, "The Sweet Smile of Success," in the *New York Times,* 7 June 1992.

Darnton, Nina, "The Rainbow Coalition," in *Newsweek,* 13 July 1992.

Walt, Vivienne, "From Rags to Riches," in the *San Francisco Examiner,* 9 August 1992.

Piaggi, Anna, "By Air," in *Vogue* (Milan), August 1992.

Jaffe, Deborah, "Great Style," in *Elle* (New York), September 1992.

"Working It!" in *Essence,* September 1992.

Baker, Martha, "(Byronic) Poses," in *New York,* 12 October 1992.

Donovan, Carrie, and Ruven Afanador, "New York," in the *New York Times Magazine,* 1 November 1992.

Rubenstein, Hal, "Return to *Gilligan's Island,*" in the *New York Times Magazine,* 17 January 1993.

Donovan, Carrie, and Mark Peterson, "It's Lyrical on Seventh Avenue," in the *New York Times Magazine,* 28 March 1993.

Praeger, Emily, "Neither Virgin Nor Siren," in the *New York Times,* 14 November 1993.

Bellafante, Ginia, "En Vogue in Vogue?" in *Time,* 6 December 1993.

MacIntosh, Jeane, "His Dance Cards are Full," in *DNR,* 28 February 1994.

Johnson, Eunice W., "Spotlightin' Legs," in *Ebony,* April 1994.

Houston, Ruth, "The All-Important Jacket," in *Black Elegance,* April 1994.

Menkes, Suzy, "A Touch of Modern Exotica," in the *New York Times,* 24 April 1994.

Dunn-Lee, Ionia, "Well Suited," in *Black Elegance,* October 1994.

White, Constance C.R., "Patterns," in the *New York Times,* 28 February 1995.

———, "Patterns," in the *New York Times,* 4 April 1995.

"New York: Byron Lars," in *WWD,* 4 April 1995.

White, Constance C.R., "Fur Tradition Versus Fur Fun," in the *New York Times,* 23 May 1995.

———, "Vision for Changing Times," in the *New York Times,* 4 November 1995.

———, "Patterns," in the *New York Times,* 23 January 1996.

———, "Three Successes, and So American," in the *New York Times,* 3 April 1996.

White, Renee Minus, "Byron Lars Designs for Dolls—Barbies and Real Ones," in the *New York Amsterdam News,* 20 April 1996.

Dunn-Lee, Ionia, "Fashion Innovators on Seventh," in *Black Elegance,* September 1996.

"Bryon Lars Sues San Siro Over Contract, Trademark," in *DNR,* 27 December 1996.

"Byron's Secret," in *WWD,* 18 February 1997.

"Byron Loves Barbie," in *WWD,* 7 May 1997.

Gite, Lloyd, "Breaking into the Fashion Biz: Career Opportunities," in *Black Enterprise,* June 1997.

Williamson, Rusty, "Byron Lars Comes Back with Spring Green T Line," in *WWD,* 20 July 2000.

Williamson, Rusty, "Back in the New York Groove; Hot 1990s Designer Byron Lars…," in *WWD,* 3 August 2000.

* * *

The career of Byron Lars took wing with his fall 1992 collection inspired by legendary aviatrix Amelia Earhart, but Lars had already been one of the most closely watched and praised newcomers in New York for several years. Mary Ann Wheaton, who worked with Patrick

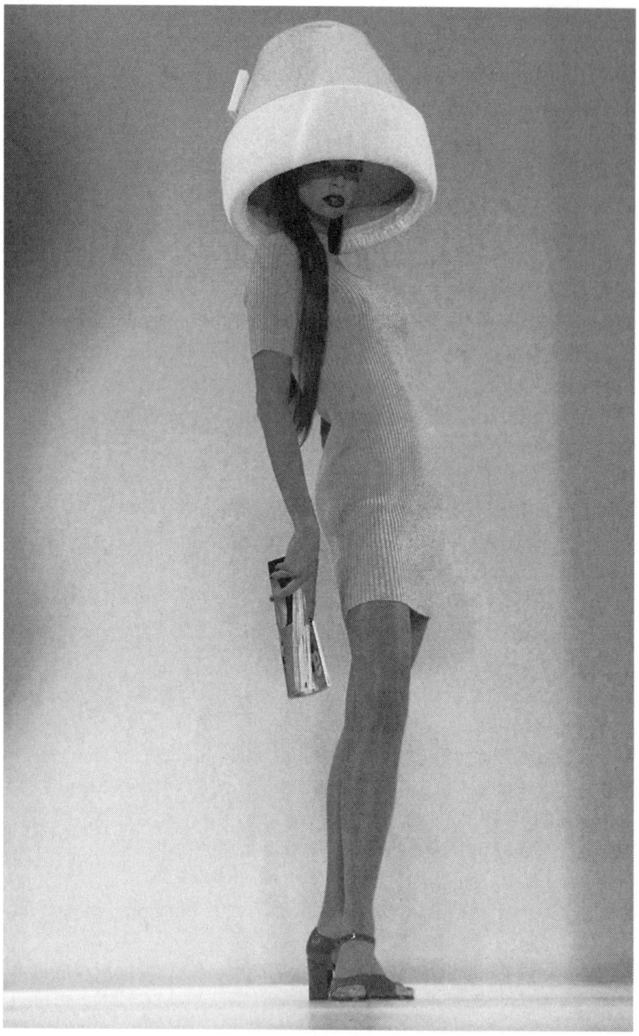

Byron Lars, fall 1996 collection: ribbed knit dress with a hairdryer hat. © AP/Wide World Photos.

Kelly during his Paris years and took him from $700,000 in business to $7.5 million in 18 months, took Lars under her wing in February 1991 and placed his clothes in top stores within a week.

The fall 1992 collection, Lars' first full-scale New York show, consolidated his reputation (and, not coincidentally, his business circumstances, including backing from C. Itoh & Company) and was built on the same strengths that had characterized his earlier work. In an interview in *Essence* (September 1992), Lynn Manulis, president of Martha International (which became one of the first stores to carry Lars' work), said, "It was the best and most original collection that happened during the entire fashion week." Lars also attracted the attention of dance legend Merce Cunningham, with whom he became friends.

Appropriating from menswear, with a special interest in the men's dress shirts and in stripes and patterns especially associated with menswear, melding isolated elements of exaggeration with conventional dress in a dry irony, and responding to high fashion and street influence, Lars developed a signature style while still in his twenties. According to Anne-Marie Schiro (*New York Times,* 7 June 1992), stores "love his clothes, which can be quirky yet classic, streetwise but never vulgar. His inspiration may come from baseball or aviation, from rappers or schoolgirls. And the accessories are outrageous: caps with oversize crowns and two foot-long peaks, lunch boxes or boom boxes as handbags. They make you smile."

Designer Jeffrey Banks called Lars "the African-American Christian Francis Roth," relating the former's incongruity with the latter's paradoxes of sophisticated innocence in clothing. Roth and Lars share yet another characteristic: they are both consummate masters of the cut, enjoying the construction of the garment almost in the manner of the couture. Lars is not merely making a joke of men's shirts cross-dressed for women, but took the shirttail as a constructive element, reshaped the bust, and deconstructed the shirt to be worn by a woman. It is as much a tour de force in construction as it is an apt idea of 1990s gender transaction. If Lars' clothes were merely facetious, they would succeed as great fun; but they succeed as great fashion because they are beautifully cut.

In adapting menswear, Lars is attentive to feminine outcomes, offering a kind of enhanced sensuality in the presence of male and female in one garment. In many instances, peplums emphasize waist and hips (but not with the 1980s power look), and the sartorial nuancing of shirt and jacket for women directs attention to a broadened expanse of the bust. Often including even men's ties, the result is unequivocally feminine when Lars includes a built-in bra for shaping. Even as he used airplane motifs in textiles in his epochal fall 1992 collection, his fantasy was not a little boy's—aviator jackets had a curvaceous femininity approximating Azzedine Alaïa while shorts, short skirts, and leggings emphasized the female. A duck hunter's outfit in plaid (with a duck decoy made into a handbag), seemingly destined for the L.L. Bean catalogue before a perverse, savvy drollery rendered it chic, and it was featured in the *Tribute to the Black Fashion Museum* exhibition at the Fashion Institute of Technology, New York, in spring 1992.

Even before the Earhart collection, Lars was influenced by the 1940s. His twists of menswear in the best Rosie-the-Riveter tradition and his fascination with the sarong recall the period. Both shirts and sarongs depended upon tying, a sense of the improvised wrap, that the designer built into the garment. In this, Lars seemed an antecedent in Claire McCardell, whose lifelong interest in casual wraps is similar to Lars' fascination with the shaping and informality afforded by tying. He has also been influenced by pop singers, such as the 1993 En Vogue collection, inspired by the group of the same name. The following year, he created a collection based on African themes; the next, 1995, he had fun with fur, joining other designers such as Yeohlee Teng, Ben Kahn and various others in designing fur collections; and in 1996 Mattel asked Lars to design a collectible Barbie doll, complete with her own fashion wardrobe. His collection that year was a result of being inspired by Barbie, with charcoal gray and cocoa brown colors gracing the line. The Barbie foray proved so successful Mattel asked Lars in 1997 to develop an entire line of African American Barbie dolls, all dressed in designer duds. The same year Lars negotiated with Victoria's Secret to design a collection of sexy, fun cotton lingerie separates and silk robes bearing the firm's logo.

Unfortunately for Lars, the walls came crashing down in late 1997 despite a slew of promising licensing deals. After his financial backing was withdrawn, Lars had little more than the Mattel Barbie collaboration to keep him going. Commenting on the dry period to *Women's Wear Daily* (20 July 2000), "I freelanced with lots of different types of companies and stretched my creative wings." Yet the times were far from rosy, and he learned a tough lesson on licensing deals. "I'd rather flip burgers at McDonald's than go through that again," he declared. Lars did, however, orchestrate a comeback with a new funky collection in 1999, called Green T, with his name conspicuously absent from the label. "With Green T, we intentionally left my name off the label because we wanted to see if it could fly without a designer angle. We just wanted to do a really great product with design integrity at a really great price."

Lars is only one of many African American designers achieving prominence in New York in the last decade. Others include C.D. Greene, Gordon Henderson, Michael McCollum, Tracy Reese, and Kevin Smith, all inspired by the works of previous designers such as Stephen Burrows, Patrick Kelly, Thierry Mugler, and Willi Smith. If still considered a prodigy today, since he is only in his thirties, Byron Lars is making clever yet important clothes, wearable ideas, wondrous social transplants and mutations, and some of the most sensitively and sensuously cut garments in America.

—Richard Martin; updated by Daryl F. Mallett and Owen James

LAUG, André

French designer working in Rome

Born: Alsace, France, 29 December 1931. **Career:** Moved to Paris, 1958, to begin working for Raphäel fashion house; designer, Nina Ricci, Paris, early 1960s; worked freelance, from 1962, selling designs to Venet; collaborated with Courrèges until 1963, when he moved to Rome; designed nine collections of haute couture and five of ready-to-wear for Maria Antonelli, 1964–68; opened own couture house and showed own collection, Rome, 1968; house continued for a few years after his death, then closed. **Died:** December 1984, in Rome.

Publications

On LAUG:

Books

Lambert, Eleanor, *World of Fashion: People, Places, Resources,* New York, 1976.

Soli, Pia, *Il genio antipatico,* Milan, 1984.

Stegemeyer, Anne, *Who's Who in Fashion, Third Edition,* New York, 1996.

Articles

McEvoy, Marian, "Rome Laurels to Laug, Valentino," in *WWD,* 20 July 1978.

Talley, André Leon, "André Laug," in *Vogue* (Paris), January 1981.

Morris, Bernadine, "André Laug, Stylist," [obituary] in the *New York Times,* 18 December 1984.

"Milan Steers a More Balanced Course Back to Sanity After Two Seasons of Turbulence," in the *Chicago Tribune,* 17 March 1985.

"André Laug: chiaro, lieve con quel preciso stile," in *Vogue* (Milan), March 1987.

"Roma alta moda: André Laug," in *Vogue* (Milan), March 1988.

* * *

In July 1978, am enthused retailer told *Women's Wear Daily* about André Laug's latest couture collection: "The suits, the suits, the suits. His suits are divine.... These clothes are so neat, so technically perfect, so sharp." For the client of keenest interest in impeccable tailoring along with a kind of restraint and temperate elegance about her style, Laug was the perfect expression of the Roman couture. From the 1960s until his death in 1984, Laug produced definitive collections of Roman style combining expertise in tailoring and the richest materials with a sober moderation.

For the American clientèle in particular, Laug suits held a *Daisy Miller* enchantment in an equilibrium between European sensuality and luxury and American simplicity. Americans may have, in general, expected the fireworks of extravagant Roman couture in the 1970s, but Laug provided an aesthetic closer to *Roman Holiday*—a reserved beauty. Moreover, the designer's success in the couture occasioned a lively, if somewhat less characteristic ready-to-wear business in the late 1970s and 1980s.

Tailored clothing by Laug was sufficiently elegant to move from cocktails to evening. A simple Laug black jacket with mushroom-like shoulders would have worked for daywear, but clearly would pass as evening dress. In his final collection, a charcoal quilted wool and silk evening jacket with black velvet trousers certainly would have sufficed for an elegant day as much as for evening. Laug knew the ethos of casual clothing in the 1970s and created an eveningwear that accommodated the social change of the period toward informality.

His American clientèle was typically old-guard and even conservative, the high-quality and high-comfort sense of the Philadelphia Main Line (his discreet good taste sold especially well at Nan Duskin in Philadelphia). As Bernadine Morris noted, "His designs were not the spectacular kind that change the shape of fashion. They were conservative day and evening clothes, which made women feel comfortable. They reflected the way Mr. Laug himself dressed, like a banker."

Trustworthy chic of Laug's kind was often compared to menswear in opposition to the fluctuations of women's fashion in the 1970s. By avoiding excess, in allowing for a mix of day and evening elements, Laug allowed his clients to develop a sensible, abiding wardrobe. Like menswear, trousers and jackets were basic for both day and evening. Jackets were clearly tailored for women with a defined waist. Ironically, Laug's design interests and his personal sense of forbearance were pursued by many other designers by the time of Laug's death at the age of 53. His love of black was almost the same as the prevalence of fashion black in the 1980s. The swanky luxury of his understated garments began with the textiles, lining jackets with rich and vivid textiles to inflect the relative moderation of the exterior. Further, the abstemious chic of a Laug suit would assume apparent luxury as accompanied by its silk blouse.

In the subtle distinctions among those designers who influence their colleagues and establish wardrobes for the most stylish women, as opposed to the most flamboyant and visible, André Laug represented the achievement of fashion as a well-bred, well-made design art. His catwalk shows were extravagant and showy, but not so the clothing. He sought no vanguard and claimed no new invention, but he made undeniably beautiful clothing for the most selective clients practicing a lifestyle of utmost urbanity and discretion.

At the time of his death, Laug had completed more than a dozen design sketches for his next fall/winter collection. His staff reproduced these designs, which were, according to the *Chicago Tribune*

(17 March 1985), "in the designer's timeless tradition of classic, elegant, ladylike suits and dresses…distinguished by waist definition and the use of bright jewel tones." After the collection debuted, Laug's staff sought a French-speaking designer to continue the late designer's legacy. Though the fashion house remained in business for a few years, no one ever filled the void left by André's death, and the company closed.

—Richard Martin

LAUREN, Ralph

American designer

Born: Ralph Lifschitz, Bronx, New York, 14 October 1939. **Education:** Studied business science, City College of New York, late 1950s. **Military Service:** Served in the U.S. Army, 1962–64. **Family:** Married Ricky Low-Beer, circa 1964; children: Andrew, David, Dylan. **Career:** Part-time sales assistant, Alexanders Stores, New York, 1956–57; assistant menswear buyer, Allied Stores, New York, 1958–61; salesperson, Bloomingdale's and Brooks Brothers, New York, 1962; traveling salesperson in New England for A. Rivetz, neckwear manufacturer, Boston, circa 1964–66; designer, Polo Neckwear Division, Beau Brummel, New York, 1967; founder/designer and chairman, Polo Fashions, New York, from 1968; Ralph Lauren Womenswear, from 1971; Polo Leather Goods, from 1979; Polo/Ralph Lauren Luggage, from 1982; Polo Ralph Lauren Corp., from 1986; introduced diffusion line, Chaps, 1972; introduced Ralph, Double RL, and Polo Sport lines, 1993; established Polo/Ralph Lauren stores in Beverly Hills, 1971, Lawrence, MA, 1983, Paris, 1986, flagship store in New York, 1986, Costa Mesa, CA, 1987, East Hampton, NY, 1989; Polo Sport, New York, 1993; launched fragrances *Polo* and *Lauren,* 1978, *Chaps* and *Tuxedo,* 1979, *Safari,* 1990, *Polo Crest,* 1991; new line of contemporary casualwear launched by Polo Jeans Co., 1996; offered collection of 400 colors of house paint, 1996; Polo Ralph Lauren became a publicly traded company on the New York Stock Exchange (NYSE: RL), 1997; introduced Polo Sport RLX line, 1998; opened RL restaurant, Chicago, 1999; introduced RALPH line, 1999; acquired Canadian-based Club Monaco, 1999; launched Pink Pony Campaign to help reduce disparities in cancer care, 2000; established Ralph Lauren Center for Cancer Prevention and Care at North General Hospital in Harlem, 2000; Ralph Lauren Media opened Polo.com, 2000. **Exhibitions:** Retrospective, Denver Art Museum, 1983. **Collections:** Fashion Institute of Technology, New York. **Awards:** Coty American Fashion Critics award, 1970, 1973, 1974, 1976, 1977, 1981, 1984; Neiman Marcus distinguished service award, 1971; American Printed Fabrics Council "Tommy" award, 1977; Council of Fashion Designers of America award, 1981; Coty Hall of Fame award, 1981; Retailer of the Year award, 1986, 1992; Museum of American Folk Art Pioneering Excellence award, 1988; Council of Fashion Designers of America Lifetime Achievement award, 1992; Woolmark award, 1992; CFDA Womenswear Designer of the Year, 1996; Honorary Doctorate of Letters from Brandeis University, 1996; Nina Hyde Center for Breast Cancer Research Humanitarian award presented by Diana, Princess of Wales, 1996; CFDA Menswear Designer of the Year, 1997; CFDA award for humanitarian leadership, 1998; inducted into the Fashion Walk of Fame, 2000. **Address:** 650 Madison Avenue, New York, NY 10022, USA. **Website:** www.Polo.com.

Ralph Lauren, fall 2001 collection: cashmere coat over a cashmere dress. © AP/Wide World Photos.

PUBLICATIONS

On LAUREN:

Books

Morris, Bernadine, and Barbara Walz, *The Fashion Makers,* New York, 1978.

Diamondstein, Barbaralee, *Fashion: The Inside Story,* New York, 1985.

Milbank, Caroline Rennolds, *Couture: The Great Designers,* New York, 1985.

Perschetz, Lois, ed., *W, The Designing Life,* New York, 1987.

Coleridge, Nicholas, *The Fashion Conspiracy,* London, 1988.

Trachtenberg, Jeffrey, *Ralph Lauren: The man Behind the Mystique,* Boston, 1988.

Milbank, Caroline Rennolds, *New York Fashion: The Evolution of American Style,* New York, 1989.

Canaedo, Anne, *Ralph Lauren: Master of Fashion,* Ada, Oklahoma, 1992.

Stegemeyer, Anne, *Who's Who in Fashion, Third Edition,* New York, 1996.

Ralph Lauren, fall 2001 collection: cashmere blend coat over a cashmere turtleneck and leather skirt. © AP/Wide World Photos.

Le Dortz, Laurent, and Muriel Lartigue, *Profil et dynamique du groupe Polo Ralph Lauren,* Paris, 1999.

Le Dortz, Laurent, and Béatrice Debosscher, *Stratégies des leaders américains de la mode: Calvin Klein, Donna Karan, Liz Clairborne, Polo Ralph Lauren, et Tommy Hilfiger,* Paris, 2000.

Articles

Wohlfert, Lee, "What Do Woody, Bob, and Diane Have in Common? Money, Yes, But Designer Ralph Lauren Too," in *People,* 6 February 1978.

Ling, F., "Ralph Lauren's Polo Game," in *Forbes,* 26 June 1978.

"Profile of a Designer: Ralph Lauren," in the *Sunday Times* (London), 13 September 1981.

Langway, L., and L. R. Prout, "Lauren's Frontier Chic," in *Newsweek,* 21 September 1981.

Ettorre, Barbara, "Give Ralph Lauren All the Jets He Wants," in *Forbes,* 28 February 1983.

"Beyond the Name Game: New Design World from Halston and Ralph Lauren," in *Vogue,* September 1983.

Feretti, Fred, "The Business of Being Ralph Lauren," in the *New York Times Magazine,* 18 September 1983.

Trachtenberg, Jeffrey A., "You Are What You Wear," in *Forbes,* 21 April 1986.

Cocks, Jay, "Born and Worn in the U.S.A.," in *Time,* 16 June 1986.

Infantino, Vivian, "Interview: Ralph Lauren," in *Footwear News* (New York), July 1986.

Koepp, Stephen, "Selling a Dream of Elegance and the Good Life," in *Time,* 1 September 1986.

Skenazy, Lenore, "Lauren Gets Honorable Mansion," in *Advertising Age,* 20 October 1986.

Tornabene, Lyn, "The World According to Ralph Lauren," in *Cosmopolitan,* February 1987.

Brubach, Holly, "Ralph Lauren's Achievement," in *Atlantic Monthly,* August 1987.

"Ralph Lauren: The Dream Maker," in *U.S. News & World Report,* 8 February 1988.

Aronson, Steven M. L., "High Style in Jamaica," in *House & Garden,* October 1988.

Dowling, Claudia Glenn, "Ralph Lauren," in *Life,* May 1989.

"A Big Time Safari for Ralph Lauren," in *WWD,* 27 October 1989.

Mower, Sarah, "The Unspeakable Chic of Summer," in the *Independent* (London), 19 April 1990.

Hume, Marion, "In the Swing," in the *Sunday Times* (London), 29 April 1990.

Parola, Robert, "Polo/Ralph Lauren," in *DNR,* 17 October 1990.

———, "Polo/Ralph Lauren: At the Crossroads," in *DNR,* 29 October 1990.

Buck, Joan Juliet, "Everybody's All-American," in *Vogue* (New York), February 1991.

Spevack, Rachel, "Polo and Izod: Adding New Luster to Knit Logos," in *DNR,* 12 March 1991.

Born, Pete, "Polo Crest Takes Fashion Approach to Fragrance," in *DNR,* 26 July 1991.

Forbes, Malcolm S., Jr., "Dressing Us with His Dreams," in *Forbes,* 2 September 1991.

Slonim, Jeffrey, "Ralph Lauren: October 14," in *Interview* (New York), October 1991.

Talley, Andre Leon, "Everybody's All-American," in *Vogue,* February 1992.

Born, Pete, "New Men's Lauren Fragrance to Debut," in *DNR,* 6 March 1992.

Siroto, Janet, "Ralph Lauren—Looking Back," in *Mademoiselle,* May 1992.

Moin, David, "Ralph Lauren is Back at Saks in a Big Way," in *WWD,* 14 October 1992.

Donaton, Scott, and Pat Sloan, "Ralph Lauren Sets Magazine Test," in *Advertising Age,* 2 November 1992.

Gross, Michael, "The American Dream," in *New York,* 21 December 1992.

Goldman, Kevin, "More Made-in-the-USA Claims, Surprisingly, are Showing Up," in *Wall Street Journal,* 15 January 1993.

Gross, Michael, "Ralph's World," in *New York,* 20 September 1993.

Mower, Sarah, "Ralph Lauren's New World of Sport," in *Harper's Bazaar,* October 1993.

Rutberg, Sidney, "Goldman, Sachs Buys into Ralph," in *WWD,* 24 August 1994.

Gill, Brendan, "Lauren's Home Movies," in the *New Yorker,* 7 November 1994.

Schiro, Anne-Marie, "Ralph Lauren Does What He Does Best," in the *New York Times,* 6 April 1995.

Menkes, Suzy, "Lauren: An Oscar for Polish," in the *International Herald Tribune,* 9 April 1995.
"Einer fur alle: Ralph Lauren, der Lifestyle-Spezialist," in *Vogue Manner* (Munich), April 1995.
Malone, Maggie, and John Leland, "Of Walls and Wanting," in *Newsweek,* 8 January 1996.
Goldstein, Lauren, "Ralph Lauren, Prince Charles, and You!" in *Fortune,* 9 November 1998.
"Polo Ralph Lauren Gets License Agreement with Danskin," in *United Press International,* 2 February 1999.
Keith, Andrew, and Elaine Marshall, "Ralph's Rough Ride," in *Time,* 15 March 1999.
"Food is Fashion," in *Restaurants & Institutions,* 15 April 1999.
Furman, Phyllis, "Ralph Lauren Teams with NBC for E-Commerce Company," in the *Daily News,* 7 February 2000.
Baker, John F., "A Fashion Statement," in *Publishers Weekly,* 27 March 2000.
Weldon, Kristi, "Polo Sprints into the 21st Century," in *Apparel Industry Magazine,* June 2000.
Rubenstein, Hal, "The Look of Ralph Lauren," in *In Style,* 1 September 2000.
Geller, Adam, "Luxury Retailer Closing Polo Stores," in *AP Online,* 5 October 2000.
"Style Guides," in *Forbes,* 9 October 2000.
"Lauren Creates the Polo Line, October 18, 1969," in *DISCovering U.S. History,* available online at galenet.gale.com, 17 October 2000.
"Ralph Lauren," in *DISCovering U.S. History,* online at galenet.gale.com, 17 October 2000.
Deeny, Godfrey, "Ralph's Riders," in *Fashion Wire Daily,* online at fashionwindows.com, 14 February 2001.
Horyn, Cathy, "For Kors and Lauren, A Fondness for the Paddock," in the *New York Times,* 15 February 2001.
Limnander, Armand, "Fall 2001 Ready-to-Wear," online at Style.com, 17 February 2001.
Davis, Boyd, "Ralph Lauren," online at fashionwindows.com, 2 June 2001.
Redstone, Susan, "Menwear Spring 2001," in online at fashionwindows.com, 2 June 2001.

* * *

Style, as opposed to fashion, is the major imperative underlying Ralph Lauren's work. Initially a designer of the high-quality ties that started the Polo label, Lauren soon directed his talents to menswear. Inspired by such notable dressers as the Duke of Windsor, Cary Grant, and Fred Astaire, he began to produce classic lines derivative of the elegant man about town or the country squire of a bygone age. A love of the fashions of the F. Scott Fitzgerald era led him to introduce wide neckties and bold shirt patterns. In 1974 Lauren achieved world acclaim as the designer of the men's fashions in the film version of F. Scott Fitzgerald's novel *The Great Gatsby.*

When he turned to womenswear, Lauren applied the same qualities of timeless elegance to his designs. By using uniformly high-quality tweeds, tailoring down men's trousers and jackets, and producing shirts in finer cottons, Lauren created clothes for the active woman of the 1970s, as epitomized in the Annie Hall look. These classic, tailored garments have changed little since they were first introduced but continue to epitomize long-lasting quality and style.

Another side of Lauren is seen in his Roughwear clothing. Directly inspired by the tradition of America's past, Roughwear takes the form of long tweed or plain skirts combined with colorful, hand-knitted, Fair Isle or sampler sweaters, tartan scarves, trilby hats, and lumberjack's wind cheaters and brushed cotton shirts. The origins are easy to trace, but the result is an updated, truly American style. Romantic touches of Edwardian and Victorian times occur in lace-trimmed jabots and large collars delicately held together with aging cameo brooches. Shades of the classic English riding costume appear in his tailored tweed jackets. Lauren's contribution to fashion can perhaps best be summed up on the names that he gave to his cosmetics introduced in 1981: Day, Night, and Active.

In the 1990s, Lauren continued to tune into contemporary life. The Double RL label featured new, high-quality clothes that looked old as a response to the craze for the vintage and second-hand. For increasingly fitness-conscious women, he produced informal clothes with a strong fashion input. To appeal to the youthful interests of younger customers, Polo Jeans launched a line of contemporary casualwear in 1996. Two years later, Lauren's trademark aesthetic sensibility and superior craftsmanship was applied to the Polo Sport RLX line of high-performance athletic apparel.

As the new millennium approached, the Ralph Lauren Company began moving from Ivy League to pop culture by acquiring Canadian-based Club Monaco, marketing contemporary apparel, home furnishings, accessories, and cosmetics for the hip, urban crowd. In 2000, Ralph Lauren Media launched the Polo.com website, offering "comprehensive online access to the Ralph Lauren American lifestyle with clothing, accessories, fragrances, vintage items, travel, style tips, multimedia information and entertainment, world-class customer service and more." With son David Lauren as creative director, Polo.com aimed to "spread the upper-crust Ralph Lauren image to a new generation of shoppers," wrote Phyllis Furman in a February 2000 article in the *Daily News.*

Still, Lauren's womenswear for fall 2001 came full circle, offering the classic styling of equestrian looks from the country estate such as hacking jackets, taupe and ebony pants with suede knee patches, sleek crocodile belts with thoroughbred buckles, and riding boots with oilcloth spats. For the menswear spring 2001 collection, the timeless Polo line was updated with slim polo shirts and lime green, Nantucket red, and hot orange fuchsia-front trousers. The more dressed up Purple Line offered suits with sculpted waists and soft natural shoulders, paired with striped ties, creating the classic Lauren look.

Lauren's skill and experience has enabled him to design for women and men, their children, and their homes. As a native New Yorker, Lauren has promoted a truly American casual style in his prairie look while developing classic, uncluttered lines that have brought him international fame. Along with colleagues Bill Blass, Geoffrey Beene, and six other designers, Lauren earned a white bronze and granite marker along the Fashion Walk of Fame in New York City. This worldwide notoriety will also be the subject of a new biography of Lauren, the story, according to a March 2000 article in *Publishers Weekly,* of "a poor Russian Jewish immigrant boy who began in Seventh Avenue fashion house stock rooms and became a billionaire."

For Ralph Lauren, fashion is something that lasts for more than one season. It is this timelessness, abetted by inspirations deep in the soil of America's past, that distinguishes his work and won him a Lifetime Achievement award from the Council of Fashion Designers of America in 1992.

—Hazel Clark; updated by Jodi Essey-Stapleton

LAURENT, Yves Saint

See SAINT LAURENT, Yves

LEATHERS, Peter

See PETER HOGGARD

LEE, Mickey

Chinese designer

Education: Graduated in commercial and industrial design from Hong Kong Polytechnic, 1973, interior design from Leeds Polytechnic, England, 1976, and advanced fashion and illustration, St. Martin's School of Art and Design, London, 1977. **Career:** Fashion designer for various Hong Kong garment manufacturers, 1978–83; established own design studio, mainly providing fashions and illustration for promotional projects, 1983; fashion consultant, then head of design and merchandise, Hwa Kay Thai Development Company for Puma; graphic and interior designer of Puma boutiques; director/fashion consultant of own company, Highmax International Ltd.; launched fashion and lifestyle product range for young people, Living Basic. **Address:** Highmax International Ltd., 13/F Zoroastrian Building, 101 Leighton Road, Hong Kong.

PUBLICATIONS

On LEE:

Articles

"The Puma Suede," in the *New York Times,* 21 February 1993.

"Doyle Swaps Sneaker Accounts," in the *New York Times,* 29 April 1994.

"Puma AG: Pretax Profit is Reported for Year's First Five Months," in the *Wall Street Journal,* 21 June 1994.

McAllister, Bob, "Can Hollywood Raise Puma's U.S. Growl?" in *Footwear News,* 2 December 1996.

Lefton, Terry, "Puma Nears Four-Year NBA Deal; Reborn Browns Ink McD's and BK," in *Brandweek,* 31 May 1999.

Carr, Debra, "To The Max: Athletic Companies are Taking Sporty Design to the Next Level," in *Footwear News,* 31 July 2000.

"Closing In," in *Footwear News,* 20 November 2000.

Feitelberg, Rosemary, "Labels Try the Training Game," in *WWD,* 22 March 2001.

* * *

In 1983, Hwa Kay Thai (Hong Kong) Ltd. bought the design and merchandising licence for Puma Hong Kong from its Herzogenaurach, Germany-based parent company, Puma AG Rudolph Dassler Sport. Mickey Lee was employed as their design consultant and so began a design success story. The business has expanded geographically to encompass Thailand, Singapore, and China, and the product range has developed likewise. Lee has taken Puma from basic sportswear into a complete range of leisurewear and accessories. He created the concept of a healthy and energetic lifestyle especially, for Hong Kong young people. "Live the Puma life," is the slogan catching on with Hong Kong's younger generation.

Lee became director, in charge of the design of the products, merchandising, and even the window displays of the Puma shops, with five assistants at his beck and call. For the greater part of his time with the company, he did most of the designing, consisting of two annual fashion collections and an accessory collection, plus promotional materials. Lee spearheaded the creation of a market-orientated image very different from Puma AG's original vision. Germany now controls only the quality of the workmanship and influences technological aspects, like the composition of sports shoes.

From the original tracksuits and swimsuits, Puma's clothing range grew to include jeans and other forms of leisurewear. The clothes are medium priced and mass-market, functional, but enlivened with fashion details and up-to-date cutting. The original bags gave way to lively accessories suited to the particular demands of Hong Kong. Backpacks and weekend bags in bright colors or sensible black are much in demand in a place where people tend to go away for short trips, such as nearby Macau or China. Around 80 percent of Puma's merchandise is for men; black and white are the staple colors, with sprinklings of seasonal color trends. The image is masculine and sporty, and the womenswear aims to project a feminine but equally healthy look. Lee pays attention to international design directions but does not consciously follow trends; his strongest inspiration comes from Japan, whose young people provide style models for Hong Kong.

Puma offers a totally coordinated image—everything relates. The garments and accessories have their own color scheme, characterized by brights. The first Puma boutiques were opened in Hong Kong, and there one experiences the full impact of Lee's total design image. In addition to the clothing design and store decor, he was also responsible for the promotion and publicity materials. Television commercials and brochures have an annual theme; set in faraway locations such as Kenya, Egypt, or Moscow, they are exciting and create an impact.

Lee has complete artistic control; his varied background, in graphic, interior, and fashion design has served Puma well. He credits himself with developing the swimsuit, jeans, and accessory ranges, but this is underplaying his influence. He has increased the company's profits by creating a lively design image. It has proved just right for its target market, but is strong enough to be equally successful further afield.

Due to the ever-prevailing influences of Lee, Puma has made great strides in capturing more of the global footwear and activewear trade. Although not as popular in the U.S. as the company is abroad, Puma has been moving in the fast lane of the athleticwear market. In 1996 film producer Arnon Milchan supplied investment capital to help place Puma into the mainstream athletic footwear scene via Hollywood connections. The producer of such well known films as *Free Willy, JFK,* and *A Time to Kill,* Milchan had the power to help boost Puma's sales in America.

In 1998, with a quarter stake of Logo Athletic clothing, Puma leapt into the licensed sports clothing market. The "jumping cat" logo of Puma progressed as far as the NBA courts and the NFL, stepping in where their predecessor, Starter, had failed (Starter declared bankruptcy in 1999, providing a golden opportunity for the Lee-enhanced Puma image). In addition, Puma sponsored sports camps and clinics targeted at young male and female athletes, and signed high-profile athletes, including tennis star Serena Williams, to endorse its products.

With their NBA move, Puma began competing with its rival German brand, Adidas (owned by the brother of Puma AG's CEO Rudolf Dassler), and was instantly catapulted into the U.S. retail limelight. Puma opened two concept stores in California, the first in Santa Monica and the second in San Francisco, to great success. The company also began offering signature collections and limited editions, entrenching itself as a staple of footwear and apparel suppliers. Puma continues to be known for the quality, comfort, and durability of its products; even its up-to-date lacing systems are in keeping with the fashionable quest for the perfect all-terrain shoe. Thanks to the innovative contributions of a modest designer, Mickey Lee, Puma regained its status as not only a Western and European phenomenon but also as a global contender in the athleticwear arena.

—Hazel Clark; updated by Sandra Schroeder

LÉGER, Hervé

French fashion designer

Born: Bapaume, Pas de Calais, France, 30 May 1957. **Education:** Studied in Paris until 1975. **Career:** Designed hats for Venus et Neptune, Pablo Delia, Dick Brandsma, 1975–77; assistant for Tan Giudicelli, couture and ready-to-wear, 1977–80; assistant to Karl Lagerfeld, furs, ready-to-wear, swimsuits, and accessories at Fendi, 1980–82; designer for Chanel, 1982–83; designer for Cadette, Milan, 1983–85; founded own company, MCH Diffusion, 1985; opened boutique on rue Pelican, Paris, assistant at Lanvin for couture and ready-to-wear, and assistant to Diane von Furstenberg, 1985; designed fur collection for Chloé, 1987; created accessory collection for Swarovski (Vattens, Austria) and ready-to-wear collections for Charles Jourdan, 1988–92; partnership with G.H. Mumm & Compagnie, 1992; designed theatre costumes for *Les Troyens,* Milan, 1992; first ready-to-wear collection for Hervé Léger S.A., 1993; costumes for *Trois Ballets,* Opéra de Paris, 1994; Mumm controlling interest sold to BCBG Max Azria, 1998; Léger left company, 1999; opened boutique in Left Bank, 2000.

Hervé Léger walking down the catwalk with his models after showing his autumn/winter 1999–2000 ready-to-wear collection. © AFP/CORBIS.

Publications

On LÉGER:

Books

Stegemeyer, Anne, *Who's Who in Fashion, Third Edition,* New York, 1996.

Articles

"Day for Night Body Dresses Make All the Right Moves," in *Elle* (New York), May 1991.
Carter, Charla, "Hervé Legér, Paris' Newest Design Talent Proves He Knows How to Throw a Curve," in *Vogue,* March 1992.
Spindler, Amy, "Alaïa and Legér Loosen Up a Bit," in the *New York Times,* 20 March 1993.
Deitch, Brian, "Hervé's Legerdemain," in *Women's Fashion Europe,* December/January 1993–94.
Quick, Harriet, "Legér Wear," in *Elle* (London), April 1994.
Doe, Tamasin, "Splashing Out on that Curvy Feeling," in the *Evening Standard* (London), 21 June 1994.
Min, Janet, and K. Nolan, "King of Cling: Fashion Designer Hervé Legér," in *People Weekly,* 31 October 1994.
Menkes, Suzy, "Paris Silhouette in Flux," in the *International Herald Tribune,* 15 October 1996.
White, Constance C.R., "Azria Backs Hervé Léger," in the *New York Times,* 11 August 1998.
Avins, Mimi, "L.A.'s BCBG Takes Control of France's Hervé Léger," in the *Los Angeles Times,* 11 August 1998.
Walton, A. Scott, "Paris Fashion Week: Valentino, Celine and Léger: The End—For Now," in the *Atlanta Journal-Constitution,* 19 October 1998.
Menkes, Suzy, "Yohji Yamamoto Defines the Spring Season with Tenderness and Wit," in the *International Herald Tribune,* 20 October 1998.
Lowthorpe, Rebecca, "Designer Loses His Own Label," in the *Independent* (London), 21 April 1999.
"The Chic of It! Ex-Model Gets the Designer Boot," in the *The Guardian* (London), 17 September 1999.
Menkes, Suzy, "For 'Young' Designers, 40 is a Dangerous Age," in the *International Herald Tribune,* 7 October 1999.
Walton, A. Scott, "Fashion Week: Léger's New Look Emphasizes Youth," in the *Atlanta Journal-Constitution,* 5 October 1999.
Donnally, Trish, "Shop Talk," in the *San Francisco Chronicle,* 4 January 2000.

Menkes, Suzy, "The Comeback Kids: Customers, Old and New, Track Down Fashion's Hidden Assets," in the *International Herald Tribune,* 13 June 2000.

———, "In Paris, a Craving for the Exotic," in the *International Herald Tribune,* 17 July 2001.

*

In interviews I try systematically to dodge the connotation "artist, designer." The French word *créateur* seems to me particularly bombastic. I usually avoid theories on fashion in terms of "art" and I hate definitions on style. On the other hand, I always insist on the quality of my work. People will always appreciate quality. Quoting Madeleine Vionnet, to her niece, I used to say, "We are not rich enough to buy cheap."

The quality "hand-sewn," or "good investment," or "good value," is a rather original attitude when one thinks about it. The dissertation on fashion has a tendency to glorify the short-lived, the novel, the whim, ostentatious consumption rather than the everlasting. I think it's a pity.

Two consumer types exist for me: the first, "crazy about fashion," or "fashion victim," will irrevocably conform to the fashion of the designers and systematically adopt their outlook. The second type of woman, the one I prefer, is fed up with the vagaries of fashion. She will not act as a guinea pig for the designer's "experiments." She does not give a damn about the trends, she refuses to be a feminine clothes hanger. My fashion is made for that woman, to help her to express herself. I do not use women to express my world vision.

—Hervé Léger

* * *

If any designer heralded the shift away from the deconstructed, loose, long shapes of the early 1990s it was Hervé Léger. His clothes, based on the deceptively simple principles of Lycra and spandex-rich fabrics pulling the body into the desired hourglass shape, have made him the darling of the fashion world. Tired of the austerity of recession dressing and eager for a contrary style that would revive a sense of glamor and flatter the wearer with its overblown femininity, Léger's work was warmly embraced during the 1990s both by fashion opinion-makers and the rock stars, models, and minor royalty who are his most publicized clients.

His dresses have the properties formally associated with foundation garments: the ability to mold the body and keep it in place. They enhance the figure, metamorphosing the wearer into cartoonlike proportions with full bust and hips. If this exaggeratedly feminine image is in direct contradiction to the narrow adolescent silhouette that had preceded and has run parallel with Léger's vision, it has nevertheless struck a chord with women wishing to relish their sexuality and are unafraid of displaying their redefined body in the modern equivalent to tight-laced corsetry.

Chiming in with the postfeminist doctrine of Naomi Wolf and Camille Paglia, which promotes the reclaiming of the right to enhance and emphasize the figure, this trend, labeled new glamor, is unashamed in its devotion to the female form. It is the latter that undoubtedly inspires Léger, his creations geared toward maximizing the purity of the curving lines of his models. His most obvious predecessor is the Algerian designer Azzedine Alaïa, who rose to fame in the late 1980s with his clingy Lycra creations, which Léger so clearly referred to in the overt sexiness of his own work.

Léger, however, developed the style further, exploiting the stretchy qualities of Lycra and spandex to the full, so that the dresses became more restrictive and better able to maintain the desired shape. His signature outfits, known as "bender" dresses, are composed of narrow strips of these elastic materials combined with rayon, which are sewn horizontally like bandages to form the whole shape of the garment, sometimes with extra bands curving over the hips and across the bust to add emphasis. Even on the hanger, therefore, they have a three-dimensional quality, so reliant are they on the Olympian figure they at once create and emulate.

Léger produces innumerable variations of this "bender" style, all equally flattering, the fabric eliminating any faults in the figure to produce smooth hourglasses. For all their glamor, his clothes avoid brashness through their lack of any unnecessary detail or decoration; their interest is in their shaping and the subtle Parisian tones in which they are produced. He concentrates on classic black, navy, white, and cream, tempered by stripes of burnt orange on halter dresses reminiscent of 1930s swimwear and delicate pastels with dark bodices.

By the middle of the 1990s, Léger had softened the banded look a bit. His 1997 spring/summer line included dresses with elegant cutout midriffs and sailor suits with light organza jackets. Léger's evening line has always been strong, so during this time his challenge was to create a daywear line to hold its own. Transforming women into Amazonian figures or goddesslike nymphs, his name gained importance with the increasing desire to express rather than obscure the potential sexuality of clothing. His dresses have adorned the likes of Halle Berry, Tyra Banks, Celine Dion, Fran Drescher, Christine Lahti, and Gillian Anderson. The downside, however, to creating such a well-defined signature style is the perception of becoming repetitive. Léger was able to adapt his look to the latest trend but was still seen by some critics as being in a rut.

In 1998 Los Angeles-based BCBG Max Azria purchased a controlling interest in the Hervé Léger fashion house from G.H. Mumm & Compagnie (itself a subsidiary of Seagram & Co.). Azria felt the addition of Léger's line would strengthen his company's global presence. Léger remained the designer of his line and was promised "unconditional support." The relationship soured, however, when BCBG cut the budget and Léger refused to cooperate. He was fired just six months after the takeover, forcing him to start from scratch. Léger initiated a lawsuit to regain his name and set out in a new direction; he signed a contract in 1999 to design clothing for Wolford, an Austrian company known for its hosiery. The line debuted in the company's first store, based in San Francisco, in the spring of 2000 with ready-to-wear designs made of merino wool and viscose.

The following year, 2001, marked the opening of Léger's own shop under the name Hervé L. Leroux in Paris. Former clients, still enthusiastic about his work, have managed to locate him by word of mouth. The designer remains focused on eveningwear and creates custom pieces for clients who have the desire and the means (which usually run around $7,000). Leroux (Léger) continues to spotlight his innovative designs, now with an even fresher outlook. His summer 2001 presentation in Paris featured draped dresses, cut with tucks in the bodice, forcing the fabric to hug the neck, leaving the back strikingly bare.

Léger's concentration on the ability of clothing to create the desired flattering silhouette, through manipulation of fabrics and eye-arresting details, owes its legacy to his couture background. His time at great houses like Chanel, Fendi, and Chloé enabled him to witness the power of a thoughtfully cut ensemble to transform the wearer. His homage to the goddesslike form touched on the desire to demonstrate beauty through strong, clear lines and sexually charged imagery that his clinging dresses so literally embodied.

—Rebecca Arnold; updated by Carrie Snyder

LEHL, Jürgen

German designer working in Japan

Born: Poland, 1944. **Education:** Trained as textile designer, 1962–66; freelance designer in France, 1967–69; moved to New York, 1969; moved to Japan, 1971. **Career:** Textile designer, 1970–74; formed Jürgen Lehl Co. Ltd., 1972; showed first ready-to-wear collection, 1974; also designer, bed and bath Tint collections. **Exhibitions:** *Contemporary Fabric Exhibition,* Kyoto International Conference Center, 1992; *Seasonal Exhibition,* Tokyo; Cooper-Hewitt Museum, New York; *Koromo-Stoffe Zwischen Zwei Welten (Fabrics Between Two Worlds),* Museum für Angewandte Kunst, Cologne, 1998; *Fashions by Jürgen Lehl,* Gemeentemuseum den Haag (The Hague), 2000; *Jürgen Lehl: A Personal View,* London, 2001. **Awards:** Creative prize, 1991; Best Advertisement award, 1993. **Address:** 3–1–7 Kiyosumi, Koto-ku, Tokyo 135, Japan.

Publications

On LEHL:

Books

Tadanori, Yokoo, *Made in Japan—The Textiles of Jürgen Lehl,* Tokyo, 1983.

Koren, Leonard, *New Fashion Japan,* Tokyo, 1984.

Martin, Richard, and Harold Koda, *Flair: Fashion Collected by Tina Chow,* New York, 1992.

Fleischmann, Isa, and Brigitte Tietzel, *Koroma-Stoffe Zwischen Zwei Welten,* [exhibition catalogue], 1998.

Fashion by Jürgen Lehl, [exhibition catalogue], 2000.

Articles

"Fashions by Jürgen Lehl," available online at Gemeentemuseum Den Haag, www.gemeentemuseum.nl, 25 July 2001.

"Artist Biographies," Museum of Modern Art, online at www.moma.org, 25 July 2001.

Featured in "Japan Newsletter," Embassy of Japan in the U.K., Japan Information and Culture Center, online at www.embjapan.org.uk, 17 October 2000.

* * *

Jürgen Lehl represents a cultural amalgam that is reflected in his design philosophy. Born in Poland of German nationality, he has lived in Japan since 1971. He founded his textile design company, Jürgen Lehl Co. Ltd., in 1972, producing a ready-to-wear line of clothing in 1974.

His clothes convey united elements of both Eastern and Western fashion. In 1982 Lehl's contemporaries Yohji Yamamoto and Rei Kawakubo of Comme des Garçons founded a fashion revolution when they showed their respective collections in Paris, introducing clothes that were Asian in origin and inspiration, with few concessions to traditional Western ideas of dressing. The clothes presented a design theory that contradicted established Western modes yet immediately became essential dressing for any serious follower of 1980s fashion.

The Japanese invasion permanently altered concepts of fashion in the West. These clothes seemed to owe nothing to trend, reaction, or retrospection but were rather a constantly evolving and refined version of the traditional kimono shape. Multilayered and elaborate in its simplicity, the kimono represents the basis of all Japanese fashion thinking. Lehl's clothing married Eastern and Western fashion. A man's jacket in black wool from 1986 combined the notion of Western tailoring with the band neckline of a kimono jacket. His radical minimalism is reflected with a single button that fastens the jacket, with a simplistic buttonhole created logically between the band and the body of the jacket. Lehl is intellectually reductive in his approach to design, reexamining and reducing details to produce unpretentious simplicity.

Lehl is also culturally eclectic in his textile designs, introducing concepts from high art or native idioms in both Western and Asian customs. He is inspired by the unexpected; chance discoveries of old shop signs or even an upturned shoe are applied to his design mechanism of refinement and reduction.

Japanese designers often seem subtle when compared with their Western contemporaries. Their logical, controlled approach has a mathematical precision, a calculation accurately solved. Fabric, texture, and proportion are of supreme importance to the designer. Kansai Yamamoto admits to spending as much as seventy-percent of his time working with textiles, which explains perhaps why Lehl's career expanded into clothing from his textile design origins.

Lehl's creations are popular in Japan and are sold there in 44 boutiques. His garments are always made of natural materials—cotton, linen, silk, and wool—and he uses the traditional Japanese dyeing techniques of ikat and *shibori.* When a major assessment is made of the influence of Japanese designers on contemporary fashion, it should be remembered that the East-to-West design passage is not all one way. Lehl represents the rare phenomenon of a Western designer working in the East.

—Kevin Almond; updated by Carrie Snyder

LEIBER, Judith

American handbag and accessories designer

Born: Judith Peto in Budapest, 11 January 1921; immigrated to the U.S. and moved to New York, 1947. **Education:** Studied in England, 1938–39; apprenticed with Hungarian Handbag Guild, 1939, became journeyman and first woman Meister. **Family:** Married Gerson Leiber, 1946. **Career:** Designer in New York for Nettie Rosenstein, 1948–60, Richard Kort, 1960–61, and Morris Moskowitz Co., 1961–62; launched own firm, 1963; added costume jewelry, mid-1990s; opened Madison Avenue boutique, 1996; retired, 1998; sold business to Time Products, Inc., 1998; resold to Pegasus Apparel Group, 2000; Pegasus Apparel Group became The Leiber Group, 2001. **Exhibitions:** *The Artist and Artisan: Gerson and Judith Leiber,* Fine Arts Museum of

Long Island, 1991; Judith Leiber, *The Artful Handbag,* Museum at the Fashion Institute of Technology, New York, 1994; *Spring Retroactive,* Atlanta, GA, 2001; **Collections:** Permanent displays in the Metropolitan Museum of Art (New York), Smithsonian Institution (Washington, D.C.), and the Victoria and Albert Museum (London). **Awards:** Swarovski Great Designer award; Coty American Fashion Critics award, 1973; Neiman Marcus award, 1980; Foundation for the Fashion Industries award, New York, 1991; Silver Slipper award, Houston Museum of Fine Arts Costume Institute, 1991; Handbag Designer of the Year award, 1992; Council of Fashion Designers of America award, 1993; Council of Fashion Designers of America Lifetime Achievement award, 1994; Dallas Fashion award for Excellence. **Address:** 20 West 33rd Street, New York, NY 10001, USA.

Publications

On LEIBER:

Books

Martin, Richard, *The Artist & Artisan: Gerson and Judith Leiber,* [exhibition catalogue], Hempstead, NY, 1991.

Nemy, Enid, *Judith Leiber,* [exhibition catalogue], New York, 1994.

———, *Judith Leiber: The Artful Handbag,* New York, 1995.

Stegemeyer, Anne, *Who's Who in Fashion, Third Edition,* New York, 1996.

Articles

Jakobson, Cathryn, "Clutch Play: In Judith Leiber's Line of Work, the Fun Is in the Bag," in *Manhattan, Inc.,* February 1986.

Newman, Jill, "Judith Leiber: The Art of the Handbag," in *WWD,* August 1986.

Johnson, Bonnie, "Judith Leiber's Customers are left Holding the Bag," in *People Weekly,* 20 April 1987.

Harris, Leon, and Matthew Klein, "Judith's Jewels," in *Town & Country,* December 1988.

Van Gelder, Lindsey, "It's in the Bag," in *Connoisseur* (New York), April 1990.

Morris, Bernadine, "Flights of Fancy Take Shape in Lush Evening Bags," in the *New York Times,* 18 December 1990.

"Houston Costume Museum to Honor Leiber Saturday," in *WWD,* 25 January 1991.

Peacock, Mary, "The Whimsy of Judith Leiber's Handbag Designs Comes Through in the Clutch," in *Departures,* December/January 1991–92.

"Splurge: Judith Leiber's Handbags," in the *New Yorker,* 25 May 1992.

Newman, Jill, "Judith Leiber; Leader in Luxury," in *WWD,* 6 November 1992.

———, "British Watch Giant Buys Judith Leiber," in *WWD,* 8 March 1993.

Menkes, Suzy, "Just a Handful of Art," in the *International Herald Tribune,* 22 November 1994.

Morris, Bernadine, "The Portable Art of Leiber Handbags," in the *New York Times,* 25 November 1994.

White, Constance C.R., "A Leiber Jewelry Line," in *New York Times,* 9 May 1995.

Witchel, Alex, "Handbags That Make Headlines," in the *New York Times,* 1 May 1996.

———, "Handbag Designer Leiber Proves Talent More Than Skin-Deep," in *Commercial Appeal* (Memphis, TN), 9 June 1996.

"Judith Leiber," in *Current Biography,* September 1996.

Klensch, Elsa, "Leiber's Delightfully Deluxe Bags," available online at CNN Style, www.cnn.com, 19 December 1997.

Bold, Kathryn, "Accessories: For Many Women, Dressing to Impress is Simply in the Bag," in the *Los Angeles Times,* 26 December 1997.

Schiro, Anne-Marie, "Judith Leiber is Retiring," in the *New York Times,* 13 January 1998.

Barron, Susannah, "Style: Off the Cuff," in *The Guardian* (London), 21 January 1998.

Brown, Hero, "Is it Worth it?" in the *Independent Sunday* (London), 24 May 1998.

"Prize Purses," in the *Tampa Tribune,* 23 March 1999.

"Bag Maker for Sale," in the *Times* (London), 19 June 1999.

"Time Products Pounds 9m Disposal," in the *Times* (London), 29 September 2000.

"Diary of a Dainty Duffel: Laura Bush's Bag Lady Has Lots of Experience Accessorizing First Ladies," in the *New York Post,* 18 January 2001.

Walton, A. Scott, "Style: Leiber Bags Reign as Fine Art Holdings," in the *Atlanta Journal-Constitution,* 18 March 2001.

"New Name and CEO for Troubled Pegasus," in *Fashion Wire Daily,* online at Tradeweave Retail Network, www.insight.-tradeweave.com, 22 May 2001.

*

I love to design beautiful objects that can be worn of course, whether it is made of alligator, ostrich, lizard or silk, or a great metal box/minaudière that can be held in the lady's hand. Top quality is a great concern and it pleases me greatly to keep that paramount. Today's fashions really cry out for beautiful accessories, be they belts, handbags or great jewelry.

—Judith Leiber

* * *

Judith Leiber talks of herself as a technician and prides herself on the Budapest-trained craft tradition she exemplifies and continues. But her skill and the consummate perfection of her workshop are only one aspect of the recognition of her work. She is steadfast in advancing the artistic possibility of the handbag, and she is unceasing in her own artistic pursuits of this goal. Yet, as Mary Peacock averred, "A sense of whimsy is integral to Leiber's vision," as the committed pursuit of craft is matched with a stylish wit and the cultural cleverness that is akin to craft's creativity. A Leiber handbag is an item of expert handiwork and engineering, but it is also a charm, a potent amulet, and a beguiling object of beauty. Each bag takes six to seven days to create and can range in price from $700 to $7,000. The names of Leiber admirers are far too long to list but include Queen Elizabeth and every First Lady from Pat Nixon through Laura Bush.

Technique is central to the Leiber concept. A Leiber minaudière, for example, might seem at first glance like a Christmas tree ornament but in technique is more like an ecclesiastical censer, an object of perfection intended for long-lasting use. Her watermelon and citrus slices are farm fresh in their juicy handset rhinestone design, but these fruits will never perish. Cathryn Jakobson, writing in *Manhattan Inc.* in February 1986, described the sound and impeccable impact of closing a Leiber handbag, "The engineering is perfect: it is like closing the door on an excellent automobile."

Leiber's product may be jewellike and ladylike in scale, but her collectors are rightly as proud and avid about these small objects as any possessor of a Rolls Royce. There is perhaps one drawback to the Leiber evening bags: they hold very little. But Leiber's aesthetic more than mitigates the possible problem. If going out is a matter of saddlebags and gross excess, then Leiber's sweet purses and precious objects are not the answer. But if there is any truthful measure that the best things come in small packages, Leiber's beautiful clutches make the maxim true. Leiber's characteristic evening bags, in fact, compound their delicacy in scale with their solid form: these hardly seem, despite their elegance, to be places of cash and chattel. Leiber has achieved a carrier that is neither wallet nor winnings—it is something intimate and personal.

The ideas for her bags come from a variety of sources. Arguably, little is invented ex nihilo in Leiber's work, but is instead understood and applied from other arts. She acknowledges her love of finding objects in museums and even the objects in paintings that lend themselves to her imaginative formation as the handbag, realizing the capability of an object to serve as a container. Leiber's version of Fabergé eggs at substantial (but less than Romanov) prices are inherently about containment, but her inventions of the three-dimensional bunch of grapes or the frogs that open up or Chinese foo dogs with hollow insides are her own invention. Leiber has also looked to the arts of the East, especially netsuke purse toggles, for their wondrous world of invented objects and miniatures from nature. Leiber's first jeweled evening bag was a metal teardrop purse, an ironic play on the soft shape of the purse or money bag converted into a hard form.

Handbags by Leiber for the day employ beautiful reptile and ostrich skins, antique Japanese obis, and extraordinary embroideries. In the daytime bags she uses not only the softest materials and a colorist's palette, even in skins, but lightens the touch with supple pleats, braid, and whimsical trims and closings. Leiber makes elegantly simple envelope bags accented by a single point or line of decoration.

As attention-getting as her designs might be, the designer herself tends to be understated. As a young woman in Budapest, Leiber narrowly escaped the Nazi concentration camps. She was accepted to Kings College in London and intended to study chemistry, with a goal of developing skin creams. But World War II began, forcing her to remain in Hungary. She instead became an apprentice to a handbag maker, and from that point, her course was set. Alex Witchel of the *New York Times* wrote that after escaping the Nazis as a teen, "She has considered it a virtue to avoid the spotlight ever since. It seems only in her designs, whether the rich leather bags for daytime or the lush, detailed bags for evening, that the disparate elements of her own personality find release: whimsical yet functional (a yellow rose of Texas), stylish yet silly (a jeweled slice of watermelon), majestic yet devastatingly simple (a perfect seashell). She is a beguiling contradiction—a rather severe-looking matron with the artistic imagination, and freedom, of a girl."

Leiber never makes a subservient bag, but an autonomous object that whether egg, minaudière, or piggy, is the finality and finesse of style. In this, Leiber observes fashion as critically and cognizantly as she scours art for her selection of objects, but she never creates a tartan to be coordinated to a textile or a frog or other animal to fit into an established environment of garments. Rather, she creates commodities that enhance dress and create style because they are self-sufficient. Leiber creates objects that are undeniably, despite the creator's modesty, unique sculptures on a small scale.

—Richard Martin; updated by Carrie Snyder

LELONG, Lucien

French designer

Born: Paris, 11 October 1889. **Education:** Studied business, Hautes Études des Commerciales, Paris, 1911–13. **Military Service:** Performed military service, 1914–17, awarded Croix de Guerre. **Family:** Married Princess Natalie Paley (second wife). **Career:** Designed first collection, 1914; joined father's dressmaking firm, 1918; house of Lelong established, 1919; showed designs under own name, from 1923; Parfums Lucien Lelong established, 1926; Éditions Lucien Lelong ready-to-wear established, 1933; president, Chambre Syndicale de la Couture, 1937–47; retired from couture, 1948. **Died:** 10 May 1958, in Anglet, France.

Publications

On LELONG:

Books

Picken, Mary Brooks, and Dora L. Miller, *Dressmakers of France,* New York, 1956.

Latour, Anny, *Kings of Fashion,* London, 1958.

Lynam, Ruth, ed., *Couture,* Garden City, New York, 1972.

Ewing, Elizabeth, *History of Twentieth Century Fashion,* New York, 1974.

Howell, Georgina, *In Vogue,* Middlesex, England, 1975.

Glynn, Prudence, *In Fashion,* New York, 1978.

Carter, Ernestine, *Magic Names of Fashion,* Englewood Cliffs, New Jersey, 1980.

Garnier, Guillaume, *Paris couture années trente,* Paris, 1987.

Stegemeyer, Anne, *Who's Who in Fashion, Third Eiditon,* New York, 1996.

Monsen and Baer Memories of Perfume: The Perfumes of Lucien Lelong and Masterpieces of Today, [auction catalogue], Vienna, 1998.

Articles

"And the Winner is...," in *Global Cosmetic Industry,* December 1999.

* * *

While Lucien Lelong dressed many a fashionable lady during the 1920s and 1930s, he is most remembered for his heroic diplomatic efforts to sustain Parisian couture during World War II. He was, in every respect, a hero of both world wars fought during this century.

He received his call to serve during World War I two days short of showing his first collection at his father's already established dressmaking shop. He served from 1914 until 1917 when he was severely wounded. He was one of the first seven Frenchmen to be decorated with the Croix de Guerre for his heroism.

In 1918, after recuperating, he rejoined his father's firm. By 1923 he was designing under his own name. As a contemporary of such designers as Chanel, Vionnet, Molyneux, Lanvin, and Patou, he designed for café society during the 1920s and 1930s. His designs were characterized by classic lines, following the major silhouettes of each period. He was not particularly innovative, choosing rather to concentrate on fine workmanship and fabrication. He was, however, the first designer to introduce a lower priced line—he called it Édition—to cater to less wealthy clients in 1933. During the height of his career he employed 1,200 workers.

His election as president of the Chambre Syndicale de la Couture in 1937 proved to be his greatest challenge and contribution to fashion. Faced with threats to move the entire couture to Berlin and Vienna, Lelong negotiated, cajoled, and lied to the Germans throughout the occupation of Paris. "One of the first things the Germans did was break into the Syndicate offices and seize all documents pertaining to the French export trade. I told them that *la couture* was not a transportable industry, such as bricklaying."

When not one foreign buyer appeared in Paris after war was declared, Lelong sent an emissary to New York with gowns and models to prove couture was still a viable industry. In January 1940, despite having to be routed through Italy, 150 buyers appeared for the showings. By 1941 the Germans had issued textile cards, comprised of a point system, to every design house. It was obvious that compliance with these regulations would spell the end of Paris couture. Lelong, through difficult negotiations, obtained exemptions for 12 houses. "Unfortunately the Germans noticed at the end of six months that 92 houses were operating, which led to more discussions. Finally we succeeded in keeping 60." Madame Grès and Balenciaga both exceeded their yardage requirements one season and were ordered to close for two weeks. Banding together in a show of unity and force, the remaining houses finished these two collections so they could be shown on time.

Lelong is credited with saving over 12,000 workers from deportation into German war industries. "Over a period of four years, we had 14 official conferences with the Germans…at four of them they announced that *la couture* was to be entirely suppressed, and each time we avoided the catastrophe." Paris couture had won its own, private war.

Lelong, much as Hattie Carnegie did in the United States, employed talented young designers and gave them the opportunity to grow professionally. Christian Dior, Pierre Balmain, Hubert de Givenchy, Jean Ebel, Serge Kogan, and Jean Schlumberger were all employed by Lelong at one time or another. "It was from Lucien Lelong that I learned fabrics have personality, a behavior as varied as that of a temperamental woman," said Christian Dior.

Exhausted from his efforts during the war and his earlier wounds, Lelong retired in 1948 and died a decade later near Biarritz. He showed a total of 110 collections during his career, and though closed his couture business, he continued the fragrance business. While Lucien Lelong's clothes were elegantly conceived and executed, he will be remembered as fashion's leading diplomat during the German siege on Parisian couture.

More than half a century after Lelong retired, his exquisitely designed perfume bottles are among the most collected in the world. The fragrances themselves are still popular today, continuing the Lelong legacy.

—Mary C. Elliott; updated by Sydonie Benét

LEMPICKA, Lolita

French fashion designer

Family: Married to business partner Joseph-Marie; children: Elisa. **Career:** Showed first collection, 1984; introduced Lolita Bis junior line, 1987; introduced signature leather collection and lines of knitwear, jewelry, and glasses; ready-to-wear designer, Cacharel. **Awards:**

Lolita Lempicka, fall/winter 2001–02 ready-to-wear collection: leather slip dress. © AP/Wide World Photos.

Package of the Year award, 1998. **Address:** c/o Leonor International, 78 Avenue Marceau, 75008 Paris, France.

PUBLICATIONS

On LEMPICKA:

Articles

Hochswender, Woody, "Young French Designers Stretch Fashion's Rules," in the *New York Times,* 19 October 1990.

"Accent on Comfort: A Parisian Designs with Real Lives in Mind," in the *Chicago Tribune,* 12 January 1992.

Solis, Robbin Raskin, "Liquid Memory," in *Harper's Bazaar,* November 1998.

"Package of the Year 1998 and the Winner Is..." in *Global Cosmetic Industry* (New York), December 1998.

* * *

Pert, gamine, nostalgic, playful: these are just some of the words used to describe Lolita Lempicka collections. Since her debut in 1984, she has reintroduced a discarded Parisian elegance to fashion. Although her look is of the moment, young and modern, it has often echoed 1940s themes and styling: turbans, pearl chokers, tiny floral prints on viscose crêpes, piping, polka dots teamed with tiny stripes, contrast trims, pearl trims, and wedged shoes. Even the sepia-colored tones used in a distinctive promotional booklet for her 1991 spring-summer collection suggest the discovery of a utility frock, produced to the British government's austere guidelines for goods in World War II, in grandmother's attic, and the subsequent restyling and alteration of the garment to give it a naughtier, more risqué 1990s feel.

Lempicka places greatest importance on the use of meticulous detailing and the finest materials from international textile manufacturers. She is renowned for her precise and exquisitely-cut tailored suits that are never hard-edged but gently flatter the customer. Her look is very French, and she was the first of a new generation of female designers to emerge in Paris during the 1980s. Myrène de Premonville, Martine Sitbon, and Sophie Sitbon were others who promoted a fresh Parisian femininity with a classical base.

Lempicka's business has expanded into several areas since its inception. She created a junior diffusion line, Lolita Bis, in 1987, designed for nice and naughty young girls. She dedicated the line to her daughter, Elisa, whom she described as both "cute and feminine," like the Lolita Bis image. The company expanded rapidly in the international marketplace as well, aided by two agreements for fabrication and distribution; one with the Guy Laroche group for the main line collection and the other with the CGP group for Lolita Bis. She also had contracts with the Rinel group for Lolita Lempicka leather collections and the Italian company Alma for knitwear. Her other lines of jewelry and eyewear are licensed by Kashiyama, which directs Lolita Lempicka boutiques in Japan.

Lempicka sees her customers as ranging from schoolgirls and students, their mothers, and grandmothers. Her clothes need to be interesting and accessible for all ages. She dresses women gently and does not compromise characteristically clever detailing and sculptured cuts to fashion's whims. Her naughty but nice nature, however, doesn't stop at fashion. Tom McGee, a scientist at Givaudon Roure perfume house, released the contradictory licorice fragrance, *Lolita Lempicka* in 1998. In the U.S., licorice is thought of as the cherry red ropes people love and a candy of tradition; it was just as popular in the

Lolita Lempicka, fall/winter 2001–02 ready-to-wear collection. © AP/Wide World Photos.

1950s as it is today. In France, however, licorice often evokes the anise-flavored liquor commonly served at traditional French cafés and restaurants, hence giving the fragrance its "naughty" edge.

Not long after the naughty-and-nice fragrance was released it won DCI's Package of the Year award for 1998. The award was attributed to the fact that women respond to the scent, whereas other perfumes or colognes on the market were released with the idea of attracting the opposite sex. Described as the "fruit of our dreams," *Lolita Lempicka* comes in an apple-shaped bottle with the Lempicka name engraved on it—a portrayal of the fine details she puts into her clothing. A combination of licorice flower, anise seeds, amarena, violets, vetiver, and tonka bean, the fragrance complements Lempicka's femininity and playful style.

While Lempicka had some lines that were deemed successful, the Lempicka fragrance has undoubtedly made Lolita Lempicka a name to remember. Because smell is the most primitive sense, scientists believe the scent alone has had a bigger impact on her career than any collection ever could.

—Kevin Almond; updated by Diana Idzelis

LENOIR, Jacques

See CHLOÉ

LESER, Tina

American designer

Born: Christine Wetherill Shillard-Smith in Philadelphia, Pennsylvania, 12 December 1910. **Education:** Studied art at the Pennsylvania Academy of Fine Arts, the School of Industrial Arts, Philadelphia, and at the Sorbonne. **Family:** Married Curtin Leser, 1931 (divorced, 1936); married James J. Howley, 1948; children: Georgina. **Career:** Sold designs through her own shop in Honolulu, Hawaii, 1935–42; also formed a company in New York, 1941–43; designer, Edwin H. Foreman Company, New York, 1943–53; designer, Tina Leser, Inc., New York, 1953–64; designed Signet men's ties, 1949, Stafford Wear men's sportswear, 1950, and industrial uniforms for Ramsey Sportswear Company, 1953; retired briefly, 1964–66; retired permanently, 1982. **Awards:** Fashion Critics award, New York, 1944; Neiman Marcus award, 1945; Coty American Fashion Critics award, 1945; *Sports Illustrated* Sportswear Design award, 1956, 1957; U.S. Chamber of Commerce citation, 1957; Philadelphia Festival of the Arts Fashion award, 1962. **Member:** National Society of Arts and Letters Fashion Group. **Died:** 24 January 1986, in Sands Point, Long Island.

Publications

On LESER:

Books

Stuart, Jessie, *The American Fashion Industry,* New York, 1951.
New York and Hollywood Fashion: Costume Designs from the Brooklyn Museum Collection, New York, 1986.
Milbank, Caroline Rennolds, *New York Fashion: The Evolution of American Style,* New York, 1989.
Steele, Valerie, *Women of Fashion,* New York, 1991.
Fashion for America! Designs in the Fashion Institute of Technology, New York, Haslemere, Surrey, 1992.
Stegemeyer, Anne, *Who's Who in Fashion, Third Edition,* New York, 1996.

Articles

"Southern Resort Fashions," in *Life* (New York), 14 January 1946.
"Women Designers Set New Fashions," in *Life* (New York), 14 January 1946.
Robin, Toni, "Global Fashions," in *Holiday* (New York), November 1949.
"Industrial Uniforms Get Beauty Treatment," in *American Fabrics* (New York), Summer 1953.
"Designer Tina Leser Dies; Services Will Be Held Today," [obituary] in *WWD,* 27 January 1986.
"Tina Leser, a Designer, Dies," [obituary] in the *New York Times,* 27 January 1986.
"Tina Leser," in *Current Biography,* March 1986.

* * *

Tina Leser was an early and very successful proponent of an American design aesthetic inspired by textiles and clothing from non-Western cultures. She traveled through Asia, India, and Africa as a child, and lived in Hawaii after her first marriage in 1931, which may explain the ease with which she later adapted influences from those areas into her designs. Although she is remembered today primarily for this gift, her success was not confined to that genre, but also encompassed references to other folk and historical traditions.

Her earliest work was done in Hawaii, where she opened a shop in 1935 selling high quality ready-to-wear and playclothes of her own design. She used Hawaiian and Filipino fabrics, and even hand block-printed sailcloth. In 1940 she brought her work to New York where she was to open her own firm, but only began to be a force in fashion in 1943, when she joined the Edwin H. Foreman sportswear firm as designer.

Leser's work during World War II reflected the fabric scarcities of the wartime economy, and the limits of wartime travel. From Mexico she derived a printed flannel jacket with sequined trim; from Guatemala a strapless dress made from a handwoven blanket. Sarong-styled dresses and wrap skirts were an important part of her design vocabulary at this time, possibly stemming from her years in Hawaii. She varied these with less exotic styles, such as a tartan cotton playsuit with a matching shawl and kilted skirt, and wonderful wool flannel calf-length overalls—offspring of a very American idiom.

From the first Leser emphasized an uncluttered mode, and by the end of the war she had won awards from both Neiman Marcus and Coty for her contributions to American fashion. She had also widened her horizons to include India—very much in the news in the immediate postwar years—with her *dhoti* pants-dress, available in several versions for a variety of occasions. The facility with which she could adapt one model into many styles can be attributed to her artist's eye for proportion, and clean balance between line and form.

What was, in theory, an around-the-world honeymoon trip with her second husband in 1949 became, in practice, a way for Leser to collect fabrics, clothing, and antiques from a multitude of cultures. She based designs on objects as varied as an English game table, Siamese priest robes, an Italian peasant's vest, and a Manchu coat. Her mature work, from this date on, displayed a consistent sense of humor and intelligence in her choice of references.

Her collections included many "play" pieces but also contained relaxed day and evening clothes eminently suited to the needs and budgets of many postwar American women. Her variation on the ubiquitous 1950s sweater twinset was a halter with an embellished cardigan, and she is also credited with introducing the cashmere sweater dress. Sensitivity to the realities of life for working women induced her, in 1953, to design a line of industrial uniforms for Ramsey Sportswear Company. The trim fitting separates included a skirt to be worn over uniform slacks on the way to or from work.

Her fabric choices as well as her fashion inspirations were wide-ranging. Indian sari silks, Pringle woollens, Boussac floral prints, and embroidered Moygashel linens shared her stage with the "Modern Masters" print series made of Fuller cottons, Hope Skillman wovens, Galey & Lord ginghams, and Wesley Simpson prints. She championed denim as a fashion fabric, using it in 1945 for a two-piece swimsuit trimmed with chenille "bedspread flowers," in 1949 for coolie trousers and sleeveless jacket, and in the mid-1950s for a strapless bodice and wide cuffed pants. American bandanna prints or tablecloth fabrics were as likely to show up in her work as copies of Persian brocades, and they might equally be used for playsuits or cocktail dresses. One butterfly patterned batik print turned up as a swimsuit and cover-up skirt, capri trousers and strapless top, a sarong dress, and even as binding on a cardigan sweater.

Leser was active throughout the 1960s and into the 1970s, maintaining her flair for sportswear, loungewear, and bathing suits. Some of her best pieces from this period were slim toreador or stirrup trousers worn with long, boxy sweaters or baby-doll tunics, and her coordinated bathing suits and cover-ups remained strong. The details of her designs, however, are rather less important than the spirit she brought to them. Many young American designers carry on the referential style Leser helped establish—creating, as she did, something uniquely American from a melting-pot of cultural sources.

—Madelyn Shaw

LEVI-STRAUSS & CO.

American clothier company

Founded: by Levi Strauss (1829–1902) in the 1850s. **Company History:** Levi Strauss arrived in San Francisco in 1853, and began selling dry goods to gold prospectors. Strauss made and sold "waist-high overalls" out of material originally intended for sale as tent canvas; rivets used to reinforce seams and pockets, 1873; company passed to four nephews after Strauss' death, 1902; beige twill introduced, 1960s; corduroy jeans introduced, 1961; stretch jeans and Sta-Prest® slacks introduced, 1964; womenswear introduced, 1968; began manufacturing and marketing in Hong Kong, early 1970s; company went public, 1971 (family members retained controlling interest); official outfitters of U.S. Winter and Summer Olympic teams, and Los Angeles Olympic Games staff, 1984; publicly-held shares repurchased by family members, 1985; casual Dockers line of pants introduced, 1986; Slates dress slacks first marketed, 1996; Original Spin, custom jeans program, initiated 1998; first nonfamily member CEO takes reins, 1999; jeans and jackets with "wearable electronics" marketed in Europe, 2000. **Collections:** Smithsonian Institution, Washington, D.C. **Awards:** Coty Special award, 1971. **Company Address:** 1155 Battery Street, San Francisco, CA 94111, USA. **Company Website:** www.levistrauss.com.

Publications

On LEVI STRAUSS & CO.:

Articles

Kurtz, Irma, "Levis: Not So Much a Pair of Pants, More a Nation's Heirloom," in *Nova* (London), September 1970.
Willat, N., "The Levitation of Levi Strauss," in *Management Today* (London), January 1977.
"Levi Strauss & Co.," in *American Fabrics & Fashions* (New York), No. 109, 1977.
"Market Manipulation: The Levis 501 Experience," in *International Textiles* (London), July 1987.
"Denim: Is the Party Over?" in *Fashion Weekly* (London), 14 January 1988.
Bradley, Lisa, "A Modest Success," in *Fashion Weekly* (London), 14 January 1988.
Simpson, Blaise, "Levi's Makes Push in Women's Wear," in *WWD,* 2 March 1988.
Rowlands, Penelope, "Vintage Power: Levi's," in *WWD,* (London), 10 February 1992.
Elliott, Stuart, "The Media Business: Levi's Two New Campaigns Aim at Who Fits the Jeans," in the *New York Times,* 27 July 1992.
Magiera, Marcy, and Pat Sloan, "Levi's, Lee Loosen Up for Baby Boomers," in *Advertising Age,* 3 August 1992.
"Fashion Statement," in *San Francisco Business Magazine,* October 1992.
Elliott, Stuart, "The Media Business: Going Beyond Campaigns and into Sales and Marketing," in the *New York Times,* 18 November 1992.
Ellsworth, Jo, "Engineering a Revival for Levi's," in *Marketing* (London), 19 October 2000.
Kastor, Elizabeth, "Smarty-Pants Pants...and Shirts," in the *Washington Post,* 28 December 2000.
Skolnik, Lisa "Once and Again American Ingenuity Puts a New Spin on Classic Designs," in *Chicago Tribune,* 15 April 2001.
"Levi Strauss Reacquires A Pair of Jeans, at Markup," in the *Wall Street Journal,* 29 May 2001.

* * *

Levi's are an American icon; people of all ages, from countries as diverse as Japan, Russia, and the U.S. wear Levi's, buying them new or used. They are valued for both their enduring quality and wide array of designs.

Levi Strauss & Company was established in the 1850s in San Francisco, California, to sell the finest domestic and foreign dry goods, clothing, and household furnishings. Levi and his brothers Jonas and Louis as well as two brothers-in-law, William Sahlein and David Stern, ran the company. They had a ready market for their wares in the goldminers, cowboys, and lumberjacks, who had moved West to make their fortunes. Especially popular were the company's sturdy pants that stood up to the rugged work.

"The Original Levi's Store" in New York, 1999. © AP/Wide World Photos.

The pants were further improved thanks to Jacob W. Davis, a tailor who lived in Reno, Nevada. Davis sewed horse blankets, wagon covers, and tents from an off-white duck cloth bought from Levi Strauss & Co. He also made work clothes, though the miners and cowboys complained about pockets ripping off. As a result he tried riveting the pockets on the pants with the same copper rivets he used to attach straps to horse blankets. Davis made more riveted trousers using a 10-ounce duck twill and, by word-of-mouth advertising, a steady business grew.

Davis could not finance the patent necessary to protect his idea so he offered Levi Strauss & Co. half the right to sell all such riveted clothing in exchange for the $68 patent fee. The patent was granted to Davis and the Levi Strauss company on 20 May 1873. Levi Strauss & Co. soon made and marketed trousers, vests, and jackets using the rivets at stress points. White and brown duck twill and denim were used in the trousers Strauss called waist pantaloons or overalls, not "jeans."

The term jeans referred to trousers constructed from a fabric woven in Genoa, Italy, or "Genoese" cloth, while denim was derived from "serge de Nimes," or cloth from Nimes, France. The fabrics were all shrunk to fit as a snug fit was desirable because wrinkles caused blisters when riding in a saddle. Suspender buttons, two in back, and four in front were used. There were no belt loops, though cinch straps and a buckle were sewn onto the back of the trousers to tighten the waist.

Strict price and quality standards were established at Levi Strauss, and fabric was furnished by Amoskeag, a New England mill. Orange linen thread was used for stitching because it matched the copper color rivets, and two curving Vs were stitched on back pockets to distinguish the Levi pants from those of competitors (this arcing row of stitches, however, did not become a registered clothing trademark until 1942). An oilcloth guarantee with the "Two Horse Brand" was tacked to the seat of the trousers. It had an engraving of two teamsters whipping a pair of dray horses trying to pull apart riveted trousers.

In 1886 a leather label with the two horse logo was permanently affixed with orange linen thread, and due to the quality of manufacturing and fabric, Levi Strauss was able to charge more than its competitors. The original XX 10-ounce denim trousers were known as the 501, and became the hallmark to be measured against. Levi's, as they became known, were functional, simple and above all durable.

The company grew and evolved to meet changing economic and societal needs brought about by world wars, the Depression, and unionization of the labor force. Clothing was sized to fit children as well as women; linen thread was replaced with a fine gauge version of the cord used to stitch shoes to make seams stronger, belt loops replaced suspender buttons on the original 501 design, the cinch belt was removed, 13.5-ounce denim came into use, a zipper fly was introduced, preshrunk fabric became the norm, and the red Levi tag was added to further distinguish the jeans from the competition. New lines of more dressy yet casual clothes were also introduced, such as Dockers and Slates.

The mystique and marketability of Levi's received a boost throughout the 20th century when worn by men and women with high profiles. James Dean wore Levi's in *Rebel Without a Cause*, and Marlon Brando was similarly outfitted in the *Wild One.* Director Steven Spielberg and software mogul Bill Gates both appeared frequently in jeans, while the corporate world's casual Fridays and even former President Bill Clinton have given Levi's both exposure and status.

Yet during the 1990s the market was inundated by branded jeans, from popular designers such as Calvin Klein, Ralph Lauren, Tommy Hilfiger, Dolce & Gabbana, Donna Karan, and many others, as well as store brands like Gap and Old Navy. Though Levi Strauss marketed a myriad of styles—from boot cut to flare to "loose" or wide-legged pants to stretch—distribution problems, discounters, and a weakened textile industry contributed to a serious loss in market share. To combat the slump, the company initiated a series of hip print and television ads, some with winning results. The introduction of the computerized Original Spin program in 1998, to help create the perfect custom-made pair of jeans, also brought a new market segment to the Levi's fold.

In the 21st century Levi's remain a staple in the wardrobes of many consumers worldwide, yet the company's overall sales and profits continued to slide. Japan and the U.S., once the company's strongest markets, were sadly lacking in 2000 and 2001. On a more positive note, the company acquired an original pair of work pants made in the early 1880s (probably sold for about $1 at the time) for more than $46,500 in 2001, from the eBay auction site. Additionally, the home of company founder Levi Strauss was restored and opened for touring in San Francisco.

The jeans of Levi Strauss & Co. will never go out of style and have achieved an iconic stature in the U.S. and around the world. For its part, the Levi Strauss company has created dozens of styles and variations of its stalwart products to transcend trends. More recent innovations included ergonomically engineered jeans as well as Levi's with built-in gadgets such as MP3 players and voice-activated cellular phones. Levi's—originally intended for use by goldminers and cowboys—have become an integral part of the American way of life. Yet as the world's number-one manufacturer of branded clothing, Levi Strauss is a name known and beloved in more than 80 countries.

—Nancy House; updated by Owen James

LEWIN, Lucille

See WHISTLES

LEWIS-CROWN, Peter

See LACHASSE

LEY, Wolfgang and Margarethe

See ESCADA

LIBERTY OF LONDON

British department store

Founded: by Arthur Lazenby Liberty (1843–1917) in 1875. **Company History:** Founded as oriental import emporium, "East India House," 218A Regent Street, London; expanded, 1876, 1878, 1883, 1924; produced Liberty Art Fabrics, from 1878; introduced Umritza Cashmere, 1879; opened furnishing and decoration department, 1883; debuted costumes, 1884; introduced jewelry and metalwork, 1899; opened Birmingham branch, 1887; Paris, 1890; became public company, 1894; opened branch in Manchester, 1924; established Liberty and Company Ltd., wholesale company, 1939; acquired Dutch firm, Metz and Company, 1973; expanded men's offerings in flagship store, late 1990s; opened U.S. distribution center in Fort Worth, Texas, 2000; acquired by real estate company Marylebone Warwick Balfour, 2000. **Exhibitions:** *Liberty's, 1875–1975,* Victoria & Albert Museum, London, 1975; *Art Nouveau, 1980–1914,* Victoria & Albert Museum [traveling exhibit], 2000. **Awards:** Silver Medal, Rational Dress Exhibition, 1883; Gold Medal, Amsterdam Exhibition of 1883; Arthur Lazenby Liberty knighted, 1913. **Company Address:** Lasenby House, 32 Kingly Street, London W1R 5LA, England.

Publications

By LIBERTY OF LONDON:

Periodicals

Aglaia (journal of the Healthy and Artistic Dress Union), 1894.
Liberty Lamp (in-house magazine), 1925–32.

On LIBERTY OF LONDON:

Books

Laver, James, *The Liberty Story,* London, 1959.
Adburgham, Alison, *Liberty's: A Biography of a Shop,* London, 1975.
Liberty's 1875–1975 [exhibition catalogue], London, 1975.
The Liberty Style, London, 1979.
Milbank, Caroline Rennolds, *Couture: The Great Designers,* New York, 1985.
Levy, Mervyn, *Liberty Style, the Classic Years: 1898–1910,* London, 1986.
Morris, Barbara, *Liberty Design, 1874–1914,* London, 1989.
Calloway, Stephen, ed., *The House of Liberty: Masters of Style and Decoration,* London, 1992.

Arwas, Victor, *Art Nouveau: From Mackintosh to Liberty,* Windsor, England, 2000.

Articles

Amaya, Victor, "Liberty and the Modern Style," in *Apollo* (London), February 1963.
Boyd, A., and P. Radford, "The Draper Who Made History," in the *Observer Magazine* (London), 6 April 1975.
Williams, Antonia, "Liberty Quality Centenary: At the Sign of the Purple Feather," in *Vogue* (London), June 1975.
Banham, Reyner, "A Dead Liberty," in *New Society* (London), 7 August 1975.
Nichols, Sarah, "Arthur Lazenby Liberty: A Merc Adjective?" in the *Journal of Decorative and Propaganda Arts* (Miami, Florida), Summer 1989.
"Liberty of Regent Street in Big Men's Wear Push," in *DNR,* 3 April 1996.
Curan, Catherine, "Liberty of London," in *DNR,* 27 September 1996.
Menkes, Suzy, "Downsizing for the Upscale—Stores Cope with Consumer Caution in a Chilly Retail Climate," in the *International Herald Tribune*, 17 November 1998.
"Liberty of London Unveils New Collection at Gift Fair," *Trade Partners New Products Press Release,* 2 July 2000.

* * *

Sir Arthur Lazenby Liberty, the founder of Liberty of London, contributed in 1894 to the Healthy and Artistic Dress Union's journal *Aglaia,* which stated his declared aim to "promote improvements in dress that would make it consistent with health, comfort and healthy appearance, but [dress] should not obviously depart from the conventional mode." Lazenby Liberty had left the Oriental Warehouse, famous among the leading artists and aesthetes of the day for its collections of blue and white porcelain and oriental fabrics in 1874 to set up on his own in half a shop in London's Regent Street. Lazenby Liberty presided over the shop's transformation from an Eastern bazaar to a department store that commissioned and sold modern design of all kinds.

"Liberty art fabrics" in subtle tones, which soon became known worldwide as "Liberty colors," (produced in collaboration from 1878 with the dyers and printers of Thomas Wardle) were the first step toward the creation of the shop's new image, and by the end of the century, *Stile Liberty* was synonymous in Italy with art nouveau. The quintessential fabric of the Aesthetic Movement was Liberty or Art silk and, aided by such popular successes as the Gilbert and Sullivan opera *Patience* (where the clothes were made from Liberty fabrics and Liberty artistic silks were advertised in the program) and the cartoons of George du Maurier—Liberty soon to became a household name.

In 1884 Lazenby Liberty opened the costume department, appointing as its first director the celebrated architect E.W.E. Godwin, whom Oscar Wilde once described as being "the greatest aesthete of us all." Godwin had made a study of historic dress and approached his task with almost missionary zeal, aiming to "establish the of dressmaking fame hygienic, intelligible and progressive basis."

Godwin's death three years later did not mean the end of his influence on Liberty dress, and the catalogues showed a wide range of Liberty Art costumes, ranging from a Grecian costume in Arabian cotton, to a peasant dress in thin Umritza cashmere, embroidered and smocked (a skill revived by Liberty and used on the finest materials). Smocking was also a striking feature of the Kate Greenaway-influenced artistic dress for children, a range of clothes hugely popular with Liberty's customers from the late 1880s onwards.

In the 20th century, Liberty fabrics were used by the best known designers of each decade, from Paul Poiret to Yves Saint Laurent, from Cacharel to Jean Muir. The famous Liberty silk scarves and ties are sold all over the world, and the distinctive fabrics are still used by home dressmakers to create their own "Liberty style" in a fashion familiar from the time of their 19th-century forebears. Liberty also relaunched its own clothing collections, described as "contemporary yet classic. Simply yet beautifully styled, they could be worn by the modern girl or she of between-the-wars-era alike."

Of all the major London department stores, the character of Liberty's Regent Street flagship store and the quality and range of the goods it offers have changed least in recent years. In fashion terms, Liberty's offers a unique combination of its own entirely distinctive and yet ever-changing fabric and clothing designs for womenswear and menswear and the fashion collections of such distinctive contemporary designers as Nicole Farhi, Kenzo, Issey Miyake, and Paul Smith.

During the 1990s, Liberty of London expanded its Liberty consumer brand from mainly soft goods and apparel into a broader range of products encompassing home furnishings, decorative accessories, and gifts. At the same time, the Liberty brand has maintained as its centerpiece the colorful prints with which it has long been associated. To remain fresh, the company has continuously updated its designs under the Liberty of London label to achieve a more modern look, as it did with its men's ties and scarves (licensed to Salant in the U.S. and Mitchelson's in the UK) in 1997.

Although the company's brand division—which operates separately from its retail unit—drove significant sales and profit for Liberty in the late 1980s, its performance fell off in the 1990s. This trend had begun to reverse itself by 2001, thanks to the company's efforts to invigorate the brand. As of the early 2000s, the company was trying to rebuild its brand by focusing on three main product categories: women's fashions, gifts, and home furnishings. An in-house design team created Liberty of London-branded products for distribution in Liberty's own stores as well as in other retail locations throughout the world. The goal is to set trends with Liberty of London merchandise designs yet to remain true to the sensibility of founder Arthur Lazenby Liberty.

Liberty's 2000 giftware collection, shown at the New York International Gift Fair, was emblematic. Fifteen products, ranging from sleepwear to kitchen, bed, and bath products, featured floral-based prints in pinks and greens. Some favorite Liberty products, including kimonos and cosmetic bags, were focal points of the line. And as part of its objective of solidifying sales in the North American market, Liberty opened a Fort Worth distribution center in 2000 to enhance fulfillment in its U.S. operations.

The printed patterns highlighted in the Liberty of London giftware line typically reflect those in the company's fashion range. The label's spring 2001 women's apparel collection, as described in a review on the website supporting London Fashion Week, featured beachwear and daywear in a wide variety of colors, from solids to avant-garde prints to stripes. The site made note of the 1960s-influenced themes on the collection, which were updated for 2001.

Liberty has also been active in its department store operations, which comprise its largest division in terms of sales. Its flagship store on Regent Street—other Liberty stores are located in Windsor and at London's Heathrow Airport—expanded its men's offerings in the late 1990s, focusing on cutting-edge designers. These included names such as Dries van Noten, Helmut Lang, and Alexander McQueen, as well as designers considered classics "in Liberty's terms" such as Yohji Yamamoto and Jean-Paul Gaultier, according the *Daily News Record* in April 1996. It also expanded its sportswear selection, which featured lines such as Mossimo and Griffin Laundry, and maintained its strong designer suit business featuring Ralph Lauren, Giorgio Armani, Hugo Boss, and others.

Despite all its activity in both its branded merchandise unit and its stores, Liberty suffered financial losses throughout the 1990s and, in 2000, was acquired by London property company Marylebone Warwick Balfour. The purchase marked the end of 125 years of family ownership. Marylebone set out first to renovate the Regent Street store and made clear its intention to rejuvenate and further develop the Liberty of London brand.

—Doreen Ehrlich; updated by Karen Raugust

LINARD, Stephen

British designer

Born: London, England, 1959. **Education:** Studied at Southend College of Technology, 1975–78, and St. Martin's School of Art, London, 1978–81. **Career:** Designer, Notre Dame X, 1981–82; showed first two womenswear collections, 1982; introduced menswear line, 1983; designer, Bigi, Japan; designer, Georges Sand Range for Jun Co., Japan; designer, Beyond Stephen Linard range for Bazaar; designer for Powder Blue, 1986; assistant designer, Drakes.

Publications

On LINARD:

Articles

"Cue: Future Talent," in *Vogue* (London), October 1981.
Grieve, Amanda, "Quids In," in *Harper's & Queen* (London), April 1983.
"Da Londra: Moda Come Provocazione Eclettica," in *L'Uomo Vogue* (Milan), December 1985.
Mower, Sarah, "It's Westwood Redux in London 1980s Time Warp," in the *International Herald Tribune,* 14 March 2001.

* * *

It would be difficult to exaggerate the impact of Stephen Linard's degree collection when his models appeared on the catwalk at St. Martin's School of Art in London in the summer of 1981. Linard was a menswear student, and his models were real men, with real muscle, stubble, tattoos, and the demeanor of East End toughs about to enter the boxing ring. The Reluctant Emigrés collection was a subtle mix of solid and transparent, the safely known and the unpredictable. Traditional pinstripe trousers had contrast patches at the derriére, solid dark waistcoat fronts and shadowy organza backs. Striped city shirts were seen to have curious underarm patches, and all was concealed beneath swirling black greatcoats. The clothes were instantly covetable, thoroughly masculine in an entirely new way, and electrifying in the way that only the truly innovative can be.

Linard was famous overnight, and his charisma and photogenic air ensured him an enthusiastic press. He joined a leading young design team known as Notre Dame X, with Richard Ostell and Darlajane Gilroy, among others. When he split from this group, backers set him up in a city studio, where he produced sought-after garments in esoterically titled collections—Angels with Dirty Faces, Les Enfants du Chemin de Fer. He was an early revivalist of bias cutting, and showed underwear as outerwear. He continued with an anarchic mix of fabrics and influences appealing to the glam-sex clubbers always in search of new heroes, and labels with cachet. These were great days of club couture, with punters in fierce competition over their evening toilettes. New heights of sartorial extravagance were scaled, with Linard and art-world personality Leigh Bowery in the running for chief mountaineer.

British rag-trade backing is notoriously fickle, however, and when Linard's company collapsed, he went to Japan to join the stable of eccentric models at Men's Bigi. The Japanese are always swiftly attracted to high-profile talent with high-profile personality, and Linard was soon designing the prestigious Georges Sand range for Jun Company selling in Japan, the Far East, and the United States. At home, he designed the Beyond Stephen Linard ranges for Bazaar in South Moulton Street, London. Starting Powder Blue in 1986, he designed the Chess and Innocents Abroad collections, the latter an eclectic mix of leopard skin, broderie Anglaise and Edwardian schoolgirls. Since teaching at Southend, his former college, and Middlesex, he has been the assistant designer at Drakes, producing exclusive menswear accessories in silk and cashmere.

Linard has long been involved in the fashion and music mix, designing for singers David Bowie and Boy George and for pop groups such as Fun Boy 3, Spandau Ballet, and the Pet Shop Boys. Neil Tennant of the Pet Shop Boys says on their website, "I wore [a black coat] in the first *Opportunities* video and for *West End Girls.* It's designed by Stephen Linard who, interestingly enough, played Envy in the *It's a Sin* video. Eric Watson, a friend of mine who does most of our photography, had one first; I loved it and got one, the last one they had. It's made of black linen, so it creases all the time. I liked it because it was very, very severe, and I wanted to look a bit like a preacher from the Wild West. It's what people associated us [the Pet Shop Boys] with in the beginning."

Linard also hosted the "Total Fashion Victims" theme nights at the Wag club, introducing Sadé and Swing Out Sister, with John Maybury's light installations dazzling the crowd. He has styled for *The Face* and interviewed for *Blitz,* two top London style magazines. In short, for more than a decade, he has lived and worked a life of glamour and style.

Though the industry has become accustomed to real men on the catwalk, some agencies—So Dam' Tuf, for example—deal in nothing else. Yet back in the early 1980s, all this was new, and therein lies Linard's contribution to his time—he did it first. At the dawn of the 21st century, two decades after his first collection stunned the fashion world, Linard is enjoying a resurgence of interest in his work. Along with the likes of designers and firms such as Bodymap, Boy, PX, Richmond/Cornejo, and Vivienne Westwood, Linard's work has come to the forefront as retro, gaining a whole new band of followers. The works of these seminal 1980s designers has also been catching the interest of new designers such as Maria Chen and Anthony Symonds, who grew up in the heyday of the fashion-industry-meets-music-industry-meets-the-club-scene era.

—Alan J. Flux; updated by Daryl F. Mallett

LITTMAN, Helen and Judy

See ENGLISH ECCENTRICS

L.L. BEAN

American clothing manufacturer and mail order company

Founded: in 1912 by Leon Leonwood Bean (1872–1967), in Freeport, Maine. **Company History:** Company founded for mail order sales of Maine Hunting Shoe, patented 1911. Camping and fishing equipment offered, from 1920s; bicycles, cookware, watches, luggage offered, from 1930s; casual apparel offered, from 1980s; retail salesroom added to manufacturing plant, 1945; offered 24/7 service from 1951; first branch store opened, in Japan, 1991; began offering separate catalogues for men, 1998; opened first full-line retail store outside of Freeport, 2000; launched first women's skin care line, 2000; introduced SUV in partnership with Subaru, 2000. **Awards:** Coty American Fashion Critics award, 1975; American Catalogue Awards Gold award, 1987, 1989, for hunting specialties catalogue; American Catalogue Awards Silver award, 1989; American Catalogue Awards Gold award for women's outdoor specialties catalogue, 1989. **Company Address:** L.L. Bean, Inc., Freeport, Maine, 04033, USA. **Company Website:** www.llbean.com.

Publications

On L.L. BEAN:

Books

Montgomery, M. R., *In Search of L.L. Bean*, Boston, 1984.

Griffin, Carlene, *Spillin' the Beans*, Freeport, Maine, 1993.

Articles

Dickson, Paul, "L.L. Bean," in *Town and Country* (New York), February 1977.

Crews, Harry, "L.L. Bean Has Your Number, America!" in *Esquire* (New York), March 1978.

Longsdorf, Robert, "L.L. Bean: Yankee Ingenuity and Persistence Transformed This Little Maine Boot Shop into a Veritable Sportsman's Candy Store," in *Trailer Life* (Agoura, CA), May 1986.

Kerasole, Ted, "L.L. Bean: 75 Years," in *Sports Afield* (New York), October 1987.

Zempke, Ron, and Dick Schaaf, "L.L. Bean," in the *Service Edge* (Minneapolis, MN), 1989.

"Bean Sticks to Its Backyard," in the *Economist,* 4 August 1990.

Kaplan, Michael, "Gumshoe," in *GQ (Gentlemen's Quarterly),* October 1992.

Hirano, Koji, "L.L. Bean's First Japan Store," in *Daily News Record (DNR),* 13 November 1992.

Symonds, William C., "Paddling Harder at L.L. Bean," in *Business Week,* 7 December 1998.

Hays, Constance L., "L.L. Bean Casts About for Ways to Grow," in the *New York Times,* 14 August 1999.

Palmieri, Jean E., and Melonee KcKinney, "L.L. Bean Set to Open Second Full-Line Unit in Virginia," in *DNR,* 21 April 2000.

Dodd, Annmarie and Jean E. Palmieri, "L.L. Bean Warms to Its Male Customer," in *DNR,* 12 November 2000.

* * *

The assimilation of the work of L.L. Bean into the world of fashion design is a direct result of the eclecticism in late 20th-century culture. Sportsman, businessman, and inventor Leon Leonwood Bean stood outside the world of fashion during his lifetime. His mail order company, based in Freeport, Maine, began before World War I selling sporting garments and accessories which were innovative, durable and, once perfected, consistant in appearance over many decades. They were, initially, the epitomé of antifashion.

Founded on the innovative design of the Maine Hunting Shoe, patented in 1911, L.L. Bean's range of clothing came to include traditional articles such as leather moccasins, based on American Indian footwear, long red woollen underwear, and collections of well-made weekend clothes for sportsmen and sportswomen. The appeal was their comfort, durability, and timelessness of appearance.

Bean's early business success was aided by the U.S. Post Office's introduction in 1912 of a cheap parcel post service. Similarly, the construction of the national highway network and the expansion of private car ownership in the 1910s and 1920s promoted recreational travel for sportsmen and helped to create a need for the specific kinds of garments sold by Bean. Their shop in Freeport was open for business around the clock, 365 days a year, demonstrating a genuine devotion to customer service and an understanding of the particular needs of their specialist clientèle. Through its marketing policies, L.L. Bean came to represent solid, ethical values of conduct in commerce. The personification of integrity, L.L. Bean tested his own equipment prior to marketing, as the company president does today.

A notion of the L.L. Bean style had developed by the 1920s, when the company's catalogue was known worldwide. The catalogue had, from the start, a unique look and quality. Written in L.L. Bean's personal descriptive style, it was presented in a casual, scrapbook format, with its familiar Cheltenham typeface, plain wholesome models, and cover illustrations by America's foremost painters of outdoor life. By the 1980s, the catalogue had become an institution and a symbol for a particular lifestyle. It attracted references in publications such as Lisa Birnbach's *The Preppy Handbook*, which dubbed Bean "Preppy Mecca," and it was parodied in a National Lampoon "Catalogue" which featured a range of items including an "Edible Moccasin" and a "Chloroform Dog Bed." The genuine catalogue layout has contained such surrealist juxtapositions as jackets, trousers, and duck decoys.

Following the death of L.L. Bean in 1967, the business passed into the hands of his grandson, Leon Gorman, who expanded and modernized both the operation and its products while maintaining its essential character, rooted in Down East hunting and fishing culture. But modernization had its dangers. Enthusiasm for their newly developed synthetic fibres, useful in extreme weather conditions, had carried over to the range of casual clothing of the 1960s and 1970s. During the 1980s, however, in keeping with the rising tide of environmentalism and a new public appreciation of the natural, as opposed to the synthetic, L.L. Bean returned to 100-percent natural materials in their traditional clothes.

Expansion from shoes and outdoor clothing to accessories and equipment such as snowshoes, fishing gear, and canoes showed a keen awareness of links between apparel and the utilitarian accoutrements of modern life. Later catalogues acknowledged the rise of the fitness movement, with new lines of garments for exercising, water sports, and accessories for activities such as roller skating and cross-country skiing.

In 1975 L.L. Bean was recognized as a bona fide member of the fashion world when it received the prestigious Coty award. This accolade signified an expansion of the meaning of fashion and confirmed its role as a mirror on contemporary culture. The genius of L.L. Bean had been to recognize the recreational potential in his local surroundings and to invent ways to cater, through clothing, first for the growth of outdoor sporting activities and, later, to the booming leisure market.

Since its founding, L.L. Bean clothes have reflected the social attitudes, leisure pursuits, and health awareness of America while also embodying a dream about the unspoiled American landscape and the values it represented. Yet in the late 1990s, L.L. Bean ran into financial trouble. Its sweaters, parkas, khakis, and boots were no longer perceived as fashion-forward, but rather as clinging to the same outdoor and preppy looks that had been behind the company's success in the 1970s and 1980s. Analysts felt Bean's management had not kept up with changes in the mail-order and apparel industries. Many of its competitors—of which there were an ever-growing number—had moved into the children's market, for example, but Bean had not. It also was out of sync with the industry in its continued direct response-only strategy. Therefore, despite a strong brand name, a high level of service and customer satisfaction, a reputation for quality, and a sophisticated warehousing system, sales were flat.

The company took several steps to effect a turnaround. While its original product, the Bean Boot, remained one of its bestsellers, it undertook to update its apparel and footwear styles. It also began to put profitability on an equal footing with customer service—as opposed to its traditional belief that with good service, profit would follow—and increased marketing expenditures. Bean began to release catalogues for specific market niches, such as the Freeport Studio casual clothing and accessories catalogue targeted female Baby Boomers. Separate men's catalogues were introduced in 1998 and, by 2000, Bean issued six men's-only catalogues per year, emphasizing detailing and color palettes. The company similarly segmented children's and home products and now publishes 50 catalogues per year.

Meanwhile, Bean added new products and product categories that tied in with its brand image. In 2000 it introduced skin care products to its women's catalogue, focusing on items that protect the skin in the midst of an outdoor lifestyle. One of Bean's more unusual product extensions is a sport utility vehicle, the Subaru Outback Limited Special L.L. Bean Edition, also introduced in 2000. Bean also began expanding its distribution. In 2000, Bean opened its second full-line store (after its Freeport flagship). The launch marked the first step in a conservative retail strategy encompassing three to five new stores in the Northeast U.S. over three or four years. L.L. Bean also operates 10 outlet stores in the U.S. and 20 retail shops in Japan. Its stores feature both soft and hard goods, including the L.L. Bean Home collection. The company was an early entrant into e-commerce and has seen success with its Internet program, being rated among the top sites for sales and customer satisfaction.

Despite all the changes, Bean has remained focused on its core brand attributes. It is not attempting to become a designer brand—which it feels would alienate its loyal customers—but rather to create a more cohesive presentation and a greater emphasis on lifestyle. L.L. Bean had parlayed this focus into sales well above $1 billion by the turn of the century.

—Gregory Votolato; updated by Karen Raugust

LLOYD, Alison

See ALLY CAPELLINO

LORCAN MULLANY

See BELLVILLE SASSOON-LORCAN MULLANY

LOUIS VUITTON

French luxury retailer and part of LVMH

Founded: by Louis Vuitton (1811–92) in Paris, 1854. **Company History:** Vuitton was apprenticed to several luggage makers; began designing flat luggage for use on new railways, diverging from traditional iron hooped trunks used on horse-drawn coaches; LV monogram introduced, 1896; opened stores in England, then in the U.S., 1897–1900; Henry Racamier became director, 1977; merged

Louis Vuitton, spring/summer 2002 ready-to-wear collection. © Reuters NewMedia Inc./CORBIS.

with Moët-Hennessey to become LVMH, 1987; LVMH bought Givenchy, 1988; Bernard Arnault acquired firm and became chairman, 1989; Recamier departed and started Orcofi SA, 1990; acquired many design houses and brands, from 1993; Marc Jacobs signed as artistic director, 1997; ready-to-wear line launched, 1997; introduced menswear, and opened megastores in New York, Paris, and London, 1998; opened second Hong Kong flagship, 2000. **Company Address:** 2 Rue du Pont Neuf, Paris 75001, France. **Company Website:** www.vuitton.com; www.lvmh.com.

Publications

On LOUIS VUITTON:

Books

Lartigue, Jacques-Henri, *125 Years of Louis Vuitton,* Paris, 1980.
A Journey Through Time: A Louis Vuitton Retrospective Exhibition, Paris, 1983.
Louis Vuitton, Traveling Through Time, Paris, 1984, 1996.
Vuitton, Henry L., *La malle aux souvenirs [A Trunkful of Memories],* Paris, 1984, 1989.
Forestier, Nadège, *The Taste of Luxury: Bernard Arnault and the Moët-Hennessy Louis Vuitton Story,* London, 1992.
Sebag-Montefiore, Hugh, *Kings on the Catwalk: The Louis Vuitton and Moët-Hennessy Affair,* Chapmans 1992.

Louis Vuitton, spring/summer 2002 collection. © AFP/CORBIS.

Articles

"French Capital Markets: Bags of Bubbly," in *Euromoney,* January 1987.
"Fashionable Takeover," in the *Economist,* 16 July 1988.
Toy, Stewart, "Avant le Deluge at Moët Hennessy Louis Vuitton," in *Business Week,* 24 April 1989.
Carson-Parker, John, "Dese, Doms and Diors," in *Chief Executive,* November/December 1989.
Toy, Stewart, "Meet Monsieur Luxury," in *Business Week,* 30 July 1990.
Berman, Phyllis, and Zina Sawaya, "Life Begins at 77," in *Forbes,* 27 May 1991.
Caulkin, Simon, "A Case of Incompatibility," in *Management Today,* February 1993.
"Vuitton's 100-Year Dash," in *WWD,* 22 January 1996.
Singer, Natasha, "The Rush to Russia," in *WWD,* 20 January 1998.
Raper, Sarah, and Katherine Weisman, "Vuitton's Big Adventure," in *WWD,* 19 February 1998.
Barrett, Amy, "Vuitton Aims Makeover at Youth: Leather House Launches Megastores," in the *Wall Street Journal,* 10 March 1998.
"First Look at Louis Vuitton Menswear," in *DNR,* 23 March 1998.
Edelson, Sharon, "Vuitton: Upscale Downtown," in *WWD,* 15 September 1998.
Lloyd, Simon, "Louis Vuitton Breezes Along in an Expansive Mood," in *Business Review Weekly,* 29 October 1999.
Hammond, Teena, "On Rodeo: A Bigger, Better Vuitton," in *WWD,* 23 December 1999.
Daswani, Kavita, "Louis Vuitton's Asian Rise," in *WWD,* 29 March 2000.

* * *

The French firm of Louis Vuitton, making prestigious luggage and leather accessories since the middle of the 19th century, has been much overshadowed by its merger with Moët-Hennessey to become Moët-Hennessey Louis Vuitton (LVMH). Yet long before the merging of like-minded luxury companies, Louis Vuitton had established itself as an enduring purveyor of quality goods for the most discerning clientèle.

Young Louis Vuitton first came to Paris in 1837, in the year in which stage and mail coach travel was to be transformed by the opening of the first railway line in France, from Paris to St. Germain, to passenger traffic. Vuitton became an apprentice *layetier,* or luggage packer, to the prominent households of Paris at a time when journeys could take many months and require endless changes of wardrobe. He established such a reputation in this work that he was appointed by the Emperor of France, Napoleon III, as official *layetier* to his wife, the Empress Eugenie.

Vuitton acquired expert knowledge of what made a good traveling case and started to design luggage, opening his workshops to the general public in 1854 to provide luggage suitable for a new age of travel. Vuitton designed the first flat trunks that could be easily stacked in railway carriages and in the holds of ocean liners. Made of wood and covered in a new distinctive canvas called "Trianon Grey," this particular traveling trunk superseded the dome-shaped, cumbersome trunks originally designed for the stage coach.

So successful and prestigious was this luggage that other trunk makers began to copy Vuitton's style and designs, a problem the firm bearing his name was still dealing with over a century later. In 1876 Vuitton responded to the imitators by changing the Trianon Grey canvas to a striped design in beige and brown. The problem, however, persisted and in 1888, Vuitton adopted another canvas—a checkerboard pattern with the words "Marque deposée Louis Vuitton" interwoven through the material.

When George Vuitton took over the family firm on his father's death in 1892, imitation of company products was still a major problem, and four years later he designed and took out worldwide patents on the now legendary Louis Vuitton canvas featuring his father's initials against background motifs of stars and flowers. This innovative design had the effect of stopping all imitations until the 1960s, when counterfeiting became a serious problem once again. The firm launched an offensive, employing a team of lawyers and special investigation agencies to actively pursue offenders through law courts all over the world, which continues to this day.

Methods of manufacture have changed little since the 19th century. Suitcases are still made by hand; the craftsmen line up the leather and canvas, tapping in the tiny nails one by one and securing the five-lever solid pick-proof brass locks with an individual handmade key, designed to allow the traveler to have only one key for all his or her luggage. The wooden frames of each trunk are made of 30-year-old poplar dried for at least four years. Each trunk has a serial number and can take up to 60 hours to make, and a suitcase as many as 15 hours.

Although the luggage collection has always offered extensive choice, Louis Vuitton has been creating special made-to-order hard-sided luggage since 1854. Congo explorer Pierre Savorgnan de Brazza (1852–1905) commissioned a combined trunk and bed from the company, and in 1936 for American conductor Leopold Stokowski's travels, Gaston Vuitton designed a traveling *secrétaire.* When opened, the extraordinary design revealed two shelves for books, three drawers for documents and musical scores, and a vertical compartment to store a typewriter. The gate-legged table which completed the instant workstation folded into the door.

To celebrate the 100th anniversary of the Louis Vuitton logo, the founder's son George invited a who's who of designers to create items from its trademarked striped fabric. Azzedine Alaïa, Manolo Blahnik, Helmut Lang, Isaac Mizrahi, Romeo Gigli, Vivienne Westwood, and Sybilla all fashioned limited edition carry-alls, from small cases to large bags for sale at select Vuitton stores, as well as other items.

In the 21st century some 200 Louis Vuitton boutiques in the major cities of Europe, the U.S., and Far East supplied prestigious luggage, elegant apparel, and a wide range of accessories to its distinguished clientèle. As part of the LVMH empire, the Vuitton brand was nestled among an ever-expanding number of design houses including Christian Lacroix, Givenchy, Emilio Pucci, Kenzo, Fendi, Michael Kors, and Donna Karan.

—Doreen Ehrlich and Owen James

M

MA, Walter

Chinese designer

Born: Hong Kong, China, 28 August 1951. **Education:** Graduated from Hong Kong Institute of Design, 1975. **Family:** Married to Joyce Ma; children: Adrienne. **Career:** Worked for a fashion company for eight months before opening his own first shop, Vee Boutique; founder/owner, with wife Joyce, Hong Kong-based Joyce Boutique Holdings, circa 1980; sold interest in Joyce to Holding di Partecipazioni Industriali, 1998; Ad Hoc younger collection introduced by Joyce Ma; agreed to sell majority stake in Joyce to Wheelock & Company, 2000; also served as vice chairman, Hong Kong Fashion Designers Association. **Address:** Unit 11, 8/F, Tower 1, Harbour Centre, Hok Cheung Street, Hunghom, Kowloon, Hong Kong, China. **Website:** www.Joyce.com.

Publications

On MA:

Articles

"HDP Builds Its Presence in Far East," in *WWD,* 1 December 1998.

"Sincere Celebrates 100 Years," in the *South China Morning Post,* 24 January 2000.

Sito, Peggy, "Investment Firm Takes Joyce Control," in the *South China Morning Post,* 5 April 2000.

Daswani, Kavita, "Internet Firm to Control Joyce Boutique," in *WWD,* 17 April 2000.

Chung, Yulanda, "Business Buzz: A Hong Kong Family Affair," in *AsiaWeek,* 1 July 2000.

Walton, Chris, "Fashion in Motion," available online at TotallyHK.com, www.totallyhk.com, 2001.

* * *

Walter Ma, fall/winter 2001 collection. © AP/Wide World Photos.

Walter Ma is very much a home-grown designer. Born and educated in Hong Kong, he has been a pillar of fashion for the young and fashion-conscious for more than a quarter-century now. One of the first graduates of Hong Kong's Institute of Fashion Design, Ma began working immediately to establish himself as one of the foremost local designers.

At the time he graduated from the Institute, it was the normal practice for graduates to work within the industry or to go abroad for further training. But after a very short stint working for an export company, Ma took the risky step of opening his own shop. It paid off—his boutiques, Gee and Vee, are now found in major shopping locations, and his workshops employ over a hundred people. He, along with Judy Mann, was among the first local designers to create his own label, became a pioneer in the field, and helped transform Hong Kong from a cheap garment factory into an upscale fashion cosmopolitan. He also served as vice chairman of the Hong Kong Fashion Designers Association, which was cofounded by Judy Mann.

Ma designs for four labels: Gee, Vee, Front First, and Walter Ma. Each offers a distinct look: Vee is the most up-market and offers sophisticated party and daywear, the clothes are feminine, detailed, and dressy; Gee is an easy-to-wear, middle-priced line aimed at the career woman with an emphasis on quality fabric and neutral shades that mix and match; Front First line is Ma's most outrageous, a casual, fun line providing mainly separates for fashionable young men and

Walter Ma, fall/winter 2001 collection. © AP/Wide World Photos.

women; and the Walter Ma line, which is designer clothing. Together they cater to the needs of Hong Kong people, from leisurewear to clothes for special occasions such as graduate parties and the annual Chinese New Year celebrations. As a consequence, Walter describes himself as being client-led. His regular customers are women whose ages range from 20 to 40 and over. "She is a career woman who knows what she wants," he says. He also designs one-off eveningwear for regular customers, who include local film stars, pop singers, and society figures.

Designing for the Hong Kong market is no easy task, for although there is a regular demand for new items, it is a small clientèle and they are quite difficult to please. Ma, along with other local designers such as Bonita Chung, Lulu Cheung, Vivienne Tam, William Tang, Cecelia Yau, Danny Yu and others, dominate the local scene. Giorgio Armani, Ferragamo, and Prada also are quite visible with their modern twists on the classic figure-hugging cheongsam.

Ma designs around a dozen basics produced in very small quantities, on average from 6 to 24 pieces per design. Comfort is always an important consideration in his work, but the clothes are never safe or dowdy. Ma's look is distinctive with inspiration coming from European fashion capitals like Paris and Milan, modified for the local market. Pinstripes and checks are popular fabrics, suits are a staple. Unusual cutting reveals unexpected parts of the body.

His "two-in-one" look coalesces the case of a single garment with the appearance of two. Combinations of black and white have become another part of his signature. This is applied, somewhat unusually, to jumpsuits and other leisurewear, rather than to business attire. Embroidery and beading are other constant features Ma employs, and locally he has become so influential others frequently mimic his look. He regards this both as an irritation and a compliment. Copyists can threaten a designer's reputation, but they also represent the success of a look or a direction. Hong Kong has also been infamous for designer rip-offs, which also damage the reputation of the credible designers.

Ma has long created fashionable clothing for a market he knows and understands; both he and wife Joyce are preeminent representatives in the Asian design world. The two founded Joyce Boutique Holdings, a Hong Kong-based luxury goods distributor, bringing Giorgio Armani, Hugo Boss, Dolce & Gabbana and Jil Sander clothes into Asia. Yet due to a retail slump in the Far East, Walter and Joyce decided to sell a 20-percent stake in Joyce to Italy's Holding di Partecipazioni Industriali (HdP) in 1998. The infusion of cash helped the struggling firm, but not enough—its star import line, Giorgio Armani, withdrew its lines from Joyce stores. This in turn led to selling a majority interest in Joyce to Strategic Capital Group (SCG), an investment group, in 2000. Yet this too went sour, and the Mas finally found a buyer in Wheelock and Company.

For Walter and Joyce Ma, the move to sell most of the family's shares in Joyce was a firm step into the future—since the errant SCG as well as the new white knight Wheelock specialized in commerce over the Internet. As Joyce Ma told *Women's Wear Daily* (17 April 2000), "We will continue to be a fashion retailer," she explained, "The advantage...from this is that we will not be just an old-economy retailer, but we will also have e-commerce which, in essence, is much wider exposure for our brand name. We were the first to bring luxury European brand names to Asia," she continued, "Now we will be the first to bring the same level of service to our Asian consumers, online, in the new economy."

—Hazel Clark; updated by Daryl F. Mallett and Owen James

MACKIE, Bob

American designer

Born: Robert Gordon Mackie in Monterey Park, California, 24 March 1940. **Education:** Studied advertising and illustration at Pasadena City College; costume design at Chouinard Art Institute, Los Angeles, 1958–60. **Family:** Married Marianne Wolford in 1960 (divorced, 1963); children: Robin. **Career:** Sketch artist for film designers Frank Thompson, Jean Louis, and Edith Head, 1960–63; worked in television as assistant designer to Ray Aghayan, receiving his first screen credit for *The Judy Garland Show,* 1963; designer for *The King Family Show,* 1965, Mitzi Gaynor's night club acts, from 1966, *The Carol Burnett Show,* 1967–78, *The Sonny and Cher Comedy Hour,* 1971–74, and *The Sonny and Cher Show,* 1976–77; designed swimwear for Cole of California, 1976; independent designer of ready-to-wear fashions, with own label Bob Mackie Originals, New York, from 1982; created 1950s costumes for *Moon Over Buffalo,* 1995; introduced fall collection, 1996; designed 1970s

Bob Mackie posing with some of his designs at the "Unmistakably Mackie" retrospective at the Fashion Institute of Technology in New York, 1999. © AP/Wide World Photos.

costumes and scenery in the Cleveland San Jose Ballet's *Blue Suede Shoes,* 1997; designed late-1960s costumes for musical *Pete & Keely.* **Awards:** Emmy award, 1967 (with Ray Aghayan), 1969, 1976, 1978, 1985; Costume Designers Guild award, 1968; American Fashion award, 1975. **Address:** Bob Mackie Originals, 225 West 29th Street, New York, NY 10001, USA

Publications

By MACKIE:

Books

Dressing for Glamor (with Gerry Brenner), New York, 1979.

On MACKIE:

Books

Morris, Bernadine, and Barbara Walz, *The Fashion Makers,* New York, 1978.

Maeder, Edward, et al., *Hollywood and History: Costume Design in Film,* New York, 1987.

Pecktal, Lynn, *Costume Design: Techniques of Modern Masters,* New York, 1993.

Stegemeyer, Anne, *Who's Who in Fashion, Third Edition,* New York, 1996.

DeCaro, Frank, *Unmistakably Mackie: The Fantasy and Fashion of Bob Mackie,* New York, 1999.

Articles

Thomas, Kay, "Spotlighting Two Designers Who Took Broadway by Storm," in the *New York Daily News,* 28 November 1971.

"Bob and Ray," in *Newsweek,* 11 June 1973.

Moore, Didi, "Designing Man," in *US,* 19 January 1982.

Rittersporn, Liz, "Bob Mackie: The World's Most Visible Designer," in the *New York Daily News,* 5 May 1985.

Oney, Steve, "Bob Mackie: Daring, Dazzling Designer to the Stars," in *Cosmopolitan* (London), April 1986.

Milbank, Caroline Rennolds, "Bob Mackie," in *Interview* (New York), December 1986.

Michaels, Debra, "Bob Mackie: Cashing in on the Glamor," in *WWD,* 19 April 1988.

"Bob Mackie," in *Current Biography* (New York), October 1988.

Mansfield, Stephanie, "Bob Mackie, the Boogie-Woogie Bugle Bead Boy of Seventh Avenue, Wants to Be Taken Seriously," in *Vogue* (New York), February 1990.

Finke, Nikki, "Trouble in the House of Mackie," in *Vanity Fair,* June 1993.

Chase, Anthony, "Designer Sketchbook: Moon Over Buffalo," in *TCI* (New York), November 1995.

Schiro, Anne-Marie, "Into the Evening with Elegance," in the *New York Times,* 2 April 1996.

Slingerland, Amy L., "Blue Suede Shoes," in *TCI* (New York), March 1997.

DeCaro, Frank, "Fashion Chat," in *TV Guide,* 22 March 1997.

"Bob Mackie," in *People,* 16 February 1998.

Barbour, David, "ED Designer Sketchbook: Stayin' Alive," in *Entertainment Design* (New York), February 2001.

Szabo, Julia, "All Hams on Deck," in the *New York Times Magazine,* Spring 2001.

* * *

Bob Mackie is one of a handful of designers to work with success in the related but disparate fields of theater and fashion design. He is probably best known for the wittily revealing, glamorous beaded and feathered ensembles he designed for actress and singer Cher since the early 1970s. This collaborative image remains so strong that to visualize Cher is to see her dressed by Mackie. His true genius as an interpretative designer, however, can best be seen in his work for comedian Carol Burnett.

For 11 years, Mackie designed costumes and wigs for Burnett's weekly variety show, including full-scale production numbers to showcase guest artists in elaborate parodies of such classic cult films as *Sunset Boulevard* or *Mildred Pierce.* These character sketches were written for Burnett's company of regular performers, with ongoing stories starring Burnett as one of her various alter egos. In Mrs. Wiggins, for example, Mackie and Burnett created the archetypal "keep busy while doing nothing" secretary, complete with overlong fingernails, brass spittoon-colored perm, stiletto heels, and a skirt so tight walking seemed doubtful and sitting impossible. In this case, the costume first defined the character and thus gave direction to the ensuing scripts. Visually, audiences were led away from the personality of the performer and toward that of the character portrayed. In contrast, Mackie's designs for guest artists always enhanced their

Bob Mackie, fall 2001 "Foreign Intrigue" collection: beaded slip top minidress with an ostrich coat. © AP/Wide World Photos.

visual trademarks, so their personalities remained the focus, supported by wig and costume, even when they played comic or character roles.

When he turned to ready-to-wear in 1982, Mackie's name had been before the television viewing public for 15 years. Women who had admired the casual but elegant tailored outfits Burnett wore to open and close her show or the dramatic allure of Cher's gowns formed an eager and ready market for the first designs from Bob Mackie Originals. The fashion press took rather longer to convince that the aptly dubbed "sultan of sequins, rajah of rhinestones" had the necessary seriousness of purpose to sustain a career on Seventh Avenue. Yet Mackie has always designed day and evening clothing in addition to his theatrical work. As early as 1969, he and partners Ray Aghayan and Elizabeth Courtney established their Beverly Hills boutique, Elizabeth the First, which in turn spawned the short-lived wholesale firm Ray Aghayan/Bob Mackie.

In his 1979 book, *Dressing for Glamor,* Mackie states his belief that glamor is "a state of mind, a feeling of self-confidence." His strength as a designer is an intuitive understanding of what makes a woman feel self-confident and well dressed—solid craftsmanship, attention to detail, clothes that combine wit and artistry with a sense of flair and drama.

In 1995 *Moon Over Buffalo* took to the stage. With Mackie's outstanding costume design and makeup artistry, the Broadway production became a hit. Directed by Tom Moore, the play featured Carol Burnett and Philip Bosco yearning for Hollywood careers. It takes place in the 1950s, in a time where actresses never went anywhere without being made up. Mackie had his work cut out for him: costumes were bold in color and contrasted with room schemes. Referring to a purple-and-white ensemble and a bright green suit, Mackie says, "Those colors are accurate to the period. Clothes were a lot more flamboyant in the 1950s than we're used to seeing now."

In March 1997 *TV Guide* sat down with Mackie to discuss the importance of shock value in fashion. "It gives you something to talk about at the office the next day," the designer explained. But when it comes to hairstyles, Mackie said to stick with what you know, "It's like on your wedding day, don't try a new hairdo. You should look like yourself. My idea of a real movie star is someone who you know who they are, no matter what they play or where they are."

With costuming Vegas showgirls, disco divas, Cher, and numerous Broadway productions in his past, Mackie took his career to a new and different level—ballet. Danced to master recordings of Elvis Presley songs, the Cleveland San Jose Ballet's *Blue Suede Shoes* was the first project in which Mackie designed not only costumes but the sets as well. He is, in fact, one of the few costume designers who has expanded his work into set design.

Responsible for 230 costumes and 12 sets, Mackie's flashy style fit right in with the 1970 trends. With men in bell-bottomed pantsuits and showgirls in brightly sequined body stockings, the show's well-deserved applause speaks for itself. In the off-Broadway musical *Pete & Keely,* Mackie once again nailed the era—the 1960s—perfectly in his designs.

Renowned for costume design after costume design and even set design after set design, Mackie is the first to admit he can't take all the credit. The modest legend claims, "I was showing lingerie while everybody else was showing evening gowns. I was rather well known because of all the people I dressed at the time." That may be true, Mackie, but now perhaps, *you're* the reason others become known.

—Whitney Blausen; updated by Diana Idzelis

MAD CARPENTIER

American design house

Founded: by Mad Maltezos and Suzie Carpentier in Paris, 1939 (taking over from Vionnet after her retirement). **Company History:** House closed, 1957.

Publications

On MAD CARPENTIER:

Books

Perkins, Alice K., *Paris Couturiers and Milliners,* New York, 1949.
Picken, Mary Brooks, and Dora Loues Miller, *Dressmakers of France: The Who, How and Why of the French Couture,* New York, 1956.

Mad Carpentier, 1946 collection: chiffon evening gown. © Genevieve Naylor/CORBIS.

Articles

"Carpentier Likes to Work with Folds," in *WWD,* 14 April 1948.

* * *

There were matters far more urgent in the late 1930s than that which led to the creation of the house of Mad Carpentier in January 1940. The firm's two partners—Mad Maltezos and Suzie Carpentier—banded together when Madeleine Vionnet, their former employer, closed in 1939.

In the unexamined cliché in fashion history and for a number of clients, the two women represented a continuation of Vionnet's bias cut and elegance in fashion combined with a discreet social model, always proper. Twins seized from a most inspired rib, two women balanced to equal one, and perseverance through the war years established an interesting mystique around Mad Carpentier. As Mary

Mad Carpentier, 1946 collection: silk blouse. © Genevieve Naylor/ CORBIS.

Brooks Picken and Dora Loues Miller, authors of *Dressmakers of France: The Who, How, and Why of the French Couture* (New York, 1956) passionately enthused, "When it was almost impossible to think of luxury, of the richness of colors, of the beauty of fabrics, in a city without joy and without light...these two talented women carried on."

Like Antoine de Saint-Exupéry heroines, Maltezos, designer and creative spirit, and Carpentier, refined and cordial proprietress, formerly a Vionnet *vendeuse,* sustained some of the ideas of Vionnet in soft evening clothes, but there were two special and autonomous distinctions for Mad Carpentier. In the late 1940s, Mad Carpentier created evening dresses of extraordinary historical fantasy, attenuating the body with faux bustles and creating the new sumptuousness of postwar evening clothes determined chiefly by silhouette. If these gowns did not achieve the flamboyant success of Fath and Dior in the same years, it is because the Mad Carpentier gowns are too redolent of the past and failed to capture the spirit of the "new" necessary to the marketing and imagination of the postwar era. Though Fath and Dior were both influenced by the past, the belle époque could scarcely be revived in this era without, at least, the veneer of the newest and most extravagant. A Mad Carpentier gown photographed in *L'Officiel* at Christmas in 1947 has New Look traits, but maintains the aura of a Victorian past.

Another hallmark of the house of Mad Carpentier were its remarkable coats, long surpassing the Vionnet tradition. The bravura shapes of Mad Carpentier coats in robust textures were immensely popular in the 1940s and 1950s independent of the Vionnet tradition. In particular, the coats were much imitated by Seventh Avenue, New York manufacturers, often rivaling the ever-popular Balenciaga coats for copying. B. Altman & Co., New York, for example, advertised a romantically sweeping long coat with high collar as "Mad Carpentier's famous coat...beautifully copied in all-wool fleece" in *Vogue,* January 1947. Amplitude, rugged materials, and the swaggering grandeur of riding coats gave both assertiveness and grace to the Mad Carpentier creations.

At Mad Carpentier, the Vionnet tradition was maintained in ease, a desire for easy shaping and even for tying. In the dresses, the full three-dimensionality emphasized by Vionnet was often compromised by an interest in details at the side, as if to reinstate planarity, but in the coats, the effect was to create soft, large volumes. *Women's Wear Daily* (14 April 1948) commented, "the firm has gone its quiet way, and now ranks as a house for clothes of distinctive character rather than one taking an active or publicized role in the general development of the Paris couture. Carpentier clothes have the handmade air of Vionnet, but do not always follow the bias technique of that school of dressmaking."

Linked to Vionnet's innovations in dressmaking, but in fact functioning with little inclination to their inventiveness, Mad Carpentier turned out to be a house of the most traditional dresses, genteel tailoring, and of sensational coats. Its understated, highly proper sensibility was at odds with advanced and aggressive postwar fashion and only in the exuberance of its sculptural coats did the imagination and reputation soar.

—Richard Martin

MADRAZO, Mariano Fortuny y

See FORTUNY (y MADRAZO), Mariano

MAINBOCHER

American designer

Born: Main Rousseau Bocher in Chicago, Illinois, 24 October 1890; adopted name Mainbocher, circa 1929. **Education:** Studied at the Lewis Institute, Chicago, 1907; Chicago Academy of Fine Arts, 1908–09, and at the Art Students' League, New York, 1909–11; attended University of Chicago, 1911, and Königliche Kunstgewerbemuseum, Munich, 1911–12; studied painting with E. A. Taylor, Paris, 1913–14. **Military Service:** American Ambulance Corps, and Intelligence Corps, Paris, 1917–18. **Career:** Lithographer, part-time, New York, 1909–11; sketch artist for clothing manufacturer E.L. Mayer, New York, 1914–17; illustrator, *Harper's Bazaar,* Paris, 1917–21; fashion correspondent, then editor, French *Vogue,* 1922–29; established couturier firm, Paris, 1930–39, and New York, 1939–71; also designed stage costumes, from 1932, and uniforms for American WAVES (U.S. Navy), 1942; American Girl Scouts, 1946; American Red Cross, 1948; U.S. Women's Marine Corps, 1951. **Exhibitions:** *Fashion on Stage: Couture for the Broadway Theater, 1910–55,* New York, 1999. **Collections:** Mainbocher

Mainbocher, 1949 collection: satin gown. © Genevieve Naylor/CORBIS.

sketchbooks, Costume Institute at the Metropolitan Museum of Art.
Died: 27 December 1976.

PUBLICATIONS

On MAINBOCHER:

Books

Levin, Phyllis Lee, *The Wheels of Fashion,* New York, 1965.

Lee, Sarah Tomerlin, editor, *American Fashion: The Life and Lines of Adrian, Mainbocher, McCardell, Norell, and Trigère,* New York, 1975, 1987.

Milbank, Caroline Rennolds, *Couture: The Great Designers,* New York, 1985.

———, *New York Fashion: The Evolution of American Style,* New York, 1989.

Stegemeyer, Anne, *Who's Who in Fashion, Third Edition,* New York, 1996.

Mainbocher, spring 1958 collection: wool suit with a halter top of lace over shantung. © Bettmann/CORBIS.

Articles

"Mainbocher," in *Current Biography,* February 1942.

"Mainbocher," special monograph issue of *Harper's Bazaar,* July 1967.

"Mainbocher: Great Gentleman of Fashion," in *Harper's Bazaar,* June 1971.

"Mainbocher," [obituary], in the *Times* (London), 5 January 1977.

"The Career of Mainbocher Discussed," in the *Times,* 14 January 1977.

Lawford, Valentine, "A Look Back in Fashion," in *Architectural Digest* (Los Angeles), September 1988.

Cunningham, Bill, "An Elegant Blast From the Past," in the *New York Times,* 24 September 2000.

* * *

The snob appeal of patronizing an American couturier with a French sounding name—extremely successful in Paris for a decade before his arrival in the United States—appealed to the socially élite trade in 1940 New York. No less appealing was the fact that Mainbocher had designed the Duchess of Windsor's trousseau upon her marriage in 1937. In 1930, after several years as editor of French *Vogue,* Mainbocher suddenly decided to channel his artistic sensibilities into the establishment of a couture salon in Paris. Editorial experience enabled him to sense what would become fashionable and to package himself as an exclusive designer to the wealthy and the titled.

From the start, Mainbocher specialized in simple, conservative, elegant, and extremely expensive fashions, the luxury of cut, materials, and workmanship that could only be recognized by those in the know. Most importantly, the clothes, exquisitely finished inside and out, gave self-confidence to the women who wore them.

Mainbocher considered his contemporary Chanel too plebeian, and Schiaparelli too avant-garde. Instead, he admired Vionnet and borrowed her bias-cut technique for his own simple slip evening dresses in the 1930s. Twenty years later, a very similar slip design was employed by Mainbocher, produced in a signature elegant silk velvet fabric. From Augustabernard, another 1920s French dress designer, Mainbocher was inspired not only to form his name, but to use godets in skirts, and shoulder bows to catch the folds of draped bodices. Frequent Mainbocher suit treatments in the 1930s included short capelet effects or dropped shoulders widening into full sleeves. The designer knew his clientèle personally and designed for the lives they led, specializing in evening clothes. For resort wear he ventured into a mix-and-match ensemble consisting of matching top, skirt, bathing suit, and hat. Slim, demure black wool dresses for daytime would sport white chiffon interest at the throat.

While Mainbocher did use some Japanese-like kimonos as eveningwear during this period, his hallmark was nonaggressive, not exaggerated or period dressing. A touch of labor-intensive luxury would be bestowed by all-over sequins on an evening jacket or on a bare top worn discreetly under a jacket. The grayish-blue, "Wallis blue," of the Duchess of Windsor's wedding dress, as well as the long, fluid crêpe dress itself, was widely copied. The simple, conservative elegance of Mainbocher's style, feminine but not fussy, perfectly suited the slim, severe good looks of the Duchess and wealthy women like her. Additionally, she was honoring a fellow American.

In 1934 Mainbocher introduced the boned strapless bodice, and before the war forced him to leave Paris, a waist cincher, forming tiny waisted, pleated and skirted dresses that presaged Dior's postwar New Look. Mainbocher's arrival in New York coincided perfectly with the city élite's love for French couture, for though he epitomized it, he satisfied their patriotism because he was actually an American. Society matrons such as C.Z. Guest and the Vanderbilts, and stage actresses such as Mary Martin, avidly patronized this "most expensive custom dressmaker" who made women look and feel exquisitely well-bred.

Accedance to wartime economies resulted in Mainbocher's short evening dresses, and versatile cashmere sweaters—beaded, lined in silk, and closed by jeweled buttons—designed to keep women warm in their bare evening gowns. Another practical wartime innovation, the "glamor belt," an apron-like, sequined or bead-encrusted accessory, could be added to embellish any plain costume. Practically gratis, Mainbocher designed uniforms for the U.S. Women's Marine Corps, the WAVES (Navy), the American Red Cross, and the Girl Scouts.

As the years progressed, Mainbocher continued to design exclusively on a made-to-order basis, refusing to license his name. La Galerie, a department in his salon, did produce clothes in standard sizes, a compromise for busy women without time for lengthy fittings. The reverse snobbery of the humble pastel gingham or cotton piqué used for fancy dresses appealed to Mainbocher's clientèle, as did refined tweed suits with subtle dressmaker touches such as curved bands or fabric appliqués, worn with coordinating bare-armed blouses. A Mainbocher standby was the little black "nothing" sheath dress.

By the 1950s and 1960s, old guard Mainbocher customers enjoyed wearing impeccably made classic coats and suits of wool, often furlined, in the midst of nouveau-riche ostentation. The typical ladylike daytime Mainbocher look was accessorized by a plain velvet bow in the hair instead of a hat, a choker of several strands of real pearls, white gloves, and plain pumps with matching handbag. The integrity of luxurious fabrics, intricate cut, quality workmanship and materials, elegance and classicism, were cherished and worn for years by Mainbocher's upper crust customers.

—Therese Duzinkiewicz Baker

MALDEN MILLS INDUSTRIES, INC.

American textile manufacturer

Founded: in Malden, Massachusetts, by Henry Feuerstein as Malden Knitting, 1906. **Company History:** Malden Knitting expanded to include Malden Spinning and Dyeing, 1923; provided U.S. Army uniforms during World War I and II; company moved to Lawrence, Massachusetts, 1950s; developed synthetic fabric (later named Polarfleece), 1979; betted heavy on fake fur and lost, 1981; Polarfleece products selling under Polartec label flourish, 1980s; clothed the U.S. Winter Olympics team, 1992; fire wiped out major operations, 1995; opened rebuilt state-of-the-art mill facility, 1996; closed upholstery division and satellite mill, 1998; settled suit against company, 2000; forced to declare bankruptcy, 2001. **Awards:** citation from President Clinton, 1996; *Workforce* Magazine Optimas award for Managing Change, 1997. **Company Address:** 46 Stafford Street, Lawrence, MA 01841.

Publications

On MALDEN MILLS:

Articles

"Performance Fleece Fabrics Force New Insulating Frontiers," in *Sporting Goods Business,* September 1991.

Rotenier, Nancy, "The Golden Fleece," in *Forbes,* 24 May 1993.

Diesenhouse, Susan, "A Textile Maker Thrives by Breaking All the Rules," in the *New York Times,* 24 July 1994.

Lee, Melissa, "Malden Looks Spiffy in New England Textile Gloom," in the *Wall Street Journal,* 10 November 1995.

Herszenhorn, David M., "A Plume of Hope Rises from Factory Ashes…" in the *New York Times,* 16 December 1995.

Witkowski, Tim, "The Glow From a Fire," in *Time,* 8 January 1996.

Jerome, Richard, and Stephen Sawicki, "Holding the Line," in *People,* 5 February 1996.

Teal, Thomas, "Not a Fool; Not a Saint," in *Fortune,* 11 November 1996.

Owens, Mitchell, "A Mill Community Comes Back to Life," in the *New York Times,* 26 December 1996.

Goldberg, Carey, "A Promise is Kept," in the *New York Times,* 16 September 1997.

Luscombe, Belinda, "Good Old Factory Values," in *Time,* 29 September 1997.

"Malden Mills Workers Sue Employer," in *Claims,* February 2000.

* * *

Henry Feuerstein, a Hungarian immigrant, bought a small mill in Malden, Massachusetts, in 1906. At Malden Knitting, Feuerstein set about making wool "workmen's" sweaters and bathing suits. His enterprise flourished and expanded, adding Malden Spinning and Dyeing in 1923 to produce uniforms for the U.S. Army throughout World Wars I and II. By the end of the World War II, Feuerstein's son Samuel had taken the reins of the company, and Malden Knitting had begun exploring new kinds of textiles to increase production.

In the mid-1950s the company moved to Lawrence, Massachusetts, and within a decade had opened several branch mills. Samuel was succeeded by his son, Aaron, who took Malden Mills into the future with automation and increased research into synthetic fabrics. Though going into fake fur proved a near-fatal blunder and the company was forced into Chapter 11 in 1981, Aaron Feuerstein and Malden Mills soon revolutionized the textile industry with a new product called Polarfleece. Originally created in 1979, Polarfleece was 100-percent polyester, capable of drawing moisture away from the body while providing warmth, and became the fabric of choice for high-performance athletic and aerobic apparel. Among Malden's first major customers was outerwear producer Patagonia, which ordered a myriad of garments made from the unusual shearling knit. Soon outfitters from across the country were bombarding Malden with orders.

With its Chapter 11 woes behind it and an incredible surge of business due to Polarfleece, Malden created several new lines of high-performance, technically advanced fabrics to service the outdoor crowd. Customized colors, thicknesses, and textures were made for clients, though imitators were many. By the end of the 1980s Malden Mills had expanded into Europe; by the end of the following decade Polarfleece, marketed and trademarked Polartec, was available in over 1,000 patterns, 5,000 colors, and 100 products—from underwear, bike shorts, and sweatshirts to jackets, wet suits, and gloves. Polartec was the industry leader; its Polarfleece was fast wicking, easily dyed, durable, partially made from recycled materials, and had one of the only nonpilling finishes. Clients like Eddie Bauer, Land's End, L.L. Bean, Ralph Lauren, and many others often based their entire outdoor or athletic collections on Polartec fabrics.

Malden began producing natural jacquard velvets in 1992, which were used in clothing as well as a number of upholstery applications, including furniture and car and infant seats. Sold the world over, the upholstery business rivaled the Polarfleece operations, but the latter initiated the Polartec Performance Challenge, sponsoring outdoor adventures like the Trango Towers Expedition in Southern Pakistan and a 4,000-mile trek in China. Malden also supported the 1992 Winter Olympics by providing Polartec fabric for the official garments worn by U.S. athletes.

Everything changed in 1995; the U.S. Consumer Products Safety Commission televised reports of fleece fabrics catching fire in March, and though the products were not Polartec, consumers across the nation began returning Polartec products. Malden fired a salvo of its own, launching a massive ($8.5 million) advertising campaign outlining the company's standards and its government inflammability tests (passed with flying colors). Not long after the company solidified plans for the textile manufacturing plant in Germany (as a companion to an existing Rotterdam facility), tragedy struck in December 1995.

Aaron Feuerstein was celebrating his 70th birthday in a Boston restaurant when there was a tremendous explosion at Malden Mills. Fire swept through three of the company's nine buildings, injuring 33 employees and causing some $500 million in damage. Feuerstein had rushed to the scene and immediately vowed to rebuild; within a few days he had set 2 January 1996 as the company's reopening date. Feuerstein stated he not only would pay all employees their regular salaries for the next month or more, while continuing health benefits for the next three months during rebuilding, but would give all employees a small Christmas bonus.

Some called Feuerstein a saint; others a fool for not taking the insurance money and running. But most were so impressed, including Malden clients and neighboring businesses, that they too chipped in to rebuild and support the community's workers. All in all, it was a risky endeavor, but within three weeks the factory was reopened and half of Malden's workforce was in place. The new Malden Mills complex reopened in September 1996 and all was well for about a year. Then came the closure of its upholstery division in 1998, which had lost its footing after being completely destroyed. With a mild winter and an overseas recession that rocked the usually stalwart Polartec sales, Feuerstein was forced to close a satellite mill in Bridgeton and lay off hundreds of workers (who were, true to the Malden spirit, given generous severance packages).

The story of Malden Mills continued to be an eventful one; in January 2000, employees who had been injured in the 1995 fire bit the hand that had fed and clothed them—suing Feuerstein and the company for negligence. The employees had just days earlier settled an $18 million lawsuit against several Malden suppliers who they blamed for the fire. Malden itself had been cleared in a 22-month investigation by the Massachusetts Fire Marshal and in a similar investigation by the Industrial Accidents Board. Feuerstein and the disgruntled employees settled the lawsuit in December 2000; terms were not disclosed. Though Feuerstein valiantly tried to prevent it, Malden Mills was forced to declare bankruptcy in late 2001. Given the firm's history of rising from its ashes, hopefully this is another temporary lull from which Feuerstein and his employees would emerge anew.

Malden Mills will forever be remembered for two things: the generosity of Aaron Feuerstein and his unswerving belief in his company and its products. Polartec fleece products, which are now made from 100-percent recycled materials, revolutionized the textile industry and remain the fabric of choice among discriminating clothiers.

—Owen James

MALTEZOS, Mad

See MAD CARPENTIER

MANDELLI, Mariuccia

Italian fashion designer

Mariuccia Mandelli, designed for Krizia's fall/winter 2001–02 Top luxury line collection. © AP/Wide World Photos.

Born: Bergamo, Italy, 1933. **Family:** Married to Aldo Pinto. **Career:** Elementary school teacher, Milan, 1952–54, designer/founder, with Flora Dolci, of Krizia fashion firm, Milan, from 1954; showed first collection, Krizia, 1957; first major fashion show, 1964; founded Kriziamaglia knitwear, 1966, and Kriziababy children's clothes, 1968; subsequently established Krizia boutiques in Milan, Tokyo, London, New York, Detroit, Houston; owner, the K Club, West Indies, from 1996; launched home collection, 1997; signed with Grace Silver to open three Krizia stores in China, 1998; several new licensing agreements, including Krizia World, Krizia Eyewear, Segreti di Krizia, and Krizia Kids, 1999; introduced new fragrance, *Easy Krizia,* 1999; Alber Elbaz hired as design consultant, then replaced by Jean-Paul Knott, 2000; new boutique opened in Moscow, 2000. **Exhibitions:** *Italian Revolution*, La Jolla Museum of Art, California, 1982; *40 Years of Italian Fashion,* Trump Towers, New York, 1983; traveling retrospective, Grey Art Gallery, New York, 1999. **Awards:** Fashion Press award, Florence, 1964; made a Knight of the Italian Republic, Rome, 1986; named "Ideal Woman Leader of the Year," St. Vincent, Italy, 1987. **Address:** Krizia SpA, Via Manin 19, 20121 Milan, Italy. **Website:** www.krizia.net.

PUBLICATIONS

On MANDELLI:

Books

Lambert, Eleanor, *The World of Fashion: People, Places, Resources,* New York & London, 1976.

Mariuccia Mandelli, designed for Krizia's fall/winter 2001 collection. © AP/Wide World Photos.

Mulassano, Adrianna, *I Mass-Moda: Fatti e Personaggi dell'Italian Look,* Florence, 1979.
Aragno, B.G., compiler, *40 Years of Italian Fashion* [exhibition catalogue], Rome, 1983.
Kennett, Frances, *The Collector's Book of Twentieth Century Fashion,* London & New York, 1983.
McDowell, Colin, *McDowell's Directory of Twentieth Century Fashion,* London, 1984.
O'Hara, Georgia, *Encyclopedia of Fashion from 1840 to the 1980s,* London, 1986.
Sparke, Penny, et al., *The Design Source Book,* London, 1986.
Vercelloni, Isa, *Krizia: A Story,* Milan, 1995.
Stegemeyer, Ann, *Who's Who in Fashion, Third Edition,* New York, 1996.

Articles

"Nostalgia and Romance in Italy," in the *New York Times,* 11 March 1992.
"Sleek as a Leopard, Bold as a Zebra: When Animal Prints are Your Second Skin," in *Harper's Bazaar,* September 1992.
Lindbergh, Peter, "Don't Be Fooled by the Small Prints," in *Harper's Bazaar,* March 1993.
Morris, Bernadine, "Soft, Sexy Fashion in Milan," in the *New York Times,* 10 March 1993.
Gellers, Stan, "Expanding on Krizia's Platonic Ideal," in *Daily News Record,* 13 December 1993.
Forden, Sara Gay, "Krizia's Mandelli Details Story of Forced Payoff," in *DNR,* 22 September 1994.
Salfino, Catherine, and Sara Gay Forden, "Designing Women," in *DNR,* 18 January 1995.
Ashby, Don, "Dressing Long and Lean," in the *New York Times Magazine,* 26 February 1995.
Menkes, Suzy, "Berets are Off to Krizia," in the *International Herald Tribune,* 7 March 1995.
Alhadeff, Gini, "La Beauté Platonicienne de Krizia," in *Vogue* (Paris), April 1995.
Forden, Sara Gay, "Some Top Italian Designers Facing Criminal Indictments Over Bribes," in *DNR,* 8 June 1995.
———, "Milanese Designers to Present United Defense in Bribe Case," in *DNR,* 11 September 1995.
"Krizia's Spring Collection Hits All the Right Buttons," in *Elle,* March 1996.
Brown, Alix, and Jennifer Jackson, "Special K(rizia)," in *Harper's Bazaar,* May 1996.
Forden, Sara Gay, "Designer Bribe Trial Gets Started in Milan," in *WWD,* 8 July 1996.
Conti, Samantha, "Ferré, Santo Versace and Mandelli Sentenced to 14 Months; Under Italian Law, Prison Terms Will be Suspended," in *DNR,* 5 May 1997.
———, "Verdict Against Milan Designers Overturned," in *WWD,* 26 January 1998.
"Krizia," in *WWD,* 24 February 1998.
Ilari, Alessandra, "Krizia's 45-Year Variety Show," in *WWD,* 14 April 1999.
Socha, Miles, "Krizia Eyes U.S. Comeback," in *WWD,* 2 February 2000.
"Krizia Bows in Moscow," in *WWD,* 22 November 2000.
Colavita, Courtney, "Elbaz Leaves Krizia After Three Months," in *WWD,* 30 November 2000.
"Sexpots and Prairie Babes...Mariuccia Mandelli's Krizia and Jean-Paul Knott's Krizia Top Collections," in *WWD,* 1 October 2001.

* * *

The success of the Milanese firm Krizia and, in fact, the prominence of Milanese fashion that occurred during the 1980s and 1990s are both largely due to the efforts of Krizia's founder and designer, Mariuccia Mandelli. Originally an elementary school teacher, Mandelli cofounded the company in 1957 with Flora Dolci and took its name from Plato's dialogue on female vanity. Mandelli was an originator of the major contrast trend in which simple, classic tailoring was punctuated with original and amusing accents to create a new face for stylish ready-to-wear that was both eminently wearable and exuberantly youthful.

Among Krizia's early, important presentations was a showing at Orsini's on the invitation of Jean Rosenberg, vice president of Bendel's. It was on this occasion that Mandelli was labeled Crazy Krizia by the fashion press for her combinations of simple shapes with madcap details. In 1976 Bergdorf Goodman featured stock by Krizia and other Milan designers, providing the final step necessary for the Italians' rise to the forefront of the fashion industry.

Representative of what has been called Krizia's "rough and sweet" look are Mandelli's 1977 outfittings consisting of nylon undershirts topped by matching rose-colored, dove-gray mohair bed jackets, or cardigans in open-knit weaves worn with dropped-waist ballerina skirts of scalloped lace. Mandelli's daywear tends toward the practical. She has, for example, put elastic waistbands on her skirts for comfortable ease of movement, and her 1982 group of sports suits of loose tweeds and checks were plain, loose, and stylized. Mandelli's use of her signature "improbable contrasts," however, abound most openly in her evening clothes, such as the mixes of satin skirts with sporty Angora sweaters. She has also presented simple slip dresses accompanied by characteristic touches of humorous flamboyance such as a long, feathered stoles or quilted jackets of satin faced in a different shade of the same color.

Mandelli has often used jodhpur pants. One 1977 outfit consisted of loose, draping jodhpurs in silk charmeuse worn with a lacy mohair camisole, the whole enlivened by the glowing berry colors she featured that year. Also among Mandelli's original fashion accomplishments is her development of what she named "harmonica pleats," which combine vertical and horizontal pleatings. Outstanding among Mandelli's designs are her knits, which include items such as her 1977 lacy, mushroom-colored evening sweater teamed with silk and eyelet taffeta and jodhpur pants. In 1981, she showed subtly sophisticated shiny knits and white Angoras bedecked with yokes of pearls.

Often appearing on Mandelli's knitwear have been her signature animal motifs, such as a jacquard crêpe blouse with the front view of a tiger on its front and rear tiger-view on its back. Not limiting herself to knitwear, Mandelli has also put highly colorful birds and parrots on that season's summer tote bags and shoulder purses. For 1984 it was the Dalmatian, sharing the scene with more streamlined suits and double-dresses such as a back-buttoned flare over a bit longer slim skirt.

In the mid-1990s, the Italian fashion world was rocked by the exposure of a bribery scandal that supposedly occurred in 1990. Top officials from Italian design houses, including Giorgio Armani, Santo Versace, Gianfranco Ferré, Mandelli, and Giralomo Etro were investigated for bribing tax officials, but the designers argued the money was nothing more than extortion by those same officials. The nasty court battle ended in 1997 when Mandelli, Versace, and Ferré were convicted and sentenced; luckily for the defendants, the sentences were suspended and in 1998 the convictions overturned.

During the infamous court proceedings, Mandelli continued to do what she did best—showing in 1996 a collection based on traditional Chinese shapes, Indian saris, Mongolian leather, and Japanese design. "It's all about very pure, simple straight lines," Mandelli said in a CNN interview. Around the same time, Mandelli fell in love with the Caribbean island of Barbuda. There she built the K Club, described by TravelWizard.com as "a personalized retreat of square, white bungalows with louvered windows and characteristic spired roofs." The cottages were designed by architect Gianni Gamondi, and the interiors reflected "Krizia's design taste right down to the doorknobs. Wooden cathedral ceilings, 14 feet high, and white ceramic tile floors add to the sense of spaciousness in the rooms."

In the fashion world, many men design clothing for women; the reverse, women designing clothing for men, is not so prominent. Mandelli is among the few women who are well known for their men's clothing lines. The small sorority of designers includes Jhane Barnes, Laura Biagiotti, Katharine Hamnett, Donna Karan, Rei Kawakubo, and Nicole Miller. Mandelli repeatedly delivers though, as the *Daily News Record* (15 January 1997) enthused over a Milan menswear showing, "This collection showed what buyers really come to Milan for—sharp, comfortable clothes that make any man look good."

In the last years of the century, Mandelli sought design help from several sources. The most high profile was Alber Elbaz, formerly of Yves Saint Laurent, who was hired as a consultant in 2000. The collaboration, however, lasted only three months; Elbaz left, citing his wish to return to Paris and denying any friction with Mandelli. Elbaz was soon replaced by Jean-Paul Knott, who had also worked at Yves Saint Laurent before launching his own label. For nearly five decades, Krizia has remained an integral part of the Italian fashion scene, and one of the few independent design houses left. Mariuccia Mandelli and her Krizia empire, with close to 60 worldwide boutiques and more than three-dozen licensing agreements, combines highly original designs with nervy eccentricity and wit.

—Barbara Cavaliere; updated by Owen James and Daryl F. Mallett

MANN, Judy

Chinese designer

Born: Mann Lai-Yin in Hong Kong, China, 13 August 1946. **Education:** Good Hope School, Hong Kong, 1962–65. **Family:** Married David Hsu Kin, 1974. **Career:** Model; Fashion coordinator and merchandiser, 1972, junior stylist, 1973, chief designer for Roncelli and R-2 labels, 1974–77; formed own company, Cheetah Management, June 1977, with Judy Mann, J.M. Diffusion, and Cheetah labels; showed first collection in London and Paris, 1979; opened first boutique, Taipei, 1984; cofounder, 1984, chair, 1984–85, 1989–95, Hong Kong Fashion Designers Association; marketing, advertising and promotion consultant, Continental Jewellery Ltd., Hong Kong, 1989–91; chief editor, Videofashion (Chinese version), Hong Kong, 1990–91; fashion consultant, Romano Group, Hong Kong, 1991–92; formed Beijing Charisma Fashion Co. Ltd., a joint venture company with the Chinese government, with outlets in Beijing & Shanghai, a production factory in Canton, 1993; formed the Consultant Group, 1998; signature fragrance, *Judy Mann.* **Exhibitions:** Hong Kong Design Gallery (permanent collection). **Awards:** Ten Best Dressed Personalities award, 1977. **Address:** Cheetah Management Co. Ltd., 5/F East Wing, 14–24 Wellington Street Central, Hong Kong, China; **Website:** www.judymann.com.

PUBLICATIONS

On MANN:

Articles

Russell, Tara, "Judy Mann Builds on Her Reputation," in *Style,* July 1987.

Cheung, Raymond, "Sketches of Designers: Judy Mann," in *New Wave,* June 1988.

"Hong Kong Designers: Perseverance Is Paying Off," in *WWD* (Asia), 22 July 1988.

Gopinath, Sharmila, "Vanity under the Rose, Vanity on the Go," in *Lifestyle Asia,* September 1988.

"Winter Fashion: Back to Classics," in the *Bulletin* (Hong Kong), September 1989.
Chen, Kent, "Cultural Obstacles Block Local Talent," in the *South China Morning Post,* 22 April 1990.
Bartlett, Frances, "Settings for Love: Judy Mann," in *Beautiful Home,* October 1990.
Allemann, Angela, "Hong Kong: Frauen Ganz Oben. Fünf mal Erfolg," in *Annabelle,* 13 November 1990.
Bourke, Marion, "Designs on Hong Kong," in *Eve Magazine* (Hong Kong), January 1991.
Chu, Kennis, "Top Designer Prepares for Fashion Week," in the *Sunday Morning Post* (Hong Kong), 13 January 1991.
Stravinsky, Sonya, "Judy Mann: Designing," in *Boutique,* Summer 1991.
McDonald, Claire, "Image is Everything," available online at TimesNet Asia, www.web3.asia1.com.sg, 1999.
Crampton, Thomas, "Master Mimics of Hong Kong," in the *International Herald Tribune,* 16 March 2001.

*

I design for young executive women who are alert to fashion trends, but by no means a slave to them; who know what suits them and want to look presentable and efficient, yet stylish and sophisticated. My objective is to offer quality clothes at affordable prices.

My designs have to reach most women, not just a limited number.... My collection very much reflects my own lifestyle, a working woman of the modern days. I like very simple silhouettes with perfect cut, quality fabric, and good color coordination. I prefer separates and coordinates to dresses, as they give customers more flexibility; colors you don't easily get tired of, which will last more than one season, and still look elegant and stylish; clothes that you can always change the look of by adding different accessories.

I don't believe that only intricately designed clothes can make a woman look outstanding. A well-coordinated, simple outfit can achieve the same effect, or better.... As a designer, it is important to know your clientèle, to know how to put a collection together—concept, sampling, fabrication, coloring—and make sure it can be put into production. We are not from the tailoring era. We are the age of mass- or semimass production. My design inspiration comes mainly from the lifestyle of modern women, things happening around me, and the culture of my own race and that of others.

—Judy Mann

* * *

Judy Mann is an influential figure in Hong Kong fashion. As a designer, fashion merchandiser, and coordinator, cofounder and two-time former chair of the Hong Kong Fashion Designers Association, she knows her business very well. After graduating from the Good Hope School in Hong Kong in 1965, Mann became a model, a job that helped her learn the importance of market awareness and of being aware of her clientèle. As Mann herself says, "Most women are not built like catwalk models, so I believe in workable styles, easy to make and easy to wear." She quickly moved behind the scenes, taking a job as a fashion coordinator and merchandiser at Thayer International New York in 1972, and worked her way up the chain to junior stylist (1973), and then becoming the chief designer for the Roncelli and R-2 labels of that company from 1974 to 1977. Along the way, however, she did find time to get married, to David Hsu Kin, in 1974. Three years later, Mann formed her own company, Cheetah Management Co. Ltd., beginning with the Judy Mann, J.M. Diffusion, and Cheetah labels. She showed her first collection, mostly made of silk, in London and Paris in 1979. Mann worked hard over the next five years, designing her own lines and eventually opening her own boutique in Taipei, Taiwan, in 1984.

Mann has also worked hard to help promote Hong Kong as a creative fashion center. In 1984 she was a founding member of the Hong Kong Fashion Designers Association, which she has chaired twice. The group has done enormous work over the last 15 years to dispel the image of Hong Kong as a production base by encouraging and promoting local fashion designers. Annual fashion shows, its "Young Talent award," Hong Kong Fashion Week, and regular contact between members have helped strengthen the designer's position in the industry. "Being a designer in Hong Kong is not easy—you have to struggle and struggle," for although there is a regular demand for new items, it is a small clientèle and they are quite difficult to please. Mann's position as a role model and a champion for more support of the local industry has paid off in spades with greater encouragement by the local media and increased financial backing than in years past. The worldwide exposure gained by local talent on the Internet has also helped immensely. Now, designers like Bonita Chung, Lulu Cheung, Arthur Lam, Walter Ma, Vivienne Tam, William Tang, and Danny Yu dominate the local scene and enjoy some international success as well. Hong Kong fashion has come a long way in a short time and is poised to achieve much more in the new century.

Designing fashion garments has not been the only focus of Mann's career. She was the first Hong Kong designer to have her own perfume, *Judy Mann,* produced for her in Switzerland. She spent two years working with Continental Jewelery Ltd. as a part-time consultant responsible for marketing, advertising, and promotion. She had a brief stint as the chief editor of the Chinese edition of *VideoFashion.* She started her own fashion consultancy with the Romano Group, which owned over a dozen retail outlets in Hong Kong specializing in European menwear and womenswear. At the same time, she licensed her label to a local garment manufacturer, who produced three collections a year, founded a joint venture with the Chinese government called Beijing Charisma Fashion Co. Ltd., and opened outlets in Beijing and Shanghai and a production factory in Canton.

Although a businesswoman as well as a designer, Mann does know her customers very well. They are young professional women who want to appear efficient yet stylish. She specializes in coordinated daywear, separates, and informal eveningwear. It is a young, sophisticated look, which she calls "casual chic." The image reflects her own way of dressing. Simple silhouettes, quality fabrics, and colors that can mix and match are her trademark. Although her collections reflect seasonal trends and colors, half are classics, in neutral easy-to-match colors that are guaranteed to sell. And yet, because Mann is a professional woman herself, sales are her motivation. "Every sketch I make has to be thought out, rethought, and then designed with a view to selling."

Mann works for export, chiefly to Europe, where she is fast gaining a reputation. Japan, Australia, and the Middle East are other major foreign markets where her garments can be found in specialty boutiques and stores. She designs a little for the U.S., but only in silk, a fabric not subject to quota restrictions. For the same reason, her first European collection under her own label, Cheetah, was also in silk. Nowadays she likes working in jersey, Swiss cotton, and Italian linens and wools, fabrics that are comfortable and travel well. Designing for export poses creative challenges; colors have to be chosen carefully to complement different skin tones. A neutral palette provides the basis for each season. In winter, black dominates, and in summer, white is heightened by brighter shades. The designs of Judy Mann continue to represent and champion the Hong Kong fashion scene.

—Hazel Clark; updated by Daryl F. Mallett

MANSON, Glen

See FENN WRIGHT MANSON

MARA, Max

See MAX MARA SpA

MARAMOTTI, Achille

See MAX MARA SpA

MARC, Andrew

American designer

Family: Married Suzanne Schwartz. **Career:** Launched the Andrew Marc line, 1981; developed leather and fur bomber jacket designs, 1981; founded Precision International for watch manufacture and distribution, 1986. **Address:** 390 Fifth Avenue, Suite 606, New York, NY 10018, USA.

Publications

On MARC:

Articles

"Marc's New Man," in *WWD,* 1 September 1998.
"Andrew Marc Said Near Pact for Levi's Dockers Outwear," in *Daily News Record,* 23 September 1998.
Gilbert, Daniela, "The Newest Faces," in *WWD,* 3 January 2001.

* * *

Fine leather apparel and luxurious watches are the trademarks that put Andrew Marc in the luxury fashion industry. Beginning in 1981 with the introduction of his famous leather and fur bomber jacket, Marc has climbed the fashion ladder by setting his designs apart from the rest. He quickly developed leather and cloth outerwear collections based on the concepts driven by his jackets. By doing so, he has become a leader in setting style rather than following the trends of the time.

Marc's company performs all design work in-house and generally begins the design process up to one year in advance of the selling season. His apparel is described as upscale, but secondary labels such as Marc and Andrew Marc Additions are used for upper-moderately priced and bridge designs. With this marketing strategy, Marc is best known for having a strong sense of his customers.

Andrew Marc Schwartz is partnered with his wife, Suzanne Schwartz. Together they combine their unique abilities to cater to the masculine and the feminine. The result is high-quality, mass-appeal fashion. When working with leather, the Andrew Marc collection uses all techniques for designs, including waxing, distress, tie-dye, and watercolor. With today's technology, Marc can produce a very thin and supple coat of wax, which gives the skin a smooth polished finish to the touch, but which is still sturdy. In 2000, as wearing suede and leather became more of a year-round fashion trend, Marc's jackets and skirts were in higher demand. For the spring 2001 collection, Marc will offer the waxed leathers in a variety of pastel colors.

In 1986 Marc began producing elegant timepiece watches under the Precision International company. The look and design of the rugged yet exquisite watches were inspired by the Marc bomber jackets. The watches are unique by virtue of their styling and quality is assured by its Swiss-made components and stainless steel construction. Jewels such as synthetic sapphires and rubies are located in the places most subject to wear due to friction. All watches are water-resistant to 330 feet and targeted to consumers who are fashion-oriented, yet want a watch to be sporty, refined, and with easy-to-read features.

By 1998 Marc ventured out to produce a collection of leather and cloth outerwear under the Levi's Dockers label. The new line consisted of women's leather and cloth Dockers outerwear, as well as men's leather Dockers outerwear. Marc continues to develop leather and cloth apparel as well as his unique and elegant watches. His style is modern and chic. Hehas always been a trendsetter, never a follower in the fashion industry. He takes both the masculine and the feminine to create looks that are unique and appealing to all customers. Andrew Marc designs are created to last through time.

—Kimbally A. Medeiros

MARCASIANO, Mary Jane

American designer

Born: Morristown, New Jersey, 23 September 1955. **Education:** Attended Montclair State College, Montclair, New Jersey; graduated from Parsons School of Design, New York, 1978. **Career:** Showed first collection, 1979; launched Mary Jane Marcasiano Company, New York, from 1980; introduced menswear line, 1982; licenses from 1985 include shoes and jewelry; business bought by Hampshire Designs, New York, 1995; Marisa Christina, Inc. acquires label, 1998. **Exhibitions:** *All American: A Sportswear Tradition,* Fashion Institute of Technology, April-June 1985. **Collections:** Fashion Institute of Technology, New York City. **Awards:** Cartier Stargazer award, 1981; Wool Knit Association award, 1983; Dupont Most Promising Designer award, 1984; Cutty Sark Most Promising Menswear Designer award, 1984. **Address:** 138 Spring Street, New York, NY 10018, USA.

Publications

On MARCASIANO:

Books

Stegemeyer, Anne, *Who's Who in Fashion, Third Edition,* New York, 1996.

Articles

"Making It Big in Prime Time," in *Harper's Bazaar,* April 1988.

Boyes, Kathleen, "Mary Jane Marcasiano: Staying in the Arts," in *WWD,* 6 June 1988.

Starzinger, Page Hill, "Smart Women, Smart Clothes," in *Vogue,* September 1988.

Matousek, Mark, "Mary Jane Marcasiano," in *Harper's Bazaar,* October 1988.

Socha, Miles, "Marcasiano's Luxury Revival," in *WWD,* 25 February 1998.

D'Innocenzio, Anne, "New Designs for Marcasiano," in *WWD,* 12 May 1999.

*

My design philosophy and how I want to look as a woman have always been intertwined. My first collection came out of a desire to wear something that didn't exist yet. There is always a dual purpose when I design—the aesthetics of the line and color have to coexist with wearability. Therefore, I test all the yarns and fabrics first on myself.

Color is where I start when I'm working on a new collection, simultaneously matching color with the surface of the yarn or fabric to enhance the color impact. My goal is to create a wearable surface of color, texture, and light. My shapes are simple. I like the ease of knitwear, giving enough room for the garment to move around the body, both covering and revealing it. Necklines are very important to my designs. I use simple geometric shapes to create a presentation of the face, neck, and decolleté.

I am designing for the lifestyle of the modern woman who needs clothes that can take her from day into evening, cold to warm weather, sexy to serious. I want a woman to be as comfortable in all of my designs as she is wearing her favorite sweater. Complete knitwear dressing combined with Lycra-blend stretch fabrics are how I achieve this.

I don't impose a "look" on my customer—my customer has her own style or I help her to discover her own. This is one of the great satisfactions in designing.

—Mary Jane Marcasiano

* * *

Mary Jane Marcasiano began her business as primarily a sweater knit house, a focus she has maintained throughout her years in business. The company, located in the SoHo district of New York, has grown and now includes woven fabrics as well as knits. When beginning a new collection, Marcasiano starts with color, simultaneously matching the color with the yarn or fabric to enhance the impact of the completed look. The yarns she prefers are rayon, cotton, silk, linen, and blends of these fibers. In woven fabrics, rayons and silks are favored, owing to their lightness and draping ability.

At a more experimental level, she also utilizes yarns and fabrics with Lycra and superior uses of polyester and nylon. Her ultimate goal is to create a wearable surface of color, texture, and light. Shapes are always simple, as required by the needs of her specific knitwear designs. Beginning with the neckline, Marcasiano uses a variety of geometric shapes to create a pleasing presentation of the face, neck, and decolleté. The ease of wearing her knitwear as well as the woven elements of the collection allow the garments to flow around the body, both covering and revealing it.

Throughout the years Marcasiano's designs have been influenced by a wide variety of historical and artistic movements. The ancient cultures of Egypt, North Africa, Greece, and Rome, with clothes that were the ultimate in simplicity, are an obvious influence on her minimalist designs. Etruscan and Roman jewelry and the Neo-Etruscan movement in Europe have also influenced her designs.

Her target market is women who buy designer-price clothing and appreciate quality, comfort, and ease in their garments. Many professional women, women in the arts, and women involved in the fashion industry wear the Marcasiano label. Exclusive department stores such as Bergdorf Goodman in New York and Neiman Marcus in Dallas have recognized Marcasiano's talent for understanding and designing for the American woman.

Marcasiano and her designs began receiving more exposure, due to business deals that launched her label into new retailers. First, in 1995, Hampshire Designs, a New York sweater firm, bought Marcasiano's business. Then in 1998, Marisa Christina, Inc. acquired the label. Under the new ownership, Marcasiano is producing products accessible to a spectrum of consumers in a range of prices and has been able to penetrate new markets, introducing her quality knit designs to a wider audience.

In her desire to create beautiful and wearable knitwear, Marcasiano follows in the footsteps of women designers such as Coco Chanel, Sonia Rykiel, and Jacqueline Jacobsen (Dorothée Bis)—typical of women designers in Europe who have influenced her work. Her personal innovations in the advancement of knit dressing in America, through the use of unusual yarns, stitches, and simplification of the shape of sweaters, is an inspiration to a new generation of young independent designers working on their own.

—Roberta Hochberger Gruber; updated by Megan Stacy

MARCIANO, Paul, Georges, Maurice, and Armand

See GUESS, INC.

MARGIELA, Martin

Belgian designer

Born: Louvain, Belgium, 9 April 1957. **Education:** Royale Académie of Fine Arts, Antwerp, 1977–80. **Career:** Freelance designer, Milan, 1980–81; freelance fashion stylist, Antwerp, 1982–85; design assistant to Gaultier, 1985–87; showed first major collection under own label in Paris, 1988; launched knitwear line manufactured by Miss Deanna SpA, Italy, 1992; appointed artistic director for Hermès' ready-to-wear women's division, 1997. **Exhibitions:** *Le monde selon*

Martin Margiela, fall 2001 collection. © AP/Wide World Photos/ Fashion Wire Daily.

ses créateurs, Musée de la Mode et du Costume, Palais Galliera, Paris, 1991; *Infra-Apparel,* Metropolitan Museum of Art, 1993; *Belgian Fashion: Antwerp Style,* Fashion Institute of Technology, New York City; *Martin Margiela: 9/4/1615,* Rotterdam, 1997. **Address:** 13 Boulevard St Denis, 75002 Paris, France.

Publications

By MARGIELA:

Books

Margiela et al, *Martin Margiela: 9/4/1615,* [exhibition catalogue], Rotterdam, 1997.
Maison Martin Margiela Street, Special Edition, Volumes 1 & 2, Paris, 1999.

On MARGIELA:

Books

Le monde selon ses créateurs [exhibition catalogue], Paris, 1991.
Martin, Richard, and Harold Koda, *Infra-Apparel* [exhibition catalogue], New York, 1993.
Stegemeyer, Anne, *Who's Who in Fashion, Third Edition,* New York, 1996.
Borthwick, Mark, *2000–1: La maison Martin Margiela,* Paris, 1998.

Articles

Allen, Elizabeth, "Marvelous Martin," in *WWD,* 22 March 1989.
Cunningham, Bill, "The Collections," in *Details* (New York), March 1989.
Paz, Ricardo Martinez, "Los Margenes de Margiela," in *Impar* (Spain), No. 3, 1991.
Voight, Rebecca, "Martin Margiela Champions the Seamy Side of French Fashion," in *Blitz* (London), March 1991.
O'Shea, Stephen, "Recycling: An All-New Fabrication of Style," in *Elle* (London), April 1991.
"La Mode Destroy," in *Vogue* (Paris), May 1992.
Betts, Katherine, "La Nouvelle Vague," in *Vogue,* September 1992.
Spindler, Amy M., "Coming Apart," in the *New York Times,* 25 July 1993.
———, "Four Designers in the Vanguard Hold the Line," in the *New York Times,* 11 October 1993.
Zahm, Olivier, "Before and After Fashion," in *ArtForum* (New York), March 1995.
Spindler, Amy M., "Beyond Sweet, Beyond Black, Beyond 2001," in the *New York Times,* 17 March 1995.
Evans, Caroline, "The Golden Dustman," in *Fashion Theory,* Vol. 2, 1998.
Mead, Rebecaa, "The Crazy Professor: Why Was Paris Persuaded That the Radical Martin Margiela Was Right for the Venerable House of Hermès" in the *New Yorker,* 30 March 1998.
Mower, Sarah, "Margiela Does Hermès," in *Harper's Bazaar,* June 1998.
Braunstein, Chloe, "Martin Margiela, Couturier," in *L'Architecture d'aujourd'hui,* January 1999.
Alexander, Hilary, "At Last: Margiela by Mail Order," in the *Daily Telegraph* (London), 19 July 1999.
Murphy, Robert, "Margiela: Time to Step Up," in *WWD,* 15 February 2001.
White, Jackie, "The Belgian Influence on Display: Designers Focus on Innovation and Design," in the *Kansas City Star,* 18 February 2001.

*

a creativity: unfailing and inexhaustible (force) where everything fits
an energy: that makes things move
an extremity: that calls into question again
an action: carried out and provoking reactions
a force: that every time again provokes emotions
a fantasy: that makes one dream
a sensitivity: that makes you want to be part of it
a proposal: everyone has the choice to interpret
a subtlety: that makes everything possible
a sensuality: that makes everything acceptable
an authenticity: that restores the true or right values of things again
a professionalism: that makes one interested, curious, and inquisitive
a positivity: that gives hope for the future.

—Jenny Meirens for Martin Margiela

Martin Margiela, fall 2001 collection. © AP/Wide World Photos/ Fashion Wire Daily.

* * *

Martin Margiela is a powerful talent in avant-garde fashion. Formerly an assistant to Jean-Paul Gaultier, the Belgian-born Margiela showed his first collection in 1989 and immediately achieved cult status. He was heralded as fashion's latest bad boy genius and the most notorious exponent of *la mode destroy.* He dislikes the term "destroy fashion" and has insisted he does not regard it as destructive when he slashes old clothes. On the contrary, he told *Elle* in April 1991 that it is his way of "bringing them back to life in a different form."

The idea of cutting up clothes goes back to the ripped t-shirts of the Punks and the subsequent street style of slicing jeans with razor blades. But the new deconstruction goes much further. Margiela has unravelled old army socks and made them into sweaters, transformed tulle ball gowns into jackets, recut secondhand black leather coats in the form of dresses, even made plastic laundry bags into clothes. He has designed jackets—beautifully tailored and lined with three different kinds of fabrics—with the sleeves ripped off.

Although conservative members of the fashion industry cringed, young trendsetters enthusiastically embraced Margiela's radical look, which had nothing to do with traditional forms of ostentatious elegance and everything to do with creativity and what he calls "authenticity." Exposed linings and frayed threads testify to the internal construction of the garments, whereas the deliberate deconstruction of garments implicitly raises questions about our assumptions regarding fashion. Detached sleeves, for example, hark back to the way clothes were made in the Middle Ages, when mercenaries first slashed their silken garments. A cloven-toed boot-shoe and fingers laced in ribbons are rebellious statements in a world of high fashion orthodoxy.

The freedom of Margiela's imagination also evokes the sartorial liberty of the 1970s (a decade Margiela views in a positive light), especially in contrast to the opulent and conservative 1980s. Like the hippies who pillaged flea markets, Margiela gave a second life to old and rejected garments, recycling them, and giving a priority to individual creativity rather than consumerism. Opposed to the status-hungry cult of the designer so ubiquitous in the 1980s, Margiela chose for his label a blank piece of white fabric, and resisted talking to the press about what his clothes "mean."

Clothing per se interests him less than how styles are created and interpreted. In this respect, he is very much a conceptual and postmodern designer. Yet, like his former mentor Gaultier, Margiela is an excellent tailor who really knows how to sew, and his clothes, although undeniably strange, are beautifully (de)constructed. Margiela's aesthetic also extends to his fashion shows. He staged one show in an abandoned lot in a poor immigrant neighborhood of Paris, with local children dancing down the improvised catwalk along with the models. Another show was held at a Salvation Army hall, at the edge of the city, so that an international crew of fashion journalists found themselves wandering around, hopelessly lost, trying to read the hand-drawn map—and when they finally made it there, they had to perch on secondhand furniture and drink wine in plastic cups. Further, he held two simultaneous shows (one of all-black clothes, the other white) at the edge of a cemetery, with crowds of admirers fighting to get in.

Symbolically powerful colors like black, white, and red have dominated Margiela's palette. In his atelier are posted dictionary definitions of these colors, with red, for example, being associated with wine, blood, and rubies. His atelier itself, on the Boulevard Saint Denis, is near the red-light district of Paris. Like his clothes, his studio is a masterpiece of *bricolage.* Graffiti decorates the walls, and the floors are covered with copies of old magazine and newspaper articles, which on close inspection turn out to be reviews of his collections.

With Margiela steeped so deeply in the avant-garde sensibility, it came as a perplexing surprise in 1997 when he was appointed artistic director of womenswear for Hermès (which also happens to own a third of Gaultier's business), long associated with luxury and restraint. But the pairing has proved successful, with Margiela continuing the Hermès tradition of quality craftsmanship while playing with conventions of clothing construction and function. His collections for Hermès have been luxurious and subdued but still push the conceptual limits of structure. Dresses are soft and minimalist, sweaters are reversible, and coats double as capes.

Margiela has also continued with his own label, and revenues in recent years have steadily increased, allowing La Maison Martin Margiela to expand. The label moved into mail order sales in 1999 and opened its first freestanding boutique in Tokyo in 2000, with further openings projected.

Margiela himself is famously reclusive, communicating infrequently with the press and then only by fax. In keeping with his ideological convictions, he prefers not to become a public fashion personality, allowing the craftsmanship and design aesthetic of all his fashion collections to communicate his conceptual visions for him.

—Valerie Steele; updated by Megan Stacy

MARIMEKKO

Finnish textile and clothing design firm

Founded: by Armi Ratia (1912–79) and Viljo Ratia in Helsinki in 1951. **Company History:** Fabrics introduced in the U.S. by Design Research stores, from 1951; ventured into the U.S., early 1960s; signed licensing agreement with Dan River company for bed linens, 1976; wallpaper and home furnishing lines introduced, 1978; firm acquired by Amergroup, Finland, 1985, stopped selling directly to U.S., 1989; sold to Kristi Paakkanen, in 1991; new Helsinki flagship shop opened, 1993; opened store in Mexico City, 1994; signed new licenses for rugs and children's dinnerware, 1994; exclusive product placement with Mervyn's and Crate & Barrel, 1996; launched new bed linen collections exclusively with Crate & Barrel, 1998; signed with DelGreco Textiles for fabrics in U.S., 1999; new wallcovering and coordinating fabric agreement with Imperial Home Decor, 2000. **Company Address:** Marimekko Oy, Puusepankatu 4, Helsinki 00810, Finland.

Publications

By MARIMEKKO:

Books

Marimekko-Printex Oy, *The Marimekko Story,* Helsinki, 1964.
Marimekko, New York, 1980, 1989.
Marimekko Oy Architect Colleciton, Helsinki, 1982.

On MARIMEKKO:

Books

Beer, Eileene Harrison, *Scandinavian Design: Objects of a Life Style,* New York, 1975.
Lambert, Eleanor, *World of Fashion: People, Places, Resources,* New York & London, 1976.
Suomen Taideteollisuusyhdistys, *Women Who Create,* Helsinki, 1984.
Suhonen, Pekko, *Phenomenon Marimekko,* Helsinki, 1986.
Ainamo, Antti, *Industrial Design and Business Performance: A Case Study of Design Management in a Finnish Fashion Firm,* Helsinki, 1996.

Articles

Davies, David, "Fabrics by Marimekko," in *Design* (London), August 1968.
Lintman, Jaako, "Finland Marches Forward," in *Design,* No. 245, May 1969.
"Bright Spell Forecast," in *Design,* October 1973.
Tulberg, Diana, "That Old Marimekko Magic," in *Designed in Finland 1975* (Helsinki), 1975.
Holm, Aase, "Marimekko," in *Mobilia* (Amsterdam), No. 284, 1979.
Apple, R.W., "Finland's Spirited Designer," in the *New York Times,* 2 August 1979.
Slesin, Suzanne, "Finnish and Muted," in the *New York Times,* 16 September 1979.
"Armi Ratia, Marimekko Founder and Innovator in Printed Fabrics," [obituary] in the *New York Times,* 4 October 1979.
Furman, Phyllis, "Marimekko's Designs on a Turnaround," in *Crain's New York Business,* 5 September 1988.
Fraser, Mark, "Marimekko on the Move in America," in *HFN (Weekly Home Furnishings Newspaper),* 20 November 1989.
Boyle-Schwartz, Donna, "Thoroughly Modern Marimekko," in *HFN (Weekly Home Furnishings Newspaper),* 26 July 1993.
———, "Marimekko Inks Newmark, Selandia," in *HFN (Weekly Home Furnishings Newspaper),* 24 October 1994.
Orenstein, Alison F., "Marimekko Revs Up," in *HFN (Weekly Home Furnishings Newspaper),* 24 June 1996.
Boyle-Schwartz, Donna, "A Crate & Barrel Exclusive...for Bedding with Marimekko Designs," in *HFN (Weekly Home Furnishings Newspaper),* 26 January 1998.
Gilbert, Daniela, "Marimekko Back in Spotlight," in *HFN (Weekly Home Furnishings Newspaper),* 13 July 1998.
———, "Marimekko Set to Re-Cover North America in Fabric," in *HFN (Weekly Home Furnishings Newspaper),* 25 January 1999.
"The Finnish Line," in *Interior Design,* November 1999.
"Marimekko Ready for Spring," in *HFN (Weekly Home Furnishings Newspaper),* 17 January 2000.
Stevens, Kimberly, and William L. Hamilton, "Trying on Those Supergraphics Again," in the *New York Times,* 31 July 2001.

* * *

A strong Finnish design movement emerged after World War II and was given decisive impetus by the International Triennales of 1951 and 1954 which defined the concept of "Finish design." By formally integrating design into manufacturing, textiles from Marimekko acquired international attention through their identification of an exclusive market responsive to the strong Finnish design aesthetic.

Marimekko was founded by Armi and Viljo Ratia in 1951 and has since established a reputation for producing quality textiles for home furnishings and clothing. The Finland-based company actually began in 1949 by acquiring Printex Oy—an oilcloth factory in the suburbs of Helsinki. After a refit, the factory reintroduced the craft-based technique of hand silk-screen printing on cotton sheeting. The technique, which was recognized by resulting irregularities and repeat lines, evoked a human feel to each design. Although production techniques at Marimekko were mechanized long ago, the company maintains hand-crafted quality in its printing. Its use of decorative designs and natural fibers strengthened its commitment to the Scandinavian affinity to nature.

Under the design direction of Armi Ratia, the company broke ranks with conventional Finnish textile designers and implemented a range of nonfigurative patterns, using abstract graphic designs of art colleagues. The first collection of simply cut dresses, introduced in 1951 in Helsinki, originated as a promotional vehicle for the company's printed cotton fabrics. Wraparound and front-buttoned garments were included, accentuating the textiles rather than the styling of the garments. The collection was called Marimekko, combining the old-fashioned Finnish girl's name of Maria and the term *mekko* which described a tow shirt, open at the back and worn like a pinafore. Since then "Maria's little dress" expanded into home furnishing textiles, with overseas licensing agreements (initiated in 1968) for wall coverings, bedding, decorative fabrics, paper products, table linens, kitchenware, ceramics, glassware, rugs, and wallcoverings.

The textile patterns used by Marimekko have given the firm a unique identity throughout the world; inspired by elements, forms, and colors taken from Finland's landscape and national heritage. At the same time, however, Marimekko's textile designs embrace experimental ideas and contemporary graphic thinking, often resulting in bold patterns and saturated colors. Marimekko designs are based on an understanding of modernity, rather than concerns for contemporary fashion trends.

Marimekko's garments sought to incorporate functionalist ideas; comfort and timelessness were strikingly evident in the design of the fabrics themselves. Designs produced in the 1950s by Maiha Isola and Vuokko Nurmesniemi (founder of Vuokko in 1964) included small, simple stripes and nature-inspired graphic prints in black and white. By the 1960s there were oversized decorative graphics, flowers, and Op-Art-inspired prints, reflecting the playful and opulent mood of the period. By the end of the 1970s stripes were rendered primarily in bold primary colors as exemplified by the Peltomies series (1975–79). Similar designs continued to be produced through the next decade, with geometric patterns scaled for furniture in shades including mauve, opal, and midnight.

Marimekko's designs came full circle in the 1990s collections—Fujiwo Ishimoto (prints in celebration of the 75th anniversary of Finnish Independence), Jukka Rintala (womenswear), and Elina Helenius and Jatta Salonen (prints and patterns) returned to the natural patterns and colored world of Finland's seasons and landscape, which inspired original designs of the 1950s. By 1994 there were two dozen Marimekko stores worldwide, with 22 in Finland, one in Germany, and its first shop outside Europe opening in Mexico. The company, which had stopped direct selling to the U.S. at the end of the 1980s, staged comeback with two new licensing agreements with Selandia Designs and the Newmark Rug Company.

Selandia signed on to produce children's dinnerware, snack trays, and lunchbags coordinated to Marimekko's textile designs, while Newmark created rugs or all sized and shapes matching Marimekko kitchen and bath collections. Further U.S. exposure came from product placements with Mervyn's and Crate & Barrel in bed linens through its American distributor, Revman. Mervyn's began displaying Marimekko bed linens in its 297 stores in 1996; Crate & Barrel used simple leaf-designed collections of sheets, pillow cases, and comforters to showcase their beds. "Marimekko is what we use to decorate," Betty Kahn, a spokesperson for Crate & Barrel told *HFN (Weekly Home Furnishings Network Newspaper)* (24 June 1996). The popular ensemble, Kahn explained, became the "basic design element in our stores, so it's more than just selling [Marimekko's] sheets; we have a symbiotic relationship."

Marimekko and Crate & Barrel continued their association and in 1998 five new bedding ensembles and accessories debuted exclusively at Crate & Barrel stores. "Marimekko represents something unique and special," Carole Newton, product manager and textiles buyer for Crate & Barrel stated to *HFN* (26 January 1998). "Marimekko and Crate & Barrel go together very well; we have a similar philosophy.... There's a real synergy between our classic contemporary points of view."

By the end of the 20th century, Marimekko had engineered a major comeback in the U.S., with fabric (for both indoor and outdoor use), wallcoverings, bed linens, rugs and much more available to American buyers through a series of licenses. Though not as well known in America as many other textiles firms, Marimekko's bold, simple, classic print designs and characteristic use of color have established a permanently recognizable and highly individualistic identity that remains to this day.

—Teal Triggs; updated by Owen James

MARINA RINALDI SRL

Italian plus-size fashion company

Founded: by Achille Marmotti in Reggio Emilia, Italy, within the Max Mara Group, 1980 (named after his great-grandmother, Marina Rinaldi). **Company History:** Launched first collection of larger-sized fashions, 1980; Persona line introduced, 1985; Marina Sport launched, 1986; knitwear line, 1987; set up U.S. division and headquarters, 1993; opened flagship stores in New York and Beverly Hills, 1998; launched first U.S. magazine ads, 1998. **Company Address:** Via Mazzacurati 4, 42100 Reggio Emilia, Italy.

Publications

On MARINA RINALDI/MAX MARA:

Books

Alfonsi, Maria Vittoria, *Leaders in Fashion,* Bologna, 1983.
Soli, Pia, *Il genio antipatico,* Venice, 1984.

Articles

"Che cosa di chi: Max Mara," in *Vogue* (Milan), October 1984.
"Pianoforte di Max Mara: giunco e sabbia da turismo coloniale," in *Vogue* (Milan), February 1986.
Mower, Sarah, "Chasing the Wise Monet," in *The Guardian* (London), 3 July 1986.
Rumbold, Judy, "Grey Cells: Bright Ideas," in *The Guardian,* 7 September 1987.
"Altre scelte da Max Mara," in *Vogue* (Milan), October 1987.
Armstrong, Lisa, "The Max Factor," in *Vogue* (London), October 1988.
Tredre, Roger, "A Piece of Cake," in *Fashion Weekly* (London), 1 December 1988.
Livingston, Jennifer, "Big Stores, Big Opportunities," in *WWD,* 6 Sept 1995.
Edelson, Sharon, "Once in Not Enough on Madison Avenue," in *WWD,* 19 August 1997.
"Counter Punch," in *WWD,* 9 March 1998.

Edelson, Sharon, "Marina Rinaldi Opens on Madison Avenue," in *WWD,* 28 October 1998.

Curan, Catherine, "Clothiers See the Plus Side," in *Crain's New York Business,* 17 April 2000.

Singer, Natasha, "Luxury Boutiques Start Pouring into Russia," in *WWD,* 28 November 2000.

* * *

Marina Rinaldi originated as part of the Max Mara group, named for its founder's great-grandmother, who once had her own atelier in Reggio Emilia, Italy. The firm's purpose, however, was to answer the needs of the vast population of Italian women sized 46 and over. The group's other ranges, including Weekend and Penny Black, already catered for larger sizes, until it was recognized that there was a significant gap in the market for a separate label specializing in plus sizes.

The aim was and continues to be about producing a womenswear range with the same fashion content as other Max Mara lines. Marina Rinaldi has the same quality of cut, manufacture, fabric, and color as other fashion brands but is only available from size 16 upwards. Established as a separate company, there are now several labels under its umbrella including Marina Rinaldi, Marina Sport (launched to target a younger clientèle) and Persona. The label serves 400 points of sale worldwide, 100 of these are franchised, 80 being in Italy and 20 abroad (Paris, Tokyo, Brussels, and Amsterdam).

Marina Rinaldi has an ongoing Image Project aimed to establish a thorough understanding of its product, its customers, and the company's relationship to these customers. Larger women were identified as having very classic tastes, yet too afraid or too timid to try younger styles and modern silhouettes. For Rinaldi, sales personnel became recognized as an important link in establishing a trustworthy relationship with clients. The goal is make their customers feel good about themselves and to do so through fashionably forward, stylish clothing in a range of bigger sizes.

Designs are made to flatter heavier figures and the firm tries to incorporate as many fashion trends and styles as possible yet always with a range of classic items such as a sheepskin or suede jackets, cashmere overcoats, stretch jersey turtlenecks, brushed flannel suits, and jeans in many colors. An eveningwear look is always included with elegant smoking jackets and lounging suits, embroidered wraps and white evening shirts with assorted cufflinks. A summer beachwear collection incorporates essentials from the swimsuits to the terry cloth bathrobes and wraps.

Rinaldi also produces its own catalogue, *MR Characters,* designed to accompany the customer throughout the fashion seasons and intended as an introductory guide to a fashion lifestyle for women not entirely used to having a wide selection of outfits and separates. As well as advice on how to interpret High Street trends with the Marina Rinaldi look, it gives advice on cookery, personal problems, and travel.

It is often difficult to see much difference in Rinaldi's style from its sibling Max Mara collections, which is exactly the point. The quality of workmanship, styling, and fabrics are all there; the only real difference is in the sizing and the slightly rounder (but no less stunning) model used in the advertising. From a consumer point of view this is a measure of Marina Rinaldi's success. Figure-hugging basques and fitted strapless dresses are not included in the range, but then sexy, revealing dressing wasn't traditionally part of the Max Mara look either. Rinaldi represents a breakthrough in accessible fashion for all sizes, a business concept many other companies soon recognized.

By the 1990s, Rinaldi apparel was given much more space in high-end department stores like Saks Fifth Avenue, Bergford Goodman, Bloomingdale's, and Nordstrom due to the increased demand for retailing for larger women. With celebrity spokespersons like actor Camryn Mannheim and musician/television host Queen Latifah, plus sizes finally garnered respect from U.S. retailers and prominent fashion designers as well. Liz Claiborne, Givenchy, and Mondi were all offering plus-size collections, and Rinaldi was doing so well the firm opened two U.S. flagship stores in 1998. In New York, the first Rinaldi flagship was located just a block from sibling Max Mara's store on Madison Avenue. The second freestanding store, nestled snugly on Rodeo Drive in Beverly Hills, opened as part of a two-unit powerhouse, with Max Mara next door. To promote its new stores, Rinaldi also launched its first U.S. magazine advertising campaign, using the slogan, "Style is not a size, it's an attitude."

Marina Rinaldi in the 21st century was a respected womenswear design firm, offering plus-size women a myriad of stylish, exceptional apparel from eveningwear to casual separates. With stores around the world, from its flagships in the U.S. to shops in Russia where there is virtually no competition—Marina Rinaldi has been a pioneer in giving larger women fashion options in a retail world where there were few available.

—Kevin Almond; updated by Owen James

MARINO, Manuel Roberto

See VERINO, Roberto

MARKS, Stephen

See FRENCH CONNECTION

MARMOTTI, Achille

See MARINA RINALDI SrL

MARONGIU, Marcel

French designer

Born: Paris, France, 9 February 1962. **Education:** Studied economics and fashion design in Stockholm, Sweden. **Career:** Fashion illustrator for newspapers and magazines, 1980–82; assistant to France Andrevie, Paris, 1982–88; first signature collection, 1988; first catwalk show, Paris, 1989; founded company Permanent Vacation, Paris, 1989; showed collection at Cour Carré du Louvre, October

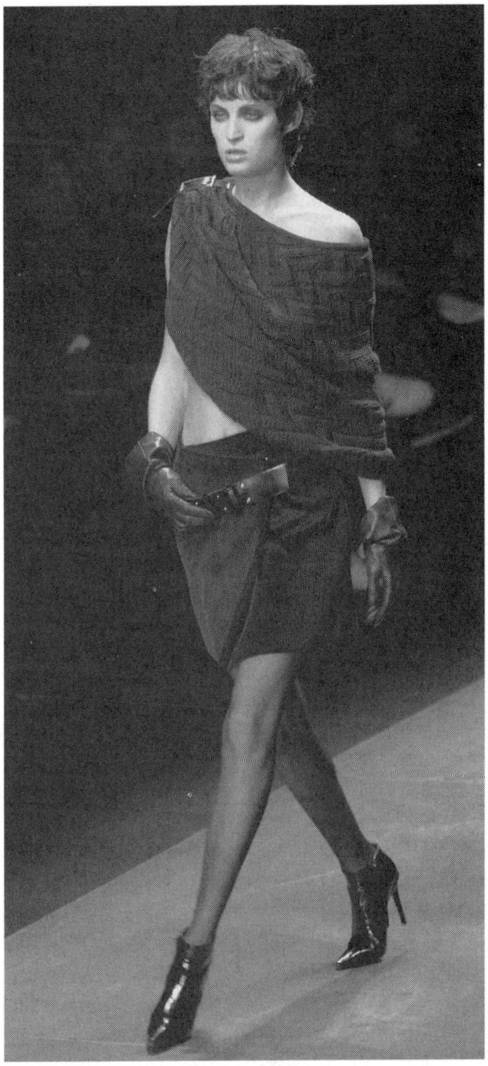

Marcel Marongiu, fall/winter 2001–02 ready-to-wear collection. © AP/Wide World Photos.

1991; received new backing, from Japan, 1996; opened Paris boutique, 1998; ended launched ceramics collection, 1999. **Exhibitions:** Stockholm Design Museum, retrospective, 1998. **Awards:** "Venus" Best Young Designer award for spring/summer collection, 1993; Designer of the Year, *Elle Sweden,* 1999. **Address:** 9 rue Scribe, Paris 75001 France. **Website:** www.marcel-marongiu.com.

Publications

On MARONGIU:

Articles

Nilard, Sita, "Sita Nilard Meets Fashion Upstart," in *Fashion Weekly* (London), 28 February 1991.

Baker, Lynsey, "Glad Rags to Riches," in *The Guardian* (London), 13 January 1992.

Menkes, Suzy, "The North Wind Doth Blow," in the *International Herald Tribune,* 13 March 1993.

Gordon, Mary Ellen, "Marongiu's Spare Shapes," in *WWD,* 13 September 1993.

Spindler, Amy, "In Paris, Clothes That Look Tough and Dangerous," in the *New York Times,* 16 March 1995.

Radsken, Jill, "Fashion; One World of Fashion," in the *Boston Herald,* 17 September 1999.

Stephans, Laura, "White-Out," in the *Minneapolis-St. Paul Magazine,* April 2000.

"Diversity Training," in *WWD,* 11 October 2000.

Biography Resource Center, available online at www.galenet.com, October 2001.

"From Style Correspondent Elsa Klensch," available online at CNN.com, www.cnn.com, October 2001.

"Pleins Feux Sur la Femme de l'été," online at Absolu Féminin, www.absolufeminin.com, October 2001.

"Marcel Marongiu," online at First View, www.firstview.com, October 2001.

"La Scandinavie a Paris," available online at Planet@Paris, www.planetaparis.com, 4 October 2001.

*

I believe the 1980s was all about appearance, money and "power dressing." The consumer was suddenly unimportant as media, photographers, and stylists went too far in seeking to shock and surprise each other through unreal supermodels.

We are facing a new era where a designer has once more to be in contact with the consumer and make them feel fashion can be fun and easy. Therefore I try to do interesting, personal clothes—easy to mix and at affordable prices. There is a new generation of women with a completely new attitude toward fashion. I believe clothes are an important and interesting way of communicating; therefore it is important to make the "user" comfortable and secure, to bring out the best in them.

Silhouette is my main preoccupation and everything is in the cut and the fabric. Details are secondary and should be avoided as much as possible.

—Marcel Marongiu

* * *

Marcel Marongiu sees fashion design as a genuine means of communication. He wants people to be able to live out their fantasies by wearing his clothes and to discover what he terms "la vie plus belle," the beautiful life.

Marongiu designs clothes that are classically elegant yet also up to date, sexy, and carefree. His style is always strong and pronounced, the cut always clean and streamlined, emphasizing the contours and shape of the human body. Stretch fabrics and natural classic fabrics, often with a small Lycra percentage, help him achieve these silhouettes. His customer is a young, modern women, slightly tongue-in-cheek and sexy, who refuses to dress expensively. Marongiu targets this clientèle in a logical, businesslike way, and in the short time since the company's inception in 1991, the clothes are now sold in many boutiques throughout Sweden, Great Britain, Italy, France, Japan, and the United States.

Marongiu draws his inspiration from various sources; his favorite designers are Jacques Fath and Christian Dior, two men who had a

Marcel Marongiu, fall/winter 2001–02 ready-to-wear collection. © AP/Wide World Photos.

huge influence on 1940s and 1950s fashion, a period to which Marcel particularly adheres when designing. He adores hard rock music and in 1991 even named his company after the title of an Aerosmith album, *Permanent Vacation.* Other favorite muses are painter Nicholas de Stael, writer Graham Greene, and filmmakers Martin Scorsese and Peter Greenaway.

Comparing two Marongiu collections perhaps gives an indication of the designer's style. The spring-summer 1994 collection was a mixture of three styles: renaissance in the fluidity and lightness of the materials, baroque in its generous volume, and classical in its Greek and Roman influences. Constructed mainly around a basic dress shape, Marcel wanted to create a collection that was soft, serene, and human, in colors making reference to nature—reds and chestnuts, the blues of dusk and twilight, and the colors of sand, beige, and white. The fall-winter collection for 1994–95 moved on from the ruralistic feeling of spring-summer and was inspired by the lifestyle and atmosphere of European cities between World War I and World War II and contrasted with shapes inspired by the Ottoman Empire. Using striped fabrics, Prince of Wales checks, mock astrakhan, and pleats, Marongiu created baggy silhouettes and distinctively superimposed tunics, smocks, or waistcoats on dresses or trousers. He also introduced colors of orange, green, and saffron yellow to his usual palette of burgundies, aubergines, and grays.

Marongiu prides himself on the fact that his clothes are 100-percent French in production. The sample collection is produced in his Paris studio but is manufactured in the Vendée, retail prices are very reasonable for a designer label. As well as clothes, the company has diversified by producing a small line of accessories, shoes, necklaces, belts, boots, bags, and hats, all in the distinctive Marongiu style. As Paris is the base of Marongiu's activities, he is now established as one of the city's leading young designers. He looks set to expand his business further, because Paris, as he describes it, is a present-day city, full of energy and romance.

Marongiu reached the breaking point with Swedish backers in 1996 when he vacated his contract and reestablished his firm with Japanese backing. Within two years, he opened a Paris boutique on the exclusive rue Saint-Honoré and established his first vendor in Nagoya, Japan. In his ninth year in the business, he debuted a first collection of leather goods. In support of the Swedish fashion maven and his impact on world tastes, Stockholm's Design Museum honored him with a retrospective exhibit.

In 1998, when the emerging trend aimed for minimalism and dressing down with flair and attitude, Marongiu lauded a new freedom from tradition. His wearable European day outfits produced the ease and comfort that women demanded. Of the push for simplification, CNN cited his faith in a voguish breeziness, "It enabled us...to have a new approach to fashion."

The year 1999 saw Marongiu at his best. He branched out into understated asymmetrical Artoria porcelainware for Limoges, plus cushions and lingerie, and snagged *Elle Sweden's* Designer of the Year award. In Paris, he celebrated the first decade of his Composites brand. He insisted on New York City for unveiling his 10th fashion collection. According to the *Boston Herald,* he expressed confidence in the switch from European venues, "You just have to be in the right place at the right moment. And New York is the right moment."

In the trendy new millennium, when he introduced a secondary line, Marongiu avoided artistic pretension to focus on chic that sells. Layering military with rock, he centered jersey frocks with soldier belts, the indispensable accessory for the with-it Marongiu look. For everyday attire, he topped crisp cotton skirts with wrapped bodices. His theme held steady for affordable goods that span the seasons.

—Kevin Almond; updated by Mary Ellen Snodgrass

MATSUDA, Mitsuhiro

Japanese designer

Born: Tokyo, 1934. **Education:** Graduated from Waseda University, 1958; graduated with degree in fashion design from Bunka College of Fashion, 1961. **Career:** Ready-to-wear designer, Sanai Company, Japan, 1961–67; traveled to Paris and the U.S., 1965; freelance designer, then formed own company, Nicole, Ltd., Tokyo, 1971; introduced divisions Monsieur Nicole, 1974, Madame Nicole, 1976, Chambre de Nicole, 1978, formed Matsuda, USA, and opened New

York City store, 1981; opened boutique in Hong Kong, 1982; launched Nicole Club, 1982, and Nicole Club for Men, 1984; Séduction de Nicole, 1986; cosmetics line introduced and Paris store opened, 1987; closed original New York showroom and reopened on Fifth Avneue, 1989; hired Yukio Kobayashi as menswear designer; Kobayashi took over womenswear, 1995; hoped to open U.S. boutiques, including a flagship in New York, 1997. **Awards:** So-en prize. **Address:** 3–13-11 Higashi, Shibuya-ku, Tokyo 150, Japan.

PUBLICATIONS

By MATSUDA:

Books

Men & Women: Images From Nicole, with Bruce Weber, Tokyo, 1983.

On MATSUDA:

Books

Koba, Matsuda, et al., *Matsuda,* Tokyo, 1985.

Stegemeyer, Anne, *Who's Who in Fashion, Third Edition,* New York, 1996.

Articles

Kidd, J.D., "Matsuda Collects His Dues," in *DNR,* 1 November 1982.

Morris, Bernadine, "From Japan: New Faces, New Shapes," in the *New York Times,* 14 December 1982.

"Big, Bold and Black: The Japanese Fashion Invasion," in *Life,* April 1983.

Trucco, Terry, "Behind the Japanese Look," in *Across the Board* (New York), December 1983.

Kidd, J.D., "Matsuda: The Other Japanese," in *WWD,* 10 April 1984.

Vogel, Carol, "A Boutique as Glamorous as the Clothes Inside (Matsuda, New York)," in the *New York Times,* 14 September 1989.

"Matsuda," in *WWD,* 29 November 1989.

Ozzard, Janet, "Matsuda Moves to Build U.S. Volume," in *WWD,* 19 July 1995.

"Fall 1996 Sportswear Collections—New Republic's Bookish Look and Matsuda's Future Feature," in *DNR,* 6 March 1996.

White, Constance C.R., "Getting Real at Matsuda," in the *New York Times,* 11 June 1996.

Ozzard, Janet, "Matsuda Out to Stake a Bigger Claim in U.S.," in *WWD,* 12 Feburary 1997.

* * *

Mitsuhiro Matsuda's designs are picturesque, evoking historical passages and a profound sense of connection with the past and place—but at the same time are transformed through Matsuda's personal style. In a November 1989 article, *Women's Wear Daily* commented, "Few can tread the fine line between sophistication and adventure the way Mitsuhiro Matsuda does." The designer who probably comes the closest, Romeo Gigli, brings a similar transfiguration to his clothing.

Matsuda, of course, precedes Gigli and also differs from him in an essential way: despite the whimsical romance of his clothing which could seem to suit a Brontë heroine, Matsuda observes a stern rule of practicality borrowed from menswear. His basic canon of separate elements—the signature Matsuda silk blouse, jackets (generally elongated), trousers of various kinds, vests, and sweaters often elaborated with embroidery or other textural play—affords a versatile set of components in the sportswear tradition. He is eminently pragmatic but irrepressibly romantic and sensuous, even in appropriations of menswear to womenswear. Matsuda defined a kind of practical aesthetic dress of the late 20th century, and continued to make unique fashion inroads in the early 2000s.

In the mid-1960s, Matsuda and Kenzo sailed from Japan to Europe to make their way to Paris, the great beacon of fashion. After some six months, Matsuda returned to Japan with no money, while Kenzo stayed. Matsuda's aesthetic and cultural allegiance outside of Japan is not to Paris, but to England and America. His first company outside of Nicole Company in Japan was Matsuda USA which opened a Madison Avenue boutique in 1982. Matsuda has delved into the Anglo-American sportswear traditions as ardently as any designer, even as much as Ralph Lauren. What differentiates Matsuda from Lauren, though, is his critical, slightly adverse edge on examining traditions.

Matsuda's famous fall 1982 collections showed the impeccable tailoring of the English jackets, heavy trousers, layering, and indulgent textiles of the English countryside for men adapted for women, but with the almost impish heterogeneity of canvas aprons serving as a sign of the working class and as a reminder of the transference from male to female, female to male. As an apron customarily signified the female, Matsuda both broke and then reemployed the image of the apron from female to male and back again.

In fall-winter 1984 Matsuda's collections were seemingly inspired by Edwardian England; in fall-winter 1985, the collections seemed to step out of Burne-Jones paintings; the Moroccan embroideries of 1989 could seemingly have costumed a Paul Bowles novel. There is a further literary aspect to Matsuda's work in his preoccupation with words and letters. His clothing has been favored by artists, writers, and other creatives who have recognized a kinship with this most literary image-making style and who enjoy the practicality of clothing that mixes so easily, even improvisationally, with other separates.

There seemed to be a continuous synthesis about Matsuda's work; in fall-winter 1992, he created a homage to jazz saxophonist Miles Davis. His collections have often been presented as performance and were even affiliated with dance or visual arts. His advertising and photography have been collaborative art, presenting the clothing in secondary status to the picture. Matsuda boutiques, too, projected the absolute austerity of the design and yet showcased the lasciviousness of the designer's details. In the mid-1990s Matsuda sought to cxpand its brand throughout the U.S. and Europe, which included moving menswear designer Yukio Kobayashi, who had begun designing some womenswear, to the head all of the women's labels (Madame Nicole, Nicole Club, Nicole Sport and Zelda) in 1995. Matsuda himself also continued to design for women, but for the Asian markets.

In 1996 the *Daily News Records* (6 March 1996) praised the latest Matsuda collection by Kobayshi, stating, "Synthetics rule, and there is an unabashed modern edge. But rather than being simply a techno-driven line, Matsuda offers a sensualist's version of classic silhouettes rendered in fabrics that are light years beyond most other designer lines." There were, as well, classic or "vintage" Matsuda separates which were also warmly received. The following year, on a trip to New York, Matsuda scouted locations for possible stores. Though the Nicole brands (Madame Nicole, Nicole Sport, Boutique Nicole and others) were available in Saks Fifth Avenue and Barneys, as well as 500 stores in Asia and Europe, Matsuda hoped to bring his unique designs and growing licensed products to the U.S. in company-owned boutiques. Matsuda clients are ardently loyal, and his creations are profoundly progressive—the perfect combination for New York fashion and beyond.

—Richard Martin; updated by Nelly Rhodes

MAXFIELD PARRISH

British design firm

Founded: by designer Nigel Preston, 1972. *Preston* born in Reading, Berkshire, 1946; studied painting and graphic art at Dartington Hall, then interior design; by late 1960s was designing for popular musicians. **Company History:** Maxfield Parrish cloth collection launched, 1983; signed Fashion Stage as distributor, 1991. **Company Address:** 5 Congreve St., London SE17 1TJ, England.

Publications

On MAXFIELD PARRISH:

Books

McDowell, Colin, *McDowell's Directory of Twentieth Century Fashion,* Englewood Cliffs, New Jersey, 1985.

Articles

d'Aulay, Sophie, "Cologne Delivers the Crowds; Three-Day German Show Had Excitement…," in *DNR,* 12 August 1994.

Socha, Miles, et al., "New York Trade Shows: Getting Fancy for Spring," in *WWD,* 30 September 1999.

* * *

For centuries it was believed that by adorning the body with the skin of an animal, the wearer was thereby encouraged to develop its attributes. Accordingly, a lion denoted strength and courage, while a rabbit implied a rather inferior metamorphosis. In time certain types of fur, especially those more difficult to find such as ermine, became symbols of wealth, power, privilege, and—ultimately—in Western culture, eroticism. The history of wearing animal skin is varied and responses to it differ from culture to culture and have changed with time. In contemporary Western culture, there is still a certain amount of prestige attached to the fur, yet less due to pressure by groups such as Lynx, the Green movement, and PETA (People for the Ethical Treatment of Animals).

Leather, however, and its more "well-bred" counterpart suede, are still generally acceptable; in fact a whole mythology exists for the rebellious black leather jacket. These seemingly arbitrary distinctions and distortions can be set against the continuing success of the company Maxfield Parrish, whose name for some brings to mind the production of well-cut and crafted suede, sheepskin, and leather garments. The company was founded twenty years ago by designer Nigel Hayter Preston who was born in Reading, Berkshire in 1946. After studying painting and graphic design at Dartington Hall, Devon, Preston moved into interior design, toyed for a time with music, and in turn began designing clothes for his friends in the record industry.

This low-key venture took off so successfully that by the end of the 1960s Preston was producing stage outfits for names such as Suzy Quatro and Emerson, Lake & Palmer. From these humble beginnings Maxfield Parrish was to become an international label, synonymous in womenswear with the design and production of suede, leather, and sheepskin clothing which displayed unusual combinations of color—thanks to Preston's studies in fine art—and classic relaxed styles whose defined cutting betrays the discipline of a training in graphic design.

During the production cycle of the company's definitive garments it is the choosing of the skins which is of the utmost importance for the designer. Those of the softest, supplest kind are selected so they can be cut into and shaped like cloth, one of the company's trademarks. Preston handles the materials confidently, using the same methods other designers would utilize with more malleable wool, seen in classically styled outerwear such as the 1982 voluminous loose coats and jackets in soft blues, faded rose or beige, worn over softly draped skirts and cropped trousers. One of his more innovative methods is to overlap several skins to produce a montaged patchwork textured effect. This is used as a bolt of cloth from which he cuts various garments such as tubular or sarong skirts and tops.

For years, Preston and partner Brenda Knight worked in a design studio based in a Normandy chateau to creates sample collections of elegant, easy to wear garments which are then manufactured and distributed from the company's administrative base in London. By the middle 1990s Maxfield Parrish had become an international brand name in retail; the goods bearing the name were available in boutiques and stores in Europe and the United States.

Despite the fragmented nature of women's fashion at the end of the 20th century with its changing styles and alternative looks, there have always been lower profile designers more interested in producing elegant styles in the most refined materials. Maxfield Parrish is one such firm; it has relied on the ongoing development of new techniques in the cut and construction of leather, suede, and sheepskin, using only the finest materials, and availing its luxurious garments to a certain segment of society for which wearing fur or related accoutrements is of the utmost importance.

—Caroline Cox; updated by Owen James

MAX MARA SPA

Italian fashion design company

Founded: in 1951 by Achille Maramotti. **Company History:** Launched Commerciale Abbigliamento Company, 1976, and Marina Rinaldi,

Max Mara SpA, fall/winter 2001–02 collection. © AP/Wide World Photos.

1980; comprised of five companies by 1990; opened shop in Tokyo, 1993; opened flagship store, New York, and first South American store, in Caracas, 1994; launched cosmetics line, 1997; acquired stake in Marzotto, 1997; introduced Max Mara S, and Sportmax lines, 1999; opened new SoHo flagship and celebrated 50th annual collection, 2001. **Company Address:** Via Fratelli Cervi 66, 42100 Reggio Emilia, Italy.

Publications

On MAX MARA:

Books

Alfonsi, Maria Vittoria, *Leaders in Fashion,* Bologna, 1983.
Soli, Pia, *Il genio antipatico,* Venice, 1984.

Articles

"Che cosa di chi: MaxMara," in *Vogue* (Milan), October 1984.
"Pianoforte di MaxMara: giunco e sabbia da turismo coloniale," in *Vogue* (Milan), February 1986.
Mower, Sarah, "Chasing the Wise Monet," in *The Guardian* (London), 3 July 1986.
Rumbold, Judy, "Grey Cells: Bright Ideas," in *The Guardian* (London), 7 September 1987.
"Altre scelte da Max Mara," in *Vogue* (Milan), October 1987.
Armstrong, Lisa, "The Max Factor," in *Vogue* (London), October 1988.
Tredre, Roger, "A Piece of Cake," in *Fashion Weekly* (London), 1 December 1988.
Pogoda, Dianne M., "Max Mara Takes Madison," in *WWD,* 7 September 1994.
Conti, Samantha, "Conquering New Worlds," in *WWD,* 29 August 1995.
"Max Mara Buys into Marzotto," in *WWD,* 12 June 1997.
Hammond, Teena, "Max Mara's Double Life on Rodeo," in *WWD,* 14 December 1998.
Edelson, Sharon, "Max Mara Joining the SoHo Brigade," in *WWD,* 27 October 1999.
Zargani, Luisa, "The Family Business," in *WWD,* 22 February 2000.
Singer, Natasha, "Luxury Boutiques Start Pouring into Russia," in *WWD,* 28 November 2000.
"Easy and Breezy—Spirited Sportswear Starred at Both Max Mara and Sportmax," in *WWD,* 1 October 2001.

* * *

The brainchild of Achille Maramotti, Max Mara was founded in 1951 and has since become one of Italy's most successful fashion companies. Like many Italian firms, Max Mara remains a family company although, interestingly, no member of the family is a fashion designer. Instead Max Mara operates by the highly successful formula of employing well-known fashion designers to create their collections—a method described by fashion critic Colin McDowell as a form of designer "moonlighting" and which is characteristic of a number of Italian ready-to-wear companies. Designers who have created collections for Max Mara include Anne Marie Beretta, Karl Lagerfeld, Luciano Soprani, Guy Paulin, and Jean-Charles de Castelbajac. The identity of more recent Max Mara designers was a jealously-guarded secret; they were, however, acknowledged in retrospect.

The first Max Mara shop was opened in Reggio Emilia in northern Italy in 1951 and the first collection consisted of two coats and a suit which were copies of Paris couture designs. Although Achille Maramotti was officially trained as a lawyer, his family background was firmly entrenched in dressmaking since his mother had founded a tailoring school in 1923. Maramotti's vision to produce designer fashion for the mass market was remarkably farsighted at a time when haute couture still dominated fashion and high fashion ready-to-wear clothing did not exist. Like the whole fashion industry during the early 1950s, Max Mara looked to Paris as inspiration for its designs and produced garments which combined Parisian designs with their quality manufacturing techniques.

By 1969 Maramotti introduced a new line called Sport Max to cater for its younger customers, an early forerunner of diffusion lines which were not an established part of most major fashion companies. Today the company has many labels, catering to clients of all ages and sizes. Max Mara proved to be as astute in its attitude towards the importance of advertising its product as it was in the early production of fashionable ready-to-wear. As early as 1970 the company commissioned photographer Sarah Moon to capture the mood of their

Max Mara SpA, fall/winter 2001–02 collection: suede jacket and pants. © AP/Wide World Photos.

collections for a series of advertisements. Since then the essence of Max Mara has been captured by prominent fashion photographers including Paolo Roversi, Oliviero Toscani, Steven Meisel, and Peter Lindbergh.

The basis of the Max Mara design philosophy is understated, easy to wear clothes in luxury fabrics, with an emphasis placed on quality of cut and production. The company consistently emphasizes the requirements of the Max Mara customer and the importance of innovation has always been carefully balanced by wearability. Luigi Maramotti, Achille's son and a director of the Max Mara group, maintains, "Our customers are led by fashion, but are never its slaves." Tailoring is one of the company's strong points, although in the softer Italian mode as opposed to the stiff British style of tailoring. Max Mara is perhaps best recognized for its coats; these garments best illustrate the firm's simplicity of style, cut in soft wools or cashmere mixes.

According to Luigi, "Clothes must be designed with an understanding of the women who wear them and the demands of their life. Max Mara's highly successful policy of employing design consultants results in clothes which serve an international demand within an Italian design concept. It has always been Max Mara's aim to give the consumer a worthy product with a high ratio of content, price, and quality." By the dawn of the 21st century, the firm was certainly serving these needs, with 700 stores in 90 countries, most recently Russia, and a recent U.S. expansion which opened shops in New York, Los Angeles, Las Vegas, Chicago, Dallas, Boston, Beverly Hills, Houston, Miami, Palm Beach, San Francisco, and Seattle. Offering three dozen lines under the Max Mara umbrella, customers are sure to find apparel and a growing mix of accessories to their liking.

—Catherine Woram; updated by Nelly Rhodes

MAXWELL, Vera

American designer

Born: Vera Huppe in New York, 22 April 1903. **Family:** Married Raymond J. Maxwell, 1924 (divorced, 1937); married Carlisle H. Johnson (divorced, 1945); children: R. John Maxwell. **Career:** Danced with the Metropolitan Opera Ballet, 1919–24; studied tailoring in London and worked as a fitting model before beginning to design in 1929; designed for New York wholesale firms, including Adler & Adler, Max Milstein, Glenhurst, 1930s and 1940s; designer of sports and tailored clothes, Brows, Jacobson & Linde, from 1937; launched firm, Vera Maxwell Originals, New York, 1947; closed firm, 1985; designed collection for Peter Lynne division, Gulf Enterprises, 1986; retired to write her memoirs. **Exhibitions:** Smithsonian Institution, Washington, D.C., 1970 [retrospective]; Museum of the City of New York, 1978 [retrospective]. **Awards:** Coty American Fashion Critics award, 1951; Neiman Marcus award, Dallas, 1955. **Died:** 14 January 1995, in Rincon, Puerto Rico.

Publications

On MAXWELL:

Books

Milbank, Caroline Rennolds, *Couture: The Great Designers,* New York, 1985.
New York and Hollywood Fashion: Costume Designs from the Brooklyn Museum Collection, New York, 1986.
Milbank, Caroline Rennolds, *New York Fashion: The Evolution of American Style,* New York, 1989.
Fashion for America! Designs in the Fashion Institute of Technology, New York, Haselmere, Surrey, 1992.
Stegemeyer, Anne, *Who's Who in Fashion, Third Edition,* New York, 1996.

Articles

Curtis, Charlotte, "Vera Maxwell: The Designer with Many Interests," in the *New York Times,* 1 June 1961.
Morris, Bernadine, "Fashion Retrospective at the Smithsonian for Vera Maxwell," in the *New York Times,* 2 March 1970.
"Vera Maxwell," in *Current Biography,* July 1977.
Morris, Bernadine, "Timeless Fashions at Vera Maxwell Retrospective," in the *New York Times,* 12 December 1980.
Shapiro, Susan, "A Classic on Seventh Avenue," in the *New York Times Magazine,* 2 December 1984.

Design by Vera Maxwell, 1963. © Bettmann/CORBIS.

Schiro, Anne-Marie, "Vera Maxwell, 93, Dies; Was Early Leader of American Sportswear Designs," in the *New York Times,* 20 January 1995.
Obituary, "Died, Vera Maxwell," in *Time,* 30 January 1995.

* * *

Throughout her long career, Vera Maxwell held steadfastly to her belief that good design is timeless; decade after decade her collections bore the fruit of this philosophy. In 1935 her career was launched with the goal of achieving softer tailoring in women's suits. The silhouette of those early designs would be quite fashionable today. In 1937 she joined Brows, Jacobson & Linde as a designer of sports and tailored clothes. Active sportswear was her specialty with emphasis on skiing and riding, and her shorts, jackets, slacks, and skirts became the foundation of American sportswear separates and the staple of the industry.

Maxwell was most famous, however, for her suits and topcoats, worn for both the city and the country and characterized by excellent tailoring, choice fabrics, beautiful colors, and pragmatism. One suit, designed under her own label in 1948, a year after she opened her own business, was designed for traveling. Called "the original flight suit," it consisted of a brown and white Irish tweed coat with a plastic-lined pocket for carrying a washcloth and toothbrush, worn over slacks and blouse of a coordinating cocoa wool jersey. Ease of movement and comfort while traveling were of great importance, but the effectiveness of the design with the close fitting jersey and the fingertip length full coat, gave this particular suit a timeless modernity.

Influences on Maxwell's designs came from many sources. One of her early memories was of a visit to Vienna with her father, an aide-de-camp to the Emperor Franz Joseph, where she was impressed with the beautifully dressed military officers. Chanel was also an important influence. Long considered a classicist by the industry, Maxwell's clothes were usually described as "handsome, interesting, and eminently wearable," according to a *New York Times* article from November 1964. In 1960, on the occasion of the 25th anniversary of her entry into the fashion business, Maxwell pulled together her favorite designs of the past and discovered she had trouble identifying them by year, an indication of the constancy of her work.

In 1935 Maxwell visited Albert Einstein and was inspired by his Harris tweed jacket which she adapted and paired with a gray flannel skirt and pants, giving an important boost to the concept of separates and what she called the "weekend wardrobe." During the 1940s she designed a coverall, which she considered the first jumpsuit for the women doing war work at the Sperry Gyroscope Corporation. In 1951 she was honored with a Coty Special award for coats and suits, and in 1955 came the Neiman Marcus award, both during one of her most prolific decades. In 1970 she was given a retrospective at the Smithsonian Institution.

Ever concerned with attractive and convenient clothes and wardrobes that could travel well, and always on the lookout for new means to achieve them, she took a significant risk in 1971 to purchase 30,000 yards of a new fabric called Ultrasuede produced by a company in Japan. Initially buyers were afraid to purchase clothes made of the new material, but time proved Maxwell right and the fabric became identified with her designs. Though Maxwell closed her business in 1985, she was again designing in 1986. Then she once again announced her retirement to set about writing her memoirs, which were never completed.

Vera Maxwell inspired a loyal following of fashion-conscious women who sought the timeless wearability of her clothes. She ranked among the top of the group of craftspeople-designers who flourished during the 1930s and 1940s in New York and who created the well-tailored but casual look long associated with American fashion.

—Jean Druesedow

McCARDELL, Claire

American designer

Born: Frederick, Maryland, 24 May 1905. **Education:** Attended Hood College, Maryland, 1923–25, and Parsons School of Design, New York and Paris, 1926–29. **Family:** Married Irving D. Harris, 1943. **Career:** Fashion model, knitwear designer, Robert Turk, Inc., New York, 1929–31; designer, Townley Frocks, New York, 1931–38; designer, Hattie Carnegie, New York, 1938–40; designer, Claire McCardell for Townley Frocks, New York, 1940–58; children's line, Baby McCardells, introduced, 1956. **Exhibitions:** Retrospective, Frank Perls Gallery, Beverly Hills, California, 1953; *Innovative Contemporary Fashion: Adri and McCardell,* Smithsonian Institution, Washington, D.C., 1971; *Three Women: Madeleine Vionnet, Claire McCardell and Rei Kawakubo,* Fashion Institute of Technology, New York, 1987. **Awards:** *Mademoiselle* Merit award, 1943; Coty American Fashion Critics award, 1944, 1958; Neiman Marcus award, 1948; Women's National Press Club award, 1950; Parsons

Claire McCardell in 1940. © Bettmann/CORBIS.

medal for Distinguished Achievement, 1956. **Died:** 22 March 1958, in New York.

Publications

By McCARDELL:

Books

What Shall I Wear? The What, Where, When, and How Much of Fashion, New York, 1956.

On McCARDELL:

Books

Williams, Beryl, *Fashion is Our Business,* Philadelphia, 1945.

Lee, Sarah Tomerlin, editor, *American Fashion: The Life and Lines of Adrian, Mainbocher, McCardell, Norell, Trigère,* New York, 1975.

Milbank, Caroline Rennolds, *Couture: The Great Designers,* New York, 1985.

New York and Hollywood Fashion: Costume Designs from the Brooklyn Museum Collection, New York, 1986.

Koda, Harold, Richard Martin and Laura Sinderbrand, *Three Women: Madeleine Vionnet, Claire McCardell, and Rei Kawakubo* (exhibition catalogue), New York, 1987.

Milbank, Caroline Rennolds, *New York Fashion: The Evolution of American Style,* New York, 1989.

Steele, Valerie, *Women of Fashion: Twentieth Century Designers,* New York, 1991.

Stegemeyer, Anne, *Who's Who in Fashion, Third Edition,* New York, 1996.

Articles

"Claire McCardell," in *Current Biography* (New York), November 1954.

"Designers Who Are Making News," in *American Fabrics and Fashions* (New York), No. 38, 1956.

"Claire McCardell" obituary, in the *New York Times,* 23 March 1958.

Morris, Bernadine, "Looking Back at McCardell: It's a Lot Like Looking at Today," in the *New York Times,* 24 May 1972.

Beckett, Kathleen, "Designing Women," in *Vogue* (New York), March 1987.

Weinstein, Jeff, "Vionnet, McCardell, Kawakubo: Why There Are Three Great Women Artists," in *Village Voice* (New York), 31 March 1987.

Drier, Deborah, "Designing Women," in *Art in America* (New York), May 1987.

Yusuf, Nilgin, "Form and Function," in *Elle,* June 1990.

"Claire McCardell: Designer of Fashion for All-American Beauties (The 100 Most Important Americans of the 20th Century)," *Life,* Fall 1990.

Als, Hilton, "Suited for Leisure," in *Artforum* (New York), 4 November 1994.

* * *

Claire McCardell was the founder of American ready-to-wear fashion, and in doing so defined what has become known as the American Look. She created casual but sophisticated clothes with a functional design, which reflected the lifestyles of American women. McCardell's design philosophy was that clothes should be practical, comfortable, and feminine. Capitalizing on the World War II restrictions on the availability of French fashions and fabrics, McCardell designed simple, inexpensive clothes under the label Townley Frocks by Claire McCardell and later Claire McCardell Clothes by Townley.

The first successful silhouette McCardell designed was the Monastic, a dartless, waistless, bias-cut, tent-style dress that could be worn with or without a belt. McCardell had several other successful designs which stayed in her collections, with slight changes, for years. In 1942 McCardell introduced the Popover, a wrap around, unstructured, utilitarian denim dress to be worn over smarter clothes. This garment was made in response to a clothing request by *Harper's Bazaar* for women whose hired help had left for wartime factory work. The Popover evolved in later collections into dresses, coats, beach wraps, and hostess dresses.

McCardell was known for many other innovations and she experimented with unconventional fabrics for various silhouettes. Her wool jersey bathing suits and cotton-diaper swimsuit are examples of nontraditional fabric use. Madras cotton halter-style full-length hostess gowns were shown for evening. Her design trademarks were

Design by Claire McCardell, 1946. © Genevieve Naylor/CORBIS.

double top-stitching, brass hardware replacing buttons with decorative hooks, spaghetti ties, large patch pockets, and Empire waists. McCardell also brought denim to the fashion forefront as a dress fabric, as well as mattress ticking, calicos, and wool fleece. Manmade fibers, too, were a source of innovation. She also loved leotards, hoods, pedal pushers, and dirndl skirts. Surprising color combinations were indicative of McCardell's work.

Ever resourceful, McCardell viewed the 1940s wartime restrictions as challenging. Shoes were heavily rationed, so McCardell promoted the ballet slipper as street wear, often covered in coordinating or matching fabrics to her clothing ensembles.

The inspirations for McCardell's designs were many. She relied primarily on her own intuition as a woman, believing that many other women had the same needs for their wardrobes. "Most of my ideas," stated McCardell, "come from trying to solve my own problems." She sought to find solutions by analyzing the various needs of women, concluding that essentially clothes must be functional. While skiing she found her head became quite cold and thus designed winter playclothes with hoods. She also recognized how cars and airplanes had changed the American travel lifestyle dramatically; women needed clothes that would travel well. Accordingly, McCardell designed a six-piece interchangeable and coordinated wardrobe of separates, enabling traveling woman to produce many combinations from just a few garments.

McCardell rarely looked to contemporary French fashion for inspiration, as many other American designers did before and after World War II. She recognized the differing needs of American women from the European couture client and the potential of the larger ready-to-wear market in the United States. In this way she was able to define the American style of casual elegance. Back in 1926 during her sophomore year at Parsons School of Design, McCardell studied in Paris. While there she was able to buy samples from the French couturier Madeleine Vionnet and study the pattern and cut of her garments. Vionnet's influence was evident in McCardell's work; though McCardell did not work in the couture tradition, she was able to create ready-to-wear clothing by simplifying Vionnet's cut. She incorporated the bias cut into her designs, both for aesthetic as well as functional effects. From Vionnet, McCardell said she learned "the way clothes worked, the way they felt."

The beauty of McCardell's clothes lay in the cut which then produced a clean, functional garment. Her clothes accentuated the female form without artificial understructures and padding. Rather than use shoulder pads, McCardell used the cut of the sleeve to enhance the shoulder. Relying on the bias cut, she created fitted bodices and swimsuits which flattered the wearer. Full circle skirts, neatly belted or sashed at the waist without crinolines underneath, a mandatory accessory for the New Look, created the illusion of the wasp waist. McCardell clothes often had adjustable components, such as drawstring necklines and waists, to accommodate many different body types.

Claire McCardell's greatest contribution to fashion history was in creating and defining the American Look. Her inspiration is evident in the work of the many fashion designers who followed her.

—Margo Seaman

McCARTNEY, Stella

English designer

Born: Notting Hill, England, 1972. **Education:** Attended Central St. Martin's College of Art & Design, London, graduated in 1995. **Family:** Daughter of musician Paul and photographer Linda (deceased) McCartney. **Career:** Interned for Christian Lacroix, apprenticed with Knightsbridge tailor Edward Sexton; launched her first line, "Stella," of lingerie-modeled dresses in London, 1995; became head designer of Chloé in Paris, 1997; first Paris show at the Ritz included her spring-summer collection, 1997; introduced spring collection, 1997; moved to Gucci, 2001; launched her own label, 2001. **Awards:** VH1 and *Vogue* Designer of the Year, 2001. **Address:** Eighth arrondissement near the Palais de L'Elysse, Paris, France.

Stella McCartney, spring/summer 2002 ready-to-wear collection. © Reuters NewMedia Inc./CORBIS.

Publications

By McCARTNEY:

Articles

"My Chloé Diary," in *Harper's Bazaar* (New York), January 1998.

On McCARTNEY:

Articles

"Magical Mystery Couture," in *People,* 3 July 1995.
Mower, Sarah, "Chloe's Girl," in *Harper's Bazaar* (New York), June 1997.
"Stella McCartney," in *People,* 29 December 1997.
Bellafante, Ginia, "Romance," in *Time,* 6 April 1998.
Chambers, Veronica, "She Grooves; Will She Go?" in *Newsweek,* 18 October 1999.
"Women on Top," in *Harper's Bazaar,* April 2001.
Menkes, Suzy, "A Move to Gucci for McCartney," in the *International Herald Tribune,* 10 April 2001.

Stella McCartney, spring/summer 2002 ready-to-wear collection. © Reuters NewMedia Inc./CORBIS.

* * *

The name itself implies fame, but it can't all be attributed to the ever-popular Beatles legend, Paul McCartney, or his photographer wife, the late Linda Eastman McCartney. Barely in her 30s, the British designer Stella McCartney had already introduced several clothing lines of her own, not to mention becoming head designer of the House of Chloé.

Living in her Notting Hill flat, McCartney seemed to have it all. Guests flocked to experience the inviting atmosphere and sensual modeling episodes. Sexpot slips, metal-mesh minis, and revealing knit dresses were McCartney's greatest accomplishment up to 1997. But her carefree, living-for-the-moment lifestyle came to an end when the offer to head Chloé was presented before her—an offer any young designer couldn't refuse.

Hired only 18 months out of design school, McCartney's flirtatious style was a perfect fit with Chloé. Although young and inexperienced, her determination and bold personality earned her quite the success she deserved. In 1999 Chloé pulled in an amazing $421.4 million, not including the opening of its first subsidiary in 20 years, a Chloé boutique in Manhattan.

With the help of high-profile friends Naomi Campbell and Kate Moss, McCartney successfully took over veteran designer Karl Lagerfeld's place at Chloé. Whether it was for a fitting, fashion show, photo shoot, or merely moral support, Campbell and Moss helped pave the road for McCartney. "Stella's a friend of mine. I wanted to help her out on this," Campbell said in 1995 at the start of McCartney's career. While Chloé continued to thrive with newcomer McCartney, rumors still swirled about the young designer's path. People thought she was too young, didn't have an understanding of the design world, and even worse, was hired based on her father's name. "I don't think the Chloé chiefs would be stupid enough to ride a whole company on me because of who my father is. I'm the breath of fresh air that Chloé needs," McCartney told *People* in January 1998.

As McCartney transitioned from London to Paris, she kept a diary describing in detail her day-to-day experiences. Some inserts focused on Paris life in general, and some on what she was feeling. Learning the ins and outs of Paris seemed to come quickly for her; it was in the designing world she had yet to prove herself. Near the end of the journal, dated the morning of 5 October 1997, McCartney wrote: "To me, this spring-summer 1998 collection is more than a fashion show, it is a statement. Fashion shows come and go, don't they? They don't change the world, do they? But these clothes that you see parading by are my way of speaking to women, to the girls of my own generation, but even more to the women who are old enough to be my mother, and especially to my mother, Linda, to whom this collection is dedicated."

McCartney often commuted back and forth between London and Paris and also did a fair amount of travel within Paris. As she met more people and visited more design studios, it became clear she needed to reduce the gap between male and female clothing. The idea may not have surfaced completely, but what did develop was her 1998 spring-summer collection. The line resembled those of her London days yet with a flare of sophistication and modern maturity. Although other designers would agree that McCartney's designs portray a "girlish" and feminine style, the designer herself believes her collections have grown since her time in London and are based on romantic tradition. "My mom always collected thrift-shop stuff—especially Italian slips," McCartney commented in an April 1998 *Time* magazine article. "I've always loved underwear and antique fabrics and lace for all their soft texture."

Probably the greatest challenge McCartney faced at Chloé was her ability to appeal to both 25-year-olds as well as 45-year-olds. In her spring 1998 collection, McCartney featured garments that indicated sensuality. Wide-leg pantsuits, delicately patterned knee-length day dresses, lace-trimmed slip dresses, spaghetti-strap tops, and translucent minis are at the heart of what the designer loves most—femininity. But the look appealed to a much more youthful audience. With the influence of President Mounir Moufarrige and Lagerfeld, McCartney's level of detail helped her address the age-insensitive issue. Her styles became as popular among 20-somethings as they were to women in their 40s and 50s. McCartney's clothing portrays more than a fashion statement; her fashions often characterize a woman's personality, intellect, and sexuality. McCartney's young, flirtatious style has slowly transformed into elegant fun.

The question hanging in the air, however, was how long McCartney planned to stay at Chloé. The young and inspiring designer had only begun to set out on her career; opportunities were already bombarding the once "girlish" designer. As for her role at Chloé, some said it would soon diminish, as she has been known to move from one pursuit to another rather quickly in the past. McCartney took Chloé to a level most people never anticipated, which was exactly the reason many foresaw another major career move in the youthful designer's life. Industry insiders speculated there wasn't enough room for McCartney to grow at Chloé—at least not to the extent she desired. And they were right: life at Chloé was short-lived for McCartney. The designer's bold, captivating style intrigued Domenico De Sole, president and chief executive of the Gucci Group. In April 2001, Gucci announced it had signed McCartney, who would soon launch her own label under its banner.

—Diana Idzelis

McCLINTOCK, Jessica

American designer

Born: Jessica Gagnon in Presque Isle, Maine, 19 June 1930. **Education:** Studied at Boston University; received Bachelor of Arts degree, San Jose State University, California, 1963; no formal training in design. **Family:** Married Al Staples, 1949 (died, 1964); married Fred McClintock (divorced, 1967); children: Scott. **Career:** School teacher, Marblehead, Massachusetts, 1966–68, Long Island, New York, 1968, and Sunnyvale, California, 1964–65 and 1968–69; partner/designer, Gunne Sax Company, San Francisco, from 1969, company renamed Jessica McClintock, 1986; girls line and Jessica McClintock Contemporary line introduced, 1979; Romantic Renaissance bridal collection introduced, 1980; Scott McClintock line of women's clothes introduced, 1982; first sleepwear collection presented, 1985; Scott McClintock sportswear line introduced, 1986; Jessica McClintock Collection introduced, 1987; first boutique opened, San Francisco, 1980; second shop opened, Costa Mesa, California, 1986; signature fragrance introduced, 1987; Beverly Hills store opened, 1991; introduced fabrics; new Young at Heart bed and bath line, 1996; signed license with Barth & Dreyfuss for kitchen accessories line, 1996; opened two new strores, 1998; had 27 shops by 30th anniversary, 1999; signed license for 50-piece furniture collection, 2000; introduced area rugs, 2001; fragrances include *Jessica McClintock, Jessica,* and *Jess.* **Awards:** Ernie award, 1981; California Designers award, 1985; American Printed Fabrics Council Tommy award, 1986; Press Appreciation award, 1986; Dallas Fashion award, 1988; Merit award in Design, 1989. **Address:** 1400 16th Street, San Francisco, CA 94103, U.S.A. **Website:** www.jessicamcclintock.com.

Publications

On McCLINTOCK:

Books

Delgado, Gary, *How the Empress Gets New Clothes: Asian Immigrant Women Advocates vs. Jessica McClintock Inc.,* Oakland, California, 1994.

Stegemeyer, Anne, *Who's Who in Fashion, Third Edition,* New York, 1996.

Articles

Wilhelm, Maria, "Jessica McClintock Weaves Romantic Fashion," in *People Weekly,* 17 September 1984.

Mercer, Marilyn, "Space to Dream," in *Working Woman,* May 1986.

Evans, Karen, "Meet Designer Jessica McClintock," in *Seventeen,* April 1987.

Simpson, Blaise, "Jessica McClintock: Marketing Romance," in *WWD,* 5 January 1988.

Dunhill, Priscilla, "Jessica McClintock: An Endearing Quality," in *Victoria* (New York), August 1989.

Frinton, Sandra, "The Younger Set: Bibb Gets McClintock to Woo the Girls," in *HFN (The Weekly Newspaper for the Home Furnishing Network),* 15 April 1996.

Orenstein, Alison F., "A Brand Launch: Barth Label to Include New Licenses," in *HFN (Weekly Newspaper for the Home Furnishing Network),* 23 September 1996.

Barrett, Joyce, "Labor Dept. Releases Quarterly Violations List," in *WWD,* 22 November 1996.

"Pretty in Pink," in *Time,* 2 June 1997.

"The Top 100," in *WWD,* 19 November 1997.

Wilson, Eric, "Jessica McClintock at Thirty: From Rickback to Riches," in *WWD,* 9 March 1999.

Power, Denise, "McClintock Revises its Web Site Strategy," in *WWD,* 19 January 2000.

Goldbogen, Jessica, "McClintock: From Dresses to Dressers," in *HFN (Weekly Newspaper for the Home Furnishing Network),* 11 September 2000.

"Bashian to Unveil Jessica McClintock Rug Collection at High Point Market," in *HFN (Weekly Newspaper for the Home Furnishing Network),* 17 September 2001.

* * *

At the height of the hippie movement, Jessica McClintock joined the San Franciscan Gunne Sax Company to design their long, calico, lace-trimmed dresses, very popular with the young. Besides "granny" dresses, McClintock also designed lace-trimmed denim clothes and combined lace with linen. By the 1970s she had added prom dresses and wedding gowns, continuing to use lavish lace trim, which had become her trademark.

When the more contemporary Jessica McClintock line was introduced in 1979, Gunne Sax became the little girls' division, for which the calico, ruffled lace trimmed dresses were eminently suitable. In her San Francisco shop McClintock sold accessories, cosmetics, and her higher-priced designs, but it was for her feminine alternative to the hard-edged emerging high tech trends in fashion that she became known. A moderately priced Scott McClintock line specialized in misses' dresses and sportswear, all with the romantic McClintock look, but more sophisticated than Gunne Sax.

Gunne Sax dresses for teenagers featured ribbons, ruffles, Victorian lace collars, ballerina length skirts. In the mid-1980s McClintock drew her inspiration for misses' dresses from the 1920s, combining straight silhouettes, loose enough for maternity wear, with Victorian details of lace insertions, peplums, or high collars. McClintock designed 2,500 outfits per year, each with her unique romantic touches and femininity. The Jessica McClintock label, aimed at women in their 20s and 30s, offered special occasion ready-to-wear at relatively moderate designer label prices.

The use of man-made materials (polyester, acetate, nylon, rayon) made the lavishly decorated heirloom looks possible at a lower price. Cotton and linen are also used by McClintock, resulting in tea-gown-length Edwardian-inspired dresses in ecru, suitable not only for attendance at weddings, but for wear by the bride for a second or third, less formal, occasion. McClintock expanded into sleepwear, also romantic and nostalgic.

McClintock studied what teenagers wore to incorporate new trends, such as sundresses or the can-can skirts of 1987, and interpreted them in her own manner. Unlike Jeanne Lanvin's matching mother-daughter outfits, McClintock designed coordinating little girl-mother or older sister dresses. The fabrics, colors, and trims might be the same, but the styling and placement of trimmings differed. In keeping with mainstream fashion's more opulent evening looks, McClintock began adding deep color and black velvets into her collection, creating long, unabashedly romantic gowns. Tight décolleté bodices edged with heavy white or metallic gold Venetian lace contrasted with lush velvets falling to the floor, sometimes with a bustle effect, were more demurely echoed in little girls' dresses reminiscent of *The Little Princess.*

McClintock dresses were the sort that might be taken out of a trunk to be worn over and over again when a woman tires of her mundane everyday clothes. For juniors, the Scott McClintock line even offered short black velvet halter dresses, without any lace, paired with black velvet jackets. Additional sophistication was developed by the use of velvets brocaded with metallic, stiff bouffant taffeta skirts topped by metallic floral brocade jackets. More recent additions were a short sexy strapless black lace dress sparkling with all-over *paillettes.*

The McClintock name ran into some trouble in the middle 1990s due to sweatshop allegations, especially with the group Asian Immigrant Women Advocates. One of the McClintock's contractors was investigated by the U.S. Department of Labor, and due to several violations the McClintock business was listed among the violators published in the quarterly Garment Enforcement Report. McClintock vowed to investigate the charges and problems, and in subsequent Dept. of Labor reports was on both the violatiors list as well as the Trendsetter's list of businesses setting an excellent labor example. Commenting to *Women's Wear Daily* (22 November 1996) on the firm's presence on both lists simultaneously, McClintock said, "You can try your best to solve all the problems, but it's almost impossible to monitor them all the time."

By the end of the 1990s McClintock frocks were still in style—both as new apparel and even more so as retro fashion. Prom gowns were a major hit in 1997 as pastels and flowers were again the favorites of young women. Even the *Jessica McClintock* fragrance, introduced years earlier, remained a perennial bestseller among new scents like Clavin Klein's *CK One* and *CK Be,* and Tommy Hilfiger's *Tommy Girl.* In a *Women's Wear Daily* survey of the Top 100 most recognized apparel and accessories brands in the industry, Jessica McClintock ranked a surprising seventh, behind such varied powerhouses as Cartier, Tiffany, and Timberland.

In the 21st century the McClintock look continued to be nostalgic dresses with a sense of mystery, appropriate for both mothers and daughters. Yet over the ensuing three decades, the McClintock brand had come to emcompass far more than its well known dresses; the name graced a myriad of products including sportswear, separates, sleepwear, hosiery, baby bedding, fragrances, linens, bath collections, kitchen textiles, upholstery fabrics, furniture, and area rugs. Additonally, the company had joined of ranks of Internet retailers, introducing a website with style updates, store locations, and online sales.

—Therese Duzinkiewicz Baker; updated by Sydonie Benét

McFADDEN, Mary

American designer

Born: New York City, 1 October 1938. **Education:** Studied at the École Lubec, 1955–56, at the Sorbonne, Paris, 1956–57; studied fashion at the Traphagen School of Design, 1956; studied sociology at Columbia University and at the New School for Social Research, New York, 1958–60. **Family:** Married Philip Harari, 1965 (divorced); married Frank McEwan, 1968 (divorced, 1970); married Armin Schmidt, 1981 (divorced); married Kohle Yohannan, 1988

Mary McFadden, fall/winter 1999 collection: Mongolian wedding gown with beading and embroidery. © AP/Wide World Photos.

(divorced); children: Justine. **Career:** Director of Public Relations, Dior New York, 1962–64; merchandising editor, *Vogue,* South Africa, 1964–65; travel and political columnist, *Rand Daily Mail,* South Africa, 1965–68; founder, Vukutu sculpture workshop, Rhodesia, 1968–70; also freelance editor for *My Fair Lady,* Cape Town, and *Vogue,* Paris, 1968–70; special projects editor, American *Vogue,* New York, 1970; freelance fashion and jewelry designer, New York, from 1973; Marii pleated fabric patented, 1975; president, Mary McFadden Inc., from 1976; home furnishings line introduced, 1978; lower priced line manufactured by Jack Mulqueen, from 1980; Mary McFadden Knitwear Company, launched 1981; also costume designer for *Zooni,* 1993; launched Mary McFadden Studio, 1995; began designing neckwear, 1999; Mary McFadden Collection, debuted 2001. **Exhibitions:** *A Passion for Fashion: The Mortimer Collection,* Wadsworth Atheneum, Hartford, Connecticut, 1993. **Awards:** Coty American Fashion Critics award, 1976, 1978, 1979; Audemars Piquet Fashion award, 1976; Rex award, 1977; Moore College of Art award, Philadelphia, 1977; Pennsylvania Governor's award, 1977; Roscoe award, 1978; Presidential Fellows award, Rhode Island School of Design, 1979; Neiman Marcus award, 1979; Doctor of Fine Arts, Miami International Fine Arts College, 1984; American Printed Fabrics Council Tommy award, 1991. **Address:** 240 West 35th St., New York, NY 10001, U.S.A.

Publications

On McFADDEN:

Books

Morris, Bernadine, and Barbara Walz, *The Fashion Makers,* New York, 1978.

Milbank, Caroline Rennolds, *Couture: The Great Designers,* New York, 1985.

Diamonstein, Barbaralee, *Fashion: The Inside Story,* New York, 1985.

Milbank, Caroline Rennolds, *New York Fashion: The Evolution of American Style,* New York, 1989.

Stegemeyer, Anne, *Who's Who in Fashion, Third Edition,* New York, 1996.

Articles

Tucker, Priscilla, "Mary Had a Little Dress," in the *New York Daily News,* 6 April 1980.

Foley, Bridget, "Mary McFadden: A New Type of Tycoon," in *New York Apparel News,* March 1983.

Rafferty, Diane, "Beyond Fashion," in *Connoisseur* (New York), October 1988.

Thurman, Judith, "Power Gives You an Aura, Says Mary McFadden," in *Mirabella,* September 1989.

Gross, Michael, "Mary, Mary, Quite Contrary: The Life and Loves of Mary McFadden," in *New York,* 26 March 1990.

"The Designers Talk Passion, Whimsy and Picassos," in *ARTnews* (New York), September 1990.

Horyn, Cathy, "A Mary-Tale Romance," in the *Washington Post,* 9 June 1991.

"New York: Mary McFadden," in *WWD,* 4 November 1994.

Mary McFadden, fall/winter 1999 collection: sheared mink coat with a stenciled leopard print. © AP/Wide World Photos.

Friedman, Arthur, "McFadden Exits Seventh on Sixth...," in *WWD,* 21 March 1995.

"MMCF's New Society," in *WWD,* 25 July 1995.

"Mary McFadden Launches Better Special-Occasion Line," in *WWD,* 19 September 1995.

Monget, Karyn, "McFadden, Boutique Industries Renew Licensing Agreement," in *WWD,* 20 October 1997.

McKinney, Melonee, "Women's Designer Mary McFadden to Do First-Ever Neckwear Collection," in *WWD,* 19 March 1999.

"Joan Blumberger Olden Rejoins Mary McFadden," in *WWD,* 11 August 2000.

Greenberg, Julee, "McFadden Expanding," in *WWD,* 5 September 2001.

* * *

With an artist's sensitivity to color, harmony, and proportion, Mary McFadden successfully designed original clothing for nearly 20 years. Her distinctive garments reflect an avid study of ancient and ethnic cultures. Inspired by the art and artifacts of Greece, Byzantium, South America and China, among others, as well as the distant cultures encountered during her own travels around the world,

McFadden built a foundation of pure, timeless silhouettes to which she added exotic details, decorations, in stunning fabrics, to culminate in elegant and flattering results.

When *Vogue* featured McFadden's simple tunics made of African prints and Oriental silks, clothes she had fashioned for herself out of necessity during her years spent in South Africa, the effect created sensation. While trousers had become accepted as daytime workwear during the 1970s, women were resigned to spongy polyester double-knits in mundane sherbet colors. McFadden's tunics, worn over silk Chinese pants, offered the comfort of natural fabrics and the eye appeal of vibrant colors and patterns. McFadden's first collection included quilted kimono-shaped jackets, flowing silk or chiffon trousers topped by loose togas made of stylized batik prints depicting Indonesian flowers and dragons, themes she was to repeat in a more luxurious manner in the fall of 1992. Bold, chunky, African-inspired jewelry made from various metals, plastic, and coral accented the eclectic mix.

Shimmering tunics resembling the shapes and patterns of butterfly wings followed, as McFadden developed her famous "*Marii*" pleating, recalling Fortuny's silk pleated fabrics, which were, in turn, based upon ancient Greek and Egyptian pleating. McFadden's pleated evening gowns were ideal for her wealthy, jet-setting clientèle since they were made of satin-backed polyester, which retained the pleats through hand-washing and travel. McFadden's awareness of modern technology had succeeded in making the pleats permanent.

Even her less expensive clothes, offered in the late 1970s, maintained an exotic feeling through the use of hand-painting on challis and suede, macramé yokes, quilting, and grosgrain ribbon binding. Herself a striking model for her creations, McFadden presented some black and white outfits in every collection, echoing her own straight black hair and very pale skin. Drama was created by the contrast, texture, and richness of fabric. The same sense of sophistication was imbued into McFadden's bedding and table linen licensing.

During the late 1970s her more expensive line of dresses included chiffon embroidered in gold, silver, and gold lamé, gold washed silks, foreshadowing the opulence of the 1980s. McFadden continued to design bold sculptured jewelry and braided belts to tie her gowns closer to the body or to use as edgings. Bolero jackets featured details from Portuguese tiles, an example of McFadden's ability to focus on a detail of a work of art, enlarge the motif, and incorporate it into her design.

Ever sensitive to the interplay of textures, the designer punctuated her columns of fine vertical pleating with beaded cuffs and collars, jewel encrusted panels, draped diagonals. Many of her garments came close to the surface richness of the art-to-wear movement but, eschewing the social statements inherent in the movement, her work was instead wearable art, to be collected and taken out to wear as one might precious jewelry. As evocative of the past as some of McFadden's designs may be, they stop short of looking like costumes. Pattern-upon-pattern mosaics of gold embroidery on sheer silk may highlight a Gustav Klimt-inspired collection, but the clothes have always been modern.

Despite the vagaries of fashion, McFadden maintained a consistent aesthetic. Her clothes offered something for almost everyone who could afford them. McFadden herself recommended, "chiffons for the heavy figures, the pleats for the thin ones, the velvets for everyone." By the end of the 1980s, McFadden had experimented with showing slits of bare skin in between swaths of pleated strips composing the bodices of her gowns. The columns closely outlined the curves of fit figures, for the cult of the body was in full swing. The designer shortened her skirts to above the knees, flippy skirts of rows of layered pleats dancing beneath sequined tops. A striking short dress in the spring of 1992 had a skirt encrusted with beads forming a panel from a Tiffany wisteria window, belted with a beaded belt beneath a diagonally Marii-pleated sleeveless bodice. Her Japanese collection followed, the mystery of the Orient conveyed through embroidered snakes and sinuous blossoms.

In 1995 McFadden shifted her secondary line from daywear to more occasion dressing and dresses wearable for day and evening, then created two new lines: the value-priced Mary McFadden Studio, featuring classic dresses and eveningwear, and Mary McFadden Collection, consisting of better suits and sportswear for younger women, which debuted in 2001. Additionally, McFadden, like other designers, had also become a popular guest on QVC. The McFadden accessories featured on the television shopping channel sold exceedingly well.

It may well be said of Mary McFadden that "she walks in beauty," especially since she wears her own designs. She has proven, however, that she is far more than a pretty face. As a preeminent designer she has used her unique skills to fashion an empire, supporting various charities, and overseeing numerous licenses for womenswear, sleepwear, footwear, eyewear, neckwear, and home furnishings.

—Therese Duzinkiewicz Baker; updated by Sydonie Benét

McQUEEN, Alexander

English fashion designer

Born: Lee McQueen, London, England. **Education:** Left school at the age of 16; apprenticed as a tailor with Saville Row tailors Anderson & Shepard and later Gieves & Hawkes, 1990–92; M.A., St. Martin's School of Art, 1992. **Career:** Briefly worked with Koji Tatsuno, 1992; assistant to Romeo Gigli, Milan, 1993–94; launched his own line, 1994; succeeded John Galliano as head designer of Givenchy, 1997; sold 51 percent of his own label to Gucci, 1997; fashions currently available in London, New York, Paris, and Japan. **Awards:** British Designer of the Year, 1996, 1997, 2001. **Address:** 47 Conduit Street, London, England, W1R 9FB. **Website:** www.alexandermcqueen.com.

Publications

On McQUEEN:

Articles

"London Finale: Royalty and Rebellion," in *WWD,* 14 March 1995.

Fallon, James, "Totally British: A Trio of UK Apparel Designers Take the Plunge into Shoe Design," in *Footwear News,* 1 January 1996.

"McQueen Signs with Givenchy," in *WWD,* 11 October 1996.

Alexander McQueen, autumn/winter 2001–02 collection. © AP/ Wide World Photos.

Frankel, Susannah, "Bull in a Fashion Shop," in *The Guardian,* 15 October 1996.

Foley, Bridget, "The Word from McQueen," in *WWD,* 16 January 1997.

Luscombe, Belinda, "What Would Audrey Think?" in *Time,* 21 July 1997.

Foley, Bridget, "McQueen Renews Givenchy Contract," in *WWD,* 11 May 1998.

Raper, Sarah, "McQueen Eyes Shifting Show to New York," in *WWD,* 5 October 1998.

Horyn, Cathy, "McQueen's Audacity, Beene's Impishness," in the *New York Times,* 18 September 1999.

"African McQueen and Classic Burberry," in *WWD,* 17 February 2000.

Horyn, Cathy, "In London, Ho-Hum Ends in Smash Finale," in the *New York Times,* 1 October 2000.

Bellafante, Ginia, "Gucci Secures a Deal with Alexander McQueen," in the *New York Times,* 5 December 2000.

Givhan, Robin, "Givenchy's Loss, Gucci's Gain," in the *Washington Post,* 5 December 2000.

Menkes, Suzy, "A Farewell from McQueen," in the *International Herald Tribune,* 20 March 2001.

Fallon, James, "Alexander McQueen," in *WWD,* 5 June 2001.

"YSL Beaute Secures Alexander McQueen Perfume License," in *PR Newswire,* 13 June 2001.

"YSL Still Gets Backing of Gucci Despite Significant Losses," in *Cosmetics International,* 10 July 2001.

Banks, Jeff, "The Top Brass," in the *Independent on Sunday* (London), 22 July 2001.

"Worldwatch Trade Fairs & Exhibitions," in *Financial Times Business Limited,* 1 November 2001.

* * *

Alexander McQueen is most notably known as the genius of various tailoring techniques. He has audaciously set a different fashion stage in England, where his outlandish fashion shows have brought energy and attention to a fairly quiet and conservative fashion market. The last extreme attention London received was back in the 1960s when Mary Quant entered with the mod look. McQueen's clothes are beautiful and wearable, but he receives most of his attention for his outrageous personality and vibrant character. He is a designer with the stamina to pursue and conquer the world of fashion; by the dawn of the 21st century, McQueen was a fashion icon in the making.

McQueen grew up in London, one of six children of a cab driver and a homemaker. His family struggled financially while McQueen was growing up, so to help the family along, he starting making dresses for his three sisters. At this point, his desire to become a fashion designer began to evolve. He expressed an interest to his parents about a career in fashion, and they were against it. "I was the pink sheep of the family!" McQueen told *Elle* magazine. His parents later became extremely supportive of his career and very proud of his accomplishments.

McQueen has truly grown up in the eyes of the fashion press. He left school at the age of 16 and landed an apprenticeship with Saville Row tailors Anderson & Shepard, later working for Gieves & Hawkes. McQueen has said, "It is important to learn the basics of cut and proportion." Through his apprenticeships, he mastered six methods of pattern cutting, from the 16th century to the present; his talented tailoring techniques are well known within the fashion industry.

At 20, McQueen worked as an assistant to designer Romeo Gigli in Milan, who was extremely impressed with his skills. After a short period working for Gigli, McQueen returned to London to study at Central St. Martin's College of Art and Design. He wanted to be admitted into the Masters of Art program but lacked a formal education. He showed his portfolio to the director of the school, who was very impressed with the work, and admitted the fledgling designer immediately. McQueen's first international exposure came while presenting his final collection at St. Martin's, and he received an enormous amount of press coverage.

McQueen launched his own line in 1992 and on one occasion used crushed beetles and human hair in a fashion show. His presentations have always been full of unpredictable magic and madness. "In the past, he has dressed models in chadors and hoisted them into the air, where they did somersaults and pirouettes until finally miming their own electrocution," wrote the *Washington Post* in December 2000. In

Alexander McQueen, autumn/winter 2001–02 collection. © AP/Wide World Photos.

1996 McQueen replaced John Galliano, ready-to-wear head designer at Givenchy's Haute Couture, but he was not embraced by the fashion press as a designer who was sophisticated enough to handle the Givenchy customer. He was viewed as too controversial and the same month he replaced Galliano, he also received notoriety as British Designer of the Year.

Within two years, McQueen was unhappy at Givenchy, and in an interview in *Arena* magazine, dared his employers to fire him. But before his contract expired, he sold a 51-percent stake in his own label to rival Gucci. Owning the remaining interest in his company still allowed him to have full creative independence. During the breakup with Givenchy, McQueen produced some of his most beautiful clothes to date in his career. The show once again was very controversial, with the setting in an insane asylum. The show, however, confirmed his reputation of producing fashion with an edge.

In the early 2000s, McQueen was concentrating on his own label under a Gucci-McQueen partnership. He was quoted in an article in *WWD* (5 June 2000) saying, "It hasn't been as easy as it seems leaving Givenchy and being able to focus strictly on McQueen. Now I'm seeing all the mistakes we made in the past.... At some stage, you have to grow up. It's important now that people focus on the clothes rather than someone in a clown suit." McQueen continued working on his own line, redesigning the label and packaging, a new store design, preparing the launch of a fragrance in 2003, considering a cosmetics line under the Gucci Group, as well as overseeing the licensing of his eyewear.

Alexander McQueen is a designer who has carved his own career path in the fashion industry. He is a workaholic who keeps moving forward despite the sometimes negative media surrounding him. He is an artist, not just a fashion designer, who does not let the commercial value of his clothing take away from the controversial presentation necessary to draw attention to his creations.

—Donna W. Reamy

MEDINA del CORRAL, José Luis

See VICTORIO Y LUCCHINO

MEISTER, David

American designer

Born: 23 February 1962 in Cincinnati, Ohio. **Education:** Bachelor of Design, magna cum laude, University of Cincinnati College of Design, Architecture, Art, and Planning, 1985. **Career:** Assistant Designer, Danskin 1986–88; designer, Silk Studio, Macy's Corporate Private Label, 1988–91; designer, Oleg Cassini Silk, 1992–93; designer, evening wear for Laundry, 1993; joined with ENC, a division of Kellwood Industries, to create a signature evening wear collection, 1998; introduced day dresses into his David Meister line, 2001. **Address:** 1307 East Temple Avenue, City of Industry, CA 91746; Showroom: 214 West 39th Street, Suite 203, New York, NY 10018.

Publications

On MEISTER:

Articles

"Market Basket," in *WWD,* 29 December 1998.
"SOS: Working the Next Wave," in *WWD,* 13 April 1999.
Williamson, Rusty, "The Party Meister," in *WWD,* 19 May 1999.
Hall, Len, "Running Hot and Cold on the Millennium," in *WWD,* 20 July 1999.
Turk, Rose-Marie, and Eric Wilson, "In Day Dress Revival, a Starring Role for L.A.," in *WWD,* 31 August 1999.
Wilson, Eric, "For Evening Vendors, the End Isn't Near," in *WWD,* 23 November 1999.
Haber, Holly, and Rusty Williamson, "Stores Foresee a Strong Summer," in *WWD,* 12 January 2000.
Wilson, Eric, and Rusty Williamson, "The Ups and Downs of Building a Dress Line," in *WWD,* 7 March 2000.

David Meister: jersey backless gown with rusching and front slit. © Gale Group.

Greenberg, Julee, "Eveningwear's Next Millennium," in *WWD,* 22 August 2000.
McCants, Leonard, "New Day for Meister," in *WWD,* 22 August 2000.
Greenberg, Julee, and Leonard McCants, "Dollars and Dresses: The Ladies are Back and Sales Are Stirring," in *WWD,* 9 January 2001.

*

My collection is clean, modern, glamorous and sexy. It compliments the needs of today's woman and her lifestyle.

—David Meister

* * *

David Meister understands many things. He understands fabrics and the way they flow over the female figure. He understands that a young heart might reside in a mature body. He is aware of the need for good, contemporary dresses for day and evening with price tags less than the national debt. He knows versatility is important. He understands what women want.

The M Collection by David Meister debuted for fall 1999. The 32-piece holiday and resort line included dresses and a wide range of evening separates. The sweater sets, multiple silhouettes in skirts and pants, tanks and novelty shirts, permit tremendous flexibility in evening dress. "The spectrum of styles shows that we're not addressing an age group but a state of mind. Women who appreciate fashion, but don't like fickle trends and those who love opulence but don't want to look over-the-top, will appreciate my line. It's a 21st century mind-set."

Meister's garments are feminine and elegant and cut with strong, clean, sexy silhouettes. Blatantly revisiting eras of glam and glitz with beading and sequins, his first collection offered the perfect attire for the modern siren. Fabrics ranged from simple matte jersey and crêpe to crinkled silks and organza. Outerwear included luxurious faux fur wraps. Stepping outside the usual black for evening, his palette included lilac, moss, dusty gold, ivory, peach and gray. Pegged as "a young designer to watch," the launch was an unqualified success, far outselling expectations.

A 12-year veteran of the fashion industry, Meister previously worked for Danskin, Macy's Corporate, and Oleg Cassini Silk. He spent the next six years at Podell Industries' Laundry Division building the social occasion and bridal area. In the fall of 1998, ENC, a division of Kellwood Industries, approached him about creating a signature evening collection. M by David Meister was introduced to the market in March 1999.

In his second year of business, Meister added a day dress line, "taking the next step in his desire to dress women while the sun is shining." Though he admits eveningwear is his first love, the new collection presented the opportunity to branch out. More tailored than his soft evening styles, the line is clean and modern. He plans to eventually expand to about 60 looks, but the premiere was primarily dresses and two-piece outfits with sweaters and skirts.

Maintaining his signature spare lines, Meister's spring 2001 day collection offered garments in linen, linen tweed, denim, and cotton. Some of the print dresses have a bold 1960s feel with strong graphic elements. His contemporary day dresses fill a void left by collections that have become too young, and the public response has been outstanding. Nieman Marcus' Gerald Barnes said, "The line is pretty and clean and on target," and Beverly Rice at Jacobsen's added, "The collection is very versatile and well made. The styling is updated and the fabrics are great. David Meister represents the fashion leadership and value that we love." Meister commented, "I want to take it as far as we possibly can. Hopefully with the success of the day dress line, I will be able to do sportswear. So you're dressing the same customer from day to evening to sportswear." His spring 2001 evening collection included little crêpe "classic cocktail" selections that were flying out the door, and his evening wear has continued to sell well.

David Meister has met a very difficult challenge: he has managed to understand women want well-made, beautiful clothing that show them at their best. They want garments that will be right for social occasions and versatile enough to be worn more than once, with a silhouette that will enhance a good figure, but with enough forgiveness to help conceal imperfections. Women want to feel pretty and feminine and sexy, at an affordable price. Not only does Meister understand, he delivers.

A native of Ohio, David Meister is well spoken and personable. He graduated magna cum laude from the fashion design program at the University of Cincinnati College of Design, Architecture, Art and Planning. A serious and committed student, Meister excelled academically and artistically. Remembered fondly by his professors, he retains his humility and approachability. In a competitive and fickle industry, it's refreshing to see that nice guys don't always finish last.

—Christina Lindholm

METT, Madame Torrente

See TORRENTE

MILLER, Nicole

American designer

Born: 1952, in Lenox, Massachusetts. **Education:** Graduated from Rhode Island School of Design, Providence; spent third year attending the École de la Chambre Syndicale Parisienne. **Family:** Married Kim Taipale, 1996; child: Palmer.**Career:** Designer, Rain Cheetahs, New York, 1975; head designer for Bud Konheim, P.J. Walsh women's fashion company, New York, 1975–82; in partnership with Konheim, company renamed Nicole Miller, 1982; launched line of men's accessories, circa 1987; began licensing agreements for socks, tights, jeans, handbags, and men's formal wear; debuted footwear, 1992; fragrance and cosmetics collection, 1993; bridalwear 1995; Nicole line 1997; men's and women's at-home wear 1999; men's sportswear 2000. Opened boutiques in New York (1987), Mexico City and Naples, Florida (1991), Barcelona, Tokyo, Osaka, and Seville (1992), Los Angeles (1993). **Awards:** Dallas Fashion award, 1991; Girl Scouts of America award, New York, 1994. **Address:** 525 Seventh Avenue, New York, NY, 10018, USA. **Website:** www.nicolemiller.com.

Nicole Miller, spring 2001 collection. © Reuters NewMedia Inc./ CORBIS.

PUBLICATIONS

On MILLER:

Articles and Video

Schulte, Lucy, "A Real Fashion Outlaw," in *New York,* 16 February 1987.

Hochswender, Woody, "A First Show with the Right Flair," in the *New York Times,* 3 November 1990.

"Nicole Miller: Fashion's Wittiest High Roller," in *People,* 29 April 1991.

Shand, Gayle, "Miller's Crossing," in *Footwear News* (New York), 3 February 1992.

Rockwell, Abigail, and Sally V. Beaty, *A Different Look: The Nicole Miller Story* (video), RMI Productions, 1993.

Ball, Aimee Lee, "Thoroughly Modern Miller," in *New York,* 8 March 1993.

Drake, Laurie, "Can Nicole Eat Lunch in This Town?," in *Los Angeles Magazine,* May 1993.

"Miller Time: Nicole Goes Retail," in *Crain's New York Business,* 15 June 1998.

Mui, Nelson, "Nicole Miller Launches Sportswear Collection for Fall 2000," in *DNR,* 20 December 1999.

Curan, Catherine, "Nicole Miller Redresses Strategy," in *Crain's New York Business,* 12 June 2000.

Johnson, Hillary J., "A Fashionable Address," in *InStyle* (New York), November 2000.

* * *

Immense talent as a designer, fun, and an astute sense of fashion are the key to Nicole Miller's success. Miller is a hands-on designer, who pays particular attention to clothing construction throughout the entire design process. Her studies at a haute couture school in Paris taught her the importance of a well-engineered and well-fitting garment. Realizing that few women have perfect bodies, she has always made certain every body looks its best, camouflaging problem areas. Because of simple but unique details and superior cut, a woman wearing a Nicole Miller garment is assured of looking her best.

Nicole Miller has had her own women's line of clothing since 1982. The company is primarily known for great looking dresses in both solid and printed fabrics. However, due to an over-abundance of leftover fabric from a line of unsuccessful dresses, she opted to make

Nicole Miller, spring 2001 collection. © Reuters NewMedia Inc./CORBIS.

the conversational black silk print, featuring colored ticket stubs in the foreground, into the Nicole Miller necktie sensation; hence the birth of the Nicole Miller men's accessories line. A dark cloud turned out to have a platinum lining and Miller blossomed into a leading men's accessory manufacturer. In the mid-1990s, the Miller ties, shirts, boxer shorts, and robes accounted for 20 percent of business.

Inspiration for Miller prints can come from anywhere. After seeing the off-Broadway hit *Song of Singapore,* Miller decided to create a special silk print in honor of the show. The company employs dozens of artists who develop a wide range of graphics. Designs incorporate everything from assorted candy, animals, or vegetables to the sports collection, which has featured basketballs, footballs, and baseballs. These prints have become so influential that knockoffs can be found at every level of the marketplace.

Miller has been prolific in other areas of design as well. She was involved in designing costumes for the Brooklyn Academy of Music's New Wave festival tribute to the late Carmen Miranda. Inspiration for the costumes was the peasant clothing of the Bahia region of Brazil visited by Miller.

Although she received a great deal of publicity for her prints, Miller's reputation was actually built with her dramatic pared-down silhouettes and her striking use of graphics. Some examples are her curvy, strapless pale linen chambray dresses, and her short white rompers and dresses stitched in red like a baseball. Flattering fit and drop-dead designs are not Miller's only strong points. She is one of the few American designers with fashion's sixth sense for setting the trends without resorting to fads; her clothes are young and fresh. In a time where many of the baby boomers have become more conservative, the Miller customer remains forever young.

While Miller's cocktail dress and men's novelty ties were the mainstays of her business in the 1980s, she oversees an extensive product line. Miller keeps close watch on her customers and expands her offering to meet their needs. While the core business for the Nicole Miller line remains the dress and dinner suit, she created a bridal line in 1995 after noticing prospective brides were ordering several copies of a particular dress for their bridesmaids. She also launched the Nicole line in 1997 to serve her younger buyers with more contemporary styles like t-shirt dresses.

Drawing on her relationship with the men who buy her ties, Miller launched a sportswear line in 2000 offering trendy clothes priced at a lower-bridge level, including pants, sweaters, shirts, and pajamas, all in characteristically bright, catchy colors. In addition, Miller's prodigious design talent has been applied to many more nontraditional products, including hospital gowns for Hackensack University Medical Center, ties for the NFL as well as the Komen Foundation to fight breast cancer, and a line of premium cigars and accessories.

The growth of the Nicole Miller line accelerated the company's move into retail. Responding to changes in the retail market during the 1990s, department stores began carrying more private labels than designer lines and turned to promotional techniques which some designers believed hurt their image and profits. By establishing Nicole Miller stores which would carry the entire collection, the company could control its identity to the customer. In 1998, Nicole Miller opened many stores outside of New York by licensing the designer's name and giving local owners a great deal of latitude to operate their businesses. Although some of the stores remain successful, the company also faced problems from bad locations, stores selling merchandise that wasn't Nicole Miller, and a case of credit card fraud. The company met the need for another expansion in 2000 more cautiously. All new stores were company-owned and a new director of retail coordinated their operation. In 2001, the company has 30 stores within the United States. Nicole Miller launched its web site for information only in 1994 and began selling online in 1998 at the Nicole Miller website and other sites dedicated to specific products, like its skincare line. Nicole Miller's design talent and her understanding of her customers will make her an important part of the fashion scene for years to come.

—Roberta H. Gruber; updated by Janette Goff Dixon

MISCHKA, James

See BADGLEY MISCHKA

MISSONI

Italian knitwear and fashion house

Founded: in Gallarate, Varese, Italy, 1953, by Ottavio Missoni (born in Dalmatia, 11 February 1921) and Rosita Jelmini Missoni (born in Lombardy, 20 November 1931). **Company History:** First collection produced for Rinascente Stores, 1954; Missoni label introduced, from 1958; first Paris showing, 1967; Missoni SpA workshop and factory established, Sumirago, 1968; first New York showing, 1969; first boutiques opened, Milan and New York, 1976; fragrance line introduced, 1981; Missoni Uomo and Missoni Sport lines introduced, 1985; Angela Missoni collection introduced, 1992; Angela took control of firm, 1997; launched footwear line, 1998; M Missoni debuted, spring-summer 1999; new flagships opened in New York and Paris. **Exhibitions:** Solo exhibition, Il Naviglio Gallery, Venice, 1975; retrospective, La Rotonda Gallery, Milan, and the Whitney Museum, New York, 1978; solo exhibition, Galleria del Naviglio, Milan, and the University of California, Berkeley, 1981; retrospective, Ridotto/Pergola Theatre, Pitti Immagine Filati, Florence, 1994. **Awards:** Neiman Marcus award, 1973; Bath Museum of Costume Dress of the Year award, 1974; American Printed Fabric Council Tommy award, 1976; Gold Medal of Civic Merit award, Milan, 1979; Fragrance Foundation award, 1982; Tai Missoni given Arancia award, 1986; Rosita Missoni named Commendatore al Merito della Repubblica Italiana, 1986; Fashion Group International Design award, 1991; Munich Mode-Woche award, 1992; Dallas Historical Fashion Collectors Stanley award, 1999. **Company Address:** Via Luigi Rossi 52, 21040 Sumirago (Varese), Italy. **Company Website:** www.missoni.com.

Missoni, fall/winter 2001–02 collection. © AP/Wide World Photos.

PUBLICATIONS

On MISSONI:

Books

Mulassano, Adriana, *The Who's Who of Italian Fashion,* Florence, 1979.

Alfonsi, Maria Vittoria, *Leaders in Fashion: I grandi personaggi della moda,* Bologna, 1983.

Giacomozzi, Silvia, *The Italian Look Reflected,* Milan, 1984.

Aragno, Bonizza Giordani, *Moda Italia: Creativity and Technology in the Italian Fashion System,* Milan, 1988.

Tutino Vercelloni, Isa, editor, *Missonologia: The World of Missoni,* Milan, 1994.

Stegemeyer, Anne, *Who's Who in Fashion, Third Edition,* New York, 1996.

Articles

Buck, Joan Juliet, "The Missoni Way," in *WWD,* 12 March 1975.
Klensch, Elsa, "Knit Together for 25 Years," in the *New York Post,* 24 May 1978.
Morris, Bernardine, "Missoni's Clothes a Hit As Milan Showings Open," in the *New York Times,* 26 March 1979.
Buckley, Richard, "Tai and Rosita: Designing Missoni for the Future," in *DNR,* 4 January 1984.
Piaggi, Anna, "Ottavio e Rosita Missoni: legati a doppio filo," in *L'Uomo Vogue* (Milan), October 1987.
"Missoni in mostra: freschi di stampa," in *Donna* (Milan), February 1988.
"In diretta da Milano: l'energia concentrata di Missoni," in *Donna,* October 1988.
"The Missoni Story," in *Donna* supplement, October 1988.
Menkes, Suzy, "Missoni: First Family of Knits," in the *International Herald Tribune,* 12 July 1994.
Muir, Lucie, "Italian Designers Bring Body Conscious Looks Center Stage," in *WWD,* 18 September 1996.
"Missoni," in *WWD,* 24 February 1998.
Zargani, Luisa, "Missoni Planning New Bridge Line for Women," in *WWD,* 23 July 1998.
Williamson, Rusty, "Missonis Win Stanley Award," in *WWD,* 20 May 1999.
Sloan, Carole, "Missoni on a Mission," in *Home Textiles Today,* 13 November 2000.
Jensen, Tanya, "Missoni's Fiery Femininity," online at Fashion Windows, www.fashionwindows.com, 2 October 2001.

* * *

Missoni exemplifies success in a specific fashion area, knitwear for men and women. In the knitwear business since 1953, the business begun by Ottavio (Tai) and Rosita Missoni took off with recognition by Anna Piaggi in 1965 and was one of the landmark enterprises of the Italian renaissance in postwar fashion products through the 1960s and 1970s. In 1968 and 1969, Missoni garnered worldwide attention for knit dresses, coats, and sweaters that revived the sensational appeal of knits in the 1920s. From a start in producing the finest knits, the Missoni repertory came to include pullovers, long coats, chemises, trousers, and skirts. Even more, in the 1970s, the Missonis' deliberate allegiance to Milan heralded that city's eminence as a fashion center and helped create Milan fashion week.

Primarily creators of exceptional knitwear, Missoni has been noted as an art as much as a business. Technology provides a range of fluid knits and special effects, but the identifying and indescribable aspect of the Missoni knits is color, the affinity to art. Most importantly, Missoni brought a vivid sense of imagination to knits, rescuing them from the heirlooms and old-fashioned aspects of handknits and from the conventional sameness of many machine-knitted products. Like many Italian products of the postwar period, the value of the product was not in its handwork, but in the unquestionable supremacy of design attained through machine. Today computers and sophisticated machines make the Missoni knits, yet they remain exceptional in their colors and texture and have become a staple in both menswear and womenswear.

Missoni, fall/winter 2001–02 collection: wool lame top and matching plaid pants. © AP/Wide World Photos.

Tai Missoni's introduction to the knitwear business was as an athlete. Knitwear was for active sports, but by 1958 a striped Missoni knit shirtdress was produced and the crossover from sports to casual living was underway. The sports heritage remains in some graphic boldness, including stripes and zig-zags and even patchwork. What enhances Missoni for daywear and even for evening (especially with Lurex) are the subtleties within. Rosita told Elsa Klensch, writing for the *New York Post* (24 May 1978), "Our philosophy since we went into business has been that a piece of clothing should be like a work of art. It should not be bought for a special occasion or because it's in fashion, but because a woman likes it…and feels she could wear it forever."

Little the Missonis have produced ever depended upon fashion. Instead, their knits seem perennial: a Missoni design might be worn with a favored color one season and still be compatible with other colors in other seasons. Bernadine Morris of the *New York Times* (26 March, 1979) believed the Missonis "elevated knitted clothes to a form of art," and as such they were recognized as visible status symbols in the 1970s and 1980s. By the middle 1990s the Missoni name graced a sexier style of apparel, brought about by Angela Missoni, who had begun designing her own signature collection in 1992. Celebrities flocked to buy the sensual knitwear, the new enthusiasts including Nicole Kidman, Jennifer Lopez, Ashley Judd, and Julia Roberts.

In 1997 Angela took the reins of the company and over the next few years increased brand awareness through a wide range of licensing, from rugs to footwear. New flagships in New York and Paris were opened, while a new bridge line, M Missoni, was introduced for spring-summer 1999. By the early 2000s, Missoni was more than a vital force in knitwear; the firm had gone far beyond its founders' original vision to encompass Missoni designs for an entire lifestyle.

—Richard Martin; updated by Owen James

MIYAKE, Issey

Japanese designer

Born: Kazumaru Miyake in Hiroshima, Japan, 22 April 1938. **Education:** Studied at Tama Art University, Tokyo, 1959–63, and at École de la Chambre Syndicale de la Couture Parisienne, 1965. **Career:** Design assistant, Guy Laroche, 1966–68, and Givenchy, 1968–69; designer, Geoffrey Beene in New York, 1969–70; established Miyake Design Studio in Tokyo, 1970; theater designer, from 1980; first U.S. boutique opened, New York, 1988; director, Issey Miyake International, Issey Miyake and Associates, Issey Miyake Europe, Issey Miyake USA, and Issey Miyake On Limits; lines include Issey Sport, Plantation, Pleats Please (introduced, 1993), and A-POC (introduced, 1999); A-POC stores opened in Tokyo and Paris, 2000; new HQ and store in TriBeCa, 2001; fragrances include *L'Eau d'Issey,* 1992; *L'Eau d'Issey pour Homme,* 1995; *Le Feu d'Issey,* 1998. **Exhibitions:** *Issey Miyake and Twelve Black Girls,* Tokyo and Osaka, 1976; *Issey Miyake in the Museum,* Seibu Museum, Tokyo, 1977; *A Piece of Cloth,* Tokyo, 1977; *Fly With Issey Miyake,* Tokyo and Kyoto, 1977; *East Meets West,* International Design Conference, Colorado, 1979; *Les Tissus Imprimés d'Issey Miyake,* Musée de l'Impression sur Étoffes, Mulhouse, 1979; *Intimate Architecture: Contemporary Clothing,* Massachusetts Institute of Technology, 1982; *Bodyworks,* international touring exhibition, 1983; *A New Wave in Fashion: Three Japanese Designers,* Phoenix Art Museum, Arizona, 1983; *Issey Miyake Bodyworks: Fashion Without Taboos,* Victoria and Albert Museum, London, 1985; *Á Un,* Musée des Arts Decoratifs, Paris, 1988; *Issey Miyake Pleats Please,* Touko Museum of Contemporary Art, Tokyo, 1990; *Ten Sen Men,* Touko Museum of Contemporary Art, Tokyo, 1990; *Twist,* Naoshima Contemporary Art Museum, 1992; *Making Things,* Paris, 1999. **Awards:** Japan Fashion Editors Club award, 1974; Mainichi Newspaper Fashion award, 1976, 1984; Pratt Institute Design Excellence award, New York, 1979; Council of Fashion Designers of America award, 1983; Fashion Oscar, Paris, 1985; Mainichi Fashion Grand Prix, 1989, 1993; Officier de l'Ordre des Arts et Lettres, France, 1989; Asahi prize, 1992; Honorary Doctorate, Royal College of Art, London, 1993; Hiroshima Art prize, 1991; Chevalier de l'Ordre National de la Legion d'Honneur, Paris, 1993; Tokyo Creation award, 1994; Shiju Housho from the Japanese Government, 1997. **Address:** 1–23 Ohyamacho, Shibuya-ku, Tokyo 151, Japan. **Websites:** www.isseymiyake.com, www.pleatsplease.com

PUBLICATIONS

By MIYAKE:

Books

East Meets West, edited by Kazuko Koide and Ikko Tanaka, Tokyo, 1978.
Bodyworks, edited by Shozo Tsurumoto, Tokyo, 1983.
Issey Miyake and Miyake Design Studio 1970–1985, Tokyo, 1985.
Pleats Please, Tokyo, 1990.
Inspired Flower Arrangements, with Toshiro Kawase, Tokyo, 1990.
Madeleine Vionnet, with Betty Kirke, San Francisco, 1998.
Making Things, Paris, 1999.

On MIYAKE:

Books

Deslandres, Yvonne, *Les Tissus Imprimés d'Issey Miyake* [exhibition catalogue], Mulhouse, 1979.
Hayden Gallery, Massachusetts Institute of Technology, *Intimate Architecture: Contemporary Clothing Design* [exhibition catalogue], Cambridge, 1982.

Issey Miyake, spring/summer 2001 ready-to-wear collection. © AFP/CORBIS.

Issey Miyake, spring/summer 2001 ready-to-wear collection. © AP/Wide World Photos.

Phoenix Art Museum, *A New Wave in Fashion: Three Japanese Designers* [exhibition catalogue], Phoenix, 1983.

Koren, Leonard, *New Fashion Japan,* Tokyo and New York, 1984.

Milbank, Caroline Rennolds, *Couture: The Great Designers,* New York, 1985.

Sparke, Penny, *Japanese Design,* London, 1987.

Calloway, Nicholas, ed., *Issey Miyake: Photographs by Irving Penn,* Boston, 1988.

Coleridge, Nicholas, *The Fashion Conspiracy,* London, 1988.

Howell, Georgina, *Sultans of Style: Thirty Years of Fashion and Passion 1960–1990,* London, 1990.

Miyake Design Studio, eds., *Ten Sen Men,* Tokyo, 1990.

Miyake Design Studio, eds., *Issey Miyake by Irving Penn 1991–1992,* Tokyo, 1992.

Miyake Design Studio, eds., *Issey Miyake by Irving Penn 1993–1995,* Tokyo, 1995.

Hiesinger, Kathryn B., and Felice Fischer, *Japanese Design: A Survey Since 1950,* New York, 1995.

Jouve, Marie-Andrée, *Issey Miyake,* New York, 1997.

Holborn, Mark, introduction, *Irving Penn Regards the Work of Issey Miyake: Photographs 1975–1998,* Boston, 1999.

Watson, Linda, *Vogue Twentieth Century Fashion: 100 Years of Style by Decade and Designer,* London, 1999.

Articles

Lewis, J., "The Man Who Put Show in Fashion Shows," in the *Far East Economic Review* (Hong Kong), 22 January 1979.

Bancou, M., "Issey Miyake Revisited," in *American Fabrics & Fashions* (Columbia, SC), Spring 1979.

"Issey Miyake," in the *New Yorker,* 8 and 15 November 1982.

"Issey Miyake," in *Art and Design* (London), March 1985.

Popham, Peter, "The Emperor's New Clothes," in *Blueprint* (London), March 1985.

"Issey Miyake's *Bodyworks,*" in *Domus* (Milan), May 1985.

White, Lesley, "Miyake's Marvelous But Issey Art," in *Cosmopolitan* (London), August 1985.

"Issey Miyake: Dateless Fashion," in *Art and Design* (London), October 1986.

Angel, Sally, "Zen and the Art of Fashion," in *Blueprint,* October 1987.

Knafo, Robert, "Issey Miyake is Changing the Way Men View Clothes," in *Connoisseur* (New York), March 1988.
"Eye of the Artists: Issey Miyake," in *Vogue,* October 1988.
Brampton, Sally, "Modern Master," in *Elle* (London), June 1989.
Martin, Richard, "The Cubism of Issey Miyake," in *Textile & Text* (New York), 12/4, 1990.
Penn, Irving, and Ingrid Sischy, "Pleats Please," in *Interview,* September 1990.
Tilton, Mary, "Issey Miyake: Designer for the Millennium," in *Threads* (Newtown, CT), June/July 1991.
Gross, Michael, "Issey Does It," in *New York,* 22 July 1991.
Bucks, Suzy, "Clothes That Grow on You," in the *Independent on Sunday* (London), 3 July 1994.
Spindler, Amy M., "Art or Vanity? Fashion's Ambiguity," in the *New York Times,* 13 December 1994.
Schiro, Anne-Marie, "Photogenic, But Out of Focus," in the *New York Times,* 20 March 1995.
Menkes, Suzy, "Show, Not Clothes, Becomes the Message," in the *International Herald Tribune,* 20 March 1995.
Wood, Dana, "Miyake's Lust for Life," in *WWD,* 18 December 1996.
Edelson, Sharon, "Miyake Rides SoHo Wave," in *WWD,* 27 August 1997.
Simon, Joan, "Miyake Modern," in *Art in America* (New York), 2 February 1999.
Dam, Julie, "Issey Miyake," in *Time International,* 23 August 1999.
Edelson, Sharon, "Miyake Moves Downtown: New Store, New Concept," in *WWD,* 19 July 2000.

* * *

Architect Arata Isozaki began an essay in Issey Miyake's *East Meets West* with the question, "What are clothes?" The question, perhaps too fundamental and unnecessary for most designers, is the matrix of Issey Miyake's clothing. Possibly more than any other designer of the 20th or 21st centuries, Miyake inquired into the nature of apparel, investigating adornment and dress functions from all parts of the world and from all uses and in all forms, to speculate about clothing. Aroused to question fashion's viability in the social revolution he observed in Paris in 1968, Miyake sought a clothing of particular lifestyle utility, of renewed coalition with textile integrity, and of wholly reconsidered form. In exploring ideas emanating from the technology of cloth, Miyake created great geometric shaping and the most effortless play of drapery on the bias to accommodate body motion since his paragon Madeleine Vionnet.

Miyake's highly successful Windcoats wrap the wearer in an abundance of cloth but also generate marvelously transformative shapes when compressed or billowing and extended. In these efforts, Miyake created garments redolent of human history but largely unprecedented in the history of dress. As a visionary, he often seemed to abandon commercial ideas of dress for more extravagantly new and ideal experiments, such as a 1976 knit square with sleeves, which became a coat with matching bikini; or fall/winter 1989–90 pleated collection which was a radical cubist vision of the human body and of its movement. Miyake has also worked with traditional kimonos, and has even experimented with paper and other materials to find the right medium for apparel. Despite unusual and some thoroughly utopian ideals, Miyake appeals to a clientèle of forward thinkers and designers who wear his clothing with the same zeal and energy from which they were created.

Miyake gives his work interpretative issues and contexts that contribute to their meaning, acknowledging the garments as prolific signs. His two earliest books *East Meets West* (Tokyo, 1978) and *Bodyworks* (Tokyo, 1983), were both accompanied by museum exhibitions of his many creations. Miyake can be anthropologically basic; again and again, he returns to tattooing as a basic body adornment, rendered in clothing and tights and bodysuits. He relishes the juxtaposition between the most rustic and basic and the most advanced, almost to prove human history a circle rather a linear progression. No other designer—with the possible exception of the more laconic Geoffrey Beene, for whom Miyake worked briefly and with whom he maintains a mutual admiration—interprets his work as deliberately and thoughtfully as Miyake.

Such allusiveness and context would have little value were it not for the abiding principles of Miyake's work. He relies upon the body as unerringly as a dancer might. He demands a freedom of motion that reveals its genesis in 1968. If Miyake's concept of the body is the root of all of his thinking, it is a highly conceptual, reasoned body. His books have customarily shown friends and clients—young and old—wearing his clothing. They come from East and West; they do not possess a perfect anatomy or the streamlined physique of body sculptures, but they are in some way ideals to Miyake.

Miyake's works have placed him in the worlds of both clothing designer and artist. His designs explore space and natural forms but are grounded in the understanding that they are to be worn. They exist in one form, only to be transformed when a body gives the piece a third dimension. This transforming power is evident in the endless variations of his pleats collection, which first appeared in his 1989 and was expanded into the Pleats Please line in 1993. Garments were constructed first and then pleated, a reversal of the standard process. Huge garments made of lightweight polyester were fed into a pleating machine and the resulting clothing was easy to wash, quick to dry, and wrinkle-resistant. This practicality reflected Miyake's dedication to the universality of his designs and proved to be a great commercial success. He opened the first Pleats Please store in SoHo in 1998, and the line is one of his most widely recognized.

Miyake's continual questioning and exploration of his own work led to another revolutionary concept in clothing design—mass-produced clothes designed to be individualized by each wearer. In 1999 he introduced the A-POC line, an abbreviation for A Piece of Cloth. In this line, the wearer takes scissors to a section of a continuous knitted tube with cutting guides to fashion her own garment, varying hem, sleeve lengths, and the neckline. The first store dedicated to the A-POC line opened in Tokyo in 1999. The A-POC line is but one example of how Miyake's designs originate with the fabric. His fascination with textiles continues to be the springboard for his work; whether the textiles are natural or synthetic, handwoven or high tech, Miyake transforms fabric into clothing that brings its wearer the joy of beauty and movement.

—Richard Martin; updated by Janette Goff Dixon

MIZRAHI, Isaac

American designer

Born: New York City, 14 October 1961. **Education:** Attended New York High School for the Performing Arts; graduated from Parsons School of Design, New York, 1982. **Career:** Assistant designer,

Isaac Mizrahi taking a bow after showing his spring 1997 collection. © AP/Wide World Photos.

Perry Ellis, New York, 1982–83; womenswear designer, Jeffrey Banks, New York, 1984; designer, Calvin Klein, New York, 1985–87; formed own company, 1987; menswear collection introduced, 1990; began designing costumes for ballet and modern dance productions, from 1990; designed accessories line, 1992; handbags, 1993; shoes, 1997; lost backing and closed business, 1998; debut of one-man show, *LES MIZrahi,* 2000. **Awards:** Council of Fashion Designers of America award, 1988, 1989, 1991; Fashion Industry Foundation award, 1990; Michaelangelo Shoe award, New York, 1993; Dallas Fashion award for Excellence.

Publications

On MIZRAHI:

Books

Martin, Richard, and Harold Koda, *Bloom,* Metropolitan Museum of Art, 1995.

Stegemeyer, Anne, *Who's Who in Fashion, Third Edition,* New York, 1996.

Articles

"Mr. Clean: New Designer Isaac Mizrahi," in *Vogue,* February 1988.

Slonim, Jeffrey J., and Torkil Gudnason, "Retro-Active: Back to the 1960s with Isaac Mizrahi," in *Interview,* March 1988.

Foley, Bridget, "Isaac Mizrahi: Setting Out for Stardom," in *WWD,* 18 April 1988.

"Color Me Chic," in *Connoisseur* (New York), October 1988.

Hoare, Sarajane, "Vogue's Spy: Isaac Mizrahi," in *Vogue* (London), November 1988.

Bender, Karen, "Isaac Mizrahi," in *Taxi* (New York), February 1989.

Mansfield, Stephanie, "Nobody Beats the Miz," in *Vogue,* February 1989.

Mower, Sarah, "Isaac Mizrahi," in *Vogue* (London), September 1989.

Jeal, Nicola, "The Divine Mr. M.," in the *Observer Magazine* (London), 1 April 1990.

Hepple, Keith, "Plum in the Middle of the Pomegranate," in *The Independent* (London), 12 April 1990.

Menkes, Suzy, "Mizrahi: The Shooting Star," in the *International Herald Tribune,* 17 April 1990.

Wayne, George, "Brooklyn Kid K.O.s Couturiers," in *Interview,* June 1990.

Talley, André Leon, "The Kings of Color," in *Vogue,* September 1990.

Gross, Michael, "Slaves of Fashion: Isaac Mizrahi, the Great Hip Hope," in *New York Magazine,* 1 October 1990.

DeCaro, Frank, "Mizrahi Loves Company," in *Mademoiselle* (New York), January 1991.

"Isaac Mizrahi," in *Current Biography,* January 1991.

Bernhardt, Sandra, "I and Me," in *Harper's Bazaar,* March 1993.

Foley, Bridget, "Hard Acts to Follow: Isaac Mizrahi," in *WWD*, 24 October 1994.

Spindler, Amy M., "Cocktails, Anyone? Clothes that Strut," in the *New York Times*, 2 November 1994.

Menkes, Suzy, "Mizrahi's All-American Swirls," in the *International Herald Tribune*, 3 November 1994.

Ezesky, Lauren, "Isaac Unbound," in *Paper* (New York), March 1995.

Spindler, Amy M., "Luxurious Armor by Karan, Klein, Mizrahi," in the *New York Times*, 8 April 1995.

"Dueling Isaacs," in *WWD*, 10 April 1995.

Pogrebin, Robin, "Mizrahi, Once Again the Main Attraction, Sings it Like it is," in the *New York Times*, 3 October 2000.

Mattingly, Kate, "From Off the Rack to Off the Wall," in *Dance Magazine*, October 2000.

Malkin, Marc S., "Isaac Mizrahi's Next Stage," in *US Weekly*, 6 November 2000.

Comita, Jenny, "Life After Isaac," in *Vogue*, May 2001.

* * *

Isaac Mizrahi worked, upon graduation from Parsons School of Design, for Perry Ellis, Jeffrey Banks, and Calvin Klein. When he started his own business in 1987, he intimately knew the world of American sportswear at its best, but his work refined the sportswear model by a special sense of sophistication and glamor. His ideals, beyond those he worked for, were such American purists as Norell, Halston, Beene, and McCardell, each a designer of utmost sophistication. Suzy Menkes analyzed in the *International Herald Tribune* in April 1990: "The clean colors and Ivy League image of Perry Ellis sportswear might seem to be the seminal influence on Mizrahi. But he himself claims inspiration from his mother's wardrobe of all-American designers, especially the glamorous simplicity of Norman Norell."

It is as if Mizrahi was challenged by distilling the most well-bred form of each garment to an understated glamor, whether tartan taken to a sensuous evening gown but still buckled as if Balmoral livery; pocketbooks and luggage ingeniously incorporated into clothing with the practical pocket panache of McCardell; or versions of high style in adaptations of men's bathrobes or sweatshirting used for evening. While Mizrahi was often commended for the youthfulness of his clothing, the praise was for the freshness of his perception, his ability to recalculate a classic, not just a market for young women. His interest in the Empire waistline; his practicality of wardrobe separates in combination; and his leaps between day and evening addressed all women equally. In the early 1990s, many designers and manufacturers saw the value of simplification: Mizrahi sought the pure in tandem with the cosmopolitan.

When Sarah Mower of *Vogue* described Mizrahi in September 1989 as "that rare thing in contemporary design: a life-enhancing intelligence on the loose," she rightly characterized his revisionist, rational, distilling, pure vision. With his fall 1988 collection Mizrahi was immediately recognized by the *New York Times* as "this year's hottest new designer" in unusual color combinations (such as rust and mustard and orange-peel and pink) as well as the diversity of silhouettes from baby-doll dresses to evening jumpsuits to long dresses.

Mizrahi had clearly demonstrated the range of a commercially viable designer while at the same time demonstrating his simplifying glamor and the cool nonchalant charm of his smart (intellectually and aesthetically) clothing. The spa collection of 1988 included rompers and baseball jackets and playsuits as well as the debonair excess of trousers with paperbag waist. His spring 1989 collection assembled sources from all over the fashion spectrum to create a unified vision of elegance and appeal. The fall 1989 collection featured tartan (later developed by Mizrahi for a Twyla Tharp American Ballet Theater production in 1990) with most extraordinary accompaniment. In a notable instance, *New York* (21 August 1989) showed Mizrahi's tartan dress with his raccoon-trimmed silk taffeta parka in a perfect assembly of the wild and the urbane.

In 1990 Mizrahi showed a short-lived menswear line and sustained his color studies, creating double-faced wools and sportswear elements in watercolor-like colors, delicate yet deliberate. Spring 1990 was a typical Mizrahi transmogrification: black and white patterns recalling both art déco and the 1960s was, in fact, derived from costume for the Ballets Russes. In 1991 Mizrahi's themes were American, creating a kind of Puritan revival in dresses with collars and bows in spring/summer 1991 and an American ethnic parade in fall 1991, including Native American dress and a notable totem-pole dress inspired by Native American art.

Mizrahi's drive to find the most sophisticated version of each concept he developed was the *leitmotif* of his work. His spring 1991 collection examined motifs of the 1960s, but with a clever sharpness not observed in other designers of the same year looking back to the period. In 1991 his tube dresses with flounces were inspired by Norell, but given proportion. McCardell's audacious applications of cotton piqué are extended by Mizrahi's love of the same material and Halston's radical simplicity is inevitably a source for any designer longing to return to essential form. Mizrahi's color fields owed their consciousness to Perry Ellis, but the particular color sensibility was Mizrahi's own. Mizrahi's immaculate, ingenious modernism was as clearly aware of sources as it was pushed toward the clarification of form.

Mizrahi had referred to his style as a "classic New York look," which presumably meant a casual American idiom, but inflected with big-city reserve and refinement. Mizrahi captured something of Manhattan chic and glamor of the 1940s and 1950s. His fashion was indescribably beautiful in subtlety and sophistication. Yet Mizrahi soon gave it all up to pursue another dream—performing. From the early 1990s Mizrahi had begun collaborating with choreographers like Twyla Tharp and Mark Morris, and designed costumes for an increasing number of ballets, modern dance productions, and even film.

Mizrahi himself was the subject of a documentary film, *Unzipped*, detailing the assemblage of his 1994 fall collection, working with Douglas Keeve, who directed, and Michael Alden, who produced. Released commercially to raise funds for varied AIDS programs, the experience must have helped crystallize Mizrahi's direction for the future. In 1998, after Chanel pulled its backing, Mizrahi closed his fashion business and was suddenly with little to do. Within a year he turned in a new direction, writing a one-man show about his life. The funny, satiric cabaret show was *LES MIZrahi*, yet the only similarity to the long-running and much honored show, *Les Misèrables* was in name only. *LES MIZrahi*, debuted in Greenwich House Theatre in New York in October 2000, and was well received by critics and audiences.

For those yearning for the perfectly designed Mizrahi dress or outfit, a former protégée, Behnaz Sarafpour, garnered raves for her debut collection in 2001. Amid the praise for the black and white collection, however, were comments about Mizrahi's obvious influence on her style. For his part, Mizrahi declared in the May 2001 *Vogue*, "She knows what people really want to wear.... She's a great editor of her own accord. I learned as much from her as she did from me."

Generous, funny, immensely talented—that's Isaac Mizrahi. Whether on the stage, behind it designing costumes, or dressing Hollywood's elite, he made an indelible mark on the fashion scene. When asked by *US Weekly* in November 2000 if he missed designing, Mizrahi admitted this was so but countered, "I don't miss the business side of it. Just the idea of doing that makes me cringe." But would he ever return to designing? "I can't say never," he told *US*'s Marc Malkin, "There are all sorts of ways to sell clothes that feel more like me."

—Richard Martin; updated by Owen James

MOLINARI, Anna

See BLUMARINE

MOLYNEUX, Edward H.

British designer

Born: Hampstead, London, 5 September 1891. **Military Service:** Served as captain in the British Army, World War I. **Career:** Worked for couturier Lucile in London and the U.S., 1911–14; opened own house, Paris, 1919; added branches in Monte Carlo, 1925, Cannes, 1927, and London, 1932; moved business to London, 1939–46; returned to Paris, added furs, perfume, lingerie, and millinery, 1946–49; turned business over to Jacques Griffe and retired, 1950; reopened as Studio Molyneux, Paris, 1965; retired permanently soon thereafter. Fragrances included *Numéro Cinq,* 1926, *Vivre,* 1930, and *Rue Royale,* 1943. **Died:** 23 March 1974, in Monte Carlo.

Publications

On MOLYNEUX:

Books

Balmain, Pierre, *My Years and Seasons,* London, 1964.
Carter, Ernestine, *Magic Names of Fashion,* New York, 1980.
Milbank, Caroline Rennolds, *Couture: The Great Designers,* New York, 1985.
de Marly, Diana, *The History of Haute Couture,* London, 1988.
Stegemeyer, Anne, *Who's Who in Fashion, Third Edition,* New York, 1996.

Articles

"Captain Edward Molyneux," [obituary] in the *Times* (London), 25 March 1974.
Dobbs, Michael, "National Gallery Vulnerable to Provenance Questions," in the *Washington Post,* 20 May 2000.

* * *

Captain Edward Molyneux embodied the style he created in the 1920s and 1930s—an idle, slim ("never too rich or too thin"), elegant style on the verge of dissipation, at the edge of the outrageous, and always refined. His friendship with Noel Coward was *kismet,* two personifications of the sophisticated style that made both drawing-room comedy and its grace. Caroline Milbank, writing in *Couture: The Great Designers* (1985), described Molyneux "as the designer to whom a fashionable woman would turn if she wanted to be absolutely 'right' without being utterly predictable in the 1920s and 1930s."

Molyneux's ineffable decorum had come as a privilege of his own style liberation from Lucile, Lady Duff Gordon. Lucile's trademark was her rich proliferation of fine details and adornment. One would not characterize Lucile as florid, but one would certainly characterize Molyneux as chaste. His military self-presentation and English background did, however, make him seem even more Spartan in the world of French couture. Molyneux banned all superfluous decoration in an early and intuited version of modernist international style akin to the architecture of the period. He was a "modern' in his adoration of line, avoidance of excessive decoration, as well as in his engaging manner; he was undeniably modern in his love of luxurious materials and his embrace of modern circumstances, including the automobile.

While his work was most often in black, navy blue, beige, and grey, he had the sophistication as an art collector to collect late Impressionist and post-Impressionist paintings, shown in 1952 at the National Gallery of Art in Washington, D.C., sold to Ailsa Mellon Bruce, and later bequeathed to the National Gallery. Unfortunately, in early 2000s the origin of many of Molyneux's paintings came into question, after it became known that his principal dealer had collaborated with the Nazis. While it was not discovered how much if any of the collection had been stolen, Molyneux was not named as a knowing member of any scheme.

Molyneux loved bourgeois scenes of beauty, but he also created motoring outfits and easy-to-wear slip-like evening dresses for the leisure class of his time and superbly cut evening pajamas that could have costumed any Noel Coward comedy. Molyneux would be a designer successful at designing for and determining the lifestyle of his own social class, participant-observer in what Pierre Balmain called Molyneux's international set. His curious Franco-English snobbism belonged to a time and place; his two post-World War II business enterprises were of limited success, so fully was he the product and model of a world already forgotten.

The modern charm of Molyneux's creation was appreciated by Balmain who apprenticed with Molyneux in Paris. Balmain wrote in *My Years and Seasons* (London, 1964) of his regret on departing his first fashion job in the late 1930s, at Molyneux's, what he described as a "temple of subdued elegance… [where] the world's well-dressed women wore the inimitable two-pieces and tailored suits with pleated skirts, bearing the label of Molyneux." Balmain further praised Molyneux's consistent, reserved, understated couture, one often barely noticed by the fashion press, yet which was the manifestation of a conservative, continuous style.

Molyneux also designed for the theater and was a friend of Gertrude Lawrence who wore his clothing with a West End and Broadway panache, but the costumes never subsumed the actress. Molyneux's international set wore his tailored suits by day, but also could be seen at night in one or both nightclubs owned by Molyneux in partnership with hostess Elsa Maxwell wearing furs, long gowns, beaded chemises, and other elegant outfits by the designer.

Today designers who mingle with their clients are often criticized for social climbing. There is no evidence that such charges were placed against Molyneux as he moved so effortlessly and with *soigné* flair among the ladies he dressed. Ernestine Carter, writing in *Magic*

Names of Fashion, called Molyneux "dashing and debonair," comparing him to Fred Astaire. That he dressed women of the greatest propriety and restraint made it clear that, in dwelling among them, he was of like sensibility and shared spirit. It was Molyneux's place in international café-society that allowed him to cavort with Noel Coward and gave the sobriety of his design its sense of belonging. Given that fashion went through so many changes and excesses in the 1920s and 1930s, Molyneux was a constant model of cool elegance.

—Richard Martin

MONDI TEXTILE GMBH

German fashion and accessory firm

Founded: in Munich by Herwig Zahm, 1967. **Company History:** Accessory collections added, 1970s; fashion lines, mainly women's ready-to-wear, included Elementi, Mondi, Portara, Patrizia S, Braun, and Chris (by Christa Zahm); opened freestanding shops in Budapest, 1989, and New York, 1993; company purchased by Investcorp, 1993; issued its own credit cards in U.S., 1997; lost Investcorp backing and forced into bankruptcy, 1999; Mondi trademarks and worldwide licensing rights bought by Fehmi Chama, 1999; Gilmar Group signed license for women's apparel line, launching in 2000; Patrizia S collection set to debut with new German licensee, 2001. **Awards:** Forum prize of the textile industry, 1986; Igedo's International Fashion Marketing award, 1988; Fashion Oscar, Munich, 1991.

Publications

On MONDI:

Articles

Morais, Richard, "Who is First in the Market, Sells," in *Forbes,* 16 September 1991.
"Investcorp Buys Stake in Mondi, and Pushes Ahead with Circle K," in the *Middle East Economic Digest,* 8 January 1993.
Dreir, Melissa, "Mondi Making Major Revamp," in *WWD,* 5 January 1995.
"Telling It Like It Is," in *WWD,* 21 July 1995.
Ozzard, Janet, "Mondi Recharges Battery," in *WWD,* 21 February 1996.
"Mondi of U.S. Starts to Offer its Own Plastic," in *WWD,* 18 February 1997.
Drier, Melissa, "Two German Houses Update for Spring 1999," in *WWD,* 21 July 1998.
Socha, Miles, "Mondi Goes Soft and Modern," in *WWD,* 23 December 1998.
Drier, Melissa, and Miles Socha, "Mondi Seeks Backer, Files for Insolvency," in *WWD,* 10 September 1999.
"Without Financing, Mondi Cancels Spring Collection," in *WWD,* 1 October 1999.
Drier, Melissa, and Vivki Young, "Mondi Signs Licensing Pact for a Women's Apparel Line," in *WWD,* 3 November 1999.
Manning, Margie, "Closing," in the *St. Louis Business Journal,* 29 November 1999.

* * *

The fashion house of Mondi was established in Munich in 1968 by Herwig Zahm, selling exclusive fashion coordinates and accessory goods. By 1995 Mondi sold products in over 54 countries worldwide, through 2,300 independent speciality stores, almost 100 company-owned stores and 200 franchised stores, including a capsule collection on the prestigious cruise liner *Queen Elizabeth II.* The fates were not kind to the German firm, however, and it lost its footing at the end of the 20th century.

The Mondi group once emcompassed six major labels, yet in its later years had began expanding. The early powerhouse labels were Portara (sophisticated fashion); Mondi (the main label); Chris by Christa Zahm (designer collection); Patrizia S by Mondi (larger-sized fashions) and Braun (sport and golf wear). The overall appeal was cosmopolitan, designed for American, European, and Asian markets. The Mondi woman herself was difficult to categorize; she was undoubtably strong, individual, and successful but also ageless.

There had always been a multicultural feel to Mondi collections, brought about by a diverse design team at the Munich headquarters, as well as at the company's American unit. The designers' varied backgrounds and experiences combined to create a look that was cosmopolitan, formal, and informal, adapting to the demands of city and country. Mondi collections were easily mixed and matched; different fashion themes were explored in each collection, then combined with each other. The customer had the freedom to interpret each look according to her own personality or the occasion for which she was dressing. The company's goal was always to ensure that customers were in control and felt confident, yet individual, in Mondi outfits.

In the expanding but unstable fashion market, Mondi maintained a belief in strong design, bold color, and fashionability. Its wide appeal and distinctive multicultural approach was repeated in every collections, when several strong yet interrelated themes were available to the buyer. Spring/summer 1991 was just such an example, with Pure Paris (fresh summer elegance, with a distinctive Coco Chanel influence), Neo Geo (graphic, chic black-and-white combining lace, dogtooth check, and severe geometric lines), Colorissima (street-smart city silhouettes in primary colors and florals), and Polo Club (nautical, sporty looks in water colors, with embroidered polo emblems). Mondi style was modern yet traditional casual elegance, in sporty yet wearable designs.

In the late 1990s the European recession and Asian slump took its toll on many fashion houses; Mondi was no exception. The firm as well as its Amercian unit, Mondi of America—which accounted for around half of its worldwide sales—suffered setbacks despite innovations to bolster sales. In an effort to revamp its image and retool operations in 1998, Mondi gave in to the increasingly casual atmosphere of apparel, carrying more sportswear and separates, especially at its nearly 50-freestanding U.S. stores. The American division hired a new designer, Maggie Norris, formerly of Ralph Lauren, expanded eveningwear, cut back on logos, and spruced up its advertising as well.

Although Mondi seemed well on its way to a turnaround, the company's owner, Investcorp, had neither the patience or the inclination to see it through. In 1999 Investcorp pulled its financial backing and Mondi was forced to look elsewhere. No immediate backers were found, the firm cancelled its spring-summer 2000 showing, and filed for bankruptcy in quick succession. The American unit remained solvent for slightly longer, then fell into bankruptcy as well. There was, however, a bit of brightness—two licensing pacts were announced, one with the Italian Gilmar Group for a Mondi women's apparel line designed by freelancer Vera Schaal, and another for the Patrizia S larger-sized women's collection. The new Mondi collections were set to debut in 2000 and 2001, and their licensees had high hopes to carry on the Mondi tradition of elegant, wearable fashion.

—Kevin Almond and Nelly Rhodes

MONTANA, Claude

French designer

Born: Paris, 29 June 1949. **Education:** Studied chemistry and law. **Family:** Married Wallis Franken, 1993 (died 1996). **Career:** Freelance jewelry designer, London, 1971–72; designer, with Michelle Costas, ready-to-wear and accessories line for Idéal-Cuir, Paris, 1973; assistant designer, 1973, and head designer, 1974, MacDouglas Leathers, Paris; freelance designer, Complice, Ferrer y Sentis Knitwear, Paris, from 1975; founded own company, 1979; Hommes Montana presented, 1981; first boutique opened, Paris, 1983; *Montana Pour Femme* fragrance introduced, 1986; signed with Gruppo GFT to license womenswear, 1987; *Parfum d'Homme* introduced, 1989; *Parfum d'Elle* introduced, 1990; designer in charge of haute couture, Lanvin, 1989–92; continues ready-to-wear collections under own name, diffusion line introduced, 1991; Parums Montana acquired by Clarins SA, 1995; left Gruppo GFT for Groupe Mendes, 1996; launched leather accessories, 1996; launched *Just Me* fragrance, 1997; sought protection from creditors, 1997; firm and name sold, 1998; Montana Blu collection introduced, 1998; *Montana Blu* fragrance debuted, 2001. **Exhibitions:** *Intimate Architecture: Contemporary Clothing Design,* Hayden Gallery, Massachusetts Institute of Technology, 1982. **Awards:** Prix Medicis, 1989; Fragrance Foundation award, 1990; Golden Thimble award, 1990, 1991. **Address:** 54 avenue Marceau, 75008 Paris, France. **Website:** www.claude-montana.com.

Claude Montana, fall/winter 2001 ready-to-wear collection: faux fur coat with a matching mini-skirt. © AP/Wide World Photos.

Publications

On MONTANA:

Books

Hayden Gallery, Massachusetts Institute of Technology, *Intimate Architecture: Contemporary Clothing Design* [exhibition catalogue], Cambridge, 1982.

Perschetz, Lois, ed., *W, The Designing Life,* New York, 1987.

Articles

Talley, André Leon, "The State of Montana," in *WWD,* 13 March 1978.

McCarthy, Patrick, "Claude Reigns," in *WWD,* 4 September 1979.

"Paris Advance: Claude Montana," in *WWD,* 2 October 1980.

Brantley, Ben, "I, Claude," in *WWD,* 18 May 1984.

Brampton, Sally, "La règle du jeu," in the *Observer* (London), 5 May 1985.

Filmer, Denny, "Claude Montana," in *Cosmopolitan* (London), October 1988.

Knafo, Robert, "Claude Montana," in *Connoisseur,* November 1988.

Brubach, Holly, "Selling Montana," in the *New Yorker,* 23 January 1989.

Petkanas, Christopher, "Chez Claude," in *Harper's Bazaar* (New York), June 1989.

Gross, Michael, "The Great State of Montana," in *New York,* 31 July 1989.

"Montana: Then and Now," in *WWD,* 19 October 1989.

Thim, Dennis, "The New State of Montana," in *WWD,* 29 May 1990.

Vernesse, Francine, "Viva Montana," in *Elle* (Paris), 13 August 1990.

Mulvagh, Jane, "Lanvin c'est moi," in the *Sunday Times Magazine* (London), 4 November 1990.

Spindler, Amy M., "Claude's New Adventure," in *WWD,* 26 February 1992.

James, Laurie, "The State of Montana," in *Harper's Bazaar,* October 1992.

Schiro, Anne-Marie, "Photogenic, But Out of Focus," in the *New York Times,* 20 March 1995.

"Montana Leaves GFT for Mendes," in *WWD,* 9 May 1996.

Weisman, Katherine, "Montana Leather Accessories Lines to Debut," in *WWD,* 9 September 1996.

Claude Montana after showing his fall/winter 2001 ready-to-wear collection. © AP/Wide World Photos.

Wilson, Eric, "Trademark Dispute Pits State of Montana vs. Claude Montana," in *WWD,* 21 March 1997.

———, "Ortenbergs Back Little Guy in Montana Wars," in *WWD,* 22 April 1997.

Aktar, Alev, "Just Me: Montana's Next Fragrance Foray," in *WWD,* 27 June 1997.

Raper, Sarah, and Katherine Weisman, "Claude Montana Files for Credit Protection; Restructuring Planned," in *WWD,* 19 November 1997.

Pogoda, Dianne M., "The Year in Fashion," in *WWD,* 15 December 1997.

Raper, Sarah, "Montana Has Possible Buyer in Ex-Ricci VP," in *WWD,* 18 March 1998.

———, "Claude Montana Hits Comeback Trail," in *WWD,* 13 April 1998.

Weisman, Kathering, "Montana's New Blu," in *WWD,* 1 October 1998.

"...Claude Montana Did Sexy Leathers and Glam Furs...," in *WWD,* 19 March 2001.

"Fresh and Fragrant 'Blu' Breath of Air," in the *New Straits Times,* 24 May 2001.

* * *

In the late 1970s and 1980s Claude Montana was known for an *outré* silhouette and commanding sense of aggression that made him both *enfant terrible* in a cultural sense and yet fashion's most devoted adherent in design. Padded shoulders and leathers seemed to some observers a misogynist's view of women in the manner of a cartoon. To others, however, the same style renewed the shoulder-accented horizontal of Constructivism, or even the influence of Balenciaga's surgically acute cut. Little wonder, then, that Montana said in an interview in 1989, "I'm like a battlefield inside, a mass of contradictions." More than ever, Montana has proved in the late 1980s and 1990s how contradictory and how complex his style is, incapable of the kinds of knee-jerk reactions that many critics had initially. Few designers have been as virulently attacked as Montana has, sometimes for "gay-clone" proclivities to leather, for supposed misogyny, for impractical clothing, for excessive accoutrements. Leather jackets borrowed from menswear—bikers and the military—caused strong controversy in the American press and market in the 1980s when Montana appropriated them. A decade later, Ralph Lauren, Donna Karan, Calvin Klein, and Byron Lars were working with similar looks to no protest (and Saint Laurent had long borrowed from the male wardrobe to only mild demurral).

Few designers today can be equally admired for the surety of cut, the sensuousness of appearance, the femininity that is beneath the bold forms, the luxurious seductions of fabrics more varied than leather alone, and the continuous and consummate mastery of a fashion design that always plays between the abstract forms of art and the conventions of clothing. Indeed, Constructivism is a strong influence on Montana's work. Top-heavy geometry twirling into a narrow skirt or pencil-thin trousers was not commonplace until Montana offered the option. Reductive by nature, Montana has vacillated in terms of accessorizing, particularly in the mid-1980s, but by the 1990s he clearly preferred an austerity about clothing, approximating the linear probity and arc-based sculptural form. Like Constructivist drawings for the stage, Montana's designs come to life in the animation of gyrating proportions, often with exaggerated shoulders or collars, almost invariably with a very narrow waist, and the spin of a peplum over a narrow skirt. Cocoon coats could seem to be the nimbus of abstraction; spiralling line, alternately clinging to the body and spinning away, seemed a gesture of whole cloth, unpieced.

Montana's principal aesthetic contribution is silhouette; nonetheless, his materials, beginning historically with leather, and his color palette are beautiful and sensuous. What became the power look in women's clothing in the mid-1980s is derived from Montana's aesthetic, so persuasive was it as an option for assertive presence without sacrifice of the female form. Based on circuiting spirals and a few strong lines realized on the body, Montana's aesthetic was described by some critics as being too Space Age or futuristic, but recognized by its advocates for its invocation of the principles of Futurist abstraction. Moreover, after a signal collection for fall-winter 1984, in which Montana toned down the most extreme aspects of his style, he remained true to his aesthetic principles and interests, demonstrating that they were not merely the radical forms they had seemed at first, but the fundamental forms that fashion had known since Thayatt and Exter, Adrian and Balenciaga. As early as 1979, when many might have dismissed him as an iconoclast, Montana admitted to André Leon Talley of his admiration for Vionnet and Madame Grès, likewise two designers of utmost simplicity of form (*Women's Wear Daily,* 13 March 1978).

What had been extreme now seems pure. Even in that convention, Montana has emulated avant-garde art. As an artist-designer, he sustains his own predilections. For example, the gargantuan shoulders are reduced in the late 1980s and great, oversized collars keep the outspoken gesture to the top. Robert Knafo (*Connoisseur,* November 1988) describes that transition: "casting out the sharp-shouldered, fearsomely assertive Montana woman, installing in her place a mellower, softer-edged, more romantic figure, although no less self-assured." Indeed, it is some of the referentiality of fashion—association we make with clothing types and image—that has attributed the controversial profile to Montana as a designer. More importantly, he has been a steadfast practitioner of a kind of isolated, non-referential abstraction, obdurately and passionately and compellingly exploring fashion at its most distinct cut. Montana's design survival as a classic figure and a model with lasting impact on other advanced designers in modern fashion attests to that design primacy and perseverance.

After his Lanvin stint, Montana maintained his precise, inimitable approach to fashion. His fall 1995 Paris womenswear collection was presented in stunning, futuristic white. *Women's Wear Daily* (17 October 1995) applauded the line's "sharp edges, swirling seams and strict silhouettes,"concluding "nobody beats Montana for his precision tailoring." The following year Montana moved the licensing of his two prominent womenswear lines, Montana Femme and State of Montana, from Gruppo GFT to French fashion firm Groupe Mendes. Montana menswear, however, remained with GFT. Additionally in 1996 Montana introduced a new leather collection including handbags, belts, travel bags, and other smaller accessories.

Unfortunately for Montana, brewing legal battles overshadowed his fashion contributions. The imbroglio stemmed from a 1995 tiff with a small firm named Montana Knits, which sought to trademark its name. Claude objected, having already trademarked his apparel lines (Montana, Claude Montana, and State of Montana), and believing Montana Knits would confuse buyers. The owners of Montana Knits, Tom and Ann Doolings, decided to take Claude to court over the matter. Suddenly, it was a cause célèbre, with high profile fashion icons like Liz Claiborne championing the underdog Doolings. The case was decided in favor of the Doolings; Montana then subsequently renamed his diffusion line, State of Montana, to Montana White Label.

If the lawsuit was troubling for Montana, what occurred on its heels was much more vexing: his firm was forced to seek protection from creditors in 1997 after several years of sliding sales, setbacks, and just plain bad luck. His woes had included lower margins after switching his Japanese licensee, losing prominent retailers Bloomingdale's and Henri Bendel, and being forced to close several stores for underperformance. The Montana name and the designer's skills, however, were never in question; he was still roundly praised by buyers and critics alike.

Montana finally decided it was time to sell, a decision many of his fellow designers had faced. He told *Women's Wear Daily* (12 December 1997), "There comes a moment in your life when you say, 'Now, what really interests me is my work and creating.' And so I'm ready now to open up…to an investor with whom I get along, and with whom I share the same ideas about future strategy." That investor turned out to be Jacques Berger, formerly of Nina Ricci, and two partners who paid $670,000 for 51-percent of the struggling fashion firm. Ironically, part of the agreement called for Montana to give up the rights to his name, something he had fought so vehemently for in the past. The designer would, however, maintain the right to design for the house for another ten years.

Montana seemed happy with his prospects, "This is going to give me much more freedom to travel, to sit down and talk with others in the studio about designs," he told *Women's Wear Daily* (13 April 1998). "Isolation is not very healthy for creativity…. In the end, my biggest role hasn't really changed," Montana explained, "I'm the artistic director for the house and now I will have more energy to throw into my work. That should be stimulating for everybody."

Free from the pressures of running a business, Montana rebounded quickly and unveiled Montana Blu, a younger, hipper collection for women in late 1998. The line seemed to stem from Montana's passion for contemporary art. "Sculpture and painting are inexhaustible inspiration sources," he noted in a biographical sketch at his website. In Montana Blu he has created perhaps the most profound designs bearing his signature; it was successful enough to spawn its own fragrance in 2001, while his signature line was praised by *Women's*

Wear Daily (19 March 2001), "Whatever the Claude Montana collection should be, whatever it could be or once was, for fall, the designer stuck to stuff he knows well—sexy leathers and glamorous furs."

—Richard Martin and Nelly Rhodes

MORENI, Popy

French designer

Born: Annalisa Moreni in Turin, Italy, 3 December 1947. **Education:** Istituto Statale d'Arte, Moda e Costume, Turin, 1961–64. **Family:** Children: Amour, Aimée. **Career:** Moved to Paris, 1964; design assistant to Maïmé Arnaudin, 1964; designer in Arnaudin's Mafia design studio, Paris, 1965–67, and in Promostyl, Paris, 1967–73; designer, Timmi, 1972; established own design and consulting office (working for Rhone-Poulenc Textile and Rasurel), from 1973; first boutique opened, Paris, 1976; first fashion collection, 1980; first creations for Swiss catalogues, 1981; ready-to-wear licensed, from 1982; childrenswear licensed, from 1987; introduced housewares, linens, furniture, and rugs; launched first signature fragrance, 1996; second scent, 1997; third fragrance, *Cirque,* 2000. **Exhibitions:** *Popy Moreni, Collerettes x 13,* Galerie des Femmes, Paris, 1985; *Les Années 80,* Musée des Arts de la Mode, Paris, 1989–90; *Mode et Liberté,* Musée des Arts de la Mode, Paris, 1992. **Awards:** Named Chevalier de l'Ordre des Arts et des Lettres, 1986. **Address:** 13, place des Vosges, 75004 Paris, France.

Popy Moreni, spring/summer 1996 ready-to-wear collection. © AP/Wide World Photos.

Publications

On MORENI:

Books

Deslandres, Yvonne, *Histoire de la mode au XXme siècle,* Paris, 1986.

Benaim, Laurence, *L'Année de la mode,* Paris, 1988.

Articles

Godard, Colette, "La mode comme le souvenir d'un bonheur," in *Le Monde* (Paris), April 1986.

Seraglini, Marie, "Carte noire et blanche à Popy Moreni," in *Maison Française* (Paris), July 1986.

Perrier, M.J., "Designer Close Up," in *Interior* (London), March 1987.

Mont Servan, N., "Les 100 poids lourds de la mode," in *Passion* (Paris), February 1990.

Born, Pete, "Scent Spout Wide Open," in *WWD,* 11 October 1996.

"Martin Gras: A Master Perfumer at Work," in *Soap & Cosmetics,* January 1999.

"Popy Moreni," available online at Fashion Windows, www.fashion-windows.com, March 2001.

*

I hope to love everything, unfortunately I cannot yet do so. In fact, I tell myself that what I do not love is simply what I do not understand. So, potentially, I love everything: the real and the false, the authentic and the copied, the straight line and the curve, elegance and vulgarity, the good and the bad, the law-abiding and the outlaw. I would like to do everything! Not necessarily in order to do but in order to search.... I'm rather inquisitive and dissatisfied on the whole...so I persevere! I am active because the unknown is so potent...

For my work I like silence, white and black, open countryside, concrete, the morning, thick pencils...the ideas are in the pencil.... It is through drawing a lot that one makes discoveries.... You rarely get surprising results early on...

Work keeps me busy and prevents me asking myself too many questions. I am short of time to do everything I would like to.... So it is just a matter of choice and chance...

—Popy Moreni

* * *

Popy Moreni is an Italian designer working in Paris who has managed to combine distinctive style elements from both countries—a strong Italian sense of color and coordination, with a chic French practicality. She was born into an artistic family in Turin, Italy; her mother was a sculptor and her father a painter. She studied costume and design in Italy at L'Istituto Statale d'Arte, Moda e Costume, then moved to Paris at 17 to pursue a career in fashion. Her first job was at Mafia, the design studio of Maïmé Arnaudin; next she worked for the Promostyl Organization and the Italian firm Timmi until 1972.

She opened her own design studio in 1973 and worked on consultancies with a range of clients that included Rhone-Poulenc Textile and Rasurel. In 1980 she showed her first collection on the catwalk. She quickly became known for her witty, carefree clothes. A taste for theatricality and the baroque gave her collections the recurrent theme of *commedia dell'arte* with harlequin prints and jagged-cut details, satin capes and Pierrot collars, all translated into inventive sportswear shapes. She has also been inspired from her artistic heritage, looking to abstract painters like Jackson Pollock and Hans Hartung when designing and choosing prints.

By 1985 the collections had grown in size and breadth, incorporating such details as petal shapes, corollas, and plush velvets. More recent innovations were oversize crisp white cotton shirts decorated with ruffled cuffs and necklines. Cheeky sleeveless striped suits again decorated with a huge ruff collar of satin, plus fun linen suits, printed with an asymmetric leaf detail. Her collection for autumn-winter 1993–94 showed a stark paring down of her carefree theatricality, with severe charcoal and black fit-and-flare dresses with unusual details like tiny cap sleeves or asymmetrical seaming. Accessory details like fingerless gloves, black nail polish, and a no-make-up look contributed to the austerity.

Expansion of the Moreni business began with the opening of her first boutique in the Les Halles district of Paris in 1976. In 1980 she began a joint collaboration with a French mail order firm, Les Trois Suisses, to design children's and women's clothes. She also developed a distinctive eveningwear line, as well as hat, shoe, and jewelry ranges. Of particular interest were her plastic shoes dyed to bright colors. A licensing agreement with Mitsukoshi Ltd. in Japan gave Moreni a lucrative Asian exposure and marketing of her name and products.

By the turn of the century Moreni continued to expand her business, introducing a wide range of products from housewares, linens, furniture, and rugs. Additionally, the third Moreni fragrance, *Cirque,* was launched in 2000.

—Kevin Almond

Popy Moreni, spring/summer 1996 ready-to-wear collection. © AP/ Wide World Photos.

MORI, Hanae

Japanese designer

Born: Tokyo, 8 January 1926. **Education:** Graduated in literature from Tokyo Christian Women's University, 1947. **Family:** Married Kei Mori; children: Akira, Kei. **Career:** First atelier in Shinjuko, Tokyo, 1951; costume designer for films, 1954–circa 1961; first New York fashion show, 1965; showed in Monaco and Paris, 1975; established haute couture collection and fashion house in Paris, 1977; member of Le Chambre Syndicale de la Haute Couture Parisienne, 1977; opened Hanae Mori Boutique in Faubourg St. Honor, Paris, 1985; designed costumes for La Scala, Milan; designed costumes for Paris Opera Ballet, 1986; launched Hanae Mori Boutique, Monte Carlo, 1989; shows in Paris, Budapest, Moscow, and Kuala Lumpur, 1990; shows in Lausanne and Taipei, and member of Japan Olympic Committee and chairman of Cultural Affairs Promotion Committee of Tokyo Chamber of Commerce and Industry, 1991; eyewear added, 1993; fragrances added: *Butterfly,* 1995; *HM* (for men), 1997; *Haute Couture,* 1999; also designed accessories, home furnishings, textiles, and skiwear. **Exhibitions:** *Avant-garde Japon,* Centre Pompidou, Paris, 1986; *Hanae Mori: 35 Years in Fashion,* Tokyo, 1989, Monte Carlo, 1990, and Paris, 1990; *Diana Vreeland: Immoderate Style,* Metropolitan Museum of Art, New York, 1993–94; *Japonism in Fashion,* Kyoto Costume Institute, 1994; *Japanese Design: A Survey Since 1950,* Philadelphia Museum of Art, 1994; *Orientalism,* Metropolitan Museum of Art, New York, 1994–95. **Awards:** Neiman Marcus award, 1973; Medaille d'Argent, City of Paris, 1978; The Symbol of Man award, Minnesota Museum, 1978; Croix de Chevalier des Arts et Lettres, 1984; Purple Ribbon Decoration, Japan, 1988; Asahi prize as pioneer of Japanese Fashion, 1988; named Chevalier de la Légion d'Honneur, 1989; Person of Cultural Merit, Japan, 1989; Order of Culture, Japan, 1996. **Address:** 6–1, 3 Chome, Kita-Aoyama, Minato-ku, Tokyo, Japan. **Website:** www.morihanae.co.jp.

Hanae Mori, spring/summer 2001 haute couture collection: embroidered lace jacket over a tulle sheath. © AP/Wide World Photos.

Hanae Mori, spring/summer 2001 haute couture collection. © AP/Wide World Photos.

Publications

By MORI:

Books

Designing for Tomorrow, Tokyo, 1979.
A Glass Butterfly, Tokyo, 1984.
Hanae Mori 1960–1989, Tokyo, 1989.
Fashion—A Butterfly Crosses the Border, Tokyo, 1993.
Hanae Mori Style: Highlights from a Lifetime in Fashion, Tokyo, 2001.

On MORI:

Books

Marcus, Stanley, *Quest for the Best,* New York, 1979.
Koren, Leonard, *New Fashion Japan,* Tokyo, 1984.
Sparke, Penny, *Japanese Design,* London, 1987.
Fairchild, John, *Chic Savages,* New York, 1989.
Stegemeyer, Anne, *Who's Who in Fashion, Third Edition,* New York, 1996.

Articles

"Hanae Mori: Legend in Her Own Time," in *American Fabrics and Fashions* (Columbia, South Carolina), Spring 1974.
Whitehead, Ron, "Japan's Queen of Haute Couture," in *Femina,* May 1979.
Lohse, Marianne, "Hanae Mori," in *Madame Figaro* (Paris), April 1987.
Lalanne, Dorothee, "Hanae Mori Première!," in *Vogue* (Paris), March 1989.
Beurdeley, Laurence, "Hanae Mori," in *L'Officiel* (Paris), June 1989.
Menkes, Suzy, "Hanae Mori: Fashion that Fuses the East and West," in the *International Herald Tribune,* June 1989.
Bumiller, Elizabeth, "Japan's Madame Couturier," in the *Washington Post,* February 1990.
Davy, Philippe, "Un souffle nouveau," in *L'Officiel,* February 1990.
Davidson, Monique, "Univers Hanae Mori: Un Empire au Soleil Levant," in *Joyce,* March/April 1991.

"Kei Mori, Chief of Hanae Mori, Dead at 84," in *WWD,* 22 October 1996.

Menkes, Suzy, "For Hanae Mori, a 20th Birthday," in the*International Herald Tribune,* 15 July 1997.

———, "A New Spirit Takes Wing with Madame Butterfly," in the *International Herald Tribune,* 11 May 1999.

Reitman, Valerie, "Daughter-in-law of Founder Slowly Inserts a Youthful Look into the Line," in the *Los Angeles Times,* 14 May 1999.

Weil, Jennifer, "Saujet's Entrepreneurial Odyssey," in *WWD,* 19 January 2001.

Young, Clara, "Hanae Mori," available online at Fashion Live, www.fashionlive.com, 19 March 2001.

"Hanae Mori Style," available online at the Japan Page, www.thejapanpage.com, 23 August 2001.

*

I design primarily to enhance our lifestyle and make it richer and more enjoyable. Expression changes with the times; but the essence does not change. The history of the world is the story of men and women—how men relate to women and how they live. I would like to express that great sense of existence in clothing. I have been in pursuit of that all through my life.

I am true to my identity; I keep trying to be myself. I am Japanese, in Japan there is this beauty by itself which has been nurtured by tradition—fashion is an international language. What I have been trying to do is to express the wonderful beauty of Japan using international language.

—Hanae Mori

* * *

A delicate sense of feminine beauty, stemming from Hanae Mori's Japanese heritage, is married to an artistic use of color and fabric in all her work. She treads a careful line, balancing Eastern influences with Western ideals to produce consistently successful couture and ready-to-wear lines with international customers. If her clothes lack the more outrageous, attention-grabbing qualities of some of her couture counterparts, they compensate with the economy of their cut and base their appeal on the practical needs of the wealthy metropolitan women who wear them.

By stepping outside current trends and concentrating on conservative but always feminine daywear, Mori has established a niche for herself in the Parisian fashion arena. Integral to this is the sense of the longevity of her easy-to-wear separates, which even in the ready-to-wear line retain a delicacy of touch through the textiles used. Mori elaborates on the basic tenets of combining fine fabrics and flattering cut, adding her own feel for the dramatic to her eye-catching eveningwear. For this she makes optimum use of the lustrous printed textiles produced by her husband until his death in 1996. Although there is an air of restrained elegance to much of her design, symbolized by the fragile butterfly motif by which she is known, her eveningwear often breaks into more vibrant realms.

In 1981 Mori produced a languorous silk mousseline dress, the vampish leopard print and deep *décolleté* of which were balanced by the soft, sinuous fall of the fabric. Other examples used bright hot colors, juxtaposed in one ensemble to provide interest, bringing a strong Japanese feel to their narrow hues, frequently harking back to the kimono for their silhouette and cut. It is in this area that her work is most inspired, bringing together European tailoring and Japanese color and ideals of beauty. She uses the Japanese love of asymmetry to further develop her style and the linear patterns she prints onto her distinctive silks. She exploits the natural appeal of such fabrics with a well-defined sense of cut to illuminate her realistic styles. By doing so, Mori is providing both an alternative to and a definite rejection of the type of elaborate couture confections that mold the female form into fantastical shapes, ignoring the woman beneath the fabric.

The other main strand to Mori's design is her close involvement in the arts. Her early costuming of innumerable Japanese films enabled her sense of color to evolve, using each primary-hued textile to represent a different emotion, and sharpened her sense of the dramatic effect of dress. This has grown in her work for opera and ballet, the clothing full of delicacy and poise counterpointed with strong coloration, the arresting mixes representing the two worlds her design principles straddle.

Mori's wedding dresses are in particular demand and are always made to order. The designer is also a favorite of the Japanese royal family and Thailand's Queen Sirikit. A new influence is beginning to work its way into Mori's collections with the addition of her daughter-in-law, Pamela, as creative director of the ready-to-wear line since 1999. The younger Mori favors simpler, more understated clothing. She helped usher in the newer Studio Line to reach the next generation of Mori customers, both in Japan and internationally. Hanae Mori, despite her advancing years, remains actively involved with the company's daily affairs and still heads up the couture line and the more expensive ready-to-wear.

A firm grasp of the value of these cross-cultural reference points has enabled Mori to establish herself in Paris couture and develop an international market. Her understanding of the needs of contemporary women has lent a practical slant to her simply shaped, wearable clothes, while her theatrical preoccupations and Japanese background have inspired her love of rich, tactile fabrics in the vibrant prints and colors that are the hallmark of her design.

—Rebecca Arnold; updated by Carrie Snyder

MORRIS, Robert Lee

American jewelry and accessories designer

Born: Nuremburg, Germany, 7 July 1947. **Education:** Graduated from Beloit College, Beloit, WI. **Family:** Married Susan; children: Taylor. **Career:** Showed first collection in 1972; owner, Robert Lee Morris Gallery, since 1974; owner/manager, Artwear Gallery, 1977–93; introduced Robert Lee Morris Necessities mail order catalogue, 1993; also packaging designer, Elizabeth Arden, New York, from 1992. **Exhibitions:** Artwear Gallery, New York, 1992; *Good as Gold: Alternative Materials in American Jewelry,* Smithsonian Institution (international touring exhibition), 1981–85; retrospective, Museum of the Fashion Institute of Technology, New York, 1995. **Awards:** Coty American Fashion Critics award, 1981; Council of Fashion Designers of America award, 1985, 1994; International Gold Council award, 1987; Woolmark award, 1992; American Accessories Achievement award, 1992; Grand Prix, Tahitian Pearl Trophy, North America, Necklace Category, 2000; Site of the Week award,

Professional Jeweler, January 2001. **Address:** Robert Lee Morris Gallery; 400 West Broadway; New York, NY 10012, USA. **Website:** www.robertleemorris.com.

PUBLICATIONS

By MORRIS:

Articles

"Nature as Inspiration," in *Professional Jeweler,* January 2000.

On MORRIS:

Books

Untracht, Oppi, *Jewelry Concepts and Technology,* Garden City, New York, 1982.
Cartlidge, Barbara, *Twentieth Century Jewelry,* New York, 1985.
Shields, Jody, *All That Glitters,* New York, 1987.
Mulvagh, Jane, *Costume Jewelry in Vogue,* London, 1988.
Blauer, Ettagale, *Contemporary American Jewelry Design,* New York, 1991.
Cera, Deanne Farneti, *Jewels of Fantasy: Costume Jewelry of the 20th Century,* New York, 1992.
Stegemeyer, Anne, *Who's Who in Fashion, Third Edition,* New York, 1996.

Articles

"Artwear: Redefining Jewelry with a Modern Style," in *Vogue* (New York), January 1984.
Gross, Michael, "Jewelry Mirrors Its Designer," in the *New York Times,* 7 April 1987.
Johnson, Bonnie, "Jewelry Designer Robert Lee Morris Sinks His Claws Into Heavy Metal," in *People,* 11 May 1987.
Hochswender, Woody, "Attention-Getter," in the *New York Times,* 25 April 1989.
Hamilton, William L., "What Becalms a Legend Most," in *Metropolitan Home,* May 1989.
Greendorfer, Tere, "Going for the Bold," in the *Sunday Star Ledger* (London), 2 July 1989.
Newman, Jill, "On the Cutting Edge with Robert Lee Morris," in *WWD,* 19 August 1989.
"Freedom Saunters into Style; Polar Opposites, Isaac Mizrahi and Romeo Gigli Lead a Runaway Renaissance," in *People,* Spring 1990.
Myers, Coco, "Icon Maker," in *Mirabella* (New York), October 1990.
Sikes, Gini, "World Apart," in *Harper's Bazaar,* October 1990.
Greco, Monica, "Portrait of the Artist," in *Sportswear International* (New York), 1991.
Mower, Sarah, "Robert Lee Morries: A Multi-Faceted New York Jeweller Finds Inspiration in the British Isles," in *Vogue* (London), November 1991.
Slesin, Suzanne, "Inspiration is Only a Room Away," in the *New York Times,* 9 January 1992.
Schiro, Ann-Marie, "Paying Tribute to a Wearable Art," in the *New York Times,* 26 April 1992.
Spindler, Amy M., "Piety on Parade: Fashion Seeks Inspiration," in the *New York Times,* 5 September 1993.
Goodman, Wendy, "Breaking Ground," in *Harper's Bazaar,* February 1994.
Menkes, Suzy, "A Jeweler's Creed: Value is in the Design," in the *International Herald Tribune* (Paris), 17 April 1995.
Reif, Rita, "A Fashion Maker Looks Beyond Seventh Avenue," in the *New York Times,* 3 December 1995.
Blauer, Ettagale, "Robert Lee Morris," in *American Craft,* April-May 1996.
"Sugar and Vice," in *Cosmopolitan,* March 2000.
"New Money," in *International Jeweler,* April-May 2000.
Marx, Linda, "Wear Art Thou?" in *Simply the Best,* December 2000.
D'Annunzio, Gracia, "Isn't Jewelry Art?" in *Vogue Gioiello* (Italy), March 2001.
Karimzadeh, Marc, "Bridging the Gap," in *WWD,* Summer 2001.

*

My jewelry is a distant cousin of ancient armor—those smooth, sensual body-conscious constructions that employ ingenious mechanics to allow for fluid movement. My inspiration has never been clothing or fashion trends, but rather the human need for personal intimacy, with tokens of spiritual potential that amulets and talismans provide.

I constantly seek to fine-tune, focus, purify, and strengthen my style, to make it more clear, more recognizable, and more understandable by people of any and all cultures. Mass fashion jewelry, in my mind, is purely decorative, employing a cacophony of glittery values to achieve a dazzling effect. This is as much a part of human culture as the bright plumage of birds, and will remain with us, as it should. But it has always been against this world that I design my work; placing value on classicism and heirloom status over the thrill of temporary trends. My forms and shapes lead my concepts. My concepts are generally anthropological and my attitude is "less is more."

—Robert Lee Morris

* * *

"Wearable art," as created by Robert Lee Morris, has become a symbol of style among young, modern, rebellious, sexy, and chic individuals. Morris has redefined the way people perceive jewelry. He entered the fashion scene some 20 years ago and has transformed the contemporary jewelry industry by drawing on symbols from antiquity in ways that underscore their relevance to our lives today. He remains fascinated by the meaning of art, the role of jewelry as a talisman of the spirit. Morris maintains a keen appreciation of a pure, powerful aesthetic.

Born in wartorn Nuremburg, Germany, the son of a U.S. Air Force colonel and a former fashion model, Morris was a world traveler at a young age. He was schooled in places like Brazil and Japan, as the family followed Morris' father from post to post, moving over 25 times before Robert turned 18. Morris graduated from Beloit College in Wisconsin in 1969 with a degree in art. Soon thereafter, he joined an artists' commune near Beloit and began designing jewelry.

Originally planning a career in anthropology, but recognizing his artistic talents, Morris combined his favorite discipline and added art, history, sculpture, filmmaking, and much more into the craft of jewelry making. As a self-taught artist, Morris developed a distinctive "Etruscan" gold finish by layering pure 24-carat gold over brass. As opposed to the high shine of 18-carat gold jewelry, the matte yellow gold has an unusual muted glow. Along the same lines, Morris created a green patina—a crude finish with the look of weathered stone. These creations not only established his style but filled a gap between costume jewelry and the "really real stuff."

When the commune accidentally burned down, Morris fled to shelter for the winter at the home of his friend Tony in Vermont. As luck or fate would have it, the forced flight turned out to be quite fortuitous. While in Vermont at a local crafts fair, a prominent gallery owner purchased one of Morris' necklaces. Within weeks, Morris was offered a contract to be represented by the chic gallery of famous artist jewelry, Sculpture to Wear, located in the lobby of the Plaza Hotel in New York City.

Morris relocated to New York in 1972 and found his work being displayed as artwork next to the likes of sculptor Alexander Calder (1898–1976), American pop artist Roy Lichtenstein (1923–97), and artist Louise Nevelson (1899–1988). It was here that his bold, minimalistic, sculptural forms quickly became popular. Sales of his designs immediately outpaced such masters as Picasso, Braque, Calder, Max Ernst, and Man Ray. His Celtic crosses, cuffs, collars, disk belts, and heart-shaped brooches are treasured by the stylish glitterati, ranging from Hollywood celebrities and musicians—like Candice Bergen, Lisa Bonet, Cher, Bianca Jagger, Grace Jones, and Ali McGraw—to rich urban bikers and businessmen and women who are eager to express their individuality.

He opened his own gallery store, the Robert Lee Morris Gallery, described as "the very first 'designer store' of its kind," in 1974 on West Broadway in New York City, just down the street from the famous SoHo Grand Hotel. Two years later, he was featured on the cover of *Vogue,* and has been a cornerstone of fashion and jewelry design since, winning just about every major award in the field.

In 1977, three years after he moved to New York, Morris launched an entire modern jewelry movement when he opened his own gallery, called Artwear. At Artwear, Morris created a showcase "for artists focusing on jewelry as their prime medium" and attracted public interest through merchandising techniques as unique as the gallery's overall concept. The jewelry was displayed on dramatic plaster body casts resembling sculptural relics of ancient civilization. This concept was based on his belief that jewelry "comes alive on the body." He also developed an image catalogue, featuring models covered in mud, sand, and flour, which instantly became a collector's item. For 16 years, up to 1993, Morris' Artwear provided a haven and at least three showcase locations for young, new talent in the jewelry industry.

The following year, 1994, Morris began collaborating with a wide variety of famous designers including Geoffrey Beene, Anne Klein, Calvin Klein, Michael Kors, Karl Lagerfeld, and Kansai Yamamoto. When Donna Karan went solo, she turned to Morris to accessorize her collection with his jewelry, beginning thus far a two-decade on and off collaboration. Karan's fall 2001 collection featured Morris' jewelry as featured items.

In October 2000 the World Gold Council launched a major new multipage, four-color co-op print campaign titled, "The Gold Fashioned Girls." The $3-million media push featured Morris, Chimento, Roberto Coin, Tissot Watch, and AngloGold and appeared in various fashion, luxury, and lifestyle consumer magazines and jewelry trade publications.

In addition to being a successful jewelry designer and businessman, Morris designs handbags, belts, scarves, amulets, sconces, candlesticks, picture frames, packaging for beauty products (the latter for Elizabeth Arden), as well as his own fragrance, *Verdigris,* named for the ancient color that has become a signature of his mythic style.

Throughout his career, Morris has continually sought out new avenues for expression, collaborating with designers and contemporaries. In his own collections, he has invented a clean, pure, uniquely American style, launching such trends as "bold gold" and the green patina verdigris. Today Morris still lives in SoHo, New York, with his wife, Susan, and their daughter Taylor. A much sought-after lecturer, his philosophy has matured into "a synergy of anthropology, art, and spirituality shaped by a true and abiding love and understanding of beauty, and guided by the principles of Shamanism."

—Roberta H. Gruber; updated by Daryl F. Mallett

MORTON, Digby

Irish designer

Born: Digby (Henry) Morton in Dublin, 27 November 1906. **Education:** Studied architecture at the Metropolitan School of Art and Architecture, Dublin, 1923; London Polytechnic. **Family:** Married Phyllis May Painting, 1936. **Career:** Worked as sketch artist, Jay's fashion store, Oxford Street, London, 1928; founded tailoring firm of Lachasse in Farm St, Mayfair, London, 1928; own house established, 1934, closed, 1957; founded Reldan-Digby Morton, 1958; founding member of the Incorporated Society of London Fashion Designers, 1942; designer of Utility clothing for British government, 1942; film costume designer in Hollywood during World War II; established Digby Morton (Exports) Ltd. for marketing British womenswear to the U.S., 1947; Digby Morton for Jacqmar collection, 1950; designer, and vice president, 1955–58, Hathaway Shirt Company, New York; designer/director, Reldan-Digby Morton, 1958–73; designed Women's Voluntary Services uniform, 1939. **Awards:** Aberfoyle International Fashion award, New York, 1956. **Died:** 1983, in London.

Publications

On MORTON:

Books

Amies, Hardy, *Just So Far,* London, 1954.

Carter, Ernestine, *Tongue in Chic,* London, 1974.

Lambert, Eleanor, *World of Fashion: People, Places, Resources,* New York & London, 1976.

Ginsburg, Madeleine, and Prudence Glynn, *In Fashion,* London, 1977.

Amies, Hardy, *Still Here,* London, 1984.

Mulvagh, Jane, *Vogue History of 20th Century Fashion,* London, 1988.

* * *

The fashion for sportswear during the 1920s was the ideal environment for Digby Morton to establish the London house of Lachasse, which specialized in the tailored sporting suit for women. Morton was brought in as chief sportswear designer of a dress establishment owned by businessman Fred Singleton. Morton later claimed his decision to call the new house Lachasse was because at that time British women would not consider anything but French labels in their wardrobes.

Morton transformed the classic tweed suit into a fashionable garment through the carefully planned placing of seams that gave a more decorative line to the native Irish tweeds he used. Sir Hardy Amies acknowledges that Morton's intricate cutting technique and designs made the ordinary country tweed suit into a fashionable garment, worn confidently in town as well as the country. Morton's first collection, in 1929, featured Ardara tweeds, large herringbone wools, and diagonal stripes and checks in the then-unusual color combinations such as pale lime green and duck egg blue with dark brown. Morton used French printed silks by Rodier for blouses and linings which were clean cut and spare for detail, and far removed from what he called "postmistress blouses."

Morton's belief that British women could not successfully wear conspicuous clothes was evident in designs where he endeavored to "translate the trends of feminine fashion into the masculine medium of tailoring." His theory was that it was more difficult to eliminate details than to decorate garments, which resulted in simple lines that relied for effect upon his use of fabrics. Morton's preference for uncluttered designs was also reflected in his dislike of designing eveningwear, which he referred to as debutante clothes. When he began to introduce eveningwear into his collections in the late 1940s his designs were based on the tailored evening dress.

After five years at Lachasse, Morton established his own couture house in 1934. In 1939 he was invited to design the Women's Voluntary Service uniform and during World War II was an active member of the Incorporated Society of London Fashion Designers, established in 1942 to promote exports of British fashion. Morton also designed a collection of garments for the British government's Utility clothing scheme (no-trim standards for wartime clothing and household goods), which went into production anonymously in 1942.

Morton became more closely involved in the field of ready-to-wear clothing in the postwar period and enjoyed particular success in the American market during the 1950s. In 1953 he was asked to design the Lady Hathaway shirt collection for the Hathaway company—a manufacturer of top quality men's shirts. By copying the cut of men's shirts, with slight adjustments for the female form, Morton created the collection in brilliant colors and patterns with contrasting bowties. The success of this venture earned him the title of *Daring Digby* by *Time* magazine. This may have prompted Morton to close his couture house in 1957 and enter the field of ready-to-wear on a full-time basis. Morton always acknowledged he felt constrained by couture, and his real design career began when he started designing clothes for the average woman.

In 1958 Morton formed the company Reldan-Digby Morton with Nadler, a large fashion producer owned by Cyril Kern. Morton's ready-to-wear designs for Reldan-Digby Morton introduced ready-made garments with a couture image to the British public. The collection of separates was renamed Togethers and produced at the company's High Wycombe, Buckinghamshire factory. They were also successful in America where some of the more adventurous designs such as bright yellow-and-black striped suits and jet black beach coats appealed to a particular market.

In 1963 Morton began designing menswear, an area that had always appealed to him—he had personally adopted the neo-Edwardian style so fashionable for men in the 1950s. Morton designed his first menswear collection in Trevira cloth for the Cologne Fair, one of the most widely publicized garments of which was the *Mesh-Over-Flesh Vestshirt* which featured string vest fabric with formal shirting. Other designs played on the traditional image of the male suit, with unusual features such as curved side slits on formal trousers.

Primarily a designer of tailored clothes, Digby Morton was recognized for his use of traditional fabrics in unusual color combinations. His couture designs for women reflected his belief that the British couture customer required unobtrusive suits in good tweeds that were wearable rather than dramatic.

—Catherine Woram

MOSCHINO, Franco

Italian designer

Born: Abbiategrasso, 1950. **Education:** Studied fine art, Accademia delle Belle Arti, Milan, 1968–71. **Career:** Freelance designer and illustrator, Milan, 1969–70; sketcher for Versace, 1971–77; designer for Italian company Cadette, 1977–82; founded own company Moonshadow in 1983; launched Moschino Couture!, 1983; fragrance for women *Moschino* introduced, 1987; introduced diffusion line, Cheap & Chic, 1988; launched Uomo, menswear collection, 1986,

Franco Moschino, fall/winter 2001–02 collection. © AP/Wide World Photos.

and Cheap & Chic Uomo, 1991; *Ok-Ko* men's fragrance, 1991; firm continued after his death in 1994; formation of Franco Moschino Foundation, to help children with HIV and AIDS, 1994; *Cheap & Chic* fragrance debuted, 1995; opened shops in Rome and Beverly Hills, late 1995; *Oh! de Moschino* launched, 1996; opened New York Madison Avenue store, 1996; introduced Moschino Life sportswear, 1999; opened new London boutique, and hired Vincent Darre as designer, 2000; bought by Aeffe SpA, 2001. **Exhibitions:** *X Years of Kaos!* [retrospective], Museo della Permanente, Milan, 1993–94. **Died:** 18 September 1994. **Company Address:** Moonshadow SpA, Via Ceradini 11/A, 20129 Milan, Italy. **Company Website:** www.moschino.it.

PUBLICATIONS

By MOSCHINO:

Books

X Anni di Kaos! 1983–1993 [exhibition catalogue], with Lida Castelli, Milan, 1993.

Franco Moschino, fall/winter 2001 collection: patent leather suit. © AP/Wide World Photos.

On MOSCHINO:

Books

Martin, Richard, and Harold Koda, *Jocks and Nerds: Men's Style in the Twentieth Century,* New York, 1989.
Stegemeyer, Anne, *Who's Who in Fashion, Third Edition,* New York, 1996.
Mazza, Samuele and Mariuccia Casadio, *Moschino,* Cort Madera, California, 1997.

Articles

Webb, Iain R., "Il Cattivo: Franco Moschino...," in *Blitz* (London), August 1987.
Eastoe, Jane, "Designer Chaos," in *Fashion Weekly* (London), 23 February 1989.
"Franco Moschino," in *i-D* (London), May 1989.
Mower, Sarah, "Dressing Down with the Joker," in the *Independent* (London), 16 November 1989.
Ducas, Jane, "An Italian in Love with All Things English," in the *Sunday Times* (London), 29 April 1990.
Born, Pete, "Frankly Franco," in *WWD,* 14 June 1991.
Casadio, Mariuccia, et al., "I Am Proud of the Odor of Garlic and Tomato in My Clothes," in *Interview* (New York), September 1991.
Goodman, Wendy, "Surrealist at Work," in *House & Garden,* March 1993.
Hochswender, Woody, "Pins and Needles," in *Harper's Bazaar,* October 1993.
"Moschino," in *Mondo Vomo,* July-August 1994.
Talley, André Leon, "Franco Moschino, 1950–1994," in *Vogue,* December 1994.
"Florence: Moschino," in *DNR,* 18 January 1995.
Hari, Alessandra, "Moschino's Troops March On," in *WWD,* 2 March 1995.
Conti, Samantha, "Moschino at the Crossroads," in *WWD,* 27 August 1996.
Zargani, Luisa, "Moschino Puts Some Life in Line Made for Comfort," in *WWD,* 2 June 1999.
Menkes, Suzy, "Aeffe Buys Moschino," in *International Herald Tribune,* 26 October 2001.
Ellism Kristi, "Moschino's Artistic Moment," in *WWD,* 27 October 1999.

* * *

"Fashion is full of chic," Franco Moschino once commented, was an ironic statement coming from one of Europe's most successful designers. Based in Milan, Moschino originally studied fine art, with ambitions to be a painter, but came to see that tailoring and fabrics could be just as valid a means of expression as paint and canvas. Consequently, his first job in fashion was with the Cadette label, for whom in 1977 he produced a simple range of stylish clothes.

Starting his own label in 1982, Moschino used his experience in the Italian fashion industry as a source for his philosophical ideas evolving a set of tactics designed to shake the fashion establishment out of its complacency. Much to his amazement, he was embraced with open arms as a new iconoclast by the very people he despised. Essentially Moschino was picking up where Schiaparelli had left off, displaying an interest in the surrealist tactic of displacement—he has for a long time professed a love of Magritte's use of the juxtaposition of incongruous imagery to produce a surreality. This is aptly shown in designs such as his quilted black denim mini with plastic fried eggs decorating the hemline, quilted jacket decorated with bottle tops, plug-socket drop earrings, and bodices made out of safety pins. Moschino's 1989 fun fur collection included a winter coat of stitched together teddybear pelts and a scorch-mark printed silk shirt saying "too much ironing."

Although dubbed the Gaultier of Italian fashion, Moschino responded to fashion differently. Unlike Jean-Paul Gaultier who was interested in playing around with the shapes and the fabrics of fashion, Moschino used basic forms and traditional methods of construction to produce wearable, sexy clothes, cut to flatter and beautifully made. Dismissing his approach as visual and superficial, Moschino stressed he was a decorator, completely disinterested in clothing construction.

Believing he could criticize the business more effectively from the inside, the underlying theme of his work was the parodying of so-called fashion victims, those prepared to be seen in the most ridiculous clothes if they were the latest style, and a general protest against the materialism of capitalism. He did this with visual gags like a triple pearl choker with attached croissant or the Rolex necklace—the pearls and Rolex being traditional ways of displaying wealth—and by mixing cheap plastics with expensive fur.

This parodying of the conspicuous consumers of fashion was continued in 1990 with his use of jokey logos on a series of garments like the cashmere jacket with the words "Expensive jacket" embroidered in gold across its back, or "Bull chic" on a matador-styled outfit. Designs such as these were supposed to make the wearer feel duped into spending vast amounts of money on designer clothing, but after achieving a vast amount of publicity, the people he was attacking flocked to buy his clothes. The iconoclasm of Moschino was destined to become the choicest thing on the catwalk.

Calling for a "Stop to the Fashion System" through his advertising in high fashion magazines, Moschino displayed a classic Dada stance—for an end to the fashion system would mean the destruction of his own empire which came to encompass not just Moschino Couture! but the successful Cheap & Chic range—a diffusion line which was not actually all that cheap—and ranges of underwear, swimwear, jeans, children's clothes, accessories, and fragrances (the men's sold in a double-ended bottle so it can't stand up and the women's advertised with a model drinking it through a straw rather than dabbing it behind her ears).

Known for his theatrical fashion shows (in the past his models impersonated Tina Turner and Princess Margaret), Moschino mixed up and twisted classic styles and wrenched them into the present by using humor. A fine example was a Chanel-type suit restyled with gold clothes pegs for buttons. Interestingly enough, his insults were rarely taken seriously. At one collection he pointedly mocked the top fashion editors by leaving moo-boxes on their seats, implying they were dull bovines with not an original thought in their heads, but they applauded all the more.

Moschino's ambition was to destroy the dictates of fashion so people could please themselves with what they chose to wear, and to produce more anonymous clothes once he completed the downfall of the industry. The irony is that Moschino became his own fashion-as-antifashion status symbol; yet his belief that fashion should be fun was valid and remains so today. Unfortunately for Franco Moshino, he was not around to see his plans to fruition—he died in 1994. His funky design firm was carried on after his death, and to dizzying heights of popularity. Soon after Moschino's death, the Franco Moschino Foundation was founded to help children battling HIV and AIDS, and the Moschino firm would routinely design for charities and fundraisers like Artwalk New York.

Fashionwise, Moschino designs lacked the sharpness of Franco's razor wit yet still provided laughs and sales. The company segued into fragrances with the launch of *Cheap & Chic* in 1995, and opened wildly funky boutiques in Rome and Beverly Hills near the end of the year. More hip shops, in New York City and London, bowed in 1996 and 2000 respectively, while a new sportswear range, Moschino Life, was introduced in 1999. Yet the biggest Moschino news was the firm's acquisition by Aeffe SpA, the burgeoning fashion empire founded by Alberta Ferretti in 2001, which had already produced several Moschino lines.

—Caroline Cox; updated by Sydonie Benét

MOSES, Rebecca

American designer

Born: New Jersey. **Career:** Developed her first collection at age 21; closed her New York-based design company, 1992; replaced Gianni Versace as designer for Donnatella Girombelli's clothing label Genny Collection and Genny Platinum, 1993; continued as a consultant for Genny and Genny Platinum for some years; developed her current label, 1996; designed for the Gerani line, 2000; continues her clothing label to date. **Address:** 588 Broadway, New York, NY 10012, USA.

Publications

On MOSES:

Articles

Biggs, Melissa E., "Carry-On Classics," in *Town & Country.*

Gross, Michael, "The Subject is Moses: The Name Game," in *New York,* 14 March 1988.

Mansfield, Stephanie, "In the World of Fashion, a Designer's Name Can Be Her Most Important Asset," in *Vogue,* December 1989.

Quick, Harriet, "Rebecca Moses," in *Harpers & Queen,* January 1997.

"Rebecca Moses: Keeping it Simple, in *Eve,* July 1997.

"BG, Rebecca Moses Thinking Big," in *WWD,* 1998.

Ilari, Alessandra, et al., "Rebecca Moses: The Bag Solution," in *WWD,* February 24, 1998.

Ellis, Kristi, "Moses Show Brings $100,000 for Jeri Rice," in *WWD,* July 28, 1999.

Zargani, Luisa, "Gilmar and Marzotto Take Different Paths," in *WWD,* November 9, 2000.

"Sure Things," in *WWD,* 7 March 2001.

"Elegance Made Easy," in *Simply the Best,* April 2001.

Rebecca Moses, fall/winter 2001–02 collection. © AP/Wide World Photos.

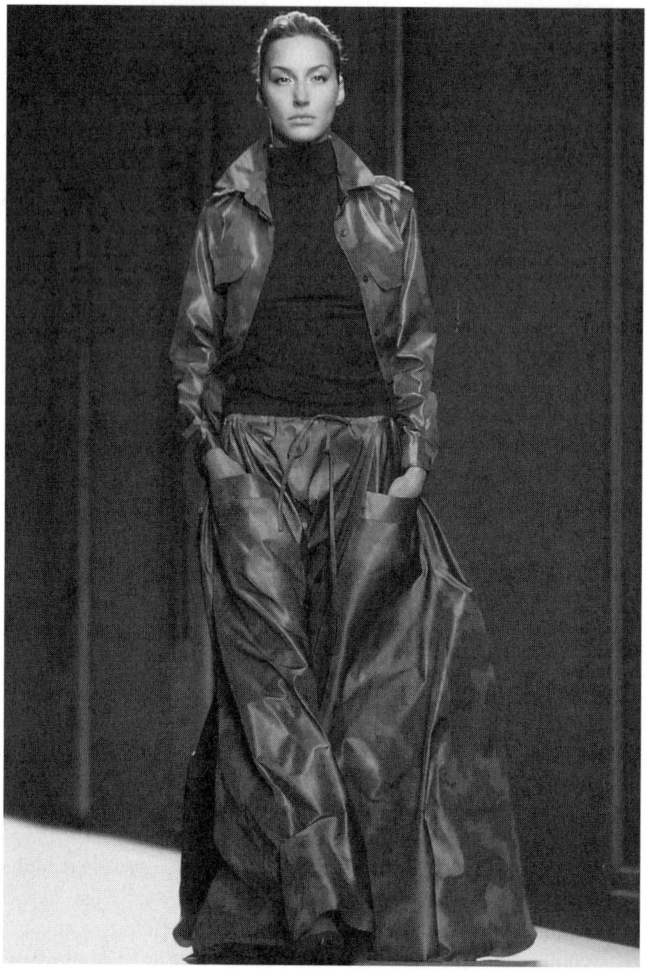

Rebecca Moses, fall/winter 2001–02 collection. © AP/Wide World Photos.

* * *

Women who are on the go and looking for simple style can always look to Rebecca Moses' designs for their fashion needs. Moses has developed a unique way of combining sheer elegance with ready-to-wear fashion by creating relaxed fits with sexy and womanly designs. Bias-cutting and plunging necklines in fine cashmere fabric is a trademark of Moses. She prides herself in using the finest quality cashmere in all her fashions and says that comfort should not negate looking sexy.

Moses' lines are always exquisite and seemingly weigh nothing on the body. They are comfortable and cool, lively and eye-popping. She uses cashmere almost exclusively in her newer collections, year-round. The secret to warmth in cashmere is to layer the paper-thin fabric during the chilling winter months. In 1997, Moses took the cashmere V-neck sweater to 30 opalescent shades, including pink, melon, lavender, and blue ice.

Moses uses vibrant colors, as well as neutrals, to balance women's wardrobes so that pieces can easily be mixed and matched. The colors and hues are inspired by everything around her, especially the flowers in her gardens. Hydrangeas, wisteria, red and pink roses, geraniums, rhododendrons, and azaleas are just a few of the inspiring florals for her creations. Large Scotch pines and a large American maple tree are also sources for inspirational color.

In the summer 1997 collection, Moses created colors of stone, glass, and classic black. The outfits were cool and fresh, and never tight-fitting. The collection included sexy halters and one-shouldered tops. For pants, jackets, and skirts, she enjoyed using neutral colors so that other pieces of the outfit could be used to add vibrant color. She believes a woman should have a base to her wardrobe and then work around the base by adding color. To go along with her sexy yet simple style, Moses created a sling-in-a-bag, cashmere roll-in-a-ball dress, which she called the "va-va voom" dress, to make traveling easier for the busy, modern woman.

Still paying close attention to working women, in 1998, Moses developed a collection of functional yet stylish bags. Practicality was the motivation for her designs, which meant there were compartments for cellular phones, calculators, and glasses. The bags were made out of either deer, lamb napa, or calfskin, and lined with flannel. Colors included black, mud, and toffee brown next to bronze, gray, and copper metallics.

Spring/summer 1999 marked the beginning of a new line of bigger sizes for Moses. She struck a deal with Bergdorf Goodman to develop a collection for plus sizes. The line was created to give plus-sizes the opportunity to feel sexy and modern, and included all of Moses' regular designs: cashmere knits with plunging necklines, cardigans, bias-cut dresses, tunics, and cigarette pants. To enhance the line, she used colors such as white, sand, stone, saturated pastels, and ocean blue.

For regular sizes, the spring/summer 1999 collection continued to address busy, on-the-go women. There were pieces of sportswear, a twinset, a clutch coat, the Capri, and sundresses. Accessories such as slipper shoes, bags, and scarves played a more significant role in the designs. Colors included saturated pastels highlighted against neutrals.

The spring/summer 2001 collection gave the feel and look of being on a leisurely vacation. The colors produced a warm, neutral and sensual glow. The silk and cashmere knits captured the feeling of tropical life. Moses also added one more touch to her cashmere designs: delightful brooches.

Rebecca Moses is a designer of versatility, sensuality, and comfort. She has made her mark as "the" designer of light cashmere clothes for busy, working women. Her attention to details, comfort, and style has given her the reputation as a designer who creates seemingly effortless luxurious styles.

—Kimbally A. Medeiros

MUGLER, Thierry

French designer

Born: Strasbourg, Alsace, France, 1948. **Education:** Studied at the Lycée Fustel de Coulange, 1960–65, and at the School of Fine Arts, Strasbourg, 1966–67. **Career:** Dancer, Opéra de Rhin, Strasbourg, 1965–66; assistant designer, Gudule boutique, Paris, 1966–67; professional photographer, from 1967; designer, André Peters, London, 1968–69; freelance designer, Milan, Paris, 1970–73; created Café de Paris fashion collection, Paris, 1973; founder, Thierry Mugler, 1974, owner, from 1986; published *Thierry Mugler, Photographer,* Paris, London & New York, 1988; Thierry Mugler Perfumes, created 1990; *Angel* fragrance introduced, 1992; first couture collection shown, 1992; worked on film *Prêt-à-Porter,* 1994. **Address:** 130 rue du Faubourg St. Honoré, 75008 Paris, France.

Thierry Mugler, spring/summer 2001 collection. © AP/Wide World Photos.

Publications

By MUGLER:

Books

Thierry Mugler, Photographer, Paris, London & New York, 1988.

On MUGLER:

Books

Polhemus, Ted, and Lynn Proctor, *Fashion and AntiFashion,* London, 1978.

Martin, Richard, *Fashion and Surrealism,* New York, 1987.

Martin, Richard, and Harold Koda, *Infra-Apparel,* New York, 1993.

Stegemeyer, Anne, *Who's Who in Fashion, Third Edition,* New York, 1996.

Wargnier, Stéphanie, *Thierry Mugler,* Paris, 1997.

Baudot, François, *Thierry Mugler,* London, 1997, 1998.

Deloffre, Claudi, *Thierry Mugler: Fashion Fetish Fantasy,* Los Angeles, 1998.

Articles

Kuka, John, "Notes on Fashion," in the *New York Times,* 4 August 1981.

Morris, Bernadine, "The Directions of the Innovations," in the *New York Times Magazine,* 27 February 1983.

LaLanne, Dorothee, "Thierry Mugler et Macbeth," in*Vogue* (Paris), November 1985.

Trittoleno, Martine, "Thierry Mugler: L'Homme qui aimait les lègendes," in *L'Officie* 1 (Paris), November 1986.

Morris, Bernadine, "Japanese Excitement in Paris," in the New York Times, 20 March 1987.

Gasperini, Nicoletta, "Traveling Goddesses," in *Joyce* (Hong Kong), March 1988.

Mory, Frederique, "De la mode à la photo," in *Madame Figaro* (Paris), 2 July 1988.

Baudot, François; "Double objectif de Thierry Mugler," in *Elle* (Paris), 7 November 1988.

Hochswender, Woody, "Thierry Mugler: Nuts, Bolts and Sequins," in the *New York Times,* 18 March 1989.

———, "Stripping Down to Basics," in the *New York Times,* 24 October 1989.
Moutet, Anne-Elisabeth, "Hocus Focus," in *Harper's Bazaar,* June 1990.
Gross, Michael, "The Wild One," in *New York,* 4 June 1990.
Wrobel, Catherine, "Mugler à Moscou," in *France-Soir* (Paris), 26 June 1990.
"Mugler, Clarins Link for a Scent," in *WWD,* 28 September 1990.
Forestier, Nadège, "Thierry Mugler: L'Art de se faire une griffe," in *Le Figaro* (Paris), 6 October 1990.
Polan, Brenda, "Mugler," in *Elle* (Paris), December 1990.
von Unwerth, Ellen, "How to Look Good in Thierry Mugler," in *Interview* (New York), March 1991.
Martin, Richard, "Fashion License: Clothing and the Car," in *Textile and Text,* 13 April 1991.
Morris, Bernadine, "Voyages into Uncharted Waters," in the *New York Times,* 19 October 1991.
"Mugler's Monster Show," in *Elle* (New York), November 1991.
Morris, Bernadine, "Designer in Paris Seeks a Shake-Up," in the *New York Times,* 27 March 1992.
Yarbrough, Jeff, "Thierry Mugler Talks Trends," in the *Advocate* (USA), 21 April 1992.
Spindler, Amy, "Monsieur Mugler," in *WWD,* 22 July 1992.
Morris, Bernadine, "Calm and Classy vs. Bluntly Sexual," in the *New York Times,* 31 July 1992.
Casadio, Mauriccia, "Six Haute Designers: Pure Allure," in *Interview* (New York), December 1992.
Brubach, Holly, "Whose Vision is It, Anyway?" in the *New York Times Magazine,* 17 July 1994.
Spindler, Amy M., "Thierry Mugler on a Roll," in the *New York Times,* 18 October 1994.
———, "Waiting for Mugler," in the *New York Times,* 27 December 1994.
"The Paris Collections: The Ideas of March: Thierry Mugler," in *WWD,* 17 March 1995.
Spindler, Amy M., "A Mature Mugler, Demeulemeester, and Lang," in the *New York Times,* 18 March 1995.
Luscombe, Belinda, "Running Wild on the Runway," in *Time,* 27 March 1995.
Gaudoin, Tina, "Very Thierry," in *Elle* (London), April 1995.
Spindler, Amy M., "In Paris, Ready for Their Close-Ups," in the *New York Times,* 14 October 1995.
———, "Giving More Weight to Lightness," in the *New York Times,* 24 January 1997.
"Clarins in Talks with Fashion House," in the *New York Times,* 18 April 1997.
White, Constance C. R., "Touches of Spice in a Tepid Stew," in the *New York Times,* 27 January 1998.
———, "Breezy Gaultier and Yamamoto," in the *New York Times,* 17 March 1998.

* * *

Rich in iconography, the work of Thierry Mugler has, since 1974, exploited wit and drama to convey an imaginary narrative that is at once erotic, amusing, and unsettling. His clothing spans the spectrum from vulgar ornamentalism to the most rigorous minimalism, denying the possibility of defining a Mugler style.

Born in 1948 in Strasbourg, Mugler was a child prodigy at the city's School of Fine Arts. At the age of 14, he began dancing with the Rhine Opera Ballet. By 20, he had moved to Paris to begin work as an assistant designer for the Gudule boutique. Later he would design for André Peters in London before freelancing for other fashion houses in Milan and Paris. In 1973, he created his first label, Café de Paris, which featured dresses made of muslin and trimmed with fox. Mugler founded his own brand the following year and opened his own shop.

Thierry Mugler, fall/winter 2001–02 ready-to-wear collection. © AP/ Wide World Photos.

It is Mugler's imagery that most clearly identifies him within high fashion. His sources include Hollywood glamor, science fiction, sexual fetishism, political history, Detroit car styling of the 1950s, and various periods in the history of art and decoration. In this way, his work reflects the eclecticism of the art world during the 1970s and 1980s. Mugler has taken a particular delight in industrial styling, which he displayed in the precise geometries of ornamental detail and through his vocabulary of thematic references, which have included the jet age forms used in the fantastic automobiles devised by Harley Earl for General Motors during the 1950s.

Clothing designs that operate as costumes in a dramatic narrative have reinforced the importance of Mugler's link with the cinema and particularly with the American film costumes of designers such as Edith Head, Travis Banton, and Adrian. A love of glamor was evident in his extravagant 1992 collection, redolent of 1950s fashion at its most lavish and photographed among the Baroque roof sculptures of the old city of Prague. His interest in romance and the bizarre has often run counter to political ideologies. Against a backdrop of feminist reinterpretation of the female image, Mugler adopted an ironic, postmodern stance and exploited an array of erotic icons as themes for his collections.

Women who favor Mugler are often those who find themselves encased in rigid materials such as leather, latex, rubber, plastic, plexiglas, and chrome. Therefore, it is no surprise that Mugler is a big favorite of those involved in the corset and fetish worlds. His designs range from the insectoid to the medieval, from the fantastic to the science fictional. His "Carapace" ensemble, created from sculpted and embossed leather and silk chiffon, trimmed with beads and feathers, upon which he collaborated with leather designer Abel Villareal, resembles nothing if not the body armor of a medieval knight.

The London-based House of Harlot often works with Mugler to create outfits and accessories for his catwalk shows. Few if any designers have used rubber in such a provocative and consequential way. He has also worked with everything from taffeta, lace, muslin, and raffia to coconut fibers, chrome, latex, and color-changing, temperature-sensitive plastic. Difficult to characterize and appearing to work in opposition to current fashion and intellectual trends, Mugler has remained a controversial figure on the fashion scene.

Mugler's photographic talent may prove to be as important as his fashion designs. A book of his photographs, *Thierry Mugler, Photographer,* published in 1988, contained images comparable in their artifice, explosive glamor, and formal control to the cinematic images of Peter Greenaway. His photographs exploit grand vistas, deep interior spaces, and heroic monuments as settings upon which models perch like tiny ornaments, strongly defined by the extravagant outline of their costumes and asserting their presence through dramatic pose and gesture. His fashion photographs provide a narrative framework for Mugler's clothes, while relegating them to the role of costume within a larger dramatic context.

The broad-shouldered Russian collection of 1986, for example, was presented against backgrounds of heroic Soviet monuments or sweeping landscapes reminiscent of earlier 20th-century Social Realist painting and poster art. Mugler has also made photographic collages repeating and emphasizing the formal elements of his clothes in kaleidoscopic compositions that revealed his interest in abstract aesthetics. These images were conceived as pure works of art, in which the clothing became an element of the creative whole.

Not content to dabble just in clothing design and photography, Mugler introduced his first fragrance in 1993. Called *Angel,* it is a blue-hued, oriental scent with essences of chocolate, caramel, honey, and vanilla with sensual wooded notes. Favored by music diva Diana Ross, the scent comes in a five-pointed star-shaped bottle. A second fragrance, *Amen,* followed some years later.

In 1994, Mugler worked on the film *Prêt-à-Porter,* starring Julia Roberts and Tim Robbins, a complicated film following about a half-dozen plots, all circling around the death of a much-hated leader in the fashion world.

Mugler's clothes are designed to be performed in. His major catwalk shows—featuring top models such as Esther Canadas—beginning in 1977, have been choreographed like the great Hollywood musicals of Busby Berkeley. Later exhibitions were held in huge sports stadiums, emulating the highly charged atmosphere of rock concerts. Mugler designs the offstage wardrobes of rock celebrities such as Madonna, as well as dressing famous women like Danielle Mitterand, who require a more dignified appearance. His fall 2000 showing at the Louvre mixed demure organza and georgette evening dresses with outlandish latex and fluorescent creations.

Whether aggressively vulgar or caricatures of sobriety, Mugler's designs are consistently body conscious. His clothes can be read as essays in the aesthetic potential of extreme proportions; shoulder widths three times head height, wasp waists, and panniered hips are among the repertoire of distortions and exaggerations of the human figure to be found among his designs. Mugler's annual collections, for both women and men, consistently aim to provoke through their challenging themes and flamboyant formal qualities.

—Gregory Votolato; updated by Daryl F. Mallett

MUIR, Jean

British designer

Born: Jean Elizabeth Muir in London, circa 1930. **Education:** Dame Harper School, Bedford. **Family:** Married actor Harry Leuckert.

Jean Muir, autumn/winter 2001 collection. © Reuters NewMedia Inc./CORBIS.

Career: Sales assistant in lingerie and made-to-measure departments, Liberty, London, 1950–55; studied fashion drawing and modeled at St Martin's School of Art, London; joined Jacqmar then Jaeger, 1956–63; studied knitwear design and manufacture, especially jersey, and visited Paris collections; worked at Courtaulds, 1966–69; created own label, Jane & Jane, 1967; formed Jean Muir Ltd. with husband, 1986; sold majority interest to Coats Paton group; bought back 75-percent stake in company, 1989; Jean Muir department in Jaeger's flagship store, London. **Awards:** British Fashion Writers Group Dress of the Year award, 1964; *Harper's Bazaar* trophy; Ambassador award for Achievement, 1965; Maison Blanche Rex awards, 1967, 1968, 1974, 1976; Churchman's Fashion Designer of the Year award, 1970; Royal Society of Arts Royal Designer for Industry, 1972; elected fellow of RSA; Neiman Marcus award, 1973; elected fellow of Chartered Society of Designers, 1978; Bath Museum of Costume Dress of the Year award, 1979; named Honorary Doctor, Royal College of Art, 1981; appointed to the Design Council, London, 1983; made a Commander of the Order of the British Empire, 1984; awarded Hommage de la Mode, Fédération Française du Prêt-à-Porter Féminin; British Fashion Council award for Services to Industry, 1985; Chartered Society of Designers medal; Textile Institute Design medal, 1987; Australian Bicentennial award, 1988; The Ford award, 1989. Honorary Degree, Doctor of Literature, University of Newcastle. **Died:** 28 May 1995, in London.

Jean Muir, autumn/winter 2001 collection: silk multicolored dress. © Reuters NewMedia Inc./CORBIS.

Publications

By MUIR:

Books

Jean Muir, London, 1981.

Articles

"Getting Going," in *The Designer* (London), October 1979.

On MUIR:

Books

MacCarthy, Fiona, and Patrick Nuttgens, *Eye for Industry: Royal Designers for Industry, 1936–1986,* exhibition catalogue, London 1986.
Stegemeyer, Anne, *Who's Who in Fashion, Third Edition,* New York, 1996.

Articles and Video

"Jean Muir Designs," in *The Times* (London), 4 November 1971.
"1979 Design for Bath Museum," in the *Sunday Times,* 2 September 1979.
"Great British Design: Jean Muir," in *Vogue* (London), August 1981.
Green, Felicity, "The Gospel According to St Muir," in the *Sunday Telegraph Magazine* (London), 8 March 1987.
"Designers Take Two," in *Good Housekeeping* (London), March 1988.
Lambert, Elizabeth, and Derry Moore, "The Essential Jean Muir: Composition in White for Her London Apartment," *Architectural Digest,* September 1988.
Maitliss, Nicky, "A Day in the Life of Jean Muir," in the *Sunday Times Magazine* (London), 13 November 1988.
Dutt, Robin, "Jean Muir Interview," in *Clothes Show* (London), February 1989.
"Winter '89," in *DR: The Fashion Business* (London), 4 March 1989.
Klensch, Elsa, "*Style* with Elsa Klensch," (video), CNN Special Reports, 6 May 1989.
McCooey, Meriel, "The Prime of Miss Jean Muir," in the *Sunday Times Magazine* (London), 13 January 1991.
Webb, Ian R., "Secure with Miss Muir," in *Harpers & Queen* (London), March 1991.
van der Post, Lucia, "The Queen of Simple Chic," in the *Financial Times* (London), 9 March 1991.
Rawlinson, Richard, "Pure Miss Muir," in *DR: The Fashion Business* (London), 11 May 1991.
Menkes, Suzy, "Twenty-Five Years of Disciplined Design," in the *International Herald Tribune* (Paris), 21 May 1991.
———, "Muir's Classical Rigor," in the *International Herald Tribune* (Paris), 30 May 1995.
Fallon, James, "UK Designer Jean Muir Dead at 66," in *WWD,* 30 May 1995.
Obituary, in *Time,* 12 June 1995.
Bowles, Hamish, "The Prime of Miss Jean Muir," in *Vogue,* September 1995.

* * *

Jean Muir was noted for simple, flattering, and extremely feminine clothes that were sophisticated yet retain a handcrafteded look with diligent attention to detail. Her favorite fabrics—jersey, angora, wool crêpe, suede, and soft leather—reappeared time after time, regardless of trends. Her more famous clients included actresses Joanna Lumley and Patricia Hodge and writers and artists such as Lady Antonia Fraser and Bridget Riley.

Muir was renowned for producing clothes women really wanted to wear and felt comfortable in. She achieved this by modeling all the clothes and toiles herself at fittings, an advantage she believed she had over male designers. "If you're going to make clothes, the first thing you have to understand is the female anatomy. When I try on a dress, I can feel if something is wrong; I can tell if it's not sitting properly on the shoulders or the bust or the hip. I couldn't tell these things if I saw it on a stand," she had explained.

There was an air of the fashion headmistress in Jean Muir's approach; her steadfast opinions could not be budged. Her tone was unrelenting when she stressed a need to restore a sense of pride in the technique of making clothes and her passion for "art, craft and design and the upholding of standards and quality, maintaining them and setting new ones." She believed fashion was not art but industry. The word fashion, she said, suggested the "transient and the superficial," hardly the best attributes for a commercial business. Muir described her work as being based on intuition, aesthetic appreciation, and mathematical technical expertise. Never at the cutting edge of fashion, the clothes were timeless, understated, and often dateless. Like Fortuny or Chanel, the company based its look on the evolution of a singular theme, a soft, supple fluidity of cut which created the form of a garment.

In person Muir epitomized the type of woman for whom she liked to design. Writer Antonia Fraser described her as a "modish Puck" with a white, powdered face with a mouth slashed in crimson lipstick. Muir had a wiry, bird-like frame and was always dressed in navy calf-length jersey dresses, with black stockings and Granny shoes. In her studio Muir had a reputation for perfectionism and exacting standards in all aspects of production. "There are tremendous activities involved in the making of clothes," she declared in a television interview, with such conviction that the viewer was left in no doubt about her sincerity.

In the annals of fashion history Jean Muir should be remembered as a designer who liberated the body. While many designers have forced bodies into structured tailoring, boning, or restrictive interfaced fabrics, Muir's fluid and easy clothes always provided an emancipated alternative; devoid of structure and underpinning, the clothes nevertheless remained womanly and melodious.

—Kevin Almond

MUJI

Japanese design firm

Founded: in 1983 by retail conglomerate Seiyu. **Company History:** Joint venture with Liberty Plc, 1991–97; opened first European outlet, London, 1991; spun off as part of Ryohin Keikaku Ltd., 1997; announced intention to open 40 stores in Germany over next decade, 1997; majority stake in Ryohin sold by Seiyu, 1999; launched company websites for online sales, 2000. **Awards:** D&AD Silver award, 1994; *Design Week* award for Retail Design, 1994. **Company Address:** Nikko Ikebukuro Building, 4–26–3 Higashi-Ikebukuro, Toshima-ku, Tokyo, Japan 170. **Company Websites:** www.muji.net (in Japan); www.MujiOnline.com (in North America).

Publications

On MUJI:

Articles

Glancey, Jonathan, "No Labels, No Brand Names, No Nonsense," in the *Independent,* July 1991.

Nakamoto, Michiyo, "Life With Liberty in the Pursuit of Happiness and Joint Profits," in the *Financial Times,* July 1991.

Furness, Janine, "The Brand With No Name," in *Interior Design* (London), September 1991.

Louiek Elaine, "If You Want to Make an Understatement," in the *New York Times,* November 1991.

van der Post, Lucia, "New Worshippers for Japan's Muji Cult," in the *Financial Times,* June 1992.

Thompson, Elspeh, "Selling a Lifestyle Without a Label," in *The Guardian,* July 1992.

Horsham, Michael, "Adoration of the Muji," in *The Guardian,* 21 October 1994.

"Japanese Retailing—Look Out (Japanese Supermarket Chain Seiyu's Restructuring Plans," in the *Economist,* 24 October 1998.

Nusbaum, Alexandra, "Seiyu to Sell Shares to Offset ¥88bn Charge," in the *Financial Times,* 23 February 1999.

"Japanese Retailing—A Yen for Cheap Chic," in the *Economist,* 3 June 2000.

"Muji Online Bows in North America," in *WWD,* 6 November 2000.

Nicksin, Carole, "Japan's Muji Launches E-Commerce Site for U.S., Canada," in *HFN (Weekly Newspaper for the Home Furnishing Network),* 13 November 2000.

Terazono, Emiko, "Growing Pains are Natural as Muji Enters the Major League," in the *Financial Times,* 5 April 2001.

"New Daiei Store Heats Up Ginza Clothing War," in *Yomiuri Shimbun/Daily Yomiuri,* 9 November 2001.

* * *

The company name signals its policy—Muji, short for Mujirushi Ryohin, is represented by four characters meaning "no-brand quality goods." The concept is Japanese; its success has been international. Muji is proving a workable design formula for the 1990s and well into the 2000s.

In providing an antidote to the 1980s designer label obsession, Muji is consciously self-effacing; the policy is to sell quality products at reasonable prices. Clothes, household goods, food, and stationery are staples and the emphasis is on necessity, not superfluity—Muji caters to needs, not wants. The Muji concept is about lifestyle. "Kanketsu," the belief in simplicity which forms the heart of the Japanese art of living, guides the design and retail of the products. Packaging is in simple brown paper bags, swing tags are made of recycled paper and clearly describe the product, in Japanese. The shops are strictly utilitarian: each one is different, but most of the materials and objects used in the construction are taken from local sources, such as scrapyards. The interiors, like the products, are pared down and intended to survive. Typical merchandise includes strongly-woven undyed towels, notebooks made from unbleached paper, reusable storage bottles, rice crackers sold in plain see-through packaging; each item is the result of a philosophy clearly echoed in the clothes.

Muji garments have been described as an "alternative to fashion." Elegant and classic, they are, in the company language, "meant to be worn, not to adorn." White cotton shirts, West Point trousers, Californian cotton rugger shirts, tracksuit bottoms, polo shirts, and Peruvian cotton socks are representative of the range. Clothes are designed to feel comfortable, to be easy to wear, pleasant to the touch and convenient to launder, sound almost anathema to fashion. The company does not use the term, "We would not call them fashion because they might make you think they are expensively designed with bits here and there thrown in for good measure," company materials note. In Tokyo the garments have become an acceptable alternative to fashion; this phenomenon increasingly happened elsewhere.

Since 1983, when it was founded by the Japanese retail giant Seiyu, Muji has achieved cult status. When the first London shop opened in the summer of 1991, at the back of Liberty's of Regent Street, consumer response was instantaneous. Items sold too rapidly to be immediately restocked from Japan. The next summer a second, bigger store followed and Muji clothing featured a strong development in "one mile wear," meaning they were the comfortable clothes worn at home, or within a mile radius, for leisure or for popping out to the local shop. Traditional Japanese workwear inspired relaxed, deconstructed coordinates in comfortable, natural fabrics. Muji clothes are sensible, but not boring, austere but not dull. They mix well with other labels and their no-brand clothes have had designers, such as Masuro Amano, who trained at St. Martin's School of Art in London.

The first ten years of trading in Japan provided Muji with a firm base and an established design philosophy; the next decade brought recognition and rocketing sales of its "spare chic" and accessories, with nearly 300 worldwide stores and dozens planned for the U.S. and Canada. But before the newest stores debuted, Muji brought its wares to North America via the Internet. Muji's first website was launched exclusively in Japan, and a second was tested in America in 1999 and officially went online in 2000, as many Japanese retailers were recovering from a years-long recession. Even Muji's ultimate parent, Seiyu, had been forced to sell all but five-percent of its stake in Muji's immediate parent, Ryohin Keikaku Ltd., to offset losses in 1999.

As Muji expanded outside its home base of Japan, especially in the U.S. and Canada, its biggest competition came from brands like Gap and Abercrombie & Fitch. Both Gap and A&F were immensely popular with young men and women from teens to thirties, the same segment Muji had so enthralled in Asia. Yet even Muji finally succumbed to competition in Japan, as upstarts followed its lead into pared-down clothing and accessories. In 2001 Muji suffered its first loss since its creation, as two rivals—Y100 and Fast Retailing—lured away teenaged customers. Muji executives reacted quickly, reducing its products line (which had grown from 40 to over 6,000 items in 12 years) and shored up its image. Further, Muji decided to move from cult status to well-known retailer through advertising, not unlike the transformation of Gap years before.

Given Muji's track record and emphasis on tradition and longevity, the Japanese no-brand leader would rally from its temporary woes. In the U.S., the firm was scouting locations to build its freestanding, no-nonsense stores in New York City, Los Angeles, and San Francisco. Muji stands for quality at reasonable prices; its message and its products have a broad international appeal, and the firm poses a healthy challenge to established preconceptions of fashion. Ironically, no-brand became *the* brand of the 1990s and beyond.

—Hazel Clark; updated by Sydonie Benét

MULBERRY COMPANY

British fashion and accessory firm

Founded: by Roger Saul and his mother, Joan, to produce leather accessories, 1971. **Company History:** Opened factory, Chilcompton, Bath, England, and set up wholesale operation in Australia, 1973; Mulberry Ltd. formed, 1974; London and New York showrooms open, and clothing line introduced, 1976; three-year contract signed with Sisheido, Japan, and first women's ready-to-wear clothing collection introduced, 1978; freestanding shop opened in Paris, and first men's shoe collection, 1982; men's ready-to-wear collection introduced, 1985; launched men's toiletry range, 1989; added home furnishings, 1991; Mulberry shops opened in Tamagawa and Hankyu Osaka, Japan, 1991, and in Russia, 1992; first edition *Muberry Life* magazine, 1993; public offering marks 25th anniversary, 1996; Madison Avenue, New York, store opens, 1997; marketing gambit with Motorola, 1999; operated stores in 21 countries, 2000. **Awards:** Queen's award to Industry and Export, 1979; Queen's award for Export, 1987, 1989; British Knitting and Clothing Export Council award, 1988, 1991; Business in Europe "Best Consumer Company" award, 1989; Classic Designer of the Year, 1992, 1993. **Company Address:** 11–12 Gees Court, St Christopher's Place, London W1M 5HQ, England.

Publications

By MULBERRY:

Books

Mulberry at Home: A New Approach to Luxurious Country Style, London, 1999.

On MULBERRY:

Articles

"Business in Europe Awards, 1989," in *Management Today,* May 1989.

McDougall, Mary, "Rich and Romantic," in *Connoisseur* (London), March 1991.

"Fashion into Furniture," in *Elle Decoration* (London), September/October 1991.

"English Clothier Mulberry Plans Expansion into U.S.," in *Chicago Tribune,* 17 March 1996.

Menkes, Suzy, "It's Their Party…Mulberry at 25, Redefines the English Country Look," in the *International Herald Tribune,* 21 May 1996.

* * *

Mulberry was founded in 1971 by Roger Saul through a gift of 50-pounds sterling from his mother Joan. Roger began by selling his own designs for leather chokers and belts to such high fashion shops as

Biba in London. His first collection of belts in suede and leather demonstrated the influence of saddlery techniques and traditional English crafts, and were worked to Saul's designs by local craftsmen housed in what was once an old forge in his parent's garden in Chilcompton, near Bath. The following year Saul made Mulberry's first significant export—an order of a thousand belts from the Paris department store Au Printemps, while Saul created a subsequent belt collection for Jean Muir. By 1975 Mulberry had expanded into Europe, with handbag designs for Kenzo in Paris and a special range for Bloomingdale's in New York.

The definitive English "hunting, shooting and fishing" look which is the hallmark of Mulberry's style was enhanced in 1976 by an expansion from accessories to clothes, with the first jacket design. Consisting of a cotton blouson with a leather collar, the distinctive Mulberry jacket was a worldwide success. The first women's ready-to-wear collection followed in 1978, and within a decade Mulberry was the largest manufacturer of designer quality leather accessories in Britain, with exports, including those to the United States, accounting for the majority of its production. Unfortunately, Mulberry's success in the U.S. market was shortlived, as the dollar drastically lost its value against the pound. Yet Mulberry rallied and was sustained by its European growth, were the company's tree logo was an established status symbol.

The end of the 1980s brought the Queen's award for Export in both 1987 and 1989 and by 1991 a new At Home collection of home furnishings was launched at Harvey Nichols, in Knightsbridge, London. Soon after, two shops opened in Japan, followed by stores in Russia, Italy, Chile, and South Africa. Mulberry continued to win awards and gain exposure, including the opening of another shop in London, on Bond Street.

In the late 1990s, Mulberry ventured back into the U.S. with renewed vigor, and toyed with a public offering on London's Alternative Investment Market to celebrate its 25th anniversary. By the end of the 20th century the English country elegance of Mulberry was increasingly well known, with a savvy marketing deal with Motorola (buy a phone, get a Mulberry leather wallet) and Saul writing a coffee-table book about the company's home furnishings. *Mulberry at Home: A New Approach to Luxurious Country Style* was published in 1999 and was enthusiastically received. With Mulberry stores in 21 countries worldwide, what Roger Saul characterized as the "spirit of Mulberry, with its witty English nostalgia, amusing eccentricity and uncompromising devotion to quality," had become synonymous with refined elegance in clothing, accessories, and home furnishings. As Saul so aptly put it, Mulberry has come to represent "a romantic but robust lifestyle."

—Doreen Ehrlich; updated by Nelly Rhodes

MULLANY, Lorcan

See BELLVILLE SASSOON-LORCAN MULLANY

MUSCARIELLO, Rocco

See BAROCCO, Rocco

N

NATORI, Josie Cruz

American designer

Born: Josie Cruz in Manila, Philippines, 9 May 1947. **Education:** Studied at Manhattanville College, Bronxville, New York, 1964–68, B.A., Economics. **Family:** Married Ken Natori, 1973; son: Kenneth. **Career:** Piano soloist, Manila Philharmonic Orchestra, 1956; stockbroker, Bache Securities, New York, Manila, 1968–71; investment banker, vice president, Merrill Lynch, New York, 1971–77; founder/president and designer, Natori Company, women's lingerie and daywear, from 1977; introduced at-homewear, 1983; introduced boudoir accessories and footwear lines, 1984; introduced bed and bath collections, 1991; delegate, Clinton Economic Summit Conference, and commissioner, White House Conference on Small Business, 1990s; Manhattanville College Board of Trustees; numerous licenses, including Avon, Bestform Foundations. **Exhibitions:** Asia Society's Philippine Style, New York, 2000. **Awards:** Harriet Alger award, 1987; Girls' Clubs of America award, 1990; Laboratory Institute of Merchandising award, 1990; National Organization of Women Legal Defense and Education Fund Buddy award, 1990; Philippine Independence Ball award, 1999. **Address:** 40 East 34th Street, New York, NY 10016, USA.

Publications

On NATORI:

Books

Martin, Richard, and Harold Koda, *Infra Apparel* [exhibition catalogue], New York, 1993.

Enkelis, Liane, et al., *On Our Own Terms,* San Francisco, 1995.

Stegemeyer, Anne, *Who's Who in Fashion, Third Edition,* New York, 1996.

Crisostomo, Isabelo T., *Filipino Achievers in the USA & Canada,* Midlothian, VA, 1996.

Bautista, Veltisezar, *The Filipino Americans (from 1763 to the Present): Their History, Culture and Traditions,* Midlothian, VA, 1998.

Kim, Hyung-Chan, ed., *Distinguished Asian Americans: A Biographical Dictionary,* Westport, CT, 1999.

Articles

Ballen, Kate, "Josie Cruz Natori," in *Fortune,* 2 February 1987.

Haynes, Kevin, "Three SA Women: How They Built Their Business Niches," in *WWD,* 10 April 1987.

Hochswender, Woody, "Lounge Wear for Cocooning," in the *New York Times,* 3 January 1989.

Klein, Fasy, "Beyond the Paycheck," in *Dun & Bradstreet Reports,* March/April 1989.

Morris, Bernadine, "Lingerie is Visible: So are its Designers," in the *New York Times,* 5 June 1990.

Goodman, Wendy, "Paris Ensemble," in *HG* (New York), September 1990.

Hofmann, Deborah, "Movie Star Pajamas for a VCR Public," in the *New York Times,* 21 October 1990.

Retter, Nancy Marx, "The Pajama Game," in *Savvy Women* (New York), February 1991.

Monroe, Valerie, "The Natori Story," in *Mirabella* (New York), March 1991.

"A Touch of Lingerie in Outerwear," in the *New York Times,* 28 April 1991.

Weisman, Katherine, "Cementing a Marriage," in *Forbes,* 22 July 1991.

"Josie Natori: Queen of the Nightgown," in *Cosmopolitan,* December 1991.

Dohrzynski, Judith H., "The Metropolitan's Natori-ous Display," in *Business Week,* 5 April 1993.

Hassan, Wendy, "The Mark of Natori," in *WWD,* 23 April 1993.

Willen, Janet A., "Fashioning a Business," in *Nation's Business,* February 1995.

Medford, Sarah, and Michel Arnaud, "Natori's Glory Days," in *Town & Country,* March 1995.

"Making a Fashion Statement that Revolutionized Lingerie," in *Diversity Suppliers & Business Magazine,* Fall 1996.

Schiro, Anne Marie, "Going Sheer But Not Going Overboard," in the *New York Times,* 14 January 1997.

Seno, Alexandra A., "It's My Party and I'll Spend if I Want to," in *Asianweek,* 6 June 1997.

"Ebony and Ivory: Not Just Negligee Colors," in *Asianweek,* 26 December 1997.

* * *

"I never think of men when I design my lingerie or my fragrances. My desire is to encourage women to appreciate and pamper themselves," Josie Cruz Natori told the Fragrance Foundation. The tiny Filipino-American designer has created a new model in the business of fashion. Founder and chief executive officer of the Natori Company, Natori eschews the designation "designer," though others have described her as an "international fashion magnate." It is not surprising, considering the unprecedented degree of her vision and tenacity.

Battling puritanism and body reticence, which stifled the concept of fashion developing from the inside out, Natori has taken lingerie from a barely visible inner layer of fashion to the entirety of fashion and, in the process, built a multimillion-dollar worldwide business, featuring numerous major international licenses. To build a major fashion house from the base of lingerie is unparalleled, visionary, and a sign of the very late 20th century in its ambition and success. Yet contemporary culture has taken to Natori's vision of exposing the beautiful details of lingerie within a fashion vocabulary, which previously denied such ornamentation.

The stunning growth of Natori's empire is due to her vision. In the 1980s, she realized her lingerie was increasingly exposed by the women who purchased it, so she created publicly wearable garments inspired by her lingerie. The resulting neologist crossover category "innerwear-as-outerwear" was never her corporate slogan, though it might serve. Natori brought boudoir apparel out of the bedroom, perhaps inevitably so at a moment in culture when all heretofore privileged and private matters of the bedroom seemed to become public discourse. As a visionary, she simply answers a client's question of "how or where should I wear this?" with "wherever you want," granting lingerie an opportunity to enter into every aspect of attire. It is an ironic turn of success for Natori since she first approached a Bloomingdale's buyer about making shirts; her destiny was set when the buyer recommended she make them longer to be sold as nightshirts.

Natori brought a richness of detail back to apparel, one she remembered from Philippine embroideries and appliqúes. Natori shrewdly assesses the culture of the body, bringing stretch and bodysuits to the realm of lingerie and back to playwear, as well as the possibilities of feminine self-expression to dress for public circumstances. She neither suppresses nor proposes that the clothing she designs be mistaken for career wear, the operative description for much apparel of the 1980s. Instead she realizes the affiliation between private clothing, body expression, and eveningwear, all committed to comfort and to some degree of seduction and sensual pleasure.

To some, Natori might seem antifeminist; she argues, of course, that she is the true feminist delighting in and extending the category endemic to feminine traits and the female body. Talking with Woody Hochswender of the *New York Times* in January 1989, Natori said, "It's really a way for a woman to express herself. We've made women feel good without feeling sleazy." Indeed, all apparel addresses wearer and spectator; Natori's reassessment of the innerwear category has been refreshing for both men and women.

"Think of Katherine Hepburn, answering the doorbell," Natori offered to Deborah Hofmann, giving evocative pedigree to the ease-without-sleaze that she makes of her innerwear-as-outerwear. Natori is a perfect example for the woman who asserts authority in contemporary fashion: her first career was in investment banking; she herself wears couture (generally a tailored jacket and skirt) in impeccable taste; and she makes her way and her company's way in the fashion market with unmistakable respect for the women who wear her clothing. Natori's business acumen and design sensibility seem unerringly and culturally right—she created a fashion that satisfies women's feelings and practical needs in a culture and era of precious privacy and of women's expressions of themselves.

By the 1990s, Natori was involved in almost every aspect of fashion. Besides camisoles, thongs, panties, briefs, bras, and other lingerie items, Natori further developed her line of clothing to include chic pajamas, robes, pants, tank tops, tunics, sleepshirts, and more, made in a wide variety of fabrics, from cotton and satin to silk and polyester. Realizing the relationship between the feel of classy lingerie and scents, Natori began designing fragrances to complement her clothing, including her namesakes, *Josie* and *Natori.* "When I wear lingerie and fragrance, it's being sexy for me, not for someone else," she commented to the Fragrance Institute. "I never could use the word 'sexy'—for many years I was brought up to think it meant 'dirty,' but I've come to realize…it means feminine and sensual. There's nothing wrong with being both 24 hours a day." The company also manufactures home furnishings, accessories, jewelry, and eveningwear.

As one of the few early Asian designers to attain prominence in the international fashion world, Natori serves in a variety of roles, from businesswoman (in 1999, she was named number 40 in the Goldsea 100, America's 100 Top Asian Entrepreneurs list) to role model, from advocate for women's rights to delegate for business conferences (during the Clinton administration, she served as a delegate to the Economic Summit Conference in Little Rock, Arkansas, and as a commissioner to the White House Conference on Small Business).

—Richard Martin; updated by Daryl F. Mallett

NAVARRO, Sara

Spanish fashion designer

Born: Elda, Alicante, Spain, 17 August 1957. **Education:** Studied psychology, University of Valencia, Spain, 1974; shoe styling at Ars Sutoria Institute, Milan, 1978; fashion design, under Gianfranco Ferré, Domus Academy, Milan, 1987; business management at Escuela de Organizacion Industrial, Madrid; classical art at Dante Alighiere School, Florence. **Career:** Director of fashion, Kurhapies Group; head stylist, Sara Navarro Company, Alicante; launched first shop in Madrid, 1979; specializes in footwear, handbags, belts, and ready-to-wear in leather; collaborated with Fernandez, Vittorio y Luccino, and Robert Verino for footwear; first international collection, 1988; official designer for V-Centenario, 1991, and Expo 92, 1991–92; launched shoe collection with Martine Sitbon, Paris, 1992; director of fashion team Creaciones Exclusivas S.A. and Komfort Spain SL (now Komfort Spain SL); introduced Pretty Shoes and Via Sara Navarro lines. **Exhibitions:** GDS Show, Dusseldorf, 1985; Premiere Classe Show, Paris, 1987; Expo Universal, Seville, 1992; *Luz Blanca* Collection, Galeria Nieves Fernandez, Madrid, 1992. **Collection:** Museu del Calzado de Elda, Alicante, Spain. **Awards:** Fashion Oscar for footwear, 1978; Alipac de Oro award, 1979; Catalog-81 prize, 1981; Master International award, 1985; Premio Valencia Innovacion award, 1989. **Address:** c/o Komfort Spain, SL, P.O. Box 83; CP: 03600 Elda (Alicante), Spain.

Publications

On NAVARRO:

Books

Coad-Dent, Elizabeth, *Spanish Design and Architecture,* London, 1990.

McDowell, Colin, *Shoes: Fashion and Fantasy,* New York, 1989, 1994.

The Fashion Guide, Paris, 1990.

Articles

Barker, Barbara, "Two Spanish Designers Open Stores in Madrid Center," in *Footwear News,* 5 June 1989.

———, "Bad Timing Puts Spain Fairs in Fix," in *Footwear News,* 16 October 1989.
———, "Spain's FICC Shows Off With Complicated Shoes," in *Footwear News,* 2 April 1990.
Ilari, Alessandra, "Vergelio Operates Ten Shoe Stores in Milan," in *Footwear News,* 11 June 1990.
Barker, Barbara, "Elda Vendors Make Winter Statement," in *Footwear News,* 24 September 1990.
"109 Anni Vissuti Intensamente," in *Vogue Pelle* (Milan), May-June 1991.
"Pasos Decivos," in *Vogue* (Madrid), June 1991.
Barker, Barbara, "Madrid International Fair Trots Out Cowboy Boots, Rugged Looks," in *Footwear News,* 6 April 1992.
Weisman, Katherine, "Premiere Classe Brings Accessories Back to Earth," in *Footwear News,* 26 October 1992.
"Identità di Gusto," *Vogue Pelle,* (Milan), July/August 1993
Barker, Barbara, "Sara Navarro: Profile of a Professional," in *Footwear News,* 9 August 1993.
Weisman, Katherine, "Premiere Classe Enjoys Traffic Bonus," in *Footwear News,* 18 October 1993.
———, "Shoes Play Leading Role at Premiere Classe Show," in *Footwear News,* 14 March 1994.
"World Footwear Production," in *Economic Review,* November 1995.
Barker, Barbara, "Spain Makers Pin Hopes on Far East," in *Footwear News,* 23 September 1996.
"Spanish Fly," in *Footwear News,* 1 November 1999.
"Fashion Fair," in *Footwear News,* 29 May 2000.
Mullins, David Philip, "Showing Off: The Latest New York Shoe Expo…," in *Footwear News,* 29 May 2000.

*

I view creating with an outlook onto the future, spending a great deal of time researching cultural trends to gather information for the purpose of finding an underlying concept or thread tying together each collection. [I try to] reflect society's current cultural scene, so my designs may serve as a response to the questions, desires, or needs of those purchasing these items, but will also be a response, reaching them by getting over a message that is never void of content. I like to play with the imagination, to create a story told through my designs, to have them include playful aspects with a certain touch of irony (hence my collaboration in Almodovar's film, *Mutant Effect*). I place a great deal of importance on quality and comfort.

—Sara Navarro

* * *

Born in Elda, Alicante, Spain, in 1957, Sara Navarro is a third-generation shoemaker in her family. Dedication to hard work and craftsmanship were central to the family philosophy. Navarro's father, Juan Navarro Busquier, believed that in business, although the ultimate might be impossible, a "fervent desire for perfection" can lead to the greatest success. Juan's company, Kurhapies, was founded on the meager savings of his father, a modest artisan shoemaker. Forty-five years later, the company, now known as Komfort Spain SL, is an empirical leader in volume Spanish footwear.

Sara joined the design department of her father's company in 1979. She was only 21 years old but had already majored in industrial psychology at the University of Valencia, Spain, and had studied classical ballet, fine arts, and several languages at prestigious schools all over the world. She studied design and shoe styling at the Ars Sutoria Institute in Milan and fashion design under Gianfranco Ferré at the Domus Academy. Navarro also obtained a B.A. in business management from L'Escuela de Organizacion Industrial in Madrid. Clearly, her decision to join the family business was not motivated by any lack of career choices. Her broad range of interests, from literature to piloting aircraft, typifies her dedication to study and work, in her own words: "There are few geniuses, only professionals. I've risked much with some pretty surprising collections."

Navarro has been conscious of her Mediterranean heritage throughout her career, incorporating the Spanish tradition of fine leatherwork and handcrafted finishes into her design work. Study of her work reveals an equally important commercial versatility. The Sara Navarro collections are nonrisk styling for the domestic market; Pretty Shoes are an everyday leisure line for "the woman who does not want to grow up." To find Navarro at her most creative and surprising, it is best to look at the Via Sara Navarro lines. Launched in 1988, the Via styles were designed and targeted at the export fashion market. Carried by Komfort Spain SL, this wider market brief has given Navarro the opportunity to explore and develop her own ideas about materials and techniques. The result is the emergence of a very personal design signature as the Via lines have become stronger over the years, encompassing evening, cocktail, and wedding footwear.

The trend of fashion in the 1990s to embrace recycled looks, distressed textures, and hand-rendered natural finishes is perfectly in harmony with Navarro's interest in her native Mediterranean heritage. She has explored derivatives of traditional constructions such as clogs, espadrille shoes, and boots. The silhouettes are strong, often irregular, echoing the clean classic lines of early Via collections; but the use of materials and chaotic color combinations is often surprising. In the mid-1990s, Navarro experimented more with the antique look, crafting granny boots, 1940s-styled walking shoes, and riding boots out of crinkled and oiled, redyed leather and damask fabrics mixed with aged leather. Her styles have attracted the interest of other designers, for example, John Galliano and Martine Sitbon, who find Navarro's styling in harmony with their own ideas.

It is a fortunate designer who can explore her interests and generate international acclaim for her work, and it is tempting to assume the fashion climate is simply in tune with this designer. Yet this would ignore the simpler truth that Navarro is a professional who can react to the fashion demands of both her domestic and export market. Jumping on the Swarovski crystals bandwagon, along with Ecoral, Stuart Weitzman, Sonia Rykiel, and Celine, Navarro nevertheless incorporates traditional Spanish craft skills such as hand-stitching into her work, making the Sara Navarro style instantly recognizable.

Navarro's work is so recognizable, in fact, that her designs were picked up by the Gusac Corp., based in Miami, Florida, for distribution in the U.S., alongside works by Uad Medani and Looky. In 2000 Navarro continued to be one of the top designers in the Spanish shoe industry, along with Panama Jack and Vincente Pastor's Bright Election, helping Spain hold its position among the top five shoe-producing countries in the world, especially in the textile shoe segment—espadrilles, leather shoes, and Western boots.

—Chris Hill; updated by Daryl F. Mallett

NEIMAN MARCUS

American retail store

Opened: in Dallas in 1907. **Company History:** Ready-to-wear retailer was established by Herbert Marcus, Carrie Marcus Neiman, and Abraham Lincoln (Al) Neiman. Through Herbert, his son Stanley, and grandson Richard, management remained in the Marcus family over 80 years. Over the years many events and activities were established and became part of the fabric of contemporary fashion. Originally known for excellent service and unique merchandise, the company struggled to redefine itself under new ownership. **Company Address:** 1618 Main Street, Dallas, TX 75201. **Company Website:** www.neimanmarcus.com.

PUBLICATIONS

On NEIMAN MARCUS:

Books

Marcus, Stanley, *Minding the Store,* Boston, 1974; reissued, 2001.
———, *Quest for the Best,* New York, 1979, reissued 2001.
———, *His & Hers: The Fantasy World of the Neiman Marcus Christmas Catalogue,* New York, 1982.
Farmer, David, *Stanley Marcus: A Life with Books,* Fort Worth, TX, 1993.
Marcus, Stanley, *The Viewpoints of Stanley Marcus: A Ten-Year Perspective,* 1995.
Wilson, Robert A. and Stanley Marcus, eds., *American Greats,* 2000.

Articles

Marcus, Stanley, "My Biggest Mistake," in *Inc.,* July 1999.
"Not Nearly Shelved at 94 (Stanley Marcus)," in the *New York Times,* 22 August 1999.
"Who's News: Neiman Marcus Group Inc.," in the *Wall Street Journal,* 26 June 2001.
A&E Biography Series (Arts and Entertainment Channel television series), *Neiman Marcus: Last of the Merchant Kings.*
Pacer, Eric, "Stanley Marcus, the Retailer, is Dead at 96," in the *New York Times,* 23 January 2002.

*

There is never a good sale for Neiman Marcus unless it's a good buy for the customer.

—Herbert Marcus

* * *

As one of only a handful of luxury retailers in the United States, Neiman Marcus is perhaps best known for their extravagant Christmas catalogue. Featuring annual his and her gifts of great imagination, several of these improbable items have actually sold. Since the first Christmas catalogue in 1939, Neiman Marcus has offered his and her Beechcraft planes (selling hers to a Texas rancher for his wife; he already had one), Chinese junks, eight of which were delivered to five different bodies of water, matching buffalo, and a female camel.

Herbert Marcus was a buyer of boys' clothing for Sanger Brothers in Dallas, while his sister, Carrie Marcus Neiman, was a blouse buyer and saleswoman for A. Harris and Company. Carrie's husband, Abraham Lincoln (Al) Neiman, persuaded the pair to accompany him to Atlanta to set up a special events business. After two years of success, the trio had a couple of offers to buy their business, one for $25,000 cash and another for a franchise in a new company. American retail would have been very different had they chosen the Coca Cola franchise.

They returned to Dallas and on 10 September 1907 opened the doors of Neiman Marcus. Though all were under 30, with not a high school diploma among them, they set out to offer ready-to-wear clothing of quality and value in an era when most clothing was still custom made. The apparel industry had not yet evolved into any sort of organized mass production, and issues of sizing, quality control, and style kept most fashionable women returning to their private dressmakers.

The young owners recognized that the world was changing and were determined to establish a unique business in the new era. They worked closely with manufacturers, demanding excellence, and offered to pay more for improved and finer garments. Customer satisfaction was paramount, and the sales staff was trained to accommodate clientèle and gently guide them toward good taste. Dallas was a thriving city of 84,000 people, many of whom possessed wealth from cotton. Oil money would come later, and Neiman Marcus was positioning itself to be the most fashionable store in the Southwest.

Herbert's son Stanley joined the store in 1926, after a Harvard education. His three younger brothers eventually followed him into the business. Two years later, Carrie and Al Neiman divorced, leaving the store owned by the Marcus family. Stanley Marcus instituted many events and practices that became standard for department stores, such as the first luncheon fashion show, personalized gift wrapping, bridal shows, and national advertising in *Vogue* and *Harper's Bazaar.* His immaculate taste and genius for merchandising are legendary, and stories about his sales ability abound. He has been asked to select gifts for royalty and heads of state as well as the difficult to please; he once sold an electric blanket for a pet lion and had a toupee made for a mounted lion's head whose mane had been ravaged by moths.

Stanley Marcus assumed the rank of CEO and president in 1950 and stayed with the store until 1979, retiring as chairman of the board (he died in January 2002 at the age of 96). His son Richard, who served as CEO and chairman until 1988, succeeded him.

Neiman Marcus opened a suburban store in 1948, beginning a slow expansion in the U.S. that would eventually spread across nearly half the nation. The first public sale of common stock occurred in 1959, the same year Neiman Marcus by Mail was launched. Carter Hawley Hale of Broadway Hale bought the stores in 1969. A difference in philosophy created poor sales and damaged Neiman Marcus' reputation as unique.

In 1987 Carter Hawley Hale traded controlling interest in the Neiman Marcus Group to General Cinema (renamed Harcourt General in 1993). The Group included the prestigious Bergdorf Goodman stores (two) in New York and the mass-market chain Contempo Casuals. The Group purchased Horchow Mail Order of Dallas, a high-end home items retailer in 1988. Contempo Casuals was sold to Wet Seal in 1995, and the Group bought Chef's Catalogue, a purveyor of fine cookware in 1998. The Group also opened three Galleries of Neiman Marcus, smaller stores specializing in gifts and fine jewelry.

In 1998 the Group acquired controlling interest in the company that makes Laura Mercier cosmetics. The next year, they purchased more than 50 percent of Kate Spade, manufacturer of luxury shoes and handbags. Harcourt General spun off most of its stake in the Neiman

Marcus Group to its own shareholders in 1999, with Richard Smith, his son Robert, and his son-in-law, Brian Knez, controlling about 23 percent of Neiman Marcus.

It remains to be seen whether the Neiman Marcus Group can continue to provide the superb special events, exotic one-of-a-kind items, and the personal attention that made the store one of the great retailers in America.

—Christina Lindholm

NEW REPUBLIC

American fashion firm

Founded: in 1981 by Thomas Oatman (born 1953). **Company History:** Established as a vintage clothing trading company and opened first store on Greene Street, SoHo, New York; store moved to Spring Street, New York, 1986; company produced two collections per year; clothing sold to better department stores and specialty stores throughout the U.S., Europe, and Japan; began offering custom services, 1995; signed licensing agreement with Ingram Company, Inc., 1996; collaborated with Pinky Wolman to create Soup + Fish formalwear collection, 1997; designed restaurant uniforms for Jean Georges, 1997. **Company Address:** 93 Spring Street, New York, NY 10012, U.S.A.

Publications

On NEW REPUBLIC:

Articles

Shields, Jody, "Everything Old is New Again," in *Vogue,* April 1989.
"New York Collections," in *DNR,* 10 February 1995.
"New Republic's Bookish Look and Matsuda's Future Feature," in *DNR,* 6 March 1996.
Socha, Miles, "Sportscast," in *DNR,* 13 March 1996.
———, "New Republic," in *DNR,* 2 October 1996.
Matsumoto, Janice, "Uniform Elegance," in *Restaurants & Institutions,* 15 December 1997.

* * *

Long before the current vogue for retro fashion, New Republic—founded by Thomas Oatman—has kept alive the flame of American menswear design that burned bright from the 1930s through the 1960s. New Republic, however, is not about promoting any particular era. Oatman added a few different styles to the line's roster every season, changing only the fabrics and colors, and updating the sizing. What the company does manage is to always be in style, because the premise of New Republic is simply about good style.

Thomas Oatman has said: "The difference is that I'm downdating, not updating. I'm not interested in classics with a twist. I want to remain true to the real classics, not the modern knockoffs." New Republic's interpretations are exacting, dealing with more than just the images from those eras that other designers rely on. The company is able to appeal simultaneously to both an avant-garde audience as well as to a more conservative customer. Thus a 1950s Ivy League sack suit exists alongside a pair of 1960s plain-front pegged trousers. Fashion icons are, after all, in the eye of the beholder. New Republic manifests a postmodern sensibility, mixing clothes from different eras in their presentations, which, ultimately, only make fashion sense in an era that coincides with the end of the century.

Oatman is the utmost connoisseur of fine vintage men's clothing. As such, he designs by accessing the index cards in his memory. Every item in the collection can be placed in an elaborate mental stage set that recalls its glory days. And so, a belted leather jacket—as worn by Marlon Brando in the movie *On the Waterfront*— is endearingly called The Strikebreaker. A 1950s-inspired cabana shirt recalls one's parents' honeymoon photos in Havana.

New Republic weaves romantic dreams that span the decades: a khaki bellows-pocket jacket in Palm Beach cloth conjures up the image of a gentleman on safari in the 1930s. A linen-blend three-button plaid jacket with solid sleeves recalls the look that American soldiers sported when they returned from World War II.

During their leisure time, men in this period wore a pajama-collar rayon gabardine shirt with flap pockets—which happens to be New Republic's trademark, and one of its first styles. Then later, when those soldiers went on vacation, they would wear clamdiggers and cabana shirts at the shore—just like the ones New Republic designed in Creamsicle colors. The late 1950s and early 1960s are also alive and well at New Republic in a natural-shoulder three-button madras sport coat with a hooked center vent and full lap seaming that could have come straight out of Brooks Brothers or J. Press.

America's icons have been inextricably tied with Hollywood, for Hollywood has given us with countless images from which to draw. New Republic, for its part, supplied menswear with a treasure trove of refined American looks. The enduring attraction of New Republic's style has been simple class; as the *Daily News Record* (10 February 1995) concurred, commenting on a new collection, "New Republic, designed by Thomas Oatman, sent out its signature classics," albeit this time "with a decidedly dandy flavor."

New Republic took commitment to its clientèle a step further in 1995 when it began offering custom services out of its SoHo store. The practice was successful enough that the firm expanded its services the following year, around the same time New Republic inked a 10-year joint venture with Ingram Company Inc., a subsidiary of Network Corporation. The agreement concerned opening three freestanding boutiques in Japan to start, then to continue opening stores throughout Asia.

Oatman also segued into different facets of fashion, teaming up with Pinky Wolman for a rather unusual formalwear collection called Soup + Fish, and then designing uniforms for Jean Georges, a 1950s-styled restaurant. Janice Matsumoto, writing for *Restaurants & Institutions* (15 December 1997), described the uniforms, five black suits, as "ranging from boxy Nehru jackets for back waiters to eye-catching double-breasted jackets for captains." New Republic's elegant, classically tailored menswear—whether for uniforms, entertaining, or formal occasions—will never go out of style.

—Vicki Vasilopoulos; updated by Sydonie Benét

NEXT PLC

British fashion company

Established: May 1981 by George Davies in conjunction with J. Hepworth & Son. **Company History:** First womenswear chain opened, 1982; first dual Next/Hepworth store in Reading, Berkshire,

1984; Next for Men launched, 1984; first Next mini department store, Edinburgh, 1984; home furnishings range, Next Interior store, Regent Street, London, 1985; name change to Next plc, 1986; launched Next Cosmetics, 1986; merged with Grattans mail order company, 1986; womenswear divided into Next Too and Next Collection, 1986; lingerie introduced, 1986; boys- and girlswear launched, 1987; Next Directory mail order and Next Originals, 1988; jewelry stores opened, 1988; Department X stores in London and Glasgow, 1988; David Jones appointed CEO, 1988; retail and mail order merged, 1993; first U.S. Next store, Boston, 1993; joint venture with Bath & Body Works, 1994–96; opened Paris store, 1995; signed licensing deal with Shekem for three stores in Israel, 1996; sold seven company stores, 1998; sold credit-card unit, 2001. **Exhibitions:** *All Dressed Up: British Fashion in the 1980s,* British Council Touring Exhibition, 1990. **Company Address:** Next plc, Desford Road, Enderby, Leicester LE9 5AT, England. **Company Website:** www.next.co.uk.

Publications

On NEXT PLC:

Books

Davies, George, *What Next?,* London, 1989.

Huygen, Frédérique, *British Design: Image & Identity,* London, 1989.

Wilson, Elizabeth, and Lou Taylor, *Through the Looking Glass: A History of Dress from 1860 to the Present Day,* London, 1989.

Articles

"The Rise and Fall of Next," in the *Daily Telegraph* (London), 14 December 1990.

Gilchrist, Susan, "Next Fights Recession with 88% Profits Rise," in the *Times* (London), 30 March 1994.

"Buying British Pays Off for Fashion Firm," in the *Daily Mirror* (London), 30 March 1994.

Bethell, James, "Next Goes Streets Ahead of Its Rivals," in the *Sunday Times* (London), 3 April 1994.

Reed, Paula, "Good Value Ousts Designer Gloss," in the*Sunday Times,* 3 April 1994.

"Next (Company Profile)," in *Retail Business: Retail Trade Reviews,* September 1995.

Fallon, James, "Next Has a Knack for Hits," in *WWD,* 28 September 1995.

"Next to Shut Five U.S. Stores," in *WWD,* 26 June 1998.

"Performance of Next," in *Investors Chronicle,* 23 October 1998.

"Next Trading Update," in *UK Retail Report,* May 2000.

Fallon, James, et al, "British Retail Stocks Get Hammered," in *WWD,* 12 January 2001.

"Next Homes in on Bigger Stores," in *In-Store Marketing,* October 2001.

* * *

The brainchild of retail entrepreneur George Davies, the initial success of the British chain of Next shops during the 1980s is credited with having prompted greater awareness of the importance of good design in both clothing and fashion retailing on the High Street by traveling around the country to check out the existing competition. It is interesting to note that the two concepts he most admired were the upmarket German brand, Mondi, and the Italian company, Benetton. Elsewhere he found a lack of inspiration with what he described as the "buy it all approach to stock…in the hope that something would sell."

Davies' vision of what the High Street required was firstly, a strong store identity and, secondly, a high level of quality control over the garments, from raw materials to finished product. Davies believed the tailored jacket was the garment that could establish Next, so long as it represented high quality and fantastic value for the price. The first seven Next shops opened in February 1982 and the sales were two-and-a-half times what the company had originally estimated. Davies' philosophy of providing what he called "affordable collectables" found a ready market for his merchandise, which represented good design at reasonable prices.

Next offered the "power suit" at an accessible price when it was desired by female customers. Authors Elizabeth Wilson and Lou Taylor, writing in *Through the Looking Glass: A History of Dress from 1860 to the Present Day* (London, 1989), maintained that during the 1980s, Next brought together "…a fantasy of old-time shopping and 'aspirational buying'—the desire of newly affluent members of the 25 to 35 age group to wear an approximation of designer clothes."

Textile expert Brenda Azario believed Next's success was because, "Quality is what a customer expects or desires at any price point; this expectation has to be met. Next came in very strongly in this aspect, giving the public a better product. It wasn't a particularly expensive one but it was better—the designing was better and it was certainly better presented to the customer." There followed Next for Men, Next shoes, Next Interior (home furnishings), Next Two, Next Collection, lingerie, Next Boys & Girls, and Next Directory.

Next Directory represented what was perhaps the most significant achievement as it was the first company to try to raise the rather downmarket image of the mail order business. The catalogue itself was a beautifully-produced book with a matte black cover, featuring well-recognized faces from the modeling world, captured by established photographers in great locations. The early numbers even included fabric swatches of certain garments, all of which contributed to the widespread media coverage attracted by the Directory's launch, which revolutionized home shopping in January 1988.

The story of Next during the latter years of the 1980s to the early 1990s is renowned—a victim of over-zealous expansion paired with the recession that hit Britain during this period. Another factor contributing to the firm's demise was the failure of Next Directory to achieve the success predicted by Davies who invested £24.1 million into its launch. The fall of Next was as dramatic as its meteoric rise—a profit warning came in December 1988 and within two weeks there followed the unceremonious sacking of George Davies.

A dramatic restructuring ensued under the guidance of the newly-appointed CEO, David Jones. A large number of stores were sold off and the company raised cash by selling off its Grattan mail-order business. These measures, however, were not enough to fuel the relatively rapid rise of Next to its astounding profits, which doubled from 1992 to 1993. Improved customer service, new clothes displays, and larger fitting rooms were not enough to entice the customer to buy; the clothes themselves effected the turnaround. Next succeeded in recapturing the British customer of the 1990s, and by 1994 there were over 300 Next-owned stores across Britain and nearly half a million Next Directory customers.

According to journalist Paula Reed of the *Sunday Times* (3 April 1994), at Next clients received "basic, honest merchandise without pretension to status or glamour. What makes Next sexy these days is not a glossy image but a quick response to catwalk trends and a canny anticipation of what is next in style." A year later, Jones concurred in *Women's Wear Daily* (28 September 1995), "We have never been a fashion business. We sell good taste, good design and good quality." Near the end of the decade, however, Next faltered once again, having gone too trendy and neglecting its classics base. Sales in its stores as well as its mail-order business suffered declined, and the firm sold seven (five in the U.S., one each in Paris and Brussels) underperforming company-owned stores in 1998.

The new century brought a rollercoaster ride for British retailers; first a brief resurgence early on, then another decline with disappointing holiday sales in 2000. In 2001 Next sold its consumer credit business, about the same time the company's former CEO, George Davies, joined competitor Marks & Spencer to turnaround its womenswear division. Next garnered a turn of its own, however, with climbing sales for the Directory as well as its retail outlets. In the boardroom, Jones moved up to chairman, while Simon Wolfson assumed the duties of chief executive. By the end of 2001, Next was expansion-minded once more, closing smaller shops in favor of larger stores able to carry both clothing and its growing home furnishings collection.

—Catherine Woram; updated by Sydonie Benét

NIKOS

Greek designer working in France

Born: Nikos Apostolopoulos in Patras, Greece. **Education:** Studied at the Sorbonne, Paris, diploma in political science, doctorate in international law. **Career:** Designed first collection of intimate wear for men, 1985; line expanded to include intimate wear for women, swimwear, and men's and women's ready-to-wear, 1987; designed costumes for theatre and opera, including Monsigny's *Cadi Dupe,* Paris Spring Festival, 1989, and Richard Strauss' *Salome,* Montpellier Festival, 1990; created Nikos Parfums and introduced first fragrance *Sculpture Femme,* 1994; created men's fragrance *Sculpture Homme,* 1995. **Address:** 6 rue de Braque, Paris 75003, France.

Publications

On NIKOS:

Books

Pronger, Brian, *The Arena of Masculinity,* New York, 1990.

Articles

"Paris Now," in *DNR,* 7 February 1990.
"Nikos Eyes U.S. Market," in *DNR,* 26 June 1990.
Spindler, Amy M., "Tarlazzi, Nikos Cancel Paris Men's Showings," in *DNR,* 29 January 1991.
Deschamps, Mary, "Le retour de Nikos," in *Vogue Hommes International* (Paris), Fall 1992.
"Lancaster to Try on New Scents," in *Advertising Age,* 4 July 1994.
Fallon, James, "After Sculpture's Success, Nikos to Mold Men's Scent," in *WWD,* 7 April 1995.
———, "Latest Introductions in England Drive Department Store Sales," in *WWD,* 12 April 1996.

* * *

Homoerotic masculinity is the motive of Nikos fashion. Invoking an idealism of gods and demigods, stretching and flexing on Olympus wearing versions of jock straps, ergonomic t-shirts and tank tops, and some street clothing, Nikos projects a similar image of apparel. Beginning with his first collection in 1985, Nikos employed cotton and Lycra for the stretchy, minimalist, erotic clothing of the gods and all who aspire to their condition of pumped-up muscles and physique divinity.

In 1988 Nikos worked with American photographer Victor Skrebneski in an ideal collaboration of like-minded fashion erotics. Denizens of South Beach and Venice, California, were logical candidates for this self-assured, body-flaunting clothing driven by heat, narcissism, and sexuality. Men who might dress for the evening in Gianni Versace might choose Nikos for activewear. While the line diversified to some street clothing for men and swimwear and exercise wear for women, Nikos still primarily addresses the homoerotic male.

Nikos' clothing template is the jock strap. He customarily provides a band (including many in the late 1980s that, like the underwear of competitors, included the designer name) around the waist from which an extended cod-piece or pouch distends. The designer's phallic primacy is complemented by bared sides and minimal coverage of buttocks, offering voyeurism (and implied accessibility) front and rear to the male. His tanks stress angularity almost as if to clothe men of granitic triangulation, rather than the ordinary soft body.

Further, two devices frequent in Nikos' work exacerbate the homoerotic content. In effectively using stretch materials, Nikos often opens apertures in the briefs and tops, allowing a peek-a-boo spectatorship more often associated with female undergarments. Additionally, Nikos relishes piecing and visible seams, the stretchy activewear taking on something of the aspect of a virile Vionnet or an Azzedine Alaïa transferred to Muscle Beach. The effect, of course, is to promote even further the sense of the garment as strapping, swaddling, a slight covering for muscles and body movement. In instances when Nikos uses stripes, his only pattern, line enhances the verticality and size of the phallic pouch.

In the early 1990s collections emphasized more moderate clothing for the street, including the graphically strong spring/summer 1993 collection with outfits in black-and-white for exercise and shirts with bold designs inspired by Matisse cutouts. The spring/summer 1994 collection stressed sportswear for the street and offered a repertoire of loose, long knits and colorful shorts and white and black oversized trousers. Whenever Nikos had shown streetwear in the late 1980s and 1990s, the look was still of extremism, with see-through tank tops, faux leopard skins, and tailored clothing with zoot suit bravado. In the street clothes, Nikos did not abandoned fetishes, but moved toward mainstream menswear, ironically leaving many other designers from Dirk Bikkembergs to Gianni Versace to fill his gap on the wild side.

One can either dismiss Nikos for his marketing of the most blatant homoerotic clothing, of which probably a considerable portion is purchased but seldom worn, or worn only for the private circumstance. Or one can understand that Nikos stands, with many designers of men's underwear and related athletic wear, as one who cultivates specific and definable traits of the homoerotic to develop garments possessing their own brand of beauty.

Nikos ventured into fragrances in 1994 with, oddly, a women's scent rather than one for men. *Sculpture Femme* launched amidst much fanfare did well enought to encourage Nikos to develop a complementary men's scent, preferably one as iconoclastic as its creator. *Sculpture Homme,* introduced in 1995, didn't disappoint with its sexy mythical connotations and spicy base, rolled out with widespread media advertising. Both Nikos incarnations sold very well at a time when upscale retailers were in a slump. The designer pondered additional fragrances as well as bath and body lines.

—Richard Martin; updated by Nelly Rhodes

NINA RICCI

French couture house

Founded: by Maria "Nina" Ricci (1883–1970) and son Robert Ricci (1905–88) in Paris, 1932. **Company History:** First ready-to-wear collection shown, 1964; men's collection introduced, 1986; first boutique opened, Paris, 1979; men's boutique, Ricci-Club, opened, Paris, 1986; cosmetics line, *Le Teint Ricci,* introduced, 1992; several new designers brought in, beginning 1993; Ricci products placed in luxury hotels as guest amenities; designer Nathalie Gervais hired, 1999; Gervais departs, 2001. Fragrances include *Cœur de Joie,* 1945, *L'Air du Temps,* 1948, *Capricci,* 1961, *Farouche,* 1974, *Signoricci,* 1975, *Fleur de Fleurs,* 1980, *Nina,* 1987, *Ricci-Club,* 1989. **Awards:** Mme. Ricci awarded Chevalier de la Légion d'Honneur; Fragrance Foundation Hall of Fame award, 1982; Fragrance Foundation Perennial Success award, 1988; Dé d'Or award, 1987; Bijorca d'Or award, 1987, 1988; Vénus de la Beauté, 1990; Trophée International Pardum/Couture, 1991; Prix d'Excellence "Créativité" 1992; Trophée de la Beauté de Dépêche Mode, 1992; Prix Européen de la P.L.V., 1992; l'Oscar du Mécénat d'Entreprises, 1993. **Company Address:** 39, avenue Montaigne, 75008 Paris, France.

Nina Ricci, fall/winter 2001–02 collection designed by Nathalie Gervais. © AP/Wide World Photos.

PUBLICATIONS

On NINA RICCI:

Books

Milbank, Caroline Rennolds, *Couture: The Great Designers,* New York, 1985.
O'Hara, Georgina, *The Encyclopaedia of Fashion,* New York, 1986.
Guillen, Pierrre-Yves, and Jacqueline Claude, *The Golden Thimble: French Haute Couture,* Paris, 1990.
Pochna, Marie-France, *Nina Ricci,* Paris, 1992.
Skrebneski, Victor, *The Art of Haute Couture,* New York, 1995.
Stegemeyer, Anne, *Who's Who in Fashion, Third Edition,* New York, 1996.

Articles

Carter, Ernestine, "The New Boys at Nina Ricci," in the*Sunday Times Magazine* (London), 15 December 1963.
Morris, Bernadine, "Robert Ricci, Couturier, 83, Dies...," in the *New York Times,* 10 August 1988.
Davy, Philippe, "Le charme romantique des succès de Nina Ricci," in *L'Officiel* (Paris), February 1990.
"Ricci Cruise," in *WWD,* 6 July 1990.
Deeny, Godfrey, "Ricci's Pipart: Staying Power," in *WWD,* 26 January 1995.
White, Constance, C.R., "Refreshing Nina Ricci," in the *New York Times,* 25 April 1995.
"Nina Ricci Gets Luminous," in *Cosmetics Products Report,* September 1999.
"Guest Amenities," in *Hotel & Motel Management,* 20 September 1999.
Sulic, Diana, "Nina Ricci," [profile] online at Fashion Live, www.fashionlive.com, 5 August 2000.
"New York: A Delicate Balance," in *WWD,* 16 February 2001.
Deeny, Godfrey, "From Russia with Ricci as Designer Bows Out," available online at Fashion Windows, www.fashionwindows.com, 10 March 2001.
Patterson, Suzy, "Luscious Furs and Fabrics at Nina Ricci," available online at www.theage.com.au, 12 March 2001.

*

To make women beautiful, to bring out the charm of each one's personality. But also to make life more beautiful...that has always been my ambition, and that is the underlying philosophy of Nina Ricci.

—Robert Ricci

Nina Ricci, fall/winter 1966 collection: "El Moroco," a North African-inspired cocktail djellaba. © AP/Wide World Photos.

* * *

Nina Ricci is established as one of the longest running Parisian couture houses. Unlike her peers, Elsa Schiaparelli and Chanel, Ricci's reputation does not rest on a revolutionary fashion statement. Instead, she was successful because she provided an understated, chic look for elegant and wealthy society women, always classic, yet intoxicatingly feminine.

When it came to designing clothes, Nina Ricci relied greatly on her feminine intuition. She worked directly on the model and designed by draping the actual fabric, which she felt gave her the answer to what the dress would become. Creating clothes was simply a matter of solving problems and in the 1930s she described several of them—she had to find an extra special, elegant detail that would render a dress a client's favorite and achieve a maximum ease and lightness that did not encumber the wearer when moving or dancing.

Much of the detailing in Nina Ricci clothing reflected the designer's ultrafeminine approach, the flattering effects of gathers, tucks, and drapery and an attention to décolleté and figure-hugging details like fitting dresses below the waist. She was clever and original in her use of fabric, cutting plaids and tartans on the bias for evening dresses and a black silk border print fabric so the print was avidly displayed over the bust, leaving the rest of the dress to become a straight column of fabric.

Ricci had been a successful designer for other houses before she decided to open her own with her son Robert in 1932. At the age of 49, this could have been a risky venture but the gamble paid off as the company rapidly grew in size and stature during its first decade. By 1939 they occupied eleven floors in three buildings, a stark contrast to their humble beginnings in one room at 20 boulevard des Capucines, Paris.

Nina retired from the business in the early 1950s, leaving the field open to her son Robert who pursued his own ambitious plans for the house. An excellent businessman, Robert Ricci established many divisions and licensees for the Ricci name. A fragrance, *Cœur de Joie,* was introduced in 1945, followed by the now classic *L'Air du Temps.* Later such fragrances as *Fleur de Fleurs,* and *Nina* were successively marketed. Sunglasses alone were reported to be grossing $6 million in the late 1970s and by 1979 the house had become firmly established in the former Kodak Mansion, opposite the House of Dior on avenue Montaigne, Paris.

Robert Ricci had also been successful in his choice of designers for the house. Belgian designer Jules-François Crahay was named head designer in 1954 and made his debut with a collection paying homage to Nina's trademark feminine look. Carrie Donovan from the *New York Times* described it as "a collection that was feminine in the extreme—beautiful of coloring and fabric, unbizarre and elegant." Crahay was succeeded in 1963 by Gérard Pipart, who remained as designer of both the couture and boutique collections for 30 years. After Pipart, there was a succession of designers, including Christian Astuguevielle and Myriam Schaeffer but the label had fallen out of favor with young Parisians.

Canadian Nathalie Gervais, formerly of Gucci and Valentino, was brought in in 1999 to reinvigorate the Nina Ricci name. Her luxe and trendy designs, along with a flashy new ad campaign, put the label back on solid ground. Gervais' early 2001 collection did not disappoint; her Indian and Russian-inspired collection featured slim pants, slinky tops and tunics, and leathers and furs.

In the 21st century Nina Ricci remains best known for its fragrances, especially the enduringly classic *L'air du Temps,* as well as a growing number of other fragrances and skincare products. Its haute couture, however, has struggled to maintain its identity. Nathalie Gervais seemed to have captured and updated the elegance long associated with the Nina Ricci name, then stunned the fashion world by announcing her departure from the venerable house in 2001. Nina Ricci was once again looking for a designer left by the void of longtime trendsetters Crahay and Pipart.

—Kevin Almond; updated by Owen James

NORDSTROM

American retail company

Founded: as a shoe retailer by Carl F. Wallin and John W. Nordstrom as Wallin & Nordstrom in Seattle, 1901. **Company History:** Second store established, 1923; Nordstrom retires, sells his share of the company to his sons, 1928; Wallin retires, sells interest to Nordstrom sons, 1929; Lloyd Nordstrom, another son, joins the company, 1933; expansion throughout Washington, and into Oregon and California; purchased Best Apparel, 1963; acquired Nicholas Ungar retailer and renamed new store Nordstrom Best, 1966; opened a Nordstrom Best in Tacoma, Washington, 1966; changed name to Nordstrom Inc., 1973; Nordstrom Rack stores opened in Seattle, 1975; company restructured, 1999. **Company Address:**

1617 Sixth Avenue, Suite 700, Seattle, WA 98101, USA. **Company Website:** www.nordstrom.com.

PUBLICATIONS

On NORDSTROM:

Books

Spector, Robert, and Patrick D. McCarthy, *The Nordstrom Way* (2nd edition), New York, 2000.

Articles

Palmieri, Christopher, "Filling Big Shoes," in *Forbes,* 15 November 1999.

"Nordstrom Launches New Retail Cards," in *PR Newswire* (Seattle), 5 April 2000.

Bond, Jeff, "What's Inside Nordstrom's Reinvention?" in *Washington CEO,* July 2000.

"Nordstrom to Buy Faconnable, a Top Seller in Its Stores," in the *New York Times,* 7 September 2000.

* * *

Carl F. Wallin, a Seattle shoemaker, and John W. Nordstrom opened a shoe store, Wallin & Nordstrom, in Seattle in 1901. The partners built their business on the philosophy of offering customers the best in service, selection, quality, and value. Today, Nordstrom continues to grow and thrive on that very same philosophy through its family-controlled business. Nordstrom believes in service with a smile and wants to project an image of smalltown modesty—that's the corporate culture and it sells. An example of this phenomenon is Patrick McCarthy, who retired in 2000, and was the top salesperson for 15 consecutive years, selling over $1 million per year in the downtown Seattle store. Because of his accomplishment, McCarthy was the subject of an article called, "Personal Touch: Service Makes Salesman a Legend at Nordstrom."

Wallin and Nordstrom opened a second shoe store in Seattle's University District in 1923. The stores did well and in 1928 Nordstrom retired and sold his share of the company to his sons, Everett and Elmer. The following year Wallin retired, and sold his interests to Nordstrom sons. A third Nordstrom son, Lloyd, joined the company in 1933, and the company continued to expand throughout Washington and the surrounding states. Nordstrom soon had eight shoe stores in Washington and Oregon, and 13 leased shoe departments in Washington, Oregon, and California. The company's flagship store, in the downtown Seattle, was the largest shoe store in the country.

In the 1960s, Nordstrom began acquiring other companies, such as Best Apparel. Best Apparel was a Seattle-based clothing store with an outlet in Seattle and another at the Lloyd Center in Portland, Oregon. Nordstrom purchased Nicholas Ungar, a Portland fashion retailer, and merged the store with the existing shoe store in downtown Portland, and renamed the new store Nordstrom Best in 1966. Another Nordstrom Best was opened in Tacoma, Washington, and the company continued expanding and changed its name to simply Nordstrom, Inc. in 1973. Two years later, the first Nordstrom Rack stores opened in Seattle, and the company continued to grow as an all-purpose retailer through the rest of the 1970s and into the 1980s.

The course for Nordstrom has been to modernize, adding brands such as Caslon, DKNY, and EMME for women and Faconnable (which it later acquired), Kenneth Cole, and Tommy Bahama for men to its racks. After the company was restructured in 1999, Nordstrom decided to sharpen its image with consumers. In May 2000, Nordstrom declared "Reinvent Yourself" as its advertising campaign: when customers entered stores, they no longer saw piano players wearing tuxedos (a former trademark) and instead found modernized displays with hip, brighter, flashier colors, and the more casual apparel. Nordstrom also changed its advertising style, airing trendy commercials during hit shows like *ER* and *Ally McBeal.*

Following trends to make shopping easier for its customers, Nordstrom entered the Internet world in the spring of 1999 with its own website (www.nordstrom.com). The website was created to announce fashion shows, augment advertising, and often showcases select window and store displays. Further, it echoes trends of the season and is full of photos of Nordstrom's clothing, shoes, jewelry, gifts, and accessories available at stores. Customers can easily click to items to buy, add them to their shopping bag, visit customer service, request a catalogue, and use their credit card. Nordstrom's catalogue, like its website, is another exceptional convenience—available 24 hours a day, with toll-free phone operators and personal shoppers.

Nordstrom took customer convenience a step further when they hired Jennifer Morla in April 2000 to help redesign the company's proprietary credit card. Morla, a renowned designer based in San Francisco, helped Nordstrom depart from its conservative look to a more upbeat, fresh style for the company. For customers' credit ease, Nordstrom added the Nordstrom Retail, Nordstrom Legacy, Nordstrom Platinum, and Nordstrom Platinum Legacy proprietary cards.

One thing customers notice about Nordstrom, in its 72 full-line stores and 28 Nordstrom Rack stores, is the continued personal touch of the company's customer service. Nordstrom is still controlled and owned by a family, whose commitment and philosophy are the foundation of its success. Nordstrom may move forward with the trends of technology, but the needs of today's consumers will always come first.

—Kimbally A. Medeiros

NORELL, Norman

American designer

Born: Norman David Levinson in Noblesville, Indiana, 20 April 1900. **Education:** Studied illustration at Parsons School of Design, New York, 1919; fashion design at Pratt Institute, Brooklyn, New York, 1920–22. **Career:** Costume designer, Paramount Pictures, Long Island, New York, 1922–23; theatrical costume designer, 1924–28; designer, Hattie Carnegie, New York, 1928–40; partner/designer, Traina-Norell company, New York, 1941–60; director, Norman Norell, New York, 1960–72. **Exhibitions:** Norman Norell retrospective, Metropolitan Museum of Art, New York, 1972. **Awards:** Neiman Marcus award, Dallas, Texas, 1942; Coty American Fashion Critics award, 1943, 1951, 1956, 1958, 1966; Parsons medal for distinguished achievement, 1956; *Sunday Times* International Fashion award, London, 1963; City of New York Bronze Medallion, 1972. Honorary Doctor of Fine Arts, Pratt Institute, 1962. **Died:** 25 October 1972, in New York.

Norman Norell, fall 1968 collection: sequined, fur-trimmed cossack shirt over a narrow skirt. © AP/Wide World Photos.

PUBLICATIONS

On NORELL:

Books

Epstein, Beryl Williams, *Fashion is Our Business,* Philadelphia and New York, 1945, 1970.
Ballard, Bettina, *In My Fashion,* New York, 1960.
Roshco, Bernard, *The Rag Race,* New York, 1963.
Fairchild, John, *The Fashionable Savages,* New York, 1965.
Sotheby's, *Property of Norman Norell et al., Public Auction Catalogue,* New York, 1973.
Morris, Bernadine, "Norman Norell," in Sarah Tomerlin Lee, editor, *American Fashion: The Life and Lines of Adrian, Mainbocher, McCardell, Norell, and Trigère,* New York, 1975.
Glynn, Prudence, *In Fashion,* New York, 1978.
Milbank, Caroline Rennolds, *Couture: The Great Designers,* New York, 1985.
New York and Hollywood Fashion: Costume Designs from the Brooklyn Museum Collection, New York, 1986.
Mulvagh, Jane, *Vogue History of 20th Century Fashion,* London, 1988.
Milbank, Caroline Rennolds, *New York Fashion: The Evolution of American Style,* New York, 1989.
Stegemeyer, Anne, *Who's Who in Fashion, Third Edition,* New York, 1996.

Articles

"Designer Honoured by Fashion Critics," in the *New York Times,* 23 January 1943.
Pope, Virginia, "Designer Stresses Simple Silhouette," in the *New York Times,* 24 January 1944.
"Laurels Anew for Norell," in *Life* (New York), 8 October 1956.
Cushman, Wilhela, "American Designers," in *Ladies' Home Journal* (New York), March 1957.
Levin, Phyllis Lee, "Paris Sets Pace but Creative Talent, Critics Agree, Exists in US," in the *New York Times,* 19 June 1958.
"Four Inside Views of Fashion," in the *New York Times Magazine,* 19 June 1960.
Donovan, Carrie, "Stylist Gives Detailed Aid to Imitators," in the *New York Times,* 21 July 1960.
"Norell Styles Raise Ruckus All Their Own," in *Life* (New York), 26 September 1960.
Donovan, Carrie, "Norman Norell: Fashion Is His Life," in the *New York Times,* 28 June 1961.
"American Collections: Norell Shows Tailored and Femme-Fatale Designs," in the *New York Times,* 11 July 1962.
"Where the Shape Lies," in *Newsweek* (New York), 23 July 1962.
Frank, Stanley, "Style King of Ready-to-Wear," in *Saturday Evening Post* (New York), 20 October 1962.
"The Socko American Pair," in *Life* (New York), 1 March 1963.
"Backstage Notes at Norell," in *Vogue* (New York), March 1963.
"The Great Norell," in *Vogue* (New York), 1 October 1963.
Taylor, Angela, "Everything from Coats to Pants Cheered at Norman Norell Show," in the *New York Times,* 1 July 1964.
"Norman the Conqueror," in *Time* (New York), 10 July 1964.
"He's a Fashion Purist with the Golden Touch," in *Business Week* (New York), 12 September 1964.
"Norman Norell," in *Current Biography,* (New York), 1964.
Morris, Bernadine, "Parsons Honors Celebrated Dropout," in the *New York Times,* 30 April 1965.
Tucker, Priscilla, "Norman Norell," in the Metropolitan Museum of Art *Bulletin* (New York), November 1967.
Morris, Bernadine, "A Talk with Norman Norell," in the *New York Times,* 15 October 1972.
———, "At Retrospective Hundreds Salute an Ailing Norell," in the *New York Times,* 17 October 1972.
———, "Norman Norell Dies; Made Seventh Avenue the Rival of Paris," in the *New York Times,* 26 October 1972.
"Homage to Norell," in *Newsweek* (New York), 30 October 1972.

Norman Norell, fall 1968 collection. © AP/Wide World Photos.

Morris, Bernadine, "Recollections: Norell in Kansas City," in the *New York Times,* 23 September 1986.
Elliott, Mary C., "Norman Norell: Class All the Way," in *Threads* (Newtown, Connecticut), October/November 1989.

* * *

Simple, well-made clothes that would last and remain fashionable for many years became the hallmark of Norman Norell, the first American designer to win the respect of Parisian couturiers. He gained a reputation for flattering design while Traina, whose well-heeled clientèle appreciated the snob appeal of pared-down day clothes and dramatic eveningwear. From his early years with Hattie Carnegie, Norell learned all about meticulous cut, fit, and quality fabrics. Regular trips to Paris exposed him to the standards of couture that made French clothes the epitome of high fashion. Norell had the unique ability to translate the characteristics of couture into American ready-to-wear. He did inspect each model garment individually, carefully, in the tradition of a couturier, and was just as demanding in proper fabrication and finish. The prices of "Norells," especially after he went into business on his own, easily rivaled those of Paris creations, but they were worth it. The clothes lasted, and their classicism made them timeless.

Certain characteristics of Norell's designs were developed early on and remained constant throughout his career. Wool jersey shirtwaist dresses with demure bowed collars were a radical departure from splashy floral daydresses of the 1940s. World War II restrictions on yardages and materials coincided with Norell's penchant for spare silhouettes, echoing his favorite period, the 1920s. Long before Paris was promoting the chemise in the 1950s, Norell was offering short, straight, low-waisted shapes during the war years. For evening, Norell looked to the flashy glamor of his days designing costumes for vaudeville.

Glittering *paillettes,* which were not rationed, would be splashed on evening skirts—paired with sweater tops for comfort in unheated rooms—or on coats. Later, the lavish use of all-out glamor sequins evolved into Norell's signature shimmering "mermaid" evening dresses, formfitting, round-necked and short-sleeved. The round neckline, plain instead of the then-popular draped, became one of the features of Norell's designs of which he was most proud. "I hope I have helped women dress more simply," was his goal. He used revealing bathing suit necklines for evening as well, with sable trim or jeweled buttons for contrast. Variations on these themes continued throughout the years, even after trousersuits became a regular part of Norell's repertoire.

Striking in their simplicity, Norell suits would skim the body, making the wearer the focus of attention rather than the clothes. Daytime drama came from bold, clear colors such as red, black, beige, bright orange, or pale blue, punctuated by large, plain contrasting buttons. Stripes, dots, and checks were the only patterns, although Norell was credited with introducing leopard prints in the 1940s, again, years before they became widespread in use. Norell's faithful clients hailed his clothes as some of the most comfortable they had ever worn.

Early exposure to men's clothing in Norell's father's haberdashery business no doubt led to the adaptation of the menswear practicality. An outstanding example was the sleeveless jacket over a bowed blouse and slim woolen skirt, developed after Norell became aware of the comfort of his own sleeveless vest worn for work. As in men's clothing, pockets and buttons were always functional. Norell created a sensation with the culotte-skirted wool flannel day suit with which he launched his own independent label in 1960. His sophisticated clientèle welcomed the ease of movement allowed by this daring design. As the 1960s progressed Norell presented another masculine-influenced garment, the jumpsuit, but in soft or luxurious fabrics for evening. Just as durability and excellent workmanship were integral to the best menswear, so they were to Norell's. Men's dress was traditionally slow to change; Norell stayed with his same basic designs, continually refining them over the years. He developed the idea that there should be only one center of interest in an outfit, and designed only what he liked.

What he liked was frequently copied, both domestically and overseas. The short, flippy, gored, ice skating skirt was copied by Paris. Aware of piracy in the fashion business, Norell offered working sketches of the culotte suit free of charge to the trade to ensure that at least his design would be copied correctly. This integrity earned him a place as the foremost American designer of his time. Unlike most ready-to-wear that would be altered at the last moment for ease of manufacture, no changes were allowed after Norell had approved a garment. His impeccable taste was evident not only in the clothes, but in his simple life: meals at Schrafft's and Hamburger Heaven, quiet evenings at home, sketching in his modern duplex apartment, and unpublicized daily visits to assist fashion design students at Parsons School of Design.

As the designer whose reputation gained new respect for the Seventh Avenue garment industry, Norell was the first designer to receive the Coty Award, and the first to be elected to the Coty Award Hall of Fame. True to his innate integrity, he attempted to return his third Winnie award when he learned that judging was done without judges having actually seen designers' collections. Norell promoted American fashion as founder and president of the Council of Fashion Designers of America, but also by giving fledgling milliners their start in his black-tie, special event fashion shows. Halston and Adolfo designed hats for Norell, for, as in couture, Norell insisted upon unity of costume to include accessories.

As the "Dean of American Fashion," Norell was the first to have his name on a dress label, and the first to produce a successful American fragrance, *Norell,* with a designer name. Some of his clothes can be seen in the films, such as *The Sainted Devil, That Touch of Mink* and *The Wheeler Dealers.* Show business personalities and social leaders throughout the country treasured their "Norells" for years.

—Therese Duzinkiewicz Baker

NOTT, Richard

See WORKERS FOR FREEDOM

O

OATMAN, Thomas

See NEW REPUBLIC

OLDFIELD, Bruce

British designer

Born: London, 14 July 1950. **Education:** Ripon Grammar School, Yorkshire, 1961–67; studied at Sheffield City Polytechnic, Yorkshire; studied fashion design at Ravensbourne College of Art, Kent, 1968–71; St. Martin's School of Art, London, 1972–73. **Career:** Designed freelance from 1973–75, including capsule collections for Liberty and Browns, London, and collection for Henri Bendel store, New York, 1974; established own fashion house, Bruce Oldfield, Ltd., London, from 1975; visiting lecturer at the Fashion Institute of Technology, New York, 1977; couture division established, 1978; guest lecturer, Los Angeles County Museum of Art, 1983; opened flagship store in Beauchamp Place, Knightsbridge, London, 1984; reintroduced ready-to-wear line, 1984; lectured at Aspen Design Conference, Colorado, 1986; columnist, *Welt am Sonntag* (Hamburg), 1987–91; first diffusion collection, 1988; moved to only custom designing; created uniforms for Alexandra Corporate Clothing, 2000; designed home accessories for St. James Homes, 2001. **Exhibitions:** Metropolitan Museum of Art, New York; Victoria & Albert Museum; Bath Museum. **Awards:** Bath Museum of Costume Dress of the Year award, 1985; the *Times* Designer of the Year award, London, 1985; named Honorary Fellow, Sheffield City Polytechnic, 1987; Honorary Fellow, Royal College of Art, London, 1990; Honorary Fellow, Hatfield College, Durham University, 1990; OBE, 1990. **Address:** 27 Beauchamp Place, London SW3 1NJ, England.

Bruce Oldfield. © Geray Sweeney/CORBIS.

PUBLICATIONS

By OLDFIELD:

Books

Bruce Oldfield's Season, with Georgina Howell, London, 1987.

Articles

"Nothing to Do with Greed or Vanity," in the *Independent* (London), 9 September 1989.

On OLDFIELD:

Books

Coleridge, Nicholas, *The Fashion Conspiracy,* London, 1988.

Stegemeyer, Anne, *Who's Who in Fashion, Third Edition,* New York, 1996.

Articles

Tuohy, William, "Chic Guru of European Society," in the *Los Angeles Times,* July 1983.

Scobie, W., "Star Dresser," in the *Observer* (London), 19 February 1984.

Moore, Jackie, "Men About Town: Bruce Oldfield," in *Women's Journal* (London), April 1985.

Kendall, Ena, "A Room of My Own," in the *Observer Magazine,* 8 June 1986.

"Bruce Oldfield Makes Clothes for (Future) Queen," in *People Weekly* (New York), April 1987.
Lasson, Sally Ann, "A Life in the Day of Bruce Oldfield," in the *Sunday Times Magazine* (London), 10 May 1987.
Nadelson, Regina, "Bruce Oldfield—A Profile," in *European Travel & Life,* September 1987.
Gross, Michael, "A London Designer Leaves Poverty Behind," in the *New York Times,* 9 October 1987.
Stead, Kate, "Couturier to the Stars," in the *Morning Herald* (Sydney), January 1988.
Dutt, Robin, "G'day Bruce," in *Clothes Show* (London), Spring 1988.
Lambert, Elizabeth, "Modern Glamour for His London Flat," in *Architectural Digest,* September 1988.
Samuel, Kathryn, "Rags to Rag-Trade Riches and Home Again," in the *Daily Telegraph* (London), 31 October 1988.
Leston, Kimberley, "Oldfield's New Pastures," in the *Daily Express DX Magazine* (London), May 1989.
Eyers, Anthony, "The Conversion of St. Bruce," in *Isis* (Oxford University), 1989.
D'Silva, Beverly, "The Affordable Essence of Oldfield," in the *Daily Telegraph* (London), 18 January 1990.
Tredre, Roger, "Bruce Stoops to Conquer," in the *Independent* (London), 18 January 1990.
D'Silva, Beverly, "A Middle-Class Man of the Cloth," in the *Sunday Times* (London), 21 January 1990.
———, "The Bruce Oldfield Show," in the *Telegraph Magazine,* 3 March 1990.
Deane, April, "Bruce Oldfield: An All Round Touch of Quality," in the *Journal,* 17 April 1991.
Reed, Paula, "Bruce is Back," in the *Sunday Times,* 14 February 1993.
Himes, Winsome, "Guru of High Style," in *The Voice,* 19 October 1993.
Tyrrel, Rebecca, "Bruce Oldfield: Twenty Years of Fashion Success," in the *Tatler,* November 1993.
Spackman, Anne, "Oldfield Shows How Far Estate Chic Has Come…," in the *Financial Times,* 27 January 2001.
Curtis, Chris, "Wear and Stare," in *Leisure & Hospitality Business,* 22 February 2001.

*

My approach to fashion is, and always has been, through couture-orientated technique in cut and detail. I like the idea of producing a garment where the actual technique and the cut are the integral design elements. For me, this approach in designing clothes allows a greater scope for developing ideas from season to season. I am not enamoured of ad hoc superfluous detailing and would always prefer to use a good quality plain fabric over a print, because if I should need to have a surface detail, I would rather create it myself.

I love quality and finesse and continuity and am horrified by the concept of "in one season and out the next." It seems to devalue the whole creative process. This is not to say that fashion could or should stand still, we need new ideas and a rolling out of attitudes to the way that we see ourselves, but the speed of change and the polarization of successive trends show an insecurity that to me is quite undesirable. It would make me very happy if, in 2050, someone came across a Bruce Oldfield dress in a thrift shop and simply had to buy it.

—Bruce Oldfield

* * *

"It would have been better for me to have lived at an earlier period," Bruce Oldfield told journalist and writer Georgina Howell (who collaborated with Oldfield on *Bruce Oldfield's Season,* London, 1987), "because I care about the technique of making clothes." During the 1970s and 1980s there was an increasing disregard for quality and workmanship in dress manufacturing, and it was this very sloppiness, readily accepted by retailers and customers alike, that Oldfield reacted against. He was attracted to the traditional high standards and technical workmanship of couture and the private client.

In the 1970s and 1980s, crazy fashion was very popular but Oldfield declared he could never create such fantasy clothes. To him they were totally unconvincing. He recognized there was an established market for understated, flattering clothes and targeted an identifiable, timeless look towards this customer, someone he described as being expensive, sexy, body-conscious, a great looking woman in a flattering dress. Avoiding the need to make seasonal fashion statements he has remained a staunchly classic designer. "There have been times when I have been in fashion and times when I have been out of fashion, but I have always had six pages a year in *Vogue,* sometimes [more]," he once declared.

After leaving St. Martin's School of Art with a fashion degree in 1973, Oldfield worked as a freelance designer for several high-profile fashion companies, ranging from an exclusive collection for Henri Bendel in New York to selling shoe designs to Yves Saint Laurent in Paris. He established his own company in 1975 with a bank loan and a grant from Dr. Barnardo's, the children's home where Oldfield grew up. The business began as a ready-to-wear operation that produced two seasonal collections a year. Concentrating on occasion clothing, the range was available at prestigious stores such as Harvey Nichols in London, and Bergdorf Goodman, Saks Fifth Avenue, and Bloomingdale's in New York. He also worked on specialist commissions, such as designing the film wardrobe for Charlotte Rampling in *Le Taxi Mauve* and Joan Collins in *The Bitch.*

The success of the business led to an increasing emphasis on the private customer, resulting in the decision to provide an exclusively couture service by 1983, producing unique and glamorous evening and wedding dresses. In 1984 the first Bruce Oldfield shop opened at 27 Beauchamp Place, London, selling a total look, both to the ready-to-wear and the couture customer. Oldfield is perhaps best known for his couture and ready-to-wear evening dresses, often worn by high-profile clients such as the late Princess of Wales or actresses Joan Collins and Anjelica Huston.

Sumptuous fabrics like crushed velvets, taffeta, mink, printed sequins, crêpe, chiffon and lamé are used to design traditional sculpted shapes that are exquisitely manufactured. A ruched bodiced dress in velvet, with a huge *fischou* collar, is completed with a vast swathed taffeta bow on the hip. A velvet double-breasted coat dress is enhanced by an exaggerated mink collar. Particularly distinctive is Oldfield's use of color blocking; simple jersey dresses are slashed asymmetrically and blocked in various vivid color combinations. His tailoring is always curvaceous and womanly, with seams and darts significantly placed to flatter the feminine physique, in soft leathers and wool crêpes.

Oldfield's career has covered a wide span of activities and he has recently received awards acknowledging his contribution to fashion. In 1990 he was awarded the OBE and made an honorary fellow of both the Royal College of Art and Durham University. The same year he was also the subject of a television documentary on his life and career, *A Journey into Fashion,* which was subsequently sold to television companies around the world.

If success can be measured by public recognition, then Oldfield has achieved it. His name is synonymous with style; he is universally acknowledged as having a unique understanding of how to make a woman look and feel her best. Yet in the 21st century Oldfield took his particular fashion sense into alternate fields of design. Signing on with Alexandra Corporate Clothing, Oldfield designed staff uniforms for the Warren Village Cinemas, then Oldfield segued into interior design in a new St. James housing development in Kew, where he designed furniture and furnishings for two homes and two apartments of the 400-house Kew Riverside neighborhood.

Looking to move more firmly into interiors, the opportunity with St. James was a welcome respite from the demands of fashion designing. As Oldfield told Anne Spackman of the *Financial Times* (27 January 2001), "The idea that you spend three months making a collection of clothes which should be useless in six months' time makes a mockery of all the effort." For this reason Oldfield cut back to only custom orders, yet home furnishings, on the other hand, "are more of a worthwhile investment for me and for the customer.... The British have always been reluctant to spend money beautifying themselves, but when it comes to their homes, it's a different matter."

Brits with a taste for Bruce Oldfield style can seek him out for private orders, but his design skills now adorn the employees of Warner cinemas, the furnishings of select St. James homes, and if the designer gets his wish—perhaps restaurants and hotels as well.

—Kevin Almond; updated by Nelly Rhodes

OLDHAM, Todd

American designer

Born: Corpus Christi, Texas, 22 November 1961. **Education:** No formal training in design. **Career:** Worked in the alterations department, Polo/Ralph Lauren, Dallas, Texas, 1980; showed first collection, in Dallas, 1981; partner/designer, L-7 company, New York, incorporating Times 7 women's shirt collection, from 1988; reintroduced signature Todd Oldham collection with backing from Onward Kashiyama Company, 1989; introduced line of handbags, 1991; produced Todd Oldham patterns for *Vogue Patterns,* 1992; footwear line introduced, 1993; opened SoHo store with his father, Jack, 1994; signed on as creative consultant, Escada, 1995; began appearing on MTV's *House of Style,* 1995; directed first music video, 1997; designed complete renovations for The Hotel, Miami, 1999; published two books, 1997, 2000. **Awards:** Council of Fashion Designers of America Perry Ellis award, 1991; Dallas Fashion award, 1992; Fashion Excellence award, 1993. **Address:** 120 Wooster Street, New York, NY 10012, USA. **Website:** www.toddoldhamjeans.com.

PUBLICATIONS

By OLDHAM:

Books

Todd Oldham: Without Boundaries, New York, 1997.
Suits: The Clothes Make the Man, with Dave Hickey and Shaila Dewan, New York, 2000.

Todd Oldham, spring 1997 collection. © Mitchell Gerber/CORBIS.

On OLDHAM:

Books

Stegemeyer, Anne, *Who's Who in Fashion, Third Edition,* New York, 1996.

Articles

Robinson, Rob, "Todd Oldham," in *Interview* (New York), October 1982.
Morris, Bernadine, "Two Young Designers Decorate Their Clothes with Wit," in the *New York Times,* 27 November 1990.
Hochswender, Woody, "Flights of Fancy: Todd Oldham's Magic Carpet Ride," in the *New York Times,* 11 April 1991.
Darnton, Nina, "The New York Brat Pack," in *Newsweek,* 29 April 1991.
"Great Expectations," in *WWD,* 12 June 1991.
Schiro, Anne-Marie, "The 3-Year Leap of Todd Oldham," in the *New York Times,* 29 December 1991.
Lender, Heidi, "Hot Toddy," in *WWD,* 8 May 1992.
Servin, Jim, "Todd Oldham: This Year's It," in the *New York Times,* 10 May 1992.
"Hot Designer: Todd Oldham," in *Rolling Stone,* 14 May 1992.

Todd Oldham, spring 1995 collection. © Mitchell Gerber/CORBIS.

James, Laurie, "Hot on the Trail," in *Harper's Bazaar* (New York), August 1992.

Orlean, Susan, "Breaking Away," in *Vogue* (New York), September 1992.

Mower, Sarah, "How Does Todd Do It?" in *Harper's Bazaar,* December 1994.

Ferguson, Sarah, "Natural Force," in *Elle* (New York), March 1995.

Spindler, Amy M., "Oldham and Tyler Look Super," in *WWD,* 6 April 1995.

Ingrassia, Michelle, "All Todd, All the Time," in *Newsweek,* 12 June 1995.

Colman, David, "Fashioning a Collection," in *ARTnews,* September 1997.

Bussel, Abby, "Haute Hotel," in *Interior Design,* January 1999.

Wasserman, Ted, "Designer Oldham Aims Snappy Duds at Polaroid," in *Brandweek,* 25 October 1999.

* * *

Todd Oldham's eclectic and electric fashion fuses a traditional avant-garde premise to an abiding love of the crafts. Acknowledging in *Women's Wear Daily* in 1992 that his "total hero" is Christian Lacroix, Oldham indicates his wild sense of rich pastiche and cultural mix. At the time of his show for fall 1991, Woody Hochswender of the *New York Times* wrote, "The young Texas-born designer is on his own strange trip, and Tuesday afternoon he whisked editors and buyers on a whirlwind round-the-world tour—by plane, flying carpet and Greyhound."

Oldham's irrepressibly mischievous design takes fashion very seriously, bringing to dress a range of visual references. In 1990, in a collection called Garage Sale, he showed a black satin suit embroidered with items that might be found at a garage sale, including a lamp with its electrical cord, a clock, and crossed knife and fork. For fall 1992, he showed a coy "Old Masters—New Mistress" skirt with a beaded Mona Lisa on the front and a Picasso on the back. In between, he showed a black silk shantung trouser suit with sequined and embroidered travel patches, African-inspired embroidered tops, and Lamontage (synthetic-fiber felting) designs akin to Byzantine mosaics.

His vernacular references have strayed to the backyard for a 1991 hammock dress and to the kitchen for what he described to *People* magazine as "embroidered shirts that look like they've been iced by cake decorators" and his memorable "potholder suits" with pockets resembling the potholders of elementary crafts. In such gestures, Oldham gives literal meaning to "everything but the kitchen sink," but never with desperation, only with a charming surrealism. Another art-for-art's sake suit for 1990 used the motif of paint-by-numbers for its beaded pockets. Oldham's ever-present sense of ornament is not, however, for resplendence alone (although the decoration plays an undeniable role) but for its contribution to the narrative, the ironic information dispatched in each garment.

Oldham disavows kitsch, an almost inescapable epithet for his idiosyncratic talent, but his enthusiasm for naive crafts and his juxtapositions of good and highly uncertain taste encourage the description, however inadequate. Kitsch implies, however, no intervention or interpretation, only laconic appropriation. Oldham's aesthetic power is a willful perversity, a zest for twisting and changing the original source, whether kitsch or Mediterranean mosaic. His buttons are curious and quirky; his well-tailored suits are saved from conformity by their odd pockets; and his canny knowledge of fashion sources is saved from being scholastic by his whimsical juxtapositions.

For all of its personal taste, Oldham's fashion extends the tradition of Schiaparelli in its bold thematic development, delicate equilibrium between propriety and aesthetic anarchy, overt decoration, and annexation of related arts (including theater, film, and such street-inspired elements as using drag queen Billy Erb and the rock group B-52's Kate Pierson in his catwalk shows). Oldham's 1992 mirror dress pursued a Schiaparelli ideal, as does his preoccupation with the unexpected and seemingly autonomous pockets of suits.

Big-city, high-style savoir faire is key to Oldham's chic tongue in cheek, as it was for Schiaparelli. But Oldham's Texas roots and his family-based manufacturing give the work roots in the American Midwest as well as in the dry wit of capital cities. Born in Corpus Christi, Texas, in 1961, Oldham began his fashion business 20 years later, following a brief stint in alterations at the Polo/Ralph Lauren boutique in Dallas. He moved to New York in 1988 and started the women's shirt collections Times 7 at the time.

Spring 1992 headlines for Oldham as "Hot Toddy" in *Women's Wear Daily* (8 May 1992) and the "It" guy according to the *New York Times* (10 May 1992) might be the kiss of death for some designers, but Oldham possesses the characteristics of lasting, needed style, however outré or idiosyncratic it may seem. His persistent technical investigation—he was, for example, unique in experimenting with

Lamontage as an apparel fabric—gives added meaning to his comment in the *New York Times* in 1991: "I haven't had any formal training, but that's worked to my advantage. People don't know what to expect." If cool whimsy is ever unexpected, so is the technology of the clothing endemic to Oldham's interest in the crafts. Likewise, his keen interest and perceptions in contemporary culture, beyond fashion, have provided him with a wealth of images for the work.

Oldham's aesthetic is bold and self-assured but far less transitory than it might initially seem. Oldham's creativity is in tune with fashion's constant striving to achieve ironic involvement in matters outside of dress and attempts, with irony, to understand the phenomena of clothing and contemporary life. A good example of his appeal was "Todd Time," irreverently goofy monthly segments filmed for MTV's *House of Style,* seen by nearly five million teens and young adults around the world. This exposure in turn led to Oldham directing a music video for jazzy hip-hop trio, US3.

In the late 1990s Oldham continued to branch out, this time in writing, with a book entitled *Todd Oldham: Without Boundaries* and into interior design by remodeling The Hotel, located on Miami's South Beach. The Hotel, formerly known as the Tiffany, is an old landmark given a glam new transformation thanks to Oldham. Glowing in chrome, blues, greens, and beiges, Oldham found the experience fun but not really challenging. He told Abby Bussel of *Interior Design* in January 1999, "I've been putting things on people for years, so putting things under people was no big deal." Everything used in renovation, including the furniture, tile, cabinetry, linens, and even bathrobes, were produced in Oldham's factory, which is overseen by his brother, Brad (Oldham also employs his father, mother, grandmother, and sister).

Of Oldham's literary career, *Todd Oldham: Without Boundaries* featured many of today's top fashion photographers capturing some of the world's most famous personalities—all wearing Oldham designs. His next book, *Suits: The Clothes Make the Man,* is an often hilarious account of two artists who spent a year touring the country wearing Oldham-designed suits. On the suits, they sold advertising space to fifty-six companies. The story is told through interviews, photos, and firsthand accounts.

Miles Socha, in an article in *Women's Wear Daily,* quoted Oldham from a speech he gave at Career Day at the Fashion Institute of Technology. Oldham talked of his decision to close the collection part of his business and focus on his line of Todd Oldham Jeans. "I elected to stop wholesaling my collection line because my heart wasn't in it anymore. I just didn't want to be part of $1200 blouses.... It was just not modern anymore." Oldham urged students to discover their own path. "The one thing we can really count on is change," he said. Oldham also told the students to "cultivate freethinking" and to be "singular in your vision," about what the market wants.

—Richard Martin; updated by Andrew Cunningham and Nelly Rhodes

ONG, Benny

Singaporean/British designer working in London

Born: Singapore, 1949 (one source says 1956); moved to London, 1968. **Education:** Graduated in fashion from St. Martin's School of Art, London. **Career:** Formed own company, Benny Ong Ltd., 1977; represented Britain in the Fashion Extravaganza in Milan, 1978; lectured in fashion at St. Martin's School of Art and Newcastle Polytechnic, England, 1979; introduced Private Label business designs for Austin Reed, London, 1983; launched Sunday and Ong by Benny Ong lines, 1988; produced private label designs for House of Fraser stores, 1988; created International Collection diffusion line, ONG, 1989; introduced third label, Bene, 1992; opened two Benny Ong boutiques in Singapore, 1992; guest lecturer to BA honors program fashion majors, Surrey Institute, 2001; also corporate uniform designer from 1986 with clients including BAA and British Telecom. **Address:** 3A Moreton Terrace, London SW1V 2NS, England.

Publications

On ONG:

Books

Mulvagh, Jane, *Vogue History of Twentieth Century Fashion,* London, 1988.

Articles

Hyde, Nina S., "No One Takes a Vacation Just to Shop," in the *Washington Post,* 17 April 1977.

Freedman, Lisa, and Barbara Griggs, "Secrets of Diana's Wardrobe," in the *Sunday Express Magazine* (London), 12 June 1983.

Theis, Tammy, "Wearing Linen to the Office? Here's a New Wrinkle for You," in the *Dallas Morning News,* 11 June 1986.

"Hot Fashion—Stolen Seat Belts—Causes Problems for Airline," in the *AP Newswire,* 29 June 2000.

"The Belgian Wave," in the *AP Newswire,* 22 January 2001.

"Benny Ong," available online at the Fashion Page, www.fashionz.co.uk, 20 August 2001.

"The Premier Collections," available online at the Fashion Page," www.fashionz.co.uk, 20 August 2001.

"Undergraduate Programmes," available online at the Surrey Institute," www.surrart.ac.uk, 20 August 2001.

* * *

Benny Ong is a designer of pretty, relaxed clothes that are charming and flattering to wear. Born in Singapore of Chinese descent, he moved to London in 1968 to study fashion design at St. Martin's School of Art. Today he retains his Singaporean connections with twice yearly visits that consolidate his successful design combination of Eastern philosophy with Western glamor.

He formed Benny Ong Ltd. in 1977 and presented a well-received debut collection quickly snapped up by two of London's top stores, Harrods and Selfridges. The collection set the tone for Ong's later work, with exquisite loose fitting, hand-sprayed silk chiffons, and jerseys. His successful debut year also saw Ong becoming a founding member of the prestigious London Designer Collections, which now represents the cream of British designers.

Expansion of the business has proved no problem, owing to the avid press interest and acclaim for the label since its inception. In addition to the designer range, the company began producing several diffusion lines for the middle price market. The first, in 1980, the International Collection, featured predominantly silk special occasion clothes; this was followed by Sunday, which presented less formal occasion clothes. The Ong by Benny Ong range was produced in 1988 and sells throughout Europe.

Fabrics for Ong are always classical, traditional, and stylish. As well as glamorous silk eveningwear fabrics, he has easy handkerchief linens, plain or in tiny checks; crisp white cottons and voiles for pretty, oversize shirts; or stonewashed crêpes for simple jackets. In 1983 the company began promotions for the European Silk Commission, with major fashion shows and wide coverage in international fashion magazines. Simple and graceful knitwear and cashmere ranges were added to the collection in 1985 and were immediately snapped up in huge quantities by the New York retailer Barneys.

Diana, the late Princess of Wales, was a frequent Ong customer. She commissioned dresses and suits for her first official visit to Australia in 1985. The exposure generated by having possibly the most prestigious customer in the UK led to an invitation to participate in a fashion show on the BBC television program *Pebble Mill at One,* that same year.

As well as producing ranges of clothes for the more glamorous end of the fashion market, Ong has worked on several corporate clothing commissions. In 1986 he was invited, along with five other eminent British designers, to tender for the British Airports Authority corporate clothing project. He won the contract, which led to further invitations to design for a new corporate clothing image for British Telecom and a prestigious clothing contract for the reopening of the internationally famous Raffles Hotel in Singapore.

Ong's other activities have included guest lecture programs in fashion design at St. Martin's College of Art and invitations to speak at various fashion forums for students and the trade, covering a range of topics from design to management. After the presentation of a first full fashion show to top buyers and press in 1979, his company further expanded into the private label business, designing a young and well-made range for Austin Reed in 1983 and branded merchandise for the designer section of the popular catalogue of Great Universal Stores, along with designers like Roland Klein, Jasper Conran, and Jean Muir. With colleagues Owen Gastor and Steve Stewart, in 2001, Ong guest lectured at the Surrey Institute to students in the BA honors program in fashion.

Ultimately, Benny Ong is best known for his eveningwear. He can handle beautiful fabrics in a sensitive and refined manner, producing conventional yet becoming garments for a wealthy clientèle.

—Kevin Almond; updated by Mary Ellen Snodgrass

OSTI, Massimo

See C.P. COMPANY

OZBEK, Rifat

British designer

Born: Istanbul, Turkey, 11 July 1953. **Education:** Studied architecture at Liverpool University, 1970–72; fashion design at St. Martin's School of Art, London, 1974–77. **Military Service:** National military service in Turkey, 1977. **Career:** Worked with Walter Albini for Trell, Milan, 1978–80; designer for Monsoon, London, 1980–84; established own firm, Ozbek, 1984; established second line, O, renamed Future Ozbek, 1987; production under licence by Aeffe SpA, Italy, from 1988; launched New Age collection, 1989; debuted *Ozbek,* signature fragrance, 1995; designed carpet for Christopher Farr, 1999. **Exhibitions:** *Fellini: I Costumi e le Mode,* Pecci Museum, Prato, Italy, and Stedeligk Museum, Amsterdam, both 1994; *V&A: Street Style, From Sidewalk to Catwalk, 1940 to Tomorrow,* 1994–95; *Customised Levi's Denim Jacket for Benefit for Diffa/Dallas Collection,* 1990, 1991, 1992. **Awards:** *Woman* Magazine Designer award, 1986; British Fashion Council Designer of the Year award, London, 1988, 1992; British Glamour award, 1989. **Address:** 18 Haunch of Venison Yard, London W1Y 1AF, England.

Rifat Ozbek, spring 2001 collection. © Fashion Syndicate Press.

Publications

On OZBEK:

Books

Coleridge, Nicholas, *The Fashion Conspiracy,* London, 1988.

Stegemeyer, Anne, *Who's Who in Fashion, Third Edition,* New York, 1996.

Rifat Ozbek, spring 2001 collection. © Fashion Syndicate Press.

Articles

Brampton, Sally, "Wizard of Ozbek," in the *Observer* (London), 12 May 1985.

Hoae, S., "Out of the Playpen," in the *Observer,* 23 March 1986.

Thackara, J., "Hooked on Classics," in the *Creative Review* (London), June 1986.

Etherington-Smith, Meredith, "Street Smart," in the *Observer,* 21 September 1986.

"Designer of the Year," in *DR: The Fashion Business* (London), 15 October 1986.

Jeal, Nicola, "The Wizard of Ozbek," in the *Observer,* 16 October 1986.

"Designer of the Year: Rifat Ozbek," in *Woman* (London), 8 November 1986.

Aitken, Lee, "Designer Rifat Ozbek, London's Young Turk, Dazzles the Rag Trade with a Theme for All Seasons," in *People,* 17 November 1986.

Ducann, Charlotte, "The Designer Star: Rifat Ozbek," in *Vogue* (London), February 1987.

"Rifat Ozbek," in the *Sunday Times Magazine* (London), 22 November 1987.

"View: London's Young Turk," in *Vogue,* June 1988.

Rumbold, Judy, "Ozbek Out on Top," in *The Guardian,* 11 October 1988.

"Ozbek on Top," in *DR: The Fashion Business,* 15 October 1988.

Jeal, Nicola, "The Wizard of Ozbek," in the *Observer Magazine* (London), 16 October 1988.

"Rifat Ozbek," in *Vogue* (London), December 1988.

Gross, Michael, "The Wizard of Ozbek," in *New York,* 23 January 1989.

Campbell, Lisa, "Ozbek on the Fringe," in *Vogue,* January 1989.

Jobey, Liza, "Rifat Madness," in *Vanity Fair* (London), February 1989.

Brampton, Sally, "Aspects of Ozbek," in *Elle* (London), May 1989.

Perry, Beverly, "The Rifat Ozbek Collection," in *Marie Claire* (London), July 1989.

Bakjer, Caroline, "Beyond the Veil," in the *Sunday Times Magazine* (London), 26 November 1989.

Reed, Paula, "Ozbek: The Movie," in *Correspondent Magazine* (London), 11 March 1990.

"The Designers Talk Passion, Whimsy and Picassos," in *ARTnews* (New York), September 1990.

Alderson, Maggie, "Rifat Ozbek's Hot Stuff," in *Elle* (New York), October 1990.

Fallon, James, "Ozbek Will Show in Milan in October," *WWD,* 20 August 1991.

Daspin, Eileen, "Rifat Ozbek, Milan's New Turk," in *WWD,* 16 October 1991.

Orlean, Susan, "Breaking Away," in *Vogue* (New York), September 1992.

Morris, Bernadine, "A Little Bit Exotic, But Soothingly So, the *New York Times,* 7 October 1992.

Johnson, Marylin, "Copycat Chic: Military Look Takes Charge for Fall," the *Atlanta Journal & Constitution,* 15 August 1993.

McSweeney, Eve, "The Story of Ozbek," in *Vogue UK,* August 1993.

Morris, Bernadine, "At Lacroix, Hollywood Meets Paris," in the *New York Times,* 7 March 1994.

Reed, Paula, "The Sultan of Style," in the *Sunday Times Magazine,* 5 June 1994.

"Paris...Milan: Prettiness Peeks Through in Lines for Spring '95, in the *Atlanta Journal & Constitution,* 16 October 1994.

Middleton, William, and Godfrey Deeny, "Mugler Model Gambit Shreds Paris RTW Slate; Miffs Ozbek," *WWD,* 3 March 1995.

"Schedule Changes Put End to Furor Over Thierry Mugler's Stealth Show," in *WWD,* 9 March 1995.

"The Paris Collections—The Ideas of March: Rifat Ozbek," in *WWD,* 17 March 1995.

Barone, Amy B., "Ozbek's Fragrance to Make London Debut," in *WWD,* 28 July 1995.

Fallon, James, "Barney's Gets Ozbek Exclusive," in *WWD,* 17 November 1995.

Spindler, Amy M, "Treating History with a Sense of Pride," in the *New York Times,* 17 March 1997.

Everett, Rupert, "Rifat Ozbek," in *Interview,* July 1997.

White, Constance C.R., "Finding the Sanctity in Magic," in the *New York Times,* 8 November 1997.

"New York Globe Trotters," in *WWD,* 10 November 1997.

"Dyed in the Wool," in *Interior Design,* July 1998.

Theis, Tammy, "Sweater Weather," in the *Dallas Morning News,* 28 October 1998.

"Shopping for Turkish Delights," in *Travel Agent,* 19 April 1999.

"New York: A Delicate Balance," in *WWD,* 16 February 2001.

Klensch, Elsa, "The Turkish Touch: Ozbek's Sporty, Mystical Styles for Winter," available online at CNN.com, www.ccn.com, 20 August 2001.
"Rifat Ozbek," available online at Fashion Live, www.fashionlive.com, 20 August 2001.

*

My collections always have an element of ethnic and modern feeling.

—Rifat Ozbek

* * *

One of Britain's few truly international designers, Rifat Ozbek draws on London street style and his own Turkish origins to produce sophisticated clothes that successfully amalgamate diverse sources and keep him at the forefront of new developments in style. Ozbek restyles the classic shapes of Western couture, using multicultural decorative references like the traditional stitching of the djellaba and caftan to outline garments such as A-line linen dresses. He became renowned in the 1980s for a series of lavishly embroidered black cocktail suits that appeared with different themes each season, such as gold bows and tassels or Daliesque lips.

After leaving Turkey at the age of 17, Ozbek trained as an architect at Liverpool University, cutting his studies short after deciding he was more interested in decorating the surfaces of buildings than learning the methods of construction needed for his architectural projects to remain standing. This interest in the decoration of classic shapes, rather than breaking the barriers of garment construction, was expressed in his first clothing designs, which appeared in 1984.

Ozbek graduated from St. Martin's School of Art in 1977 and went on to work for three years at Monsoon, a company known for creating popular styles based on non-Western originals. Ozbek assimilated all these ideas and became known in the mid-1980s for his combinations of motifs and shapes from different cultures and juxtapositions of unusual fabrics, creating not just a straight pastiche of ethnicity but an arresting amalgamation of eclectic sources such as Africa, the Far East, ballet, and the Ottoman Empire.

At this time, his skillfully tailored clothes were fashioned out of luxurious fabrics like moiré silks and taffeta, with an amazing palette of colors of turquoise, purples, and fuchsia. His sophisticated and understated designs developed into an easily recognizable style, using heavy fabrics like gabardine or cashmere to structure the top half of an outfit combined with lighter materials below, like silks or jersey. This elegant look was supplanted by a more overtly sexy one in 1988, where the multicultural aesthetic was taken to new levels with the use of a diverse array of eclectic material. His confidence in dealing with a number of different non-Western sources was displayed in this significant collection, with garments showing their origins in Senegal, Tibet, and Afghanistan, an ethnic look made urbane for the fashion consumer. The collection included sarong skirts and gold chain belts, midriff tops, and boleros embroidered with crescent moons and stars, hipster trousers, and tasselled bras worn on the catwalk by models who resembled Turkish belly dancers.

In the 1990s Ozbek became more heavily influenced by the club scene, and his White Collection of 1990 caught the mood of the times. Acknowledging the New Age and Green consumerist tendencies of his audience, Ozbek created a range of easy-to-wear separates based on track suits and other sports clothing to be worn as club gear. This collection was in complete antithesis to the hard metropolitan chic of 1980s power dressing and paved the way for hooded sweatshirt tops and trainers appearing in the catwalk collections of other designers that year. The clothes were a stark bright white, displaying New Age slogans like "Nirvana." Unlike designers who have used white before, such as the "yé yé" designers of the 1960s who employed white to glorify science and technology, Ozbek used the color, without irony, to profess a faith in the concept of a New Age and a belief that a return to the spiritual would improve the quality of life and save the planet.

Antifashion soon became the fashionable look of the early 1990s. Casual, baggy clothes, making reference to sports and black youth subcultures, were worn with sequined money belts and baseball caps, and Ozbek was lauded as a designer in touch with the street. His popularity continued with the urban cowgirl look of fringed suede tops, hot pants, and North American Indian jewelry, his mock bone fronts on waistcoats and evening gowns, and the Confederate look incorporating tailed or cropped military jackets.

In 1995 Ozbek guarded his turf by inaugurating *Ozbek,* his signature women's fragrance manufactured in Milan by Proteo Parfumi. After three years of work developing the glamorous, heady blend of pittosporum with freesia, peach, and touches of jasmine and ylang ylang, he bottled it in an aluminum-topped flask reminiscent of a Turkish minaret and launched it in the U.S. exclusively at the Barneys chain in New York and Los Angeles. In England, he marketed *Ozbek* at Harrods, Liberty, and Selfridges. Of its appeal, he remarked, "I wanted something traditional yet modern… I wanted it to be quite floral, but not too strong. It's supposed to be very feminine and sensual." Paralleling his coup in the perfume market, Ozbek did not hesitate to clash publicly with Thierry Mugler for professional sabotage in block-booking such top models as Naomi Campbell and usurping Ozbek's space on the fashion calendar with an unscheduled showing.

Ozbek asserted his individualism in 1997, complaining that the era's design standards forced him to think of his hobby as a business. To old friend writer-interviewer Rupert Everett, who labeled Ozbek "an independent, an inventor, and an inveterate puncturer of pomposity," he said, "I still love designing, but it just moves too fast. Fashion has become sort of a relentless Ferris wheel, and you can't get off it—you know, it's one collection after the other."

Ozbek joined English stylist Christopher Farr's stable of carpet designers in 1998 and added vibrant prints reminiscent of Ottoman tile motifs to his clothing line. For city silhouettes, he stressed long romantic skirts mixed with energized, sporty jogging pants in Polartec fleece. He declared his exuberant, sensual chiffons, flocked velvet, devores, jerseys, and metallics a return to his Turkish roots.

—Caroline Cox; updated by Mary Ellen Snodgrass

P

PACKHAM, Jenny

British designer

Born: Southampton, England, 3 November 1965. **Education:** Studied at Southampton Art College, 1982–84; studied textile and fashion design at St. Martin's College of Art, London, 1984–88 (1st class honors). **Career:** Designer/director, Packham Anderson Ltd., from 1988. **Exhibitions:** London Designers Exhibition, 2001. **Address:** Zoomphase Ltd., The Imperial Works, 2nd Floor, Perren Street, London NW5 3ED England.

Publications

On PACKHAM:

Articles

Hepple, Keith, "Jenny Packham," in *DR* (London), September 1991.

Yusuf, Nilgin, "Designer's Inspirations," in *Joyce* (Hong Kong), 1991 Holiday Issue.

Tait, James, "Don't Change a Thing, Carol," in the *Sunday Mirror* (London), 12 December 2000.

Dent, Grace, "Who the Nell Would Wear This?" in the *Sunday Mirror* (London), 8 July 2001.

* * *

British designer Jenny Packham's early training as a textile designer became an important influence on her later eveningwear. Her first collection of 12 short evening gowns was created entirely in black and white silk, with a bold print of musical instruments. The short evening dress continued to be the principal style in her collections, although full-length dresses were introduced in 1992. She also began designing wedding gowns in the 1990s.

Although the shapes of Packham's dresses remain essentially simple, their construction is complex and owes much to Christian Dior's designs of the 1950s, featuring intricate seaming, linings, and boning. Dress panels were lined with stiff organdy to create fullness, bodices had boned seams for a corseted effect, and full skirts were created with layer upon layer of stiff netting. A typical example of Packham's short evening dresses was a fitted torso, full skirt, and fichu neckline or short sleeves. Her theory that women want to look glamorous by night, with emphasis placed on the bustline and waist, has been a recurring feature of Packham's designs. She also placed an emphasis on comfort, which she believes is vital for eveningwear.

Although the styling of Packham's designs evolves gradually from one season to the next, the colors and textiles change dramatically. The designer acknowledges that eveningwear by tradition is less susceptible to major changes in fashion and thus unusual colors and fabric combinations play a central role in her designs. Packham often draws upon the works of famous artists, including Gaudi, Miro, and van Gogh, as inspiration for her use of color. Bold prints decorate the full skirts of her gowns, with designs based on such themes as harlequin checks, playing cards, and giant florals. Packham's use of rich fabrics and colors has been likened to that of Christian Lacroix, and costly fabrics such as embroidered brocades, silk taffetas, satins, and silk gazars have featured heavily in her collections.

Traditional styling married to contemporary prints and color combinations is the essence of Packham's design formula, and this theme is continued through to the Jenny Packham Sequel collection of less expensive dresses, which echoed the shapes and colors of the main collection. Like the latter collection, Jenny Packham Sequel items are also produced in the United Kingdom by a small factory, supplemented by out-of-factory workers. The Sequel collection opened up a new market for her designs in the U.S., already one of her principal export markets, where her collection is sold through prestigious stores such as Neiman Marcus and Bergdorf Goodman. Packham's designs are favored by stars such as Sharon Stone, Shirley Bassey, and Nell McAndrew, the six-foot Amazon model who was the original face of *Tomb Raider*'s Lara Croft. McAndrew showed up at the British premiere of Arnold Schwarzenegger's movie, *The Sixth Day* in a Packham creation.

Packham's success in the American market, where her collections are widely sold, proved her theory that there was a gap in the middle market for eveningwear which was sophisticated yet still youthful, and sexy in a humorous way. In the last six or so years, however, Packham has become best known for her wedding dress lines. Her Desire collection focuses on cut, shaping, attention to detail, and understated glamor. The white, shimmery dresses range from off-the-shoulder wrapped fronts to a meshed blouse look. Packham obviously designs these lovely dresses to make the bride feel special and comfortable, and they allow the bride to be enhanced rather than distracted while wearing her creations.

In October 2000, Packham was the guest designer for Evangeline Rose Exclusive Bridal Designs, and her creations have been carried by the best London couture houses (Harrods, Harvey Nichols, Selfridges, Debenhams), next to those of Mori Lee, Rena Koh, Katherine Jane, Sally Bee, and Lady Grace. She also created the Empire line of bridal dresses, including a stylish number called Kansas, a short-sleeved Empire-line dress with delicate beading around the neckline and a fine georgette overlay on the skirt. The Empire line also features organza and organza-and-rose skirts.

Highly active in England, France, Italy, and the U.S., Packham is represented by Flax PR, a public relations firm specializing in the design industry. Their client list includes not only Jenny Packham but also Agatha, Ballantyne, BHS, Fenn Wright Manson, Petit Bateau, Jane Packer, Katharine Hamnett, Land's End, Marilyn Moore, Toast, and Bridgewater.

—Catherine Woram; updated by Daryl F. Mallett

PARNIS, Mollie

American designer

Born: Sara Rosen Parnis, in Brooklyn, New York, 18 March 1902. **Education:** Briefly studied law, Hunter College, New York. **Family:** Married Leon Livingston (originally Levinson) in 1930. **Career:** After high school, worked in sales for a blouse manufacturer, then as stylist for David Westheim Company, New York, circa 1928–30; Parnis-Livingston ready-to-wear established, New York, 1933; launched own label, 1940s; boutique line added, 1970; Mollie Parnis Studio Collection ready-to-wear line added, 1979; firm closed, 1984; first loungewear collection, Mollie Parnis at Home, designed for Chevette, New York, 1985; Molly Parnis Livingston Foundation established, 1984. **Died:** 18 July 1992, in New York.

Mollie Parnis, 1955 collection. © Bettmann/CORBIS

Publications

On PARNIS:

Books

Levin, Phyllis Lee, *The Wheels of Fashion,* Garden City, New York, 1965.

Bender, Marylin, *The Beautiful People,* New York, 1967.

Morris, Bernadine, and Barbara Walz, *The Fashion Makers,* New York, 1978.

Diamonstein, Barbaralee, *Fashion: The Inside Story,* New York, 1985.

New York and Hollywood Fashion: Costume Designs from the Brooklyn Museum Collection, New York, 1986.

Milbank, Caroline Rennolds, *New York Fashion: The Evolution of American Style,* New York, 1989.

Fashion for America! Designs in the Fashion Institute of Technology, New York, Haslemere, Surry, 1992.

Stegemeyer, Anne, *Who's Who in Fashion, Third Edition,* New York, 1996.

Articles

"It Can Happen to the President's Wife," in the *New York Times,* 1 April 1955.

"Blue-Green on the National Scene," in *Life* (New York), 25 April 1955.

"Molly Parnis," in *Current Biography* (New York), May 1956.

"Molly Parnis, Designer, Dies in Her Nineties," in the *New York Times,* 19 July 1992.

"A Woman of Many Modes: Mollie Parnis Dead at 93," in *WWD,* 20 July 1992.

"Died, Mollie Parnis," in *Time* (New York), 3 August 1992.

Friedman, Arthur, "Memories for Mollie Parnis," in *WWD,* 16 September 1992.

* * *

Mollie Parnis belongs to the first generation of American fashion designers to be known to the public by name rather than by affiliation to a department store. Her clothing became standard in the wardrobes of conservative businesswomen and socialites of the mid-20th century. Parnis herself was one of these women; she understood what women wanted to wear and what they required to appear appropriately dressed, yet feminine.

Parnis was a success in the fashion industry from the start. During her first job as a salesperson for a blouse manufacturer, she showed a keen interest in design details, as well as a good sense of what might sell. She was promoted to a design position with the firm in a short period of time. Her ability to determine what fashion would be successful served her throughout her career, spanning over 50 years in the industry. When she and her husband, Leon Livingston, started their own business just prior to World War II, the prospects for any new clothing wholesaler seemed dim. They knew, however, that one of the keys to success was specialization, so Parnis-Livingston limited its line to women's dresses and suits, which were immediately successful.

The look of Mollie Parnis clothes was conservative and classic. In the 1950s she was known for her shirtwaist dresses and suits in luxurious-looking fabrics that spanned seasons and made the transition from office to dinner. She also employed whimsical, all-American combinations such as menswear wool with silk fringe in some of her evening dresses. Though not always a design innovator, she was a consistent provider of well-made, highly wearable clothes. She interpreted the contemporary silhouette with her conservative good taste and her sensibility to the busy American woman's desires and needs.

United States First Ladies, from Mamie Eisenhower to Rosalyn Carter, were Parnis customers. One dress in particular received national attention in April 1955 when Mrs. Eisenhower arrived at a Washington reception wearing a Mollie Parnis shirtwaist of blue and green printed taffeta, only to be greeted by another woman in the same dress. Parnis expressed her embarrassment over the situation, but explained to the *New York Times* in April 1995: "I do not sell directly to any wearer, nor do I usually make one of a kind; that is what makes this country a great democracy. But I do feel that the First Lady should have something special." There had been minor variations made to Mrs. Eisenhower's dress alone, but approximately 90 dresses of the similar style were shipped to U.S. stores.

Though other designers were hired by the firm eventually, Parnis remained the originator of themes and ideas, and the final editor of her design staff's creations. Eleanor Lambert described her as having "an architect's eye for proportion" and the ability to endow mass-produced clothing with a custom-made look. Like many designers who were successful in the long run, she avoided trendy looks in the service of her customers who came to expect fashionable clothing that would last for more than one season. Mollie Parnis used her own life as inspiration and guide for her work. She stated her design philosophy in Barbaralee Diamonstein's *Fashion: The Inside Story* (1985): "Being a designer is being a personality. It's creating a look you like, that your friends like, that belongs to the life that you know."

Parnis' life exemplified the successful and civic-minded businesswoman in New York. In addition to her career as an award-winning fashion designer, she founded several philanthropic organizations. Through her design work and her membership in such organizations as the Council of Fashion Designers of America, she played a role in the promotion and success of the American fashion industry.

—Melinda L. Watt

PARRISH, Maxfield

See MAXFIELD PARRISH

PATOU, Jean

See JEAN PATOU

PAULIN, Guy

French designer

Born: Lorraine, France in 1946. **Career:** Freelance designer for Prisunic, Jimper, Dorothée Bis, Paraphernalia, Mic Mac, Byblos, and others, prior to establishing own house, 1970s–84, and 1986–89; designer, Chloé, 1984–86; designer, Tiktiner, 1990. **Died:** June 1990, in Paris.

Publications

On PAULIN:

Articles

"Designer Guy Paulin Dies in Paris at Age 44," in *WWD,* 15 June 1990.

"Guy Paulin, Fashion Designer," [obituary], in *Chicago Tribune,* 17 June 1990.

* * *

Guy Paulin began his career as a freelance designer of women's ready-to-wear in Paris. Though he had no formal training he was hired as a design assistant to Jacqueline Jacobson at Dorothée Bis, where he first worked with knits. He then signed a contract with Paraphernalia, a chain of franchised stores in New York, where he rubbed shoulders with other young designers of the time, including Mary Quant, Betsey Johnson, Emmanuelle Khanh, and Lison Bonfils.

A shy, quick-witted conversationalist and lover of 1950s American Abstract Expressionist paintings, Paulin believed fashion to be part of life, an essential component of the French l'art de vivre. He claimed to be most inspired by Katherine Hepburn—a mature, free-spirited soul who eschewed fashion trends and projected her own sense of personal style, and his clothing designs were often acclaimed for their gentle and unpretentious lines, reminiscent of classic American sportswear.

On returning to Paris after his New York sojourn, Paulin received an enthusiastic press response for the simple, feminine clothes he designed for various clients. He worked for the next two decades in France and Italy, designing for Bercher, Biga, P. Blume, Byblos, Sport Max for Max Mara, Mic-Mac, PEP, and Rodier. Before establishing his own business, he was known to juggle as many as thirteen different ready-to-wear collections, designed anonymously, in a single season. His designs were marked by simplicity of line, softness of color, and ease of movement—from loose sportswear separates to classic suits and cocktail dresses.

In 1984 Paulin succeeded Karl Lagerfeld as director of design at Chloé, claiming this appointment was "a dream." At Chloé he adapted his unerring fashion sense into a look he called "as French as French cuisine—an image of a young couture, of ready-to-wear with the finesse of couture but with a very young spirit behind it." But his casual, relaxed, and individualistic styles were not completely welcomed by Chloé's tradition-minded customers, and he resigned after overseeing only a few collections.

The disappointment he experienced at Chloé did not deter Paulin—between 1985 and 1990 he created S.A. Guy Paulin design studio, the principal clients being Byblos and Mic-Mac; took back the direction of his own house and signed two licensing contracts with the groups Kanematsu Gosho and Yoshida, establishing himself in Japan; and signed on as part-time artistic director of Tiktiner, a French ready to-wear manufacturer. During this period he designed a range of classic garments, including clingy knit dresses, feminine pinstriped suits, pretty floral 18th-century-inspired dresses, and simple one- and two-piece swimsuits. His clothes never strove for shock value, but remained reserved and feminine, with only the occasional theatrical accessory for emphasis, such as a "waistcoat" of multicolored cords draped across the breasts, or an oversized fringed straw hat.

Though not strictly an avant garde designer, Paulin considered himself one of a creative generation of createurs including Thierry Mugler, Claude Montana, and the younger Jean-Paul Gaultier. Towards the end of his career he was investigating retro looks, such as 1940s-inspired tweed suits and neo-Baroque velvet gowns strewn with embroidery. His death in 1990 at the young age of 44 prompted waves of regret among his peers at the loss of such a talented, industrious, and benevolent designer and colleague.

—Kathleen Paton

PEDLAR, Sylvia

American designer

Born: Sylvia Schlang in New York, 1901. **Education:** Studied art and fashion illustration, Cooper Union school, and at the Art Students League, New York. **Family:** Married William A. Pedlar. **Career:** Founder/designer, Iris Lingerie, 1929–70 (business closed in 1970). **Awards:** Coty American Fashion Critics award, 1951, 1964; Neiman Marcus award, 1960. **Died:** 26 February 1972, in New York.

PUBLICATIONS

On PEDLAR:

Books

Lambert, Eleanor, *World of Fashion: People, Places, Resources,* New York, London, 1976.

The Undercover Story [exhibition catalogue], Fashion Institute of Technology, New York, 1982.

Stegemeyer, Anne, *Who's Who in Fashion, Third Edition,* New York, 1996.

Articles

Bender, Marylin, "Lingerie Can Be Sensibly Elegant," in the *New York Times,* 17 December 1963.

* * *

For 41 years American women relied on Sylvia Pedlar for sleep and loungewear to suit their every mood. Fine fabrics, careful workmanship, and imaginative styling distinguished the Pedlar gown. Some of her designs were based on traditional favorites; others were strikingly original, sometimes pleasingly provocative, but always in good taste. Pedlar designed to suit many scenarios. She understood a woman might prefer to dress in a certain way for the street, yet play a wider variety of roles in the privacy of her own home. She saw no reason why a wardrobe for sleeping should not be as versatile as one for day.

Pedlar was the cofounder and designer of Iris Lingerie, from its inception in 1929 until she closed the business in 1970. In all that time, according to Marylin Bender, writing in the *New York Times* in December 1963, the company employed no salesmen and bought no paid advertising. The product spoke for itself. Pedlar was said to have created the baby-doll look, a phrase she disliked and did not use herself, as a response to the wartime fabric shortages of 1942. She interpreted the classic flannel Mother Hubbard nightgown in sheer cotton batiste, giving it a more sophisticated, bateau neckline and open, flowing sleeves. Deep borders of Cluny lace finished the neck, sleeves, and hem.

For women who preferred to sleep in the nude, Pedlar offered the "bedside toga," a column of crêpe slit entirely up one side which fastened with a single tie at the shoulder and one at the waist. Originally designed as a novelty item for friends, the bedside toga was photographed for the cover of *Life* magazine in 1962 and became a bestseller. Although she was trained as an illustrator, Pedlar preferred draping directly to sketching her ideas. Many of her designs relied on simple, bias cut shapes with a minimum of seaming, cut from solid shades of crêpe or chiffon. A trio of Iris gowns from the mid-1960s pictured in *The Undercover Story,* the catalogue for an exhibition held in 1982–83 at the Fashion Institute of Technology, New York, and the Kyoto Costume Institute in Japan illustrate Pedlar's gift as a cutter. An asymmetrical layered gown in turquoise georgette both conceals and reveals; an off-white one shouldered gown in crêpe charmeuse evokes the prewar years with its diaper hem and bias cut. A pair of coral lounging pajamas have trousers cut wide like a *dhoti.* Each is as wearable today as when they were first produced.

A winner of two Coty awards, Pedlar was cited by the American Fashion Critics committee for "her talent in combining luxury, beauty, and femininity with modern fabric developments and contemporary silhouettes."

—Whitney Blausen

PEPE

British jeans/casualwear manufacturer

Founded: Pepe brand jeans began on London's Portobello Road market. **Company History:** Lines have included Basic, BSCO, Hardcore, Buffalo, and Tommy Hilfiger labels; Pepe Group Plc. bought by SEL International Investments Corp. (in turn owned by Apparel International Holdings Ltd., the parent company of Tommy Hilfiger), 1993; entered U.S. market with Pepe Jeans USA, 1993; acquired license for new Tommy Hilfiger line of jeans, 1995; separate units for women's and men's Hilfiger jeans formed, 1996; signed deal to distribute Tommy Hilfiger lines in Europe, 1997; signed licensing agreement with Keystone Industries, 1997; Pepe Jeans USA unit sold to Tommy Hilfiger Corp., 1998; opened first U.S. Pepe stores, 2001. **Company Address:** Pepe House, 11 Lower Square, Old Isleworth-on-Thames, Middlesex TW7 6HN, UK. **Company Websites:** www.pepejeans.com.

Publications

On PEPE:

Articles

Lippert, Barbara, "Clean Jeans, Dirty War," in the *Chicago Tribune,* 16 December 1988.

Wall Street Journal, (New York), 10 April 1989.

Bidlake, Suzanne, "Pepe Strides Upmarket with Branding U-Turn," in *Marketing,* 11 April 1991.

Fallon, James, "Maurice Marciano Seeks Interest in Pepe Group," in *DNR,* 6 January 1993.

———, "Restructuring Done, Pepe Group is Set to Go," in *WWD,* 3 February 1993.

Gordon, Maryellen, "New Owners, New Power for Pepe," in *WWD,* 10 February 1993.

Ozzard, Janet, "Margolis Cuts a New Pattern at Pepe," in *WWD,* 19 January 1994.

Walsh, Peter, "Margolis Joins Hilfiger as Vice-Chairman, President; Succeeded at Pepe by Lewis," in *DNR,* 10 March 1994.

Lockwood, Lisa, "More Suitors Seen Pitching for CK Jeans," in *WWD,* 14 April 1994.

Moore, M. H., "Pepe Jeans May Be Loose, Seeking Fit," in *Adweek,* 22 August 1994.

Ozzard, Janet, "Pepe's New Fashion Flavor," in *WWD,* 1 February 1996.

"Pepe Forms Two Units for Hilfiger Lines," in *WWD,* 5 December 1996.

Socha, Miles, "Tommy Taking Department Store Jeans Biz by Storm," in *DNR,* 8 September 1997.

"Hilfiger Holders Okay Pepe Jeans USA Deal," in *DNR,* 6 May 1998.

Caplan, David Grant, "Pepe Jeans to Launch Stores," in *WWD,* 19 April 2001.

* * *

In the notoriously competitive denim sales market, Pepe has been able to maintain its profile as much through witty and eclectic marketing as through design details. The company and its various casualwear lines have carved a niche by concentrating on prompting a contemporary, directional image which has enabled them to establish an identity distinct from the nostalgia-led promotional strategy of many jeans companies.

A potent mix of references has marked out Pepe and its sister ranges as fashionable and different. The attention to detailing, with double stitched seams and copper rivets, so important to serious denim wearers, has underpinned their success and enabled Pepe to prosper. The range of different denims it produces has also been significant; the firm has maintained a reputation for quality, both in its staple Basic line, which established Pepe's classic straight-cut shapes for jeans and jackets, and its production of a changing array of washes and dyes to pick up on current fashion trends for its other lines.

Having started life in London's Portobello Road market, Pepe has always had an affinity with street fashion and urban life, and it is this ability to chime in with the *Zeitgeist* that brought them to the fore in the 1980s. After the dip in denim's popularity at the start of the decade, the slick advertising of the market leader, Levi Strauss, dominated by retro 1950s cool, sent jeans sales rocketing, partly triggered by the obsession with so-called design classics and media hype. If Pepe was lacking the long history of the main American labels, it certainly made up for it with its originality of approach.

Pepe recognized its own strengths as a British-based name and employed strong, innovative advertising to promote its ranges. The company understood that it was just as important to generate an aura of streetwise cool about its product, as to keep up with trends in fabric washes and design details. From 1986 Pepe sidestepped the traditional American imagery associated with jeans and produced a series of ads which ultimately led to an almost complete brand awareness by the end of the decade. Pepe's advertising achieved cult status; two of its most successful campaigns produced a soundtrack of contemporary music fitted together with well-known club images for the usually-resistant younger market. The "Wears Pepe" series cut images of avant-garde nightclub figure Leigh Bowery with shots of natural-looking models in Pepe denims and increased Pepe's status as a company which could both encapsulate and define the times.

Along with the memorable "Raindance" advertising, which also brought together maverick elements, looking more like a clip from a film than a piece of marketing, and "Laughter," which simply showed a group of people smiling and talking in a park in Pepe clothes, the company created a precedent. Pepe had recognized a crucial element of the 1990s youth market, seeing that the video generation was not taken in by straightforward name-plugging, but wanted to feel in on the joke, as though they were part of the street culture which Pepe represented.

Pepe has defined its role within the denim market and built on its strengths by clever advertising and an empathy with street fashion. If never quite in the same league as the biggest names in denim, it chose to strike out in a different direction, leaning on the contemporary rather than exploiting its own history to promote its ideals, such as the now legendary SoulHole parties. This approach has since been mimicked by other British casualwear names, but never with Pepe's originality and quality of research, in marketing or design.

From the early 1990s, Pepe became inextribably linked with Tommy Hilfiger, when it was bought by SEL International Investments Corp., which in turn was owned by Apparel International Holdings Ltd., the corporate parent of Hilfiger. Then Pepe Jeans USA secured the license for the new Tommy Jeans line, which debuted amidst much fanfare. The momentum of Hilfiger did much for Pepe, long considered a European jeans brand, to break into the American market and challenge such titan Levi Strauss. By 1997 the Tommy Jeans collections were the top-selling brand in over 1,200 U.S. departments stores, many of which had in-store Hilfiger boutiques, and Pepe London had signed exclusives agreements with Tommy Hilfiger to market products throughout Europe, as well as another licensing deal with the Montreal-based Keystone Industries to produce and distribute Pepe's own jeans in Canada.

The following year, 1998, Pepe Jeans USA was bought by Tommy Hilfiger Corp., just as the division planned an expansion of its women's denim collection and added styles to Tommy Jeans for men and boys. In 2001 Pepe Group Plc., sans its American subsidiary Pepe Jeans USA, announced plans for stores to open in Los Angeles, Miami, and New York carrying Pepe denim, outerwear, and accessories for both sexes. Though the company was already established in London, elsewhere in Europe and in Latin America, these were the company's first U.S. stores. Pepe clothes were successfully sold in

American specialty and department stores, but as Pepe executive Jonathan Cea told David Grant Caplan of *Women's Wear Daily* (19 April 2001), opening the firm's own shops was "the best form of advertising. It solidifies you as a brand."

—Rebecca Arnold; updated by Nelly Rhodes

PERETTI, Elsa

Italian designer working in New York

Born: Florence, Italy, 1 May 1940. **Career:** Language (French) teacher in Gstaad, Switzerland, 1961; ski instructor; studied interior design in Rome; modeled in London, Paris, New York, mid-1960s; began designing jewelry for Halston and Georgio di Sant'Angelo, New York, 1969; designer, Tiffany & Co., New York, from 1974; packaging designer, Halston fragrances (including *Elsa Peretti*) and cosmetics. **Exhibitions:** *Fifteen of My Fifty with Tiffany,* Fashion Institute of Technology, New York, 1990; retrospective, Tiffany's stores worldwide, 2001. **Awards:** American Fashion Critics Coty award, 1971; President's Fellow award, Rhode Island School of Design, 1981; Fashion Group "Night of the Stars" award, 1986; Cultured Pearl Industry award, 1987; Council of Fashion Designers of America's Accessories Designer of the Year, 1996. **Address:** Tiffany & Co., 600 Madison Avenue, New York, NY 10022.

Elsa Peretti in 1969. © Colita/CORBIS.

Publications

By PERETTI:

Books

Elsa Perretti, Tenth Anniversary, New York, 1984.

Elsa Perretti: Fifteen of My Fifty with Tiffany [exhibition catalogue], New York, 1990.

On PERETTI:

Books

Morris, Bernadine, and Barbara Walz, *The Fashion Makers,* New York, 1978.

Stegemeyer, Anne, *Who's Who in Fashion, Third Edition,* New York, 1996.

Loring, John, *Tiffany's 20th Century: A Portrait of American Style,* New York, 1997.

Articles

Kent, Rosemary, "Elsa Peretti...Real Things with a Thought," in *WWD,* 29 December 1971.

Talley, André Leon, "Elsa Peretti: Style is to Be Simple," in *WWD,* 11 June 1976.

"Jewelry's New Dazzle," in *Newsweek,* 4 April 1977.

"The Peretti Obsession," in the *New York Times Magazine,* 26 February 1978.

Blair, Gwenda, "Elsa Peretti at 40," in *Attenzione,* August 1980.

McAlpin, Heller, "Designing Women," in *Savvy* (New York), October 1981.

Caminiti, Susan, "Selling: Jewelers Woo the Working Woman," in *Fortune,* 8 June 1987.

Rice, Faye, with Laurie Kretchmar, "Competition: Tiffany's Tries the Cartier Formula," in *Fortune,* 20 November 1989.

"A Look at Peretti's Work and Life," in *WWD,* 27 April 1990.

Shain, Michael, and Pat Weschler, "Inside New York," in *Newsday,* 13 October 1993.

Rosenberg, Joyce M., "Karats, Trademarks are Gold Symbols to Assure You Get What You Pay For," in the *Minneapolis Star Tribune,* 18 December 1996.

Kovel, Ralph, and Terry Kovel, "Rare Kites Can Bring Sky-High Prices," in the *St. Louis Post-Dispatch,* 4 January 1997.

Levins, Harry, "People," in the *St. Louis Post-Dispatch,* 27 February 1997.

Okun, Stacey, "Tiffany's 20th Century: A Portrait of American Style," in *Town & Country,* 1 September 1997.

Pittel, Christine, "Tiffany's 20th Century: A Portrait of American Style," in *House Beautiful,* 1 November 1997.

McRee, Lisa, "Treats from Tiffany's," from ABC's *Good Morning America,* 19 November 1997.

Berry, Warren, and Kathy Larkin, "A Bright Time for Gift Ideas," in *Newsday,* 22 November 1998.

Robson, Julia, "Style: Chokers Let Off the Leash," in the *Daily Telegraph,* 11 January 1999.
Papakonstantinou, Irene, "Give Them a Gift with All Your Heart," in the *Toronto Sun,* 9 February 1999.
Woods, Judith, "Features: Cherie's Cry from the Heart is Highlighted in Silver," in the *Daily Telegraph,* 5 May 1999.
Johnson, Marilyn, "In Style Trends, Shows, Shopping, Tips: Peretti, A Jewel in Tiffany's Crown," in the *Atlanta Journal and Constitution,* 30 May 1999.
Stanley, Kathleen, "It's Not the Thought That Counts, It's the Box," in the *Washington Post,* 16 December 1999.
"Chanel's Burning Issue Brings Tears to My Eyes," in the *Toronto Star,* 23 November 2000.
Eldredge, Richard L., "Gifting Braxton," in the *Atlanta Constitution,* 1 May 2001.

* * *

"Style," Elsa Peretti says, "is to be simple"—an ironic statement from a designer described as "the most complicated person I know. She's volatile, explosive, obstinate, and as difficult as any artist trying to achieve perfection"—according to Tiffany's vice president and long-time Peretti colleague, Frank Arcaro (from the *Toronto Star,* 2000). He adds: "But she is also charming and kind and very, very shy."

Peretti can deliver a brusque maxim in her husky voice with a Chanel imperiousness and a Montesquieu-like incisiveness. Her knowledge of style is perhaps so vivid because it comes intuitively from a career in modeling, friendships with fashion designers, interest in sculptural adornment, and a fascination with the crafts that go into jewelry. Her quest is for expressive, perfect form, even if it happens to look imperfect at first. Touch—the hand of making and of holding—is foremost. She has brilliantly expanded the materials and repertory of jewelry, ensuring that it is a modern tradition but also guaranteeing it preserves special crafts of the past. Her art evades any particular place in the world, drawing upon Japanese traditions, surrealism, and modernist design; it is an art so vagrant its only home is in the heart.

Peretti explores nature with a biologist's acumen and an artist's discrimination. The simplicity of her forms resides in the fact that she selects the quintessential form from among those found in nature, never settling on the median or most familiar, but striving for the essence. Her hearts, for instance, are never of a trite Valentine's Day familiarity; rather, they cleave to the hand with shaped, hand-held warmth. That the heart necklace, described by Tiffany's Melvyn Kirtley as "a wonderful free-form heart," hangs "on a woven mesh chain" in asymmetry as the chain passes through the middle, gives it the quirk of love and the aberration of art that Peretti admires. John Loring of Tiffany's and editor of *Tiffany's 20th Century: A Portrait of American Style,* on ABC's *Good Morning America* television show described Peretti's floating heart as "probably [her] best-known piece of jewelry." Additionally, her 18-carat gold mesh bracelet flows like water and "wears like silk," according to her fans.

Reminding us that Chanel never forgot she was a peasant, Peretti too never forgets the simple things of life. Her suite of beans is ineffably ordinary, yet they are extraordinary in their craft, in their scaling to hand, and in their finest materials. Her bottles are common; Peretti transfigures the crude practicality into an elegant simplicity. "The design," said Peretti, "is full of common sense. Of course I'm slow. I have to crystallize a form, find the essence."

In June 1974, Peretti joined Tiffany & Company. That year, her first collection, featuring "sinuous," "sensual," and "sculptural" shapes and forms, debuted, causing a sensation in the accessories world. Sixteen years later, in the 1990 catalogue of *Elsa Perretti: Fifteen of My Fifty with Tiffany,* Richard Martin wrote: "A transcendental aspect haunts Peretti's work; she hints at our affinity to nature even as she plucks the perfect form from the cartload of nature's abundance and art's options. Peretti returns us in her absolute objects to a Garden of Paradise. There, all form has its lingering memory and every shape is the definitive best."

Peretti's sensibility is deeply touched by her professional and personal friendships with Halston and Georgio di Sant'Angelo, no less so after the death of both designers. As a model, Peretti had known both. In 1999 she explained how it all started to the *Atlanta Journal and Constitution,* "In 1969, I found a tiny flower vase in a junk shop and was inspired to design a bottle on a chain for designer Giorgio di Sant'Angelo," from whom Peretti drew a spirit of incorporating regional materials in an aggregate at once a composite of many sources and a refinement of them in modern terms. She went on to design belts for Halston—whose minimalism is a touchstone for Peretti, not only in the opportunity for her demonstrative forms to stand out in the ensemble of such simple luxury in dress but also in the obdurate minimalism of her own design—before joining Tiffany's.

Generous in acknowledging such designers and in expressing her pleasure in cooperating with craftspeople in the fulfillment of her work, Peretti cannot disguise her own remarkable ability, which she sometimes passes off as craft, to distill form and ideas. The sabotage of her belts is that their sources are in the stable, not in haberdashery: Peretti's attention in 1969 to a leather horse girth inspired a belt without mechanisms, working by the unadorned looping to fulfill the function of the belt. Her tableware is fit for a peasant table, before chopsticks or other utensils: she has created the perfect setting for Picasso's *Blind Man's Meal* to transform it to Tiffany grace without ever compromising its rudimentary, manual presence, which is ironic, since her colleague at Tiffany's is none other than Paloma Picasso, daughter of the famous painter. Other Tiffany's colleagues have included Angela Cummings and Jean Schlumberger.

Characteristically, when Peretti confronted diamonds, she flouted convention and offered the affordable—and revolutionary—"Diamonds by the Yard," giving even the desired stone a degree of access and of animation. Of that insouciant success, a landmark of 1970s design, Peretti says modestly, "My objective is to design according to one's financial possibilities." Few would earlier have imagined a leading jewelry designer to come up with such a frank and sensitive view of the product or the consumer. In fact, it is one of Peretti's triumphs to restore to jewelry a vitality it had lost in the 1960s and early 1970s.

"My love for bones has nothing macabre about it," Peretti says. Indeed, Peretti's sensibility is one of unmitigated joy. Her fruits are prime produce; her sea life is a miracle of abundance; her scorpions and snakes are never scary but seem instead to be mementos of exhilaration; her handbags long to be clutched; her angels and crosses evoke respect for religion making it "touchable" by the masses; even her teardrops adapted for earrings, pendants, and even pen clips are never melancholic. They are tears of joy created by a designer who zealously celebrates life, and enjoys it, as evidenced by her "Alphabet," a series of sterling silver pendants in loopy representations of the alphabet.

Her fragrances are no different. For Tiffany, Peretti released a fragrance named after herself, described as "a spicy woodsy fragrance composed of narcissus, wood, magnolia, the Japanese flower, daphne, nutmeg, and pepper." She also designed a beautiful cobalt blue glass heart-shaped paperweight reminiscent of her jewelry hearts; a crystal apple candy dish, which floats like an iridescent bubble on the table; lacquered pens that evoke images of chopsticks and yet can be worn like jewelry; "Thumbprint" pottery bowls and glasses with a very oriental flavor; sterling silver punch ladles; candlesticks and candle snuffers; wine coasters; and many other items.

In 1996 the Council of Fashion Designers of America named her the Accessories Designer of the Year. The same year, one of Peretti's belts showed up in the Jackie Kennedy Onassis estate sale, going, with another belt, for $7,475. Other famous women drawn to Peretti's work include Mona Williams, Diana Vreeland, Gwyneth Paltrow, and Demi Moore. Peretti's career and designs have inspired a whole new generation of accessory designers, including Jennifer Miller, who designs "replica" jewelry in the style of Peretti and others.

—Richard Martin; updated by Daryl F. Mallett

PERRIS, Bernard

French designer

Born: Millau, France, 5 October 1936. **Education:** Studied fashion design at Cours Bazot School. **Career:** Assistant to Marc Bohan, assistant designer, Guy Laroche, 1960–61; designer, Jacques Heim, 1961–63; designer, Dior, 1963; designer, Paul Bon, 1964–69; opened ready-to-wear firm, Bernard Perris Nouvelle Couture, 1969; opened New York shop, 1986; opened two Paris shops, 1988; introduced bridge line, 1989; business closed briefly, reopened, 1992; hired by Jean-Louis Scherrer as head designer, 1994 (later replaced by Stephane Rolland). **Exhibitions:** Musée des Arts Decoratifs, Paris, 1988; Musée de la Mode, Marseille, 1994. **Awards:** Best Fashion Designer, Houston, Texas, 1988; Best Fashion Designer, Tokyo, 1988; Silver Slipper award, Houston, 1995. **Address:** 5 rue de Magdebourg, 75116 Paris, France.

Publications

On PERRIS:

Articles

"International Ethnic is the Big News from Paris," in *WWD,* 19 March 1990.

"Bernard Perris Liquidates Two Main Holding Companies," in *WWD,* 12 July 1991.

"Perris to Reopen with New Partners," in *WWD,* 13 October 1992.

Godfrey, Deeny, "House of Scherrer Names Perris Couture, Ready-to-Wear Designer," in *WWD,* 7 September 1994.

Bernard Perris, fall 1995 collection. © AFP/CORBIS.

Griffin, Linda Gillian, "Not the Retiring Type, Perris Goes Back to the Drawing Board," in the *Houston Chronicle,* 25 May 1995.

Additional articles in *Vogue, L'Officiel, Elle, Figaro, Madame, Town & Country, Harper's Bazaar,* as well as *Joyce* and *Mode x Mode* (both Japan).

*

What has been mainly distinctive of my work…is an atmosphere of high standard elegance with a glance to independence of mind and fun toward "les ideés reçues." I have been many times called the most "couturier" of the "createurs," probably because my line was more a nouvelle couture than a deluxe RTW. As everyone, I have a double personality and am reflecting the influence of the "austerité" and "grandeur" of a Balenciaga, as well as the "glamour," "sexy touch," and "joie de vivre" of a Jacques Fath.

—Bernard Perris

* * *

It has been said that the women's ready-to-wear designs by Parisian Bernard Perris embody the philosophy "more is more." From the moment he opened his own Paris showroom in 1969, Perris favored dramatic, almost theatrical fare, incorporating luxurious fabrics, intricate construction, and extravagant trim into his creations. He was even accused of cramming enough ideas for a dozen dresses into one garment, loading his designs with high voltage, eye-popping details.

As a young boy in the south of France, Perris was strongly influenced by the women's fashions he saw in his mother's ready-to-wear clothing boutique. At age 16, he ventured to Paris, where he eventually was hired as a couture assistant for Guy Laroche. He then went on to design debutante and wedding dresses under the Jacques Heim and Paul Bon labels, where he learned ready-to-wear techniques. After a short stay at Dior, Perris opened his own house and showed his first collection of Nouvelle Couture, a collection based on techniques that allowed him the creative freedom of haute couture but whose prices were accessible to more women.

The designer's fortunes rose and fell precipitously, causing him to suffer bouts of nervous exhaustion and from about 1971–77 he remained out of the fashion spotlight. But as the interest in ethnic revivals and the "hippy look" waned and a renewed taste for glamorous dressing arose toward the end of the 1970s, Perris again emerged, promoting his special brand of opulent ready-to-wear deluxe. His fur-trimmed and embroidered velvets, gathered capes and evening gowns, tiered and ruffled cocktail dresses, and appliqued resort wear garnered a newly appreciative audience, and he opened his own Paris boutique in 1985.

Perris became particularly popular in America, appealing as he did to the big-spending, flashy customer who wanted to be seen in his bold yet high-quality clothing, and he established a Madison Avenue shop in New York. He did not shrink from personally promoting his clothes in the U.S., presenting trunk shows for wealthy buyers from Beverly Hills to Las Vegas and often appearing at in-store events and charity dinners.

Chosen in 1985 by the "Best" committee as one of the 10 most elegant men in the world, Perris created clothing for a high-profile, international clientèle, including several film stars. He designed all the women's costumes for the 1986 film *Max, My Love,* in which actress Charlotte Rampling wore 10 different Bernard Perris ensembles. Clothing from the 1980s stressed strong lines, saturated color, and a kind of dazzling, urban chic—these were powerful clothes made for grand entrances, completely in step with the period's emphasis on wealth and conspicuous consumption.

Later styles found the designer embracing less show-stopping ideas without sacrificing his essential devotion to luxury or glamor, as in his wool daytime suits trimmed with sheared beaver, drapey silk georgette lounging ensembles, cashmere separates, and extravagant accessories. He remained true to his reputation for fabulous eveningwear, however, as seen in his sumptuous 1988 all black-white-and-red collection featuring swaths of fur, rustling silks, and liberal lace trim.

His acceptance into the Chambre Syndicale du Prêt-à-Porter des Couturiers and des Crèateurs de Mode finally validated Bernard Perris' long and fruitful, if uneven, career. In early 1994, he closed his business to regroup after a business partner's retirement, but his absence from the fashion world did not last long. In August of 1994, Perris was appointed as the couture and haute couture designer for the Paris house of Jean-Louis Scherrer. While in the position, Perris received critical praise and expanded his reputation for designing elegant and sumptuous clothing. The Scherrer house was bought by François Barthes in 1997 and Stephane Rolland took over designing in 1998.

—Kathleen Paton; updated by Megan Stacy

PER SPOOK

See SPOOK, Per

PETER HOGGARD

British design firm

Founded: by Michelle Hoggard (born in West Yorkshire, England, 1962) and Peter Leathers (born in Tyneside, England, 1962) in Tyneside, 1983. **Company History:** Sells clothes to local retail outlets; opened own outlet in Hyper Hyper store, London, 1985; first catwalk collection presented at British Fashion Week, London, 1986; opened shop in Rupert Court, London, 1987; established small factory in Yorkshire, England, to manufacture own label, 1987; established retail chain selling own label and other small designer labels, with shops in Leeds and Manchester, England, 1992; label falls from fashion, late 1990s; "Air" home furnishings shops opened by Michelle Hoggard, 2000s. **Awards:** Yorkshire Television Young Business Entrepreneur of the Year, 1985; Fil d'Or Linen award, Paris, 1991.

Publications

On PETER HOGGARD:

Articles

"Fresh Blow to City as Store Quits Its Home," available online at Bradford & District, www. thisisbradford.co.uk, 1 October 2000.

Poole, Suzy, "Good Taste in the Air," available online at Bradford & District, www.thisisbradford.co.uk, 1 October 2000.

* * *

When Oscar Wilde wrote, "One should either wear a work of art or be a work of art," little did he imagine it would one day appear embroidered on the sleeve of a Peter Hoggard jacket. Ideas such as this, not to mention coats made from a Bayeux tapestry print or Peter Rabbit appliqués on skirts, have been a staple of Peter Hoggard collections since their inception in the early 1980s. This was the age of do-it-yourself fashion, street credibility being the latest in media hypes, with style bibles such as *i-D* and *The Face* eagerly documenting the wild and outrageous sartorial antics of British youth.

Amid this heady atmosphere and fueled by their joint passion for clothes and dressing up, Peter Leathers and Michelle Hoggard formed their fashion company, Peter Hoggard. Hoggard explained, "We were both very visual people—I think that's why we were attracted to each other—I made my own clothes while Peter customized his." Their first collection was inspired by Leathers' innovative idea of making couture one-offs from hotel laundry, which were then sold to friends. Big, baggy shirts, each one sprayed with an individual pattern, were customized with de rigueur designer rips and tears. The skirts were spotted by television presenter Leslie Ash when the duo appeared suitably attired on the set of the pop music show *The Tube.* She promptly placed an order, as did guest artist Gary Glitter.

Encouraged, the duo decided to take the bull by the horns and approach the fashion world in a serious and businesslike way. Becoming their own agents, they sold clothes to various retailers through a trunk show. This success led in turn to the opening of their own retail outlets and a stall in Hyper Hyper, the thriving and bustling center for London's young and avant-garde designers in Kensington High Street.

Concentrating on womenswear with strong yet eclectic themes that were both interesting and inspirational to research, Peter Hoggard collections have evolved to embody a sophisticated designer interpretation of street fashion, in tune with the 1990s customer who demanded quality and superb cut. Working in fabrics that often opposed and contradicted—linen and raffia, venetian wool and plastic, waxed cotton piping and rayon—themes have included prints based on dollar and pound signs and ship rigging, which incorporated jackets and sheath dresses with waxed-cotton piped sleeves or inserts. Bomber jackets in plastic with Dada-inspired imagery were appliquéd and reembroidered to create a cornucopia of reference, and crushed velvet minidresses and jackets were trimmed in new age crystal.

Peter Hoggard has been part of a similar breed of talented British designers and design duos emerging in the early 1980s—Bodymap, Richmond/Cornejo, and Mark and Syrie—being contemporaries. Compared to the vast success of international designers such as Gianni Versace or Calvin Klein, Peter Hoggard and company run the risk of being shackled by what Michelle Hoggard calls "the great British disease," being the traditional difficulties smaller designers have with production. When public relations officer Richard Titchner described Peter Hoggard as being "the best kept secret in fashion," his ironic statement served only as a reminder that many talented individuals had to go abroad to be taken seriously as creative designers. Peter Hoggard viewed itself as an endangered species, determined to retain its design integrity and a very English look to its product—and unfortunately, its status was right on the mark. By the end of the 20th century, the Peter Hoggard label was virtually extinct.

The new millennium found Michelle Hoggard, a permanent resident in the West Yorkshire area, still dedicated to a sense of place and distinctive English style. In an interview for the "This is Bradford" website, she discussed her reason for opening two city center housewares stores to offer hard-to-find items. With 14 years in fashion retail and manufacturing behind her, she established the "Air" shops at the Wool Exchange in Bradford to reflect her taste in interior design. "When I bought my new house," she explained, "I was very conscious of wanting to put my own stamp on things, but there wasn't an awful lot around. I started going to trade shows but then I put the focus on smaller items to suit the market."

Hoggard's eye for business saw opportunity in high-end gifts and home decoration. Her shops on Hustlergate and Market streets stocked aromatherapy products, oil burners, picture frames, storage units, table decoration, and clocks. Her criteria for new additions to the household and giftware lines focused on unique global sources such as salt crystal lamps and candleholders from Germany and on items that were both natural and attractive. Her pledge to remain viable in Bradford's business district accompanied the opening of the second Air shop, a boon to a city center hard hit by business reorganizations and closures.

—Kevin Almond; updated by Mary Ellen Snodgrass

PEZZUTTO, Graziella Ronchi

See ERREUNO SCM SpA

PFISTER, Andrea

Italian footwear designer working in Paris

Born: Pesaro, Italy, 30 August 1942. **Education:** Studied art and languages at University of Florence 1960–62, shoe design at Ars Sutoria, Milan, 1962. **Career:** Designed collections for Lanvin, Patou, in Paris, 1963; showed first collection under own label, 1965; opened first shop, Paris, 1967, and began production of own line, 1968; collaborated with Anne Klein, 1973–94; started shoe factory and introduced accessory line (belts, bags, scarves, jewelry), 1974; introduced ready-to-wear line, 1976; introduced lower-priced shoe range, 1990; invented colors and new finishings or prints for the Italian tannery Stefania, from 1990; artistic director of Bruno Magli Shoes since 1993. **Exhibitions:** *Mostra d'epoca della calzatura,* Vigevano, Italy; *Andrea Pfister: Trente ans de création,* (traveling exhibition), Musée International de la Chaussure, Romans, France, 1993–94; UBS-Brugg, Switzerland, 1994; Palazzo degli Affari, Milan, 1994–95; Fashion Institute of Technology, New York, and Bata Shoe Museum, Toronto, 1996; Fashion Institute of Design and Merchandising, Los Angeles, 1998; Fashion Institute of Design and Merchandising, San Francisco, 1999. **Collections:** Metropolitan Museum, New York. **Awards:** Fashion Footwear Association of New York, Gold Medal, 1988; Designer of the Year, 1990 (for Anne Klein); first prize, shoe designer international competition, Amsterdam. **Address:** Viale dei Mille, 47, Vigevano 27029 (PV), Italy.

Publications

On PFISTER:

Books

Liu, Aimee, and Rottman, Meg, *Shoe Time,* New York, 1986.
Trasko, Mary, *Heavenly Soles,* London, 1989.
McDowell, Colin, *Shoes: Fashion and Fantasy,* New York & London, 1989.
Hirmer, S., *Schuhe,* Munich, 1992.
Andrea Pfister: Trente ans de création [exhibition catalogue], Romans, France, 1993.
Mazza, Samuele, *Andrea Pfister,* Milan, 1998.

Articles

"Dateline Milan," in *Footwear News* (New York), 25 March 1985.
"Andrea Pfister," in *Footwear News,* 11 February 1991.
McKay, Deirdre, "Pflights of Pfancy: A Tribute to Andrea Pfister's Creative Passion," in *Footwear News,* 29 January 1996.

McKinney, Melonee, "Shoe Designer Andrea Pfister Does Accessories," in *DNR,* 23 April 1999.
Spindler, Amy, "The Two Gentlemen of Priano," in the *New York Times,* 23 January 2000.
"Pfister Acquired by Italian Fin. Part Group," in *Footwear News,* 5 March 2001.
Articles in *Donna, Grazia, Panorama,* (Italy), October 1993; further articles in *Ars Sutoria,* December 1993; *Mode Pella* January 1994; and *Bazaar Italy,* February 1994.

*

My shoes are feminine, sexy, full of humor and perfectly made. But a shoe cannot only be pretty—it has also to fit, not hurt. Colors, materials and clear lines are very important to me. I love flat heels and very high heels.

—Andrea Pfister

* * *

"If a beautiful woman's feet hurt, she becomes ugly." This is a typically robust statement from a designer whose opulent creations have been variously described as frivolous, witty, and even in dubious taste. Yet the success of his creations depends on the combination of proportion and line with comfort: "I always think shoes should be very feminine and sexy. Compromises are often necessary. It's easy to make wonderful looking shoes, but they also have to fit and be comfortable."

Andrea Pfister's shoes are essentially Italian in their craftsmanship and attention to detail. But there is an element of lightness and irreverence about his creations not usually associated with the traditional shoemaker. He improvises on themes—starry skies, the sea, music, circuses, and Las Vegas—designing shoes such as Martini Dry, with cocktail glass heels supporting slices of lemon. He uses applique motifs, so that when a sandal is called Jazz, it really does have a snakeskin saxophone on the upper.

Another reason for the originality of his work may be that unlike most footwear designers, Pfister is a colorist. Twice a year, he retreats for two months to prepare new collections. The starting point is always color, then he works on shape, proportion, and styling. He is involved with several tanneries, creating seasonal color charts and matching colors in diverse materials such as reptile and suede as a basis for his collections. Pfister's commitment to color also explains his copious use of ornamentation. Jewels, sequins, and glitter catch the light bouncing color off upper and heel as the shoes trip lightly along. The fullest ranges of materials are used to create the desired effects. He will use sumptuous handcrafted embroidery and silks and yet is equally at home with plastics and paste stones.

Despite the occasional jokiness of his themes, the shoes are true couture creations. Pfister has always been a couturier; he began his career at the top with Lanvin and Jean Patou at the age of 21. More recently, he created shoes for Italian dress designer Mariuccia Mandeli, whose Krizia collections are also often quirky, and for the Bruno Magli label. Pfister's business has evolved as well; in 2001 his company was acquired by Fin. Part Group, allowing the designer to retain creative control while reaching new markets.

Like all original designers, his ideas were plundered by others. Snakeskin, a favorite material, was used in multicolored patches over white kidskin on a court shoe called Mosaique. This style, from the early 1980s, is instantly recognizable because it has been copied so often. His most famous style must be the Birdcage shoe of 1979. This was a closed-back, opened-toed flat pump, with the main body constructed in an open latticework of thin leather straps. It spawned millions of copies. Its final form, far removed from the finely crafted snakeskin original, is as a molded plastic beach shoe. Pfister's style in his later collections became less ornate and subtler. Even as his personal style continues to evolve, museums across the globe have hosted retrospectives of his work, honoring his enduring influence and originality.

Pfister diversified into handmade handbags, scarves, leatherwear, gloves, neckwear, and even picture frames, but remains committed to producing beautiful shoes. His attitude toward fashion is relaxed. Pfister styles complement current trends but can also stand alone. He looks for this independence in his customers, including stars from Elizabeth Taylor to Madonna. For him the client is "the woman who mixes different pieces—an Armani top, for instance, with a Donna Karan skirt, and a jacket by Ferré. My shoes work best on the woman who's sure enough of herself to create her own combination."

Andrea Pfister creates truly original footwear; though it may not be fashionable in a trendsetting sense. It may not always appeal to the mainstream idea of good taste, but the styles are extraordinary, often eccentric, and frequently enchanting, making him one of the most innovative designers of footwear.

—Chris Hill; updated by Megan Stacy

PICASSO, Paloma

French designer

Born: Paris, France, 19 April 1949, daughter of Pablo Picasso and Françoise Gilot. **Education:** Attended University of Paris, Sorbonne, and University of Nanterre; studied jewelry design and fabrication. **Family:** Married Rafael Lopez-Cambil (aka Lopez-Sanchez), 1978. **Career:** Fashion jewelry designer for Yves Saint Laurent, 1969; designed jewelry for Zolotas, 1971; designed costumes and sets for Lopez-Cambil's Parisian productions *L'Interprétation,* 1975 and *Success,* 1978; teamed with Lopez-Cambil to create Paloma Picasso brand, including jewelry for Tiffany & Company, from 1980; introduced fragrance and cosmetics line, 1984; designed men's and women's accessories for Lopez-Cambil, Ltd., 1987; began designing fabrics and wall coverings for Motif, 1993; celebrated 20 years with Tiffany, 2000; designed hosiery for Grupo Synkro; eyewear for Carrera; bone china, crystal, silverware, and tiles for Villeroy & Boch; household linens for KBC; Paloma Picasso boutiques throughout Europe, and in Japan and Hong Kong; fragrances include: *Paloma,* 1984; *Minataure,* 1992; *Tentations,* 1996. **Award:** MODA award for design excellence, 1988. **Address:** Lopez-Cambil Ltd., 37 West 57th Street, New York, NY 10019 USA.

Publications

By PICASSO:

Books

Paloma Picasso: Galleria d'Arte Cavour, with Roberto Sanesi, Milan, 1972.

Paloma Picasso in 1985. © Bettmann/CORBIS.

Designwelt Paloma Picasso (The Design World of Paloma Picasso), with Wilhelm Siemen, Hoccheim, Germany, 1997.

On PICASSO:

Books

Mulvagh, Jane, *Costume Jewelry in Vogue,* London, 1988.
Stegemeyer, Anne, *Who's Who in Fashion, Third Edition,* New York, 1996.
Loring, John, *Tiffany's 20th Century: A Portrait of American Style,* New York, 1997.

Articles

Irvine, Susan, "Paloma's Pink Period," in the *Sunday Express* magazine (London), 7 August 1988.
Fusco, Ann Castronovo, "Paloma's Classic Touch," in *House Beautiful* (London), February 1989.
Samuel, Kathryn, "The Look That Says Picasso," in the *Daily Telegraph* (London), 7 September 1989.
Beckett-Young, Kathleen, "Design for Living," in *Working Woman* (New York), October 1990.
Gandee, Charles, "Paloma Picasso Has Mass Appeal," in *House & Garden,* November 1990.
Stern, Ellen, "The Prolific Paloma," in *House Beautiful* (London), March 1992.
Landis, Dylan, "Paloma Picasso's Signature Style," in *Metropolitan Home* (New York), September/October 1993.
Gendel, Debra, "With a Red Kiss, Picasso Tours," in the *Los Angeles Times,* 13 August 1993.
Jolis, Alan, "Matisse, Picasso, Disney, and Paloma: Paloma Picasso Talks About Life With—and Without—Her Father," in *ARTnews,* November 1996.
Nightengale, Cyndi Y., "Wall Falls," in the *Los Angeles Times,* 2 May 1998.
"Paloma Picasso," in the *Los Angeles Times,* November 1998.
Ceballos, Chris, "Focus: Orange County Community News," in the *Los Angeles Times,* 26 August 1999.
Musselman, Faye, "The Softer Side of Paloma Picasso," in *HFN (Home Furnishings Network),* 20 March 2000.
Hessen, Wendy, "Tiffany Celebrates 20 Paloma Years," in *WWD,* 2 October 2000.
"Charles Tiffany's 'Fancy Goods' Shop and How It Grew," from the *Biography Resource Center,* the Gale Group, 2001.
"Paloma Picasso," from the *Biography Resource Center,* the Gale Group, 2001.

* * *

With such a name, one could hardly fail to be noticed. And since her marriage, her name has an even more exotic ring—Paloma Picasso Lopez-Sanchez. The daughter of Pablo Picasso, however, is undoubtedly a personality and exciting talent in her own right. Visually arresting with striking features, she always wore bright red lipstick to emphasize her white skin and thick, black hair; when she reached her fifties, however, she no longer cared for such scrutiny and wore less noticable cosmetics. "For 20 years, I put it on every day," Picasso told Faye Musselman of the Home Furnishings Network's weekly newspaper, *HFN,* in March 2000. "When I was younger, I wanted to make an impression, to look older. But now that I've turned 50, I obviously don't want to look older anymore."

Picasso has, however, continued to be a newsworthy and photogenic participator in the world's fashion circuit—and not because she is the daughter of Pablo Picasso. Picasso *fille* has earned her reputation through a myriad of creations, from fragrances, bath and body products, and cosmetics to sought-after jewelry and home furnishings.

Picasso was born and educated in Paris. Formally trained as a jewelry designer, her interest was possibly kindled by childhood memories of the glass beads seen on the island of Murano in Venice and an early fascination with sparkling colors. Initially, she was involved in costume design for the theater, where her originality and exotic pieces attracted much attention. An invitation from Yves Saint Laurent to create a collection of jewelry for his couture house ensured that her work was widely seen, and in 1972 her gold designs for the Greek company Zolotas achieved further recognition and acclaim.

In 1980 Picasso began designing jewelry for Tiffany & Company of New York, the legendary jeweler. Her early creations mixed color and varying gemstones in bold designs, demonstrating a modernity and panache that singled them out as something special. Her name (meaning "dove") and the color red were long used as essential ingredients of her work. Picasso's also began experimenting with fragrance, creating the very successful and distinctive *Paloma,* with its dynamic red and black packaging and strikingly shaped bottle. Described by its creator as "jewelry for the senses," the floral, wood, and amber scent was formulated in 1984 along with a cosmetics and bath line including body lotion, powder, shower gel, and soap.

The year 2000 marked a time for commemoration and change for Picasso. She had stopped wearing her trademark red lipstick, and underwent an artistic transformation as well. Her home furnishings collections, consisting of wallpaper and fabrics, had always been awash in bold, vibrant colors. But the new patterns and colors available in 2000 were softened and subtle, especially in a shimmering silk collection awash in silvery-grays, blues and greens. Moreover, there was more emphasis on texture and less on pattern.

While Picasso's jewelry has been available in the U.S. since the 1980s, her home accessories collections (except for a stint in linens) were sold in Europe. In the new millenium, however, the designer considered broadening both her product line and market. Style for the home, she commented to HFN's Musselman, "has become the new fashion statement. People are spending [much] more time thinking about their surroundings." Like a true connoisseur, though, she eschewed trends. "I don't like fashion that changes every six months. It's like the icing on the cake—but you still have to have a very good cake." Picasso's designs, whether for the body or its environment, continue to evolve.

—Margo Seaman; updated by Kimbally A. Medeiros

PIGUET, Robert

Swiss/French designer

Born: Yverdon, Switzerland, 1901; immigrated to France, 1918. **Education:** Trained as a banker; studied fashion design under Redfern and Paul Poiret, 1918–28. **Career:** Founded own fashion house, 1933; sold designs by Dior, Balmain, Bohan, Givenchy, and Galanos; introduced perfume, *Bandit,* 1944, then *Fracas,* both of which remained successful for years; retired and closed his business, 1951. **Died:** 22 February 1953, in Lausanne.

Publications

On PIGUET:

Books

McDowell, Colin, *McDowell's Directory of Twentieth Century Fashion,* Englewood Cliffs, NJ, 1985.

O'Hara, Georgina, *The Encyclopaedia of Fashion,* New York, 1986.

Stegemeyer, Anne, *Who's Who in Fashion, Third Edition,* New York, 1996.

* * *

Robert Piguet headed his own couture house for nearly two decades, and the years were the culmination if not the sum of his career in fashion. He learned his craft in two of the more important houses of the early 20th century, Poiret and Redfern. Both houses were fashionable and influential, but they espoused widely divergent philosophies of fashion and appealed to very different customers. In developing his own style, Piguet combined the imagination and awareness of Poiret at his peak with the quality and stability of Redfern. The resulting look was youthful but not girlish; the clothes echoed, flattered, and enhanced the body beneath them. There was an essential effortless wearability to garments from Piguet, which the vantage point of more than half a century has neither diminished nor obscured.

Design by Robert Piguet, 1937. © Austrian Archives/CORBIS.

Like Poiret, Piguet understood and employed the links between high fashion and the arts. His collections often reflected his sensitivity to the cultural environment of the moment. An example is his response to the historical romanticism of the 1930s, an important movement fed by theatrical and motion picture costume dramas. These provided Piguet with inspiration for everything from suits to evening gowns. Particularly notable was the spring 1936 collection, which featured high, gathered-sleeve caps, bold up-flaring collars, or wide shoulder yokes based on 16th century modes used in the hit play *Margot.*

Just a short time later, during the early years of World War II, Piguet produced collections with a different, darker mood, influenced by political circumstances. In these, models were accessorized with such wartime essentials as gas masks, or given topical names referring to the realities and hardships of wartime life. Even his fabric choices reflected his surroundings. In 1945 Piguet joined many fellow Paris designers in the Théâtre de la Mode. With an eye to the scarcities and rationing of the immediate postwar years he used synthetics for several of his models.

No matter what Piguet's mood or inspiration, however, his creations always remained clothing, and never descended into costume—or they would now be considered camp, not classic. Some of Piguet's most timeless designs include the post-New Look evening dresses which harkened back to the romantic silhouettes he used in the 1930s. These were in sync with his contemporaries, but, in a way, cleaner, with less ornamentation.

Since several different designers worked for Piguet, it is difficult to isolate elements of cut or construction as hallmarks of his house. There was, instead, an overarching impression of ease, comfort, and femininity. Piguet clothes, however fitted, never seemed to constrict or restrict the wearer. Allowance was made for movement: a narrow waist expanding into pleats or gathers above or below, a sheath skirt topped by a dolman-sleeved bodice. Tailored garments were rarely hard-edged; the severity of a pleated shirtwaist dress was mitigated by a short, cascading bolero top. Slim suit-skirts might be side draped sarong-style, or pegged with a gathered waistline; jackets could have rounded peak lapels, or tulip hems. Even a post-liberation suit, styled on the lines of an Allied forces military police uniform, had a shawl collar, long gloves crushed around the wrists, and white detailing to lift the khaki linen outfit out of the masculine realm.

It might be said that Piguet's most lasting contributions to postwar fashion were the designers he employed and encouraged. Dior, Givenchy, and Balmain each worked for or sold designs to Piguet in the 1930s and 1940s, and went on to open houses of their own. Whether Piguet hired them because an inherent romanticism in their work agreed with his fashion sense, or they learned from him traits which each would use to advantage in his own business is not a matter of record. Piguet's wisdom in choosing able designers, however, was more than matched by his skill in maintaining the identity of his house and collections, no matter who produced the actual sketches.

All Piguet's clothes provide distinction without constraint, and comfort without disorder. The fashions he fostered bespoke a mature editorial talent, ranging freely with his times and of his times. After retiring due to health problems in 1951, Piquet died two years later in Lausanne, Switzerland.

—Madelyn Shaw

PIPART, Gérard

French fashion designer

Born: Near Paris, 25 December 1933. **Education:** Studied at the École de la Chambre Syndicale de la Couture Parisienne. **Career:** Began selling sketches to Balmain and Jacques Fath; sketched for Marc Bohan and Givenchy; became chief designer for Nina Ricci, from 1963; freelanced for London's Germaine et Jane, Jean Baillie-Itemcey, and Chloé. **Awards:** De d'Or, or Golden Thimble, for best couture collection, 1987; National Knight Cross Badge, 1995.

Publications

On PIPART:

Books

Lambert, Eleanor, *World of Fashion: People, Places, Resources,* New York, 1976.

McDowell, Colin, *McDowell's Directory of Twentieth Century Fashion,* New Jersey, 1985.

O'Hara, Georgina, *The Encyclopaedia of Fashion,* New York, 1986.

Skrebneski, Victor, *The Art of Haute Couture,* New York, 1995.

Stegemeyer, Anne, *Who's Who in Fashion, Third Edition,* New York, 1996.

Articles

"Ricci Cruise," in *WWD,* 6 July 1990.

"Gianfranco's Couture Chic Revs Up Dior," in *WWD,* 29 January 1991.

Deeny, Godfrey, "Ricci's Pipart: Staying Power," in *WWD,* 26 January 1995.

Menkes, Suzy, "Divine Madness: Galliano True to Himself at Dior Debut," in the *International Herald Tribune,* 21 January 1997.

"New York: A Delicate Balance," in *WWD,* 16 February 2001.

"Alta Costura vs. Prêt-â-Porter," available online at Tendencia.com, www.tendencia.com 20 August 2001.

"Gerard Pipart," available online at International Culture Festival, www.sh.com, 20 August 2001.

Gérard Pipart, designed for the house of Nina Ricci's 1995 collection. © AFP/CORBIS.

Gérard Pipart, designed for the house of Nina Ricci's spring 1965 "Java" collection: linen with a shantung bodice. © Bettmann/CORBIS.

* * *

Before the age of 30, Gérard Pipart had become the most vital women's ready-to-wear designer in Paris. His clothes were already great sellers abroad. He made his mark with snappy, colorful sportswear, well-tailored, detailed, and with a deceptively casual simplicity that only good seams and a fine cut can guarantee. He became known for his inspired use of fabrics, as he skillfully manipulated every material he chose into amusing, wearable chic. His work as a freelancer at Chloé and other houses gained him widespread visibility, and he was hired by Nina Ricci in 1963 to replace designer Jules-François Crahay. His move to Nina Ricci's Haute Couture Studio was closely watched, and indeed, the young, fresh-faced designer brought new life to Ricci with his lively, youthful designs.

As a young designer, Pipart considered Balenciaga an important influence and greatly admired the designs of Norell. His background as an assistant at Balmain, Fath, and with Marc Bohan at Patou gave him a solid grounding in haute couture before he became a bright young star in ready-to-wear and then back again to couture. His couture collections have included elegant daytime wear, sumptuous coats, extravagant evening looks, furs, and bridal wear. Early collections focused on supple lines and a fit close to the body without being overly confining, and his clothes were praised as "never, never too haute." Later collections investigated the long, languid lines of the bias-cut dress, played with loose, theatrical capes, feminized the culotte for daytime wear, and toyed with 1940s and 1950s retro looks.

His penchant for no-holds-barred glamor can be seen in evening dresses of frothy chiffon and bright, opulent taffeta, long-waisted and cinched, with high trumpet sleeves and luxuriant folds billowing to the floor, or exquisite embroideries requiring hundreds of hours of work. He dared to defy the "bride wore white" norm with his design for a Provençal-printed, multicolored mélange of a bridal dress, wrapped at the waist with a wide cummerbund, topped with a short jacket splashed with rhinestones. Fur trim, feathered hats, ruffles, lace, long gloves—Pipart has never shied away from a certain feminine, Parisian elegance in his designs and use of accessories.

His 1990s collections included bright, crisp cruise wear, including short skirts and swimsuits with matching floor-length skirts in shades of hot orange, fuschia, and kelly green. Fabrics ranged from cotton pique and satin to embroidered linen and cotton jersey, affording comfortable and cheerful warm-weather looks. Other collections have highlighted pleats, with pastel skirts under pleated safari jackets for day and long iridescent taffeta dresses for evening. Pipart also received praise for his white linen suits and two-toned, draped crêpe dresses.

Not really an innovator, Pipart's strength at Ricci has been his ability to take stock of fashion trends throughout each season and then to imbue them with freshness and youthfulness without sacrificing his unerring sense of French good taste. Pipart earned much respect in the early 1990s for his three decades as Nina Ricci's couturier designer of classic, ultrafeminine costumes. Reminiscing of the mid-1960s, he recalled, "I was only thirty, young and full of new ideas, so it was all pretty different and I had to adjust." He numbered among his fans the queens of Thailand and Norway, Grand Duchess Josephine-Charlotte of Luxembourg, Marcella Perez de Cuellar, and Mai Hallingby.

Looking back with pride in his staying power, Pipart admitted that he was initially hesitant to throw in with Ricci. Of the flux of the fashion world, he remarked, "I'm amazed I stayed so long. When I arrived everyone was predicting the death of couture, so I was keen to get in for what were meant to be the final few years." Marking his 30th anniversary, he showed a collection of multicolored caftans and harem pants, ostrich plumes, and pleated column shapes with bustiers or lace bodies, his homage to impressionist painter Eugene Delacroix. He stated his objective: "My goal is to make a woman beautiful. In the evening, it's a great pleasure when a woman makes a man happy, hopefully in my clothes." By 1997 the irrepressibly romantic Pipart was off in poufs of pink taffeta. Of his elevation of women into birds of style, Suzy Menkes of the *International Herald Tribune* remarked, "His polished technique is at its best in floaty evening dresses as fine as a mille-feuille pastry and twice as sweet."

—Kathleen Paton; updated by Mary Ellen Snodgrass

PLATT, Johnathan

See ALLY CAPELLINO

POLLEN, Arabella

British designer

Born: London, England, 21 June 1961. **Education:** Self-taught in design. **Family:** Married Giacomo Algranti, 1985 (separated, 1992); children: Jesse, Sam. **Career:** Worked as a personal assistant in advertising and on film scripts in France, 1979–81; established own business, Arabella Pollen, Inc., 1981; introduced Pollen B diffusion range, 1992; ceased trading, 1993; freelance hosiery designer, Courtaulds Textiles, for Aristoc, Rech, and Lyle & Scott, 1993. **Address:** 8 Canham Mews, Canham Road, London W3 7SR, England.

Publications

On POLLEN:

Articles

Wansell, Geoffrey, "Buzz about Miss Pollen," in the *Sunday Telegraph Magazine* (London), 5 June 1983.

Modlinger, Jackie, "Bella la Bella," in the *Daily Express* (London), 14 July 1985.

Jobey, Liz, "Designing Women," in *Vogue* (London), July 1987.

Samuel, Kathryn, "Pollen: A Success Story Not to Be Sneezed At," in the *Daily Telegraph* (London), 14 December 1987.

"Soul Sister," in the *Sunday Times Magazine* (London), 6 May 1990.

Haggard, Claire, "Getting an Education in the Borders," in the *Independent* (London), 26 May 1990.

Smith, Liz, "In Her Own Image," in the *Times* (London), 3 July 1990.

Tredre, Roger, "A Designer Prepared to Meet Her Maker," in the *Independent,* 11 August 1990.

Collier, Andrew, "Pollen's Body English: A British Designer Puts Her Own Twist on the Classics," in *WWD,* September 1990.

Smith, Liz, "Putting New Faith in Pollen," in the *Times* [Saturday Review,] 27 October 1990.

Armstrong, Lisa, "Stuff the Purple Satin Tabards! It's Pollen B, Honey!" in the *Independent,* 20 February 1992.

Morris, Bernadine, "A Reality Check for British Designers," in the *Dallas Morning News,* 25 March 1992.

Flett, Scarth, "Arabella Pollen," in the *Observer Magazine* (London), 23 February 1993.

"Textiles Giant Axes Designer Fashion Firm," in the *Independent,* 20 May 1993.

Samuel, Kathryn, "From Cheers to Tears for Arabella Pollen Label," in the *Daily Telegraph,* 20 May 1993.

Fallon, James, "Arabella Pollen Closes Business," in *WWD,* 20 May 1993.

"New York: A Delicate Balance," in *WWD,* 16 February 2001.

"Arabella Pollen," available online in the *Vogue* Archives, www.cntraveller.co.uk, 20 August 2001.

* * *

Arabella Pollen established a reputation as the bold colorist of British fashion. She became known for her snappy, classic, and wearable suits that were always trimmed with witty and unexpected touches—braid, velvet, or combinations of vivid orange, turquoise, and pink on a black jacket shape. Her special occasion wear was described by Harvey Nichols' buying director Amanda Verdan as "brilliant, perfect and never fuddy duddy." Traditional gold laces were made into slinky, long-sleeved tunics teamed with matching hot pants; short shifts of scarlet sequins were edged with pink velvet and wrapped in hooded velvet robes.

Pollen entered the world of fashion without formal training in design. She had hated drawing and sewing as a child but started making clothes for herself and friends at the age of 19. She found that she could survive on the money her clothes were making and began to expand. After designing and making a collection of clothes based on the hunting styles of the early 1900s, she showed the clothes to the wealthy publisher Naim Attallah, who was impressed by her enthusiasm and talent and agreed to provide financial backing.

Pollen's customers have tended to be like herself: young, energetic, with a relaxed style. She realized quickly to survive she had to find an identifiable look that was innovative but not too daring. She recognized there was a niche for chic elegant sportswear, telling the *Sunday Telegraph Magazine* in June 1983, "I try to do clothes that you can more or less slum around in, but that look elegant at the same time." The look instantly appealed to a particular group of upper-class women and their daughters christened by the press as "Sloane Rangers." Diana, the late Princess of Wales, was one of Pollen's first customers, wearing a number of her well-cut tweeds and dresses from her early collections. This proved a great publicity coup for the young designer and convinced Attallah he had made a wise investment.

Pollen was often her own best advertisement for the clothes, inspiring an affinity between designer and customer by incorporating many of her designs into her own personal wardrobe. This image was strengthened when she agreed to be photographed in the clothes she designed for the fashion manufacturers Windsmoor. The company recognized in Pollen a designer with a strong identity who could adapt her style to updating the Windsmoor image. Although Windsmoor suffered from its overly genteel reputation in the early 1980s, Pollen's youthful styles sharpened the company's identity and boosted sales.

In 1990 Courtaulds Textiles bought a minority stake in Pollen's business, a link that gave her the resources to make a huge international impact. Unfortunately, while sales grew rapidly in the UK, this was not the case in other parts of the world. After reviewing the situation, both parties felt it was inappropriate at this stage to provide further resources, and Arabella Pollen Ltd. announced that it had ceased trading in May 1993, though Pollen retained her link with Courtaulds as a design consultant.

As a woman designing for women, Pollen proved she had no preconceived ideas about what women wanted to wear. Wearing the clothes herself gave her insight into how women actually felt about them, their likes and dislikes—a major contribution to fashion that was accompanied by close attention to detail, quality, cut, and fit. An independent spokeswoman for women, Pollen had summarized her outlook years before in *Vogue,* stating: "I think modern women are tired of being dictated to by faddish whimsy. Fashion should be alive, expressing, not swamping, personality." From designing for the Princess of Wales and earning £1.2 million in 1990 at the top of her form, Pollen departed the first phase of her career to serve as design consultant for Courtaulds, including hosiery by Aristoc, Rech, and Lyle & Scott.

—Kevin Almond; updated by Mary Ellen Snodgrass

POLO

See LAUREN, Ralph

POMODORO, Carmelo

American designer

Born: New York, 20 March 1956. **Education:** Studied painting, then fashion design at Parsons School of Design, New York, graduated in 1978. **Career:** Assistant to designers Ralph Lauren, Stan Herman, and Bill Haire, mid-1970s to 1981; showed first collection, working from home, 1981; designer, Betty Hanson company, New York, 1982–86; established Carmelo Pomodoro Design Studio, Inc. for freelance work, 1985; formed Carmelo Pomodoro Sportswear, Ltd., 1986; introduced lower priced line, 1987, and line of bodywear, 1991; licenses included jewelry, from 1989, furs, from 1990, and Toyota sportswear line, from 1990; first of seven Carmelo Pomodoro boutiques, joint ventures with Takashima Company, opened in Tokyo, 1989; dressed television commentators for Winter Olympics, 1992. **Died:** 1 October 1992, in New York.

Publications

On POMODORO:

Books

Milbank, Caroline Rennolds, *New York Fashion: The Evolution of American Style,* New York 1989.

Ewing, Elizabeth, *History of Twentieth Century Fashion,* New York 1992.

Articles

Buck, Genevieve, "Two 'Overnight Successes' Spring Forth—With 26 Years Between Them," in *Chicago Tribune,* 22 July 1987.

Behbehani, Mandy, "Young, Hip Believers in Affordable Fashion," in the *San Francisco Examiner,* 26 June 1990.

Hayes, Tracy Achor, "Young Designers with Big Potential," in the *Dallas Morning News,* 3 October 1990.

Hix, Charles, "The 'Hot Tomato' of Cornwall Hollow: Fashion Designer Carmelo Pomodoro Carves High-Profile Niche with His Forward Fashions," in the *Litchfield County Times* (Connecticut), 22 February 1991.

———, "Carmelo Pomodoro," in *Collections Tokyo-New York,* Spring/Summer 1991.

White, Constance C.R., "Sportswear Report SCOOP," in *WWD,* 25 September 1991.

Blissard, Mardi, "Autumn Fashions on the Runway at Bolo Bash IV—New York Designer Carmelo Pomodoro," in the *Arkansas Times,* 11 June 1992.

Lambert, Bruce, "Carmelo Pomodoro, 37, Designer Who Led New York Fashion Firm," [obituary] in the *New York Times,* 2 October 1992.

White, Constance C.R., "Carmelo Pomodoro Dead at 37: Energetic and Talented, He Helped Lead Young Designer Pack," in *WWD,* 2 October 1992.

* * *

The November 1992 cover of *Harper's Bazaar* was redesigned at the last moment to pay homage to one of the most promising fashion designers of his generation, Carmelo Pomodoro. The cover spoke gently of Pomodoro's œuvre—an elegant neo-1930s-type woman wearing an ivory colored chenille open-work gridded robe. The words describing this image were soft, sensual, and just a little bit Hollywood. From his first independent collection in 1987, it was clear Pomodoro had an unclassifiable sense of style that was at once romantic yet ruthlessly contemporary.

Pomodoro had thought of becoming an actor, an architect, and a painter, before discovering his natural affinity for the fashion arts through the guidance of Frank Rizzo, chairman of the fashion design department at Parsons School of Design, New York. After stints with Stan Herman, Ralph Lauren, Bill Haire, and Betty Hanson, Pomodoro established his own design studio in 1985 where he carried out freelance projects. With characteristic good energy and optimism he started Carmelo Pomodoro Sportswear Ltd., and produced a collection in 1986. His business partner John P. Axelrod supported Pomodoro's career, even after it received substantial Japanese backing.

His first signature collection was memorable and indicative of his greatest strengths as a designer. What could be called "the white resort collection" of 1987, featured drapy fabric, simple lines, and virtually no color. Akin to the paintings of Agnes Martin, the fabrics of Pomodoro's collection revealed subtle and delicate details at close range. The textures of his unusual fabric blends, or the quiet wit of an almost surreal self-scarf sweater, characterized his ability to balance artistic self-consciousness with a paradoxical sense of reverence and fun. This blend resulted in perhaps the best-ever designed trapeze tunic from the same collection, which seemingly floated over a tight tube skirt.

Throughout his all too brief career, Pomodoro continued to develop this series of women in white, and these were arguably his most successful artistic and commercial fashions. From the eggshell cotton crochet cover-up, both a tribute to the 1960s and an avant-garde prefiguration of the 1993 crochet craze, from his resort 1990 collection, to virginal white cotton organza overshirts and cotton silk lace tank dresses also appearing that year, Pomodoro brought forth inspirational designs that made women feel and project their most beautiful selves. Whether or not his attraction to monochromatic compositions came from his skills as a black-and-white photographer (he did much of the photography for his company's advertising campaigns himself), it is clear this propensity distinguished him among other artists of his generation such as Charlotte Neuville, Zang Toi, Jennifer George, and Rebecca Moses.

If white was his best noncolor, knitted fabric was his best medium for making art (dresses). A master technician, he understood not only pattern making and construction but also his materials. In knitting, with its ability to hold a shape, to drape, to cling, and to stretch, Pomodoro gave his designs a comfort quotient not possible from any other technique. What made his knits extraordinary was the mixture of mostly natural fibers, with a minuscule amount of the newest microfibers developed for him in Japan.

Softness permeated Pomodoro's work, even his much heralded leather designs. His use of leather, which he considered a very modern no-fuss fabric, was at times biker-chic but usually tempered when paired with flowing double-layered georgette short skirts or pastel leggings. The fall 1992 line featured a leather bathrobe coat mixed with fake fur, and jackets that gracefully followed the natural contour of the torso. Menswear collections developed as adjunct to the women's lines, but the intellectually savvy androgyny of his men's sleeveless undershirt with sequined evening skirt of 1992 reminds us that Carmelo Pomodoro was a gifted thinker with a lot to say about our sartorial lives.

Pomodoro's last collection was inspired by one of the world's most alluring women, Sophia Loren. A blend of camel hair and velvet pieces, the tailored glamor was eroticized by the leopard prints in the form of scarves, vests, and blouses. The look conjured up images of Rome, and the *dolce vita* of Federico Fellini. The formal elements, however—the colors, lines, and fabrics—were of-the-moment and Pomodoro world view.

Carmelo Pomodoro's love of the female was paramount. He demonstrated an uncanny knack for knowing how to interpret the ideal dress for his clients, women 25 to 45, part girl, part femme fatale, self-assured. The power of his clothing was its emotional connection to its designer. Early in his career he said, "If women wear my fashions and smile, I'll be happy." Mission accomplished summa cum laude.

—Marianne T. Carlano; updated by Nelly Rhodes

PORTER, Thea

British designer

Born: Dorothea Naomi Seale in Jerusalem, 24 December 1927; raised in Damascus, Syria. **Education:** Studied French and Old English at London University, 1949–50; studied art at Royal Holloway College, Egham, Surrey. **Family:** Married Robert Porter, 1953 (divorced, 1967); children: Venetia. **Career:** Lived in Beirut, 1953–early 1960s; established Greek Street, Soho, boutique selling textiles from the Near East and clothing of her own design, 1967–69; also maintained a shop in Paris, 1976–79; in-store Thea Porter boutique created at Henri Bendel, New York, 1969; freelance fashion, textile and interior designer, London, from 1969. **Awards:** English Fashion Designer of the Year award, 1972. **Died:** 24 July 2000 in London.

Publications

On PORTER

Articles

"Thea Porter to Design Knitwear," in the *Times* (London), 1 April 1973.
"Back to Bakst," in the *Times,* 18 December 1973.
"Dressed to Vote," in the *Times,* 8 September 1974.
"Porterama," in the *Times,* 21 September 1975.
McColl, Patricia, "Couture Arabesque," in *Aramco World* (New York), March/April 1977.
Shapiro, Harriet, "In Style: Porter," in *People,* 9 January 1978.
Gibb, Frances, "Top Fashion Designers to Go Out of Business," in the *Times,* 5 February 1981.
"Thea Porter is Back," in the *Times,* 18 July 1982.

Trebay, Guy, "Thea Porter, 72; Dressed the Elite of the 1960s in Hippie Chic," in the *New York Times,* 27 July 2000.
Obituary, "Thea Porter, Designer, 72," in *WWD,* 28 July 2000.
"Deaths Last Week," [obituary], in *Chicago Tribune,* 30 July 2000.

* * *

Having lived in the Middle East as a child, Thea Porter based her fashion aesthetic upon the ethnic clothing she encountered there. During the late 1960s, fashion revolutions of many kinds were taking place, one of which was the new romanticism mirroring the romantic view of the East common to Victorian England. Hippie types went to Porter's store in Greek Street, London, to purchase Middle Eastern imports to decorate their homes, true to the spirit of 19th-century artists who created a complete atmosphere in their immediate environment that included loose aesthetic robes echoing distant lands and other time periods. Porter's shop offered pillows and cushions made from fancy Middle Eastern textiles as well as antique caftans. These dresses sold so well that Porter began to design them herself to meet the demand.

An ancient, loosely cut ankle-length garment, the caftan lent itself to opulent decoration and luxurious fabrics. Porter's evening gowns were made from silks, brocades, velvets, even crêpe de chine and filmy chiffon, embellished with metallic embroidery and spangles or braid. While not strictly native costume reproductions, the caftans captured the spirit of mysterious harem allure. Wealthy international clients like Elizabeth Taylor, Raquel Welch, Charlotte Rampling, Barbra Streisand, and Iranian royalty comprised Porter's clientèle, as much for the exoticism of the clothes, as no doubt for the comfort. Porter had long admired Arabic clothing, entranced by the rich embroideries and fabrics, in shapes producing a protected and secure feeling of being able to hide in one's clothes while feeling like a princess, in the richness of execution of her romantic fantasies.

Porter's nostalgic sensibilities also extended toward the Renaissance and the Edwardian periods. During the 1970s she offered high-waisted midi- or maxi-dresses with voluminous sleeves. These simple historic shapes also lent themselves to luxurious brocades, tapestries, velvets, and embroidery. Her Edwardian looks featured vintage trimmings, and sailor-collared or lacy dresses recalling the last days of the Imperial Russian Grand Duchesses. Porter claimed Chekhov as an influence as well as art déco. Gypsy dresses with their full-flounced skirts allowed for romantic play of colorful patterned fabrics. Again, the shapes were easy, flattering.

Much as Poiret brought Eastern exoticism to a turbulent era, so Porter reflected rapid fashion change toward individuality, coupled with comforting escapism. Even her knit collection, developed for the chilly English climate, included caftan-type dresses, skirt and cardigan sets, and culottes in bright, cheerful colors. By the 1980s Porter had dressed many well-known personalities in her couture and expensive ready-to-wear, including members of the Beatles and Rolling Stones, Donovan, Princess Margaret, and Jessye Norman. Her designs allowed the expression of artistic inclinations, while giving the wearer a shield from the too-scrutinizing eyes of the public.

In the 1990s the Porter look was found in secondhand stores and as with most fashions of earlier decades, enjoyed a bit of a renaissance. Porter's stores in New York and London, however, were long gone. Porter, who had been diagnosed with Alzheimer's, died in July 2000 in London.

—Therese Duzinkiewicz Baker; updated by Owen James

PRADA

Italian fashion house

Founded: by Mario Prada (born in Milan, Italy in 1913) and his brother as a luxury leather goods company; taken over by granddaughter Miuccia Bianchi Prada, 1978. *Miuccia Prada* began designing for company, early 1980s; married Patirizio Bertelli, 1989. **Company History:** Ready-to-wear added, 1989; launched Miu Miu line, 1992; first London boutique, 1994; opened Miu Miu shop in SoHo, New York, and Prada shops in San Francisco, New York, and Paris, 1996; bought stake in Gucci, 1998; introduced innerwear, cosmetics, home furnishings, athleticwear, 1998–99; resold Gucci to LVMH, and acquired stakes Helmut Lang, Church, and Jil Sander, 1999; teamed with LVMH to buy Fendi, 1999; formed partnership with Azzedine Alaïa, 2000; bought stake in Carshoe, sold Fendi stake to LVMH, 2001; postponed IPO indefinitely. **Awards:** Miuccia Prada named *Footwear News* Footwear Designer of the Year, 1996; Special Achievement award, National Italian American Foundation, 2000; Patirizio Bertelli given the Pitti Immagine Uomo award, 2001. **Company Address:** Via Andrea Maffei 2, 20135 Milan, Italy. **Company Website:** www.prada.it.

Publications

On PRADA:

Articles

Alford, Lucinda, "Modern de Luxe," in the *Independent* (London), 19 June 1994.
"New York: Miu Miu," in *WWD,* 31 October 1994.
Spindler, Amy M., "Cool Rises to Intimidating Heights," in the *New York Times,* 7 April 1995.
Edelson, Sharon, "Prada to Open Miu Miu Unit in New York," in *WWD,* 29 September 1995.
Forden, Sara Gay, "Prada Using Star Status to Expand its Role on Global State," in *WWD,* 15 February 1996.
Baber, Bonnie, "Prada Power," in *Footwear News,* 23 December 1996.
Forden, Sara Gay, "Prada on the Prowl: Seeking Growth via Acquisitions, Stores," in *WWD,* 10 December 1997.
Conti, Samantha, "Prada Buys Five-Percent Gucci Stake," in *WWD,* 8 June 1998.
Luscombe, Belinda, "Catfight on the Catwalk," in *Time,* 22 June 1998.
Weisman, Katherine, "It's Getting Serious: LVMH Buys Prada's 9.5-Percent Stake in Gucci," in *WWD,* 13 January 1999.
Conti, Samantha, and Lisa Lockwood, "Prada, Helmut Lang Plan Joint Venture to Build Lang Name," in *WWD,* 29 March 1999.
Goldstein, Lauren, "Prada Goes Shopping," in *Fortune,* 27 September 1999.
Menkes, Suzy, "Prada and LVMH Join Forces to Buy Italian Fashion House Fendi," in *International Herald Tribune,* 13 October 1999.
Conti, Samantha, "The End of the Affair," in *WWD,* 25 January 2000.
Socha, Miles, et al., "There's Something About Miuccia," in *WWD,* 10 July 2000.
Zargani, Luisa, "Bertelli Takes Prada to the Public," in *WWD,* 10 November 2000.
Conti, Samantha, "Prada Postpones IPO," in *WWD,* 20 September 2001.

Prada, spring/summer 2002 ready-to-wear collection. © Reuters NewMedia Inc./CORBIS.

"Prada Sells Stake in Fendi for $265 million (to LVMH)," in *New York Times,* 26 November 2001.

* * *

Fratelli Prada was established as a purveyor of fine quality leather goods and imported items in Milan, Italy, in 1913, by Mario Prada and his brother. For most of this century, affluent clients were offered the requirements of fine living, in an atmosphere immersed in the refined opulence of Milan's Galleria Vittorio Emmanuele boutique. The *oggetti di lusso* or luxury items have included steamer trunks, Hartman luggage made in America, handbags from Austria, silver from London, crystal, tortoise, and shell accessories as well as now obsolete articles made from exquisite materials. Mario Prada traveled throughout Europe in order to familiarize himself with those materials and elements which would build his essential concepts of style and luxury.

Prada, spring/summer 2002 ready-to-wear collection © Reuters NewMedia Inc./CORBIS.

Attracted to these same aspects but integrating her own design philosophy, his granddaughter, Miuccia Prada, proceeded to enrich and expand this inherited legacy in 1978. Initially she had dismissed any involvement with the family business as less important than the goals she had set for herself. She received a degree in political science, followed by a period of study in mime at the Piccolo Teatro di Milano in preparation for a career in acting. By her mid-20s she was a committed participant in the political activities of the 1970s in Milan. Though one who had always drawn inspiration from history, "she also refused to reject that part of herself." She was taught to value quality materials and craftsmanship, in a city noted for traditional tailor's ateliers and elegant fabric showrooms.

Miuccia's personal convictions and this serious aspect of her education probably attributed to her belief that women are successful designers because clothing today must express what many women deeply feel. This philosophy has resulted in clothing not preoccupied with sex appeal. What appears to be restrained design quite surprisingly feels exceptional on the body. There has continued to be a nonconforming aspect of beauty in all her collections. This was important to the continuance of Mario Prada's vision of fashion in a full and creative context, capable of making the artisan's qualities come alive in a contemporary spirit.

In the 1980s Miuccia Prada, with her distinctive regard for clothing, accessories, and footwear, began to develop and market an innovative line of fashion accessories eventually followed by a line of ready-to-wear clothes and footwear. In a magazine article, she was quoted as saying that her designs had freedom of movement, freedom from definition, and freedom from constriction. Bohemians, the avant-garde, the beatniks had been constant motifs in her designs. Her philosophy of dress also includes aspects developed and influenced by her own free-spirited personality. A fashion writer once remarked that "her clothes don't necessarily have misfit connotations, nor are particularly for young women, they're like uniforms for the slightly disenfranchised."

She was among the first to produce a practical, lightweight, nylon backpack and other hand-held bags of the same waterproof material. Disregarding season and occasion, the metal stamped Prada logo and brilliant palette combined tassels and leather trim. Black was, without a doubt, the stylish choice. Miuccia has stated she does not focus on inventing but rethinks the company's traditions in a different fashion, "I believe that every form is an archetype of the past."

In their Milanese headquarters, Miuccia Prada and her husband, business partner Patrizio Bertelli, oversee all aspects of the company. Collections are presented there as well as at cultural events. In their Tuscan factory, near Arezzo, prototypes are sampled and all stages of design and technology are controlled. The firm, I Pelletieri D'Italia SpA (IPI), produces and distributes the various lines. It was to this Bertelli-owned factory that Miuccia Prada was originally attracted when she researched improved manufacturing techniques. The firm continues to research all possible methods to make an industrial product look like the unique work of an artisan.

The company Fratelli Prada continues to manufacture leather goods; suede trimmed with *passementerie* and silk tassels, leather wallets embossed with constructivist motifs, jewelry rolls in suede-lined calf skin, boxy pigskin suitcases, and key rings with leather medallions. Beginning with autumn-winter 1989, ready-to-wear was presented in the calm and stately atmosphere of the Palazzo Manusardi headquarters. Admittedly inspirational to her first collections of black and white dresses and sportswear, were the predominantly stylish and lonely characters in films by Michelangelo Antonioni. "Prada is a reflection of Miuccia's taste, about being a connoisseur rather than a consumer," was an excerpt from a magazine interview. Her first footwear collections combined classicism with elements of the avant-garde in such styles as spectator oxfords and embroidered and bejeweled suede slippers.

Signora Prada begins developing her seasonal repertory with the concept that no single style is appropriate for one occasion. She offers her international clientèle an openminded regard for style. In 1994 there were 45 Prada retail stores worldwide and two Miu Miu (a newer apparel line bearing Miuccia's nickname) stores. In the Prada store in the Galleria, the original mahogany and brass fittings reflect luxury and tradition. On two floors, garments, accessories, footwear, and the addition of menswear, express refinement, grace and gentility as they fuse the past with the modern present.

In commenting on design, she confesses that combining opposites in unconventional ways such as refinement with primitive, and

Prada, fall/winter 2001–02 collection. © AP/Wide World Photos.

natural with machine-made helped produce the collections in her namesake store Miu Miu. In 1992, inspired by items in her own wardrobe closet, she created this bohemian, artsy-craftsy collection of patchwork and crocheted garments, saddle bags, and sheepskin jackets, clogs, and boots. She based the new and fresh line on rough finishes, natural colors, and materials reflecting the artisan's craft, stylish in the small boutiques of the 1960s. Her choices of fabrics usually associated with haute couture have been cut into streamlined sportswear such as silk *faille* trenchcoats, double faced cashmere suits, and nylon parkas trimmed in mink. "In the end," she says, "fabric is fabric. What is really new is the way you treat it and put the pieces together."

In the later 1990s, the Prada empire grew in size and scope due in part to the growing popularity of the Miu Miu range. The first Miu Miu stores, in Paris and Milan, were joined by another in New York's SoHo in 1996, while new Prada stores in opened in Beverly Hills, New York, San Francisco, and Paris. Additionally, Prada licensed a cosmetics line with Estée Lauder, began designing innerwear, and rolled out a home furnishings collection in 1999. Prada further expanded through acquisitions, buying stakes in Church & Co., a UK footwear manufacturer, as well as in designer brands Helmut Lang, Jil Sander, and bitter rival Gucci. Building a relationship with LVMH, Prada then sold its Gucci stake to the French luxury giant and formed an alliance to acquire Fendi in 1999. Further moves included a partnership with Azzedine Alaïa, buying Carshoe, selling its Fendi stake back to LVMH, and postponing an initial public offering originally planned for early 2001.

Prada, a fashion conglomerate in the 2000s, is still an exciting fashion label best known for its elegant accessories and breath-of-fresh-air Miu Miu apparel line.

—Gillion Skellenger; updated by Nelly Rhodes

PRÉMONVILLE, Myrène de

See de PRÉMONVILLE, Myrène

PRESTON, Nigel

See MAXFIELD PARRISH

PRICE, Anthony

British designer

Born: Bradford, England, 1945. **Education:** Studied at Bradford School of Art and the Royal College of Art, 1965–68. **Career:** Designer, Stirling Cooper, 1968–74; Che Guevera Plaza, 1974–79; formed own company incorporating Plaza, 1979; opened boutiques in London. **Address:** 15 Cranmer Road, London SW9 6JE, England.

Publications

On PRICE:

Articles

Yates, Paula, "Glamour at A. Price," in *Cosmopolitan* (London), April 1981.

Eggar, Robin, "Style at Any Price," in *You* magazine of the *Mail on Sunday* (London), 11 March 1984.

Webb, Ian R., "Price," in *Blitz* (London), April 1987.

Coleman, Alix, "The Frock Prince," in the *Sunday Express Magazine* (London), 10 April 1988.

"The Price of Stardom," in *Vogue* (London), August 1988.

Bell, Jaki, "Anthony Price," in *DR: The Fashion Business* (London), 10 February 1990.

Mower, Sarah, "Leader of the Glam," in *Vogue* (London), March 1990.

DiSilva, Beverly, "Adam on Eve," in *Mirabella,* November 1990.

Blanchard, Tamsin, "Working Magic With Feathers and Visor," in the *Independent,* 1 March 1996.

Sharkey, Alix, "Fashion Victim," in the *Independent,* 9 March 1996.

Rayner, Abigail, "As Seen at…the New Look Party," in the *Independent,* 14 February 1997.

"Top Designers Bemoan Lack of Materials," in *Mirror Regional Newspapers,* 1998.

Williams, Cayte, "The Intelligent Consumer: The Fashion Month," in the *Independent,* 1 March 1998.

"A Model Wears a Dress by Anthony Price," in the *Times of London,* 21 May 1999.
"Some Leading Designers and Influencers of Sixties Fashions," available online at www.sixtiescity.velnet.com, 2001.
"Anthony Price," from the *Biography Resource Center,* Gale Group, 2001.

* * *

Anthony Price, who designs glamorous clothes for glamorous people, was born during the swan song of Hollywood's starstruck years. The last great screen goddesses loomed large in suburban theatres, with scarlet lips and arched eyebrows under pompadour hairstyles—their square shoulders emphasized wasp waists and shapely hips swathed in pleated lamé. By the time Price was attending the fashion course at London's Royal College of Art in the mid-1960s, these celluloid masterpieces of noir sex-kitsch were daytime television oddities. The shapely heroines gliding across the screen could not have been further removed from the London Twiggies in their flared Courrèges-style minidresses. It was the old-style glamor of these magical, sassy sirens—as embodied by Rita Hayworth—that inspired Price then and continues to do so today.

Soon the golden boy at Stirling Cooper, Price designed clothes to fit and flatter: his skin-tight snakeskin tailoring found its way onto the backs of the Mick Jagger and Dave Clark. A fortuitous association with Roxy Music and their elegant front man, Bryan Ferry, led Price to design stage sets and costumes, as well as album covers, considered classics of their time.

Producing successful commercial ranges for Che Guevera and Plaza, icon fashion labels of the day, Price laid claim to inventing the ubiquitous cap-sleeved t-shirt, flatteringly cut for muscle appeal, and suggestively revealing trousers. While designing largely for men, Price's clothes nevertheless had a contemporary unisex attraction. Price's personal style emerged in his King's Road, Chelsea, shop—a starlet's fitting room of celestial blue and gold, with scalloped 1930s-style vases spilling luxuriant flowers. No clothes rails here—garments were displayed on boards like sculptures in a gallery. In his South Molton Street shop, the Price style came to a baroque climax in a crescendo of dove gray velvet drapes, gilt-framed mirrors, crystal chandeliers, and golden scallop-shell fauteuils.

From hipster to couturier, Price's client list read like a who's who of pop and fashion stars: Duran Duran, Annie Lennox, Lucy Ferry, Joan Collins, and Jerry Hall. He also forayed into royal territory, designing for the Duchess of York's Canadian tour. Price's love of camp cabaret culminated in unforgettable party shows, each a stunning revue of set pieces staged in front of his own gold monogrammed velvet cinema curtains.

Price's gowns were also remarkable, not just for the way they looked, but for the way they were made. Attaining the Hollywood hourglass silhouette in these uncorseted days necessitated built-in structure, and his clothes became intricate masterpieces of boning and interfacing beneath the silks and taffetas. His wide-shouldered men's suits, with their narrow waists and snakelike hips, were equally flattering and apt to attract and allure.

Only a true craftspersons could produce such collectable apparel for his devoted clients. Price once told a student audience that his pattern-cutting skills stemmed from his days as a dry-stone waller in his native Yorkshire. Price most certainly is that rare animal, a designer of unparalleled flair who can also cut, drape, and sew. He cuts his own patterns, mathematically piecing together intricate toiles on his secret system of client-shaped dummies. Practical in many ways, Price is as likely to be found rewiring his studio or laying down the law on the cultivation of the exotic *Gunnera Manicata* as cutting an evening gown.

His clients, transformed by sculptured curves into beings from a higher plane, may walk with the well-postured assurance that springs only from the knowledge that one is clothed by a master of his craft.

When he's not designing, Price spends his time as a socialite, hobnobbing with the likes of Hollywood's celebrities, Britain's high society, and the fashion industry's best. From 1996 to 1998, Price never missed a single London Fashion Week annual event. In 1996 Price was noticeable at Philip Treacy's hat show; in 1997, dressed in his a Diorish waistcoat and hat, Price attended the launch party for "Forties Fashion and the New Look." The show, commemorating the 50th anniversary of the New Look, was a star-studded event. "It was the most revolutionary fashion statement this century," Price commented. "People wanted to go out the next day and throw their clothes away. As an exercise in commercial design it was the best. It was like a number one hit album, it was beyond the Spice Girls."

By 1998 London Fashion Week was focused more on practicality than the usual outrageousness. Rather than only adhering to their creative desires, designers were concerned with cost and the need to sell their garments. Shows were better organized and designs more. Reflecting on the trend away from the outlandish to the more subdued, Price admitted to the *Independent,* "Putting on a catwalk show is like asking the world to a fantastic party and spending the next five years paying it off."

—Alan J. Flux; updated by Kimbally Medeiros

PRINGLE OF SCOTLAND

Scottish design house

Established: by Robert Pringle in Cross Wynd, Hawick, Scotland in 1815 and known worldwide for quality sweaters. **Company History:** Acquired by Dawson International Plc., 1967; segued into luxury goods market and aggressively opened retail shops, 1993–94; scaled back and converted stores to franchises, 1995; incurred substantial losses and reduced workforce, 1997–98; sold to S.C. Fang & Sons Company, Ltd., Hong Kong textile group for $8.8 million, 2000; Kim Winser brought in as CEO and new diffusion line introduced, 2000; began opening retail outlets, 2001–02. **Company Address:** Glebe Mill, Noble Place, Hawick TD9 9QE, Scotland, UK. **Company Website:** www.pringle-of-scotland.co.uk.

PUBLICATIONS

On PRINGLE of SCOTLAND:

Books

Houck, Catherine, *The Fashion Encyclopedia,* New York, 1982.
O'Hara, Georgina, *The Encyclopaedia of Fashion,* New York, 1986.

Articles

Richards, Amanda, "The Knitwear Brand that stretched Too Far," in *Marketing,* 6 April 1995.

Fallon, James, "Pringle to Cut 290 Factory Workers," in *DNR,* 24 October 1997.

Moffat, Alistair, "Sold Off to Hong Kong," in the *New Statesman,* 21 February 2000.

"Pringle joins the fashion elite," available online at BBC News, www.news.bbc.co.uk, 21 February 2001.

"The Lion Prepares to Roar," in the *Drapers Record,* 2 April 2001.

Hall, Emma, "Fashion's Old Guard Aim to Generate Youth Appeal," in *Campaign,* 7 September 2001.

* * *

Founded in Cross Wynd, Hawick, Scotland in 1815 by Robert Pringle as a family business making hosiery, Pringle of Scotland became known throughout the world as an established brand and leader in fine cashmere and other high quality knitwear and sportswear, and a pioneer of modern knitwear technology and systems.

Although its origins were in the production of hosiery and underwear, Pringle is more well known for its particular emphasis on leisurewear and sportswear. The emphasis on knitwear as outerwear is a comparatively recent one, dating from the earlier years of the 20th century when its use by sportsmen, particularly in golf, as nonconstricting yet striking-style garments made it fashionable. Up until 1934 Pringle was known primarily as a company producing fine quality undergarments and a limited selection of knitted outerwear. In June 1934 the appointment of Otto Weisz, an Austrian refugee, as the first full-time professional designer to work within the British knitwear industry, brought a revolutionary attitude to the importance of design and a flair for color to an insular industry. Weisz's designs included the concept of the twinset, which became a classic. It has been said that few industries did more than Scottish whiskey and the Hawick knitwear industry to earn dollars for Britain.

Many Scottish crafts families worked for generations in the Pringle mills and a substantial investment program resulted in these factories being equipped with the latest state of the art technology and machinery, employing thousands and ranking with the most up-to-date production units in Scotland. Some of the finest fibers in the world were used, including cashmere from the mountains of East Asia, lambswool and the best quality Geelong from Australia, and the native Scottish wools, such as those from the Shetland Isles.

The men's and womenswear collections took their inspiration from the wools themselves, current color trends, lifestyles, and surroundings. These collections included patterned, textured, plain, and highly-styled garments in the latest shades to meet the requirements of an ever-changing fashion scene, and complementary woven accessories for both men and women, mainly in natural fibers. Active and leisure sportswear were of particular importance to Pringle products; the Nick Faldo Collection of knitwear and coordinates sold very well in the UK, Europe, Japan, and the U.S., as well as the Ladies Golf and sports Classic collections.

Pringle of Scotland became part of Joseph Dawson (Holdings) Limited, later renamed Dawson International Plc. in 1967. The strong international style of the company's products allowed expansion and the Pringle name was soon established in over 45 countries throughout the world. An aggressive expansion in the early 1990s took the company into a myriad of luxury products and put Pringle shops in many European outlets, and into Japan and South America. In addition, Pringle held two Royal Warrants, as Manufacturers of Knitted Garments to both Her Majesty the Queen and Her Majesty the Queen Mother. Yet the turbulent mid- and late 1990s took their toll on the venerable kntiwear producer.

The too-rapid expansion of 1993 and 1994 came back to haunt Pringle; it was forced to cut back and sell shops to franchisees in 1995. There was, however, a glimmer of hope during a brief turnaround in 1997 and 1998, only to have the company clobbered by surge in the pound's value. The weakened export market (which accounted for two-thirds of Pringle's business) forced the manufacturer to scale back operations, first through a shortened work week, then through increasing layoffs. The once mighty brand then suffered a devastating blow in 2000 when Dawson International, wanting to concentrate solely on cashmere operations, sold the ailing Pringle to the Hong Kong-based S.C. Fang & Sons Company, Ltd. Alistair Moffat, writing in the *New Statesman* (21 February 2000), didn't mince words, stating, "Half the workforce will go, with 140 losing their jobs and 60 being transferred to another company. That is a disgrace, and a very damaging act."

While its future seemed in doubt, Pringle rallied in the early 21st century under the leadership of new chief executive Kim Winser, formerly of Marks & Spencer. The firm was further invigorated by sales of a diffusion line launched in 2001. A company spokesperson told Emma Hall of *Campaigns* (7 September 2001), "The Diffusion collection has a more casual feel and will establish a new attitude for the brand, aimed at the cutting edge of the youth market." Hall commented that the knitwear producer had already made much progress, producing advertising with a "rough-and-ready appeal that would have been anathema to the Scottish knitwear house a couple of seasons ago." Though Pringle of Scotland suffered the loss of longtime workers, plant closings, and a change of ownership—the 187-year-old company more than endured, it triumphed with a new look and a broader appeal.

—Doreen Ehrlich; updated by Owen James

PUCCI, Emilio

Italian designer

Born: Marchese Emilio Pucci di Barsento in Naples, 20 November 1914. **Education:** Attended the University of Milan, 1933–35, University of Georgia, 1935–36, Reed College, Portland, Oregon, 1936–37; M.A., 1937; Ph.D., University of Florence, 1941. **Family:** Married Cristina Nannini di Casabianca, 1959; children: Alessandro, Laudomia. **Military Service:** Bomber pilot in the Italian Air Force, 1938–42. **Career:** Oylmpic skier, 1934; women's skiwear designer, White Stag, for Lord & Taylor department store, 1948; freelance fashion designer, from 1949; first Pucci shop established in Capri, 1949, Rome, Elba, Montecatini, from 1950; president, Emilio Pucci SrL, Florence, and Emilio Pucci, New York, from 1950; vice-president for design/merchandising, Formfit International, 1960s; business run by family after death, 1992; daughter Laudomia assumed design duties; men's ties, swimwear reintroduced, 1998; new womenswear designed by Stephan Janson, 1998; majority share acquired by LVMH,

Emilio Pucci, 1976: printed silk dresses. © Bettmann/CORBIS.

2000; launched website, 2001. **Awards:** Neiman Marcus award, 1954, 1967; *Sports Illustrated* award, 1955, 1961; Burdines Fashion award, 1955; the *Sunday Times* award, London, 1963; Association of Industrial Design award, Milan, 1968; Drexel University award, Philadelphia, 1975; Italy-Austria award, 1977; Knighthood, Rome, 1982; Medaille de la Ville de Paris, 1985; Council of Fashion Designers of America award, 1990. **Died:** 29 November 1992, in Florence, Italy. **Company Address:** Palazzo Pucci, via dei Pucci 6, Florence, Italy. **Company Website:** www.emiliopucci.com.

Publications

On PUCCI:

Books

Mulassano, Adriana, *I mass-moda: fatti e personaggi dell'Italian Look,* Florence, 1979.

Aragno, B.G., editor, *40 Years of Italian Fashion* [exhibition catalogue], Rome, 1983.

Emilio Pucci, spring/summer 2002 ready-to-wear collection. © AFP/ CORBIS.

Kennedy, Shirley, *Pucci: A Renaissance in Fashion,* New York, 1986, 1991.

Casadio, Mariuccia, *Emilio Pucci,* New York, 1998.

Articles

Schiff, F., "If You Knew Pucci," in *Interview,* September 1974.

"Founding Father of the Signature Print," in the *Times* (London), 1 September 1976.

Shields, Jody, "Pucci," in *Vogue,* May 1990.

Hochswender, Woody, "Pucci Redux," in the *New York Times,* 8 May 1990.

Porti, Anna Gloria, "Mai come adesso è Pucci," in *Vogue* (Milan), September 1990.

Young, Lucie, "The New Pucci Coup: Psychedelic Swirls Back," in *Metropolitan Home* (London), December/January 1990–91.

Morris, Bernadine, "Emilio Pucci, Designer of Bright Prints, Dies at 78," in the *New York Times,* 1 December 1992.

"Prince of Prints," [obituary] in *People,* 14 December 1992.

"Emilio Pucci," [obituary] in *Current Biography,* January 1993.

Goldstein, Lauren, "Pucci Adds New Punch to Spring Presentation," in *DNR,* 1 December 1997.

Forden, Sara Gay, "Tribute to Pucci Leads to Birth of a Collection," in *WWD,* 22 December 1997.

Braunstein, Peter, "Pucci Conquers Cyberspace," in *WWD,* 30 July 2000.

Menkes, Suzy, "Pucci Picks an Eclectic Designer," in the *International Herald Tribune,* 31 October 2000.

* * *

Rising out of the ashes of European fashion after World War II, Emilio Pucci brought a spectrum of carefree colors to the rationed continent. His sportswear beginnings lent a casual air to his work, a welcome relief from recent austerity and a new meaning to the term "resort wear." The swirling freestyle patterns and fluid fabrics he used became internationally recognized and desired, copied by many but rivaled by few.

American Tina Lesser may have been earlier with her hand-painted silks, but Pucci quickly made them his own, covering the fine lustrous fabric with optical fantasies of geometric shapes. His color range came straight from an Aegean horizon, turquoise and ultramarine set against sea green and lime, or hot fuchsia and sunflower yellow. Pucci swept away the repetitive sailor styles and tailored linens of cruisewear and brought in a new air of ease and luxury with his breezy separates. He capitalized on the lull in British and French couture after the war that benefitted many American and Italian designers, and dressed the fashionable *mondaine* in bold ready-to-wear.

The government-backed presentations of Italian designers of the late 1940s provided an aristocratic Florentine backdrop for Pucci's collections, which were soon internationally popular, and he became increasingly aware of the importance of the American market to his success. His characteristic style was best seen in slim-legged trousers in fruity shades, which provided a sexy foil to loose-hanging tunics and classic shirts left to hang outside the waistband.

His collections encompassed more than just stylish but jaunty daywear. In 1961 he showed simple evening dresses with deep V-shape panels set into their sophisticated bias-cut silhouette. Pucci saw his greatest success in the 1960s; his psychedelic-patterned printed silks were seen everywhere. They were, and continued to be worn by celebrities, from early clients Marilyn Monroe and Jackie Kennedy to Madonna, all seduced by the light touch of his designs.

As his reputation grew, Pucci's distinctive patterns were aspired to by many; a Pucci scarf or vivid silk handbag provided the cachet of luxury. His name was seen on everything from gloves to small ornaments, yet by the 1970s his work, like that of other big fashion houses, seemed less in tune with the times. During the 1980s, Pucci ranges seemed irrelevant to the weighty tailored severity that preoccupied the fashion world. It was not until the start of the 1990s that the pure whirling colors of the Pucci label (by then directed by his daughter, Laudomia) were again universally embraced. His signature shapes and vivid patterns had already inspired a generation of Italian designers, notably Gianni Versace and Franco Moschino, and in 1991 the reinvigorated Pucci look was everywhere. It had been translated into the modern essentials—clingy leggings, catsuits, and stretch polo necks which continued the sexy feel of his work and contrasted perfectly with his airy shirts. His clothes sold out across the world as a new, younger audience took up the label, perpetuating its popularity, albeit on a less high profile level after the initial Pucci mania earlier in the year.

The eclectic use of surface pattern and innovative color combinations distinguishing Pucci's work have been widely emulated throughout the fashion strata. His use of color added a feeling of movement to his clothes, while the quality fabrics enhanced the fluid line. The classic separates he designed continued to be successful, while the addition of newer styles ensured that the label would continue as a vibrant note to fashion in the later 1990s after Pucci's death in 1992.

A rebirth of Pucci's distinctive prints for men, including swimwear, sleepwear and ties, was scheduled to arrive in U.S. in 1998, but not before a new collection of womenswear debuted in Florence in January. At a time when original Pucci designs brought in premium prices at vintage shops, the reissue of menswear was inspired. The fall/winter womenswear line, however, grew out of different circumstances. "The whole idea started during the Biennial exhibition in Florence last fall," Laudomia Pucci, a company's director, told *Women's Wear Daily* in December 1997. The tribute, arranged by her mother Crista, had garnered so much attention the family decided to introduce a 50-piece collection, mostly for women, designed by Milan-based designer Stephan Janson. "We decided on Stephan Janson to do the collection because he's young, well-traveled, and well-cultured," Laudomia commented, and Janson "will be able to live well in the Pucci universe."

In the 21st century, change came to Pucci by way of new ownership. In Feburary 2000 luxury conglomerate LVMH bought a controlling stake in the firm and initiated a rehaul of the Pucci image. Four new Pucci stores opened in Milan, Portofino, St. Moritz, and Palm Beach, followed by a segue into home furnishings. Next came the appointment of Puerto Rican designer Julio Espada as artistic director (Laudomia was named Image Director), and in 2001 came the launch of a snazzy Pucci website.

The online Pucci forum blended archival photos with newer images, with collections past and present. Laudomia believed the mix of "classic and contemporary" was worthy of special notice. "I don't think any fashion house with a history has tried to convey that dimension to an online audience," she remarked to *Women's Wear Daily* in July 2001. "They focus solely on now." The "now" of Pucci may be firmly rooted in the past, but is securely focused on the future.

—Rebecca Arnold; updated by Owen James

PULITZER, Lilly

American designer

Born: Lillian McKim in Roslyn, New York. **Family:** Married Herbert (Pete) Pulitzer (divorced, 1969); married Enrique Rousseau (died 1993); children: Peter, Minnie, Liza. **Career:** Formed business in Palm Beach, Florida, for sale of women's shifts, 1959; president, Lilly Pulitzer, Inc., 1961–84; children's dresses, called "Minnies," introduced, 1962; Pulitzer Jeans introduced, 1963; Men's Stuff line introduced, 1969; nearly three dozen stores nationwide, late 1970s; Chapter 11 filed and business closed, 1984; new line of Lillys designed by Marty Karabees, 1986; rights to line purchased by Sugartown Worldwide, Inc., 1992; relaunched and expanded Lilly lines, mid-1990s; sleepwear introduced, 1998; signed licensing deal with Dan River Home Fashions, 2000; profiled in the *New Yorker,* 2000.

Publications

On PULITZER:

Books

Fairchild, John, *The Fashionable Savages,* Garden City, New York, 1965.

Bender, Marylin, *The Beautiful People,* New York, 1967.

Lambert, Eleanor, *The World of Fashion: People, Places, Resources,* New York, London, 1976.

Articles

Moin, David, "Lilly Pulitzer's Prizes: A 'Shift' into the 1980s," in *New York Apparel News,* February 1984.

Reed, Susan, "Lilly Pulitzer's Preppy Prints to Get a Second Life," in *People,* 23 June 1986.

Staples, Kate, "Pulitzer's Prizes," in *Mademoiselle,* May 1993.

Koski, Lorna, "The Return of Lilly," in *W,* October 1993.

Monget, Karen, "Lilly Pulitzer's Latest—Sleepwear," in *WWD,* 27 April 1998.

Yazigi, Monique P., "The Pink-and-Green Police…," in the *New York Times,* 17 May 1998.

"Textile Briefs," in *HFN (Weekly Newspaper for the Home Furnishing Network),* 28 February 2000.

"Beachy Keen…Lilly Pulitzer Rousseau Enjoys a Second Blossoming…," in *People,* 4 September 2000.

MacFarquahar, Larissa, "Everything Lilly," in the *New Yorker,* 4 September 2000.

* * *

According to the legend, it all began with an orange juice stand begun by a bored (and rich) housewife in October 1959. The boss brought a dozen dresses made by her dressmaker from fabric bought at a nearby Woolworth's (in bright colorful prints that wouldn't show orange juice stains) and sold them off a pipe-rack. "I started it as a lark," Pulitzer remembered years later to Lorna Koski of *W,* "I just knew what I liked." Within five years, it seemed as if every woman in America had at least one sleeveless, back-zippered "Lilly"and more or less lived in the comfortable lifestyle of the the dress represented.

The Lilly designed by Pulitzer was a simple shift or chemise, an unarticulated little dress that caught the attention of women everywhere, including boarding-school chum Jacqueline Bouvier Kennedy. John Fairchild, writing in *The Fashionable Savages* (New York, 1965) explained, "Watch the chemise make a comeback with the masses… Just look at the Lilly, those chemises designed by Lilly Pulitzer, who has a gold mine in those little nothing, beautiful print chemises… All the top stores clamor for them—the same fashion they had on their markdown racks a few years back. The only difference is the Lilly is lined and [its] shape controlled."

There is, however, always a big difference between the uncomplicated Diane Von Furstenberg wrap dress, the Halston Ultrasuede shirtwaist or other icons of style, and all the competition. Pulitzer invented nothing; she wasn't really a designer—but she provided a uniform of sorts to women of the early and mid-1960s. The nondesign of the Lilly was its allure; a perky, bright, and unpretentious shift in polished cotton chintz met an American need for personal style amidst homogenous culture. Eleanor Lambert, writing in *The World of Fashion,* (New York, 1976) describes its evolution, "first a 'snob' uniform, then a general fashion craze."

Pulitzer had long been a powerful family name in America, and its associations with Palm Beach grandeur made vague allusions to wealth and aristocracy, but the dress was easily accessible. One of the elements of its popularity was it appealed not only across class lines, but across all ages of women, serving young women who might aspire to more than *Laugh-In* shifts, and style to women of a certain age who found the simplified form a kind of chaste elegance. Especially in an era influenced by the easy and unadorned grace of Jackie Kennedy, who became First Lady. As Marylin Bender reported in *The Beautiful People* (New York, 1976), "the fact that Jacqueline, Ethel, and Joan Kennedy were Lilly-fans didn't hurt at all."

Bender quoted Pulitzer as saying, "The great thing about the Lilly is that you wear practically nothing underneath." In this inner simplicity as well as the outward simplicity in silhouette and bold tropical print, Pulitzer understood her time as much as she understood herself. Pulitzer was said to have worked with her dressmaker to come up with an alternative to trousers for the leisure life of Palm Beach, as she felt she didn't look good in pants. The alternative arrived at was nothing more than the classic housedress, sanctioned a little by Balenciaga's 1950s chemise, brightened by the tropical palette, and rarefied by the connection to grand lifestyle.

Only in America could the "Lilly" have happened as it did—a triumph of nondesign, an aristocratic aura bestowed on a distinctly unaristocratic idea, a dress that at a modest $30 to $75 retail exemplified its time. The mid-1960s youthquake, however, with its extreme minis followed by paper dresses and other experiments made the Lilly recede somewhat from fashion. In the 1970s Pulitzer opened retail shops across the U.S., numbering nearly three dozen by late in the decade. The Lilly, which had waxed and waned, was rediscovered in the 1980s and again became the chicest shift; yet by 1984 sales had fallen off so sharply Pulitzer was forced to close her boutiques and filed for Chapter 11 bankruptcy.

In fashion, where everything old is new again, the Lilly experienced another renaissance in 1986 when designer Marty Karabees introduced a line, then again in the early 1990s when the Lilly Pulitzer label was acquired by Sugartown Worldwide Inc., run by entrepreneur James B. Bradbeer, Jr. and his partners. Bradbeer reintroduced the Lilly chemise and a host of other designs including sportswear and swimwear for women and girls, and planned a foray into men's products as well. Pulitzer sleepwear was launched in 1998 at luxury retailers like Saks Fifth Avenue and specialty chains, and the following year a new housewares collection was slated for release. The Pulitzer home collection became a reality in early 2000 through a licensing deal with Dan River Home Fashions. Luxury bed linens and a bath collection debuted in April, marking a new era for the Lilly-inspired prints designed more than three decades before.

—Richard Martin; updated by Owen James

PUMA

See LEE, Mickey

Q

QUANT, Mary

British designer

Born: Kent, 11 February 1934. **Education:** Studied art and design at Goldsmith's College of Art, London University, 1952–55. **Family:** Married Alexander Plunket Greene, 1957 (died, 1990); children: Orlando. **Career:** Fashion designer, from 1955; established Bazaar boutique and Alexander's restaurant, London, 1955; founder/director, Mary Quant Ginger Group wholesale design and manufacturing firm, 1963, and Mary Quant, Ltd., 1963; cosmetics line introduced, 1966; launched hot pants, 1969; member, Design Council, London, from 1971; Mary Quant Japan franchise shops established, 1983; has designed for J.C. Penney, Puritan Fashions, Alligator Rainwear, Kangol, Dupont Europe, Staffordshire Potteries, and many more; authored several books; opened Mary Quant Colour Shops, 1990s; stepped down from firm bearing her name, 2000. **Exhibitions:** *Mary Quant's London,* Museum of London, 1973. **Awards:** Woman of the Year award, London, 1963; the *Sunday Times* International Fashion award, London, 1963; Bath Museum of Costume Dress of the Year award, 1963; Maison Blanche Rex award, New Orleans, 1964; Piavola d'Oro award, 1966; Chartered Society of Designers medal, 1966; Officer, Order of the British Empire, 1966; Fellow, Chartered Society of Designers, 1967; Royal Designer for Industry, Royal Society of Arts, 1969; British Fashion Council Hall of Fame award, 1990; Senior Fellow, Royal College of Art, London, 1991. **Address:** 3 Ives St., London SW3 2NE, England. **Website:** www.maryquant.com.

PUBLICATIONS

By QUANT:

Books

Quant by Quant, Bath, 1966, 1974; New York, 1967.

Mary Quant's Daisy Chain of Things to Do, Glasgow, 1975.

Colour by Quant, with Felicity Greene, London, 1984; New York, 1985.

Quant on Makeup, with Vicci Bentley, London, 1986; New York, 1987.

The Ultimate Beauty Book, Ontario, 1996.

Classic Makeup & Beauty Book, with Maureen Barrymore and Dave King, London, 1998.

Articles

"A Personal Design for Living," in the *Listener* (London), 19–26 December 1974.

"Things I Wish I'd Known at 19," in the *Sunday Express Magazine* (London), 21 June 1982.

On QUANT:

Books

Halliday, Leonard, *The Fashion Makers,* London, 1966.

Bender, Marylin, *The Beautiful People,* New York, 1967.

Morris, Brian, and Ernestine Carter, *An Introduction to Mary Quant's London,* [exhibition catalogue], London 1973.

Bernard, Barbara, *Fashion in the Sixties,* London, 1978.

Carter, Ernestine, *Magic Names of Fashion,* Englewood Cliffs, NJ, 1980.

Mary Quant, 1965 collection: "Catamaran" (left), "Raleigh" (center), and "Centre-half" (right). © AP/Wide World Photos.

Mary Quant (right) with three of her designs, 1968. © AP/Wide World Photos.

MacCarthy, Fiona, and Patrick Nugent, *Eye for Industry: Royal Designers for Industry 1936–1986* [exhibition catalogue], London, 1986.

Whiteley, Nigel, *Pop Design: Modernism to Mod* [exhibition catalogue], Design Council, London, 1987.

Lobenthal, Joel, *Radical Rags: Fashions of the Sixties,* New York, 1990.

Stegemeyer, Anne, *Who's Who in Fashion, Third Edition,* New York, 1996.

Cawthorne, Nigel, *Key Moments in Fashion,* London, 1998.

Strodder, Chris, *Swingin' Chicks of the Sixties,* New York, 2000.

Articles

"British Couple Kooky Styles," in *Life* (New York), 5 December 1960.

"Brash New Breed of British Designers," in *Life,* 8 October 1963.

Davis, John, "Mary, Mary, Quite Contrary, How Does Your Money Grow?" in the *Observer* (London), 19 August 1973.

De'Ath, Wilfred, "The Middle Age of Mary Quant," in the *Illustrated London News,* February 1974.

Kingsley, H., "How Does Her Empire Grow?," in the *Sunday Telegraph Magazine* (London), 29 March 1981.

Jackson, Jan, "Interview with Mary Quant," in the *Leicester Mercury* (England), 12 November 1984.

Lowe, Shirley, "Mary's Quantum Leap into the 1980," in the *Sunday Times Magazine* (London), 10 August 1986.

Savage, Percy, "Mary Quant," in *Art & Design* (London), September 1986.

Orr, Deborah, "Minis to the Masses," in the *New Statesman & Society* (London), 19 October 1990.

Kay, Helen, "Uppers and Downers: British Entrepreneurs of the Past 25 Years," in *Management Today* (London), 9 October 1991.

Gandee, Charles, "Mod Mary," in *Vogue,* July 1995.

Terry, Elizabeth, "Beauty Black Book—Proud Mary," in *In Style,* 1 March 1996.

"All Revolutions Start Somewhere," in *Management,* September 1997.

Gillan, Audrey, "Mary Quant Quits Fashion Empire," in *The Guardian,* 2 December 2000.
Holmes, Lee, "A to Z of Fashion—Q is for Quant," in the *Independent on Sunday,* 7 October 2001.

* * *

The name Mary Quant is synonymous with 1960s fashion. Quant's designs initiated a look for the newly emerging teen-and-twenties market enabling young women to establish their own identity and put Britain on the international fashion map.

Quant did not study fashion; following parental advice she enrolled in an Art Teacher's Diploma course at Goldsmith's College, London University, but she was not committed to teaching. In the evenings she went to pattern cutting classes. Her fashion career began in 1955, in the workrooms of the London milliner, Erik, the same year she opened her boutique, Bazaar in King's Road, Chelsea, in partnership with her future husband, Alexander Plunket-Greene. The idea was to give the so-called Chelsea Set "a *bouillabaisse* of clothes and accessories." Quant was the buyer, but she soon found the kinds of clothes she wanted were not available. The solution was obvious, but not easy—21 years old, with little fashion experience, Quant started manufacturing from her home. Using revamped Butterick patterns and fabrics bought retail at Harrods, she created a look for the Chelsea girl. Her customers were hardly younger than herself and she knew what they wanted; her ideas took off in a big way, on both sides of the Atlantic.

Americans loved the London Look, so much so that in 1957 Quant signed a contract with J.C. Penney to create clothes and underwear for the wholesale market. American coordinates convinced her that separates were versatile and ideal for the young. To reach more of the British market in 1958 she launched the Ginger Group, a mass-produced version of the look, with U.S. manufacturer Steinberg's. In the same year she was nominated as Woman of the Year in Britain and the *Sunday Times* in London gave her its International Fashion award.

Quant created a total look based on simple shapes and bold fashion statements. She hijacked the beatnik style of the late 1950s: dark stockings, flat shoes, and polo necks became obligatory for the girl in the street. The pinafore dress, based on the traditional British school tunic, was transformed as one of the most useful garments of the early 1960s. Hemlines rose higher and higher; Quant's miniskirts reached thigh level, in 1965, and everyone followed. Courrèges confirmed that the time was right by launching his couture version in Paris but Quant needed no confirmation—1965 was the year of her whistlestop tour to the United States. With 30 outfits and her own models, she showed in 12 cities in 14 days. Sporting miniskirts and Vidal Sassoon's five-point geometric haircuts, the models ran and danced down the catwalk. It was the epitome of Swinging London and it took America by storm.

Quant's talents did not go unnoticed in higher places. In 1966 she was awarded the OBE for services to fashion and went to Buckingham Palace wearing a miniskirt. Her cosmetics line was also launched this year, and recognizable by the familiar daisy logo, Quant cosmetics were an international success. Later taken over by Max Factor, they were retailed in 90 countries. Additionally, she experimented with new materials including PVC and nylon, to create outerwear, shoes, tights, and swimwear.

In the early 1970s Quant moved out of mass market and began to work for a wider age group, chiefly for export to the U.S. and Europe. Her range of merchandise expanded to include household goods, toys, and furnishings. Mary Quant at Home, launched in the U.S. market in 1983, included franchised home furnishings and even wine. By the end of the 1980s her designs were again reaching the British mass market, through the pages of the Great Universal Stores/Kays mail order catalogues.

Mary Quant remained a genuine fashion innovator well into the 1990s and into the 2000s. She adjusted to change—the 1960s designer for the youth explosion became a creator for the 1980s and beyond lifestyle boom. Her market had grown up with her and she was able to anticipate its demands. Along the way she began publishing books, autobiographical to start, and later on beauty and cosmetics. It wasn't until she was in her 60s that Mary Quant stepped down as director of Mary Quant Ltd., in 2000. She did, however, remain a consultant for the myriad of products she pioneered over the last four decades.

—Hazel Clark; updated by Owen James

R

RABANNE, Paco

French designer

Born: Francisco Rabaneda Cuervo in San Sebastian, Spain, 18 February 1934; raised in France. **Education:** Studied architecture at l'École Nationale des Beaux-Arts, Paris, 1952–55. **Career:** Presented first haute couture collection, "Twelve Unwearable Dresses," Paris, 1966; home furnishing and tableware lines introduced, 1981; launched men's ready-to-ear line, 1983; men's skin care line launched, 1984; debuted women's ready-to-wear line, 1990; opened first shop, Paris, 1990; introduced leather goods, 1991; began condominium development in Miami beach, 1994; launched Champagne Lanson Noble Cuvee, 1998; parent company Puig closes Rabanne fashion, 1999; fragrances include *Calandre,* late 1960s, *Paco Rabanne pour Homme,* 1973, *Metal,* 1979, *La Nuit,* 1985, *Sport,* 1985, *Tenere,* 1988; *Ultraviolet,* 2000. **Exhibitions:** *Body Covering,* Museum of Contemporary Crafts, New York, 1968; *Paco Rabanne,* Musée de la mode, Marseille, 1995; *Une vision plastique: rencontre de la plastique et de la Haute-Couture,* Musée du Peigne et de la Plasturgie, Oyonnax, 1998. *Folies de dentelles,* Musée des Beaux-Arts et de la Dentelle, Alençon, 2000. **Awards:** Beauty Products Industry award, 1969; Fragrance Foundation Recognition award, 1974; L'Aiguille d'Or award, 1977; Dé d'Or award, 1990; Chevalier de la Légion d'Honneur, 1989; Officier de l'Ordre d'Isabelle la Catholique (Spain), 1989. **Address:** 6, boulevard de Parc, 92523 Neuilly, France. **Website:** www.paco.com.

Paco Rabanne, fall 1968 collection: "The Water" (left) and "The Fire," (right) minidresses made of gold and silver plates. © AP/ Wide World Photos.

PUBLICATIONS

By RABANNE:

Books

Trajectory, Paris, 1991.
Collections Paco Rabanne: 200 modèles de haute couture, 1966–1994, [catalogue], with Herve Chayette and Laurence Calmels, Paris, 1994.
Paco Rabanne: Musée de la mode, 9 juin–17 septembre 1995, [exhibiton catalogue], Marseille, 1995.
La force des Celts: l'heritage druidique, with Philip Carr-Gomm, Paris, 1996.
Paco Rabanne: A Feeling for Research, with Lydia Kamitsis, Paris, 1996.
La leçon indienne: les secrets d'un homme-médecine, conversations avec Wallace Black Elk, with Wallace Black Elk, Paris, 1996.
The Dawn of the Golden Age: A Spiritual Design for Living, Barcelona & Shaftsbury, Dorset, 1997.
Paco Rabanne: Une vision plastique—rencontre de la plasturgie et de la Haute-Couture, [exhibition catalogue], Oyonnax, France, 1998.
Journey: From One Life to Another, Shaftsbury, Dorset, 1999.
1999: Fire from the Heavens, Paris, 1999.
Folies et dentelles, [exhibition catalogue], Alençon, France, 2000.

On RABANNE:

Books

Bender, Marylin, *The Beautiful People,* New York, 1967.
Clemmer, Jean, *Canned Candies: The Exotic Women and Clothes of Paco Rabanne,* Paris & London, 1969.

Loebenthal, Joel, *Radical Rags: Fashions of the Sixties,* New York, 1990.

Stegemeyer, Anne, *Who's Who in Fashion, Third Edition,* New York, 1996.

Kamitsis, Lydia, *Paco Rabanne,* London, 1999.

Articles

Sharp, Joy, "Fashion Foibles of 1967," in *Costume,* No. 2, 1968.

Tretiak, Philippe, "Paco le visionnaire," in *Elle* (Paris), 24 October 1988.

Dutt, Robin, "Metal Guru," in *Clothes Show* (London), December/January 1989–90.

Bourdley, Laurence, "Paco Rabanne," in *L'Officiel* (Paris), February 1990.

Silver, Vernon, "Label Living: You've Worn the Perfrume, Now Live in the Condo," in the *New York Times,* 20 February 1994.

Louie, Elaine, "Here's a Rainy Day Project (but Watch for Lightning)," in the *New York Times,* 30 May 1996.

Whitney, Craig R., "An Old Prediction Speeds France's Annual Exodus," in the *New York Times,* 6 July 1999.

Young, Clara, "Paco Rabanne," [profile] online at Fashion Live, www.fashionlive.com, 5 August 2000.

* * *

It comes as no surprise, on viewing the designs of Paco Rabanne, to hear that he prefers to be described as an engineer rather than a couturier. Son of the chief seamstress at Balenciaga (famed for his intricate techniques of construction), Rabanne, after studying architecture, made his name in the 1960s with a series of bizarre, futuristic garments made out of incongruous materials. When viewed on the catwalk they seemed space-age prototypes rather than high fashion garments.

Believing that the only new frontier left in fashion was the discovery and utilization of new materials rather than the old couture method of changing lines from season to season, Rabanne totally broke with tradition, experimenting with plastic and aluminium, to create some of the most eccentric yet influential garments of the 1960s. It was estimated that by 1966 Rabanne was using 30,000 metres of Rhodoid plastic per month in such designs as bib necklaces made of phosphorescent plastic discs strung together with fine wire and whole dresses of the same material linked by metal chains. When he had exhausted the possibilities of plastic, Rabanne created a contemporary version of chainmail using tiny triangles of aluminium and leather held together with flexible wire rings to construct a series of simple shift mini dresses.

The delight of his designs comes in the use of disparate materials not previously considered appropriate for use in clothing, or the displacing of traditional materials in order to produce strange juxtapositions of color and texture. He was, for instance, one of the first designers to combine knits, leather, and fur, using combinations like a cape made of matte silver leather triangles with black ponyskin or a coat teaming curly white lamb and white leather.

It could be said that in the 1970s and 1980s the name Paco Rabanne became associated with male toiletries rather than for the intriguing experimentation he had been carrying out. Rabanne relies on the sales of his successful line of skinscents—including *Calandre, Paco,* and *Metal*—to finance his more technological projects. In 1971 he collaborated with Louis Giffard, an authority on flow-molding techniques, to produce a raincoat molded entirely in one piece of plastic. Even the buttons were part of the same process, molded directly into the garment and fitting into pressed-out pieces on the other side of the coat.

In the 1990s, with a 1960s renaissance in full swing, the inventive caliber of Rabanne has been rediscovered. His latest collections are concentrating on stretch jersey, cotton, and viscose fabrics in metallic hues, still accessorized by enormous pieces of jewelry. The high modernism of his 1960s designs seems touchingly innocent when viewed through the jaded eyes of the 1990s. Science and technology in contemporary culture signify something far removed from the faith and hope in the future Rabanne was expressing with his self-consciously space age materials. His designs give less a sense of the future than imbue us with feelings of nostalgia for the optimism in new technology he embraced so fully in decades past.

By the end of the 20th century, Rabanne had broken ground on condominiums in Miami's South Beach, introduced a prciey champagne, a new fragrance (*Ultraviolet*), and published several new Age books, including a bestselling doomsday-ish tome based on his interpretations of several Nostradamas prophecies regarding 1999. On the fashion scene, however, Rabanne designed his last collection in July 1999, preparing to leave his various labels in the hands a cadre of assistants. Yet Rabanne's backer, Spain's Puig Fashion & Beauty, pulled its support, effectively shutting down the label. While Rabanne's clothing may have become less controversial over the years, his often audacious beliefs and outspokenness will probably continue to shock and amuse for years to come.

—Caroline Cox; updated by Owen James

RATIA, Armi and Viljo

See MARIMEKKO

RAYNE, Sir Edward

British footwear designer and manufacturer

Born: London, 19 August 1922. **Education:** Studied at Harrow School. **Family:** Married Phyllis Court, 1952; children: Edward, Nicholas. **Career:** Trainee in family shoemaking firm, H&M Rayne Ltd. (founded 1889), 1940–50; managing director, 1951–87; purchased half share in Delman, formed Rayne-Delman Shoes, Inc., 1961, president, 1961–72, and executive chairman, 1972–86; Paris shop opened, 1970; firm acquired by Debenhams, 1973 (itself acquired by the Burton Group, 1985); director, Debenhams, London, 1975–88; chairman, Harvey Nichols Stores, London, 1978–88; Burton Group sold off H&M Rayne to David Graham, 1987 (Rayne himself broke off ties with company); Graham sold firm to Richard Kottler, 1990; retired as chair of British Fashion Council, 1990; Rayne firm dissolved, 1994. **Awards:** *Harper's Bazaar* trophy, London, 1963; Fellow, Royal Society of Arts, London, 1971; Commander of the Victorian Order, 1977; Chevalier, l'Ordre National du Mérite, France, 1984; received Knighthood, 1988. **Died:** 7 February 1992, in London.

Sir Edward Rayne, spring/summer 1955 collection: workers inspect a pair of gold-studded luster calf shoes. © Hulton-Deutsch Collection/ CORBIS.

PUBLICATIONS

On RAYNE:

Books

Lambert, Eleanor, *The World of Fashion: People, Places, Resources,* New York & London, 1976.

Swan, June, *Shoes,* London, 1982.

McDowell, Colin, *Shoes: Fashion and Fantasy,* London, 1989.

Articles

Tyrrel, Rebecca, "The Face of British Fashion," in the *Sunday Times Magazine* (London), 16 October 1989.

"Edward Rayne," [obituary] in *The Guardian,* 8 February 1992.

McDowell, Colin, profile in *The Guardian,* 10 February 1992.

"Edward Rayne," [obituary] in the *Times* (London), 10 February 1992.

"Edward Rayne," [obituary] in the *Independent,* 11 February 1992.

Fallon, James, "Britain's Rayne, 69, Dies in Fire at Home," in *Footwear News* (New York), 17 February 1992.

MacDonald, Laurie, "The Great Fashion Merchants," in *Footwear News,* 17 April 1995.

Baber, Bonnie, et al., "The Great Design Houses (Shoe Designers Gucci, Rayne, Delman, Bally and I. Miller)," in *Footwear News,* 17 April 1995.

LoRusso, Maryann, "1940–49—Stylish Sacrifices," in *Footwear News,* 26 April 1999.

———, "Walk of Fame—Celebrities Have Been Among Shoe Designers' Best…," in *Footwear News,* 26 April 1999.

* * *

In 1918, when the second generation of Raynes took over the family firm, the idea of shoes as an article of fashion was a novel one. "The only people who bought stylish footwear were actresses and ladies of easy virtue," said Edward Rayne of the type of customer to patronize the first New Bond Street, London shop. This changed rapidly as the flapper age of the 1920s produced a breed of liberated and fashion-conscious women who demanded shoes like those worn by their idols of stage and screen. An H&M Rayne Ltd. advertisement of the time used popular actress Lily Langtry to promote the Langtry Shoe and the company won fashion credibility in a 1920s issue of *Vogue* when their button boots were described as the "smartest footwear in town."

Long before stars of stage and screen were fashion leaders, trends were set by monarchs and aristocracy in the courts of Europe. When H&M Rayne received its first royal warrant from Queen Mary it was a sign the company had shed its risqué theatrical past and was respectable within the fashion world. Other royal warrants followed and a new generation of rich, famous, and aristocratic women patronized the company. These ladies were indeed well heeled, as H&M Rayne was the first British firm to introduce machinery from the U.S. to make the sole of the shoe more flexible.

With American-style multiple fittings and sizes, a Raynes shoe had the comfort and fit found previously only in bespoke shoes. H&M Raynes' success as a British footwear fashion house to rival those of Charles Jourdan, Bally, and Miller came about in the 1950s. At age 28, Edward Rayne was still a young man when he took control of the family firm, and he led a hectic social life in Paris, enjoying night clubs and the company of fashion editors and glamorous diplomatic socialites. French and Italian design led the field in the 1950s and Rayne, from early on in his career, took an interest in promoting British design. In the 1950s when the buyers from important U.S. department stores came increasingly less often to London, Rayne courted them in the Paris couture houses and the fashionable night spots.

Edward Rayne became chairman of the Incorporated Society of London Fashion Designers (ISLFD) in 1960 and within two years *Vogue* was hailing his remarkable success in persuading American press and buyers to view British collections. Other members of the ISLFD included Hardy Amies, John Cavanagh, and Norman Hartnell, who all designed shoes for Rayne. During the 1950s H&M Rayne produced classic styling that perfectly matched the rigid dress codes of the day. Times were changing, however, and the 1960s saw a fashion revolution in clothes, music, and dance. Edward Rayne called dancing the "language of the legs" and knew full well that what a woman wore to dance, and how she danced, would influence her choice of footwear. In response to the changing trends he contracted new British designers to contribute to the Miss Rayne range.

Mary Quant designed her first leather stacked stiletto heels and Shirley Temple-style ankle-straps for Rayne in 1960. Later she was commissioned to design her own range, along with other young British designers such as Jean Muir and Gerald McCann, to produce collections in synch with the Swinging Sixties. Rayne made sure that alongside the sophisticated styling for one generation there was sufficient fashion and frivolity for the next.

The quality of the footwear designs was matched by their production. Rayne was a shoemaker himself, having served an 11-year apprenticeship. He was, said Jean Muir, the "best British shoemaker of his age. He worked to a quality that matched anything from abroad." It is not surprising that in 1963 shoes by Roger Vivier were being made and sold exclusively by Rayne. In the 1970s shoes by Rayne were being used by leading French couturiers including Lanvin and Nina Ricci. The 1970s saw the fulfilment of one of Edward Rayne's personal ambitions, his first shop in Paris. It was the first British shoe-shop to open in Paris since John Lobb, which specialized in bespoke footwear. By 1985 H&M Rayne had some 70 retail outlets throughout the world.

It was the Americans, Rayne claimed, who taught him to sell shoes, and he used his transatlantic talents to promote fashion design at the same time. Fashion writer Colin McDowell, writing in *Shoes: Fashion and Fantasy* (London, 1989) described Rayne as "a mover and a shaker to whom the British fashion industry owes a permanent debt." Before the ISLFD was formed, the idea that one could sell a fashion industry to a world market was unheard of—but Edward Rayne changed this outdated mode of thinking. For over 40 years, first through the ISLFD and then the British Fashion Council, he was involved in any scheme that would improve the image of British fashion. He used his contacts with royalty and governments to stage fashion shows, banquets, and receptions to promote British collections. British Fashion Week became a glamorous affair which helped persuade overseas buyers and press to visit London. In launching the British Fashion Awards in 1989, he brought catwalk shows to the public and, through television coverage, brought fashion to the attention of millions.

Edward Rayne's contribution to the development of the British Fashion Council was the culmination of a lifetime's diplomatic pioneering—and partying—in aid of British design. He did more than any other businessman to persuade overseas buyers and press to take British fashion design seriously. By the time he retired from chairing the British Fashion Council in 1990, the Council had success and recognition worldwide as a promotional body, and Rayne had received a well deserved knighthood for his services to the industry.

—Chris Hill

RED OR DEAD

British footwear and clothing design firm

Founded: in London, 1982, by Wayne and Geraldine Hemingway (both born 1961); incorporated in 1983. **Company History:** Specialized in customized second-hand clothing and Doc Marten shoes and boots; produced Space Baby collection, 1989; approached by Marks & Spencer to consult on shoes, 1993; introduced Dead Basic collection, 1994; opened store in Tokyo, 1994; participated in Cool Britannia, 1998; debuted website. **Company Address:** 17–19 Popin Commercial Centre, South Way, Wembley, Middlesex HA9 OHB, England. **Company Website:** www.redordead.co.uk.

Publications

On RED OR DEAD:

Books

Kingswell, Tamsin, *Red or Dead: The Good, the Bad, and the Ugly*, London, 1998.

Articles

Collier, Andrew, "Red or Dead Becomes London Cult Happening," in *DNR*, 7 November 1988.

Red or Dead, spring 1998 collection. © AP/Wide World Photos.

———, "Two UK Retailers Refuse to Sell Acid House Clothing," in *Footwear News,* 5 December 1988.
———, "Red or Dead: This British Chain is Red Hot," in *DNR,* 6 March 1989.
Haggard, Claire, "Alive and Kicking," in *Sportswear International* (New York), July 1990.
"Going to Greater Lenghts—Those Unpredictable British Designers Take the Lead in Feminine, Wearable Fashions," in *Chicago Tribune,* 31 October 1990.
Heath, Ashley, "Sole Survivors," in *The Face* (London), March 1992.
Tredre, Roger, "What's Red, Dead, Alive and Kicking?" in the *Independent* (London), 15 March 1992.
Warren, Rachael, "My First Break," in the *Evening Standard* (London), 25 March 1992.
"Fashion, Fascism and Dead Old Doc," in *Management Today* (London), April 1992.
Fallon, James, "Red or Dead Finds 'Easy Does It' Works," in *Footwear News,* 17 August 1992.
"The Doctor is In," in *DNR,* 28 May 1993.
Stretton, Lynda, "Red or Dead," [profile] at the Fashion Page website, available online at www.fashionz.co.uk, 1995.
———, "Interview with Wayne Hemingway," at the Fashion Page website, online at www.fashionz.co.uk, 1995.
"Shopping Europe," in *Footwear News,* 30 September 1996.
Freedman, Cheryl, "King of the Catwalk," in *Estates Gazette* (Manchester, England), 22 March 1997.
Brooks, Libby, "Let's Help British Design Cut It (British Fashion Designer Wayne Hemingway)," in *The Guardian,* 4 February 1998.

*

Red or Dead is a London-based design company producing innovative clothing and footwear at affordable prices. Consisting of a dynamic group of young talent, the Red or Dead team has worked closely to create fashion with a refreshing sense of humour and individuality. In the space of 10 years, Red or Dead grew into an internationally known design label with shops in England, Copenhagen, Amsterdam, and Hong Kong. There is an extensive wholesale network selling to shops worldwide and a thriving mail order service with a biannual catalogue.

—Red or Dead

* * *

There are those who have described Wayne Hemingway as the shrewdest man in fashion. In the 1980s, while other British footwear companies were closing or retreating into safely classic styling, Hemingway, with his keen market trader's sense of street fashion, launched Red or Dead (the name came from Hemingway's father, Billy Two Rivers, a Mohawk Indian chief, and former heavyweight champion).

In the mid-1980s, formative years for Red or Dead, the well tailored young executive look dominated the London High Street stores. This was power dressing, clothes to make money, the yuppie uniform. In contrast to the serious adult dressing there was a "hard times" student style, sometimes dubbed "recession chic." The poverty stricken but style-conscious dressed in jumble sale bargains and 1940s or 1950s cheap secondhand clothes. Heavy fabrics combined with a long layered look evoked the workwear of a proletariat still engaged in a class war.

This was a street fashion which seemed to be suggesting some hidden socialist agenda within a mode of dress. Suddenly, politics and fashion could be mixed. The first designer t-shirt by Katherine Hammett proclaimed "58% Don't Want Pershing,"and a fashion label was named Workers for Freedom. Yuppies really were conservative and socialists were chic.

The footwear of choice for the young, idealistic, and working class at heart was the classic steel-toe boot originally aimed at postmen and construction workers. The Doc Marten (DM) boot was designed for those who wanted to make an antifashion statement, and it quickly became popular with punk rock devotees. Hemingway introduced the basic DM through his Camden Market stalls and shop. They were immediately taken up by young men and women and customized by cutting in metal toe-caps, putting safety pins through them, sewing on beads and threading them with brightly colored laces. The basic black DM was sprayed in a multitude of colors and could be made as individual as the owner.

The DM boot was the only footwear available at the time with the heaviness of silhouette required to make a woman's foot look really

Red or Dead: autumn/winter 1998–99 collection: sheepskin coats. © AP/Wide World Photos.

weighty. This went against all the traditional ideas of dainty feminine footwear for ladies who wanted their feet to look smaller, not bigger. The idea of a heavy, functional shoe for women was not initially a fashion statement; it came out of the whole recession chic concept, but it soon became an obligatory accessory for those who would never have bought secondhand.

Red or Dead produced styles with jagged soles, platform soles, bigger and heavier than the basic DM. They made boots in perspex, bright orange patent, silver, and other colors. Hemingway had found a winning formula and could have continued selling chunky shoes from his now rapidly expanding retail empire. He was, however—his own words—easily bored. Moving into clothing was an obvious progression.

The Red or Dead clothing collections were as antifashion establishment as the footwear. Not for Hemingway the traditional middle-class, middle-aged values of made-to-last quality—the idea behind Red or Dead was, he states, "to wear the stuff for a few months, and then it either drops to bits or becomes unfashionable." Hemingway recognized that fashion changed very quickly for young people and didn't believe in taking it terribly seriously. His collections have become somewhat more tailored since the Space Baby or Kaleidoscope days and more professional than the notorious Animals collection, where the prints simply dropped off the garments. And since Hemingway long refused to court what he saw as the "la-di-da" fashion editors and stylists, his catwalk collections were not reviewed in the mainstream fashion bibles.

Yet what the fashion editors thought of Red or Dead was irrelevant; more than a third of the company's international business came from clothing, and Hemmingway's reputation as a shrewd businessman earned him an invitation to sit on the British Fashion Council. For many this was the height of irony; but Hemingway and Red or Dead had—like it or not—joined the fashion parade. By the middle of the 1990s Red or Dead had stores around the world, from several in the UK to Tokyo, Tel Aviv, Copenhagen, and Ontario. Its uncanny ability to straddle fashion and antifashion continued to make it a sought-after commodity, in both apparel and shoes. Such was confirmed once again when Red or Dead made the "Hot List" put together by *Footwear News* (30 September 1996) naming shoe designers "who had buyers buzzing in Paris, Milan and Dusseldorf."

Hemingway's legacy to the fashion world will be twofold: first, in footwear, because Red or Dead changed the silhouette of women's feet, along with our preconceptions of how they should look; and second, in apparel for transcending and creating trends simultaneously. Hemingway's own mission statement said, "At Red or Dead our mission is to produce challenging clothing at an affordable price on a nonelitist level. We want fashion and high fashion for everybody." Whether making a statement through chunky-soled shoes or in "nonelitist" clothes, Red or Dead is and will remain, according to the Fashion Page website, "one of London's most innovative labels."

—Chris Hill; updated by Nelly Rhodes

REESE, Tracy

American designer

Born: 12 February 1964, in Detroit, Michigan. **Education:** Cass Technical High School; Parsons School of Design, graduated 1984. **Career:** Design assistant, Martine Sitbon, New York, 1984–87; started own company, 1987–89; designer for Perry Ellis, 1990; freelance designer for Gordon Henderson, 1990; design director, Magaschoni, 1990–95; designed exclusive line for The Limited, New York, 1995; started own company, Tracy Reese Meridian, 1995.

Publications

On REESE:

Books

Stegemeyer, Anne, *Who's Who in Fashion, Third Edition,* New York, 1996.

Articles

Chua, Lawrence, "Tracy Reese," in *WWD,* 8 September 1987.
Rosenblum, P., "Three Strike Out," in *WWD,* 30 November 1988.
Lockwood, Lisa, "Duffy is Named President of Perry Ellis Women's Unit," in *WWD,* 26 January 1989.
Gregory, Deborah, "Tracy Reese," in *Essence,* July 1993.
Holch, Allegra, "Tracy Reese," in *WWD,* 6 January 1994.
Cain, Joy Luckett, Interview, *Essence,* May 1995.
Fashion brief, in *Essence,* September 2000.

* * *

Tracy Reese's designs have been inspired by a wide variety of sources: a piece of music, a painting, a book, a vacation spot, or a particular city. Reese is known for combining unusual textures and colors, often with a touch of vintage. She claims that she designs for "a smart shopper," but actually designs for shoppers who want no-nonsense sportswear. "My clothes are not basics, and they're not really classics either, but they are, hopefully, essentials." Reese has further stated that she would never design anything she would not wear herself.

Reese hails from Detroit, where as a youngster her mother enrolled her in art classes on the weekends so she wouldn't be bored. Reese's mother, a modern dance teacher, would challenge Tracy by staging sewing contests to see who could finish an outfit first—the loser had to pay for the fabric. Reese attended the well-known Cass Technical High School, where she took her first fashion design class. While she was in high school, she was encouraged to apply for a scholarship to a summer program at the Parsons School of Design. After receiving the scholarship and participating in the program at Parsons, she realized clothing design was the career choice for her, "That's when I knew I wanted to be involved in every aspect of this business, not just stuck in some back room sketching and draping for days." Reese later earned her B.A. from Parsons, graduating in 1984.

After Parsons, Reese was an apprentice to French designer Martine Sitbon for the Arlequin line of clothing. While working at Arlequin, Reese became more than an apprentice, as Sitbon allowd her to sketch designs. With encouragement from friends and family, and financial backing from Reese's father, Claud, she started her own company in 1987. She designed and manufactured a full line of clothing shipped in the autumn of that year, but after the release of her fall 1988 line, the company folded. Her designs were well received and sold at boutiques and specialty stores, as well as upscale stores such as Barneys New York, Bergdorf Goodman, and Ann Taylor. Although Reese was successful as a designer, she did not have enough capital to keep up with the demand, and like many other designers in the late1980s, her company failed.

Reese moved on to design for the Perry Ellis Portfolio line with Marc Jacobs. She also worked as a consultant with the sportswear designer Gordon Henderson, from whom she learned several key elements about how to succeed in the fashion design business. After about a year, Reese sought a job designing for Magaschoni, the company owned by Magdalena Lee. At first, Reese continued to work on the company's existing line of clothing, which was "not my style," but Magaschoni was a new company with an open mind and growth potential, and after two years, Reese was designing her own label. Lee, who had worked with several prominent designers, said of Reese: "What really impressed me so about Tracy is she knows how to make a better garment." One of Reese's friends, Ellen Greenberg (president of Magaschoni), who offered moral support in Reese's early career, called her line "the jewel in the crown."

Reese typically sketches her design ideas late at night while at home listening to music, and has admitted she cannot "put paper to pencil unless I'm listening to music." She is very impressionable and gets her design ideas from a variety of sources, including fashion designs from previous eras, films, different cities. A recent trip to New Orleans was incorporated and reflected in a subsequent collection. Her eclectic taste in music and her passionate desire to experience new things and visit new places continues to pervade her designs.

After several successful years designing for Magaschoni, Reese left the company to work on her own. She designed an exclusive line of clothing for The Limited in 1995, which funded her first contemporary sportswear label, Tracy Reese Meridian. The Meridian line debuted in the spring of 1996 and the following year she established a second sportswear line, Plenty, inspired by a trip to India. Her collections have been shown at Saks, Nordstrom, Fred, Segal-Ron Herman, and Anthropologie.

—Christine Miner Minderovic

RENÉ LEZARD

German fashion company

Founded: René Lezard Mode GmbH founded in 1978, Schwarzach, Wurzburg, by Thomas Schaefer. **Company History:** Specializes in womenswear, sportswear, and menswear; main lines are Classic, Excess, Sophisticated, plus Denim House; licensee products include shirts (Asoni), ties (Albisetti), belts (Condor), and leather accessories (Traveller); added footwear line, 2000; exports to Europe, U.S, and Asia; annual show at Herren-Mode-Woche (Cologne). **Company Address:** Industriestrasse 2, D-97359 Schwarzach, Germany. **Company Website:** www.rene-lezard.de.

PUBLICATIONS

On RENÉ LEZARD:

Articles

Erlick, June C., "René Lezard Establishes U.S. Group," in *DNR,* 13 August 1991.

"Jennifer Nichols Joins René Lezard Fashion Group Inc. as Director of Sales and Marketing," in *DNR,* 8 January 1992.

Gellers, Stan, "Suit Makers Doubling Up for Fall," in *DNR,* 15 April 1993.

D'Aulnay, Sophie, "Suitably German," in *DNR,* 8 July 1996.

Conti, Samantha, "U.S. Still a Tasty Carrot for Hungry German Companies," in *DNR,* 11 February 1998.

Mui, Nelson, and James Fallon, "René Lezard to Make a Splash in 2000," in *DNR,* 8 November 1999.

"Multiple Choice: If a Little of What You Fancy Does You Good, Then the Fall New York Collections Should Benefit Many," in *WWD,* 8 February 2000.

Boye, Brian, and Brian Scott Lipton, "Spreading the Nudes," in *DNR,* 16 June 2000.

Gellers, Stan, "From Power Suits to Power Sportswear," in *DNR,* 28 August 2000.

Weldon, Kristi, "The Men's Business Suit: Extinct, or Just Evolving?" in *Apparel Industry Magazine,* October 2000.

McCants, Leonard, and Julee Greenberg, "Bold Blueprints to Boost Brands," in *WWD,* 5 December 2000.

Cunningham, Thomas, "Old World Elegance with New Twists Stars at Cologne," in *DNR,* 7 February 2001.

*

Company philosophy—planned growth, team work and strong relationships with our clients are our top priorities. Product philosophy—offering a unique collection, using the highest quality fabrics available, the prerequisite for a smart mix of fashion.

—René Lezard

* * *

René Lezard is a medium-sized German fashion group making clothes for men and women. Neither high fashion nor cheap mass-market, René Lezard makes quality outfits and separates for High Street shops throughout Germany in what's known as the "gold" range—a bit less than designer but above bridge collections. René Lezard is a top German fashion brand and company, making quality, everyday clothes for practical lives. The clothes have a very practical, Northern European look and feel: thick, warm, heavy-duty office, leisure, and outdoor wear, distinctively German or middle European. The accent is on tailoring, not cut; fabrics are expensive but not flashy. The look is smart-somber, like a Northern European city in the rain or snow.

Fabrics used by the company include soft fleeces and refined leathers, warm corduroys and smooth velvets, thick tweeds, heavy lambswool and cashmere. Colors include all the darker shades of brown, gray, green, and blue, some dark mustard, some burgundy, and more recently denim and bright colors were added to the mix. The occasional item or outfit shines out in mother-of-pearl or cream. Though the styles are very classical, René Lezard seems more influenced by English fashion than French. The overall composition is pure German, with homegrown lines and styles. Shoulders are soft; upper parts are unrestricted and loose. There are many buttons and buttonholes, turnups, dark linings, high collars. The overall look is soft and loose, dry and warm. The smart chic of the clothes comes through the choice of refined color and fine fabric.

The company's range is comprehensive—for men, there are suits, jackets, vests, trousers, coats, sport jackets, shirts, neckties, belts, knitwear, t-shirts, polo neck sweaters, leathers, and most recently footwear. These are split into three lines: Classic, the basic elements of the collection; Excess, the young, approachable, commercial range; and Sophisticated, the fashionwear and experimental items. Similarly for women the range covers suits, trousers, skirts, blazers, coats, leatherwear, knitwear, blousons, and belts. Denim House is a mass-market brand, with jeans, shirts, jackets, and waistcoats clearly aimed at the High Street and a young adult market that buys one or more items to build or expand an existing wardrobe. In addition to the above, René Lezard uses licensee products within the collection: Asoni shirts, Albisetti ties, Condor belts, Traveller leather accessories.

René Lezard's strength is in finding its niche both in Europe and the U.S.—adults in the middle-age range who are willing to pay for stylish, practical, quality clothing that delivers as promised. The strategy paid off with strong growth in New York's SoHo district, which was treated to the company's first American store in September 1997, and corporate leaders are now looking toward Florida or the West Coast for future boutiques. The women's apparel is especially strong in the U.S. and sold in many Saks and Bergdorf Goodman locations. Men's apparel is primarily found in independent specialty stores, although the company is working to expand in the market.

René Lezard is actively seeking growth, particularly in the U.S., with increased spending for advertising, a "virtual showroom" website to interact with customers and professionals, sponsored trips for art students to Normandy, and by building ties with the art community, such as through sponsorship of the New York Academy of Arts benefit event "Take Home a Nude." The high quality and fit of René Lezard, coupled with its gold-level niche status, is sure to grow in popularity.

—Sally Anne Melia; updated by Carrie Snyder

RENTNER, Maurice

American designer and manufacturer

Born: Warsaw, Poland, 3 March 1889; immigrated to the U.S. in 1902. **Family:** Married Dorothy Fineberg; children: two daughters. **Career:** Worked as an errand boy, traveling salesman and jobber, 1902–12; partner, M&H Rentner, 1912–23; owner, Maurice Rentner, Inc., 1923–58; company merged with sister's firm, Anna Miller & Company, then run and eventually renamed by Bill Blass, 1970. **Died:** 7 July 1958, in New York.

PUBLICATIONS

On RENTNER:

Books

Ballard, Bettina, *In My Fashion,* New York, 1960.

Milbank, Caroline Rennolds, *New York Fashion: The Evolution of American Style,* New York, 1989.

Maurice Rentner, 1952 collection: silk satin evening gown with an abbreviated beaded bodice superimposed on top. © Bettmann/CORBIS.

Articles

Profile, in *New York World Telegram,* 11 May 1945.

"Maurice Rentner," in *National Cyclopaedia of American Biography,* 1957.

"Maurice Rentner is Dead at 69; Noted as Dress Manufacturer," [obituary] in the *New York Times,* 8 July 1958.

* * *

According to Bettina Ballard's *In My Fashion* (New York, 1960), Maurice Rentner styled himself the "King of Fashion." It is perhaps more accurate to call him a prince of American ready-to-wear. In his boyhood he worked briefly for his father's button-making company, then advanced from errand boy to salesman for a shirtwaist manufacturer by 1906. As ready-made clothing became more respectable, Rentner perceived its potential for growth, and began to develop the higher-priced end of the emerging industry.

Between 1912 and 1923 Rentner was associated with his brother in M&H Rentner, establishing his own company under his own name after the partnership was dissolved. From the very first, Rentner was careful to establish an air of exclusivity around his company. Advertisements were discreet but not inconspicuous, with text declaring Maurice Rentner gowns were only to be seen in the finest shops. He offered high quality merchandise at prices to match, setting standards of excellence for other ready-to-wear manufacturers.

Suits and daydresses made up most of the company's output, but eveningwear was also produced. Rentner said that he could not "sketch, sew, drape, pin or cut" and counted on design assistants to realize his ideas, which were rooted in the belief that "clothes should never decorate," as he told the *New York World Telegram* in May 1945, "but should always frame." As a result, silhouettes were generally uncomplicated, with spare detailing which was often innovative and sometimes unexpected. A narrow ruffle down the placket of a suit jacket resolved into a pocket flap at the hipline, or a smooth wool sheath dress was paired with a shirt-jacket having a hand-crocheted body. Fabrics were generally kept simple but sumptuous; wool or silk crêpes and jerseys, fine Rodier tweeds, silk prints. And, at least for a while, Rentner published and wrote the majority of the copy for his fashion periodical, *Quality Street.*

Rentner's prevailing theme was femininity, expressed in soft suits and graceful dresses. He further claimed to have pioneered the use of casual styling in formal clothing, introduced in the 1930s with a gold lamé shirtwaist-styled dinner gown. His efforts to meld style with comfort helped to establish an American fashion identity, in which casual need not mean unkempt, nor formal signify stuffy. At his level of workmanship, detail, and fabric quality, ready-made clothing was not for the working gal, but for the society or business woman who did not care to spend much of her free time in fittings. Garments by Maurice Rentner, Inc. were available as exclusives at stores like Bonwit Teller, I. Magnin, Rich's, Lord & Taylor, and Kaufmann's.

As one of the upmarket manufacturers who supported an in-house design staff, Rentner was very aware of the plague of design piracy. In 1933 he formed the Fashion Originator's Guild, which established a design registration bureau for its members. The Guild grew from 12 original members to 60 by the end of its first year. Cooperating retailers agreed to refrain from buying or selling copies of garments created by Guild members. It seems to have been a laudable experiment, but consensus on the terms of the agreements rapidly broke down, and by 1936 the Guild was being sued by several retailers for restraint of trade. It was disbanded in 1941.

Rentner tried always to foster the interests of the garment industry, as a member of the New York Dress Institute Couture Group and other garment center organizations, and by serving on the advisory board of the Fashion Institute of Technology in New York. His company was among those that profited, in terms of consumer recognition, by the isolation of American fashion during World War II. It may be that his success with high quality name ready-to-wear inspired the rush of European couturiers to lend their own names to the market in the late 1940s.

Although Rentner died in 1958, his business, in a way, lived on. Maurice Rentner, Inc. merged with Anna Miller & Company, owned by Rentner's sister, in 1958, with Miller's head designer, Bill Blass, maintaining the position in the joined company. Bill Blass for Maurice Rentner was successful through the 1960s, while Blass became vice-president and then owner of the firm. He organized the company under his own name in 1970. It is a tribute to Rentner's achievement in making his name synonymous with quality and style that, even through the turbulent 1960s, his name endured.

—Madelyn Shaw

RESTIVO, Mary Ann

American designer

Born: South Orange, New Jersey, 28 September 1940. **Education:** Studied retailing at College of St. Elizabeth, Morristown, New Jersey, 1958–60, and design at Fashion Institute of Technology, New York, 1960–61, with associate degree in Applied Arts. **Family:** Married Saul Rosen, 1978. **Career:** Trainee, Abby Michael junior sportswear house, New York, 1961; designer for New York firms Bernard Levine, Petti for Jack Winter, Something Special, Sports Sophisticates, and Mary Ann Restivo for Genre, 1962–74; head designer, women's blouse division, Dior New York, 1974–80; launched own firm, Mary Ann Restivo, Inc., 1980; sold company to Leslie Fay Corporation, 1988; designer, Mary Ann Restivo division, Leslie Fay Corporation, 1988–92; division closed, 1992; independent design consultant, for clients including Saks Fifth Avenue and Burberrys, from 1993; launched new scarf line, 1999; began designing home accessories, 1999–2000. **Awards:** Hecht Company Young Designers award, Washington, D.C., 1968; Mortimer C. Ritter award, Fashion Institute of Technology, 1973; awarded Honorary Doctor of Humanities, College of St. Elizabeth, 1986; Alumnus of the Year award, American Association of Community and Junior Colleges, 1992; Ellis Island Medal of Honor award, 1993.

Publications

On RESTIVO:

Books

Milbank, Caroline Rennolds, *New York Fashion: The Evolution of American Style,* New York, 1989.

Fashion for America! Designs in the Fashion Institute of Technology, New York, Surrey, 1992.

Articles

Larkin, Kathy, "Meet Two Designers Who Are Changing Establishment Fashions," in the *New York Daily News,* 14 January 1973.

Foley, Bridget, "Mary Ann Restivo Marches to Her Own Drummer," in *New York Apparel News,* April 1983.

Morris, Bernadine, "Working Women: A Designer's Focus," in the *New York Times,* 30 June 1987.

Daria, Irene, "Mary Ann Restivo: Targeting the Working Woman and Herself," in *WWD,* 26 October 1987.

Vespa, Mary, "Designer Mary Ann Restivo Walks on Fashion's Mild Side...," in *People,* 23 November 1987.

Michals, Debra, "Dresses from Sportswear Firms: Plusses and Problems," in *WWD,* 28 February 1989.

Schiro, Anne-Marie, "From Restivo, a New Look of Softness," in the *New York Times,* 3 November 1989.

Morris, Bernadine, "Building Wardrobes Around Jackets," in the *New York Times,* 8 May 1990.

Buck, Geneviève, "Barneys, Buddy and Bo—New Style, Old Style and No Style," in *Chicago Tribune,* 15 July 1992.

Johnson, Tish, "Restivo Returns," in *WWD,* 12 July 1999.

"Robert Allen Event Combines Fashion, Charity," in *HFN (Weekly Newspaper for the Home Furnishing Network),* 6 December 1999.

* * *

"People need fashionably sensible clothes," Mary Ann Restivo commented to *People* magazine in the midst of the late 1980s excesses, to which *People* asserted that Restivo was "emerging...as the savior of the stylish but sane professional woman." Career and professional dressing have been the appropriate context for Restivo's work, not only in terms of her clientèle, but of the clothing's emphasis on good fit, excellent materials and manufacture, personal luxury without ostentation, and wearable good taste.

Bernadine Morris, a likely champion of Restivo's work in her commitment to American sportswear, wrote of Restivo that she "tries to walk the tightrope between clothes that are subdued and those that attract attention." The attention a Restivo garment attracts is primarily for its flattering image to the client. Restivo emphasizes fit, with some camouflage to the hips, appealing to women in sizes six, eight, and ten. As the designer argues in the tradition of sportswear, no woman should feel squeezed into the clothing, but should have mobility for her own sense of elegance and self-confidence, as well as the functions of dressing for careers in which one outfit may suffice from home to office to evening. In the 1980s, Restivo's work directly coincided with the perceived need of women of middle- and upper-management to wear sensible clothing to the office without merely adapting menswear. Other American designers came to the same conviction in the 1980s, but Restivo was one of the first to create stylish careerwear and to establish it as the cornerstone of her business.

Through the 1980s jackets were an important element of all Restivo collections, even for resort. Like most designers of the period, Restivo made her jackets softer and softer, choosing the textiles for unconstructed jackets still capable of the fresh self-confidence required by career women. Restivo told the *New York Times* (8 May 1990) at the apogee of the well-tailored business jacket: "The jacket is the key. When you start to develop your collection, you begin with the jacket then build everything else around it. You work out the skirts or the pants and the blouses and sweaters." Further, Restivo commented, "It is interesting to me that when store buyers come to buy the collection, they follow the same procedure. When customers go shopping for their fall clothes, they will probably do the same thing."

Restivo's acuity to the customer has always been an essential part of her business, begun in 1981. The loyalty of her clients is legendary—when the Restivo line was abruptly dropped by Leslie Fay in the early 1990s, clients pursued the designer herself to be sure they would not be cut off from their favorite clothing. Restivo's client empathy is undeniably important in the success of a woman designer creating for like-minded sensible women of business and style. Gloria Steinem once described Restivo's designs as "the kind of clothes that, after you've died, another woman would find in a thrift shop and like." Such enduring good taste and clothing recycling may thwart the image of fashion as a place of excess and fickle change. Yet Restivo's clothing fosters another more sensible, purposeful, and undeniably beautiful concept of fashion.

Restivo has long been a fan of exquisite textiles and a fixture at fabric fairs like Moda In and the European Textile Selection, scouring their wares for the best materials and often permitting the textiles to determine her designs. By the end of the 1990s Restivo had turned away from her consulting duties for Saks Fifth Avenue and Burberrys to again design under her own name. A new line of scarves and shawls, in bright colors and patterns, came in a variety of fabrics including cashmere, silk, tulle, and velvet. The new accessories were sold to high-end retailers and department stores, some of the very same stores Restivo targeted with her next launch of home accessories, including small lingerie dressers and decorative pillows. Commenting on her new direction, Restivo told *Women's Wear Daily* (12 July 1999), "I like the freedom that accessories offers in terms of the scale of design."

—Richard Martin; updated by Nelly Rhodes

RHODES, Zandra

British designer

Born: Zandra Lindsey Rhodes in Chatham, Kent, England, 19 September 1940. **Education:** Studied textile design, Medway College of Art, 1959–61, and Royal College of Art, 1961–64. **Career:** Established dressmaking firm with Sylvia Ayton, London, 1964, and textile design studio with Alexander McIntyre, 1965; partner/designer, Fulham Clothes Shop, 1967–68; freelance designer, 1968–75; director, Zandra Rhodes U.K. Ltd, and Zandra Rhodes Shops Ltd., from 1975; launched ready-to-wear collections, in Australia, 1979, and in Britain, 1984; also designed bed linens and household textiles; opened a studio in California for interior design and fine art, 1995; launched Zandra Rhodes fur collection for Pologeorgis, 1995; featured designer with Lady Thatcher for *U.K. Utah* British promotion in Salt Lake City, 1996; featured designer for *Designing Women,* Costa Mesa, with accompanying book signing, 1996; launched Zandra Rhodes II, hand-painted silk ready-to-wear collection made in Hong Kong, 1996; created bed linens for Grattons mail order catalogue in the U.K., 1996; launched Zandra by the Sea ready-to-wear collection, California, 1997; launched Zandra Rhodes eyewear collection with Lygo Merx, 1998; created exclusive collection for Liberty of London, 1998; active in the British Invasion at Saks Fifth Avenue, New York, 1998; conducted Riga-Latvia Show and headed Fashion Forum,

Zandra Rhodes in 1989. © Eric Crichton/CORBIS.

1999; groundbreaking ceremony for the Fashion and Textile Museum, London, 1999; trunk show at Lilly Dodson, Dallas, 2000; opened Melbourne Fashion Week, 2000. **Exhibitions:** *Zandra Rhodes: A Retrospective with Artworks,* Art Museum of Santa Cruz, California, 1983; retrospective *Works of Art,* Seibu Seed Hall, Tokyo, Japan, 1987; exhibition of watercolors, Dyansen Gallery, New York, 1989; exhibition of scarves, dresses, and watercolors, Westbury Hotel in London, 1989; exhibition of watercolors, Dyansen Gallery, Los Angeles, 1989; exhibition of watercolors, printed textiles, and sketchbooks, Seibu Hall, Tokyo, 1991; *Fabrics and Their Inspiration* show and lectures, Goldstein Gallery, Daytons, Minneapolis, 1991; exhibition of watercolors, Dyansen Gallery, New Orleans, 1991; retrospective garment show, Mint Museum, North Carolina, 1992; *Dressed to Kill,* National Gallery of Australia, 1993; *Street Chic,* Victoria and Albert Museum, London, 1994; *Couture of Chaos,* Auckland Art Museum, New Zealand, 1997; *Punk Kulture,* South Melbourne, Australia, 1997; *Cutting Edge Fifty Years of Fashion,* Victoria and Albert Museum, London, 1997; *The Surface and Beyond,* Victoria and Albert Museum, 1997; *Best Dressed,* Victoria and Albert Museum, 1997; *The Surface and Beyond,* San Diego, 1998; *Costume of the Ancient Egyptians,* Manchester Museum, 1998; *Exotisme,* Musee de la Mode et du Textile, Paris, 1998; Grace Barrand Design Centre, Surrey, 1998. **Awards:** English Fashion Designer of the Year award, 1972; Royal Designer for Industry, 1974; Moore College of Art award, Philadelphia, 1978; DFA, International Fine Arts College of Miami, 1977; Royal Designer for Industry, Royal Society of Arts, 1977; Best Costume award for *Romeo and Juliet on Ice,* British Association of Film and Television Emmy award, 1979; "Britain's Designer", Clothing and Export Council and the National Economic Development Committee, 1983; Alpha award for Best Show of the Year, Saks Fifth Avenue, New Orleans, 1985; Woman of Distinction award, Northwood Institute, Dallas, 1986; Number One Textile Designer in the U.K. by the *Observer* magazine, 1990; Alpha award for Best Show of the Year, Saks Fifth Avenue, New Orleans, 1991; Hall of Fame award by the British Fashion Council, 1995; Golden Hanger award for lifetime achievement, Fashion Careers of California College, San Diego, 1997; Commander of the British Empire, 1997; Leading Woman Entrepreneur of the World by the Star Group U.S.A., 1998; Honor award from the National Terrazzo and Mosaic Association Honor for Del Mar Terrace, 1998. **Address:** Zandra Rhodes Head Office, 79–85 Bermondsey Street, London, SE1 3XF. **Website:** www.zandrarhodes.com.

PUBLICATIONS

By RHODES:

Books

The Art of Zandra Rhodes, with Anne Knight, London, 1984; New York, 1985, 1994.

Articles

"A Life in the Day of Zandra Rhodes," with Anne Whitehouse, in the *Sunday Times Magazine* (London), 24 January 1982.
"My Country, Right or Wrong," in the *Sunday Telegraph Magazine* (London), 10 May 1987.

On RHODES:

Books

Santa Cruz Art Museum, *Zandra Rhodes: A Retrospective with Artworks,* Santa Cruz, CA, 1983.
Milbank, Caroline Rennolds, *Couture: The Great Fashion Designers,* London, 1985.
McCarthy, Fiona, and Patrick Nuttgens, *Eye for Industry: Royal Designers for Industry, 1936–1986,* [exhibition catalogue], London, 1986.
Loebenthal, Joel, *Radical Rags: Fashions of the Sixties,* New York, 1990.
Mendes, Valerie, and Claire Wilcox, *Modern Fashion in Detail,* London, 1991.
Steele, Valerie, *Women of Fashion,* New York, 1991.
Stegemeyer, Anne, *Who's Who in Fashion, Third Edition,* New York, 1996.
Crane, Tara Christopher, *Elements of an Era: A Postmodern Interpretaton of the Art of Zandra Rhodes,* Columbia, Missouri, 1998.

Articles

"Zandra's Fantasies," in *Viva* (New York), February 1974.
Perschetz, Lois, "On the Rhodes," in *WWD,* 26 April 1974.
Kavanagh, Julie, "All Rhodes Lead to Zandra," in *WWD,* 31 December 1975.
Walkley, Christina, "Zandra Rhodes," in *Costume* (London), 1976.
"British New Style," in *Vogue* (London), 15 March 1976.
Howell, Georgina, "The Zandra Rhodes Dossier," in *Vogue* (London), July 1978.
Bakewell, Joan, "Zandra Rhodes: A Profile," in the *Illustrated London News,* October 1978.
"Schooldays," in *Vogue* (London), October 1981.
"Zandra Rhodes at Home," in *Connoisseur* (London), December 1981.
Williams, Antonia, "Zandra, the Non-Stop Rhodes Show," in *Vogue* (London), August 1982.
Fallon, James, "At Long Last Friends: Dress Designer Zandra Rhodes and Her Sister Beverly," in the *Sunday Times Magazine* (London), 8 May 1983.
"Zandra Rhodes," in *Art and Design* (London), February 1985.
Burnie, Joan, "We'll Tak' the High Rhodes," in *You* magazine of the *Mail on Sunday* (London), 28 February 1988.
"The Fashion Fatigue of Zandra Rhodes," in *Design Week* (London), 11 March 1988.
Niesseward, Nonie, "Ware-ability," in *Connoisseur,* June 1988.
"Zandra Rhodes," in *Pins and Needles* (London), July 1988.
"The Correspondent Questionnaire: Zandra Rhodes," in the *Correspondent Magazine* (London), 21 October 1990.
Schaeffer, Claire B., "Zandra Rhodes Couture," in *Threads* (Newtown, CT), June/July 1990.
O'Kelly, Alan, "The London Home of Zandra Rhodes," in *House Beautiful* (London), November 1990.
Fallon, James, "Rhodes Shutters London Workroom," in *WWD,* 14 July 1992.
Loper, Mary Lou, "Overdue Celebration for Nobel Laureate," in the *Los Angeles Times,* 28 January 1993.
Gendel, Debra, "Cutting Runaway Runway-Model Fees," in the *Los Angeles Times,* 24 September 1993.
Robinson, Gaile, "Mannequins or Humans?" in the *Los Angeles Times,* 29 September 1994.
Goodwin, Betty, "Tiaras, Anyone," in *Los Angeles Times,* 3 November 1994.
Lederer, Edith M., "The Present and Future are Here and Now," in the *Los Angeles Times,* 16 March 1995.
Williamson, Rusty, "Flight of Fancy: The Colorful Whimsy of Designer Zandra Rhodes Floats into Dallas," in *WWD,* 9 March 2000.
Gale Group, "Zandra Rhodes," in *Biography Resource Center* (Farmington Hills, MI), 2001.
Herman-Cohen, Valli, "Wolfgang, Meet Zandra," in the *Los Angeles Times,* 12 January 2001.

* * *

Zandra Rhodes is an artist whose medium is printed textiles. Working in a calligraphic style uniquely her own, she designs airy prints from which she produces floating, romantic garments whose cut evolves from the logic and placement of the print itself. Rhodes has no imitators and her work is instantly recognizable.

In a field where novelty is prized, Rhodes' work over the years is remarkable for its consistency. Because the shapes of her garments are fanciful and fantastical, using volume to display the textile to its best advantage, her clothes do not date. Her references are timeless: T-shaped gowns of printed chiffon belted in satin; the full-pleated skirts and long gathered sleeves of Ukrainian festival dress; off-the-shoulder tabards finished with a fringe of dagging; children's smocking reinterpreted in silk jersey. Rhodes' clothes are extravagantly feminine, delicate, and mysterious—created, as one writer observed, for "contemporary Titanias."

Each collection of prints evolves as a thoughtful response to a personal vision. Drawing on traditional historic sources, on images from nature, from popular culture, and from her own past, Rhodes sketches an object over and over, entering into a dialogue with it as the sketches become increasingly abstract and a personal statement emerges. Only at that point are a series of these personal images combined until the right composition presents itself to be translated into the final screen print. The print determines how the garment will be cut. Rhodes was not trained as a draper or cutter, and she has not been bound by the concept of symmetry, conventional seam placement, or internal shaping. Many of her dresses are cut flat or with minimal shaping, sometimes incorporating floating panels that follow the undulations of the patterned textile. She favors large repeats on silk chiffon or silk net, and as the garment falls in on itself against the body, it creates mysterious shapes and soft, misty layers not easily known. Rhodes is without doubt one of the most gifted and original designers of the late 20th and early 21st century.

Rhodes began taking her artistry to much larger material. Pink and orange concrete walls, rotating exhibits, and lavish interiors are part of Rhodes' latest constructive endeavor for the fashion industry. She calls it the Fashion and Textile Museum, her lifelong dream. Located in Bermondsey on the South Bank of the River Thames near London Bridge, Rhodes is building the museum to exhibit local and international fashion and textile designers and to educate students of contemporary fashion and textile design. Rhodes planned to open the museum's doors in 2002.

In January 2001, Rhodes provided the San Diego Opera with her imaginative and brilliant style for the production of Mozart's *The Magic Flute.* She designed 127 costumes, which, according to Valli Herman-Cohen of the *Los Angeles Times,* included everything from a rhinoceros with mirrored mosaic paws to a fantastic Queen of the Night cloak. The extraordinary costumes were such a success for Rhodes that she also launched a *Magic Flute*-themed eveningwear collection.

Even with the success of her collections, Rhodes finds time to venture into other fashion and artistic territories such as furs, interior and exterior design, and even etched and cut-glass windows. Rhodes teamed up with artist David Humphries for her interior and exterior work; together they have fashioned a number of terrazzo designs such as the Global Plaza at Harbourside, Sydney, and the Del Mar House Terrazzo Project. Rhodes' unusual and exceptional designs are just as breathtaking today as they were when she began as a textile designer almost 40 years ago. Highly admired, Rhodes continues to be "the" designer for cutting-edge fashion in a variety of forms.

—Whitney Blausen; updated by Kimbally Medeiros

RIBES, Jacqueline de

See de RIBES, Jacqueline

RICCI, Nina

See NINA RICCI

RICHMOND, John

British designer

Born: Manchester, England, 1960. **Education:** Graduated from Kingston Polytechnic, 1982. **Family:** Married Angie Hill; children: Harley, Phoenix. **Career:** Freelance designer in England for Lano Lano, Ursula Hudson, Fiorucci, Joseph Tricot, and Pin Up for Deni Cler, 1982–84; designer/partner with Maria Cornejo, Richmond-Cornejo, London, 1984–87; introduced John Richmod Man and John Richmond Woman collections, 1987; introduced lower-priced Destroy collection, 1990; introduced Destroy Denim collection, 1991; opened first London boutique, 1992; launched own ready-to-wear and accessories line, 1995; signed on to design womenswear and accessories for Valextra, 2000–03. **Address:** 25 Battersea Bridge Road, London SW11 3BA England

John Richmond, fall/winter 2001–02 collection. © AP/Wide World Photos.

PUBLICATIONS

On RICHMOND:

Books

Thackara, John, ed., *New British Design,* London, 1986.

McDermott, Catherine, *Street Style: British Design in the 1980s,* London, 1987.

de La Haye, Amy, ed., *The Cutting Edge: Fifty Years of British Fashion, 1947–1997,* New York, 1997.

Debrett's People of Today, London, 2001.

Articles

"All Right John?" in the *Sunday Express Magazine* (London), 3 August 1986.

John Richmond, spring/summer 2001 ready-to-wear collection. © Reuters NewMedia Inc./CORBIS.

"Design Duo Separate," in *Fashion Weekly* (London), 12 November 1987.

"Richmond/Cornejo," in the *Sunday Times Magazine* (London), 22 November 1987.

Scott-Gray, Chris, "Designing Contradictions," in *Fashion Weekly* (London), 6 October 1988.

Collen, Matthew, "Maximum Impact," in *i-D* (London), December/ January 1989–90.

Ferguson, Sarah, "Cyclist," in *Elle* (New York), April 1991.

"John Richmond," in *Face* (London), September 1991.

Fallon, James, "Richmond the Destroyer," in *DNR,* 6 July 1992.

Gordon, Mary Ellen, "Rock 'n' Roll Control," in *WWD,* 18 November 1992.

Clemente, Alba, "Limelighting John Richmond," in *Interview,* January 1993.

"Real Shopping: Style Police—Look, No Hands," in the *Independent,* 7 March 1999.

Bonas, Maurizio, "Milan Men's Wear Schedule," in *DNR,* 7–12 January 2000.

Zargani, Luisa, "Notebook from Milan: Valextra New Line," in *Women's Wear Daily*, 27 November 2000.

"John Richmond," available online at the Fashion Page, www.fashionz.co.uk; Fashion View, www.fashionview.com; Moda Online, www.modaonline.it; and at British Fur, www.british-fur.com; 5 October 2001.

* * *

The twin icons of popular rebellion—rock music and biker chic—are combined with good tailoring and attention to detail to make John Richmond's designs a success, commercially and critically. He is one of the most business-minded of his British counterparts, steadily building up his clothing range while others have fallen prey to financial and production problems. His designs have developed along the lines initiated during his partnership with Maria Cornejo, with certain motifs being carried through. These make his work instantly recognizable and, he says, justify the use of the "Destroy" slogan as a brand name for his cheaper lines, instead of promoting it as a diffusion range.

Richmond's womenswear shows the use of sharp tailoring with subversive twists that carry out the motto of "Destroy, Disorientate,

Disorder," so often emblazoned on his garments, as he tries to challenge accepted design conventions and expectations. Richmond's clothes are always sexy and brazen, leading many stylists and pop stars to reach for his styles when wanting to create a memorable and striking image. Well-cut jackets, often in hot fruity colors, are combined with fetish motifs. Bondage chains, zips, and leather inserts hark back to punk, although the sophistication of the style and the quality of the fabric make the overall look far more contemporary. His tattoo-sleeve tops and biker jackets were seen everywhere, even inspiring a vogue for the real thing among some London clubbers.

These design details also highlighted another side of his more subversive work. The macho tattoos he juxtaposed with transparent georgette wrap tops in the late 1980s questioned sexual stereotypes, something he continued in his menswear, where bright shiny fabrics were used for long-jacketed suits, and net was set against hard leather. These were perhaps a reflection of the vulnerable, slightly camp edge possessed by many of the rock heroes who inspired Richmond; impossibly masculine images, at the same time tempered by a glam-rock glitziness or the feminine twist of a soft shiny fabric. Although the anarchy symbols he so often used challenge, they never led to his creating unwearable or unsellable clothes. A suit might have been made with bondage trousers as a witty edge to a traditional design, but the fine Prince of Wales check of the fabric still made it seem stylish and desirable.

Richmond's Destroy and Destroy Denim labels had the same pop star/rock chic feel yet retained the quality of design of his main line, relying mainly on Lycra, denim, and splashes of leatherette to produce a sportswear influence and clubby feel. Jeans in denim and biker jackets formed the basis of this collection, although sharp suits also featured, with 1970s glam rock again an influence: feather boalike trim around coats and jackets and tight sequin tops for both men and women. Later collections showed a growing maturity in style and widening of influences, in couture-inspired jackets with gilt buttons and quilted linings and sleek slit skirts, still with the distinctive Richmond elements like shiny leggings and the contrast platform heels of the boots designed for Shelly's, the popular London footwear chain.

For the 1996–97 winter season, Richmond's second Milan showing stressed a distinctive sophistication merging sensuality with a cosmopolitan flair. He refined classic ensembles to suit a mature, worldly buyer who wanted to appear tasteful yet alluring. His dresses, which Forlì Red Falcon made and distributed, succeeded primarily because of Richmond's fabric and detailing savvy. For the modish, self-confident woman, he underscored uncomplicated lines.

Richmond made his mark on the season with devoré velvets, metallic woolens, delavé taffetas, and optical prints. The collection of skirts and day costumes tended to be well-fitted and long; tapered pants complemented crêpe georgette blouses. For casual wear, he relaxed the silhouette with twin sets, trapeze skirts, low-slung pant lines, and tight, figure-revealing tops. His choice of animal prints and skins, bi-tone gabardine, satin, suedes, and vinyl, and velvet for dresses provided texture and variety to suit more occasions and settings. His palette centered on black, dark umber, and navy, often offset by diagonal slashes of pink and burgundy. For some ensembles in his winter 2001–02 collection, Richmond, like Dior, Gucci, Chanel, Prada, Armani, and numerous other of the fashion world's top designers, chose fur, a material that Brenda Polan of the *London Evening Standard* connected with wealth, sex appeal, luxury, and glamor.

Additionally, in 2000, Richmond signed a three-year contract with Valextra, the Italian accessories firm, to design a new womenswear collection and coordinating accessories line featuring footwear and handbags. "I didn't want to work with just my company, and I don't really plan to do any other consulting," Richmond told *Women's Wear Daily* (27 November 2000), "I'm thinking of clothes that fit with the bags; I thought this was the easiest way to change people's perception of Valextra, to show how accessories fit into modern life."

—Rebecca Arnold; updated by Mary Ellen Snodgrass

ROBERTS, Patricia

British designer

Born: At Barnard Castle, County Durham, England, 2 January 1945. **Education:** Studied at Queen Mary's School, Lytham St. Anne's, Lancashire, 1961–63; Fashion Diploma, Leicester College of Art, 1963–67. **Family:** Married John Christopher Heffernan, 1982; children: Amy. **Career:** Knitting editor, IPC Magazines, 1967–71; director/designer, Patricia Roberts Knitting, Ltd., from 1971, and, through *Vogue,* supplied knitwear for London shops; designer, Patricia Roberts Yarns and Woollybear Yarns, from 1976; director/designer, Patricia Roberts shops, from 1976; *Patricia Roberts* perfume, 1990. **Exhibitions:** *Knit One, Purl One,* Victoria & Albert Museum, London, 1986. **Collections:** Victoria & Albert Museum, London; Whitworth Museum, Manchester. **Awards:** Duke of Edinburgh's Designer's prize, 1986; Design Council award, 1986. **Address:** 60 Kinnerton St., London SW1X 8ES, England.

PUBLICATIONS

By ROBERTS:

Books

Patricia Roberts Knitting Patterns, London, 1977.
Patricia Roberts Knitting Book, London, 1981.
Patricia Roberts Second Knitting Book, London, 1983.
Patricia Roberts Collection, London, 1985.
Patricia Roberts Style, London, 1988.
Patricia Roberts Variations, London, 1991, 1993; New York, 1992.

On ROBERTS:

Books

O'Hara, Georgina, *Encyclopedia of Fashion from 1840 to 1980s,* London, 1986.
Sutton, Ann, *British Craft Textiles,* London, 1991.

Articles

Raven, Susan, "Patterns for Patricia," in the *Sunday Times Magazine* (London), 8 December 1984.
Brampton, Sally, "A Priceless Pearl among the Plain Set," in the *Times* (London), 31 March 1986.

McDowell, Colin, "Never Out of Fashion," in *Crafts* (London), May/June 1986.

*

My knitwear is identifiable by its sophisticated stitchcraft. I love to push the technical limits of hand knitting into new areas, but always within the context of casual, easy to wear fashion. I am inspired by the creative possibilities of hand knitting and enjoy inventing new stitches and amalgamating them with colours, textures and form.

For each collection I think of a theme and then imagine ways of interpreting it into colour, Aran or lace work, or a combination of these. There is often something completely new about the way they are worked. The inspiration comes from anywhere and anything—holidays, nature, the sea, art exhibitions, bric-a-brac, etc. I work in natural fibres, often luxury ones, like cashmere and angora. We have developed our own range of cottons, specially for hand knitting, in a myriad of colours.

I want people to feel comfortable and enjoy wearing my sweaters at almost any time and anywhere from the city office, to the country, the sea, or the fashionable ski resort.

—Patricia Roberts

* * *

The 20th century saw a revolution in hand knitwear and this fresh interpretation of knitting tradition was made by a small number of designers. Foremost in the field was Patricia Roberts who had trained in fashion at Leicester College of Art. On leaving college as an enthusiastic hand knitter in the early 1960s, she worked for a group of women's magazines making up patterns, and quickly learned the value of technical accuracy. Frustrated by the general outlook of hand knitting for economy's sake and magazines wanting Marks & Spencer copies, she realized knitwear must go in a different direction to justify knitting by hand at all.

At the age of 26 she launched herself as a freelance designer and put together a collection of entirely fresh-looking handknits which were sold to Browns of London and Bloomingdale's in the United States. She opened her first shop in London's Knightsbridge in 1976, selling both made up garments and knitting kits for the home knitter. Noting the lack of quality and limited color of available yarns, she sold her own range wholesale. Roberts soon had a thriving mail order business and had produced the first of her annual pattern books in a short time. More than a dozen were published in paperback and several in hardback as well. Roberts designed the books herself, stylish volumes of glamorous sophistication, many of which often sold out almost overnight.

Texture and colour have always been dominant features of her work—she was one of the first to make the British Spinning Industry confront the challenge for more creative yarns for the burgeoning talents among British knitwear designers. Roberts skilfully explored new techniques to achieve textural bobbles and bas relief, taking images from nature like bunches of grapes and cherries or, more mundanely, novelties like children's sweets or even a Scrabble board. Her grapes and cherries were huge bestsellers. Aran castes thin as trellises intersected areas full of different pattern, color, and stitchery. The yarns themselves further increased surface interest with fluffy mohair, smooth silks, and other luxury yarns like cashmere and angora.

Roberts has long used only natural fibers and designed her own range of cottons. Her plainer garments made use of thick linens, tweeds, and marls. These highly textured, one-color designs vied for attention with the more dramatic, multicolored, intricately-patterned garments in bright primaries or jewel tones. For the home knitter, these were not garments for the faint-hearted. Roberts continually designs on the needles, "I keep knitting it up," she has said, "and unravelling it because I keep changing my mind." It is then written down and sent to outworkers to be made up. Ready-made garments have definitely been at the top end of the market and customers have included stars of stage and screen.

Designer Jean Muir, who chaired the Knitting Committee of the Design Council, compared Roberts' work to that of a painter or sculptor, calling her "a craftsman who has made her work commercial.... [she is] a leader in the resurgence of artists and craftsmen who are bringing about the most exciting movement that has happened in this country for a century." Roberts regards herself as primarily a designer, very interested in the product design, and claims to be not at all "arty crafty." She has often been referred as the most commercial of Britain's hand knitters; with no loss of originality and quality, her ready-made collections, patterns, and yarns have been available to a wide international public.

In 1986 Roberts was awarded the Design Council award and subsequently the supreme accolade, the Duke of Edinburgh's Designer's prize of the year, never before awarded to a clothing designer. The Design Council described her achievement as "an outstanding example of British design success," and added, "despite a considerable growth of sales, the best design standards had been maintained throughout the growth of the company." Her work was included in exhibitions at the Victoria & Albert Museum twice in that same year, and her work was added to the museum's permanent collection.

In the mid-1990s Roberts showed two collections each year to buyers in Paris, Milan, and London. Retail shops bearing her name were opened in London and franchised shops in Hong Kong, Cyprus, and Melbourne. As much as three-quarters of her garment business was exported, primarily to Italy. Roberts was probably the first to see the commercial possibilities in what had started in the early 1960s as a fairly obscure craft revival. She remained seemingly untouched by her success, "I've always been a worker," she has said, "a plodder. I tend to think I'm not ambitious but I must be; other people seem to think I am." She progressed steadily from designing knitting patterns to masterminding an internationally acclaimed empire of haute couture knits and designs.

Roberts has raised handknitting to an artform and pioneered a way for others to follow. Although self-effacing by nature, she is matter of fact about her success: "I'm not surprised because nothing has happened overnight. It's all been just one stage after another."

—Elian McCready

ROBINSON, Bill

American designer

Born: circa 1948. **Education:** Graduated from Parsons School of Design, New York. **Career:** Chief designer of menswear collection,

Calvin Klein, 1977 to early 1980s; went to Yves Saint Laurent and updated men's collection; premiered own collection, fall, 1986; introduced complete suit, dress shirt, and neckwear collections, 1988; signed deal with Kindwear Company of Tokyo for the distribution of the Bill Robinson collection in Japan, 1987; label relaunched through three licensing agreements, 1996; new collections debuted, 1997. **Awards:** Student of the Year award, Parsons School of Design, 1969; Cutty Sark menswear award nomination, 1987; Most Promising U.S. Designer award, 1987. **Died:** 16 December 1993, in New York.

Publications

On ROBINSON:

Articles

Various reviews and coverage in the *Philadelphia Inquirer, USA Today, Manhattan Inc., Daily News Record, Toronto Globe & Mail,* June to November 1986.

Hochswender, Woody, "Making One's Mark (Designer Bill Robinson)," in the *New York Times,* 14 June 1988.

Cameron, Victoria Pearson, "Why So Blue? (Men's Fashions)," in *Esquire,* March 1991.

Laxton, William, "Mister America: A Salute to Designer Bill Robinson," in *Esquire,* May 1991.

Furman, Phyllis, "Resuiting American Men," in *Crain's New York Business,* 15 July 1991.

Pace, Eric, "Bill Robinson, 45, Pioneering Designer of Fashions for Men," [obituary] in the *New York Times,* 17 December 1993.

"Deaths Last Week," in *Chicago Tribune,* 19 December 1993.

Socha, Miles, "Robinson's Crusade: Bill Robinson Label Resurfaces as Contemporary Mainfloor Label," in *DNR,* 19 August 1996.

* * *

Bill Robinson was a rare breed of designer—articulate, modest, and enormously intuitive. He was one of the few American menswear designers to achieve a worldwide reputation in the 1980s. His clothes had their roots in classic American styles but also reflected a tradition of European design. They were an amalgam of fashion basics and sophisticated, elegant sportswear.

Robinson was inspired mainly by the period of the 1930s through the 1950s, considered the golden age of American sportswear. Yet he always strived to be "up-to-date, contemporary, modern," in his own words. The innate American character of his philosophy was expressed in a quote in the May 1991 issue of *Esquire* regarding his spring-summer 1991 collection, "My summer collection tells little stories, from Main to Florida."

Ironically enough, having once designed uniforms for Avis and TWA, Robinson set his sights on eradicating uniforms for men and opening up the horizons of menswear design. Wearing an unconstructed suit to work is fine, he seemed to say. And rather than donning a run-of-the-mill denim shirt and jacket, one could wear an indigo washed silk shirt and blazer—a casual yet eminently sophisticated ensemble that sacrificed nothing to comfort. Taking the classics as his starting point, he designed modern clothes for forward-thinking, creative men who were unafraid of their sensuality.

Robinson's formative years were spent working on the menswear collection for Calvin Klein. "Somehow, by fate, when I moved into menswear, I really took off," he said. Robinson made his reputation with sleek leather jackets and body-conscious knits, setting the standard against which other menswear designers were judged in these categories. He himself wore one of his signature looks, a black turtleneck, and managed to look chic yet down-to-earth, setting the tone for his collection.

He put his individual stamp on schoolboy ties, CPO shirts, regatta striped blazers, and mackinaw jackets. Robinson was a master of subtlety and a superb colorist, qualities brilliantly expressed in a seminal show staged at New York's Plaza Hotel for the fall 1989 season, when he launched his Japanese license with Kindwear. A velvet corduroy suit from the fall 1991 collection is among the best examples of his work, combining the utilitarian quality of a common fabric with the plush and rich color associated with luxury clothing. The collection was also the start of a new direction for the designer, who adopted a softened approach casting aside the excesses and "power looks" of the 1980s.

Having brought American design to a world-class level, Robinson also collaborated on advertising campaigns with such equally renowned figures as photographers Steven Meisel, Kurt Markus, and Guzman, raising the level of fashion photography in the United States. For his fall 1992 collection, Robinson included such classic as pea coats, slim, flat-front pants, a host of knits, short overcoats, and a generally slimmer silhouette. He combined the rugged with the urbane in a mackinaw jacket shown over a one-button business suit and a mock turtleneck. As he had commented, "The lines between work and play are blurring."

With his backer, Bidermann Industries Corp., Robinson was also forward thinking in his pricing structure, making the collection accessible to a wide range of customers and emphasizing the value-price relationship way before it was in vogue in the post-Ronald Reagan era. The fashion world, however, was robbed of this forward-minded designer in 1993, when Robinson died at the age of 45. Robinson's modesty was reflected in his designs, clothing separates easily incorporated into any man's wardrobe. They weren't block-buster looks with a limited shelf life, but modern classics that would never go out of style. A testament to these qualities and Robinson's skills came in 1996, three years after the designer's untimely death, when his longtime companion and business partner, Leo Chiu, as well as other principals of Bill Robinson International, decided to save the floundering company through several new licensing agreements.

Three companies picked up the Robinson mantle: Male Concepts Inc. signed on to relaunch Robinson menswear in spring 1997, with suits, sports coats, full coats, and a range of trousers, from dress to casual; the Dino di Milano Corporation, headquartered in Miami, took the license for Robinson knit, woven, and dress shirts; and the New York-based Roffe Accessories company was slated to release Robinson neckties and socks. Chiu told Miles Socha of the *Daily News Record,* (19 August 1996), "This is something [Robinson] always wanted. We wanted to find suitable licensees we could trust, and [I] think we've found them." Though Robinson designs had been licensed in the past to backer Bindermann Industries and the Plaid Clothing Group, both companies had gone into bankrupcty proceedings.

—Vicki Vasilopoulos; updated by Nelly Rhodes

ROCCOBAROCCO

See BAROCCO, Rocco

ROCHAS, Marcel

French designer

Born: Paris, 1902. **Career:** Opened fashion house in rue Faubourg St-Honoré, Paris, 1924; moved to avenue Matignon, 1931; first perfume launched, 1936; fragrances lab scents discontinued, during World War II; Parfums Rochas S.A. established, 1945; Helene Rochas took over after Marcel's death, 1955; factory moved to Poissy, 1969; acquired by Wella AG, 1987; couture relaunched with designer Peter O'Brien, 1990; debuting spring-summer collection after three-year absence, 2000; fragrances include *Air Jeune, Avenue Matigon,* and *Audace,* 1936 (latter was reintroduced 1972); *Femme,* 1945, *Chiffon* (later renamed *Poupee*), 1946; *Madame Rochas,* 1960, *Monsieur Rochas,* 1969; *Mystère,* 1978; *Eau de Rochas,* 1970; *Eau de Rochas pour Homme,* 1973; *Macassar,* 1980; *Lumière,* 1984; *Globe,* 1990; *Tocade,* 1994; *Byzantine,* 1995; *Fleur de L'eau,* 1996; *Tocadilly,* 1997; *Alchimie,* 1998; *Aquaman,* 2001. **Died:** 1955, in Paris. **Company Address:** 33 rue François 1er Paris F-75008, France.

Marcel Rochas, 1950 collection. © Bettmann/CORBIS.

Publications

By ROCHAS:

Books

Twenty-Five Years of Paris Elegance 1925–50, n.d.

On ROCHAS:

Books

Picken, Mary Brooks, and Dora Loues Miller, *Dressmakers of France: The Who, How, and Why of the French Couture,* New York, 1956.
Garland, Madge, *The Changing Face of Fashion,* London, 1970.
Kennett, Frances, *Collector's Book of Twentieth Century Fashion,* London, 1983.
Mohrt, Françoise, *Marcel Rochas: 30 ans d'élégance et de créations, 1925–1955,* Paris, 1983.
Milbank, Caroline Rennolds, *Couture: the Great Designers,* New York, 1985.
Stegemeyer, Anne, *Who's Who in Fashion, Third Edition,* New York, 1996.
Robert, Guy, *Les sens du parfum,* Paris, 2000.

Articles

Noel, Lucie, "Marcel Rochas Stresses Youth in New Styles," in the *New York Herald Tribune,* 3 August 1948.
Alexander, Hilary, "The Face that Relaunched Rochas," in the *Daily Telegraph* (London), 16 November 1989.
Weisman, Katherine, "Rochas' *Tocade* to Bow in September," in *WWD,* 6 May 1994.
Weil, Jennifer, "Rochas' New Brew," in *WWD,* 19 June 1998.
"Lavender Goes Green for Rochas," in *Cosmetics International,* 10 March 1999.
Rein, Anne, "Rochas Sees the Light," in *WWD,* 28 April 2000.
Loyer, Michele, "The Sleeping Beauties of Couture are Waking," in the *International Herald Tribune,* 11 October 2000.
Jensen, Tanya, "Rochas: Classic & Refined,"in *WWD,* 8 October 2001.

* * *

In the sometimes indeterminate world of fashion, Marcel Rochas was determined and decisive. He operated with a business acumen and cultural strategy (including the fashion designer as a conspicuous social mixer) that caused him in the postwar period to doubt the continued vitality and interest of couture—and to turn resolutely to his boutique operation and lucrative fragrance business. His motto was "Youth, Simplicity, and Personality," alternatively reported in the *New York Herald Tribune* (3 August 1948) as "elegance, simplicity, and youth," but it was in many ways the characteristic of personality that differentiated Rochas from other designers of his era. His initial fame came in the 1920s and rested on his *tailleur,* accompanied with full, supple skirts.

In 1942, five years before the Dior New Look, Rochas had offered a new corset to create the *guépière,* or wasp-waist, anticipating the return of the extreme femininity that enchanted him. Caroline Rennolds Milbank, writing in her book *Couture: the Great Designers* (New York, 1985), said Rochas and his skill were "characterized by a calculated originality." Originality was very important for Rochas, if only as a sign of rights and attribute of value rather than of real creative initiative.

In the 1930s, he was already selling ready-to-wear and made-to-order clothes in his New York store. He claimed to have invented the word "slacks" in the early 1930s, along with originating the idea to include gray flannel slacks as part of a suit. In an era when women's trousers were limited to extreme informality or recreation, Rochas trousers were highly advanced if not revolutionary. His clothing was not cautious, and for him "original" and "invention" were key words in the vocabulary of selling fashion.

The wide shoulders of the 1930s were created by several designers more or less simultaneously. He continuously played on the shoulders as a sign of the feminine—a fall-winter 1947 evening gown, for instance, invents broad shoulders through a capelet-like scarf attached to the bodice. Bolero jackets of the 1940s were lighter in construction than Balenciaga's inspirations direct from Spain; Rochas was more interested in the effect of the enhanced shoulders to pad and to frame. Likewise, a 1949 *robe du soir* dipped to a bouquet of silk camellias at the bust, but capped the shoulders and framed the face with a flaring lightness. In other instances, grand white collars performed the same role and in providing a sweet, portrait-like framing for the face.

In January of 1948, *Women's Wear Daily* reported of Rochas, "this house is very modern but with the modernity which carries with it a tradition linking it with the fashion picture of the day. There is always an air of excitement in his collections which are designed to enhance the charm of women." If Rochas' anatomical obsession was the shoulder, his second favorite was the arm. He often embellished the sleeves in suits and coats, and his coats from the 1940s, which tended to be voluminous and drapey, were characterized by large sleeves. Loose blouson effects were more than carried over into the excess of sleeves as well as an interest in full backs.

Picken and Miller, in their book, *Dressmakers of France* (New York, 1956), stated, "Conscious of the changes in fashion, Rochas was the first to give up his heavy burden of the haute couture collections and to restrict his activities to his boutique which specializes not only in accessories, but also in separates." Anticipating Cardin and the marketing orientation of fashion and beauty, Rochas was a visionary. Though his firm had quit creating fragrances during World War II, a separate company, Parfums Rochas S.A. was set up in 1945 to handle the burgeoning interest in perfumes.

Upon his death in 1955, Marcel Rochas had not fully achieved the synthesis of design and marketing that would become the dynamic of late 20th-century fashion, but he had more than proven himself one of its pioneers. His business was taken over by family members who concentrated on developing fragrances. The Rochas name became synonymous with intriguing and evocative fragrances for women and men throughout the next several decades. The company was acquired by the Darmstadt, Germany-based Wella AG in 1987, and went back into couture with the hiring of designer Peter O'Brien 1990. Rochas couture remained overshadowed by its ever-increasing fragrance line until the market was flooded with signature scents. At the dawn of the 21st century, however, Rochas was once seeking recognition for its apparel as it prepared to show a spring/summer 2001 collection by O'Brien.

—Richard Martin; updated by Sydonie Benét

RODIER

French fashion house

Founded: by Eugene Rodier, 1848. **Company History:** Entered ready-to-wear knit wear, 1956; U.S. subsidiary, Rodier USA set up and stores opened, from 1983; acquired by Paris-based Group Vev; began selling to department stores, 1995; hired designer Christophe Lebourg, 1996; new flagship store in New York, 1996; signed licensing deals with Pierre Lannier (watches), Royer SA (shoes), Renown Group (in-store boutiques in Japan), 1997; set up wholesale operations in U.S., 1998; signed licensing agreement with Bella Donna Group, 2001. **Company Address:** 44, Avenue Georges Pompidou, 92300 Levallois-Perret, France. **Company Website:** www.rodier.tm.fr.

PUBLICATIONS

On RODIER:

Articles

"French Clothier Picks Chief for Its Assault on the U.S.," in the *New York Times,* 28 March 1988.

Edelson, Sharon, "Rodier Spices Up Lines with New Looks, and Plans for More Stores," in *WWD,* 22 November 1994.

———, "Rodier to Open Up its Distribution," in *WWD,* 8 December 1995.

———, "Rodier: One More Time in U.S.," in *WWD,* 14 November 1996.

"Rodier Licenses Shops in Japan, Line of Watches," in *WWD,* 19 June 1997.

Socha, Miles, "Rodier's Modified American Plan," in *WWD,* 2 September 1998.

"Ready-to-Wear Rodier Grants License to Egyptian-Lebanese Bella Donna Group," in the *European Report,* 10 January 2001.

* * *

Long known for fine knits and woolen clothes, the House of Rodier continues a tradition which began when Eugene Rodier was commended by the Comte de Montaliner, Minister of the Interior under Napoleon. Rodier's distinction was won by reinterpreting the shawls of Kashmir for the contemporary woman of the 1800s at home and abroad, making his contribution to French commerce as well as to the nascent fashion industry.

Eugene Rodier formally established the house in 1848. Under his direction, and later under the direction of his son Paul and grandson Jacques, the firm continued to produce inventive and experimental textiles, informed by a study of past traditions. A collection introduced in the early 1920s was inspired by the decorative arts of French colonial territories shown at the 1922 *Exposition Nationale Coloniale de Marseilles.* Rodier adapted and edited motifs from French Indo-China (Vietnam, Cambodia, and Laos) and from French Equatorial Africa (Tunisia, Algeria, and Morocco). These were woven into a series of soft, winter-white cloths of wool and cashmere in such a way that when the dress was made up, the motifs formed a border or band of trimming.

In the early part of the 20th century the Rodier mills developed such new fabrics as *senellic,* an early experiment in spun rayon, and the copyrighted Kasha, which remained a staple in their line. Perhaps the best known fabric developed by Rodier is the knitted jersey which Coco Chanel rescued from its warehouse oblivion in 1916. The combined visions of Jacques Rodier and Coco Chanel transformed a humble fabric, intended primarily for men's underwear, into a textile inextricably linked with 20th-century style.

During the 1920s and 1930s, Rodier was also associated with such couturiers as Jean Patou, for whom the firm produced new textures and distinctive colors of unusual depth and subtlety. According to his biographer Meredith Etherington Smith, Patou's expansion in the mid-1920s was partially financed by the Rodier family. It was also during the mid-1920s that the house expanded its range to include fabrics for interiors designed by such luminaries as Pablo Picasso.

For Rodier, the first function of the mill was to act as a laboratory for the production of new yarns, new textures, and above all inventive designs reflecting the spirit of their age. Paul Rodier and his family were not only master weavers, but artists and editors. As such, they naturally studied the arts of the past and kept current with contemporary movements in painting, ballet, and anything else which might provide inspiration for their hand-operated looms. Rodier entered the ready-to-wear field in 1956 with a collection of fine knitwear.

Rodier rarely changed its design sensibilities, other than expanding into different areas, such as coats and accessories. Collections in the 1990s centered around color-related separates for women in distinctive patterns, rich colors, and with fine detailing, continuing Rodier's tradition of excellence. Buyers in the U.S. were given more opportunity to buy such clothes when Rodier began selling its products to high-end specialty stores and department stores in 1995, in addition to the dozen firm-owned boutiques nationwide and stores in over 20 countries worldwide. In revmping its image, Rodier hired Christophe Lebourg, who had worked with GFT Group, Joseph, and Claude Montana, as its new designer in 1996 and closed its store Fifth Avenue in New York to make way for a new flagship store at Rockefeller Center. Similarly styled stores were planned for Chicago, Beverly Hills, and San Francisco.

As the century came to a close, Rodier had restructured its operations with high hopes for the future. Part of its new focus was on bringing wholesale operations to the U.S. and boosting brand awareness through several licensing agreements. Pierre Lannier, in its first licensing deal, signed on to produce Rodier watches; Royer SA began manufacturing shoes; the Tokyo-based Renown Group was slated to open over 200 in-store Rodier boutiques in Japan from 1998 through 2002. In addition, Rodier and the Egyptian-Lebanese fashion firm Bella Donna Group inked a deal in 2001 for apparel and accessories.

—Whitney Blausen; updated by updated by Sydonie Benét

RODRÍGUEZ CARO, José Victor

See VICTORIO Y LUCCHINO

ROEHM, Carolyne

American designer

Born: Jane Carolyne Smith in Kirksville, Missouri, 7 May 1951. **Education:** Graduated from Washington University, St. Louis, 1973. **Family:** Married Axel Roehm, 1978 (divorced, 1981); married Henry Kravis, 1985 (divorced). **Career:** Designer, Mrs. sportswear by Kellwood Co. for Sears, Roebuck & Co., circa 1973; designer, Oscar de la Renta licensees, including Miss "O" line, New York, 1974–84; launched own deluxe ready-to-wear firm, New York, 1985, added couture line, 1988, footwear, 1989, closed house, 1991; launched mail order clothing, accessories, and gift collection, 1993, with related in-store boutiques at Saks Fifth Avenue, closed business again, 1994; president, Council of Fashion Designers of America, 1989. **Awards:** Pratt Institute award, 1991. **Address:** 550 7th Avenue, New York, NY 10018, USA.

Publications

By ROEHM:

Books

A Passion for Flowers, New York, 1997.
Summer Notebook: Garden Hearth Traditions Home, New York, 1999.
Carolyne Roehm's Fall Notebook, with Alan Richardson (Photographer), New York, 1999.
Carolyne Roehm's Winter Notebook: Garden Hearth Traditions Home, New York, 1999.
Spring Notebook: Garden Hearth Traditions Home, with Melissa Davis, New York, 2000.
Seasonal Notebooks: Summer, Fall, Winter, Spring, New York, 2000.
At Home With Carolyne Roehm, New York, 2001.

On ROEHM:

Books

Milbank, Caroline Rennolds, *New York Fashion: The Evolution of American Style,* New York, 1989.
Steele, Valerie, *Women of Fashion: Twentieth Century Designers,* New York, 1991.
Stegemeyer, Anne, *Who's Who in Fashion, Third Edition,* New York, 1996.

Articles

Kornbluth, Jesse, "The Working Rich: The Real Slaves of New York," in *New York,* January 1986.
Jobey, Liz, "Vogue's Spy: Carolyne Roehm," in *Vogue* (London), September 1987.
Gross, Michael, "Roehm's Forum," in *New York,* 7 November 1988.
Mehle, Aileen, and Karen Radkai, "Carolyne Roehm: An Opulent Aesthetic for the Designer's Manhattan Residence," in *Architectural Digest,* September 1989.
Menkes, Suzy, "Couture's Grand Ladies," in the *Illustrated London News,* Spring 1990.
"Those Gilded Moments..." in *Esquire (Special Issue),* June 1990.
Howell, Georgina, "Roehm's Empire," in *Vogue* (New York), August 1990.

"The Designers Talk Passion, Whimsy and Picassos," in *ARTnews* (New York), September 1990.
"End of a Dream," in *Time,* 23 September 1991.
"Carolyne Roehm," in *Current Biography,* February 1992.
Ginsberg, Merle, "Henry and Carolyne Hit Hollywood," in *WWD,* 28 May 1992.
Norwich, William, "Roehm's Return," in *Vogue,* March 1993.
———, "The Roehm Report," in *Vogue,* December 1993.
Bowles, Hamish, "Paris and Roehm," in *Vogue,* June 1996.
"In Full Flower," (interview) in *Vogue,* October 1997.
Mehle, Aileen, "Carolyne Rohem in Manhattan: The Fashion Designer's Rooms on Sutton Place," in *Architectural Digest,* December 1997.

* * *

Carolyne Roehm is an American designer who created clothes for men to love and women to find flattering. She is a person with a passion for designing beautiful, feminine clothes in luxurious materials, who took great care with the details. She opened the doors of her own ready-to-wear and couture design firm in 1985, only to close them six years later.

Designing clothes was a lifelong passion for Jane Carolyne Smith Roehm. After studying fashion design at Washington University, she spent a year designing polyester sportswear for Kellwood Co., a supplier for Sears, before working for Oscar de la Renta, holding pins and serving as his fitting model. She learned the details of classic couture from him and later designed the Miss "O" line. After 10 years with de la Renta, she formed her own design firm known as Carolyne Roehm, Inc.

Roehm designed for women, like herself, who had money and an active life, involved with benefits and social events, but who might also work outside the home. She is known for well-detailed, finely constructed, feminine clothes created to make women feel elegant. Fabrics were rich: cashmere, satin, velvet, and suede. Details might include trapunto stitching, embroidery, or leather trim. Roehm's eveningwear was glamorous, fairytale-like, to be seen in at social occasions and photographed at charity events. The dresses could be cut full and made of rich fabrics, reminiscent of those worn in the aristocratic portraits of the artist Franz Winterhalter, or sleek, sensuous columns recalling John Singer Sargent's *Madame X.* Although best known for her glamorous eveningwear, half of her design work was in everyday wear. She created sporty separates, dresses, coats, hats, and shoes. In all circumstances, Roehm's design work was known for quality and fit. She was numbered among the working rich; her second husband, Henry Kravis, financed her design firm before they were married. After their marriage she certainly didn't have to work, but she was driven. She designed her collections and used her organizational skills to support charity events. As president of the Council of Fashion Designers of America, Roehm guided the organization as it became a major supporter of AIDS research. She also served as her own fitting model and appeared in her own advertising campaigns.

In 1991 after the death of stepson, Roehm closed her design business. Afterwards she maintained a small office and staff, creating a mail-order business, produced an exclusive catalogue for Saks Fifth Avenue, and designed clothes for private customers. In 1994, despite her success with Saks, Roehm again closed her business.

In the late 1990s Roehm turned from fashion to flowers and began publishing a number of books on flower arranging and garden design. Her first, *A Passion for Flowers,* instructs the reader on arranging flowers in a way to accentuate their beauty. She organizes flowers by season, to make the reader aware that flowers can be enjoyed at any time of the year. Roehm has also written a series of "Notebooks," one for each season of the year. Each book comes with graph paper, pockets for notes or clippings, tips for flower arranging, recipes, and photographs. Roehm includes projects and decorating ideas for seasonal holidays in the books as well. It remains to be seen whether Roehm will return to glamorous, feminine clothing she so beautifully designed in the past.

—Nancy House; updated by Andrew Cunningham

RONCHI, Ermanno

See ERREUNO SCM SpA

ROTH, Christian Francis

American designer

Born: New York City, 12 February 1969. **Education:** Special student, Fashion Institute of Technology, New York, 1986–87; studied fashion design at Parsons School of Design, New York, 1987–88. **Family:** Married; children: two daughters. **Career:** Apprentice, later employee, of Koos Van den Akker; produced first small collection in Van den Akker studio, 1988; showed first full collection, 1990; closed couture business, 1995; initated bridge designs with backing of Equal 4 Inc., 1995. **Awards:** Honoree, Cotton Inc. "Celebration of American Style" show; Council of Fashion Designers of America Perry Ellis award, 1990. **Address:** 18 East 17th Street, New York, NY 10003,USA.

Publications

On ROTH:

Books

Martin, Richard, and Harold Koda, *Infra-Apparel,* New York, 1993.
Stegemeyer, Anne, *Who's Who in Fashion, Third Edition,* New York, 1996.

Articles

Chua, Lawrence, "Christian Francis Roth," in *WWD,* 27 June 1989.
"A New York Upstart Puts a Smile on the Face of Fashion," in *People Weekly,* 30 October 1989.
Brubach, Holly, [fashion column] in the *New Yorker,* 29 January 1990.
Starzinger, Page Hill, "New Faces," in *Vogue* (New York), March 1990.
"Word is Out: SA [Seventh Avenue] Has a New Boy Wonder," in *WWD,* 10 April 1990.
Buck, Genevieve, "New Designer is Creating a Stir with His Quirky, Kid-Stuff Collection," in *Chicago Tribune,* 1 July 1990.
Boucher, Vincent, "The New Youthquake," in *Vogue* (New York), September 1990.

Shaw, Daniel, "New Kid on the Block," in *Avenue* (New York), September 1990.
Morris, Bernadine, "Two Young Designers Decorate Their Clothes with Wit," in the *New York Times,* 27 November 1990.
"Card Company Says Designer Went Out of Line in Using Crayola Motif," in *Chicago Tribune,* 5 December 1990.
"Great Expectations," in *WWD,* 12 June 1991.
Coffin, David Page, "Stitching Fabric Puzzles," in *Threads* (Newtown, Connecticut), June/July 1992.
"Arts and Crafts," in *WWD,* 1 September 1992.
White, Ken, "New York Designer Making His Lighthearted Designs More Affordable," in the *Las Vegas Review-Journal,* 22 April 1997.

* * *

In 1990, a week after his first show and at the young age of 21, Christian Francis Roth was heralded by *Women's Wear Daily* as Seventh Avenue's latest boy wonder. Acclaim came stiflingly early for Roth; *Vanity Fair* had already photographed Roth with his ingenious dress-form dress (now in the collection of the Metropolitan Museum of Art) in August 1989 and in the *New Yorker* of January 1990, Holly Brubach proclaimed of Roth's designs, "These clothes would look first-rate in Paris or Milan or Timbuktu. It is already too late to call him promising. There is, in his clothes, nothing more to wait for." Such immoderate and unanimous praise could only be withering to many young artists, but Christian Francis Roth earned the adulation and has only gone on to warrant further accolades.

Yet after the last hurrah and congratulations, there is the designer who works as a consummate technician in a tightly circumscribed aesthetic. He reaches not for the gold ring of commercial success and recognition like other designers, but instead for a level of virtuosity and quiet quality in his work. Roth is an artist as evidenced by his vocabulary of forms conversant with such artistic elements as Surrealist *trompe l'oeil,* used in the dress-form dress (1989) and his wool jersey dress with illusionistic inset collar, cuffs, and belt (1991). Pop Art-derived concepts from consumer culture are represented in the spring 1990 Cartoon collection featuring daffy squiggles and suits with buttons looking as though they were spilled out of M & M candy bags.

Roth's breakfast suit (1990) breaks some eggs and prepares them sunny-side up, while his "Rothola" crayon outfits play with the children's toy for making art, and his scribbles and pencil-shaving skirt and jacket provide the means for artistic delineation. His 1990–91 wrought-iron (or, as he says, "Roth-iron") fence dress (also a jacket and jumpsuit) was partly indebted to the artist Jim Dine, while the dollar bill dress, which wraps the body in oversized bills, owes more than a buck to Andy Warhol. His spring/summer 1991 collection included a suite of brilliantly colored dresses inspired by Matisse's *découpages.*

While Roth's whimsical and artsy clothing was a hit with women, not everyone was amused with his creative borrowings. In late 1990 Hallmark Cards Inc., which owned Crayola, threatened to sue the designer for trademark infringement. Hallmark's unhappiness was two-fold: not only had Roth appropriated the trademarked Crayola crayon design, but the company had plans for its own clothing line through mail-order giant Speigel. Although the Speigel Crayola clothing was intended for young children, the companies felt Roth's designs were too close to their own intended collection. Roth disfused the imbroglio by agreeing to become a licensee and pay fees for the Caryola/Rothola motifs.

Admitting such debts did not diminish Roth's luster and originality, however, for each artistic enterprise is different, and Roth has scrupulously chosen to take from art only what he accommodates to the construction of clothing. His inlaid panels, sometimes compared to the finest marquetry, are a skilled fabrication in the pattern of the garment. While some fashion designers have sought to poach on art's prestige and to steal some aesthetic thunder, Roth has committed only the most discriminating larceny, flattering both art and fashion. His concern in integrating scribbles into the form of a garment is more integral to his medium than the cartoon appropriations of Pop Art. When he brings Matisse's cutouts to dressmaking, he does so not as surface decoration, but as pattern pieces to create the three-dimensional shape of the garment.

Roth's small collections were likewise developed with the concentration and formal intensity of musical form. His fall 1992 collection studied menswear. The lyrical spring 1992 collections included cocktail dresses that set up a 1950s bar and became the drinks themselves as well as a black cotton sateen dress with a diamond ring homage to Marilyn Monroe. In fall/winter 1991, his principal studies were Amish quilts which Roth translated from the spiral concentricity of flat quilt patterns into the piecing of dresses and circle skirts. Combining some techniques of color blocks with the rich harmonies of American quilts, the collection emphasized Roth's handmade warmth and beauty. Accompanying the quilt patterns, Roth provided a congenial coterie of hoboes in a trickle-up theory of fashion for clients not accustomed to a trackside way of life.

In the 1990s Roth changed his tune, closing his couture business in favor of lower-priced clothing. He told Ken White of the *Las Vegas Review-Journal,* "I just didn't think it was worth doing anymore." Roth further explained that the high-end couture collections were not a prime moneymaker. "Not that money has ever been my motivation to do what I do, but there comes a time [when] you make a career on what has been a successful craft for you. So, I more or less put the word out that I was interested in a different kind of situation." This new "situation" has been designing bridge clothes for young women and teens with a lower price tag, usually more than half the cost of his previous collections. The sweaters, skirts, pants, and shirts, still colorful and lighthearted, are sold in department stores.

Having matured and reached his 30s in the new century, Roth is still as quirky and fresh in his designs as when he vaulted to the top echelons of fashion barely into his 20s. Though he gave up the couture lifestyle and even settled into fatherhood, he still thinks fashion should be fun and functional. "You're in charge of your own destiny.... You have to make it work for yourself," he told White of the *Las Vegas Review-Journal* in 1997. "As long as you make great clothes, there's really nothing that can go wrong, particularly. It's always nice to have a good backer, a good situation, good promotion and merchandising. But that all comes from making nice clothes. I believe if you make beautiful things, people are going to want to get behind you."

Like Geoffrey Beene, whom he admires, Roth is an American designer of extravagant gift who has chosen the almost scholastic life of precious technician and exacting artist. Dubbed the "next Franco Moschino"or the "Schiaparelli of the '90s," Roth has worked with the unceasing patience and the quest of an artist to achieve in measure and modesty what others cannot attain in magnitude.

—Richard Martin; updated by Nelly Rhodes

ROUFF, Maggy

French designer

Born: Maggie Besançon de Wagner in Paris, 1896. **Career:** Designer for company owned by parents, Drécoll; own house opened, 1929, specializing in sportswear and lingerie; retired, 1948; daughter, Anne-Marie, took over; retired, 1960; house turned briefly to ready-to-wear; closed, 1960s. **Awards:** Chevalier de la Légion d'Honneur; Conseilleuse du Commerce Exterieur. **Died:** 7 August 1971, in Paris.

Publications

By ROUFF:

Books

Ce que j'ai vu en chiffonnant la clientèle, Paris, 1938.
La philosophie de l'elegance, Paris, 1942.
L'Amérique vue au microscope, Paris, circa 1948.

On ROUFF:

Books

Latour, Anny, *Kings of Fashion,* London, 1958.
Milbank, Caroline Rennolds, *Couture: The Great Designers,* New York, 1980.
Steele, Valerie, *Women of Fashion,* New York, 1991.

* * *

Harmony and simplicity were cornerstones of Maggy Rouff's belief in elegance as a way of life, and the way of fashion. A truly elegant woman was in harmony with her environment and herself, and to Rouff this meant being properly dressed for every occasion. Even in her early work at Drécoll in Paris, Rouff addressed a basic longing in the relationship between many women and their clothes. Patrons of her salon were secure in the knowledge that they would emerge with the right clothes, clothes that were fashionable, flattering, and appropriate. This did not mean she was conservative; rather, she believed novelty, and even surprise, were good for fashion. Novelty when allied with taste yielded chic, but novelty without taste was only eccentric.

As a result, a Rouff design considered "too much" was rare. She took care to establish a focal point in every costume. An evening gown in which the skirt was trimmed with a crossover hip wrap and little side puffs had simply-cut sleeves and bodice. Afternoon dresses with plain skirts might have an asymmetrical cowl neckline with a jeweled clip at one side, or a platter collar and shaped belt in a contrasting color. She enriched some surfaces with shirring, quilting, or trapunto, as in her 1936 "plus four" playsuit and 1938 button-quilted evening dress, but very lush fabrics and furs were handled in accordance with her less-is-more philosophy.

Common themes ran through Rouff's designs, always enhancing the underlying sense of femininity. She had a fondness for draped details, whether the sarong-like side drape of a skirt panel or soft cowl folds at the neckline. Rouff often highlighted the upper body, drawing attention toward the face with a few favorite devices such as wrapped and tied surplice fronts, unusual necklines, and dramatic sleeves. Accents were important: belts and sashes were wide, buttons were bold, silk flowers were substantial, yet somehow they were always in proportion. Contrasts of color, texture, or luster were also used as accents, and with the same sense of balance.

Historical allusions were frequent, but true to her beliefs she used historicism as a tool and not a crutch. The Directoire collection she showed in 1936 was striking for its theme, with variations on cutaway and frock coats turning up in corduroy with a bias-cut plaid skirt, in printed floral shantung with a black crêpe skirt, and in velvet with a wool skirt and an oversized watch chain pocket detail. Usually her references to the past were less direct, perhaps expressed in gigot sleeves, or apron and bustle effects.

In 1942 while Paris was occupied by German troops, Rouff wrote *La Philosophie de L'Elégance.* Her justification for what might have been considered in such circumstances a frivolous topic, was her belief that even in darkest times there must be faith in the future. An intelligent woman who had already lived through one world war, she could not help but understand that a different world than the one she had known would emerge from the second. Her book was, in a sense, an affirmation of the value and substance which the arts of elegance had given to her life and her success. Within the framework of her expertise—fashion—Rouff gave her readers a thread to tie the future to the past.

Rouff's daughter, Anne-Marie Besançon de Wagner, took over the designing upon her mother's retirement in 1948. The house maintained the attitudes toward dress it had always expressed, and the clothes were still elegant and feminine. For the first few years she was inclined to overdo, and some designs seem to have been fussy or hard-edged. As the 1950s progressed, however, she found her own sense of focus and greater sureness of line. Particularly beautiful were her full-skirted organdy evening and cocktail dresses from 1952 and a group of short, bouffant gowns with floor-length trains from 1959. Engaging day ensembles included, from 1953, a sleek tweed sheath with standaway cornucopia-shaped pockets at the bust and from 1952, a fur-trimmed swing coat worn over a pleated wool dress belted at the waist.

The house of Maggy Rouff did not survive the make-or-break period of the 1960s. Three designers worked for the house in the 1960s, during which time the business was transformed into a ready-to-wear house. The collections seem to have been aimed at a younger customer, but the original precepts of the house may have made it difficult to become established with a clientèle more interested in the pursuit of youth than the pursuit of elegance. The company was closed before Rouff's death in 1971.

—Madelyn Shaw

ROWLEY, Cynthia

American designer

Born: Barrington, Illinois, 29 July 1958. **Education:** Studied art at Arizona State University, graduated from the Art Institute of Chicago, 1981. **Family:** Married Tom Sullivan, 1988 (died, 1994). **Career:**

Cynthia Rowley, spring 2001 collection: ensembled called "String Fever." © AP/Wide World Photos.

Senior at the Art Institute when she sold an 18-piece collection to Marshall Fields; moved to New York, 1983, incorporated business, 1988; designed costumes for dance troupes and films (including *Three of Hearts* and *Dream Lover*); produced shoes, ready-to-wear, sportswear, dresses; introduced line of girl's dresses, 1991; taught at Parsons School of Design, New York, 1992–93; critic, Fashion Institute of Technology, New York, 1992–94, and Marist College, New York, 1994; coauthored *Swell: A Girl's Guide to the Good Life,* 1995; opened Chicago store, 1995; opened Los Angeles store, 1996; signed licensing deal with Cheil Industries for Asia, 1996; introduced menswear, 1997; teamed up with Keds for shoe line, 1998; announced partnership with Pegasus Apparel Group, 2000. **Exhibitions:** *Objects of Their Appreciation,* Interart Center, New York, 1993; linen exhibition, Fashion Institute of Technology, New York, 1993; Dupont/Lycra exhibition, Fashion Institute of Technology, New York, 1994. **Collections:** Metropolitan Museum of Art Fashion Video Library, New York; Fashion Institute of Technology Permanent Collection, New York; Fashion Resource Center, Chicago Art Institute. **Awards:** New York Finalist, Entrepreneur of the Year, *Forbes* magazine, 1994; Council of Fashion Designers Perry Ellis award for New Fashion Talent, 1994. **Address:** 550 Seventh Avenue, 19th Floor, New York, NY, USA.

Publications

By ROWLEY:

Books

Swell: A Girl's Guide to the Good Life, with Ilene Rosenzweig, New York, 1999.

On ROWLEY:

Books

McBride, Mary, *Wedding Dress,* New York, 1993.

Bartlett, L., *Feast for Life,* Chicago, 1994.

Stegemeyer, Anne, *Who's Who in Fashion, Third Edition,* New York, 1996.

Articles

Finkelstein, Anita J., "Rowley Revs Up," in *WWD,* 6 January 1992.

"Cynthia Rowley Rises and Shines," in *Mademoiselle,* March 1992.

Goodman, Wendy, "Living with Style," in *HG* (New York), May 1992.

Levine, Lisbeth, "A Sense of Whimsy," in the *Chicago Sun-Times,* 3 May 1992.

Goodman, Wendy, "Fashion Designer Cynthia Rowley Serves Up 1940s Tablecloths...," in *HG,* May 1993.

Spindler, Amy M., "Fresh Talents Dish Up Tasty Design," in the *New York Times,* 5 November 1993.

Cawley, Janet, "Designer Makes Splash in New York," in the *Chicago Tribune,* January 1994.

Infantino, Vivian, "Rowley's Big Adventure," in *Footwear News* (New York), January 1994.

Trebay, Guy, "FTV," in *Harper's Bazaar,* August 1994.

Glusac, Elaine, "Rowley's Retail Homecoming," in *WWD,* 7 June 1995.

Ingrassia, Michele, "Dress for Success," in *Newsweek,* 13 November 1995.

Shae, Dan, "A Designer Original: Fashion Designer Cynthia Rowley," in *Working Woman,* March 1996.

Pogoda, Dianne M., "Rowley Expands in Asia," in *WWD,* 9 July 1996.

Anniss, Elisa, "Design Champion: Keds and Cynthia Rowley...," in *Footwear News,* 25 August 1997.

"Cynthia Rowley" in *DNR,* 3 August 1998.

Wilson, Eric, "Rowley's Aim for the Good Life" in *WWD,* 17 May 2001.

*

The underlying thing about my clothing is that I always think about a woman's shape. Sometimes it is a basic shape that everyone understands, but I try to make it a bit more fun. I definitely have a sense of whimsy with everything. I like clothes that are very feminine, but with an added twist. I also think a woman shouldn't have to spend a lot for great clothes; maybe it's my Midwestern practicality coming through, but I feel there's always a need for great dresses at good prices.

Cynthia Rowley, fall 2001 collection. © AP/Wide World Photos.

For me, inspiration is very personal. A lot of what I design is inspired by where I grew up. I often do a play on the classics: tiny crop twin sets, mixed-match plaids, and polo dresses. Like everyone growing up in the suburbs, television was my link to fashion coolness—it's where I got my first sense of glamor. My clothing reflects these classics but with wit and originality.

—Cynthia Rowley

* * *

Cynthia Rowley does not think clothes should be taken too seriously; nor does she believe style and individuality must necessarily go hand in hand with a high price tag. Rowley is known for a line of dresses that are charming, easily affordable, and utterly distinctive. This winning combination enabled her sales to double twice within three years during the mid-1990s while some of her better-known colleagues had to retrench.

Rowley's clothes reflect her well-developed sense of play. Drawing on shared and familiar elements of popular American culture, she elevates the mundane, rethinking and transforming the cliché to produce garments that arrest and amuse. Yet she is careful not to push a joke too far—her clothes, though with a sense of humor for daily use, are not novelty items to be quickly discarded. Instances of her quirky style include a long, snap-fronted sleeveless dress of quilted rayon and acetate satin worn over a matching ribbed cotton turtleneck for fall 1992, with a reference to the classic hunter's vest simultaneously reinforced and subverted by a six-pack of Budweiser slung low on the model's hip.

To commemorate the 100th anniversary of the bottle cap, Rowley scattered them across the front of a sleeveless cotton sweater, one half of a twin set with an eye-catching twist. Her spring 1993 collection included sundresses of classic red and white tablecloth checks, supported by straps made from plastic fruits and vegetables. "I definitely like to have a little sense of whimsy with everything," she said in a 1992 interview with the *Chicago Sun-Times.*

Rowley's more traditional dresses also incorporate styling elements not often seen at her end of the market. A halter dress becomes suitable for the office when cut from classic pinstripes and paired with a white shirt. She understands that the basics need not bore and that an imaginative dialogue between cut and fabric can produce distinctive clothing in any price range. She captured renewed attention in 1995, dubbed The Year of the Dress, for her feminine, fun to wear dresses. The Council of Fashion Designers awarded her the Perry Ellis award for New Fashion Talent in 1994, even though she had been in the business for 12 years.

Rowley's approachable collections move from down-to-earth casual to fanciful fun. In 2001, Rowley explored the popular interest in denim by presenting new shapes in puffed-sleeve dresses and also mixed jeans with dressier pieces. In her fall 2001 show, she produced a circus complete with mimes and jugglers and showed two-tone skirts and mismatched stockings. While always comfortable, Rowley's clothes can also be more sophisticated, like coordinated tailored jackets, skirts, and trousers or linen suits in 1998. Rowley designs dresses and sportswear and holds licensing arrangements for lingerie, coats, shoes, handbags, and other accessories. Her lines are sold in five company-owned stores in the U.S., department stores, and in-store boutiques in Japan.

For years, Rowley has been designing clothes for a woman with a carefree life loaded with style and bravado. In 1995 Rowley and friend Ilene Rosenzweig, a *New York Times* writer, packaged this ideal woman in their book *Swell: A Girl's Guide to the Good Life.* The popular book went through five printings and was translated into five languages. Rowley and Rosenzweig were preparing two sequels and making plans for a television spin-off. Rowley, of course, welcomes the opportunity to design the television wardrobes.

—Whitney Blausen; updated by Janette Goff Dixon

RUGGERI, Cinzia

Italian designer

Born: Milan, Italy, 1 February 1945. **Education:** Studied design at Accademia delle Arti Applicate, Milan, 1963–65. **Career:** Freelance designer in Milan, from 1966. **Exhibitions:** Galleria del Prisma, Milan, 1963; Venice Biennale, 1981; *Italian Re-Evolution,* La Jolla Museum of Contemporary Art, La Jolla, California, 1982; *Per Un Vestire Organico,* Palazzo Fortuny, Venice, 1983; *Italia: The Genius of Fashion,* Fashion Institute of Technology, New York, 1985; *Dopo Gondrand: Cinzia RuggeriDenis Santachiara,* Il Luogo di Corrado Levi, Milan, 1986; *Extra Vacanze di Cinzia Ruggeri,* Galleria Tucci Russo, Turin, 1986; *Internationale Mobel Messe,* Cologne, 1987; *Fashion and Surrealism,* Fashion Institute of Technology, New York, 1987 (toured); *Pianeta Italia,* Kaufhof Stores, Cologne, 1988; Salon del Mobile, Milan, 1988. **Collections:** Museo della Moda, Parma. **Awards:** Fil d'Or award, Confederation Internationale du Lin, 1981, 1982, 1983. **Address:** Corso Buenos Sires 2, Milan 20124, Italy. **Website:** www.cinziaruggeri.com.

Publications

By RUGGERI:

Articles

Casa Vogue (Milan), April 1980.

On RUGGERI:

Books

Amendola, Paola, *Vestire Italiano,* Rome, 1983.
Branzi, Andrea, *The Hot House: Italian New Wave Design,* London, 1984.
Soli, Pia, *Il Genio Antipatico,* Milan, 1984.
Manzini, Ezio, *La Materia Dell'Invenzione,* Milan, 1986.
Martin, Richard, *Fashion and Surrealism,* New York, London, 1987.
Soli, Pia, *Pranzo alle 8,* Milan, 1988.
Yajima, Isao, *Fashion Illustrators of Europe,* Tokyo, 1989.
Contemporary Designers, Third Edition, Detroit, 1997.

Articles

"Suggestioni Antoillogiche," *Il Giorno,* 3 May 1998.
Gandini, Manuela, "Ombre di Cinzia Ruggeri," *Il Sole 24 Ore,* 31 May 1998.
Muritti, Elisabetta, "Alice nel Paese della Post-Meriviglie," *Elle,* June 1998.
Davide, Paolini, "Ma il Grana e' in Galleria," *Il Sole 24 Ore,* 21 June 1998.
Piccoli, Cloe, "Specchi e Poltrone," *La Repubblica,* 22 June 1998.
Carloni, M. V., "Essere Dandy nel XXI Secolo," *Specchio della Stampa,* 27 June 1998.
"Cinzia Ruggeri," available online at her company website, www.cinziaruggeri.com, October 2001.

* * *

Following her studies in the applied arts at the Accademia delle Arti Applicate in Milan, Cinzia Ruggeri obtained a position in the atelier of Carven in Paris. On her return to Italy, she served as director of design for the ready-to-wear firm of Unimac SpA, owned by her father, Guido Ruggeri, and based in Milan.

The Ruggeri firm was founded in 1963 and ceased operations in 1975. It had been controlled by the family and, under the label Guido Ruggeri, produced women's suits and coats. Unimac SpA was one of the foremost manufacturers in the booming Italian ready-to-wear industry of the 1960s. Signor Ruggeri and his daughter integrated the artisan's aesthetics and sartorial traditions with new techniques of production and distribution. During the 1960s, radical changes were occurring in the Italian garment industry. Good design, improved manufacturing methods, and competition diminished the pervasive antipathy to mass production. New ideas and reorganization were fused in collaborative efforts between manufacturer and small but specialized companies.

Around 1966, Unimac SpA began investigating alternatives such as synthetic fur detailing and novelty fasteners. It was possibly Cinzia Ruggeri's developing sense of design that was responsible for linking diverse fashion elements with the new manufacturing methods. During the 1970s, when Milanese designers were involved more than usual with "things English," Ruggeri worked for the manufacturer Bumblebee, which produced a line of women's blouses labeled Bloom. On the Via Gandino in 1977, she proceeded to build her own line, labeled Bloom SpA, and presented her first collection to the press in 1978.

In 1979 the atelier was moved to the Via Crocefisso. From 1980 through 1984, Ruggeri presented her singular, thematic ready-to-wear collections with other Milanese designers at the Fiera di Milano. On one occasion, outside the seasonal venue, her 1985 collection was presented in a building formerly used for religious services. The lighting installation was designed by the English musician Brian Eno. In 1982, she added the label Cinzia Ruggeri to her existing Bloom SpA line, and in 1986 she introduced menswear.

Throughout the 1980s, Ruggeri continued to apply thematic appliqués to traditional styling, employing contemporary fabrics. A 1981 winter ensemble included a jacket of synthetic fur strips, ornamented with a fabric appliqué of three pigs covering the entire back of the garment. At an early stage in her career, Ruggeri established her sense of global responsibility by refusing to use animal fur, and both the wool trousers and the crêpe de chine blouse also featured the threesome appliqué. The pièce de résistance in this case was a perfectly constructed three-dimensional shoulder bag in the shape of a pig.

Ziggurat 1984–85 was a two-piece synthetic evening dress. The garment was appliquéd with scattered two-dimensional fabric bows, knotted as if clutching the three-dimensional feathers. The ruffle-edged jacket was traditional in design, and the floor-length skirt was three tiered, recalling the stepped towers of ancient civilizations. Subsequent garments have included these ziz-zag elements and structuring to form a volume independent of the wearer's body. She refers the stepped pattern to a personal symbol, which she has also repeated in other artistic expressions. *Artform Magazine* featured an illustration of a glass container that incorporated the pattern at right angles to each other.

The fantasy of nature itself was compelling to the Surrealists and to Ruggeri. Her 1983 Surrealist vision of marine life was titled "Dress with Octopus." The long-sleeved, boxy jacket was the surface for randomly placed cascading square fabric forms, and the straight shift worn underneath involved the same protrusions, including a neckline cut as an ocean's horizon. Her broken ground print dress, quite traditional in style and fit, was pierced with oversized blossoms and crawling with three-dimensional lizards. Most recently, in her Milanese studio, she proceeded to design prototypes for various projects that combined fashion with photography, anthropology, geology, and ecology by incorporating photographs of grass, cobblestones, and marble in her textile designs.

Ruggeri has developed "behavioral" garments, printed with material that changes color according to body heat, and designed a "rain coat" with images of lightning and wind. A fitted dress, printed with Scottie dogs and edged with a cantilevered structure from which the dogs appear to be running, is, of course, not surprisingly featured in a magazine accompanied by a set of three-dimensional Scottie dog suitcases. "Abito Tovaglia," tablecloth gown, illustrates a seated woman wearing a floor-length gown. She wears a collar as napkin, at first rolled up to the waist and attached at the sides of the garment. When unrolled, the panel reveals a cloth set with the utensils of an entire meal. For the Milanese firm Poltrona Frau, Ruggeri designed a chair ornamented with whiskered cats and illuminated eyes. A shower head is illustrated in the shape of a human hand with water spraying out from the ringer tips.

As an artist, Ruggeri has challenged herself in designing theatrical productions, ballets, and artistic events and has ventured into interior and furniture design. She has exhibited at the Triennale di Milano and the Biennale di Venezia, and performances involving her fantastical costumes have clearly reflected her poetic tendencies when given such titles as *Performance Adanamica* (Performance Without Movement), *La Casa Onirica* (The House Where I Dream), and *Per Vestire Organico* (To Dress Organically), all from 1983. *La Neo Merce, Il Design dell'Intensione e dell'Estasi Artificiale* were new products design and artificial ecstasy in 1985, and *Vestiti al Video,* videowear, in 1986. Also presented in 1994 were *Verona Neo Eclettismo,* Verona new eclecticism, and an exhibit at the Bacini Meridionale Museo Nuova Era.

Firmly entrenched in the world of interior design in the 1990s, Ruggeri created chairs, wardrobes, glassware, mirrors, and other avant-garde furniture and home accessories for such firms as Bic, Colombra, Driade, Ferrari Champagne, Glass Design, Mirror Schatzi, Poltrone Frau, Rapsel, and Wardrobe Rocco. Her work was exhibited at the Krizia Studio in Milan as well as venues in Frankfurt, Paris, London, Tokyo, and New York.

—Gillion Skellenger; updated by Mary Ellen Snodgrass

RYKIEL, Sonia

French designer

Born: Sonia Flis in Paris, 25 May 1930. **Education:** Attended high school in Neuilly-sur-Seine. **Family:** Married Sam Rykiel, 1953; children: Nathalie, Jean-Philippe. **Career:** Freelance designer for Laura boutique, Paris, 1962; first Paris boutique opened, 1968; household linens boutique opened, Paris, 1975; Sonia Rykiel Enfant

Sonia Rykiel, fall/winter 2001 ready-to-wear collection. © AP/ Wide World Photos.

boutique opened, Paris, 1987; cosmetics line introduced in Japan, 1987; Rykiel Homme boutique opened, Paris, 1989; Inscription Rykiel collection, designed by Nathalie Rykiel, introduced, 1989; new flagship boutique opened, Paris, 1990; menswear collection, Rykiel Homme introduced, 1990; second Inscription Rykiel boutique, Paris, 1990; Rykiel Homme boutique opened, Paris, 1992; footwear collection launched, 1992; Sonia Rykiel fragrance introduced 1993; also columnist for *Femme,* from 1983; 30th anniversary celebration, Bibliothèque Nationale, 1998. **Exhibitions:** *Sonia Rykiel, 20 Ans de Mode* (retrospective), Galeries Lafayette, Paris, and Seibo Shibuya department store, Tokyo, 1987; retrospective, the Orangerie, Palais du Luxembourg, 1993. **Awards:** French Ministry of Culture Croix des Arts et des Lettres, 1983; named Chevalier de la Légion d'Honneur, 1985; Fashion Group, "Night of the Stars" award, 1986; Officier de l'Ordre de Arts et des Lettres, 1993. **Address:** 175 boulevard Saint Germain, 75006 Paris, France.

Publications

By RYKIEL:

Books

Et je la voudrais nue, Paris, 1979.
Rykiel, Paris, 1985.
Célébrations, Paris, 1988.
La collection, Paris, 1989; Tokyo, 1989.
Colette et la mode, Paris, 1991.
Collection Terminée, Collection Interminable, Paris, 1993.
Tatiana Acacia, Paris, 1993.
(contributor) Spengler, Franck, ed., *Plaisirs de femmes: nouvelles,* Paris, 1998.
Paris: sur les pas de Sonia Rykiel, Paris, 1999.

On RYKIEL:

Books

Fraser, Kennedy, *The Fashionable Mind. Reflections on Fashion 1970–1981,* New York, 1981.
Chapsal, Madeleine, Hélène Cixous, and Sonia Rykiel, *Rykiel,* Paris, 1985.
Milbank, Caroline Rennolds, *Couture: The Great Designers,* New York, 1985.
The Power of Paris: Frankly French, (video), New York, 1991.
Marion, Sylvie, *L'école de la vie, ou La France autodidacte,* Paris, 1993.
Chapsal, Madeleine, *La jalousie,* Paris, 1994.
Benstock, Shari, and Suzanne Ferriss, *On Fashion,* New Brunswick, New Jersey, 1994.
Stegemeyer, Anne, *Who's Who in Fashion, Third Edition,* New York, 1996.
Lemoine, Bertrand, and Jean Gaumy, *Regards: L'art des grands travaux,* Paris, 1997.
Mauries, Patrick, *Sonia Rykiel,* Paris, 1997; New York, 1998.

Articles

"Sonia Rykiel, ambigue, célèbre et solitaire," in *Elle* (Paris), 25 October 1976.
Tournier, Françoise, "Sonia Rykiel sa vie, de fil," in *Elle* (Paris), 17 June 1985.
Schoonejans, Sonia, "Autour de l'album Rykiel," in *Vogue* (Paris), August 1985.
Menkes, Suzy, "Sonia Rykiel—Winning at Life," in the *International Herald Tribune* (Neuilly, France), 18 October 1988.
Sacase, Christiane, "Sonia Rykiel, les 20 ans de la dame en noir," in *Biba,* November 1988.
de Turckheim, Hélène, "Mes rendez-vous," in *Madame Figaro* (Paris), 11 February 1989.
Chapsal, Madeleine, "Les vingt ans de Sonia Rykiel," in *Elle* (Paris), 20 February 1989.
Tredre, Roger, "Touch of the Grande Dame," in *The Independent on Sunday* (London), 25 February 1990.
"Sonia Rykiel," in *Current Biography* (New York), May 1990.
Nolin, Dominique, "En visite chez Sonia Rykiel," in *Marie-France* (Paris), March 1991.
Raulet, Sylvie, "Sonia Rykiel: une femme d'atmosphère," in *Vogue* (Japan), March 1991.
Lender, Heidi, "Rapping with Rykiel," in *WWD,* 18 November 1991.
Schwarm, Barbara, "Sonia Rykiel, la compil," in *L'Officiel* (Paris), June 1993.
Lender, Heidi, and Godfrey Deeny, "Sex, Sweaters and Sonia Rykiel," in *WWD,* 7 July 1993.
Menkes, Suzy, "Rykiel in Retrospect: The Unfinished Work of a Designer," in the *International Herald Tribune,* 13 July 1993.
Webb, Ian, "Capital Elle," in *The Times Magazine,* 1994.
Rafferty, Jean Bond, "The Leading Lady of the Left Bank," in *Town & Country* (New York), December 1994.
Ozzard, Janet, "Rykiel Sips Tea, Seeks N.Y. Store," in *WWD,* 28 December 1994.
Schiro, Anne-Marie, "Lacroix and Rykiel: Classics," in the *New York Times,* 18 March 1995.
Menkes, Suzy, "Sonia Rykiel: Still Whipping Up the Culturual Broth," in the *International Herald Tribune,* 28 April 1998.

*

First I destroyed, undid what I had made. I wasn't satisfied with it, it wasn't me. It didn't relate to me. It was fashion, but it wasn't my fashion. I wanted to abolish the laws, the rules. I wanted to undo, overflow, exceed fashion. I wanted to unfold, unwind it. I wanted a lifestyle appropriate to the woman I was…this woman-symphony who was living the life of a woman mingled with the life of a worker.

I wanted airplane-style, travel-style, luggage-style. I saw myself as a woman on the go, surrounded by bags and children…so I imagined "kangaroo-clothes," stackable, collapsible, movable, with no right side, no wrong side, and no hem. Clothes to be worn in the daytime I could refine at night. I put "fashion" aside to create "non-fashion."

—Sonia Rykiel

* * *

French ready-to-wear designer Sonia Rykiel is a compelling presence whose intellect and individuality are apparent in her clothes. With her small bones and trademark mane of hair, she is probably her own best model, projecting assurance and energy. She began designing with no previous experience when, as the pregnant wife of the owner of Laura, a fashionable boutique, she was unable to find maternity clothes she liked. Continuing to design knitwear for Laura,

Sonia Rykiel, fall/winter 2001 ready-to-wear collection. © AP/ Wide World Photos.

she soon carved a niche for herself designing for well-to-do and sophisticated modern French women.

By 1964, Rykiel had been nicknamed "The Queen of Knitwear" in the U.S., where an ardent following developed for her knits, which were sold in trendsetting stores like Henri Bendel and Bloomingdale's in New York. For women who were rich and thin enough to wear them, these skinny sweaters, with their high armholes, imparted instant chic. Part of their appeal was in their distinctive colors and striped patterns. Black, navy, gray, and beige are still standards, but there was also a unique Rykiel palette of muted tones—stripes of grayed seafoam green and grayed teal. Although she herself does not wear red (she wears black, considering it a uniform), Rykiel still uses it consistently, with the shade changing from season to season.

Rykiel continues to design a complete range of clothes and accessories for women in the 1990s, drawn from her experiences and her fantasies, which she encourages women to appropriate and adapt whilst inventing and reinventing themselves. In addition to knits and jerseys, she uses crêpe for soft clothes, and woven tweeds and plaids for a more structured day look. Evening fantasies are best expressed in lightweight black luxury fabrics, often combined with sequins, metallic thread, embroidery, or elaborate combinations incorporating velvet.

Physical fitness is implicit in Sonia Rykiel's idea of modern femininity, so it is no surprise that the innermost layers of the knitted or jersey separates at the heart of her collections continue to be body conscious, if not figure hugging. They range in style from skimpy, narrow-shouldered pullovers with recognizable Rykiel detailing, to drop-shouldered tunics, to cardigans both short and boxy, and long and flowing. The detailing itself can be as soft as ruffles and bows, or as hard as nail heads. Although certain themes like cropped wide-leg trousers recur, the skirts and trousers that accompany the sweaters sometimes reflect the fashion of the moment, as in the short skirt worn with a classic Rykiel sweater which was featured by the *New York Times Magazine* in Patricia McColl's 1988 spring fashion preview, titled "The Byword is Short." The sweater is a fine example of another important facet of Rykiel's work: the dress, sweater, or accessory as bulletin board.

As befits the author of several books, Rykiel began to incorporate words into her designs. "I feel more like a novelist than a fashion designer," she commented to the *International Herald Tribune*'s Suzy Menkes. "Someone who writes a new chapter each season, including everything I see around me." And what she has seen around her becomes emblazoned on slinky dresses and the fronts or backs of sweaters variously inscribed "Moi," "Fête," and "Plaisir," among others. Nor has English been slighted: "Artist," "Ready," "Black Tie," and "Black is Beautiful" have also been included. Not even eveningwear is sacrosanct: a 1983 ensemble with a sheer black lace bodice and black crêpe sleeves and skirt was encircled with a rhinestone studded belt reading, "Special Edition Evening Dreams." Nonetheless, the most frequent words to appear are "Sonia Rykiel," or simply "Rykiel."

Rykiel was an early exponent of deconstruction. Made of the finest quality wool yarns, sometimes mixed with angora, her knits are frequently designed with reverse seams. She also innovated the use of lockstitched hems. Since the early 1980s Rykiel has also produced at least two casual lines a year in cotton velours, a fluid, sensual fabric well suited to uncluttered silhouettes. Each season there is at least one dress, in addition to trousers, pullovers, cardigans, and jackets, many with reverse seams. They are offered in several solid colors, in stripes and, occasionally, in prints. Like other clothes of illusory simplicity, they have often been unsuccessfully copied.

Another Rykiel specialty is outerwear. Her coats, whether in fine woolens, or in highly coveted fake fur, tend to be voluminous. Along with these and her accessories line, other Rykiel enterprises include children's and menswear lines and perfumes. The entire Rykiel design output is available in the lifestyle boutique on Boulevard Saint Germain, which opened in 1990.

As the century came to a close, Rykiel looked forward and back. She celebrated the 30-year anniversary of her first Paris boutique with a gala at the Bibliothèque Nationale in 1998, remembering the Parisian student riots that forced her to close temporarily. Yet this particular French revolution ushered in both political upheaval and a shift in fashion—one Rykiel was only too happy to espouse. Her passion for artistic design is undiminished; yet it is now a family affair, involving daughter Nathalie, her husband, and Nathalie's three daughters who have modeled new Rykiel designs. And family is ever important to Rykiel, as she told Menkes in April 1998: "I wrote the story of women across the world. We all have the same needs and desires, the demands of work and family life. The Rykiel woman? She always has a bag on her shoulders so she can stride forward—with a child in each hand."

In 2000 and 2001 Rykiel continued what she did best: fluid, fashionable clothing in a variety of fabrics and styles. She produced taut tops, skirts, and dresses in geometic patterns for a cruise line collection in early 2000, including her perenially popular matelot stripes. And black, of course, always black, her personal favorite. Though older and wiser, her tenets have remained the same: clothing should be sophisticated, and as she told Menkes, a "kind of *bouillon de culture [a cultural broth]*. To be modern is to be aware of what is going on."

Sonia Rykiel, once called "Coco Rykiel," is a worthy successor to the Chanel tradition: she is a strong, ultrafeminine, articulate intellectual with a flair for simplicity and self-promotion, who has shown herself capable of both refined innovation and commercial success.

—Arlene C. Cooper; updated by Nelly Rhodes

S

SACHS, Gloria

American designer

Born: Gloria Harris in Scarsdale, New York, circa 1927. **Education:** Graduated in fine arts, Skidmore College, New York, 1947; studied textile design, Cranbrook Academy of Art, Michigan, 1947; studied painting with Fernand Léger, Paris, 1949; studied architecture with Giò Ponti and Franco Albini, Italy. **Family:** Married Irwin Sachs, 1953; children: Nancy, Charles. **Career:** Worked as a model for Balenciaga and Balmain, Paris, 1949; textile designer, Hans Knoll, Herman Miller, 1948–49; apprentice, *Domus* magazine, Milan, 1949–50; executive trainee, assistant buyer, then fashion coordinator, Bloomingdale's, New York, 1951–56; preteen clothing designer, Gloria Sachs Red Barn company, 1958–60; fashion director for children's wear, Bloomingdale's, 1960–62; preteen clothing designer, Saks Fifth Avenue, New York, 1962–65; formed own sportswear company, Gloria Sachs Designs, Ltd., 1970; showed first evening collection, 1983; private label introduced, 1986; closed firm, 1991–92; also paints, sculpts, and weaves. **Exhibitions:** paintings and sculpture shown at Pratt Institute, Brooklyn, New York, 1949, Art Alliance of Philadelphia, 1950, Art Institute of Chicago, 1950, Museum of Modern Art, New York, 1951. **Awards:** Saks Fifth Avenue Creator award, 1969; Woolknit Design award, 1974, 1976.

Publications

On SACHS:

Books

Milbank, Caroline Rennolds, *New York Fashion: The Evolution of American Style,* New York, 1989.

Articles

Morris, Bernadine, "Low-Key Elegrance by Gloria Sachs," in the *New York Times,* 22 September 1984.

Green, Wendy, "Gloria Sachs: Designing Her Own Business," in *WWD,* 14 July 1986.

Morris, Bernadine, "Sportswear Steps Up to Gold, Lace, and Velvet," in the *New York Times,* 15 April 1988.

Buck, Geneviève, "Barneys, Buddy and Bo—New Style, Old Style and No Style," in *Chicago Tribune,* 15 July 1992.

* * *

Gloria Sachs' intensive artistic education played a major part in her fashion work and its development. A fine arts graduate of the Skidmore College, she went on to study textiles at the Cranbrook Academy of Art in Michigan in 1947. Her first job was as a textile designer, noted for designing her own yarns in distinctive and individual color combinations. She used her earnings from this job to finance a cultural year in Europe. She was lucky enough to study painting at the atelier of Fernand Léger in Paris and architecture with both Giò Ponti and Franco Albini in Italy, which further developed her sense of color and proportion.

Returning to New York, Sachs worked in textiles at Bloomingdale's department store, eventually becoming their fashion coordinator. She later joined Saks Fifth Avenue as an in-house designer and her success there gave her the confidence to establish her own business on Seventh Avenue in 1970. Her first designs established her as a smart, casual separates designer. Mix-and-match pleated skirts, jackets, and coats, teamed with tailored shirts, were particularly distinctive. A glamorous, sporty evening look was another favorite with buyers. She later made glossy ensembles of color-blocked sweaters, teamed with uncoordinated skirts and trousers. Alongside other New York designers, including John Antony and Calvin Klein, she pioneered the New York look for casual sportswear shapes in supple and expensive fabrics.

Sachs is famous for her clever development of textile designs in her fashion. She worked very closely with the mills that produced her fabrics and even opened her own mill in Scotland to produce contrast trim and embroidered cashmere sweaters. She often used classic and antique patterns, developed with her own particular twist. Paisleys and plaids were reworked in unusual color combinations to be fresh and unexpected, always subtle and never brash. Experimentation with English gentlemen's neck-tie prints further allowed Sachs to originate and rescale exciting new patterns and shapes; in turn the fabrics served as inspiration for the creation of new clothing designs.

In her later work in the 1980s Sachs continued her development of signature, revamped textiles in beautiful fabrics. She also introduced looser, more unstructured clothing. Supple, fluid shapes that were simply cut and balanced were very flattering to wear and proved extremely popular. She sold her work through many top retailers, including Saks Fifth Avenue. Unfortunately, the early 1990s proved difficult for Sachs and a number of talented designers, including Mary Ann Restivo and Rebecca Moses, who were forced to close their businesses.

Gloria Sachs' major contribution to fashion was her easy, glamorous sportswear, dressed up for the evening or down for the day. These clothes were for professional, executive women who wanted to retain their femininity in the boardroom with taste and style. More relaxed than power dressing, it is dressing for success with dash and individuality.

—Kevin Almond; updated by Nelly Rhodes

SAINT LAURENT, Yves

French designer

Born: Yves Henri Donat Mathieu Saint Laurent in Oran, Algeria, 1 August 1936. **Education:** Studied at L'École de la Chambre Syndicale de la Couture, 1954. **Career:** Independent clothing stylist, Paris, 1953–54; designer/partner, 1954–57, chief designer, Dior, Paris, 1957–60; began designing for theater and film, 1959; founder/designer, Yves Saint Laurent, Paris, from 1962; Rive Gauche ready-to-wear line introduced, 1966; menswear line introduced, 1974; firm purchased by Elf-Sanofi SA, 1993; designer Elber Albaz hired, 1998–2000; acquired by Gucci Group NV, 1999; Tom Ford took over as creative director, 2000; renovated Madison Avenue store reopened, 2001; retired from designing, 2002; fragrances include *Y* 1964; *Rive Gauche,* 1971; *Opium,* 1978; *Paris,* 1983; *Champagne,* (renamed *Yvresse,* 1996) 1993; *Opium* relaunch, 1995; *Opium for Men,* 1996; *Baby Doll,* 1999; *Nu,* 2001. **Exhibitions:** *Yves Saint Laurent,* Metropolitan Museum of Art, 1983; *Yves Saint Laurent et le Théâtre,* Musée des Arts de la Mode, Paris, 1986; *Yves Saint Laurent, 28 Ans de Création,* Musée des Arts de la Mode, 1986; retrospective, Art Gallery of New South Wales, Sydney, Australia, 1987. **Awards:** International Wool Secretariat award, 1954; Neiman Marcus award, 1958; *Harper's Bazaar* award, 1966; Council of Fashion Designers of America award, 1981; CFDA Lifetime Achievement award, 1999; Fifi Fragrance award (for *Baby Doll*), 2000. **Address:** 5 avenue Marceau, 75116 Paris, France. **Website:** www.yslonline.com.

Yves Saint Laurent after showing his spring/summer 2000 high fashion collection. © Reuters NewMedia Inc./CORBIS.

PUBLICATIONS

By SAINT LAURENT:

Books

Yves Saint Laurent, New York & London, 1984.

Yves Saint Laurent par Yves Saint Laurent, Paris, 1986.

Bergé, Pierre, and Yves Saint Laurent, *Yves Saint Laurent,* London & New York, 1996, 1997.

Yves Saint Laurent: Forty Years of Creation, New York, 1998.

Love, by Yves Saint Laurent, New York, 2000.

On SAINT LAURENT:

Books

Lynam, Ruth, ed., *Couture: An Illustrated History of the Great Paris Designers and Their Creations,* New York, 1972.

Madsen, Axel, *Living for Design: The Yves Saint Laurent Story,* New York, 1979.

Milbank, Caroline Rennolds, *Couture: The Great Designers,* New York, 1985.

Musée des Arts Décoratifs, *Yves Saint Laurent et le Théâtre* [exhibition catalogue], Paris, 1986.

Art Gallery of New South Wales, *Yves Saint Laurent, Retrospectives* [exhibition catalogue], Sydney, New South Wales, 1987.

Perschetz, Lois, ed., *W, The Designing Life,* New York, 1987.

Yves Saint Laurent: Images of Design [exhibition catalogue], New York, 1988.

Howell, Georgina, *Sultans of Style: 30 Years of Fashion and Passion 1960–1990,* London, 1990.

Benaïm, Laurence, *Yves Saint Laurent,* Paris, 1993, 1995.

Martin, Richard, and Harold Koda, *Orientalism: Visions of the East in Western Dress* [exhibition catalogue], Metropolitan Museum of Art, 1994.

Stegemeyer, Anne, *Who's Who in Fashion, Third Edition,* New York, 1996.

Rawsthorn, Alice, *Yves Saint Laurent, A Biography,* London, 1996, 1997.

Duras, Marguerite, *Yves Saint Laurent and Fashion Photography,* Munich, 1998.

Tierney, Tom, *Yves Saint Laurent Fashion Review,* Mineola, New York, 1999.

Articles

"YSL Models *Rive Gauche* for Men in His Marrakesh Home," in *Vogue* (London), 1 October 1969.

"Yves Saint Laurent: His Very Special World," in *McCall's* (New York), January 1970.

"Mary Russell Interviews Saint Laurent," in *Vogue* (New York), 1 November 1972.

"Yves Saint Laurent Talks to Bianca Jagger," in *Interview,* January 1973.

Julian, P., "Les années 20 revues dans les années 70 chez Yves Saint Laurent," in *Connaissance des Arts* (Paris), December 1973.

Heilpern, John, and Yves Saint Laurent, "Yves Saint Laurent Lives," in *The Observer Magazine* (London), 5 June 1977.

"Designers of Influence: Yves Saint Laurent, the Great Educator," in *Vogue* (London), June 1978.

"Bravo: 20 Years of Saint Laurent," in *Vogue* (London), April 1982.

Yves Saint Laurent, 1999 special show of Moroccan high couture. © AFP/CORBIS.

"A Salute to Yves Saint Laurent," in the *New York Times Magazine,* 4 December 1983.

Brubach, Holly, "The Truth in Fiction," in *The Atlantic Monthly* (Boston, Massachusetts), May 1984.

Savage, Percy, "Yves Saint Laurent," in *Art and Design* (London), August 1985.

Berge, P., "Yves Saint Laurent der Modezeichner," in *Du* (Zurich), No. 10, 1986.

"Un équilibre définitif: Saint Laurent *Rive Gauche*," in *Vogue* (Paris), February 1986.

Griggs, Barbara, "All About Yves," in *The Observer* (London), 25 May 1986.

Mauries, Patrick, "Yves," in *Vogue* (Paris), June 1986.

"Le triomphe de Saint Laurent," in *L'Officiel* (Paris), June 1986.

Pringle, Colombe, "Saint Laurent: sanctifié il entre au musée," in *Elle* (Paris), June 1986.

Worthington, Christa, "Saint Laurent: Life as a Legend," in *Women's Wear Daily* (New York), 18 July 1986.

"Yves Only," in *Vogue* (London), September 1987.

"Prince Charmant. Bernard Sanz: L'homme de Saint Laurent," in *Profession Textile* (Paris), 27 May 1988.

"Saint Laurent pour toujours," in *Profession Textile* (Paris), 30 September 1988.

Duras, Marguerite, "Saint Laurent par Duras," in *Elle* (Paris), 31 October 1988.

Hyde, Nina, and Albert Allart, "The Business of Chic," in the *National Geographic* (Washington, D.C.), July 1989.

Howell, Georgina, "The Secrets of Saint Laurent," in *The Sunday Times Magazine* (London), 2 July 1989.

———, "Best Couturier: Yves Saint Laurent," in *The Sunday Times Magazine* (London), 16 July 1989.

Rafferty, Diane, Charles van Rensselaer and Thomas Cunneen, "The Many Faces of Yves: The Designer of the Half Century," in *Connoisseur,* February 1990.

Menkes, Suzy, "Yves of the Revolution," in the *Sunday Express Magazine* (London), 22 April 1990.

Germain, Stephanie, "All About Yves," in *Paris Passion* (Paris), October 1990.

Roberts, Michael, and André Leon Talley, "Unveiling Saint Laurent," in *Interview* (New York), June 1991.

Smith, Liz, "Thirty Years at Fashion's Cutting Edge," in *The Times* (London), 27 January 1992.

"Yves Saint Laurent, King of Couture," interview, in *Elle* (New York), February 1992.

Brubach, Holly, "Fanfare in a Minor Key," in *The New Yorker,* 24 February 1992.

White, Lesley, "The Saint," in *Vogue* (London), November 1994.

Kramer, Jane, "The Impresario's Last Act, in the *New Yorker* (New York), 21 November 1994.

Schiro, Anne-Marie, "Yves Saint Laurent's Shocking New Color: Black," in the *New York Times* (New York), 22 March 1995.

Menkes, Suzy, "YSL Plays Safe While Valentino Shines at Night," in the *International Herald Tribune* (Paris), 22 March 1995.

"Saint Laurent: A Fitting End," in *WWD,* 22 March 1995.

Menkes, Suzy, "A New Generation in Ready-to-Wear: Alber Elbaz Gets Aboard at YSL," in the *International Herald Tribune,* 9 June 1998.

"YSL Coming to Receive CFDA Award," in *WWD,* 29 March 1999.

Menkes, Suzy, "Gucci Buys House of YSL for $1-Billion," in the *International Herald Tribune,* 16 November 1999.

———, "New Team, Same Theme at YSL," in the *International Herald Tribune,* 20 January 2000.

Socha, Miles, "Ford's YSL: Full Steam Ahead," in *WWD,* 12 January 2001.

"At Yves Saint Laurent, Tom's Triumph," in *WWD,* 15 March 2001.

Menkes, Suzy, "YSL and the Secrets of Classic Couture," in the *International Herald Tribune,* 12 July 2001.

Ozzard, Janet, "Tom's Rive Gauche," in *WWD,* 6 September 2001.

Ozzard, Janet, et al, "Tom Ford Expands YSL Store," in *DNR,* 10 September 2001.

Diderich, Joelle, "Fashion Legend Yves Saint Laurent Retires," from Reuters Newswire, 7 January 2002.

Cowdy, Hannah, "YSL: Adieu to a Fashion Generation," available online at ABCNews, www.ABCNews.com, 7 January 2002.

* * *

A great adaptor, Yves Saint Laurent responds in his designs to history, art, and literature. Vast ranges of themes are incorporated into his work, from the Ballet Russes to the writings of Marcel Proust, who inspired his taffeta gowns of 1971; the paintings of Picasso to the

Yves Saint Laurent, autumn/winter 2001–02 haute couture collection. © Reuters NewMedia Inc./CORBIS.

minimalist work of Mondrian and the de Stijl movement, shown in the primary colors of his geometrically blocked wool jersey dresses of 1965.

Saint Laurent has a great love of the theatre. He has designed costumes for many stage productions during his long career and the theatre is an important source of ideas for his couture collections. Flamboyant ensembles, such as the Shakespeare wedding dress of brocade and damask of 1980 and his extravagant series of garments inspired by a romantic vision of Russian dress, reflect his passion for theatrical costume.

Less successful have been his attempts to engage with countercultural movements such as the 1960 collection based on the bohemian Left Bank look. The criticism leveled by the press on being confronted with the avant garde on the couture catwalk led to Saint Laurent's replacement as head designer for Dior, even though his 1958 trapeze line had been an enormous success and he had been fêted as the savior of Parisian couture. At this time the House of Dior was responsible for nearly half of France's fashion exports, so there was a heavy burden of financial responsibility on Saint Laurent's shoulders.

The 1960 collection appropriated the Left Bank style with knitted turtlenecks and black leather jackets, crocodile jackets with mink collars, and—a design which was to crop up again and again in his repertoire—the fur jacket with knitted sleeves. In 1968 Saint Laurent produced a tailored trouser collection reflecting his sympathy with the cause of the student marchers who had brought the streets of Paris to a standstill. The clothes were black and accessorized with headbands and fringes.

Where Saint Laurent sets the standards for world fashion is in his feminizing of the basic shapes of the male wardrobe. Like Chanel before him, he responded to the subtleties of masculine tailoring seeking to provide a similar sort of style for women. He produced a whole series of elegant day clothes, such as the shirt dress, which became a staple of the sophisticated woman's wardrobe of the 1970s. Saint Laurent is justly acclaimed for his sharply tailored suits with skirts or trousers, *le smoking* (a simple black suit with satin lapels based on the male tuxedo, which became an alternative to the frothily feminine evening gown), safari jackets, brass buttoned pea jackets, flying suits—in fact many of the chic classics of postwar women's style.

Saint Laurent's designs contain no rigid shaping or over-elaborate cutting but depend on a perfection of line and a masterful understanding of printed textiles and the use of luxurious materials. He worked with silk printers to produce glowing fabric designs incorporating a brilliant palette of clashing colors such as hot pink, violet, and sapphire blue. A sharp contrast is produced with his simple, practical daywear and romantic, exotic eveningwear, which is more obviously seductive with its extensive beadwork, embroidery, satin, and sheer fabrics such as silk chiffon.

Less interested in fashion than in style, Saint Laurent is and will always be a classicist, designing elegant, tasteful, and sophisticated apparel, perfectly handcrafted in the manner of the old couturiers. He did, however, use industrial methods to produce his Rive Gauche ready-to-wear line, created in 1966, and sold in his own franchised chain of boutiques. The popular line was later taken over by Alber Elbaz, who had worked for Guy Laroche, in 1998, and then by Tom Ford in 2000.

There was been a radical change in the small company founded by Yves Saint Laurent and business partner Pierre Bergé in 1961. It became a massive financial conglomerate, listed on the Paris Bourse, the result of profitable licensing deals. In the 1990s the firm changed ownership several times, ending up as part of the Gucci Group in 1999. Called "fashion's shiniest trophy," by the *International Herald Tribune* (16 November 1999), the YSL acquisition was another example of the fashion industry's tightening consolidation.

In the 21st century, YSL remained an acclaimed couture house, though its namesake and Rive Gauche designer Tom Ford rarely saw eye to eye. In January 2002, however, such creative differences were moot: Saint Laurent announced he was leaving the firm that bore his name and retiring. Roundly considered the last of the true haute couturiers, the industry lost one of its most elegant and inspired purveyors.

—Caroline Cox; updated by Nelly Rhodes

SAKS FIFTH AVENUE

American retail store

Opened: in 1924 as a joint venture between Horace Saks of Saks & Co. and Bernard Gimbel of Gimbel Bros. **Company History:** Targeting upscale customers, it was the first specialty store to expand across the

Saks Fifth Avenue, New York City, 1996. © AP/Wide World Photos.

nation; financial stresses precipitated the sale of Saks Fifth Avenue to the U.S. subsidiary of British American Tobacco in 1973; company changed hands again in 1990; was acquired by Alabama-based Proffitt's, 1998. **Awards:** Fifth Avenue store earned a Gold Medal award from the Fifth Avenue Association and remains a New York landmark. **Company Address:** 12 East 49th Street, New York, NY 10017, USA. **Company Website:** www.saksfifthavenue.com.

PUBLICATIONS

On SAKS FIFTH AVENUE:

Books

Marcus, Stanley, *Quest for the Best,* New York, 1979.
Leach, William, *Land of Desire,* New York, 1993.

Articles

Benbow-Pfalzgraf, Taryn, "Saks Fifth Avenue," in the*International Directory of Company Histories,* Detroit, MI, 1999.
"Saks Inc. in Store Deals," in *WWD,* 7 November 2001.

* * *

Saks Fifth Avenue evokes images of style and elegance. One of the most famous luxury retailers in the world, Saks Fifth Avenue has long been the destination for fashion-conscious men and women. The flagship store at 611 Fifth Avenue at 50th Street opened in 1924 and has served the stylish for over three-quarters of a century.

Andrew Saks was born in Baltimore, Maryland, and moved to Washington, D.C., to make his fortune. He established a clothing business there in 1867 that grew to include stores in other cities. He moved to New York and opened Saks & Company in 1902 at Sixth Avenue and 34th Street with the help of his brother Isadore and his sons Horace and William. When Andrew died in 1912, he was succeeded by the Princeton-educated Horace.

Saks & Company joined with Gimbel Bros. in 1922. Bernard Gimbel gained ownership of the store two years later, although it continued to operate under the Saks name until 1965. Looking for a higher class of clientèle, Horace pushed his new associate to open an upscale store on Fifth Avenue. Gimbel and Saks opened Saks Fifth Avenue in 1924. The beautiful building was awarded a Gold Medal from the Fifth Avenue Association and is now on the designation list of the New York Landmarks Preservation Commission.

Horace Saks died suddenly of septic poisoning in 1926. Bernard Gimbel's cousin Adam had been Horace's assistant and was named president of Saks Fifth Avenue. Handsome, charming, and gregarious, Adam created small specialty shops within the store, which he had redecorated in the dramatic Art Moderne style. He filled Saks Fifth Avenue with exclusive merchandise from Europe and the U.S. and established small boutiques that made custom men's shirts and ladies' made-to-order dresses. He built the dominant fine shoe business and believed in a large stock, even in difficult economic times, so customers could have a large range of choices. He opened the company's first Resort store in Palm Beach, Florida, becoming the first specialty store to expand nationally. Both chains prospered, with Gimbel's and Saks & Company supplying all income levels, while Saks Fifth Avenue appealed to the well-heeled. By 1969, the year Adam retired, there were 28 Saks Fifth Avenue stores in 16 states. In addition to the geographic expansion, Saks Fifth Avenue branched into direct mail sales by introducing Folio in 1970.

In 1973 the U.S. subsidiary of British American Tobacco (B.A.T.) offered to purchase Gimbel Bros. As the company was experiencing financial woes, it was a welcome bid. They renovated the Fifth Avenue store in 1978, closed the Gimbel chain in 1986, and planned a $300 million expansion the following year. Rather than face an unwelcome takeover, Saks Fifth Avenue was sold in 1990 for $1.6 billion. Bahrain-based Investcorp was an international investment group that also owned Gucci Group and Tiffany & Co. Phillip B. Miller, formerly of Neiman Marcus (1977–83) was named CEO of Saks Fifth Avenue.

Financial circumstances caused the firm to open Clearinghouse (Off 5th since 1995), an outlet store for Saks Fifth Avenue merchandise in 1992. In an effort to enhance its West Coast presence, the chain acquired four I. Magnin stores in 1994, though the chain was phased out in 1995. Also in 1995, Saks Fifth Avenue opened the largest store in Beverly Hills, Saks West. The following year, 1996, the holding company, Saks Holdings, went public and Main Street, more compact stores, opened to address the demand of small but wealthy areas.

Saks Holdings was purchased by Proffitt's, based in Birmingham, Alabama, in 1998 for $2.1 billion. The company, which already owned department store chains Carson, Pirie, Scott and Parisian, changed its name to Saks Incorporated to capitalize on the higher prestige of its new acquisition. Christina Johnson became the company's first female chief executive when she assumed the office of president and CEO of Saks Fifth Avenue in 2000. Phillip Miller remained chairman.

Saks Holdings plans to spin off Saks Fifth Avenue and Saks Off 5th, while the catalogue and online Saks Direct were abandoned in early 2001 because of poor sales of luxury items. The $6-billion enterprise operated 62 Saks Fifth Avenue, 50 Saks Off 5th, Saks Direct, 40 Parisian, and 203 stores under the names of Proffitt's, McRaes, Younkers, Herbergers, Carson, Pirie, Scott, Bergner's and Boston Store.

—Christina Lindholm

SANCHEZ, Fernando

Spanish designer working in New York

Born: Spain, 1934. **Education:** Studied fashion, École de la Chambre Syndicale de la Couture Parisienne, 1951–53. **Career:** Assistant designer, Maggy Rouff, Paris, 1953–56; designer, Hirsh of Brussels, circa 1956–58; designer for Dior boutiques, and Dior lingerie and knitwear licensees, Paris, Germany, Denmark and the U.S., 1960s; designer, Revillon, New York and Paris, 1961–73 and 1984–85; established own lingerie firm, New York, 1973; introduced ready-to-wear line, 1980; also designer for *Vanity Fair,* from 1984; regular attendee of the Igedo Dessous and Beach Show, Dusseldorf. **Awards:** Winner, International Wool Secretariat Competition, 1954; Coty American Fashion Critics award, 1975, 1981; Coty Special award for Lingerie, 1974, 1977; Council of Fashion Designers of America award, 1981. **Address:** 5 West 19th Street, New York, NY 10011, U.S.A.

Publications

On SANCHEZ:

Books

Milbank, Caroline Rennolds, *New York Fashion: The Evolution of American Style,* New York, 1989.

Stegemeyer, Anne, *Who's Who in Fashion, Third Edition,* New York, 1996.

Articles

Krenke, Mary, "Frivolous Fernando," in *WWD,* 16 September 1965.

Gross, Michael, "Glamor Guys," in *New York,* 23 May 1988.

McDowell, Colin, "Origin of the Species," in *The Guardian* (London), 18 October 1988.

Urquhart, Rachel, "Minimalism with a Flourish: Spanish Austerity and Oriental Fantasy Merge in Fernando Sanchez's Style," in *Vogue,* January 1989.

Romano-Benner, Norma, "Shaping the '90s," in *Americas,* September/October 1990.

Morris, Bernadine, "A Touch of Lingerie in Outerwear," in the *New York Times,* 28 April 1991.

Koski, Lorna, "The Survivor: Designer Fernando Sanchez Has Seen, Done—or Outlived—It All," in *W* (New York), July 1994.

Drier, Melissa, "U.S. Makers Enjoy Warm Welcome at Igedo," in *WWD,* 19 September 1994.

Munk, Nina, "The Beauty and the Beast," in *Forbes,* 23 October 1995.

"Autumn in New York," in *WWD,* 2 April 1998.

"Presidential Picks," in *WWD,* 6 September 2000.

* * *

Born of a Spanish father and a Flemish mother, Sanchez began his career in high fashion ready-to-wear in Paris after studying at the École de la Chambre Syndicale de la Couture. He started out at the house of Dior, where he produced knitwear, lingerie, and accessories for the prestigious company's chain of boutiques. From there he moved to design assistant at Yves Saint Laurent before starting up his own company in 1974, after a period of working in both New York and Paris.

With a name already established for extravagant and exotic fur designs for Revillon, he rapidly built on his reputation through the creation of elegant, easy separates with an ambiguous functionality—they had no obvious place in the formal etiquette of dress. Such clothes as his soft, fluid camisoles with matching pyjama trousers and wrapped jackets or overshirts could be worn just as easily to bed as to dinner at an upmarket restaurant. He was quickly assimilated into the circle of New York fashion designers, which at the time included Halston, Calvin Klein, and Mary McFadden.

Sanchez's experimentation with separates dressing struck a chord among affluent American women in the 1970s and seemed to fit the notion of independent femininity that had filtered into fashion imagery and marketing. The ideal of self-reliant womanhood was superficially acknowledged in the whole concept of separates—the idea of putting together garments in one's own individual way, rather than being dictated into sporting a designer look from head to toe. Sanchez's separates were, however, like those of other American designers, always created with an organic whole in mind.

In the 1980s Sanchez was recognized for his use of lace appliqué which appeared extensively on his nightwear, and the fan motif became his trademark as was the bold use of synthetics and vibrant color. His more contemporary forays into the ready-to-wear market followed the same lines as his original, understated, and elegant ensembles—with their basis in the language of lingerie, for which he received Coty Special awards in 1974 and 1977.

The entire concept of underwear as outerwear, what Sanchez himself referred to as "homewear," was especially suited to the designer. He continued to experiment for the remainder of the 1970s and well into the 1990s, although in a less obvious fashion than Jean-Paul Gaultier or Dolce & Gabbana. Designs in middle and late 1990s were sleek, flirty slip dresses for the same sort of fashionably wealthy woman who, like her counterpart in the 1970s, didn't want to stand out from the crowd. Yet some Sanchez designs, like brightly colored ostrich-feather jackets, were intended for the opposite effect. Such creations also caught the eye of animal rights activists, who continued to protest the use of any animal or bird parts. Sanchez, like many of his fellow designers, including Nicole Miller, Karl Lagerfeld, and Ralph Lauren, wasn't terribly concerned about being politically correct—as long as the designs were selling.

Sanchez exhibited at the 1994 Igedo Dessous and Beach show in Dusseldorf, Germany, at a time when many American designers stayed home. After a seven-year absence of the German show, the Igeldo trade fair nevertheless provided participants, like Sanchez, with a chance to hook up with European distributors. Expansion continued to be an important factor for Sanchez, especially since many had jumped on the innerwear-as-outerwear bandwagon. Yet Sanchez's designs were still among the best in the business. Anne Stegemeyer, writing in *Who's Who in Fashion, Third Edition,* (New York, 1996), described his designs as "Seductive, luxurious, trendsetting, and expensive…[he] has been given credit for reviving interest in extravagant underthings," long before Victoria's Secret came onto the scene. *Women's Wear Daily* similarly enthused in April 1998, "Sanchez sent out the beautiful silk slips and quilted kimonos his customer can't lounge without, and the evening looks—full-skirted taffeta dresses, velvet opera coats, and stretchy bodysuits with embroidered organza and tulle skirts—that make her feel grand."

—Caroline Cox; updated by Owen James

SANDER, Jil

German designer

Born: Heidemarie Jiline Sander in Wesselburen, Germany, 27 November 1943. **Education:** Graduated from Krefeld School of Textiles, near Düsseldorf, 1963; foreign exchange student, University of Los Angeles, 1963–64. **Career:** Fashion journalist, *McCall's,* Los Angeles, and for *Constanze* and *Petra* magazines, Hamburg, 1964–68; freelance clothing designer, 1968–73; opened first Jil Sander boutique, Hamburg, 1968; founded Jil Sander Moden, Hamburg, 1969; showed first women's collection, 1973; founded Jil Sander GmbH, 1978; introduced fragrance and cosmetics line, 1979; launched Jil Sander furs, 1982; debut of leather and eyewear collections, 1984; Jil Sander GmbH converted to public corporation, Jil Sander AG, 1989; opened Paris boutique, 1993; showed first menswear collection, 1993; opened flagship store, Hamburg, 1997; Prada bought stake in firm, 1999; departed the company bearing her name, 2000; barred from designing a competing Sander line, until 2003; fragrances include *Woman Pure, Woman II, Woman III, Man Pure, Man II, Man III, Man IV,* and *Feeling Man.* **Awards:** Fil d'Or award, 1980, 1981, 1982, 1983, 1984, 1985; City of Munich Fashion award, 1983; Vif-Journal Silberne Eule, 1983; Fédération Française du Prêt à Porter Feminin award, 1985; Aguja de Oro award, Madrid, 1986; Forum Preis, 1989. **Address:** Osterfeldstrasse 32–34, 22529 Hamburg, Germany. **Website:** www.jilsander.com.

Jil Sander, fall/winter 2001–02 collection. © AP/Wide World Photos.

Jil Sander, fall/winter 2001–02 collection. © AP/Wide World Photos.

Publication

On SANDER:

Books

Stegemeyer, Anne, *Who's Who in Fashion, Third Edition,* New York, 1996.

Articles

Mayer, Margit J., "Soft und Sander," in *Deutsch Vogue* (Munich), January 1990.
Gomez, Edward, "Less is More Luxurious," in *Time,* 25 June 1990.
Drier, Melissa, "Jil Sander," in *Mirabella* (New York), June 1991.
Mayer, Margit J., "Jil Sander: Ganz Privat," in *Marie Claire* (Germany), August 1991.
———, "A Walk with Jil Sander," in *W* (New York), 30 September–7 October 1991.
Livingston, David, "A Vision of Strength: Jil Sander," in the *Toronto Globe & Mail,* 2 January 1992.
Miller, Annetta, "The Selling of Jil Sander," in *Newsweek,* 16 November 1992.
Schaenen, Eve, "Minimalist No More," in *Harper's Bazaar,* March 1993.
Rubenstein, Hal, "The Glorious Haunting of Jil Sander," in *Interview,* September 1993.
La Ferla, Ruth, "Pure Style: Jil Sander Talks About Clothes...," in *Elle* (New York), February 1994.
Bellafante, Ginia, "Lessons in Lessness," in *Time,* 7 November 1994.
Spindler, Amy M., "Luminous Design from Jil Sander," in the *New York Times,* 8 March 1995.
"Jil Sander: Coming on Strong," in *WWD,* 8 March 1995.
Ozzard, Janet, "Jil Power," in *WWD,* 17 May 1995.
Drier, Melissa, "Jil Goes Home," in *WWD,* 29 September 1997.
"Milan's Minimal Man," in *DNR,* 14 January 1998.
Bowles, Hamish, "More for Less," in *Vogue,* September 1998.
"Jil's Smart Set," in *WWD,* 9 October 1998.
"Technologically Speaking," in *WWD,* 5 March 1999.
Cohen, Edie, "Minimalism with Mouldings," in *Interior Design,* April 1999.
"Faded Glory," in *WWD,* 1 October 1999.
Mui, Nelson, and Luisa Zargani, "Retailers Still See Viability of Sander's Men's Line," in *DNR,* 26 January 2000.
Horyn, Cathy, "Up and Out, Jil Sander Makes a Clean Sweep," in the *New York Times,* 25 February 2000.
Givhan, Robin, "Jil Sander and Prada: A Clash of Colors," in the *Washington Post,* 3 March 2000.
"No Mending Fences for Jil Sander," in *DNR,* 7 April 2000.
"The Council of Fashion Designers of America Honors the Year's Most Influential Designers at the American Fashion Awards 2000 Gala," in *PR Newswire,* 16 June 2000.
"Jil Sander Profits Up," in *WWD,* 6 September 2000.
Conti, Samantha, "Prada's Wild Ride," in *WWD,* 18 December 2000.
Ball, Deborah, "The Brand Rules Fashion's New World," in the *Wall Street Journal,* 12 March 2001.
"The Sander Saga," in *WWD,* 9 July 2001.
Davis, Boyd (ed.), "Jil Sander," available online at Fashion Windows, www.fashionwindows.com, 3 October 2001.
Guerrero, Clare, "Jil Sander," online at First Cut, www.firstcut.com, 3 October 2001.
"Project Profile: Jil Sander Headquarters," online at Rambusch, www.rambusch.com, 3 October 2001.

* * *

Jil Sander has often been described as the Queen of German fashion, but her style and ambitions have always been international. Her company headquarters were located in the north German city of Hamburg, but her clothes were manufactured in Milan, where she showed for almost a decade before changing her venue to Paris. A self-made success story, Sander designed for independent, intelligent women around the world. She also created fragrances for both men and women, and began producing a menswear line in 1993.

Sander has a strong, modern sensibility, and her style has been described as luxurious minimalism, on the edge of forward. There were no frills or fads in Sander's world; everything irrelevant is eliminated. Like Giorgio Armani, she is one of the fashion world's most austere purists, a creator of designs so clean they seem stripped down to the bone. Yet it is not entirely accurate to describe her clothes as classic, because this would imply they are static, and Sander has never repeated bestselling designs from the previous collections.

"I find 'timeless' classic terribly boring," Sander told German *Vogue* in January 1990. "A classic is an excuse, because one is too lazy to confront the spirit of the time." Her own style of classicism always had a modern edge, and the woman who wears Sander's clothes "knows perfectly well what is 'in' this season, and has consciously reduced [it] to suit herself." Sander loves fashion and change and believes other women feel the same way. "We don't buy a new coat because we are cold. We buy things that animate, that give us a good feeling."

Sander has been one of the most important women designers working in both the 20th and 21st centuries, believing there are definite differences between male and female design sensibilities. Male designers, Sander told *Mirabella* in June 1991, tend to "see things more decoratively—more from the outside. I want to know how I feel in my clothes." She tries on all the clothes in her women's collection herself, to ensure they look and feel exactly right. They consistently have the high quality of the best menswear; they are beautifully tailored, and made from menswear-derived fabrics, often her own luxury fiber blends such as wool-silk or linen-silk. Yet her palette tends toward pale neutrals, which read as both strong and feminine.

Sander's combination of masculine and feminine design elements results in clothes that feel comfortable and look powerful but are also sexy in a subtle way. Her version of understated chic is not cheap, however. "If you want quality, it costs," she bluntly told *Mirabella*'s journalist. (Her women's suits range from $1,500 to $6,500.) Think more and buy less, she advised. "People have already consumed too much." But as journalist Melissa Drier observed, Sander's clothes give women the same confidence that a hand-tailored suit gives a man.

The words "strong" and "powerful" occur frequently in Sander's conversation, revealing something of her own personality, as well as her design aesthetic and her ideal customer. "A powerful woman, a woman who knows who she is—I would say that is more interesting than a doll with the most beautiful nose in the world," she told *Marie Claire* in August 1991. And as if to complement the strong modern woman, Sander has called her men's fragrance *Feeling Man.*

Sander has had no sympathy for the old-fashioned concept of woman as sex kitten or status symbol. "It is possible to have a very sexy feeling without looking like a sex kitten," she commented to *W* in fall 1991. A woman wearing an austere, brown wool trouser-suit can look and feel sexy, she believes. The typical *alta-moda* woman might not be happy in Sander's clothes, but many women today do want clothes that express a liberated sensibility and a modern sensuality.

Sander's intuition, too, has guided her into unusual modes, which *Women' Wear Daily* typified as the "bold and controversial punch" that is her trademark. In 1997, she opened a Hamburg flagship on Neuer Wall, which she dubbed the city's emerging "Madison Avenue." *Interior Design* applauded her collaboration with American architect Michael Gabellini and characterized the two visionaries as "masters of minimalism." Her ambition turned to locations in Osaka, Zurich, Basel, St. Moritz, London, New York, Miami, and Costa Mesa, California.

In 1999 Sander abandoned the airy femininity of 1998 with its drapey rayons, metallic threads, and mesh and invigorated her line with vinyl tunics. Later in the year, she paired top and skirt in contrasting patterns. To soften the look, she reversed fabrics to present the faded underside. She detailed with ruching and pintucking and experimented with felted or rubber-coated wools. For a new men's line, she replaced the power suit with pared-down tweeds, cashmere, and boiled wools. For herself, she commissioned Renzo Mongiardino to refurbish her 19th-century villa in Hamburg.

Just as Sander was revolutionizing unyielding, cookie-cutter men's businesswear, her unforeseen exit from Hamburg-based Prada in January 2000 bemused the fashion hierarchy with more questions than answers. The dust-up with moneyman Patrizio Bertelli occurred five months after Prada invested in her fashion house. At the time, Sander saw Prada as a partner and looked to Bertelli for strength as she aimed at introducing a line of fashion accessories.

Chief executive Bertelli obviously discounted the element that sold Jil Sanders clothes. His refusal to budget her choice of fine fabrics and trims for her $3,000 suits, $6,000 coats, and $1,000 sweaters irrevocably destroyed their synergy. Critics tended to take her side on the issue of marketing versus quality. In March, the *Washington Post* mourned, "Sander's cool dedication to business, smart women and fine tailoring will be sorely missed."

Of Sander's instinct for fashion, Nancy Pearlstein of Louis in Boston stated, "I think she's probably one of the most talented people in the business. She has an exquisite sense of fine fabric and that knowledge is irreplaceable." Appropriately, the Council of Fashion Designers of America nominated Sander for the 2000 International award. Fashion analyst Boyd Davis crowed her the Queen of German Fashion.

Ironically, Sander's exit her company occurred when the firm was showing strong sales and profits. Milan Vukmirovic, formerly with Gucci, eased into Sander's place but without replicating her knack for style and luxe. Exuding confidence in Sander's replacement, Bertelli stated to *Women's Wear Daily,* "A brand that's as strong as Jil Sander doesn't need to rely on the name of a designer." A legal settlement prohibited Sander from designing a competing line until January 2003. Speculation envisioned her making up with Bertelli and paired her with Hèrmes as a replacement for Martin Margiela, but both rumors proved untrue. As models hit the runway wearing spring 2002 designs, the fashion world missed Sander's élan.

—Valerie Steele; updated by Mary Ellen Snodgrass

SANT'ANGELO, Giorgio

American designer

Born: Count Giorgio Imperiale di Sant'Angelo in Florence, 5 May 1933; raised in Argentina; immigrated to the U.S., 1962. **Education:** Studied architecture in Florence, industrial design in Barcelona, and art at the Sorbonne. **Career:** Animator, Walt Disney Studios, Hollywood, 1962–63; textile and jewelry designer, 1963–67; designer, Sant'Angelo, New York, from 1966; launched Sant'Angelo Ready-to-Wear, 1966; di Sant'Angelo Inc. established, 1968; began licensing for sportswear, outerwear, suits, neckwear, fragrances, home furnishings; firm continued after his death, 1989. **Exhibitions:** Metropolitan Museum of Art, Costume Institute, 1999. **Awards:** Coty American Fashion Critics award, 1968, 1970; Inspiration Home Furnishings award, New York, 1978; Knitted Textile Association Designer award, New York, 1982; Council of Fashion Designers of America award, 1987; Fashion Designers of America award, 1988. **Died:** 29 August 1989, in New York. **Company Address:** 611 Broadway, New York, NY 10012, U.S.A.

PUBLICATIONS

On SANT'ANGELO:

Books

Morris, Bernadine, and Barbara Walz, *The Fashion Makers,* New York, 1978.

Milbank, Caroline Rennolds, *New York Fashion: The Evolution of American Style,* New York, 1989.

Stegemeyer, Anne, *Who's Who in Fashion, Third Edition,* New York, 1996.

Articles

Mazzaraco, M., "Di Sant'Angelo's Head," in *WWD,* 16 October 1968.

Nemy, Enid, "It Takes a Little Bit of Being Yourself," in the *New York Times,* 4 March 1969.

"Restless Count from Italy Who Took Picasso's Advice," in *Life,* 7 March 1969.

Klensch, Elsa, "Sant'Angelo Superstar," in *WWD,* 4 February 1972.

Haber, Holly, "Sant'Angelo, a Master of Fantasy, Dies," in *WWD,* 31 August 1989.

Polan, Brenda, "Sant'Angelo: Lycra Looks," [obituary] in *The Guardian* (London), 1 September 1989.

Moore, Jackie, "Obituary: Giorgio Sant'Angelo," in the*Independent* (London), 4 September 1989.

"Giorgio di Sant'Angelo: 1933–1989," [obituary] in *Vogue,* November 1989.

Wilson, Eric, and Rusty Williamson, "The Ups and Downs of Building a Dress Line," in *WWD,* 7 March 2000.

Gilbert, Daniela, "What Gives? The Continuing Popularity of Stretch Fabrics in the Fashion Industry," in *WWD,* 12 June 2001.

* * *

Giorgio di Sant'Angelo (the "di" was later dropped) was a child of the 1960s. Unlike many of the decade's talented new designers—including Pierre Cardin, André Courrèges, and Rudi Gernreich—who suffered symptoms of career burnout as the 1960s came to a close, Sant'Angelo soared on a creative high. His formative years, leading up to his move to New York, included an education in the arts in Florence and a studio apprenticeship with Picasso who urged Sant'Angelo to trust his own restless creativity and to keep trying new artistic ventures.

Sant'Angelo, who had an affinity for the new plastics developed with futuristic technology, designed Lucite jewelry and accessories in colorful geometric shapes. Diana Vreeland, editor of *Vogue* from 1963–71, found his designs to be in step with her own ideas and gave him carte blanche as a stylist. The results of their association during the late 1960s were stunning examples of the breadth of Sant'Angelo's originality. His concoctions of colored Veruschka were the peak of fashion fantasy. This option of make-believe went beyond mere merchandise shown in a magazine layout. His work was theatrical, exotic, and on some level could be considered performance art; this taste for escapism through dress coincided with the escalation of the Vietnam War beginning in 1968.

Inspired by hippie and street fashions, Sant'Angelo also translated ideas that would fit the marketplace. His love of ethnic clothing was evident, and his gypsy looks included elements of romanticism. Introducing a modern component, he incorporated Lycra body suits with these varied influences. He offered women a chance at self-expression through dress. In 1972 Sant'Angelo left behind his gypsy and Native American inspirations and concentrated on body-conscious designs combining knits and wovens. His 33-piece collection was shown at the Guggenheim Museum and further emphasized Sant'Angelo's commitment to fashion design as an artform. "To me, soul means freedom and inner confidence," Sant'Angelo commented on the collection. "I express it in happy, bright colors, and in simplicity of design." He presented matching knit shirts, tops, trousers, and bras that folded into an envelope for travel. These pieces were based around a body stocking and formed the 1970s American fashion silhouette.

An old advertisement read, "Giorgio Sant'Angelo Spoken Here," a true statement as how he saw his work as a new language in fashion. He admired the ideas of Rudi Gernreich, whose work also contributed key elements to modern design. He also respected the work of Halston, Elsa Peretti, Betsey Johnson, Stephen Burrows, Oscar de la Renta, Yves Saint Laurent, Pierre Cardin, and Valentino. Throughout the 1980s fashion shifts, Sant'Angelo worked on classical refinements of his own concepts. Poised for a timely reemergence as a name in fashion, Giorgio Sant'Angelo died in 1989. A truly original free spirit was lost forever, yet his name lived on with his company, and as inspiration for a new generation of designers making retro the hottest trend of the late 1990s and early 2000s. Among his admirers were David Meister, whose spring 2002 collection was reminiscent of Sant'Angelo styles from throughout the 1970s, as well as Marc Jacobs who winked at the hip decade's duds in his spring 2002 showing.

—Myra Walker

SARNE, Tanya

See GHOST

SARVEA, Jimmy

See TRANSPORT

SASSOON, David

See BELLVILLE SASSOON-LORCAN MULLANY

SAUL, Joan and Roger

See MULBERRY

SAVINI, Gaetano

See BRIONI

SCAASI, Arnold

American designer

Born: Arnold Isaacs in Montreal, Canada, 8 May 1931. **Education:** Studied fashion design at École Cotnoir Capponi, Montreal, 1953, and at the École de la Chambre Syndicale de la Haute Couture Parisienne, 1954–55; apprenticed one year with Paquin. **Career:** Moved to New York, worked with Charles James, 1951–53; freelance designer in New York working for Dressmaker Casuals and Lilly Daché, 1955–57; opened own business, 1957; president/designer, Arnold Scaasi Inc., from 1962; designer, Scaasi couture collections, from 1962; designer, ready-to-wear collections, 1962–63, 1969, and from 1984; introduced signature fragrance and dressed First Lady Barbara Bush for inauguration, 1989; inked licensing deal with Warnaco for leisurewear, 1995; began designing for First Lady Laura Bush, 2001; debuted new leisurewear collection for QVC, 2001. **Exhibitions:** Retrospective, New York State Theater, Lincoln Center, New York, 1975; *Scaasi: The Joy of Dressing Up,* New York, 1996, then Ohio State University, 1998. **Awards:** Coty American Fashion Critics award, 1958; Neiman Marcus award, 1959; Council of Fashion Designers of America (CFDA) award, 1987; Pratt Institute Design award, 1989; Girl Scout Council of Greater New York Salute, 1990; Dallas International Apparel Fashion Excellence award, 1992; CFDA Lifetime Achievement award, 1996. **Address:** 681 Fifth Avenue, New York, NY 10022–4209, U.S.A.

Arnold Scaasi, spring 1968 collection: white feather ball gown. © AP/Wide World Photos.

Publications

On SCAASI:

Books

Morris, Bernadine, and Barbara Walz, *The Fashion Makers,* New York, 1978.

Diamonstein, Barbaralee, *Fashion: The Inside Story,* New York, 1985.

Milbank, Caroline Rennolds, *New York Fashion: The Evolution of American Style,* New York, 1989.

Daria, Irene, *The Fashion Cycle,* New York, 1990.

Morris, Bernardine, *Scaasi: A Cut Above,* New York, 1996.

Stegemeyer, Anne, *Who's Who in Fashion, Third Edition,* New York, 1996.

Articles

Schwartzbaum, Lisa, "The Dramatist of Elegance," in *Connoisseur* (New York), July 1984.

Reed, Julia, "Little Big Man," in *Vogue,* April 1989.

Milbank, Caroline Rennolds, "Scaasi's New Stars," in *Connoisseur,* June 1989.

Sporkin, Elizabeth, "Scaasi," in *People,* 23 April 1990.

Shaeffer, Claire, "American Haute Couture," in *Threads* (Newtown, CT), December/January 1991–92.

Goodman, Wendy, "Palm Beach Story," in *House & Garden,* August 1992.

Pogoda, Dianne M., "Scaasi: $50,000 at Saks Bridal," in *WWD,* 5 March 1996.

"Blum & Fink Gets Scaasi Fur License," in *WWD,* 2 April 1996.

White, Constance C.R., "Scaasi Revisited," in the *New York Times,* 28 May 1996.

Sullivan, Robert, "Capitalist Tulle," in *Vogue,* October 1996.

Witchel, Alex, "A Polka-Dot Defender at Glamor's Gate," in the *New York Times,* 3 October 1996.

Brubach, Holly, "The Social Fabric," in the *New York Times Magazine,* 13 October 1996.

"Scaasi: A Cut Above," [review] in *Publishers Weekly,* 14 October 1996.

Vienne, Veronique, "The Scaasi's the Limit," in *Town & Country,* November 1996.

Luscombe, Belinda, "Seen & Heard," in *Time,* 10 February 1997.

DeCaro, Frank, "Fashion Chat," in *TV Guide,* 22 March 1997.

Taub, Bernadine, "Arnold Scaasi—A Conversation About the Evolution in Fashion," in *WWD,* 13 September 1999.

Sheehan, Susan, "The Scaasi Perspective," in *Architectural Digest,* November 2000.

"Dowdy No More?" in *Time,* 4 June 2001.

Monget, Karyn, "QVC Hits: Scaasi, Herman," in *WWD,* 11 June 2001.

"Mrs. Bush, Making it Scaasi in Europe," in the *Washington Post,* 29 June 2001.

Menkes, Suzy, "Scaasi: A Glitzy Tribute to 40 Years of Couture," available online at Style.com, www.iht.com, 3 October 2001.

"The Scaasi Exhibit," online at Ohio State: The College of Human Ecology, www.hec.ohio-state.edu, 3 October 2001.

*

Clothes should be worn to make one feel good, to flatter and as a statement of personality. The overall effect should always be a well-groomed look, not sloppy…. This is not a matter of self-indulgence; when you know you look your best, you face the day and the world with great self-assurance.

It's most important that one chooses clothes that work for their lifestyle, both financially and psychologically…I try to design clothes that will flatter the female form. I create clothes that are pretty, usually with an interesting mix of fabrics. I like luxurious fabrics, great quality for day, opulence for evening dresses. I am definitely not a minimalist designer! Clothes with some adornment are more interesting to look at and more fun to wear.

I believe clothes should touch and define the body at least in one spot. Most of my clothes have a defined waist and hipline, with some movement below the hip. Bustlines are always defined and I am known for low décolletage—either off-the-shoulder, strapless or simply scooped-out necklines. Sweetheart necklines are also flattering and I use them constantly. I prefer using color to black and white though sometimes black and/or white are most dramatic. Shades of red, pink, turquoise, violet and sapphire blue can be more flattering and exciting to look at.

At one point in my career I used an enormous amount of printed fabrics and found them wonderful to work with. However, in recent seasons my eye has changed and the prints seemed to have faded from fashion. Before long, the print craze will probably return as women—and designers—get bored with solid fabrics. In place of prints we are using more embroideries to give texture and life to the fabrics.

Lastly, clothes should be fun with a dash of fantasy. Scaasi creations are the champagne and caviar of the fashion world, as a very prominent Queen once said, "Let them eat cake!" I do hope I won't have my head chopped off for these thoughts!

—Arnold Scaasi

* * *

As a young apprentice to Charles James during the early 1950s, Arnold Scaasi was imprinted by James' concentration on "building" an evening dress as a sculpture. This early training led Scaasi to construct dresses in the round and to approach design as three-dimensional form. The influence of James has been a lifelong inspiration for Scaasi; another was the richness of the fabrics and furs used during the 1950s, when the prerequisite for women was to be perfectly dressed from head to toe.

Scaasi began to rethink his objectives after juggling a career during the late 1950s and early 1960s that included menswear, children's wear, and costume jewelry, in addition to ladies' ready-to-wear and custom designs. He decided to focus strategically on couture dressmaking at a time when Paris couture was beginning to suffer. It was 1964 when Scaasi debuted his collection of eveningwear. He was able to take the freedom of the youth-obsessed 1960s and channel the energy into designs that featured keen attention to details and the workmanship of couture dressing.

Scaasi emphasized sequins, fringe, and feathers as trims, substituting new fabrics to create an ostentatious signature style that included minidresses, trouser suits, and the use of transparency. Barbra Streisand wore a memorable Scaasi creation to the 1969 Academy Awards. His customers have often been the celebrated rich and famous—Elizabeth Taylor, Ivana Trump, Blaine Trump, Joan Rivers, Barbara Walters, and many other glamorous clients have favored Scaasi for years.

During the 1970s, styles changed to a more body-conscious, pared-down way of dressing. Scaasi, true to form, turned to dressing women who still loved to be noticed, such as artist Louise Nevelson. It made sense to Scaasi to continue creating what he was known for and what he loved to do. The basis of his work has been a combination of cut, color sensibility, and fabric selections recalling a past elegance yet which continue to speak to his clients' most current desires.

The 1980s, the Reagan era, ushered in a renaissance of upscale dressing perfect for the Scaasi touch. He dressed First Lady Barbara Bush for the inaugural ball and designed her wardrobe for the week of festivities. Never one to concern himself with everyday dressing, Scaasi dressed the urban woman who attends parties, galas, charity balls, and elaborate dinners. His customer is affluent and has a personality enabling her to wear a Scaasi creation. Often described as lavish, sumptuous, and magical, Scaasi's evening gowns are worn for making a sensational entrance.

Fashion editor Bernardine Morris' book, *Scaasi: A Cut Above* (1996) traced the designer from his beginnings to wardrobing such elite clientèle as singer Aretha Franklin, actresses Joan Crawford and Elizabeth Taylor, and socialites Brooke Astor and Charlotte Ford. Simultaneous with the publication of the book, the New York Historical Society presented *Scaasi: The Joy of Dressing Up,* a showcase of Scaasi's four decades accommodating the varied tastes of actresses, First Ladies, and many other memorable clients. Featured in the collection were two drop-waist off-the-shoulder gowns, a wedding dress, and an afternoon suit trimmed in fur with matching hat.

Drawing on his 75 scrapbooks for past successes, Scaasi expressed his delight in seeing people enjoy the experience of dressing well in couture ensembles, which tends to require numerous tedious fittings. The 1996 New York retrospective coincided with his Lifetime Achievement award from the Council of Fashion Designers of America, presented by Barbara Bush. Two years later, Ohio State's College of Human Ecology opened a three-month exhibit, a reprise of the New York tribute. Curator Gayle Strege accented the line's elegance and rich taffetas, lace, chiffons, velvets, satins, and jerseys.

In 1999 Scaasi helped satisfy the spunky American buyer hungering for a change. In explanation of his philosophy, he stressed to *Women's Wear Daily* writer Bernadine Taub that designers must listen to their clientèle. He summarized his own philosophy of assisting women to appear at their best: "A look doesn't happen out of the air—it comes from what someone wants or needs." One needy customer brought Scaasi immediate media acclaim. He reportedly rescued Laura Bush from the fashion scrap heap in 2001 after the inauguration of her husband, George W. Bush. To upgrade her down-home Texas wardrobe to a snappier, more photogenic look, he made suits and a coatdress for a state tour of Europe. To enhance her appearance for the media, he created ensembles stressing vivid, cheerful shades of tomato red, green, lapis, and turquoise.

Midyear 2001 was a financial success for Scaasi's Leisure Collection for QVC, which sold 4,500 pieces netting $250 million. His line showcased rose prints, leopard stripes, and tropical flora in at-home caftans and patio dresses. According to the *Washington Post,* he informed critics that he aimed for a feminine, pretty look, warning, "If you don't want those kinds of clothes, don't come to me."

—Myra Walker; updated by Mary Ellen Snodgrass

SCHAEFER, Thomas,

See RENÉ LEZARD

SCHERRER, Jean-Louis

French designer

Born: Paris, circa 1936. **Education:** Studied ballet, Conservatoire de Danse Classique, Paris, and fashion, Chambre Syndicale de la Couture Parisienne. **Career:** Assistant at Christian Dior, 1955–57, and to Saint Laurent at Dior after Dior's death, 1957–59; left to design for Louis Féraud, 1959–61; founded Jean-Louis Scherrer label, 1962; ready-to-wear collection and Scherrer Boutique ready-to-wear lines introduced, 1971; signature fragrance, 1980; *Scherrer 2* perfume, 1986; bath line, 1981; bought by Japanese firm, Sebu-Saison Group, 1990; diffusion line, Scherrer City, 1992; Scherrer replaced by Erik Mortensen and forced out of company, 1992; signed menswear license with Société Korn, 1994; Bernard Perris hired to head design department, 1994–97; Stéphane Rolland hired as designer, 1998; opened shop in Beijing, 2001; Parfums Jean-Louis Scherrer spun off, 2001. **Awards:** Dé d'Or award, Paris, 1980. **Address:** 51 avenue Montaigne, 75008 Paris, France.

Publications

On SCHERRER:

Books

Lambert, Eleanor, *World of Fashion: People, Places, Resources,* New York, 1976.

McDowell, Colin, *Directory of 20th Century Fashion,* London, 1984.

Articles

"In Paris, a Squabble over M. Scherrer's Good Name," in the*Times* (London), 24 June 1969.

"Scherrer: Third Time Round, But No Revolution," in the *Times,* 26 January 1971.

"...And Why Haute Couture is Still Fun," in the *Sunday Times,* 28 July 1974.

"Le point sur les collections: Jean-Louis Scherrer," in *L'Officiel* (Paris), March & September 1986.

"Beauty—Daughters with Dash: Laetitia Scherrer," in *Vogue,* September 1988.

Petkanes, Christopher, "Flair à la Scherrer," in *Harper's Bazaar,* December 1988.

"Scherrer Deal for Japanese," in the *New York Times,* 12 April 1990.

"Hearing in Scherrer v. Scherrer Delayed," in *WWD,* 23 March 1994.

"Jean-Louis Scherrer S.A.," in *DNR,* 18 May 1994.

Godfrey, Deeny, "House of Scherrer Names Perris Couture, Ready-to-Wear Designer," in *WWD,* 7 September 1994.

Weisman, Katherine, "Emmanuelle Khanh Said to Be in Talks to Buy Jean-Louis Scherrer," in *WWD,* 5 June 1997.

"Scherrer Skips Spring, Readies Fall Collections," in *WWD,* 13 January 1998.

"Fashion Extravaganza: A Fashion-Full December Beckons...," in the *Bangkok Post,* 4 December 2000.

"Tantalising Scherrer: The Latest Fashion Show at the Oriental Was a Shimmering Display of Elegance and Decadence...," in the *Bangkok Post,* 28 December 2000.

* * *

His early training as a dancer exposed Jean-Louis Scherrer to theatrical costumes and prepared him to design clothes that would suit the public roles of women connected with politics, theatre, and the arts, as well as the more private roles lived by the wives of wealthy Arabs, whose patronage once accounted for up to a third of the House of Scherrer's income.

From an early apprenticeship with Christian Dior in Paris, Scherrer learned the basics of cutting and draping, alongside a young Yves Saint Laurent. When Saint Laurent inherited the house of Dior, Scherrer successfully started his own haute couture establishment during a period when critics foretold the demise of traditional couture. He quickly became known for designs described as classic, restrained, sophisticated, and sexy but not vulgar. His customers read like a roster of the world's wealthiest women: Mme. Anne-Aymone Giscard d'Estaing, wife of the then-President of France, as well as his daughter, Valerie-Anne Montassier; Baronness Thyssen; Olympia and Nadine de Rothschild; Queen Noor, the wife of the then-King of Jordan; Patricia Kennedy Lawford; Isabelle d'Ornano; Ann Getty; Nan Kempner; Françoise Sagan; Michèle Morgan; Raquel Welch; and Sophia Loren.

In the mid-1970s dozens of American stores, including Bergdorf Goodman in New York, carried Scherrer. Chiffon evening dresses, often accented with sequined embroideries, were a staple, as was deluxe ready-to-wear. These were simpler clothes, more moderately priced than the thousands of dollars of the couture, but still expensive-looking. One such boutique outfit, modeled by Scherrer's daughter Laetitia, featured a leopard print shaped blazer jacket with matching leopard cloche hat, worn with a slim black leather skirt.

Scherrer was not a maker of trends, but of refined deluxe versions of trends. When everyone was showing tiered flounced skirts during the 1980s, Scherrer made a restrained version that just grazed the knee and was topped by a long-sleeved shirt-collared bodice, in luxurious silk. A prime example of Scherrer's hallmark "exotically pampered appearance" was a lavishly embroidered coat in mink-bordered beige cashmere, hooded, reminiscent of Anna Karenina and following in the footsteps of Saint Laurent's revolutionary Russian-inspired looks of the late 1970s. Scherrer, in fact, often borrowed exotic details from the East. Chinoiserie and Mongolian-inspired coats and jackets frequently appeared in his collections. At the apex of 1980s opulence in couture, Scherrer indulged in pearl-decorated rajah jackets, tunics, and trousers. In a spirit of Arabian Nights fantasy much like Paul Poiret's, jeweled and feathered turbans completed the ensembles.

Even Scherrer's day clothes featured opulent touches: velvet appliqués on wool, or gold piping on trenchcoats. Chiffon and silk were used for dresses and skirts; leathers and furs decorated coats. While hemlines rose during the remainder of the decade, Scherrer continued to show calf-length skirts. For him, surface texture and sumptuous workmanship were more important than innovative lines. The longer covered-up fashions satisfied his customers' modesty requirements, dictated by Islamic law, while also proclaiming their wealth and status.

Into the 1990s Scherrer continued to employ luxury materials and to explore a variety of trends—long, short, bright colors (a departure from conservative beiges, grays, and white), patchwork prints, plaids, jumpsuits, feminine versions of men's suits and hunting attire. The Scherrer boutique continued to offer sleek toned-down versions of the high fashion items in over 100 markets in 25 countries. In Europe and Japan scores of Jean-Louis Scherrer accessories could be obtained, and a bestselling signature perfume launched in 1979 was followed by a spicy floral haute couture perfume, *Scherrer 2,* in 1986.

Financial difficulties resulted in the late 1992 firing of Scherrer from the firm he founded, and he fought back in the following year in court, winning a cash settlement but not the use of his name. The company, Jean-Louis Scherrer S.A., however, continued by hiring Erik Mortensen as couture designer, then announced a licensing agreement for a new menswear collection with Société Korn in 1994. Mortensen was replaced by Bernard Perris, and soon rumors of a possible sale of the embattled house circulated in the industry. Denied by both Seibu-Saison (which owned 95-percent of the company) and Hèrmes (which owned the remaining 5-percent), the rumors persisted, and in 1997 Groupe Emmanuelle Khanh bought the ailing fashion house.

Soon after the acquistion, Perris departed as artistic director and Stephane Rolland was appointed new designer in 1998. By the 21st century, the house of Jean-Louis Scherrer had bounced back with a flashy showing in Bangkok and the opening of a new location in Beijing. The Bangkok show, commemorating the golden wedding anniversary of the King and Queen of Thailand, showcased Rolland's bright, nature-inspired prints as well as the sophisticated, feminine dresses and separates for which the company was renowned.

—Therese Duzinkiewicz Baker; updated by Nelly Rhodes

SCHIAPARELLI, Elsa

French designer

Born: Rome, 10 September 1890. **Family:** Married Comte William de Wendt de Kerlor, 1914 (separated); children: Yvonne ("Gogo"). **Career:** Lived in New York working as scriptwriter and translator, 1919–22 and 1941–44; immigrated to Paris, 1923; showed first collection, 1925; house of Schiaparelli operated, 1928–54; London branch opened, 1933, girls' debutante department added, 1935; Schiaparelli Paris boutique opened, 1935; lecturer on fashion, 1940, and volunteer in U.S. for French war effort, 1941–43; fragrances include *Salut, Soucis,* and *Schiap,* 1934; *Shocking,* 1937; *Sleeping,* 1938; *Snuff* for men, 1939; *Le Roi Soleil,* 1946; *Zut,* 1948;*Succès Fou,* 1953; *Si,* 1957; and *S,* 1961. **Exhibitions:** *Hommage à Elsa Schiaparelli,* Pavillon des Arts, Paris, 1984; *Fashion and Surrealism,* Fashion Institute of Technology, New York, and Victoria and Albert Museum, London, 1987–88; *Elsa Schiaparelli,* Brooklyn Museum, 1995–96. **Awards:** Neiman Marcus award, 1940. **Died:** 13 November 1973, in Paris.

Publications

By SCHIAPARELLI:

Books

Shocking Life, London, 1954.

On SCHIAPARELLI:

Books

Flanner, Janet, *An American in Paris,* New York, 1940.
Bertin, Celia, *Paris à la Mode: A Voyage of Discovery,* London, 1956.
Latour, Anny, *Kings of Fashion,* London, 1958.
Hommage à Elsa Schiaparelli [exhibition catalogue], Paris, 1984.

Elsa Schiaparelli, 1937: lamé dihabille. © Bettmann/CORBIS.

Elsa Schiaparelli, 1949 collection. © Genevieve Naylor/CORBIS.

Milbank, Caroline Rennolds, *Couture: The Great Designers,* New York, 1985.
White, Palmer, *Elsa Schiaparelli,* New York, 1986.
Martin, Richard, *Fashion and Surrealism,* New York, 1987.
Leese, Elizabeth, *Costume Design in the Movies,* New York, 1991.
Steele, Valerie, *Women of Fashion: Twentieth Century Designers,* New York, 1991.
White, Palmer, *Elsa Schiaparelli: Empress of Fashion,* New York, 1995.
Stegemeyer, Anne, *Who's Who in Fashion, Third Edition,* New York, 1996.
Baudot, François, *Schiaparelli,* New York, 1997.
Cawthorne, Nigel, *Key Moments in Fashion,* London, 1998.

Articles

Wilson, Bettina, "Back to Paris with Elsa Schiaparelli," in *Vogue* (London), October 1945.
"Schiaparelli the Shocker," in *Newsweek,* 26 September 1949.

Sheppard, Eugenia, ''Schiaparelli's Dim View of Today,'' in *The Guardian,* 11 August 1971.

"Elsa Schiaparelli," [obituary] in the *New York Times,* 15 November 1973.

"Berry—We Called Her Schiap," in *American Fabrics and Fashions* (New York), No. 100, Spring 1974.

"Schiaparelli sa vie en rose—shocking," in *Elle* (Paris), 6 August 1984.

Moutet, Anne Elizabeth, "A Shocking Affair," in *Elle* (London), October 1986.

Lawford, Valerie, "Encounters with Chanel, Mainbocher, Schiaparelli, Valentina, and Charles," in *Architectural Digest,* September 1988.

White, Edmund, "The Jewelry Designer's Crush on Schiaparelli...," in *Architectural Digest,* September 1989.

McCooey, Meriel, "Strung Along," in the *Sunday Times Magazine* (London), 21 April 1991.

Menkes, Suzy, "Elsa Schiaparelli: Shocking Life on the rue de Berri in Paris," in *Architectural Digest,* October 1994.

Smith, Roberta, "In Schiaparelli's Hands, Women as Works of Art," in the *New York Times,* 18 December 1995.

Cuccio, Angela, "Elsa Schiaparelli: The Roman Who Was the Sensation of Paris Through the 1930s, Looks Forward," in *WWD,* 13 September 1999.

* * *

Elsa Schiaparelli considered designing an art rather than a profession, making the unconventional acceptable. Born into a high ranking Italian family, her creativity was influenced by accepting the visually rich and rebelling against her extremely regulatory and proper upbringing. Much of her extravagance was inspired by the proper yet dramatic vestments of the priests and nuns remembered from her youth in Rome, combined with the city's architecture, magnificent medieval manuscripts, and ancient Greco-Roman mythology from the library where her father worked. The opulent and fanciful beadwork and embroidery Schiaparelli later produced in Paris was reminiscent of stained glass windows and had its roots in her youth in Italy. Other influences in her work were the futurists, cubists, New York dadaism, Parisian surrealists, and art déco.

Schiaparelli began designing gowns for herself and friends in 1915, with help and influence from Paul Poiret. She was an inventor of clothes; her clothes were immediately considered avant-garde, individualistic, eccentric, yet easy to wear. Sportswear, coordinated beachwear, and matching bags and shoes characterized her early work. Unusual fabrics such as upholstery material and terrycloth for beachwear and zippers on ski ensembles were characteristic.

Schiaparelli was a contemporary of Chanel. They worked during the same period and both started out designing sweaters—yet these are the only similarities they shared. Schiaparelli's initial success came with her *tromp l'oeil* sweater featuring a knitted-in bow at the neckline. So influential were these sweaters that additional designs followed, which included belts, handkerchiefs, and men's ties, all utilizing the unique methods of Armenian knitters. The immediate success of her sweaters allowed Schiaparelli to open her own shop on the rue de la Paix, the most fashionable street in Paris in 1927. An amazing success, it was estimated that by 1930 her company's income was approximately 120 million francs per year and her workrooms employed more than 2,000 people. She introduced good working-class clothes into polite society and understood how snob appeal worked through pricing.

After the Great Depression, fashion was in desperate need of excitement. Schiaparelli was to answer this call—she shocked as well as entertained the public, believing good taste was less important than creativeness, outrageousness, and fun. It was her belief that women should dare to be different, and through wearing attention-seeking clothes, a woman became chic. Utilizing wit and shock tactics to arm modern women, Schiaparelli believed they would gain equality and independence.

The extraordinary and unusual were expected of Schiaparelli; she didn't disappoint. She was the first couturier to use brightly colored zippers, using them initially on sportswear, beginning in 1930, and reintroducing them in 1935 on evening dresses. She collaborated with fabric houses to develop unusual novelty prints and unique materials. When Rhodophane, a cellophane material, was invented, she made glass-like tunics. Schiaparelli was known for such fabrics as "anthracite," a coal-like rayon; "treebark," a matte crêpe crinkled in deep folds to look like bark; and fabrics printed with newsprint.

Her commissions of contemporary artists were legendary—they included Christian Bérard, Jean Cocteau, and Salvador Dali. Their collaborations led to such eccentric designs as the lamb-cutlet hat, the brain hat, the shoe hat, and the suit with pockets that simulated a chest of drawers. She also incorporated oversized buttons in the shape of peanuts, bumblebees, and rams' heads. Her basic silhouettes were often simple and easy-to-wear, but through witty embellishments on a variety of themes such as the military, the zodiac, and the circus, they became unique. Through the study of Tunisian methods of sewing, draping, and veil twisting, Schiaparelli brought Arab breeches, embroidered shirts, and wrapped turbans to Paris fashion, as well as huge pompom-rimmed hats, barbaric belts, jewelry, and the "wedgie"—a two-inch-soled shoe that would be a trend throughout the 20th century and into the next.

There was also a more cautious side to Schiaparelli, which appealed to the somewhat more conservative woman. For this woman, her severe suits and plain black dresses were appealing. To her tailored ensembles she added trousers and unconsciously influenced the mix-and-match sportswear concept which wasn't fully recognized for the next 40 to 50 years. She showed her trouser suits for every occasion—travel, citywear, evening, and sports. After the acceptance of these slimmer, more slender divided skirts as they were called, she took the next step and shortened them, thus creating the culotte.

Black and the combination of black with white were favorites of Schiaparelli. In 1936 she launched shocking pink, a brilliant pink somewhere between fuchsia and red, and it became the hallmark of her couture house. Schiaparelli's influence can still be seen today in the masculine chic looks, the surrealistic accessories, and ornate buttons. She broke down the walls dividing art and fashion and anticipated the 21st century's eclectic approach to designing. Elsa Schiaparelli remains an everlasting influence on contemporary fashion.

—Roberta H. Gruber; updated by Nelly Rhodes

SCHÖN, Mila

Yugoslavian designer working in Italy

Born: Maria Carmen Nutrizio Schön in Trau, Dalmatia, Yugoslavia, 1919; raised in Trieste and Milan, Italy. **Career:** Opened atelier, Milan, 1958; first showed own custom designs, 1965; first boutique

Mila Schön, spring/summer 1967: silk damask suit (left) and striped linen suit (right). © AP/Wide World Photos.

for womenswear opened via Montenapoleone, Milan, 1966; launched Linea Uomo line of menswear, alongside opening of new boutique, Mila Schön Uomo, at via Montenapoleone, 1972; Mila Schön 2, second company, set up in 1973 to produce and distribute Alta Moda Pronta, Miss Schön, and Mila Schön Uomo lines; launched perfume, *Mila Schön,* 1978; established Mila Schön Japan; took over running of company in Como, Italy, for the manufacture and distribution of textiles for all Mila Schön lines, 1983; Aqua Schön swimwear collection introduced, 1984; opened first U.S. shop, Beverly Hills, 1986; Schön retired; company bought by Japanese firm Itochu Fashion Systems and distributor Coronet; Andrea Pinto appointed director and new design team hired, 1994; Schön returned to help design, 1996; opened second shop in Russia, 1998; acquired by Mariella Burani Fashion Group SpA, 1999; Pinto departed, 2000; launched menswear line, 2001; also produces shoes, stockings, furnishings, eyewear. **Address:** Via Montenapoleone, Milan.

Publications

On SCHÖN:

Books

Lambert, Eleanor, *World of Fashion: People, Places, Resources,* New York, 1976.

Alfonsi, Maria Vittoria, *Leaders in Fashion: i grandi personaggi della moda,* Bologna, 1983.

Soli, Pia, *Il genio antipatico* (exhibition catalogue), Venice, 1984.

Stegemeyer, Anne, *Who's Who in Fashion, Third Edition,* New York, 1996.

Vergani, Orio, *Birignao: piccolo lessico del palcoscenico,* Udine, 1997.

Articles

Pertile, Marina, "Roma: la primavera di Mila Schön," in *Vogue* (Milan), March 1985.

"Rigorosamente femminile: grande moda a Roma: Mila Schön," in *Vogue* (Milan), September 1986.

"Mila Schön, lo chic," in *Donna* (Milan), July/August 1987.

Forden, Sara Gay, "Pinto Brings in Mila Schön in Attempt to Save House," in *WWD,* 29 June 1995.

"Mila Schön," in *WWD,* 24 February 1998.

Wilson, Eric, "Andrea Pinto Gives Up Directorship," in *WWD,* 21 June 2000.

Singer, Natasha, "Luxury Boutiques Start Pouring into Russia," in *WWD,* 28 November 2000.

"Far and Away—Fun and Games at Moschino to Dainty, Ruffled Romance at Mila Schön," in *WWD,* 3 October 2001.

* * *

Mila Schön's interest in high fashion began when she became a personal client of Balenciaga. Her family were wealthy Yugoslav aristocrats who had fled to Italy to escape the communist regime. Living the life of a wealthy Italian demanded an elegant wardrobe and Schön's natural grace and good taste made her an excellent couture client. She must have studied the business thoroughly during her fittings because, when the family fortunes were lost, she turned to the fashion industry in order to make a living.

Business began in 1959 when Schön was 35, with a small atelier in Milan, where Parisian models were basically adapted and copied, combining Balenciaga's austerity of cut with Dior's versatility, plus a hint of Schiaparelli's wit. By the mid-1960s Schön was showing more original work at trade fairs in Florence and Rome, establishing a reputation as a perfectionist who worked within the constraints of a classic design structure. Her tailoring was particularly distinctive, executed with faultless attention to detail and cut in her favourite double-faced wools. The resultant clothes were highly sophisticated and sold at the top end of ready-to-wear or in the Mila Schön boutiques in Rome, Florence, and Milan. Small wonder clients included wealthy socialites like Jacqueline Kennedy Onassis, her sister Lee Radziwill Ross, and Babe Paley.

Schön described her company slogan as "Not how much, but how." This was reflective of her attitude towards high quality and taste. The company decided to translate the DOC (controlled origin denomination), a quality mark used in the wine business, for use on their clothes, denoting the company's attitude towards perfection. Schön was also very selective when it came to choosing clients in order to retain quality. She traded on what she described as a "medium circulation basis," so that when any side of her business was seen to make a marked profit, therefore operating beyond its limits, she started a new company to accommodate it.

There have been several diffusion lines and licensees since the company's inception. In line with the Schön business philosophy, these products have been marketed and sold through separately formed companies. Mila Schön Due is a less expensive ready-to-wear line; Mila Schön Uomo is the men's range. There is also a swimwear range, Aqua Schön, and a sunglasses range, Schön Ottica. Ties,

Mila Schön, autumn/winter 2001–02 ready-to-wear collection. © AFP/CORBIS.

scarves, fabrics, handbags, belts, and the perfume *Mila Schön,* were also produced.

By the mid-1990s Mila Schön, the designer, had retired, and her firm had been acquired by the Japanese trading company, Itocha, and the Coronet distribution firm. In 1994 the new owners hired Andrea Pinto, son of Pinto clan owning Krizia, to return the house to a higher profile, since it had lost much of its cache and was no longer profitable. Anna Domenici, also of Krizia, was brought over to help as a design consultant, and Pinto approached Schön herself to come back in 1996. The move was inspired, and so were the resulting collections. When the firm was acquired by Mariella Burani Fashion Group SpA in 1999, the Schön name was once again at the forefront of fashion, with new boutiques opening worldwide, including two in Russia, another in Prague, and plans for a third Russian store.

In 2001 Mila Schön was alive and well. In its coverage of the Milan fashion shows, *Women's Wear Daily* (3 October 2001) enthused over the firm's ability to add a hint of feminity to its traditionally tough-as-nails chic, "The hard edges of sculptured shapes were softened with cutout lace motifs and discreet ruffling. From day into evening, the delicate detailing appeared on almost everything, and, when it wasn't on the clothes, it found its way onto the accessories, from belts to boots."

Some 45 years after its founding, Mila Schön remains one of the most respected and established names in Italian fashion, representing design standards that are classic, flattering, and sometimes highly imaginative. Though Schön herself is no longer a fixture, her design sensibility ranked her among the finest Italian design houses in clientèle and prestige.

—Kevin Almond; updated by Nelly Rhodes

SCHNURER, Carolyn

American designer

Born: Carolyn Goldsand in New York City, 5 January 1908. **Education:** Studied at the New York Training School for Teachers; received B.S. from New York University, 1941; studied fashion at the Traphagen School of Design, New York, 1939–40. **Family:** Married Harold Teller (Burt) Schnurer, 1930 (divorced, late 1950s); children: Anthony. **Career:** Taught music and art before turning to sportwear design, 1940; clothes originally manufactured by Burt Schnurer Cabana Co., sold only at Best and Co., New York; company renamed for Carolyn Schnurer, 1946; left fashion design, became textile consultant to J.P. Stevens Company, circa 1956. **Awards:** New Orleans Fashion Group award, 1950.

Publications

On SCHNURER:

Books

Milbank, Caroline Rennolds, *New York Fashion: The Evolution of American Style,* New York, 1989.
Steele, Valerie, *Women of Fashion: Twentieth-Century Designers,* New York, 1991.

Articles

"Southern Resort Fashions," in *Life* (New York), 14 January 1946.
"Women Designers Set New Fashions," in *Life,* 14 January 1946.
Carlyle, Cora, "Carolyn Schnurer's Flight to Japan," in *American Fabrics,* No. 20, Winter 1951–52.
———, "Carolyn Schnurer's African Trip," in *American Fabrics,* No. 24, Winter 1952–53.
"From Natives to Natives," in *Time,* 11 January 1954.
"Carolyn Schnurer," in *Current Biography,* March 1955.

* * *

Carolyn Schnurer was a rather late bloomer in the field of fashion design. After teaching for a time in the state school system, she attended the Traphagen School of Design in New York and began working for her husband's bathing suit company, Burt Schnurer, Inc., in 1940. Her timing was perfect. As one of a handful of American designers whose creativity filled the vacuum left by the war-enforced absence of European fashion, Schnurer capitalized on her Traphagen training in methods of adaptive design. She became so well known for her casual clothes that in 1946 the company name was changed to Carolyn Schnurer, Inc.

Schnurer was a product of a persistent theme in American design between the World Wars: the need for freedom from the dictates of Europe. To this end, fabric and garment designers were encouraged to do original research in museum collections. Schnurer embraced the practice, picking a country on which to base a collection and then examining relevant objects at the Brooklyn Museum or Metropolitan Museum of Art in New York.

She enjoyed an advantage over her predecessors in that as air travel became more common, the countries she studied became readily accessible. In 1944 she made her first trip, to the Andes Mountains, returning with the theme for her Serrano collection, and her first enormous success, the Cholo coat. So strongly did she become associated with the idea of foreign inspiration that it overshadowed the real diversity in her work.

One of Schnurer's biggest boosters was *American Fabrics* magazine, founded in 1946. Its editors denounced what they perceived as a fundamental lack—and fear—of originality within most of the North American textile industry. Praise and publicity were lavished upon the few innovators. Each issue included a survey of some textile or decorative arts tradition, to educate and inspire subscribers. Schnurer's methods were in accord with the *American Fabrics* editorial policy, and her trips abroad, together with the designs they inspired, received substantial coverage.

Schnurer's career travel included visits to Brittany and Normandy, Ireland, Portugal, Greece, India, Japan, South Africa, Turkey, and Norway. Many of these were sponsored by stores such as Peck & Peck or Franklin Simon, with some secondary support coming from textile companies who then produced Schnurer's designs. She differed from some of her contemporaries in how she made use of the references she chose for garments. Schnurer preferred to graft an element or two of an ethnic style onto an otherwise Western silhouette. The Japanese-inspired collection, for instance, featured kimono sleeves, padded hems or wide, *obi*-like sashes on conventional full skirted dresses, pagoda-shaped shoulder and hem details on a bathing suit, beach coat, and shorts, and necklines which left the nape bare in virtually every outfit. The African collection of a year later showed cropped jackets with Hausa style embroidery and dress-bodices styled along the lines of tops worn by native women.

The African-inspired work, however, depended much more on the fabrics she derived from native sources than on the shapes of native costume. Earlier, Schnurer had originated a wrinkle-resistant cotton tweed as a result of the trip to Ireland. Dan River, Fuller, Bates, Arthur Beir, and Hollander were among the companies she worked with to develop textiles based on the motifs which filled her travel notebooks. A love of texture was apparent in all her fabric choices. Print designs came from Japanese ink paintings, African wood carvings, and Islamic architecture. A knotted-fiber rain cloak from Japan and an African mud cloth were translated into all-over embroidery patterns. Supple fibers such as linen, cotton, cashmere, and alpaca, as well as fabrics with character, including glazed chintz, sueded jersey, or velvet, distinguished her work. Schnurer's most creative fabric designs and developments adapted the look of the original into a form better suited to the American environment and lifestyle.

It is not surprising that when Schnurer left fashion design after her divorce in the late 1950s, she spent some time as a consultant with the J.P. Stevens textile company. Although she had a relatively short career in fashion, Schnurer left a considerable legacy. With others of her generation who gained prominence in the 1940s, she gave credibility to American design, even at the level of "popular" pricing. Her casual wear enhanced the leisure time of the average woman, while the fabrics and styles she introduced opened the minds of both consumers and those in the industry to the variety awaiting them outside the borders of the nation.

—Madelyn Shaw

SENNEVILLE, Elisabeth de

See de SENNEVILLE, Elisabeth

SHAMASK, Ronaldus

Dutch designer working in New York

Born: Amsterdam, Netherlands, 24 November 1945; raised in Australia. **Education:** Trained as an architect, self-taught in fashion design. **Career:** Window display designer, Melbourne, Australia, 1963–66; fashion illustrator for the *Times* and *Observer,* London, 1967–68; theatrical designer, Company of Man performance group, Buffalo, New York, 1968–71; freelance interior and clothing designer, New York, 1971–77; designer, Moss Shamask fashion company, New York, 1978–90; opened Moss on Madison Avenue boutique, New York, 1979, closed, 1986; introduced first menswear collection, 1985; showed new collection under his own name, and formed new company, SUSA (Shamask USA), 1990; signed on with Revlon for cosmetics line, 1993; created costumes for dancer Lucinda Childs, 1994; began designing womenswear again, for Barneys New York, 1995; showed collection in Greenwich Village loft, 1998; has also designed furniture. **Exhibitions:** *Intimate Architecture: Contemporary Clothing Design,* Massachusetts Institute of Technology, Cambridge, 1982; *Infra-Apparel,* Metropolitan Museum of Art, New York, 1993. **Awards:** American Fashion Critics Coty award, 1981; Council of Fashion Designers of America award, 1987; Confédération Internationale du Lin Fil d'Or award, 1987, 1989; Woolmark Award, 1989. **Address:** c/o Revlon, 625 Madison Avenue, New York, NY 10022, U.S.A.

Publications

By SHAMASK:

Articles

"Commentary," in *Details* (New York), April 1989.

On SHAMASK:

Books

Massachusetts Institute of Technology, *Intimate Architecture: Contemporary Clothing Design* [exhibition catalogue], Cambridge, 1982.

Diamonstein, Barbaralee, *Fashion: The Inside Story,* New York, 1985.

Milbank, Caroline Rennolds, *New York Fashion: The Evolution of American Style,* New York, 1989.

Stegemeyer, Anne, *Who's Who in Fashion, Third Edition,* New York, 1996.

Articles

"Shamask: High Technique," in *WWD,* 3 November 1980.

Duka, John, "New Architects of Fashion," in the *New York Times Magazine,* 16 August 1981.

Shapiro, Harriet, "Ronaldus Shamask's Wearable Architecture," in *People,* 24 August 1981.

Carlsen, Peter, "Ronaldus Shamask," in *Contemporary Designers,* Detroit, 1984.

Sturdza, Marina, "Ronaldus Shamask," in *Fashion 85* (New York), 1984.

Sinclaire, Paul, and Lesley Jane Nonkin, "Designer, Client: The Modern Equation," in *Vogue,* November 1987.

Boehlert, Bart, "Who's That Shamasked Man?" in *New York,* 8 February 1988.

Parola, Robert, "The Anatomy of Design," in *DNR,* 17 October 1988.

Schiro, Anne-Marie, "Three U.S. Designers, Less or More in the Mainstream," in the *New York Times,* 4 November 1988.

Chua, Lawrence, "Ronaldus Shamask Enjoying a Sense of Pleasure," in *WWD,* March 1989.

"Designing Men," in *GQ,* July 1989.

Boucher, Vincent, "The Two Mr. Shamasks," in *Seven Days* (New York), 7 March 1990.

"The Word to Men: Hang Looser," in *People,* Spring 1990.

Fenichell, Stephen, "The Look of the Nineties: Four Designers Lead the Way," in *Connoisseur* (New York), March 1991.

Sloan, Pat, "Ron Shamask: Streetwise Designer Has His Finger on Pulse of American Culture for Revlon," in *Advertising Age,* 8 February 1993.

Pogoda, Dianne M., "Shamask Gets Back into Fashion," in *WWD,* 26 September 1995.

Spindler, Amy M., "What a Difference A Zip Makes," in the *New York Times,* 3 October 1995.

———, "The Cut of One Seam Coiling," in the *New York Times,* 12 August 1997.

White, Constance C.R., "New Wave of Designers Opening Stores in SoHo," in the *New York Times,* 2 September 1997.

Schiro, Anne-Marie, "For Dancing the Night Away," in the *New York Times,* 10 November 1998.

* * *

Peter Carlsen, writing in *Contemporary Designers* (1984), perceived Ronaldus Shamask's designs in a most interesting and prophetic way. Carlsen claimed, "Shamask dresses an élite—the largely self-appointed élite comprising the devotees of high style. Certainly, his work is part of a way of life that is bound up with living in Manhattan; his clothes are meant to be worn in lofts, to downtown openings, are meant to signal to other members of what might be called the esthetic establishment their wearers' good standing in its ranks.… What Charles James was to 1940s New York, Shamask was to the late 1970s and early 1980s." Shamask creates intellectual, aesthetic clothing and perhaps inevitably, he has dressed intellectuals and aesthetically-minded individuals.

Recognized initially in a August 1981 feature article by John Duka in the *New York Times Magazine,* and subsequently in an exhibition, *Intimate Architecture: Contemporary Clothing Design,* at the Massachusetts Institute of Technology in 1982, Shamask was the wunderkind of the architectural rubric. But people do not wear buildings; nor is Shamask's design genuinely analogous to architecture. Rather, he is an immensely idiosyncratic and adventuresome designer with a sensibility for minimalism, a cant to the East, and a depth of conviction about fashion that often makes his work seem more utopian than commercially viable.

Shamask seeks a purity in fashion that others would not even warrant: his pursuit can seem too severe to some and austerely perfect to others. Anne-Marie Schiro wrote in the *New York Times* (4 November 1988), "At a time when many American designers are sticking to the classics, Mr. Shamask went a different route, showing styles that most women do not already have in their closets. Of course, they are not clothes for most women but for those with a flair for fashion and a desire to look different." His design has always been deliberate, but its visual rewards can be equally deliberate as well.

His fall 1981 two-piece coat with a visible spiraling seam may be more sophisticated in construction than most wearers or viewers would wish to know, though others such as Balenciaga and Geoffrey Beene have similarly designed to the utmost chastity of form. A 1979 linen ensemble literally unbuttons pockets down their sides to become part of the fold of the garment. His Japanese-inspired *hakima* trousers were featured in the Japonisme exhibition of the Kyoto Costume Institute at the Kyoto National Museum in 1994; his sensibility has often been shaped by Japanese esthetics. Shamask participates in a rarefied international culture that recognizes fashion as an art and seeks its participation with dance, theater, architecture, and all visual arts. He creates fashion worthy of such a status.

In the 1990s, Shamask devoted himself to menswear, where his talent for building clothes was shown to advantage. Ruth Gilbert, writing for *New York Magazine* in February 1992, claimed Shamask's tailored clothing "perfect fits." Years earlier, Shamask had told *Esquire* (September 1987), "Men are less interested in applied decoration than in the logical engineering of clothes." Even in menswear, Shamask had ardent admirers and a circle of devoted wearers without having vast commercial impact. His may not be an easily likable aesthetic, but it has definitely been a high art of dress informed by intelligence.

Making a comeback to women's fashions, Shamask didn't focus on the design, fabric, or fit—but on the zipper. Unzipped, the articles of clothing take on a rectangular form, shapeless, and don't even appear as if they can be worn. Once the zipper is fastened, however, this seemingly useless piece of fabric becomes a three-dimensional shape. In some instances, the zipper has been used as spaghetti straps; at other times, it forms a slit from the neck to shoulders, or just slightly above the neck.

Some say Shamask reinvented the use of the zipper. Others claim it was not a reinvention at all; merely an expansion of his ever-popular spiral jacket. Created in 1981, the jacket was based on one piece of fabric and emphasized the seam. Nearly two decades later, Shamask is still known for the jacket that gained him recognition. Like all of Shamask's creations, it was based on intellect rather than trend. Though trendy is not a word most would ascribe to Shamask, he was continually at the forefront of style.

In the early 1990s Shamask began designing fragrance packaging for Revlon, as well creating his own line of cosmetics. Then, after a five-year absence, Shamask was once again designing womenswear in 1995. Through a deal with Barneys New York, Shamask's new 25-piece collection was sold in exclusive in-store boutiques. In late 1998 Shamask took over the Greenwich Village studio of the abstract artist Jennifer Bartlett to display his new collection. Along the runway, paintings of Bartlett were shown to illustrate Shamask's appreciation for her, especially her color palette. The spring collection featured pleated pieces in trapezoidal shapes and dresses with spiral seams—another extension of the most notable spiral jacket.

Shamask continued to focus on architectural design late in his career, using mathematics and geometry to create each single piece of fabric. "The only decorative element is my clothes is the cut, the only detail is the seams," Shamask told the *New York Times* in 1997. Since Shamask's reinventing of the zipper, he has has a vast and varied design career—from working with Revlon to studying furniture design, while continuing to design extraordinary clothes for men and women.

—Richard Martin; updated by Diana Idzelis

SHILLING, David

English milliner and designer

Born: London, England, 27 June 1956. **Education:** St. Paul's School, Hammersmith, London. **Career:** Underwriter, Lloyd's of London, 1973–75; established millinery business, 1974; established own shop for couture hats, 1976; introduced women's ready-to-wear collection, 1984; other lines include menswear collection, 1986–89, and hand-painted ties, 1988–90; fashion correspondent, Radio London, 1982–86; Senior Consultant on Design and Product Adaptation, United Nations, from 1990; created symbol for Britain's Festival of Arts and Culture, 1995; designed the logo for the Consortium for Street Children; organized a millinery course in one of Her Majesty's prisons. **Exhibitions:** *David Shilling—The Hats,* toured the United Kingdom, 1981–84; Edinburgh College of Art, 1982; *David Shilling: A Decade of Design,* Chester Museum, England, 1991; exhibition of paintings, Richard Demarco Gallery, Edinburgh, 1991; *Unique Insight Into David Shilling,* Hatworks Museum, Stockport, 2001; *Mrs. Shilling Outfits,* National Horseracing Museum, Suffolk, 2001. **Collections:** Metropolitan Museum, New York; Los Angeles County Museum; Philadelphia Museum of Art; Victoria and Albert Museum, London; and Musee de l'Art Decoratif, Paris. **Awards:** President for Life of Valdivia, Ecuador. **Address:** 5 Homer Street, London W1H 1HN, England. **Website:** www.davidshilling.com.

PUBLICATIONS

By SHILLING:

Books

Thinking Rich, London, 1986.

On SHILLING:

Books

Hickey, Ted, and Elizabeth McCrumb, *David Shilling: The Hats* [exhibition catalogue], Belfast, 1981.

Polan, Brenda, ed., *The Fashion Year,* London, 1983.

Ginsburg, Madeleine, *The Hat,* Hauppauge, New York, 1990.

McDowell, Colin, *Hats: Status, Style, Glamour,* London, 1992.

Articles

Neustatter, Angela, "Cheeky Chapeaux," in *The Guardian* (London), 15 March 1978.

Glynn, Prudence, "A Sense of Occasion," in the *Times* (London), 16 March 1978.

"The Shilling Hat Man," in the *Observer,* 30 April 1978.

Cleave, Maureen, "Over 21," in *Woman's Day,* June 1979.

"Simply Shilling, My Dear," in *Woman's Day,* 23 July 1979.

Clemeneigh, Mirella, "Capelli in Mostra," in *Casa Vogue,* December 1980.

McKay, Peter, "Man with a Head for Hats," in *Woman's Journal* (London), December 1980.

Heron, Marianne, "Shilling, the Man Who Makes Headlines," in *Irish Independent,* Summer 1981.

Blume, Mary, "David Shilling, Wild Hatter of Ascot," in the *International Herald Tribune,* 5 June 1982.

Webster, Valerie, "A Shilling's Worth of Extravagance," in the *Scotsman,* 15 February 1984.

Mercer, Tim, "A Room of My Own: David Shilling," in the *Observer,* 18 March 1984.

Benchy, Maeve, "Not Like the Ones He Used to Make for His Mother," in the *Irish Times,* 15 May 1984.

"Hats Off to Shilling," in *World of Interiors* (London), August 1984.

Hillier, Bevis, "David Shilling Hat Trick," in the *Los Angeles Times,* 13 October 1985.

"Haute Hats," in *Cosmopolitan,* November 1986.

"Who Needs Money to Be a Millionaire," in the *Sunday Express,* 2 November 1986.

"A Head for Hats," in *Woman's Journal,* February 1987.

Weber, Bruce, "The Milliner's Tale," in the *New York Times Magazine,* 24 April 1988.

"David Shilling, Hatmaker to the Rich and Famous," in *Hello* (London), 22 April 1989.

"A Hat Man's Day at the Races," in the *Herald-Sun,* 9 September 1990.

Smith, Liz, "David Shilling," in the *Times,* 6 February 1991.

Kuandika, Giyil, "David Shilling," in *Business Times* (Dar-Es-Salaam), May 1991.

Owens, Susan, "The Item to Top it All Off," in the *Sydney Morning Herald,* 25 August 1992.

Gibbs, Warren, "The Mad Hatter," in *New Idea,* 24 October 1992.

Cawthorne, Zelda, "Hats That are Ahead of the Rest," in the *South China Morning Post,* 28 November 1992.

Bunoan, Vladamir S., "Hats Off to David," in *Philippine Business World,* 2 February 1993.

Gusman, Susan A., "Hats Off," in the *Philippine Daily Enquirer,* 14 February 1993.

*

I have chosen to communicate not in words but in shapes and tones. In the catalogue to the 1981 Ulster Museum exhibition of my hats, I was quoted as saying that the work should speak for itself, that words about it are superfluous. I still believe this is true. If I thought I could express in words any meaningful essays or insights into my work, I might be able to save myself all the hard work that goes into creating whatever it may be that I am creating in all its glorious color and form.

The passion has always been there; as a child I knew what I wanted to be. I redesigned my room constantly but I didn't earn a penny from my designing until I sold soft toys to my local toy shop at 13. From then on I was hooked on fashion. I am very motivated by the challenges of my work, whether in art or design, and I always want to do better than before. I challenge myself; I love what I'm doing, and I guess if I find that much pleasure in it, so will my clients.

I knew my work would change over the years. What I had not expected was that enormous changes would occur at the heart of fashion itself. When I first started, you thought of fashion as clothes. Now, in every consumer purchase there is an element of fashion.

Success has not been an end in itself but the key to other things. Although I received no formal art education, it has enabled me to work in all sorts of areas, from interior design to working with the United Nations in developing countries.

I particularly enjoy innovation, but novelty alone is never enough. One of the keys of successful designing is getting your timing right. When I started designing hats commercially, I never dreamed they would have the global and continuing influence they have, but I knew I was on the right track. I knew women should enjoy again the pure indulgence of wearing hats. What I didn't foresee were the generations of young people who would imitate my success. Luckily, I still love making hats.

The deeper messages of my work I express in my paintings, examining conflicts and relationships. The message when I design is simply that to be alive is a gift, so every day should be a celebration.

—David Shilling

* * *

David Shilling's interest in millinery was first inspired by a visit to his mother's hatmaker at the age of 12. He resolved to design a hat for his mother to wear to that year's Royal Ascot. Mrs. Gertrude Shilling, who was already noted for her eccentric and flamboyant taste in occasion dressing, caused such a sensation that her appearance made front-page news. The press adored her, and for 30 years her appearance at Ascot was a national institution until her death in 1999. "Once my mother had got into the papers, she was determined to be in each subsequent year," Shilling later recalled. To gratify his mother's determination, Shilling was faced with the task of creating gimmick after gimmick, a process that led him to establish his own millinery business in 1974.

In contrast to his extravagant creations, Shilling has a vulnerable and sensitive approach to his work. This attitude led him to anonymously send his first collection of millinery to the London department stores Liberty and Fortnum & Mason. He opened his first shop in Marylebone High Street, London, where everything was designed and made on the premises. Noted for always looking in on his shop to see the results of his efforts and to advise anyone unaccustomed to wearing hats, he has an eye for detail and design flair that ensures that many of his devoted clients return each season.

No two Shilling hats are ever made exactly the same. Bloomingdale's, Bergdorf Goodman, and Nieman Marcus have all bought collections from Shilling in the past. The volume of work requested by his private clients, however, led Shilling to stop the wholesaling of his hats. Shilling's hats are more than fashion accessories; they are works of art and as such they have been exhibited in art galleries and museums around the world. According to Elizabeth McCrum from the Ulster Museum, "His hats have achieved the status of objects d'art... They also function most effectively, being both flattering and comfortable for the wearer."

Actress Susan George declared, "I only wear hats if it is a hat occasion; otherwise I tend to feel rather self-conscious." She was so overwhelmed by her choice of a Shilling wide-brimmed, veiled hat for Ascot that her self-consciousness quickly gave way to enthusiasm. As Shilling himself acknowledged, "I love women to look beautiful and could never let a woman walk out of my shop wearing a hat that I didn't think suited her." In contrast, another customer, journalist and painter Molly Parkin, admits to being a hat fetishist. "I wear hats all the time, even in bed," she said. "In fact, I can't do anything without a hat on." Shilling saw this as an ideal creative opportunity to encourage Parkin's idea that her hair is an accessory to his hats.

Shilling's basic design philosophy is simple. He believes if you pay attention to every detail of the hat from the initial design to the finishing touches, the hat will flatter the customer. His hats are created from a variety of fabrics and trimmings, including black lacquered feathers, felting, antique velvets, silk veiling, tulle, and artificial flowers. In many ways, he established a niche in the British millinery market for fantasy, with fashion hats that were witty yet stylish.

Shilling's hats reflect both a sculptural and architectural quality. In the early 1990s when he started working with all-white canvasses, his paintings were also more like sculptures. Shilling soon moved away from works with fabric and trim to create his sculptural designs. He now works with large, freestanding, mirror-polished stainless steel and a blowtorch. He completed his first commissioned sculpture in 1999, *Between the Two Blues,* in Nassau, Bahamas. Shilling's most recent commissioned sculptures are both in France.

Although Shilling never had any formal education in art, he has lectured all over the world on art and design at public gathering, art colleges, and universities. He has also worked with several government agencies, such as the United Nations, to promote the importance of excellence in design worldwide. His touch of design can be seen in the British Festival of Art and Culture 1995 symbol and in the logo for the Consortium for Street Children in London. He also served on the development committee for the Royal Academy.

"I'm the best hatmaker there is," Shilling once declared, but added modestly, "I don't know whether it is a good thing or not."

—Kevin Almond; updated by Kim Brown

SIMON, Fabrice

See FABRICE

SIMONETTA

Italian designer

Born: Duchess Simonetta Colonna di Cesarò, Rome, Italy, 10 April 1922. **Family:** Married Count Galaezzo Visconti di Modrone, 1944 (divorced, 1959); married Alberto Fabiani (divorced); children: Verde, Bardo. **Career:** Opened design studio, Rome, 1946–62, 1965; partner/designer, Simonetta et Fabiani, Paris, 1962–65; introduced fragrance *Incanto,* 1955; traveled in India, 1960s–70s, establishing a colony for the care of lepers and a craft training program, 1973–76. **Exhibitions:** Rome, 1946; *Homage and International Celebration of Italian Designers,* Center for Italian Fashion, Florence, 2001. **Address:** 8 Via Cadore, 41012 Caroi, Italy.

Publications

On SIMONETTA:

Books

Lambert, Eleanor, *World of Fashion: People, Places, Resources,* New York, London, 1976.

Steele, Valerie, *Women of Fashion: Twentieth Century Designers,* New York, 1991.

Vergani, Guido, *The Sala Bianca: The Birth of Italian Fashion,* Milan, 1992.

Stegemeyer, Anne, *Who's Who in Fashion, Third Edition,* New York, 1996.

Mormorio, Diego, *Dressed: The Style of the Italians,* Turin, 2000.

Articles

Sheppard, Eugenia, "Simonette," in the *New York Herald Tribune,* 14 November 1951.

"Simonetta," in *Current Biography,* December 1955.

"Bonjour Paris, Addio Rome," in *WWD,* 3 April 1962.

Forti, Anna Gloria, "La Lady dell'alta Moda: Simonetta," in *Vogue* (Milan), December 1991 supplement.

Brady, James, "In Italian Fashion Murder Case, Even the Psychic Gets Jail Time," in *Advertising Age,* 30 November 1998.

Goldstein, Lauren, "Valentino's Day," in *Time Europe,* 31 July 2000.

* * *

Eugenia Sheppard, writing in the *New York Herald Tribune,* in November 1951 called Simonetta the "youngest, liveliest member of the up and coming Italian Couture,"commending the breadth of her collection from a two-part playsuit with cummerbund and bloomer shorts to a silk shantung dress-suit with tiered collar to her short and long eveningwear. By 1951, with ardent advocacy from American *Vogue* and Bergdorf Goodman, Simonetta was one of the best-known names in America for the new Italian postwar fashion.

Simonetta had presented her first collection in Rome in 1946, two years after her marriage to Count Galaezzo Visconti and a year before the birth of their daughter, Verde. An aristocrat, Simonetta had been interned by the Mussolini government for antifascist activities. The further pluckiness of starting up her couture business so immediately after the war was a sign of Simonetta's dauntless determination. A press release for her 1946 collection read in part: "To understand how difficult it was to open a *maison de couture* and have a show with 14 models just after the liberation of Rome by the Allies, one must remember the general situation at that time. Materials and trimmings were very scarce. The most surprising and common materials had to be used to make the extraordinary collection—dish cloths, gardeners' aprons, butlers' uniforms, strings and ribbons, and everything that could be found on the market." It was a humble beginning for an aristocrat dreaming of a high style.

But Simonetta was not alone. Other aristocratic Italian couturiers joined her, including her future second husband, Alberto Fabiani, as well as Roberto Capucci, Marquis Emilio Pucci, Princess Marcella Borghese, Federico Forquet, Ognibene and Zendman. They turned the attention of the international fashion world away from Paris, where they had been rebuffed, to Rome, with their elegant yet comfortable ensembles, created from new and innovative textiles and set in striking color combinations. The glamor of a politically correct aristocrat improvising an Italian postwar renaissance was of hypnotic charm to the American market. Moreover, Simonetta's youthful style held a special appeal, especially in the buoyant silk cocktail dresses, elegant debutante dresses, and ball gowns she created in the 1950s, with their emphasis on the bust.

Equally popular were the daywear and sportswear lines, as well as Simonetta's coats, with the coats in particular providing a favored inspiration for Seventh Avenue copying. She could rival Balanciaga in creating coats and suits made in robust materials, cut with precision and minimal detailing to draw attention to one salient feature. Like Balenciaga, she favored capelike sleeve treatments that gave the coats a dramatic sense of volume, especially in photographs. Further, she shared with Balenciaga a preference for the seven-eighths sleeve in coats, allowing for the display of gloves and jewelry. For the American market, these popular attributes constituted an idea of ease and mobility, but they also lent themselves to facile imitation and copying.

Famed Italian filmmaker Federico Fellini helped the fledgling Italian designers by making their clothing visible in his *La Dolce Vita* (1960), and other films, like Joseph Mankiewicz's *Barefoot Contessa* (1954), also featured Italian style. Suddenly, Simonetta, Fabiani, Pucci, Armani, Jole Veneziani, Marucelli, and Emilio Schubert were enjoying international attention, though France still snubbed these Italians. In fact, in 1962, when Simonetta and Fabiani moved to Paris and established Simonetta et Fabiani, the enterprise was less successful. But for a time, Rome was a locus of fashion.

Simonetta's distinguished international clientèle included the likes of Audrey Hepburn, Clare Booth Luce, Eleanor Lambert, Lauren Bacall, and Jacqueline Kennedy Onassis. As Aurora Fiorentini Capitani and Stefania Ricci observed in the *Sala Bianca* (Milan, 1992), "The collections by Simonetta were invariably met with success, in terms of the public and in terms of sales, because they translated the image of a naturally chic woman, with essential lines, elevated by one simple feature, a knot or a raised neck, and corresponded in every way to the personality of the Roman designer."

Modern Italian designers have paid homage to Simonetta and her husband, describing the two of them, along with the Fontana sisters,

Design by Simonetta, 1952. © Genevieve Naylor/CORBIS.

Veneziani, Marucelli, and Pucci as being among the pioneers who gave international wings to the then fledgling Italian fashion industry, paving the way for the likes of Valentino, Gucci, and Armani. Archives of her work, and that of Fabiani, are held at the New York Public Library's Manuscripts and Archives Division.

Simonetta was often photographed in her clothing and served in some ways as her own best model. She lived the life Americans dreamed of as portrayed in such movies as William Wyler's *Roman Holiday* (1953). If Simonetta was the ideal model for her clothing in the 1940s and 1950s, exemplifying practicality and young elegance, and a famous designer of clothing in the 1950s and 1960s, she later epitomized another cultural transformation as she forsook fashion to devote herself to philanthropy and spirituality, working with lepers in India in the 1970s and 1980s. Eventually, she moved to the Himalayas, where she studied Eastern spirituality and mysticism. In the 1990s, she returned to Rome, interested in reviewing and collecting her fashion work for a museum, and her works influenced those of future designers like Anna Municchi.

Simonetta's life seems to have been, more than most, culturally keyed. If it was in any way a destiny granted with privilege, it was also a destiny seized. Her fashion recognized the possibility of renewed elegance in postwar Italian and American life as well as the practicality of designing for distinctly modern women.

—Richard Martin; updated by Daryl F. Mallett

SIMPSON, Adele

American fashion designer

Born: Adele Smithline, in New York City, 28 December 1904. **Education:** Studied dressmaking at Pratt Institute of Design, Brooklyn, New York, 1921–22. **Family:** Married textile manufacturer Wesley William Simpson, 1930 (deceased); children: Jeffrey, Joan. **Career:** Assistant designer, 1922, then head dress designer, 1923–26, Ben Gershel's ready-to-wear fashion house, New York; chief designer, William Bass, New York, 1927–28; designer of Adele Simpson fashions, at Mary Lee Fashions, New York, 1929–49; president and director of Adele Simpson Inc. (bought out Mary Lee Fashions), New York, beginning in 1949. Member of the New York Couture Group; treasurer and board member, Fashion Group, New York; co-founder and board member, Fashion Designers of America. **Collections:** Brooklyn Museum, New York; Metropolitan Museum of Art, New York; Dallas Public Library, Texas. **Awards:** Neiman-Marcus award, 1946; Coty American Fashion Critics Winnie award, New York, 1947. **Died:** 23 August 1995, in Greenwich, Connecticut.

Adele Simpson, spring 1965 collection. © AP/Wide World Photos.

Publications

On SIMPSON:

Books

Celebrity Register, New York, 1963.

Moritz, Charles, ed., *Current Biography Yearbook 1970,* New York, 1970.

Watkins, Josephine Ellis, *Fairchild's Who's Who in Fashion,* New York, 1975.

Babbitt, Marcy, *Living Christian Science: Fourteen Lives,* Englewood Cliffs, New Jersey, 1975.

Walz, Barbra, and Morris, Bernadine, *The Fashion Makers,* New York, 1978.

Houck, Catherine, *The Fashion Encyclopedia,* New York, 1982.

O'Hara, Georgina, *The Encyclopaedia of Fashion,* New York, 1986.

Stegemeyer, Anne, *Who's Who in Fashion, Second Edition,* New York, 1988.

Calasibetta, Charlotte Mankey, *Fairchild's Dictionary of Fashion, Second Edition,* New York, 1988.

Milbank, Caroline Rennolds, *New York Fashion: The Evolution of American Style,* New York, 1989.

Stegemeyer, Anne, *Who's Who in Fashion, Third Edition,* New York, 1996.

Articles

"First Lady Selects Spring Wardrobe," in the *New York Times,* 25 March 1966.

"Mrs. Johnson to Wear Slim Tunic for Easter," in the *New York Times,* 9 April 1966.

Morris, Bernadine, "Mrs. Nixon's One Midiskirt," in the *New York Times,* 14 March 1970.

———, "Cheerful Designs for Winter Sun," in the *New York Times,* 27 August 1975.

———, "Joyful Fashions with a Folkloric Flavor," in the *New York Times,* 6 November 1976.

———, "Designers Softly Changing the Way Women Will Dress," in the *New York Times,* 23 April 1977.

———, "Fashion: Serious About Summer," in the *New York Times,* 18 January 1978.

———, "For Resort Wear: Trousers Are Shorter and Waistlines Easier," in the *New York Times,* 19 August 1978.

Bancou, Marielle, "Adele Simpson," in *American Fabrics and Fashions* (New York), Fall 1978.

Anster, Linda, "Simsoniana on Display," in the *New York Times,* 15 November 1978.

Morris, Bernadine, "Long Reach of the Reagan Style," in the *New York Times,* 24 February 1981.

———, "Four Designers Present Easy-to-Wear Clothes," in the *New York Times,* 29 October 1982.

———, "Seventh Avenue Winners: Coat Dresses, Suits," in the *New York Times,* 1 March 1983.
———, "Short Gowns Shine for Night," in the *New York Times,* 17 May 1983.
Obituary, *Time,* 4 September 1995.
Profile and obituary, *Current Biography,* October 1995.

* * *

The longevity of Adele Simpson's fashion business might be attributed to her acute awareness of the needs of her clientele: busy women who were frequently in the public eye, traveled quite a bit, and who required practical, well-made clothes to please not only their husbands and their observers, but themselves. Avant-garde or bizarre fashions would not do for these women. Simpson consistently offered conservative, yet pretty and feminine versions of current trends. The garments were made of ordinary fabrics such as cotton—Simpson was the first American designer to treat cotton seriously as a fashion fabric—or sumptuous fabrics inspired by the textiles she saw and collected on her frequent world travels. Her inspiration might have come from close to home as well, as in her adaptation of a New York City public school child's drawing of a cityscape at dusk, which Simpson interpreted in a silk dress and jacket ensemble that was later displayed at the Fashion Institute of Technology.

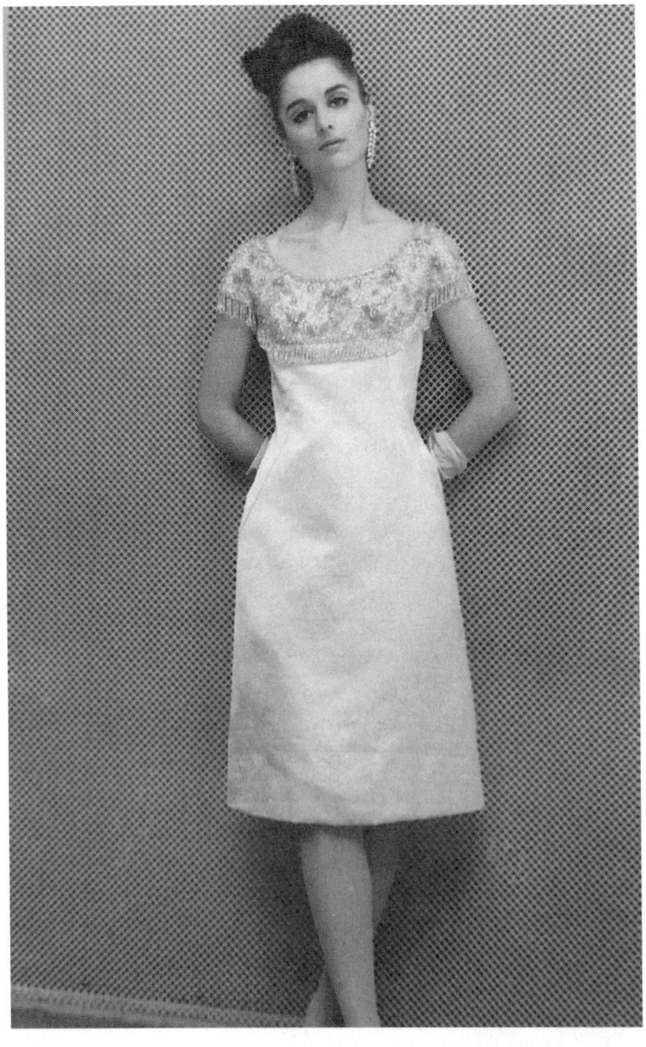

Adele Simpson, fall 1964 collection: satin princess dress. © AP/ Wide World Photos.

From the beginning of her career, Simpson dedicated herself to what she described as "realistic" fashion. During a time when women's dresses were developing a radically simpler silhouette, Simpson went even further and devised clothing that could be stepped into rather than pulled over the head. She concentrated on creating dresses and coats, blouses and suits, or dress and jacket combinations, all of which could coordinate and allow the wearer to be well dressed from daytime into the evening with a minimum of effort. An ingenious design consisted of a woolen cape and skirt teamed with a luxurious brocade blouse, and a separate underskirt made of the brocaded blouse material. When the cape and outerskirt were removed for evening, the resulting costume would be an elegant two-piece dinner dress. Political wives with busy itineraries and traveling schedules (including four First Ladies), and international performers such as Dame Margot Fonteyn, appreciated the practicality of Simpson's clothes, as well as their quality and artistic merits. As if to compensate for the basic conservatism of the styles, Simpson often rendered them in unusual, often sensuous fabrics.

Credited with "taking cotton out of the kitchen" during the 1940s, Simpson proved the fiber's suitability for street dresses and full-skirted evening gowns. Although known for her pretty prints in delicate colors, Simpson often used black for spring or summer, and made unusual pairings of fabrics, such as velvet over gingham. Silhouettes would generally be modified versions of prevailing shapes. There would usually be a defined waist and gentle overall curvaceousness that proved flattering to her somewhat more mature customers. Even the Simpson version of the chemise in the 1950s came with an adjustable tie belt.

Simpson often looked to the East for exotic touches to her designs. In the early 1960s, one collection featured day and evening clothes for summer that were made of linen and silk embroidered with Turkish patterns or printed in Byzantine mosaic motifs. Simpson also employed authentic Indian cotton sari fabrics, some embroidered in gold, for a dress collection that was exhibited at the New York World's Fair. Japanese silk prints also proved to be elegant and feminine sources of inspiration.

Drawing from the collection of foreign costumes she amassed during world travels, Simpson might conceive a fabric design from a single decoration, color scheme, or detail to create fashion that she would then display next to the original native piece. A printed evening gown might be inspired by a delicately embroidered Chinese jacket, or a vested outfit by a South American gaucho costume. Clothes such as these would appeal to clients who traveled, or merely wished to enliven their wardrobes with a touch of the exotic.

Adele Simpson, Inc. had long been one of the most successful manufacturers of women's better ready-to-wear. Prices of the designs ranged from about $100 in the 1940s, through $200 for a dress or suit in the 1960s, and from $400 to $1,000 in the 1980s, although a simple "ladylike dinner dress" could be had for $325. In 1990 Gump's catalogue (San Francisco, California) offered two versions of Simpson's "little black dresses" for around $400 each. First Ladies Mrs. Eisenhower, Mrs. Johnson, Mrs. Nixon, and Mrs. Carter included Simpson designs in their public and private wardrobes. When Mrs. Johnson selected a Simpson sand-beige coat and black silk dress ensemble to wear on Easter Sunday, the item made the news. Mrs. Nixon wore Simpson designs to Russia, China, and Africa, and one of the second Inaugural balls.

While for years the designer favored only pure silk, wool, and cotton in their many variations, she later did admit the merits of synthetic fibers. Simpson always made a point of asking women about their needs and desires in clothing; she credited her belief in Christian Science for setting the standard for beauty and excellence in her work.

After Adele Simpson donated her vast collection of artifacts, costumes, and fashion magazines to the Fashion Institute of Technology in 1978, she continued to oversee the designing, but Donald Hobson became the official designer for the company. His work maintained the Simpson aesthetic, but it evolved into even softer, more fluid and youthful lines.

In August 1995, Adele Simpson died at her home in Greenwich, Connecticut.

—Therese Duzinkiewicz Baker

SITBON, Martine

French designer

Born: circa 1952 in Casablanca; raised in Casablanca and Paris. **Education:** Graduated in fashion design from the Studio Bercot, Paris, 1974. **Career:** Fashion consultant, then freelance designer, 1974–84; signature ready-to-wear collection debuted in Paris, 1984; also ready-to-wear designer, Chloé in Paris, 1987–91; opened Paris store, 1995; licensing deal with Gibo and launched Martine Sitbon Tricot, 1998; introduced menswear collection, 1999; debuted punk collection, March 2000; named creative director for women, Byblos, 2001. **Address:** 6 rue de Braque, 75003 Paris, France.

Martine Sitbon, spring 2001 collection. © AP/Wide World Photos/ Fashion Wire Daily.

Publications

On SITBON:

Books

Steele, Valerie, *Women of Fashion: Twentieth Century Designers,* New York, 1991.

Articles

Webb, Ian R., "Martine Sitbon," in *Blitz* (London), April 1986.
"Chloé Unveils New Design Team with Martine Sitbon," in *WWD,* 14 May 1987.
Maiberger, Elise, "Sitbon Pretty," in *The Face* (London), June 1988.
Voight, Rebecca, "Martine Sitbon: France's Best Kept Fashion Secret," in *i-D* (London), March 1989.
Gross, Michael, "Paris Originals: Chloé in the Afternoon," in *New York,* 15 May 1989.
Quick, Harriet, and Louise Chunn, "Beauty and the Beastly" in *The Guardian,* 10 March 1994.
Forden, Sara Gay, "Italy Smokes Paris," in *WWD,* 24 April 1996.
Drake, Alicia, "Fashion Lights Up the Town," in *WWD,* 10 March 1997.
"Sitbon Signs License Pact with Gibo," in *WWD,* 15 June 1998.
Dodd, Annmarie, and Nelson Mui, "Martine Sitbon Hones in on Homme…," in *DNR,* 12 April 1999.
Murphy, Robert, "French Designers are Determining Own Approach to Sportswear from Slimane to Sitbon…," in *DNR,* 19 January 2000.
"Byblos Appoints Martine Sitbon as Women's Creative Director," in *WWD,* 19 March 2001.

* * *

Although her early collections bore fairytale titles like Cinderella, it is rock music, especially of the 1970s, that has often been Sitbon's strongest inspiration. Her sculptural suiting, often based on masculine lines, underpins each season's looks but leathers, studs, and swirling sequins were present, emphasizing both her affinity with the music scene and her skilled use of luxury fabrics.

Sitbon's manipulation of delicate textiles, mixing soft pastel and metallic shades as artistically as fruitier colors, is seen in both her own name line and the work she produced to breathe life back into the Chloé label from the mid-1980s to the early 1990s. Her use of fine organzas, left to flow and ruffle in petal-like folds at the cuff and collars of blouses, was a recurring element in her work. Such ruffling reached its apex in the cascading frills that flowed down the back of blouses dotted with overblown silk flowers in her spring/summer 1992 collection. The delicate femininity was tempered by the cool shine of slim satin trousers, abbreviated skirts, and elongated jackets.

The freedom to use these sensuous fabrics comes from her strong Italian financial backing, enabling her to experiment with expensive 1970s decorative favorites like sequins and embroidery. In 1989 she punctuated cropped leather waistcoats with gold studs, manipulating Hell's Angel motifs to achieve more luxurious results. The idea was developed further in olive suede waistcoats with looped chains that hung down to the bright gold velvet skirts with which they were teamed, demonstrating the subtle use of color and shade pervading her work.

In the middle 1990s, Sitbon's rock preoccupations came into their own, in tune with retrospective trends that gave an edge to her signature use of flares and bell bottoms. She has shown them in everything from intricate pink and charcoal cut velvet to dazzling gold sequins. In her spring/summer 1993 collection, her look became more attenuated. Slate grey hipster flares were worn with thigh-skimming jackets, severely cut away and held together by black thongs bound across the body, a look which was very influential. This collection contrasted bondage motifs with fluid chocolate-brown satin and organza skirts, and raised her already impressive profile in Europe, linking as it does with the main elements of current deconstructed styles putting proportions off balance and dress-down luxury textiles with rougher detailing and accessories.

Martine Sitbon, fall 2001 collection. © AP/Wide World Photos/ Fashion Wire Daily.

Sitbon's work has always been carefully accessorized, with perspex-heeled platform sandals with black straps criss-crossing up the leg or with stringy leather or satin chokers. Her attention to detail inspires the trimmings she uses; a futuristic bent is also a recurring undercurrent with stretch fit leggings, tops and jackets in soft leather, stitched in circles and stripes, which emphasize the wearer's physique and give a starkly postmodern feel. A sculptural form continues in her suits, tailored to accentuate the shape of the body, like the soft Prince of Wales trouser suits in 1987 that exploited the cut of men's suits and, more severely, in fitted black jackets and miniskirts defined by white borders and flap pocket edges in 1990. Along with the simple raw silk trousers and supple blouses, they provided a classic foil to her more dandyish designs for Chloé and the more fantastic elements of her main line.

This ability to design strong daywear items as well as more luxurious garments has provided Sitbon with a wide customer base in Europe. She has skillfully manipulated fabrics and the mixing of very contemporary themes, masculine and feminine, or what *Women's Wear Daily* (10 March 1994) termed "roughness...combined with richness." Sitbon's duality has made her an important force in fashion, with a successful record of collections, including a new menswear line in 1999. Fashioned after Brit rockers, the suits and separates had hints of feminity, just as her womenswear usually had underlying masculinity.

Sitbon next dove into men's sportswear, telling the *Daily News Record* (19 January 2000), "I've been highly influenced by sportswear in the measure that comfortable clothes are part and parcel with today's zeitgeist. But at the same time, Paris is not about pure sportswear, it's about elegance. I like to mix diverse elements to give my man the freedom to dress in a personal way." Another mix came in early 2000 when Sitbon surprised everyone at the Paris showings with a fall punk collection.

A new collaboration arrived in the 21st century when Sitbon signed with Byblos to become its womenswear director in 2001. The appointment came at a time when Sitbon's own collections were increasingly well received. Her spring 2002 womenswear showing in Paris was another stunner with delicate shirts and camisoles, cinched dresses, and wide trousers for day, and eveningwear in darker shades of gold, coral, and black with elaborate beading and embroidery. Karin Nelson, writing for the Fashion Windows website, reported, "It was a collection so simply poetic, so acutely appropriate that the crowd did something they rarely ever do—stood up and applauded the designer."

—Rebecca Arnold; updated by Sydonie Benét

SITBON, Sophie

French designer

Born: Paris, France, 29 June 1961. **Education:** Attended the Lycée Victor Hugo, Paris; followed a one-year course in screenwriting,

Paris, 1980; studied fashion design, 1981–83, Paris. **Career:** Launched own fashion line, Sophie Sitbon, 1985; lauded for unusual designs, early 1990s; designed Academy Awards dress for Juliette Binoche, 1997. **Exhibitions:** *Modes Gitanes,* Carousel des Sources, 1994. **Address:** 10 Rue Charlot Paris, 75003 France.

Publications

On SITBON:

Books

Modes Gitanes, Paris, 1994.

Articles

Véran, Sylvie, "…Et les bonheurs de Sophie," in *Gap* (Paris), February 1986.
"Sophie Sitbon," in *Elle* (Paris), May 1987.
"Stylistes: Sophie Sitbon," in *20ans* (France), September 1989.
"Designers' Inspirations: Sophie Sitbon," in *Joyce* (Hong Kong), Summer 1991.
Schiro, Anne-Marie, "In Paris, Escapism is in Fashion for the 1990s," in the *New York Times,* 15 October 1992.
Avins, Mimi, "Fashion: Lessons That Oscar Taught Us," in the *Los Angeles Times,* 24 March 1997.
Johnson, Marylin, "Pre-Oscar Preening: What'll They Wear?" in the *Atlanta Journal-Constitution,* 24 March 1997.
Avins, Mimi, "Calendar Goes to the Oscars," in the *Los Angeles Times,* 25 March 1997.
Johnson, Marylin, and Miriam Longino, "Oscar Night: The 1997 Academy Awards," in the *Atlanta Journal-Constitution,* 25 March 1997.
Levine, Lisbeth, "Fashion Parade Actresses Stop Traffic in Starry Battle of the Cleavage," in the *Chicago Tribune,* 25 March 1997.
Colman, David, "Abandon Ship: Fashion Follies of the Year," in the *New York Times,* 4 January 1998.
Thomas, Barbara, "Magazine Review: Guides to Help You Dress with Success," in the *Los Angeles Times,* 18 December 1998.
Swanson, James L., "Three Hot Colors: Gray, Black and a Touch of Pink…," in the *Chicago Tribune,* 11 April 1999.
"Sophie Sitbon," available online at Get Chic, www.getchic.com, 5 October 2001.
"Sophie Sitbon," online at First View, www.firstview.com, 5 October 2001.
"Sweet Scent of Success," online at Contessa Helena, www.contessa-helena.com, 7 October 2001.

* * *

Fashion, to Sophie Sitbon, is functional. Clothes are not a means of artistic expression but a liaison between proportion and harmony and their sole reason for being is to be worn. Clothes are an individual means of expression for the person who wears them; they send out messages that can describe the complex range of subtleties and distinctions making up the human persona, a signal to other people about the essence of another person.

Sitbon describes her signature look as being seductive. In contrast to sexiness, seduction is subtle and has the power to attract in many directions. She particularly admires the seductive power of writer Tennessee Williams and the complex, often subversive repression of his heroines. Her designs reflect this, being always provocative yet never blatant. Movies and television are another strong influence; Sitbon regards her generation as being more audiovisual than literary. The visual impact of glamorous movie stars and their wardrobes often tell a more potent story than the written word. She sees clothes as a visual medium for reinterpreting the excitement and vibrancy of movies in real life.

Sitbon loves the drama of black and red, colors she adopted as her own: "I love black. I loved it before it became fashionable and I will always love it. Black is perennial," she said in an interview with *Joyce* magazine in Paris. Her clothes are simple yet dramatic, classic yet eccentric—a stark, black shift dress, suspended by spaghetti straps, is punctured by tiny holes that follow the dart positions of a dress block and is teamed with matching opera gloves. Another shift dress has a scalloped neckline and is splashed with an asymmetrical contrast color shape reminiscent of a Matisse cutout. Always energetic in her approach, Sitbon creates designs that are whimsical yet vital and impudent without being aggressive.

A graduate of the Esmode School of Fashion in Paris, in her final year she was awarded a Gold Medal by a jury of designers including Jean-Paul Gaultier and Thierry Mugler at the International Style Competition in Osaka, Japan. She produced her own collection in 1985, financed by a Japanese group and manufactured from a showroom in the Marais district of Paris, aiming to provide a simple, high-quality couture look for modern women at affordable prices. Seven years later, she declared herself happy with her design success, although her admiration for movie heroines has left her with one unfulfilled ambition—to direct her own movie.

In the 21st century, Sitbon continues to create clothes for an independent, self-confident woman who is what she is, rather than what she wears. Her clothes are a proposition rather than an imposed ideal. Her customer interprets Sitbon clothes to create her own independent look. "I prefer people to see someone in my designs and say 'doesn't she look wonderful,' not 'she's wearing Sophie Sitbon,'" the designer declared. Though she may not be as well known as some of her contemporaries, Sitbon remains a sought-after designer for such high profile events as the Academy Awards, for which she has produced several show stoppers.

—Kevin Almond; updated by Mary Ellen Snodgrass

SLIMANE, Hedi

French menswear designer

Born: Paris, France, 1969. **Education:** No formal training in fashion; studied art history at the École du Louvre. **Career:** Hired as assistant at José Lévy, 1990; became assistant at Yves Saint Laurent, 1997, quickly becoming designer of Rive Gauche Homme and then YSL menswear; took over as designer of Dior Homme, 2000. **Address:** Dior Homme, 30 Avenue Montaigne, 75008 Paris, France.

Hedi Slimane, designed for the house of Christian Dior's spring/summer 2002 ready-to-wear collection © Reuters NewMedia Inc./CORBIS.

Publications

On SLIMANE:

Articles

Plewka, Karl, "A Hedi New Experience," in *Interview,* March 1999.

Horyn, Cathy, "An Electric Moment for a Men's Designer," in the *New York Times,* 1 February 2000.

Raper, Sarah, and Robert Murphy, "Is Hedi Slimane Leaving Yves Saint Laurent?" in *DNR,* 18 February 2000.

Socha, Miles, "Slimane Talks About Dior, YSL," in *WWD,* 5 July 2000.

Horyn, Cathy, "A Short, Creative Trip," in the *New York Times,* 18 July 2000.

Bowles, Hamish, "Hedi Times," in *Vogue,* May 2001.

Sischy, Ingrid, "The French Connection," in *Vanity Fair,* June 2001.

Menkes, Suzy, "Dior's Fashion Warriors Amid the Luxury," in the *International Herald Tribune,* 3 July 2001.

Horyn, Cathy, "Erotic Undercurrents," in the *New York Times,* 11 July 2001.

* * *

Hedi Slimane, designer at Dior Homme since late 2000, has achieved nearly universal positive reviews for his collections, both at Dior and before that at Yves St. Laurent. This young man has made his way in just a few years from a virtual unknown to the highest profile menswear designer in France.

The fashion press and his fellow designers alike find Slimane's upscale designs stand out from the competition. Colleagues such as Karl Lagerfeld and Slimane's former boss, Yves St. Laurent (with whose brand he now competes), attend his shows; in fact, St. Laurent caused a stir when he made a rare appearance at one of Slimane's first shows for Dior, whose parent company, LVMH, is a bitter rival of YSL's parent, the Gucci Group.

Slimane's silhouettes are based on classic menswear but with a modern twist. He is known for preferring black (sometimes with hints of bright color); for narrow lines, low-cut and sheer shirts and thin-waisted suits; and for a certain femininity that appeals to men and women alike. After women such as actress Cate Blanchett and entertainer Madonna requested versions of his men's suits, Slimane began selling certain items for women as well, not modified at all from the men's designs except being available in smaller sizes.

Slimane has a reputation for high-quality tailoring, attention to detail, and minimalist designs, his pieces have frequently been termed "architectural" and "slightly subversive." He also is interested in the idea of matching, whether a tuxedo and a swimsuit or a pair of sunglasses and a ring. Although his designs appeal to youthful men—and his very young runway models emphasize this slant—Slimane has commented that his clothes are much more about attitude the wearer's age.

Slimane's work for Dior has been a continuation of his progression at YSL, where he first designed the Rive Gauche Homme ready-to-wear brand, later taking over the reins at YSL menswear. He became known for pieces that have been called slim and sexy, elegant and erotic, subtle and simple. He has a modern take on fashion yet a respect for and inspiration from the work of leading menswear designers throughout history. After leaving YSL, Slimane had many options, from designing his own label for YSL's owner, Gucci Group, to designing Prada's Jil Sander women's collection. He opted for LVMH's Dior because he liked the idea of creating a men's business practically from the ground floor; Dior Homme had focused only on suits for some time, with distribution limited to Europe and Asia.

Slimane's move to Dior in 2000 at age 32—caused in part by his dissatisfaction in reporting to another designer after Tom Ford was hired to oversee all of Gucci's brands—was acclaimed, but some observers wondered about the ramifications to the Dior brand, especially given the fact that John Galliano, Slimane's polar opposite, was designing the women's collection. Critics wondered how Dior could put forth a cohesive brand image when its women's and men's lines were so divergent, even taking into account that the two were never merchandised or advertised together.

Yet Slimane felt comfortable, at this point in his young career, with the idea of creating new designs within the established Dior framework. He told *Women's Wear Daily* (5 July 2000) that he liked facing the challenge of creating something new within the vocabulary of a firm with a long history. So far, given the way the fashion world has continued to embrace the shy designer and his work, the fit seems perfect.

—Karen Raugust

SMITH, Graham

British milliner

Born: Bexley, Kent, 19 January 1938. **Education:** Studied at Bromley College of Art, 1956–57, and the Royal College of Art, London, 1958–59. **Career:** Worked for Lanvin, Paris, 1958–59; milliner, Michael of Carlos Place, London, 1960–67; own firm established, 1967–81, and from 1991; consultant design director, Kangol Limited, 1981–91; created hat collection for BHS stores, 1990s. **Address:** 22 Crawford Street, London W1H 1PJ, England.

Publications

On SMITH:

Books

McDowell, Colin, *Hats: Status, Style, Glamour,* London, 1992.

Articles

"Haute Hats," in *Cosmopolitan* (London), November 1986.
Rowe, Gillian, "Heads He Wins," in *You* magazine of the *Mail on Sunday* (London), 6 November 1988.
Fallon, James, "Storehouse to Sell BHS Clothing Again," in *WWD,* 28 March 2000.

* * *

Graham Smith is a milliner's milliner; one examines his hats and finds outstanding craftmanship. These featherweight pieces appear untouched by human hand; no irregularities mar the sheen of the fine straw crowns, and snow-white felts remain pristine after the rigorous hand-blocking which sets them irrevocably into shape. Invisibly-stitched brims and seemingly effortless draping belie hours of pains-taking handwork for which there is no substitute if one requires the genuine article.

Nor does Smith's work exhibit technical mastery alone—to walk into his showroom is to be amazed and amused by the combination of color, texture, and shape, and by the witty inventiveness of the trims. Smith's shows during the decade of his design directorship of Kangol were stunning parades of the milliner's art and a gift to fashion editors, whether the chosen theme followed a traditional floral path, swooped up into outer space or dived to the bed of a tropical ocean. The staid Kangol beret suddenly emerged as a hot fashion item, whether studded, colored or trimmed whimsically with buttons.

Smith left London's Royal College of Art early to work in Paris with Lanvin. After returning to work with Michael, the English couture house, he ran his own business off Bond Street, which soon attracted a distinguished clientèle. Royalty and media stars have worn his hats; every leading London store carries them. He has worked with many leading designers, amongst them Zandra Rhodes and Jean Muir, and has often designed for the screen—notably for *Help, The Ruling Class, Goodbye Mr. Chips,* and the Bondish face, *Casino Royale.*

Smith hats have also literally traveled the world, adorning the heads of British Airways flight attendants. Additionally, his work is represented in the permanent collection at the Victoria & Albert Museum, and has been photographed for Pirelli calendars by Norman Parkinson. To use an inelegant term for an elegant man, Smith might be termed a workaholic; given the time, one could well imagine he would prefer to do all his own work. Of this he would certainly be more than capable, and he is an exacting master—which does not deter his loyal staff, some of whom have worked with him for decades. His wit and entertaining teaching style have endeared him to many fashion students during his time as millinery tutor on the degree course at Kingston Polytechnic.

Graham Smith has thrived on design talent and technical excellence, running a successful business through years when hats were far from obligatory as high fashion accessories. As hats wax and wane in importance, Smith's faithful clients continue to wear his creations in the knowledge that they are simply of the highest possible quality; and to reach these heights there are no short cuts.

—Alan J. Flux

SMITH, Paul

British designer

Born: 1946. **Family:** Married Pauline Denyer, 2000. **Education:** Attended Beeston Fields Grammar School, Nottingham, England. **Career:** Opened first menswear shop, Nottingham, 1970; opened in London, 1979; opened New York store, 1987; opened flagship Tokyo shop, 1991; introduced womenswear collection, 1993; opened first women's boutique, Paris, 1994; opened first children's shop, London, 1994; first Jeans shop, London, 1994; introduced watch collection, 1994; offered custom tailoring, 1998; new London flagship, 1998; 13 worldwide stores, sold in more than 40 countries, by 2001. **Exhibitions:** *Observation,* Victoria & Albert Museum, London, June-November 1995; Paul Smith True Brit exhibition, Design Museum, London, October 1995–April 1996. **Awards:** British Design for Industry award, 1991; named Honorary Fellow, Chartered Society of Designers, 1991; named Commander of the British Empire, for services to fashion industry, January 1994; Queens award for Industry, for export achievement, April 1995; invited to join the Labour government's Department of Culture, Media and Sport Creative Industries Taskforce, 1997; knighted for services to the British fashion industry, November 2000. **Address:** Riverside Building, Riverside Way, Nottingham NG2 1DP, England. **Website:** www.paulsmith.co.uk.

Publications

On SMITH:

Books

Jones, Dylan, *Paul Smith True Brit,* Italy, 1995.

Articles

York, Peter, "The Meaning of Clothes," in *Blueprint* (London), October 1983.

Paul Smith, fall/winter 2001 collection. © AP/Wide World Photos.

Paul Smith, fall/winter 2001 collection. © AP/Wide World Photos.

"Harris Tweed, Campaign Sign; Paul Smith," in *Fashion Weekly* (London), 13 June 1985.
"Cue: Paul Smith," in *Vogue* (London), 15 September 1985.
"Face to Face," in *Creative Review* (London), June 1986.
Boehlert, Bart, "Mr. Smith Comes to New York," in *New York,* 20 April 1987.
Rumbold, Judy, "The Man of Paul Smith's Dreams," in *The Guardian* (London), 9 November 1987.
Mower, Sarah, "The Gospel According to Paul," in the *Observer Magazine* (London), 29 November 1987.
Schneider-Levy, Barbara, "Paul Smith, Anti-Fashionist," in *Footwear News* (London), 14 December 1987.
"After Nottingham, the World for Smith," in *Blueprint* (London), December 1987.
"Wearing Mr. Smith," in the *Economist* (London), 9 January 1988.
Jeal, Nicola, "Smith Said 'Cotton'," in the *Observer* (London), 21 February 1988.
Hamilton, William L., "The Schoolboy's Revenge," in *Metropolitan Home,* August 1988.
Dutt, Robin, "Paul Smith," in *Clothes Show* (London), July/August 1989.
Emmrich, Stuart, "The Hip Little Shop Around the Corner," in *Manhattan, Inc.,* February 1990.
Harris, Martyn, "The Designer Guru Who Suits Himself," in the *Sunday Telegraph* (London), 11 March 1990.
Gandee, Charles, "Mr. Smith Goes to Italy," in *House & Garden* (London), April 1990.
Fairchild, Gillian, "A Day in the Life of Paul Smith," in the *New York Times Magazine,* 9 June 1990.
Jordan, Mary Beth, "I Am a Camera: Designer Paul Smith Shoots his New York," in *Metropolitan Home,* August 1990.
Omelianuk, Scott, "Mr. Smith Goes Global," in *GQ,* August 1993.
Morais, Richard C., "We're Finally Ready…," in *Forbes,* 24 April 1995.
Clarke, Michael, "Suitable Opportunity," in the *Times Educational Supplement,* 6 October 1995.
Spindler, Amy M., "Slim, Sophisticated Men's Wear in Paris," in the *New York Times,* 9 July 1996.
———, "In Paris, Men's Wear Sizzles," in the *New York Times,* 28 January 1997.
———, "The Gutsy, the Greedy, the Humble," in the *New York Times,* 8 April 1997.

———, "Strength in Diversity at Men's Shows," in the *New York Times,* 9 July 1997.
Fallon, James, "London's Hip Notting Hill Neighborhood is Now Home to Paul Smith," in *DNR,* 15 June 1998.
Mower, Sarah, "Smith's Open House," in *Harper's Bazaar,* August 1998.
Goldstein, Lauren, "Paul Smith Brings Designer Credentials to Custom Tailoring," in *Fortune,* 26 October 1998.
Friedman, Vanessa, "Paul Smith Steps Out," in *Travel & Leisure,* September 1999.
"Queen Knights Paul Smith," in *WWD,* 19 June 2000.
Hiscock, Jennifer, "Different Cloth," in *Marketing,* 1 February 2001.
Freed Carlson, Janet, "The Day-Tripper," in *Town & Country,* May 2001.
"Sir Paul Smith," in *Financial Times,* 9 October 2001.

* * *

The much-used phrase "classics with a twist" was the original design philosophy behind Paul Smith's menswear collections, where the element of classicism did not frighten traditionally conservative British male dressers. With no formal training in fashion design, Smith's fashion career began with his shop in Nottingham in 1970. The shop sold mostly other designers such as Kenzo and Margaret Howell, but it also stocked some early Paul Smith shirts, trousers, and jackets that he made in nearby workrooms. With the encouragement of Pauline Denyer, an RCA graduate in fashion, then his girlfriend, and evening classes at the local polytechnic, Smith was able to create more of what he wanted for his shops. His first collection was introduced in Paris in 1976; unable to find the type of clothes he wanted, he introduced his own designs for shirts and jackets, which he had made up in local workrooms.

The evolution of the Paul Smith label away from classicism, which began in the early 1980s, was prompted by the proliferation of copyists springing up on the heels of his initial success. The Paul Smith style was imitated both in England and abroad by companies such as Next, Façonnable, and Henry Cotton's. Smith admits his decision to become a more fashion-oriented label resulted in confusion about the company's image. Although the classic phase of the label gave way to a higher fashion emphasis, the designer says he is often likened to America's Ralph Lauren because of his earlier image. Later designs are best characterized by wit and humor, with offbeat fabrics and colors creating a hint of excitement in the essentially practical styles. Smith's attention to detail is easily seen in the functional buttons in his men's suits and the inside pockets, hand-stitching, and vivid lining found in the women's suits.

Smith continues to be the chairman of his company as well as the designer of the clothes. "At the moment, while I still have my health and my sanity, there is somebody called Paul Smith behind the label. And I am really behind the label. I am involved in every shop decision, every design decision, the way the advertising looks, the way the window dressing looks, the way the clothes look," Smith stated during an interview with Jennifer Hiscock of *Marketing* (1 Feburary 2001). Fiercely committed to his customers, Smith continues to work in his Nottingham Hill Gate Shop on Saturday afternoons when he is in London. It is his attempt to stay in contact with his customers and understand what they want. "I think a lot of designers or company bosses lose touch with the reality of their customers, or where they earn their wages. They surround themselves with subservients, have ivory-tower offices and chauffeur-driven cars, and eventually they just lose touch, especially in a fickle industry like fashion."

Smith attributes his personal success to the fact that his early designs were representative of the company's classical phase. His jackets were traditionally styled, but he lowered the armholes to make them easier to wear and subtly changed the shape of the trousers. Using wools, tweeds, and fine cottons, Smith's designs retained just the right element of English tailoring traditions with a hint of eccentricity that appealed not only to conservative city types but also to the newly-emerged yuppie of the 1980s, for whom a Paul Smith suit became an important status symbol. By gradually introducing changes to the male wardrobe, Smith says he found his customers slowly became less nervous about adding a patterned tie or a colored sweater. Richly patterned or embroidered waistcoats, colored braces, and decorative socks are also examples of Smith's subtle changes to basic menswear items.

Smith's own shops are an integral part of his design strategy and form the backdrop for his fashion designs. His was one of the first fashion shops to sell items other than clothes; they included watches and pens, modern sculpture, candlesticks, mirrors, and glassware. The selling of a lifestyle was also greatly imitated during the 1980s, when ordinary everyday objects achieved cult status in the right environment. Smith was responsible for the revival of the Filofax and men's boxer shorts during this period.

A strong British pride has fueled Smith's work to establish design as a vital component in British industry. Recognition for his work in this area has won him numerous awards, placed him on the government's official list of ambassadors, and brought suitors like luxury conglomerates LVMH and Gucci Group to his door. He has refused all offers of consolidation, content to maintain his firm and its independence.

Paul Smith, paragon of style, was rewarded for his unique brand of service to his country and the British fashion industry when he received the coveted title of "Sir," and earned a knighthood from HRH Queen Elizabeth II in November 2000.

—Catherine Woram; updated by Kim Brown

SMITH, Willi

American designer

Born: Willi Donnell Smith in Philadelphia, 29 February 1948. **Education:** Studied fashion illustration, Philadelphia Museum College of Art, 1962–65; studied fashion design, Parsons School of Design, New York, 1965–67. **Career:** Worked as fashion illustrator with Arnold Scaasi and Bobbi Brooks, New York, 1965–69; freelance designer, working in New York, for Digits Inc., sportswear company, Talbott, Bobbie Brooks, 1967–76; with Laurie Mallet established company, WilliWear, Ltd., 1976; added WilliWear men's collection, 1978; began lecturing in art history at the Fashion Insitute, London; first store opened posthumously, Paris, 1987; WilliWear reintroduced with Michael Shulman as designer, 1996. **Exhibitions:** Featured in Harlem Museum, New York, 1987; among permament collections of Black Fashion Museum, Washington, D.C., 1998. **Awards:** International Mannequins Designer of the Year award, New York, 1978; Coty American Fashion Critics award, 1983; 23 February named "Willi Smith Day" in New York City, 1988. **Died:** 17 April 1987, in New York.

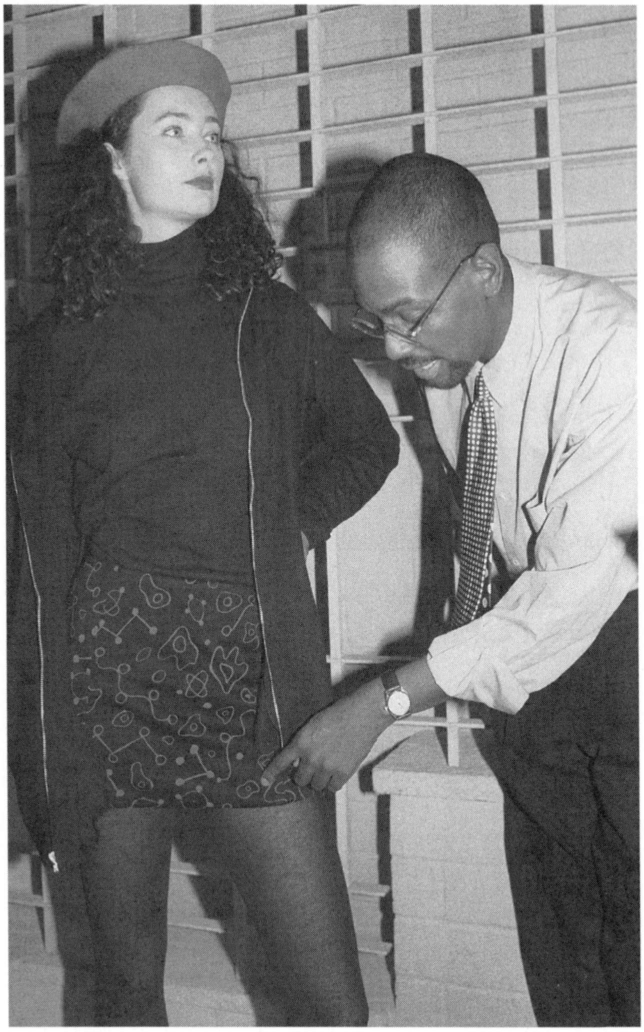

Willi Smith in 1987 © Bettmann/CORBIS.

Publications

On SMITH:

Books

Lambert, Eleanor, *World of Fashion,* New York, 1976.
Alexander, Lois K., *Blacks in the History of Fashion,* New York, 1982.
Milbank, Caroline Rennolds, *New York Fashion: The Evolution of American Style,* New York, 1989.
Stegemeyer, Anne, *Who's Who in Fashion, Third Edition,* New York, 1996.

Articles

Rogers, Susan, "Willi Smith, a Man with Missions," in *Amsterdam News,* 16 June 1979.
"Willi Smith: noir et blanc et en coton," in *Elle* (Paris), September 1984.
"Da New York: Off Off Fashion," in *L'Uomo Vogue* (Milan), March 1985.
"Designer Willi Smith Suits Groom, Ushers at Kennedy Nuptials," in *Jet,* 4 August 1986.
"Talents: WilliWear," in *Depêche Mode* (Paris), January 1987.
Filmer, Denny, "Just William," in *Fashion Weekly* (London), 12 February 1987.
Horwell, Veronica, "The Wonder of Willi," in the *Observer* (London), 8 March 1987.
James, George, "Willi Smith, Clothes Designer, Creator of Vivid Sportswear," in the *New York Times,* 19 April 1987.
Rittersporn, Liz, "Designer Willi Smith Dead," in the *New York Daily News,* 19 April 1987.
"Willi Smith," [obituary] in the *Daily Telegraph* (London), 22 April 1987.
O'Dwyer, Thom, "Willi Smith is Dead," in *Fashion Weekly* (London), 23 April 1987.
Als, Hilton, "Willi Smith, 1948–87," in the *Village Voice,* 28 April 1987.
Buck, Genevieve, "Though The 'Real' is Gone, Williwear Plans to Forge Ahead," in *Chicago Tribune,* 29 April 1987.
Parikh, Anoop, "The Man Who Had Attitude," [obituary] in *The Guardian* (London), 30 April 1987.
Lebow, Joan, "WilliWear Without Willi: His Partner, Petite, French and Tough, Looks Ahead," in *Crain's New York Business,* 4 May 1987.
Smith, Marguerite T., "Sustaining Williwear's Spirit," in the *New York Times,* 17 May 1987.
"For Willi, 1948–87," [obituary] in *Essence* (New York), July 1987.
Campbell, Roy H., "Black Creations Long Overlooked, Fashions by Black Designers Find a Home in a Harlem Museum," in *Chicago Tribune,* 16 September 1987.
"Designer Collection: Garments by Willi Smith," in *Elle* (London), October 1987.
"Willi Smith Day Held to Aid Needy N.Y. Groups," in *Jet,* 20 March 1989.
Davis, Stephania H., "The Return of Willi: Company Revives the Stylish, Comfortable Designs of Willi Smith," in *Chicago Tribune,* 13 June 1996.
White, Constance C.R., "A Paris Store for de la Renta; Willi Smith Meets T.J. Maxx…," in the *New York Times,* 27 August 1996.
Burch, Audra, "D.C.'s Black Fashion Museum Traces Untold Story," in *Chicago Tribune,* 20 December 1998.
Johnson, Eunice W., "Black Designers—Shaping the Future," in *Ebony,* February 2000.

* * *

Without respect for race, Willi Smith was one of the most talented designers of his era. With respect to race, he was indisputably, as the *New York Daily News* fashion writer Liz Rittersporn declared upon his death in 1987, that he was "the most successful black designer in fashion history." Smith chafed at the attention given to the anomaly of his being a black designer, yet he acknowledged some advantages in the sensibility of being an African-American: "Being black has a lot to do with my being a good designer. My eye will go quicker to what a pimp is wearing than to someone in a gray suit and tie. Most of these designers who have to run to Paris for color and fabric combinations should go to church on Sunday in Harlem. It's all right there." It was all right there for Smith as a quintessentially American designer, of the people and for the people, with a vivid sense of style democracy and eclectic mix.

Perhaps in part due to his Indian cottons and colors, or to his inexhaustible appeal to youth, or maybe just due to his own wit and sense of loose fit, Smith excelled in clothing for summer. His winter collections, too, were especially notable for oversized coats based on classic shapes. His WilliWear News for fall 1986 proclaimed with irony his intention to get "serious" with the fall collection. In a sense, Smith never was serious, preferring instead a lively incongruity he had learned from observation and refined from affordable clothing made in India.

WilliWear, the company he founded with Laurie Mallet in 1976, went from $30,000 in sales in its first year to $25 million in 1986. His soft, baggy looks did not require sophisticated tailoring and benefitted from the Indian textiles that he chose for their supple hand, easy care and comfortable aging, and indescribably indefinite colors. Smith's slouchy softness was a "real people" look, marketed at modest costs with great impact in the 1980s as the informality of designer jeans and other casual wear was replaced by the kind of alternative Smith's designs offered—a drapey silhouette for comfortable clothing with style.

While primarily a designer of women's clothing, WilliWear was also influential in men's clothing. In July 1983 he created the clothes for Edwin Schlossberg's marriage to Caroline Kennedy, including blue-violet linen blazers to be worn with white slacks and white buck shoes for the groom's party; the groom wore a navy linen double-breasted suit with a silver linen tie, outfits that were both traditional and slightly spoofy and outrageous enough to notice and enjoy.

Smith's tenure in the fashion world, however, was terribly short-lived. He died, young and at his prime, in 1987. George James quoted Smith in an obituary written in the *New York Times* (19 April 1987): "I don't design clothes for the Queen, but for the people who wave at her as she goes by." In Smith's designs there was no equivocation—sportswear was for fun and comfort. He knew this, having first worked for Arnold Scaasi in a rarefied world of fancy dress. Later, he worked for Bobbie Brooks and Digits, among others, but it was on his own, first in a business with his sister Toukie, and later in WilliWear, that Smith found his own voice designing what he affably called "street couture" without apology.

Smith created uniforms for the workers on Christo's Pont Neuf, Paris wrapping in 1985. His work even anticipates much that became casual style in America in the late 1980s and 1990s through the Gap and A/X—loose, slouchy oversizing and mixable possibilities. Hilton Als eulogized Smith in the *Village Voice* (28 April 1987), "As both designer and person, Willi embodied all that was the brightest, best, and most youthful in spirit in his field.... That a WilliWear garment was simple to care for italicized the designer's democratic urge: to clothe people as simply, beautifully, and inexpensively as possible."

In his short life, terminated by an AIDS-related death at 39, Smith made little issue or complaint of the social disadvantages and difficulty of being an African-American committed to making a mass-market clothing business—he simply proceeded to make an exemplary life of innovative design that both earned him the Coty award in 1983 and countless fans of his sportswear style who may never have known—or cared—whether he was black, white, or any other color. These fans found his designs available for a short time after his death, and then in 1996 WilliWear was relaunched. Available exclusively at T.J. Maxx stores, the new lines were produced by designer Michael Shulman.

—Richard Martin; updated by Owen James

SNOEREN, Rolf

See VIKTOR & ROLF

SPOOK, Per

Norwegian fashion designer

Born: Oslo, Norway, 1939. **Education:** Studied at School of Fine Arts, Oslo, and École de la Chambre Syndicale, Paris. **Career:** Arrived in Paris, 1957, and joined house of Dior soon afterwards; worked as freelancer with Yves Saint Laurent and Louis Féraud; opened own house, 1977; acquired by Haifinance Corp., 1991; lost funding, 1994; produces haute couture and ready-to-wear. **Awards:** Golden Needle (Chambre Syndicale, Paris), 1978; Golden Thimble, 1979. **Address:** 6 rue François 1er, 615008 Paris, France.

Publications

On SPOOK:

Books

McDowell, Colin, *McDowell's Directory of Twentieth Century Fashion,* Englewood Cliffs, New Jersey, 1985.
O'Hara, Georgina, *The Encyclopaedia of Fashion,* New York, 1986.
Guillen, Pierre-Yves, and Jacqueline Claude, *The Golden Thimble: French Haute Couture,* Paris, 1990.
Stegemeyer, Anne, *Who's Who in Fashion, Third Edition,* New York, 1996.

Articles

Greene, Elaine, and Bent Reg, "Coming Home to Norway," in *House Beautiful,* May 1988.
"Paris: C'est Tout!" in *WWD,* 22 July 1993.
Ramey, Joanna, "Backer Pulls the Plug on Per Spook Couture," in *WWD,* 27 June 1994.
"Haute Couture-Behind the Scenes," available online at www.diplomatie.fr, 5 October 2001.
"Os Negócios da Moda," online at www.centroatl.pt, 6 October 2001.
"Per Spook," online at www.afaa.asso.fr, 6 October 2001.

* * *

Per Spook came to Paris in the late 1950s after graduating from the Oslo School of Fine Arts. For him, Paris had been a lifelong ambition, the place to go for anyone wanting to work in the fashion industry. After studying at L'École de la Chambre Syndicale de la Couture in Paris, he embarked on a long career as an apprentice and freelance designer. Experience with revered houses like Yves Saint Laurent, Christian Dior, and Louis Féraud gave him a taste for haute couture and the specialized fashion that created a sensation when he opened his own house at the age of 38 in 1977.

Spook clothes were instantly applauded for their new, soft shapes and color. He established a hallmark for well-cut clothes that were elegantly understated but upheld the characteristics of quality, individuality, and wearability. Distinctive innovations have been his versatile long dresses with a device allowing them to be taken up for daywear, then let down again for an evening look; his Ile de Wight dress, a square-cut white linen dress embroidered with abstract black squares; and his Crumple clothes, made from a fabric that allows the clothes to fold into a small bundle and pack away without creasing. He also likes to design versatile mix-and-match outfits that can unite to create ensembles ranging from glamorous cocktailwear to daywear.

When it comes to ready-to-wear, the ideal Spook customer has been a woman who is both realistic and practical. She is active, up to date and, with her international lifestyle and career, needs clothes that are graceful and polished but also witty and lively. With his couture clothes, Spook likes to combine his own creativity with the individual personality of a client. He recognizes that each client has a different set of needs and fantasies about how she wants to look. Even if designer and client have opposing ideas, it is always possible to create a united design.

Spook collections have often been fanciful and evoked romantic images of society lifestyles in the 1920s and 1930s. The clothes have had a strong resort feel, suggesting leisured times at Deauville or on the Lido at Venice. Figure prints on expensive crêpes and asymmetric details on crossover crêpe minidresses have been popular, as have saucy nautical stripes, abstract polka dots, and geometrics, like black-and-white checkerboard jackets or long sequin shift dresses in geometric-patterned fabrics. They evoked references to fashion icons of the past, an updated Duchess of Windsor, Marlene Dietrich, or the 1950s model Dovima.

Spook's other artistic interests are noteworthy and undoubtedly inspirational when it comes to fashion design, and his design interests have not been exclusively fashion oriented. He is an accomplished painter, sculptor, and photographer. Interiors, textiles, and product design capture his imagination and have been barometers of inspiration and observation helping form and develop his creative fashion ideas. In his career, Spook has been recognized with several fashion awards, including the Chambre Syndicale's Golden Needle and Golden Thimble awards. Ultimately, it is in couture that Spook has excelled. To a designer, haute couture is often the inventive lifeblood of the industry, where creativity is unhampered by the limitations of expense or market (unfortunately, financing has been a battle for Spook, who lost his backing in 1994).

Financed or not, Spook's approach has always been down to earth. He enjoys creating couture that combines practicality and realism with creativity and aesthetic vision—and his vision is genuinely appreciated.

—Kevin Almond; updated by Mary Ellen Snodgrass

SPROUSE, Stephen

American designer

Born: Ohio, 1953. **Education:** Attended Rhode Island School of Design for three months. **Career:** Worked briefly for Halston and Bill Blass; showed first collection, 1983; out of business, 1985–87; showed three lines, S, Post Punk Dress for Success, and Stephen Sprouse in own shop, 1987; opened satellite shop, Beverly Hills, 1988; out of business, 1988–92; designer, introducing Cyber Punk line, Bloomingdale's, 1992; signed licensing deal with Staff International, 1997; began working with Marc Jacobs and Louis Vuitton, 2000; designed gown for artist E.V. Day, 2000.

Publications

On SPROUSE:

Books

Milbank, Caroline Rennolds, *New York Fashion: The Evolution of American Style,* New York, 1989.

Stegemeyer, Anne, *Who's Who in Fashion, Third Edition,* New York, 1996.

Articles

"Hot Commodities: Rich Returns," in *Harper's Bazaar,* July 1987.

Goodman, Wendy, "Stephen Sprouse Tries a Comeback with a Bold New Store," in *New York,* 21 September 1987.

"Art & Commerce: Stephen Sprouse," in *Interview* (New York), September 1987.

"All Sproused Up: The Return of Stephen Sprouse," in *i-D* (London), November 1987.

Martin, Richard, "Vicious Icon: Hero and History in the Art of Stephen Sprouse," in *Arts Magazine,* December 1987.

Fressola, Peter, "Glitzy Sprouse," in *DNR,* 19 April 1988.

Cihlar, Kimberly, "The Many Sides of Stephen Sprouse," in *DNR,* 12 August 1988.

Young, Lucie, "Corporate Greed: A Fashionable Vice," in *Design* (London), August 1988.

Lender, Heidi, "The Return of Stephen: The Seventies Are Back and So is Stephen Sprouse," in *WWD,* 30 October 1992.

Norwich, William, "Back to the Future," in *Vogue,* December 1992.

Yarritu, David, and Mariuccia Casadio, "Quick! There's a Sprouse in the House," in *Interview,* December 1992.

Spindler, Amy M., "Rock-and-Roll's Designer-Curator," in the *New York Times,* 9 May 1995.

White, Constance C.R., "Licensing Deal for Sprouse," in the *New York Times,* 24 June 1997.

———, "Sprouse's American Hurrah," in the *New York Times,* 4 November 1997.

"Fashion: A Bite of the Apple," in the *Independent,* 17 January 1998.

"Joie de Mode," in *WWD,* 6 April 1998.

White, Constance C.R., "Breakaway Looks: Vintage to Cyberchic," in the *New York Times,* 7 April 1998.

"From Superfine to Chunky, Knits Take Center Stage on Milan Runways," in *DNR,* 15 January 1999.

Schiro, Ann-Marie, "Muses from Futuristic to Folk," in the *New York Times,* 19 February 1999.

"Xybernaut: Wearable PC Debuts at Fashion Week," in the *PR Newswire,* 25 March 1999.

"Sprouse on Stint at Louis Vuitton with Marc Jacobs," in *WWD,* 28 July 2000.

Cash, Stephanie, "E.V. Day at Henry Urbach Architecture," in *Art in America,* October 2000.

"Sprouse in the House," in *WWD,* 11 October 2000.

"Public Lives: It's Graffiti, by Design, and Flying Cars to Come," in the *New York Times,* 22 August 2001.

"Mercedes-Benz Revs Up Fashion Week," in the *PR Newswire,* 7 September 2001.

Hastreiter, Kim, "Stephen Sprouse," available online at www.papermag.com, 7 October 2001.

* * *

A much lauded figure on the New York fashion scene in the early 1980s, Stephen Sprouse is one of the most notorious success-failure stories in the American fashion business. One of a number of designers with their roots in the rural backwaters of Indiana, Sprouse shares his origins with Norman Norell, Bill Blass, and Halston, for whom he worked briefly in the early 1970s. Reputedly already displaying a precocious talent by the age of 12 when he designed leopard-print jumpsuits, Sprouse went on to study for a mere three months at the Rhode Island School of Design before hitting the New York scene as a rock photographer.

In the late 1970s Sprouse made his name by designing stage clothes for Debbie Harry of the pop group Blondie, having met her in the kitchen of the flats they were sharing in New York's Bowery. His designs included ripped t-shirts, minis, and leotards, paving the way for the first of his collections in 1983. Sprouse's clothes displayed a nostalgia for the New York underground of the 1960s, particularly Andy Warhol and the Factory aesthetic, and he seemingly designed with Edie Sedgewick or Ultra Violet in mind. Revisionist rather than retro, the garments were a witty caricature of the wildest excesses of 1960s fashion, harking back to the days of Betsey Johnson at Paraphernalia—yet tempered by Sprouse's New Wave sensibilities.

Sprouse used synthetic fabrics, neon hues, and striking graphic prints to give his basic shapes visual appeal, contrasting Day-Glo colors with black jersey separates such as t-shirts and minis. Press attention focused primarily on his use of sequins shown on jackets, thigh high boots, and his signature single shoulder strap dresses worn with matching bra tops. The influence of André Courrèges and Rudi Gernreich has been obvious in his use of cutout panels revealing parts of the female torso such as the waist or midriff or in his redefinition of that staple of the 1960s male wardrobe, the Nehru jacket, colored hot punk pink by Sprouse in 1985.

Acknowledging the clichés of youthful rebellion, Sprouse toyed with items of subcultural style, which through overuse in popular imagery became mainstream. A prime example of this approach is the motorcycle jacket Sprouse experimented with endlessly, covering it with sequins, 1960s iconography, or pseudoslang. His use of logos, which seemed to be making reference to some magical teenage argot, bemused audiences in 1988 when the meaningless phrase "Glab Flack" was emblazoned over clothes shown on the catwalk.

Arguably his best work, as worn and publicized extensively by Debbie Harry, was the collection in 1983 on which Sprouse collaborated with celebrated New York graffiti artist Keith Haring to produce Day-Glo prints of hand-painted scribbles, imagery lifted straight from the subway walls. Matching outfits of miniskirts and tights or shirts and flares for men made the wearer look as if he or she had been caught full force in the fire of a spray can.

Sprouse's designs were strictly club clothes, street fashion at couture prices as a result of the expensive fabrics, applied decoration, and hand-finishing applied to every garment. Following a 1997 comeback based on Andy Warhol spinoffs, Sprouse's 1998 fashion line thrust fatigue-green hooded capes with orange lining above wide-leg pants and long maxiskirts. He bolstered his showing with matte sequined evening dresses and slim-line tuxedos anchored with Velcro.

With free-flowing chutzpah, Sprouse produced a techno-chic line for fall 1999. During Fashion Week, Sprouse caught the eye of the global fashion in-crowd and rockers such as Axl Rose and Steven Tyler, energized by the designer's high-fashion shoes, 3-D microminis, and unisex pants. Taking his cue from the Mars Pathfinder Rover, Sprouse toned up the runway spectacle with silvered colors, plastic sheen, and imagery from the Warhol catalogue, to which he has exclusive rights. Sprouse outdid himself with a unique application of head gear, paneling, and body computers. According to *PR Newswire,* he exulted, "I had no idea that the computer industry has advanced to the point that people can be wearing computers. This technology is so cool." In his estimation, the melding of cyber hardware with garments set the tone for the new millennium.

In fall 2000, Sprouse supplied a silver spangled dress to artist E.V. Day for "Transporter," one of her *Exploded Couture* exhibits. Spotlighted against a marine backdrop at the heart of her show, the gown floated between disks like a celestial mirage. Day slit the fabric to enhance a semblance of earthly beauty absorbed into the cosmos. Valued for his spunky countercultural panache, Sprouse made a palette of world-class luxury items. For 2000, he moved easily from clothes to accessories. Partnering with creative director Marc Jacobs during regular commutes between New York and Paris, Sprouse returned to the Day-Glo graffiti of his 1983 debut to enhance fabrics, prints, handbags, and luggage for Louis Vuitton.

Sprouse freed himself of the retro tag, telling *Women's Wear Daily* his use of a sprinkling of squiggles and a reinterpretation of LV lettering was not looking back— "I'm more into the present, but I guess the 1980s are the present now. This stuff looks more now to me." Even more demanding than his Paris job was a sizeable painting commission for NASA. At the New York showing of spring 2002 collections, he spackled show tents with his trademark eye-popping fluorescent color.

—Caroline Cox; updated by Mary Ellen Snodgrass

STAVROPOULOS, George Peter

Greek designer

Born: Tripolis, Greece, 20 January 1920. **Family:** Married Nancy Angelakos, 1960; children: Peter. **Career:** Couturier, Athens, 1949–61; New York couture and ready-to-wear business opened, 1961–90. **Died:** 10 December 1990, in New York.

PUBLICATIONS

On STAVROPOULOS:

Books

Milbank, Caroline Rennolds, *New York Fashion: The Evolution of American Style,* New York, 1989.

Articles

"George Peter Stavropoulos," *Current Biography,* March 1985.

Milbank, Caroline Rennolds, and Peter Vitale, "George Stavropoulos: A Master of Classical Line in Manhattan," in *Architectural Digest,* September 1989.

"George Stavropoulos Dies; Known for Classic Designs," in *WWD,* 12 December 1990.

"George Peter Stavropoulos," [obituary] in *Current Biography,* February 1991.

* * *

Throughout his career, George Peter Stavropoulos maintained a relatively low but highly respected profile in the fashion world. He was one of a small number of designers in America who exclusively produced ready-to-wear clothes of the quality and caliber of Parisian haute couture. Stavropoulos presented two ready-to-wear collections, produced in his own atelier each year for 30 years and never ventured into lower priced lines, licensed products, or perfumes, as did many of his contemporaries. Nor did he venture into the further reaches of avant-garde design. While many of his designs were innovative and strikingly beautiful, they were never shocking or arresting and his innovations were subtle to the degree that they were apparent only to the wearer or noticed either upon close inspection, or when the wearer moved about.

Stavropoulos established his business in New York in 1961, having left his native Greece, and chiffon evening dresses of every variety were central to his collections. Signature chiffon looks included single shoulder asymmetrically draped toga styles, inspired by models from classical antiquity, many layered body-skimming styles, and dresses with pleats originating at the neckline or shoulders that could be tied at the waist or left flowing freely away from the body. Recurring details included intricate pleats and tucks, wrap and capelet effects, free floating panels that could be thrown across the shoulders as a scarf or wrapped around the waist as a belt, and other multipurpose convertible details.

Evident in his chiffons and central to Stavropoulos' design philosophy were the ideas of comfort, softness, and ease of movement. In 1961 he remarked, "I don't want clothes to be tight, it's not high fashion. A woman must be able to move around in a dress." In the early to middle 1960s, contrary to the prevailing tendency toward stiffness and a boxy silhouette, Stavropoulos designed unconstrained kimono-sleeved jackets and daytime wool suits cut on the bias that subtly draped over the body. Throughout his career, rather than designing evening coats to go over his gowns he preferred the soft and simple cape to finish off his evening looks, often accessorized with a single long strand of black or white pearls.

By the mid-1970s, when the trends had caught up with Stavropoulos and fluid simplicity was the rage, the designer presented the ultimate innovation in soft and simple luxury—a gently flaring tank dress in five layers of bias-cut white chiffon with a single seam at the center back. Unlike his contemporary Halston, however, who presented similar looks around the same time, cerebral, minimal modernism was not the conceptual basis for his design. Instead Stavropoulos was most interested in exploring the ideas of softness and ease of movement (despite the apparent simplicity of Halston's designs and his pretensions to minimalism, many of his garments were a challenge to wear). Although Stavropoulos was most praised for his creations in chiffon, he was adept at working with other fabrics and had a particular liking for taffeta and satin, pleated, tucked, and manipulated on the bias with the same attention to fine detail he gave chiffon.

Stavropoulos' style remained unchanged in his three decades in business in New York. Demand for his signature body-skimming layered chiffon evening look was so consistent that he found it a challenge to "make the clothes look different," yet still reflect his point of view that "classical design is forever." His clients appreciated the classic and long-lasting investment quality of his garments and many still wear his clothes today.

—Alan E. Rosenberg

STECKLING-COEN, Adrienne

See ADRI

STEFANEL SPA

Italian sportswear manufacturer and retailer

Formed: in Treviso, 1959, by Carlo Stefanel (1925–87); son Giuseppe joined firm, 1970s. **Company History:** Signed licensing agreements with Romeo Gigli, the Girbauds, Peter Handley and others; company went public; announced joint venture with Calvin Klein, 1995; formed K Service SpA and SKY Company SpA with Klein, 1996; opened first CK store, Milan, 1997; signed with Joyce Ma to license apparel in Hong Kong, 1997; expansion planned for the U.S., 2001–02. **Company Address:** 85 via Postumia, 31047 Ponte di Piave, Treviso, Italy.

Publications

On STEFANEL:

Articles

"Knitting Patterns," in the *Economist,* 3 October 1987.
Bannon, Lisa, "Stefanel's Fantasy Trip," in *WWD,* 13 March 1992.
Ozzard, Janet, "Stefanel Deal Will Put CK Stores in Europe," in *WWD,* 20 December 1995.
"Restructuring Puts Stefanel in Red," in *WWD,* 18 March 1996.
"Stefanel Loses $12.6M in Half," in *WWD,* 3 October 1996.
Forden, Sara Gay, "Restructuring and Cuttine Costs Return Stefanel to Profitability," in *WWD,* 18 March 1998.

* * *

Stefanel is one of Italy's largest fashion companies, manufacturing young, sporty, wearable separates and knitwear for the young menswear and womenswear market. Sold in shops worldwide, Stefanel clothing is synonymous with good design in quality fabrics, as well its licensing agreements and a joint venture with Calvin Klein.

The company began in 1959 as a manufacturer of knitwear in Treviso, Italy. The brainchild of Carlo Stefanel, it quickly established a reputation for lively color and quality. Carlo's son Giuseppe Stefanel entered the business in the mid-1970s, with exciting plans for expansion into the broader fashion market of casual clothing, sportswear, jeans, and ready-to-wear. Through franchising, Stefanel developed a competitive distribution system that resulted in a steady growth in international markets, particularly in the Far East and Europe. Stefanel's development strategy has supported distribution growth by introducing carefully targeted production policies within the textile and clothing sector, constantly widening the breadth of product ranges.

Knitwear still plays a dominant role in Stefanel collections. For both menswear and womenswear the look is unisex, homespun, and traditional. Fair Isles, jacquards, stripes and checks are incorporated into cozy, easy shapes and restyled into modern, young looks. For evening there are slinky gold, ribbed knits and crochet designs teamed with black drainpipes and silky white blouses for a dressed-up look. Pioneer-style denims, chambray, tartans, and tiny paisley prints are the major woven fabrics used in oversize shirts, casual shirtwaist dresses, simple jackets, and wrap over minis with fringed hems. Cuban style jackets in heavy wool coating, teamed with fisherman jerseys, can give a nautical feel to the range.

Stefanel boutiques mix high-tech with traditional in their interiors. Simple wood floors and furniture are mixed with chrome and glass to create a spacious, modernistic shopping environment. The clothing is merchandised in a logical, easy way with garments arranged in color coordinated sections making it simple for the customer to put together an outfit. Such retail outlets were sprinkled throughout the UK, including its first shops in Ireland in the 1993. Stefanel also opened stores in major cities in China, the first consumer goods manufacturer to do so.

In the 1990s the firm experienced growth and a much higher profile. In 1995 Stefanel and Calvin Klein agreed to a joint venture to manufacture and distribute the popular CK bridge lines. The agreement further called for opening CK stores across Europe and in the Middle East, for Stefanel to acquire a production facility exclusively for CK apparel, and the formation of two new companies—K Service SpA (wholly-owned by Stefanel for manufacturing) and SKY Company SpA (73-percent owned by Stefanel, the remainder to Klein, for distribution). The glow from the Klein deal dimmed quickly, however, when Stefanel experienced its first ever losses in 1995 and 1996, due mostly to restructuring its worldwide operations. Then the following year top officials of the firm were under investigation by Italian authorities for fiscal fraud and falsifying documents, though charges had yet to filed.

Stefanel and Klein opened their first CK store in Milan in early 1997, and the former finally reaped the benefits of its reorganization and debt reduction of the last two years. For 1997 Stefanel was back in the black and the Klein venture was beginning to pay off. Stefanel then turned its attention to expansion outside Europe, namely in the U.S. where operated just a few stores. Guiseppe Stefanel has carried on the tradition his father began almost 50 years ago, and their firm is one of the few remaining independent fashion empires in Italy and beyond.

—Kevin Almond; updated by Owen James

STEFFE, Cynthia

American fashion designer

Born: Sioux City, Iowa, 30 June 1957. **Education:** Parsons School of Design, 1978–81. **Family:** Married Richard W. "Rick" Roberts, 1984. **Career:** Designer for Donna Karan and Louis Dell'Olio at Anne Klein & Company, 1981; designed women's tailored separates for Spitalnick & Company, 1983–88; consultant for Crystal Brands, 1988–89; chaired Cynthia Steffe Inc., 1989–2000; joint designing of cosmetics line, 1995; produced luxury coats for the Tepper Collection, 1995; created secondary line, 1997; sold firm to Leslie Fay, 2000. **Awards:** Student Designer of the Year, 1981; Donna Karan Gold Thimble, 1981; one of *People* magazine's "50 Most Beautiful People in the World," 1991. **Address:** 550 Seventh Avenue, Floor 21, New York, NY 10018–3203 U.S.A.

Cynthia Steffe, fall 2001 collection. © Fashion Syndicate Press.

PUBLICATIONS

On STEFFE:

Books

Hodgman, Ann, *A Day in the Life of a Fashion Designer,* Mahwah, New Jersey, 1988.
Stegemeyer, Anne, *Who's Who in Fashion, Third Edition,* New York, 1996.
The Complete Marquis Who's Who, 2001.

Articles

"Steffe Leaves Spitalnick," in *WWD,* 18 January 1988.
"Steffe Joins Crystal Brands," in *WWD,* 16 March 1988.

Rosenblum, Anne, "Steffe Line Poised for Fall Debut," in *WWD,* 10 November 1988.
———, "Cynthia Steffe: A Class Act," in *WWD,* 1 February 1989.
"Cynthia Steffe Premieres," in *WWD,* 29 March 1989.
Schiro, Anne-Marie, "Cynthia Steffe," in the *New York Times,* 28 August 1989.
Delaney, Joan, "Designing Woman," in *Executive Female,* September-October 1990.
"The 50 Most Beautiful People in the World," in *People,* July 1991.
Friedman, Arthur, "Tepper Gets Coat License for Steffe," in *WWD,* 11 April 1995.
"Steffe Makes Up," in *WWD,* 25 October 1995.
White, Constance C.R., "Sleek Powerbroker Suits and Cool Characters," in the *New York Times,* 1 November 1995.
Ozzard, Janet, "Cynthia's Steady Course," in *WWD,* 20 December 1995.
"Savvy Take on Rocky Retail Era..." in *Crain's New York Business,* 4 March 1996.
Ozzard, Janet, "Cynthia Steffe Stretches Out," in *WWD,* 12 February 1997.
Bounds, Wendy, "Behind the Scenes at a Designer's First Show," in the *Wall Street Journal,* 25 April 1997.
Avery, Nicole Volta, "Cynthia Steffe Showcases Spirited Designs for Hudsons," in the *Detroit News,* 23 March 1998.
"Leslie Fay to Buy Cynthia Steffe Inc.," in *WWD,* 20 April 2000.
Homan, Becky, "Snake Charmers," in the *St. Louis Post-Dispatch,* 20 May 2000.
Mayer, Robin Long, "Tradition Honored," in *Country Living,* May 2001.
"In Cynthia's Closet," in *Ladies Home Journal,* August 2001.
"Cynthia Steffe," available online at Fashion Dex, www.fashiondex.com, 2001.
Davis, Boyd, "New Generation: Cynthia Steffe," online at Fashion Windows, www.fashionwindows.com, 10 November 2001.
Davis, Mari, "Cynthia Steffe: A View from Backstage," online at Fashion Windows, www.fashionwindows.com, 10 November 2001.

* * *

Cynthia Steffe, developer of Cynthia Steffe Collection, Cynthia's Closet, and Francess & Rita, used market savvy to ease her way into a highly competitive field. Born in Sioux City, Iowa, in 1958, she grew up in Boyden. In her teens, she emulated her mother's flair for clothes by sketching and sewing her own outfits. After Steffe chose fashion for her career, she entered New York City's Parsons School of Design at age 19. Before graduating in 1981, she snagged both the Student Designer of the Year and the Donna Karan Gold Thimble awards.

Immediately signed with Donna Karan, Steffe worked for Karan and Louis Dell'Olio at Anne Klein & Company. She began designing women's tailored separates for Spitalnick & Company in 1983 and left in 1988 to consult for Crystal Brands, maker of clothing for women, men, and youth under the Izod, Lacoste, and Ship 'n' Shore labels and Monet costume jewelry. A gift for design earned her a place among *People Weekly*'s "50 Most Beautiful People in the World." *Women's Wear Daily* classed her as one of the "New Majors," a slate of tyros including Jennifer George, Rebecca Moses, Charlotte Neuville, and Carmelo Pomodoro, the five new names fashion pundits predicted would take the place of older, fading fashion houses.

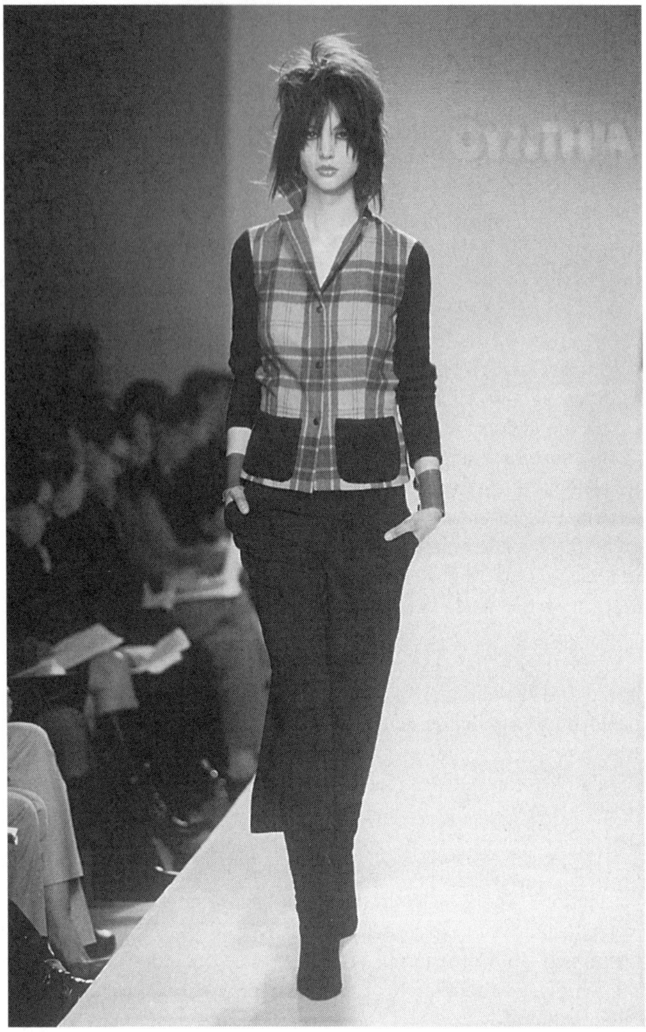

Cynthia Steffe, fall 2001 collection. © Fashion Syndicate Press.

Steffe realized the only way to impact the market with original, unedited designs was to market them herself. In partnership with Ira J. Hechler & Associates, in March 1989 she launched Cynthia Steffe Inc., a 2,500-square-foot showroom at 575 Seventh Avenue to wholesale her creations in the $100 to $400 range. She involved herself at all levels, from design and administration to production and sales. Assisting her was company president Richard W. "Rick" Roberts, formerly president of Alexander Julian Womenswear for two years and director of the Calvin Klein Studio Division for two years. She had met Roberts in her sophomore year at Parsons and married him in 1984.

Chairing her own company, Steffe aimed for the best in fabric, detail, and construction to give buyers more value for their fashion investment. In anticipation of demand for luxury items and novelty fur pieces, she showed a first 50-item collection featuring blanket coats, tunics, kimono jackets, cigarette pants, bolero jackets, and faux furs in fundamental gray, navy, and black. To punch up her line, she stressed interesting buttons, trims, and shawls. Anne Rosenblum of *Women's Wear Daily* quoted Steffe's aim: "I am designing for a woman with a high taste level, who wants quality at a price she can afford."

Steffe's interest in a less monied class of shopper caught the fashion world's attention. Joan Delaney, writing for *Executive Female,* summarized Steffe's appeal: "By skirting fashion shows, this material girl delivers designer duds for fewer dollars." Steffe pushed herself to top previous years' successes with something wearable and eye-catching, including affordable crêpes, mohair boucles, wool jacquards, and suedes. Her niche was the bridge between the mass merchandising of Evan Picone and Jones of New York and exclusive originals by Calvin Klein. In 1990 Spiegel featured her contemporary designs in its 125th anniversary catalogue.

A year later, when Steffe was named one of the world's most attractive people, she told *People,* "I want a youthful personality to my clothes." CBS fashion analyst Pat George confirmed Steffe's choice of direction and ventured a prediction: "Her clothes are right on and her colors are original. She will be another Liz Claiborne or Adrienne Vittadini." In 1995 Steffe began cautiously branching out in a joint effort with Prescriptives on the introduction of Understatements '96, a cosmetics line, and made her first venture into licensing with Jeff Tepper's collection, for which she produced luxury coats in fur-trimmed alpaca velvet, angora flannel, shearling, leather, and shimmer sateen for sale at Saks Fifth Avenue and Neiman Marcus. Accounting for around two-thirds of her wholesale business in 1995 was the office-minded Francess & Rita line. Steffe told *Women's Wear Daily,* "We went after the market of women who wanted something to wear to work but wanted a little more style."

At her headquarters, Steffe acknowledged the uphill struggle in a cooling department store market that saw the demise of Ames, B. Altman, and Bloomingdale's and the sale of Saks. Fewer department stores meant stiffer competition for those that survived the shakeout; in retrospect, she commented that the 1980s offered a more forgiving fiscal climate: "Today, you can't afford to make a mistake. You really have to know your customer."As company pilot in chancy waters, she hired Susan Portnoy from Nicole Miller as public relations manager and initiated an aggressive advertising and promotion campaign.

After steadily advancing in sales to about $22 million in wholesale goods annually, in 1997 Steffe's company added a secondary line with the security of the Frances & Rita line, the office-friendly sportswear label, anchoring the firm. To Janet Ozzard of *Women's Wear Daily,* president Rick Roberts exulted, "The company is seven-and-a-half years old, and it's been consistently profitable for the last five."

Boldly thrusting into new territory, Steffe's designs reached out to women who buy individual wardrobe items rather than whole costumes. She offered narrow coats, slim shirtdresses and skirts, boot-leg pants, and double-breasted jackets over man-tailored trousers. To put more texture into the line, she featured fake fur, leather, stretch cotton and napa satin, wool pinstripe, burnout velvet, Lycra spandex twill, wool pebble crêpe, Lurex, and rayon or chenille yarns. She held down prices by buying from the second tier of expensive mill collections. In late April 2000, Steffe sold her firm to Leslie Fay Company, Inc.

At the beginning of a new millennium, Steffe was still pursuing texture by adding reptile prints and mottled touches to her designs as well as softly draped materials to her home. Targeting twentysomethings, she captured the Jackie look of the 1960s with matching rainwear as well as retro riding gear, asymmetrical hemlines, belts, leggings, and the indispensible purse to hold makeup and cell phone. In May 2001 *Country Living* featured the mountain getaway of Steffe and her husband. Departing their New York City apartment, they retreated to Calicoon, New York, in the Catskill Mountains, where she coated walls and ceiling in creamy and ivory fabric lengths to reflect natural light.

In August 2001 *Ladies Home Journal* summarized the designer's unique sense of workable style. The choice of a monochromatic base enabled her to simplify shopping, accessorizing, and moving from 14-hour days to evening. Steffe confided, "Open my closet and it's a sea of black. I work with color all the time, so I wear black because it's the perfect backdrop to drape my fabrics against when I'm designing."

—Mary Ellen Snodgrass

STEHLE, Gerd

See STRENESSE GROUP

STEWART, Stevie

See BODYMAP

STOCK, Robert

American designer

Born: The Bronx, New York, 1946. **Education:** Self-taught in design. **Family:** Married Nancy McTague, 1982; children: two. **Career:** Apprentice designer, Paul Ressler Pants, New York, circa 1966; owner/designer, Country Britches, New York, 1967–73; design assistant, Chaps by Ralph Lauren, 1973–76; designer, Country Roads by Robert Stock, from 1976; formed Robert Stock Designs, 1978; co-owner/designer, Robert Stock Designs Ltd., 1990–99; women's line introduced, 1992; children's line introduced, 1993; licenses include men's shirts and ties, from 1991, jeans, and leather goods, from 1992; licensed overcoats, hosiery, and footwear, 1994; loungewear separates licensed, 1995; cotton jackets, 1996; Robert Stock School Gear, 1999; closed Robert Stock Ltd. and signed licensing pact with Capital Mercury Apparel, 1999. **Awards:** American Fashion Critics Coty award, 1978.

Publications

On STOCK:

Articles

"Robert Stock: Quiet on the Fashion Front," in *GQ* (New York), April 1981.
"Robert Stock," in *DNR,* 12 March 1987.
"Robert Stock Forms Firm," in *DNR,* 19 June 1990.
"Robert Stock Ltd.," in *DNR,* 4 August 1993.
"Mister Coats Gets Robert Stock License," in *DNR,* 27 January 1994.
Schneider-Levy, "Stock Adds Shoes to Fashion Lineup," in *Footwear News,* 5 December 1994.
"Robert Stock Expands Pacts with Foster," in *DNR,* 6 October 1995.
Socha, Miles, "Robert Stock Limited," in *DNR,* 29 May 1996.

"U-Got-It Gets Robert Stock License for 1997," in *DNR,* 14 October 1996.
Romero, Elena, "...Robert Stock Creates Stylish Uniforms for Back-to-School," in *DNR,* 19 April 1999.
Dodd, Annmarie, "Robert Stock to Dissolve Manufacturing Company," in *DNR,* 11 October 1999.
Curan, Catherine, "Designer Patches up Menswear Label with License Deal; Robert Stock Allies with Large Company," in *Crain's New York Business,* 29 November 1999.

* * *

As a fashion designer, Robert Stock achieved a remarkably successful about-turn. His first foray into the fashion industry, after an apprenticeship with a trouser company, was to form Country Britches, a company that produced traditional sportswear—including classic slacks and polo shirts—fitting into almost any traditional department store. Stock later sold the company and went to work with Ralph Lauren, the master of timeless dressing. He aided in the design and development of Chaps, Lauren's lower-priced men's sportswear division which later became a division of Warnaco.

Country Roads by Robert Stock, a division of Creighton Industries, was the company for which Stock designed after leaving Ralph Lauren. Appropriately, this line followed the same traditional vein—sportswear to appeal to the conventional middle American male. In 1990 Stock and a partner formed Robert Stock Designs to manufacture men's knitwear. Soon after, sandwashed silk pieces were added and the company grew swiftly from a firm worth $10 million into one valued at $100 million.

Although it would be inaccurate to credit Stock as designer of a line consisting chiefly of plain and print sandwashed silk shirts, he should be credited for recognizing that silk, considered a luxury fabric, could be sourced and manufactured in the Far East at a cheaper price than previously thought. By adding this luxury line, Stock offered consumers value at an affordable price, referred to in the market as "perceived value." Stock expanded his offering of silk luxury to both the womenswear and boyswear markets and reintroduced the leisure suit to the menswear market. His version, however, was almost active wear; a sweat- or warm-up suit offered not in the usual nylon or Goretex, but in sandwashed silk. Such an ensemble, designed for leisure or sport and manufactured in a luxurious fabric seemed incongruous, yet clients snapped them up.

The success brought by sandwashed silk apparel enabled Stock to enter into a slew of licensing agreements in other areas, including tailored clothing, furnishings, neckwear, jeans, knitwear, hosiery, footwear, loungewear, and the outerwear market, including both casual and dress outerwear. Stock took another tack in 1999, when he began designing school uniforms. Commenting on the new label, Robert Stock School Gear, to *Daily News Record* (19 April 1999) the designer said, "The collection is value driven yet it also offers tremendous quality as well as a degree of style." The range included both short- and long-sleeved button-down shirts, polo shirts, sweaters, and pants made from twill, flannel, and gabardine pants and were sold to high-end department stores.

By the end of the 20th century, Stock had decided to close his manufacturing firm, Robert Stock Ltd., in favor of his burgeoning licensing business. A subsequent licensing pact with Capital Mercury Apparel had Stock designing men's sportswear, shirts, and swim gear for a fall 2000 launch. Stock told Annmarie Dodd of *DNR* (11 October 1999), "In today's marketplace teaming up with a manufacturer like Capital Mercury can only help to elevate the brand and allow me to concentrate on design."

As an erstwhile traditional designer, Robert Stock has pushed the limits of traditional men's sportswear by changing the face of the fabrics used. Once considered the "King of Silk," an evolving market forced him to segue into less appreciated forms of fashion. Though he has referred to himself as the "Ford or Chevrolet of designers," this is an understatement of his worth—unless, of course, he meant Corvettes or Lincoln Navigators.

—Lisa Marsh; updated by Owen James

STOREY, Helen

British designer

Born: 16 August 1959 in Rome, Italy. **Education:** Graduated with degree in fashion design, Kingston Polytechnic, 1981. **Family:** Married Ron Brinkers; children: one son. **Career:** Apprenticed to Valentino and Lancetti, Milan, 1981–83; launched own label, Amalgamated Talent, 1984; partner/designer, Boyd & Storey, London, 1987–89; first catwalk show, London, 1990; designer, Jigsaw stores, 1990; introduced menswear collection, 1991; designer, Knickerbox, and Empire stores, 1991; introduced 2nd Life line of recycled clothes, 1992; opened store in King's Road, London, 1992; Edith Sitwell-inspired collection, London, 1995; began selling stakes in her stores and went into bankruptcy, 1995; authored book on fashion business, 1997; launched housewares and party favors collection, 1999. **Awards:** With Karen Boyd, British Apparel Export award, 1989; Most Innovative Designer of the Year award, 1990; Young Designer of the Year award, 1990; with sister Kate Storey, Wellcome Trust Sci-Art Initiative, cash award, 1997. **Address:** Coates & Storey Ltd., 57 Kings Road, London SW3 4ND, England.

Publications

By STOREY:

Books

Fighting Fashion, London, 1997.

Articles

"Party Like It's 1999," in *Los Angeles Magazine,* December 1999.
"It's Not the Art but the Taking Part," in the *Times Educational Supplement* (London), 5 May 2000.
"My Best Teacher: Helen Storey," with Hilary Wilcein, in the *Times Educational Supplement* (London), 20 July 2001.

On STOREY:

Articles

Wheeler, Karen, "Five Survivors," in *DR: The Fashion Business* (London), 26 August 1989.
Wolford, Lisa, and Mark Borthwick, "West End's Storey," in *Interview,* December 1989.

Hume, Marion, "Shock Tactics," in the *Sunday Times* (London), 17 December 1989.
Armstrong, Lisa, "Success Storey," in *Vogue* (London), May 1990.
Curtis, Anne-Marie, "Love Storey," in *Sky* (London), June 1990.
Bull, Sandra, "Multi Storey," in *Fashion Weekly* (London), 13 September 1990.
Rowe, Gillian, "Storey Lines," in *Shop in Town,* 14 March 1991.
"Great Expectations," in *WWD,* 13 June 1991.
Chunn, Louise, "Bettering by Design," in *The Guardian* (London), 20 May 1992.
Mulvagh, Jane, "From the Rag Trade to Riches," in the *European* (London), 3–6 December 1992.
Dutt, Lalla, "True Storey," in *City Limits* (London), 21–28 January 1993.
Underhill, William, "The Roaring 1990s: America's Resurgent Economy," in *Newsweek,* 22 February 1993.
Schiro, Anne-Marie, "Small Houses: Holding in the 1980s, or Back to the 1970s," in the *New York Times,* 23 February 1993.
Armstrong, Lisa. "One Girl's Storey," in *Vogue* (London), November 1994.
Spindler, Amy M., "From Young Designers, Familiar Echoes," in the *New York Times,* 14 March 1995.
Brampton, Sally, "From Catwalk to Dole Queue (Interview of British Fashion Designer Helen Storey)," in *The Guardian,* 14 June 1995.
"Fighting Fashion," [book review] in the *Economist,* 15 March 1997.
Riddell, Mary, "Interview: Helen Storey," in the *New Statesman* (London), 12 September 1997.

* * *

Helen Storey is one of Britain's most innovative and controversial designers. She has been described as "the next great British hope," and rationalized her success in characteristic style: "One of the reasons that I am here and a lot of my contemporaries aren't is because I sit on the knife edge between good and bad taste, fashion and theatre, business and imagination."

Trained at Kingston Polytechnic in Surrey, Storey was encouraged by one of her tutors, Richard Nott (of Workers for Freedom) to apply to Valentino, as her work seemed out of step with the fashion course at Kingston. Storey says of her work as a student at the time, "I was designing wildly theatrical outfits—I doubt if they could even be made up, let alone washed. I tried to think Marks & Spencer but it always came out wrong." She stayed with Valentino's design studio for two years and was much struck by the contrast between the experience in Rome and her student training: "Valentino designed 65 collections a year and was treated like a lord. I felt sick that this kind of sky's-the-limit attitude could never happen at home."

When she returned to London, at the high point of international interest in young British designers in 1984, Storey became one of a group to join forces under the umbrella title of Amalgamated Talent, where she showed six highly successful collections. In 1987 Storey opened Boyd & Storey in West Soho, London, together with fellow designers Karen Boyd and Caroline Coates. Two years later, Helen Storey and Karen Boyd (who were to go their separate ways within the year) won the British Apparel Export award in recognition of their outstanding export achievements. By May 1990 the Helen Storey for Jigsaw collection was available in Jigsaw stores throughout Great Britain, and in October of the same year Storey won the Most Innovative Designer of the Year award with her first solo catwalk show during London Fashion Week.

In 1991 Storey designed her first full menswear collection, which was launched at SEHM, Paris. The same year she was commissioned by the underwear chain Knickerbox to design a range and by Empire stores to endorse and design for their mail order catalogues. In the following year, Showroom Seven was appointed as Storey's American agent, and the fall-winter 1992 collection "Dreams and Reality" was shown in New York, London, Paris, and Düsseldorf.

Storey has been preoccupied with recycling: "Fashion is a wasteful image—full stop! So there's a limit to how much you can fly the eco-flag. As a fashion company my problem is how do I keep selling and respond to environmentalism. We must tackle the problem slowly." In June 1992, Storey introduced a range of recycled clothes under the name 2nd Life, and in the same year she began another significant foray into eco-fashion when she became the first British designer to launch and use the most recent Courtauld's fiber Tencel, the so-called cashmere of denim, for her October 1992 collection. Tencel is the first new synthetic textile fiber in 30 years, and Storey described it as having extraordinary possibilities. "It can be as floppy as silk but has all the robust characteristics of denim." In 1993 Storey continued her innovatory fiber association and marketing with the use of Tencel, Tactel (ICI), and Acetate Novaceta Ltd.

Storey believes "the fashion industry is really a very funny place for me to be," and attempts to explain her work in the following terms: "Basically, people want to see a bit of the impossible in the clothes because it confirms their own sense of reality. I am an instinctual designer; I see that I am attached to the energy of creation, but it also makes me want to give up sometimes because of the amount of unnecessary items we churn out for the sake of another season."

The innovative and controversial Storey did a show in London in 1995. Inspired by English eccentric Edith Sitwell, the bohemian poet and intellectual of the 1920s, Storey's collection included androgynous pinstripe suits entailing fake fur boas, as well as 1920s gowns also showing long trains of fake fur. A year or so later, the award-winning British designer spoke up about the strains of running a fashion business while supporting her husband during his fight against cancer. Selling parts of her shops here and there, Storey believes it is a lack of professionalism that forces designers to be on the move. Brand-building is probably the weakest element in the fashion industry, according to Storey, especially in Britain, where the designer got her start.

But Storey is known well beyond that of the design world. Along with her sister Kate, they won an award from the Wellcome Trust's Sci-Art Initiative, an organization that supports cross-fertilization between art and science. Storey's focus in this cause was to ensure that her designs were an accurate representation of the scientific process. From studying the first 1,000 hours of human life to studying the division of cells under a microscope, Storey underwent a whole new aspect of education most designers never experience in their lifetime. The idea of the cross-fertilization between art and science is that those who are passionate about fashion will also pick up lessons in human biology. Storey describes it as "New Fashion."

Although Storey said she did not miss straying away from the fashion world to accommodate for and learn more about science, she did return to what she knew best in 1999. It was not clothing but instead party essentials she introduced, including Arts & Letters designed to enhance invitations, the Empty Vase for any array of flowers, and Illume for candles. Due to the fact that it was presented before the millennium, the products were highly successful.

—Doreen Ehrlich; updated by Diana Idzelis

STRAUSS, Levi

See LEVI-STRAUSS & CO.

STRENESSE GROUP

German fashion house

Founded: from family clothing company by Gerd Strehle in Nordlingen, 1968. **Company History:** Joined by wife Gabriele Strehle as designer, from 1973; launched Strehle Collection, 1976; Strenesse Blue, sportswear line debuted, 1993; opened flagship store, Dusseldorf, 1995; launched ready-to-wear in the U.S. at Bergdorf Goodman, 1995; introduced footwear, 1996; took footwear line to U.S., 1997; launched first fragrance *Strenesse Gabriele Strehle,* 2001; opened New York showroom, 2001; introduced first menswear line, 2002; opened Tokyo flagship, 2002. **Awards:** European Fashion Diamond for Marketing Excellence (to Gerd Strehle), 1999. **Company Address:** Eichendorffplatz 3, 8860 Nordlingen, Germany. **Company Website:** www.strenesse.com.

Strenesse Group, fall/winter 2001–02 collection. © AP/Wide World Photos.

Publications

On STRENESSE:

Articles

Drier, Melissa, "Strenesse: Making Marks with Minimalism," in *WWD,* 2 February 1993.

"Skirmishing in Asia," in *WWD,* 29 November 1994.

"Shopping Europe," in *Footwear News,* 30 September 1996.

LoRusso, Maryann, "Feisty Fern...Fern Dembicer Sets Out...to Make German Brand Strenesse an American Staple," in *Footwear News,* 26 May 1997.

Socha, Miles, "Strenesse Takes Aim at U.S.," in *WWD,* 19 November 1997.

"Milan Going for Glamour," in *WWD,* 5 March 1998.

Conti, Samantha, et al., "Connolly, Strenesse Eyed for HDP's Expansion List," in *WWD,* 30 November 1998.

"Sense and Sensibility," in *WWD,* 4 March 1999.

Socha, Miles, "The New Gold Rush," in *WWD,* 21 April 1999.

Ilari, Alessandra, "The Main Event...Accessories are Stealing the Spotlight from the Clothes," in *WWD,* 1 May 2000.

"New Strenesse USA CEO," in *WWD,* 21 July 2000.

"Study in Contrasts: Designer Gabriele Strehle," in *WWD,* 4 October 2000.

Drier, Melissa, "A Classic Turn for German RTW," in *WWD,* 13 February 2001.

Wilson, Eric, "Strenesse Subsidiary Maps U.S. Growth Plan," in *WWD,* 28 February 2001.

Drier, Melissa, "Strenesse to Launch First Fragrance," in *WWD,* 1 June 2001.

Wilson, Eric, "Strenesse, Strehle Open in U.S.," in *WWD,* 3 August 2001.

* * *

The Strenesse group designs clothes aim to show the personality of a woman in a way that suits her own style. It is for this reason that the company promotes its label as a style label rather than a designer label, so often only a platform for the creative personality of the designer. A group collection like Strenesse is concerned with providing the modern woman with a versatile, stylish wardrobe created by a united team of fashion experts.

The company was originally established in 1948 and produced a wearable but unadventurous line of coats and suits. Gerd Strehle took over the company from his parents in 1968 and, with the help of freelance designers and stylists, established it as a popular fashion label. In 1973 a design graduate from the fashion school in Munich became responsible for the collection. Gabriele Strehle eventually married into the company and became its creative director.

Gabriele Strehle established a stylish collection—a mixture of luxury materials, quality workmanship, and a purist, minimalistic look intended to emphasize the aura and personality of its wearer. Strenesse collections became timeless and classic, with a design principle that each new piece could be combined and worn with the previous season's look, to create a harmonious continuity of style. It also emphasizes Gabriele's ecological and cultural sense in for a definitive style that will not date. The clothes themselves are simple and luxurious, sensuous knits, hacking jackets, tailored skirt and trouser suits, and roomy, comfortable coats. Fabrics include tweeds, leathers, chiffons, pinstripe flannels, and cashmeres.

Strenesse Group, fall/winter 2001–02 collection. © AP/Wide World Photos.

Photographers such as Jacques Olivar and Ellen Von Unwerth have been responsible for creating many of the visuals that represent the Strenesse look in both publicity and advertising. Classic tailored, mannish looks and elongated, sexy basque dresses are generally photographed in sharp black and white. Classic movie star references abound: Sophia Loren on a Vespa in Rome, Marlene Dietrich languidly smoking in a darkened railway station, or Ingrid Bergman in a beret from *Arch of Triumph.* These looks suggest to the customer the many different roles she can adopt with her versatile Strenesse wardrobe.

The ideal Strenesse woman is both erotic and confident in her pared-down chic. She does not use fashion as a means to flaunt her success, wealth or status. Like Gabriele Strehle, she believes in the phrase "Less is more." In a world often taut with recession and environmental constraints, this philosophy has a creative longevity. Fashion gimmicks and short-lived trends are rejected in favor of a forward-looking fashion style that adapts to, but does not radically alter, the personality of its wearer.

Teamwork is very important at Strenesse. Strehle sees her role as catalyst for her design team's many ideas. The company views group work as being the chief motivation for creativity and, ultimately, productivity. Teamwork is a unity of interpersonal relations and common interests with one aim in mind, that being the extended development of new ideas for the evolution of the Strenesse look. Strenesse began in the 1990s to introduce accessory products—belts, shoes, and handbags—to encourage customers to adopt the Strenesse lifestyle. In autumn 1993 the company introduced Strenesse Blue, a more casual holiday and leisurewear collection. By 1995 the firm had approximately 900 worldwide clients, among them new customers in the U.S. after the exporting its ready-to-wear line to Bergdorf Goodman in New York. Acceptance from Americans only further confirmed Strenesse's established popularity and influence on international style.

In the late 1990s while other German design firms had less than stalwart sales, Strenesse continued to sell well both in Germany and abroad. Capitalizing on its name and brand awareness, Strenesse introduced a new footwear line in Germany, Europe, and Asia, then launched the collection in the U.S. in 1997, with the help of consultant Fern Dembicer, president of the Fern Monica marketing company. The Strenesse collection was made up of more than three dozen comfortable yet stylish shoes, footwear Dembicer told *Footwear News* (September 1997) would "work with a whole wardrobe of stylish looks, from suits to pants to long and short skirts."

"We say Strenesse is an intelligent collection," Gabriele Strehle told Miles Socha of *Women's Wear Daily* back in 1997. "Our philosophy is that we are a modern luxury brand. Modern means with a much more realistic approach to the market." Apparently, its ever-increasing clientèle agreed; for luxury retailers in the U.S., Strenesse represented what Saks Fifth Avenue called "the gold range" between the highest priced designer collections and bridge lines. At both Saks and Bergdorf Goodman, Strenesse had been achieving record sales since debuting in the U.S., and the Strehles continued to roll out new products from accessories and a new jeans line, to a fragrance launch and Gabriele's first menswear collection. To help with the growing demand, the firm created a new division, Strenesse USA, and hired Deb Maxwell (formerly of Gruppo GFT) as chief executive officer.

In 1998 *Women's Wear Daily* had praised the enduring elegance of Strenesse, stating, "Classics have always been the backbone of Strenesse, and it's been a formula that has worked for this German powerhouse." The message was the same in February 2001, when Elke Giese, director of the German Fashion Institute, said of Strenesse's newest collection to *WWD*'s Melissa Drier, "It has a stunning clarity." Drier concurred, stating, "The collection harked back to Strenesse's roots with the kind of streamlined tailoring and rich fabrics with which the label originally made its mark." Such high praise wasn't lost on Europe's luxury conglomerates, as both Gruppo GFT and LVMH had expressed an interest in acquiring the German firm. The Strehles, however, had yet to find the right combination of funds and creative control, and loathed to have Strenesse lose its most valuable asset—excellence in both design and quality.

—Kevin Almond; updated by Nelly Rhodes

STUART, Jill

American fashion designer

Born: Daughter of Lynn Stuart, New York City designer-merchandiser. **Education:** Dalton School; the Rhode Island School of Design.

Jill Stuart, fall 2001 collection. © AP/Wide World Photos.

Family: Married Ron Curtis, 1986. **Career:** Opened a belt and handbag boutique on New York's Upper East Side, 1988; worked out of a design studio/showroom on East 68th Street, 1990; introduced Skinclothes, 1993; designs featured in the movie *Clueless,* 1995; thrived in the Japanese market with stores in Tokyo and Osaka, mid-1990s; showed the Jill Stuart International Collection at her shop at 100 Greene Street in SoHo, 1998; opened third Japan store in Kobe, 1998; signed several licensing deals and launched jeans collection, 2000; new lingerie line, 2001. **Exhibitions:** Debuted at the Plaza Hotel, New York, 1990. **Address:** 550 Seventh Avenue, Fifth Floor, New York, NY 10018 U.S.A.

Publications

On STUART:

Articles

Brill, Eileen B., "Designers Support U.S. Production," in *WWD,* 25 October 1985.
Botton, Sari, "Jill Stuart Opens Shop," in *WWD,* 12 October 1988.
Newman, Jill, "Stuart Takes New Direction," in *WWD,* 4 May 1990.
———, "Showroom Seven to Represent Leather Line by Jill Stuart," in *WWD,* 10 May 1991.
Gaut, Halle, "Jill Stuart to Unveil Lower-Priced Jill Line," in *WWD,* 31 July 1992.
"Jill Stuart Opens Skinclothes Lines," in *WWD,* 24 November 1993.
Schiro, Anne-Marie, "Leather, Shapely and Pretty," in the *New York Times,* 28 February 1995.
White, Constance C.R., "Two Soothing Visions of Clothes for the 1990s," in the *New York Times,* 1 April 1996.
"Jill Stuart Goes In-Store," in *WWD,* 12 June 1996.
Socha, Miles, "Whipping Up an American Frenzy: Jill Stuart Opens Store in Japan," in *WWD,* 23 March 1998.
"Joie de Mode," in *WWD,* 6 April 1998.
"New York Rolls On," in *WWD,* 17 September 1998.
Schiro, Anne-Marie, "Cutting Loose with Colors and Grace," in the *New York Times,* 17 September 1998.
"Girl Talk...Anna Sui, Victor Alfaro and Jill Stuart are Taking a Sweeter Approach," in *WWD,* 17 September 1999.
Wilson, Eric, "Jill Stuart's Licensing Streak," in *WWD,* 28 September 2000.
"Jill Stuart Launches Jeans Line," in *WWD,* 30 November 2000.
Monget, Karyn, "Jill Stuart Gets Intimate," in *WWD,* 30 April 2001.
"In Brief," in *WWD,* 24 May 2001.
"Party On," in *WWD,* 18 July 2001.
Czarra, Kerstin, "White Out? The Much-Maligned White Pump is Waging a Fashion Comeback (Jill Stuart Brings Back Trend)," in *Footwear News,* 30 July 2001.
Davis, Boyd, "Jill Stuart Spring 2002," available online at Fashion Windows, www.fashionwindows.com, 11 November 2001.
"Jill Stuart," available online at Fashion Windows, www.fashionwindows.com, 11 November 2001.
"Jill Stuart Runway Fashion Photos," available online at Fashion Showroom, www.fashionshowroom.com, 11 November 2001.
Johnson, Phillip D., "(Le) Smokin'!" online at Lucire, www.lucire.com, 11 November 2001.
Kim, Eri, "Jill Stuart's Sensual Vision," online at Fashion Windows, www.fashionwindows.com, 11 November 2001.
Knight, Molly, "Jill Stuart's Black Out," online at Fashion Windows, www.fashionwindows.com, 11 November 2001.

* * *

Since her introduction of trendy handbags, belts, and leather kilts, the star attraction among her girlish sportswear and dresses in 1993, Jill Stuart has maintained a steady business in the U.S. and a robust demand for her goods in Europe and Asia. She received her first nudge into fashion design in childhood from observing her parents, makers of tailored clothing for Mister Pants in Manhattan's Garment District. Her mother, Lynn Stuart, earned recognition by creating costumes for Lucille Ball and Sheila MacRea. To fashion writer Eric Wilson, Stuart explained, "I was born into this business. It's in my blood and my genes. I live for it and I'm very passionate about it. As a child, I remember hearing about the business at the dinner table every night, from the designers of the fabric to the collection to the ad campaign and the contractors." By age 15, she was selling her first line of bags and belts to Bloomingdale's.

Educated at the Dalton School and the Rhode Island School of Design, in 1986 Stuart asserted her creative bent by marrying a fellow artist, Ron Curtis, producer of an off-Broadway play. In 1988 she

Jill Stuart, fall 2001 collection. © AP/Wide World Photos.

opened her first boutique, a 400-square-foot shop on New York's Upper East Side, at 22 East 65th Street, between Madison and Fifth Avenues. From one-on-one interaction with customers, she got to know shoppers and their needs. Interviewer Eileen Brill reported the designer's motivation to succeed: "I've always believed in my designs. I'm pretty aggressive and pretty persuasive and I won't stop once I've started on something."

Stuart's modest beginnings prefaced a rapid rise in name and style recognition. By 1990 her low-priced line of belts, evening bags, stoles, and fur accessories quickly found choice spots at Neiman Marcus and in Bergdorf Goodman stores and catalogues. Working out of a design studio/showroom on East 68th Street, she gave a formal exhibition at New York City's Plaza Hotel and distributed her fashions through Showroom Seven on 37th Street. She demonstrated pride in American goods by lauding U.S. crafting, which she correctly envisioned would impact the rest of the world's shoppers.

Stuart made a splash in the fashion world in fall 1993 with Skinclothes, a flirty line of leather slip-dresses, jeans, shirts, jackets, and kilts with matching shirts distributed by Annett B, Barneys, New Signatures, and Macy's East. *Women's Wear Daily* quoted the excitement of Benny Lin, Macy's East fashion director: "It's great fashion at great value. We've always done well with Jill's accessories, so it's a great tie-in.... We've wanted her to do sportswear for some time."

As Stuart's company CEO, husband Curtis estimated sales of her label had reached $100 million in 1993, one quarter of which was derived from Europe. The showcasing of Jill Stuart outfits on star Alicia Silverstone in the Paramount movie *Clueless* (1995) enhanced the first nationwide spurt of interest in Stuart designs. By 1996 Stuart had introduced in-store goods at Bloomingdale's on the East and West Coasts.

When the American clothing market fizzled in mid-1990s, Stuart had begun looking to Pacific Rim outlets for her sensual, bouncy fashions. To Eric Wilson with *Women's Wear Daily,* Curtis remarked confidently, "We've always thought of Jill Stuart as a global brand." For department store shoppers, she introduced more goods priced under $100. Curtis reported there were 70 Jill Stuart in-store shops in Japan and announced plans for several dozen more over the next few years. Already successful at flagship locations in Osaka and Tokyo, her outlets carried a variety of goods, from footwear to handbags.

In fall 1998 *Women's Wear Daily* characterized the Jill Stuart look as cute and sugary "girly-wear." Departing Cinderella fantasies, Stuart developed a frontier look with burlap and showed open-backed smock dresses, cropped pants, and full skirts teamed with peasant blouses and chiffon aprons. She acquired a 5,000-square-foot store in SoHo at 100 Greene Street, where she could display the entire Jill Stuart International Collection, produced by Sanei International of Hong Kong. For the gala premiere, she crafted a luxurious, mohair- and cashmere-rich collection intended to boost U.S. sales. Her models strutted in wide pants, pleated skirts, thick knits, chinchilla coats, and off-the-shoulder dresses embroidered with blossoms. For evening, she coordinated cashmere skirts with embroidered velvet bodices.

This same era saw a boom in Stuart labels in Japan, where young buyers snapped up items displaying the designer's signature cuteness. She told *Women's Wear Daily,* "Their enthusiasm is amazing. It's really a high to be there; they love to shop, the Japanese, and when they catch on..." A reader poll conducted by *Ryuko-Tushin,* a Japanese fashion magazine, placed her in the top spot shared with Vivienne Woodward for favorite international designer. A third Stuart flagship opened in Kobe in 1998.

The year 2000 was Stuart's venture into licensing deals in Japan, where Itochu Fashion System Company Limited managed distribution. Fans exalted her to cult status, stalked her in public, and begged autographs. Carrying her label were lingerie, eyewear, denim, and shoes. Stuart maneuvered forays into a spring eyewear collection with Eyewear Designs, two shoe lines debuting with Schwartz Benjamin, and another footwear collection with Japan's Moda Clea. Scoring with Bergdorf Goodman, Stanley Korshak, Neiman Marcus, and Fred Segal were Stuart's fur-trimmed pumps and gold mesh footwear. Kuipo of Japan introduced Jill Stuart handbags and shoes at 40 locations. The year 2000 also saw plans for further expansion into watches, fragrances, skincare products, and home furnishings.

To advertise her fashion goods, Stuart hired Ellen von Unwerth as photographer and Doug Lloyd of Lloyd Company as art director. CEO Curtis explained the need for collaboration as an outgrowth of the broadening of mid-level marketing. In Japan, eight-foot-high billboards splashed the Jill Stuart label and generated a sell-out business. To fashion analyst Miles Socha, Stuart chuckled, "They know how to do it in Japan." Keeping the Stuart name before the public were dolls sporting scaled-down outfits made by Itochu and Sanei. For full-sized wearers of the Stuart label, the designer relied on top-of-the-line fabrics and a wide variety of styles to catch shoppers' attention.

At the same time, Stuart pursued serious negotiations with Sara Lee Corporation to buy the Jill Stuart company. Curtis, who admittedly was not a business mogul, justified his wife's interest in a corporate connection as a relief from business concerns so she could concentrate on creativity. Of their team approach, he summarized to Eric Wilson, "Jill works on the collection, I work on the creative campaign. The demands on our time are backbreaking and overwhelming." Contributing to those demands were new lingerie designs distributed in fall 2001 by Host for Her.

In May, headlines blared Stuart's appearance in court to settle a lawsuit by Vicki Ross for nonpayment of $2.9 million in the licensing of Stuart designs in Japan. Ross sought finder's fee, royalties, and compensation. Undeterred by the action, two months later Stuart reprised her sugary basics at a designers party, where she served raspberry lemonade at her roof deck. Parading among guests, models displayed Stuart's signature peasant blouses, lacy-sleeved jersey frocks, and puff-sleeved tops with trousers.

For fall 2001, Stuart dressed models in Edwardian finery—ivory-and-white lace and cotton dresses with matching jackets, vests, slips, and leggings and rounded out the look with calf-high lace-up sandals. She balanced ultra romanticized femininity with hot pants and vest, lilac or green cargo pants, voluminous cotton shorts, patchwork skirts, voile suit, ethnic belts, and roomy peasant blouses. To *Women's Wear Daily,* she pegged her familiar style as pretty, feminine, and never retro: "The collection is playful and dainty. It has a certain sweetness with little touches of young and feminine detail."

Some fashion mavens were confused by Stuart's mixed signals in 2001. Rather than her usual tunnel vision on confection-rich clothes, she intermingled a variety of looks with a heavy tough of black. Phillip D. Johnson, writing for *Lucire,* found her "terribly erratic." He brightened that her fall-winter 2001 collection was more cohesive and classy—sleeveless knee-length coat and a cropped one-button jacket with nods to the pared waistlines of Prada and Yves Saint Laurent.

—Mary Ellen Snodgrass

SUI, Anna

American designer

Born: Dearborn Heights, Michigan, circa 1955. **Education:** Studied at Parsons School of Design, New York, circa 1973–75. **Career:** Stylist for photographer Steven Meisel and junior sportswear firms in New York, 1970s to 1981; sportswear designer, Simultanee, New York, 1981; also designed own line, from 1980; formed own company, New York, 1983; first runway show, 1991; added menswear line, opened in-store boutique Macy's, 1992; first freestanding store, SoHo, New York, 1992; opened shop in Hollywood, 1993–95; launched bridge line, SUI by Anna Sui, 1995; opened two boutiques in Japan, 1997; formed Anna Sui Shoes and added cosmetic line, 1997; introduced first fragrance, *Magic Window,* and opened Los Angeles store, 1999; introduced jean collection and second fragrance, *Sui Dreams,* 2000. **Exhibitions:** Part of the *Fashion in Motion* series, Victoria & Albert Museum, London, 2000. **Awards:** Perry Ellis award, 1993. **Address:** 275 West 39th Street, New York, NY 10018, U.S.A. **Websites:** www.annasui.com, www.annasuibeauty.com.

Anna Sui, fall 2001 collection: chiffon caftan over glittery corduroy pants. © AP/Wide World Photos.

Publications

On SUI:

Books

Steele, Valerie, *Women of Fashion—Twentieth Century Designers,* New York, 1991.

Stegemeyer, Anne, *Who's Who in Fashion, Third Edition,* New York, 1996.

Watson, Linda, *Vogue Twentieth-Century Fashion: 100 Years of Style by Decade and Designer,* London, 1999.

Articles

Casadio, Mariuccia, "Anna Sui: Spectacular Ingredients," in *Interview,* July 1991.

Anna Sui, fall 2001 collection: wool knit dress. © AP/Wide World Photos.

Goodman, Wendy, "Anna Sui Suits Herself," in *House & Garden,* March 1992.
Allis, Tim, "The Sui Smell of Success," in *People,* 13 July 1992.
James, Laurie, "Sui Success," in *Harper's Bazaar,* September 1992.
Shiro, Anne-Marie, "On Opposite Sides of the Cutting Edge," in the *New York Times,* 6 November 1992.
"Designer Dish," in *WWD,* 29 March 1993.
"Anna Sui," in *Current Biography,* July 1993.
Shiro, Anne-Marie, "Anna Sui Pounds Out the Beat," in the *New York Times,* 5 November 1993.
Foley, Bridget, "Anna's Time," in *W* (New York), September 1994.
Spindler, Amy M., "Saluting—or Doing In—The Suburban Muse," in the *New York Times,* 4 November 1994.
DeCaro, Frank, "Hairy Situations and Hula Baloos: Anna Sui," in *New York Newsday,* 4 November 1994.
Spindler, Amy M., "Cool Rises to Intimidating Heights," in the *New York Times,* 7 April 1995.
"New York: Anna Sui," in *WWD,* 7 April 1995.
Sitbon, Martine, "Oui, Sui!" in *Interview,* May 1999.
Spindler, Amy M., "Behind the Seams," in the *New York Times Magazine,* 14 November 1999.
LoRusso, Maryann, "The Sui and Lowdown," in *Footwear News,* 26 June 2000.

* * *

When Anna Sui started her own apparel company in 1980, her mission was to sell clothes to every rock 'n' roll store in the country. "It was right after the punk rock thing and I was so into that," said the designer, who has earned a reputation for bringing a designer's sensibility to wild-child, rocker clothes with a vintage spin.

One of three children of Chinese immigrants, Sui knew she wanted to be a clothing designer since she was a little girl growing up in Detroit in the late 1950s and 1960s. She came to New York to attend Parsons School of Design after graduating from high school in the early 1970s—an era whose music-inspired fashion scene, mix-it-up attitude, and free-spirited energy influenced Sui to a great degree. At Parsons, Sui met photographer Steven Meisel—her counterpart in styling ventures then and now.

Upon graduation from Parsons, Sui's first job was with the now defunct junior sportswear firm Bobbie Brooks, where she worked as a design assistant for about a year. After working for other firms over several years, Sui landed at Glenora, a firm the designer described as "very hip at the time." There she was able to experiment with her interest in clothing having a historical bent, made modern by mixing fresh colors and new shapes with vintage elements.

In 1980, prompted by friends and the praise she received as a stylist for Meisel's shoots for the Italian fashion magazine *Lei,* she started her own company. Greatly influenced by New York's punk scene of the 1970s, Sui's main focus was on selling her funky styles to music stores, though she continued as a stylist for Meisel. This changed around 1987, when the designer decided to "get serious about being a designer," as she recalled. She moved her line into the Annette B showroom, owned by Annette Breindel, a no-nonsense woman known for nurturing young designers. "Annette helped me enormously," said Sui. "She helped me build my dress business first because that's what she saw as a worthwhile area."

Building up her dress category is what allowed Sui to move her business out of her apartment and into a loft workspace in the garment district of New York. In 1991 Sui staged her first major fashion showing during New York Fashion Week. Her friends—supermodels Naomi Campbell, Linda Evangelista, and Christy Turlington—walked Sui's runway for free, in exchange for clothes. Influenced by the shows of Thierry Mugler and Jean-Paul Gaultier, the designer created a showing that was as much about music and theater as about clothing. She soon reigned as the queen of fashion show extravaganzas.

Sui's designs mixed styles and time periods. She explained her creative focus in an interview with Maryann LoRusso in *Footwear News* in June 2000: "My designs are a combination of nostalgia and trendiness and rock 'n' roll and flea markets. And fantasy and dress-up. I'm a product of American pop culture, and my designs really show that." She is a fanatical researcher with an insatiable desire to learn. She draws inspiration from art exhibits, films, flea markets, museums, music, and street fashion. She does not simply pluck ideas from the past or another culture, but instead pulls together themes from many sources and seeks to relate them to what people are currently experiencing. She understands that her customers want to express themselves through their clothing and not feel as if they were wearing a costume.

Sui's business continues to expand; she has over 200 boutiques worldwide, in such locations as New York, Los Angeles, Tokyo, and

Osaka, and her collections are sold in many major department and specialty stores. She formed Anna Sui Shoes in 1997, and her cosmetic and fragrance line is now a global brand. Even as her business branches out, Sui's commitment to fashion that is fun to wear hasn't diminished. Her 2001 collection included 59 feminine t-shirts decorated with printed designs, fabric flowers, lace, and sequins, and were as fashionable as they were affordable. Never interested in haute couture, Sui's work reflects her ongoing concern to "continue to make these clothes accessible to the people I want wearing them."

—Mary Ellen Gordon; updated by Janette Goff Dixon

SUNG, Alfred

Canadian designer

Born: 26 April 1948, in Shanghai, China; immigrated to Paris, 1966; immigrated to Canada, 1972. **Education:** Studied fashion design at Chambre Syndicale de la Couture Parisienne, Paris; studied one year at Parsons School of Design, New York, 1967–68. **Career:** Worked in New York City Garment District, late 1960s-early 1970s; moved to Toronto, 1972; worked on Spadina Avenue for Lindzon Ltd.; opened own boutique, Moon; partnered with Joseph and Saul Mimran to form Monaco, 1979; first women's fragrance, 1986; licensed with Etac Sales Ltd. to make and market the Alfred Sung line and Sung sportswear, 1991; Etac went bankrupt, 1994; Sung and the Mimran Group formed Alfred Sung Collections Ltd. and bought back licensing agreements from Etac, 1994–95; signed new bridge licensing agreement, 1994; Alfred Sung Collections Ltd. filed for bankruptcy, 1997; fragrances include: *Sung,* 1986; *Forever,* 1995; *Pure,* 1997; *Shi,* 2000. **Awards:** Named one of the Top Ten New Designers by Saks Fifth Avenue, 1981; HBA International Package Design award, for *Shi* fragrance, 2000.

Publications

On SUNG:

Articles

MacKay, G., "Alfred Sung: The New King of Fashion," in *Macleans,* 22 August 1983.

Bennett, J., "Designs for an Empire," in *Macleans,* 15 December 1986.

Hastings, N.J., "Sung Style: Like His Fashions," in *Chatelaine,* January 1989.

Wickens, B., "Sung Also Rises," in *Macleans,* 12 September 1994.

Socha, Miles, "Sung Returns to Apparel with Bridge License Deal," in *WWD,* 3 August 1994.

Larsen, Soren, "Sung's *Forever* Slated for Fall," in *WWD,* 31 March 1995.

"Sung Staying Pure with Latest Fragrance," in *WWD,* 27 June 1997.

"Scents and Senses," in *WWD,* 18 July 1997.

Born, Pete, "Alfred Sung's *Shi*—Balance of Nature," in *WWD,* 28 July 2000.

"The HBA Show in New York Claims Another Record," in *Cosmetics International,* 10 July 2001.

* * *

Alfred Sung is a Canadian designer with an international following. Based in Toronto, Sung created designs primarily for women, though he has on occasion produced for men. The most recognized of Sung's creations, however, are his fragrances, as well as bridal collections and accessories.

The hallmark of this Shanghai-born designer was simple, chic design created to be worn by women who needed stylish yet wearable clothes for busy lifestyles. Sung's designs evinced a classic feeling for line and detail, and his clothes were made from high-quality fabrics he himself had been known to design. He created separates, dresses, evening clothes, and jeans. His simple shapes were easy to wear and chosen by people in the public eye because they are neither trendy nor outrageous, and because they were somewhat conservative. His designs always complemented rather than overwhelmed their wearer; he worked towards an understated chic for real life, not for the runway.

Sung has long been a perfectionist who lived and breathed the world of fashion design and often eschewed other concerns of life. He has, however, faced more than his share of challenges as his career developed. A native of Shanghai, Sung was originally named Sung Wang Moon, which meant "a door in the cloud." When his family moved to the British colony of Hong Kong, his father changed his son's name to Alfred. From an early age he painted, drew, and wanted to continue study in this field. His father sent him to Paris, though not to study painting but fashion design at the Chambre Syndicale de la Couture Parisienne. Sung soon learned draping, cutting, and sewing garments by hand, obtaining a sound grounding in design and clothing construction basics.

Sung studied at the Parsons School of Design for a year, and worked on Seventh Avenue in New York City for several years, eventually moving to Toronto, Canada, where he worked on Spadina Avenue for Lindzon Ltd. Wanting to be self employed, he opened a boutique named "Moon." For three years, he was responsible for all aspects of the design process, from designing, cutting and sewing, to marketing. He developed a devoted following of young people who delighted in his well-designed clothes.

Fortuitously, in 1979 Sung formed a partnership with Joseph and Saul Mimran. The brothers took over the business end of the operation, allowing Sung to concentrate on designing. Based in Canada, the three men developed an operation that at one point included boutiques under the Alfred Sung name in Boston, Washington D.C., and Short Hills, New Jersey. In 1981 Sung was named one of the top new designers by Saks Fifth Avenue. Sung licensed luggage designs, sunglasses, and created his first fragrance in 1986. Unfortunately, the group licensed to manufacture Sung's clothing designs went bankrupt, creating a void in the production and distribution of his work. In spite of these problems, Sung continued to design and formed a new firm, Alfred Sung Collections Ltd., with the Mimran brothers and Michael Waitzer, formerly of Marks & Spencer.

All seemed bright for the latest Sung enterprise; the designer had new apparel lines, a bridal collection, and eyewear and fragrance deals. His three women's fragrances had been highly successful, especially the original and aptly named *Sung* (1986). A new scent, *Forever,* debuted in 1995, followed by *Pure* in 1997. Yet while Sung fragrances were perennial bestsellers, the designer was not so fortunate. After more lows than highs, Sung was forced once again to confront bankruptcy. His longtime backer and partners, the Mimrans, terminated his licensing agreement in 1996 and Alfred Sung Collections Ltd. had to file for bankruptcy in 1997. Three Sung stores in Toronto were closed and assets liquidated to cover more than $1 million in debt.

Despite his financial woes, Alfred Sung remained an integral part of the fashion industry. His bridal collections and accessories, licensed by the Algo Group, experienced booming sales at the end of the century, as did his stable of six fragrances. Sung's latest women's scent, *Shi,* was released in 2000 and won an HBA International Package Design award in 2001.

—Nancy House; updated by Nelly Rhodes

SYBILLA

Spanish designer

Born: Sybilla Sorondo in New York City, 1963, to Polish/Argentinian parents; moved to Madrid, age 7; moved to Paris, 1980. **Family:** Married Enrique Sirera, 1992; children: Lucas. **Career:** Apprentice cutter and seamstress, Yves Saint Laurent, 1980; returned to Madrid, 1981, making made-to-measure clothes for friends; introduced first collection, Madrid, 1983; signed production/international distribution agreement for women's ready-to-wear, 1985; presented first collections in Milan, Paris, New York, 1985; head designer, Programas Exterioras SA, Madrid, from 1985; opened Sybilla boutique, Madrid, 1987; signed with Italian company Gibo for women's ready-to-wear, 1987; began producing knitwear with Italian company ICAP, 1988; began producing women's shoes and bags with Farrutx, and carpets with Vorwerk, 1988; agreed to exclusive license in Japan with Itokin, 1989; opened new shops in Paris and Tokyo, 1991; opened 20 in-store shops in Japan; launched second line for younger people, with 20 shops, called Jocomomola, autumn/winter 1993–94; left fashion for several years, then returned with new Noche line, 1999; also designs housewares, accessories, and costumes for Blanca Li ballet company. **Exhibitions:** *50 Años de Moda,* Cuartel de Conde Duque, Madrid, 1987; *Le Monde Selon ses Créateurs,* Musée de la Mode et du Costume, Paris, 1991. **Collections:** Museo de la Moda, Barcelona; Musée de la Mode et du Costume, Paris; Fashion Institute of Technology, New York. **Awards:** Premio Balenciaga, Best Young Designer of the Year, Spain, 1987; Prix Fil d'Or, France, 1987. **Address:** Callejon de Jorge Juan 12, Madrid, Spain.

PUBLICATIONS

On SYBILLA:

Books

Benaim, Laurence, *L'Année de la Mode,* Lyons, 1988.

Steele, Valerie, *Women of Fashion: Twentieth-Century Designers,* New York, 1991.

Stegemeyer, Anne, *Who's Who in Fashion, Third Edition,* New York, 1996.

Articles

"Profile: Sybilla," in *Harper's & Queen* (London), January 1987.

Dreier, Deborah, "Designing Women," in *Art in America* (New York), May 1987.

Chua, Lawrence, "Sybilla: Designing Lady of Spain," in *WWD,* 28 September 1987.

Gordon Lennox, Sarah, "Sybilla Reigns in Spain," in *W* (London), March 1988.

Fuente, Ada de la, "El Inevitable Éxito de Una Niña Salvaje," in *Vogue* (Spain), August 1988.

Benaim, Laurence, "L'Ange Couturier," in *Vogue* (Paris), October 1988.

Cocks, Jay, "A Look on the Wild Side: Two Young Designers Liven Up a Groggy Fashion Scene," in *Time,* 16 January 1989.

"Deux Grands d'Espagne: Sybilla et Javier Valhonrat," in *Jardin des Modes* (Paris), 1–8 April 1989.

Brantley, Ben, "Spain's New Flame," in *Vanity Fair,* November 1989.

Naeto, Maite, "El Triunfo de Una Chica Precoz," in *El Pais* (Madrid), November 1989.

Armstrong, Lisa, "She's a Wizard of Aaahs," in *Harper's Bazaar,* August 1990.

Mower, Sarah, et al., "The Reign of Spain," in *Metropolitan Home* (New York), February 1991.

Oku, Emiko, "Sybilla's 77 Answers," in *Ryuko Tsushin* (Tokyo), February 1992.

Alvarado, Antonio, "Sybilla, ¡Jo, Cómo Mola!" in *El Mundo* magazine (Madrid), March 1994.

Weisman, Katherine, "Vuitton: A Quality Harvest," in *WWD,* 11 January 1996.

"Brand Newsline," in *Euromarketing,* 20 February 1998.

"Consumer Goods Euro," in *MarkIntel,* 1 April 2000.

Barker, Barbara, "Loewe Show in Madrid: Under the Big Top Sybilla: Lazarus," available online at Fashion Click, www.fashionclick.com, 5 October 2001.

"Candelabro," online at Cerebella, www.cerabella.com, 7 October 2001.

"Shopping Fashion Designers," online at Time Out, www.timeout.com, 7 October 2001.

"A Short Shopping Guide for Madrid, Spain," online at www.blackwhite.freeserve.co.uk, 7 October 2001.

*

I guess people try to dress up in a way that represents themselves. Somehow we all "paint" our skin with clothes, copying an inner image of ourselves. If you're able to get to this point, you can forget what you're wearing, you can overcome your own image.... At this moment the peace and serenity you show outside can be considered elegance.

—Sybilla

* * *

Sybilla has been widely acclaimed as the most exciting designer to have emerged from Spain since Balenciaga. She was born in 1963 in New York City, the daughter of an Argentine diplomat. Her mother was a Polish aristocrat who worked as a fashion designer under the name Countess Sybilla of Saks Fifth Avenue. When Sybilla was seven years old, her family moved to Madrid, and she considers herself thoroughly Spanish; her clothes, she has said are also very Spanish—"not olé, olé," but Spanish in the classical sense.

She served a brief apprenticeship in Paris at the couture atelier of Yves Saint Laurent, but recoiled at what she regarded as the "snobbish, cold, and professional" aspects of French fashion, saying, "Paris scares me. 'Fashion' is too serious. In Spain, you can still play." Like filmmaker Pedro Almodovar, Sybilla is a member of the post-Franco generation that launched a creative explosion in the 1980s. "We were the first generation after Franco died, and we tried to be different and creative," recalled Sybilla. With success came greater professionalism. In 1987 Italian fashion manufacturer Gibo began producing Sybilla's clothes en masse in Italy.

At the end of the 1980s Sybilla became famous for creating what she called "weird and outrageous designs"—such as sculpted dresses with wired hems. But there is also a soft feeling to many of her clothes, which derives both from the colors (tobacco, pumpkin, pale green) and from a tendency toward biomorphic shapes. "The dresses of Sybilla remind you of when you were a child and your mother would tell you fairy stories," commented Almodovar actress Rossy de Palma. "But in her dresses you live that, like a dream."

Once the celebrity *maga* (sorceress) of the Movida, Sybilla withdrew from media-centered fashion for seven years, then returned in 1999 to a quiet alley off the ready-to-wear center of Madrid. For her new Noche line from her bridal and couture shop, she produced chic but subdued elephantine pants and free-form, easy-wear dresses. Stressing red, green, violet, blue, olive, champagne, black, and terracotta, she gowned her models in feminine sweeps of silken, gauzy layers above Minorcan platform sandals and wedgies. Fashion analyst Barbara Barker of Fashion Click quoted her statement of intent to make clothing "as easy to wear as pajamas."

Selling largely in Japan with an eye to outlets throughout Spain, Sybilla kept before her the tastes and needs of Generations X and Y. The sculpted crêpes and silks for long and short ensembles expressed a womanly vulnerability beneath a quiet show of self-confidence. Her media extended from her own daywear, Louis Vuitton bags, and vases for Alessi to candles for Cerabella and film costumes for the Blanca Li ballet company. With a mounting interest in the home, she intended to encompass flatware, place settings, carpets and rugs, and lamps.

—Valerie Steele; updated by Mary Ellen Snodgrass

T

TAKADA, Kenzo

See KENZO

TAM, Vivienne

American designer

Born: Yin Yok Tam in Guangzhou, China, 1957. **Education:** Graduated from Hong Kong Polytechnic University; also studied in London. **Career:** Designer, New York, 1982; established East Wind Code, and designed first collection, 1982; designed Vivienne Tam signature collection, 1993; launched first collection under the East Wind Code label, 1994; designed controversial Mao collection, 1995; Mao collection subsequently incorporated into the permanent archives of the Andy Warhol Museum, Pittsburgh, PA, and Museum of FIT, New York; signed with Candie's to create line of spring shoes, 1996; opened New York store, 1997; signed exclusive licensing agreement with Itochu Corporation for distribution in Japan, 1998; announced plans for two freestanding stores in Japan, 1998; designed interior for the new Alero from Oldsmobile, 1999; opened Tokyo store, 2000. **Awards:** *People Weekly*'s 50 Most Beautiful People, 1995; Outstanding Alumnus, Hong Kong Polytechnic University, 1997; nominated for Council of Fashion Designers of America Perry Ellis award, 1997. **Address:** 550 Seventh Avenue, New York, NY 10018, USA.

Vivienne Tam, fall 2001 collection. © AP/Wide World Photos.

Publications

By TAM:

Books

China Chic, with Martha Huang, New York, 2000.

On TAM:

Books

Stegemeyer, Anne, *Who's Who in Fashion, Third Edition,* New York, 1996.

Articles

Gordon, Maryellen, "East Wind Code by Vivienne Tam," in *WWD,* 29 March 1993.

Eng, Victoria, "Vivienne Tam," in *Asian Magazine,* 31 March 1995.

Parnes, Frances, "Vivienne Tam's SoHo Splash," in *WWD,* 29 March 1996.

Pointer, Nandi, "A New Fashion Sensibility," in *Asian Weekly,* 13 August 1998.

Ma, Fiona, and Heather Harlan, "Fusion Fashion," in *Asian Weekly,* 25 March 1999.

Harlan, Heather, "Y2K: A Fusion of Time & Place," in *Asian Weekly,* 7 October 1999.

———, "Downtown Funky in New York City," in *Asian Weekly,* 29 September 2000.

Landler, Mark, "An Empire Built on China Chic," in the *New York Times,* 31 December 2000.

"Vivienne Tam Defines China Chic as Fashions with a Western Twist," in *Associated Press,* 6 January 2001.

* * *

By combining culture, classic style, and an offbeat flair to her fashion design, Vivienne Tam has become one of the 21st century's most unusual and successful contemporary designers. The key to her achievement is her ability to design with an eye for East meets West, an inspiration that comes from her current home, New York City, and her childhood home, Hong Kong. Bringing these cultural inspirations together in her designs, she is able to design clothing of traditional elements with a modern edge. Her collections are perceived with the idea that each person's personality will bring out different aspects from within each design.

Tam's success was preceded by a childhood of turmoil in China. In an effort to find a better life after the 1949 revolution and to rid themselves of the Communist political system, the Tam family moved to Hong Kong. At first, Tam stayed behind with her grandparents, but soon relocated to Hong Kong to be with her parents. She entered a Catholic school, where she became Vivienne Tam instead of her birth name, Yin Yok Tam. At age eight, she learned to sew by watching her parents stitch clothing. She remained with her parents until 1982, when she moved to New York. There, she hawked her designs from a duffel bag to Henri Bendel and a couple of the city's shops.

By the end of the 1980s Tam had created her own company, East Wind Code, and was designing in earnest. She gained acclaim and controversy with her early 1990s collections, including the notorious "Mao" collection where she and Chinese artist Zhang Hongtu added unusual touches to the former Chinese leader such as a bee on his nose or putting his hair in pigtails. Chinese customers were outraged; Americans found the t-shirts and jackets amusing and the height of fashion.

Tam's collections in the late 1990s were lively and awash in color, often mixing religious symbolism with Asian art, silver, red, and beautiful embroidery becoming her trademarks. With her spring 2001 collection, aptly titled the Year of the Dragon, came varied images of dragons adorning the clothes, clearly portraying her Asian inspiration. During the fashion show, "Birdsong" played as the models glided down the runway in embroidered fabrics, again in bright color combinations. Susan Redstone, writing for the online fashion site FashionWindows, applauded the "the exotic fringed mint pointelle camisole and dress" paired with "a lime silk eyelet skirt," as well as the "chartreuse metallic halter tee and turquoise sequin dragon embroidered skirt."

In an interview with Heather Harlan from *Asian Weekly* about her spring 2001 collection, Tam told her, "Many of the prints and patterns in the collection are the result of the views from my terrace [in New York City]. I love watching the light shimmering as it plays with the architectural corners and angles of buildings against a grey and bluish evening sky." The results included a Chrysler building-inspired black and white print dress, sequined skirts mimicking city lights sparkling in the darkness, and a pink metallic dress Redstone likened to "sidewalks glittering under the pink glow of street lamps." The collection also artfully mixed hard and soft, uptown and downtown, grunge and glamor, black and stunning color. Tam and several fashionistas designated blue as the new black for their spring collections.

Tam's unique talent for bringing Asian and American culture together in fashion attracts many to her East Wind Code (meaning good fortune and prosperity) shops in New York, Los Angeles, Japan, and Hong Kong. Clients who admire her elegant, unconventional style include movie stars and musicians, such as Alanis Morissette, Bjork, Britney Spears, Fiona Apple, Lauryn Hill, Madonna, Neve Campbell, Sandra Bullock, and Julia Roberts. Roberts commented to *People Weekly* in November 1998, "Tam's clothes are the perfect balance of being simple but also unique."

Vivienne Tam, fall 2001 collection. © AP/Wide World Photos.

At the New York SoHo store, with the help of a feng shui master, Tam recreated her Chinese heritage for a distinctly Asian atmosphere, though with Western touches. The Chinese character of double happiness dominates the shop, along with Fu dogs, Ming chairs, an antique carved screen, and a "red" wall. Red, as one of Tam's favorite colors, features heavily in her décor and her designs. Zany, imaginative clothing adorned with Mao, buddhas, dragons, peonies, or mums combined with shimmering metallic or black fabrics and sequins epitomize Tam's style. The prints and characters mark a spiritual journey, one that has made Tam an accomplished trendsetter for bicultural fashion design.

For those seeking insight into Tam's life and inspiration, she wrote a book with Martha Huang entitled *China Chic*. Published in 2000 by Regan Books, the red coffee-table styled hardcover is full of illustrations, photographs, and Tam's brand of East-meets-West wisdom. To promote the book, Tam took over the Luk Yu Tea House in Hong Kong, and invited both Eastern and Western luminaries. "People think this book is about my fashion, but it's not," Tam told Mark Landler of the *New York Times* in December 2000. "It's about all the things I love: furniture, gardens, spirituality, the body, health, city life." The world of designer and author Vivenne Tam, like her book, is far reaching and filled with the union of Eastern wisdom and Western synergy.

—Kimbally A. Medeiros and Sydonie Benét

TAMOTSU

Japanese fashion designer

Born: Tokyo, Japan, 29 July 1945. **Education:** Kuwazawa Design School, Tokyo; Fashion Institute of Technology, New York City, 1960s. **Career:** Fabric designer, Itida, 1960s; pattern maker, Norma Kamali, mid-1960s; sewer, Karl Lagerfeld, mid-1960s; designer for Ann Taylor, 1980s; designer, Vogue pattern company, 1987; introduced the Hana line, 1999. **Awards:** D.I.V.A. (Design Impact Vision Atlanta) Bridge Designer of the Year award, Atlanta Apparel Mart, 1997. **Address:** 214 West 39th Street, Suite 305, New York, NY 10018 U.S.A. **Website:** www.tamotsu.com.

Publications

On TAMOTSU:

Books

Stegemeyer, Anne, *Who's Who in Fashion, Third Edition,* New York, 1996.

Articles

Perman, Stacy, "Stores Set to Scout Fall," in *WWD,* 7 February 1994.

Wiltz, Teresa, "Plus No Longer a Minus," in the *Chicago Tribune,* 23 March 1997.

Foderaro, Lisa W., "Made in New York is Coming Back Into Fashion," in the *New York Times,* 13 January 1998.

Swartz, Nikki, "Big is Beautiful for Tamotsu: New York-Based Manufacturer Finds Niche in Plus-Size," in *Apparel Industry Magazine,* 1 February 1998.

"She Says Tamotsu," in *WWD,* 29 December 1998.

Donovan, Carrie, "Carry On, Carrie," in the *New York Times,* 17 January 1999.

Stein, Jeannine, "Fashion Police; Spots Where Petite or Tall is a Plus," in the *Los Angeles Times,* 25 June 1999.

"Market Basket," in *WWD,* 12 October 1999.

Bellafante, Ginia, "Fashion Meets Politics," in the *New York Times,* 29 February 2000.

Buccholz, Barbara, "Dressing Down Businesses Favor Substance Over Style," in the *Chicago Tribune,* 31 December 2000.

Kleinman, Rebecca, "Size Matters; Manufacturers and Retailers are Finally Taking Notice of Two Long-Overlooked Categories: Pluses and Petites," in *WWD,* 7 June 2001.

Barr, Vilma, "The Lucrative Plus-Size Market," in *Display & Design Ideas,* July 2001.

"Designs on Success," available online at Small Business Opportunities, www.sbomag.com, 12 November 2001.

Gold, Donna, "An Elegant Spirit: Tamotsu," and "Tamotsu: The Spirit of Understatement," online at Tamotsu, www.tamotsu.com, November 2001.

* * *

In a fashion world overwhelmed by sylphs in bikinis, wrap skirts, and capri pants, Tamotsu is the one holdout, the designer who envisions consistently polished, wearable garments for a variety of female shapes. From the pursuit of a growing niche market share in pluses, talls, and misses, his vision, which he calls "The Elegance of Understatement," is gaining acceptance in more department stores, including Saks Fifth Avenue, Bloomingdale's, Harrods, House of Fraser, Jacobson's, Marshall Fields, Neiman Marcus, and Nordstrom. Tamotsu's sales manager Ellen Mullman explained to *Women's Wear Daily* fashion reporter Rebecca Kleinman, the concept was "not to make clothes for big people, but just to make clothes." Tamotsu's timeless, U.S.-sewn designs in gentle, body-flattering fabrics have found champions in Senator Hillary Clinton, television hostess Joan Lunden, and actresses Rosie O'Donnell, Star Jones, and Camryn Manheim, who have modeled dresses and suits for the company.

A native of Japan and graduate of Tokyo's Kuwazawa Design School, Tamotsu designed for Itida, the nation's prime fabric manufacturer. After a visit to New York, he took up permanent residence in a small West Side New York apartment in the 1960s. He studied at the Fashion Institute of Technology while earning a living freelancing in the fashion industry. By day, he made patterns for designer Norma Kamali; in the evening, he sewed uniforms for Karl Lagerfeld.

Tamotsu got his start as a private-label couturier late in the 1960s while stitching up jumpsuits to order for friends. To introduce his designs, he let the clothes speak for themselves. Late in the 1970s, a retailer saw someone wearing one of Tamotsu's simple, elegant suits and placed an order. Advanced from one sewing machine, the operation rapidly needed a pattern maker, cutter, seamstresses, sales staff, and office. To ensure quality, Tamotsu hired employees but monitored each production stage. In the 1980s Ann Taylor swamped his small firm with orders for as many coats as his staff could produce. By 1987 he became the top designer of the Vogue Pattern Company's wardrobe division and an alumnus of the Fashion Institute of Technology, for which he has served as a mentor.

Tamotsu's influence on the market grew from customer loyalty. In October 1997, Southeastern retailers voted him the Atlanta Apparel Mart's D.I.V.A. (Design Impact Vision Atlanta) Bridge Designer of the Year award. By the following year the Tamotsu label grew into a $16-million enterprise in suits, rain coats, careerwear, dresses, dress slacks, and sportswear sized 4 to 22. To meet demand, he assembled a close-knit staff of 200 to complete 10,000 to 15,000 garments per month in up to 40 styles.

Untrendy and uninterested in fashion buzz, Tamotsu focused on neutral tones as well as the red, navy, and black that suited urban needs. Introducing four to eight pieces each month, he reduced length, hem, and sleeves from standard sizes to fit women with high waistlines and short strides. Most appreciative of his unfussy basics were large women and petite larger women, ones the toney designers had long ignored.

In business terms, Tamotsu targeted buyers wearing size 14 and above, who make up 60 percent of clothing purchases. To flatter a range of body sizes, he chose Italian viscose acetate for its fluidity, as well as imported silks, cottons, and wool blends for quality and durability. For spring 1998, he created "wedding cake" pieces, textured rayon acetate garments in soft praline, cream, caramel, and oyster. Comfortable and functional, the basic pieces harmonized classic lines that suited career and social occasions.

Tamotsu's company has earned respect for consistency and quality, which he maintains through carefully controlled growth. He respects employees, a tight coterie who think of themselves as family. The staff work out problems jointly, including times when the designer is not present to guide them. To *Small Business Opportunities,* he remarked, "I don't ask them too many questions as long as they are doing business." Generous and unpretentious, he distributes bonuses unexpectedly and is so devoted to his workers that he flew them to Hawaii to visit his new house.

In mid-1999 Tamotsu perked up his image with more vibrant color, more variety, and a younger, more playful silhouette. He took his cue from his customers, who indicated an interest in relaxed clothes, he embellished without compromising texture and comfort. Without alienating faithful clients, he enhanced his Tamotsu line to include a second tier called Hana, a washable, long-lived collection made from tencel, nylon, and Lycra in black and ivory. The line bore the name of his cat, who he called by the Japanese word for flower. The decision to update Tamotsu's sell-out clothing collection required his usual caution. He told fashion writer Donna Gold his philosophy of change: "In the past I would try different things, but the fans didn't always accept them. Now they are giving me more freedom to experiment, and I'm very happy about that. It gives me the opportunity to discover something new, something different."

Design was only the beginning of Tamotsu's innovations. To his staff, he added Steve Jacobson as Chicago sales representative. Tamotsu increased his outreach by plotting an August ad campaign for the *New York Times Magazine, Mode, Town & Country,* and *Harper's Bazaar.* He field-tested designs for Saks at stores in Louisiana, Massachusetts, Michigan, Missouri, New York, Texas, and Virginia and sent in-house teams to educate sales staffs on fitting the "Tamotsu woman." The initial outlay of $1 million also covered trade show promotions, two color brochures, and an appealing and informative company website.

Overall, Tamotsu's career has flourished from a steady balance of familiar, enduring garment shapes in minimalist style with a hint of newness and adventure. To *Small Business Opportunities* magazine he confided one of the joys of popular success: "Sometimes I see people wearing my designs of 10 years ago. They still look good—I like that." He also explained his method of selecting materials, "I have a good eye; I know fabric and I look very quickly. I catch the little things people miss."

Tamotsu has summarized his business style: he began with simple, understated elegance and based his business on fabrics and designs he liked; over decades, he built a one-owner empire to suit the large female shopper; valued staff and customer loyalty and shared proceeds with his staff; chose his niche and made it a reality by developing a home business into a fabled element of the clothing world. Unconventional in managerial style and principle, he has disdained corporate hierarchy and has remained honest and responsible about paying bills, avoids incurring debt, and keeps his word.

Essential to the Tamotsu business paradigm is another element—knowing how much he needs. The control of his operation stems from his attitude toward money. In February 2000, Nikki Swartz of *Apparel Industry Magazine* quoted Tamotsu's haiku-like thoughts on self-enrichment: "I ask myself, 'How much do I need?' not, 'What more can I get?'"

—Mary Ellen Snodgrass

TANG, William

Chinese designer

Born: Hong Kong. **Education:** Graduated in Economics and Business, University of Guelph, Canada; studied fashion design, London School of Fashion. **Career:** Returned to Hong Kong, 1982, to design for a number of labels, including Sahara Club, Michel René, and Daniel Hechter; opened own company, W. Tang Co. Ltd., 1985, designing womenswear and menswear; labels include William Tang, and W by William Tang; opened Paris boutique, Presence II; generated controversy for drug-themed runway show, 1997; created uniforms for Hong Kong's Miramar Hotel, 1997; designed uniforms for Dragonair Airlines, 2000; created interior designs for Villa by the Park, Hong Kong housing development, 2001. **Address:** Flat E, Upper Ground Floor, 14/16 Aberdeen St. Central, Hong Kong, China.

William Tang, fall 2000 collection. © AFP/CORBIS.

PUBLICATIONS

On TANG:

Articles

Marshall, Samantha, "Shenzhen: A Look across the China Border," in *DNR,* 10 January 1994.

Farley, Maggie, "Another Kind of Streetwear," in the *Los Angeles Times,* 1 May 1997.

Seno Alexandra, "People: Hong Kong Designer Redefines High Fashion," in *Asia Week,* 1 August 1997.

Cheng, Scarlet, "Dressed to Kill," in the *Far Eastern Economic Review,* 4 September 1997.

"Dragonair Enters the Tang Dynasty," in *Inflight Asia,* October 2000.

"SHKP Recruits Famous Fashion Designer William Tang," in Sun Hung Kai Properties press release, 2 May 2001.

*

Fashion itself is an art form that moves and lives with the human body. The fashion business is also art, a form that is based on creative ideas where various commercial aspects are taken into consideration.

—William Tang

* * *

Known as the bad boy of Hong Kong fashion, William Tang has never been one to take the conventional route. After studying economics and business and then hotel management, he decided on a career in fashion. He wanted to further develop his interest in the arts, and the choice was between fashion and architecture. To him, fashion seemed closer to the fine arts and fulfilled his childhood love of drawing people. His arrival in London as a fashion student coincided with the style era of the New Romantics. Tang was in tune with their retro brand of flamboyance and glamor.

History and culture have been very important to Tang's work. In Western art and design, his particular interests have included art déco and Georgia O'Keefe. The Mediterranean has been his greatest geographical influence: he holds a special place for Venice, and ancient Greece and Egypt. Tang revived the unique technique of fine pleating originated by Mariano Fortuny to create elegant shift dresses inspired by the ancient Greek chiton. For Tang, fashion must be a means of expression, not purely concerned with commercialism. Artistic and personal fulfillment have been his major lifetime goals.

Tang has always gone his own way. Never sticking to one look, he prefers to experiment and innovate. But he has a practical side; his business education provided a sound base for the more pragmatic aspect of fashion. W by William Tang and William Tang are his two of his retail labels in Asia, where he sells through major department stores, including the Japanese Seibu and Daimaru. He has worked with the Betu Company in Hong Kong and with Seibu to produce contemporary silk collections aimed at the Japanese and Taiwanese markets. He also opened his own workshop in his home base of Hong Kong and operated a shop, Presence II, in Paris. Another shop was opening in Hong Kong's fashionable Lan Kwai Fong area. His aim is to encompass the extent of his creativity, including individual couture designs, contemporary daywear, and also his paintings.

William Tang, fall/winter 2001 collection: man's hooded full-length gown. © AP/Wide World Photos.

Tang's enthusiasms fuel his work. He reinterpreted clothes photographed by Man Ray to coincide with an exhibition of the artist's work. He has awakened others to the significance of fashion through his designs, lectures, books, and articles and his collections have echoed his knowledge of Chinese history and culture. Shanghai in the 1930s inspired a shocking pink cheong-sam dress, trimmed with ostrich feathers and worn with platform shoes, which stunned the catwalks of Hong Kong. Exquisite lace eveningwear, created from fabric handcrafted in the Shandong Province of China, was declared the triumph of the 1989 Hong Kong Fashion Week. As evidence of his diversity, the following year he showed tie-dyed coordinates topped with overvests and leggings made from rubber bands.

Tang's versatile young look is not as well known as many of his contemporaries. Insufficient financial backing and the need for better promotion have proved hurdles to wider recognition, yet Tang is relaxed about the future. He enjoys his work too much to be concerned about what lies ahead. He has been accused of "stirring things up on the Hong Kong fashion scene" by frequently playing the wild card. But Tang knows his business; he knows "good fashion should be a combination of artistic ideals and expression and the commercial process involved in producing a line of clothes that will sell well." In Hong Kong he has long been a darling of the press. His personality and presence set him apart from some of his older and more reserved contemporaries, but Tang is no mere showman. His work is lively, fresh, and worthy of greater recognition.

Tang, in the 21st century, is still one of the best-known designers in Hong Kong and Asia, but his distribution is limited primarily to China, Southeast Asia, Australia, and Europe. He has not yet broken into key markets such as Japan or the United States in a significant way, either with his proprietary William Tang and Chi Chi labels or with his products for Tienlan, where he serves as design director. His collections are popular in Asia and increasingly commercial, although he manages to solidify his "bad boy" reputation with some attention-attracting designs.

Tang continues to be inspired by the art and people of the streets, for example incorporating calligraphic graffiti (by a renowned Hong Kong street artist) into fabrics highlighted in a collection. He also holds shows in malls and housing projects, in an effort to bring his fashion "to the streets."Tang talks to Hong Kong's homeless about how they dress, and sometimes incorporates their ideas into his collections. "These people are truly original," he told the *Los Angeles Times* in May 1997. "The rest of us only care about how others look at us, but they don't care what people think. They dress only for themselves."

His controversial fall 1997 collection took the street images too far for some critics. It featured models poking themselves with syringes, which led observers to accuse him of promoting "heroin chic." To *Asia Week,* Tang argued that the theatrics were intended to show drug use as what he called "a deformed lifestyle."

Aside from his work in design, the well-rounded Tang is a short story author and a travel, culture, and fashion writer for a number of newspapers and magazines in Hong Kong, as well as the host of a television program. He even considered retiring from fashion in the late 1990s but ultimately decided to continue. Much of his revenue comes from large-scale custom work such as uniforms and interior designs for organizations such as the Hong Kong airport, the Miramar Hotel, IBA Bank, a housing development, and Hong Kong Dragon Aviation (Dragonair).

Tang combines East and West, ancient and modern. He can take styles from Chinese peasant villagers of the past and recreate them in Day-Glo colors, or fashion cheong-sams with a modern, sexy flair. His collections walk the line between the avant-garde and the commercially acceptable.

—Hazel Clark; updated by Karen Raugust

TARABINI, Gianpaolo

See BLUMARINE

TASSELL, Gustave

American designer

Born: Philadelphia, Pennsylvania, 4 February 1926. **Education:** Studied at Pennsylvania Academy of Fine Arts. **Military Service:** Served in the U.S. Army. **Career:** Joined Hattie Carnegie, late 1940s, as window-dresser, later designer; designer, Elfreda Fox; designed custom clothes, Philadelphia; sketch artist for Mme. Fath and freelance sketch artist, Paris, 1952–54; designer, Hattie Carnegie fashion house, New York, 1954–55; managed own design firm, Los Angeles, 1956–72; took over design at Norman Norell, New York, after death of Norell, 1972–76; designer, Michael Forrest Furs, 1976; reestablished own firm, from 1976. **Awards:** International Silk Association award, 1959; Coty American Fashion Critics award, 1961; Cotton Council Fashion award, 1963.

Publications

On TASSELL:

Books

Levin, Phyllis Lee, *The Wheels of Fashion,* Garden City, New York, 1956.

Lambert, Eleanor, *World of Fashion: People, Places, Resources,* New York, 1976.

Morris, Bernadine, and Barbara Walz, *The Fashion Makers,* New York, 1978.

Milbank, Caroline Rennolds, *New York Fashion: The Evolution of American Style,* New York, 1989.

Stegemeyer, Anne, *Who's Who in Fashion, Third Edition,* New York, 1996.

Articles

Fashion profile, in *Holiday,* June 1962.

Several articles in the *New York Times,* 24 January 1974, 6 August 1974, 8 August 1975, 12 July 1976.

Houser, Dave G., "The Attic Spirit; Gustave Tassell's Paean to Greece in Los Angeles," in *Architectural Digest,* September 1983.

* * *

White gloves and pearls were the accessories one needs to wear with the refined, graceful designs of American Gustave Tassell. He designed for women who had a built-in serenity and who were not out to shock. His designs went beyond fringe and ruffle and were noted for their sense of proportion, simplicity of line, and refined detail.

Among the notable people who have worn Tassell designs were Princess Grace of Monaco and Jacqueline Kennedy Onassis—especially the latter who very influential in the fashion field when she was First Lady of the United States. She wore simple clothes, favoring sleeveless dresses without a defined waistline or much detail. Tassell's creations were perfect for the First Lady; they were youthful, elegant, without unnecessary details or defined waistlines. They would glide over the body rather than hugging it, his designs were elegant and easy to wear.

Tassell had a New York showroom, but the base of his operation was in Los Angeles. There he maintained a small organization and workroom which insured top notch quality at relatively low cost. He did not produce the extremes of fashion. In *Holiday* magazine (June 1962) he said "forget fashion, you can't go around startling people all the time." Fabrics were important, *peau d'ange* and quilted cotton damask added interest; bugle beads were used, in an understated manner, for eveningwear.

Through the use of seams, tucks, and gathers, Tassell was able to create sculptural forms which skimmed over the body, rather than a tight fit. The look was graceful and feminine. Skirts could be bell shaped, or gathered gently. The seams of a princess-style dress curved to suggest the bust and waistline. He designed clothes for both evening and daytime wear—separates, dresses, and coats. He designed versions of the black dinner dress, the shirtwaist, culottes, and the reefer coat. His interpretation was always graceful and feminine. In 1961 he received the Coty American Fashion Critics award.

Tassell did not start out to be a fashion designer, but studied painting at the Pennsylvania Academy of Fine Arts. Moving to New York, he worked in the advertising and display department for Hattie Carnegie, who was well known in the fashion design world for both custom-made and ready-to-wear clothes. Seeing the design work of Norman Norell inspired Tassell's decision to create clothes for women.

In the early 1950s Tassell moved to Europe where he did fashion sketches for Geneviève Fath and became acquainted with American designer James Galanos. It was through the encouragement of Galanos that Tassell eventually began his own business in 1956 in California, though the designs Tassell produced were closer in concept to those of Norell than Galanos. In 1972, when Norman Norell died, Tassell was asked to come to New York to maintain the line. He did this under the name House of Norell, Gustave Tassell. The Norman Norell line was permanently closed in 1976 and Tassell returned to California where he again turned out his sophisticated designs for a small group of customers.

Tassell's design sensibility changed little from the 20 to the 21st century—he sought to create forward-looking fashion appropriate for elegant, confident women. He envisioned designs in natural fibers able to serve many purposes, with changing silhouette according to how the garment was buttoned, seamed, or tucked. Tassell aimed to produce affordable clothing with a sense of proportion, grace, and design.

—Nancy House

THOMASS, Chantal

French designer

Born: Chantal Genty in Malakoff, Seine, France, 4 September 1947. **Family:** Married Bruce Thomass, 1967; children: Louise, Robin. **Career:** Freelance designer selling to Dorothée Bis, 1966–71; partner, Ter et Bantine boutique, Paris, 1967, renamed Chantal Thomass, 1975; introduced lingerie and hosiery collections, 1975, maternity wear, 1981, children's clothing line, from circa 1982; signed partnership with World Co. for distribution, licensing, and boutiques in Japan, 1985; opened second boutique for clothing and household accessories, Paris, 1991; fired from namesake label, owned by World Co. of Japan, 1995; original label went into bankruptcy, 1996; acted as consultant to companies such as Victoria's Secret and Wolford, 1995–98; repurchased rights to her name from World Co. and relaunched label with backing from Sara Lee's Dim division, 1999; first U.S. trunk show, at Saks Fifth Avenue, 2001. **Exhibitions:** *Chantal Thomass: 30 ans de Créations,* Musée de la Mode, Marseille, 2001. **Awards:** Named Chevalier des Arts et Lettres. **Address:** 346 rue Saint-Honorè, 75001 Paris, France.

Chantal Thomass, fall/winter 1996–97 collection: angora sweater and crêpe skirt. © AP/Wide World Photos.

PUBLICATIONS

On THOMASS:

Books

Slesin, Suzanne, and Stafford Cliff, *French Style,* New York and London, 1982.

Steele, Valerie, *Women of Fashion: Twentieth-Century Designers,* New York, 1991.

Stegemeyer, Anne, *Who's Who in Fashion, Third Edition,* New York, 1996.

Articles

"Les Stylistes," in *Elle* (Paris), 23 May 1977.

"Chantal Thomass: La Renouveau du Froufrou," in *Jardin des Modes* (Paris), October 1982.

Depardieu, Gérard, "Chantal Thomass," in *La Mode en Peinture,* Winter 1982–83.

"Chantal Thomass," in *Profession Textile* (Paris), 18 September 1987.

White, Constance C.R., "Patterns," in the *New York Times,* 19 March 1996.

"Chantal Thomass Studio Firm Reported to Be in Liquidation," in *WWD,* 26 August 1996.

"Chantal Thomass, Dim in Deal," in *WWD,* 17 February 1998.

Benoit, Ruth, "Chantal Thomass Back in Lingerie," in *WWD,* 28 December 1998.
Weisman, Katherine, "Chantal Thomass Show Stops Traffic, Starts Protests," in *WWD,* 23 April 1999.
Monget, Karyn, "Breaking into the American Boudoir," in *WWD,* 22 January 2001.
Murphy, Robert, "Bring Back That Sex Appeal," in *WWD,* 9 July 2001.
"Dentelles et Froufrous de Chantal Thomass sur la Canebière," in *Le Monde,* 20 July 2001.

* * *

Chantal Thomass has built a reputation for her tantalizing, flirtatious clothes. Much of her work pays a titillating homage to exotic underwear; there is, however, never a blatant display of overt sexuality. Instead there is always a hint of the naughty schoolgirl or a sensuous allusion to the charms of the teenage seductress, like Carole Baker in *Baby Doll* or Sue Lyon in *Lolita.* The clothes are often fitted or skimpy, trimmed in frills, ribbons, and flounces, and always produced in the most sophisticated fabrics.

Thomass had no formal training in fashion design, but as a child, dressing up proved enough of a motivation for her to design her own clothes, which were made by her mother. She began her fashion career at 18, designing clothes for girls of her own age. A year later, she married Bruce Thomass, who had studied at the École des Beaux Arts in Paris. Together they formed a small fashion company called Ter et Bantine manufacturing and selling young and unusual clothes. They created dresses from hand-painted scarves, designed by Bruce, and succeeded in selling them to Dorothée Bis. Thomass also designed dresses with flounced pinafores, schoolgirl collars, and balloon sleeves that were sold from their first boutique on Boulevard Saint Germain in 1967. Actress and French cultural symbol Brigitte Bardot became a regular customer, as did designer Jacqueline Jacobson, who ordered over a hundred dresses in one season alone.

The business was sufficiently successful for the pair to found the Chantal Thomass label in 1975, with Chantal as creative director and Bruce as licensing and sales director. As the profile of the company rose, so did the price of the clothes, although they retained their young, enchanting, and highly feminine style. Thomass has often been motivated by the progression of her own life. Her pregnancy in 1981 led her to develop a line of maternity clothes. As her daughter began growing, Thomass developed a childrenswear division that retained many of the distinctive and theatrical elements of her mainline collections. The company moved into licensing in 1985, joining forces with the Japanese group World as a financial partner. Licensed products were available throughout Europe and Japan and included fine leather goods, tights, women's shoes, eyewear, watches, children's ready-to-wear, scarves, lingerie, and swimwear. There were soon a dozen Thomass boutiques throughout France.

Thomass retains her eminence by reflecting fashion changes and adapting her look to suit the prevalent mood. A youthful feel to her clothes has kept her in the forefront of leading Paris-based designers. Yet the mid- to late 1990s were a turbulent time for Thomass. In 1995 she was fired from her own label, of which she owned a minority interest, in a dispute with Japanese majority owner World Company. World planned to continue the label, publicizing aggressive expansion plans, and released further designs, which were considered more commercial than Thomass' typical work. A year later, however, the label went into bankruptcy and liquidated its assets.

Thomass, meanwhile, stopped designing lingerie for a time, leaving the category that had become her main focus. She spent the next four years as a consultant to companies such as Austrian hosiery maker Wolford (where she designed a swimwear line), Victoria's Secret, Antinéas, and Rosy, often in categories outside lingerie. In late 1998 after a lawsuit against World was resolved, Thomass reacquired the rights to her name and found a backer, the Dim division of Sara Lee, which took a two-thirds ownership of her company and assumed manufacturing duties for the core lingerie lines. Her first products under the relaunch were available in 1999. Her reentry into lingerie design was marked by controversy when a Galeries Lafayette window display featuring live models wearing her lingerie drew protests from feminists and other groups in Paris.

Among the best-known designers in France—a retrospective of her work at Marseille's Musée de Mode in 2001 included 230 pieces—Thomass also has a strong business in Japan and began her entry into the U.S. market in the late 1990s and early 2000s, with her first Saks Fifth Avenue trunk show taking place in April 2001. Licensed lines, distributed primarily in Europe and Japan, include eyewear, among other categories.

Thomass remains best known for her sexy, comfortable lingerie, often done in black but sometimes pastels or white, or with a layering of different colors and materials. She often shows her line to retail buyers using live dioramas featuring models doing everyday tasks in their lingerie. *Women's Wear Daily* (5 February 2001) termed her display at the Salon International de la Lingerie as "a naughty peep show featuring saucy vignettes of boudoir voyeurism." In the future, Thomass planned to expand into apparel again, focusing on lingerie-inspired looks.

—Kevin Almond; updated by Karen Raugust

TIEL, Vicky

American designer

Born: Washington, D.C., 21 October 1943. **Education:** Studied fashion design at Pratt Institute, 1961–62, and at Fashion Institute of Technology, 1962–64. **Family:** Married Ron Berkeley, 1971 (divorced, 1986); children: Rex, Richard. **Career:** Film costume designer 1960s; settled in Paris, 1964; opened boutique, Mia & Vicky, later renamed Vicky Tiel; introduced fragrance line, 1990; introduced eveningwear bridge line, 1992; launched first men's fragrance, *Ulysse,* 1998. **Address:** 159 East 63rd Street, New York, NY 10021 USA. **Website:** www.vickytiel.com.

Publications

On TIEL:

Books

Leese, Elizabeth, *Costume Design in the Movies,* New York, 1991.

Articles

de Leusse, Claude, "Vicky Tiel: Gentleness on Her Mind," in *WWD,* 3 March 1972.
Grassi, Adriana, "Vicky, Elizabeth and Richard," in *WWD,* 27 June 1972.

Morris, Bernadine, "An American in Paris: The Eclectic Spirit," in the *New York Times,* 18 May 1978.
"Tiel Goes Hollywood," in *WWD,* 31 May 1978.
Johnson, Bonnie, "American in Paris," in *People,* 1 September 1986.
Stephens, Suzanne, "Vicky Tiel: American Élan in Paris Apartment," in *Architectural Digest,* September 1989.
Hunter, Catherine Ellis, "Vicky Tiel: An American in Paris," in *Drug & Cosmetic Industry,* August 1990.
Pagoda, Dianne M., "Tiel Lowers Prices as Business Drops," in *WWD,* 30 July 1991.
Diamond, Kerry, "Tiel's Launch: You Have Male," in *WWD,* 5 June 1998.
"The Cinderella Treatment," available online at the *Washington Post,* www.WashingtonPost.com, 9 January 2001.

* * *

Vicky Tiel is a unique phenomenon in the international world of fashion. She is perhaps the only American to operate her own fashion design business in Paris and to do so longer than many of her French contemporaries. She holds a unique place in the history of fashion as one of the early boutique/ready-to-wear designers in Paris. Her clothes now occupy a special place between ready-to-wear and couture, both in manufacture and in marketing.

In 1964, having graduated from the Fashion Institute of Technology in New York, Tiel arrived in Paris with the intention of designing costumes for films. During her school years in New York, she had already been actively creating youth-oriented clothes, sold in Greenwich Village boutiques. Her designs in this early period included leather skirts with matching fringe vests and a prototypical miniskirt designed in fall 1963, a full season ahead of Mary Quant's mini, introduced in London in the spring of 1964.

While looking for film work in Paris, Tiel, together with her friend Mia Fonssagrives, created innovative "youth-quaker"-style ready-to-wear. These clothes caused a stir among the fashion press, and in 1965 Tiel and Fonssagrives even appeared on the *Tonight Show* with Johnny Carson. At this time, fashion in Paris was still dominated by the great couturiers, and only a few designers, such as Emmanuelle Khanh and Michele Rosier, were exclusively designing ready-to-wear clothes. Subsequently Fonssagrives married couturier Louis Féraud, who, in a highly unusual move, permitted Tiel and Fonssagrives to use sample-hands and seamstresses from his atelier to produce their ready-to-wear for sale in their own boutique called Mia & Vicky.

Fonssagrives later dropped out and the boutique was renamed Vicky Tiel. As a direct result of this series of events, Tiel's clothes have come to hold a unique place between ready-to-wear and couture—they are meticulously crafted clothes of the finest fabrics, sewn in the tradition of haute couture. By 1972 Tiel's clothes had moved away from the radically young, kooky 1960s look toward a traditionally feminine style with a sexy twist, as seen in floral printed garden party dresses closely gathered through the bodice, skinny navy jersey tops with white piqué collar and cuffs, and long skirts worn with ruffled shirts.

By the mid-1970s, dramatically draped dresses in matte jersey had become a major component of Tiel's collection. From this period onward, her style has reflected her point of view that a woman can be glamorous, sexual, powerful, and feminine all at the same time. Her exemplar for the reification of this concept was the Hollywood screen goddess of the 1940s and 1950s. Her clothes appeal to the consumer's basic fantasy desire, a fantasy of glamor and sexuality mediated by quality and a refined sensibility.

In 1978, inspired by a 1940s Frederick's of Hollywood catalogue, Tiel designed a collection with the theme Fun Hollywood Trash but remarked that "the look is done in very good taste and in the most expensive fabrics." The collection featured backless tuxedo dresses and evening dresses of contrasting colored chiffon layered over jersey, creating an iridescent look. Her description of the development of her perfume could also serve as a description of her clothes: "I wanted it to reek of femininity and sensuality, but to be soft and romantic, with subtle, not overpowering sex." More recent designs continued to reflect this point of view, with a large portion of her collection devoted to eveningwear, especially her signature draped jerseys, often enhanced with appliquéd sequins and embroidery.

Tiel's clothes are sold in her own boutique in Paris and in fine department stores and specialty stores where she often makes personal appearances at trunk shows. Special and custom orders account for a large percentage of Tiel's sales, and her personal style of marketing is consistent with the caliber of these uniquely luxurious, sensual clothes. Throughout the late 1990s and early 2000s Tiel placed an increased emphasis on eveningwear. She is perhaps better known in many circles for this portion of her business than for the ready-to-wear that made her famous. Her gowns, rendered in jersey, organza, and lace, in a rainbow of rich colors as well as elegant black, are often worn by celebrities to high-profile events. She even designed dresses for several of the politically connected who were invited to the balls surrounding the 2001 inaugural of U.S. President George W. Bush. A significant percentage of her clothing business continues to be custom orders.

While her designs are popular among the rich and famous, they are not for everyone. Tiel favors tight-fitting silhouettes best suited to women in top physical condition. Even among this consumer segment, those who choose Vicky Tiel have the confidence to show their bodies to the world. And with the expansion of her fragrance line, Tiel has become more recognized, to many in the general public, for her scents than for her apparel. Manufactured by Five Star Fragrances and distributed by Riviera Concepts, the Parfums Vicky Tiel Paris label is in upscale distribution in outlets such as Neiman Marcus and Bergdorf Goodman stores, which are also key customers for her apparel. In 1998 Tiel launched *Ulysse,* her first men's scent.

Tiel described her women's scents, which include *Originale* and *Sirene,* to *Women's Wear Daily* in June 1998 as "feminine" and "seductive." These words also accurately describe her apparel designs.

—Alan E. Rosenberg; updated by Karen Raugust

TIFFANY & COMPANY

American luxury goods company

Founded: in New York City in 1837 by Charles Lewis Tiffany and John Young as a stationery and "fancy goods" emporium. **Company History:** Began jewelry sales, 1840s; added the manufacture of silver, 1850s; purchased the Tiffany Diamond, one of the world's largest yellow diamonds, 1878; introduced a six-prong diamond engagement ring, exhibiting what became known as the "Tiffany" setting, 1886; company moved to its present Fifth Avenue location, 1940; Tiffany family sells to the Hoving Corporation, 1955; company sold to cosmetics giant Avon Products, 1979; management repurchased

Jewelry designs by Tiffany & Company, 2000. © AP/Wide World Photos.

the company in a leveraged buyout, 1984; Tiffany & Company becomes a publicly traded company, 1987; wholesale distribution of products to independent retailers discontinued, 1999; purchased stake in Canadian diamond miner Aber Resources, 1999. **Company Address:** 727 Fifth Avenue, New York, NY 10022, USA.

Publications

On TIFFANY & COMPANY:

Books

Purtell, Joseph, *The Tiffany Touch,* New York, 1971.
Carpenter, Charles Hope, *Tiffany Silver,* New York, 1978.
Proddow, Penny, *American Jewelry: Glamour and Tradition,* New York, 1987.
Loring, John, *Tiffany's 20th Century: A Portrait of American Style,* New York, 1997.
Snowman, A. Kenneth, ed., *The Master Jewelers,* New York, 1990.

Articles

Cohen, Daniel, "Charles Tiffany's 'Fancy Goods' Shop and How It Grew," in *Smithsonian,* December 1987.
———, "Splendor in Glass," in *Historic Preservation* (New York), 1987.
Loring, John, "Tiffany & Company Celebrating 150 Years," in *Architectural Digest,* No. 10, 1987.
Safford, Frances Gruber, and Ruth Wilford Caccavale, "Japanesque Silver by Tiffany & Company in the Metropolitan Museum of Art," in *Magazine Antiques* (New York), October 1987.
Trachtenbert, Jeffrey, "Cocktails at Tiffany," in *Forbes,* 6 February 1989.
Lorge, Sarah,, "A Priceless Brand: Strategic Marketing at Tiffany & Company," in *Sales & Marketing Management* (New York), October 1998.
Curan, Catherine, "Multifaceted Success: After Years of Gains, Wall Street Notices Tiffany," in *Crain's New York Business,* 18 October 1999.

* * *

Tiffany & Company is a name that, throughout its long history, has epitomized luxury. It is part of America's cultural lexicon, referenced in film, literature, and public discourse to signify the good life and social refinement. While linked in the popular imagination with cascades of diamonds, the firm retails a variety of selective items, including jewelry, glassware, flatware, china, writing materials, fashion accessories, and fragrances. Tiffany & Company's status as an iconic American institution is predicated on product quality and an authoritative marketing strategy promising exclusivity. All this is wrapped up in a trademark blue box, whose symbolic cachet is as valuable as the gift it holds.

Tiffany & Company trades not only in luxury products but also in a certain image. The famed ambience of the New York City flagship store, with its discreet sales staff, as well as company publications on etiquette and gem selection, are meant to position the company as far more than a retail store. Throughout its history, wealthy Americans have gone to Tiffany's to put a stamp on their own affluence and social respectability.

Part of the company's enduring legacy is its ability to draw on disparate sources for artistic inspiration while creating a distinctly

Pearls in a Chicago, Illinois, Tiffany & Company display window, 1996. © Kevin Fleming/CORBIS.

American product. Tiffany's was a preeminent silver producer in the late 1800s, and its silver pieces reflected many of the influences of the time, from ornate Victorianism to simpler classical revival designs, to the growing fascination with the Orient and the Middle East. Craftspeople rigorously trained in the Tiffany apprenticeship program produced a tremendous amount of silverwork to supply the demands of a culture in which the dining room and its silver were paramount to social life and status. At exhibitions throughout the 19th century, the company won acclaim from European audiences skeptical of American ability in the decorative arts.

Innovative designers produced exclusively for the company, including Edward Moore, whose Japanese-influenced silver containers are still critically acclaimed and admired today. Moore also oversaw a celebrated collection of jewelry and silver inspired by Native American art. During this same period, a set of 25 enamel orchids designed by Paulding Farnham contributed to a European revival in enamels. With the efforts of mineralogist George Frederick Kunz, Tiffany popularized the decorative use of American gems, semiprecious stones, and freshwater pearls in jewelry design. At the same time it was promoting fine silver and jewelry, Tiffany & Company was also creating several popular sterling silver flatware lines, some of which are still produced. The late-19th century was a period of incredible design innovation for the company, and this combination of fine craftsmanship and artistic quality secured Tiffany's reputation among affluent American and international clientèle.

Charles Tiffany's son Louis Comfort Tiffany dominated Tiffany style in the early 20th century. Louis Tiffany was a leading proponent of art nouveau in America, taking themes from nature (emphasizing American flowers as well as animal and insect life) and rendering them in jewelry and glass. Louis Tiffany's hand-blown Favrile glass vases and bowls, his stained glass mosaics and lamps, his exuberant use of color combinations and innovative techniques were heralded in his day. Due to the growing trend of modernism, however, interest waned in Louis Tiffany's style and by his death in 1933, Tiffany & Company had entered a period of stalled artistic innovation.

Tiffany's so-called second Golden Age commenced under the management of Walter Hoving in 1955. He hired Jean Schlumberger, whose imaginative designs uniquely combined gems in highly detailed designs. Van Day Truex became design director and redesigned Tiffany's silver, crystal, and china lines. The company continued to hire design luminaries, including Donald Claflin in 1965, known for pieces based on imaginary or fictive creatures. The work of Elsa Peretti was introduced in 1974, followed the next year by the work of Angela Cummings. Designer Paloma Picasso's jewelry was introduced in 1980. Well-known designers were also commissioned to design Tiffany tableware. Current Tiffany design director John Loring commented, "I see a thread linking all the most worthwhile of Tiffany productions, however great the successive changes in taste. They are all an authentically American phenomena, derived from but not imitating the set ideas of European and Oriental sophistication. All Tiffany pieces are emphatically New World."

Despite a period in the 1980s under the management of Avon Products in which lower-quality, inexpensive goods were introduced to the Tiffany stock, Tiffany & Company continued to symbolize a specific American refinement and sumptuousness. Marketing strategies since the 1990s have sought to retain the upper-class patina of the Tiffany name while expanding into the middle-class and younger markets with affordable items, touring jewelry collections, and a sleek website. Even though the company successfully weathered economic recessions and years when fashion trends bypassed expensive jewelry, Tiffany now seems committed to negotiating the fine balance between exclusivity and accessibility. The company has slowly established its own retail locations across the U.S.; the goal is to have 75 locations across the country, bringing Tiffany style to a broader audience. Expansion has also included several international locations and the company's mail-order business, with slick catalogues further spreading the Tiffany name.

Tiffany & Company endures, in part, because its products promise far more than quality craftsmanship: they promise to lift the possessor up into an exclusive circle of social privilege and to identify a Tiffany client as having that most elusive quality of all, good taste.

—Megan Stacy

TIFFEAU, Jacques

French designer

Born: Chenevelles, Loire Valley, France, 11 October 1927. **Education:** Early training in Paris couture house until World War II. **Military Service:** Served in the French Army Air Force, 1939–40. **Career:** Tailor; assistant to Dior, 1945–50; immigrated to the U.S.; studied figure drawing, Art Students' League, New York; pattern maker, then designer, Monte-Sano & Pruzan coat and suit manufacturers, circa 1952–58; partner/designer, Tiffeau & Busch Ltd. for Monte-Sano & Pruzan, New York, 1958–66; launched own firm, 1966–71; taught fashion design, Paris, 1970s; supervisor, Rive Gauche collections, Yves Saint Laurent, 1972–76; designer, Originala, and Blassport lines, New York. **Awards:** Coty American Fashion Critics award, 1960, 1966; National Cotton award, New York, 1961; *Sunday Times* International Fashion award, London, circa 1966; Tobe-Coburn Fashion award New York. **Died:** 1988.

Publications

On TIFFEAU:

Books

Bender, Marylin, *The Beautiful People,* New York, 1967.

Lambert, Eleanor, *World of Fashion: People, Places, Resources,* New York & London, 1976.

Milbank, Caroline Rennolds, *New York Fashion: The Evolution of American Style,* New York, 1989.

Articles

Sheinman, Mort, "Jacques Tiffeau Dies in Paris," in *WWD,* 7 March 1968.

"The Decades (Fashion in the 1960s)," in *WWD,* 28 September 1998.

Brady, James, "Scoops, Scandals, and Scalawags; Merry Memories of a Giddy, Glorious Era," in *WWD,* 16 July 2001.

* * *

Writing about designer Jacques Tiffeau in the 1960s, fashion doyenne Diana Vreeland once grandly declared, "He's in tune." She was referring to a Tiffeau collection comprised of simple, nonchalant, elegant dresses and daytime suits, most without bust-darts or extraneous frills, many cut on the bias. The gifted designer, who once turned down an offer to replace Yves Saint Laurent at Dior, excelled at creating pared-down, sophisticated, gimmick-free clothes that derived their strong visual impact purely from the designer's manipulation of cut, shape, and color. He was one of the prescient few who understood the importance of trousers for women, including basic trousers in nearly every collection until they were no longer seen as inappropriate for certain occasions. He was also known for his uncluttered coat designs with their clean, graphic silhouettes.

A Frenchman transplanted to America, Tiffeau belonged to the 1960s pantheon of American designers which included Geoffrey Beene, Bill Blass, Donald Brooks, and James Galanos. He embraced the advanced manufacturing technologies of the post-World War II era, eagerly investigating the properties of new materials in his garments: double-knits, rayons, plastics, and polyesters. His clothes were designed with a young, affluent, fashion-conscious consumer in mind, and his styles found ready buyers in America who saw reflected in his streamlined designs the modern spirit they wished to project.

Tiffeau spent many years learning his trade. During the German Occupation of France, the teenaged Tiffeau left his small Loire village and ran off to Paris, where he apprenticed himself to a men's tailor. There he skillfully mastered the art of cutting a toile, the muslin pattern which designers used as a model for the finished pattern. He next moved to New York and became protégé and chief stylist for Max Pruzan at Monte-Sano & Pruzan, an Italian artisan tailor who had built up one of the most expensive women's coat-and-suit houses in the trade. A friendship with Christian Dior led to an offer to design at Dior New York, but Tiffeau felt his future lay in ready-to-wear. Tiffeau teamed up with Beverly Busch, Pruzan's daughter, and formed Tiffeau & Busch, a successful ready-to-wear line of young, lower-priced coats, dresses, and sportswear separates. The designer spent nearly a decade creating six collections a year between the two concerns before dedicating himself exclusively to Tiffeau & Busch.

Life-drawing art classes combined with his inspired manipulation of toiles as a tailor's apprentice had given the young Tiffeau an excellent comprehension of the body as a mobile, three-dimensional object in space. This in-depth knowledge of clothing construction came to set him apart from many other American designers of his generation. Unlike his contemporaries, who would simply give their assistants a sketch to translate into three dimensions, Tiffeau was able to cut, shape, drape, and sew a garment from start to finish. Buyers loved that Tiffeau's clothing truly fit and rarely needed alterations; but he preferred to think of himself merely as a technician, never as an artist.

Tiffeau was an inspired designer, however, often using staid gray flannel for elegant separates, making cocktail dresses of zebra-striped velveteen—and he was among the first to use wool for evening dresses. He was an avid collector of ancient Near-Eastern and Asian art, from which he claimed to derive ideas about purity of line. He always sought refinement in his designs, an endless paring down, saying, "the secret of good clothes is to keep taking off, simplifying, trimming down—yet to capture the shape of the human body." Besides his mentor Christian Dior, he admired Balenciaga, Beene, Courrèges, and Norell. His minimalist, almost severe style made him one of the most renowned designers of the 1960s, but as tastes changed in the 1970s he was accused of merely "rehashing" his old styles and was never again able to regain the spotlight.

In 1972 Tiffeau left New York and returned to France, where he worked for a time for Balmain and Yves Saint Laurent. An attempt to revive his career designing coats at Originala in New York was short-lived, though he was praised for his soft, unconstructed styles in tweed, alpaca, and cashmere. Eventually he found himself again in France, this time as a fashion design instructor. He left behind the legacy of a strong-willed and talented man whom his friend artist Robert Motherwell once said was "like having a beautiful leopard in the room."

—Kathleen Paton

TIKTINER

French fashion firm

Company History: Began as family business in Nice, 1949, expanded into sportswear with factories in the South of France. **Company Address:** 14 avenue de Verdun, 06000 Nice, France.

Publications

On TIKTINER:

Books

McDowell, Colin, *McDowell's Directory of Twentieth Century Fashion,* Englewood Cliffs, New Jersey, 1985.

Articles

"Tiktiner Fall," in *WWD,* 26 February 1990.

* * *

The owners of Tiktiner, a family-run fashion house based in Nice, France, never really considered their position outside the urban fashion center of Paris a liability. The principles, Henri and Dina Viterbo and their daughters Miquette and Vivian, occasionally admitted to the need for stimulation beyond the French Riviera in order to inspire new ideas. But the Viterbos remained committed to their own brand of high-quality, classic-styled, resort-oriented ready-to-wear, and felt no need to leave Nice or tamper with the relaxed attitude toward clothing that supported them handsomely for decades.

The Tiktiner family members each played an important role in the company: Henri was the founder and owner; Dina was the head designer; eldest daughter Miquette, an international attorney married to American Mort Schrader, represented the company in the United States; and younger daughter Vivian helped designed collections with her mother. Together the Viterbos created and promoted dependable ready-to-wear collections with their own, recognizable "Tiktiner look,"—a look based essentially on tailored sportswear separates, with a focus on knits, basic colors, rich weaves, and youthful lines.

The combined inspiration of Vivian and mother Dina resulted in fashion-forward clothes mitigated by classicism, and Vivian often chided her mother for excessive conservatism. Yet the pair worked well together. Early collections emphasized the sleek lines in vogue during the 1960s, with clingy jersey tops over slim, hip-hugging trousers and mini-skirts. Tiktiner favored the natural fiber fabrics used in active wear, often experimenting with stretch jerseys and printed piques in their youth-oriented clothes. The polo shirt, that icon of French sportswear popularized by René Lacoste, was even fair game, given a clever twist by Vivian and Dina in their one-piece shirt dress with a polo top and faux skirt designed to look like separates. The Tiktiner style, though essentially casual, relied on the buyer's familiarity with design classics, and the look was equally at home at a beachside tennis court or a Parisian salon.

The family firm, however, did not design only garments meant for warm weather resorts. The biannual collections included autumn-winter lines with thick knits and cold-weather layered looks. In the 1970s Tiktiner made fashion news with their sweater tunics and bulky multicolored sweater coats over plaid shirt jackets in lieu of the traditional cloth coat. Each knitted sweater layer was designed to coordinate, so a lightweight, slim jersey top might slip over a matching skirt under a fuller mohair coat, all in various shades of amber or other compatible hues. These loose, comfortable, mix-and-match cold weather knits fit perfectly into the youthful fashion mood of the period of the 1970s, when even a simple cloth coat could be seen as bourgeois and confining. But Tiktiner was not averse to more traditional coat designs, and were lauded for their updated, shaped "redingote" of rosy wool chinchilla in 1979.

Tiktiner never wavered from the Viterbos' dedication to style combined with comfort. One clothing group comprised of over 200 pieces highlighted slim waists with drawstring closures, shirred shoulders, and back yokes for easy movement. The collections were frequently hailed for their coordinating palettes; muted earth tones, dusty blues and greens, pale pastels, and paired intensities of the same color figured largely in the Viterbos' vision. The notion of comfort also emerges when considering Tiktiner's attention to travel-minded clothes made from lightweight and packable wool challis, mohairs, and double-knits. Underlying the designs was a philosophy based on ease—ease of fit, of combining colors, of simply getting dressed.

—Kathleen Paton

TIMNEY FOWLER LTD.

British textile design firm

Founded: in London in 1980 by husband and wife team Sue Timney (born 9 July 1950) and Grahame Fowler (born 12 January 1956). *Timney* educated at Carlisle College of Art, 1966–67; Newcastle-upon-Tyne Polytechnic 1971–76, B.A.; Heriot Watt University, Edinburgh, postgraduate diploma, textiles, 1976–77; Royal College of Art, M.A., Textiles, 1977–79. **Company History:** Incorporated, 1985; partnership developed Japanese market for print design, clothing and accessories consultancy, 1980–84; clients included Issey Miyake and Yohji Yamamoto; opened UK retail outlets and Print

Studio Workshop; interior fabric range, 1984; expanded design services to Yves Saint Laurent, Chloé, and Agnes B., produced for Italian designers Bini and Mantero; exports to Europe and U.S., and designed for Calvin Klein, Kamali, Saks Fifth Avenue, 1985–88; designed tableware and giftware for Wedgwood, 1991; fashion accessories launched in U.S., 1993; signed textile license with Linda McCartney, 1994; contracted to hotels for interior design, 1997; opened office and showroom in New York, 1999; began offering online sales, 2000; members of Chartered Society of Designers, London; Textile Institute, London; Interior Designers and Decorators Association, London. **Exhibitions:** *Period Homes and Interiors,* Olympia, London, 1992. **Collections:** Victoria & Albert Museum, London; Cooper-Hewitt Museum, New York City; Art Institute of Chicago. **Awards:** Roscoe award, Interior Fabrics, USA, 1988, 1989; Textile Institute Design gold medal, 1991. **Company Address:** 355 King Street, London W6 9NH, UK. **Company Website:** www.timneyfowler.com.

Publications

On TIMNEY FOWLER:

Books

McDermott, Catherine, *Street Style: British Design in the 1980s,* London, 1987.

Gordon-Clark, J., *Paper Magic,* London, 1991.

Articles

"Timney Fowler Prints," in *Country Life* (London), 16 September 1984.

"England's Fabric," in *WWD,* 3 June 1985.

"Two's Company," in the *Sunday Express Magazine* (London), 15 September 1985.

Hall, Dinah, "Family Classics," in *World of Interiors* (London), April 1988.

Hawkins, Heidi, "Culture Club," in *Graphics World,* September/October 1988.

Crawford, I., "Artists in Residence: Mission Impossible," in *Elle Decoration* (London), October 1990.

Heinrich-Jost, Ingrid, "Alte Römer und Junge Englander," in *Frankfurter Allemein,* March 1991.

"Duo Tones," in *Metropolitan Home,* December/January 1991–92.

Fitzmaurice, Arabella, "Appearing in Print," in the *Sunday Times Magazine* (London), 1 March 1992.

Malone, Scott, "Prints' Future is Colorful," in *WWD,* 26 January 1999.

Gilbert, Daniela, "Dots Key at Print Shows, Embroideries Still Hot," in *WWD,* 25 January 2000.

Caplan, David Grant, "Black and White Stars at Shows," in *WWD,* 30 January 2001.

"Modernart Editions Debuts New Collection," in *Art Business News,* March 2001.

*

Timney Fowler's distinctive designs draw on the rich symbolism of European art. Neo-classical, architectural and Egyptian images are placed together in unexpected ways to create modern prints. Other designs use hand-drawn symbols to give a softer, more ethnic look. Animals, leaves and other images from the natural world are also used in unexpected ways.

—Timney Fowler Ltd.

* * *

Sue Timney and Graham Fowler are a design team of international repute who began working together after graduating in textiles from London's Royal College of Art. Timney had earlier studied fine art and Fowler, graphics and textiles. They launched themselves as freelance fashion designers in 1979, selling printed fabric on the roll. In 1985 they produced their own range of interior furnishings to sell in their first London showroom in Portobello Road.

Self-confessed "20th-century vultures," their inspiration has been drawn variously from photography, mythology, classicism, and European history, and from the arts and crafts and aesthetic movements—this eclecticism expressed with bold graphic imagery and in an uncompromising monochrome. "Image rather than color is our main vehicle for expression," Timney explained. "Black and white keeps color to its absolute classical minimum."

If design hype were to be believed, they virtually invented black and white. This striking classical modernism was taken up avidly by the style conscious avant-garde in the early 1980s. From the early years strong links were established with Japan, from where their work derived many influences. Clients included Yohji Yamamoto and Issey Miyake and the Japanese market has remained an important business connection.

The company's design criteria could be said to be embodied in the Neo-Classical Collection, the core of the Timney Fowler fabric range, produced in 1984–85. Drawing extensively on the history and symbolism of European art, the designs were presented in the company's distinctive graphic style, black on white. Greek, Roman, and Florentine objects led by the bestselling Emperor's Heads; twisted columns, sections of architectural buildings plans, elaborate montages of stonework and foliage scrolls, the unexpected and witty juxtapositions of paisley dolphins teamed with acanthus plasterwork. To complement these classical borrowings was a range of Regency stripes, latticed Victorian ironwork, and small scale heraldic repeats. Linked to all this was a small group of wallpapers, friezes, and borders.

Timney Fowler's aim has always been to produce "20th-century classics, contemporary and exciting in mood but making few concessions to instant fashion." The Neo-Classical Collection has been featured in some of the world's leading museums of modern design. Over the years the duo have become truly international, supplying specialist design consultancy services to leading fashion and household names. Their position in the forefront of British design has been recognized in the UK and internationally with the prestigious Textile Institute Design Medal for "outstanding contributions to textile design and management." Twice they have been the recipients of the Roscoe award in the United States.

In the late 1980s, Timney Fowler expanded into fashion, with a range of scarves and shawls in wool and silk, silk shirts, ties and t-shirts, waistcoats, and bags. New fabrics included velvet and plastic-coated cotton. Design features included images from Greek and Roman works of art, French tapestries, nautical instruments, along with a strong architectural theme; Russian maps, mosaic floor plans, and in the scarf range what over the years virtually became the company's logo—the clock—all used in a thoroughly modern way. Surprisingly, having traded for so long on their black and white signature, Timney Fowler at this stage introduced color for the first time into its fashion range. Their shirts and fashion accessories sell worldwide through retail outlets, as well from a New York showroom opened in 1999.

New products continue to emerge, including umbrellas, jewelery, shoes, furniture, lights, and a collection of black and white clothes. Noteworthy is the range of ceramics, mainly neo-classical and paralleling the fabrics. But while the source remains historical, there is also wit and a sense of the surreal. Strongly inspired by the etchings of Piranesi, the 18th-century Venetian architect, they capture the romantic characteristics of his work. On a much larger scale yet maintaining the same imagery are the Timney Fowler gun-tufted rugs—manifestly intended to be centerpieces, perennial designs like Coinhead and Timepiece, all resolutely in black and white, which speak for themselves.

The company fast outgrew its original premises in Portobello Road and in 1986 moved to the highly fashionable Chelsea where they concentrated on key products suited to this more sophisticated mileu—fashion, scarves, ceramics, tableware and interiors. Timney Fowler describe its design philosophy as "a process of evolution, working through one set of ideas in a kind of natural progression, but without any ups and downs."

Although there has been no let up in the appeal and saleability of Timney and Fowler's original style theme, much plagiarized by lesser talents, there have been moves to get away from visual typecasting. To this end a major development was the expansion of the Interiors Collection in the early 1990s, from the original black and white neo-classical themes into new fabrics and color, including a range of deep dyed cottons and velvets. New themes have emerged based on Rococo and Toiles, 15th-century European fashion portraits and 18th-century Byzantine paintings.

Color has been creeping into the Timney Fowler scheme of things and, as the designers would have it, not before time. There is also a distinct softening of the edges. Timney has described her earlier work as "clinical and calculated," and believes the new ecological awareness, lowering of international barriers, and the recession make for less ostentation in the 1990s and again in the early 2000s. Although interiors followed fashion's lead towards purer, simpler lines, by the end of the century texture, embroidery, and metallics played a prominent role. Micro and miniaturized prints were popular, and Fowler noted to *Women's Wear Daily* (26 January 1999), "Simple geometrics in fresh colors have gotten a great response from buyers," while dots and horizontal borders gained as well. The following year at the English Accents show in January 2000, batik prints with wood-blocked borders and Japanese screen designs were the rage.

The dynamic couple of Timney Fowler had created a stunningly unique look; their contrasting approaches of the formal intellectual on the one hand and flamboyant practicality on the other have been the recipe for an ever-evolving success story which has yet to slow down.

—Elian McCready; updated by Owen James

TINLING, Ted

British designer

Born: Eastbourne, 23 June 1910. **Military Service:** Served in the British Army, 1939–47, Lieutenant Colonel. **Career:** Designed custom dresses and sportswear, London, 1931–39 and 1947–75; liaison committee member, Wimbledon Tennis Association, London, 1927–49, 1982–90; chief of protocol, International Tennis Federation, 1973; immigrated to the U.S., 1975; designer, Virginia Slims Tournament, 1971–78. **Awards:** British Clothing Institute Designer of the Year award, 1971; International Tennis Hall of Fame award, 1986. **Collections:** International Tennis Hall of Fame, Newport, Rhode Island. **Died:** 23 May 1990 in Cambridge, England.

Ted Tinling, 1966 collection: dacron souffle tennis catsuit with a vinyl miniskirt decorated in a racquet motif. © AP/Wide World Photos.

PUBLICATIONS

By TINLING:

Books

White Ladies, London, 1963.
Love and Faults, London, 1979.
Sixty Years in Tennis, London, 1983.

Articles

Numerous columns for *British Lawn Tennis.*

Ted Tinling, 1967 collection: tennis ensembles with racquet motif. © AP/Wide World Photos.

"From Bustles to Bodysuits," with Camille Peri, in *Women's Sports & Fitness* (Boulder, Colorado), U.S. Open special advertising section, September 1986.
"Stay Back to Get Ahead," in *World Tennis* (New York), June 1987.
"The Goddess and the American Girl," [book review] in *Tennis* (New York), April 1988.
"Tennis Idol of the Twenties," [book review] in *Tennis,* April 1988.
"Who's the Best Ever?" in *World Tennis,* March 1989.

On TINLING:

Books

Glyn, Prudence, *In Fashion: Dress in the 20th Century,* New York, 1978.
Wade, Virginia, *Ladies of the Court,* London, 1984.

Articles

"An Interview with Teddy Tinling," in *World Tennis,* December 1954.
Glynn, Prudence, "That Tinling Feeling," in the *Times* (London), 11 June 1971.
Cox, Sue, "Teddy Tinling: The Go-Between," in the *Sunday Express Magazine* (London), 26 June 1983.
Flink, Steve, "The Professor of His Profession," in *World Tennis,* June 1985.
———, "You Must Remember This," in *World Tennis,* February 1986.
Bodo, Peter, "Why Tinling Worries About the Women," in *Tennis,* May 1986.
Griggs, Barbara, "Wimbledon's Other Champion," in the *Daily Telegraph* (London), 19 June 1986.
Ciampa, Gail, "Tinling's Shocking Tennis Togs Now Tame Stuff," in the *Providence Journal Bulletin* (Rhode Island), 23 July 1987.
Rothlein, Lewis, "Combining Form with Fashion," in *Women's Sports & Fitness* (Boulder, Colorado), August 1988.
Thomas, Robert, "Ted Tinling, Designer, Dies at 79; A Combiner of Tennis and Lace," in the *New York Times,* 24 May 1990.
Cullman, Joseph F., "Tinling: Patrician Sage for the World of Tennis," in the *New York Times,* 27 May 1990.
Bodo, Peter, "Ted Tinling, the Doyen of Women's Tennis," in *Tennis,* June 1990.
"Died, Ted Tinling," in *Time,* 4 June 1990.
Finn, Robin, "Ted Tinling, Couturier and Critic, is Remembered at Service," in the *New York Times,* 25 June 1990.
Pignon, Laurie, "Ted Tinling: 1910–1990," in *Women's Tennis* (New York), July 1990.
Flink, Steve, "He Left Them Tinling," in *World Tennis,* August 1990.

* * *

Teddy Tinling was a major presence in the world of international tennis from the late 1920s until his death at the age of 79 in 1990. Among the roles he filled were player, umpire, announcer, ombudsman, raconteur, historian, and designer to generations of champions.

Tinling's entrance into the professional side of tennis came about wholly by chance. In the absence of a club official, he was asked to referee a match in Nice starring the legendary Suzanne Lenglen when he was only 13 years old. The unlikely combination of smitten teenager and temperamental tennis star gelled and Tinling accompanied Lenglen to Wimbledon. In 1927 he became Wimbledon's official liaison between the tournament's players and its committee members. He held the position until 1949.

At the age of 21, Tinling decided on dressmaking as a profession, setting himself up in South Kensington, London. His first collection was shown in 1931, and by 1939 Tinling had moved to Mayfair where a staff of 100 worked on the wedding gowns and evening dresses that were his specialty. After serving in World War II, Tinling sought to resume his business yet postwar utility regulations combined with a shortage of raw materials prevented him from creating luxurious gowns for the carriage trade. Tinling turned instead to the new phenomenon, sportswear. Standard wear at the time for women on the tennis court was a blouse or jersey and a pair of culottes, an outfit which Tinling thought utterly lacking in femininity or style. His heroine Suzanne Lenglen always looked glamorous on or off the court, always dressed as the star she was. Tinling determined to bring these qualities to women's tennis clothes.

His designs were controversial from the outset—Tinling's first commission, for Joy Gannon's Wimbledon debut in 1947, was a dress with a small colored border at the hem. A similar design the following year for champion Betty Hilton's Wightman Cup match so outraged

Hazel Wightman she threatened to ban color—if not Tinling—from future Wimbledon games. Into this brewing storm blew Gertrude "gorgeous Gussy" Moran. Could Ted, she wrote from California, design her a dress for Wimbledon? A very colorful dress?

Tinling correctly predicted that an all-white rule would prevail for the 1949 games and so he designed instead a dress in proper white of satin-trimmed rayon, which shimmered, he said, as did Moran herself. Came the fitting, it was apparent that a pair of panties would be required to complete the ensemble. As legend has it, Tinling finished off the pants with a bit of lace edging and with this act inadvertently secured his place in fashion history. Moran was besieged by the press; photographers crawled behind her on their stomachs to achieve the most advantageous camera angle. Tinling was accused of introducing sin and vulgarity to a gentleman's game and was banned from Wimbledon for the next 33 years.

Tinling's clothes, however, were not banned, and they continued to provoke Wimbledon officialdom as they continued to bring a sense of flair and glamour to center court. Tinling had an easy rapport with the stars of the game. He designed to suit the playing style and personality of the players he came to know so well, matching fabric, trim, and cut to the individual. Between 1952 and 1961 every female champion at Wimbledon and most winners of the U.S. Women's Open wore Tinling's dresses. In 1973 he dressed the winners of every major international tournament.

Tinling continued to subvert the all-white regulations, which he felt led to clothing lacking spectator appeal and contributing nothing to a player's individuality. In 1950 he conceived a shirt and shorts ensemble of *broderie anglaise* which the United Press dubbed the "peekaboo" suit, thus assuring its later success in the retail market. A few years later Lea Pericoli sported a pink petticoat under her dress for the 1955 Wimbledon games. In 1962 Tinling's designs for Maria Bueno proved too provocative to escape censure—Bueno's Wimbledon costumes were enhanced with colored diamond-shaped petals which appeared in a sunburst pattern on her skirt lining and across her panties. One costume came suspiciously close to the official tournament colors; Bueno's semifinal match was lost amidst outbursts of temper and flashes of hot pink. The committee closed ranks and banned color for a second time.

From 1971 to 1978 Tinling was the official designer for the Virginia Slims circuit. It was here that he was able to introduce color to the game in a significant way. For the Slims circuit Tinling might design 100 dresses per season, each unique to the player, with color as the unifying factor. When the occasion called for it, Tinling could bring a sense of drama and flamboyance to the game. For Rosie Casals, he created a three-piece ensemble in, of all things, black velvet. Billie Jean King's "battle of the sexes" match against Bobby Riggs was fought in a sequined dress which perfectly suited the frivolity of the event, even as it made sure she would be visible to spectators at the top of Houston's vast Astrodome.

Largely because of the Virginia Slims tournament and owing to the efforts of the women themselves, women's tennis in the late 1970s became popular enough for sportswear manufacturers to offer lucrative endorsement contracts to the players. Unfortunately for Tinling, this ended his career as a custom designer for the women's tennis circuit.

Within the profession Tinling was respected as the supreme arbiter who represented players to management in an official capacity not only at Wimbledon, where he was reinstated in 1982, but at the other three Grand Slam events as well as on the Slims tour. His encyclopedic knowledge of tennis and tennis players made him an oral historian of the game, and keeper of its traditions. For six decades Ted Tinling and tennis were synonymous.

—Whitney Blausen

TISE, Jane

See ESPRIT

TOI, Zang

American designer

Born: Malaysia, 11 June 1961. **Education:** Studied fashion design at Parsons School of Design, New York, 1981–83. **Career:** Production associate, Mary Jane Marcasiano, New York, 1982–87; freelance designer, Ronaldus Shamask, New York, 1988; opened own business, 1989, introduced diffusion line Z, 1992. **Exhibitions:** Fashion Institute of Technology Museum. **Awards:** Mouton-Cadet Young Designer

Zang Toi, fall 2001collection: silk/wool/cashmere/mohair handknit cardigan wrap and turtleneck with a cashmere mini-kilt. © AP/Wide World Photos/Fashion Wire Daily.

award for Outstanding Achievement in the Arts, 1990. **Address:** 30 West 57th Street, New York, NY 10019, USA.

Publications

On TOI:

Books

Stegemeyer, Anne, *Who's Who in Fashion, Third Edition,* New York, 1996.

Articles

Starzinger, Page Hill, "New Faces," in *Vogue,* March 1990.
Baker, Martha, "Back to School," in *New York Magazine,* 17 September 1990.
De Caro, Frank, "Fashion New Kids: On the Block," in *Newsday,* 3 October 1990.
Darnton, Nina, "The New York Brat Pack," in *Newsweek,* 29 April 1991.
"Great Expectations," in *WWD,* 12 June 1991.
Goodman, Wendy, "Couture Cuisine," in *House and Garden,* December 1991.
Ezersky, Lauren, "Going for the Glitz," in *Paper* (New York), October 1992.
Pan, Esther, "Zang Toi's Zzzerious Couture," online at Newsweek.WashingtonPost.com, 20–21 February 1999.
Redstone, Susan, "Zang Toi," at FashionWindows.com, 31 December 2000.
Kee, William K.C., "Grand Entrance," at TheStar.com, 3 January 2001.
Elkins, Laura Lee, "Designer Zang Toi at Gus Mayer," in the *City Paper,* 25 January 2001.
Ong, Shirley, "Louis XVI Meets the Last Emperor," at TheStar.com, 31 January 2001.
Marsh, Lisa, "Zang Toi is Rolling Out Men's Line," in the *New York Post,* 13 February 2001.
Stern, Jared Paul, "Otherwise, How Was the Show?" in the *New York Post,* 17 February 2001.
"Infinite Variety," in *WWD,* 20 February 2001.
Townsend, Catherine, "Zang Toi's Scottish-Asian Fantasy," in *Fashion Wire Daily* (New York), 21 February 2001.

*

At the house of Toi, it all starts with color. Lavish hues of chartreuse, red, and hot pink...which, theoretically, should never be seen together. Here they have been combined masterfully with a flair and wit that has won the hearts of both critics and customers alike. Breaking the rules is what I do best. I try not to limit my thinking to the way things have been done before—my customers have come to expect the unexpected. Pioneering in dressing up good old all-American denim—in splashy red and hot pink stitching—and [adding] metalic gold stitching to sexy suits and little bustier dresses is the chicest way to dress.

The Zang Toi formula is creating glamorous, tailored, classic sportswear with a dramatic twist; with a surprising mixed palette and signature design finishes. Evening at Zang Toi means haute fantasy with a dash of old Hollywood glamor.

It is always a dream of mine to merge my fashion sense with fine food.... Food is like fashion; clothes are just a piece of cloth until you add the decoration and the look, then it becomes fashion. The same with food—once you start decorating it becomes appetizing. My personal philosophy is that beautiful food and clothes should always be a part of life.

—Zang Toi

* * *

Zang Toi has the dubious distinction of being a featured designer in a *Newsday* article of October 1990, "Fashion's New Kids: On the Block," and of being a principal in Nina Darnton's article "The New York Brat Pack," in the April 1991 issue of *Newsweek.* In the *Newsweek* article, Zang Toi had the last word, telling Darnton, "I think women are looking for good prices and styles that are new—not just young people in the same mold as the current stars." Likewise, in the *Newsday* article, Toi's pragmatic and sensible remarks form the article's conclusion when he says, "There are so many young designers who are eager to be stars right away. But ego can be the worst killer to any young designer. You can't let the press and the hype go to your head. If the work doesn't meet the demand and the quality, it doesn't mean anything."

Toi's work resoundingly meets demand and determined desires and styles in the early 1990s. The gifted young designer has demonstrated a color sensibility related not only to Asian textiles (the collection that earned him the Mouton-Cadet Young Designer award was inspired by Southeast Asian textiles, with rich batiks and embroideries) but perhaps equally to Matisse in his vibrant palette. Toi's color is often and aptly compared to Christian Lacroix's, but Toi has brought his tinted exuberance to serviceable sportswear separates while Lacroix tends toward almost baroque forms of highly elaborated couture. For Lacroix, the pleasure is in the whole and design by ensemble; in Toi's work, the delights are in the elements. Even within, his ingenious and extravagant details give punctuation with whimsy. Well-cut jackets, saucy skirts and shorts, spunky sarong skirts with ornament, wonderful vests and trousers provide a sensible dressing from constituents rich in color and texture. As much as Toi loves glamor, he also created a diffusion line, Z, launched in 1992, that luxuriates in denim and less expensive fabrication.

Toi did not set out to be a designer. Growing up as the youngest son of seven children of a grocer in a small town in Malaysia, he loved sketching and drawing but dreamed of being an architect or interior designer. His love of fashion came later and always in conjunction with cuisine and other pleasurable arts. He admits to wanting to combine fashion and running a restaurant. Like many designers, however, a lifetime interest in classic movie glamor and stars such as Audrey Hepburn encouraged his fashion interests. The Malay tradewinds have always brought rich interactions of British colonialism (apparent in Toi's schoolboy stripes), Chinese, Indonesian, and other converging possibilities. Exoticism and pragmatic synthesis seem to come effortlessly to Toi.

In the West, we have traditionally enjoyed an adulation of the new, and Zang Toi is a new designer. But his merit and interest reside in the fact that his design is distinguished not by novelty but by his intense commitment to color. His fashion draws eclectically and with an absorbing anachronism on history and global fashion, always keeping his international eye for color. His practicality and sensitivity to the consumer are hallmarks of smart design for the 1990s and the 21st

Zang Toi, fall 2001 collection: silk/cashmere shirt and cigarette pants with a stole. © AP/Wide World Photos/Fashion Wire Daily.

century beyond. Infinitely personable and charming, Toi, like many Western designers, is a social mixer and has a gregarious personality. Lauren Ezersky wrote, "I love Zang. Everybody loves Zang. He truly is one of the nicest designers on the scene today. And his designs are as fabulous as his gams, which he displays on a regular basis by wearing shorts."

In a fiercely competitive and fickle industry, Toi has flourished as a high society and movie star fashion designer. His commitment to luxury, beauty, and glamor continued to be evident in his designs, which made him the obvious choice to create a millennium gown for Melinda Gates (Mrs. Bill Gates). Whether the theme is the wild, wild West, inspired by a Montana trip (spring 2001), or "An Asian in Scotland" (fall 2001), his collections are executed in the finest fabrics and characterized by his signature use of color and attention to detail. His fall showing was one of the few to receive a standing ovation and praise from the New York fashion critics.

A favorite of Madonna, Sharon Stone, Ivana Trump, and Kirstie Alley, Toi is reaching out to their significant others by introducing a limited men's line for fall 2001. "This is really for the husbands and boyfriends of my private customers. They *are* the ones who pay for the clothes." Like his women's clothes, the new line is handmade or hand-knit and uses luxury fibers like cashmere and silk.

Zang Toi has held fast to his vision of fashion, despite an era of increasing informality and casual dress. "It is not a separate thing outside you, but something that flows out from inside you. That is why my clothes, my home, and my showroom all reflect a core that comes from the same source—a beauty that I see and feel and which takes its form in the look and feel of my creations and in the space where I live and work." No longer the new kid on the block, Zang Toi continues to inspire and delight and remind us of what fashion and glamor are really all about.

—Richard Martin and Christina Lindholm

TOLEDO, Isabel

Cuban designer working in New York

Born: Cuba, 9 April 1961. **Education:** Studied painting and ceramics, then fashion design, at the Fashion Institute of Technology and Parsons School of Design, New York. **Family:** Married Ruben

Isabel Toledo, fall 1998 collection. © Fashion Syndicate Press.

Toledo, 1984. **Career:** Showed first collection, 1985; stopped showing collections in traditional runway shows, 1988; opened first store, Isabel Toledo Lab, 1998; returned to regular showings of her collections, late 1990s. **Exhibitions:** *Toledo/Toledo: A Marriage of Art and Fashion,* Fashion Institute of Technology (traveling to other museums), 1999; *Interpretation: 20th Century Clothing and Illustration,* Ohio State University/Ohio Arts Council, 2000. **Awards:** Coty American Fashion Critics "Winnie" award; Women's Wear Designer of the Year, Hispanic Designers Inc.; Otis Critics' award named for her at the Los Angeles-based Otis School of Fashion Design. **Address:** 277 Fifth Avenue, New York, NY 10016, USA

Publications

By TOLEDO:

Books

Toledo/Toledo: A Marriage of Art and Fashion, with Ruben Toledo, New York, 1999.

On TOLEDO:

Books

Steele, Valerie, *Women of Fashion: Twentieth Century Designers,* New York, 1991.

Stegemeyer, Anne, *Who's Who in Fashion, Third Edition,* New York, 1996.

Articles

Schiro, Anne-Marie, "Hot New Young Designers," in *Cosmopolitan,* June 1987.

"Storm Over Toledo," in *Connoisseur* (New York), February 1992.

Rosenblum, Anne, "Partners in Style," in *Harper's Bazaar,* March 1992.

Gordon, Mary Ellen, "Isabel Toledo's Cottage Industry," in *WWD,* 27 May 1992.

"What Do Women Want?" in *Mirabella* (New York), October 1992.

"The Toledos," in *Mirabella,* January 1993.

Wadyka, Sally, "A Structured Life," in *Vogue,* February 1995.

Mason, Christopher, "A Pair of Muses, Above It All," in the *New York Times,* 27 February 1997.

Spindler, Amy, "The Gutsy, the Greedy, the Humble," in the *New York Times,* 8 April 1997.

Granados, Christine, "Memories and Culture Inspire Isabel Toledo's Clothing Designs," in *Hispanic Magazine,* January-February 1998.

Edelson, Sharon, "Isabel Toledo's First Store: Staying on the Edge," in *WWD,* 11 March 1998.

Hastreiter, Kim, "Isabel Toledo," in *Paper,* Fall 1998.

Bissonnette, Anne, "Introducing Isabel Toledo," in *Threads,* November 2000.

* * *

The United States is better known for the mass production of clothing than for nourishing avant-garde talent. Isabel Toledo was one of the few cutting-edge designers working in New York, and financial success has been a long time coming. When she began designing professionally in 1986, Toledo was immediately recognized as a powerful talent; her clothes were featured in magazines like *Vogue* and *Harper's Bazaar* and sold in prestigious stores like Bendel's of New York. Since then, however, she has had legal difficulties with financial backers, as well as problems with American retail store executives.

Toledo did not sell a single piece of clothing at retail in the U.S. for three years in the early 1990s. She and her husband, artist Ruben Toledo, told *Women's Wear Daily* that they just could not afford to take orders from stores that refused to provide half payment up front. Meanwhile, store buyers worried that her line was too "experimental" for the American market. She survived on the business from sales in Japan and Paris. "It makes sense for us to sell to Japanese and European accounts because when they give you an order, they give you the money," she said. She also had the patronage of about 60 devoted private clients, who were attracted by what she calls her penchant for "practicality disguised as fantasy."

Through it all, Toledo was a cult figure among fashion enthusiasts. Her fellow designers admired her tremendously; Todd Oldham called her "one of America's greatest resources." Both Marc Jacobs and Christian Francis Roth have praised her "incredible" talent and urged retailers to advance her money. Journalists, too, agreed: "Best overall collection for our money was Isabel Toledo, who ignored the market and concentrated on a well-edited, very weird, internal vision," raved a reporter for the *Village Voice.* Toledo is a "great designer...traveling on that new American highway of fashion," argued Kim Hastreiter of *Paper.* She had finally begun to achieve the financial recognition she deserved in the middle and late 1990s, and her clothes were available in Barneys New York (Manhattan, Chicago, and Beverly Hills).

Toledo designs clothes that are structured, even architectural, and sometimes (as she says) "rather severe—a lot of black and strong shapes." She has always started with a shape, usually a circle or a curved line: a circle skirt, a curved bra, a flared apron overskirt, the sweeping arc of a coat. "I'm not a fashion designer," insists Toledo. "I'm a seamstress. I really love the technique of sewing more than anything else." She believes it is crucial to know fashion from the inside: through cutting, draping, pattern making, and sewing. Among the designers she admires are women like Madeleine Vionnet and Madame Grès, who also worked in three dimensions rather than from a flat sketch. Toledo sees definite advantages in being a woman designer, because they "experience" the way the clothing feels. Men, she believes, tend to be more "decorators of clothing."

Like Claire McCardell, creator in the 1940s of the "American look," the Cuban-born Toledo has used classic materials such as denim and cotton flannel plaid in a modern way. Although inventive tailoring is characteristic of her work, her clothes are not for "an office type of person," she admits, but for someone like herself—artistic and feminine. There is also a futuristic element in her work, which she sees as being related to her experiences as an immigrant to a new country. Unlike many designers, Toledo has never been interested in recycling styles from the past, preferring to experiment with the basic materials of her art and to explore the future of fashion.

Toledo's work has remained critically acclaimed—especially by avant-garde fashion publications such as *Paper* and *Visionaire*—but not readily adapted by the bulk of fashion consumers. Despite this lack of mass appeal, Toledo has managed to maintain a successful business by selling to an upscale clientèle embracing her nontrend-dependent creations. From her Zigzag Dress and Jellyfish Blouse to her Gym Teacher, Kangaroo, and twisting Caterpillar Dresses, Toledo's

Isabel Toledo, fall 1998 collection. © Fashion Syndicate Press.

sense of shape, color, fabric, architecture, and movement have remained at the forefront of fashion.

Toledo stopped showing her collections in traditional seasonal runway shows in 1988. She believed designers rushed to get ready for such shows, ending up with unfinished pieces. She prefers to let her designs develop in their own time. In addition, to be noticed at runway shows, a designer must be "loud"—Toledo believes designs should develop organically rather than being created to attract attention. Her business even improved after she stopped showing, which she attributed to the fact that her designs were fully formed by the time they were seen by her customers. In the late 1990s, however, Toledo began to show again.

In 1998 Toledo—still without a corporate backer—opened her first store, called the Lab, in New York near Madison Square Garden. The shop featured children's clothing, menswear, home furnishings, and the womenswear for which she is known. The Toledos felt the location, atypically located on the fifth rather than ground floor and far away from other designer shops, suited Toledo well by allowing her customers privacy and by reflecting her lack of interest in following trends. The designer's latest efforts were roundly praised, by the *New York Times,* which had already labeled her a fashion original in 1997—"Only great designers can dispense with themes and theatrics and let the work speak instead. Ms. Toledo does just that, letting fashion itself be the theme, and the theatrics come from the improbable cuts, drapes and drawstrings that hike dresses here and there."

Toledo and her Lab shop continued to gain exposure and accolades from the fashion press. In March 1998 *Women's Wear Daily* commented that Toledo showed "artsy, sometimes silly pieces...[but] when she does make sense, she makes beautiful clothes." Kim Hastreiter, writing for *Paper* in the fall of 1998, captured the essence of Toledo's career when she noted, "Isabel Toledo is without a doubt one of America's most talented designers. Her work is so far removed from mass marketing, unfortunately, it seems she may only become recognized in museums and art books." For Toledo, however, the ambiguities of fame and widespread recognition recall a battle she won long ago.

—Valerie Steele; updated by Karen Raugust

TOMALIN, Lewis

See JAEGER

TOMPKINS, Susie and Doug

See ESPRIT

TORII, Yuki

Japanese fashion designer

Born: Tokyo, Japan, 3 January 1943. **Education:** Studied at the Bunka College of Art, Tokyo, 1958–61. **Family:** Married Takao Torii, 1974; children: Maki. **Career:** Freelance designer, working in Torii Ginza Boutique, Tokyo, founded by her grandmother, 1952 (now belonging to Yuki Torii); presented first designs within her mother's collection, 1962; established Torii Company Ltd., ready-to-wear firm, Tokyo, 1972; first Paris collection, autumn 1975; launched Yuki Torii Deux label and Yuki Torii International, 1983; opened Yuki Torii Design Studio, Tokyo, 1984; established Yuki Torii France S.A., 1985; designed costumes for theatre and television; designs include ready-to-wear for men and women, printed fabrics, kimonos, lacquerware, accessories, interior design items, and childrenswear; member of NDC (Nippon Designer Club), from 1984. **Awards:** Fashion Editors Club award, Paris, 1976; Japan Fashion Editors Club, Best Designer of the Year, 1988. **Address:** Yuki Torii Design Office, Daito Building, 1–5–1 Minami Azabu Minato-ku, Tokyo 106, Japan.

Publications

On TORII:

Books

The Tokyo Collection: Graphic Sha, Tokyo, 1986.

Yuki Torii, spring/summer 2001 ready-to-wear collection. © AP/ Wide World Photos.

Articles

Monique, "They Have a Yen for Traditional Japanese Styles," in the *New York Daily News,* 1975.
———, "Paris' New Household Word: Yuki," in the *New York Daily News,* 1975.
de Turckheim, Hélène, "Le Travail c'est la Santé de la Mode," in *Le Figaro* (Paris), 9 December 1975.
"Yuki Torii," in *WWD,* 19 December 1975.
"Mais Qu'est-ce qui fait courir les Japonais?" in *Gap,* December/ January 1977–78.
Klensch, Elsa, "Cool Kimonos: Torii's Creations are Feminine and Fun," on CNN, 25 November 1998.
Saito, Mayumi, "Yuki Torii," in *Japan Today,* 19 April 2001.

*

I create clothes which make women beautiful, happy, and gay. My clothes are easy to wear. They are made in beautiful colors, vivid or tender. Reflecting well the *air du temps,* [my clothes] are trendy and modern, but never provocative. I like femininity and *le charme* based on nature and harmony.

There is no age to wear my clothes; they are for women of any age. At first sight, my clothes give the impression of being destined for the very young, because of the bright colors. But they give successfully a young and modern allure to any woman. My philosophy—the clothes should make the person who wears them beautiful and happy as well as the people who look at her.

—Yuki Torii

* * *

As a child, Yuki Torii had ambitions of becoming a painter. Pattern and color had always excited her, and when she became a professional designer in the early 1960s, her approach always began with the textile or color, with a defined choice of palette that ranged from pastels to brights. These bold, vivid color have been an enduring and recognizable quality in Torii's work. One distinctive collection was autumn/winter 1986, which mixed rigorously colored tartans and

Yuki Torii, spring/summer 2001 ready-to-wear collection. © AP/ Wide World Photos.

checks for menswear, womenswear, and childrenswear. The collection consisted of lively, wearable separates; oversize tartan shirts, tartan trousers, and comfortable cardigans for men; long tartan flounced skirts for women, teamed with long, skinny rib jumpers or oversized Argyle patterned sweaters; tartan pinafore dresses for girls and a weatherbeaten, mountaineering look for boys, layering tartan overshirts over tartan Levi-style jackets.

The vibrant Yuki Torii collection sold as part of Liberty of London's *Japan at Liberty* promotion in 1991 and displayed a more sophisticated air, paying homage to the style of Coco Chanel combined with the color combinations of Christian Lacroix. Vibrant tweeds in unities of orange, lime green, red, grass green, yellow, pale pink, and fuchsia were made into neat, boxy suits, and separates. Much of the fabric was fringed at the hems of garments, and flower-shaped tweed emblems were interesting details appliquéd on pockets and trims.

Torii was the youngest student to have enrolled at the Bunka Gakuin College of Art in Tokyo when she was 15. This precocious talent led her to sell her first creations in her grandmother's haute couture boutique Ginza in Tokyo. By 1972 she had established her own ready-to-wear business, Torii Co. Ltd., and by 1975 had shown her first collection in the prestigious Paris ready-to-wear collections.

Torii has often been told her clothes look best on herself, and it is from this perspective that she begins designing. The approach is similar to that adopted by many other female designers, in particular Jean Muir, who is renowned for producing clothes women really want to wear and feel comfortable in. Torii thinks it natural that female designers conceive ideas from themselves and their roles and needs as women. She likes to project an overall image of sweetness in her clothes, a sweetness retained in images of childrenswear but is often lost in adult fashion. She achieves this by never presenting themes that threaten or provoke controversy. Her look instead is a harmonious combination of contrasting color and fabric that is wearable and flattering but often incorporates the unusual detailing found in children's clothes, for instance, Western cowboy detailing on children's shirts or the naïve flower emblems in her tweed collection.

In 1983, two new brands were created, Yuki Torii Deux and Yuki Torii International. Licensed products like scarves, furs, gloves, belts, eyewear, neckties, and umbrellas were produced from the Yuki Torii Design Studio established in 1984. By the following year, the company was operating from both Japan and France when Yuki Torii France S.A. was established, together with the opening of the boutique at 38–40 Galerie Vivienne in Paris.

A continuing theme in Torii's work has been the kimono. Kimonos and obis have been included in her lines and influenced items in her collections for decades. Typically, she bases these designs on the traditional kimono, which is a complicated and rule-governed garment, but adds a flexibility that allows today's women to adapt them to their lifestyle. She also incorporates modern fabrics, such as polyester, which does not wrinkle.

Torii told CNN in 1998 that "the classic, traditional kimono, with all its detailing, sometimes frightens women. They're not sure exactly how to wear a kimono. So I try to push the idea that they should start simply, wear a kimono casually, and not get too bogged down with the traditional implications." Her kimono designs often combine unusual pattern combinations or unexpected fabric choices, such as creating sleeves from a men's pinstripe. Yet her kimonos, like all her designs, are as feminine as they are comfortable.

Torii's haute couture and ready-to-wear similarly feature unique mixes of fabrics and patterns, such as checks with velvet or leather with gold lamé. Her collections are often critically acclaimed, with the term "classy" frequently used. The fashion press and customers alike find them innovative yet wearable. In addition to her collections, Torii designs school uniforms, as well as licensed accessories.

—Kevin Almond; updated by Karen Raugust

TORRENTE

French fashion house

Established: in Paris by designer Rosette Torrente-Mett, in 1969. **Company History:** Licensing contract for men's ready-to-wear signed with French factory, 1971; signed licensing deal with Japan, 1972; childrenswear, leather collection, luxury accessories such as

Torrente, fall/winter 2001–02 ready-to-wear collection. © AP/Wide World Photos.

neckties, scarves, glasses, jewelery, and household linens introduced; signed with La Callonec and Murier for corporate wear; sells both couture and ready-to-wear lines; signed licensing pact with Perfumer's Workshop for fragrance line, 2000. **Company Address:** 1, rond-point des Champs-Elysées 75008 Paris, France.

Publications

On TORRENTE:

Articles

d'Aulnay, Sophie, "Vestra Weaves Its Global Web," in *DNR,* 25 January 1993.
"Paris: Disco Finale," in *WWD,* 22 July 1994.
Singer, Natasha, "Testing theWaters in Russia: Couture's Mission to Moscow," in *WWD,* 4 December 1995.
"News in Brief," in *Cosmetics International,* 25 January 2000.
Laushway, Ester, "The Haute and Mighty," in *Europe,* November 2000.

* * *

Torrente is a French haute couture and ready-to-wear label. The essence of the company's style is represented by its longstanding reputation in Paris as one of the finest couture houses. Torrente couture and ready-to-wear lines are made from the most exquisite, luxurious, and individual fabrics in the world. Many of the clothes are hand-finished, which although adding to the cost of the garments, gives the customer a unique and personalized purchase.

Popular and influential Torrente styles have included the satin collar in an abstract floral print on a shapely, turquoise, short-skirted suit or a classic cream collar and cuffs on elegant, checked wool coat dresses and two-pieces. Unusual, stiff, gauzy silk fabrics are used on stoles, edged in bead embroidery and thrown over short, strapless bell-skirted raw silk dresses, with matching beading on the hems. Lace is another popular fabric, used mainly in eveningwear and ranging from heavily beaded and encrusted for sculpted looks, to a soft drapable lace used in short empire dresses in cream, with décolleté necklines. The drape is positioned centrally at the cleavage and secured with the palest of pink roses. The overall look is very feminine, aimed not at fashion's vanguard, but designed for a woman secure and established in her own style, whose schedule demands a quantity of individualistic, smart occasion wear.

The company was established by its first designer Rosette Torrente-Mett in 1969 and the upper echelons of Paris society soon recognized a formidable design talent. Torrente creations began to be seen in places like Maxim's and at the Opéra; stylish names like Claudia Cardinale and Marlene Dietrich became regular clients at the Haute Boutique. Since the 1960s the company steadily expanded. In 1971 a licensing contract for men's ready-to-wear was signed with a French factory and in the following year a lucrative deal was clinched with Japan. Childrenswear, a leather collection, and luxury accessories like neckties, scarves, glasses, jewelry, and household linens have since been introduced. The company even branched out into corporate wear, signing a licensing deal with La Callonec and Murier in France.

Torrente, spring/summer 2001 haute couture collection. © AFP/ CORBIS.

Madame Torrente-Mett was elected a member of the Chambre Syndicale de la Haute Couture in 1971. Her other activities in the fashion world include being founder and vice-president of the French Fashion Institute and lecturing at the Paris business school, Hautes Études Commerciales. Her fashion pedigree comes not only from her father, who was a tailor, but from working with her brother, Ted Lapidus, at his design firm before venturing out on her own.

Items from the Torrente couture range are available in hundreds of shops worldwide, while the less expensive ready-to-wear line, Miss Torrente, is found in shops throughout Europe. The firm's menswear retailed in some 500 worldwide outlets. Helping Torrente's expansion were recent forays into the burgeoning Russian market in the mid-1990s through Haute Couture Week in Moscow. "It's very important for us to come to Russia…with its extraordinary youth and energy, with its new generation besotted by fashion," Torrente-Mett told *Women's Wear Daily* (4 December 1995). "It's up to us to show them the best of what we have to offer…. My role is to demonstrate, to reveal to them what is beautiful and at the same time wearable."

At the turn of the century the venerable Torrente tested uncharted waters with its first fragrance, under license to Perfumer's Workshop

International. The new women's scent, part of a long-term association between the perfumery and Torrente, debuted in 2001. Yet it was still Torrente's couture line that remained the anchor and essence of Torrente style—denoting quality with an international sophistication equally at home at a society wedding in the south of France or at an opera gala in Milan.

—Kevin Almond; updated by Sydonie Benét

TRACY, Ellen

See ALLARD, Linda

TRANSPORT

British footwear firm

Founded: by Jimmy Sarvea. **Company History:** Opened first shop, Reading, Berkshire, 1970; firm bought by Allied Shoes Ltd. **Company Address:** Allied Shoes, 77–79 Great Eastern St., London EC2A 3HU, UK.

* * *

Transport shoes probably epitomized the growth of modern footwear fashion and the looks we took for granted as the street level expression of the young. The originator of the label, Jimmy Sarvea, previously a boxer, was first a shoe repairer, became an assistant manager for a major footwear retailer, and went on to become one of the leading shoe entrepreneurs of the 1970s and 1980s. From the opening of his first shop in Reading, Berkshire, in 1970 to his continued presence on the High Street, Sarvea helped ensure that the avant-garde, trend-conscious customer was well served.

Whether classic or high fashion, the original Transport shoes, manufactured in Italy, created an impressive turnover. One of the most famous outlets for their men's shoes was Succhi, a mecca for the discriminating. The menswear market in general had become increasingly aware of fashion as the decade progressed, and the individuality of the footwear sold under the Transport label became an essential ingredient of a positive statement. Sarvea was joined by Carol Sullivan and the influence they found from streetwear added charisma and a new visual freedom to their shoes. The collection continued to grow, with exciting and innovative designs for both sexes. Many styles were unisex, with wide use of the unexpected, including glitter fabrics, stinging shades of orange and purple, unforgettable last and heel shapes, platform soles, chunky silhouettes, and interesting and unusual use of laces and buckles.

Transport shoes were featured on *Top of the Pops,* a BBC television musical program for the young, and potential customers eagerly sought out the shoes. Transport had created the most anticipatory underground footwear fashion statement of the 1980s. Their ultimate goal, total originality, assisted in attracting celebrities of the period, and George Michael, Five Star, Duran Duran, and Ian Dury were the pioneers for those who desired, for personal or professional reasons, that their footwear be the center of attention.

—Angela Pattison

TREACY, Philip

Irish designer working in London

Born: County Galway, Ireland, 1967. **Education:** Attended National College of Art and Design, Dublin, 1985–87; Royal College of Art, 1988–90. **Career:** Hat designer; worked with John Galliano and Rifat Ozbek, 1989; opened showroom in London, 1991; began working with Karl Lagerfeld and Chanel, from 1991; began designing diffusion line for Debenhams, 1992; shows sponsored by Harvey Nichols, Debenhams, Rolls Royce, British Fashion Council, Swarovski Crystal, Max Factor, and others, 1993–98; launched accessories line, 1997; participated in British Invasion at Saks Fifth Avenue, 1998; showings in Singapore and Vienna, 1999; moved to 12 Elizabeth Street, 1999; Paris couture week appearance, 2000; signed with

Philip Treacy, spring/summer 2000 haute couture collection. © AP/ Wide World Photos.

Trussardi for an exclusive women's hat collection, 2001. **Exhibitions:** Biennale di Firenze exhibit, Italy, 1996; *Cutting Edge* and *One Woman's Wardrobe* exhibits, Victoria & Albert Museum, London, 1997; *Addressing the Century, 100 Years of Art and Fashion,* Hayward Gallery, London, 1998; *Satellites of Fashion,* Crafts Council, London, 1998; Hyper Hall exhibit, Copenhagen, 1998; Fragile House, Soho, London, 2000; London Designers Exhibit, Natural History Museum, 2000; La Beauté Exhibition, Avignon, France, 2000. **Awards:** British Accessory Designer of the Year, 1991, 1992, 1993, 1996, 1997. **Address:** 12, Elizabeth Street, Mount Barrow House, London, SW1 W9RB, UK. **Website:** www.philiptreacy.co.uk.

Publications

On TREACY:

Articles

Fallon, James, "Philip Treacy: The Shape of Things to Come," in *WWD,* 6 July 1990.
Killen, Mary, "Hats Off to Philip Treacy—His Fanciful Designs are Turning Heads," in *Vogue,* October 1991.
"Treacy: Another Feature at BG," in *WWD,* 15 November 1991.
McKenna, Joe, "The Big Fat Hat," in *Interview* (New York), November 1991.
Overland, Martha Ann, "Style Makers: Philip Treacy," in the *New York Times,* 5 April 1992.
Bowles, Hamish, "The New Enlightenment," in *Vogue,* March 1993.
Moore, Alison, "London Calling," in the *New York Times Magazine,* 19 December 1993.
"Glad Hatter," in *People,* 4 July 1994.
Luscombe, Belinda, "Mad About Hats: Milliner Philip Treacy's Fantastic Creations are Real Head Turners," in *Time,* 1 March 1999.
Fallon, James, "Treacy's Hat Show is Going Couture," in *WWD,* 13 December 1999.
Armstrong, Lisa, "The Mad Hatter of London," in the *Times* (London), 10 January 2000.
"Closing Remarks: Spring Couture Season Came to a Close With a Dazzling Show by Milliner Philip Treacy..." in *WWD,* 20 January 2000.
"Classic Beauty or Divine Madness," in *WWD,* 12 July 2001.

* * *

Former Royal College of Art student Philip Treacy was recognized as a talented milliner even before graduating from college where his final show was sponsored by *Harper's & Queen* magazine, London. In the years since leaving college, the Irish-born Treacy has moved to the forefront of the fashion world, producing hats for some of the most prestigious couture and ready-to-wear designers, including Chanel, Versace, Givenchy, Valentino, and Rifat Ozbek. Described as the Rembrandt of millinery by established hat designer, Shirley Hex, Treacy's monumental creations for the fashion catwalks often receive as much publicity as the outfits for which they were designed.

Treacy's millinery designs reflect his unquestionably vivid imagination, drawing upon diverse subjects such as surrealism, the dance of Martha Graham, or religious and historical imagery. Creating a hat, Treacy asserts, does not require space age influences; he prefers to plunder the past for inspiration and then make it appear totally new. A floral Treacy hat is a crash helmet covered in flowers and butterflies; a towering turban is created by an intricately wrapped blanket with fringed edging; a large cluster of black coq feathers are tied together with white feathers to form a brim and crown.

Treacy's hats, like those of other British milliners, are often described as eccentric. The designer attributes this eccentricity to the British being associated with idiosyncrasy, but says he does not set out to create deliberately unusual hats. Using what he describes as "boring" fabrics, Treacy begins working upon these materials with different treatments—feathers, for example, are singed so they take on the appearance of very fine gossamer.

An important factor in Treacy's work is his mastery of highly skilled traditional millinery techniques which ensure the correct balance, fit, and proportion for the hat which he concedes are as much mathematical as aesthetic. It is this artisan approach, with the emphasis on craft and technique, that characterizes much of Treacy's work. He produces hats for many different companies, both couture houses and ready-to-wear firms, and his annual shows in London and New York have been sponsored by a who's who of fashion and business, from Debenhams and Rolls Royce to Swarvorski Crystal and Max Factor. Treacy's ability to work at all levels of the market, from the

Philip Treacy, spring 2001 collection. © AP/Wide World Photos.

costly couture creations to the less expensive ready-to-wear field, illustrates his versatility as a designer for whom price barriers are seen as a challenge rather than an obstacle.

While Treacy's use of imagery and visual effects for his millinery creations is a vital element in his success, fashion critic Brenda Polan claims Treacy's mastery of technique is what singles him out as a great milliner, stating, "The balance of his hats, their swooping and curving, is perfect. A Treacy hat sits naturally upon the head, its proportions complementing those of the body, its horizontal and vertical lines extending and dramatizing the planes of the face. It is a perfection only an obsessive can achieve."

Obsessive or not, Treacy creations are unique and in demand. The designer branched out into accessories in 1997, and in 1999 was asked by the Federation Françoise dc la Couture to show his hats during the spring-summer haute couture presentations. Treacy, honored and excited by the prospect, put together a small, specialized collection, telling *Women's Wear Daily* (13 December 1999) "I can't compete with the multizillionaire designer companies, so I plan to do a very small, discreet collection…. It's important to give a profile to hat making; hats and headdress have been around since the beginning of time, despite the fact that many people say hats are finished."

Response to Treacy's highly anticipated catwalk collection were enthusiastic, with *Women's Wear Daily* (20 January 2000) declaring, "Treacy's hats were sculptural, exquisite…. This season, he's fallen head over heels for orchids, and he delivered a hothouse full of exotic hand-painted blooms that were fabulous." Succeeding shows continued to be the rage for critics and fellow designers alike, placing Treacy firmly in the upper echelons of fashion royalty. His aim, however, is simple—"The object of the exercise is to beautify women," Treacy had explained to *Women's Wear Daily* (20 January 2000). "I want to inspire young people to wear hats and to think of hats as something new and modern. In our parents' generation, to wear a hat used to be to conform. Now, to wear a hat is to rebel." Well said by the master.

—Catherine Woram and Sydonie Benét

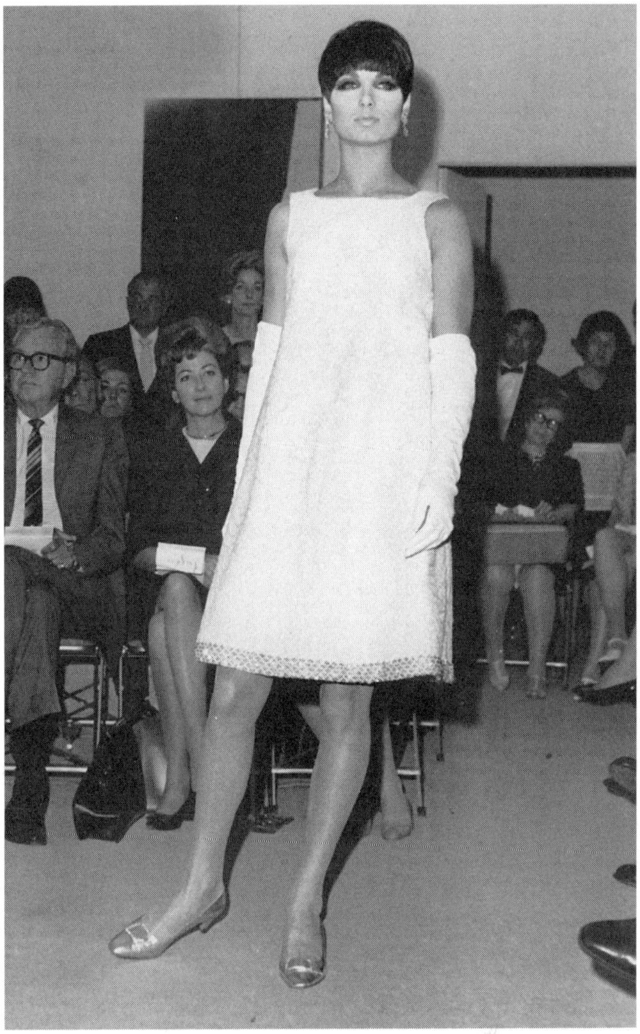

Pauline Trigère, fall 1966 collection: American broadtail dinner dress with a rhinestone border. © AP/Wide World Photos.

TRIGÈRE, Pauline

American designer

Born: Paris, 4 November 1912; immigrated to the U.S., 1937, naturalized, 1942. **Education:** Jules Ferry and Victor Hugo Colleges, Paris, 1923–28. **Family:** Married Lazar Radley, 1929 (separated); children: Jean-Pierre, Philippe. **Career:** Trainee clothing cutter, Martial et Armand, Paris, 1928–29; assistant cutter, fitter, in father's tailoring business, Paris, 1929–32; freelance designer, Paris, 1933–36; design assistant, Ben Gershel, New York, 1937; assistant to Travis Banton, Hattie Carnegie fashion house, New York, 1937–42; cofounder/designer, House of Trigère, from 1942; one of the original cofounders of the Council of Fashion Designers Association, 1962; closed firm, 1993; launched jewelry collection, 1994; introduced fragrance, *Liquid Chic,* circa 1995; retired 1997; worked for various charities, including Citymeals-on-Wheels; launched accessories line with Gold Violin web company, 2000. **Awards:** Coty American Fashion Critics award, 1949, 1951, 1959; Neiman Marcus award, Dallas, 1950; National Cotton Council of America award, 1951; Filene award, Boston, 1959; Silver Medal, City of Paris, 1972, 1982; CFDA Lifetime Achievement award, 1993; placed on Fashion Walk of Fame, 2001. **Died:** 13 February 2002.

Publications

On TRIGÈRE:

Books

Lee, Sarah Tomerlin, *American Fashion: The Life and Lines of Adrian, Mainbocher, McCardell, Norell, Trigère,* New York, 1975; London, 1976.

Morris, Bernadine, and Barbara Walz, *The Fashion Makers,* New York, 1978.

Diamonstein, Barbaralee, *Fashion: The Inside Story,* New York, 1985.

Milbank, Caroline Rennolds, *Couture: The Great Designers,* New York, 1985.

Pauline Trigère, fall 1966 collection: chiffon ensemble with plumes. © AP/Wide World Photos.

New York and Hollywood Fashion: Costume Designs from the Brooklyn Museum Collection, New York, 1986.

Milbank, Caroline Rennolds, *New York Fashion: The Evolution of American Style,* New York, 1989.

Stegemeyer, Anne, *Who's Who in Fashion, Third Edition,* New York, 1996.

Articles

"Designers Who Are Making News," in *American Fabrics & Fashions* (New York), No. 38, 1956.

Alexander, J., "New York's New Queen of Fashion," in the *Saturday Evening Post,* 8 April 1961.

"Pauline Trigère Takes John Fairchild to Task for a Three-Year Snub from *Women's Wear Daily,*" in *Chicago Tribune,* 24 August 1988.

Greene, Gael, and Peter Vitale, "The Style of Pauline Trigère," in *Architectural Digest* (Los Angeles), September 1988.

Woods, Vicki, "Vicki Woods Crosses Paths with the Eccentric Pauline Trigère—and Comes Away with an Earful," in *Vogue,* October 1989.

Brady, James, "Most Elegant Pauline," in *Advertising Age,* 21 November 1994.

"Fashion, Beauty Gala Will Help Fund Citymeals," in *WWD,* 21 April 1999.

Wilson, Eric, "Declaration of Independence: CFDA's Founders Sought to Shed Light on American Design," in *WWD,* 13 June 2000.

———, " Never Too Old to Accessorize," in *WWD,* 27 November 2000.

"Designing Women, Meet Golden Girls," in *Business Week,* 25 December 2000.

Goff, Lisa "Dot-coms' Senior Circuits; Surfers are Older Than People Think, " in *Crain's New York Business,* 22 January 2001.

McCants, Leonard, "Fashion Walk of Fame to Induct Second Class," in *WWD,* 1 February 2001.

Fabrikant, Geraldine, "It's Never Too Late to Accessorize (Designer Pauline Trigère)," in the *New York Times,* 25 February 2001.

McCants, Leonard, "Trigere Talks Tailoring at Walk of Fame Event," in *WWD,* 19 July 2001.

*

I've always found it difficult to talk or write about FASHION. I think FASHION—clothes, garments—should be enjoyed and worn, and certainly fill a certain purpose in one's life… I love my work, I love designing, I love folding, draping, molding the fabric in my hands and producing new shapes, new designs.

I have never gone up-up, or down-down like a yo-yo. I have tried to keep my women, my customers, happy in their Trigère clothes—hoping they bought them and wore them with pleasure, and that they were right for their lives—PTA, business meetings, concerts, theater, etc. In thinking back, I don't think that I would have enjoyed anything else but doing collection after collection, four to five times a year…(oh yes, maybe I could have been an architect, or most certainly a surgeon…).

—Pauline Trigère

* * *

Pauline Trigère was more than a designer of women's clothing, she was a fabric artisan. Trigère left her native France in 1937 and arrived in New York with practical training gathered from her parents' tailoring shop and the Parisian couture house of Martial et Armand, plus a natural talent for working with fabric. She started her own business in 1942 with a collection of just 12 dresses. During World War II, when the American fashion industry was cut off from inspiration normally coming from Paris, Trigère's combination of French elegance and American practicality proved successful. Her constant commitment to excellent design and workmanship kept her in business for 60 years.

During the 1940s Trigère become known especially for her impeccable and imaginative tailoring of women's suits and coats. She made use of all weights of wool, from sheer crêpes for eveningwear to thick tweeds for daytime coats. She was recognized early in her career as an innovator for such fashions as evening dresses made of wool or cotton, reversible coats and capes in all shapes and sizes. Another characteristic Trigère feature is the luxurious touch of fur trim at necklines, cuffs, and hems. Before the 1960s, her palette was fairly subdued and she rarely used printed fabrics; during the 1960s and 1970s she began to use more prints and softer fabrics, always retaining a tailored touch. Her use of prints is bold and deliberate, the pattern is often used to complement the structure of the piece. Notwithstanding her extensive use of wool and tailoring techniques, Trigère's clothing has always been unmistakably feminine.

While she was an acknowledged innovator of fashions, she was also known for repeating and perfecting her most successful themes. For example, her princess line dress has consistently been considered to have no equal, and her rhinestone bra top, first introduced in 1967, was revived in 1985 and again in 1992. Throughout the evolution of fashion in the six decades, Trigère worked within the mainstream while retaining her signature style. Simple elegance and timelessness are descriptions often applied to her work, but style was not her only concern. She insisted on the highest quality of materials to assure her clothing served her customers for years to come. Her collections were carefully planned so many pieces worked together, and complement past seasons' collections.

Trigère's work has been compared to that of two legendary French couturiers, Cristobal Balenciaga and Madeleine Vionnet. These designers were known for employing complex and unusual construction techniques to create simple, elegant silhouettes. Trigère herself rarely sketched her ideas; like Balenciaga and Vionnet she designed by draping and cutting the actual fabric on a dress form or live model. The fabric itself is an important part of Trigère's design process; it is her inspiration and her guide as it reveals what it is capable of doing. Trigère's continued involvement with the creative process and her insistence on quality made her unique on New York's Seventh Avenue.

Though she officially retired in 1997 at age 85, amazingly, Pauline Trigère was still going strong in the 21st century. In her 90s, she organized benefits, was inducted into the New York Fashion Walk of Fame, and launched an accessories line for seniors with Internet company Gold Violin in 2000. Time finally caught up with Trigère in February 2002 when the 93-year-old died at her New York City home; in true Trigère style she has asked to be cremated wearing her trademark red lipstick.

—Melinda L. Watt; updated by Nelly Rhodes

TRUSSARDI, SPA

Italian leathergoods and accessories manufacturer

Founded: in Bergamo, Italy, as a glove making firm by Dante Trussardi, 1910. **Company History:** Firm taken over by nephew Nicola Trussardi, 1970; first boutique opened, Milan, 1976; jewelery collection introduced, 1976; fragrances introduced, *Action Uomo* for men and *Action Donna* for women, early 1980s; men's and women's ready-to-wear collections and Trussardi Junior line introduced, 1983; Trussardi Jeans, Trussardi Action, and Trussardi Sport collections introduced, 1987; designed Italian Olympic team uniforms, 1988; new fragrance, *Trussardi Action Sport,* launched, 1993; Balenciaga designer Nicolas Ghesquière creates two collections, 1997; Jeremy Scott hired as design consultant, 1999; Francesco and Beatrice Trussardi take over after Nicola's death, 1999. **Awards:** Nicola Trussardi named Cavalier of the Great Cross, Italy, 1987. **Company Address:** Piazza Duse 4, 201 22 Milan, Italy.

Trussardi, SpA, fall/winter 2001–02 collection. © AP/Wide World Photos.

Publications

On TRUSSARDI:

Books

Gasperini, Nicoletta, and Giovanni Gaspel, *Trussardi estate 1985,* Milan, 1985.

———, *Il mondo di Trussardi: nelle immagini di Giovanni Gastel,* Milan, n.d.

The Fashion Guide: International Designers Directory, London, Paris, New York & Tokyo, 1990.

Casadio, Mariuccia, and Samuele Mazza, *Trussardi,* Milan & Corte Madera, California, 1998.

Articles

Frosh, Jennifer, "Camping in with Trussardi," in *WWD,* 8 July 1977.

Trussardi, SpA, fall/winter 2001–02 collection. © AP/Wide World Photos.

"La Maison Trussardi: A Distinctive Style," in *Esquire,* February 1998.

Cohen, Edie, "Trussardi alla Scala: Gregotti Associati Renovates a Palazzo in Milan's Center for the Global Fashion Concern," in *Interior Design,* April 1998.

Nemy, Enid, "Nicola Trussardi, 56, Who Led Family Fashion House in Italy," [obituary] in the *New York Times,* 16 April 1999.

"Nicola Trussardi," [obituary] in the *Washington Post,* 17 April 1999.

"Trussardi," available online at Fashion Live Interviews, www.FashionLive.com, 19 March 2001.

* * *

For over 60 years the Italian family firm of Trussardi manufactured high quality leather gloves. Opened in 1910 by Dante Trussardi in Bergarmo, the company had a limited but well-respected reputation for its goods. In 1970 Nicola Trussardi, a graduate of business and economics from the University of Milan, joined the family firm and worked alongside his father, Giordano, and his older brother, Dante. After Dante died in a car accident, Nicola ran the family business with his father. With high ambitions for broadening Trussardi's scope and production and after comprehensive research, Nicola introduced a wide range of luxury goods made to the highest possible standards. Top-quality leather goods like belts, wallets, bags, and luggage were followed by umbrellas, ties, and shoes.

By 1976 the first exclusive Trussardi boutique opened in Milan and further accessory products, together with gold and silver jewelry, were presented. All merchandise was stamped with a trademark greyhound, the sleek symbol of nobility and antiquity, now well established as a mark for Italian quality. By the end of the 20th century, there were well over 50 boutiques in Italy alone, plus international boutiques throughout Europe, the U.S., and the Far East as well as exports to many luxury department stores.

By 1983 Nicola Trussardi was devoting much energy to the launch of the company's first ready-to-wear collection. Clean-cut and essentially classic, the ranges of men's and womenswear soon diversified to include knitwear, skiwear, eveningwear, and Trussardi Junior, a children's clothing line. The clothes reflected the exclusive luxury of the established leather and accessory goods, yet were modern in feel, casual, and wearable. Favored fabrics included leathers (often embossed or treated), velvets, wool jerseys, and furs. Some collections adopted more avant-garde trends such as Empire line suits in oversize plaids, sleeveless A-line leather slipovers or a side-split plaid skirt dangerously perched at hipster level. Such an approach kept the collection youthful and provided a healthy fashion content, while retaining the ever-present sense of lavish expense and exquisite taste.

Trussardi has been noted for presenting collections in prestigious sites, organized and participated in by the most noted international names in theatre, cinema, and opera. The first ready-to-wear collection was presented in La Scala in Milan; another was shown in an enormous mostly transparent cube constructed in Piazza Duomo in the heart of Milan. The theatricality of these showings was obviously designed to attract the maximum media coverage for the Trussardi name.

In 1987 Trussardi segued into jeans and sport lines, then designed Italy's team uniforms for the 1988 Olympics in Seoul, Korea. Fervently nationalist, Trussardi had also sponsored the building of the Palatrussardi in 1986, an important center for sports and entertainment ventures in Milan. The launch of a new fragrance, *Trussardi Action Sport,* reinforced the company's sporty image in 1993 (previous scents included *Action Uomo* and *Action Donna*), while a new 70,000-square-foot headquarters in Milan's Piazza della Scalla in 1996 reflected Trussardi's enduring legacy of luxury.

Frenchman Nicolas Ghesquière, who designed for Balenciaga, created two popular collections for Trussardi for 1997, and was followed in 1999 by American Jeremy Scott, who was hired to spice up Trussardi's jeans and sports lines. Yet the deal with Scott had barely been made when tragedy again struck the Trussardi family—Nicola was in a coma following a car accident. Two days after the accident, on 15 April 1999, Nicola died from his injuries.

Nicola Trussardi's family, including his wife Maria Luisa, and children Beatrice, Francesco, Gaia, and Tomaso had all been involved in the family business in one way or another for several years. After Nicola's death Beatrice and Francesco supervised Trussardi's design department, opting to end the planned collaboration with Jeremy Scott. Collections for 2000 and 2001 were as luxe and conservative as those of previous years, including a myriad of leathers and suedes, chamois, bright neoprene, as well as crocodile and python.

—Kevin Almond; updated by Owen James

TUFFIN, Sally

British designer

Born: 1938. **Education:** Studied at the Walthamstow School of Art; graduated from the Royal College of Art, 1961. **Family:** Married. **Career:** Partner, Foale & Tuffin, 1962–72; opened retail store, 1965; designer, Sally Tuffin, Ltd., from mid-1970s.

PUBLICATIONS

By TUFFIN:

Books

Children's Wardrobe with Ann Ladbury, London,1978.

On TUFFIN:

Books

Lobenthal, Joel, *Radical Rags: Fashions of the Sixties,* New York, 1990.

Articles

"Tuffin Alone," in *WWD,* 10 July 1972.
"Being There," in *WWD,* 16 July 2001.

* * *

Sally Tuffin was one of several designers to emerge from Professor Janey Ironside's talented stable of fashion design graduates at London's Royal College of Art in the 1960s. In company with Ossie Clark, Zandra Rhodes, and Bill Gibb she and her business partner Marion Foale (also a RCA graduate) fast came to epitomize the street style and culture of what became the trademark phrase of the decade, "Swinging London."

Based in the hotbed of trendy 1960s happenings, Carnaby Street, Tuffin and Foale produced clothes celebrating youth culture. "We were dressing ourselves and our friends and it just happened to be the things people wanted," Tuffin reminisced in the 1980s. The pair recognized that the sudden predominance of street fashion was a reaction to a previous generation's reliance on Paris for ideas. To the young, the couture direction seemed tired and inaccessible. Tuffin and Foale noted there was a fast-growing younger market which wanted something inexpensive in which to have fun and wear to dance clubs.

As designers, they incorporated both modernist and nostalgic ideas into their clothes. Beginning with the Pop Art movement that spawned prints and "keyhole"shift dresses, they moved through Op Art, into an art déco phase, and next the romantic dressing made popular by the hippie movement. They created hipster trousersuits, clean-cut crêpe dresses like cycle shirts, or vigorously banded into rugby stripes. They even printed giant Ys across a group of shift dresses intended as a pun on the male undergarment, in many ways a forerunner to the witty tactics employed by Moschino today.

Tuffin and Foale's partnership came to symbolize the greater opportunities available to young people with ideas and energy in the 1960s. Initially inspired by a lecture on garments given by Mary Quant at the Royal College of Art, the pair realized business could be fun and approached it in a lighthearted way. "As students we were trained to see, to explore, to enjoy ourselves. We felt as though we could go off and do anything without restriction," enthused Tuffin.

Tuffin and Foale's clothes sold in many outlets; their first big break came in 1962 when buyer Vanessa Denza purchased their designs for the Woolands 21 shop in London. This was followed by the opening of their one showroom in Carnaby Street and the retailing of their clothes in the famous Countdown boutique on the King's Road, Chelsea, and at various department stores throughout England. In 1965 the partners were among the first designers to be stocked in Paraphernalia in New York, where designer Betsey Johnson recalled they sold out of Tuffin and Foale's clothes almost immediately.

In 1972 the design duo dissolved their partnership. Tuffin went on to produce some collections under her own name label, which closely adhered to the cutting-edge young fashion look she and Foale had established in the 1960s. Yet Tuffin tired of designing clothes and turned to another form of art, establishing a pottery business with her husband.

—Kevin Almond

TYLER, Richard

Australian designer working in Los Angeles

Born: Sunshine, Australia, circa 1948, son of a factory foreman and a seamstress. **Family:** Married Doris Taylor (divorced); married Lisa Trafficante, 1989; children: Sheriden, Edward. **Career:** Opened store, Zippity-doo-dah, in Melbourne, Australia, late 1960s; designed outfits for rock stars, early 1970s; designed and traveled with Rod Stewart's Blondes Have More Fun tour, 1978; started the Richard Tyler collection with wife and partner, Lisa Trafficante, late 1980s; opened Los Angeles showroom, Tyler Trafficante, 1988; opened New York City showroom, 1992; named head designer for Anne Klein & Company, 1993; left Anne Klein & Company, 1994; reintroduced menswear line, 1995; hired as designer for Byblos, 1996–98; initiated bridal line, 1999. **Awards:** Council of Fashion Designers of America (CFDA) New Talent award, 1993; CFDA Womenswear Designer of the Year, 1994; Designer of the Year Award (CFDA), 1996; Gumleaf award by Australian American Chamber of Commerce (contribution to Australian and American Culture), 2001.

PUBLICATIONS

On TYLER:

Books

Stegemeyer, Anne, *Who's Who in Fashion, Third Edition,* New York, 1996.

Articles

Beckette, Kathleen, "Runway Report: My One and Only Hue—Richard Tyler," in the *New York Post,* 4 November 1994.
"New York: Richard Tyler," in *WWD,* 4 November 1994.

Richard Tyler, fall 2001 collection: cashmere chenille lace tuxedo. © AFP/CORBIS.

Schiro, Anne-Marie, "The V-Shaped Jacket of the 1940s Makes a U-Turn," in the *New York Times,* 5 November 1994.

Spindler, Amy M., "Anne Klein's Designer Departs," in the *New York Times,* 20 December 1994.

Campbell, Roy H., "Richard Tyler Takes the High Fashion Moments with the Lows," in *Knight-Ridder/Tribune News Service,* 2 February 1995.

LaFerla, Ruth, "Richard Tyler, Perfectionist," in *Elle* (New York), March 1995.

"New York: Richard Tyler," in *WWD,* 5 April 1995.

Spindler, Amy M., "Oldham and Tyler Look Super," in the *New York Times,* 6 April 1995.

Anniss, Elisa, "Richard Courts," in *Footwear News,* 29 July 1996.

Conti, Samatha, "Behind the Purge at Byblos," in *DNR,* 4 December 1996.

Sanchez, Eurydice, "Richard Tyler Exclusive Interview," in *Men Mode Magazine,* Spring 1997.

"Richard Tyler," in *Current Biography,* May 1997.

Ginsberg, Merle, "Golden Moments in Fashion," in *WWD,* 8 January 2001.

Young, Kristin, "Tyler Receives Gumleaf Award," in *WWD,* 1 February 2001.

Haber, Holly, "Too, Too Tyler," in *WWD,* 3 March 2001.

Rubenstein, Hal, "The Look of Richard Tyler," in *In Style,* 1 July 2001.

Townsend, Catherine, "Bridal Collection 2002, Brides Who Rock," available online at www.fashionwindows.com, 8 August 2001.

Various articles and reviews in *GQ,* October 1990; *Harper's Bazaar,* October 1992; *New York,* 12 October 1992; *Vogue,* August 1993; *New York,* 13 September 1993; *People,* 21 February 1994; *Newsweek,* 4 April 1994; *New York,* 11 April 1994; and *Vogue,* October 1994.

* * *

"At my age, I'm thrilled," 46-year-old Richard Tyler told *People* magazine when he won the Council of Fashion Designers of America New Talent award in 1993. Just one year later, he walked away with the Council's Womenswear Designer of the Year award—one of the fashion world's highest honors. Although Tyler's fame may have come later in life than other designers, it quickly grew, earning him the respect of his peers and the devotion of his customers.

Much of Tyler's initial success was due to his celebrity clients. Julia Roberts, Janet Jackson, Sigourney Weaver, and Oprah Winfrey are just a few of the stars who have publicly praised the exemplary quality and fit of his clothes. "That's the age-old recipe for success in fashion: get the right people to wear your clothes," Patrick McCarthy, the executive editor of *Women's Wear Daily,* told *Newsweek.* Although his famous clients might have drawn new customers in, Tyler's attention to detail and fine tailoring have kept his business growing. Everything on a Richard Tyler design is done by hand. Identical and precise buttonholes are a hallmark of his collection, and his fabrics—the finest wools, silks, and linens—boast such details as individual stripes sewn onto the cloth with silk threads.

Tyler was born in Sunshine, Australia, just outside Melbourne. His mother was a costumer with the Melbourne Ballet and sewed wedding dresses, men's suits, and clerical robes as well. Tyler's father was a plastics factory foreman with one of the best wardrobes in town. It was through his mother that Tyler learned his love for fine quality tailoring. At age 16, Tyler dropped out of school and began work as a tailor at a shop known for outfitting the Australian prime minister. He also spent some time at a factory, cutting out bras. At the age of 18, with his mother's help, Tyler opened his own store, Zippity-doo-dah, in a rundown section of Melbourne. His father paid the bills and his mother sewed his designs in the back room.

By the 1970s, Tyler's shop was beginning to attract a steady clientèle. Australian celebrities, and such touring musicians as Cher, Elton John, and Alice Cooper, began to seek out his Lycra and sequined outfits. During this time, Tyler married Doris Taylor. The marriage lasted 10 years, and they had a son, Sheriden, born in the late 1970s. After Tyler's mother died in 1976, he made many trips to London, continuing to dress a growing cadre of musicians.

In 1978 Rod Stewart asked Tyler to design his Blondes Have More Fun tour. When the show stopped in Los Angeles, Tyler fell in love with the city and decided to make it his home. He continued to design for performers, including Supertramp, the Bee Gees, the Go-Gos, and Diana Ross. But as costume demands became increasingly outrageous in the mid-1980s, Tyler began to drop his work for the stars. He stayed in Los Angeles, doing odd jobs and trading his gardening and sewing skills for rent at the guest houses of friends.

Richard Tyler, fall 2001 collection: silk chiffon diagonal pintucked/stitched dress. © AFP/CORBIS.

Tyler then spent two years in Oslo, Norway, but ended up back in Los Angeles in 1987, with his last $100 and a plane ticket home to Australia. The night before he was to fly home, he met Lisa Trafficante, an actress and businesswoman, who would change his life forever. Together, Tyler and Trafficante formed a partnership enabling them to establish the Richard Tyler line of clothing. Trafficante urged Tyler to follow his strengths and design finely-tailored menswear. She took it upon herself to come up with a business plan and the necessary capital.

Tyler's clothes were so bold that many buyers thought their customers wouldn't buy them. It was during their last appointment of the day, at the boutique If in SoHo, that Tyler and Trafficante received their first order. If's customers were immediately drawn to Tyler's work, and within two years Chativari in New York City and Wilkes Bashford in San Francisco were also buying from Tyler. In 1988 Trafficante persuaded Tyler that they needed to open their own showroom in Los Angeles. With the backing of Trafficante's sister Michelle and investor Gordon DeVol, they bought a drapery manufacturing building in an out-of-the-way part of town. They gutted the interior of the art deco building and created a bare, contemporary setting for Tyler's fashion-forward designs.

The store was named Tyler Trafficante, and it was there that Tyler first became known for his trademark fitted jackets. Diana Rico, writing for *GQ,* described the transformation felt after trying on a Tyler jacket: "Its dashing cut and construction are so comfortable that you feel as though you're barely wearing anything at all. The sensuous silk lining and luxurious hand-tailored details bespeak an old-world emphasis on fine craftsmanship, while the stagy lapels, offbeat colors and elongated silhouette give the piece a daring rock and roll edge." Although the showroom started without a women's section, so many women came in off the street requesting clothes that the next season Tyler began designing for them.

It was the demand for women's clothes that really sparked the growth of Tyler Trafficante. Within five years, they had one of the hottest stores in Los Angeles. In 1992 Tyler decided it was time to introduce his line to New York. The New York fashion world welcomed him and the press lauded his debut show in March of 1993. The reviews were barely in when he was contacted by the upscale women's sportswear line Anne Klein & Company, asking him to sign on as their new design director. Many in the fashion world questioned the pairing of Tyler—known for his bold, sexy designs—with Klein, a label manufacturing traditional, conservative career clothes for women. The first year Tyler began designing for Anne Klein, store orders rose 30 percent. Despite the immediate jump in sales, the reviews of the Anne Klein line were mixed.

In December of 1994, Anne Klein and Tyler parted company. There were a number of problems that plagued his tenure with Anne Klein. Tyler had difficulty controlling quality and price: his demand for impeccable quality raised the price of an Anne Klein jacket by 15 percent. In addition, he was not used to overseeing a huge staff of pattern makers, tailors, design assistants, and dressmakers. Many speculated that the overriding reason for Tyler's termination, however, was that in his attempt to attract a younger customer, he made too many changes too soon and turned off Klein's traditional customers.

Industry insiders had no doubt, however, of Tyler's rebound. He left Anne Klein with a reported $2.1 million buyout of his contract. In the near future, Tyler planned to launch a secondary line, with a lower price point so that more women can afford his clothes. In 1995, Tyler relaunched his men's line. "The timing was right for coming back to menswear. I felt that at this point we could fill a niche that has opened up. I also think men are tired of wearing big baggy clothing—a look I personally hate," Tyler told *Mode Magazine* in the spring of 1997.

In 1996 Donatella Girombelli hired Tyler as the chief designer at Byblos, the famous Italian label. He was hired for the job because, according to Girombelli, he was both a designer and a craftsman. He produced four women's collections and two men's collections for Byblos while at the same time producing similar lines in America under his own name. Also in 1996, he joined forces with Rossimoda, a shoe manufacturer based in Italy. Tyler creates sketches with his staff and then sends them to Rossimoda for prototypes to be made. The shoes match his womenswear collections and sometimes inspire his collections because they are produced first.

Tyler was replaced at Byblos by John Bartlett in 1998 and returned to his Tyler Trafficante home base. His lines include Richard Tyler Couture, a designer sportswear line, and the most recently added Richard Tyler Bride in 1999. The bridal debut line featured quilted embroidery with handmade roses, which has become his signature on his bridal gowns. Tyler remains a choice designer for Hollywood celebrities to wear to various functions, including award shows. His clothes are well received, fashion-forward, and wearable. He describes his business as a life investment, and although he thrives on challenges, he has found his place in the fashion world and is currently has no plans for further expansion.

—Molly Severson; updated by Donna W. Reamy

U

UNDERWOOD, Patricia

British millinery designer working in New York

Born: Patricia Gilbert in Maidenhead, England, 11 October 1947. **Education:** Trained in millinery at Fashion Institute of Technology, New York, 1972. **Family:** Married Reginald Underwood, 1967 (divorced, 1976); married Jonathan Moynihan, 1980; children: Vivecca. **Career:** Clerk/typist at Buckingham Palace, 1966–67; secretary, United Artists, New York, 1968–69; manufactured hats with Lipp Holmfeld (Hats by Lipp), 1973–75; president/designer in own company Patricia Underwood, New York, 1976; launched Patricia Underwood Knit Collection, 1983; opened in-store shop in Saks Fifth Avenue; Patricia Underwood Too line of women's ready-to-wear introduced, 1990; featured collections in *Vogue,* has designed for Bill Blass, Oscar de la Renta, Carolyne Roehm, Donna Karan, Calvin Klein, and others. **Exhibitions:** *Hats,* Philadelphia Museum of Art, 1993. **Awards:** Coty American Fashion Critics award, 1982; Council of Fashion Designers of America award, 1983, American Accessories Achievement award, 1992. **Address:** 242 West 36th Street, New York, NY 10018, U.S.A.

PUBLICATIONS

On UNDERWOOD:

Books

Khornak, Lucille, *Fashion 2001,* New York, 1982.
Steele, Valerie, *Women of Fashion,* New York, 1991.
McDowell, Colin, *Hats: Status, Style, Glamour,* London, 1992.
Muller, F., *Les chapeaux: une histoire de tête,* Paris, 1993.
Smith, R., and Smolan, L., *The Hat Book,* New York, 1993.
Stegemeyer, Anne, *Who's Who in Fashion, Third Edition,* New York, 1996.

Articles

Meadus, Amanda, "Major Gripe: The Minimalist Wave," in *WWD,* 14 February 1994.
Gault, Ylonda, "A Crowning Achievement in Hats: Designer Builds Heady Reputation with Stylish Toques in Hatless World," in *Crain's New York Business,* 18 January 1999.
Karl, John, "Mad About Hats," in *Sarasota Herald Tribune* (Saradota, Florida), 18 April 2000.

*

I design hats which complement clothing, flatter the wearer, and rely on shape and proportion rather than ornamental trim to achieve this effect. My designs are characterized by clean, elegant lines that enhance a silhouette and complete a sophisticated look. A simplicity of design avoids the pitfalls of a hat becoming a distraction on a wearer. I create hats in a variety of materials since there are also the practical weather-related aspects to hat wearing. A hat must be comfortable and easy to wear; this is achieved by using high quality, malleable materials and handcrafted workmanship.

My inspiration for a collection comes from my travels, art, and the international world of fashion. Beautifully tailored clothing, innovative uses of materials and application of finishing details are constant sources of new ideas. Collaborations with talented designers including Bill Blass, Marc Jacobs, the late Perry Ellis, and many others, are a tremendous source of inspiration for me. I am always intrigued by color and certain tones that flatter a complexion to enhance beauty.

We are lucky today that one may choose to wear a hat or not, unlike 50 years ago when a hat was considered a necessity of good grooming. Now hat wearing has become a matter of personal style and a way of stimulating response… Hats create amazing possibilities.

—Patricia Underwood

* * *

The outstanding characteristic of millinery designer Patricia Underwood's hats is they are, for the most part, completely unadorned. There are no added trimmings, no flowers, ribbons, or even hatbands on her pieces. The shape and the materials are the statement, they provide all the texture and color she feels is necessary. Underwood works with a variety of traditional millinery materials; various straw braids, fur felts, real fur, and knitted yarns, in addition to more unusual materials such as fake furs and her signature sewn strips of leather and suede.

Underwood's hats are designed specifically to work with clothing and to complement it. She strives to avoid overwhelming the wearer, and to avoid crossing the fine line between the flattering and the absurd in millinery. She is described by Colin McDowell in *Hats: Status Style, Glamour* (1992) as, "Probably the most skilful of the middle-market milliners…Underwood's approach is entirely practical. Her paramount concern is how the hats will relate to clothing." Underwood herself explains, "Why bother to have a hat…if it doesn't go with the clothes?"

Underwood's strength lies in transforming traditional hat shapes and types and creating new interpretations of these classic forms. The change may be made by the use of an unexpected material, or by her subtle manipulation of the form, giving a familiar shape an entirely new look. A cowboy hat, for example, for her 1991 collection was made of fine straw braid, the brim slightly wider than normal, the curve of the brim more subtle, the curl of the edge was slightly exaggerated. The overall effect of the hat was more feminine and sophisticated than a cowboy hat has ever been before. A 1920s-style cloche from the same year was transformed in a similar manner—the crown was squared and the brim became a small visor off the front; the feminine cloche was given a sportier character, suggesting a modern baseball cap. Other familiar hat types she has reworked include boaters, nun's coifs, and the wide-brimmed picture hat.

By changing the expected relationships between the elements of the hat, the crown, and the brim, Underwood creates modern versions of virtually any forms. Her aesthetic is in concert with the minimalist fashions of designers such as Giorgio Armani and Calvin Klein; she takes the forms we are familiar with and eliminates detail until they are reduced to their essential shape.

In response to the frequent pronouncements that "hats are back" as mandatory fashion accessories, Underwood maintains that the hat will not return as a fashion staple, but will continue to exist as an optional accessory. The art of the milliner will therefore survive in modern fashion. Underwood's inspiration is derived from the arts, her travels, and historical fashion. Her palette for the fall-winter 1994 collection was inspired by the work of the painter Modigliani. In general, her preferred colors are muted, natural tones.

In the middle 1990s she added coordinating scarves, shawls, and gloves to her collection. Her work is mostly ready-to-wear, available through department and specialty stores such as Saks Fifth Avenue and Bergdorf Goodman, and has her own in-store boutique in the latter. Additionally, Underwood continues to do custom work for a select clientèle and has expanded her horizons into Europe and Japan.

Besides her own collections, Underwood has collaborated with many of the top American fashion designers who appreciate her purity of form. Upscale retailers appreciate Underwood's creations as well. Nicole Fischelis, vice president and fashion director of Saks Fifth Avenue, a longtime admirer of Underwood told *Crain's New York Business* (19 January 1999), "She is very successful because she has a complete understanding of the couture customer. She has a great sense of proportion, keen color sensibility, and the style is pure, never ornamental."

—Melinda L. Watt; updated by Nelly Rhodes

Emanuel Ungaro, fall/winter 2001–02 ready-to-wear collection. © AP/Wide World Photos.

UNGARO, Emanuel

French designer

Born: Aix-en-Provence, 13 February 1933. **Family:** Married to Laura Ungaro. **Career:** Worked in his father's tailoring business, Aix-en-Provence, 1951–54; stylist, Maison Camps tailors, Paris, 1955–57; designer, Balenciaga, Paris, 1958–64; head of design, Balenciaga, Madrid, 1959–61; designer, Courrèges, 1964–65; established own firm, 1965; Ungaro Parallèle ready-to-wear collection introduced, 1968; menswear collection added, 1975; sportswear line, Emanuel, introduced, 1991; launched bed and bath collection, then plus-size line, 1995; firm bought by Ferragamo, 1996; opened new Palm Beach store, 1998; Gianbattista Valli hired as creative director, 1998; launched Fever denim line, 2000; Valli took over all designs but couture, 2001; fragrances include *Ungaro,* 1977; *Diva,* 1982; *Senso,* 1987; *Ungaro pour l'homme III,* 1993; *Fleur de Diva,* 1997; *Desnuda,* 2001. **Awards:** Neiman Marcus award, Dallas, 1969; Dallas Fashion award, 1995, 1996; first fashion designer asked to address Oxford Union, 2001. **Address:** 2 avenue Montaigne, 75008 Paris, France. **Website:** www.emanuelungaro.fr.

Publications

By UNGARO:

Books

Emanuel Ungaro, Paris, with Yves Navarre, Paris, 1988.
Emanuel Ungaro, with Frederico Fellini, Milan, 1992.

On UNGARO:

Books

Lyman, Ruth, ed., *Couture: An Illustrated History of the Great Paris Designers and Their Creations,* New York, 1972.
Perschetz, Lois, ed., *W, The Designing Life,* New York, 1987.
Loebenthal, Joel, *Radical Rags: Fashions of the Sixties,* New York, 1990.

Emanuel Ungaro, spring/summer 2001 haute couture collection. © AP/Wide World Photos.

Guillen, Pierre-Yves, and Jacqueling Claude, *The Golden Thimble: French Haute Couture,* Paris, 1990.

Stegemeyer, Anne, *Who's Who in Fashion, Third Edition,* New York, 1996.

Orban, Christine, *Emanuel Ungaro,* Paris & London, 1999.

Articles

Arroyuelo, Javier, "La haute couture: Ungaro," in *Vogue* (Paris), March 1985.

"The Allure of Ungaro," in *Vogue* (New York), April 1985.

Salinger, Pierre, "Emanuel Ungaro, un homme et artiste," in *Vogue* (Paris), September 1985.

Brubach, Holly, "Theme and Variations: Expression of a Unique Style at Ungaro," in *Vogue* (New York), December 1985.

Salinger, Pierre, "Emanuel Ungaro, un homme et un artiste," in *Vogue* (Paris), February 1986.

Salvy, Gérard Julien, "Créer c'est rêver d'une femme," in *Vogue* (Paris), February 1986.

Premoti, Francesca, "Emanuel Ungaro: un'eleganza discreta," in *L'Uomo Vogue* (Milan), October 1986.

Bernasconi, Silvana, "Ungaro la seduzione: *Senso,"* in *Vogue* (Milan), September 1987.

Williamson, Rusty, "Rapping with Ungaro: He Talks of Couture, Fashion and Texas Women," in *WWD,* 16 January 1990.

Howell, Georgina, "Ungaro Fortissimo," in *Vogue* (New York), November 1991.

Prey, Nadine, "Prints Charming," in *Harper's Bazaar* (New York), November 1991.

Gerrie, Anthea, "Sex, Style and a Man Called Ungaro," in *Clothes Show* (London), January 1992.

Yusuf, Nilgin, "Emanuel Ungaro: The British Are So Exotic," in *Marie Claire* (London), January 1992.

Morris, Bernadine, "House of Ungaro at 25: Seductiveness without Vulgarity," in the *New York Times,* 25 March 1992.

Aillaud, Charlotte, "Chez Emanuel Ungaro," in *Architectural Digest* (Los Angeles), July 1992.

Menkes, Suzy, "Chanel: Beauty Without Gimmicks," in the *International Herald Tribune,* 25 January 1995.

Haber, Holly, "Emanuel Line Wins Dallas Award," in *WWD,* 13 June 1995.
"Ferragamo Acquires the House of Ungaro; Emanuel Keeps Reins," in *WWD,* 3 July 1996.
Ozzrad, Janet, "Ungaro's American Face," in *WWD,* 20 May 1997.
Weisman, Katherine, "Ungaro's New Global Approach," in *WWD,* 16 July 1998.
Zargani, Luisa, "Ferragamo Chooses Ungaro Licensees," in *WWD,* 14 July 1999.
Pogoda, Dianne M., "Emanuel Ungaro—On Freedom, Obsession and Pleasing Women," in *WWD,* 13 September 1999.
Folpe, Janet M., "Will Bestiality Sell Dresses? How About S&M?" in *Fortune,* 21 February 2000.
Socha, Miles, "Ungaro: Time to Catch the Fever," in *WWD,* 3 August 2000.
———, "Ungarro's New Design," in *WWD,* 11 January 2000.
Fallon, James, "Professor Ungaro of Oxford," in *WWD,* 18 May 2001.
Socha, Miles, "Do the Rite Thing: Emanuel Ungaro Passes Control to Giambattista Valli," in *WWD,* 9 October 2001.

* * *

Approaching 50 years in fashion, Ungaro can look back and see he had indeed accomplished his goal of "seducing the woman." His early training in the atelier of Balenciaga taught Ungaro about line and color. He still refers to what he learned about draping directly on the model. Later, working with Courrèges, Ungaro participated in the Space Age hard chic of his mentor.

It was later suggested that many of Courrèges's successful designs might have been attributed to Ungaro, who created metal bras, skimpy cutout A-line dresses, and white boots in a hard, futuristic manner Ungaro himself later dismissed as "false modernism." The influence of two years with Courrèges carried over into the early years of Ungaro's work on his own. He continued to make young, "kicky" fashions, dresses, and coats in bold, interlaced geometrics. His turtleneck and leggings worn underneath a sleeveless pinafore was a 1960s look that was resurrected by other designers to great popularity 20 years later. With the advantage of textile designer Sonia Knapp's artistic fabric designs, Ungaro gradually developed a softness of line that was to fully develop a decade later. Of his early designs, Ungaro prefers to say little, but chenille daisy appliquéd see-through trousersuits speak for themselves.

Toward the end of the 1970s, Ungaro began to experiment with the then-taboo mixing of textures and prints, of which he has become the master. Knapp's fabrics had evolved into more painterly, impressionistic florals, abstract smears, luminous colors. In daytime clothing Ungaro would pair a paisley blouse with a plaid suit, or a striped top worn under a tweed jacket with glen plaid trousers. In 1980 this daring approach found full expression in a collection of casual but complex ensembles, featuring fantasy printed, gold-edged jackets over sheer lace blouses, luxuriant paisley shawls wrapped over quilted, fur-lined cardigans, solid chiffon blouses paired with half-patterned, half-striped skirts.

For evening, there were embellished velvet burnooses or wrapped paisley dresses, trimmed in black lace, completed this unusual eclectic look, offered through Ungaro's expensive ready-to-wear line, Parallèle. This risk taking had its early appearance in Ungaro couture, and has continued to the present day. The clothes were designed for women who chose and combined their outfits without regard to what others would think. In the wake of the drab "dress for success" uniform, Ungaro's vision offered the self-confident woman, or one who was not dependent upon conformity for job security, the opportunity for a more personal, individual look. Knapp's special fabrics made the mixtures work. Her colors were rich, with underlying coordinate properties hard to duplicate. Over the years many designers have borrowed from Ungaro's ideas, with varying degrees of success.

Borrowing from the East, in 1981, Ungaro layered fluid chinoiserie patterned tunics over contrasting colorways skirts, draped with tasseled shawls of tiny floral and undulating lines in a riot of colors. The sensual, covered-up looks suggested Gustav Klimt's paintings in their profusion of mosaic colors and patterns. Cummerbund-bound floral skirts topped with lacy blouses under boleros showed a folkloric influence, though less literal than Saint Laurent's Russians a few years before.

Ungaro's designs have been intended to convey sex appeal without being vulgar. He has said that when doing a dress he would always ask himself if the woman in the dress would be seductive. Women and music are his inspiration. One can only guess if a particular collection has been created while Ungaro was listening to Mozart, Beethoven, Wagner, Stravinsky, or Ravel. Certainly his designs possess the contrast and harmony, repose and counterpoint of a musical composition. By the mid-1980s an Ungaro dress could be immediately identified by its diagonally draped and shirred skirt, wide shoulders gathered into gigot sleeves buttoned at the wrist, wrapped V-neckline, or jewel-toned silk jacquard fabric.

Ungaro wedding dresses were of pale pastel crêpe, sculpted, diagonally draped and caught with self-fabric flowers. At this time he introduced the short black-skirted suit with colorful jackets, both printed and plain—this look continues to be universally chic. To add to the seductiveness of his ensembles, Ungaro's models wore veiled elongated pillbox hats, pushed down over the eyes, an accessory resurrected a decade later for fall.

By 1985 Ungaro seemed to achieve a new serenity, the result of his thoughts and dreams. Since then he has repeated with variations the sleek curvaceous silhouettes, the fluid construction, ingenious cut, original color sense, and print and pattern mixtures without ever becoming boring. The self-confident Ungaro customer is also appealingly vulnerable because the fabric and cut subtly reveal her body. A flirtation with the short bubble floral skirt followed Lacroix's introduction of that silhouette, but Ungaro became even more wildly successful with his short, tightly wrapped dress. Late 1980s spring dresses featured short flounced skirts, big puffed sleeves, and bold solids or florals. Ungaro called his style a "new Baroque."

Fall 1989 ball gowns were gypsy inspired, with floor-length bouffant floral skirts trimmed with polka dotted ruffles and black lace, puffed sleeved jackets of contrasting florals trimmed with velvet and jewels. In 1990 folkloric flowers trimmed a cape worn over a short black leather skirt and deep red jacket. Voluminous Victorian-bustled plaid skirts on strapless evening dresses highlighted Ungaro's 1991 couture, while padded Asian coats were offered through his ready-to-wear line. After a cheerful, bouffant skirted spring, Ungaro presented a more somber, but no less luxurious, collection for the fall of 1992. Ungaro Parallèle continued to produce feminine floral brocade dresses and vibrant plaid suits interwoven with gold threads. In 1991 the lower priced Emanuel line was launched, with the famous tight and short Ungaro silhouette typified by a thigh-high shirred houndstooth dress with high neck and long sleeves.

Certainly the body-hugging Ungaro designs require a trim figure, but all the shoulder and hip emphasis can also be flattering to many figures by simulating an hourglass shape. Diagonal lines have a slimming effect. Some of Ungaro's spring dresses have merely skimmed the body, hiding flaws. Slit skirts have flatteringly shown off still-good legs.

At the end of the 20th century Ungaro was a name and brand increasingly recognized worldwide. The designer's 17th freestanding boutique opened in Palm Beach, Florida, and all remaining stores were renovated to reflect a new, hipper style. The outward changes reflected some internal struggles over the last few years, including the loss of longtime designing team Ken Kaufman and Isaac Franco, who went to Anne Klein. Esther Chen took over, then Gianbattista Valli was hired in 1998.

Ungaro ignited a storm of controversy in 2000 after new ads featured model Kirsten Owen and a large German Shepard wearing unusual accoutrements and assuming unusual positions. Most laughed at the resulting bestiality and S&M jokes, and Ungaro himself was unfazed. When the new Ungaro swimwear collection was introduced a few months later, there was nary a wag about the dog.

Ever in search of pleasing women, Ungaro has endured because his clothes show profound appreciation and respect for women (with the exception of that silly canine ad). Though Ungaro stepped back a bit to design only his couture line, turning the rest of the responsibilites over to Valli, he will continue to do what he does best: make women feel beautiful.

—Therese Duzinkiewicz Baker; updated by Owen James

UNGER, Kay

American designer

Born: Chicago, Illinois, 22 May 1945. **Education:** Studied at Washington University, Missouri, and Parsons School of Design, New York. **Career:** Worked for Pattullo-Jo Copeland, Gayle Kirkpatrick, and Geoffrey Beene; became designer of Traina Boutique and Traina Sport collections, 1971; created own collection; became partner at Gillian Group, 1972, with Howard Bloom and Jon Levy; lines include Gillian, Gillian Dinner, Gillian Suits, Gillian Petites, Woman, and two other prominent dress lines, A.J. Bari and GiGi By Gillian; shut down Gillian and A.J. Bari labels, 1995; launched own company with labels Kay Unger New York and Phoebe, 1995; created eveningwear division, Unger Mindel, 1996; began separates collection, 1999; started producing lower-priced Pamela Dennis line, 2000. **Awards:** J.C. Penney scholarship and Irish Linen Association scholarship, Parsons School of Design. **Address:** Kay Unger Phoebe Enterprises, 575 Eighth Avenue, New York, NY 10018 USA. **Website:** www.kayunger.com.

Publications

On UNGER:

Books

Lambert, Eleanor, *World of Fashion: People, Places, Resources,* New York, 1976.

Articles

Stiansen, Sarah, "Staying on Top," in *Savvy Woman,* November 1990.

Wilner, Rich, "Unger's Back on Seventh Avenue as Chief Designer for Phoebe," in *WWD,* 7 March 1995.

"Kay's Evening Bag," in *WWD,* 15 October 1996.

Rath, Paula, "Island Style," in *Honolulu Star Advertiser,* 27 December 2000.

Haber, Holly, "Oh, Kay," in *WWD,* 24 May 2001.

* * *

Kay Unger epitomizes the customer for whom she designs—with a clear understanding based on her own busy lifestyle. Using herself as the customer, she understands the needs of an active lifestyle, whether a woman is involved in a career or not. The specific needs of her clientèle are rooted in lifestyle dressing, primarily dresses that can be worn from the office to dinner or appropriate for luncheons or charity functions.

In 1989, recognizing a void in the marketplace for "clean dinner dresses," Unger set out to reinvent the little black dress. She designed a group of understated, tasteful, less embellished restaurant dresses, brought hemlines down—some to mid-calf and ankle length—and successfully replaced the overly opulent, short, and ornamented looks of the 1980s dress market. In addition to the void in evening dresses, she also filled a void in the daywear market with city short sets or rompers. To unite day and evening, she created ensemble dressing: two- or three-piece outfits sold as one rather than as sportswear separates. This allowed the customer a certain freedom to alter the look of a garment, depending on the occasion.

Selling her wares under the Gillian label, Unger's signature fabric was silk, in many guises and in various weaves. Other fabrics used were wool crêpe for fall and linens and linen weaves for spring and summer, always incorporating novelty fabrics and innovative color mixes. Unger's eye for color and design was honed during early training as a painter and influenced the prints appearing in every line, designed in-house by her design team and exclusive to the Gillian Group. They were often influenced by her knowledge of art history as well as home furnishings. Color was the primary strength of the Gillian line, due to its innovative and saleable quality.

Unger's clothes were categorized as bridge, falling between top-quality ready-to-wear and designer apparel, feminine and classic rather than trendy, streetwise, or masculine, and dresses following trends. Her customers were adult women, fairly affluent, with good taste, interested in the classic rather than trendy but definitely not traditional. The Gillian collection included a wide variety of classic designs for daytime, career, and dinner dressing. Comfort and affordability were important considerations for a customer whose day demanded polish and professionalism, from early meetings to late night dinners or entertaining. Bold color combinations, quality fabrics, and striking prints were consistent Gillian trademarks. Certain styles such as the longer shirt dresses, easy chemises, coat dresses, savvy suits, and understated dinner dresses met with great success.

The Gillian Group was one of the largest suppliers of women's apparel in America. Recognizing the various needs of women spanning from the Northeast to the South and to the West, these regional differences were addressed through a large variety of fabrics and colorations within the different fashion divisions bearing the signature Gillian style and value. They included Gillian, Gillian Dinner, Gillian Suits, Gillian Petites, Woman, as well as the A.J. Bari and GiGi By Gillian labels.

Unger and her partners shuttered Gillian and A.J. Bari in 1995 after more than two decades in business. Within a few months, in 1995, Unger set up shop for herself as a bridge resource, establishing the brands Kay Unger New York, for misses' sizes, and Phoebe, consisting of dresses and eveningwear for younger women. The higher-priced Kay Unger New York line consists of both classic styles and more innovative pieces. In 1996 Unger launched an eveningwear division in partnership with Wendy Mindel, an assistant designer for Phoebe, under the Unger Mindel moniker. Then in 1999, Unger started a line of separates for daytime, allowing her customers to shop for mix-and-match coordinates rather than exclusively for sets.

Unger's designs are recognized for their attention to detail and for utilizing a variety of prints, nearly all created in-house. From stripes to florals, Unger's fabrics claim a central role in her designs; some pieces layer fabrics in a variety of prints. The fact that the company makes its own fabrics also gives it the flexibility to quickly react to changes in the market and to focus on bestselling items, a trait appreciated by key customers, including Neiman Marcus and Saks (for whom Unger creates some exclusive items to differentiate the line from store to store).

In 2000 the Lieber Group retained Unger to produce a lower-priced line of eveningwear under the Pamela Dennis label (although the line, designed by Lieber staffers, is thought to be in some jeopardy as of 2001 due to the Lieber Group's financial problems). Unger has also designed a line of leather goods for Vericci and has created several licensed accessories lines under her own labels.

Unger prides herself on her readiness to listen and respond to her customers. She is on the road for appearances 20 weekends a year, not only to publicize her line but to collect customer feedback. She has a following among the famous; she created Tipper Gore's gown for the 1997 inaugural ball and has designed custom attire for stars at various awards shows, including the Grammy Awards. Unger's designs have received a boost through publicity in fashion publications, particularly *In Style* magazine, and through product placement in television shows and films such as *Bounce.* Indeed, many of her designs are influenced by looks from Hollywood's heyday, with Unger claiming Audrey Hepburn as one of her muses.

Kay Unger's philosophy is "less is more." She counsels women to eschew bulky clothing and to dress appropriately but without regard to age or shape; she sometimes creates designs in the same fabrics for different figures so all customers will find something in which they feel comfortable. She urges her customers to emphasize their femininity, and she creates affordable clothing that enables them to do so.

—Roberta Hochberger Gruber; updated by Karen Raugust

V

VALENTINA

American designer

Born: Valentina Sanina in Kiev, Russia, 1 May 1904. **Education:** Studied drama in Kiev, 1917–19. **Family:** Married George Schlee, 1921 (died, 1971). **Career:** Dancer, Chauve Souris Theater, Paris, 1922–23; moved to New York, 1923; opened small couture house, 1925, incorporated as Valentina Gowns, Inc., 1928; introduced perfume *My Own,* 1950; designed for the theatre, gowns for leading ladies, 1934–54; firm closed and retired, 1957. **Died:** 14 September 1989, in New York.

Publications

On VALENTINA:

Books

Milbank, Caroline Rennolds, *Couture: The Great Designers,* New York, 1985.

Owen, Bobbie, *Costume Designers on Broadway: Designers and Their Credits 1915–1985,* Westport, Connecticut, 1987.

Milbank, Caroline Rennolds, *New York Fashion: The Evolution of American Style,* New York, 1989.

Steele, Valerie, *Women of Fashion,* New York, 1991.

Articles

Diesel, Leota, "Valentina Puts on a Good Show," in *Theatre Arts,* April 1952.

Pope, Elizabeth, "Women Really Pay Her $600 for a Dress," in *Good Housekeeping,* February 1955.

Lawford, Valentine, "Encounters with Chanel, Mainbocher, Schiaparelli, Valentina, and Charles James," in *Architectural Digest,* September 1988.

"Valentina," [obituary] in *Current Biography,* September 1989.

Morris, Bernadine, "Valentina, A Designer of Clothes for Stars in the Theater, Dies," in the *New York Times,* 15 September 1989.

"Valentina," [obituary] in *WWD,* 18 September 1989.

"Valentina," [obituary] in the *Independent* (London), 28 September 1989.

Anderson, Lisa, "Garbo Walks Her Companion on Many a N.Y. Stroll...," in *Chicago Tribune,* 25 October 1991.

Fraser, Kennedy, "The Valentina Vision," in *Vogue,* March 1995.

* * *

Madame Valentina was as exotic as her name. A Russian emigrée, she attracted attention in New York after her arrival in 1923 by looking like a woman at a time when women were trying to look like young boys. For dining in fashionable restaurants or attending the theatre with her theatre-producer husband George Schlee, Valentina wore her own designs—full-length, high necked, long sleeved gowns with natural waistlines, made of flowing black velvet—in contrast to the short, waistless, beaded flapper fashions that prevailed at the time. Instead of bobbed hair, Valentina emphasized high cheekbones and large soulful eyes by wearing her long blonde hair in a high chignon. Slavic reserve, thick Russian accent, expressive hands, and movement with a dancer's grace completed her personality. She was her own best model and maintained a consistency of appearance throughout her long career.

Interest in Valentina's unusual clothes led to the establishment of Valentina Gowns, Inc. in 1928, on New York's upper East side. Success was immediate; Valentina's clients included luminaries from the theatre, opera, ballet, society, and film. Greta Garbo, whom Valentina was said to resemble ("I'm the Gothic version," she once said) was one of her customers. Each of Valentina's clients, who numbered no more than 200 at any one time, was granted personal attention. Valentina insisted that she alone knew what was best for these women and made last-minute changes in color or detail if necessary. Fashion editors were exasperated by Valentina's insistence upon selecting and modeling her clothes herself, but, ultimately, Valentina was right. Her business remained successful for 30 years.

Valentina's sophisticated color sense, influenced by Léon Bakst, gravitated toward subtle earth tones, "off-colors," monochromatic schemes, and the ubiquitous black. An evening dress with a bolero might be made of three shades of grey. In the 1950s Valentina began using variations of deep colors of damask and brocade. From a visit to Greece, she learned proportion, which lent an architectural dignity to her gowns. Her couture was original, intricately cut and fitted, and avoided the popular practice of copying French haute couture.

With an innate flair for the dramatic, Valentina successfully designed for the theatre. Beginning with a play starring Judith Anderson in 1933, Valentina was known for her ability to suit the character, whether on or off the stage. Critic Brooks Atkinson had commented, "Valentina has designed clothes that act before a line is spoken." The clothes she created for Katherine Hepburn in the 1939 stage play, *The Philadelphia Story,* remained in demand by her customers for five years. Timelessness of design was essential. In the 1930s and 1940s Valentina introduced hoods and snoods as headcoverings, wimple-like effects (flattering to mature throats) swathed around tall, medieval-inspired head-dresses. The diamond and emerald Maltese cross brooch she wore almost constantly was widely copied. Drawing inspiration from the art of European galleries, Valentina created striking evening ensembles along Renaissance lines such as a white crêpe floor-length gown fastened down the bodice with small fabric bows, topped by a three-quarter length beige wool cape.

Only the wealthy could afford Valentina creation. A minimum price of $250 dollars was charged per dress in the 1930s, with an average price of $600 dollars in the mid-1950s. Valentina preferred to sell entire wardrobes, presenting a unified look from formal to casual. For ease of travel she introduced coordinating pieces, like a blouse, bare top, skirt, shorts, and scarf that could be mixed and matched. She disdained fussy, frilly ornamentation, silk flowers, or sequins, relying instead on exquisite line. During the 1930s she borrowed Oriental details such as *obi* sashes and Indian striped embroidery used as sleeve accents. A favorite casual accessory was a coolie hat tied under the chin. In the 1940s she promoted a look that was slightly softer than the popular, mannish, broad-shouldered silhouette, and she introduced the short evening dress, while promoting ballet slippers, which were not rationed, worn with dark rayon stockings.

Valentina's working costume often consisted of a simple black long-sleeved dress with a versatile neckline, cut so it could be pinned high with a contrasting brooch, or folded down and worn with a long scarf draped about the head or shoulders for evening. A slice of colored satin lining would be turned *en revers* for contrast with the black. By the 1950s Valentina's evening gowns featured increasingly *décolletage* necklines. Her casual ruffled handkerchief linen blouses, worn with pleated skirts, were widely copied, as were her aproned organdie party dresses.

The supple matte fabrics favored by Valentina included crêpe cut on the bias for daytime, wool and satin crêpes, chiffons and damasks. Elegant wraparound silhouettes were created for coats, one of which featured three layers of progressively longer capes falling from the shoulders. Valentina's idiosyncratic, though classic, fashions also included evening gowns with one bare shoulder, the other long-sleeved, dolman sleeves, large fur hats made from sable, the only fur she would accept. Plain necklines lent themselves well to showcasing a client's jewelry.

Often called "America's most glamorous dressmaker," Valentina was recognized to be one of the top U.S. couturiers and theatre costume designers. She retired in 1957, and died in 1989.

—Therese Duzinkiewicz Baker

Valentino, spring/summer 2002 ready-to-wear collection. © AFP/ CORBIS.

VALENTINO

Italian designer

Born: Valentino Garavani in Voghera, Italy, 11 May 1932. **Education:** Studied French and fashion design, Accademia dell'Arte, Milan, to 1948; studied at the Chambre Syndicale de la Couture, 1949–51. **Career:** Assistant designer, Jean Dessès, 1950–55, and Guy Laroche, 1956–58; assistant to Princess Irene Galitzine, 1959; business established, Rome, 1960; showed first ready-to-wear collection, 1962; ready-to-wear boutique established, Paris, 1968; company owned by Kenton Corporation, 1968–73, Rome shop opened and menswear collection introduced, 1972; repurchased by Valentino, 1973; Valentino Più established, 1973; signature fragrance introduced, 1978; opened Milan shop, 1979; London store, 1987; founded Valentino Academy as well as LIFE, an AIDS assistance program and fund, 1990; launched *Vendetta* and *Vendetta Pour Homme* complementary fragrances, 1993; opened new boutiques in Rome and New York, 1996; V Zone sportswear launched for fall 1997; introduced new fragrance *Very Valentino,* 1997; sold firm to Holding di Partecipazioni Industriali (HdP), 1998; *Very Valentino Homme* debuted, 1999; Valentino Roma line launched, 2000; rehauled Milan store, 2001; considered buying firm back from HdP, 2001. **Exhibitions:** *Italian Re-Evolution,* La Jolla Art Museum, California, 1982; *30 Years of Magic* traveling exhibit and retrospective, 1991; retrospective, Capitoline Museum, Rome, 1991, and New York, 1992. **Awards:** Neiman Marcus award, 1967; National Italian American Foundation award, 1989; CFDA Lifetime Achievement award, 2000. **Address:** Piazza Mignanelli 22, 00187 Rome, Italy. **Website:** www.valentino.it.

Publications

On VALENTINO:

Books

Mulassano, Adriana, *I mass-moda: fatti e personaggi dell'Italian Look,* Florence, 1979.

Ricci, Franco Maria, ed., *Valentino,* Milan, 1982.

Sartogo, Piero, editor, *Italian Re-Evolution: Design in Italian Society in the Eighties* [exhibition catalogue], La Jolla, California, 1982.

Valentino, autumn/winter 2001–02 haute couture collection. © AFP/ CORBIS.

Alfonsi, Maria-Vittoria, *Leaders in Fashion: i grandi personaggi della moda,* Bologna, 1983.
Cosi, Marina, *Valentino che veste di nuovo,* Milan, 1984.
Soli, Pia, *Il genio antipatico* [exhibition catalogue], Venice, 1984.
Talley, André Leon, *Valentino,* Milan, 1984.
Milbank, Caroline Rennolds, *Couture: The Great Designers,* New York, 1985.
Aragno, Bonizza Giordani, *Moda Italia: Creativity and Technology in the Italian Fashion System,* Milan, 1988.
Howell, Georgina, *Sultans of Style: 30 Years of Fashion and Passion 1960–1990,* London 1990.
Pelle, Marie-Paule, and Patrick Mauries, *Valentino: Thirty Years of Magic,* Rome & New York, 1991.
Martin, Richard, and Harold Koda, *Orientalism: Visions of the East in Western Dress* [exhibition catalogue], New York, 1994.
Morris, Bernadine, *Valentino,* New York, 1996.
Stegemeyer, Anne, *Who's Who in Fashion, Third Edition,* New York, 1996.
Sozzani, Franca, *Valentino,* New York, 2001.

Articles

Pertile, Marina, "Valentino: 25 anni nella moda compiuti," in *Vogue* (Milan), September 1984.
Buck, Joan Juliet, "An Affair Called Valentino," in *Vogue,* March 1985.
Etherington-Smith, Meredith, and Caroline Clifton-Magg, "Palace Evolution," in *Harpers & Queen* (London), June 1989.
Ducci, Carlo, and Lele Acquarone, "Valentino 1959–89," in *Vogue* (Milan), September 1989.
Rafferty, Diane, "Valentino," in *Connoisseur* (New York), August 1990.
"Viva Valentino...Marking 30 Years in Fashion," in the *Chicago Tribune,* 19 June 1991.
Casadio, Mariuccia, "Valentino, Take a Bow!" in *Interview* (New York), September 1991.
Koenig, Rhoda, "When Valentino Fêtes His Anniversary, There's No Place Like Rome," in *Vogue* (New York), September 1991.
Mulvagh, Jane, "The Sultan of Style," in the *European* (London), 1 November 1991.
Lesser, Guy, "Our Funny Valentino," in *Town & Country* (New York), September 1992.
Shields, Brooke, "Hello, Valentino?" in *Interview,* September 1992.
Schiff, Stephen, "Lunch with Mr. Armani, Tea with Mr. Versace, Dinner with Mr. Valentino," in the *New Yorker,* 7 November 1994.
Menkes, Suzy, "Craft is in the Details: Artistry is In, Supermodels are Out," in the *International Herald Tribune,* 24 January 1995.
"Valentino: For the Sophisticated Lady," in *WWD,* 21 March 1995.
Menkes, Suzy, "YSL Plays Safe While Valentino Shines at Night," in the *International Herald Tribune,* 22 March 1995.
Forden, Sara Gay, "Valentino—Destination 2000," in *DNR,* 1 January 1996.
Born, Pete, "Valentino Back in Scent Scene," in *WWD,* 1 August 1997.
Forden, Sara Gay, "Valentino's Big Move: He Agrees to Sell Firm to HdP, Parent of GFT," in *WWD,* 12 January 1998.
"Name Swapping (Valentino Garavani and Giancarlo Giammetti Complete Sale of Valentino)...," in the *Economist,* 11 April 1998.
Conti, Samantha, "The New Valentino," in *WWD,* 19 October 1998.
———, "House of Valentino Makes Plans to Begin a New Life at Forty," in *WWD,* 28 June 1999.
Herman-Cohen, Valli, "Valentino's Ageless Designs Still Shine," in the *Financial Times,* 3 November 2000.
Medina, Marcy, "Painting Tinseltown Red," in *WWD,* 16 November 2000.
Jewel, Dan, "Valentino Valentine," in *People,* 4 December 2000.
de Courtay, Romy, "Fashion's Favorite Roman: Valentino...," in *DNR,* 15 January 2001.
Conti, Samantha, "Valentino Said to be Exploring a Buyback of House from HdP," in *WWD,* 18 April 2001.
Deeny, Godfrey, "Valentino: Great Glamorous Clothes," available online at Fashion Windows, www.fashionwindows.com, 8 July 2001.

* * *

Both a reverent hush and an excited clamor simultaneously surround the Italian designer Valentino. He enjoys the patronage of a long established clientèle of wealthy and aristocratic women, yet his clothes are never staid and always express a fresh, current style. His collections and his lifestyle embody the grandeur and serenity of eternal Rome, where he works from his salon near the Spanish Steps, and at the same time represents the point of view of a jetsetting citizen

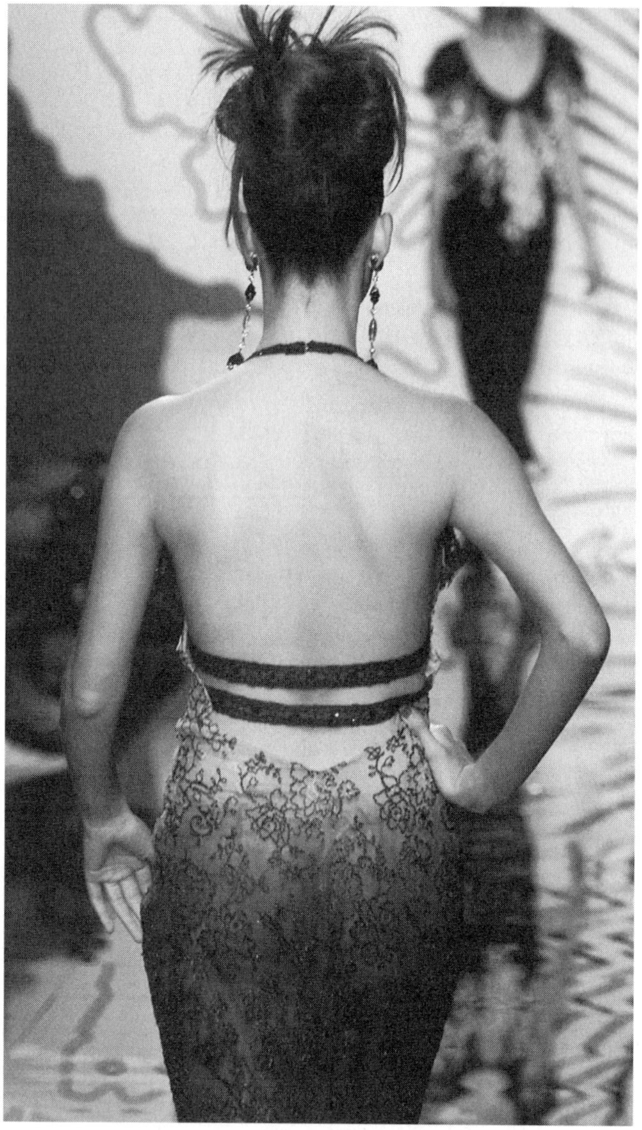

Valentino, autumn/winter 2001–02 haute couture collection. © Reuters NewMedia Inc./CORBIS.

of the world. In 2000 Valentino celebrated 40 years in business. The anniversary was celebrated in characteristic Valentino style in Los Angeles, atop the Pacific Design Center with a slew of celebrities in attendance to honor him. The gala raised more than $250,000 to go to the Children's Action Network.

In 1960, when Valentino opened his first salon in the Via Condotti, Rome was the center of fashion in Italy. The ready-to-wear designers of Milan, the industrial center, did not come to prominence until a decade later. After having served as an apprentice in Paris for five years with Jean Dessès and two years with Guy Laroche, Valentino's design foundation was firmly set in the haute couture tradition of quality, luxury, and a dose of extravagance. He immediately began to attract clients who came to him for his finely crafted, colorful, and elegant designs. By the mid-1960s he introduced his signature trousersuits for day and evening.

In 1968 he created a sensation with his White Collection, featuring short dresses shown with lace stockings and simple flat shoes. The very same year Jacqueline Kennedy chose a lace-trimmed silk two-piece dress with a short pleated skirt, for her marriage to Aristotle Onassis. Yet red has since become Valentino's signature color, a rich shade of crimson with vibrant overtones of orange. He has used it throughout his collections, especially in his lavish evening designs, characterized by magnificent embroideries and meticulous detailing. A section of his retrospective exhibition was devoted to evening jackets covered entirely in elaborately beaded decorations. Typical Valentino details include scalloped trims and hems, raglan sleeves, circular ruffles, complex plays of proportion, and extravagant pattern and texture mixes—like the combination of lace, velvet, and houndstooth in a single outfit.

In 1989 Valentino celebrated 30 years of high fashion with a two-night extravaganza in Rome, and invited hundreds of his high-profile friends, from politicos and royals such as Baroness Marie-Helene Rothschild, Mme. Claude Pompidou, Georgette Mosbacher, Pat Buckley, and Nancy Kissinger to Hollywood icons Elizabeth Taylor, Gina Lollobrigida, and Marissa Berenson. The $5-million affair was a fête to remember, with a sumptuous buffet, champagne, fireworks, flowing fountains, an American 16-piece orchestra, and a retrospective of his work at the Palazzo dei Conservatori museum, designed by Michelangelo in the 16th century. Yet for all the glamour and excess, the retrospective was set to travel to Florence, then on to London, Madrid, New York City, and Tokyo. Proceeds raised from the show were earmarked for LIFE, Valentino and Giancarlo Giammetti's private fund for AIDS victims; Giammetti is Valentino's business partner who, from the late 1960s through present day, was fundamental in the worldwide expansion and success the fashion house.

Valentino's devotees flock to him for couture, ready-to-wear, and a vast array of products and accessories including menswear, leather goods, eyewear, furs, and fragrances. He reaches a younger market through his Oliver line of clothing, which is casual but still marked with distinctively refined Valentino sensibility. He produces a special collection of eveningwear called Valentino Night, in which the luxury of his couture designs is adapted for a wider audience. All of his designs, throughout all of his collections, express a singularly opulent view of the world. Valentino's sensibility embraces both timelessness and originality, filtered through a dedication to a luxurious way of life and the commitment to express that lifestyle in his collections. For many Valentino represents not just a style of dressing, but rather a style of living.

—Alan E. Rosenberg; updated by Sydonie Benét

VAN DEN AKKER, Koos

American designer

Born: The Hague, Netherlands, 16 March 1939; immigrated to the U.S., 1968, naturalized, 1982. **Education:** Studied at the Netherlands Royal Academy of Art, 1956–58; worked in department stores in The Hague and in Paris; studied fashion at L'École Guerre Lavigne, Paris, 1961. **Military Service:** Served in the Royal Dutch Army, 1958–60. **Career:** Apprenticed at Dior, Paris, 1963–65; returned to The Hague and maintained own boutique, 1965–68; lingerie designer, Eve Stillman, New York, 1969–70; freelance designer, from 1971; established first New York boutique, Columbus Avenue, 1971–75; relocated to Madison Avenue, 1975; opened second shop, Beverly Hills, 1978; opened second New York boutique, 1979; added line of handbags, 1986;

introduced diffusion line, Hot House, 1983; guest critic, Fashion Institute of Technology, 1999; created fur designs for Alixandre, from 1999; QVC showing immediate success, 2001; also designs bed linens, lingerie, and home furnishings. **Awards:** Gold Coast award, 1978; American Printed Fabrics Council "Tommy," award, 1983. **Address:** 34 East 67th Street, New York, NY, U.S.A.

PUBLICATIONS

On VAN DEN AKKER:

Books

Khornak, Lucille, *Fashion 2001,* London, 1982.
Contemporary Designers, Third Edition, Detroit, 1997.

Articles

de Llosa, Martha, "Designer Koos van den Akker: Berserk on the Surface," in *American Fabrics & Fashions* (New York), Spring 1980.
Revson, James A., "The Uncrowned King of Collage," in *Newsday,* 9 August 1984.
Coffin, David Page, "Koos, the Master of Collage," in *Threads* (Newtown, CT), December/January 1989–90.
"New York Now," in *WWD,* 9 April 1990.
Struensee, Chuck, "Koos Comes Back," in *WWD,* 23 March 1993.
White, Constance C.R., "Fashion Loses a Father Figure," in the *New York Times,* 19 September 1995.
"Koos Into Fur," in *WWD,* 4 May 1999.
"Sweaters; Chunky Knits," in the *Omaha World-Herald,* 9 September 1999.
"Best Furrier in the World," available online at Alixandre, www.alixandrefurs.com, 14 October 2001.
"Koos," online at Europa Couture, europacouture.com, 14 October 2001.
"Koos van den Akker Marks His Return to QVC with the Debut of His Spring/Summer Collection," online at Stop the Presses, www.qvc.com, 14 October 2001.
"Koos van den Akker," online at *Texas Fashion Collection,* www.web2.unt.edu, 14 October 2001.
"Mary Wore a Little Lamb," online at Humane Society of the United States, www.hsus.org, 14 October 2001.
"Silver Needle Awards & Fashion Show 1999: Designer Critics," online at Marist College, ww.marist.edu, 14 October 2001.
"*White Noise* on View at the Student Art & Design Exhibition," online at Tools for Tomorrow, www.toolsfortomorrow.com, 14 October 2001.

* * *

Koos van den Akker is known for his painterly delight in mixing colors, patterns, and textures in unusual, often one of a kind, garments. Since his arrival in the United States in 1968 with just a sewing machine, he has been delighting clients who want something a bit different to wear. His styles have not changed much, simple shapes being more amenable to rich surface manipulations. Having learned the basics of good fit and cut as an apprentice with the house of Christian Dior, van den Akker was able to proceed confidently with the fabric collages that have become his signature. Although his Koos garments recall the art-to-wear movement, they remain free of the sometimes heavy-handed messages inherent in the artifacts which seem more suitable for gallery walls—these masterpieces are meant to be worn and appreciated for their beauty.

Conservatively styled suits consisting of cardigan jackets and gored skirts might be covered with textured mixtures of fur, quilted fabric, leather strips, or pieces of wool. A dress of lace might be dramatized by bold appliqué. As many as six materials might be combined in collages of cotton, wool, furs, tweeds, sequins, and leather. Some of the results are reminiscent of grandmother's crazy quilt, but all are carried out with a true designer's skill and artistic sensitivity. Indeed, van den Akker has admitted that the designs just flow, working themselves out through the process of creation, perhaps reflecting a hereditary affinity with Dutch national costume.

Selling his own custom-made dresses in a boutique gained van den Akker enough experience to open a Madison Avenue shop, one in Beverly Hills, and a men's boutique during the 1970s. In 1983 he presented a moderately priced collection, Hot House. By 1986 he was designing lingerie, daytime and evening clothes, furs, sheets, and home furnishings. Women's clothes were made of beautiful fabrics with colorful print and lace inserts, sometimes following the lines of the garments in harmony and balance, other times contrasting shapes versus line. During the 1980s van den Akker collected a following among celebrities, including Gloria Vanderbilt, who at one point surrounded herself with patchwork, as well as Elizabeth Taylor, Cher, Barbara Walters, Glenn Close, and Bill Cosby, who wore van den Akker's sweaters on *The Cosby Show.*

Van den Akker has been eager to share the joy he attains from his craft. Designer Christian Francis Roth was his apprentice for several years before venturing out on his own. In late 1989 van den Akker showed the home-sewing public how to make their own creative clothing in a detailed article in *Threads Magazine.* The next year signaled a broadening of his range to include simpler ready-to-wear sportswear—tweed dresses and coats, coats of blanket materials, matching suede jackets and skirts, and short floral dresses with just a hint of the Koos play with fabrics in a mixed-print collar. The designer continued to refine his artistry, developing a ready-to-wear sportswear collection for DeWilde that is more subtle and interchangeable. Toned-down collage effects and texture appliqués lend interest to classic pieces in wool and cashmere, even sheer georgette.

To adoring fans of his designs, van den Akker sold all of his fall-winter 1998 collection in 27 minutes. Finding homes in closets were a big shirt, reversible silk jacket, bias patchwork skirt, pull-cord handbag, and comfy drawstring pants with cotton tee. Stop the Presses quoted his reaction to the commercial triumph, "I am delighted that people across the country will once again have the opportunity to experience my clothing."

In May 1999 he returned in triumph from Greenwich Village to Madison Avenue in uptown New York City, his former location for decades, to market unique collage and slash-technique raincoats and dresses. He extended his contributions to Alixandre, producer of elegant and fashionable fur garments, by designing Persian lamb coats and sheared beaver with one-of-a-kind glazed linen collage on the reverse side. At the Silver Needle Awards and Fashion Show 1999, he summarized his method of blending textures and weaves: "I start out simple and then I go berserk. I mix tweeds with silk. And I like lots of color, from autumn colors to nasty vibrant green."

Throughout the last months of the 20th century and into the 21st, while collectors were stocking their wardrobes with his past glories, van den Akker remained a fashion pacesetter. He served as one of four guest critics of future fashion designers at the Fashion Institute of Technology exhibit entitled *White Noise.* The 1999 segment of the spirited annual student show at Marist College in Poughkeepsie, New York, interpreted the psychological concept of white noise with 30 garments for adults and children. Despite PETA's protests of his use of fur in coutourier collections, he, along with Oscar de la Renta and Valentino, continued to design for New York-based furrier Alixandre by applying broadtail, fox, lynx, mink, sable, and sheared beaver to winter fashions. Van den Akker's spring/summer line for 2001 perpetuated his tradition of fabric collage and appliquéd couture in softly draping shapes to flatter the figure.

—Therese Duzinkiewicz Baker; updated by Mary Ellen Snodgrass

VARTY, Keith

See BYBLOS

VASS, Joan

American designer

Born: New York City, 19 May 1925. **Education:** Attended Vassar College; graduated in philosophy from the University of Wisconsin, 1942; did graduate work in aesthetics at the University of Buffalo. **Family:** Children from first marriage: Richard, Sara, Jason. **Career:** Assistant curator, drawing and prints, the Museum of Modern Art, New York; freelance editor, Harry N. Abrams publishing house, New York; columnist, *Art in America,* New York; began designing handknits in the early 1970s with sales to Henri Bendel, New York; company incorporated as Joan Vass, Inc., 1977; labels included Joan Vass Sporting, Joan Vass New York, menswear and womenswear; Joan Vass USA, lower priced women's line, introduced, 1984; Joan Vass USA for Men introduced, 1988; New York flagship store opened, 1989; opened Chicago boutique, 1992; launched jewelry line and Joan Vass Spa; opened Houston shop, 1999. **Awards:** Smithsonian Institution, Extraordinary Women in Fashion award, 1978; Coty American Fashion Critics award, 1979, 1981; Prince Machiavelli Prix de Cachet award, 1980.

Publications

On VASS:

Books

Milbank, Caroline Rennolds, *New York Fashion: The Evolution of American Style,* New York 1989.
Steele, Valerie, *Women of Fashion,* New York, 1991.
Stegemeyer, Anne, *Who's Who in Fashion, Third Edition,* New York, 1996.
Malcolm, Trisha, *Vogue Knitting, Designer Knits,* New York, 1998.

Articles

Oliver, Richard K., "Style," in *People,* 29 October 1979.
Morris, Berandine, "With a Knack for Knits (Joan Vass)," in the *New York Times,* 4 December 1988.
Etra, Johnathan, "Vass Horizons," in *House & Garden,* January 1989.
Infantino, Vivian, "A Vass Landscape: Designer Joan Vass Paints Her Fashion Philosophy," in *Footwear News,* 28 August 1989.
Howard, T.J., "Joan Vass Boutique Comes to Chicago," in *Chicago Tribune,* 1 April 1992.
Finkelstein, Anita, "The Riches of Summerville Rags," in *WWD,* 4 April 1994.
Spindler, Amy M., "The Rise of the Fashion Stylist," in the *New York Times,* 9 April 1994.
Stephens, Suzanne, "Joan Vass of Long Island: An Eye for Understanding," in *Architectural Digest,* October 1994.
Hastreiter, Kim, "Vass Appeal," in *Mirabella,* January 1995.
"Joan Vass Boutique to Bow in Houston," in *WWD,* 9 April 1999.
Wilson, Eric "A Baptism by Fire: CFDA's New Boss Meets the Members," in *WWD,* 16 August 2001.

* * *

Joan Vass is an American designer who believes the only purpose for a label in a piece of clothing is to show which way to put it on. Her easy-to-wear designs for both men and women are beautifully crafted, in simple, elegant lines.

In college, Vass studied philosophy and aesthetics. She worked as an assistant curator of drawings and prints at the Museum of Modern

Joan Vass, spring 1996 collection. © AP/Wide World Photos.

Joan Vass, spring 1996 collection. © AP/Wide World Photos.

Art in New York. At the same time she edited art books for Harry N. Abrams and wrote columns about art auctions for *Art in America.* Vass began a cottage industry in the early 1970s when she brought her personal interest in hand-knits and crochet to women who needed an outlet for their marketable skills.

Vass created designs for hats and mufflers which these women crocheted. Marketed at Henri Bendel, New York, they quickly sold out. She went on to create designs for sweaters for both men and women, having them produced under the label Joan Vass New York. Vass provided the designs, the yarns and buttons if necessary. Her cadre of workers, ranging in age from 20 to 70, came from a variety of backgrounds including housewives and artists. They would knit, crochet, or hand-loom the design, incorporating their personal style. The production for this line was limited, selective, and not accessible to everyone. The Joan Vass New York line was still popular in the late 1990s and into the 21st century. Craftspeople still create the designs provided by Vass and it remains a small-volume, selective design business which now includes woven materials. All of the designs from the past are still available to be produced.

The return to natural fibers, the individuality in American fashion expression, the use of knits for more than just the travel wardrobe, plus a new-found appreciation for handmade items during the 1970s all helped create a welcoming environment for Vass designs. Her work was unique, practical, and beautifully crafted. She established her own company in 1977. In the 1980s, a mid-priced licensed line was first produced on a large scale by the Signal Knitting Mills in South Carolina. Working with Vass designs, these clothes carried the label Joan Vass USA and were made of beautiful fine-gauged, natural fiber, knitted and woven fabrics.

A third design line called Joan Vass Sporting was created, a more casual collection with much more detail. Though natural fibers are still used, the designs also use some of the new synthetic fibers such as chinchilla, a 100-percent polyester fabric. Whether Joan Vass New York, Joan Vass USA, or Joan Vass Sporting, the designs Vass creates are simple and easy to wear. They are predominantly made of natural fibers, usually in subtle colors, in unstructured shapes. There are no extras such as shoulder pads. Besides sweaters, she designs trousers, skirts, and shorts and dresses. Her stated aim is to produce interchangeable, ageless designs which evolve from season to season. Reviews in the *Daily News Record* have described Vass' designs as classic. When the clothes are old, she wants her clients to don them for gardening.

In the 1980s and 1990s, Vass designs were perennial favorites, enough so that she opened stores across the U.S., including shops in New Orleans, Chicago, Dallas, and New York. Her designs could also be found in high-end specialty shops and better department stores as well, including newer Vass labels for plus sizes and sportswear. In addition, Vass had segued into jewelry and footwear, known for her distinctive designs.

In an interview for *House & Garden* (January 1989) Vass told Johnathan Etra, "If you notice me I am not well-dressed." She feels style is something that lasts, and does not preclude a sense of humor in her design work, as she has been inspired by iguanas and created bizarre and funny hats. Vass is an American woman with strong ideas and concerns reflected in her designs, and frequently expressed. In the later years of her career, Vass became an outspoken fixture at Council of Fashion Designers of America (CFDA) meetings, always letting fellow members know her sometimes controversial thoughts. Because of her outbursts, Vass deemed herself "an old crone," yet her views have often been seconded by CFDA members.

—Nancy House; updated by Nelly Rhodes

VENET, Philippe

French fashion designer

Born: Lyons, France, 22 May 1929. **Education:** Apprentice tailor, age 14, at Pierre Court, Lyons, until 1948. **Military Service:** Served in French Army, 1948–50. **Career:** Assistant designer for Schiaparelli, Paris, 1951–53; master tailor for Givenchy, 1953–62; established Philippe Venet couture house, Paris, 1962; launched menswear collection, 1990s. **Awards:** Dé d'Or, Paris, 1985. **Address:** 62 rue Francois 1er, 75008 Paris, France.

Publications

On VENET:

Books

McDowell, Colin, *McDowell's Directory of Twentieth Century Fashion,* Englewood Cliffs, New Jersey, 1985.

O'Hara, Georgina, *The Encyclopaedia of Fashion,* New York, 1986.

Guillen, Pierre-Yves, and Jacqueline Claude, *The Golden Thimble: French Haute Couture,* Paris, 1990.

Stegemeyer, Anne, *Who's Who in Fashion, Third Edition,* New York, 1996.

Articles

Morris, Bernadine, "The New Looks for Nightime...Venet Offers Dresses with a Timeless Quality," in the *New York Times,* 27 July 1988.

———, "New Life From Fashion's Old Guard," in the *New York Times,* 2 August 1988.

———, "Chanel is Saucier, Ungaro is Cooler, and Venet Livelier," in the *New York Times,* 24 January 1990.

Mazzaraco, Maragaret, "Cotton's Parisian Accent," in *WWD,* 1 March 1994.

"Paris: Disco Finale," in *WWD,* 22 July 1994.

Gellars, Stan, "The Big Brand Era," in *DNR,* 18 January 1995.

"Moving Day in Paris...An Emotional Farewell to Givenchy," in *WWD,* 12 July 1995.

* * *

Philippe Venet had a long apprenticeship in fashion before opening his own couture house in 1962, at the age of 33. Born in Lyons, France, he was apprenticed at 14 to an established and respected dressmaker in the town, Pierre Court, where he was taught about fabric, manufacture, and cut, as well as learning the rudiments of tailoring, a major feature of his later work. Pierre Court held the rights to the Balenciaga label and it was Venet's association with this Parisian couture house that led him to the fashion capital to pursue his design career.

His first job was at the house of Schiaparelli. Elsa Schiaparelli had been one of the most important and influential designers of the 1930s, when her witty surrealist and avant-garde designs broke new ground in fashion. By the 1950s, however, Schiaparelli's influence was waning and the house was soon to close. For Venet the job was a stepping stone in his career; it was at Schiaparelli that he met the young Hubert de Givenchy, who was also an employee. When Givenchy opened his own couture house in 1953, he employed Venet as his master tailor.

The 1950s were Givenchy's heyday, a success to which Venet undoubtedly contributed. Givenchy is perhaps most notable for his association with Audrey Hepburn, whom he first dressed in the 1954 film *Sabrina Fair.* Together, the design house and actress created a gamine look typifing the style of the late 1950s and 1960s. It was young elegance, long-legged and sophisticated, ranging from Audrey's beatnik look in the 1957 film *Funny Face,* to her little black dress look in the 1961 film *Breakfast at Tiffany's.*

Venet finally opened his own couture house in Paris in 1962. His experience and respect for the traditions of haute couture were a mainstay of his work from the beginning, as were his superb tailoring skills. His cut has always been innovative and imaginative, with a range of beautifully cut and tailored coats featured in every collection. Distinctive pieces from the 1960s were his kite coats; in the 1970s were geometric patterns, oversized capes, and jackets in flannel and reversible wools; his suits and coats in the 1980s and 1990s were fun and flirtatious, in refreshing colors. Venet's eveningwear has often been inspired by flora and fauna; the overall eveningwear look is generally romantic but sophisticated, smart but with a hint of naughtiness, and designed for a wealthy clientèle.

Philippe Venet was awarded the Dé d'Or award in January 1985. This award not only recognized his aesthetic contribution to the fashion industry but applauded the detailed attention he brought to every aspect of the business, closely monitoring the creation of each outfit and personally attending all the fittings. In the middle and late 1990s Venet divided his time between France and the United States. A third of his clients were American, and he presented annual collections in both Los Angeles and New York. Expansion near the end of the century included a new menswear line to complement his womenswear ranges.

—Kevin Almond

VENTURI, Gian Marco

Italian fashion designer

Born: Florence, Italy, circa 1955. **Education:** Studied at the Istituto Tessile Butti in Prato; degree in economics and commerce from Florence University. **Career:** Worked for Italian firms Domitilla, Lebole, Erreuno; established own label ready-to-wear, 1979, Milan; launched leather goods and accessory line, 1981; introduced men's jeans and sportswear, 1982; introduced ladies' jeans and sportswear, 1985; introduced activewear and lingerie lines, 1988. **Awards:** The Oner Best Designer award, Milan, 1983; Catherine de Medici Perfume award, Milan, 1986. **Address:** Via della Spiga 31, 20121 Milan, Italy.

PUBLICATIONS

On VENTURI:

Articles

"Gian Marco Venturi: Gessati et Jabot," *Donna* (Milan), 7 August 1987.
Muritti, Elisabetta, "Venturing on His Own," in *Donna*, March 1989.
"Italy's Coolest Shades: Maurizio Marcolin," in *WWD Italy Supplement*, January 1997.
"Manufacturers and Distributors," in *Cosmetics International*, 10 January 1997.
"Italy: Room for Improvement," in *European Cosmetic Markets*, May 1999.
"Gian Marco Venturi," available online at www.insurance-y2k.com, 14 October 2001.
"Gian Marco Venturi," online at Fashion Video, www.albertodellorto.com, 14 October 2001.
"Gian Marco Venturi," online at Moda Online, www.modaonline.it, 14 October 2001.

* * *

Gian Marco Venturi worked for many companies as a designer and stylist before his own ready-to-wear label was launched in 1979. Born in Florence, Italy, he attended the Istituto Tessile Butti in Prato, then took a degree in business and economics at the University of Florence. He did not enter the fashion business until 1974, when he was 19, instead, he spent time traveling the world, gaining a rich variety of cultural and aesthetic experience that has provided useful inspiration for his subsequent design career.

Venturi first began designing for a firm called Domitilla. The company produced jersey clothes very much in the style of Emilio Pucci. It was Venturi's task to update the range and give it the right look for the mid-1970s. The first collection was shown in the Palazzo Pitti in Florence. He then went on to work on leather garments (leather has always been a strong feature in his work) for Sander's, while at the same time he also designed knitwear for Beba. Graziella Ronchi hired Venturi in 1979 to design for her Erreuno collections. Working with the company for six seasons, it was Venturi who helped develop and establish the soft, neutral look combined with architectural correctness for which the company became known.

Venturi's women's ready-to-wear has always been stylish and expensive—sexy, sometimes suggestive, sometimes blatant or tarty. His sensuous side is perhaps best exemplified in his autumn-winter 1989–90 collection. A masculine, black snakeskin jacket with astrakhan collar and cuffs was belted over black trousers and sweater, highlighted with a white shirt collar. Black snakeskin gloves, dark glasses, and a model with a short black bob gave the impression of Louise Brooks on a black and white aviation excursion. Dark glasses were the distinctive accessory running through a collection that also included fit and flare double-breasted coats with astrakhan cuffs, then, in a softer vein, reversible cashmere with huge shawl collars and patch pockets in sand and warm gray.

Another distinctive Venturi ready-to-wear collection was spring-summer 1993. It featured hipster chain mail belts slung over skirts and tabards in a red, white, and blue color palette. There were blue leather safari jackets, boldly printed Capri trousers, skinny ribbed knits with chain mail embroidery, topped off with gold leather jerkins, belts, and lots of gold jewelry. It was a fun, dynamic, swingy look suggesting a star or opera diva lost in Miami and featured favorite fabrics such as white lace and organza.

Venturi's menswear is usually classic and traditional but is sometimes highlighted by a touch of ornamentation, such as crests and stars lifted from the naval styles or a gold ribbon-embroidered waistcoat. The clothes are disciplined and produced in seasonal colors. Favorite fabrics include linens, flannels, and gabardines. Sober jackets, waistcoats, close-fitting trousers, and blouses are the main separates, coordinated to create these looks.

Venturi has also produced lines of leather garments, jeans, casual clothing, sportswear, and perfume, all marked by the label Gian Marco Venturi Made in Italy in black on a white ground. He has been awarded several prizes during his career, including the Oner for best designer of 1983 and the Catherine de Medici prize for the greatest sales of men's aftershave in 1986. The company moved from Florence in 1983 and began occupying studios on the prestigious Via della Spiga in Milan.

For spring/summer 1997, Venturi focused on a folk-based palette of lavender blue, violet, royal blue, and Irish green in solids, stripes, and mixed tones pearlized to give his suits an air of informality. His chose blocky, undarted shaping in stretch fabric and revived the cadet look in traditional blazers with pocket insignia. His choices of viscose acetate, cotton acetate, and wool viscose crêpe with nickel buttons, zippers, and buckles supported tailored lines. Detailing with lace and grosgrain, pinstripes, checks, and chevrons revived standard black on white for a contemporary feel.

Venturi took charge of the indomitable blazer, touching up sporty styling with a military touches. For Nehru jackets, he stressed reed-matting and silk bourette. To soften jackets, he stressed a cardigan look in drapey jersey. Practical, wearable outfits in neutral tones of beige, chalk, and white suited the season. The ensemble of jackets, vests, and trousers in broiderie anglaise-style cambric added luxe to functional wardrobe standards.

—Kevin Almond; updated by Mary Ellen Snodgrass

VERDÙ, Joaquim

Spanish designer

Born: Barcelona, Spain. **Education:** Attended Feli's fashion school; studied anatomical drawing and painting; apprenticed under Pedro Rodríguez. **Career:** Became known for knitwear; own label manufactured by Pulligan, from 1991. **Address:** Riera del Pinar, 12, 08360 Carnet de Mar, Spain.

PUBLICATIONS

On VERDÙ:

Articles

Klensch, Elsa, "España!," in *Vogue*, October 1988.
"Highlights of the Spanish Cibeles Autumn/Winter 1999–2000 Fashion Shows in the Words of Pedro Mansilla," available online at Fashion Click, www.fashionclick.com, 14 October 2001.
"Joaquim Verdù Runway Fashion Photos," online at www.fashionshowroom.com, 14 October 2001.

"La Moda Nupcial Empieza en Punto," online at La Vanguardia, www.lavanguardia.es, 14 October 2001.
"Noticias: Joaquim Verdù," online at Solo Moda, www.solomoda.com, 14 October 2001.

* * *

Joaquim Verdù is rare among fashion designers in showing a preference for knitted rather than woven fabrics—to the extent that since his label began to be manufactured by Pulligan in 1991, Verdù has devoted himself exclusively to knitting. Underlying the eminently wearable collections is a philosophy of less is more. The keynotes are well-defined volumes, fluid lines, and immaculate detailing; colors are mostly plain. What interests the designer is the knitted fabric in its own right, rather than knitting as a vehicle for multicolored jacquards and intarsias. Apart from occasional stripes or prints, if Verdù combines colors it is on a large scale. He might, for example, use a different shade for each part of an outfit or for each garment of a range. That he had intended to be a painter is always apparent in the subtle choice and juxtaposition of brights, pastels, or neutrals.

Early collections were exuberant, with a clever mix of knitted and woven materials. When mixing fabrics, Verdù tends to play a teasing game of "spot the knitting." He chooses knitted fabrics that look so much like weaves that only a very close inspection reveals what they are; then he reverses traditional roles and takes us light years away from the woven suit teamed with a sweater. In a Verdù runway, knitting, identifiable or not, is always the star of the show. Weaves become complementary or, at best, equal partners.

Handling knitting in this way is a difficult exercise, especially when tailoring is involved, and Verdù has been known to dress male models in suits entirely made out of jersey. The very same qualities that make knitting feel like a second skin turn it awkward in the workroom as knitted fabrics can be unpredictable. Pressing can stretch them; some curl, others have a sideways slant, difficult to control and impossible to correct. Half the time, the fabric needs to be designed from scratch, and here lies the greatest challenge—to start a garment not from a bale of jersey but from a cone of yarn.

Verdù's designs for the straight knitting machine show him in complete control of the fabric and of the manufacturing process. This is one of the aspects that makes his work so successful, but there are others; another is his skill at producing infinite variations on a theme, however simple. Verdù devotees know for a fact that, in any given range, they will find something to fit their age, lifestyle, and bone structure. Then there is the way in which the designer combines chic with exquisite comfort, something that international models appearing in his shows have been quick to point out. Finally, there is the clearly distinctive signature, the very personal imprint Verdù leaves on everything he does, because, except for making the clothes, he actually does everything. From the moment he chooses a yarn or fabric and reaches for the sketch pad, up to the final fitting, nobody else works on the design. In the era of the franchise, a Joaquim Verdù label means exactly what it says.

As a young man, Verdù started his studies at Feli's fashion school. He had not been there more than a few weeks before his potential was spotted by one of the lecturers. Pedro Rodríguez obtained permission from the school to take Verdù to his own couture house, where he personally introduced him to the intricacies of cut and drape. On his death, many years later, Rodríguez left him his scissors. The man who shares with Balenciaga the honor of being the father of Spanish couture could not have paid Verdù a greater compliment.

Spanning the end of the millennium, Verdù welcomed the 21st century at the Spanish Cibeles. According to commentator Pedro Mansilla, Verdù avoided the fashion vapors of no-show designers and regional divas to showcase practical Spanish goods. As in the past, he presented a wearable collection of knits in contrasting colors, his signature style. In Madrid for fall 2001, his clingy, monochromatic knits presented a vulnerable, sensuous youth in thigh-hugging pants and matching bateau-neck top and ethereal slip dress.

—Montse Stanley; updated by Mary Ellen Snodgrass

VERINO, Roberto

Spanish fashion designer

Born: Manuel Roberto Marino, Verin, Spain, May 1945. **Education:** Studied business and fine arts in Paris, mid-1960s. **Family:** Children: Cristina, Jose Manuel. **Career:** Left studies to take charge of parents' leather garments business, 1967; in 1970s, worked for MARPY Jeans; launched ready-to-wear collection for women, Roberto Verino; a year later, opened his first shop in Paris; introduced cosmetics line, 1993; collections represented in over 20 countries; specializes in

Roberto Verino, fall 2001 collection. © Fashion Syndicate Press.

women's ready-to-wear. **Awards:** T for Triumph (*Telva* magazine, Spain), 1991 and 1994; Aguja de Oro (Golden Needle), Spanish Press, 1992. **Address:** Amaro Refojo 12, 36200 Verin (Orense), Spain.

Publications

On VERINO:

Articles

Mattioni, Marina, "Roberto Verino," in *Donna* (Milan), June 1990.
"Consumer Goods Euro: Womenswear in Spain," in *MarkIntel,* 1 April 2000.

* * *

Roberto Verino is a Spanish designer who first trained in Paris before returning to take over the family leather clothing business in northern Spain. Throughout the 1970s he built a small concern into a prosperous local industry; then, in 1982, he launched his first collection of prêt-à-porter. His success was almost immediate, and year by year his fame has grown so that by 1994 he was the premier Spanish fashion designer.

Roberto Verino, fall 2001 collection. © Fashion Syndicate Press.

From the beginning, Verino has set himself the highest standards of artistry. He collaborated with well-known Spanish painter Xaime Quesada and as early as 1984 designed his prototype around the work of Joan Pere Viladecans for display at the Barcelona International Cotton Institute. In more recent years, designs for his new collections have been drawn by Arturo Elenor, whose style is similar to the British political cartoonist Gerald Scarfe, so that the fashion plates are not just design drafts but art in their own right.

As well as this strong accent on artistry, Verino makes clothes that are both practical and comfortable. To these ends, he looks to masculine fashion to create feminine clothes. All his designs are a clash of male and female—masculine lines, female detail, male fabrics, feminine cuts, masculine shape, feminine colors.

Verino prides himself on his use of cotton and linen, no longer, if ever, uniquely masculine fabrics, except that Verino prefers black, gray, and brown, pinstriped, flecked, or even tartan colors and patterns. Verino's favorite clothing is jacket and trousers, double-breasted, broad lapels, wide collars, neither cuffs nor turn-ups. Eschewing the traditional suit, the cut is pure feminine, the trousers fit snugly at the waist, then flare at the ankle or hug the waist in layers of wraparound fabric that sculpt the leg down to a tight ankle fit. The jackets have tailored waists and soft shoulders to enhance feminine profiles.

Comfort and practicality should never preclude stylishness, and it is the feminine detail of Roberto Verino's creations that make his work so original. Sparkling gems and brooches replace buttons, waistcoats shimmer and shine, shirts have full-flowing sleeves and lace collars, coats have satin linings, trousers and skirts are split high to reveal first ankle, tibia, and thigh. It would be wrong to give the impression Verino uses uniquely dark colors; he has, in fact, built entire collections around white, contrasting male versus female by mixing male form with female colors. His collection includes royal blue trousers and coats, poppy red double-breasted jackets, angel white suits, and yellow gold waistcoats. For all his use of masculine materials and his adoption of male styles, Verino's clothes are pure female.

If Verino's masculine fabrics pay homage to Giorgio Armani, he is by no means a satellite of this Italian designer. Armani's reinvention of male fashion inspired designers across Europe, but Verino's genius is to twist Armani's ideas into a uniquely feminine creation. Many other influences are also apparent; Verino takes a pinch of humor from Moschino, mixes and matches colors in the style of Christian Lacroix, and draws on the same sources of subtlety and sophistication as Sybilla and Claude Montana. Further geographic influences are readily apparent to northern Europeans: the delicate jeweled sandals straight out of a souk; the flowing gowns, high necklines, and modesty-preserving tops so reminiscent of heroines from Arabian Nights. The 1994 collection showed new influences from Asia and the Far East, square jackets, long lines, intricate toggle buttons, marvelous gold, red, and orange silks.

Verino's collections have been shown in Paris and Madrid, Barcelona and London, but his work is not uniquely haute couture as he designs for three markets. First is sport and urban, where he makes maximum use of male shapes to create practical styles for women; Look Comfortable is a younger line, with emphasis on comfort where miniskirts turn out to be shorts and blouses are long, light, and full. Espadrilles, rope, and canvas sandals are de rigueur. Finally comes his Night-time collection, where elegance meets comfort and seduction is inevitable. So reads the advertising copy, but it is clear Verino designs with a woman's wants as well as needs in mind. Back in 1993 Verino launched of a line of cosmetics. Together with his clothes, they are found in shops and boutiques in the UK, Germany, France, and Japan, making Verino a truly European designer.

—Sally Anne Melia; updated by Mary Ellen Snodgrass

VERSACE, Donatella

Italian designer

Born: Reggio Calabria, Italy, 1955. Sister of internationally renowned fashion great Gianni Versace [deceased] and often named as his chief muse. **Education:** Studied literature in Florence. **Family:** Married Paul Beck, 1987; children: Allegra, Daniel. **Career:** Significant creative force in Gianni Versace's design empire as both muse and fashion consultant, 1970s and 1980s; formal role with Gianni was as Design Studio assistant, as well as product placement, development, distribution, and public relations; Gianni's fragrance *Blonde,* launched chiefly for her, 1995; with Gianni's untimely death in 1997, she assumed the role of principal designer for the Versace company. **Address:** c/o Keeble Cavaco and Duka Inc., 450 West 15th Street, Suite 604, New York, NY 10011, U.S.A.

Donatella Versace, fall/winter 2001–02 collection. © AP/Wide World Photos.

Publications

On VERSACE:

Articles

Spindler, Amy M., "Versace," in the *New York Times,* 10 October 1997.
"Donatella Versace," in *Current Biography Yearbook,* 1998.
Helter, Zoe, "Survivor," in *Harper's Bazaar,* August 2000.
"The Good, the Bad and the Ugly," in the *Washington Post,* 2 March 2001.
"Flash and Dash," in *WWD,* 12 March 2001.
"Glitter Girl," in *WWD,* 29 June 2001.
"Donatella Versace: Perfectly Wicked," in the *Washington Post,* 4 October 2001.
"Roots," in the *Fashion of the Times* (New York), Fall 2001.

* * *

Donatella Versace was born with a natural Italian flair for personal style. Her emerging creative talents were nurtured by her mother and by the majestic, wild, and sun-drenched atmosphere of the Calabrian southwest coast of Italy where she grew up. Versace's mother, Francesca, the inspired and doted-upon couturier to the Italian aristocracy of postwar Europe, had a strength of character and boldness as a designer that shaped both her son Gianni Versace's extraordinary career and the personality of her daughter.

As a teenager, Donatella was as untamed as the countryside she grew up in. She was the darling of her older brother, Gianni, who took her everywhere and whose admiration sharpened her already vivid sense of the dramatic opportunities that life might hold for her. Versace introduces herself with a vignette about her adolescent style: "When I was a teenager, I wore black fitted shirts with tight black pants and a leather jacket. This, over the years, became my signature look. This style became the basis of many of my designs." She was and remains supremely self-confident and self-assured. Her brother was both appalled by these tight clothes and high heels and fascinated by her apparent satisfaction with her body.

Donatella's clothing design today with its sexy, feminine, powerful look is as much a reflection of her early personal style as of the fashion world in which she is a major presence. Because of the enormous success of her brother and his couture line and Donatella's role as his assistant and muse, she was well known and respected in the Italian fashion world. Gianni's early years of apprenticeship in Milan were punctuated by visits from Donatella, whose opinion he sought and valued because of her strong unconventional fashion sense and her intimate connections to the very celebrities he hoped to dress.

When Gianni established his own atelier on the Via della Spiga in Milan, he invited Donatella to join the business. Although the newspapers at the time denominated her role as muse to her brother, Versace was quite insistent that hers was an active role. Indeed, it seems that her appearance, blond and lithe and very stylish, in her brother's designs was instrumental in encouraging those celebrities and the nouveau riche set to demand Versace fashion for themselves.

Donatella Versace, autumn/winter 2001–02 high couture collection. © Reuters NewMedia Inc./CORBIS.

Her natural gift for the dramatic was also instrumental in drawing vast public attention to her brother's annual shows. *Harper's Bazaar* (1995) recognized that Donatella's demand for the most famous models as a part of the publicity surrounding each season's latest designs launched "the supermodel" cult, though it must be said that she was herself the most recognizable supermodel that Gianni engaged.

Her notoriously high standards attracted precisely the attention to Versace products that guaranteed their marketability. She was dissatisfied with the fragrance *Blonde,* and, determined to ensure the Versace signature perfume's ultimate success, had the fragrance reformulated despite time constraints and an enormously expensive ad campaign completed by famed photographer Richard Avedon.

Her personal life was not entirely ignored during this period of Versace's parallel ascent with her brother's design empire. She married an American, Paul Beck, formerly a model for Versace men's clothing and together they produced two children, upon whom both she and her brother lavished their attention, love, and financial resources. As her fame and the demands on her time have escalated,

Versace insists that the important relationship with her children, "our reality, our family," provides an appropriate anchor in her personal life as well as in her marriage to Beck.

Versace's leap to national prominence came in late 1997 when she delivered and showed the Versace collections on time, just three months after her brother was murdered. The *New York Times* wrote, "in a state of mourning, with so much pressure and so much pain, [that] Ms. Versace could produce anything at all" was remarkable. Donatella reinvented herself as the strong designing presence of Versace Couture when her role as muse and collaborator with her brother, Gianni, was instantly destroyed by the same bullet that killed him. A passionate feminist in her life as well as in the designs she produces, Donatella was determined not to give up the central position Versace Couture held under her brother's reign. She continues to cultivate the celebrity crowd; designing, for example, the extraordinary palm-leaf printed gown that Jennifer Lopez wore at a Grammy Awards ceremony where a huge sensation greeted the appearance of so much of Ms. Lopez, and entertaining, either at her palazzo at Como or in the Versace family apartments in Milan, everyone who is anyone—or who wants to be seen.

Donatella's collections in recent years have concentrated on the sexy natural shape of a woman's body, which may be an ideal but is certainly exemplified by Versace herself. Her use of clinging chiffons that hug every curve, subtle designs that follow those curves like a whisper, and sparkles of sequins highlighting those curves have perfected her look as "maybe risqué, but not reckless." Her most recent ventures into giftware—Jungle from Versace (a Rosenthal fine porcelain for the table) and lifestyle hotels (a six-star establishment on the Australian gold coast is set to open in 2001)—will certainly be successful.

Versace never appears to suffer from the decline of the economy, having overcome "crippling Italian inheritance taxes" and a vast restructuring at the time of Gianni's death. She is poised, full of the energy and naughty confidence that distinguished her youth, to mature into a major fashion leader independent of her brother but upholding the high standards of elegance, sensuality, and opulence that were and remain the Versace trademark.

—Kathleen Bonann Marshall

VERSACE, Gianni

Italian designer

Born: Reggio Calabria, Italy, 2 December 1946. **Education:** Studied architecture, Calabria, 1964–67. **Family:** Brother Santo, sister Donatella, and four nieces and nephews. **Career:** Designer and buyer in Paris and London, for his mother's dressmaking studio, 1968–72; freelance designer, Callaghan, Complice, Genny, Milan, 1972–77; formed own company, Milan, 1978; showed first womenswear collection, 1978, first menswear collection, 1979; signature fragrance introduced, 1981; home furnishings collection launched, 1993; launched *Blonde* fragance and opened New York flagship store, 1996; introduced V2 diffusion line for 1997; firm continued after his death by siblings Donatella and Santo; Donatella took over designing duties, 1997; formed joint venture with Sunland Group for luxury hotels, 1999; plans to take the firm public, 2001–02. **Exhibitions:** Galleria Rizzardi, Milan, 1982; Studio La Città, Verona, 1983; Galerie Focus, Munich, 1983; *Gianni Versace: dialogues de mode,* Palais Galliera, Paris, 1986; retrospective, Fashion Institute of Technology, New York, 1992–93; Metropolitan Museum of Art, 1997. **Awards:** Occhio d'Oro award, Milan, 1982, 1984, 1990, 1991; Cutty Sark award, 1983, 1988; CFDA International award, 1993. **Died:** 15 July 1997, in Miami, Florida. **Company Address:** Via Gesu, 20121 Milan, Italy. **Company Website:** www.versace.it.

Gianni Versace, fall 1996 haute couture collection: panne velvet and silk crêpe dress. © AP/Wide World Photos.

Publications

By VERSACE:

Books

Vanitas: lo stile dei semsi, with Omar Calabrese, Rome 1991.
Versace Signatures, with Omar Calabrese, Rome 1992.
Gianni Versace, with Bruce Weber, Milan, 1994.
Men Without Ties, with Hannah Barry, New York, 1994.
Rock & Royalty, Milan, 1996.
The Art of Being You, with Germano Celant, New York & Milan, 1997.

Gianni Versace standing with two of his silk crêpe designs, 1996. © AP/Wide World Photos.

On VERSACE:

Books

Alfonso, Maria-Vittoria, *Leaders in Fashion: i grandi personaggi della moda,* Bologna, 1983.

Giacomondi, Silvia, *The Italian Look Reflected,* Milan, 1984.

Soli, Pia, *Il genio antipatico* [exhibition catalogue], Venice, 1984.

Palais Galliera Musée de la Mode, *Gianni Versace: dialogues de mode* [exhibition catalogue], Milan, 1986.

Pasi, Mario, *Versace Teatro* (two volumes), Milan, 1987.

Bocca, Nicoletta, and Chiara Buss, *Gianni Versace: l'abito per pensare,* Milan, 1989.

Martin, Richard, and Harold Koda, *Infra-Apparel,* New York, 1993.

———, *Orientalism: Visions of the East in Western Dress* [exhibition catalogue], New York, 1994.

Turner, Lowri, *Gianni Versace: Fashion's Last Emperor,* London, 1997.

Martin, Richard, *Gianni Versace,* [exhibition catalogue], Metropolitan Museum of Art, New York, 1997.

Martin, Richard, and Sophie Léchauguette, *Gianni Versace,* Paris, 1997.

Avedon, Richard, *The Naked & the Dresses: Twenty Years of Versace,* London, 1998.

Casadio, Mariuccia and Samuele Mazza, *Versace,* London, 1998.

Mason, Christopher, *Undressed: A Biography of Gianni Versace,* London, 1999.

White, Nicola, *Versace,* London, 2000.

Articles

Carlsen, Peter, "Gianni Versace: Disciplined Negligence," in *GQ,* August 1979.

Withers, Jane, "The Palace of Versace," in *The Face* (London), December 1984.

Simpson, Helen, "Gianni Versace: ordito e trama," in *Vogue* (Milan), October 1985.

Petkanas, Christopher, "A Dialogue with Gianni Versace," in *WWD,* 22 October 1986.

Del Pozo, Silvia, "Gianni Versace: l'immigrato eccellente," in *L'Uomo Vogue* (Milan), October 1987.

Phillips, Kathy, "The Satanic Versace," in *You,* magazine of the *Mail on Sunday* (London), 19 March 1989.

Martin, Richard, "Sailing to Byzantium: A Fashion Odyseey, 1990–91," in *Textile & Text,* 14 February 1991.

Servin, James, "Chic or Cruel? Gianni Versace's Styles Take a Cue from the World of S&M," in the *New York Times,* 1 November 1992.

Morris, Bernadine, "The Once and Future Versace," in the *New York Times,* 8 November 1992.

"Gianni Versace," in *Current Biography,* April 1993.

Schiff, Stephen, "Lunch with Mr. Armani, Tea with Mr. Versace, Dinner with Mr. Valentino," in the *New Yorker* (New York), 7 November 1994.

Forden, Sara Gay, "Very Versace: Making America No. 1," in *WWD,* 1 November 1994.

Gandee, Charles, "Versace's Castle in the Sand," in *Vogue,* December 1994.

Menkes, Suzy, "Versace's Pastiche Amid Couture Upheaval," in the *International Herald Tribune,* 23 January 1995.

Spindler, Amy M., "Versace: Clean and Mean for Fall," in the *New York Times,* 8 March 1995.

"Gianni Versace: The Right Stuff," in *WWD,* 8 March 1995.

Van Lenten, Barry, "Gianni's American Dream," in *WWD,* 10 April 1995.

"Gianni vs. Giorgio: Is fashion dead?" in *WWD,* 11 September 1996.

Sullivan, Ruth, "High Fashion and a Head for Figures (Profile of Santo Versace)," in the *European* 12 June 1997.

Porter, Henrym and Susannah Barron, "A Tribute to the King of Glamour," in *The Guardian,* 16 July 1997.

Marlow, Michael, et al., "Fashion World Mourns Loss of a Leader," in *DNR,* 16 July 1997.

Socha, Miles, "The Versace Legacy," in *DNR,* 16 July 1997.

Reed, Paula, et al., "Fashion Victim," in the *European,* 17 July 1997.

Forden, Sara Gay, "Versace: The Milan Farewell," in *WWD,* 23 July 1997.

Bellafante, Ginia, "La Dolce Vita: Gianni Versace," [cover story] in *Time,* 28 July 1997.

Foley, Bridget, "Donatella's First Collection," in *WWD,* 1 October 1997.

Costin, Glynis, "Gianni Versace: A Reflection on Pride, Honesty, and Women," in *WWD,* 13 September 1999.

Spindler, Amy M., "The Great Gianni," in the *New York Times,* 18 February 2001.
"The Renaissance of Gianni Versace," in the *Economist,* 7 April 2001.

* * *

Gianni Versace's work was both metaphorical opera and real clothing, the first in its larger-than-life exuberance and design bravura and the latter in its unpretentious, practical application to the comfort of the wearer and the expressiveness of the body. Versace made all the world a stage for flamboyant and fascinating costume with the knowledgeable pageantry of the Renaissance, a Fellini-like sensuality of burlesque, and the brilliant notes of operatic color and silhouette. Richly cultivated in historical materials and vividly committed to the hedonism of late 20th-century culture, Versace created distinctive, at-the-edge designs that achieved the aesthetic limit of the avant-garde and the commercial success of viable apparel.

Versace expressed his admiration for Poiret, the fashion revolutionary who in a brief *éclat* of design genius combined a theatrical fantasy with legerdemain eclecticism. Similarly, Versace functioned as a kind of impresario to his own style, commanding authority over his image and advertising, menswear, womenswear, and accessories. His apparel design was characterized by a particular interest in bias, itself a means of revealing the body in dramatic, sexy clothing for women. His embroideries (and metal mesh) harkened back to the art déco, but were as mod as magazine covers. Likewise, his fascination with black-and-white grids and alternations recalled the 1920s and 1930s.

His abundant swathings suggested Vionnet, Madame Grès, and North Africa. Line was important, with many Versace suits, dresses, and coats marked by lines as if the bound edges of fabric would in outline define waistlines, shoulders, or center front. Like any great showman on stage, Versace was also concerned with metamorphic clothing; that which could be worn or perceived in several different ways. In these respects, it is clear the Milanese designer looked to Tokyo as well as to Milan and Paris. His metallics, trousers for women (ranging from voluminous pantaloons to cigarette-trouser leg wrappings), leather for women, and chunky, glittery accessories have created an image of women as a cross between Amazon and siren.

The boldness of silhouette in his womenswear was only reinforced in his work with photographers to represent the clothing, generally against a pure white field to grant further starkness and aggressiveness. But, in person and in the individual item, Versace's clothing was far less diva and dominatrix than it might seem. Versace's jewel-like colors, his geometric line in pattern, his recurrent fascination with the asymmetrical collars engendered by bias, and his flamboyant juxtapositions of pattern were all elegant traits. Likewise, Versace employed luxurious textiles, classical references, bias cut, and such combinations as leather reversible to wool, and embroidery-encrusted bodies and soft flowing skirts, to his unmistakable fashion.

Versace's menswear was also accented by leather, body wrapping for sensuality, audacious silhouette, and oversizing for comfort. Even in menswear, Versace played with asymmetry and the bias-influenced continuous rotation around the body, rather than a disjunctive front and back. Versace's menswear in particular was sometimes criticized as being futuristic with its big shoulders and technological detailing seeming to suggest science fiction. Yet Versace employed the most elegant menswear materials in a loose, capacious drape defying any space-age references. His designs did, however, recall a futurist ideal of clothing fully realized for the first time with sensuality and practicality.

Versace was an encyclopedist of classical tradition. His insistence upon directing all aspects of his fashion, from publicity and his books to the exhibitions interpreting his work reflected a consummate craftsman. Versace was neither a secluded scholastic, though, nor merely the glittery dresser of stars and celebrities some have perceived. The truth was somewhere in between, in a design imagination of brilliant theatrical insight, probing and analytical interest in bias, and a desire to reconcile the use of fashion history with making apparel appropriate for today.

After overcoming cancer of the lymph nodes, Versace was facing life with renewed vigor. Yet on the morning of 15 July 1997, a gunman named Andrew Cunanan, after a multi-state killing spree, shot Versace on the steps of his Miami home. The fashion industry united in outrage and grief and Versace stores were shuttered for a day in his memory. Donatella and Santo vowed to carry on in their brother's name, releasing a statement that read, "It must be remembered that Gianni Versace stood for the future, and so, of course, we stand dedicated to the future of our company." And so they soldiered on, building the Versace business to new heights amidst the tragedy.

By the year 2000, three years after Gianni's death, the Versace empire had been reorganized, streamlined, and poised for a possible initial public offering. Though Gianni was prepared to take the firm public in 1997, the plans had been tabled after his death. On the design front, Donatella's expertise grew with each succeeding collection, maintaing the Versace sensationalism and colorful style. In addition to the evolving apparel and accessories offered with the Versace label, the firm's name became associated with luxury hotels and resorts through an alliance with the Sunland Group. Gianni's former South Beach home in Miami, was also turned into a hotel.

—Richard Martin; updated by Sydonie Benét

VICTOR, Sally

American milliner

Born: Sally Josephs in Scranton, Pennsylvania, 23 February 1905. **Education:** Studied painting in Paris. **Family:** Married Sergiu Victor, 1927; children: Richard. **Career:** Saleswoman, then millinery buyer, Macy's, New York, 1923–25; assistant millinery buyer, 1925, and head buyer, 1926, Bamberger's, New Jersey; designer, Serge millinery, New York, 1927–34; opened own made-to-order millinery establishment, 1934; Sally V ready-to-wear line introduced, from 1951; firm closed, 1968. **Exhibitions:** The Brooklyn Museum, 1942. **Awards:** Fashion Critics Millinery award, 1943; Coty American Fashion Critics award, 1944, 1956. **Died:** 14 May 1977, in New York.

Publications

On VICTOR:

Books

Lambert, Eleanor, *World of Fashion: People, Places, Resources,* New York & London, 1976.
McDowell, Colin, *Hats: Status, Style, Glamour,* London, 1992.

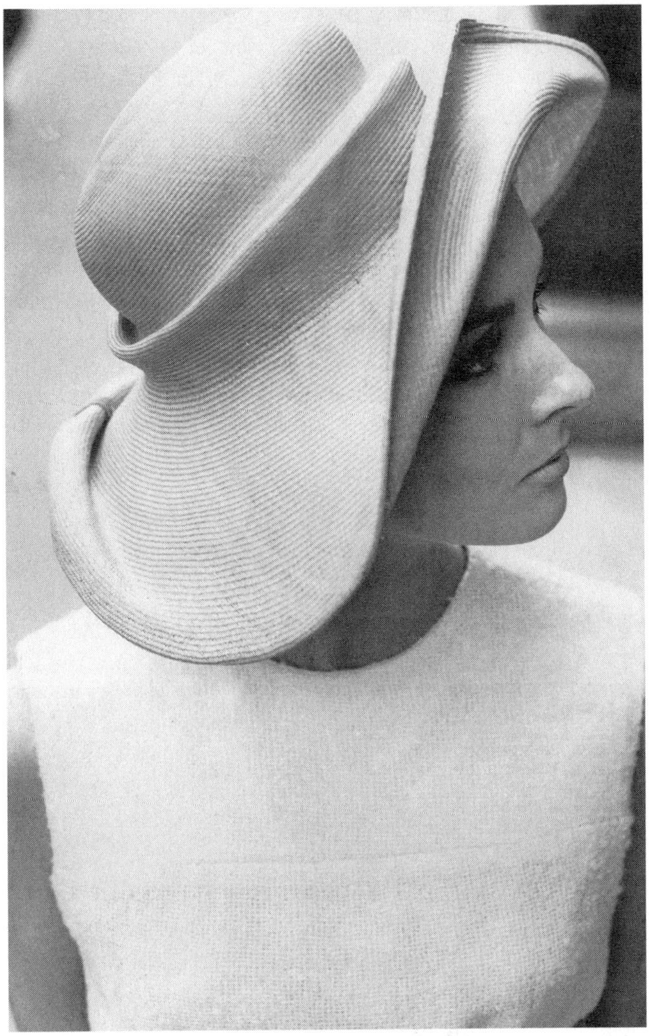

Design by Sally Victor, 1966. © AP/Wide World Photos.

Articles

"Sally Victor," in *Colliers* (New York), 11 March 1939.
"Sally Victor," in *Current Biography,* April 1954.
Sheppard, Eugenia, "Sally Victor," in the *New York Herald Tribune,* 25 March 1964.
———, "Sally Victor," [obituary], in the *New York Times,* 16 May 1977.

* * *

Just as the American sportswear designers were establishing the look of mix-and-match separates during the 1930s and 1940s, American milliners, especially Sally Victor, established the look in their own craft. Learning millinery first from the point of view of the buyer and customer, while working at Macy's in New York, Victor focused on "designing pretty hats that make women look prettier."

Victor aspirations were simple and pure; she believed women loved pretty things and liked to be noticed wearing them. Although she was occasionally denigrated for her pursuits, like when Eugenia Sheppard of the *New York Herald Tribune* (25 March 1964) said Victor was "sometimes accused of designing too pretty, too feminine, too becoming, too matronly hats," Victor was credited for reviving the Ecuadorean economy by making the Panama straw hat popular again, even with the young women of the mid-1960s.

Victor customers read like a who's who of the world's famous, including Mamie Eisenhower, Eleanor Roosevelt, Queen Elizabeth II, Judy Garland, and Helen Hayes. In addition to her designs being attractive, they were sophisticated, had clean lines, were considered especially "American." Victor was even called "a magnificent sculptress of straws and felts," by the *New Yorker* magazine in 1954.

Influences on her work were many and varied, and among those Victor readily acknowledged were art exhibitions and architecture. The 1948 exhibition of art from the museums of Berlin at New York's Metropolitan Museum of Art inspired her to create hats in a Franco-Flemish mode, with coifs and beret-like shapes taken from the paintings. In 1952 she did a series, in commemoration of Marco Polo's birth, on oriental themes using shapes inspired by fans, lanterns, and pinwheels. In the late 1950s and early 1960s she looked for inspiration to such buildings as Frank Lloyd Wright's Guggenheim Museum, which she interpreted in straw.

From early in her career she was counted with Lilly Daché and John Fredericks among the most important American milliners. Sally Victor hats were used to accessorize the catwalk models of American designers from Hattie Carnegie to Anne Klein. She was not only prolific in the variety of her made-to-order hats for each season, but was also among the first to establish a ready-to-wear line, Sally V. Her retirement in 1968 coincided with the demise of the hat as an essential fashion accessory and the increasing casualness of the American lifestyle. She died in New York in 1977.

—Jean Druesedow

VICTORIA'S SECRET

American Intimate apparel and accessories for women

Founded: by Roy Raymond in 1977, in San Francisco. **Company History:** Published first catalogue, 1978; sold for $4 million to The Limited apparel group, 1982; Cacique sibling formed to market French-styled lingerie, 1988; introduced swimwear, 1991; began selling cotton panties, 1993; launched bath and body line and introduced Miracle Bra, 1994; first runway show, 1995; spun off by The Limited, 1995; introduced seamless bras, 1996; launched legwear, 1998; went online with firm website, 1998; first live web fashion show, 1999; debuted *Dream Angels* fragrance collection, 1999; sponsored AIDS fundraiser with Miramax Films, 2000; launched first men's fragrance collection, 2001; launched *Pink* fragrance and aired first television fashion show, 2001; signed license with Shiseido Company Ltd. for cosmetics, 2001. **Company Address:** 3 Limited Parkway, Columbus, OH 43216, U.S.A. **Company Website:** www.VictoriasSecret.com.

Victoria's Secret, spring 2002 collection. © AP/Wide World Photos.

PUBLICATIONS

On VICTORIA'S SECRET:

Articles

Perman, Stacy, "Victoria's Secret Hitting the Beach," in *WWD,* 30 March 1994.

Belcove, Julie L., "Victoria's Secret—Boudoir to Bath with July Entry," in *WWD,* 6 May 1994.

Moin, David, "The Intimate Category Killer," in *WWD,* 13 March 1995.

Machan, Dyan, "Sharing Victoria's Secrets," in *Forbes,* 5 June 1995.

Brady, Jennifer L., "Victoria's Secret Seamless Bra Sews Up Sales," in *WWD,* 16 September 1996.

Palmieri, Christopher, "Victoria's Little Secret," in *Forbes,* 24 August 1998.

Moin, David, and Laura Kelpacki, "Victoria's Secret Puts Sex Appeal and Color into Cosmetics Line," in *WWD,* 18 September 1998.

Napoli, Lisa, "Bared-Bones Fashions, Fully Covered Publicity," in the *International Herald Tribune,* 11 February 1999.

Moin, David, and Pete Born, "IBI Giving Victoria's Secret Push Into Global Prominence," in *WWD,* 29 September 1999.

"Victoria's Secret to Cosponsor AIDS Benefit," in *WWD,* 9 February 2000.

Hickins, Michael, "Victoria's Secret Shifts Into Global Overdrive," in *WWD,* 5 April 2000.

Klepacki, Laura, "Victoria's Secret Takes a Brave Step," in *WWD,* 27 January 2001.

Born, Pete, "Victoria's Secret's New Interest: Guys," in *WWD,* 12 October 2001.

"Victoria's Secret Launches Something Very Sexy for Him," in *Cosmetics International,* November 2001.

"FCC Fields Complaints About Victoria's Secret Show," in *Adweek,* 19 November 2001.

* * *

Victoria's Secret made buying lingerie not only a pleasure but a must in the late 1980s and 1990s. The upscale lingerie and apparel

Victoria's Secret, spring 2002 collection. © AP/Wide World Photos.

Victoria's Secret, spring 2002 collection. © AP/Wide World Photos.

firm took shopping for lingerie from the neglected corners of department stores and put it front and center in thousands of boutiques throughout the United States. Both men and women happily flocked to the sensuous, sumptuously decorated shops and buying sexy innerwear was no longer a chore or embarrassing for either sex.

Men gladly accompanied their wives or lovers to Victoria's Secret, while women enjoyed finding a myriad of products in every size and shape imaginable. This was the experience Roy Raymond had in mind when he founded Victoria's Secret in 1977 in San Francisco. Loath to shop for lingerie or foundations for his wife in austere surroundings, Raymond envisioned an appealing shop with a stylish decor—somewhere with a Victorian-boudoir feel. The next year, Raymond took his lingerie fantasies a step further, creating a mail order catalogue to sell his growing selection of bras, panties, slips, and loungewear.

The response to the Victoria's Secret catalogue was immediate and stunning; Raymond's business mushroomed in size and scope yet he had problems meeting demand and running the mail order business. While there were rivals, such as Frederick's of Hollywood which sold many of the same products, Frederick's had a raunchy feel to its stores and looked more like an S&M supplier than intimate apparel retailer. In 1982, Raymond sold the company, which consisted of six faltering stores and its catalogue, for $4 million to Leslie Wexner, founder of The Limited women's apparel firm.

Throughout the remainder of the 1980s, the Victoria's Secret mystique grew and Wexner decided to add another lingerie maker to his fold, launching Cacique as a French counterpart to Victoria's faux English styling. While Cacique stores opened near or by Victoria's Secret stores in 1988 and 1989, the older sibling's catalogues had reached the pinnacle of popularity. The thick magazine-like editions became acceptable "girlie" material for men of all ages. Women awaited the arrival of catalogues almost as eagerly as men; soon the pages were crowded with not only intimate apparel but sportswear and accessories as well. Gone were the posed couples that had populated Raymond's catalogue, replaced by sexy, pouty, internationally known models. Being selected to pose for a Victoria's Secret catalogue became a much sought after job, a stepping stone to model superstardom.

In the early 1990s Victoria's Secret continued to broaden its product line with swimsuits (and a special swimwear catalogue reminiscent of the annual *Sports Illustrated* edition), simple, cotton panties—which suddenly made the old-fashioned underwear hip and must-have—and a bath and body line called Second Skin Satin Luxury Bath Collection. Next came the Miracle Bra in 1994, released months ahead of Warner's Wonderbra. The Limited, which had created a subsidiary called Intimate Brands to manage Victoria's Secret and its sister company, Bath & Body Works, spun the company off in 1995, retaining a majority stake when the firm went public.

Despite its similarity to its sibling, Cacique failed to gain the notoriety or clientèle of its much famed elder. Intimate Brands closed the chain in 1998, putting a new home furnishings concept into many of the stores called the White Barn Candle Company. Around the same time, Victoria's Secret introduced cosmetics into its stores and catalogue, setting the stage for Victoria's Secret Beauty, which began as in-store shops. The firm then joined the wave of the future by launching a company website. Although many retailers had websites for information, store locations, and to sell products, Victoria's Secret decided to broadcast its spring fashion show live via the Internet in early 1999. Servers were completely unprepared for the 1.5 million viewers who tried to log on; they were not only completely overwhelmed by the response but jammed for hours and eventually crashed due to the unexpected crush of web surfers.

In 1999 parent company Intimate Brands introduced additional cosmetics to Bath & Body Works and Victoria's Secret stores, and took the in-store Victoria's Beauty shops and started creating separate stores either adjacent to or near existing Victoria's Secret boutiques. Over the next two years, the company moved in several new directions. A men's fragrance collection, called *Very Sexy for Him,* was developed for a 2001 launch while the firm entered talks with Japan's Shiseido Company Ltd. to create a cosmetics line. Additionally, after the success of its website fashion show, Victoria's Secret raised the bar and took its spin on fashion to prime-time television. Its first-ever televised fashion show, aired by ABC in November, stirred controversy when concerned viewers complained to the Federal Communications Commission (FCC) about the "indecency" of the scantily clad models. Fortunately for Victoria's Secret, neither the FCC nor most of viewing public found the showing indecent. On the contrary, millions tuned in and enjoyed the provocative parade.

By 2002 there were about 2,300 Victoria's Secret boutiques in the U.S., and its racy and lacy catalogues were mailed to more than 350 million households annually. Its stores had become as much about attitude and indulgence as undergarment needs—women loved the sexy, ultrafeminine innerwear, and it made them feel sexy and beautiful regardless of their age, size, or inclination.

—Nelly Rhodes

VICTORIO Y LUCCHINO

Italian fashion design company

Founded: by José Luis Medina del Corral (born in 1954 in Seville) and José Victor Rodríguez Caro (born in 1952 in Cordoba); met in 1972, working for a Seville design group. **Company History:** Fragrances include *Carmen,* 1992, followed by *V&L* launch; introduced leather apparel and accessories; financial backing provided by the Puig family. **Exhibitions:** *Sevilla Barroca,* Museo de Ferrocariles, Madrid, 1986; British Designers Fair, Olympia, London, 1987, 1988, 1989; Cibeles Fashion Show, Madrid, 1987–91; *Festa de la moda,* Barcelona, 1988; *IGEDO,* Dusseldorf, 1989, 1990; *Mode Woche,* Munich, 1990; *Fashion Coterie,* New York, 1990; *Milanovende,* Milan, 1991; *Festival de Disenadores Hispanos,* Washington, D.C. 1991; Expo 92; Hotel Ritz, Barcelona, 1992. **Company Address:** Padre Luis Mallop, 4 Casa Natal de Velazquez, 41004 Seville.

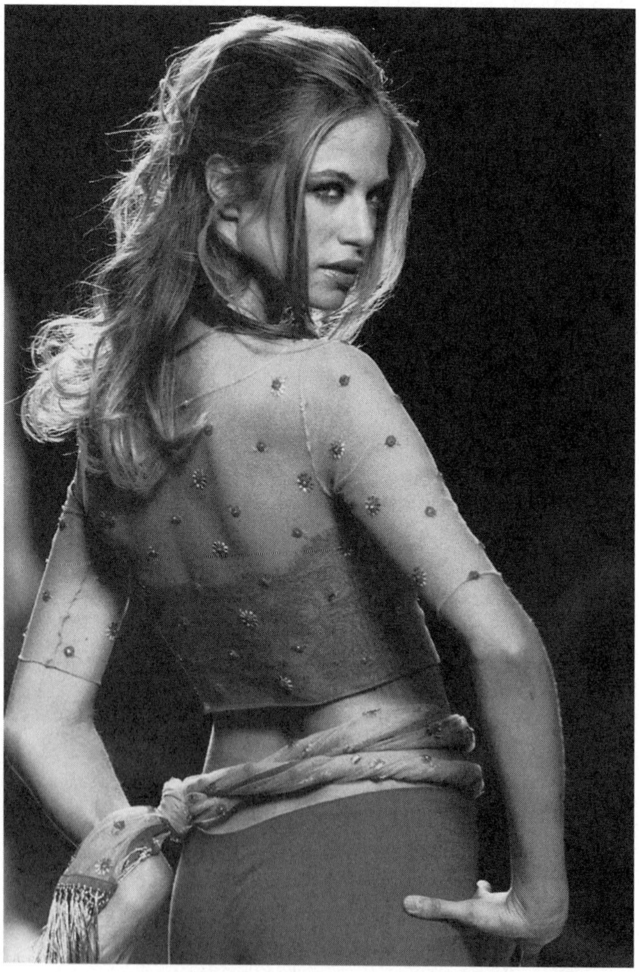

Victorio y Lucchino, spring 2001 collection. © AP/Wide World Photos.

Publications

On VICTORIO Y LUCCHINO:

Articles

"Victorio & Lucchino," in *Vanidad,* No. 1, 1992.
"Pasarela Cibeles: la moda esta de moda," in *¡Hola!,* 4 March 1993.
"Victorio y Lucchino suspiran por Espana," in *El Pais* (Madrid), 19 February 1994.
Barker, Barbara, "Fashion's Strain in Spain," in *WWD,* 2 March 1995.
Raper, Sarah, "A Younger Generation Takes Over at Puig," in *WWD,* 19 June 1998.
Corson, Alice, "Living la vida regalada," in *Soap, Perfumery & Cosmetics,* May 2001.

* * *

Victorio y Lucchino is a Spanish design duo, combining the talents of the founding partners, José Victor Rodríguez Caro and José Luis Medina del Corral. Caro comes from Palma Del Rio in Córdoba and was born during the early 1950s. He was originally inspired by the Parisian designers of the decade who dominated the pages of Spanish fashion magazines. As a teenager, he worked as an assistant for several fashion companies, collaborating in the preparation of their collections.

Del Corral, also born in the 1950s, hails from Seville. From an early age he, too, felt that his vocation was to be in fashion design. After his studies, he began work with a Seville design company where Caro was also working and, after several months at the company, the pair decided to join forces and create their own line, "Victorio y Lucchino."

The Victorio y Lucchino style is purely Spanish in origin; designs are particularly inspired by the spirit of Andalucia in the southern region of Spain where the team lives and work. The bright light creates very rich shadows, colors and textures, awakening the senses to the tastes, touches, and smells that stimulate exciting design. The visual imagery also inspires, like the religious rituals, such as the slaves of the Phoenician Goddess of Estarte as they bedeck her in heavy jewels amidst a haze of incense, myrrh and amber. The duo themselves have declared, "We create our fashions amid scents of geraniums, basil, and myrtle. Our influences are mixed and melted together to form ideas reminiscent of the streets, squares, and the river bejewelled with stars."

Luscious opulence is reflected in the type of fabrics Victorio y Lucchino choose to work with—smooth velvets in burgundies, dark olive greens, and sunlit yellows and oranges; iridescent velvets reflecting the light and ribbed and stripped velvets that shimmer; crinkled and bubbled organza, and organza with tone on tone marble effects; satin, and the luxurious effect of chenille, are other popular fabrics.

Sensuous eveningwear is a favorite look. Bustiers with long, attached sleeves leaving shoulders revealed and lots or room for full

Victorio y Lucchino, fall 2001 collection: velvet skirt and top. © AFP/CORBIS.

straps. Clingy, sculpted dresses and lily-shaped jackets are other popular innovations. The Victorio y Lucchino woman is calm, deep, and sensual; she is dressed to make an impact on a Spanish balcony or on the street. It is an outdoor, Mediterranean glamour, born of a bright and orange-scented afternoon.

The nationalistic flavor of Victorio y Lucchino collections is enhanced by recurring themes plucked from Spanish culture. Ranges have been christened with titles such as Spanish Barroca, The Comb and Manstilla, Carmen, and Vestales Hispalenses. In 1992 the design duo even launched a fragrance called Carmen, paying homage to Bizet's famous opera and his fiery heroine.

The Victorio y Lucchino design label has points of sale in Europe, Hong Kong, Japan, Kuwait, and the United States. Shows are seasonal, at the Cibeles fashion show in Madrid as well as other popular international trade shows, such as the Fashion Coterie in New York and Milanovendemoda in Milan. The design team has their own shop in Seville, and with financial backing from the Puig beauty and fashion empire, was able to expand in several directions. New in the middle and late 1990s were leather separates and matching accessories, another fragrance, *V&L,* and an increased presence in Asia, primarily in Hong Kong.

—Kevin Almond

VIKTOR & ROLF

Dutch designers

Born: *(both Viktor and Rolf)* Netherlands, 1969. **Education:** Both graduated from the Academia of Amhem, 1992. **Company History:** Created first collection, 1993; created second collection, 1994; "Winter of Love" presented at the Musée d'Art Moderne de la Ville de Paris, 1994; third collection, 1994; created photographic collection, 1995; clothing exhibition in art gallery, 1995; created the Prêt-à-Porter Catalogue, 1995; launched *Viktor & Rolf Le Parfum,* 1996; Torch Gallery installation, Amsterdam, 1996; continued developing fashion trends as art exhibitions; collection exhibited in Groninger Museum, 1998; designs turned more towards ready-to-wear, 2000. **Awards:** International Festival of Hyeres, 1993; ANDAM, 1994. **Exhibitions:** Visionaire Gallery, SoHo, 1999; Groninger Museum, Netherlands, 2001.

Publications

On VIKTOR & ROLF:

Books

Horsting, Viktor, *Viktor & Rolf,* Artimo Foundation, Amsterdam, 1999.

Articles

Martin, Richard, "Viktor & Rolf: Le Regard Noir," in *N-28,* 1997.

Goldberg, Rose Lee, "Claude Wampler [Performance Art]," *Artforum,* September 1997.

Phillips, Ian, "Fashion: 21st Century Boys Meet Viktor & Rolf," in *Newspaper Publishing PLC,* 3 October 1998.

Horyn, Cathy, "Two Dutch Designers Take Couture to the Surreal Side," in the *New York Times,* 1 June 1999.

———, "Is There Room for Fashion at the Paris Haute Couture Shows?" in the *New York Times,* 25 July 1999.

Bell, Katy, "Amsterdammer Anarchy: Viktor & Rolf are Mad as Hell and They're Not Going to Wear It Anymore," in *Metro Active,* January 2000.

Socha, Miles, "Christmas Comes Early at Viktor & Rolf Exhibit," in *WWD,* Groningen, Netherlands, 10 November 2000.

Bellafante, Ginia, "This is Paris: No Giggling, Please," in the *New York Times,* 21 March 2001.

Wilson, Eric, "Victor & Rolf to ICV," in *Women's Wear Daily*, 5 September 2001.

* * *

Viktor Horsting and Rolf Snoeren, more commonly known as Viktor & Rolf—purveyors of elaborate style and exotic design, are as much known for their works of art as they are for fashion. They sculpt their designs by distorting proportions—creating high collars and elaborate draping to hide the body, making it seemingly vanish into the sculpture. Always adding to the fabrics, Viktor & Rolf often use ornamentation that mocks accessories, including Christmas trees balls, colorful tinsel garlands, and pleated Pierrot collars. This is a clear indication of their reputation to shock and challenge fashion and remain with the forerunners of originality. Their creation of the unusual "atomic bomb," for example, was a shrewd combination of

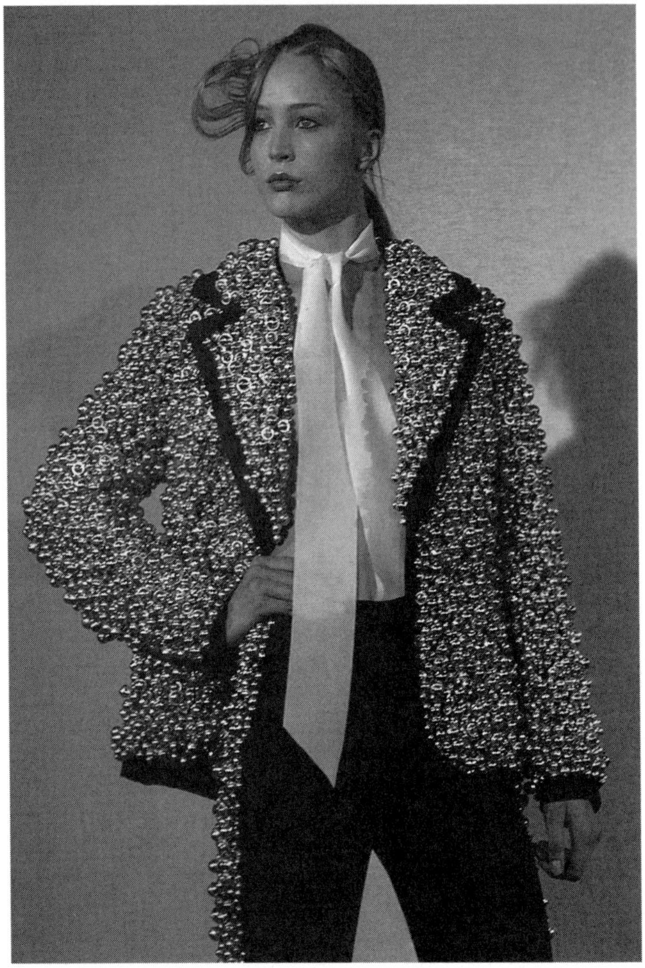

Viktor & Rolf, fall/winter 2000–01 haute couture collection: pants with bells sown down the sides and matching bell-covered jacket. © AP/Wide World Photos.

extreme fashion and art. The costume had the model's head resting on top of a huge mushroom form, a chiffon blouse inflated with brightly colored balloons, jackets with neon mink dots, and a black-and-white collection shown under scant neon light in a dark room. "Fashion doesn't hold a big value with Dutch people," Snoeren commented to the *New York Times'* Cathy Horyn. "In Holland," Horsting continued, "the mentality is you're not supposed to want to stand out. We made our collections to be noticed, but it was also a reaction."

Adhering to their reputation to intrigue and fascinate, Viktor & Rolf created *Le parfum* to awaken the fashion industry's senses with a perfume that provided no scent. The 250 limited edition bottles of *Le parfum* were never meant to be opened; another step clearly meant to integrate fashion as an art form.

Viktor & Rolf's first clothing collection was shown at a competition called Salon European des Jeunes Stylistes in 1993. The collection was comprised of preexisting pieces of garments blended into a collage, to create new clothing. In 1994 Viktor & Rolf created two collections, the first consisting of several variations of a white dress, most of which were high-waisted and long, like ballgowns, but there were also shirts blown up with balloons and confetti, giving the presentation a satirical bent. The other collection revolved around the aptly named "Black Square Dress," with squared-off shoulders to create an illusion of abstract art.

In 1995 their collection appeared at the Galerie Patricia Dorfmann in Paris, and consisted of five suspended gold garments of several different silhouettes. Next came the "Shadowdress," a dark, opaque dress which was a three-dimensional form of the pieces from the collection. Tracing back history, the "Shadow Cape" of 1996 featured the strong silhouette of an 1890s torso but in light, silk fabric. Softness and versatility were behind the addition of a grey bodysuit and supple white dress added to the collection.

Viktor & Rolf have proven that fashion and art can be interchangeable, and the Groninger Museum recognized their efforts in 1998. A permanent collection of 28 pieces from five collections exhibited fashion as an art form. The apparel, eerily exhibited on mannequins in a dark room, were illuminated as lights hit their rotating platforms. In January 1999, the designing duo created a black and white collection with firm skirts and poofy ruffs. Presentation of the collection involved ultraviolet lights so every white object glowed. Three of the 17 outfits from this collection were put on display at the trendy Visionaire art gallery and publishing house in SoHo, where fellow designers Diane von Furstenberg and Ronald van der Kemp were in attendance, along with a variety of celebrities. In a July 1999 show, the designers presented a collection by placing their model atop a revolving turntable. Dressed in a silk minidress, additional clothing was placed on the model by the designers with every revolution of the platform. By the ninth rotation, she was seemingly engulfed in Viktor & Rolf's designs—and so was the audience. Horyn decreed the show, "the most brilliant of the week."

With their reputation as fashion designers and artists, Viktor & Rolf have recently segued more into ready-to-wear collections, yet without detracting from their reputations as designers of art. Their first ready-to-wear collection, in collaboration with Gibo SpA, was launched in 2000; the lines was more wearable and functional, like jeans, ruffled shirts, and sexy pantsuits, which exhibited the designers' fondness for masculine styling for women. Yet the most popular portion of the spring collection was a stars-and-stripes motif, on jackets and shirts, inspired by the song "American Pie" by Don McLean. Several upscale retailer, including Barneys New York, placed orders.

A spring 2001 collection at the famed Louvre museum featured American classics, especially old Hollywood, and the styles from the glory days of the 1920s, 1930s, and 1940s—as modernized by Viktor & Rolf. The new line included fluid cabaret trouser suits, variations on the basic white shirt, trench coats, swinging skirts, and tap shorts. Silver seemed to be the hot accessory of the season, with metallic flashes seen on tops, shirt collars, pants, and even tuxedos. Always paying close attention to bringing art into fashion, Viktor & Rolf ended a 2000 fashion show by tap-dancing together in white tuxedos.

—Kimbally A. Medeiros

VIONNET, Madeleine

French designer

Born: Chilleurs-aux-Bois, 22 June 1876. **Family:** Married in 1893 (divorced, 1894); one child (died); married Dmitri Netchvolodov, 1925 (divorced, 1955). **Career:** Dressmaker's apprentice, Aubervilliers, 1888–93; dressmaker, House of Vincent, Paris, 1893–95; cutter, then

Viktor & Rolf, fall/winter 1998–99 haute couture collection: wool suit over puffed shirt. © AP/Wide World Photos.

head of workroom, Kate Reilly, London, 1895–1900; saleswoman, Bechoff David, Paris, 1900–01; head of studios under Marie Gerber, Callot Soeurs, Paris, 1901–05; designer, Doucet, 1905–11; designer, Maison Vionnet, 1912–14, 1919–39; retired, 1940. **Awards:** Légion d'Honneur, 1929. **Exhibitions:** *Three Women: Madeleine Vionnet, Claire McCardell and Rei Kawakubo,* Fashion Institute of Technology, New York, 1987; *Madeleine Vionnet, 1876–1975—l'art de la couture: Centre de la Vieille Charité,* retrospective, Musée de Marseille, 1991; *Madeleine Vionnet—les années d'innovation: 1919–1939,* exposition, Musée historique des tissus de Lyon, 1994. **Died:** 2 March 1975, in Paris.

Publications

On VIONNET:

Books

Latour, Anny, *Kings of Fashion,* London, 1958.
Milbank, Caroline Rennolds, *Couture: The Great Designers,* New York, 1985.
Koda, Harold, Richard Martin, and Laura Sinderbrand, *Three Women: Madeleine Vionnet, Claire McCardell, and Rei Kawakubo* [exhibition catalogue], New York, 1987.
Demornex, Jacqueline, *Madeleine Vionnet,* Paris, 1989.
Madeleine Vionnet, 1876–1975—l'art de la couture: Centre de la Vieille Charité, [exhibition catalogue], Marseille, 1991.
Kirke, Betty, *Vionnet,* Tokyo & San Francisco, 1991, 1998.
Steele, Valerie, *Women of Fashion: Twentieth Century Designers,* New York, 1991.
Alaïa, Azzedine, *Madeleine Vionnet* [exhibition catalogue], Marseille, 1991.
Madeleine Vionnet—les années d'innovation: 1919–1939, [exposition catalogue], Lyon, 1994.
Kamitsis, Lydia, *Madeleine Vionnet,* London & Paris, 1996.
Stegemeyer, Anne, *Who's Who in Fashion, Third Edition,* New York, 1996.

Articles

Chatwin, Bruce, "Surviving in Style," in the *Sunday Times Magazine* (London), 4 March 1973 (later republished as "Madeleine Vionnet" in his book, *What Am I Doing Here?,* London, 1989).
"Madeleine Vionnet, A Revolution in Dressmaking," in *The Times* (London), 6 March 1975.
Imatake, S., "Inventive Clothes 1909–39," in *Idea* (Concord, New Hampshire), September 1975.
Morris, Bernadine, "Three Who Redirected Fashion," in the *New York Times,* 24 February 1987.
———, "A New York Exhibition Traces the Evolution of Modern Fashion in the Designs of Vionnet, McCardell and Kawakubo," in the *Chicago Tribune,* 11 March 1987.
Smith, Roberta, "Three Women at the Fashion Institute of Technology," in the *New York Times,* 13 March 1987.
Weinstein, Jeff, "Vionnet, McCardell, Kawakubo: Why There are Three Great Women Artists," in the *Village Voice,* 31 March 1987.
Drier, Deborah, "Designing Women," in *Art in America* (New York), May 1987.
Kirke, Betty, "A Dressmaker Extrordinaire," in *Threads* (Newtown, Connecticut), February/March 1989.
Dryansky, G.Y., "Madeleine Vionnet: The Modest Charms of a Farmhouse in Cely-en-Biere," in *Architectural Digest,* October 1994.
McColl, Patricia, "Madeleine Vionnet: A Youth Movement for the Venerable Couturiere," in *WWD,* 13 September 1999.
Loyer, Michelle, "The Sleeping Beauties of Fashion are Waking," in the *International Herald Tribune,* 11 October 2000.

* * *

Madeleine Vionnet's inexorable synergy is the body of her extraordinary dresses. Her draping on the bias gave stretch to the fabric, a fully three-dimensional and even gyroscopic geometry to the garment, and a fluid dynamic of the body in motion as radical as cubism and futurism in their panoramas on the body. Her work inevitably prompts the analogy to sculpture in its palpable revelation of the form within. Some accused Vionnet of a shocking *déshabillé,* but Vionnet was seeking only the awareness of volume. Bruce Chatwin, writing in the *Sunday Times Magazine* in March 1973, commented, "No one knew better how to drape a torso in the round. She handled fabric as a master sculptor realizes the possibilities latent in a marble block; and like a sculptor too she understood the subtle beauty of the female body in motion and that graceful movements were enhanced by asymmetry of cut."

The only rigidity ever associated with Vionnet was her definite sense of self: she closed her couture house in 1939, although she lived until 1975. She lamented the work of other designers and disdained much that occurred in fashion as unprincipled and unworthy; she was a true believer in the modern, scorning unnecessary adornment, seeking structural principles, demanding plain perfection. Fernand Léger said that one of the finest things to see in Paris was Vionnet cutting. He used to go there when he felt depleted in his own work.

Vionnet draped on a reduced-scale mannequin. There she played her cloth in the enhanced elasticity of its diagonal bias to create the garment. In creating the idea in miniature, Vionnet may have surpassed any sense of weight of the fabric and achieved her ideal and effortless rotation around the body in a most logical way. When the same garments achieved human proportion—their sheerness, the avoidance of decorative complication, the absence of planes front and back, and the supple elegance of fabric that caresses the body in a continuous peregrination—were distinctly Vionnet.

While bias cut was quickly emulated in the Paris couture, Vionnet's concepts of draping were not pursued only by Claire McCardell (who bought Vionnets to study their technique) before World War II, but by Geoffrey Beene, Halston, and other Americans in the 1960s and 1970s, Azzedine Alaïa in France, and Japanese designers Issey Miyake and Rei Kawakubo in the 1970s and 1980s. Mikaye and Kawakubo were alerted to Vionnet by her strong presence in *The 10s, 20s, 30s* exhibition organized by Diana Vreeland for the Costume Institute of the Metropolitan Museum of Art in 1973 and 1974.

One of Vionnet's most-quoted aphorisms is "when a woman smiles, her dress must smile with her." By making the dress dependent on the form of the wearer rather than an armature of its own, Vionnet assured the indivisibility of the woman and the garment. It is as if she created a skin or a shell rather than the independent form of a dress. Like many designers of her time, Vionnet's external references were chiefly to classical art and her dresses could resemble the wet drapery of classical statues and their cling and crêpey volutes of drapery.

At Doucet, she had discarded the layer of the underdress. In her own work, Vionnet eliminated interfacing in order to keep silhouette and fabric pliant; she brought the vocabulary of lingerie to the surface in her *détente* of all structure; she avoided any intrusion into fabric that could be avoided. Darts are generally eliminated. In a characteristic example, her "honeycomb dress,"all structure resided in the manipulation of fabric to create the honeycomb, a pattern that emanates the silhouette. Elsewhere, fagoting and drawnwork displaced the need for darts or other impositions and employed a decorative field to generate the desired form of the garment. The fluidity of cowl neckline, the chiffon handkerchief dress, and hemstiched blouse were trademarks and soft symbols of a virtuoso designer.

In insisting on the presence of a body and on celebrating the body within clothing, Vionnet was an early-century original in the manner of Diaghilev, Isadora Duncan, and Picasso. But there is also a deeply hermetic aspect to Vionnet who remained, despite the prodigious research revelations of Betty Kirke, a designer's designer, so subtle were the secrets of her composition, despite the outright drama of being one of the most revolutionary and important fashion designers.

At the end of the 20th century, Vionnet's name was revived and once again adorning fashion. After the label was acquired in 1994, scarves and fragrances tested the waters for a full revival of the Vionnet name. A new boutique on the rue Montaigne, where Vionnet's own house used to reside, was planned as well as ready-to-wear and couture lines.

—Richard Martin

VITTADINI, Adrienne

American designer

Born: Adrienne Toth, in Budapest, Hungary, 1944; immigrated to the U.S., 1956. **Education:** Studied at the Moore College of Art, Philadelphia, 1962–66; received academic scholarship to apprentice with Louis Féraud, Paris, 1965. **Family:** Married Gianluigi Vittadini, 1972. **Career:** Designer, Sport Tempo, New York, 1967; designer, SW1 line for Rosanna division, Warnaco, New York, 1968–71; designer, Adrienne Vittadini collection for Avanzara division, Kimberly Knits, New York, 1976–79; with partner Victor Coopersmith, established own firm, AVVC, 1979, bought out partner, renamed company Adrienne Vittadini, 1982; designed swimsuits for Cole of California, 1984–93; formed Vopco Inc., franchising company, New York, 1987; first boutique opened, Beverly Hills, California, 1987; returned to swimwear designs with O.A.S. Industries, 1994; launched first fragrance, *AV,* 1995; introduced AV Options line (later renamed Vittadini), 1996; sold to Marisa Christina Inc. and closed Beverly Hills store, 1996; announced bath and body collection for 1997; Vittadini and husband resigned from business, 1998; launched new fragrance, *Adrienne Vittadini,* 1999; firm sold to de V&P Inc., 1999; de V&P went bankrupt, 2000; Vittadini brand bought by Casual Corner Group, 2001. **Awards:** Coty American Fashion Critics award, 1984.

Publications

On VITTADINI:

Books

Milbank, Caroline Rennolds, *New York Fashion: The Evolution of American Style,* New York, 1989.

Daria, Irene, *The Fashion Cycle: A Behind-the-Scenes Look at a Year with Bill Blass, Liz Claiborne, Donna Karan, Arnold Scaasi, and Adrienne Vittadini,* New York, 1990.

Stegemeyer, Anne, *Who's Who in Fashion, Third Edition,* New York, 1996.

Malcolm, Trisha, *Designer Knits,* New York, 1998.

Articles

Conant, Jennet, "Sweaters for the Self Assured," in *Newsweek,* 3 February 1986.

Boyes, Kathleen, "Adrienne Vittadini: From Aesthetics to Reality," in *WWD,* 25 January 1988.

Schiro, Anne-Marie, "Adrienne Vittadini: From Sweaters to an Empire," in the *New York Times,* 19 July 1988.

Pattrinieri, Anita, "A Magic Moment for Adrienne," in *Donna* (Milan), November 1989.

White, Constance C.R., "Adrienne Vittadini: The Power of Knits," in *WWD,* 7 August 1991.

Schiro, Anne-Marie, "On Opposite Sides of the Cutting Edge," in the *New York Times,* 6 November 1992.
"Vittadini Returns to Swimwear," in *WWD,* 6 July 1994.
Born, Pete, "Vittadini to Launch First Scent at Bloomingdale's," in *WWD,* 13 January 1995.
"Swimwear: Designer Views," [interviews], in *WWD,* 13 April 1995.
"Vittadini Said Restructuring for New Units, Licenses," in *WWD,* 14 June 1995.
D'Innocenzio, Anne, "Vittadini's Growth Options," in *WWD,* 25 October 1995.
Ozzard, Janet, "Expansion Strategy for Marisa Christina: Revitalizing Vittadini," in *WWD,* 22 January 1996.
"A New Vision at Vittadini," in *WWD,* 16 October 1996.
D'Innocenzio, Anne, "More Finetuning at Adrienne Vittadini," in *WWD,* 19 March 1997.
———, "Vittadinis Shuttering Business," in *WWD,* 13 October 1998.
Wilson, Eric, "The Vittadini Brand: A New Phase," in *WWD,* 14 October 1998.
"U.S. Designers Extend Fragrance Collections," in *Cosmetics International,* 10 May 1999.
Socha, Miles, "de V&P Planning Revamp, Relaunch of Vittadini Brand," in *WWD,* 7 September 1999.
"News: de V&P to Close Shop," in *WWD,* 17 November 2000.
Moin, David, "Casual Corner Buys Vittadini from de V&P," in *WWD,* 7 February 2001.

* * *

To the industry and the fashion press, Hungarian-born Adrienne Vittadini was known as the Queen of Knits. In 1979, after working with several knitwear firms, Vittadini started her own knitwear company, always asserting that knitwear was more than just sweaters. Vittadini was far more than a knitwear designer, she also created textiles and reinvented fashion. Vittadini maintained, "creating fabrics, then silhouettes, is the essence of fashion."

Vittadini began with a concept or theme for a collection, based on a mood or a feeling, which she then connected with a particular inspiration. The inspiration could evolve from an individual artist, an artistic movement, or her travels. Once she settled on a theme, came the intensive research in libraries, museums, books, and magazines. Her collections were inspired by the works of Alexander Calder, Pablo Picasso, Joan Miró, and Max Bill as well as Norwegian design and early Russian embroidery. She also tapped into contemporary pop culture for ideas, such as the line she designed based on the cartoon character Dick Tracy.

After establishing a theme, Vittadini created knit fabric by selecting and creating unusually textured yarns with Italian yarn spinners. She then oversaw the dyeing to obtain her own distinctive colorings and often supervised the initial samples off the knitting machines. Once the color and pattern were finalized, the fit, finishing, and quality were considered, which allowed her to maintain a sense of control over the design process from start to finish. Vittadini likened this entire process to painting, relating to her background in fine arts study at Moore College of Art in Philadelphia.

The Vittadini look has been characterized by knitwear of all-natural fibers, a certain practical, casual ease, and contemporary design with a feminine appeal. Her trademark knit silhouettes were loose-fit sweaters worn over short skirts, sophisticated ensembles, and sweater dresses which could all be interchanged. Vittadini has long asserted that knits are the most modern way of dressing. In her collections, she balanced her love of European elegance in design with American practicality and ease by creating clothes which were "feminine without fussiness," and possessed "a certain cleanness and pureness without hardness." Vittadini's simple knit silhouettes created seductive looks as they molded to the shape of the body.

First and foremost, Vittadini design was defined by the textile. She expanded the knitwear industry by inventing and developing new computer knitting techniques in textures, prints, and patterns as well as shapes and colors. Vittadini cites Lycra as the most important development in knitwear; she used it as a technological and functional tool to keep shape in her knits—especially trousers. Vittadini also expanded the fabrics used in her collections to include wovens, prints, suedes, and leathers. Her later lines included licensing arrangements for cotton swimwear, accessories, girlswear, sleepwear, sunglasses, home furnishings, wallcoverings, and decorative fabrics. Roughly two-thirds of her line was knits.

Vittadini always stressed the advantage she had as a woman designer. She believed because she was a woman, she innately knew what other women wanted—clothes which reflected modern lifestyles. For many years, knits were looked upon by the industry as dowdy. Vittadini, however, revolutionized the power of knits, and most all Seventh Avenue fashion firms eventually included knits in their collections. By promoting the ease and practicality of knits as well as the fact they travel well, the Vittadini customer was both suburban and city, housewife and businesswomen, with a diverse set of needs from clothes.

Unfortunately for Vittadini, her design firm suffered a series of missteps in the hands of several owners. While struggling in the middle 1990s, Vittadini was forced to cancel of 1995 show and rely on mail order to promote her collections. She then reorganized her business and launched a more competitively priced line, AV Options, for spring 1996. Vittadini explained the move to *Women's Wear Daily* (25 October 1995), "It is very frustrating as a designer these days. With all the mergers and consolidations of department stores, I am finding less pockets to sell my bridge and designer clothes. In order to grow, I have to look at other areas."

A few months after launching the AV Options line, Vittadini decided to sell her firm to Marisa Christina Inc., a publicly-owned knitwear company. The plan was to grow the Vittadini line to compete with such market stalwarts as Liz Claiborne and Jones New York. Yet Marisa Christina and its newly acquired Vittadini unit failed to meet expectations over the next 18 months, and amid rumors of discord, Vittadini and her husband/partner announced their resignation from the firm bearing her name. "For me, the company has been like a family," Vittadini told *Women's Wear Daily* (13 October 1998), "but I'm ready to do something else… I have a wonderful team in place, and they don't need my day-to-day input." The Vittadini and Adrienne Vittadini ranges, as well as the licensed footwear, were continued by Marisa Christina until the Vittadini unit was abruptly sold to de V&P Inc. in September 1999.

The acquisition, however, was a disaster. After a scant 14 months, de V&P Inc. went bankrupt; luckily for Vittadini, Claudio del Vecchio's Casual Corner came forward and bought the brand in 2001. Vittadini apparel would not be sold in Casual Corner's 1,000-plus retail outlets across the U.S., rather, the firm planned to slowly open Adrienne Vittadini shops, starting in 2002. Vittadini herself said of the new ownership, "I am extremely excited about the acquisition by Claudio del Vecchio," she told *Women's Wear Daily* (7 February

2001). "Mr. del Vecchio will do an outstanding job in maintaining the integrity, image, and the aesthetics of all the products."

—Margo Seaman; updated by Owen James

VIVIER, Roger

French footwear designer

Born: Paris, 13 November 1913. **Education:** Studied sculpture at l'École des Beaux Arts, Paris. **Family:** Adopted son, Gèrard Benoit-Vivier. **Military Service:** Performed military service, 1938–39. **Career:** Designed shoe collection for friend's shoe factory; opened own atelier, 1937, designing for Pinet and Bally in France, Miller and Delman in U.S., Rayne and Turner in UK; designed exclusively for Delman, New York, 1940–41 and 1945–47; studied millinery, 1942; opened New York store, Suzanne & Roger, with milliner Suzanne Remy, 1945; returned to Paris, 1947, designing freelance; designed for Dior's new shoe department, 1953–63; showed signature collections, from 1963; reopened own business in Paris, 1963; designs collections for couture houses, including Grès, St. Laurent, Ungaro, and Balmain; resigned with Delman, 1992–94; new licensing pact with Rautureau, 1994; opened new Paris boutique, 1995. **Exhibitions:** Musée des Arts de la Mode, Paris, 1987 [retrospective]; Nina Footwear Showroom, New York, [retrospective], 1998; *Folies de dentelles,* Musée des Beaux-arts et de la dentelle, Alençon, France, 2000.**Awards:** Neiman Marcus award, 1961; Daniel & Fischer award; Riberio d'Oro; honored by Nina Footwear, 1998. **Died:** 2 October 1998, in Toulouse, France.

Publications

By VIVIER:

Books

Vivier, Paris, 1979.

Vivier, Roger, and Cynthia Hampton, *Les souliers de Roger Vivier* [exhibition catalogue], Paris, 1987.

On VIVIER:

Books

Swann, June, *Shoes,* London, 1982.

McDowell, Colin, *Shoes: Fashion and Fantasy,* New York, 1989.

Trasko, Mary, *Heavenly Soles: Extraordinary Twentieth-Century Shoes,* New York, 1989.

Provoyer, Pierre, *Vivier,* Paris, 1991.

Pringle, Colombe, *Roger Vivier,* New York & London, 1999.

Musée des Beaux-arts et de la dentelle, *Folies de dentelles,* [exhibition catalogue], Alençon, France, 2000.

Articles

Cassullo, Joanne L., "Four Hundred Shoes," in *Next,* December 1984.

Bricker, Charles, "Fashion Afoot: Roger Vivier, the Supreme Shoemaker Comes to New York," in *Connoisseur* (New York), December 1986.

Buck, Joan J., "A Maker of Magic," in *Vogue* (New York), December 1987.

"Styles," in the *New York Times,* 9 August 1992.

Weisman, Katherine, "Rautureaus Sell Stake; Ink Vivier Deal," in *Footwear News,* 28 February 1994.

Menkes, Suzy, "Master Cobbler Sets Up Shop Again," in the *International Herald Tribune,* 24 January 1995.

Baber, Bonnie, et al., "The Design Masters," in *Footwear News,* 17 April 1995.

Weisman, Katherine, "Roger Vivier, 90, Mourned by Shoe World," in *Footwear News,* 12 October 1998.

"Died, Roger Vivier," in *Time,* 19 October 1998.

"Roger Vivier, France's Footwear Extraordinaire," [obituary] in *People,* 26 October 1998.

Carmichael, Celia, "Legendary Status: Nina Honors the Creative Genius of Roger Vivier," in *Footwear News,* 21 December 1998.

* * *

Roger Vivier was perhaps the most innovative shoe designer of the 20th century and beyond. Vivier's shoes have had the remarkable ability to seem avant-garde yet destined at the same time to become classics. He maintained an eye for the cutting edge of fashion for six decades. Vivier looked back into the history of fashion and forward to the disciplines of engineering and science for inspiration. The shoes may seem shocking at first; however, it is the way they complete the silhouette that has made Vivier so coveted by top fashion designers for decades. With a sophisticated eye for line, form, and the use of innovative materials, Vivier created footwear worn by some of the most stylish and prestigious people of both the 20th and 21st centuries, among them Diana Vreeland, the Queen of England, and Marlene Dietrich.

Vivier worked with some of the most innovative fashion designers, such as Elsa Schiaparelli, Christian Dior, and Yves Saint Laurent, at the height of their careers. Schiaparelli was the first designer to include Vivier's shoes in her collections. Vivier was working for the American firm Delman at the time; Delman rejected Vivier's sketch of the shocking platform shoe which Schiaparelli included in her 1938 collection. In 1947 Vivier began to work for Christian Dior and the New Look brought new emphasis to the ankle and foot. Vivier created a number of new heel shapes for Dior, including the stiletto and the comma heel. During their ten-year association, Dior and Vivier created a golden era of design. In the 1960s Vivier created the low heeled "pilgrim pump" with a square silver buckle, and this shoe is often cited as fashion's most copied footwear.

Vivier was one of the first designers to use clear plastic in the design of shoes. His first plastic designs were created in the late 1940s after World War II; however, in the early 1960s he created entire collections in plastic. Vivier popularized the acceptance of the thigh-high boot in the mid-1960s, a fashion considered unacceptable for women. Vivier teamed with Delman again in 1992, and the mood his later collections continued to be imaginative and forward thinking. Drawing his inspiration from nature, contemporary fashion, the history of fashion, painting, and literature, Vivier updated some of his earlier designs and was constantly creating new ones to challenge the ideas of footwear design.

Vivier studied sculpture at the École des Beaux-Arts in Paris and later apprenticed at a shoe factory. It was this solid base of training in both aesthetics and technical skills that led him to become known for precision fit as well as innovative design. A *Vogue* ad for his shoes in

1953 educates the viewer to look beyond the design. Showing the shoes embraced in callipers and other precision tools the ad read, "Now study the heel. It announces an entirely new principle—the heel moved forward, where it carries the body's weight better." In another ad from *Vogue* (1954) the experience of owning a pair of Vivier shoes was likened to owning a couturier suit or dress, "a perfection of fit and workmanship."

Vivier's shoes not only had the ability to complete a silhouette with an eloquence that made a whole, but the beauty of their line, form, and craftsmanship made them creations that stood alone as objects of art. Vivier's strong combination of design and craftsmanship allowed his shoes to stand prominently in the permanent collections of some of the world's most prestigious museums—the Costume Institute of the Metropolitan Museum of Art, New York; the Victoria & Albert Museum, London; and the Musée du Costume et de la Mode of the Louvre, Paris.

In 1994 the 86-year-old Vivier signed a new licensing agreement with Rautureau Apple Shoes, which in turn allowed him to open a boutique in Paris the following year. The Rautureau venture gave Vivier the backing to continue doing what he loved most—designing shoes. Yet three years later, in October 1998, Vivier died in Toulouse, France. He was remembered by many, including fellow shoe designer Manolo Blahnik, who told *People* magazine, "People try to copy him, but it's impossible to find that mix of technical skill and design." Kenneth Jay Lane, who had worked with the master craftsman, declared, "He was the world's greatest artist of shoe design."

—Dennita Sewell; updated by Sydonie Benét

VOLLBRACHT, Michaele

American designer

Born: Michael Vollbracht in Quincy, Illinois, 17 November 1947. **Education:** Studied at Parsons School of Design, New York, 1965–67. **Career:** Design assistant in New York to Geoffrey Beene, 1967–69, to Donald Brooks, then back to Beene and Beene Bazaar line, then returned to Brooks, 1969–71; designed for Norman Norell until Norell's death in 1972; illustrator, Henri Bendel, 1972–74, and Bloomingdale's, 1975; Vollbracht Design Studios, producing garments from hand-printed silks (by Belotti) of his design launched, 1977, New York; swimwear designer, Sofere company, 1979; launched Vollbracht Too division of Manhattan Industries, 1981; Michaele Vollbracht Sport line introduced, 1983; has also designed sheets for Burlington Industries, table linens for Audrey Company, Dallas. **Awards:** Golden Thimble award, Parsons School of Design, 1967; Coty American Fashion Critics award, 1980; American Printed Fashion Council's Tommy award, 1984.

Publications

By VOLLBRACHT:

Books

Michaele Vollbracht's Nothing Sacred: Cartoons and Comments, New York, 1985.

On VOLLBRACHT:

Books

Khornak, Lucille, *Fashion 2001,* New York, 1982.

Articles

Schiro, Anne-Marie, "And Then They Turned to Clothes," in the *New York Times,* 8 July 1978.

Langway, Lynn, "A Fashion Comet Returns," in *Newsweek,* 25 May 1981.

Heiderstadt, Donna, "The Tranquil Force Behind Michaele Vollbracht's Bold Art," in *California Apparel News* (Los Angeles), 19 August 1983.

Radakovich, Anka, "Vollbracht Perfects a 'Starring Role' for Every Fashion Fantasy," in *Apparel News South* (Atlanta, Georgia), March 1985.

Larkin, Kathy, "Michaele Vollbracht," in the *New York Daily News,* 29 December 1985.

Lavina, Bettijean, "Portrait of a New Life," in the *Los Angeles Times,* 16 October 1992.

* * *

Dubbed "a fashion comet" by *Newsweek* magazine in 1981, Michaele Vollbracht blazed across the New York fashion scene for a 10-year period beginning in 1977. When he left Parsons School of Design, New York, towards the end of the 1960s, Vollbracht logged time as a design assistant on Seventh Avenue, found it not to his liking, and turned instead to fashion illustration and graphic design. A shopping bag he created for Bloomingdale's department store in 1975 became an instant conversation piece and collector's item. It pictured an idealized woman's face, the artist's signature, and no other identifier, least of all the store name. The bag became the all-purpose tote, a symbol of reverse chic, acceptable *because* it carried no advertising, although everyone knew what it represented.

By 1977 Vollbracht was one of the top illustrators in the field. At the same time, sensing women were ready to turn away from the conservative, monochromatic look which had characterized much of the 1970s, Vollbracht established his fashion company. "We have been beiged to death," he told Priscilla Tucker for a May 1978 issue of the *New York Daily News.*

Bringing his skills as a graphic artist to the new company, Vollbracht created huge patterns in bright colors, hand screened onto lengths of silk, then cut into simple kaftan or kimono-like shapes, sometimes further embellished with sequins or bugle beads. These were entrance-making clothes with humor and panache for a confident clientèle. Vollbracht's celebrity customers included Elizabeth Taylor, Diahann Carroll, and Joan Rivers. For his first collection in 1978, many of Vollbracht's prints consisted of a single stylized element, such as a palm frond or a panther's head, enlarged to full body proportion and placed asymmetrically at the shoulder or side seam so that the motif was not quickly perceived—and the negative space of the ground formed a pattern of competing interest.

By the early 1980s Vollbracht's work included more sophisticated shaping and traditional fabrics in addition to his enormous signature prints. "I had to prove I'm not just some outrageous designer, waving fabric over women's heads," he told *Newsweek* in 1981, "I want to demonstrate that I can cut an armhole and shape a dress—maybe not as beautifully as Givenchy, but I *can* do it." Indeed he could—a black velvet dress from his 1980 collection was softly draped diagonally across the back from the left shoulder almost to the waist at right, presenting the bare back as a piece of sculpture.

At the height of his career in the mid-1980s, Vollbracht was responsible for three ready-to-wear lines, Vollbracht Too, Michaele Vollbracht Sport, and Overs by Michaele Vollbracht, as well as a line of swimwear for the American manufacturer Sofere. His licensing agreements included sheets, towels, table linens, and a line of women's blouses. Vollbracht's whimsical, eye catching prints characterized his swimwear just as they did his custom line. In 1985 Vollbracht parted company with his backer. Apparently unable or unwilling to obtain financing elsewhere, he discontinued his custom business. Two years later, in 1987, he retired from Seventh Avenue for the second time to concentrate on illustration and portraiture. His work was used in the *New Yorker* and in *Vogue* as well as in his 1985 illustrated memoir *Nothing Sacred.*

—Whitney Blausen

VON FURSTENBERG, Diane

Belgian designer working in New York

Born: Diane Michelle Halfin in Brussels, Belgium, 31 December 1946; immigrated to the U.S., 1969. **Education:** Studied at the University of Madrid, graduated in economics, University of Geneva. **Family:** Married Prince Egon Von Furstenberg, 1969 (divorced, 1983); married USA Network Chairman Barry Diller, 2001; children: Alexandre, Tatiana. **Career:** Owner/designer, Diane Von Furstenberg Studio, 1970–77, and from 1985; established couture house, 1984–88; produced signature cosmetics line, 1977–83; introduced *Tatiana* fragrance, 1977; began marketing products on QVC, 1990s; named planning director, Q2, 1994; relaunched business, 1997; published autobiography, 1998; opened in-store boutiques at Henri Bendel, 2001. **Awards:** Fragrance Foundation award, 1977; City of Hope Spirit of Life award, Los Angeles, 1983; *Savvy* Magazine award, New York, 1984, 1985, 1986, 1987, 1988; Einstein College of Medicine Spirit of Achievement award, New York, 1984; Mayor of the City of New York's Statue of Liberty medal, 1986. **Address:** 385 West 12th Street, New York, NY, U.S.A.

Publications

By VON FURSTENBERG:

Books

Diane Von Furstenberg's Book of Beauty, New York, 1976.
Beds, New York, 1991.
Diane: A Signature Life, with Linda Bird Francke, New York, 1998.

On VON FURSTENBERG:

Books

Reeves, Richard, *Convention,* New York, 1977.
Morris, Bernadine, and Barbara Walz, *The Fashion Makers,* New York, 1978.
Milbank, Caroline Rennolds, *New York Fashion: The Evolution of American Style,* New York, 1989.

Diane Von Furstenberg, spring 2002 collection. © Reuters NewMedia Inc./CORBIS.

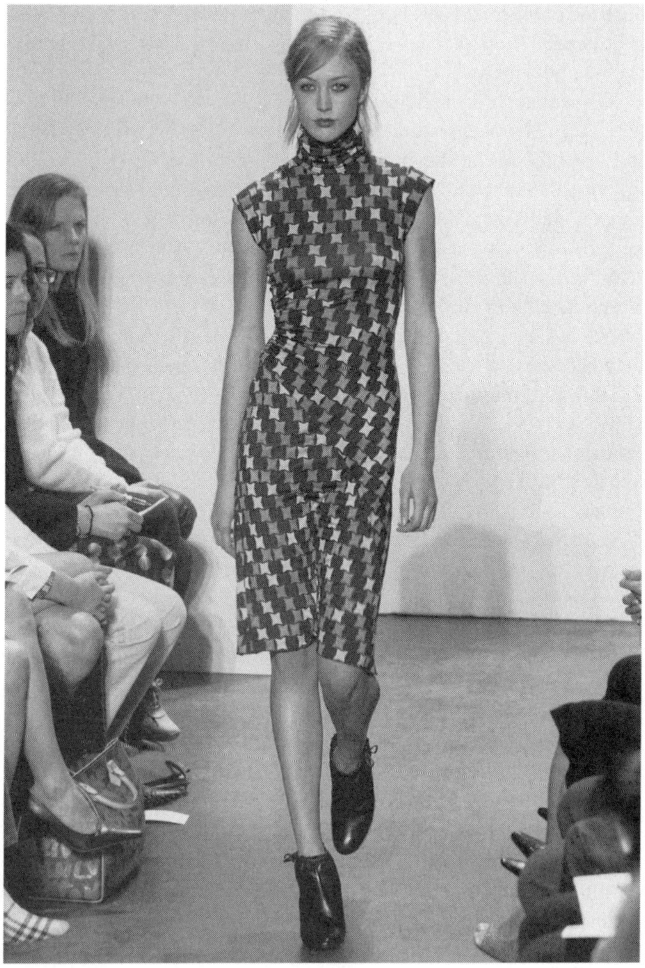

Diane Von Furstenberg, fall 2001collection: silk jersey dress. © AP/ Wide World Photos.

Stegemeyer, Anne, *Who's Who in Fashion, Third Edition,* New York, 1996.

[profile] in *Almanac of Famous People, Sixth Edition,* Detroit, 1998.

[profile] in *Encyclopedia of World Biography, Second Edition,* Detroit, 1998.

contributor, to Bonnie Miller Rubin, *Fifty on Fifty: Wisdom, Inspiration, and Reflection on Women's Lives Well Lived,* New York, 1998.

Articles

Rothmyer, Karen, "Once Upon a Time a Princess Made It with the Hoi Polloi," in the *Wall Street Journal* 17 January 1976.

Francke, Linda Bird et al, "Princess of Fashion," in *Newsweek* 28 March 1976.

Rowes, Barbara, "Women Buy, But Men Dominate...Then Came DVF," in *People,* 14 May 1979.

Wallach, Leah, "What Makes Diane Run?" in *Metropolitan Home* (New York), September 1982.

Blandford, Linda, "I Was Very Very Clever and Very Very Devious," in *The Guardian,* 9 March 1983.

Scholl, Jaye, and Paula Span, "The Savvy 60: The Top U.S. Businesses Run by Women," in *Savvy* (New York), February 1984.

Alai, Susan, "Fashion's Shy Di: DVF through the Ages," in *W,* October 1985.

Szabo, Julia, "Diane Von Furstenberg," in *Vogue,* January 1991.

Dyett, Linda, "Women of Style: Princess Di and Her Daughter," in *Lears,* June 1991.

Podolsky, J.D., "Not Lying on Her Laurels," in *People,* 7 December 1991.

Givhan, Robin D., "Cut-Rate Princess; Designer Diane Von Furstenburg Caters to the Masses—and Their Money," in the *Washington Post,* 5 January 1996.

White, Constance C.R., "Von Furstenberg's Return," in the *New York Times,* 22 April 1997.

Spindler, Amy M., "Breaking the Rules, Again," in the *New York Times,* 16 September 1997.

"In Style," in *Paris Match,* May 1998.

Barron, James, "Accidental Tourist," in the *New York Times,* 1 September 1998.

Chin, Paula, "Diane: A Signature Life by Diane Von Furstenberg," in *People,* 9 November 1998.

"DVF's Open House," in *WWD,* 27 April 2000.

Ferla, Ruth, "For Diller and Von Furstenberg, a Merger," in the *New York Times,* 3 February 2001.

"It's a Wrap," in *Harper's Bazaar,* March 2001.

Foley, Bridget, "DVF's New Life," in *W,* April 2001.

McCants, Leonard, "DVF Set to Open First Store," in *WWD,* 18 April 2001.

Czarra, Kerstin, and Anna Rachmansky, "Ladies Night; Two Powerful Forces of American Style...," in *Footwear News,* 30 April 2001.

McCants, Leonard, "DVF's New Uptown Outpost," in *WWD,* 29 May 2001.

Horyn, Cathy, "Mysteries of Inspiration: Spring 2002 in the Making," in the *New York Times,* 4 September 2001.

Menkes, Suzy, "Theater, Von Furstenberg-Style," in the *International Herald Tribune,* 11 September 2001.

"Diane Von Furstenberg: Runway Fashion Photos," available online at Fashion Showroom, www.fashionshowroom.com, 16 October 2001.

"Diane Von Furstenberg: The Queen of the Wrap," online at from Lifetime TV, www.lifetimetv.com, 16 October 2001.

"Diane Von Furstenberg," available online at Vintage Vixen, www.vintagevixen.com, 16 October 2001.

*

I got into fashion almost by accident, inspired to create the pieces I wanted, but couldn't find, in my own wardrobe. From my original 1970s' knit wrap dress, to my new 1990s' stretch "sock dress," I believe in marrying fashion and function—chic style and easy comfort, maximum impact and minimum fuss. Today I look to the modern woman; pulled in many different directions in the course of a day, she juggles multiple roles depending on the situation, but always knows who she is and what's really important in her life.

I like to say that "I design a line the way I pack a suitcase," visualizing all of the different places I'm going to be, and then creating the appropriate outfits. My clothing must be timeless and versatile, so that a few simple pieces add up to many different looks. I think building a wardrobe should be like compiling a scrapbook of your life—over the years you accumulate favorite pieces, like old friends, that you always come back to for their unfailing ability to make you feel safe or confident, sexy or secure, depending on what you need.

Fabrics are key, since they're like a second skin, and should always be soft to the touch and breathable. Colors should be beautiful and harmonious, and silhouettes simple, allowing the body to move freely. All in all, clothes should complement a woman, the perfect accessories to her beauty and lifestyle.

—Diane Von Furstenburg

* * *

When Diane Von Furstenburg married Prince Egon Von Furstenburg in 1969, she became a princess—this aristocratic title proved no mean asset when she embarked on a fashion career in 1969, after moving from Europe with her husband to the United States. The cachet of "Princess" on a label proved especially potent to American buyers, aware of the American public's fascination with titles.

Putting the preeminence of rank aside, Von Furstenburg began her career with no fashion training. Her qualifications were a degree in economics from the University of Geneva and fluency in five languages. She did, however, have knowledge of international high society and culture. For a short period after her marriage, both she and her husband were celebrities among the party-going jet set of the late 1960s, and for a time there was not a party that they did not attend. Von Furstenburg started her business during this period with a range of simple dresses she had produced in Italy. They were a reaction to the jeans dressing so prevalent at the time, providing an easy, elegant alternative for women who wanted to wear a dress. Selling the clothes herself by tugging a sample rail around various American stores, she became an immediate success and a known designer name almost overnight.

Her philosophy was simple—to create elegant ease for all women. "There was a need for my things, for very simple dresses everyone could wear," she said in an interview for the book *The Fashion Makers* (New York, 1978). Both slim and large women could wear the clothes, senator's wives or secretaries. They were sexy and chic regardless of the customer because they were designed to be sexy, accessible, and easy to wear. Von Furstenburg's business quickly flourished and expanded. Highly successful lines of cosmetics, scent, handbags, shoes, jewelry, table linens, furs, stationery, wallpaper, and designs for Vogue Patterns were produced. She even published a *Book of Beauty* in 1976 detailing many of her philosophies toward life and design. She established herself as a liberated role model for many women. When she declared, "You don't sit around in little white gloves and big hats and try to look fashionable. You have a job, a husband or lover and children," she was stressing the practicality with style needed to adapt to modern life, which in many ways sums up her design philosophy.

Von Furstenburg resumed her business in the 1990s selling via television. Her contribution to fashion rests on a universal practicality; she believes in the importance of finding a style right for the individual, which is why many of her collections have featured very simple, flattering clothes. They can be dressed up or down and versatile enough for all sorts of women to feel attractive in. "Stick with them," she advises her customers when they have found Diane Von Furstenburg clothes to suit them.

When Von Furstenberg succeeded on QVC, the home-shopping network, she and daughter-in-law Alexandra relaunched her business in 1997 at a freestanding boutique/studio/residence in West Village, New York. The store revitalized her standby, the slinky knit wrap dress, and ventured into new territory with sportswear and intimate apparel. In 1998 Von Furstenberg, with the help of Linda Bird Francke, published an autobiography, *Diane: A Signature Life,* which *New York Times* book critic Michele Orecklin described as "breezy reading for anyone who enjoys columns with a plenitude of bold-faced names," including Henry Kissinger and Jerry Brown, former governor of California. Feminist icon Gloria Steinem saluted the work as a record of Von Furstenberg's "professional struggles as well as her private ones to raise children and stay a whole person."

In late April 2001, Von Furstenburg began merchandising her expanded line in a 600-square-foot shop-within-a-shop upstairs at Henri Bendel on Fifth Avenue in Manhattan. Under one roof, she coordinated designs, showing, and sales. Amid the signature DVF inlaid frosted mirrors, black slate floors, and see-through lightboxes, her staff attempted to match fashions to womanly, self-confident customers. Supported by vintage 1972 advertising on a billboard in the meat-packing district opposite the restaurant Pastis, the new store promoted the designer's mantra: "Feel like a woman, wear a dress."

Directing retail at the Hudson River location was Nicole Martaheleur, formerly a jewelry merchandiser for Agatha. Of the store's unified effort, Von Furstenberg told *Women's Wear Daily,* "I needed to do a store to have a full showcase. This is the one place in the world where you can see the full selection." She promised a steady flow of surprises, including plans for a Paris outlet.

—Kevin Almond; updated by Mary Ellen Snodgrass

VUITTON, Louis

See LOUIS VUITTON

W

WALKER, Catherine

French designer working on London

Born: Catherine Marguerite Marie-Therese Baheux-Lefebvre, in Pas de Calais, France. **Education:** Graduated in philosophy from Lille University, and received Maître-ès-Lettres in aesthetics, Aix-en-Provence. **Family:** Married John David Walker, 1969 (died, 1975); children: Naomi, Marianne. **Career:** Worked in film department, French Institute, London, 1970; lecture department, French Embassy, London, 1971; designed childrenswear, 1977–86; opened shop, Chelsea Design Co., 1977; first womenswear collection, 1980, under Chelsea label; opened bridal shop, Fulham Road, London, 1986; favorite designer of Princess Diana (until her death); published autobiography, 1998. **Awards:** Designer of the Year award for British Couture, 1990–91, and for Glamour, 1991–92. **Address:** Chelsea Design Co., 65 Sydney Street, London SW3 6PX, England.

Publications

By WALKER:

Books

Catherine Walker: An Autobiography by the Private Couturier to Diana, Princess of Wales, New York, 1998.

On WALKER:

Books

McDowell, Colin, *A Hundred Years of Royal Style,* London, 1985.

Coleridge, Nicholas, *The Fashion Conspiracy,* London, 1988.

Debrett's Illustrated Fashion Guide—The Princess of Wales, London, 1989.

Articles

Jobey, L., "Designing Women," in *Vogue* (London), July 1987.

Alexander, H., "When Discretion Is the Better Part of Glamour," in the *Daily Telegraph* (London), 26 November 1987.

Modlinger, J., "Di's Designer Walker," in the *Daily Express* (London), 7 March 1988.

Menkes, Suzy, "Who Dresses Princess Diana?" in the *International Herald Tribune,* 8 November 1988.

Darnton, Nina, "Fashion Fit for a Princess—Di's Secret Designer," in *Newsweek,* 27 March 1989.

Jeal, N., "Catherine Walker," in the *Observer Magazine* (London), 16 September 1990.

Hauptfuhrer, Fred, and Louise Lague, "She Designs Dresses to Di For," in *People,* 6 May 1991.

"Designer Aims for Elegance of Simplicity," in the *Independent,* 16 July 1991.

Hume, Marion, "Joely Richardson Puts Sex into Catherine Walker," in the *Tatler* (London), July/August 1991.

Mower, Sarah, "The Discreet Charm of Catherine Walker," in *Vogue* (London), November 1991.

Armstrong, Lisa, "A Couture Fairy Tale (Princess Included)," in the *Independent,* 16 July 1992.

"The Undying Fascination With Di," in *Publishers Weekly,* 25 May 1998.

Mehle, Aileen, "Suzy," in *WWD,* 19 November 1999.

*

My initial interest in fashion revolved around two things: to elongate the body, and the general underlying technical composition of clothes. This took its own course towards designing glamorous, lean, fluid (1930s inspired) suits, cocktail and evening dresses, and a penchant towards couture.

I try to focus on making the above relevant to the lifestyle of today, that is to design clothes which give poise to women without being rigid, and which are poetic without being overworked.

—Catherine Walker

* * *

French-born couturier Catherine Walker established the Chelsea Design Company Ltd. in London in 1977 with no formal training in fashion design. Her educational background was in philosophy, for which she took a Maître-ès-Lettres, roughly the equivalent to a UK doctorate. Walker claims the title of her company, which did not bear her own name until 1993, was in deference to her lack of experience as a fashion designer.

The decision to start her own company was made when Walker was widowed in 1975 and left with two young children. She began making childrenswear, and the transition to making maternity wear was in fact a natural one, according to Walker, since the pregnant female form resembles the generally shapeless figure of a child. Walker affirms that it was many years before she thought of herself as a fashion designer, and that it was a purely technical interest in the construction of garments which initially inspired her.

During the first 12 years of business Walker consolidated her knowledge of pattern cutting, fitting, and sewing, and later couture dressmaking, and tailoring. As her reputation grew by word of mouth, she attracted press attention, and British *Vogue* first photographed one of her dresses for its January 1982 issue. Although the designer's clothes have been regularly featured in editorial fashion pages, Walker is renowned for her dislike of publicity and has never held a

Catherine Walker with some of her designs. © Julian Calder/CORBIS.

catwalk show. She views her personal development as a designer in a series of stages—first dressing, then tailoring, followed by embroidered decoration and, finally, draping.

It is her tailoring and decorative use of beading that have become the hallmarks of Walker's designs. There is always an emphasis on the midriff, which Walker attributes to her French background. This structured effect around the waist, which though not fitted gives the illusion of elongating it, is apparent not only in her tailored jackets but on both day dresses and evening gowns. British journalist Lisa Armstrong, writing in the *Independent* (London, 16 July 1992), believes Walker's skill as a couturier lies in her ability to create clothes possessing the subtle, unlabored tailoring that on the surface seems not to be doing anything, but somehow manages to eliminate unwanted contours and add curves.

Another characteristic of Walker's designs is her use of plain colors such as black, navy, cream, and red, which are enhanced not through the use of printed textiles but with applied decoration such as hand-embroidery, heavy beading, and frogging. Her attention to detail is

Catherine Walker-designed silk crêpe dress owned by the late Princess Diana on display at Christie's London auction house, 1996. © AP/Wide World Photos.

legendary; articles about the designer mention how she has been known to fly to Paris to find three buttons for a particular jacket.

While the bulk of her business is the made-to-measure couture collection, Walker also produced a ready-to-wear range called De Luxe and has designed hats made for her by Mailson Michel in Paris. She designs both fine jewelry and a collection of costume jewelry, which include earrings and bracelets to accessorize the clothes. Walker also designs a collection of couture bridal gowns which she launched in 1986 with the opening of a second shop on London's Fulham Road. She, along with others, was responsible for designing the wedding dress worn by Lady Helen Windsor at her marriage in July 1992.

Walker is perhaps best known for her creations for the late Princess of Wales, which attracted widespread publicity for her as a couturier, although she had always tried to avoid this aspect of the fashion world. It is important to note, however, that a close study of the

Princess of Wales' wardrobe designed by Walker would not produce an accurate image of the designer. The requirements of the public royal wardrobe that the wearer stand out from the crowd—particularly important for television cameras and photographers—meant strong, often harsh colors were used, which were not typical of Walker's style.

The draped gowns, column evening dresses, and decorated tailored jacket worn by the Princess of Wales on numerous occasions do however illustrate the designer's signature use of beading and embroidery as well as her cutting technique of emphasizing the midriff and waistline. After Diana's death, Walker was outraged when the Victoria & Albert Museum refused to display the Princess' gowns and dresses in 1999, mostly designed by Walker. Many Brits took this as an affront to Diana's memory, especially when the London museum had expressed interest in displaying a dress worn by Posh Spice, a member of the pop recording group Spice Girls, and one from Sophie Rhys-Jones was already on the premises. The imbroglio came a year after Walker published her autobiography, recounting her experiences dressing Princess Diana.

Catherine Walker's impressive clientèle, which listed not only British but foreign royalty, bears testament to her skill as a designer, despite the fact that she did not consider herself one for the first dozen years of her successful business.

—Catherine Woram; updated by Owen James

WANG, Vera

American designer

Born: New York City, 27 June 1949. **Education:** Sarah Lawrence College, B.A. in Art History, 1971; studied abroad at the Sorbonne, Paris, during her sophomore year in college. **Family:** Married Arthur Becker, 1989; children: two daughters. **Career:** Fashion editor, *Vogue,* 1971–87; design director, Ralph Lauren, 1987–89; opened Vera Wang Bridal House, 1990; took classes and taught herself design techniques, designed hand-beaded ensemble for figure skater Nancy Kerrigan, 1994 Olympics; introduced Vera Wang Made to Order couture collection, 1996; authored first book, *Vera Wang on Weddings,* October 2001; signed an exclusive license agreement with Unilever Cosmetics International to develop a signature fragrance in spring 2002. **Awards:** Chinese American Planning Council's Honoree of the Year award, 1993; Girl Scout Council's Woman of Distinction award, 1994; elected member, Council of Fashion Designers of America, 1994. **Address:** Vera Wang Bridal House, 225 West 39th Street, New York, NY 10018, U.S.A. **Website:** www.verawang.com.

Publications

By WANG:

Books

Vera Wang on Weddings, New York, 2001.

Vera Wang, 2001: evening gown with a tulle beaded bodice designed as an option for an Academy Award® nominee. © AP/ Wide World Photos.

On WANG:

Articles

Sporkin, Elizabeth M., "Wedding Belle: When the Glitterarti Get the Urge to Merge, They Flock to Bridal Expert Vera Wang," in *People,* 8 July 1991.
Carr, Debra, "Wang's World," in *Footwear News,* 5 May 1997.
Zaslow, Jeffrey, "Vera Wang," in *USA Weekend,* 8 May 1997.
"Different Strokes," in *WWD,* 24 September 2000.
"Vera Wang, by Vera Wang," in *Vogue,* March 2001.
Woods, Vicki, "Taking the Plunge," in *Vogue,* September 2001.
"Unilever Cosmetics International," in *Cosmetics International,* 10 September 2001.

* * *

Vera Wang was exposed to fashion early in her life through her mother's style and her affluent upbringing on Manhattan's East Side. Her parents were strong role models. Her mother, Florence Wu, a

Vera Wang with her gowns for the "China Without Borders" exhibition at Sotheby's in New York, 2001. © AFP/CORBIS.

United Nations translator, and her father, Cheng Ching, an oil and pharmaceuticals tycoon, gave Vera and her brother, Kenneth, a very comfortable childhood. When she was seven years old, Wang's parents bought her a pair of ice skates for Christmas. She fell in love with skating and competed during her early teens and twenties. She proved herself a talented figure skater, competing at the U.S. National Championships and placing fifth in 1968 and 1969 with her skating partner, James Stuart. "The only thing that I loved as much as skating were clothes," she once commented to *People* magazine in July 1991. It was a good thing, because not qualifying for the 1968 Olympic team and not wanting to tour with an ice show gave Wang a new career direction.

After graduation from college in 1971, Wang began working for *Vogue* magazine. At the end of her first year, she was promoted to fashion editor, the youngest in *Vogue*'s history. In a nostalgic piece written for the magazine in March 2001, editors said of Wang, "As a young fashion editor, she used the perfection she learned as a skater to produce shoots with an ice-cool edge." Despite a few fashion-shoot snafus, Wang held the position for the next 16 years.

After her stint at *Vogue,* Wang worked as a design director at Ralph Lauren; her responsibility included overseeing 13 accessory lines. Throughout her career, she wanted to be a fashion designer and this desire started to grow while she was shopping for a wedding gown for her upcoming nuptials to Arthur Becker in 1989. Frustrated with the gowns she saw, she designed her own and hired a dressmaker to create it at a cost of $10,000. Discovering a market niche for contemporary and elegant wedding gowns, in 1990 Wang opened her own bridal boutique with financial backing from her father in the upscale Carlyle Hotel on Madison Avenue in New York. She carried elegant bridal wear by well-known designers, but also to design wedding gowns herself.

Her first international attention as a designer came when she designed Nancy Kerrigan's skating outfit for the 1992 and 1994 Olympics. In her march 2001 profile in *Vogue* Wang wrote, "I felt as though my life had come full circle; I didn't make it to that level of competition, but my clothes did." Most notably, her designs are rich with luxurious fabrics and very classic lines. Her name alone conjures up images of fabulously simple wedding gowns. Brides as glamorous as Sharon Stone and as traditional as Karenna Gore have sought her out for their special day.

Wang has revolutionized the way people look at bridal dresses—transforming them in the last decade from cookie-cutter froufrou concoctions to stylish, couture-look gowns taking into consideration that brides might actually be grown up and want sophisticated dresses. "Before we brought sexuality to weddings," she said, most brides "looked like the bride on top of a cake, very decorated," she stated to *USA Weekend* in May 1997. Her ready-to-wear wedding dresses average $3,500.

The next sensible step in her career was to begin designing eveningwear. "Fashion offers no greater challenge than finding what works for night without looking like you are wearing a costume," says Wang. The world's most fashionable women, including Jane Fonda, Helen Hunt, and Kate Capshaw, quickly embraced her eveningwear. Celebrities continue to seek her advice on their most important appearances. Along with her bridal and eveningwear, Wang offers Vera Wang Made to Order, a collection of couture designs, fur, and footwear at her boutique. Her designs can also be found at Saks Fifth Avenue, Barneys, Bergdorf Goodman, and Neiman Marcus.

In 1997 Wang and Italian shoe company Rossimoda developed a line of women's dress shoes, catering to the designs of her evening and bridal gowns. The shoes have been very popular, given the design and platform heel that gives women height. "Clothes are my passion and my knowledge. I've studied fashion from every angle—historically and critically, cerebrally and emotionally." She understands how a woman wants to feel in her clothes. "Dressing celebrities gets you noticed. But I really do design for myself. And when my husband says I look sexy, I know I'm going to have a good night," she told *InStyle* magazine in December 2000.

Wang is a genius when it comes to understanding the fit of clothing. In her *InStyle* profile, she said, "For me, the magic is in weightless clothes, cutting armholes that add grace, cleverly exposing the best parts and sensuously draping fabric over less fabulous ones, offering enough internal support to allow a woman to feel secure while being totally comfortable. A woman is never sexier than when she is comfortable in her clothes."

Vera Wang's first signature fragrance launched in spring 2002, under a licensing agreement with Unilever Cosmetics International. Her first book, entitled *Vera Wang on Weddings,* became available in bookstores in 2001.

—Donna W. Reamy

WEINBERG, Chester

American designer

Born: New York City, 23 September 1930. **Education:** High School of Music and Art; graduated Parsons School of Design, 1951; B.S., Art Education, New York University. **Career:** Worked for Seventh Avenue clothing manufacturers; established own label, 1966; women's seasonal collections, 1966–75; label folded 1975; freelance designer 1975–78; consultant at Calvin Klein, 1978–81; design director of Calvin Klein jeans, 1981; critic, teacher, and member of Board of Overseers, Parsons School of Design; guest lecturer, Art Institute of Chicago. **Collections:** Texas Fashion Collection, University of North Texas. **Awards:** Coty American Fashion "Winnie" award, 1970; Maison Blanche "Rex" award, New Orleans, 1972. **Died:** 24 April 1985 in New York City.

Publications

On WEINBERG:

Books

Stegemeyer, Anne, *Who's Who in Fashion,* New York, 1980.

Milbank, Caroline Reynolds, *New York Fashion: The Evolution of American Style,* New York, 1989.

Stegemeyer, Anne, *Who's Who in Fashion, Third Edition,* New York, 1996.

Articles

Skurka, Norma, "Chester Weinberg," in the *New York Times,* 6 January 1974.

* * *

American fashion is said to have come of age in the 1960s, and Chester Weinberg is counted among those designers such as Bill Blass, Geoffrey Beene, Oscar de la Renta, and Donald Brooks who are credited with helping American fashion grow up. Specifically, Weinberg designed clothes notable enough to garner the sort of distinction and reputation that only French fashion had previously enjoyed.

A native New Yorker who attended the High School of Music and Art and went on to Parsons School of Design, Weinberg designed anonymously as an assistant at a number of clothing manufacturers on Seventh Avenue, among them Harvey Berin, Teal Traina, Leonard Arkin, and Herbert Sondheim. His first collection in 1966 was a great success and launched him into the fashion limelight. Preferring soft lines, ruffles, and an unstructured form, Weinberg designed a wide variety of evening dresses and daywear, including caftans, one-shouldered dresses with slash hems, elegant ball gowns, culotte suits, mod A-line dresses, exquisite dyed silk Japanese dresses, sweaters, jumpsuits, and soft, uniquely detailed suits with distinctive silhouettes. He was especially fond of good fabrics, using textiles from all over the world in bold, nontraditional colors. Urbane and timeless, his designs were never baroque or overwhelming.

Weinberg brought the first longer skirts to the runway in 1965, showing A-lines ending below the knee. He frequently used prints, often gigantic prints in vivid colors. He was one of the proponents of the baby-doll look and the loose, gypsy- and flower child-inspired styles of the early 1970s. Weinberg loved to travel and spent some time in Japan, adapting what he saw there into his own designs. His design range took in everything from a midi baby-doll dress with eyelet ruffles to a black-sequined mini jumpsuit over a Pierrot-collared blouse of dark green silk chiffon; from evening dresses with little tailoring at all—just an unrestrained sweep of silk chiffon from a wrapped bodice, tie-dyed lush sunset blue and cerise—to finely detailed evening dresses with rows of buttons at the wrists.

The look of a Weinberg is familiar even to those who have never heard of him, for his designs were some of the defining looks of the late 1960s and early 1970s. Black-scarfed models in swirling, long black dresses topped by smock jackets in Jackson Pollock-like yellow silk or apple green mohair, a vivid wool gabardine suit with an empire waist, cinched by a wide contrasting belt, a gray geometric print dress, all are images of "mod." At the same time, Weinberg's designs were classically simple and elegant, with details like ribbons, princess seams, inverted pleating, and his signature ruffles. From a navy blue, silk dress with an empire waist to a wool crêpe chemise dress with black lace over a lining of light cocoa, vintage Weinberg is still fashionable.

After his company folded, Weinberg designed dresses and sportswear for a company backed by Jones Apparel Group, cashmere sweaters for Ballantyne of Scotland, furs, costumes for the Twyla Tharp ballet *As Time Goes By,* and patterns for *Vogue* and Butterick. In 1978 he became a consultant for Calvin Klein, who had admired his work for many years. Weinberg went on to become the design director at Calvin Klein jeans. Throughout his career, he taught and lectured at Parsons School of Design and the Art Institute of Chicago. An award and a scholarship were named for him: the Chester Weinberg Gold Thimble award and the Chester Weinberg Scholarship, both established in 1985, the year of his death. His untimely loss to the fashion world was much mourned, and his contributions to the American look are still relevant.

—Jessica Reisman

WEITZ, John

American fashion and industrial designer

Born: Berlin, Germany, 25 May 1923; immigrated to Britain, 1934, and to the United States, 1940; naturalized American, 1943. **Education:** Studied at the Hall School, 1936, at St. Paul's School, London, 1936–39; apprenticed to Edward Molyneux, Paris, 1939–40. **Family:** Married Sally Bauner (divorced); married Eve Orten (divorced); married Susan Kohner, 1964; children: Karen, Robert, Paul, Christopher. **Military Service:** Served in the U.S. Army, 1943–46; became Captain; also worked in the OSS. **Career:** Designer of women's sportswear, working with several companies in London and New York, until 1954; founder/designer and chairman, John Weitz Designs, Inc., men's fashion designs, New York, from 1964; signed licenses with Lakeland, Gina Hosiery; also an author (from the early 1960s), yachtsman, and ex-racecar driver. **Awards:** *Sports Illustrated* award, 1959; NBC *Today Show* award, 1960; Caswell-Massey awards, 196–66; *Harper's Bazaar* Medallion, New York, 1966; Moscow Diploma, 1967; Coty American Fashion Critics award, 1974; Cartier Design award, 1981; Mayor's Liberty medal, New York, 1986; First Class Order of Merit, Germany, 1988; Dallas Menswear Mart award, 1990; Fashion Institute of Technology President's award, New York, 1990. **Address:** 600 Madison Avenue, New York, NY 10022, U.S.A.

Publications

By WEITZ:

Books

Sports Clothes for Your Sports Car, New York, 1959.
The Value of Nothing, New York & London, 1970.
Man in Charge, New York, 1974.
Friends in High Places, New York, 1982.
Hitler's Diplomat, London, 1992.
Hitler's Banker: Hjalmar Horace Greeley Schacht, New York, 1997.

Articles

"Auto Motives," in the *New York Times Magazine,* 27 March 1988.
"Jocks and Nerds: Men's Style in the Twentieth Century" (book review), in the *New York Times Book Review,* 3 December 1989.
"Home Away from Home," in *New York Magazine,* 19 February 1990.
"Fashion Statements," in *Town & Country* (New York), July 1994.

On WEITZ:

Books

Bender, Marilyn, *The Beautiful People,* New York, 1968.

Articles

Talley, André Leon, "John Weitz," in *Interview* (New York), March 1983.
Gross, Michael, "Design for Living," in *GQ,* September 1985.
Ferrari, Lynn, "John Weitz: Image of Distinction," in *Millionaire,* December 1987.
Brady, James, "In Step with John Weitz," in *Parade Magazine,* 31 July 1988.
Christy, Marian, "A Stylist with the Power of Politeness," in the *Boston Globe,* 9 April 1989.
Harris, Joyce Saenz, "The Novel Life of John Weitz," in the *Dallas Morning News* (Texas), 8 April 1990.
Simon, Cecelia Capuzzi, "Can You Explain John Weitz?" in the *New York Observer,* 10 September 1990.
Parola, Robert, "The Way It Was: John Weitz," in *DNR,* 22 May 1992.
Van Lenten, Barry, "Menswear Designer Pioneers: John Weitz," in *DNR,* 18 January 1995.
Taffin, William E., "In the Beginning...Menswear Designer John Weitz Helps Start the Men's Sportswear Revolution," in *DNR,* 18 January 1995.
Flanagan, William G., and Diana Merelman, "Tribalwear," in *Forbes,* 5 May 1997.
Murray, David, "Hitler's Banker: Hjalmar Horace Greeley Schacht," in the *New York Times Book Review,* 25 January 1998.
Horyn, Cathy, "Growing up Weitz," in New York Times Magazine, 20 February 2000.

* * *

John Weitz explained to the *Boston Globe* (9 April 1989) why he never wears a formal dress shirt with his tuxedo, "I wear white business shirts; I can't take the time to fiddle with front studs. The last thing I want is to be controlled by fashion." No one would say—and certainly no one would dare say in his presence—that Weitz is controlled by fashion. Rather he has treated fashion as a chosen field, one among many. He abandoned the competitive field of womenswear for a mannerly, self-invented calling in menswear. Even there, he stayed slightly aloof, choosing to be the debonair gentleman rather than fashion victim/victimizer. He has two rare personalities—a late New York intellectual and a natural aristocrat who has seen aristocracies disintegrate, but who persists in imagining new ones.

Since the 1940s, Weitz has spoken a gentlemanly common sense about fashion for men and women. First encouraged by Dorothy Shaver of Lord & Taylor in the 1940s to pursue women's sportswear with his demanding sense of a contemporary postwar lifestyle, Weitz carried his marrow of American practicality within the genteel spirit of his own European and English cultivation. As much a man of letters and ideas as of fashion, once an adventurer who drove race cars and was solicited to portray James Bond, Weitz is a consummate gentleman in the sometimes less than genteel world of fashion.

While his great achievements in apparel in the 1950s were of women's sportswear, he became one of the first men's fashion designers in the early 1960s, shifting his emphasis to this field for its capability to fulfill his interest in classic looks, utmost practicality, and no-nonsense durability. Until Giorgio Armani and Ralph Lauren in the late 1970s and 1980s, no designer was as faithful as Weitz to menswear. In personal style as well as his design, Weitz exemplified the refined but unpretentious good taste that comes of humane attention to what is important in life, with clothing following as a consequence of those values. Even in the extreme years of menswear in the late 1960s and early 1970s, Weitz's vision was always tempered.

If Weitz was first a visionary of the disciplines of sportswear for women in America, he transferred his allegiance to menswear in the early 1960s when a number of designers were testing the waters of menswear, among them Geoffrey Beene and Bill Blass in America, Hardy Amies in England, and Pierre Cardin in France. Weitz alone gave his primary attention to menswear, a field where his own principal ideas had first come from observing the Duke of Windsor. Long before absorbing and ultimately creating the ethos of sportswear, Weitz had been an assistant to Molyneux in London. There, he was a part of fashion that was fastidious, client-driven, and rich in protocol and money.

When asked in *Interview* (March 1983) if he considered himself a couturier, Weitz replied, "Good God, no. I'm a modern-day creature that emerged from an old couture assistant into a sort of inventive concept, which I don't mind at all." His acumen for business and licensing has enabled Weitz to build an empire in menswear with a minimum of participation from the designer. His own engaging and cosmopolitan charm establishes only the guidelines for product development. In many ways, Weitz was the first to be such a designer—god-like then thereafter far removed from the world of his own creation. Weitz makes a point, however, of wearing his own clothes; this is a matter of honor for a man of Boy Scoutish, even knightly, integrity.

At the end of the 20th century Weitz still offered a graceful conceptual model of a fashion designer, though he had significantly segued into other professions as well. As an author of several books, both novels and historical biographies, the designer had been spending more time writing than sketching

"Dress is a form of tribalism," Weitz commented to *Forbes* (5 May 1997), "People wear what their tribe wears—executives, blue-collar workers, undertakers, accountants. They want to feel tribally appropriate. Distinguishing yourself within your tribe is a matter of style, not fashion."

"...I never planned on being a great couturier," says Weitz, who switched to menswear in 1964. "To me fashion is not an art but a craft...." told *People* (Oct 26, 1992) While Weitz himself is a longtime member of internationally best-dressed Hall of Fame, his long wool coats still sell as do his tailored men's shirts, socks, and a host of other accessories.

—Richard Martin

WESTWOOD, Vivienne

British designer

Born: Vivienne Isabel Swire in Glossop, Derbyshire, 8 April 1941. **Education:** Studied one term at Harrow Art School, then trained as a teacher. **Family:** Children: Ben, Joseph. **Career:** Taught school before working as designer, from circa 1971; with partner Malcolm McLaren, proprietor of boutique variously named Let It Rock, 1971, Too Fast to Live, Too Young to Die, 1972, Sex, 1974, Seditionaries, 1977, and World's End, from 1980; second shop, Nostalgia of Mud, opened, 1982; Mayfair shop opened, 1990; first showed under own name, 1982; taught at Academy of Applied Arts, Vienna, 1989–91; first full menswear collection launched, 1990; opened Tokyo shop, 1996; introduced denim line, Anglomania, 1997; fragrances include *Boudoir,* 1998; and *Boudoir,* 2000. **Exhibitions:** Retrospective, Galerie Buchholz & Schipper, Cologne, 1991; retrospective, Bordeaux, 1992; *Vivienne Westwood: The Collection of Romilly McAlpine,* Museum of London, 2000. **Awards:** British Designer of the Year award, 1990, 1991; Order of the British Empire (OBE), 1992; Fashion

Vivienne Westwood, autumn/winter 2001–02 ready-to-wear collection. © AFP/CORBIS.

Group International awards, 1996. **Address:** Unit 3, Old School House, The Lanterns, Bridge Lane, Battersea, London SW11 3AD, England. **Website:** www.viviennewestwood.com.

PUBLICATIONS

By WESTWOOD:

Books

Vivienne Westwood: A London Fashion, with Romilly McAlpine, London, 2000.

Articles

"Youth: Style and Fashion, Opinion," in the *Observer* (London), 10 February 1985.

"Paris, Punk and Beyond," in *Blitz* (London), May 1986.

"Pursuing an Image Without Any Taste," in the *Independent* (London), 9 September 1989.

"My Decade: Vivienne Westwood," in the *Sunday Correspondent Magazine* (London), 19 November 1989.

"Vivienne Westwood Writes…," in the *Independent,* 2 December 1994.

Vivienne Westwood, spring/summer 2002 ready-to-wear collection. © AFP/CORBIS.

On WESTWOOD:

Books

Polhemus, Ted, *Fashion and Anti-Fashion,* London, 1978.

McDermott, Catherine, *Street Style: British Design in the 1980s,* London, 1987.

Howell, Georgina, *Sultans of Style: 30 Years of Fashion and Passion 1960–1990,* London, 1990.

Steele, Valerie, *Women of Fashion: Twentieth Century Designers,* New York, 1991.

Stegemeyer, Anne, *Who's Who in Fashion, Third Edition,* New York, 1996.

Vermoral, Fred, *Fashion & Perversity: A Life of Vivienne Westwood and the Sixties Laid Bare,* Woodstock, New York & London, 1996.

Krell, Gene, *Vivienne Westwood,* Paris, 1997.

Lehnert, Gertrud, *Frauen machen Mode—Coco Chanel, Jil Sander, Vivienne Westwood,* Dortmund, Germany, 1998.

Mulvagh, Jane, *Vivienne Westwood: An Unfashionable Life,* London, 1998, 1999.

McDermott, Catherine, *Vivienne Westwood,* London, 1999.

Articles

Sutton, Ann, "World's End: Mud, Music and Fashion: Vivienne Westwood," in *American Fabrics & Fashions* (Columbia, South Carolina), No. 126, 1982.

Gleave, M., "Queen of the King's Road," in the *Observer* (London), 8 December 1982.

Warner, M., "Counter Culture: Where London's Avant-garde Designers Get Their Ideas," in *Connoisseur,* May 1984.

McDermott, Catherine, "Vivienne Westwood: Ten Years On," in *i-D* (London), February 1986.

Mower, Sarah, "First Lady of Punk," in *The Guardian* (London), 11 December 1986.

Buckley, Richard, and Anne Bogart, "Westwood: The 'Queen' of London," in *WWD,* 17 March 1987.

Barber, Lynn, "Queen of the King's Road," in the *Sunday Express Magazine* (London), 12 July 1987.

Mower, Sarah, "The Triumphal Reign of Queen Vivienne," in the *Observer,* 25 October 1987.

Brampton, Sally, "The Prime of Miss Vivienne Westwood," in *Elle* (London), September 1988.

Roberts, Michael, "From Punk to PM," in the *Tatler* (London), April 1989.

Barber, Lynn, "How Vivienne Westwood Took the Fun Out of Frocks," in the *Independent,* 18 February 1990.

Fleury, Sylvia, "Vivienne Westwood," in *Flash Art* (Milan), November-December 1994.

Spindler, Amy M., "Four Who Have No Use for Trends," in the *New York Times,* 20 March 1995.

Menkes, Suzy, "Show, Not Clothes, Becomes the Message," in the *International Herald Tribune* (Paris), 20 March 1995.

Peres, Daniel, et al., "Blonde Ambition," in *WWD,* 18 September 1996.

Larsen, Soren, "Vivienne Westwood to Get her Own Scent in Deal with Lancaster," in *WWD,* 24 January 1997.

Lohrer, Robert, "Birds of Paradise: After 27 Years Vivienne Westwood Still Shocks and Rocks," in *DNR,* 16 January 1998.

Menkes, Suzy, "The Essence of Westwood," in the *International Herald Tribune,* 30 June 1998.

"Vivienne Westwood," in *Current Biography,* July 1999.

Menkes, Suzy, "Westwood: A Designer in the Wardrobe," in the *International Herald Tribune,* 9 May 2000.

Jones, Rose Apodaca, "On the Road with Viv," in *WWD,* 27 November 2000.

Jensen, Tanya, "Vivienne Westwood: Fairy Tale," at Fashion Windows, www.fashionwindows.com, 11 October 2001.

* * *

Vivienne Westwood's clothes have been described as perverse, irrelevant, and unwearable. Her creations have also been described as brilliant, subversive, and incredibly influential. She is unquestionably among the most important fashion designers of the late 20th century and beyond

Westwood will go down in history as the fashion designer most closely associated with punks, the youth subculture that developed in England in the 1970s. Although her influence extends far beyond the era, Westwood's relationship with the punk subculture is critically important to an understanding of her style. Just as the mods and hippies had developed their own styles of dress and music, so did the punks. Yet while the hippies extolled love and peace, the punks emphasized sex and violence. Punk was about nihilism, blankness and chaos, and sexual deviancy, especially sadomasochism and fetishism. The classic punk style featured safety pins piercing cheeks or lips, spiky hairstyles, and deliberately revolting clothes, which often appropriated the illicit paraphernalia of pornography.

Westwood captured the essence of confrontational antifashion long before other designers recognized the subversive power of punk style. In the 1970s Westwood and her partner Malcolm McLaren had a shop in London successively named Let It Rock (1971), Too Fast to Live, Too Young to Die (1972), Sex (1974), and Seditionaries (1977). In the beginning the emphasis was on a 1950s-revival look derived from the delinquent styles of 1950s youth culture. In 1972 the shop was renamed after the slogan on a biker's leather jacket, heralding the new brutalism that would soon spread throughout both street fashion and high fashion. Black leather evoked not only antisocial bikers like the Hell's Angels, but also sadomasochistic sex, which was then widely regarded as "the last taboo."

Westwood's Bondage collection of 1976 was particularly important. Working primarily in black, especially black leather and rubber, she designed clothes that were studded, buckled, strapped, chained, and zippered. Westwood talked to people who were into sadomasochistic sex and researched the "equipment" they used. "I had to ask myself, why this extreme form of dress? Not that I strapped myself up and had sex like that. But on the other hand I also didn't want to liberally *understand* why people did it. I wanted to get hold of those extreme articles of clothing and feel what it was like to wear them." Taken from the hidden sexual subculture that spawned it and flaunted it on the street, bondage fashion began to take on a new range of meanings. "The bondage clothes were ostensibly restricting," she said, "but when you put them on they gave you a feeling of freedom."

Sex was "one of the all-time greatest shops in history," recalled pop star Adam Ant. The shop sign was in padded pink letters and the window was covered, except for a small opening, through which one could peep and see items like pornographic t-shirts. Westwood, in fact, was prosecuted and convicted for selling a t-shirt depicting two cowboys with exposed penises. Other shirts referred to child molesting and rape, or bore aggressive slogans like "Destroy" superimposed over a swastika and an image of the Queen.

Sex was implicitly political for Westwood; when she renamed the shop Seditionaries, it was to show "the necessity to *seduce* people into revolt." She insisted sex was fashion, and deliberately torn clothing was inspired by old movie stills. She also launched the fashion for underwear as outerwear, showing bras worn over dresses. From the beginning she exploited the erotic potential of extreme shoe fashions, from leopard-print stiletto-heeled pumps to towering platform shoes and boots with multiple straps and buckles.

"When we finished punk rock we started looking at other cultures," recalled Westwood. "Up till then we'd only been concerned with emotionally charged rebellious English youth movements.... We looked at all the cults that we felt had this power." The result was the Pirates Collection of 1981, which heralded the beginning of the New Romantics Movement. The Pirates Collection utilized historical revivalism, 18th-century shirts and hats, rather than fetishism, but like the sexual deviant, the pirate also evoked the mystique of the romantic rebel as outcast and criminal. Meanwhile, in 1980 the shop was renamed World's End, and in 1981 Westwood began to show her collections in Paris, finally recognized internationally as a major designer.

Like pirates and highwaymen, Westwood and McLaren wanted "to plunder the world of its ideas." The Savages Collection (1982) showed Westwood gravitating toward a tribal look—the name was deliberately offensive and shocking—and the clothes oversized, in rough fabrics, and with exposed seams. Subsequent collections, like Buffalo, Hoboes, Witches, and Punkature, continued Westwood's postmodern collage of disparate objects and images.

In 1985 Westwood launched her "mini-crini," a short hooped skirt inspired by the Victorian crinoline, and styled with a tailored jacket and platform shoes. "I take something from the past which has a sort of vitality that has never been exploited—like the crinoline," she said. Westwood insisted that "there was never a fashion *invented* that was more sexy, especially in the big Victorian form." She also revived the corset, another much maligned item of Victoriana—and an icon of fetish fashion. Certainly her corsets and crinolines forced people to reexplore the meaning of controversial fashions. As she moved into the late 1980s and 1990s, Westwood continued to transgress boundaries, not least by rejecting her earlier faith in antiestablishment style in favor of a subversive take on power dressing. Like "Miss Marple on acid," Westwood appropriated twinsets and tweeds, and even the traditional symbols of royal authority.

As the century drew to a close, Westwood still delighted in taking the fashion world to task. While her contemporaries and a crop of new designers were concentrating on airy, fluid, feminine ensembles, Westwood took the opposite tack with revealingly tight, clinging dresses with bawdy drawings. She expanded her reach with her first store outside the UK, in Tokyo in 1996, then launched a new denim collection, Anglomania, in 1997. Her own fragrances followed, with *Boudoir* in 1998 and *Libertine* in 2000. By the time Westwood opened a flagship store in New York, appropriately located in SoHo, she already had 20 in Asia, five in England, and another slated for Los Angeles.

Though the business part of her growing empire isn't nearly as fun as designing, the Vivienne Westwood name had been attracting new generations, even cyber shoppers. Westwood accessories and her fragrances sell at various Internet sites, and the irreverent fashion queen even launched her own website. Talking with *Women's Wear*

Daily (27 November 2000), she mused on her recognition. "Most people have never seen my clothes," she said, "but they've heard of me." Indeed.

—Valerie Steele; updated by Sydonie Benét

WHISTLES

British retailing firm

Established: by Lucille Lewin, in George Street, London, 1976. *Lewin* studied fine art in South Africa, moved to the U.S., sold furniture in Cambridge, Massachusetts; joined Conran Group, London; worked for Harvey Nichols as a buyer, until 1976. **Company History:** In-house range of clothes introduced, 1985; stores in the UK and in-store boutiques at Harrods, Selfridges, and Fenwicks, all in London; began exporting to U.S., to Nordstrom, Big Drop, and Charivari; opened two stores in Japan; introduced acessories line; sought location for first U.S. store, 2000. **Awards:** Design Led Retail award, 1994. **Company Address:** 12 Saint Christopher's Place, London W1M 5HB, England.

Publications

On WHISTLES:

Articles

McDowell, Colin, "Whistling," in *Country Life* (London), 5 February 1987.
Polan, Brenda, "Lucille Has a Ball," in the *Independent* (London), 16 December 1988.
Pascal, Béatrice, "La Chaine Anglaise Whistles reve de Vendre sa Mode a Paris," in *Dossier,* 14 October 1991.
"Cost Effective: The Designer," in *Marie Claire,* November 1993.
"The Latest Wrinkle," in *WWD,* 24 November 1993.
Fallon, James, "Whistles' New Overseas Pitch," in *WWD,* 25 September 1996.
Menkes, Suzy, "What's Next—Previews from Furnishings to Fashion," in the *International Herald Tribune,* 9 August 1998.
"Whistles Looks for Sites," in *UK Retail Report,* December 2000.

* * *

Uncomplicated, classic, and comfortable are words often used to describe the clothes designed by Lucille Lewin and sold under the Whistles retail label. Lewin combines her own moderately priced designs with other top name designer garments to create individual style for what is described as the confident and independent woman. Inspired by the fine arts, history, and culture, Lewin's collection is designed along a narrow color range, setting the foundation and tone for each season in Whistles' shops. In many respects, Whistles may be compared with other British retailers such as Terence Conran and Joseph Ettedgui—all of whom are concerned with creating identities and consistency of style.

Lewin was originally a fine arts student from South Africa. After a brief period in the U.S., Lewin and her husband moved to London and opened the first of the Whistles shop in 1974. Lewin gained considerable retail experience at Harvey Nichols' 21 Shop in London, and developed an aptitude for finding new talent. Owning her own shop provided an opportunity to stock clothes by young, often virtually unknown designers. In the early 1970s the careers of British designers Wendy Dagworthy, Betty Jackson, Ally Capellino, and French designer Myrène de Prémonville were launched by Lewin and have proven to be major sales successes.

To reinforce the Whistles identity, Lewin began producing her own range of clothes in 1985. The collection consists of tailored garments, knitwear, swimwear, accessories, and shoes, with cuts ranging from classic to baggy. Natural fabrics, such as cotton and linen, were the mainstay of the collection, but Lewin is not averse to experimenting with new synthetic fabrics she deems appropriate to achieve the looks and the feel of a collection. Lewin draws inspiration from a variety of sources reinforced by her training as an artist. Morocco, India, and Tunisia have inspired desert-colored jersey sarong skirts and wrapover tops. In contrast, her designs of crisp, sporty navy-and-white garments in gabardine, linen, and cotton were influenced by baggy sailor trousers and tailored jackets from the 1920s. Another influence may be traced in her tweed suits, which are reminiscent of Chanel's simple and classic tailoring.

Lewin promotes her designs as mix-and-match pieces—not only with her own designs but with those of other designers. In effect, Lewin is acting as fashion "editor," both buying and designing garments. Her approach provides greater flexibility and choice in responding to individual preferences and budgets. In addition, through carefully considered color groups and fabric selections, overall moods may be more easily and effectively established than if garments were designed as self-contained sets. Her approach is similar in attitude to the collections of American designer Donna Karan, and has provided British women with affordable, casual apparel preserving classical appeal.

In the middle 1990s there Whistles shops dotting the UK, two freestanding stores in Japan, and growing international recognition. Exports to U.S. retailers such as Nordstrom, Scoop, and Big Drop had also grown sustantially, making the country Lewin's biggest wholesaler. To further capitalize on demand, Lewin launched a coordinating accessories line of handbags, gloves, hats, and footwear. Next on the agenda were swimwear and an innerwear collection, and a more integrated range of separates for the U.S. market. By 2000, Lewin was scouting locations in the U.S. to open Whistles' first freestanding American store.

Lucille Lewin's contribution to British fashion can be recognized on at least two levels—first, she provided a moderately priced retail shop for women who want to create an individual look without succumbing to trendy fashions; and second, her unique approach to fashion retailing has enabled her to design under the Whistles label, thereby establishing and maintaining a strong and consistent foundation for the each season's garments. This combination of retail and design distinguishes her work from other contemporary British fashion designers.

—Teal Triggs; updated by Nelly Rhodes

WORKERS FOR FREEDOM

British design firm

Founded: in 1985 by Richard Nott and Graham Fraser. *Nott* was born in Hastings, England, 3 October 1947; studied at Kingston University; design assistant to Valentino, Rome, 1972–75; principal lecturer,

Kingston University Fashion School, 1975–85. *Fraser* was born in Bournemouth, 20 July 1948; studied accountancy and fashion retailing; worked as buyer/accountant, Feathers Boutique, London, 1970–71; assistant buyer, Harrods, London, 1975–78; buyer for Wallis Shops, London, 1978–81; advertising manager, Fortnum & Mason, London, 1981–82; fashion director, Liberty, London, 1982–85. **Company History:** Nott and Fraser operated first Workers for Freedom shop, Soho, London, 1985–92; introduced menswear and womenswear wholesale collections for Littlewoods Home Shopping catalogue, beginning in summer 1993; womenswear collection for A-Wear, Dublin, summer 1994; signed licensing deal with Mark Margolis, 1996; Anthony Cuthbertson hired as designer (left in 2000). **Exhibitions:** Dayton Hudson, Minneapolis, 1991; Fenit, São Paolo, Brazil, 1992. **Awards:** British Fashion Council Designers of the Year award, 1990; Viyella Designer of the Year award, 1990. **Company Address:** 6 Spice Court, Ivory Square, Plantation Wharf, London SW11 3UE, England.

Publications

On WORKERS FOR FREEDOM:

Books

Coleridge, Nicholas, *The Fashion Conspiracy,* London, 1988.

Wilson, Elizabeth, and Lou Taylor, *Through the Looking Glass,* to accompany BBC TV series, London, 1989.

Articles

Anderson, Lisa, "London's New 'New Look' British Designers Come of Age," in *Chicago Tribune,* 22 October 1986.

Lorna, James, "Fashion Review," in the *Independent* (London), 20 February 1987.

"An Overnight Sensation in London," in *Newsweek,* 30 March 1987.

Cenac, Laetitia, profile, in *Madame Figaro* (Paris), October 1988.

Anderson, Lisa, "London Sees the Light," in *Chicago Tribune,* 19 October 1989.

Roberts, Nancy, "Workers White," in *Marie Claire* (London), April 1990.

Flett, Kathryn, fashion reviews, in the *Sunday Times Magazine* (London), 2 September 1990.

Buck, Genevieve, "…Moderately Priced Lines," in *Chicago Tribune,* 6 March 1991.

Fallon, James, "Workers Pave Wider Trail (Designers Richard Nott and Graham Fraser)," 25 September 1996.

Klensch, Elsa, "Workers for Freedom March Down the Runway in London," from Style Online, CNN.com, www.cnn.com, 9 January 1997.

* * *

Graham Fraser and Richard Nott launched their company, Workers for Freedom, in 1985 leaving behind their respective former careers as merchandising manager for fashion and accessories at Liberty in London and principal fashion lecturer at Kingston University in Surrey. Nott came from an art school background, and also worked for three years as design assistant to Valentino in Rome.

The company name was chosen to emphasize what they saw as their freedom from the large companies for whom they had previously worked. Their former experience in the fashion field left them well qualified to set up their own fashion company which, among other things, earned them the title Designer of the Year at the British Fashion Awards in 1990. The reason behind the formation of their own label, according to Nott and Fraser, was their mutual disillusion with what was happening in the field of menswear at the time and their aversion to very "preppy" styles with little or no decorative adornment.

The first Workers for Freedom collection, which was sold through their retail shop in Lower John Street in London's Soho district, was comprised solely of menswear. The garment that became their hallmark was the embroidered shirt, in black-on-white or white-on-black combinations. The success of this first collection, which attracted both male and female customers, prompted Workers for Freedom to extend the next collection to womenswear, at the request of the American and Japanese buyers who bought their apparel.

In the beginning, Nott and Fraser designs were outside mainstream fashion trends, and their customers were not concerned with being in fashion. Though not antifashion exactly, the evolutionary nature of their designs meant that each season customers could add an outfit or single garment to those from previous collections. Nott described Workers for Freedom clothing as "very gentle" and admitted that at one point during the 1980s, with the advent of designers like Christian Lacroix, their designs seemed somewhat out of place with what was happening in fashion as a whole.

According to Nott, who designed the early collections (Fraser handled the administrative and promotions side), his inspiration came from the fabric itself, which ultimately determined the shape or form of the garment. Nott viewed each garment within a collection as an individual piece, designed as a separate item and the collection is styled afterwards. The fabric for which Workers for Freedom became best known was silk, which they used either plain or in Nott's textile prints. Signature colors were subtle, with a predominant use of black, brown, ivory, and indigo blue.

In late 1991 Workers for Freedom began working for Littlewoods mail order catalogue, for whom they designed a separate collection each season. The Littlewoods connection was viewed by Nott and Fraser as a diffusion collection, produced at a lower price range which helped maintain their name at the High Street level. This left them free to make their mainline collection more "rarefied," since the sportswear element was soon incorporated into other ranges such as Littlewoods and a collection for A-Wear shops in Ireland, distributed by the company Brown Thomas.

The decision by Workers for Freedom to move to France in 1992 attracted a considerable amount of publicity from the British press. Nott and Fraser had sold their shop in Soho and considered moving the business to Toulouse where they found a château and hoped to establish the company. This fell through when the exchange rate dropped and they found themselves unable to sell their London house. During this period they kept a low profile, did not produce a collection for fall/winter 1993 and moved the company headquarters to Battersea, South London.

The six-month break from producing spurred a reevaluation period for Workers for Freedom, and succeeding collections indicated a definite change in direction, as well as limiting sales to primarily the UK. Their signature use of embroidery was dropped ("because everyone has it now," says Nott), and there was an emphasis on shape using bias-cutting Nott saw as the new softer alternative to stretch Lycra fabrics. The fall/winter collection for 1994–95 was produced entirely in black and brown, without embroidery or other form of decoration.

In 1996 Nott and Fraser took their design business in a new direction, severing ties with Littlewoods in favor of aggressive global expansion. The duo forged an alliance with the Los Angeles-based Michael Margolis, to bring a new collection of Workers for Freedom sportswear to the U.S. market. The threesome formed Workers for Freedom Inc., based in Los Angeles, to handle manufacturing and distribution of the new apparel, priced to sell alongside such hip brands as CK and DKNY in better department stores. The first collection debuted in Paris, followed by a stint at London Fashion Week, with jeans, Lycra separates, cotton and nylon skirts, and jackets.

Commenting on the new Workers for Freedom line to *Women's Wear Daily* (25 September 1996), Nott enthused, "This is an entirely new price point and market for us, and we're taking it stage by stage.... We are extremely confident about the future; this is what we have been trying to do for all these years. For me, it's true freedom at last." Elsa Klensch, writing for Style online at CNN's website (9 January 1997), praised Nott and Fraser's new direction, saying, "The constant in Workers for Freedom is the collection's casual nature—and its dare to give femininity a special flair." Workers for Freedom's flair remained intact for the remainder of the 1990s and into the 21st century, despite some changes within the firm's ranks. Anthony Cuthbertson joined Nott and Fraser, designing popular collections in 1999, but left the Workers for Freedom fold in 2000.

—Catherine Woram; updated by Owen James

WRIGHT, Trevor

See FENN WRIGHT MANSON

Y-Z

YAMAMOTO, Kansai

Japanese designer

Born: Yokohama, Japan, 1944. **Education:** Studied civil engineering and English, Nippon University; graduated from Bunka College of Fashion, 1967. **Career:** Apprenticed with Junko Koshino and Hosano; designer, Hisashi Hosono, circa 1968–71; opened firm, Yamamoto Kansai Company, Ltd., Tokyo, and showed first collection, London, 1971; first Paris showing, 1975; opened Kansai Boutique, Paris, 1977; organized program for India-Japan Mixed Cultural Cooperation Committee, 1997; worked with Junko Koshino revitalizing the kimono, 1999; took Ningensanka eyeweare line to the Middle East; signed licensing deal with Ayoyama USA for eyewear, 2001. **Awards:** Soen prize, Bunka College of Fashion, 1967; Fashion Editors award, Tokyo, 1977. **Address:** 4–3–15 Jungumae, Shibuya-ku, Tokyo 150, Japan.

Publications

On YAMAMOTO:

Books

Koren, Leonard, *New Fashion Japan,* Tokyo, 1984.
Contemporary Designers, Third Edition, Detroit, 1997.

Articles

Queen, Bobbie, "Kansai Confidence," in *WWD,* 28 January 1985.
Steber, Maggie, "Future Shock, with the Brilliant Innovators of Japanese Fashion," in *Connoisseur,* September 1986.
DuCann, Charlotte, "Zen and the Art of the Real Shirt," in the *Independent* (London), 29 June 1989.
Strauss, Frédéric, "Au Vrai Chic Wendersein," in *Cahiers du Cinema* (Paris), December 1989.
Martin, Richard, "Sailing to Byzantium: A Fashion Odyssey, 1990–91," in *Textile & Test,* 14 February 1991.
"Emerging Vision and Aoyama USA Sign Trading Partnership Contract," in *Business Wire,* 15 February 2001.
"Ajisu-cho in Yamaguchi Hosts the Japan Expo Yamaguchi 2001," available online at Japan Travel Updates, www.jnto.go.jp, 14 October 2001.
"The Investigation of the Truth of the Design and the Beauty," available online at Gifu City Women's College, www.gifu-cwc.ac.jp, 14 October 2001.
"More Opportunity Surfaces in the Gulf as Eyewear Demand Levels Up," online at Optical Middle East, www.opticalmiddleeast.com, 14 October 2001.
"1980s Kansai Yamamoto Silk Scribble Skirt," online at Enoki World, www.enokiworld.com, 14 October 2001.
"Signed Kansai Yamamoto," online at Yoko Trading Company, www.yokotrading.com, 14 October 2001.
"Yukata," online at What's Cool in Japan, www.jcic.or.jp, 14 October 2001.

* * *

Kansai Yamamoto's presentation of his fall-winter 1981–82 collection was divided into 14 parts, among them Peruvian Geometry, Sarraku (Japanese 17th-century painter), Korean Tiger, Ainu, and Sea Foam 5 Men Kabuki Play. Yamamoto declared in the accompanying program notes: "True originality is almost impossible to imitate as it is the expression of the creator's personal experience and cultural environment. As a Japanese, I always seek the 'Oriental quality' that is within me." Yet Yamamoto's personal sensibility is a single aspect of Orientalism and reflects a style relatively little known in the West in Asian forms, but comparable to many traditions of the West.

Yamamoto is Kabuki in his overt theatricality, flamboyant sense of gesture and design, and brilliant colorful design as much to be read from afar as admired at close range. Leonard Koren, writing in *New Fashion Japan,* (1984) said, "For Kansai, fashion means creating a festival-like feeling using brightly colored clothes with bold design motifs inspired by the kimono, traditional Japanese festival wear, and military clothes." Gaudy by desire, larger-than-life by theater's intensity, and virtually to Japanese culture what Pop style was to Anglo-American culture, Yamamoto has consistently cultivated a fashion of fantastic images, extravagant imagination, and sensuous approach to both tradition and a view of the future.

Unabashed entertainer and impresario (long a familiar product spokesman on Japanese television), Yamomoto achieved cult status in the 1970s for his worldly transmission of Japanese culture. His work has often been controversial in Japan inasmuch as it is thought to promote and exploit images of Japanese vulgarity internationally. Is Yamamoto creating an "airport art," expensive exoticism for the West that still thinks of an East Asia of bright colors, lanterned festivals, Kabuki masks, and fabulist stories with dragons and tigers? Yamamoto seems poised between traditional Japanese culture, the Pop sensibility of the late 20th century, and a longing for a millennial future.

Central to Yamamoto's work is his delight in mass entertainment and popular culture, a sense of both following and leading the ordinary population whether in graphic t-shirts or the convenience of knitwear. His silhouettes for both menswear and womenswear are extreme, suggesting either the most wondrous last samurai or the most magnificent first warriors for intergalactic futures; his appliqués have been in the ambiguous realm between primitive art and 20th-century abstraction.

In a West frightened by Japanese militarism (no Yukio Mishima, but no Buddhist monk either, Yamamoto has drawn inspiration from firefighter's uniforms and other easily identified work vestments

Kansai Yamamoto, 1995: Vietnamese children wearing Yamamoto-designed turtle outfits for a re-enactment of the Vietnamese Hoan Kiem Lake turtle folktale during Ciao! Vietnam Kansai Super Event, Hanoi, Vietnam. © AP/Wide World Photos.

traditional in Japanese subcultures of conformity) and prone to disregard any popular culture if not its own, Yamamoto became a designer of special but limited interest in the 1980s. His less-than-solemn work is ridiculous to some, celebratory to others. Cerebral, spiritual, aestheticized Japan (as represented by Issey Miyake or Rei Kawakubo) seemed more ideal, especially to the West. Yamamoto's plebeian flash was for many in the West the worst of two worlds.

Yamamoto's sensibility, however, is universal. If he was the first fashion designer to bring Kabuki circus-like joy, impertinence, and Japanese common culture to international fashion, and has remained a significant figure in espousing such conspicuous love of theater, a love of life, and love of exaggeration. His aggrandizements begin in delight and exuberance and end in celebration of the most universal kind. They benefit from a relationship to costume, though Yamamoto is always grounded in the wearability of his clothing. They often function as happy graphic signs, emblems of the most bold in fashion. On the opening of his Madison Avenue boutique in 1985, Kansai remarked to *Women's Wear Daily,* "My clothes are no good for someone who loves chicness." If we understand chic to be slightly haughty and narrowly sophisticated, Yamamoto misses the mark by express intention. Rather, he is seeking an earthy, populist ideal of clothing created in the grand gesture for the great audience. "I am making happiness for people with my clothes. If you walk through Central Park in them you create a 'wow.'"

In July 1999 Yamamoto explored the yukato, the traditional single-layered cotton kimono worn next to the skin. He and Japanese designer Junko Koshina helped to update and popularize the versatile garment for sale in department stores. Initially intended for after-bath and relaxing, it began to appear in outdoor styles featuring Western flower, fruit, and animal prints in black and dark green with matching obi, geta, ornamental hairpins, fans, and cloth.

At the end of the year, as demand for eyewear in the Middle East expanded rapidly, Yamamoto showed his stylish Ningensanka line at the Middle Eastern optical exhibition held at the Dubai World Trade Center in the United Arab Emirates. The exhibit targeted medium and upper-level consumers, the eyeglass shoppers for whom Yamamoto designs frames. In February 2001, Emerging Vision Inc. announced formation of a trading partnership with Aoyama USA, leading Japanese manufacturer of high-end titanium eyeglass frames and sunglasses. Employing online services to support their supply chain worldwide, Aoyama retained exclusive U.S. distribution of Yamamoto's brand.

In addition to garments and eyeglasses, Yamamoto's creative contributions influenced a variety of venues. In November 1997, following the ninth meeting of the India-Japan Mixed Cultural Cooperation Committee, he organized "Hello India," a program promoting relations between the two countries. For the Japan Expo in 2001 he designed daily performances for the main pavilion. At Gifu

City Women's College, he has served annually as designer-in-residence and delivered lectures to students who intend to specialize in fashion design, production, distribution, and advertisement.

—Richard Martin; updated by Mary Ellen Snodgrass

YAMAMOTO, Yohji

Japanese designer

Born: Yokohama, Japan, 1943. **Education:** Graduated in Law, Keio University, 1966; studied at Bunka College of Fashion, Tokyo, 1966–68, won Soen and Endu prizes; earned scholarship to Paris, 1968, studied fashion, 1968–70. **Career:** Designer, custom clothing, Tokyo, from 1970; formed ready-to-wear company, 1972; showed first collection, Tokyo, 1976; launched men's line, 1984; Yohji Yamamoto design studio, Tokyo, established, 1988; also opened Paris boutique; collaborated with Wim Wenders on film *Notebook on Cities and Clothes,* Berlin, 1989; signed licensing deal with Patou for fragrances, 1994; first fragrance, for women, *Yohji,* 1996; debuted womenswear collection in New York, 1996; opened new store in London, 1997; second women's scent, *Yohji Essential,* 1998; first men's fragrance, *Yohji Homme,* 1999; opened first freestanding boutique in SoHo, 1999; considered introducing cosmetics line, early 2000s. **Exhibitions:** *A New Wave in Fashion: 3 Japanese Designers,* Phoenix Art Museum, Arizona, 1983. **Awards:** Fashion Editors Club award, Tokyo, 1982; Mainichi grand prize, 1984, Fashion Group International, Master of Design, 1997. **Address:** San Shin Building 1, 1–22–11 Higashi Shibuya-ku, Tokyo, Japan.

Yohji Yamamoto, fall/winter 2001–02 ready-to-wear collection. © AP/Wide World Photos.

Publications

By YAMAMOTO:

Books

Yohji Yamamoto, with François Baudot, Paris, 1997.

On YAMAMOTO:

Books

Phoenix Art Museum, *A New Wave in Fashion: Three Japanese Designers* [exhibition catalogue], Phoenix, Arizona 1983.

Koren, Leonard, *New Fashion Japan,* Tokyo, 1984.

Fraser, Kennedy, *Scenes from the Fashionable World,* New York, 1987.

Sparke, Penny, *Japanese Design,* London, 1987.

Coleridge, Nicholas, *The Fashion Conspiracy,* London, 1988.

Stegemeyer, Anne, *Who's Who in Fashion, Third Edition,* New York, 1996.

Articles

"Big, Bold and Black: The Japanese Fashion Invasion," in *Life,* April 1983.

"Yohji Yamamoto: Fashion Designer," in *Blueprint* (London), February 1987.

"In Pursuit of Excellence," in *i-D* (London), May 1987.

"Mr. Yamamoto Comes Back to Town," in *Blueprint* (London), December 1987.

"Yohji Yamamoto: La vie d'artiste," in *Elle* (Paris), 19 September 1988.

Montagu, Georgina, "A Life in the Day of Yohji Yamamoto," in the *Sunday Times Magazine* (London), 26 February 1989.

Flett, Kathryn, "Yohji by Knight: Photography at Work," in *The Face* (London), April 1989.

Deslaudieres, Ainree, "Le long voyage à la recontre de Yohji Yamamoto," in *L'Officiel* (Paris), May 1989.

"Yohji Yamamoto: Les femmes et moi," in *Vogue* (Paris), November 1989.

Sudjic, Deyan, "Go Yohji, Go!," in the *Sunday Times Magazine* (London), 2 December 1990.

"Yohji Yamamoto in Deal to Develop Fragrance," in *WWD,* 5 July 1994.

Koshi, Lorna, "Yohji's New York Minute," in *WWD,* 12 December 1994.

"The Paris Collections—The Ideas of March: Yohji Yamamoto," in *WWD,* 17 March 1995.

Kerwin, Jessica, "Yamamoto Bites into the Big Apple," in *WWD,* 26 March 1996.

Aktar, Alev, "Yohji Readies Scent," in *WWD,* 12 July 1996.

Born, Peter, "Yohji Scent to Make U.S. Debut—Quietly," in *WWD,* 31 January 1997.
Foley, Bridget, "The Master Builders: Three Paris Titans Show How It's Done—Karl Lagerfeld at Chanel, Yohji Yamamoto, and Jean-Paul Gaultier)," in *WWD,* 16 March 1998.
Ozzard, Janet, "May Debut for *Yohji Homme,* in *WWD,* 2 April 1999.
Chua, Lawrence, "Yohji Yamamoto—Exploring the Yamamoto Cult," in *WWD,* 13 September 1999.
"Punk Power or Rich Romantics," in *WWD,* 29 February 2000.
"A Languid Air—Designer Yohji Yamamoto's Spring Collection," in *WWD,* 1 November 2000.

* * *

Part of a pioneering fashion sensibility that erupted onto the Parisian catwalks of the early 1980s, Yohji Yamamoto has a philosophical approach to fashion that makes him interested in more than just covering the body: there has to be some interaction between the body, the wearer, and the essential spirit of the designer. With Issey Miyake and Rei Kawakubo, Yamamoto is exploring new ways of dressing by synthesizing Western clothing archetypes and indigenous Japanese clothing. Refusing to accept traditional ideas of female sexual display and reacting against the Western notion of female glamour as expressed in titillating figure-hugging garments, Yamamoto employs a method of layering, draping, and wrapping the body, disguising it with somber, unstructured, swathed garments based on the *kimono* that ignore the usual accentuation points.

Yohji Yamamoto, fall/winter 2001–02 ready-to-wear collection. © AP/Wide World Photos.

Uncompromising to Western eyes, Yamamoto is in fact investigating the traditional Japanese conviction in beauty being not naturally given but expressed through the manipulation of the possibilities of the colours and materials of garments. Consequently, Yamamoto's clothing construction is viewed in the round rather than vertically, not from the neck down as in Western fashion, but a rectilinear, two dimensional approach that explores the visual appeal of asymmetry, the notion of the picturesque that plays an important part in Japanese design philosophy where irregular forms are appreciated for their lack of artifice and thus closeness to nature. Therefore, Yamamoto's garments have strange flaps, pockets, and layers, lopsided collars and hems, set off by the body in motion, and the labels inside are inscribed with the epithet, "There is nothing so boring as a neat and tidy look."

By not referring to Western fashion but to a fixed form of Japanese dress that has been developed and refined over the centuries, Yamamoto produces anti-fashion—non-directional garments that ignore contemporary Western developments of the silhouette but influence Western designers in turn. Beauty is more indefinable, to be found in the texture of materials rather than applied decoration, with the use of fabrics like linen and rayon that have been deliberately chosen and developed for their likelihood of wrinkling and heavy knitted surfaces. Like a number of Japanese designers, Yamamoto is interested in developing new materials.

Yamamoto's source material is idiosyncratic and derives from a vast library that he draws on for inspiration. One book to which he consistently refers is a collection of photographs by August Sander, a photographer based in Cologne in the early 20th century, who took photographs of representative types in the everyday clothes that sharply reflect their lives. Yamamoto is also inspired by utilitarian outfits such as the protective clothing worn by women munitions workers in the 1940s, and has been known to reproduce the coat lapel worn by Jean-Paul Sartre discovered in an old photograph.

Notable for his relentless use of black, a colour traditionally associated in Japanese culture with the farmer and the spirit of the *samurai,* Yamamoto's move into navy and purple in the 1980s was shortlived—he found it roused too many complicated emotions for him!

His company, launched in 1976, produces the experimental, idiosyncratic Yohji Yamamoto line, the Y & Y line for men that is moderately priced and extremely successful, made up of an easy to wear mixture of integrated separates and the Workshop line of casual leisurewear.

In 1989 Yamamoto, along with director Wim Wenders and producer Ulrich Felsberg, created a film based on his experiences of putting together one of his collections. The result, *Notebook on Cities and Clothes,* dealt with perceptions of dress, contained interviews with Yamamoto and his staff, and compared the film and fashion industries. The film was released on videocasette in 1993. The following year Yamamoto signed with Patou to produce several fragrances. The first, *Yohji,* was in development for two years and was released in France in 1996 (in the U.S. in 1997), and was followed by a second scent for women, *Yohji Essential* in 1998. Yamamoto's first fragrance for men, *Yohji Homme,* debuted in 1999, as his first freestanding U.S. boutique opened its door in New York's SoHo neighborhood. and the designer was considering a line of cosmetics in the near future.

Considered one of the brightest and most creative minds in the fashion industry, Yamamoto's showings consistently draw cheer from fellow designers and the press alike. In Paris in early 2000, Yamamoto "used his runway in an elaborate celebration of romance, from start to finish," said *Women's Wear Daily,* (29 February 2000) including coats, suede dresses, and "fabulous suits, inventively cut and draped." His spring showing in late 2000 was "infused with a quiet elegance," according to *Women's Wear Daily* (1 November 2000), which further commented, "Do designers have to shout to be heard? Not always. Yohji Yamamoto certainly doesn't."

—Caroline Cox; updated by Nelly Rhodes

YURMAN, David

American jewelry designer

Born: circa 1950. *Education:* Attended New York University. **Family:** Married to Sybil Yurman; children: one son. **Career:** Art apprentice with sculptors Jacques Lipchitz and Theodore Rozark, early years; started David Yurman, Inc. with wife and partner, Sybil, 1979; launched the Gold-Segment Collection, 1982; launched women's watch in a cable-cuff style, 1995; launched Midnight Ice Collection, 1999; launched David Yurman Thoroughbred Watch Collection, 1999; celebrated the 20th anniversary, 2000; opened flagship boutique on Madison Avenue in New York, 2000; opened a new boutique in Saks Fifth Avenue in Houston, Texas, 2000. **Awards:** Cultured Pearl Designer of the Year, 1983; InterGold Design award, 1983; Contemporary Design Guild Hall of Fame award, 2000. **Address:** 501 Madison Avenue, New York, NY 10022, USA. **Website:** www.DavidYurman.com.

Publications

On YURMAN:

Articles

"Lopez Named Yurman Sr. VP," in *WWD,* 30 October 1995.

"Yurman Sues to Restrain Price at Costco," in *WWD,* 2 December 1996.

Hessen, Wendy, "The Brand Behemoth," in *WWD,* 24 May 1999.

Brodsky, Renatt, "Fighting Copycats is a Yurman Task," in *Daily News Record,* 19 November 1999.

Nielsen, Karen Britton, "Dazzling Designs," in *Dallas Business Journal,* 17 December 1999.

Shuster, William George, "Yurman Wins $1-Million in Copyright-Infringement Case," in *Jewelers Circular Keystone,* January 2000.

Kletter, Melanie, "Yurman Flagship Opens with Strong Early Sales," in *WWD,* 14 February 2000.

Schupak, Hedda T., "Yurman's on Madison," in *Jewelers Circular Keystone,* March 2000.

"Art in the Street," in *WWD,* 11 May 2000.

Hessen, Wendy, "More Yurman in Houston," in *WWD,* 5 June 2000.

Soucy, Carrie, "Charity Becomes Them," in *Jewelers Circular Keystone,* August 2000.

"Yurman Celebrates 20 Years," in *Jewelers Circular Keystone,* October 2000.

* * *

With his signature cable look, David Yurman has created a name for himself as an artistic designer of fine, classic, and contemporary jewelry. The cable design, which was inspired by everything from simple, ordinary objects to art, is Yurman's creative use of silver or a combination of silver and gold. Then, depending on the collection, he adds stones or jewels to the pieces to add character and life. According to Yurman, inspiration for his designs has "always been touched by magical, ancient forms…There is a common thread in recognizable symbols that seems to bind people together."

Yurman does in fact make every effort to bring people together, both with his designs and within his community and business. In 1999, he presented Steven Spielberg with the first David Yurman Humanitarian award as part of the *GQ* magazine's Men of the Year awards. The award honored Spielberg's selfless contributions to both the arts and to the betterment of society. The ceremony also allowed Yurman the opportunity to launch his Thoroughbred Watch line. Each award-winner was presented with a first edition, hand-inscribed watch from the collection. To honor Spielberg, Yurman created a bronze sculpture of his inspirational angel. According to Yurman, the angel is a symbol of hope and charity, representing "the hope of the human spirit."

In 2000 the David Yurman Humanitarian award was given to Sir Elton John, who was presented an angel pin created by the designer. The pin, made of sterling silver, which can be worn by both men and women, had a signature cable bridge linking the delicate wingspan together. Hand-made replicas of the pin were also available for sale in stores to raise funds for Sir John's AIDS foundations.

Yurman's designs are stylish and clearly unique. His earrings, necklaces, bracelets, rings, and watches clearly exude luxury. The Midnight Ice Collection, introduced in 1999, featured diamonds and black onyx set in sterling silver and 18-karat gold. Yurman's popular Cable Collection has a signature look of its own, and the intertwined gold and silver have become an enduring classic—a look and style that unmistakably say Yurman. Among the Quatrefoil Collection is a beautiful gold and diamond watch, while the Silver Ice Collection is designed with diamonds in sterling silver cable. The Blue Ice Collection continues Yurman's use of cabled sterling silver, and throws 18-karat yellow gold and blue chalcedony into the mix.

In 2001 Yurman launched the Women's Thoroughbred Watch Collection, featuring soft pastels of green and pink with black and white dials. The bands, which can be accessorized, come in a variety of soft colors as well as bright orange or red, and even a cable bracelet.

David Yurman's collections are continually evolving; looking into the future, he anticipates a collection of plain gold, and perhaps another of platinum and gold. The Silver Ice Collection is being expanded to include a White Ice Collection, putting pearls and diamonds into the jewelry. One of his design trends emphasizes a much cleaner look, using a dominant hue or stone, rather than a mixture of colored jewels per piece. In addition, Yurman is also considering other accessories, such as belts and leather items, with which he has dabbled in the past.

—Kimbally A. Medeiros

ZAHM, Herwig

See MONDI TEXTILE, GmbH

ZEGNA, Ermenegildo

See ERMENEGILDO ZEGNA GROUP

ZEHNTBAUER, John A. and C. Ray

See JANTZEN, INC.

ZEIGLER, Mel and Patricia

See BANANA REPUBLIC

ZORAN

American designer

Born: Zoran Ladicorbic in Banat, Yugoslavia, 1947; immigrated to the U.S., 1971. **Education:** Studied architecture at the University of Belgrade. **Career:** Worked variously in New York as coat checker at Candy Store club, salesman at Balmain boutique, accessory designer for Scott Barrie, salesman/designer for Julio, 1971–76; freelance designer in New York, from 1976; first collection shown, 1977; Washington, D.C. showroom established, 1982; fined by FTC for not including care and content labels in garments, 1998.

Publications

On ZORAN:

Books

Milbank, Caroline Rennolds, *New York Fashion: The Evolution of American Style,* New York, 1989.

Stegemeyer, Anne, *Who's Who in Fashion, Third Edition,* New York, 1996.

Watson, Linda, *Twentieth Century Fashion: 100 Years of Style by Decade & Designer,* London, 2000.

Articles

Morris, Bernadine, "Zoran and Kamali: Success with the Offbeat," in the *New York Times,* 4 January 1983.

"Cue: Zoran Design for Living," in *Vogue* (London), March 1983.

"Zoran: The Wizard of Ease," in *Vogue,* March 1983.

Barron, Pattie, "Style: Less is Good for You," in *Cosmopolitan,* June 1983.

Watters, Susan, "Zoran Entertains at the Capital," in *WWD,* 19 October 1988.

Brantley, Ben, "Zoran Zeitgeist," in *Vanity Fair,* March 1992.

Giovannini, Joseph, "Brilliant Emptiness," in *House Beautiful* (London), March 1994.

Edelson, Sharon, "Bendel's: The Limited Version," in *WWD,* 1 July 1996,

"Designing Dior—Who's Next?" in *WWD,* 16 July 1996.

"Designer Agrees to Label Fine," in *WWD,* 27 July 1998.

"FTC Penalizes NYC's Zoran With Care Label, Fiber Violations," in the *Discount Store News,* 10 August 1998.

* * *

Zoran Ladicorbic was born in Banat, Yugoslavia in 1947. The designer, who goes by his first name, was trained in his native country as an architect, and a love of geometric shapes and straight lines is evident in his clothing design.

Zoran came to the United States in 1972. Although he had no formal education in fashion, he worked for the first few years in retail. He was also an accessories designer for the 1970s women's fashion designer, Scott Barrie.

In 1976 Zoran started his own collection, using only the best and most luxurious fabrics. Cashmere, satin, velvet, and high-quality wool are staples of his collection. He creates two collections a year, spring and fall, and shows them in his New York loft-workplace located in the downtown SoHo neighborhood.

He is obsessive about cutting and finishing a garment. His clothes create a feeling of luxury through perfect craftsmanship and materials, not through ostentatious embellishment, bright color, or showy fabrics. He uses the same muted color palette over and over: black and white, ivory, gray, and navy, with an occasional washed-out pastel such as pale pink or celery thrown in to liven the mix.

Zoran has kept to this minimalist aesthetic even during the more flamboyant 1980s. In the somewhat more abashed 1990s, his designs have gathered more momentum and his customer base has increased. His designs are not cheap, but he has a loyal following that snaps up his designs year after year. Among the Zoran devotees are model-actresses such as Lauren Hutton, Candice Bergen, and Isabella Rossellini, the painter Jennifer Hartley, socialite Amanda Burden, and Tipper Gore, the former U.S. vice-president's wife. His clothes are sold by high-level, slightly avant-garde stores such as Barney's and Henri Bendel in New York, as well as out of his workplace.

Zoran believes that his typical customer visits him once a year and buys several thousand dollars' worth of pieces at one time. Like the color palette, the silhouettes vary only slightly from season to season. Core pieces include a cardigan jacket, a T-shirt, crewneck cashmere sweaters, loose trousers, loose shorts, and a sarong skirt, which the designer claims he wore himself for a year to make sure the fit was correct.

The designer eschews the typical New York fashion life. He prefers solitude and is said to keep a constant supply of Stolichnaya vodka close at hand at all times of the day. He has an apartment in New York and a house in the resort community of Naples, Florida.

Zoran resortwear and knitwear collections remained strong sellers throughout the late 1990s. "The clientèle we see in Zoran is very interesting," Ted Marlow, president of Henri Bendel, commented to *Women's Wear Daily* (1 July 1996), "Zoran works well on every woman, no matter what size or age." Joan Weinstein, owner of Ultimo boutiques, carried Zoran in all her stores and the minimalist designs were often her top sellers. When Ultimo opened a new store in Dallas, Texas, it was Zoran's first foray in the state; the added exposure came at a time when many designers had lost their footing and were hurting for sales. Not so for Zoran, "We have a lot of Zoran," Weinstein said, "and we sell it like crazy. We never put it on sale; our sales just go up and up and up."

Zoran's minimalist designs, often called "spare luxury," appeal to a select and increasingly visible clientèle. Once hard to come by, Zoran apparel is now available at many high-end department stores, from Ultimo to Henry Bendel, Saks Fifth Avenue to Bergdorf Goodman. Zoran is popular with not only his growing client base, but with his fellow designers as well. When *Women's Wear Daily* had asked 50 designers in 1996 who should replace the departing Gianfranco Ferré at the House of Dior, Fabrizio Ferri perhaps gave Zoran the ultimate compliment: "The people who wear couture today wear it as a status symbol, rather than because they have style. In my view, if couture is going to move into the future…the designer should be someone who doesn't overpower the fabrics and the artisans—someone like Zoran who is known for the purity of his lines and doesn't overdesign."

—Janet Ozzard; updated by Owen James

NOTES ON ADVISERS AND CONTRIBUTORS

ALMOND, Kevin. Fashion director, Leeds College of Art and Design. Designer, Enrico Coveri, 1988–89, assistant designer, Woman Hautwell Ltd., 1989–90. Senior lecturer in fashion/fashion promotions, University of Central Lancashire, 1990–94. Contributor of "Camp Dressing" article to *Components of Dress,* 1988. **Essays:** Ally Capellino; John Anthony; Jacques Azagury; Sheridan Barnett; Rocco Barocco; Scott Barrie; Bellville Sassoon-Lorcan Mullany; Alistair Blair; Blumarine; Bodymap; Jean Cacharel; Oleg Cassini; Corneliani SpA; Giorgio Correggiari; Paul Costelloe; Enrico Coveri; Jules-François Crahay; Wendy Dagworthy; Oscar de la Renta; Myrène de Prémonville; Christian Dior; Erreuno SCM SpA; Escada; Luis Estévez; Louis Féraud; Gianfranco Ferré; David Fielden; John Flett; Georgina Godley; Norman Hartnell; Daniel Hechter; Betty Jackson; Bill Kaiserman; Jacques Kaplan; Donna Karan; Herbert Kasper; Christian Lacroix; Guy Laroche; Jürgen Lehl; Lolita Lempicka; Marina Rinaldi SrL; Marcel Marongiu; Mondi Textile GmbH; Popy Moreni; Jean Muir; Nina Ricci; Bruce Oldfield; Benny Ong; Peter Hoggard; Arabella Pollen; Gloria Sachs; Mila Schön; David Shilling; Sophie Sitbon; Per Spook; Stefanel SpA; Strenesse Group; Chantal Thomass; Yuki Torii; Torrente; Trussardi, SpA; Sally Tuffin; Philippe Venet; Gian Marco Venturi; Victorio y Lucchino; Diane Von Furstenberg.

ARNOLD, Rebecca. Lecturer in fashion history and cultural theory, Kent Institute of Art and Design. **Essays:** Dirk Bikkembergs; Marc Bohan; Liza Bruce; Joe Casely-Hayford; Chloé; Nick Coleman; Ann Demeulemeester; Dolce & Gabbana; Joseph Ettedgui; John Galliano; Romeo Gigli; Pam Hogg; Michiko Koshino; Karl Lagerfeld; Helmut Lang; Hervé Léger; Hanae Mori; Pepe; Emilio Pucci; John Richmond; Martine Sitbon.

ARSENAULT, Andrea. Professor of Fashion Design, School of the Art Institute of Chicago. Designer. Former chair of the Fashion Department, and the Faculty Senate, School of the Art Institute of Chicago. Contributor, *Jean Charles de Castelbajac Album;* contributor and adviser, *Contemporary Designers* and *Contemporary Masterworks.* **Essay:** Jean-Charles de Castelbajac.

BAKER, Therese Duzinkiewicz. Associate professor/extended campus librarian, Western Kentucky University, Bowling Green, Kentucky. Author of journal articles on library service for off-campus students. Book reviewer in decorative arts for *Library Journal.* Contributor to *Dictionary of American Biography.* **Essays:** Adri; Gilbert Adrian; Jacqueline de Ribes; Norma Kamali; Emmanuelle Khanh; Mainbocher; Jessica McClintock; Mary McFadden; Norman Norell; Thea Porter; Jean-Louis Scherrer; Adele Simpson; Emanuel Ungaro; Valentina; Koos Van Den Akker.

BENÉT, Sydonie. Writer currently residing in the Chicago area. Also contributor to newspapers, magazines, and books. **Essays:** Christian Aujard; Benetton SpA; Bianchini-Férier; Roberto Capucci; Pierre Cardin; Gabrielle "Coco" Chanel; André Courrèges; Christian Dior; Ermenegildo Zegna Group; Luis Estévez; Georges Rech; Jacques Griffe; Halston; Karl Lagerfeld; Lucien Lelong; Jessica McClintock; Mary McFadden; Franco Moschino; Muji; New Republic; Next Plc; Marcel Rochas; Rodier; Martine Sitbon; Vivienne Tam; Torrente; Philip Treacy; Valentino; Gianni Versace; Roger Vivier; Vivienne Westwood.

BLAUSEN, Whitney. Independent writer and researcher. Former administrator, The Costume Collection, Theatre Development Fund. Contributor of numerous articles to various periodicals, journals, and books, including *Theatre Crafts International, Fiber Arts, Surface Design Journal, Dictionaire de la mode au xxc siècle,* 1995, *50 American Designers,* 1995, and *Dictionary of Women Artists,* 1996. **Essays:** Bianchini-Férier; Donald Brooks; Bonnie Cashin; Fabrice; Elizabeth Hawes; Edith Head; Betsey Johnson; Bob Mackie; Sylvia Pedlar; Zandra Rhodes; Rodier; Cynthia Rowley; Ted Tinling; Michaele Vollbracht.

BODINE, Sarah (with Michael Dunas). Independent lecturer and writer in design and craft studies and criticism. Teacher, senior thesis studio, University of the Arts. Visiting lecturer and critic at various institutions, including Cleveland Institute of Art, Akron University, Tyler School of Art, RISD, Cranbrook Academy of Art, University of Michigan, Alfred University, Massachusetts College of Art, Parsons School of Design, Miami University, and Moore College of Art. Whitney Library of Design, 1973–79. Editor, *Metalsmith,* 1979–92; editorial director, *Documents of American Design,* 1988–91. Contributor to numerous periodicals and volumes, including *Industrial Design* and *Design Book Review.* **Essays:** Agnès B; Rei Kawakubo.

BROWN, Mary Carol. Freelance essayist based in England. **Essays:** Laura Ashley; Gabrielle "Coco" Chanel; Salvatore Ferragamo.

BURNS, Jane. B.A. in ecology and environmental studies, University of Georgia; studied fashion design at Fashion Institute of Technology. Designed Christmas windows for Hermès, New York; worked as a dresser for the Macy's Thanksgiving Day parade. **Essays:** Badgley Mischka; Patrick Kelly.

CARLANO, Marianne T. Formerly curator of costume and textiles at both the Wadsworth Atheneum in Hartford and the Museum of Fine Arts, Boston. Textile scholar. Author of catalogue essays and articles in *Art Journal* and *Arts Magazine.* **Essays:** Joseph Abboud; Gruppo GFT; Carmelo Pomodoro.

CAVALIERE, Barbara. Freelance writer on art and design, New York City. Associate editor, *Womanart* magazine, 1976–78; contributing editor, *Arts Magazine,* 1976–83. Fellowship in art criticism, National Endowment for the Arts, 1979–80. Author of exhibition catalogues. **Essay:** Mariuccia Mandelli.

CLARK, Hazel. Head of School of Design, Hong Kong Polytechnic University, Hong Kong. Contributor to various journals, including *Journal of Design History, Design, Design Week, Design Review, Monument,* and *Women's Art Journal.* Author of "Selling Design and Craft" and "Footprints Textile Printing Workshop" in *Women Designing: Redefining Design in Britain between the Wars,* 1994. **Essays:** Sylvia Ayton; Jeff Banks; Sandy Black; Sarah Dallas; Diane Freis; Ragence Lam; Ralph Lauren; Mickey Lee; Walter Ma; Judy Mann; Muji; Mary Quant; William Tang.

CLEVELAND, Debra Regan. Contributing editor and book reviewer, *The Lady's Gallery Magazine* and *The Vintage Gazette* newsletter; feature writer/correspondent, *The Antiques Journal* and *Antique Week;* freelance writer specializing in period fashion and antiques. Co-founder of the first New England vintage clothing show and sale and of *The Vintage Gazetter* newsletter. Contributor of freelance and in-house work for antiques and marketing trade publications, including *Antiques and Collecting Hobbies* and *Costume*

Society of America, Region 1 Newsletter. **Essays:** Catalina Sportswear; Jantzen, Inc.; Lacoste Sportswear.

COLEING, Linda. Freelance essayist. **Essays:** Ossie Clark; Emma Hope.

COLEMAN, Elizabeth A. Curator, Textiles and Costumes, Museum of Fine Arts, Houston, Texas; former curator of Costumes and Textiles, The Brooklyn Museum. Adjunct professor, Fashion Institute of Technology, New York. Rice University Fellow. Author of *The Genius of Charles James,* 1982, and *The Opulent Era: Fashions of Worth, Doucet, and Pingat,* 1989. **Essay:** Charles James.

COOPER, Arlene C. Consulting curator, European Textiles and Shawls, Museum for Textiles, Toronto, Ontario, Canada. President, Arlene C. Cooper Consulting (consultant to museums and private collectors of shawls, European textiles, and 20th-century fashion). Senior research assistant for textiles, Department of European Sculpture and Decorative Arts, Metropolitan Museum of Art. Author of "The Kashmir Shawl and Its Derivatives in North American Collections," 1987, and "How Madame Grès Sculpts with Fabric," in *Great Sewn Clothes from Threads Magazine,* 1991. **Essays:** Junichi Arai; Hubert de Givenchy; Sonia Rykiel.

COX, Caroline. Freelance essayist based in England. **Essays:** Azzedine Alaïa; Giorgio Armani; Pierre Cardin; André Courrèges; Jean-Paul Gaultier; Rudi Gernreich; Hobbs Ltd.; Margaret Howell; Hugo Boss AG; Hiroko Koshino; Maxfield Parrish; Franco Moschino; Rifat Ozbek; Paco Rabanne; Yves Saint Laurent; Fernando Sanchez; Stephen Sprouse; Yohji Yamamoto.

CUNNINGHAM, Andrew. Freelance writer living in Falmouth, Massachusetts. **Essays:** Todd Oldham; Carolyne Roehm.

DENNIS, Fred. Coordinator of Costume Collections, Museum at Fashion Institute of Technology, New York. **Essay:** Gabriele Knecht.

DIXON, Jeanette Goff. Freelance writer. **Essays:** Sal Cesarani; Victor Costa; Luis Estévez; John Galliano; Sandra Garratt; Nicole Miller; Issey Miyake; Cynthia Rowley; Anna Sui.

DRUESEDOW, Jean L. Director, Kent State University Museum. Associate curator in charge, The Costume Institute, Metropolitan Museum of Art, New York, 1984–92. Adjunct full professor, New York University. Author of *Jno. J. Mitchell Co. Men's Fashion Illustrations from the Turn of the Century,* 1990, and "Who Wears the Pants," chapter in *Androgyny,* 1992. **Essays:** Roberto Capucci; Vera Maxwell; Sally Victor.

EHRLICH, Doreen. Tutor in Art and Design History, Hillcroft College. Author of *Twentieth Century Painting,* 1989, and *The Bauhaus,* 1991. **Essays:** Julian Alexander; Burberry; Liz Claiborne; Nicole Farhi; Fenn Wright Manson; Brigid Foley; French Connection; Jaeger; Alexander Julian; Liberty of London; Louis Vuitton, Mulberry Company; Pringle of Scotland; Helen Storey.

ELLIOTT, Mary C. Curator of Historic Costume and Textiles, Mount Mary College, Milwaukee, Wisconsin. **Essay:** Lucien Lelong.

ESSEY-STAPLETON, Jodi. Freelance writer. **Essays:** John Bartlett; Marc Bohan; Marc Jacobs; Norma Kamali; Ralph Lauren.

FLUX, Alan J. Freelance essayist. **Essays:** Lilly Daché; Stephen Jones; Stephen Linard; Anthony Price; Graham Smith.

GORDON, Mary Ellen. Freelance writer. Associate editor, *Women's Wear Daily,* 1989–94. Contributor to periodicals, including *Elle, Self, InStyle,* and *Paper Magazine.* **Essay:** Anna Sui.

GROSHONG, Lisa. MFA earned in fiction writing from the University of Alabama. She enjoys reading nonfiction, watching lowbrow movies, and making art projects involving paper, fabric, and glue sticks. She lives in Columbia, Missouri, with her husband, Trevor, and is also a certified Kripalu yoga teacher. **Essays:** Nicole Farhi; Kaffe Fassett; Margaret Howell; Barbara Hulanicki; Joan & David; Bill Kaiserman; Kenzo; Kenneth Jay Lane.

GRUBER, Roberta Hochberger. Assistant professor, Fashion Design, Drexel University. Co-director, Design Arts Gallery, Drexel University. Freelance designer and fashion illustrator. Curator of several exhibitions, including *Fashion Imagery,* 1991, *Hat Formation,* 1993, and *Designer Sketchbook,* 1995. **Essays:** Mariano Fortuny; Mary Jane Marcasiano; Nicole Miller; Robert Lee Morris; Elsa Schiaparelli Kay Unger.

HAMADA, Yoko. (Deceased.) Fashion journalist involved in the connections between Japanese fashion and New York. Author of *HiFashion* and *Men's Club.* **Essays:** Giuliano Fujiwara; Yoshiyuki Konishi.

HILL, Chris. Senior lecturer, Cordwainers College, London. Company director, Fancy Footwork Ltd. **Essays:** Patrick Cox; Charles Jourdan; Sara Navarro; Andrea Pfister; Sir Edward Rayne; Red or Dead.

HOUSE, Nancy. Adjunct faculty, Art History, Wilmington College; also taught at Ohio State University and Salem State College, Massachusetts. **Essays:** Banana Republic; Brooks Brothers; Anne Fogarty; I. Magnin; Joan & David; John Kloss; Levi-Strauss & Co; Carolyne Roehm; Alfred Sung; Gustave Tassell; Joan Vass.

IDZELIS, Diana. Freelance writer who also has experience in news writing and advertising copywriting. She earned her B.A. in journalism and Mass Communications from the University of Iowa. **Essays:** Jeffrey Banks; Laura Biagiotti; Katharine Hamnett; Cathy Hardwick; Rei Kawakubo; Barry Kieselstein-Cord; Lolita Lempicka; Bob Mackie; Stella McCartney; Ronaldus Shamask; Helen Storey.

JAMES, Owen. Freelance writer who divides his time between Michigan and Illinois. **Essays:** Ally Capellino; Bellville Sassoon-Lorcan Mullany; Burberry; Jean Cacharel; Chloé; Mark Eisen; Perry Ellis; Esprit Holdings, Inc.; Fenn Wright Manson; Salvatore Ferragamo; Gianfranco Ferré; Andrew Fezza; Mariano Fortuny; James Galanos; Gucci; Guess, Inc.; I. Magnin; Jan Jansen; Anne Klein; Byron Lars; Levi-Strauss & Co.; Louis Vuitton; Walter Ma; Malden Mills Industries, Inc.; Mariuccia Mandelli; Marimekko; Marina Rinaldi SrL; Maxfield Parrish; Missoni; Isaac Mizrahi; Nina Ricci; Thea Porter; Pringle of Scotland; Emilio Pucci; Lilly Pulitzer; Mary Quant; Paco Rabanne; Fernando Sanchez; Willi Smith; Stefanel SpA; Robert

Stock; Timney Fowler Ltd.; Trussardi SpA; Emanuel Ungaro; Adrienne Vittadini; Catherine Walker; Workers for Freedom; Zoran.

KIRKE, Betty. Retired Head Conservator, Edwarde C. Blum Design Laboratory, Fashion Institute of Technology. Created and taught graduate curriculum in costume conservation at Fashion Institute of Technology, in the 1980s. Author of *Vionnet,* 1991. **Essays:** Jacques Griffe; Lanvin.

LEWIS, Aldarcy C. Award-winning freelance writer based in Riverside, Illinois, with an abiding interest in the arts in all forms. She has contributed to a variety of magazines, newspapers, and arts-related books. **Essay:** Max Azria.

LINDHOLM, Christina. Chairs of the Department of Fashion Design & Merchandising at Virginia Commonwealth University. She was an associate professor at the University of Cincinnati from 1980 to 1995, and is also a design and product development consultant. **Essays:** Jimmy Choo; Eddie Bauer; David Meister; Neiman Marcus; Saks Fifth Avenue; Zang Toi.

LOUWERS, Brian. Freelance writer. **Essays:** Badgley Mischka; Joseph Ettedgui.

MALLETT, Daryl F. Freelance writer, editor, publisher, actor and producer/director. He has written and edited over 50 volumes in diverse fields and has been published in the U.S., Canada, Ireland and Romania. He is one of only a handful of writers in the world to have worked on both *Star Trek* and *Star Wars.* Mallett splits his time between Phoenix, Southern California, Minnesota, and the rest of the world and is involved in the Society for Creative Anachronism. **Essays:** Azzedine Alaïa; John Anthony; Sheridan Barnett; Sandy Black; Stephen Burrows; Joe Casely-Hayford; Nino Cerruti; Nick Coleman; Dorothée Bis; Alber Elbaz; Andrew Fezza; Emmanuelle Khanh; Gabriele Knecht; Lanvin; Byron Lars; Stephen Linard; Walter Ma; Mariuccia Mandelli; Judy Mann; Robert Lee Morris; Thierry Mugler; Josie Cruz Natori; Sara Navarro; Jenny Packham; Elsa Peretti; Simonetta.

MARKARIAN, Janet. Textile specialist. Taught textile studies at many colleges and universities. Taught master's program at The Costume Institute, Metropolitan Museum of Art, and New York University. Worked in the Metropolitan Museum's Ratti Textile Center, 1995. **Essays:** Linda Allard; Kenneth Jay Lane.

MARSH, Lisa. Sportswear reporter with *Women's Wear Daily* (New York). **Essays:** Champion Products Inc.; Perry Ellis; David and Elizabeth Emanuel; Alan Flusser; Guess, Inc.; Robert Stock.

MARSHALL, Kathleen Bonann. Writer with undergraduate and graduate degrees in English from UCLA. She has taught writing at the University of Iowa and the University of Illinois at Chicago. Since 1995 she has been assistant director of the Center for Writing Arts at Northwestern University. In 2001 she joined the faculty of Northwestern's Department of Comparative Literary Studies. **Essays:** Manolo Blahnik; Oscar de la Renta; Donna Karan; Donatella Versace.

MARTIN, Richard. (Deceased.) Curator, The Costume Institute, Metropolitan Museum of Art. Among numerous other posts: Editor of *Arts Magazine,* 1974–88; editor of *Textile & Text,* 1988–92. Executive director of the Shirley Goodman Resource Center, 1980–93, and professor of art history, 1973–93, at the Fashion Institute of Technology. Taught at Columbia University, New York University, School of Visual Arts, The Juilliard School, Parsons School of Design, and the School of the Art Institute of Chicago. Books include *Fashion and Surrealism* and *The New Urban Landscape.* More than 300 essays have appeared in various journals, including *Vogue* (Munich), *Journal of American Culture, Los Angeles Times, International Herald Tribune,* and *Artforum.* **Essays:** Akira; Walter Albini; Victor Alfaro; Cristobal Balenciaga; Jeffrey Banks; John Bartlett; Geoffrey Beene; Laura Biagiotti; Bill Blass; Tom Brigance; Brioni; Stephen Burrows; Byblos; Calugi e Giannelli; Nino Cerruti; Sal Cesarani; Cole of California; Han Feng; Andrew Fezza; Fontana; Irene Galitzine; Marithé & François Girbaud; Madame Grès; Halston; Jacques Heim; Gordon Henderson; Tommy Hilfiger; Isani; Marc Jacobs; Eric Javits; John P. John; Wolfgang Joop; Gemma Kahng; Kenzo; Barry Kieselstein-Cord; Calvin Klein; Yukio Kobayashi; Michael Kors; Junko Koshino; Lamine Kouyaté; Byron Lars; André Laug; Judith Leiber; Mad Carpentier; Mitsuhiro Matsuda; Missoni; Issey Miyake; Isaac Mizrahi; Edward H. Molyneux; Claude Montana; Josie Cruz Natori; Nikos; Todd Oldham; Elsa Peretti; Lilly Pulitzer; Mary Ann Restivo; Marcel Rochas; Christian Francis Roth; Ronaldus Shamask; Simonetta; Willi Smith; Zang Toi; Gianni Versace; Madeleine Vionnet; John Weitz; Kansai Yamamoto.

McCREADY, Elian. Painter and textile designer. Churchill fellow, 1985. Design writing includes *Glorious Needlepoint,* 1987, *Kaffe Fassett at the V & A,* 1988, *Glorious Inspiration,* 1991, *Fruits of the Earth,* 1991, and *Ehrman Tapestry Book,* 1995. **Essays:** Caroline Charles; Kaffe Fassett; Bill Gibb; Patricia Roberts; Timney Fowler Ltd.

MEDEIROS, Kimbally A. Freelance writer based in Miami, Florida. Writer for St. James Press for over three years and featured in such books as *American Women Writers* and the *International Directory of Company Histories.* **Essays:** Robert Clergerie; Randolph Duke; Carol Horn; Andrew Marc; Rebecca Moses; Nordstrom; Paloma Picasso; Anthony Price; Zandra Rhodes; Vivienne Tam; Viktor & Rolf; David Yurman.

MELIA, Sally Anne. Science and culture freelance journalist and author. Contributor to *St. James Guide to Fantasy Writers,* 1994, *Larousse Encyclopedia,* 1995, *Lexus Dictionary of French Life and Culture,* 1995; author of celebrity interviews and articles for magazines in the United Kingdom and the United States, including *SF Chronicle* and *Interzone.* **Essays:** Ermenegildo Zegna Group; Sueo Irié; René Lezard; Roberto Verino.

MINDEROVIC, Christine Miner. Freelance writer for several years. She has a B.S. from Wayne State University and attended the School of Art and Architecture at the University of Michigan. **Essays:** Agnès B.; Victor Alfaro; Linda Allard; Banana Republic; Liza Bruce; Bonnie Cashin; Jasper Conran; Bella Freud; Wolfgang Joop; Helmut Lang; Tracy Reese.

MYERS, Sally A. Freelance writer/editor living in Ohio and the sole proprietor of an editorial services business. She holds a Ph.D. in American studies. **Essays:** Junichi Arai; Jacques Azagury; Dirk Bikkembergs; Betty Jackson.

OZZARD, Janet. Graduate of Bryn Mawr College; M.A. in fashion history, Fashion Institute of Technology. Reporter for *Women's Wear Daily* (New York). **Essay:** Zoran.

PATON, Kathleen. Writer, researcher, and editor specializing in cultural history. Freelance graphic designer, since 1988. M.A. in Museum Studies, State University of New York, Fashion Institute of Technology, 1993. Research and essays for *In A Rising Public Voice: Women in Politics Worldwide.* **Essays:** Christian Aujard; Franck Joseph Bastille; Jean Baptiste Caumont; Jacques Esterel; Georges Rech; Olivier Guillemin; Hermès; Guy Paulin; Bernard Perris; Gérard Pipart; Jacques Tiffeau; Tiktiner.

PATTISON, Angela. Lecturer in design. Program leader, Cordwainers College. International design consultant. Trained as a fashion designer in the early 1960s. Specializes in trend predictions, fashion forecasting, and designing footwear and accessories with major manufacturers and retailers throughout the world. **Essays:** Manolo Blahnik; Elio Fiorucci; Jan Jansen; Transport.

RAUGUST, Karen. Minneapolis-based freelance writer who contributed to publications ranging from *Publishers Weekly* to *Animation Magazine*. Her books include *The Licensing Business Handbook* (EPM Communications), *Merchandise Licensing for the Television Industry* (Focal Press), and the upcoming *Animation Business Handbook* (St. Martin's). **Essays:** Joseph Abboud; Julian Alexander; Jeff Banks; Rocco Barocco; Brioni; Bruno Magli; Byblos; Carven; Jean-Charles de Castelbajac; Caroline Charles; Cole Haan; Corneliani SpA; Paul Costelloe; Patrick Cox; C.P. Company; Angela Cummings; Wendy Dagworthy; Louis Dell'Olio; Ann Demeulemeester; Dolce & Gabbana; David and Elizabeth Emanuel; Alberto Fabiani; Han Feng; Diane Freis; French Connection; Jean-Paul Gaultier; Marithé & François Girbaud; Sylvia Heisel; Gordon Henderson; Carolina Herrera; Tommy Hilfiger; Jones New York; Yukio Kobayashi; Yoshiyuki Konishi; Michael Kors; Hiroko Koshino; Junko Koshino; Michiko Koshino; Lamine Kouyaté; Liberty of London; L.L. Bean; Hedi Slimane; William Tang; Chantal Thomass; Vicky Tiel; Isabel Toledo; Yuki Torii; Kay Unger.

REAMY, Donna W. Assistant professor at Virginia Commonwealth University in the Department of Fashion Design and Merchandising. As a visiting professor at the Univerdad de Palermo, she presented a paper entitled, "The Role of the Fashion Mechandiser," in August 2000. Research includes importing and exporting fashion, and merchandising in Latin America. **Essays:** Miguel Adrover; Liz Claiborne; Tom Ford; Calvin Klein; Alexander McQueen; Richard Tyler; Vera Wang.

REISMAN, Jessica. Fiction writer and researcher living in Austin, Texas. **Essays:** Adri; Hussein Chalayan; Kenneth Cole; Sybil Connolly; Christian Lacroix; Chester Weinberg.

RHODES, Nelly. Freelance writer based in the Midwest. **Essays:** Abercrombie & Fitch Company; Adolfo; Sir Hardy Amies; Aquascutum, Ltd.; Giorgio Armani; Laura Ashley; Badgley Mischka; Cristobal Balenciaga; Pierre Balmain; Patirizio Bertelli; Bodymap; Willy Bogner; Brooks Brothers; Oleg Cassini; Catalina Sportswear; Champion Products Inc.; Cole of California; Jacqueline de Ribes; Elisabeth de Senneville; Escada; Jacques Esterel; Joseph Ettedgui; Fabrice; Louis Féraud; David Fielden; Fontana; The Gap; Genny Holding SpA; Ghost; Romeo Gigli; Hubert de Givenchy; Gruppo GFT; Holly Harp; Edith Head; Hermès; Hugo Boss AG; Jean Patou; Charles Jourdan; Guy Laroche; Mitsuhiro Matsuda; Max Mara SpA; Mondi Textile GmbH; Claude Montana; Mulberry Company; Nikos; Bruce Oldfield; Todd Oldham; Pepe; Carmelo Pomodoro; Prada; Red or Dead; Mary Ann Restivo; Bill Robinson; Christian Francis Roth; Sonia Rykiel; Gloria Sachs; Yves Saint Laurent; Jean-Louis Scherrer; Elsa Schiaparelli; Mila Schön; Strenesse Group; Alfred Sung; Pauline Trigère; Patricia Underwood; Joan Vass; Victoria's Secret; Whistles; Yohji Yamamoto.

ROSENBERG, Alan E. Studied fashion design at The Fashion Institute of Technology and art history at Hunter College of the City University of New York. Director of the Metropolitan Historic Structures Association for several years. Studying for master's degree in museum studies, Fashion Institute of Technology. **Essays:** Adolfo; Carven; Elisabeth de Senneville; Dorothée Bis; George Peter Stavropoulos; Vicky Tiel; Valentino.

SALTER, Susan. Writer/contributor to several reference series, including *Contemporary Authors, Newsmakers,* and *Major Authors and Illustrators for Children and Young Adults.* **Essay:** Esprit Holdings, Inc.

SCHROEDER, Sandra. Freelance writer based in the Chicago area. **Essays:** Jhane Barnes; Danskin; Alberta Ferretti; Mickey Lee.

SEAMAN, Margo. Graduate of the College of Wooster; master's degrees from the Fashion Institute of Technology and Bank Street College of Education. Teacher and freelance writer. **Essays:** Pierre Balmain; Carolina Herrera; Jean Patou; Anne Klein; Claire McCardell; Paloma Picasso; Adrienne Vittadini.

SEVERSON, Molly. Freelance writer. **Essay:** Richard Tyler.

SEWELL, Dennita. Graduate of the University of Missouri and Yale School of Drama. Collections manager in The Costume Institute, The Metropolitan Museum of Art, since 1992. **Essays:** Cathy Hardwick; Roger Vivier.

SHAW, Madelyn. Collections manager, The Textile Museum, Washington, D.C. Former member of the curatorial staff, The Museum at the Fashion Institute of Technology, New York, and The Gallery of Cora Ginsburg, Inc., New York. Instructor, Boston University School of Theatre Arts, Boston, Massachusetts. Also involved in freelance exhibition consultation and preparation. Contributor to *A World of Costume and Textiles: A Handbook of the Collection,* 1988, and of "Women's Flying Clothing: 1910–1940," in *Cutter's Research Journal,* 1992–93. **Essays:** Hattie Carnegie; Jean Dessès; Tina Leser; Robert Piguet; Maurice Rentner; Maggy Rouff; Carolyn Schnurer.

SKELLENGER, Gillion. Freelance wallpaper and fabric designer, Chicago. Instructor, Fashion Department, School of the Art Institute of Chicago, beginning in 1977. **Essays:** Patirizio Bertelli; Prada; Cinzia Ruggeri.

SNODGRASS, Mary Ellen. Veteran high school teacher of English and Latin Hickory from North Carolina, and the author of some 85 textbooks and general reference works. Her awards include an American Library Association reference book of the year for *Encyclopedia of Utopian Literature.* **Essays:** Akira; Bill Blass; Blumarine; Ossie Clark; Myrène de Prémonville; English Eccentrics; Fendi; Giuliano Fujiwara; Georgina Godley; Olivier Guillemin; Eric Javits; Ragence Lam; Marcel Marongiu; Benny Ong; Rifat Ozbek; Peter Hoggard; Gérard Pipart; Arabella Pollen; John Richmond; Cinzia Ruggeri; Jil Sander; Arnold Scaasi; Sophie Sitbon; Per Spook; Stephen Sprouse; Cynthia Steffe; Jill Stuart; Sybilla; Tamotsu; Koos van den Akker; Gian Marco Venturi; Joaquim Verdù; Roberto Verino; Diane Von Furstenberg; Kansai Yamamoto.

SNYDER, Carrie. Freelance writer and editor for numerous projects. Contributor to *American Women Writers* and *Contemporary Authors.* She is a graduate of Calvin College in Grand Rapids, Michigan. **Essays:** Sylvia Ayton; Geoffrey Beene; Giorgio Correggiari; Adolfo Domínguez; Elio Fiorucci; David Hechter; Hobbs Ltd.; Emma Hope; Sueo Irié; Isani; Jaeger; Jantzen, Inc.; Stephen Jones; Lacoste Sportswear; Hervé Léger; Jürgen Lehl; Judith Leiber; Hanae Mori; René Lezard.

STACY, Megan. Freelance writer and graduate of Trinity University, where she received a degree in American History. **Essays:** Alan Flusser; Betsey Johnson; Gemma Kahng; Mary Jane Marcasiano; Martin Margiela; Bernard Perris; Andrea Pfister; Tiffany & Company.

STANLEY, Montse. Director, Knitting Reference Library, Cambridge, United Kingdom. Author of *Knitting Your Own Designs for a Perfect Fit,* 1982, and *The Knitter's Handbook,* 1986. **Essay:** Joaquim Verdù.

STEELE, Valerie. Author and professor at New York's Fashion Institute of Technology. Author of *Fashion and Eroticism,* 1985, *Paris Fashion,* 1988, *Women of Fashion,* 1991, and *Fetish: Fashion, Sex and Power,* 1995. Co-editor of *Men and Women: Dressing the Part,* 1989. **Essays:** Jacques Fath; Martin Margiela; Jil Sander; Sybilla; Isabel Toledo; Vivienne Westwood.

TRIGGS, Teal. Course leader, School of Graphic Design, Ravensbourne College of Design and Communication, London. Design historian. Editor, *Communicating Design,* 1995, and (post-conference publication) *Rear Window: American and European Graphic Design,* 1995. Author of "Framing Masculinity: Herb Ritts, Bruce Weber and the Body Perfect" in *Chic Thrills: A Fashion Reader,* 1992. Contributor of articles to numerous periodicals and books, including *Eye* magazine, *Visible Language, Contemporary Designers,* and *Contemporary Masterworks.* **Essays:** Benetton SpA; Jasper Conran; Sylvia Heisel; Marimekko; Whistles.

VASILOPOULOS, Vicki. Senior fashion editor, *Daily News Record,* Fairchild Fashion Group. **Essays:** C.P. Company; New Republic; Bill Robinson.

VOTOLATO, Gregory. Essayist. Head of Art History, Buckinghamshire College, High Wycombe. **Essays:** Adolfo Domínguez; Barbara Hulanicki; L.L. Bean; Thierry Mugler.

WALKER, Myra J. Associate professor of fashion history, School of Visual Arts at the University of North Texas in Denton. Director, Texas Fashion Collection. Curator, "The Art of Fashion: The Radical Sixties," Kimbell Art Museum, 1990. Exhibition organizer, JC Penney National Headquarters, 1993–95. Specialist in 20th-century fashion history. **Essays:** Victor Costa; Sandra Garratt; Holly Harp; Giorgio Sant'Angelo; Arnold Scaasi.

WATT, Melinda L. Study storage assistant, The Costume Institute, Metropolitan Museum of Art. M.A. in Costume Studies from New York University. **Essays:** Willy Bogner; James Galanos; Mollie Parnis; Pauline Trigère; Patricia Underwood.

WORAM, Catherine. Freelance fashion writer/stylist. Author of *Wedding Dress Style,* 1993. **Essays:** Sir Hardy Amies; Aquascutum, Ltd.; English Eccentrics; Fendi; Bella Freud; Genny Holding SpA; Ghost; Gucci; Katharine Hamnett; Lachasse; Max Mara SpA; Digby Morton; Next Plc; Jenny Packham; Paul Smith; Philip Treacy; Catherine Walker; Workers for Freedom.

NATIONALITY INDEX